GUIDE TO

INTEREST GROUPS AND LOBBYING IN THE UNITED STATES

GUIDE TO

INTEREST GROUPS AND LOBBYING IN THE UNITED STATES

Burdett A. Loomis, Editor

Peter L. Francia & Dara Z. Strolovitch, Associate Editors

Los Angeles | London | New Delhi
Singapore | Washington DC

CQ Press
2300 N Street, NW, Suite 800
Washington, DC 20037

Phone: 202-729-1900; toll-free, 1-866-4CQ-PRESS (1-866-427-7737)

Web: www.cqpress.com

Cover design: Malcolm McGaughy, McGaughy Designs
Cover image: The Granger Collection, NYC. The Original Coxey Army. The dominance of business interests in Washington is lampooned in this 1894 cartoon by W.A. Rodgers. Leading the march of businessmen on the Capitol is steel magnate Andrew Carnegie, who charges in front of bowing members of Congress. Jacob Coxey's "Army" of unemployed workers who descended upon Washington in 1894 seeking government relief during the depression of the 1890s.
Composition: C&M Digitals (P) Ltd.

Illustration credits and acknowledgements begin on page 475, which is to be considered an extension of the copyright page.

♾ The paper used in this publication exceeds the requirements of the American National Standard for Information Sciences—Permanence of Paper for Printed Library Materials, ANSI Z39.48-1992.

Printed and bound in the United States of America

15 14 13 12 11 1 2 3 4 5

Library of Congress Cataloging-in-Publication Data

Guide to interest groups and lobbying in the United States / Burdett A. Loomis, editor; Peter L. Francia & Dara Z. Strolovitch, associate editors.
p. cm.
Includes index.
ISBN 978-1-60426-457-9
1. Pressure groups—United States. 2. Lobbying—United States. I. Loomis, Burdett A., II. Francia, Peter L. III. Strolovitch, Dara Z.

JK1118.G85 2011
324'.40973—dc23

2011019847

★ SUMMARY TABLE OF CONTENTS

Contents vii
About the Editors xv
Contributors xvii
Preface xix

INTRODUCTION 1

PART I INTEREST GROUPS FROM THE FRAMING TO THE TWENTIETH CENTURY 9

PART II THEORETICAL APPROACHES TO INTEREST GROUPS AND LOBBYING 47

PART III INTEREST GROUPS AND THE GROWTH OF GOVERNMENT 99

PART IV INTEREST GROUPS BY SECTOR AND TYPE 161

PART V LOBBYISTS AND LOBBYING: TACTICS, TECHNIQUES, AND REGULATION 333

PART VI INTEREST GROUPS, CAMPAIGNS, AND ELECTIONS – AND MONEY 391

PART VII GROUPS AND LOBBYING BEYOND THE BELTWAY 443

Illustration Credits and Acknowledgments 475
Index 477

★ TABLE OF CONTENTS

INTRODUCTION 1

Interest Group Politics before the 1950s 2

Beyond Pluralism: Theoretical Approaches to Interest Groups and Lobbying 3

Groups and the Government (Parties, Too) 3

Organized Interests and Lobbying: Sector by Sector 4

Lobbying 5

Interests and Elections 6

Beyond Washington 6

Groups, Lobbying, and American Politics 6

PART I INTEREST GROUPS: FROM THE FRAMING TO THE TWENTIETH CENTURY 9

CHAPTER 1 THE EVOLUTION OF GROUPS AND LOBBYING IN 18TH CENTURY AMERICA 11

The Politics of American Interests, 1690–1750s: The English Connections 11

Interests and Colonial Legislatures through the 1760s: New Targets for Influence 13

American Interests, 1770s–1787 14

Interests and the Constitution in Theory and Practice, 1787–1800 15

Setting the Stage: Interests and Groups in Eighteenth-Century America 17

CHAPTER 2 INTEREST GROUPS AND LOBBYING IN THE 19TH CENTURY: DE TOCQUEVILLE'S AMERICA 21

From Dread of Factions to Vibrant Civil Society: The Early Nineteenth Century 22

Group Mobilization in the Antebellum Years 24

Organizing to Reform: Sabbatarian, Temperance, and Abolitionist Associations 27

The Growth of a Washington Lobbying Community: From the Civil War to the Gilded Age 31

Conclusion 33

CHAPTER 3 GROUPS IN INDUSTRIALIZING AMERICA AND THE ORIGINS OF POPULAR INTEREST GROUP POLITICS 35

The Prehistory of Interest Group Politics 36

An Age of Associations 38

The Search for Political Legitimacy and Effective Techniques 40

The People's Lobby 41

The Persistence of Interest Group Politics 43

PART II **THEORETICAL APPROACHES TO INTEREST GROUPS AND LOBBYING** 47

CHAPTER 4 GROUP FORMATION AND MAINTENANCE 49
The First Fifty Years of Political Association Research 49
Mancur Olson's Revolution 50
Organizational Factors Affecting Voluntary Political Organizations 53
Conclusion 59

CHAPTER 5 AMERICAN PLURALISM, INTEREST GROUP LIBERALISM, AND NEOPLURALISM 63
What is Pluralism? 64
Classic Critiques and Their Contemporary Relevance 66
Neopluralism 69
Is Neopluralism Old Wine in New Bottles? 70
When to Use the Pluralist Framework 71
Comparison to Alternative Frameworks 72
Unanswered Fundamental Questions 73
Conclusion 74

CHAPTER 6 INTEREST GROUPS AND SOCIAL MOVEMENTS 77
Evolving Definitions and Distinctions 77
Insiders and Outsiders 80
Divisions of Intellectual Labor 82
Interest Organizations, Contentious Politics, and other Frameworks 84
Conclusion: Implications for Representative Democracy 84

CHAPTER 7 ECONOMIC MODELS OF INTEREST GROUPS AND LOBBYING 87
A Brief Review of the Work of Mancur Olson 87
Markets and Political Activity 90
Game Theory and Interest Groups and Lobbying 90
Models with Money and Politics 91
Informational Models 92
Hybrid Models 93
New (and Old) Areas of Research into Group Activity 93
Conclusion 95

PART III **INTEREST GROUPS AND THE GROWTH OF GOVERNMENT** 99

CHAPTER 8 THE GROWTH OF GOVERNMENT AND THE EXPANSION OF ORGANIZED INTERESTS 101
The Size of the Group System 102
The Size of Government 104
Interest-Driven Explanations for Growth 104
Government-Driven Explanations of Growth 106
Conclusion 110

CHAPTER 9 INTEREST GROUPS AND THE COURTS 113
Who Participates in the Judiciary? 114

How Do Groups Participate in the Judicial Process? 115
Why Do Groups Participate? 119
Conclusion 123

CHAPTER 10 INTEREST GROUPS AND THE EXECUTIVE BRANCH 127
The Interest Group Dowry 127
Overlapping Objectives 129
Interest Groups and the White House 132
Interest Groups and Federal Agencies 138
Conclusion 141

CHAPTER 11 INTEREST GROUPS AND PARTIES: THE POLITICS OF REPRESENTATION 145
Constitutional Design and the Politics of Representation 145
Interest Groups 146
Political Parties 151
Interest Group-Political Party Collaboration and Competition 157
Conclusion 158

PART IV INTEREST GROUPS BY SECTOR AND TYPE 161

CHAPTER 12 AGRICULTURE 163
A Brief History of Agricultural Interest Groups 164
Understanding Interest Group Influence in Agriculture 168
Future Prospects of Agricultural Interest Groups 170

CHAPTER 13 BUSINESS AND ORGANIZED LABOR 173
The Logic of Collective Action 173
Formation and Early History of Labor Groups 174
Formation and Early History of Business Groups 176
Business and Labor "By the Numbers" 177
Members as a Resource: Mobilizing the Electorate 179
Financial Resources: Supporting Candidates' Campaigns 181
PACs and Independent Expenditures 182
Groups Known as 527s and 501(c)s 183
Business Versus Labor in the Legislative Arena 184
Conclusion 189

CHAPTER 14 DEFENSE AND HOMELAND SECURITY 193
National Defense 193
Homeland Security 199
Conclusion 205

CHAPTER 15 CIVIL RIGHTS 209
Early Civil Rights Action 209
The Civil Rights Movement and the Politics of Mass Participation 212
Fragmentation and Focus in the Post-Civil Rights Era 213
Follow the Funding Trail 215

The Future of Civil Rights Organizations 218
Conclusion 220

CHAPTER 16 ISSUE ADVOCACY GROUPS AND THINK TANKS 223
Think Tanks as Interest Groups 223
Think Tank Structure and Personnel 225
Tax Status of Think Tanks 225
What Do Think Tanks Think About? 226
The Birth of Think Tanks 226
War, Depression, and the Need for Expertise: Think Tanks, 1917–1945 227
Technocratic Liberalism and its Critics: Think Tanks, 1945–1969 228
The Rise of the New Right: Think Tanks, 1969–1981 231
The Age of Ideological Warfare: Think Tanks, 1981–1993 232
Think Tanks Today, 1993–Present 233
Conclusion 236

CHAPTER 17 RELIGIOUS INTEREST GROUPS 239
Development and Maintenance of Religious Groups 239
Types of Religious Lobbying Organizations 241
Electoral Involvement of Religious Organizations 242
Conclusion 247

CHAPTER 18 WOMEN'S AND FEMINIST MOVEMENTS AND ORGANIZATIONS 251
Reinterpreting the First Two Waves of Feminism 251
The First Wave Reinterpreted 252
Analyzing Second Wave Feminism 254
Developing Agenda of the Second Wave 256
The Third Wave Broadens the Feminist Agenda 257
Conclusion 258

CHAPTER 19 PUBLIC INTEREST GROUPS 261
What Are Public Interests? What Are Public Interest Groups? 261
Why So Few Public Interest Groups? The Free-Rider Problem 263
The Growing Number of Public Interest Groups 264
What Public Interest Groups Do 265
The Distribution of Organized Interest Activity 268
Conclusion 269

CHAPTER 20 PROFESSIONAL ASSOCIATIONS 271
What Is a Professional Association? 271
Professional Association Activities in Modern Politics 273
The Political Power of Professional Associations 278
Conclusion 280

CHAPTER 21 ELEMENTARY AND SECONDARY EDUCATION 283
Categories of Interest Organizations 283
Issues and Interests 286

Republican Attacks on Teachers' Collective Bargaining Rights 290
Conclusion 291

CHAPTER 22 ENERGY AND THE ENVIRONMENT 295
Group Formation 295
Organizational Maintenance 299
"Mass Membership" Environmentalism 301
Are Groups Effective? 303
New Alliances 304
The Future of Environmental Advocacy 306

CHAPTER 23 INTERGOVERNMENTAL LOBBYING 309
Empirical Research on the Intergovernmental Lobby 310
Rise of the Intergovernmental Lobby 311
Turning to the Legal System 312
Ideological Interest Representation in the Intergovernmental Lobby 313
State Offices in Washington, D.C. 313
Intergovernmental Lobby Resources and Cohesion 314
Tactics and Issues 316
Coalition Building 317
Conclusion 317

CHAPTER 24 FOREIGN LOBBYING 321
Legal Context of Foreign Lobbying 321
The Players: Foreign Governments 323
The Players: Domestic Allies and Opponents 324
Foreign Lobbying Strategies 326
Motivations for Foreign Lobbyists 327
Determinants of Success 329
Conclusion and Implications 330

PART V INTEREST GROUPS AND LOBBYING: TACTICS, TECHNIQUES, AND REGULATION 333

CHAPTER 25 LOBBYING AND LEGISLATIVE STRATEGY 335
Lobbying Congress: Following The Rules 335
The Practice of Lobbying 337
Information and Framing 340
Outside Pressure and Inside Lobbying 341
Lobbying in Coalitions 343
Lobbying and Representation 343
Conclusion 344

CHAPTER 26 LOBBYISTS: WHO ARE THEY? WHAT DO THEY DO? 347
Who Are the Lobbyists? 347
What Do Lobbyists Do? 350
Do Lobbyists Corrupt American Government? 355

CHAPTER 27 LOBBYING: TECHNIQUES AND IMPACT 359
Lobbying Definitions 359
Lobbying Tools and Techniques 361
Understanding the Impact of Lobbying 367
Lobbying: More than Influence 369

CHAPTER 28 GRASSROOTS, ASTROTURF, AND INTERNET LOBBYING 371
Competing Pressures 371
Grassroots Lobbying 372
Grass Tops Lobbying 373
Astroturf Lobbying 375
Online Lobbying 375
Online Advocacy 377
Do Grassroots, Astroturf, and Online Lobbying Work? 377
Conclusion 378

CHAPTER 29 THE FIRST AMENDMENT AND THE REGULATION OF LOBBYING 381
First Amendment Protections: A Legal History 381
The First Amendment and Early Congressional Efforts to Regulate Lobbying 382
Lobbies and the Internal Revenue Service Code 383
Campaign Finance Laws and Their Impact on Lobbying 387
Ethics Rules in the Executive Branch 388
Lobby Regulations and the First Amendment 388

PART VI **INTEREST GROUPS, CAMPAIGNS, AND ELECTIONS – AND MONEY** **391**

CHAPTER 30 INTEREST GROUPS AND FEDERAL CAMPAIGNS BEFORE THE FEDERAL ELECTION CAMPAIGN ACT 393
Groups and Federal Campaigns Prior to the New Deal 394
The New Deal to FECA: The Rise of Interest Group Money and Activity 397
Group Challenges to the Parties 399

CHAPTER 31 PACs, 527s, AND OTHER GROUPS IN CONGRESSIONAL ELECTIONS 403
What Types of Groups Invest in Elections? 403
Group Spending in Congressional Elections 408
Important Developments 409
What Motivates Interest Groups to Participate? 411
Are Interest Groups Successful? 414
What Role Should Interest Groups Play? 414
Conclusion 416

CHAPTER 32 INTEREST GROUPS IN PRESIDENTIAL ELECTIONS 419
Interest Groups and Presidential Elections 420
Endorsements and Voter Guides 422
Contributing Cash 424
Registering and Mobilizing Voters 424
Persuading Voters 426
Conclusion 428

CHAPTER 33 REGULATING AND REFORMING GROUP-BASED ELECTIONEERING 431
The Legal Context of Regulation 431
The Bipartisan Campaign Reform Act 433
A Brief History of Electioneering 434
Who Buys Electioneering Ads? 437
Why Purchase Electioneering Ads? 438
Normative Criteria for Thinking about Electioneering 439
The Future of Electioneering 440
Conclusion 441

PART VII GROUPS AND LOBBYING BEYOND THE BELTWAY 443

CHAPTER 34 INTEREST GROUPS AND STATE POLITICS 445
Organizations Active in State Politics 445
Communities of State Interest Groups 446
Lobbyists in State Politics 448
What Do These Groups and Lobbyists Do? 450
Conclusion 453

CHAPTER 35 LOCAL INTEREST GROUPS: FORGOTTEN BUT STILL INFLUENTIAL? 457
From Classic Community Power Studies to the Backwater of Political Science 457
The Challenges of Studying Local Interest Groups 459
Institutional versus Episodic Local Groups 460
Building Citizens 463
Venues for Future Research 464

CHAPTER 36 LOBBYING IN THE AMERICAN STYLE AROUND THE WORLD 467
Factors Influencing Lobbying Behavior 468
The Fundamentals of Lobbying Activity around the Globe 469
Conclusion 473

Illustration Credits and Acknowledgments 475

Index 477

★ ABOUT THE EDITORS

Burdett A. Loomis is professor of political science at the University of Kansas. A former American Political Science Association congressional fellow and recipient of a Kemper Teaching Award, he has written extensively on legislatures, political careers, interest groups, and policymaking. In 2005, he worked as director of administrative communication for Governor Kathleen Sebelius of Kansas. He is the author or editor of more than 30 books in various editions, including eight editions of *Interest Group Politics.*

Peter L. Francia is associate professor of political science at East Carolina University. He has written extensively on labor unions, campaign finance, and American elections, and is the author of *The Future of Organized Labor in American Politics*, and is co-author of *The Financiers of Congressional Elections: Investors, Ideologues, and Intimates,* and *Conventional Wisdom and American Elections: Exploding Myths, Exploring Misconceptions* (1st and 2nd eds.). His work has appeared in *American Politics Research, Political Research Quarterly, Public Opinion Quarterly, Presidential Studies Quarterly*, and *Social Science Quarterly.*

Dara Z. Strolovitch is associate professor of political Science at the University of Minnesota. She is the author of the award-winning book *Affirmative Advocacy: Race, Class, and Gender in Interest Group Politics.* Her work has appeared in journals including the *Journal of Politics*, the *American Journal of Sociology*, the *National Women's Studies Association Journal, Social Science Quarterly*, and the *Du Bois Review.* She has held fellowships at the Brookings Institution and, Georgetown University, and has received grants from sources including the National Science Foundation and the Social Sciences and Humanities Research Council of Canada.

★ CONTRIBUTORS

Scott H. Ainsworth
Former White House Aid

Gary Andres
American University and Dutko Worldwide

Robert G. Boatright
Clark University

Christopher Bosso
Northeastern University

Katharine W.V. Bradley
University of Michigan

Allan Cigler
University of Kansas

Beverly A. Cigler
Penn State-Harrisburg

Austin C. Clemens
University of Georgia

Elisabeth S. Clemens
University of Chicago

Anne N. Costain
University of Colorado at Boulder

M. David Forrest
University of Minnesota

Peter L. Francia
East Carolina University

Michael M. Franz
Bowdoin College

Elliott Fullmer
Georgetown University

R. Kenneth Godwin
University of North Carolina Charlotte

Matt Grossmann
Michigan State University

James L. Guth
Furman University

Richard L. Hall
University of Michigan

Eric S. Heberlig
University of North Carolina Charlotte

Paul S. Herrnson
University of Maryland

Ronald J Hrebenar
University of Utah

Dennis W. Johnson
The George Washington University

Paul E. Johnson
University of Kansas

Arnd Jurgensen
University of Toronto

Rogan Kersh
New York University

Beth L. Leech
Rutgers University

Suzanne Leland
University of North Carolina Charlotte

Renan Levine
University of Toronto

Burdett A. Loomis
University of Kansas

Benjamin Marquez
University of Wisconsin-Madison

Conor McGrath
Independent Scholar

Anthony J. Nownes
University of Tennessee

Karen O'Connor
American University

Susan Orr
The College at Brockport, SUNY

Mark A. Peterson
University of California, Los Angeles

Carmine Scavo
East Carolina University

Kay Lehman Schlozman
Boston College

Adam Sheingate
Johns Hopkins University

Richard Skinner
Rollins College

Jeremy Strickler
University of Oregon

Dara Z. Strolovitch
University of Minnesota

Clive S. Thomas
Foley Institute of Politics and Public Service
Washington State University

Daniel J. Tichenor
University of Oregon

Clyde Wilcox
Georgetown University

Christopher Witko
Saint Louis University

Alixandra B. Yanus
High Point University

Heather E. Yates
University of Kansas

PREFACE

A LITTLE MORE THAN FOUR YEARS AGO, Doug Goldenberg-Hart of CQ Press's reference division e-mailed me with a request to consider editing a guide to interest groups and lobbying. Such a project was not at the top of my "to-do" list. Still, it was intriguing, and I have had the experience of editing several collections in the past. The chance to help delineate a major subfield of American politics represented both a challenge and an opportunity. Doug and I arrived at a broad conception of what the *guide* would look like, and by early 2008 a contract had been signed, largely because I had convinced two great young scholars—Peter Francia and Dara Strolovitch—to join me as associate editors. Going through the e-mail record of the past three years reveals how the *Guide to Interest Groups and Lobbying in the United States* developed, with the recruitment of a wonderful group of authors, the decisions on how to structure the book, and our introduction to CQ's Andrew Boney, whose editorial and organizational skills would keep us on course and—more or less—on schedule. As luck would have it, the 2010 American Political Science Association conference was held in Washington, so I could meet Andrew in person—and could put a face (a young one) to the authoritative voice of his e-mails.

Getting almost fifty authors to write thirty-seven articles is no mean feat, but this group of busy, productive scholars has performed admirably, producing first-rate articles as they worked, individually and collectively, to define the broad field of interest groups and lobbying. Along the way, I learned a lot, whether on the nuances of pluralism or the mind-numbing development of campaign finance laws and practices. Two related incentives to put this book together were that although the field that encompasses interest groups and lobbying has always played an important part of the study of American politics, it has never been clear (1) what the field includes and (2) how central it is to understanding our political life. This volume includes more than it excludes, although the organization is by necessity a bit arbitrary. Still, as the many cross references will attest, the *guide* does address groups and lobbying with breadth and reasonable, though limited, depth.

In the end, the chapters do—as intended—offer scholars, students, and interested laypersons a good place to start in understanding the ins and outs of groups and lobbying. From eighteenth-century predecessors to modern groups to contemporary lobbying on the Internet, those who use this guide can gain a sophisticated, yet accessible, introduction to the subject at hand. Beyond Andrew's diligent work, much of the credit for the volume's quality goes to Peter and Dara, who solicited more than half the articles and shepherded them through the writing, editing, and production stages. I'm greatly in their debt for making my editorial job much simpler, and more enjoyable, than it might have been. In addition, they both wrote first-rate articles on important subjects.

Aside from Doug, Andrew, Dara, and Peter, the other essential figures in producing an excellent volume have been copyeditor Carolyn Goldinger and Elizabeth Kline, who has been in charge of production. Under great time pressure, both have done great jobs and contributed greatly to the *Guide's* overall quality.

As this four-year process comes to a close, I can honestly say that it's been personally enjoyable and, I hope, broadly useful to those who seek to understand the politics of interest groups and lobbying. As always, I thank my wife Michel, who puts up with my mutterings and mood swings, knowing that completing a project like this ultimately gives me great pleasure and a real sense of accomplishment.

Burdett A. Loomis
Lawrence, Kansas

Introduction

Interest Groups and Lobbying in American Politics: The Lay of the Land

by Burdett A. Loomis

In James Madison's drafting of the Constitution and the ratification of the First Amendment, the rights of interests to organize and petition the government were recognized and protected. This is important. As the framers sought to strengthen the national government, they simultaneously provided numerous access points for interests to make their case. To be sure, as Madison noted, factions were potentially dangerous, but they were also inevitable and in many ways energizing. Even before the Constitution's ratification, interests found ways to put forward their preferences. And the ratification itself was played out, colony by colony, as a battle among interests, culminating in New York's vigorous debate, framed by the propaganda cum political theory of the Federalist broadsides.

Over the past century the political science discipline has sought to account for the actions of organized interests in American politics. For some scholars, such as Arthur Bentley and David Truman, interests have stood center stage in the United States; for them, addressing the interplay of interests offered scholars and citizens a comprehensive, integrated understanding of our politics.[1] In the 1950s Truman and various pluralist scholars held sway, but in the wake of numerous formal, economic, and sociological studies, the emphasis on interests or groups as foundational concepts has waned. In part this diminution came as a result of E. E. Schattschneider's brief but persuasive rebuttal to pluralist conclusions in his still-valuable *The Semisovereign People.*[2] Schattschneider argued persuasively that business interests possessed a structural advantage in American politics, at least to the extent that groups dictated the action.

Still, organized interests of all kinds remain significant forces in American politics, in any number of ways. Lobbying has become more and more extensive, and increasing numbers of groups and other interests address an ever-expanding array of government policies. Likewise, organized interests have engaged ever more energetically in electoral politics, both contributing to candidates and spending money independently on their behalf. Indeed, as Jonathan Rauch, Robert Salisbury, Theodore Lowi, and others have thoroughly chronicled, organized interests of every stripe find it profitable, even essential, to lobby on their own particular concerns that are folded into thousands of federal and state programs.[3] In the end, the chances for meaningful policy change and effective governance diminish over time as the crush of interests limit the possibilities for coherent action.

The *Guide to Interest Groups and Lobbying* provides a series of foundational chapters for those among others—scholars, students, activists, and government officials—who wish to gain a fuller understanding of organized interests and their behavior. Each chapter offers a starting point for understanding a given aspect of groups and lobbying. The chapters take note of the interrelationships among the various subjects, with dozens of cross-references. For example, to address groups and elections, one must also be informed on the regulation of campaign spending by groups. And, as any organization of the subjects covered here will be arbitrary, the extensive use of cross-references allows for subject matter, not just the table of contents, to facilitate the reader's understanding.

More generally, several themes beyond those identified in the table of contents run through this volume. The lasting importance of economist Mancur Olson's 1965 *The Logic of Collective Action* can scarcely be overestimated in its influence on a host of topics included here. Addressing the maintenance, and implicitly the foundation, of groups in a rigorous assessment of membership incentives gave scholars an effective way to compare groups and examine the behaviors of individuals and firms as prospective members. Olson's insights became part of the conversation about membership, lobbying, coalition building, group patrons, and dozens of other subjects.

If Olson provides the touchstone of modern group scholarship, Madison offers a perspective in the *Federalist Papers* that has influenced group scholarship since the ratification of the Constitution. Again, writer after writer reflects on Madison's views on factions. Madison did not anticipate political parties, but his approach to interests was prescient. As a practical politician and propagandist, as well as a student of political theory, he understood the fundamental notion of interest and how it would drive politics in the new nation. So, whether they are discussing nineteenth-century interest groups, campaign finance, the constitutional basis for lobbying, or broad questions of representation (among others), contemporary political scientists still find that Madison's insights on the inevitability of factions, and their "mischiefs," shape how they think about organized interests.

A third theme found in many chapters is the question of how much influence organized interests exercise in affecting public policies. Although this question is not the immediate issue in any chapter, many authors do address the influence question because it lies at the heart of much of the attention that scholars, journalists, and citizens give to interests and lobbying. Moreover, in terms of trustworthiness, citizens rate lobbyists last among a range of occupations. The lobbyist stereotype, lately represented by convicted influence-peddler Jack Abramoff, emphasizes the story line of unethical, if not illegal, trades of favors for votes or favorable legislative actions.[4] From the perspective of almost all scholars who study interest groups, this alleged influence is difficult to pin down. To be sure, more than $3 billion is spent on lobbying each year, along with substantial campaign sums in every election cycle, and interests generally believe that their spending makes a difference. In individual cases, the impact of spending by interest groups can be substantial, but more systematic examinations find only the most modest effects.[5]

Coupled with these conclusions is a broad emphasis on the importance of information in lobbying. From the earliest days of informal lobbying in colonial America, providing high quality information has proven a core job for lobbyists. The emphasis on information relates directly to lobbying targets; scholars have found that lobbyists and interests focus their attention on friends in Congress, rather than trying to convert opponents. Even undecided legislators get no more attention than do one's friends. In a pair of influential articles, Richard Hall and colleagues found that groups—with campaign contributions and information—can elicit more activity from legislators.[6] In addition, groups subsidize legislators with cost-free information, which can subsequently be used to craft arguments on behalf of policies as well as district-oriented explanations of their votes.

In the end, organized interests and lobbyists have been part and parcel of American politics from before the founding of the Republic. Over time, groups have grown far more formalized and diverse, and lobbying has become increasingly professionalized. Still, the core issues of providing information to decision makers and finding ways to organize effectively have driven organized interests for more than two centuries. What follows is a brief introduction to the substance of this volume with its thirty-six original chapters covering the spectrum of interest group politics and lobbying.

INTEREST GROUP POLITICS BEFORE THE 1950s

The growth of pluralist analyses of American politics (Chapter 6 by Dara Strolovitch and M. David Forrest) and the publication of Truman's *The Governmental Process* in 1951 focused many scholars' attention on organized interests, but they had long played important roles in representation, lobbying, and campaign finance (see Chapter 31 by Michael Franz for the latter). Indeed, Alexis de Tocqueville's celebration of American voluntary associations is a touchstone for almost all students of organized interests. Beyond this, however, Dan Tichenor and Jeremy Strickler (Chapter 2) argue that it was the growth of government itself, especially during and after the Civil War, that helped fuel a great increase in lobbying.

The growth of organized interests in the 1800s was built upon the firm foundation of two eighteenth-century developments. As Burdett Loomis concludes in Chapter 1, by the time of the Revolutionary War, the practice of lobbying—whether targeting the Crown, colonial governors, or colonial assemblies—was well developed, and the framers were familiar with group-based lobbying (merchants, religious groups) as they drew up the Constitution. Most important, the First Amendment established lobbying as a constitutionally protected activity (speech, petition, assembly).

By the end of the nineteenth century, voluntary groups had grown in numbers, and lobbyists had become fixtures in Washington and many state capitals. In Chapter 3 Elisabeth Clemens notes an "explosion of associational activity" in the 1800s, which reflects another trend across eras: the substantial growth of groups, regardless of the time period. Per Mancur Olson's analysis, many groups were not established for political purposes, but large memberships nevertheless made them potentially powerful political forces. Indeed, one hallmark of organized interests in the nineteenth century comes in the internal debates over how much political activity is advisable. In the pre–New Deal era, groups experimented with various associational forms and pathways to influence government and politics. Broad interests came to be represented by associations with particular goals, put forward by lobbyists and politically savvy chief executives.

With the growth of government in the New Deal and World War II years, American politics changed dramatically. Although the conventional wisdom is that groups form to seek favors from government, the causal arrow from the 1930s runs largely in the opposite direction. The government takes on a task such as nuclear power, interstate highways, Social Security, or securities regulation, and interests organize to affect subsequent policies and expenditures. By the 1950s this pattern had begun to occur regularly, and the Great Society policies of the 1960s spurred further growth.

BEYOND PLURALISM: THEORETICAL APPROACHES TO INTEREST GROUPS AND LOBBYING

In many ways, the history of the study of organized interests has two phases: before and after Mancur Olson published *The Logic of Collective Action* in 1965. As an economist, Olson asked a central, but ignored question: How do large membership groups sustain themselves, given that they seek collective benefits that are often available to everyone? Individuals—whether seniors (AARP), teachers (National Education Association), farmers (Farm Bureau)—should be content to be "free riders" who obtain the benefits of group actions without the costs of membership. Olson's approach constituted a serious challenge to pluralists like David Truman, who assumed that group formation was a natural phenomenon.

Over time, as Paul Johnson notes in Chapter 4, Olson's challenge to interest group scholars was addressed by cumulative research that demonstrated how the free-rider problem could be overcome. Indeed, groups did form, and often for explicitly political purposes. But Olson made scholars ask fundamental questions about group viability and representation. Even when groups do form and persist, Strolovich argues, subgroups (poor women, people of color) may be underrepresented in various ways.[7] Moreover, as Strolovich and Forrest detail in Chapter 6, societal interests are often expressed through social movements, which overlap, both in practice and in scholarly works, with organized interests.

The overall mosaic of interests, however represented, continues to receive attention under the umbrella of pluralism as a theoretic framework. In Chapter 5 Matt Grossman offers an extensive review of pluralist theory's evolution, as well as arguments as to when pluralism or neopluralism can be best applied. Still, political scientists continue to shy away from making overarching claims for group-based theories, which have not proven highly useful in promoting broad understanding of societal politics. In some ways, a more promising general approach to organized groups and lobbying has come in the application of economic analysis. Scott Ainsworth and Austin Clemens (Chapter 7) begin with Olson and offer a summary of the strands of economic analysis that have developed in his wake. Focusing largely on individual actors, they demonstrate the possibilities for generalization across groups, although this kind of analysis is subject to its own limitations.

In the end, interests have proven resistant to generalization; and the promise of pluralism as a framework has long faded, although not entirely. Organized interests are remain salient to almost all politics in the United States, yet they rarely stand at the center of broad explanations of political behavior or policy outcomes.

GROUPS AND THE GOVERNMENT (PARTIES, TOO)

The conventional wisdom regarding interest groups is that they organize at least in part to seek favorable policies, and this is frequently true, to be sure. But government itself often leads groups to form and establish relationships with legislators and administrators. Indeed, the growth of government from the 1930s to the present has led to great increases in the number and variety of organized interests. Although groups have traditionally interacted most with Congress and state legislatures, they also have become intertwined with the other most prominent national institutions—the executive, the courts, and political parties.

Beth Leech (Chapter 8) sets the stage here with a broad discussion of the growing web of relationships between and among organized interests and various government institutions, which has been assisted by the increase in good data on campaign finance and lobbying from the 1970s and 1990s, respectively. Leech argues that focusing too much on groups and their policy preferences diverts attention from the role that government plays in generating new groups and therefore more lobbying. In his work, Jonathan Rauch has argued that the increasing entanglement of large numbers of groups with many government agencies, as well as the easily approachable Congress, leads to "demosclerosis," or the inability of the government to respond effectively to new or chronic societal problems.[8]

Although scholars have focused largely on how interests lobby Congress, groups have long used the venues of the court system and the executive branch to achieve their goals. Indeed, one consistent tactic since the 1700s has been for interests to shop for the best possible venue to make their case. In the 1940s and 1950s the NAACP sought redress of its grievances in the federal courts, knowing that the southern-dominated U.S. Congress, especially the Senate, would not welcome its arguments. In their systematic survey of interest group-court politics, Karen O'Connor and Alixandra Yanus (Chapter 9) observe that organized interests consistently approach the courts to influence policy and to maintain their organizations. Even in defeat, groups can benefit from aggressively litigating an issue or seeking the rejection or confirmation of a judicial nominee.

Lobbying the executive branch, from the president to the smallest agency, has grown steadily since the 1930s, although the evidence is less comprehensive than it might be. Still, the complex relationships between the executive and organized interests are often as important as congressional linkages. In fact, Congress has consistently delegated tremendous amounts of decision-making authority to the executive branch, as in the 2010 passage of health care reforms. Moreover, as Mark Peterson (Chapter 10) observes, not only do groups seek favored policies from the executive, but also they are often on the receiving end of executive lobbying. In the politics of health care in 2010, the drug lobby, known as PhRMA, cut a deal with President Barack Obama relatively early in the process, promising to support reform in return for a clear limit on their costs going forward.[9] Overall, as the federal government has grown, more and more lobbying initiatives focus on the executive, and often the passage of a law by Congress represents not the end point, but the start of lobbying over outcomes.

In addition to the formal institutions of government, there are the political parties. The parties are major national institutions that shape the activities of groups and lobbyists. Since the 1980s by almost all indicators, American politics has become more partisan. In the 1950s and 1960s Congress was run by Democrats, but many of them were conservative, and a fair number of Republicans were moderate or even liberal. Groups and lobbyists felt little need (with some exceptions, such as Democratic-leaning unions) to identify with one party or the other. Indeed, such a practice would likely have reduced their effectiveness. By the late 1990s Republicans, who had won control of Congress, sought to make party ties a factor in which lobbyists and groups could succeed. House Majority Leader Tom DeLay's K Street Project, in concert with leading conservative lobbyists, worked hard to ensure that lobbyists would contribute generously to GOP coffers, and party leaders attempted to sway hiring decisions to favor Republican loyalists. In the end, these tactics were not especially successful, largely because most interests have goals distinct from parties.[10]

In Chapter 11 Paul Herrnson examines the overlapping yet different politics of parties and organized interests. Groups and parties are both representative institutions, but they approach this linkage in distinct ways. Parties aggregate broad interests before an election, seeking to control the official levers of power; organized interests reflect the preferences, desires, and demands of smaller groupings. Even as parties have grown stronger in the post-1980 era, interests have tended to splinter. As Herrnson notes, "The proliferation of narrow groups has often come at the expense of larger ones; in the 2009–2010 debate over health care, dozens of specific interests, such as teaching hospitals and nurse practitioners, weighed in on the legislation, a development that reduced the impact of the American Medical Association, which has lost its dominance in representing the medical community over the past fifty years." In the end, strong parties sometimes can push legislation through, but both before and after passage, groups and their lobbyists help shape, and often blunt, the ultimate outcomes.

The institutional structure of American politics does shape the nature of interest group actions in common ways, but there is also tremendous variation among broad categories of interests. This means that organized interests often adjust differently to particular policies, or seek out the most friendly venues when faced with a policy challenge. In short, generalizations across groups and types of groups are often difficult to make.

ORGANIZED INTERESTS AND LOBBYING: SECTOR BY SECTOR

Although any listing here is by definition arbitrary, there is a long tradition of examining groups by particular categories. Indeed, much general theorizing has come from the close, long-term examination of agricultural groups, as Adam Sheingate details in Chapter 12. The agricultural sector has changed gradually over time, with more specialty groups forming, thus diminishing the influence of the broad-based American Farm Bureau Federation. In other fields, such as homeland security and defense (Carmine Scavo, Chapter 14) or the environment (Chris Bosso, Chapter 22), changes have come much more quickly, either in response to an individual event (9/11) or a strong social movement (environmentalism in the 1960s). In both instances, a major government unit—the Department of Homeland Security and the Environmental Protection Agency—was formed and subsequently served as a focal point for much group activity. In general, the time lines for different groups vary greatly across sectors. Agricultural interests formed in the late nineteenth century; think tanks and civil rights organizations have a more recent vintage. Still other sectors, such as professional groups or business, have witnessed relatively steady growth over time. In short, the overall growth of organized interests may not be reflected in any single sector, nor should we expect it to be.

Even if scholars generally find pluralism as an inadequate overall framework for understanding American politics, the number and variety of interest groups remain remarkable. Moreover, the forms taken by these organized interests are likewise varied, ranging from professional associations (see Chris Witko, Chapter 20) to the panoply of government lobbies (see Beverly Cigler, Chapter 23; and Ken Godwin, Chapter 21, on education) to a wide range of foreign lobbies (see Arnd Jurgensen and Renan Levine, Chapter 24). Indeed, the institutionalization of organized interests and the representation of institutions (corporations, think tanks, state and local governments, among many others) contribute to Rauch's "demosclerosis."[11]

Virtually all sectors of society enjoy substantial and well-connected representation, to the point that enacting broad policy change becomes more and more difficult. Susan Orr and Peter Francia (Chapter 13), in their overview of business and labor, see not only the battle lines between these sectors, but also tremendous diversity within the business community. On major issues, such as health care, business groups have rarely presented an organized front, and this proved especially true in the 2009–2010 struggle for reform; large and small businesses took different tacks, as did large insurance companies and the pharmaceutical industry, former allies in their opposition to President Bill Clinton's 1993 reform efforts.

The economics-based approach to organized interests, at least in Mancur Olson's early formulation, never would have predicted the growth and survival of groups that serve large populations often considered difficult to organize. These include civil rights organizations (Benjamin Marquez, Chapter 15), religious groups (James Guth, Chapter 17), and gender-based groups (Anne Costain, Chapter 18). Of special importance is the ability of these organizations to frame policy debates from perspectives that historically have been understated in American politics. At the same time, such well-represented points of view make policymaking more contentious and protracted than in the past. These circumstances are reinforced by the growth of think tanks, advocacy groups, and nonprofits, many of which have no membership base, but survive through the generosity of patrons and contributors.

The proliferation of these entities, well documented by Richard Skinner (Chapter 16) and Kay Schlozman (Chapter 19), offer further evidence as to the extensive reach of interest group politics. In addition, although many of these organizations provide information to decision makers, relatively few do original research. Rather, whether think tanks, nonprofits, or advocacy groups, their information is broadly "interested"—that is, presented from a point of view in order to move the debate in a particular direction. In many ways, these institutions reflect the twenty-first-century progeny of Schattschneider's 1960 observations as to expanding the scope of conflict and changing the mobilization of bias within the society at large.[12]

All in all, the expansion and diversity of groups means that they have to work hard to get their message across, whether to legislators, other policymakers, groups of citizens, or the public at large. This in turn means more lobbying, in more forms.

LOBBYING

Lobbying in America is filled with contradictions. The American people have almost no respect for lobbyists, rating them at the bottom of any grouping of occupations. Yet policymakers not only put up with lobbyists, but also often rely on their knowledge and information. Journalists and pundits frequently focus on the high costs of elections, but lobbying expenses at least double all costs of electioneering. President Obama has spoken out against the power of lobbyists and sought to exclude them from his administration, but was forced to make numerous exceptions to this rule in hiring capable executive branch officials.

Although many studies and think tanks, such as the Center for Responsive Politics, focus on money when they analyze lobbying, the more powerful coin of the realm for lobbyists is information. Various political scientists have made this point. As noted previously, Richard Hall, writing with several co-authors, has made the most powerful case, as he has developed the idea that lobbyists provide an informational subsidy to legislators.[13] In Chapter 25 he and Katherine Bradley offer an overview of legislative lobbying. Members of Congress remain the focus of Washington lobbying, even though, ironically, they possess more staff resources than any set of lawmakers in the world.

Not only are lobbyists generally disrespected, their work is largely misunderstood. In three complementary chapters (26, 27, 28), Rogan Kersh, Gary Andres, and Dennis Johnson provide a rich view of lobbyists and what they do. Kersh offers detailed portraits of who lobbyists are and what they do in a world where we both distrust lobbyists in general and support the specific interests that rely heavily on them. Andres, with experience in the White House, on Capitol Hill, as the director of a major lobbying firm (Dutko), and possessing strong academic credentials, is in a unique position to address lobbyists' tactics. Andres places lobbying in the context of the exchange of information between government officials and lobbyists, and emphasizes the different ways in which all the participants in the process use information and mutually benefit from the exchange.

Dennis Johnson explores lobbying techniques that both complement and move beyond the largely insider tactics addressed by Kersh and Andres. Grassroots lobbying, while a popular and important tactic, does not even qualify as lobbying in terms of official reporting. Groups that seek to mobilize constituents and voters may not need to register, and their expenditures largely go unreported. Even less understood is the use of social media and other Internet lobbying—techniques that have become the fastest growing and most changeable in the entire field of lobbying. Johnson does yeoman service in providing a timely assessment of a developing subfield. Indeed, the very fact of its rapid changes means that regulating lobbying, even when intentions are good, is a difficult task. Who is a lobbyist? What constitutes lobbying? To what extent is it constitutionally protected, especially by the First Amendment? Ron Hrebenar and Clive Thomas (Chapter 29) take on this subject and offer an overview of the policies and challenges presented here.

INTERESTS AND ELECTIONS

As Allan Cigler and Heather Yates note (Chapter 30) organized interests have long sought to influence elections, as a direct link to winning policy victories. Prior to 1972, despite the best efforts of some pioneering scholars, there is simply not much authoritative or systematic information about campaign finance. Other electoral efforts, such as mobilizing votes by unions and other groups, were more obvious, but increasingly campaign finance has become the name of the game. Since the Federal Election Campaign Act (1971), soon followed by post–Watergate updates, parties and candidates, along with some groups, have been required to report campaign contributions. From the mid-1970s on, political scientists have enjoyed the luxury of having reasonably good data for empirical analysis. These data, produced largely by the Federal Election Commission, proved a boon to empirical studies of contribution patterns and campaign spending. The data gave birth to institutions such as the Center for Responsive Politics and the Campaign Finance Institute, which have provided both analysis and enhanced access to the FEC information. In many ways, this pattern has been repeated in the post-1995 lobbyist reporting requirements, which have opened up new possibilities for analysis. In Chapter 31 Michael Franz details the complex and changeable rules on campaign limits and disclosure, as they apply to groups. In the end, interests can usually find ways to invest in candidates and parties in almost any form that they desire, despite consistently greater efforts at maintaining limits and transparency.

The costs of congressional and presidential electioneering have grown steadily since the 1970s. Clyde Wilcox and Elliott Fullmer chart these trends in Chapter 32. The lengthy presidential primary process and the biennial congressional elections—especially when the control of Congress is at stake—provide endless opportunities for groups to affect electoral outcomes. But as costs rise, it has become more difficult for any given interest to make a substantial impact, with some notable exceptions. Still, given the fierce partisan battles for control of the White House and Congress, the perceived stakes for interests have risen steadily since the 1980s. And with rising costs and contributions have come increased attempts to regulate campaign finance and groups' participation in electoral politics, culminating in the 2002 Bipartisan Campaign Reform Act (BCRA). Robert Boatright (Chapter 33) addresses the legal, empirical, and normative issues that surround interests' electioneering. He concludes that disclosure remains the most acceptable tool for addressing this issue, in light of recent Supreme Court decisions that have seriously weakened BCRA's regulatory goals.

BEYOND WASHINGTON

Organized interests and lobbying have grown apace in states, localities, and abroad. Indeed, states' politics often look much like smaller versions of the federal version. Lobbyists cluster around state capitols, and groups organize in myriad ways to affect state policies. Anthony Nownes (Chapter 34) provides an overview, building on a growing body of comparative state-level research that can address issues such as the nature of interest group communities. If state research is patchy, scholarship on local groups and lobbying is even less comprehensive, which is strange, given that much of the early research on pluralism derives from city-level studies such as Robert Dahl's *Who Governs?* In Chapter 35 Eric Heberlig and Suzanne Leland pull together the extant findings and argue that these local venues offer increasing potential for group-based analysis.

Finally, Conor McGrath (Chapter 36) examines how American lobbying styles have been adopted and adapted in nations around the world. Although the American government structure encourages many varieties of lobbying, McGrath finds that only some American tactics are effective in other systems, most of which do not have the number of veto points and alternative venues that exist in the United States.

GROUPS, LOBBYING, AND AMERICAN POLITICS

In the end, organized interests and various forms of lobbying are omnipresent in American politics. Many groups have great resources and seek systematic influence. Still, the study of interest groups and lobbying does not provide a coherent overall perspective on American politics. Groups do play a role in almost all politics, but they are rarely central, at least in terms of providing full-blown explanations for political behavior and policy outcomes. Groups and lobbyists are always in the mix and are continuing elements of representation at all levels of political life. This volume demonstrates the richness of group politics at a time when all interests seek to have their voices heard. This makes both for vibrant politics and frequent gridlock, a mixed blessing that continues to define our political system.

NOTES

1. Arthur Bentley, *The Process of Government: A Study of Social Pressures* (Chicago: University of Chicago Press, 1908); David B. Truman, The *Governmental Process: Political Interests and Public Opinion* (New York: Knopf, 1951).

2. E. E. Schattschneider, *The Semisovereign People: A Realists View of Democracy in America* (New York: Holt, Rinehart, and Winston, 1960).

3. Jonathan Rauch, *Demosclerosis: The Silent Killer of American Democracy* (New York: Times Books, 1994); Theodore Lowi, *The End of Liberalism: The Second Republic of the United States* (New York: W. W. Norton, 1979); Robert Salisbury, "The Paradox of Interest Groups in Washington—More Groups, Less Clout," in *The New American Political System,* 2nd ed., ed. Anthony King (Washington: American Enterprise Institute, 1993).

4. See, for example, Peter Stone, *Heist: Superlobbyist Jack Abramoff, His Republican Allies, and the Buying of Washington* (New York: Farrar, Strauss, and Giroux, 2006). In addition, Abramoff became the fodder for a commercial film, *Casino Jack.*

5. See Robert Kaiser, *So Damn Much Money* (New York: Knopf, 2009). Also, see Raquel Alexander, Susan Scholz, and Stephen Mazza, "Lobbying ROI: An Empirical Analysis under the American Jobs Creation Act of 2004," *Journal of Law and Politics* 25 (2010).

6. Richard L. Hall and Alan V. Deardorff, "Lobbying as Legislative Subsidy," *American Political Science Review* 100, 1 (2006): 69–84; Richard L. Hall and Frank W. Wayman, "Buying Time: Moneyed Interests and the Mobilization of Bias in Congressional Committees," *American Political Science Review* 84, 3 (September 1990): 797–820.

7. Dara Z. Strolovitch, *Affirmative Advocacy: Race, Class, and Gender in Interest Group Politics* (Chicago: University of Chicago Press, 2007).

8. Rauch, *Demosclerosis.*

9. Lawrence Jacobs and Theda Skocpol, *Health Care Reform and American Politics* (New York: Oxford Press, 2010), 71.

10. Burdett Loomis, "Does K Street Run through Capitol Hill," in *Interest Group Politics,* ed. Allan J. Cigler and Burdett A. Loomis (Washington, D.C.: CQ Press, 2007).

11. Rauch, *Demosclerosis;* Robert H. Salisbury, "Interest Representation: The Dominance of Institutions," *American Political Science Review* 78, 1 (March 1984): 64–76.

12. Schattchneider, *The Semisovereign People.*

13. Hall and Deardorff, "Lobbying as Legislative Subsidy."

PART I ★ INTEREST GROUPS: FROM THE FRAMING TO THE TWENTIETH CENTURY

CHAPTER 1	The Evolution of Groups and Lobbying in 18th Century America	11
CHAPTER 2	Interest Groups and Lobbying in the Nineteenth Century: Tocqueville's America	21
CHAPTER 3	Groups in Industrializing America and the Origins of Popular Interest Group Politics	35

chapter 1

The Evolution of Groups and Lobbying in 18th Century America

by Burdett A. Loomis

THE FRAMERS OF THE U.S. Constitution took the idea of faction very seriously. Much of their concern focused on what they called "majority faction"—the idea that a majority might well become tyrannical and oppress smaller groups within society. Although they did not foresee the rise of political parties (in essence, competing prospective majority factions), their perception that a wide range of minority interests needed protection proved prescient. They famously created a system of checks and balances, both in the separation of powers and in a well-defined federal system that divided responsibilities between state and national governments. With the adoption of the First Amendment, the rights of groups to organize ("the right of the people peaceably to assemble"), to speak freely, and to petition the government became institutionalized.

By the early 1790s American interest groups, either existing or potential, possessed the right to lobby the government and a host of other targets they might influence. In particular, merchants from major cities, bondholders, planters, and religious groups sought specific government actions that would work to their benefit. From the first days of the nation under the Constitution, James Madison and other framers fully expected interests to participate in the give-and-take of government, at both the state and national levels. With a long history of interacting with the English bureaucracy and Parliament, as well as with colonial governors and assemblies, interest groups in the new nation proved more than ready to take part effectively in politics and policymaking, often through lobbying or the stimulation of constituents' support at the grassroots SA: level.

This chapter examines the development of groups and lobbying in the post-1700 colonial period, during the run-up to the Revolution and in its aftermath, and in the first decade of the American experiment in democratic government. American interests became increasingly well organized over the eighteenth century, although they would scarcely pass for modern groups. Still, even in their ephemeral manifestations of this period, a host of active interests served as harbingers of the complex, resilient group-based politics that has long characterized the American political system.

THE POLITICS OF AMERICAN INTERESTS, 1690–1750s: THE ENGLISH CONNECTIONS

Understanding the growing involvement of American interests in policymaking and politics requires an initial focus on their roots in two distinct, but related, realms—English institutions and American colonial assemblies. American interests, such as merchants and religious groups, were ordinarily defined in local, or at most colony-by-colony, terms in the 1600s. Their occasional contact with government came through petitions, which could go to their nascent assemblies or to the Crown's American agents, the colonial governors, or to London.

In the twenty-five years following the Glorious Revolution (1688), English government grew in size and became more bureaucratic, and organized interests in England provided officials with a key commodity—information.[1] Trade with America was growing, as were the number and diversity of American religious groups, but the Crown did not increase the size of its colonial bureaucracy. American and English interests alike benefited from their ability to provide accurate information to the London-based bureaucracy, especially to the Board of Trade, which regulated commercial relations with the colonies. As historian Alison Olson argues, information was central to whatever influence American groups were likely to have in the 1690–1750s period.[2] British rule could not be built on coercion in the colonies; therefore, American interests, their allied English interests, and the Crown all stood to benefit if they could work together through the effective communication of accurate information about colonial needs and government actions.

High-quality information was therefore extremely important to American interests, to their English counterparts, and to various institutions of government on both sides of the Atlantic. With increased trade, growing populations, and more commercial and governmental complexity, issues such as taxes, tariffs, land disputes, and the rules for religious practice all had the potential to become highly contentious, which made accurate information essential to all participants. To deal with this growing complexity, by the early eighteenth century, interests in various colonies had begun to hire agents to address their concerns directly to Parliament and the Board of Trade. In 1712, after some years of informal representation, the South Carolina legislature appointed a permanent agent to represent the colony's mercantile interests in London. The legislation explicitly describes the representation of mercantile interests, not persons, before Parliament; in fact, the agent took on many of the colony's interests, with most of his efforts directed at the Board of Trade. Not only did South Carolina hire a lobbyist, but also one who, in modern terms, shopped for the most welcoming venue to make his case.[3]

This action did not mean that the colony's merchants were united in their requests of the Crown; indeed, squabbling among merchants was common, which made it difficult to represent their would-be collective interests. Still, the Charleston merchants, for all their disagreements, came to appreciate the power of effective lobbying, when carried out by London commercial interests. This benefit was especially apparent in lengthy debates over trade restrictions on rice, when in 1774 it finally became clear that a unified front helped them reduce the effects of policies long in place. Historian Rebecca Starr observes that the merchants might well have learned two lessons in their rice trade lobbying: first, that succeeding in winning mitigation of policies based on unequal power (Crown versus colonies) was just a step from actually lobbying to change the balance of power itself; and, second, that speaking with a unified voice was an essential precursor to convincing the Board of Trade or Parliament of the justice of their requests.[4]

More generally, Richard Brown argues that the major figures in relations between England and the colonies were "Anglo-American politicians," who needed to satisfy constituencies in both America and England.[5] Although not all of these individuals lobbied, many did, in terms of linking interests and decision makers in one venue (a colony or city) to those in another (London). Brown sees a stable system of relations developing over the mid-eighteenth century, which

Even in the early eighteenth century, colonial governments understood the importance of having agents in London to further their commercial interests. The South Carolina legislature hired such an agent in 1712 to represent the interests of the state's burgeoning trade, including merchants in Charles Towne.

begins to come apart in the decade preceding the American Revolution.

The heyday of strong relations between American and London groups came between 1721 and 1754, when British governments headed by three skillful prime ministers provided a stable framework for the useful exchange of information.[6] For American interests, the strength of their allied English groups was extremely important. To the extent that English agents could approach influential patrons within the aristocracy and important contacts within the bureaucracy, American interests could be more effectively represented as they petitioned the government on various colonial issues, ranging from tariffs to religious freedom to land disputes.

Although some interests did become reasonably well organized during this period, it would be a mistake to think of American groups of this era as modern organized interests. Churches were generally the best organized, both internally and in their relations with their British counterparts. Merchants, often loosely organized around coffeehouses as gathering spots, generated less structure than churches, and planters/farmers were even less organized, which is not surprising, given their relative isolation.

At their best, American interests worked with their English counterparts to gain information about parliamentary and ministerial actions in order to anticipate them and provide information that might enhance or mitigate the effects of decisions. These groups became part of the regular process of governance, and yet they did not lobby on causes, as modern groups would.[7] Rather, American interests were most effective in petitioning for specific actions or relief from general policies, set either by the Board of Trade or Parliament. They could affect policies on the ground in America by building bridges back to English groups and government actors, whom they could help by providing accurate information on colonial issues, desires, and concerns.

At the same time that evolving American groups became part of the London political landscape, they also interacted in significant ways with colonial governors. The most effective executives, appointed by the Crown, were those who understood that many interests had better information about London affairs than they did. Virginia governor William Gooch, who served from 1727 to 1749, succeeded in working with various groups in the largest colony to maintain his long tenure.[8] Although many new groups were forming, especially on the frontier, Gooch understood that he needed to placate the Anglican planters, who made up an elite that combined religious and economic strength within the colony. He worked with the old elite to help them understand the need to concede some power to newer groups. Keeping the peace among the various interests allowed Gooch to become well informed about their issues and anticipate the potential consequences.

The mid–eighteenth-century American interest group system, to the extent it could be described that way, was highly oriented toward specific petitions and the exchange of useful information with London interests. American groups became central to British governance in an era of economic growth that did not lead to much greater bureaucracy in the colonies. As long as strong prime ministers and a reliable Board of Trade remained in place, this system remained stable. But after 1754 the Parliament began to strengthen its role in Anglo-American affairs, and this change meant that colonial groups' access to power decreased and policymaking became more uncertain. Groups crave access and stability, and, as Parliament found its legs in the 1750s and 1760s, American interests and their London allies found themselves increasingly on the outside.

INTERESTS AND COLONIAL LEGISLATURES THROUGH THE 1760s: NEW TARGETS FOR INFLUENCE

The development of American colonial assemblies, much like the related growth of organized interests, derived directly from the British experience. Almost all British colonies created legislatures in their early years of existence, led by Virginia's House of Burgesses, established in 1619. The same lack of central control from London that encouraged the formation of organized interests also contributed to the development of legislative bodies. Moreover, pressure came from colonial landowners for Britain "to provide the same rights to security of property and civic participation that appertained to independent English property holders."[9] Historian Jack Greene concludes that colonial legislators were often men who sought to advantage themselves and their colleagues in property acquisition, business dealings, or social status.[10] At the same time, the colonial legislative elites did not represent formal, organized interests. Individuals might petition the assemblies, but groups rarely approached them with the kinds of requests or demands common in contemporary legislative politics. Still, the petitioning process did lead to real changes, in that up to half the laws of some colonies originated in this way.[11]

Given the small populations of the colonies, at least in the early eighteenth century, legislators addressed the concerns of individual constituents, or small ad hoc groups, rather than those of organized groups. "Interests" were served, in that landowners, merchants, churches, and local units of governments were often catered to, with a host of policies, such as the provision of roads, modest social services, and protection from natives or other nations' colonies.

If the forty years after 1714 witnessed the growth of American interest groups in British politics, they also saw a maturation in colonial assemblies, where increasing numbers of veteran legislators could address a new environment in which dominant elites gave way to more pluralistic interests.[12] Effective legislatures were crucial for reducing the potential for conflict. By the 1760s and 1770s, Greene concludes, "a political system emerged [with] . . . political structures for the routinization of conflict, such as interest groups or parties [and this] was peculiarly modern in form and represented a transition from traditional to modern politics."[13]

That said, the relations between interests and colonial assemblies were scarcely "modern" in the pre–Revolutionary War era, when demands upon legislative bodies were modest at best. Olson reports that just eighteen towns in Massachusetts appealed any local dispute to the assembly in the 1690–1730 period.[14] The tendency was to take disputes to England, not the provincial assembly, whose decision-making authority was less definitive because it was subject to the governor's veto.

Over the course of the eighteenth century, citizen petitions to colonial assemblies became a more common tool to propose, support, modify, or oppose prospective legislation. In earlier times, petitions were infrequent and usually came from a single individual on a highly specific matter. By the 1700s "petitions increasingly represented the appeals of informal groups for legislative action."[15] Between 1715 and 1765 the average number of legislative petitions per colony almost tripled from 26.5 per annum at the beginning of the period to 75.7 at the end.[16] Equally important, petitions addressed bills at every stage of the legislative process. Although still not modern lobbying, such activity represented the work of roughly organized interests that had come to understand how the legislative process worked.

The institutionalization of the colonial legislatures contributed to the growth of interest group actions. The speakership evolved into a more powerful office in many assemblies, and, even more important, committees, both standing and select, became integral to legislative organization.[17] In Virginia and Pennsylvania the standing committees employed subcommittees to expedite their work. Such decentralization broadly anticipated the U.S. Congress of the mid-twentieth century, and it allowed for groups to direct their attention to specialist legislators, who were often receptive and sympathetic to well-informed arguments from constituents outside the chamber. The modern parallels continue in that legislative turnover decreased substantially in many colonies, leading to a rising influence among experienced legislators serving as chairs of standing committees.[18]

Linking the committees and outside groups was their mutual need for information. Legislative committees sometimes "aggressively sought information outside the assemblies, from time to time holding hearings across their respective states."[19] Interested parties did not need to go to the legislature; instead, legislators would come to them.

These developments can all sound quite modern, and in many ways the processes do provide glimpses of a more developed system of interest group politics. But even toward the end of this period, most interests were not well organized, often building on informal contacts when an important issue arose.

Starr concludes in her assessment of the emerging South Carolina trade lobby in the first two-thirds of the eighteenth century: "[A]n elemental familiarity with the rudiments of lobbying may be . . . said to help account for the commercial lobby's ready reception into the province's political culture. However, the integration of these elements into a systematic strategy available for repeated use, failed to develop before the 1760s."[20] In short, neither the organization of most groups nor their capacity to use recognizable lobbying tactics suggests that interests in the American colonies had developed an identifiable set of organized groups or an obvious array of influence-oriented skills. But they did understand that communicating effectively to the legislature, as well as to the Crown, could pay off handsomely.

AMERICAN INTERESTS IN THEORY AND PRACTICE, 1770s–1787

As Olson details in her authoritative *Making the Empire Work*, the eighteenth-century heyday of American-Anglo lobbying, with its cooperation between interests on both sides of the Atlantic, was coming to an end in the 1750s and 1760s. The Board of Trade and influential ministers lost power to Parliament, which proved considerably less welcoming to petitions by or in behalf of American interests, whether religious, agricultural, or mercantile.[21] But across the colonies, a host of interests had gained experience in organizing, often on an ad hoc basis, and in seeking to inform or even influence decision makers, whether in London or in colonial capitals.

In addition, the idea of "interest" began to be defined more broadly both in rhetoric and practice. Cathy Matson and Peter Onuf argue that although successful American merchants benefited from the mercantilist approach to trade, such a philosophy "could not completely disguise the subordinate, dependent status of the colonies."[22] In its stead, some colonists argued in favor of free trade, which would define the American interest very differently from being a part of the British system. Broadly inclusive American nonimportation movements of the late 1760s, which sought to attack the mercantilist imbalance, represented nongovernmental group actions to restrain trade, but they had modest success in changing British commercial policy. Still, interests were being defined far more expansively than simply in terms of small groupings of merchants or manufacturers.

Along these same lines, some narrow American interests began to form coalitions among like-minded groups. In Massachusetts, merchants and mechanics joined together not only to lobby, but also to support particular slates of candidates in colonial elections. Indeed, such public action illustrates a new development for American interests—the emergence of lobbies espousing causes, either narrow (ethnic societies, such as German or Irish groups, or library supporters) or broad, such as the Sons of Liberty or extensive nonimportation groups. These "public opinion" lobbies, as Olson calls them, were organized along a new, prerevolutionary dimension of opposition to the Crown.[23] This development rapidly placed established interests at risk of fragmenting as they chose sides over a new definition of what E. E. Schattschneider calls the "scope of conflict."[24] Merchants, manufacturers, and religious adherents had to choose whether to identify with the broad, radical sentiments of the pre-Revolutionary groups or try to maintain their traditional group identities. In the end, many long-standing American interests broke apart in this period, as the decision about whether or not to join the Revolution superseded all others.

The 1786–1787 uprising of farmers, known as Shays's Rebellion, illustrated the need for a system of government that allowed groups representing varied interests access to those making the laws. Pictured here are Daniel Shays and his lieutenant Job Shattuck from an eighteenth-century pamphlet supporting the rebellion.

Although some groups did begin to function within a national context during and immediately after the Revolution, much of the representation of interests during this period came through the states within the highly decentralized framework of the Articles of Confederation and the Continental Congress. Relatively stable coalitions among the northern and southern states formed within the weak Congress, rendering it divided to the point that its stalemate led to the Constitutional Convention.[25] During the Revolutionary period, economic interests actively sought to interpret free market principles within the Continental Congress, but great divisions and the weakness of the central government prevented definitive action, and interests sometimes turned their attention to state governments, where they had better luck.[26] But until there was a stable national government, interests of all types would find it difficult, if not impossible, to defend themselves in the existing national institutions. Relying on state governments gave interests some satisfaction, but created a patchwork of policies that worked against overall coherence in either policymaking or lobbying. Still, even if interests could not agree on many policies, they could come together in expressing their need for a stronger central government, in which they could reliably press the demands and seek redress of their grievances on a national basis.

One aggrieved Massachusetts farmer, Daniel Shays, assembled an armed group of about 1,000 to march on Worcester and Springfield and provoke fear in government and economic elites. Shays's Rebellion (1786–1787) was eventually put down by local militias, but the uprising demonstrated the need for institutions that could respond to legitimate grievances and thorny issues. The Constitutional Convention of 1787 was called in part because of the clear failure of the Articles of Confederation to provide any adequate access to government for dissatisfied interests.

INTERESTS AND THE CONSTITUTION IN THEORY AND PRACTICE, 1787–1800

The members of the American political elite who framed the American Constitution also shaped its implementation over the first twenty-five years of the country's existence. Grounded in the political theory of the prior century and the practical politics of colonial legislatures, the Continental Congress, and the struggle for independence, most of the framers had participated actively within the milieu of interest groups and lobbying prior to the Constitutional Convention of 1787. Above all, James Madison's approach to interests—or factions—directly affected the structure of the Constitution, the politics of its ratification, and its impact on the nascent group and party systems that develop in the first decade of the Republic.[27]

Without question, Madison's most important contribution to the formation of organized interests and the ultimate encouragement of lobbying was to help raise the actions of speech, assembly, and petition to core rights in the First Amendment. American politicians, 200-plus years after the adoption of this amendment, frequently criticize lobbying and seek to regulate it in numerous ways, but no one seriously considers banning the practice or even severely restricting it. The First Amendment rights are clear, and the

James Madison understood the positive role interest groups could play in a democratic system, but he also advocated for a system of government that would prevent groups from obtaining an inordinate amount of power.

mix of thousands of groups and tens of thousands of lobbyists continues to reflect these basic rights. Still, much as they did not foresee the development of political parties, neither did the framers understand the full implications of the First Amendment guarantees.

In more mundane, but nevertheless important, ways, Madison actively involved himself in group politics as a private citizen and as a legislator. In addition, he helped guide one of the great public lobbying campaigns of all time in his co-authorship of the *Federalist Papers* and in his contributions to organized ratification efforts across the colonies.[28] Simultaneously, anti-Federalist forces came together as a national interest group to oppose the ratification. These opposing forces were distinctly groups, not political parties, although they developed into party-like organizations during the 1790s.

With the ratification of the Constitution and the subsequent election to the initial Congress, citizens had targets whom they could petition to address their particular concerns, seek redress of their grievances, or clarify administrative rules. At the same time, interests, even if not well organized, could put pressure on members of Congress to lobby on their behalf.

The first Congress endured a blizzard of petitions from a wide variety of sources. Although many petitions came from individuals seeking resolution of a grievance, a substantial number came from groups, such as tradesmen, mechanics, and shipwrights, and the group often reflected the interests of a specific city or town. Moreover, trade-oriented groups sometimes submitted petitions that reflected "sophisticated campaigns" based on coordination among groups in several cities.[29]

Individual members of Congress often became conduits for particular interests. Such representation was hardly surprising: the state legislatures of the 1780s had become more open to observation, and interests often sought to elect their own, largely so they could fulfill their given desires. Democracy was in full bloom, with frequent elections and broadened suffrage. Gordon Wood observes, "By the 1780s it was obvious to many, including Madison, that a 'spirit of locality' was destroying 'the aggregate interests of the community.' Everywhere the gentry leaders complained of popular legislative practices that today are taken for granted—logrolling, horse-trading, and pork-barreling that benefited *special and local interest groups.*"[30]

As much as any interest, land speculators/investors sought to influence governmental outcomes for their own benefit, even if, as with Madison, they cloaked their arguments in the rhetoric of national interest. Manasseh Cutler, a clergyman-turned-lobbyist for land speculators, may have functioned as a model for other would-be lobbyists, but he was scarcely unusual in pursuing his goal of favorable treatment for an interest-based consortium. The government's role in land transactions encouraged particular corporations or groupings to seek advantage in their speculations; indeed, positive action from Congress could prove crucial to the profitability of many ventures. In essence, as most group theories postulate, organized interests approached the government with requests for specific actions, in this case land deals. But in day-to-day policymaking, the central government also frequently sought out interests—even creating groups—that could contribute to the success of its policies (see Chapter 10).

The new nation's executive branch asserted itself in this way almost immediately, most notably as it incorporated the visions and carried out the preferences of Alexander Hamilton. Entering the cabinet as perhaps its most powerful and forceful member, Secretary of the Treasury Hamilton faced the formidable task of placing the fledgling nation on sound financial footing. Hamilton understood from the start how important it was to work with the largest and strongest financial interests, initially in establishing a national bank. This would come about by the government engaging "the monied interests immediately in it by making them contribute the whole or part of the stock and giving them the whole or part of the

MADISON, FACTIONS, *FEDERALIST* 10, AND PRACTICAL POLITICS

In *Federalist* 10 James Madison defined "factions" as:

> A number of citizens, whether accounting to a majority or a minority of the whole, who are united and actuated by some common impulse of passion, or of interest, adverse to the rights of other citizens, or to the permanent and aggregate interests of the community.[1]

Although both modern political parties and organized interests fall under this broad definition, electoral parties simply did not exist in 1787, while many early versions of interest groups did. Madison had seen many factions unite "through organizations to promote, through government, interests like . . . '[a] landed interest, a manufacturing interest, a mercantile interest, a moneyed interest.'"[2] In short, as he constructed a Constitution that would provide for centralized national power, which most interests desired, he proposed an institutional structure that would not only encourage interests to act politically but also prevent them from exercising disproportionate amounts of power.

Still, the most common Madisonian phrase drawn from *Federalist* 10 is his warning as to "the mischief of faction," and the most optimistic interpretation of his words there relies on the nature of a large republic to dilute the potentially damaging effects of faction. But Madison the practical politician proved far more accepting of a positive role for organized interests. Political scientist James Yoho notes Madison's active participation in a series of groups, ranging from student demonstrations at Princeton (1770), protest meetings in the 1770s, membership in a county "committee of safety" in Virginia, and a successful petition by planters to limit tobacco production in favor of more valuable revolutionary products.[3]

On an even more regular basis, Madison, as a state or national legislator, advocated on behalf of particular interests, including denominations that wished to disestablish the Anglican Church in Virginia and land speculators who were his constituents. In the latter case, "Madison found it easy enough to help his fellow Virginians by couching his position in terms of what was best for the country—which came to be his customary approach."[4] And these were just some of Madison's actions that helped particular groups, or so-called "special interests."

In the end, Madison as political theorist framed factions of all sorts in negative terms, arguing for their control, not their free rein. But as a politician, whether in or out of office, he recognized the legitimacy of group actions and claims, at least for those with whom he agreed. Overall, Madison anticipated group actions far more clearly than he did the formation of political parties, whose rapid development shaped the nation's future in profound and unforeseen ways.

1. James Madison, *Federalist* 10, in *The Federalist*, ed. Henry Cabot Lodge (New York: Putnam, 1907), 55.
2. James Yoho, "Madison on the Beneficial Effects of Interest Groups: What Was Left Unsaid in 'Federalist' 10," *Polity* 27, 4 (Summer 1995): 592. These paragraphs draw extensively on this article.
3. Ibid., 598.
4. Ibid., 599.

profits," thereby linking "the interests of the state in an intimate connexion with those of the rich individuals belonging to it."[31] More specifically, Hamilton sought to build his overall program of a national political economy with the assistance of an organized interest of his own creation: the Society for Establishing Useful Manufactures (SEUM).

As with many early organized interests, SEUM cannot be considered a modern interest group; it was a government corporation, established in New Jersey, which was to be a model for Hamilton's broad scheme to increase trade and bolster manufacturing. In the end, Hamilton faced considerable difficulties in catering to both domestic manufacturing interests and those oriented toward free trade. Moreover, his initial choice to head SEUM was William Duer, who knew little of manufacturing, but as Hamilton's assistant at Treasury he understood the secretary's fiscal program and possessed excellent "contacts with large merchant-creditors."[32] SEUM's ventures never got off the ground, partly because of too much focus on speculation. And Jeffersonian-Republicans found they could build on manufacturers' distaste for this Federalist policy, especially among those smaller entities that were short of capital.[33]

More generally, the Federalists sought to build networks of local support, often based on patronage. Hamilton built explicitly on the idea of interest in his attempt to create a strong central government "by increasing the number of ligaments between the Government and the interests of Individuals."[34] To be sure, on occasion the government might direct its attention to highly specific interests of a given person. Much more powerful would be an effort to address the shared interests of a group of individuals.

Whether in Madison's constitutional architecture, Hamilton's linkage of interests to the national government, the petitions of individuals and groups, or the political elite's comfort in working with established interests, the new nation of the 1790s was already one in which well-organized groups were playing major roles in politics and policymaking.

SETTING THE STAGE: INTERESTS AND GROUPS IN EIGHTEENTH-CENTURY AMERICA

To be clear, organized interests in American politics, to the extent they existed at all in the eighteenth century, did not look like the interest groups that formed in the late

THE FIRST TRUE LOBBYIST? MANASSEH CUTLER AND LAND ACQUISITION IN THE 1780s

A Congregational pastor by vocation, Manasseh Cutler demonstrated how a private interest could change government policy to its overwhelming advantage. As historian Jeffrey Pasley states, Cutler "pulled off what is arguably the greatest feat of lobbying in American history, the 1787 purchase of several million acres of public land on behalf of a group of . . . Revolutionary war veterans and land speculators calling themselves the Ohio Company."[1] The Land Ordinance of 1787 had opened up land ownership to thousands of individuals, but Cutler, acting as agent of the Ohio Company, sought an entire region of the Northwest Territory for the corporation. The government was being asked to sell a huge block of land, mostly on credit, and eventually payable in Revolutionary War debt certificates, worth pennies on the dollar.

Cutler arrived in New York, then the nation's capital, on July 5, 1787, and left twenty-two days later, his job complete. By October he had made the first of eight $500,000 payments, delivering debt certificates accumulated by the group. Remarkably, this down payment permitted the Ohio Group to occupy and develop the initial 750,000 acres without receiving a formal deed. But Cutler's job was not completed; much like modern lobbyists, he monitored the implementation of the land purchase. By 1789 the debt certificates had risen in value, and the consortium found it increasingly difficult to make their payments. Cutler returned to the capital in 1790 to press his case for a lower per-acre price and an extended payment deadline. Immediately, Cutler confronted a problem: Treasury Secretary Alexander Hamilton's ambitious set of financial proposals were dominating the congressional agenda. Like any good lobbyist, Cutler understood the virtue of timing and personal relationships. Discerning that this was an inopportune time to lobby legislators in the capital, Cutler "visited members in their homes, quietly rounding up support for a rather cheeky request that the contract price be knocked down to twenty cents per acre," which would save the company $500,000.[2] In this endeavor, Cutler ultimately failed, largely because Congress simply did not take up his proposal.

He left New York, but was back in Philadelphia, the new capital, in March 1792, when the entire deal was at risk. Again, the members disappointed him, as he found it hard to command their attention, either because committees could not mount quorums or that the legislators were caught up in the nonstop "Philadelphia entertainments." Still, Cutler prevailed, working the congressional system as well as any contemporary lobbyist. Drawing on friendships with members based on geographic or college ties, Cutler helped create a special committee whose members acted quickly on his proposal to reduce the price for the entire 1.5 million-acre tract to twenty cents per acre. Although the final legislative product was not quite as generous, the bill passed through both chambers in about six weeks, with Cutler's special lobbying target, Vice President John Adams, casting the deciding vote.

What accounted for Cutler's pathbreaking success? Pasley argues that while some questionable bargaining did occur, Cutler's lobbying victory largely derived from his style or "complaisance," which was part of a genteel culture in which the capacity to make others feel at ease was highly valued, especially given contentious circumstances. Modern lobbyists would recognize such a quality in an instant; Cutler, the well-read and personable pastor, knew how to make others feel at ease and important, and none more so than his targets with the American Congress.

1. Jeffrey L. Pasley, "Private Access and Public Power: Gentility and Lobbying in the Early Congresses," in *The House & Senate in the 1790s: Petitioning, Lobbying, and Institutional Development*, ed. Kenneth R. Bowling and Donald R. Kennon (Athens: Ohio University Press, 2002), 57–99. This summary draws heavily on the Pasley article, and all quotations come from pages 78–79.
2. Ibid., 81–82.

nineteenth century or proliferated in the late twentieth century. There was no involvement in electoral politics, nor were there scores of professional lobbyists who established strong relationships with members of Congress. Nor were there membership organizations such as trade unions or manufacturers' associations or interest-based groups such as the National Rifle Association or the Sierra Club.

Still, it is remarkable how strongly the interest-based politics of the 1700s presaged strategies and tactics that would become commonplace in group organization and lobbying as the United States government grew larger and matured. Perhaps most important, the early and continuing emphasis on providing information reflects much contemporary political science scholarship on the capacity of organized interests to affect the policymaking process.[35] Even before interests regularly hired paid lobbyists or devised extensive public relations campaigns, they understood that communicating effectively with decision makers represented a powerful tool in winning favorable treatment.

In addition, eighteenth-century interests discovered that working in coalitions was useful, as was finding the proper venue for seeking action. American groups therefore often ignored colonial assemblies in the early eighteenth century, as they chose to press their cases before the Board of Trade in London, where they could be represented by like-minded English groups, most often merchants or religious denominations. Of special importance was the ways in which legislative development in the colonies provided useful targets for organized interests. Strong Speakers and growing committee systems meant that groups could systematically work with powerful legislators, who understood that they could benefit from solid ties with organized constituencies.

Finally, influential framers such as Madison and Hamilton—regardless of their philosophical positions—became early and energetic players at interest group politics within the first few years of the ratification of the Constitution, which was itself designed to allow interests many access points within the national government. As the federal government took shape in the 1790s, the roots of interest group politics had already grown deep in American political soil. Moreover, with the Constitution's guarantee of rights to assemble, petition, and, most important, to speak, organized interests were assured of a prominent place in the politics of the new nation.

NOTES

1. Alison G. Olson, *Making the Empire Work: London and American Interest Groups, 1690–1790* (Cambridge: Harvard University Press, 1991).

2. Ibid., 57–58.

3. Rebecca Starr, *A School for Politics: Commercial Lobbying and Political Culture in Early South Carolina* (Baltimore: Johns Hopkins University Press, 1998), 26–27.

4. Ibid., 31.

5. Richard Brown, "The Anglo-American Political System, 1675–1775: A Behavioral Analysis," in *Anglo-American Political Relations, 1675–1775,* ed. Alison G. Olson and Richard M. Brown (New Brunswick, N.J.: Rutgers University Press, 1970), 14–30.

6. Olson, *Making the Empire Work,* 94ff.

7. Ibid., 124.

8. This section draws on ibid., 126–128.

9. Jack P. Greene, "Colonial Assemblies," in *Encyclopedia of the American Legislative System,* ed., Joel H. Sibley (New York: Charles Scribner's Sons, 1994), 24. The following section draws on this article in general.

10. Ibid., 28.

11. Ibid., 30.

12. Jack P. Greene, "Legislative Turnover in British America, 1696 to 1775," *William and Mary Quarterly* 39 (July 1981): 451–456.

13. Greene, "Colonial Assemblies," 34.

14. Alison G. Olson, "Eighteenth-Century Colonial Legislatures and their Constituents," *Journal of American History* 79, 2 (September, 1992): 545.

15. Greene, "Legislative Turnover," 556 (emphasis added).

16. William Sumner Jenkins's data, cited in Olson, "Eighteenth-Century Colonial Legislatures," 557.

17. Olson, "Eighteenth-Century Colonial Legislatures," 560.

18. Greene, "Legislative Turnover"; and Jack P. Greene, "Political Power in the House of Burgesses, 1720–1776," *William and Mary Quarterly* 16 (October 1959): 485–506.

19. Olson, "Eighteenth-Century Colonial Legislatures," 562. Parts of this section draw generally on this article.

20. Starr, *School for Politics,* 43.

21. Olson, *Making the Empire Work,* chaps. 10 and 11.

22. Cathy D. Matson and Peter S. Onuf, *A Union of Interests: Political and Economic Thought in Revolutionary America* (Lawrence: University Press of Kansas 1990), 21.

23. Olson, *Making the Empire Work,* 164ff.

24. E. E. Schattschneider, *The Semisovereign People* (New York: Holt, Rinehart, and Winston, 1960), 2ff.

25. For a political science reading of this era, see Calvin Jillson and Rick K. Wilson, *Congressional Dynamics: Structure, Coordination, and Choice in the First American Congress, 1774–1789* (Stanford, Calif.: Stanford University Press), 1994.

26. Matson and Onuf, *A Union of Interests,* 40ff.

27. See generally, James Madison, *Federalist* 10; and James Yoho, "Madison on the Beneficial Effects of Interest Groups: What Was Left Unsaid in '*Federalist*' 10," Polity 27, 4 (Summer 1995): 587–605.

28. Yoho, "Madison on the Beneficial Effects," 603.

29. William C. diGiacomantonio, "Petitioners and their Grievances: A View from the First Federal Congress," in *The House and the Senate in the 1790s: Petitioning, Lobbying, and Institutional Development,* ed. Kenneth R. Bowling and Donald R. Kennon (Athens: Ohio University Press, 2002), 32.

30. Gordon Wood, *Empire of Liberty: A History of the Early Republic, 1789–1815* (New York: Oxford University Press, 2009), 17. Emphasis added.

31. Quoted in John R. Nelson Jr., "Alexander Hamilton and American Manufacturing: A Reexamination," *Journal of American History* 65, 4 (March 1979): 973.

32. Ibid., 982.

33. Ibid., 984.

34. Wood, *Empire of Liberty,* 107.

35. Richard L. Hall and Alan V. Deardorff, "Lobbying as Legislative Subsidy," *American Political Science Review* 100, 1 (2006): 69–84; and Frank Baumgartner et al., *Lobbying and Policy Change: Who Wins, Who Loses, and Why* (Chicago: University of Chicago Press, 2009).

SUGGESTED READING

Bowling, Kenneth R., and Donald R. Kennon, eds. *The House and the Senate in the 1790s: Petitioning, Lobbying, and Institutional Development. Athens:* Ohio University Press, 2002.

Matson, Cathy D., and Peter S. Onuf. *A Union of Interests: Political and Economic Thought in Revolutionary America.* Lawrence: University Press of Kansas, 1990.

Olson, Alison G. *Making the Empire Work: London and American Interest Groups, 1690–1790.* Cambridge: Harvard University Press,1991.

———. "Eighteenth-Century Colonial Legislatures and their Constituents." *Journal of American History* 79, 2 (September 1992): 545.

Starr, Rebecca. *A School for Politics: Commercial Lobbying and Political Culture in Early South Carolina.* Baltimore: Johns Hopkins University Press, 1998.

Wood, Gordon. *Empire of Liberty: A History of the Early Republic, 1789–1815.* New York: Oxford, 2009.

Yoho, James. "Madison on the Beneficial Effects of Interest Groups: What Was Left Unsaid in '*Federalist*' 10." *Polity* 27, 4 (Summer 1995): 587–605.

chapter 2

Interest Groups and Lobbying in the Nineteenth Century: Tocqueville's America

by Daniel J. Tichenor and Jeremy Strickler

When French aristocrat Alexis de Tocqueville toured the United States in the early 1830s, he marveled at the propensity of Americans to organize and form groups for an astonishingly vast array of purposes. Tocqueville celebrated this striking feature of American life in *Democracy in America,* penned a few years after his journey. Indeed, one of his most famous observations in this influential work was that "Americans of all ages, of all stations in life, and all types of dispositions are forever forming associations." Tocqueville was especially captivated by the rich variety of associations he encountered in a nation little more than a half-century old. "They have not only commercial and manufacturing companies, in which all take part," he noted, "but associations of a thousand other kinds, religious, moral, serious, futile, general or restricted, enormous or diminutive." Tocqueville believed that the American tendency to organize and to join sprang from the absence of an aristocracy that in Europe performed a paternalistic, socially protective role that made it unnecessary to "combine in order to act." For Americans, however, he viewed the "art of association" as essential to facilitate meaningful collective action and citizen education. "In democratic countries knowledge of how to combine is the mother of all other forms of knowledge; on its progress depends that of all others," Tocqueville explained.[1]

The nation's founders generally viewed organized interests with an equal measure of suspicion and contempt. Yet over time Tocqueville's *Democracy in America* valorized nineteenth-century group life for Americans, who embraced his conception of the United States as "a nation of joiners" and of associations as the lifeblood of democracy.[2] "Tocqueville helped naturalize associations to later generations of Americans," historian Johann Neem aptly notes.[3] Today, rival ideological and philosophical camps make decidedly different claims about the robust world of associations that Tocqueville immortalized. Most of these debates revolve around the role and character of civil society and voluntary associations in the antebellum United States. Political conservatives have argued that the country should return to "a Tocquevillian America" in which civil society and markets flourish thanks to limited government. Romanticizing this preindustrial era, political analyst Michael Barone writes that the virtue of the Jacksonian age was that Americans were "lightly governed" and thereby gave "voluntary associations of many kinds of social functions that elsewhere and at other times have been performed by the state."[4] In response, various scholars and political progressives have asserted that Tocqueville and modern conservatives failed to recognize that voluntary associations developed as a consequence of new government structures and activities, rather than as an alternative to state power.[5] The early growth of voluntary associations, notes social scientist Theda Skocpol, "was closely tied up with the representative institutions and centrally directed activity of a very distinctive national state."[6] Meanwhile, communitarians, pluralists, and others invoke Tocqueville as gospel in quarrels over how U.S. civic engagement and voluntary associations impact social cooperation, individual and minority rights, and citizen mobilization and deliberation.[7]

Although most of these debates have fastened upon the larger, more visible voluntary associations of the nineteenth century, Tocqueville very pointedly acknowledged the significance of "commercial and manufacturing companies" and "associations of a thousand *other* kinds." To understand the range of organized interests that emerged and became politically active in Tocqueville's America requires a more encompassing approach. This chapter provides a broad view of the organized interests—from business groups and private firms to voluntary associations with large memberships—that sought to influence U.S. politics and governance from the early nineteenth century through the Gilded Age. It also discusses the rise of the lobby in national political life, a force that social critic Arthur Sedgwick insisted in 1878 was "an institution peculiar to America."[8] Whether or not Sedgwick's claim was overstated, the lobby did not receive significant public attention until after the Civil War. In the pages that follow, we trace the development of each of these vital elements of U.S. political life up to the late nineteenth century. As we shall see, interest groups and lobbying in Tocqueville-era America emerged gradually and were spurred by a variety of forces, eventually establishing themselves as fixtures in the American political system. This development would be a source of enduring ambivalence for generations to come. Americans embraced their constitutional right to form associations and petition the government for redress of wrongs, but they also lamented the impact of "special interests" on democratic representation and public policy (see Chapter 6).

FROM DREAD OF FACTIONS TO VIBRANT CIVIL SOCIETY: THE EARLY NINETEENTH CENTURY

"Liberty is to faction what air is to fire," James Madison memorably observed in *Federalist* 10, acknowledging the inevitability of factions in a free society (see Chapter 1). Because factions were fueled by "the instinct for self-preservation" and "the diversity of faculties" among any group of people, the trick was to design a republican government capable of counteracting their worst excesses.[9] Yet at the start of the nineteenth century Americans remained uneasy about private organizations and their efforts to influence public affairs. George Washington's Farewell Address set the tone. "All combinations and Associations," he said, "under whatever plausible character, with the real design to direct, control, counteract, or awe the regular deliberation and action of the Constituted authorities, are destructive . . . and of fatal tendency." In particular, the problem was that "a small but artful and enterprising minority of the Community" was able "to make the public administration the Mirror of the ill concerted and incongruous projects of faction, rather than the organ of consistent and wholesome plans digested by common counsels and modified by mutual interests."[10] Many state constitutions of the time made it a privilege rather than a right to form a corporation or association. The Massachusetts Constitution was typical in refusing to charter any "corporation or association of men" that promoted interests that were "distinct from those of the community."[11] Even Thomas Jefferson and his supporters were wary of private associations and corporations, distancing their vision of egalitarian democracy from the growth of civil society lest they "may rivalise and jeopardize the march of regular government."[12] Yet underlying these elite efforts to discourage and restrain private organizations was the

ALEXIS DE TOCQUEVILLE (1805–1859)

Alexis de Tocqueville's *Democracy in America* is an influential analysis of American popular society and politics during the Jacksonian Era of the early 1830s. To this day, his detailed account of the extent of American democracy and the active engagement of citizens in a multitude of voluntary associations remains a classic work of political science, sociology, and history. Most impressive of all, the French aristocrat was only twenty-five-years-old when he first started writing about the phenomenon of American self-government.

Raised in the political aftermath of the French Revolution, Tocqueville was yet another member of a storied family of French statesmen. His great-grandfather, Guillaume-Chretien de Lamoignon de Malesherbes, was a minister and future defense counsel for King Louis XVI, and his father, Hervé Louis François Jean Bonaventure Clérel, Comte de Tocqueville, served as a loyal prefect and peer of Charles X under the Bourbon monarchy. As a first-hand witness to the constitutional struggles of the French conservatives, young Tocqueville came to greatly admire the egalitarian nature of their rival ideology—the emerging tradition of liberalism. Upon the July Revolution of 1830 and its overthrow of the conservative regime of Charles X, the ascension of King Louis-Philippe to the French throne provided Tocqueville a perfect opportunity to further study the societal and political benefits of liberalism.

Needing an excuse to put some distance between his family's past ties to the conservatives and the new liberal regime, Tocqueville sought permission from the king to travel to the United States and Canada to study the American system of penitentiaries. Beginning in 1831, Tocqueville and his friend Gustave de Beaumont spent nine months traveling up and down the U.S. eastern seaboard. Although sent to study prisons, Tocqueville's interest quickly turned to better understanding the long-term potential for sustained liberty and equality in the present democratic American society.

Driven by his philosophical obsession with the societal influences of equality, once he returned to France, Tocqueville spent the next several years documenting the details of his travels in a multivolume work that became *Democracy in America*. The book's reputation grew throughout the nations of Western Europe and had a meaningful impact on future French citizens as they moved toward democracy. Having achieved renown for his writings, Tocqueville established a career in French politics. He served in the Chamber of Deputies, the Constituent Assembly, and later held the post of Minister of Foreign Affairs for a brief period of time. Although he served France in various capacities for more than twenty years after his return from the United States, Alexis de Tocqueville will forever be remembered for his insight on the advantages and potential dangers of liberal society and democracy.

Alexis de Tocqueville (1805–1859)

reality that ordinary Americans were forming and joining varied associations in large numbers.

The American penchant for organizing was in full display well before Tocqueville arrived on U.S. soil in 1831. The American Revolution, ratification battles over the Constitution, and the growth of popular elections all encouraged new voluntary associations. It was the spirited, pro-French democratic clubs that took root in most states that vexed Washington during his second term and led him to denounce "self-created societies."[13] In the early nineteenth century, the Second Great Awakening helped spur the formation of new associations to fulfill spiritual conceptions of personal and collective improvement. A variety of nonsectarian benevolent associations sprang up at the local, state, and national levels with leadership and funding independent of specific religious denominations. Some of the largest included the American Board of Commissioners of Foreign Missions (1810), American Bible Society (1816), American Sunday School Union (1824), American Tract Society (1825), and American Home Missionary Society (1826). They were, as historian Arthur Schlesinger Sr. put it, "a halfway house to the humanitarian reform societies of the Jacksonian period."[14] Commercial interests fueled early organizing, with local groups emerging to establish banks, build toll roads, and promote other enterprises. Agricultural improvement societies sprang up in the fledgling United States. Fraternal orders dedicated to mutual aid and brotherhood rituals left their mark across the young Republic. One of the largest was the Ancient and Accepted Free Masons, which was founded in the late eighteenth century. Threatened briefly by a popular U.S. backlash against Masons and other "secret societies," the Free Masons boasted memberships of more than 1 percent of the total U.S. adult male population from the 1810s onward.[15]

In a careful study of Massachusetts in the late eighteenth and early nineteenth centuries, social historian Richard Brown found that the number of voluntary associations soared. The number of such associations in the Bay State climbed from an estimated 24 to 1,305 between 1760 and 1830 (a staggering 5,000 percent increase), with most of this growth occurring after 1790.

According to Brown, most people remained closely tied to their families, churches, and towns, but the traditional insulation of local life was being challenged by new connections with state and national organizations. "Sometimes the contact was direct, if they traveled to a meeting or convention or if outsiders came to them as part of a political campaign, lyceum, or a temperance or missionary association," Brown notes. "More often, the contact was psychological, coming from memberships in countrywide or statewide organizations and the publications such activities produced."[16]

For the most part, the voluntary associations that took root in the early nineteenth century did not directly lobby the government. By contrast, large financial interests were anything but shy about making their presence felt in Congress and other centers of power in these years. Protective tariffs were among the most significant and contentious issues on the legislative docket, and tariff legislation inspired considerable lobbying. A variety of private commercial interests, from southern planters to northern merchants and shippers, hired representatives to monitor tariff legislation and to press for their interests. Banks also sought to influence public officials, often brazenly with major financial inducements. In the evolving economic life of the nation, banks chartered by the states supplanted local merchants as sources of credit for individuals and pressed their interests at every level of government. The Bank of the United States, a private bank chartered by the federal government, was perhaps the most notorious in its lobbying efforts. Pivotal senators were invited to serve on the bank's board of directors, a lucrative position that many accepted despite the conflict of interest.[17] The crassness of these relations between a private enterprise and elected officials was captured well when the august senator Daniel Webster of Massachusetts informed National Bank president Nicholas Biddle in 1833 that he expected financial rewards for his support. "I have had an application to be concerned, professionally, against the Bank, which I have declined, of course, although I believe my retainer has not been renewed, or *refreshed*, as

TOCQUEVILLE ON NINETEENTH-CENTURY ASSOCIATION DEVELOPMENT

"In America, the liberty of association for political purposes is unlimited. An example will show in the clearest light to what an extent this privilege is tolerated.

"The question of a tariff or free trade has much agitated the minds of Americans. The tariff was not only the subject of debate as a matter of opinion, but it also affected some great material interests of the States. The North attributed a portion of its prosperity, and the South nearly all its sufferings, to this system. For a long time, the tariff was the sole source of the political animosities which agitated the Union.

"In 1831, when the dispute was raging with the greatest violence, a private citizen of Massachusetts proposed, by means of the newspapers, to all the enemies of the tariff, to send delegates to Philadelphia, in order to consult together upon the best means of restoring freedom of trade. This proposal circulated in a few days, by the power of the press, from Maine to New Orleans: the opponents of the tariff adopted it with enthusiasm; meetings were held in all quarters, and delegates were appointed. The majority of these delegates were well known, and some of them had earned a considerable degree of celebrity. South Carolina alone, which afterwards took up arms in the same cause, sent sixty-three delegates. On the 1st of October, 1831, this assembly, which, according to the American custom, had taken the name of a Convention, met at Philadelphia; it consisted of more than two hundred members. Its debates were public, and they at once assumed a legislative character; the extent of the powers of Congress, the theories of free trade, and the different provisions of the tariff were discussed. At the end of ten days, the Convention broke up, having drawn up an address to the American people in which it declared: —1. That Congress had not the right of making a tariff, and that the existing tariff was unconstitutional. 2. That the prohibition of free trade was prejudicial to the interests of any nation, and to those of the American people especially."

SOURCE: Tocqueville, Alexis de, *Democracy in America*, vol. 1, trans. Henry Reeve (Cambridge: Sever and Francis, 1863), 245–246.

usual," he wrote. "If it be wished that my relation to the bank should be continued, it may be well to send me the usual retainer."[18] Private economic interests, rather than voluntary associations, were the most active in directly lobbying the government during this time.

GROUP MOBILIZATION IN THE ANTEBELLUM YEARS

The number of organized interests in American social and political life exploded during the "era of association," the antebellum decades of the 1830s, 1840s, and 1850s.[19] It was in this context that Tocqueville revealed in his diary that "the power of association has reached its uttermost development in America." A prominent New England theologian, William Ellery Channing, drew the same incisive conclusion several years before *Democracy in America* appeared in print. "In truth, one of the most remarkable circumstances or features of our age is the energy with which the principle of combination, or of action by joining forces, by associated numbers, is manifesting itself," he noted. "Those who have one great object find one another out through a vast extent of country, join their forces, settle their mode of operation, and act together with the uniformity of a disciplined army."[20] In her study of large, translocal groups in American political development, Skocpol describes this period as one of the most important bursts of new associations that gave form and substance to U.S. civil society.[21] Naturally, not all of these antebellum groups became national behemoths with large memberships spread across states and localities, but the depth and breadth of grassroots organizing in cities and towns throughout the country was staggering. Moreover, at a time when formal political participation was reserved for white men, American men and women—including African Americans—joined and participated in private organizations of various stripes. These included translocal African American fraternal and sororal associations, beginning with the Prince Hall Masons (1775) and Grand United Order of Odd Fellows (1843), that encouraged community solidarity, organizational experience, and civic involvement. As Skocpol, Ariane Liazos, and Marshall Ganz demonstrate, these African American organizations provided a crucial foundation for the later freedom struggles of the civil rights movement.[22] Women were prominent in the abolitionist movement before the Civil War, forming groups such as the National Female Anti-Slavery Society (1837). After being refused the right to speak at an international gathering of abolitionists, Elizabeth Cady Stanton and Lucretia Mott organized the first Woman's Rights Convention in Seneca Falls, New York. This two-day meeting of 300 women and men demanded equality and justice for women. The antislavery cause also involved former slaves, most notably Frederick Douglass, who would join firebrands William Lloyd Garrison and Wendell Phillips as the most visible leaders of the movement.

At a time when the country was "riven by factions, special interests, and political conflict," new groups proliferated to serve a vast array of public and private purposes.[23]

Some of these new associations, ranging from voluntary fire companies in the cities to larger fraternal organizations, did not pursue explicit political agendas, but they did adopt constitutions, organizational structures, bylaws, and modes of electing officers that were modeled after American political and governmental forms. These seemingly apolitical organizations would serve as important schools for democracy.[24] Joining the Free Masons among fraternal groups with large memberships in this period were the American Odd Fellows and the Improved Order of Red Men. New immigrants imported their own fraternal organizations, such as the Ancient Order of Hibernians formed by Irish Catholics in 1836 and B'nai B'rith established by German Jews in 1843. In turn, nativist and anti-Catholic secret societies arose to protect the nation from foreign influences; these groups included the Order of United Americans, the United American Mechanics, and the Order of the Star Spangled Banner. The largest of these so-called patriotic associations, the Junior Order of United American Mechanics, was founded at the end of this period (1851) and would be prominent in the movement for immigration restriction in later decades.[25]

In the economic sphere, President Andrew Jackson's successful war on the Second Bank of the United States was part of a broader effort by his fellow partisans and supporters to defeat monopolies and to promote equal competition in transportation, manufacturing, and finance. One consequence was that most states adopted laws that made incorporation rights available to business enterprises by general law rather than special legislation. This development eased the formation of business corporations, which then proliferated. The open clash of rival economic interests in Jacksonian America troubled Tocqueville deeply. Few issues were more contentious or a source of more organized struggle than the protective tariff, and an antitariff convention that Tocqueville observed in 1831 caused him considerable "alarm." By encouraging "open revolt" through state nullification, these antitariff conventions were, in Tocqueville's view, cravenly self-interested "factions" that promoted nothing short of "anarchy" by constantly challenging the legitimacy of the federal government and its policies.[26] This view was a decidedly different appraisal of the American organizing impulse than the celebratory tone he struck regarding voluntary associations *writ large*.

During the antebellum years, business interests also hired lobbyists to advance their policy agenda in Washington. Lobbying in the nation's capital during this period was often given to excess. In the early 1850s, for example, Colt's Firearms Manufacturing Company appealed to lawmakers' baser interests to secure passage of legislation that would extend the company's patent. Uncommitted senators and House members were hosted at lavish dinners by Colt's

LOBBYING FOR THE TRANSCONTINENTAL RAILROAD

Marked by the hammering of the golden spike at Promontory Point, the completion of the First Transcontinental Railroad in 1869 was one of the greatest industrial achievements in American history. Thanks to this modern marvel, the eastern states of the Atlantic coast were finally accessible to the western states of the Pacific; at last, civilization was connected to the frontier. Although finished in 1869, the beginnings of the transcontinental railroad can be traced back to the lobbying efforts of idealistic engineers and opportunistic financiers.

The first concerted attempts to get political traction on the building of a transcontinental railroad were undertaken by Asa Whitney, cousin to Eli Whitney, inventor of the cotton gin. A New York merchant who had fallen in love with the notion of train travel while on a year-long business trip in China, Asa Whitney returned to the United States determined to preach the gospel of the rail. For years, he traveled around the country on a publicity tour promoting the potential commercial benefits of a coast-to-coast railway. In spite of such efforts and the expenditure of a healthy portion of his own money, Whitney was never able to garner the necessary political support to get the railroad project up and running. But Theodore Judah, a civil engineer and future chief surveyor of the Central Pacific Railroad, was just the man for the task.

Judah's lobbying efforts on behalf of the Pacific Railroad Convention were second to none. Beginning in the late 1850s, Judah launched a lobbying blitz aimed at persuading members of Congress, cabinet secretaries, and other prominent politicians of the merits of a transcontinental railroad. Unlike Whitney, Judah was well aware that he needed more than just the political support of legislators and government officials; he also recognized the need to establish investors to back the construction of the railroad.

Theodore Judah found his investors in Mark Hopkins, James Bailey, Charles Crocker, and Leland Stanford; otherwise known as the "Big Four." Together these four businessmen financed and managed the Central Pacific Railroad. With the necessary financial and political capital secured, Judah had done his part to get one half of the transcontinental railroad on track. The result of Judah's hard work, and a bit of political glad-handing, was the Pacific Railroad Act of 1862. Signed into law by President Lincoln, this act established land grants for the Central Pacific Railroad and its twin endeavor, the Union Pacific. In a matter of a few short years, both railroads would converge in northern Utah, connecting a previously divided nation.

CRÉDIT MOBILIER

The number of congressional investigations soared during Ulysses S. Grant's eight years as president. Although the investigations were a response to well-founded dissatisfaction with the practices of the executive branch, the Crédit Mobilier scandal touched some outstanding members of Congress and tarnished the legislative branch as well.

Two committees in the House and one in the Senate investigated charges that arose during the 1872 presidential campaign of wholesale corruption in connection with construction by Crédit Mobilier of America of the final 667 miles of the Union Pacific Railroad, which had been completed three years earlier.

The charges first appeared when the *New York Sun* on September 4, 1872, reported that Rep. Oakes Ames, R-Mass., a principal stockholder in both Union Pacific and Crédit Mobilier, had used company stock to bribe Vice President Schuyler Colfax, Sen. Henry Wilson, R-Mass., Speaker James G. Blaine, R-Maine, Sen. James W. Patterson, R-N.H., Rep. James Brooks, D-N.Y., and Rep. James A. Garfield, R-Ohio. The alleged bribes represented an attempt to head off a congressional investigation of railroad transportation rates.

Blaine proposed the first inquiry, and the House on December 2 appointed a select committee headed by Rep. Luke P. Poland, R-Vt., "to investigate and ascertain whether any member of this House was bribed by Oakes Ames, or any other person or corporation, in any manner touching his legislative duty." A month later, January 6, 1873, the House appointed another select committee, this one headed by Rep. Jeremiah M. Wilson, R-Ind., to investigate the financial arrangement between Union Pacific and Crédit Mobilier.

As the House investigations proceeded simultaneously, the Poland committee discovered evidence implicating members of the Senate. Upon receiving the information, the Senate on February 4 established a select committee of its own to look into the allegations.

On February 18 the Poland committee filed a report clearing Blaine but recommending that Ames and Brooks be expelled from the House. The committee said Ames had been "guilty of selling to members of Congress shares of stock in the Crédit Mobilier of America, for prices much below the true value of such stock, with intent thereby to influence the votes and decisions of such members in matters to be brought before Congress for action." Brooks had purchased stock in his son-in-law's name but for his own benefit, the committee added. The House ultimately censured the two representatives but did not expel them.

The Wilson committee issued its report March 3, saying that Crédit Mobilier had been making exorbitant profits and that some persons connected with it were holding bonds illegally. In addition, the committee recommended that court action be undertaken to eliminate the financial irregularities. The Senate's committee had meanwhile come out with its report on March 1, saying that Patterson had bought Crédit Mobilier stock from Ames at below-market prices. The committee recommended Patterson's expulsion, but his retirement upon the expiration of his term on March 3 precluded Senate action to expel him. Colfax, whose involvement was not satisfactorily explained, had fallen from favor with Republicans before the scandal broke and was not renominated in June 1872 for a second term on the Grant ticket. Henry Wilson, who replaced Colfax as vice president, and Garfield, elected president in 1880, never explained away their connection with the affair.

SOURCE: Adapted from: CQ Press, *Guide to Congress*, 6th ed. (Washington, D.C.: CQ Press, 2008).

lobbying arm. As the company's chief lobbyist aptly quipped, "To reach the heart or get the vote, the surest way is down the throat!"[27] Lawmakers also received special Colt pistols and their wives were given presents such as French gloves. In the same decade, railroad companies and their lobbyists descended on Washington because railroad construction was fed by federal land grants and subsidies.[28]

Amidst the growth of industry and business corporations, a fledgling American labor movement began to emerge. From the start, however, labor unions met resistance, and the earliest labor federations struggled to withstand a hostile environment. Nevertheless, working men and women mobilized in the antebellum decades to secure a ten-hour workday, fair wages, and better working conditions. Most of the labor agitation centered in the nation's urban centers. In New York City new associations were created for shipwrights, coopers, masons, carpenters, printers, cabinetmakers, hatters, tailors, butchers, bakers, and others. In 1831, hundreds of women working as tailors in New York City struck for higher wages, followed a few years later by the formation of the Factory Girls' Association in Lowell, Massachusetts, to fight for improved wages and working conditions (see Chapter 13).[29]

Local crafts organized around the country sometimes established national unions for particular trades, such as the shoemakers' National Cooperative Association of Cordwainers. By 1834 these new unions succeeded in founding the country's first national labor federation, the National Trades Union. At its zenith in 1836 the National Trades Union boasted roughly 300,000 members and 160 local unions in five major cities. U.S. political leaders were, however, anything but supportive of workers' efforts to organize in response to industrializing forces and class conflict in antebellum America. Whig politicians claimed that when laborers took collective action to advance their agenda, they placed their class interests before that of the general public. If workers hoped that Jacksonian Democrats might be more responsive due to their commitment to democratization, they soon discovered that most Democratic leaders opposed labor unions on the grounds that they undermined

Rep. Oakes Ames, R-Mass, was censured by the House after he was found to have bribed members of Congress to avoid investigations into railroad transportation rates. Ames, a major stockholder in both the Union Pacific Railroad and Crédit Mobilier of America, a company hired to do construction on the railroad, sold shares of its stock at below market levels to members of Congress to sway their votes in his favor.

individual freedom in the marketplace. Faced with fierce opposition from employers and an unsympathetic reception by elected representatives and the courts, labor unions employed strikes, boycotts, pickets, closed shops, and other forms of collective action that were quite different from other associations.[30]

Various professional workers and intellectuals also organized new groups, but their principal objectives had less to do with economic security and workplace rights and more to do with establishing common professional standards, expanding research, and regularly sharing knowledge through meetings and publications (see Chapter 20). Many of these efforts began as local and state societies, before the groups banded together as national associations. Among the most notable professional and intellectual groups were the American Statistical Association (1839), American Ethnological Society (1842), American Medical Association (1847), American Association for the Advancement of Science (1848), American Society of Engineers and Architects (1852), National Education Association (1852), and the American Entomological Society (1859).[31]

The pre–Civil War groups that most enthralled Tocqueville, however, were those that engaged record numbers of Americans in the pursuit of humanitarian reform. Fusing religious and democratic ideals, these voluntary associations advanced causes that ranged from temperance and the improved treatment of the insane to woman's suffrage and the abolition of slavery. Some of the larger reform organizations that sprang up were the American Temperance Society, American Peace Society, General Union for Promoting the Christian Observance of the Sabbath, Independent Order of Good Templars, American Lyceum Association, American Anti-Slavery Society, and American and Foreign Sabbath Union. These new humanitarian and reform groups spoke to an antebellum America that was consumed by contentious debates over the protective tariff, slavery, westward expansion, immigration, warfare, and social morality.[32]

Cooperation and exchange between different reform associations was common. In Massachusetts during the 1830s, a variety of reform organizations held weeklong gatherings on the Boston Common in which large groups set up tents on the Common and smaller ones met in churches at its edges. Each day, attendees could move from one group site to the next to attend meetings and hear speeches.[33] Not all Americans favored the proliferation of these altruistic groups in their communities and nation. Some resented the intrusiveness of these humanitarian organizations. "Matters have come to such a pass," groused New England writer and intellectual Orestes Brownson, "that a peaceable man can hardly venture to eat or drink, or to go to bed or to get up, to correct his children or to kiss his wife, without obtaining the permission and direction of some moral . . . society."[34] Many of the causes that these voluntary associations championed—such as temperance, improving the penal system, or ending slavery—fueled political conflict. Indeed, some of these struggles helped push the country closer to civil war. Yet few of these reform associations engaged in direct lobbying of Washington; rather, they focused their energies on mass mobilization through publicity, grassroots organizing, and the petition. To gain a better sense of the structure, resources, and strategies of these voluntary associations, let us consider the controversial political causes of honoring the Sabbath, temperance, and ending slavery.

ORGANIZING TO REFORM: SABBATARIAN, TEMPERANCE, AND ABOLITIONIST ASSOCIATIONS

Some of the most important voluntary associations that emerged in the antebellum period were dedicated to strict universal observance of the Sabbath. The chief impetus for the Sabbatarian movement was a policy of the federal government that mail should be delivered and post offices kept open on Sundays. Inspired by previous efforts to turn the screws on national political leaders by mobilizing at the grassroots, Protestant ministers (especially Congregationalists and Presbyterians) worked together across the country to rally their parishioners. In 1815 this early grassroots effort led to more than 100 petitions being sent to Congress protesting the delivery of mail in violation of the Sabbath. But this campaign really took off a decade later after Congress renewed the rule keeping post offices open on Sundays, leading to the formation in 1828 of the General Union for the Promotion of the Christian Sabbath. Led by evangelical ministers and laity, including Lyman Beecher, an influential clergyman, the General Union sent representatives and fliers to fellow evangelicals throughout the country. The new organization also recruited supporters beyond the existing network of evangelical churches, offering membership to anyone who agreed to honor the Sabbath and to boycott transportation companies and other establishments that operated on Sundays. More than 100,000 copies of a Sabbatarian address by Beecher were distributed in newspapers or as pamphlets throughout the country. At its peak in the early 1830s, the General Union's substantial membership rolls made it one of the three largest groups in the United States. Twenty-six branch offices were maintained to coordinate local efforts to protect the Sabbath.[35]

Like other reform associations of the period, the General Union appealed directly to public opinion and counted on a particular form of grassroots political participation that it hoped would influence elected officials: the petition. The principal aim of the General Union was to generate petitions from affiliated local associations calling on Congress to revoke the rule mandating post offices be kept open and mail be delivered on Sundays. More than 900 petitions were sent to Congress between 1829 and 1831. Yet national lawmakers were unmoved. Jacksonian Democrats generally saw the General Union's demands to protect the Sabbath as undermining both civil liberties and the separation of church and state. In his committee report to the Senate on the post office controversy, Democratic senator Richard Johnson of Kentucky noted in 1829 that the Sabbatarian call to stop Sunday mail delivery would violate the First Amendment. Well aware that the General Union had delivered 467 petitions to Congress that year, Johnson underscored the need for the Senate to resist mass demands when they favored particular religious views, however popular. "The principles of our government do not recognize in the majority any authority over the minority," his report concluded. Johnson's Senate colleagues ultimately affirmed his position.[36]

Hundreds of additional General Union petitions from local affiliates across the country arrived at the Capitol in the months that followed. Yet Senator Johnson and his committee reiterated their refusal to capitulate to the popular pressure stirred up by the General Union. Johnson's opposition won support from Whigs, who, like Reverend Channing, worried that mass organizations such as the General Union led citizens to be "swept away by a crowd" and to "substitute the consciences of others for our own." If Sabbatarians succeeded in their "sway by numbers" tactics, he warned, they would "create tyrants as effectively as standing armies."[37] At the end of the day, the General Union's publicity campaign, coordinated grassroots organizing, and determined petition drives failed to push Congress to revoke its rule on Sunday mail delivery. Within a short time, the General Union dissolved, and the Sabbatarian movement faded away.

Temperance was another moral crusade that breathed life into some of the most prominent associations in American public life before the Civil War. Initially, temperance organizations avoided politics and instead focused on banding together sober members in local chapters and on preaching self-control to wayward souls. Before long, however, temperance associations embraced a "politics of social control" that, as Keith Whittington observes, "pitted churches, classes, and neighborhoods against one another over the proper use of the state and the goals of society."[38] Like the Sabbatarians, temperance groups of the antebellum period sought to arouse public opinion and participation through tracts, mass membership, and petition drives. But over time, they would employ more direct political methods to promote their cause.

The American Temperance Society was one of the most formidable voluntary associations of the Jacksonian era. By 1835 it boasted 1.5 million members, roughly one-fifth of the free adult population of the country. It modeled its structure after the U.S. federal system, with local general community affiliates joined together in state branches that selected representatives to a national body. The number of local American Temperance Society auxiliaries reached about 8,000 in 1835, with organizational branches in nearly every state. In addition to these general community auxiliaries, this leading temperance organization also inspired auxiliaries of African Americans, college students, professional groups, and others. Group meetings and oral propaganda was fortified by the distribution of printed material; in 1840 and 1841 the national organization circulated more than 430,000 leaflets and periodicals. In 1850 the Maine Temperance Union, led by Neal Dow, mobilized temperance supporters into a disciplined voting bloc that helped secure the "Maine Law," which prohibited the manufacture or sale of liquor except for medical or industrial purposes. In subsequent elections, temperance associations interviewed candidates of the major parties and endorsed them on the basis of their position on alcohol.[39] Over time, the American Temperance Society was unable to sustain its extensive

The temperance movement of the nineteenth century amassed an incredible following across thousands of local and national organizations. Prominent among those members were women who raised awareness of the detrimental effects of alcohol consumption and pressed for legislative solutions.

popular membership network and after the 1840s became what Skocpol describes as "a national center for publishing and lobbying (operating much like a modern professional advocacy group)."[40]

Several other temperance organizations gained prominence in the antebellum years. The Washington Temperance Societies emerged in the 1840s, targeting working-class members. At its highest, membership in this organization was around 600,000 and with 10,000 societies. The devotion of the Washington Temperance Societies to local democracy over national organization ultimately crippled efforts to lead and coordinate its many grassroots societies, and the voluntary association disappeared from American civil society by the end of the decade. In the 1840s the Order of the Sons of Temperance also developed a sizable membership with 2,398 local affiliates in three dozen state divisions. During the 1850s the Independent Order of Good Templars followed the same structural pattern with expansive membership rolls spread across 1,200 lodges in twenty state affiliates. Both men and women were welcomed to join as members and to hold leadership positions. All of these temperance groups advocated for their cause in the political sphere, but success eluded them for several generations.[41]

While Tocqueville was preparing to leave the United States for his native France in 1831, William Lloyd Garrison and other abolitionists formed the New England Anti-Slavery Society. Earlier in the year, Garrison followed the model of other religion-inspired crusaders of his time in relying upon the tract to agitate for reform, publishing the inaugural edition of his antislavery newspaper, *The Liberator*. Garrison viewed his newspaper not only as a means of circulating his views on slavery, but also as a way for abolitionist reformers around the country to connect and exchange ideas. *The Liberator* was, as he envisioned it, "a weekly method of communicating with each other." When his readers were particularly exercised on a subject, Garrison made sure that the newspaper was "practically given over to publication of letters, articles, speeches, statements and rebuttals from all sides of the controversy."[42] This model would not have surprised Tocqueville, as he discerned a strong linkage between newspapers and the formation of organized interests in American society. "Newspapers make associations, and associations make newspapers," he noted. "Thus, of all countries on earth, it is in America that one finds both the most associations and the most newspapers."[43] Garrison would parlay *The Liberator* into a vital instrument for antislavery organizing and ultimately abolitionist reform.

In 1833 Garrison joined with Arthur Tappan to establish the American Anti-Slavery Society (AASS) to coordinate several dozen U.S. abolitionist societies (all centered in the North). The AASS did not rely only upon the printed word to make its case. It sponsored ministers and hired agents to fan out across the North to organize local chapters and to enlist churchwomen as spearheads of petition drives. Some of its most famous leaders and speakers were Frederick Douglass, Lucy Stone, and Wendell Phillips. At the close of the 1830s, the AASS had roughly 250,000 members and its national organization stood atop 1,300 local and 7 state associations. It commanded an annual budget that ranged between $26,000 and $50,000, which it used to flood the country with 800,000 antislavery newspapers and pamphlets between 1837 and 1840. The AASS propaganda campaign was extraordinary both in its scale and impact, leading Virginia representative John Jones to curse steam power and the press—"these two great revolutionizers"—for giving abolitionists the technical means to mass produce and circulate "newspapers, pamphlets, tracts, and pictures, calculated, in an eminent degree, to rouse and inflame the passions."[44] During the summer of 1835, a mob in Charleston, South Carolina, broke into the city's post office, seized abolitionist mailings, and burned them. Postmaster Amos Kendall subsequently explained that AASS material sent to southern states would be refused because the states were akin to "twenty-six independent nations," and sovereign nations had the power to reject subversive propaganda. In his 1835 annual message to Congress, President Jackson went so far as to endorse a national censorship law that would keep "incendiary" materials from the mails[45] The AASS had foisted its polarizing abolitionist cause onto the national agenda.

As the AASS membership, budgets, and distribution of printed material grew, its petition drives infuriated southerners in the House and Senate, where the long-standing norm was for petitions of various sorts to be summarized on the floor before being referred to committee. Southern lawmakers found the language and volume of abolitionist petitions to be intolerable, and they succeeded in passing a House "gag rule" in 1836 that barred discussion of any antislavery petitions. Yet tens of thousands of abolitionist petitions continued to stream into Congress. In 1837–1838 alone, abolitionist groups generated 130,000 petitions calling for an end to slavery in the District of Columbia, 32,000 demanding repeal of the gag rule, 23,000 advocating the abolition of the interstate slave trade, and 21,000 opposing slavery in western territories. Receiving and sorting this flood of abolitionist petitions became a full-time job of several House clerks, leading the House in 1840 to adopt an additional rule that prevented it from receiving antislavery petitions. These rebuffs by the House in fact fueled support for the AASS and the abolitionist crusade in the North, where many were more outraged by the denial of sacred petitioning rights to citizens and private organizations than by the institution of slavery. John Quincy Adams, the former president who was elected by Massachusetts voters to serve in the House, regularly assailed his colleagues for adopting the gag rule. "Petition is supplication—it is entreaty—it is prayer," Adams thundered from the well of the House. "The right of petition belongs to all." In open defiance of his colleagues, Adams made a point of reading most of an antislavery petition on the floor before being silenced by the chair's gavel.[46] Significantly, middle-class and upper-class women dedicated to reform were instrumental in gathering and signing abolitionist petitions, providing an important venue for women associated with antislavery associations to exercise political leadership and participation at a time when they were denied access to the ballot box. The AASS would live on until 1870, after the Civil War and emancipation.

William Lloyd Garrison was instrumental in the founding of the New England Anti-Slavery Society in 1831. His newspaper, The Liberator, *gave abolitionist voices a national forum for discussion and a mouthpiece for reform. Newspapers and pamphlets were crucial to the abolitionists' efforts to influence congressional action.*

The Sabbatarian, temperance, and abolitionist groups were among the most significant voluntary reform associations of the antebellum period, and they each evidenced more than a few similar features. All of these associations were religiously inspired with a lineage that could be traced back to the Second Great Awakening. Publishing and distributing tracts, newspapers, and other printed material to arouse and shape public opinion was a common focus of resources. All of these groups—including the General Union for Promoting Observance of the Christian Sabbath, American Temperance Society, and American Anti-Slavery Society—developed a mass membership and a federal structure with national, state, and local units. They also placed a heavy emphasis on influencing government officials by means of petitions and memorials. As Michael Schudson observes, this quintessential element of group efforts to secure reform before the Civil War became increasingly obsolete in American politics in later years:

> The disadvantage of voluntary associations lay not in the word "association" but in the word "voluntary." . . . [W]hile the voluntary association would continue to flourish, it also would come up against social problems to which its participatory form was not a very effective solution. As the locus of authoritative decision-making

> moved increasingly to Washington, national organizations that could act quickly and, just as important, act continuously, supplemented or sometimes supplanted voluntary associations. The petition, in other words, would in time give way to the lobby.[47]

This transition, however, was not immediate. As we shall see, participatory voluntary associations thrived alongside more centralized, professional advocacy groups and lobbyists during the Civil War and the decades that followed.

THE GROWTH OF A WASHINGTON LOBBYING COMMUNITY: FROM THE CIVIL WAR TO THE GILDED AGE

Few developments endanger civil society in democracies more profoundly, Tocqueville believed, than "protracted" warfare. Yet the formation and growth of associations "boomed" during the Civil War and its aftermath. Voluntarism flourished in the North, where groups such as the Women's Central Association for Relief (which eventually became the U.S. Sanitary Commission) organized civilians to offer medical and social assistance to troops. Other groups such as the Young Men's Christian Association, founded in 1851, found new purpose and exploded in membership when it partnered with the federal government in providing support for Union soldiers. In 1864 clerks working for the federal government created a new fraternal organization focused on benevolence and "healing the wounds" of civil war; the Order of the Knights of Pythias soon became one of the largest membership groups in the country. Union veterans established associations soon after the war, the largest and most dominant of which was the Grand Army of the Republic (GAR). The GAR was more than commemorative in purpose; it later worked to secure pensions and other benefits from the federal government to support veterans and their survivors. It took local Confederate associations until 1889 to coordinate under the United Confederate Veterans. Railroad workers who grew acquainted during the Civil War established the Ancient Order of United Workmen as a fraternal benefits society that offered affordable financial protection for working-class people. Its fraternal insurance model soon proliferated. In the 1860s two national woman suffrage organizations and less radical women's cultural clubs arose and eventually banded together to become the General Federation of Women's Clubs in 1889, a group that later fought successfully for child labor laws (see Chapter 18).[48]

Voluntary associations continued to proliferate in subsequent decades. In the 1870s humanitarian reformers launched the American Prison Association, National Conference on Social Work, Society for the Prevention of Cruelty to Children, and Women's Christian Temperance Union (WCTU). The WCTU, born from grassroots women's crusades against local saloons in 1873–1874, became the nation's largest women's organization with local "unions" throughout the country and was instrumental in the struggle to prohibit alcohol. During the following decade reformers created groups such as the American Red Cross, Indian Rights Association, and National Arbitration League. The number of professional associations multiplied in the same years, with engineers, chemists, biologists, historians, artists, economists, librarians, linguists, and other specialists becoming dues-paying members of national organizations promoting their professional and research interests. More than a half-century after Tocqueville, British historian and statesman James Bryce wrote of an exceptional American "habit of forming associations." As he noted in his mammoth book, *The American Commonwealth*, "Associations are created, extended, and worked in the United States more quickly and effectively than in any other country."[49]

For all the parallels of vibrant associationalism observed by Tocqueville in the early 1830s and by Bryce in three visits to the United States starting in 1870, the role of organized interests in American politics was in fact changing as the nation shifted from the antebellum period to the Gilded Age. If most politically active groups of the Jacksonian era relied upon tracts, mass membership, and petitions to press their agendas, an unprecedented number of new interests and organizations went directly to Washington to lobby government officials. To be sure, the structure and methods of mass-based voluntary associations, such as the WCTU, GAR, or the American Protective Association, looked a great deal like their earlier counterparts. But more than ever before, citizens groups, private firms, trade associations, labor unions and federations, and professional groups were monitoring and seeking to influence the national policymaking process. A significant indication of this trend is the dramatic increase in testimony by organized interests before congressional committees after the Civil War. As Figure 2.1 illustrates, relatively few private organizations and firms testified to Congress from the 1830s through the 1860s. In the 1870s and 1880s, however, unprecedented numbers of interest groups and private firms sought to influence Congress (roughly 250 organized interests appeared at congressional hearings in these two decades, up from about a dozen over the entire preceding decades).[50] A new Washington lobbying community was beginning to take root, recasting the character of American political life.

What seems to have troubled most observers in these post–Civil War decades was not the growth and centralization of advocacy group lobbying; rather, it was the growing anxiety that business interests—and domineering monopolies in particular—were transforming U.S. economic, social, and political life in malevolent ways. A special House investigating committee summed many of these fears in its 1874 report: "This country is fast becoming filled with gigantic

FIGURE 2.1 **Organized Interests Testifying to Congress, 1830–1889 (CIS Index)**

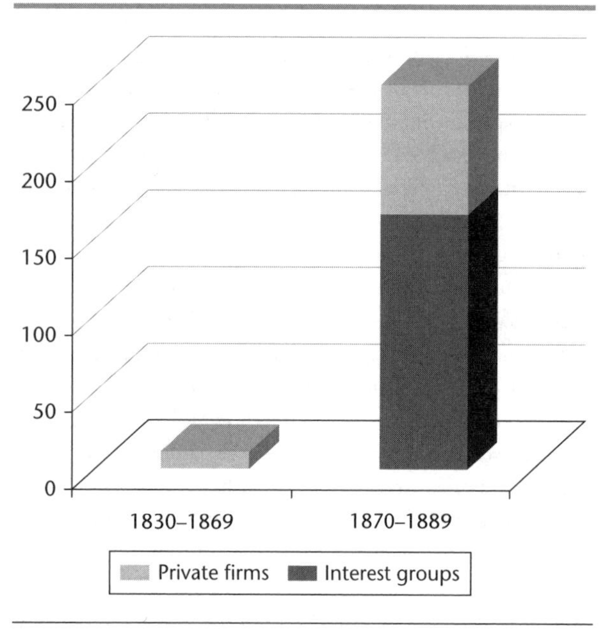

SOURCE: Congressional Information Service, *U.S. Congressional Committee Hearings Index* (Washington, D.C.: Government Printing Office, 1985).

corporations wielding and controlling immense aggregations of money and thereby commanding great influence and power."[51] Trade associations, peak business organizations, large corporations, and other private firms were anything but reluctant to use their financial resources and clout to pressure policymakers at every level of American government. These organized business interests comprised 192 (77 percent) of the 250 groups and firms who were invited to testify before congressional committees during the 1870s and 1880s.[52] Although efforts to influence governance to serve private objects were typical in democracies, as Arthur Sedgwick informed readers in 1878, the "permanent and organized form" these efforts assumed in the United States set it apart. "In forty state capitals during three months in the year, and in Washington during every session of Congress, the lobby is in full force," he wrote. "In other words, . . . an active and powerful, though indeterminate, body devotes itself to watching, furthering, or opposing the work the legislature is called into existence to do, and which it is supposed to do without supervision of any kind."[53]

Businesses of various sorts lobbied state and national officials from the Civil War through the Gilded Age. With large retainers to be had, professional lobbyists or "strikers" proliferated in Washington as rapidly as advocacy groups and corporations. Federal government subsidies for steamship lines and railroad construction were especially significant in spurring the proliferation of lobbyists and pressure groups in Washington. Lobbyists such as William E. Chandler, who later became a U.S. senator, got rich representing railroad companies in their quest for government assistance. Sometimes efforts to influence members of Congress and other federal officials took the form of lavish entertaining. As one contemporary described the scene:

> Every evening they receive, and in the winter their blazing wood fires are often surrounded by a distinguished circle. Some treat favored guests to a game of euchre, and as midnight approaches there is always an adjournment to the dining-room, where a choice supper is served. A cold game pie, broiled oysters, charmingly mixed salad, and one or two light dishes, . . . with iced champagne or Burgundy at blood heat. Who can blame a Congressmen for leaving the bad cooking of his hotel or boarding-house, with the absence of all the home comforts, to walk into the parlor web which the cunning spider-lobbyist weaves for him?[54]

In truth, officials often received far more direct compensation from corporate lobbyists for their support. Railroad magnates like Collis P. Huntington found that winning supporters in Congress yielded lucrative results but also carried a high price tag. Lawmakers expected direct payments, expensive gifts, and "free passes" to ride the railroad lines. Occasionally, these excesses became public. In 1872 the Crédit Mobilier scandal revealed that members of the House and Senate had accepted company stock in exchange for supporting particular railroad legislation. This and numerous other lobbying scandals, however, did little to diminish the prominence of lobbyists in national and state politics. Throughout the Gilded Age, businesses expended large sums in Washington on retainers for a growing population of professional lobbyists or "Third House members," as some called them. During the pivotal congressional session of 1876–1877, one railroad company alone hired nearly 200 lobbyists to pursue its interests. Huntington and his rival railroad operators resented the cost of doing business on Capitol Hill, but they ultimately accepted that "we must take care of our friends."[55]

Organized business influence in national politics encouraged mobilizations by wage earners and farmers. Although constantly under siege, dozens of new national unions were formed in the Gilded Age to fight for fair wages, ten-hour workdays, and improved working conditions. Despite fierce opposition from employer groups and government officials, new labor federations, such as the National Labor Union, Knights of Labor, and eventually the less-aggressive, craft-oriented American Federation of Labor, emerged to defend the rights of certain laborers. Farmers also established and strengthened associations guarding their interests in this period, beginning with the nonthreatening Patrons of Husbandry or Grange and later including the more radical Farmers' Alliances (see Chapter 12). Twenty-two percent of the testimony made by organized interests to congressional committees in the 1870s and 1880s was provided by labor unions, farmers associations, and citizens groups.[56] Business organizations, trade associations, and large corporations unquestionably dominated lobbying during the Gilded Age. Yet large numbers of humanitarian, labor, agrarian, veterans, moral reform, nativist, and professional groups also organized, entered the political fray, and pressed for their public policy agendas.

CONCLUSION

By celebrating the multitude of associations he encountered in the United States, Alexis de Tocqueville made Americans famous for their propensity to organize and join groups. His reflections on this subject are so widely accepted that it is easy to forget that the nation's early political leaders were anything but enthusiastic about private organizations and that politically active groups of the early nineteenth century emerged in a decidedly uneasy environment. Tocqueville also may have led us astray by suggesting that associations flourished in Jacksonian America precisely because of what he perceived as a weak national state with little or no administrative power. "Nothing strikes the European traveler in the United States more than the absence of what we would call government or administration," he wrote.[57] In a similar vein, legendary historian Arthur M. Schlesinger asserted that an American aversion to "the growth of stronger government" and "collective organization as represented by the state" fueled "the necessity for self-constituted associations to do things beyond the capacity of a single person."[58] Yet more recent studies by sociologists, historians, and political scientists offer evidence of how the early U.S. national government provided a structure that fostered the development of politically active groups and shaped their internal forms and external strategies. Moreover, as many nineteenth-century observers quickly discerned, the growth of government during the Civil War and generous public subsidies for enterprises such as railroads spurred an unprecedented expansion in lobbying by diverse interest groups, businesses, and individuals. Mass-based voluntary associations, business corporations, centralized advocacy groups, and professional lobbyists became a fixture in American political life during the Gilded Age. The Washington lobbying community would continue to evolve in scope and scale from the Progressive Era onward, but it was here to stay and would remain a source of deep ambivalence for generations of ordinary citizens and political leaders to come.

NOTES

1. Alexis de Tocqueville, *Democracy in America*, ed. J. P. Mayer; trans. George Lawrence (Garden City, N.Y.: Doubleday, Anchor Books, 1969 [1835–1840]), 511–519, 72.

2. The phrase "a nation of joiners" was coined by Arthur Schlesinger, "Biography of a Nation of Joiners," *The American Historical Review* (October 1944): 1–25.

3. Johann Neem, *Creating a Nation of Joiners: Democracy and Civil Society in Early National Massachusetts* (Cambridge: Harvard University Press, 2008), 99–121.

4. Michael Barone, "Returning to Tocqueville: Are 19th-Century Values Making a Comeback in America?" *Washington Post National Weekly Edition*, January 15–21, 1996, 23. See also Michael Joyce and William Schambra, "A New Civic Life," in *To Empower the People: From State to Civil Society*, 2nd ed., ed. Michael Novak, ed., (Washington, D.C.: American Enterprise Institute Press, 1996), 11–29.

5. Richard R. John, *Spreading the News: The American Postal System from Franklin to Morse* (Cambridge: Harvard University Press, 1995); and Theda Skocpol, *Diminished Democracy: From Membership to Managements in American Civic Life* (Norman: Oklahoma University Press, 2003).

6. Theda Skocpol, "The Tocqueville Problem," *Social Science History* (Winter 1997): 463.

7. For an excellent overview of these philosophical debates and of competing uses of Tocqueville by different camps, see Johann Neem, "Squaring the Circle: The Multiple Purposes of Civil Society in Tocqueville's *Democracy in America*," *La Revue Tocqueville* 28 (2006): 22–43.

8. Arthur G. Sedgwick, "The Lobby: Its Cause and Cure," *The Atlantic*, April 1878, 512–522.

9. James Madison, *Federalist* 10, in Alexander Hamilton, James Madison, and John Jay, *The Federalist Papers*, ed. Clinton Rossiter (New York: Signet Classic, 1999), 71–79.

10. George Rhodehamel, ed., *George Washington: Writings* (New York: Library of America, 1997), 969. Originally published in the *American Daily Advertiser* on September 19, 1796.

11. Neem, *Creating A Nation of Joiners*, 6–7.

12. Ibid., 5.

13. Quoted in Arthur Schlesinger, "Biography," 8.

14. Ibid., 6.

15. Skocpol, *Diminished Democracy*, 33–34.

16. Richard Brown, "The Emergence of Urban Society in Massachusetts, 1760–1820," *Journal of American History* 61 (1974): 29–51.

17. Robert C. Byrd, "Lobbyists," *The Senate, 1789–1989: Addresses on the History of the United States Senate* (Washington, D.C.: U.S. Government Printing Office, 1991), 491–508.

18. Daniel Webster to Nicholas Biddle, December 21, 1833, in *The Papers of Daniel Webster*, ed. by Charles Wiltse (Hanover, Conn.: 1977), vol. 3, 288.

19. The description of the pre–Civil War period as the "era of association" was made by Mary P. Ryan, *Cradle of the Middle Class* (Cambridge: Cambridge University Press, 1981), chap. 3.

20. William Ellery Channing, "Remarks on Associations," *Works* (Boston: American Unitarian Association, 1875), 139.

21. Skocpol, *Diminished Democracy*, 26–32.

22. Theda Skocpol, Ariane Liazos, and Marshall Ganz, *What a Mighty Power We Can Be: African American Fraternal Groups and the Struggle for Racial Equality* (Princeton: Princeton University Press, 2008).

23. Neem, "Squaring the Circle," 99–121.

24. Skocpol, *Diminished Democracy*, 30–44.

25. Daniel Tichenor, *Dividing Lines: The Politics of Immigration Control in America* (Princeton: Princeton University Press, 2002).

26. Tocqueville, *Democracy in America*, 193.

27. Byrd, "Lobbyists," 491–508.

28. Sedgwick, "The Lobby," 512–522.

29. Philip S. Foner, *History of the Labor Movement in the United States: From Colonial Times to the Founding of the American Federation of Labor* (New York: International Publishers, 1979).

30. Ibid.

31. Schlesinger, "Biography," 1–25.

32. Ibid.

33. Mark Schudson, *The Good Citizen: A History of American Civil Life* (New York: Free Press, 1998), 102–103.

34. Quoted in Schlesinger, "Biography," 12.

35. Richard R. John, "Taking Sabbatarianism Seriously: The Postal System, the Sabbath, and the Transformation of American Political Culture," *Journal of the Early Republic* X, (1990): 538–543. For sabbatarianism, see also Bertram Wyatt-Brown, "Prelude to Abolitionism: Sabbatarian Politics and the Rise of the Second Party System," *Journal of American History* LVIII (1971): 316–441.

36. Quoted in Neem, "Squaring the Circle," 108.

37. Channing, "Remarks on Associations," 138–158.

38. Keith Whittington, "Revisiting Tocqueville's America: Society, Politics, and Association in the Nineteenth Century," in *Beyond Tocqueville: Civil Society and the Social Capital Debate in Comparative Perspective*, ed. Bob Edwards, Michael Foley, and Mario Diani (Boston: Tufts University Press, 2001), 21–31.

39. Mark Schudson, *Good Citizen*, 99–100.

40. Skocpol, *Diminished Democracy*, 33.

41. Ann-Marie Szymanksi, *Pathways to Prohibition* (Raleigh-Durham, N.C.: Duke University Press, 2003).

42. Schudson, *Good Citizen*, 123.

43. Tocqueville, *Democracy in America*, 517.

44. Quoted in Schudson, *Good Citizen*, 105.

45. Russell Riley, *The Presidency and the Politics of Racial Inequality: Nation-Keeping from 1831 to 1965* (New York: Columbia University Press, 1999), 26–44.

46. William Lee Miller, *Arguing About Slavery* (New York: Knopf, 1996), 263–268.

47. Schudson, *Good Citizen*, 100.

48. Skocpol, *Diminished Democracy*, 46–59.

49. Viscount Lord Bryce, *The American Commonwealth* (New York: Cosimo, 2007), 273.

50. These data have been collected by the author from Congressional Information Service, *U.S. Congressional Committee Hearings Index* (Washington, D.C.: Government Printing Office, 1985).

51. Quoted in James Rhodes, *History of the United States* (New York: Macmillan, 1920), vol. II: 1854–1860, 19.

52. Ibid.

53. Sedgwick, "The Lobby," 513–514.

54. Benjamin Perley Moore, *Perley's Reminiscences of Sixty Years in the National Metropolis* (New York: AMS Press, 1971), vol. 2, 514–515.

55. Byrd, "Lobbyists," 494.

56. From data collected by the author from Congressional Information Service, *U.S. Congressional Committee Hearing Index.*

57. Tocqueville, *Democracy in America*, 513.

58. Schlesinger, "Biography," 1.

SUGGESTED READING

Byrd, Robert C. "Lobbyists," *The Senate, 1789–1989: Addresses on the History of the United States Senate.* Washington, D.C.: U.S. Government Printing Office, 1991, 491–508.

Edwards, Bob, Michael Foley, and Mario Diani, eds. *Beyond Tocqueville: Civil Society and the Social Capital Debate in Comparative Perspective.* Boston: Tufts University Press, 2001.

Gamm, Gerald, and Robert Putnam. "The Growth of Voluntary Associations in America, 1840–1940." *Journal of Interdisciplinary History* XXIX (1999): 511–557.

John, Richard. *Spreading the News: The American Postal Service from Franklin to Morse.* Cambridge: Harvard University Press, 1995.

Neem, Johann. *Creating a Nation of Joiners: Democracy and Civil Society in Early National Massachusetts.* Cambridge: Harvard University Press, 2008.

Schudson, Mark. *The Good Citizen: A History of American Civil Life.* New York: Free Press, 1998.

Skocpol, Theda. *Diminished Democracy: From Membership to Management in American Civic Life.* Norman: University of Oklahoma Press, 2004.

Thompson, Margaret Susan. *The "Spider Web": Congress and Lobbying in the Age of Grant.* Ithaca, N.Y.: Cornell University Press, 1985.

Tocqueville, Alexis de. *Democracy in America.* New York: Library of America, 2004. Translated by Arthur Goldhammer.

Twain, Mark, and Charles Dudley Warner. *The Gilded Age: A Tale of Today.* Seattle: University of Washington Press, 1968.

chapter 3

Groups in Industrializing America and the Origins of Popular Interest Group Politics

by Elisabeth Clemens

THE FOUNDING DOCUMENTS of the United States are eloquent with respect to individuals and their rights and responsibilities as citizens. In addition, charters and constitutions spelled out the institutional design of government—local, state, or national—in considerable detail. The processes and organizations that would connect citizens with government institutions, however, were left relatively unspecified. In this space, political parties emerged as a new vehicle for connecting voters to elected officials. Joining the emerging parties in the early nineteenth century, national social movements developed to promote the expansion of Christianity to the western frontier, to encourage temperance, and to demand abolition.[1] Mass petitions and a vibrant press conveyed opinions and grievances to far-flung audiences and to national officials. In different ways, each of these developments linked local networks and practices to national politics, connecting congregations and social clubs to the leading issues of the day.

As social and economic conditions changed, however, so did the forms linking citizens to state and national politics. By the second half of the nineteenth century, many of the organizing principles of earlier American politics were being undermined. The basic grid of representational politics was territorial. Members of a community elected council members to determine policy and officials to implement it and enforce the law. Local representatives, chosen by the enfranchised residents of their districts, sat in state legislatures that then selected U.S. senators. So long as most citizen concerns were generated within the bounds of an electoral district—and where national and international developments, such as tariffs and prices, impacted all residents in a similar way or divided them into competing factions—this system worked to channel public concerns into political arenas. But with the growing scale and complexity of American social and economic life, even this approximate mapping of political concerns into electoral districts was greatly eroded. Ongoing waves of new immigration, combined with relatively lenient requirements for citizenship and exercise of the franchise, created new electorates that were not integrated into existing social networks and factional alliances. Within settled portions of the older frontier, new generations headed west in search of open land and thereby injected themselves into early frontier politics or created these political systems *de novo*.

Even where the population was relatively settled and homogeneous, new economic and technological developments created problems and politics beyond the boundaries of established communities and settled networks. Long before the American Revolution, commercial networks extended out to the frontier, indeed driving it farther into the interior with demands for furs and other items for trade while creating markets for manufactured goods even in the most primitive of settlements. Just as earlier agricultural regions had understood themselves as profoundly dependent upon international commodity markets, so now industrializing and urbanizing areas recognized that their well-being depended upon a web of economic relations that stretched far beyond the scope of their formal political influence. Canals, railways, mines, and competing factories all had the potential to generate interests and grievances that could fuel political action.

In *The Public and Its Problems*, philosopher John Dewey captured the results of this unfolding process as they appeared in the decade between the First World War and the Great Depression. Industrialization, he argued, had profoundly altered the character of political life:

> The forms of associated action characteristic of the present economic order are so massive and extensive that they determine the most significant constituents of the public and the residence of power. Inevitably they reach out to grasp the agencies of government; they are controlling factors in legislation and administration. Not chiefly because of deliberate and planned self-interest, large as may be its role, but because they are the most potent and best organized of social forces. In a word, the new forms of combined action due to the modern economic régime control present politics, much as dynastic interests controlled those of two centuries ago. They affect thinking and desire more than did the interests which formerly moved the state.[2]

Dewey recognized that these changes in the character of social and economic life would generate "problems" that could not be addressed within a territorially organized polity. New problems would produce a new politics. Dewey hoped this new politics would center on expansive conversation and deliberation. The earliest effort to translate new shared concerns into political influence took the form of social movements and political parties, deploying tactics that included protests, parades, and petitions. But, historically, the specific form through which these organized social forces eventually secured political influence constitute what we now know as interest group politics (see Chapter 6).

Each term in this three-noun concept was a historical accomplishment: groups formed in ways that did not map onto traditional understandings of community or kinship; shared concerns were articulated in a language of group-specific "interest"; and new methods were found for linking the membership of groups to political actions and outcomes. Whereas much of contemporary political theory takes self-interest as given and then looks to explain "collective action"—or why individuals participate directly rather than counting on some other similarly interested actor to do the work of politics—a historical approach to interest group politics requires attention to the developments along each of these partially independent axes.

Based on economic activity, social commitments, or issue-based causes, these large social formations were not delimited by the electoral districts of formal representative politics. Instead, the response to industrialism involved the discovery of new methods of organizing across districts and outside parties in order to influence the substance of public policy. As Dewey so clearly recognized, the development of interest group politics is not the automatic outcome of a polity of self-interested rational individuals but rather of a particular phase of social development in which the response to a wide range of problems cannot be managed through inherited political forms. Instead, large-scale economic change and sustained organization innovation combined to produce what is now one of the most common features of the American political landscape: the organized interest group.

The explanation of this process begins with the explosion of associational activity that characterized much of the nineteenth century. Although these organizing efforts were not necessarily political from the outset, even the most apolitical of social groups could potentially define a group identity that then might lead to the articulation of a group interest. Religious revivals linked personal salvation to a collective interest in evangelism and the eradication of sin. These collective efforts in turn fueled efforts to distribute religious tracts throughout the western frontier, to protect the Sabbath, and to suppress vice. Many of these causes could be pursued through private actions, but given a motive for turning to politics, the most obvious path led directly into party politics. Either as a faction of one of the currently dominant parties or a third-party movement, many associational waves eventually sought to establish a foothold in electoral politics. Anti-immigrant, anti-conspiracy, anti-alcohol mobilizations, along with efforts to transform the currency system and address agrarian grievances, all found expression as third parties over the course of the nineteenth century. But with the Free Soil, later Republican, Party as the only notable success, associations and emergent groups with political grievances sought to develop new techniques for securing leverage over officials elected under the banner of other established parties. The first decades of the twentieth century saw two patterns of greatly intensified effort by large popular associations to influence public policy. One strategy emphasized the opening of access to policy through the institution of direct democracy in the form of the initiative and recall. The second worked within a party-dominated system of electoral politics, combining the opportunities afforded by party primaries and the possibility of forging tighter relationships with elected officials. By the 1920s the flurry of public condemnations of "blocs," "special interests," and "pressure boys" signaled the unquestioned establishment of interest group presence in American politics.

THE PREHISTORY OF INTEREST GROUP POLITICS

Groups are not new to either American politics or American political theory. Federalist 10 famously warned of the dangers of faction, the politics produced when "a number of citizens, whether amounting to a majority or minority of the whole, who are united and actuated by some common impulse of passion, or of interest, adverse to the rights of other citizens, or to the permanent and aggregate interest of the community" (see Chapter 1).[3] Four decades later, Alexis de Tocqueville used an extended example of an antitariff organization to illustrate his analysis of the centrality of association in American politics. But these foreshadows of interest group politics contrasted with a polity that was still largely organized around relationships of social deference or local community. Grievances motivated small farmers on the large estates of the Hudson River valley to find their way to early party politics and, in time, mobilizations of this kind would fuel the expansive partisanship of the Jacksonian era.[4] In organizational terms, the rise of the political party represented a powerful mechanism for linking local political alliances and oppositions into a national system. Through the remainder of the nineteenth century, the forms and practices of partisanship would be extended and refined, sustaining exceptionally high rates of electoral participation at least among those citizens who were both formally and effectively enfranchised.

Yet, even as the party system flourished, its capacity to channel grievances and ambitions in national politics came under new strains. By the middle of the nineteenth century, the economic development of the United States was pressing upon the neatly nested territorial units of the federal system. Westward settlement pushed the expansion of the institutions of the "General Government."[5] Each state brought new representatives and senators to Congress. Justices were added to the Supreme Court, and the circuits assigned to individual justices were enlarged. As innumerable historians have documented, each of these expansions was negotiated in light of its potential to upset one of the principal lines of division in the nation: the relationship of free states and slave states. But while political attention focused on maintaining this balance, streams of new settlement and sinews of transportation continued to cross-cut the boundaries of established electoral districts, new states, and aspiring territories. The ideas and grievances that potentially fueled political mobilization traced the same paths, creating the possibilities for social movements and ideological commitments that operated across as well as within state boundaries and congressional districts (see Chapter 6).

During the first half of the nineteenth century, these destabilizing tendencies accumulated and occasionally erupted in waves of political unrest leading to the birth of the Anti-Masonic Party of the 1820s, which feared the usurpation of democracy by a secret society, and the Know-Nothing Party of the 1850s, which had its origin in secret societies but mobilized in opposition to perceived threats from immigrants and Catholicism. In both of these cases, a new form of group politics took shape as insurgent party politics. With one major exception, this path from mobilization to political influence by way of party formation fell short. That exception was the Republican Party. The product of the cross-fertilization of the social movement for abolition and a fledgling Free Soil Party, the Republicans represented an incursion of changing social, economic, and ideological alignments into the realm of electoral politics.

This cartoon from the early 1880s caricatures the member of Congress as overwhelmed by the varied demands and interests of his constituents. His plight is juxtaposed with the idealized vision of the statesmen of yesteryear gathered to debate the fundamentals of government.

As an organizational phenomenon, the Republican Party looked both backward to the movement-like, petition-driven abolitionists and forward to the capacity of associations to serve as vehicles for politics outside—or, in this case, alongside—the major parties. The Republican Party also demonstrated how a common event or shared experience could generate not only a unifying "interest" but also expand familiarity with a shared repertoire of organizational techniques. The Civil War, particularly on the northern side, had made use of modern technology in unprecedented ways. By river and rail, steam power altered the scope of lines of supply and the movement of troops. Early forms of mass production generated streams of armaments, ammunition, uniforms, and other material accessories of war. Within both the army and the civilian organizations that supported the troops—notably the United States Sanitary Commission, which would feed into the postwar Union League movement—the experience of mobilization required new skills for coordination across lines of local networks and state governments. An indirect effect of this intensified, expanded movement of men and matériel was a further erosion of loyalties based on locality and an enhanced awareness of the impact of national politics on many aspects of life. After the war, the Grand Army of the Republic transformed itself into one of the most effective mass membership lobbies, pushing for more generous military pensions and rallying veterans across the country to support the Republican Party at the ballot box.

But since the disappearance of the Whig Party and the ascendance of the Republicans, the possibility of reconfiguring American politics through party formation has been unsuccessful in practical terms. Despite multiple efforts, particularly with the late nineteenth-century proliferation of Greenbackers, Populists, and Socialists of various flavors, the two-party system of electoral politics has consolidated and thereby limited this path for translating new kinds of political concerns into effective leverage over policy, for linking grievances directly to political decisions through the individual vote. But if movements have proven unable to become viable parties, they did begin to trace a path from grievances and mobilization to interest group politics.

AN AGE OF ASSOCIATIONS

This path began with an explosion of organizing and associating that touched almost every segment of the American population. Arriving in 1831, Tocqueville saw such activity as an intrinsic element of American political culture. But, as Johann Neem has argued, the legal framework of corporate charters and government tolerance for association outside of moments of revolutionary rupture were relatively new developments. Although the mobilization of the American Revolution had been an important seedbed of new organizing infrastructures, it was not automatically given that the associations that were hailed for their opposition to a delegitimated monarch and the British Empire would be welcomed as a normal part of a polity still learning the practices of unprecedented—but also incomplete—democracy.[6]

Once established, new legal opportunities and elite tolerance allowed for the emergence of new forms of voluntary associations and organized social movements. Michael Young argues that many of the important innovations emerged from within religious conflicts and revivals, specifically a new cultural construction that linked personal confession to national problems.[7] Abstention from the use of slave-produced goods was a practice that linked personal struggle against sin to national redemption. The importation of fraternal models, most importantly the Masons, fueled parallel and cross-cutting efforts at organizing the nation. Some sense of the scale of this effort can be found in the numbers of associations with memberships that included 1 percent or more of the relevant population (all adults, men or women). Theda Skocpol has constructed the roster of these major organizations, beginning with the Ancient and Accepted Free Masons, who crossed this membership threshold in the United States in the 1810s. The list is extensive, including other fraternal organizations, religious and social service organizations, agrarian and labor associations, and recreational groups. The peak period for the founding of these large organizations were the decades between the Civil War and the beginning of the twentieth century; almost thirty of these associations trace their origins to this time.[8]

In many of these organizations, membership fluctuated dramatically. The Grange, the model of an agrarian fraternal organization, claimed more than 450,000 members in 1875, but then collapsed to less than one-sixth that number fifteen years later, recovering to more than 300,000 only by 1930. The collapse of the Grange was offset by the meteoric growth of the Farmers' Alliance, the Populists, who claimed more than 1 million members in 1890 only to disappear almost completely within the decade. The American Farm Bureau Federation, which came to be recognized as one of the most powerful interest groups in national politics, developed in the wake of this collapse, but by 1930 had barely edged ahead of the Grange in terms of membership.[9] Despite the significant volatility in the membership of individual associations, their cumulative effect was to cultivate clear and competing understandings of what was "in the farmer's interest." Agrarian associations, in particular, were noted for their commitment to self-education and a decidedly autodidactic style. Through newspapers, lectures, and practices of debate and conversation within local groups, agrarian associations not only provided a welcome source of sociability in rural areas but also helped to define collective concerns that could then frame political efforts (see Chapter 12).

The Grange, a fraternal agricultural organization active in the nineteenth and twentieth centuries, offered farmers opportunities not only to socialize but also to discuss important issues and frame political debates.

Although the Grange and the Alliance quickly turned from sociability and economic self-help to politics, the luxuriant growth of voluntary associations in the late nineteenth century was not necessarily political in origin. Indeed, because politics was understood as potentially divisive partisanship, many associations had strict rules that effectively required members to park their party loyalties at the door. When potentially controversial issues were introduced on the program for a meeting, they would often be presented as a "report" or, as members gained more experience with public speaking, as a set debate with speakers assigned to represent both sides of the issue. But it would be a mistake to think of these expansive associations as political from the start. Instead, many associations were founded to meet desires for sociability and to organize arrangements of mutual benefit that would concentrate resources in thrift societies or share risk in mutual insurance schemes.[10] To the extent that any kind of association could potentially become a vehicle for the articulation of shared demands and the mobilization of political action, however, the proliferation of lodges and fraternals and reform associations had political consequences.

Many of these developments enrolled individuals who already had access to the polity through their standing as enfranchised and influential citizens. In such instances, the layering of private association on political participation took on a menacing appearance of elite conspiracy, which spurred outrage in forms such as the anti-Masonic mobilizations of the 1820s. Throughout the nineteenth century, elites used private association to consolidate their political influence and capacity for joint action, notably through militia units.[11] Elite clubs served as seedbeds for coalitions of industrial and financial leaders who would emerge as some of the earliest influential legislative lobbies. New forms of elite sociability and socialization, including clubs, private schools, and joint economic enterprises, contributed to the emergence of the distinct identities and interests of a rising "business class" that could exert influence at the municipal level and in national politics.[12] These elite organizing projects responded to popular associations in a defensive manner, as when employers banded together to contest union campaigns, and promoted other popular associations as means for enhancing the capacity of potential consumers. The synergy between mail order businesses and agrarian associations was particularly important, spurred by a shared interest in rural prosperity as the basis for a consumer market and better lives.[13] But aspiring elite politicians also joined more socially heterogeneous organizations, constructing ties of solidarity to larger constituencies through their membership in fraternal orders or encompassing agrarian organizations such as the Grange. For the emergence of a popular interest group politics, however, the expansive associationalism of the nineteenth century was more consequential when it involved those who were excluded from or disadvantaged within the formal electorate.

Two important lines of exclusion structured the polity: gender and, despite the Fifteenth Amendment, race. Nationally, women were largely excluded from political life even as some possessed considerable advantages due to race, class, and education. For black men, the repression of not only voting but also a wide range of civic activities in the South, seriously constrained their ability to leverage any form of organization into political influence. Nevertheless, both African American men and women (at least sporadically)[14] and women of all races (on a much larger and sustained scale) were able to use popular associations as a means for generating voice and possibly even influence despite their marginal status.

Short of full exclusion, whether *de facto* or *de jure*, other groups in the process of organizing also found themselves disadvantaged within a national polity now almost fully structured by the two major political parties. With their complex, cross-regional coalitions, both parties had a stake in suppressing issues that could divide northern elites from southern Democrats or from midwestern and western Republicans. Consequently, many issues of immediate concern to organized labor and farmers were suppressed or marginalized within national politics despite the full enfranchisement of large numbers of citizens committed to these causes. At the state level, the control of legislatures by party organizations or major corporations—notably the railroads—produced a similar dynamic with increasingly organized citizens seeking new forms of leverage over political decision making. This search was particularly intense because the well-being of farmers, workers, and other constituents in one region was becoming more dependent on decisions and struggles elsewhere in the nation. If farmers were part of a national, indeed global, market for commodities, the prices they received would be determined by the collective product of all farmers. Whereas workers might once have been able to gain leverage over employers by striking the plant in a particular community, their standards of work could now be threatened by the ability of corporations to move production elsewhere or to import new labor. Thus, there were high stakes in developing a form of political influence that was independent of the parties, capable of articulating group interests, and effective across the boundaries of electoral districts. But the search for that leverage posed challenges not only of political strategy but also political legitimacy.

THE SEARCH FOR POLITICAL LEGITIMACY AND EFFECTIVE TECHNIQUES

From the vantage point of contemporary politics, it is difficult to imagine a reason for people not to pursue their interests through collective political action. From the perspective of the late nineteenth century, however, such a practice was widely condemned. The opposition was based on a device central to centuries of liberal thought: the formation of a general will that discovered a common good. If organized workers in booming cities and farmers in scattered rural communities did not spend their time reflecting on the arguments of Locke and Rousseau, they nevertheless retained a strong sense that special interests were opposed to the general good. This linkage of uniformity and democratic values infused many areas of state and national policy, notably taxation.[15]

One result of this equation of uniformity and democracy was an uneasiness about the relationship between popular associations and political demands. Although the potential of this linkage seems obvious from the vantage point of contemporary American politics, where every imaginable association seems to have developed its own method for ranking and endorsing candidates, the etiquette of earlier associations typically required that collective self-interest and partisanship be kept under wraps. At times, such thinking resulted in organizational contortions, as members would be urged to advance their shared concerns by individually relocating to other associational venues or assuming different public identities. But if evasion and indirection were one means of lessening the friction between political involvement and associational membership, it came at the cost of a diminution of the potential leverage of the organized hundreds and thousands of members in the multiplying voluntary associations of the era. Predictably, leaders within many of those associations sought more direct means of influence. This common aspiration led to the invention of a new set of techniques and accompanying rationales.

As a consequence, members of large popular associations found it difficult to assert "their interests." They rightly understood that many would react to such proposals as incompatible with the proper deliberative character of democratic governance. As California farmers protested in 1901:

> The farmers of this country who produce so large a proportion of its material wealth and prosperity are vitally interested in both State and National legislation. They do not, however, demand and the Grange, as the representative farmers' organization, does not desire so-called *special legislation* in their behalf. We insist upon the passage of just and equitable laws that shall safe-guard all *legitimate interests,* preventing one from taking advantage of another and guaranteeing to each an equal opportunity for normal development (emphasis added).[16]

Even though these large agrarian associations would seem to exemplify the factions feared by Madison, "a number of citizens . . . united and actuated by some common impulse of passion," the farmer members were highly averse to any action that might be perceived as "adverse to the rights of other citizens, or to the permanent and aggregate interest of the community." There seemed to be no way around this legitimacy problem. Derogatory labels—blocs, special interests, lobbies—would continue to be attached to popular efforts to influence politics through the twentieth century and into the twenty-first.

Legitimacy concerns notwithstanding, the stakes in political decision making were perceived as simply too large for popular associations to stand aside in virtuous respect for the common good. But if these associations were to engage in politics, what specific interests would they promote? Two decisions by the California State Grange in 1892 illustrate this concern as well as the contested limits of group influence over individual political preferences. The Master of the State Grange offered a list of official "suggestions" for consideration by the assembled membership. The suggestions included:

> Seventh, have a committee of good men at Sacramento, during the coming session of the Legislature, to give information concerning agriculture, and to urge the passage of certain needed and reform legislation.

Eighth, let this body, at this session, examine the merits of the proposed amendments to the State Constitution, to be voted upon this fall, at the general election, and let such action be taken by this body as will inform the farmers of the State what their interest is in this matter.[17]

The "Committee for the Good of the Order" approved the first of these suggestions but denied the second, understanding it as an improper trespass of the organization on the political deliberations of its membership. This objection was not a particular quirk of this association. Any effort to articulate a shared interest also faced potential opposition from within the membership of an association. Recall, first, that many voluntary associations articulated an explicit commitment to nonpartisanship, not least as a means of welcoming a wide array of members. Even when most members did share a particular partisan inclination, there was often a strong sense that expressions of that partisanship violated the etiquette of sociability. In addition, however, was the question of which particular issues could be rightly understood as falling within the bounds of a "group interest."[18] Did labor unions have an interest in woman suffrage, particularly if organized women were suspected of supporting temperance legislation, which was believed to be opposed by many (but not all) organized working men? Even if such hotly contested cultural issues were set aside, could organized farmers or workers be said to have an interest in procedural reforms such as the initiative and referendum—particularly given that the national leadership of the American Federation of Labor was opposed to practices of direct democracy in its own self-governance? And once there had been some determination of what was a legitimate group interest in an issue, how exactly could that be linked to particular political actions by elected officials?

Cumulatively, these puzzles demanded new understandings and technologies of democratic accountability. One early form was the pledge demanded of candidates who sought the support of an association in their quest for office. In this simple form, a promise to support a piece of legislation could be the basis for renewed endorsement or opposition at the next election. For the American Federation of Labor as a whole, this method became the basis of its overall strategy of "friends or enemies" endorsement as a substitute for alliance with a major party. Officially adopted in 1906, this endorsement strategy offered an alternative to the third-party efforts of American socialists and accommodated the alliances that some unions and city federations of labor had with Republicans while others were linked to Democratic political organizations. Without a party label, however, it was not necessarily easy to identify a friend or an enemy. The identification of candidates who would promote a group's interest required information and a capacity to discriminate amongst the many votes taken during a legislative session. Consequently, by the early twentieth century, both labor and agrarian groups were experimenting with what is now known as roll call tabulation. These efforts began with the identification of specific votes on issues of interest to the group and then rated each legislator in terms of their cumulative performance. In California, organized labor also recognized that it would be possible to trade the support of their most loyal representatives on a bill of no interest to labor for support of labor issues from representatives with few union members in their districts.[19] Other efforts were directed at constituting "interests" well before a voter walked into a polling place. Years before they gained the right to vote, women's organizations actively participated in this effort to circumvent party politics. Cultivating an understanding of politics as political education, women's organizations pioneered active efforts to inform enfranchised men and to shape future voters through the introduction of required courses on issues such as temperance and sponsorship of essay contests and performances that would—it was hoped—shape opinion long before it was exposed to the direct efforts of political parties.

THE PEOPLE'S LOBBY

At some point between the late nineteenth century and the First World War, these issues of legitimacy and technique were either forgotten or resolved. Although the intensity and skill of extrapartisan, interest-based political organizations varied from state to state, this form of relationship between popular associations and elected officials was becoming a prominent, if not yet a taken-for-granted, feature of American politics. Interest-based groups mobilized to aid candidates in primary elections, to promote or oppose specific ballot proposals in the form of initiatives and referenda, and to testify and lobby in support of particular pieces of legislation. These developments were exemplified by the emergence of new kinds of organizations that sought to link multiple individuals and organizations around a particular political orientation or set of issues: the Joint Legislative Committee, which coordinated organized labor and agrarian efforts in Washington State politics; and the American Association for Labor Legislation, which linked individuals and experts to larger campaigns for labor law at state and national levels.

These new capacities represented a potential threat to the political parties and to the webs of corporate control over state and national legislatures. The threat was captured in a rumor that circulated in Sacramento during the legislative session of 1909: "Certain public-spirited citizens of Los Angeles and San Francisco would maintain at the Capitol during the session a lobby to protect the interests of the people, just as the machine lobby looks after the well-being of machine-protected corporations and individuals."[20]

These political currents of the progressive period inevitably managed to flow back into the channels of electoral politics, both through primary elections and, in an echo of many third parties past, in the form of the progressive presidential campaigns of Theodore Roosevelt in 1912 and Robert La Follette in 1924. But these efforts were largely quixotic, and the cumulative force of such political innovations was instead evident in the increasing capacity of voluntary associations to articulate policy positions and then to monitor politicians' actions with respect to them. Daniel Tichenor and Richard Harris have documented the growing numbers of individuals and association representatives who appeared in front of congressional committees to speak to different issues and specific legislation.[21] Earlier theories of representation focused on the selection of a "good man" as their representative who would join in deliberations to determine the common good, but by the early twentieth century, individual citizens and representatives of their associations insisted on speaking directly to assembled legislators in an effort to promote their particular interests in the laws under consideration.

The successes of extrapartisan, issue-based political mobilization were striking. Not one but two amendments to the U.S. Constitution—the eighteenth entrenching Prohibition as national law and the nineteenth establishing a woman's right to vote—were seen at the time as the unprecedented accomplishments of a new kind of politics. In state legislatures and Congress, a variety of associations mounted impressive lobbying operations. To have a regular presence in committee deliberations and informal persuasion, associations with headquarters scattered around the country began to open offices in Washington, D.C. The American Federation of Labor erected its national headquarters in 1916, and, after much delay reflecting antipathy to government regulation of the medical profession and public health insurance, the American Medical Association followed suit in 1943.[22]

To improve access to policymakers, many organizations began opening offices in Washington, D.C. The American Federation of Labor opened their Washington headquarters in 1916.

Imitation, however, is said to be the sincerest form of flattery. As the techniques developed by popular associations proved successful, the very forces against which these associations had mobilized in the first place began to adopt them. Whereas corporations had previously relied on the less formal "lobby" with its overtones (and often evidence) of corruption, business interests now followed the scripts established by voluntary associations and reform groups. In the 1920 presidential campaigns "the Republicans took a leaf out of the campaign procedure of the Progressive Party under Roosevelt and instituted a bureau . . . which made serious studies of the issues . . . and which, during the campaign, collated material and opinion in an effort to lift party discussion to a new and competently informed stage."[23] The Republicans also crafted policy tailored to the anticipated demands of different constituency, promising to establish a women's bureau in anticipation of the influence of a women's bloc in the electorate. As one critical, but anonymous, observer charged in 1924:

> The American woman in her activities wants, not your way, not our way, but her own way.
>
> "Group legislation" we at large have been saying to Labor for some while.
>
> "Group legislation" we're crying nowadays to the would-be Blocs, the farmer and others.
>
> "Group legislation" we'll have to cry next to the organized American woman and her lobby, the Women's Joint Congressional committee. For, of man's political weapons, the American woman has taken for her own the lobby—of all of them the most undemocratic.[24]

This critic overlooked the long record of women's organizations as innovators of the techniques of popular pressure politics, but the point is well taken. By the 1920s the methods of popular interest group politics had become widely available within the arena of American politics. Whether adopted by women who had once claimed to be free of the corruptions of partisan politics or by business interests that were the object of mobilizations for reform, these methods now shaped an ever-growing segment of political activity.

THE PERSISTENCE OF INTEREST GROUP POLITICS

The innovations that generated modern interest group politics were fueled by felt grievances with the politics of the late nineteenth century as well as the efforts of innumerable organizers to turn large-scale associations to focused political purposes. Naturally, there was no guarantee that these efforts would prove to be effective or lasting. As John Mark Hansen has argued, the entrenchment of interest group politics required not only the inventiveness of agitators and organizers but also the considerations of political elites, specifically the legislators who were the object of all this popular lobbying. Why, he asks, would legislators respond to interest group efforts out of all the possible sources of pressure and pleading intended to sway their votes? This response turns on two conditions: the greater effectiveness of interest groups in comparison to other possible sources of information and support (such as party structures or personal networks) and the expectation that issues of central concern to interest group will recur across elections and legislative sessions.

In meeting these conditions, the most formidable interest groups used recognizable variants of the linked pledges and roll call tabulations developed at the turn of the century. Gray Silver, the leading lobbyist for the American Farm Bureau Federation in the 1920s, made extensive use of "District-by-district tabulations of responses to public sentiment polls taken by county farm bureaus at the request of the headquarters in Chicago." If a congressman seemed to be wavering in advance of an important roll call or if someone had the temerity to challenge the Farm Bureau's position, Silver did not hesitate to show him the poll results. In an emergency, he would telegraph directly to state and county offices and know that a flood of wires would pour into his office as evidence that the grass roots were informed.

Technique alone, however, did not determine the influence of these interest group efforts. The alignment of group interests with partisan differences was also consequential with interest groups enjoying their greatest clout when their concerns cross-cut party lines, and their least influence under conditions such as in 1924 when Sen. Robert La Follette's independent campaign for president captured much of the impetus for agrarian insurgency.[25] The disjuncture between agrarian concerns and party loyalties gave organized groups opportunities to mobilize within party primaries and, then, to provide signals of constituent concerns to elected legislators. With farm crises recurring throughout the 1920s, legislators came to expect that agriculture issues would determine votes in future elections. With this, Hansen's two conditions—reliable information and recurring issues—required for durable interest group politics were established. Although women's groups had effectively deployed leverage from outside the parties in their campaign for the vote, the much-anticipated "women's vote" did not materialize as a coherent bloc during the 1920s, and, accordingly, the political influence of women's associations waned.[26]

The alignments of associations of social or economic groups with political institutions did not stop with the legislative branch. In a journalistic account published in 1939, *The Pressure Boys: The Inside Story of Lobbying in America*, Kenneth G. Crawford asked "Why does this piece of legislation, which seems highly desirable, get nowhere, while this other bill, which benefits only a small group, becomes law? Why does this legislator, who is a dolt at best and a crook at worst, win re-election and advancements, while this other legislator, who has all the qualifications for public service and conscientiously tries to use them, quickly fades from the national scene?" The answer, Crawford argues, could be found in "subterranean forces, whose directions cannot be charted and a day-to-day basis . . . collectively, they constitute a sort of phantom fourth branch of the government."[27] As one illustration of how the system worked through all aspects of national government, Crawford detailed the capacity of government agencies and interest groups to forestall government reorganization championed by President Franklin Roosevelt.

Crawford traced opposition to the reorganization bill to "the fuss kicked up by the Forest Service of the Agriculture Department." The motivation of civil servants to contest an efficiency-promoting reorganization flowed from ties between the federal agency and organized interest groups:

> No bureau in the government is more strongly entrenched than the Forest Service. Its representatives in the field wear snappy green uniforms. Its regional directors are lords of all they survey. They belong to civic organizations and clubs in the cities of their districts. They deal pleasantly and sympathetically with the influential lumbermen and ranchers. When the Forest Service needs anything from Congress, the regional men simply and easily turn the heat on Congressmen by explaining their problems to fellow members of the back-home Rotary Clubs.[28]

In this account, the developmental trajectory of popular interest groups turns back upon itself. If the great wave of association making had led to new kinds of pressures on political decision making, the now-established landscape of clubs and leagues and associations constituted a set of opportunities for federal officials to generate public support for the defense of their own programs and power.[29] With industry interests obscured by the veneer of professional civil servants, Crawford asserted:

> the lumber propaganda, always coupled with intense devotion to abstract principles of conservation, goes out

> to women's clubs, college and high school teachers and other groups. These trusting people live in the memory of the fight between Gifford Pinchot and [Richard] Ballinger, back in 1911, and apparently never asked themselves why the lumbering, mining and grazing interests put up money to prevent transfer of the Forest Service. From them came thousands of letters and telegrams to Congress during the reorganization controversy.[30]

The specifics of this episode notwithstanding, what is striking is how the endogenous processes of collective self-education and interest-formation that characterized association-building decades earlier were displaced—at least in part—by the consumption of opinions and positions advanced by public figures who may or may not be disinterested.

The consequences of these developments have implications for all three of the constitutive nouns: *interest* and *group* and *politics*. Whereas the recognition and understanding of interests had once been rooted in a rich set of educational practices, the recitations of women's clubs, and the hours-long lectures featured at gatherings of Populists, the shaping of interests now involved processes that were recognized as akin to advertising and propaganda. This shift was not solely the result of the appropriation of interest group politics by business lobbyists; woman suffragists had, after all, recognized much earlier that "although the proposition that women should vote is seriously and profoundly true, it will, at first, be established with this class of people much as the virtues of a breakfast food are established,—by affirmation."[31] And, if interests could be formed by affirmation and advertising, in time so would the shared identities that sustained associations be tailored to particular political agendas. The "special" but nevertheless encompassing identities of "worker" or "farmer" or "woman" would be modified with adjectives and qualifications: industrial, dairy, professional, and so forth. Finally, although this new politics emerged from the tensions with electoral politics, it did not fully escape the territorial organization of electoral districts. Rather the articulation of interests was shaped within that system, with an eye to determining who was elected or finding leverage where legislators were relatively unconstrained (or particularly conflicted) by constituency demands.

Obviously, this system did not conform entirely to John Dewey's expectations for a politics that would follow the telegraph and railroad lines instead of being contained within the boundaries of electoral districts and government jurisdictions. As popular associations morphed into popular interest group politics and then into professionalized lobbying, the lines of pressure and mobilization were woven in and out through electoral politics and the arenas in which public opinion was formed. Nineteenth-century activists had found it convenient to shift identities—appearing one day as a union official and the next as a socialist, at one rally as a woman suffragist and the next as a temperance advocate. But the complexity of the emerging system made it difficult to link positions and pressures to "authentic" constituencies as opposed to the agendas of professional lobbyists and even federal officials who either spoke in their names or educated constituencies to their own interests. What began as an effort to link popular understandings of self-interest directly to policy had become a complex, mediated, and often opaque system of influence over political outcomes.

NOTES

1. John H. Aldrich, *Why Parties? The Origins and Transformation of Party Politics in America* (Chicago: University of Chicago Press, 1995); Michael P. Young, *Bearing Witness Against Sin: The Evangelical Birth of the American Social Movement* (Chicago: University of Chicago Press, 2006).

2. John Dewey, *The Public and Its Problems* (Athens: Swallow Press/Ohio University Press, 1927 [1954]), 107–108.

3. Alexander Hamilton, James Madison, and John Jay, *The Federalist Papers,* with an introduction, table of contents, and index of ideas by Clinton Rossiter (New York: New American Library, 1961), 78.

4. Reeve Huston, *Land and Freedom: Rural Society, Popular Protest, and Party Politics in Antebellum New York* (New York: Oxford University Press, 2000); Richard L. McCormick, *The Party Period and Public Policy: American Politics from the Age of Jackson to the Progressive Era* (New York: Oxford University Press, 1986); Gordon S. Wood, *The Radicalism of the American Revolution* (New York: Vintage Books, 1991).

5. Brian Balogh, *A Government Out of Sight: The Mystery of National Authority in Nineteenth-Century America* (New York: Cambridge University Press, 2008).

6. Johann Neem, *Creating a Nation of Joiners: Democracy and Civil Society in Early National Massachusetts* (Cambridge: Harvard University Press, 2008); T. H. Breen, *American Insurgents, American Patriots: The Revolution of the People* (New York: Hill and Wang, 2010).

7. Young, *Bearing Witness.*

8. Theda Skocpol, *Diminished Democracy: From Membership to Management in American Civic Life* (Norman: University of Oklahoma Press, 2003).

9. Robert L. Tontz, "Memberships of General Farmers' Organizations, United States, 1874–1960," *Agricultural History* 14, no. 2 (1940).

10. David T. Beito, *From Mutual Aid to the Welfare State: Fraternal Societies and Social Services, 1890–1967* (Chapel Hill: University of North Carolina Press, 2000).

11. Larry Isaac, "To Counter 'The Very Devil' and More: The Making of Independent Capitalist Militias in the Gilded Age," *American Journal of Sociology* 108 (2002): 353–405.

12. Jeffrey Haydu, *Citizen Employers: Business Communities and Labor in Cincinnati and San Francisco, 1870–1916* (Ithaca, N.Y.: Cornell University Press, 2008); William G. Roy, *Socializing Capital: The Rise of the Large Industrial Corporation in America* (Princeton: Princeton University Press, 1997); Martin Sklar, *The Corporate Reconstruction of American Capitalism,* 1890–1916 (New York: Cambridge University Press, 1988).

13. Peter Ascoli, Julius Rosenwald: *The Man Who Built Sears, Roebuck and Advanced the Cause of Black Education in the American South* (Bloomington: Indiana University Press, 2006).

14. Joseph Gerteis, *Class and the Color Line: Interracial Class Coalition in the Knights of Labor and the Populist Movement* (Durham, N.C.: Duke University Press, 2007).

15. Robin L. Einhorn, *American Taxation, American Slavery* (Chicago: University of Chicago Press, 2006).

16. Quoted in Elisabeth S. Clemens, *The People's Lobby: Organizational Innovation and the Rise of Interest Group Politics in the United States, 1890–1925* (Chicago: University of Chicago Press, 1997), 171.

17. Ibid.

18. For a discussion about implications of such debates about "interests," see Dara Z. Strolovitch, *Affirmative Advocacy: Race, Class, and Gender in Interest Group Politics* (Chicago: University of Chicago Press, 2007).

19. Clemens, *People's Lobby,* 120–127.

20. Quoted in ibid, 1.

21. Daniel J. Tichenor and Richard A. Harris, "Organized Interests and American Political Development," *Political Science Quarterly* 117, 4 (2002/2003): 587–612.

22. Frank D. Campion, *The AMA and U.S. Health Policy since 1940* (Chicago: Chicago Review Press, 1984), 127–128.

23. "The Republican Victory," *Survey,* November 13, 1920, 247.

24. Quoted in Clemens, *People's Lobby,* 234.

25. John Mark Hansen, *Gaining Access: Congress and the Farm Lobby, 1919–1981* (Chicago: University of Chicago Press, 1991).

26. Clemens, *People's Lobby, 231–234;* Anna L. Harvey, *Votes without Leverage: Women in American Electoral Politics, 1920–1970* (New York: Cambridge University Press, 1998).

27. Kenneth G. Crawford, *The Pressure Boys: The Inside Story of Lobbying in America* (New York: Julian Messner, 1939), viii–ix.

28. Ibid., 195.

29. On the alliance of social movements and federal officials in the creation of agencies, see Daniel P. Carpenter, *The Forging of Bureaucratic Authority: Reputations, Networks, and Policy Innovation in Executive Agencies, 1862–1928* (Princeton: Princeton University Press, 2000).

30. Crawford, *Pressure Boys,* 199–200.

31. Quoted in Clemens, *People's Lobby,* 217.

SUGGESTED READING

Clemens, Elisabeth S. *The People's Lobby: Organizational Innovation and the Rise of Interest Group Politics in the United States, 1890–1925.* Chicago: University of Chicago Press, 1997.

Hansen, John Mark. *Gaining Access: Congress and the Farm Lobby, 1919–1981.* Chicago: University of Chicago Press, 1991.

Neem, Johann. *Creating a Nation of Joiners: Democracy and Civil Society in Early National Massachusetts.* Cambridge: Harvard University Press, 2008.

Skocpol, Theda. *Diminished Democracy: From Membership* to *Management in American Civic Life.* Norman: University of Oklahoma Press, 2003.

Tichenor, Daniel J., and Richard A. Harris. "Organized Interests and American Political Development," *Political Science Quarterly* 117, 4 (2002/2003): 587–612.

PART II ★ THEORETICAL APPROACHES TO INTEREST GROUPS AND LOBBYING

CHAPTER 4	Group Formation and Maintenance	49
CHAPTER 5	American Pluralism, Interest Group Liberalism, and Neopluralism	63
CHAPTER 6	Interest Groups and Social Movements	77
CHAPTER 7	Economic Models of Interest Groups and Lobbying	87

chapter 4

Group Formation and Maintenance

by Paul E. Johnson

The National Federation of Independent Business (NFIB) was established in 1943, breaking away from the Chamber of Commerce, where the NFIB's founder, C. Wilson Harder, had been a staff member. Following his vision to harness the political might of small businesses, Harder presided over the more or less steady growth of the organization for twenty-six years. Succeeding leaders modernized and formalized the staff and its management, cultivating and expanding the membership base. The NFIB has been widely characterized as the foremost political representative of small business in the United States. It was credited with a major political victory when Congress in 1993 rejected President Bill Clinton's plan for health care reform.

The NFIB had more than 600,000 dues-paying members in the mid-1990s. That was its high-water mark, as membership has been on the decline ever since. In 2009 the NFIB claimed a membership of 330,000, although the number may actually be lower.[1] The organization has undergone a tumultuous transition of leadership; regional offices have been closed; and administrative expenses and staff have been reduced.

For about 100 years, political scientists have searched for a theory that can explain the growth and decline of political organizations like the NFIB. The early researchers tended to view membership organizations as reflections of underlying social interests. They would probably guess that the small business segment of the economy had shrunk or that its political needs had somehow changed. More recently, some scholars have adopted more individualistic theories to interpret membership patterns. They might say that an economic recession caused the members to withdraw to save money, or that the members were unhappy with the offerings of the association and looked elsewhere to meet those needs, or that a change in the legal or economic environment made it impractical for the NFIB to maintain such a large membership base.

After looking at the problem from several points of view, political scientists have not arrived at a completely satisfactory explanation. This result may reflect the existence of so many different types of membership organizations. It is possible that one theory will explain why a small business owner joins the NFIB (an association of firms), why an aircraft factory worker joins the International Association of Machinists and Aerospace Workers (a labor union), and why a lawyer joins the American Bar Association (a professional association). Maybe that one theory will illuminate why that same person will decide to join the Izaak Walton League (a so-called citizen's group for environmentalists) or the Veterans of Foreign Wars. In short, it would be satisfying to have a single theory to provide an understanding of why organizations form, some grow large and become politically influential, while others remain on the periphery of the political conscience or die off entirely.

This chapter is divided into three parts. First, the early research that introduced political associations into political science is discussed. That period was the heyday of interest group politics and the study of pluralism. Pluralism holds that governmental decisions balance the many conflicting pressures exerted by interest groups, which are in turn seen as expressions of social and economic divisions. The second part focuses on the introduction of the more individualistic theories of organizations in the 1960s. That era is marked by the introduction of economic reasoning in political science, as a cross-fertilization of ideas led to the growth of the field of political economy. The third part digs into some organizational details. It focuses on organizational details that are likely to hold the key in the search for a more comprehensive explanation of the rise and decline of voluntary political organizations.

THE FIRST FIFTY YEARS OF POLITICAL ASSOCIATION RESEARCH

Arthur Bentley was a visionary who proposed a theory of politics based on social interests and groups in his 1908 book, *The Process of Government.* He thought of society as a mosaic of demands that were expressed through interest groups. An interest group was defined as a collection of people who were united by a shared view of public policy. Government was a balancing mechanism that compared the might of these groups and acted accordingly. "There is no political process that is not a balancing of quantity against quantity. There is not a law that is passed that is not the expression of force and force in tension." When he called for a major reorientation of political science by arguing, "The great task in the study of any form of social life is the analysis of these groups,"[2] very few scholars took any notice.

In retrospect, we can see that Bentley's behavioral theory of politics was about fifty years ahead of his time. Although Bentley did not rise to academic preeminence, his followers did. David Truman's book *The Governmental Process* accumulated the research of a generation of social scientists, including anthropologists, sociologists, and political scientists, into an over-arching "group theory of politics."[3] Also known as the "pluralist theory" of politics, Truman argued that the formation of political groups is a natural process of action and reaction driven by social, economic, and political change. Truman systematically applied his perspective to all of the "usual suspects" in American politics: elections, parties, and the branches of government (see Chapter 5).

Truman and the other pluralists did not think it was very interesting to ask "why do people join groups?" Within their mindset, such a question is as trivial as asking "why do we see with our eyes?" The answer is painfully obvious: "We just do." Truman proclaimed that "Man is a social animal," and he cited the preeminent scholar John Dewey, who contended, "Associated activity needs no explanation; things are made that way."[4]

A pluralist's explanation for the growth of organizations, then, is quite simple. When people perceive a need to coalesce and become active in politics, they do so. New interests develop because of changes in technology, the economy, or the society, and those interests are manifested by the formation of political groups. If one group exerts an unexpected amount of pressure on the system, then either it will have its way or it will be counterbalanced by exertion in the opposite direction by other groups. Public policy rests at an always tenuous balance point, reflecting the deeper changes in society. To the pluralists, it was not particularly important to explain why some particular people became active. People did become active, and that was the end of the story.

MANCUR OLSON'S REVOLUTION

In *The Structure of Scientific Revolutions*, science historian Thomas Kuhn observed that science has made major advances when scientists adopt a new world view, an *entirely* new paradigm that supplies new principles that help them understand how their observations fit together.[5] It is no overstatement to say that Mancur Olson's 1965 book, *The Logic of Collective Action*, caused a scientific revolution in political science. Indeed, it led to a comprehensive change of outlook in interest group research. Although the concepts of public finance that Olson relied upon had been known to European economists since 1898,[6] and to the mainstream of American economists in 1954,[7] they were not familiar in the least to interest group scholars in political science until Olson introduced them.

The Collective Action Problem

One can find many book-length reinvestigations of Olson's *Logic*, but Olson's theme can be summarized generally and succinctly as follows: "people don't pay for free stuff."

Casual observation would confirm this. People do sometimes give money to street musicians, to waiters, or to religious and philanthropic organizations. Nevertheless, it seems that most people, most of the time, will take free things if they are offered. Rock bands sell tickets, they do not invite partygoers to a free show and then ask for donations. For parties of six or more, most restaurants impose a standard gratuity on the group because bad tippers find security in large numbers.

How can such a simple insight be so important for interest group research? Olson said the pluralist model of human behavior did not match up with the premise that people do not pay for free stuff. The accomplishments of people who work together are collective goods, meaning that they are "nonexcludable." If a group wins congressional approval of new national holiday, a ban on handguns, or a medical care program for children, the effects of the new law will apply to all citizens. The people who do not help to produce the collective good will still benefit from it. If a collective good requires the cooperative action of thousands of people, then it seems likely each person's contribution will have a very small—perhaps negligible—effect. Under those conditions, an individual will consider "free riding" on the efforts of others. In the economic vernacular, voluntary provision of collective goods will be below the social optimum. Even Adam Smith, who in 1776 shocked the world with his advocacy of free markets, recognized that there were collective needs for which a wholly individualistic economy would not provide.[8]

At the heart of the collective action problem is the fact that the individual's contribution does not have a measurable effect on the collective good that is eventually achieved. Each person can think, "If the others are going to succeed in their effort, then I will let them. But if they are going to fail, they will probably fail whether I help or not." If every individual is considering the group's effort from that perspective, it may be that no one contributes anything. At the risk of confusing this point with economic jargon, it is worthwhile to quote the source:

> [H]owever beneficial the functions large voluntary associations are expected to perform, there is no incentive for any individual in a latent group to join such an association. . . . The traditional theory of voluntary associations is therefore mistaken.[9]

If we are to understand the aggregation of political interests into a voluntary organization, the pluralist's answer, which was "because they do," is simply unacceptable.

Olson's Account of Political Organizations

In *The Logic of Collective Action,* Olson offers a number of explanations for the formation of political organizations. First, he says that sometimes a group is "privileged" because there are donors who are willing and able to provide the collective good for themselves, and they are not bothered that others will benefit as well. Because the good is nonexcludable, everyone else free rides on the major donor's effort. A wealthy person may donate funds for new hospital wing or a school building with the understanding that the building will bear a certain person's name or follow a particular architectural style. For whatever reason, that donor is willing to cover the cost of the entire project. In some international alliances, the lion's share of the cost is born by just one or a few nations who value the collective good so dearly that will carry the whole burden.[10] Ross Perot's willingness to bankroll a political campaign and an entire political party in 1992 and 1996 might also serve as an example. Political scientist Russell Hardin cited a story about Howard Hughes, who bought a television station in Las Vegas so he could control the shows he would watch.[11] It did not matter to Hughes that all of the other residents could also watch. To Hughes, it was worthwhile to pay for the whole thing by himself. All of these examples have something in common: some donors are not powerless. They can make a difference, and so the collective action problem does not arise in its purest form. Therefore, Olson put most of his effort into understanding collective action in more difficult circumstances.

A second solution Olson considered was the "small group effect." There are a number of reasons why small groups may be more likely to muster the effort to provide a collective good. When there are just a few people who want something, and they are members of the same church or workplace, they may meet regularly and exert social pressure (coercion) on one another.

The "size effect" has been one of the most widely discussed, and most often misunderstood, components in Olson's *Logic.* The discussion of group size is tricky for a number of reasons. One source of trouble is that the term *group* has several meanings. To the pluralist, group means people who are united in an effort to achieve a common interest. For the most part, Olson uses group to mean people who would benefit if a collective good were provided. Olson believes that members of small groups are more likely to be able to find each other, to have manageable meetings, and to make a plan for collective action. The two meanings of group are frequent sources of confusion. If the members of an Olsonian group do not know about each other, it is hard to believe that it matters very much whether there are 5, 100, or 1 million members. The simple act of collecting these people together—or notifying them about each other—would be providing a collective good. If the two people who care about something happen to live in the same bedroom, however, they may be more likely to notice that their collective interest can be advanced by a mutual effort.

Another source of trouble in the debate over group size is that several variables may change as the number of members is increased. If adding users makes a collective good less valuable to the individuals involved, a "crowding effect" is said to exist. A freely available swimming pool may become less valuable to the swimmers as more and more users are added. If the collective good is truly shared, without any crowding effect, and if one person is willing to provide that good to suit his own purposes, the size of the group is completely irrelevant to the question of whether the good will be provided.[12] One might be willing to expend his whole fortune lobbying for a law that would rename the moon or officially declare that it is not made of green cheese. Whether there is one person or a million people who agree is completely irrelevant to his decision. But it is possible to design scenarios of resource collection and collective good provision that might make small groups either less likely or more likely to provide an efficient amount of the collective good.[13]

Finally, Olson offered his "by-product" theory of political organizations. This explanation is thought to apply to large groups of potential beneficiaries. Olson had in mind organizations such as labor unions, professional associations, and organizations that attempt to lobby in "the public interest." Because the free-rider problem is overwhelming to a large group of disconnected people, they will not spontaneously join together with the desire for a collective good. Rather, people who join an organization are seeking a **selective incentive,** an excludable, "members only" benefit. Organizations that try to offer only collective benefits fail because "people don't pay for free stuff." Organizations invite members by offering magazines, T-shirts, life insurance, customized credit cards, and the like.

Organizations that have clever leadership will look to the government for help. An association of professionals may seek to position itself within the licensing process in the states. The associations of doctors (American Medical

Association) and lawyers (American Bar Association) had a good deal of success with that approach until 1970 or so. Today, in twenty-eight states, an attorney is required to join a state bar association to practice law. The membership of the AMA has now declined to about one-third of all doctors, partly because state policies no longer require doctors to join the AMA when they enroll in their respective state medical associations. Leaders of labor unions also look to the government for help. They seek laws that will make it easier to organize workers and compel them to pay dues.

If organizations are framed around the marketing of selective incentives, where does political pressure come from? If an organization expends resources, by lobbying, for example, to provide a collective good—one that flows to members and nonmembers alike—the collective good is interpreted as a "by-product" of the organization's core function. According to Olson:

> The common characteristic which distinguishes all of the large economic groups with significant lobbying organizations is that these groups are also organized for some other purpose. The large and powerful economic lobbies are in fact the by-products of organizations that obtain their strength and support because they perform some function in addition to lobbying for collective goods.[14]

Organizations' publicity may claim that their main focus is providing a collective good by representing a viewpoint in politics, but if Olson is right, either they are misrepresenting themselves or they are mistaken.

The differences between the evaluation of the political "pressure system" by the pluralists and Olson could not be more stark. Where the pluralists expected spontaneous political action to emerge from newly formed interests, Olson expected no action whatsoever. Where the leading pluralists thought the political system would be a reflection of society, fairly representing all of its components,[15] Olson expected a political system that would be dominated by business and professional associations that had found ways to overcome the free-rider problem. Unlike other critics of pluralism, who claimed that the political system was somehow closed to the interests of the poor, racial minorities, women, consumers, young people, and the disabled,[16] Olson found a problem on a deeper level. The interests that are historically weak are not excluded so much as disorganized and unexpressed.[17] From within the Olsonian perspective, it appears that the would-be leaders of these weakly represented sectors have no choice but to find something they can sell in order to build a membership base. Only after that will they have the resources needed to make a major push against the political system.

Theories of Exchange and Patronage

Olson's theme struck home with many political scientists who had been seeking to develop a richer understanding of political organizations. Robert Salisbury's "exchange theory of interest groups" offered several suggestions that have served as a vocabulary and analytical framework of that research enterprise.[18] Salisbury characterized the exchange between a group organizer—an entrepreneur—and the prospective members who might enlist to obtain selective incentives. Adapting a typology of incentives from the theory of organizational management, Salisbury categorized three types of selective benefits that entrepreneurs offer.[19] First, *material* incentives are tangible members-only goods like journals, backpacks, employment licenses, and so forth. Second, *solidary* benefits flow from opportunities for interaction within the organization. An agricultural organization of the 1800s called The Grange attracted rural members by offering square dances and other social activities that were prized by farm families. Third, Salisbury proposed the idea that entrepreneurs may be able to sell *expressive* benefits to their members. The premise is that people are willing to pay some amount—probably a small amount—simply to have the psychological satisfaction of "having a say" or paying for someone to tell "those bums in Washington" what to do.

Salisbury emphasized the difficulty of maintaining an organization that is framed on expressive benefits. It may be possible to raise money by going from door to door, asking people for $50 to help hire a lobbyist to fight pollution or oppose a war. Most people will say no, but some will make a contribution. But most donors will tire of the requests and lose interest. Expressive benefits are likely to have a fleeting attraction for members, so organizations based on them may flourish, but they will as quickly die off. History is littered with organizational "flashes in the pan." Two examples are the Knights of Labor of the 1880s and the Moral Majority of the 1980s. Organizers are under pressure to either find new sources of funds or develop a new combination of more enduring material and solidary benefits.

Organizations may not be able to cover their expenses by charging dues, so entrepreneurs try to find other ways to raise funds. Behind many organizations, one will find a patron, a major donor who covers a large share of the organization's expenses. The academic focus on patrons was led by Jack Walker, who argued that the proliferation of organizations in the United States after World War II was driven by the creation of new funding sources. The growth of corporate, foundation, and government sources of grants supported an explosion in the number of interest organizations.[20] Walker contended that Olson and Salisbury exaggerated the extent to which most organizations are actually able to provide tangible selective benefits to their members. Studies of organizations, especially organizations that represent the so-called "public interest," do indicate that people who form organizations have often relied on patrons.[21] Moreover, it appears that corporate patrons, which one might have expected to support conservative or probusiness causes, may have actually been supporting many of the liberal organizations.[22]

POLITICAL SHOOTING STARS

Membership in the Knights of Labor skyrocketed from 100,000 to 700,000 in 1886, but then dwindled to a few local chapters within a few years. Historians point to a number of culprits, including bad management, bad publicity, and competition from other organizations.

There are just a few examples of organizations that have grown so precipitously and crashed so dramatically. One of them is the Moral Majority, a political organization that expressed the views of Evangelical Christians. It opened in 1979 and closed in 1989. Between those dates, the organization rose to the forefront of political debate and, at one time, boasted it had more than 4 million followers. Cofounder and public spokesman, Rev. Jerry Falwell (1933–2007), rose to national prominence as a proponent of prayer in public life and an opponent of legal abortion, protection of the rights of homosexuals, and the Strategic Arms Limitation Treaty with the Soviet Union.

An early beneficiary of the new wave of direct mail advertising pioneered by conservative consultant Richard Viguerie, the Moral Majority collected $2 million in its first year alone. In the early 1980s the organization claimed to have several million members. The actual number of donors/members was probably smaller, somewhere between 500,000 and 1 million (a significant number by any standard).

During the mid-1980s direct mail and television fundraising spigots began to run dry. Interest in the organization waned, and deficits in funds forced cutbacks in staff. As outreach activities were curtailed, the whole enterprise spiraled downward. It seems hard to deny that the collapsing supply of resources was a central cause of the organization's demise, but the leaders tried to put some positive spin on in. In his press release announcing the closure, Reverend Falwell claimed, "Our goal has been achieved."

The Knights of Labor formed in 1869 and quickly amassed an enormous membership. The Knights welcomed all laborers, including African Americans and women, and advocated for workers' rights. In this 1886 illustration, an African American delegate to the organization's annual meeting in Richmond introduces leader Terence Powderly.

It seems fair to say that many of the largest, most well-established organizations do rely on material incentives that they market to prospective members. Nevertheless, there is usually a bit of patronage involved as well. Consider the AARP, founded in 1958 as the American Association of Retired Persons.[23] The AARP claims it has more than 39 million members, which makes it the largest nonreligious voluntary organization in the United States. The AARP offers members an array of material incentives, including a monthly magazine and discounted prescriptions, insurance, travel, and more.[24] The AARP may be the poster child for the theory of material selective incentives, but its history reveals a vital role for a patron as well. The organization began with a $50,000 donation from an insurance agent named Leonard Davis, who marketed health insurance to AARP members (and paid a royalty to the AARP).[25] One may quibble with the AARP about the actual number of dues-paying members (do they have 25 million or 39 million?), but without doubt it is a huge organization.[26] In 2007 AARP's total revenue was $963 million, and about one-fourth of it was gathered from member dues. About one-half of the rest was earned from royalties, and the rest was dividends and investments. One can review the AARP's tax returns online.[27]

ORGANIZATIONAL FACTORS AFFECTING VOLUNTARY POLITICAL ORGANIZATIONS

It has been almost fifty years since Olson introduced the collective action problem. There is still quite a bit of disagreement among researchers about whether the collective action problem should be the central, driving issue in research on voluntary organizations.

One of the major challenges is putting together the general understanding of voluntary contributions with the specific understanding of many different types of organizations. The differences will affect any study of recruiters and potential members. Recruiting for a labor union occurs in a very structured, legalistic environment. It is hardly comparable to recruiting for the AARP. The response of the recruiter's target seems likely to depend on the details as well. A citizen's decision to join the Sierra Club is quite different from a corporate manager's decision to have his company pay to join the Frozen Food Locker Association.

Where Do We Stand on the "Free-Rider Problem"?

There have been many efforts to gauge the extent to which Olson's theme, summarized as "people don't pay for free stuff," describes the real world of political organizations. On the one hand, there is plenty of evidence that people often agree with causes but do not contribute to them. Many Americans agree with statements about the importance of the environment, but it is quite difficult to motivate them to actually do something that backs up their sentiments.[28] Many social groups seem to lack effective collective representation.[29] Organizations that represent children and young adults are dwarfed by the massive AARP.

On the other hand, some people do donate to some causes (at least some of the time). The United States is a large, diverse society, and if even a small fraction of the people who support a cause decide to join an organization, its membership may become substantial. Scholars have sought to understand that phenomenon on several levels—in theory, in experiments, and in the field. A highly influential group of political theorists who use mathematical models contends that people are actually individualistic (as Olson contended), and yet inclined to cooperate out of rational calculating self-interest and the anticipation of long-term benefits of cooperation.[30] In experiments, subjects sometimes make spontaneous contributions to the collective good. Some scholars conclude from those studies that Olson was simply wrong (people really will pay for free stuff!).[31] Others find the experiments unpersuasive.[32] There are studies that indicate that some organizations prosper by offering selective incentives,[33] but many offer benefits that do not seem very substantial to the outside observer.[34] Research on the use (and abuse) of collective resources indicates that behavior that advances—or at least, does not harm—the collective interest can be evoked by carefully designed institutions and procedures.[35]

Several studies of so-called "public interest" organizations, such as the League of Women Voters, Common Cause, and the American Civil Liberties Union, and environmental organizations such as the Sierra Club, observe only the most meager of selective incentives—a journal or some inexpensive logo sportswear. Walker relied on weakness of the material selective incentives as a central ingredient in his argument that organizations have to keep their dues low and rely on patrons to cover their expenses.[36] The studies of voluntary organizations by Constance Cook and Anne Hildreth observe the same thing, but they emphasize the organization's expressive benefits as motivational factors.[37]

Some studies contend that the people who join organizations simply do not feel as powerless as Olson would lead us to expect. Olson observed that people who have influence may be willing to provide a collective good for their entire group, but he felt that such a condition would not be relevant to a mass membership organization. When thousands, or perhaps millions, of people must donate for collective action to succeed, Olson thought that most group members would understand their situation. In a widely cited study of the "illogic of collective action" in American environmental organizations, Robert Mitchell contended that people contribute to environmental organizations because they believe they are advancing the welfare of their fellow citizens.[38] Terry Moe studied organizations of farmers, and the members actually believed they were making a difference.[39] In a closely related vein, studies have contended that when the members of a group feel that their interests are threatened, they are more willing to contribute to collective action.[40] On the basis of this research, one might conclude that the free-rider problem is not so serious, or that Olson may have exaggerated it.

These anomalies can be reconciled with Olson's *Logic* and Salisbury's exchange theory in a number of ways. Olson would later observe that these spontaneous contributions are so small that we should hardly expect rational analysis of costs and benefits.[41] When someone on the doorstep asks for a donation of $20, it may be easier and more satisfying to write a check than to carry on an argument about the collective action problem. If that same fund-raiser had asked for $200, the answer would likely be different. Salisbury, however, would focus on the marketing of expressive selective incentives. People may pay for a feeling of personal expression, or psychological release from a feeling of civic duty, and the organizer's main goal is to exploit that opportunity. Organizations are built on slogans that convey the idea that people who donate are virtuous people: "If you are not part of the solution, you are part of the problem." If the fund-raiser asks for $200,000, the donor may be persuaded that the money will really make a difference. If that difference in the collective objective is sufficient to justify the personal expense, then scholars from all schools of thought would agree that a donation is likely to follow.

One of the ironies of the free-rider problem is that so many scholars have tried to investigate it by studying the members of organizations. By definition, the members are not free riders. It would be more relevant to know the "mobilization rate"—the proportion of the people who agree with a point of view and who actually contribute to its political expression. While that appears to be the obvious research strategy, it is painfully difficult to carry out. Organizations are very secretive; many may well exaggerate their membership. In that vein, consider the wording of one Web page. "Welcome to the Sierra Club! You're here because, like 1.3 million of your friends and neighbors, you want. . . ."[42] It seems as though they have 1.3 million members, but the actual number is around 720,000. Their representative claims that the discrepancy results from their estimate that there are about 410,000 family members and friends affiliated with their dues-paying members.[43] Most other large organizations (including the AARP) exaggerate in that way. Another challenge for researchers is that organizations are unwilling to share the names and addresses of members with researchers (although many sell their membership lists to mass marketers and buy address lists as well). As a result, it is virtually impossible to match a roster of donors to a cause against the list of potential beneficiaries of a collective good.

Despite the challenges of research, the formula for success in building an organization is quite clear. An organization can grow as large as its leaders want, if they are willing to spend enough money. An organization should: (1) offer appealing selective incentives that people cannot find elsewhere; (2) aggressively contact nonmembers; and (3) work hard to retain current members. These steps will not necessarily make an organization profitable, but it will accumulate members. Although it may be true that some organizations survive without offering substantial selective incentives, there are also well-documented examples of organizations that do offer incentives and grow.[44]

Organizations in the modern era have many tools for contacting prospects. Recruitment by direct mail is often the cornerstone for organizations that try to grow, but direct mail advertising is costly, with a low rate of success. A typical direct mail campaign is considered a success if it recruits 1 percent to 2 percent of its targeted households, and the organization will not break even on mailing costs unless it can persuade those new members to renew their membership for a second year.[45] If an organization's leaders are willing to spend the money, they can drive up their membership even in the face of these serious disadvantages. Consider the National Rifle Association (NRA), which maintains a membership level between 2.5 million and 3.5 million. It faces heavy membership turnover—about 75 percent of new members drop out after one year.[46] Recruitment on a truly massive scale is required to sustain the organization. During the mid-1990s, when NRA leaders were resisting congressional efforts to control the purchase and ownership of firearms, the organization elected to spend into a deficit to try to maintain a high level of membership.[47] The AARP may be the strongest example of an "as big as they want to be" organization. The AARP offers a more desirable package of selective incentives—and significantly lower annual dues ($16 in 2009)—than most voluntary organizations open to the general public. The usual response rate from direct mail by the AARP is around 1.5 percent, but in the economic downturn of 2007–2008, the response rate fell below 1 percent.[48] The AARP can afford very large mailing expenses, partly because recruiting expenses are offset by the royalties earned by sales of insurance by affiliated companies.

One of the elements in this equation about which we have very little information is the retention of members. For whatever reason, it appears that all organizations face membership turnover. On average, organizations concerned about the environment keep 70 percent of their members from one time period to the next. That number masks the fact that retention of first-year members is much lower, probably around four in ten.[49] Lawrence Rothenberg characterizes members as "experiential searchers." People join to find out if an organization suits their personal needs.[50] Professional associations, which recruit members by offering them tangible incentives like insurance and business support, experience much lower rates of membership turnover.

Irrelevant and Relevant By-Products?

In his discussion of the by-product theory, Olson is quite clear that people do not join organizations to advance the collective interest, but to obtain selective incentives. The collective benefits are therefore "irrelevant" to the membership decision. The collective and political objectives of an organization might be completely irrelevant to the selective incentives that attract its members. It might as well be that people buy bread and meat, and a corporate manager then uses the profit to lobby for educational reform. Unlikely as it seems, this does happen. A conservative think tank, the Heritage Foundation, was bankrolled by beer magnate Joseph Coors, and Playboy magazine founder Hugh Hefner was an early supporter of the National Organization for the Reform of Marijuana Laws (NORML). Labor leader George Meany, who served as president of the AFL-CIO, used his position to endorse the continuation of the Vietnam War.[51]

These may be extreme examples of "irrelevant by-products," but there is a certain sense in which all effort to provide collective political representation on behalf of a group is disconnected from the membership. Virtually every large organization will include some—if not many—members who disagree with policies that their leaders advocate. The members of the AARP join because they want magazines and discounts; there is virtually no hope that all of the millions of members will agree on the big policy issues on which the AARP leaders choose to take stances. Indeed, AARP leaders understand this and proceed with caution in committing the organization to political battles.

In some cases the by-product is not completely irrelevant to the organization's basis in selective incentives. The inability to explain that connection is certainly one of the weaknesses in Olson's *Logic*. Salisbury addressed the problem in his entrepreneurial theory of organizations. Leaders may try to "farm the membership," to dredge up support for efforts to provide collective goods. Consider the National Association of Realtors (NAR), which in 2009 claimed to have more than 1.3 million members. The NAR has more dues-paying members than any other professional association, and, year in and year out, it is among the top spenders on lobbying and political campaigns.[52] The NAR has plenty of members-only benefits that entice businesspeople in real estate.[53] These offerings are part of the competitive edge that salespeople need. Only NAR members can advertise themselves as "Realtors," and they control the Multiple Listing Service (MLS), a comprehensive catalog of homes for sale. Suppose the membership of the NAR, or one of its state or local associations, has a gathering. If one of the members says, "Hey, let's all pitch in $5 to advertise for tax deductible mortgages," then many, even an overwhelming majority, might agree.[54] As long as the members who are gathered together by a selective incentive are willing to "tax themselves" to provide collective political action, the collective by-product does not seem so irrelevant. This kind of "relevant by-product" is qualitatively different from the irrelevant types that were described.

Disagreement within organizations about the pursuit of new collective goods may be highly divisive.[55] Only when an organization has an nearly irresistible selective incentive should we expect its leaders to adopt an expensive initiative without prior approval of the members.[56] In 2008 the leaders of the North Carolina chapter of the NAR developed a large-scale public education campaign on the evils of property taxes and issued each of the members a special assessment of $50. Members were outraged to learn that if they refused to pay they would be denied access to their business lifeline, the MLS.[57] For that reason, many associations avoid taking stands on issues that are controversial among their members. Some associations, such as Common Cause, solicit member feedback about their policy proposals. They do not pursue issues unless they are widely supported.[58]

The leaders of the Sierra Club, which recruits members by offering nature-related magazines and wilderness activities, have found themselves presiding over a tumultuous conflict among their members. In the 1990s the club was faced with budget shortfalls and dropping membership.[59] The leaders sought to refocus the organization on mainstream environmental issues and rebuild the membership base. Some active elements in the club wanted to make the organization's top priority a push for a ban on all immigration into the United States.[60] The opposition to immigration was driven by the view that overpopulation was causing environmental stress. Opponents of that move claimed that Sierra would be moving too far from its environmental roots and that the ban on immigration would ally the club with racist organizations. The leadership proposed to take a neutral stance, but proponents forced a referendum of the members in 1998. One might guess that would close the issue, but proponents of the immigration ban wanted to keep on fighting. More than a few eyebrows were raised in 2006, when Sierra member, and former Colorado governor, Richard Lamm, alleged that Sierra's

The National Association of Realtors not only lobbies on behalf of its members in Washington, but also offers more tangible benefits, such as the ability of members to call themselves "Realtors." In 2005 President George W. Bush addressed the association's annual meeting in Washington.

leaders "caved in" to financial pressure, agreeing to remain neutral on immigration in return for $101 million from a wealthy donor.[61]

How Organizations Can Exploit the Tax Code

Suppose a company sells stock to investors and uses the capital to manufacture logo T-shirts and backpacks (imagine a company like Aeropostale or The Gap). The company must pay federal corporate income taxes on its profits, and the stockholders expect to earn dividends.

Also consider an interest group entrepreneur who solicits donations. The entrepreneur sells magazines, backpacks, and logo T-shirts in return for membership dues (imagine the Audubon Society or World Wildlife Fund). The entrepreneur wants members not only because they will pay dues, but also because a large following confers prestige on the leaders. It also helps the organization when members "spread the word" by wearing the entrepreneur's logo.

As long as the organization does not pay dividends to stockholders, it may qualify as a nonprofit corporation that is not required to pay corporate income tax. The staff members can earn salaries; the rent, phone, and electricity bills will get paid. Nonprofits pay for everything that corporations pay for, except taxes and dividends. The money that would have been paid in taxes can be used to recruit more members, to pay salaries, or to hire lobbyists. As strange as it may seem, the AARP does not pay corporate income tax on revenues of almost a billion dollars. As long as the AARP continues to serve the interests they identify in their nonprofit charter, the association can grow as large as it wishes. Like charities and educational organizations, the NRA and AARP qualify for discount postage on mass mailings. In short, "nonprofit" does not mean "not valuable," nor does it mean nonpolitical.

For voluntary organizations, the hidden "nonprofit corporate" treasure is found in section 501(c) of the U.S. Code. On the grounds that some organizations serve a valid "public interest," Congress created exemptions from federal corporate income taxes for charitable, educational, and public service organizations, as well as for labor unions, professional and business associations, and associations of veterans. Like for-profit corporations, these organizations are forbidden from making donations to candidates for federal office out of their treasuries, but they are allowed to lobby Congress, within certain limits, and they may affect public opinion through educational messages.

Charitable, religious, educational, or scientific nonprofits are governed by section 501(c)(3). They are also free of federal corporate income tax, and their donors are allowed to deduct contributions from their personal taxable income. The deductibility of donations is thought to be a significant enticement for potential donors. If a donor would pay 30 percent of her income in federal tax, a donation of $1,000 to a 501(c)(3) saves the donor $300 in taxes. In essence, the donor can have the pleasure of giving $1,000 at the net cost of only $700.

The law gives that advantage to a 501(c)(3), but it also takes away some of its political options. These organizations may not be "substantially" involved in legislative lobbying.[62] The core function should be charity, research, or education. Influence on legislation should be a secondary activity. It is almost as if the designers of the law had an Olsonian by-product in mind. Furthermore, the organization's officials must not make explicit effort to influence federal elections nor sponsor a political action committee (PAC). These restrictions are important, but one should not forget that most of the 501(c)(3) organizations have trouble raising money; it is unlikely that most of them are able to spare a large part of their wealth for political influence. Until 1969 the Sierra Club was classified as a 501(c)(3) organization. It was famously disqualified by the Internal Revenue Service after it launched a particularly vivid and critical ad campaign in opposition to dam construction. Religious institutions fall into the 501(c)(3) category. Although their representatives may offer educational messages on public policy issues ("we oppose abortion and the death penalty," for example), they are technically forbidden from actively speaking out on federal election campaigns. They are, however, allowed to employ lobbyists and legal advisers. Similarly, the Salvation Army is a 501(c)(3) entity; its representatives may lobby, but that cannot be the organization's central purpose. All of these organizations are allowed to answer requests for information from members of Congress; answering a formal request is not considered lobbying in section 501(c).

Under the tax code, 501(c)(4) organizations—civic leagues and social welfare organizations—are allowed to lobby as much as they want, and they can use tax-exempt funds to advertise for their point of view. Donations to 501(c)(4) are not tax deductible. Most large organizations in the United States create a 501(c)(4) entity to manage member recruitment and an allegedly separate 501(c)(3) organization to receive tax deductible donations. Greenpeace, USA, has two parts. Greenpeace, Inc., is a 501(c)(4) organization that recruits members. Greenpeace Foundation is a 501(c)(3) entity that accepts tax-deductible donations. Are the activities of these two entities are actually separate? According to their IRS Form 990 reports, the same person is the executive director of both organizations; his time is split evenly, twenty hours per week assigned to each organization.

Section 501(c)(6) governs business leagues, which include trade associations, professional associations, and chambers of commerce. The IRS guidelines explain, "To be exempt, a business league's activities must be devoted to

SORRY, WE ARE NO LONGER ACCEPTING APPLICATIONS

The deadline to apply for the position of membership director at Greenpeace was August 25, 2010. The advertisement said, "We are looking for someone with a passion for fundraising and a commitment to the mission of Greenpeace. The successful candidate will have a proven track record in managing and growing a membership program in another non-profit."

That looks like a tough job. The ad mentioned that "Greenpeace employs between 300 and 500 employees spread throughout the US." The range of employee numbers seems awfully broad, but it is realistic. There is no way to be sure how many employees Greenpeace will have. The organization appears to be in serious trouble.

In 1991 Greenpeace was going strong. It had 1.2 million members in the United States and a budget of more than $50 million. But membership started to fall, dipping below 400,000 in 1997. Budget cuts followed, and membership continued to fall. The 2009 federal income tax statement from Greenpeace shows a membership of 250,000. The combined receipts of Greenpeace Inc. and the Greenpeace Foundation were about $34 million in 2009; the combined deficit of the two organizations was $12 million.

improving business conditions of one or more lines of business as distinguished from performing particular services for individual persons."[63] It is a little difficult to understand why an association that serves the needs of for-profit corporations would be exempt from federal tax. If the ad campaign that asks "Got Milk?" stimulates demand for all milk producers, then the campaign is a legitimate tax-exempt function of a nonprofit business association.

The law also allows professionals and businesses to deduct the fees they pay to these associations as business expenses. In 1993 Congress created a complicated accounting problem when it amended the law to forbid members from deducting the portion of their dues that is expended on lobbying by the association. A 501(c)(6) organization must either notify its members of the nondeductible part of their dues or pay a tax penalty on behalf of the members. Although the law created an accounting problem for business and professional associations, the reporting requirement gave researchers access to more information about political action in these organizations. The American Medical Association notified its members that 50 percent of their dues are not deductible because that amount is allocated to lobbying. For the American Nurses Association, the nondeductible part is 31.4 percent. The American Bar Association's nondeductible lobbying allocation is on the low end at 2.5 percent, while the American International Automobile Dealers Association nondeductible portion for 2009 was a bit more than 60 percent.

Labor Unions Face Different Challenges

Unions are classified as tax-free nonprofits under 501(c)(5). They are allowed to try to influence the legislative process; they may not donate to candidates out of their treasuries, but they may participate in political campaigns and can manage political action committees. Unions have the same tax status and political restrictions that are imposed on professional and business associations. Virtually everything else is different for unions.

There is no doubt that, among all organizations, labor unions are the most heavily regulated. Before the Great Depression, labor unions existed, but their main bargaining tools—collective bargaining, strikes, and boycotts, were not legal. Businesses could fire workers who attempted to form a union, and managers were not required to negotiate with union leaders. People who attempted to organize workers could be put in prison for restraint of trade. In 1935 the Wagner Act legalized unions and created guidelines that unions must follow when they seek to organize the workers in a place of business. The National Labor Relations Board (NLRB) supervises unions, enforcing a substantial body of legislation that places mandates on union leaders.

Unlike other organizations, which can contact individuals and ask them to join individually, the law requires that a union must win a "certification election" in order to represent a group of workers. The NLRB oversees the process, which involves a formalized campaign and vote among workers. From 1935 until 1947 unions in all states were allowed to negotiate "closed shop" arrangements with employers. All of the people who work under a union's jurisdiction were required to join the union as a condition of employment. In 1947 the federal law was amended to allow state governments to mandate "open shops," in which workers are not required to join a union as a condition of employment. Twenty-two states, mostly where union membership was not large, have adopted such laws. After a union has been certified, the recruitment problem more closely resembles the one faced by other associations that seek to offer selective incentives in return for dues payments (see Chapter 13).

Mancur Olson devoted a full chapter in *The Logic of Collective Action* to labor unions. Historically, factory workers were politically weak, and their inability to express themselves through political action was evidence of the deep, pervasive nature of the collective action problem. Olson argued that as long as the benefits of unionization are shared among all workers—even those who do not pay dues—the unions would remain weak. Unions that succeed in recruiting members do so by offering selective incentives, such as life insurance, or perhaps they sell "protection" to their members (who might find their cars vandalized if they refuse to join).

After unions were legalized they grew quite quickly, as workers enthusiastically supported them in certification elections, and the political power of the labor leaders grew. Union penetration into the workforce peaked in the late 1950s, when about one-third of the private sector workforce belonged to unions. Since then, the union percentage of the workforce has steadily declined. In 2008 just 7.6 percent of the workers in the private sector were members of labor unions.[64] If it were not for several decades of growth of labor union membership among government employees, which has reached 36.8 percent, unions would have almost no good news to report. But because most government employees are not allowed to go on strike, public sector unions are relatively weak organizations.

There have been many studies of the decline of the labor movement by anthropologists, economists, sociologists, and political scientists. Some researchers have seen the decline of unionism as just one more side effect of the "postmodern" economic environment of wealth and abundance. The unionization view of "us against them" is simply not relevant to modern workers.[65] Economists have been inclined to view unionization rates as a reflection of the recruiting activity of unions, the resistance campaigns of business, and the level of economic stress that motivates workers.[66] It is true that the segments of the economy in which the unions grew most quickly—industrial manufacturing, especially steel and autos—have been in decline for decades. Others point the finger at "globalization" and international competition for sealing the fate of the unions. Open markets tempt American companies to go where labor is cheap. Even so, the decline of unionization in the United States has been steeper than in other industrialized countries, a difference that may be attributable to the unique laws governing the U.S. unionization process and the somewhat lackluster organizing effort of American unions.[67]

The Ecology of Organizations

Contrary to popular reports, the *Logic of Collective Action* did not kill pluralism. Rather, it pushed it in new directions.

Some modern scholars agree that there is a grain of truth in the free-rider problem, but contend that the preoccupation with collective action stands in the way of research on other important questions. Calling themselves "neopluralists," these scholars focus on the organizational level of analysis.[68] Building on research in sociology that is known as the "ecology of organizations," neopluralists try to explain the total number of organizations and membership patterns in organizations without addressing the individualistic motivations and behavior of leaders and followers.[69] Foremost among them are political scientists Virginia Gray and David Lowery.[70] They do not claim that Olson's theory is wrong; rather, they emphasize that the ecological theory leads them to many interesting patterns that can be observed among interest organizations. One central idea is that the political-economic system imposes a "carrying capacity," an upper limit on the number of organizations that can exist at a time. The shortages of potential members and wealth weed out some organizations. They also contend that ecological theory leads to the prediction that organizations are specialized into "policy niches." Organizations specialize on policy issues in order to avoid competition and confrontation.[71] That idea matches the findings of other studies that are not based on the population ecology theory.[72] While the collective action theories cannot offer us a clear explanation for the differences in political activity levels among various social groups, such as gay and lesbian citizens, the ecological approach seems to lend some substantial insights.[73]

CONCLUSION

What should one conclude about all this research on voluntary organizations and Olson's thesis on collective (in)action? In the end, focusing on the collective action problem changed our expectations about what a randomly chosen person will do when alerted about the need to make a costly, selfless gesture to advance the collective welfare, and not in an optimistic way. Before *The Logic of Collective Action,* collaborative effort was expected, and people who did not contribute were seen as defective or unsociable. After *Logic,* the free-riding noncontributor was the expected, and people who voluntarily contributed toward collective goods were puzzling. In that way, Olson's *Logic* cut a wide swath across the academic community.

The problems that flow from failed collective action—underrepresentation, oppression, persistent poverty, pollution, war, and so forth—are found in all fields of social science. In anthropology, philosophy, sociology, economics, and political science, continuing problems came into new focus after Olson offered the community his microsope.[74] Perhaps the idea of the "free market" in the mid-1770s had a similar broad impact, but there are very few ideas that have become so pervasive in the study of societies.

The main emphasis of this essay has been on political organizations, including public interest groups and labor unions. On one side of the coin, some interests, probably widely held interests, are not effectively represented by political organizations. On the other side, however, some interests shared among substantial numbers of people do find expression. The contrast between the success of some segments (car dealers, real estate agents, gun owners) with the failures of others (homeless people, college students, children, low-paid workers) could not be more stark.

If one has trouble working up an interest in the collective action of political organizations, one could certainly find interesting work in the study of protest movements, revolution, international organizations, pollution, and management of "common pool resources."[75] In all of these areas, the challenge of dealing with free riders has been at the core. In all of these fields of study, a central question concerns whether institutions and organizations are required to aggregate the resources held by a possibly widespread set of affected parties. The core question is how much central management (that is, coercion, possibly by government) is minimally required to overcome a collective action problem.

After Edwin Banfield investigated persistent poverty in Italian villages after World War II, he proposed a theory of "amoral familism" to account for the inability of the villagers to marshal collective efforts. The villagers, he thought, were unable to foresee communal benefits; they were narrowly focused on the short-term needs of their families.[76] In light of Olson's *Logic*, the problem appears deeper than that. Individuals will free ride, even if they are not "amoral familists." If success in collective action requires contributions from many autonomous individuals, it will generally not be sufficient to explain the problem to the concerned parties. Instead, collective action needs to be "incentivized" somehow. Some sort of coercion, either by government or community, is probably needed.

There is no denying the fact that some people, sometimes, do seem to make "irrational" contributions to the collective good. A philanthropist might provide a public library building or a public monument. These "random acts of kindness" are not well situated within the collective action theory. If people do things without thinking about the benefits and costs, the theory of rational choice may have little to say. These observations do not fit in the same way that airplanes and footballs have an uneasy spot in the theory of gravity. Gravity holds many things down, but not everything. In that sense, political organizations are like airplanes: we would like to understand why some fly and some don't.

NOTES

1. Sarah Kelley, "Size Matters: Just How Big Is the Nation's Premier Small-Business Lobby, Really?" *Nashville Scene*, July 27, 2006, http://www.nashvillescene.com/2006-07-27/news/size-matters.
2. Arthur Bentley, *The Process of Government* (Chicago: University of Chicago Press, 1908), 204.
3. David Truman, *The Governmental Process: Political Interests and Public Opinion* (New York: Alfred A. Knopf, 1951).
4. Ibid., 14.
5. Thomas Kuhn, *The Structure of Scientific Revolutions* (Chicago: University of Chicago Press, 1962).
6. Joaquim Silvestre, "Wicksell, Lindahl and the Theory of Public Goods," *Scandinavian Journal of Economics* 105, 4 (2003): 527–553.
7. Paul A. Samuelson, "The Pure Theory of Public Expenditure," *Review of Economics and Statistics* 36, 4 (1954): 387–389.
8. Adam Smith, *An Inquiry into the Nature and Causes of Wealth of Nations* (London: Methuen and Co., 1776).
9. Mancur Olson Jr., *The Logic of Collective Action* (Cambridge: Harvard University Press, 1965), 58.
10. Olson Mancur Jr. and Richard Zeckhauser, "An Economic Theory of Alliances," *Review of Economics and Statistics* 48, 3 (1966): 266–279.
11. Russell Hardin, *Collective Action* (Baltimore: Resources for the Future, 1982).
12. Norman Frohlich and Joe A. Oppenheimer, "I Get by with a Little Help from My Friends," *World Politics* 23, 1 (1970): 104–120.
13. Hardin, *Collective Action*. John Chamberlin, "Provision of Collective Goods as a Function of Group Size," *American Political Science Review* 68, 2 (1974): 707–716. Koji Okuguchi. "Utility Function, Group Size, and the Aggregate Provision of a Pure Public Good," *Public Choice* 42, 3 (1984): 247–256; Joan Esteban and Debraj Ray, "Collective Action and the Group Size Paradox," *American Political Science Review* 95, 3 (2001): 663–672; R. Mark Isaac and James M. Walker, "Group Size Effects in Public Goods Provision: The Voluntary Contributions Mechanism," *Quarterly Journal of Economics* 103, 1 (1988): 179–199.
14. Olson, *Logic of Collective Action*, 132.
15. Nelson Polsby, *Community Power and Political Theory* (New Haven: Yale University Press, 1963).
16. E. E. Schattschneider, *The Semisovereign People: A Realist's View of Democracy in America* (New York: Holt, Rinehart, and Winston, 1960).
17. Arthur T. Denzau and Michael C. Munger, "Legislators and Interest Groups: How Unorganized Interests Get Represented," *American Political Science Review* 80, 1 (1986): 89–106.
18. Robert H. Salisbury, "An Exchange Theory of Interest Groups," *Midwest Journal of Political Science* 13, 1 (1969): 1–32.
19. Peter B. Clark and James Q. Wilson, "Incentive Systems: A Theory of Organizations," *Administrative Science Quarterly* 6 (1961): 129–166.
20. Jack L. Walker. "The Origins and Maintenance of Interest Groups in America," *American Political Science Review* 77, 2 (1983): 390–406.
21. Anthony J. Nownes and Allan J. Cigler, "Public Interest Groups and the Road to Survival," *Polity* 27, 3 (1995): 379–404, ISSN: 00323497; DOI: 10.2307/3235004; Anthony J. Nownes and Grant Neeley, "Public Interest Group Entrepreneurship and Theories of Group Mobilization," *Political Research Quarterly* 49, 1 (1996):

119–146; Jeffrey M. Berry, "On the Origins of Public Interest Groups: A Test of Two Theories," *Polity* 10, 3 (1978): 379–397; Robert C. Lowry, "Foundation Patronage toward Citizen Groups and Think Tanks: Who Get Grants?" *Journal of Politics* 61, 3 (1999): 758–776.

22. James T. Bennett, *Patterns of Corporate Philanthropy: Ideas, Advocacy, and the Corporation (Studies in philanthropy)* (Washington, D.C.: Capital Research Center, 1989).

23. In 1999 the name was officially changed to AARP because many members were not yet retired (the age of eligibility was fifty at the time).

24. AARP, "AARP Membership," http://www.aarpmembership.org.

25. Eric Schurenberg and Lani Luciano, "The Empire Called AARP: Under Its Nonprofit Halo, the American Association of Retired Persons Is a Feared Lobbyist and an Even More Awesome Marketer," *Money,* October 1, 1988.

26. Dale Van Atta, *Trust Betrayed: Inside the AARP* (Washington, D.C.: Regnery Publishing, 1998).

27. AARP, "Form 990: Return of Organization Exempt from Income Tax," submitted to the U.S. Department of the Treasury Internal Revenue Service, 2007 URL: http://www.guidestar.org/FinDocuments/2007/951/985/2007-951985500-04a3a6d8-9O.pdf.

28. Paul E. Johnson, "Interest Group Recruiting: Finding Members and Keeping Them," in *Interest Group Politics,* 5th ed., ed. Allan J. Cigler and Burdett A. Loomis (Washington, D.C.: CQ Press, 1998), 35–62; Christopher J. Bosso, "The Color of Money: Environmental Groups and the Pathologies of Fund Raising," in *Interest Group Politics,* 4th ed., ed. Allan J. Cigler and Burdett A. Loomis (Washington, D.C.: CQ Press, 1995).

29. Kay L. Schlozman and John T. Tierney, "More of the Same: Washington Pressure Group Activity in a Decade of Change," *Journal of Politics* 45, 2 (1983): 351–377; Kay L. Schlozman and John T. Tierney, *Organized Interests and American Democracy* (New York: Harper Collins, 1986).

30. Robert Axelrod, "The Emergence of Cooperation among Egoists," *American Political Science Review* 75, 2 (1981): 306–318; David M. Kreps et al., "Rational Cooperation in the Finitely Repeated Prisoners' Dilemma," *Journal of Economic Theory* 27, 2 (August 1982): 245–252; Claudia Keser and Frans A. A. M. van Winden, *Conditional Cooperation and Voluntary Contributions to Public Goods,* Tinbergen Institute Discussion Papers 00-011/1 (Amsterdam: Tinbergen Institute, 2000), http://ideas.repec.org/p/dgr/uvatin/20000011.html.

31. Gerald Marwell and Ruth E. Ames, "Experiments on the Provision of Public Goods. I. Resources, Interest Group Size, and the Free-Rider Problem," *American Journal of Sociology* 84 (1979): 1335–60; Donald Green and Ian Shapiro, *Pathologies of Rational Choice Theory: A Critique of Applications in Political Science* (New Haven: Yale University Press, 1996), http://www.worldcat.org/isbn/0300066368.

32. Oliver Kim and Mark Walker, "The Free Rider Problem: Experimental evidence," *Public Choice* 43, 1 (January 1984), 3–24; Thomas S. McCaleb and Richard E. Wagner, "The Experimental Search for Free Riders: Some Reflections and Observations," *Public Choice* 47, 3 (January 1985): 479–490.

33. Grant Jordan and William A. Maloney, "Manipulating Membership: Supply-Side Influences on Group Size," *British Journal of Political Science* 28.2 (1998): 389–409. ISSN: 00071234. DOI: 10.2307/194311; Johnson, "Interest Group Recruiting."

34. David C. King and Jack L. Walker, "The Provision of Benefits by Interest Groups in the United States," *Journal of Politics* 54, 2 (1992): 394–426.

35. Elinor Ostrom, *Governing the Commons: The Evolution of Institutions for Collective Action* (New York: Cambridge University Press, 1990).

36. Walker, "Origins and Maintenance of Interest Groups."

37. Constance Cook, "Participation in Public Interest Groups," *American Politics Quarterly* 12 (1984): 409–431; Anne Hildreth, "The Importance of Purposes in 'Purposive' Groups: Incentives and Participation in the Sanctuary Movement," *American Journal of Political Science* 38, 2 (1994): 447–463.

38. Robert Cameron Mitchell, "National Environmental Lobbies and the Apparent Illogic of Collective Action," in *Collective Decision Making,* ed. Clifford Russell (Baltimore: Johns Hopkins University Press, 1979). See also Kenneth Godwin and Robert C. Mitchell, "Rational Models, Collective Goods, and Nonelectoral Political Behavior," *Western Politics Quarterly* 35 (1982): 161–180.

39. Terry Moe, *The Organization of Interests* (Chicago: University of Chicago Press, 1980).

40. John M. Hansen, "The Political Economy of Group Membership," *American Political Science Review* 79, 1 (1985): 79–96; King and Walker, "Provision of Benefits."

41. Mancur Olson Jr., *The Rise and Decline of Nations: Economic Growth, Stagflation, and Social Rigidities* (New Haven: Yale University Press, 1982).

42. Sierra Club homepage, http://www.sieraclub.org/welcome.

43. Kristina Johnson, deputy press secretary, Sierra Club, personal communication, July 17, 2009.

44. Grant Jordan and Darren Halpin, "Olson Triumphant? Recruitment Strategies and the Growth of a Small Business Organisation," *Political Studies* 52, 3 (2004): 431–449.

45. Johnson, "Interest Group Recruiting."

46. Kelly Patterson, "The Political Firepower of the National Rifle Association," in *Interest Group Politics,* 5th ed., ed. Allan J. Cigler and Burdett A. Loomis (Washington, D.C.: CQ Press, 1998), 119–143.

47. "NRA Operating in the Red," *Lawrence Journal World,* June 26, 1995, 6A.

48. Stephen Driscoll, "AARP's Membership on the Rise?" *AARP Global Network,* March 31, 2009, https://www.aarpglobalnetwork.org/netzine/news/Pages/RespondingtoChangesintheEconomy.aspx.

49. Johnson, "Interest Group Recruiting."

50. Lawrence S. Rothenberg, "Organizational Maintenance and the Retention Decision in Groups," *American Political Science Review* 82 (1988): 1129–1152.

51. Taylor E. Dark, *The Unions and the Democrats: An Enduring Alliance* (Ithaca, N.Y.: Cornell University Press, 2001).

52. See, for example, the values for political spending reported by the Center for Responsive Politics, http://www.OpenSecrets.org.

53. National Association of Realtors, http://www.realtor.org/about_nar/member_reference_guide; Illinois Association of Realtors, http://www.illinoisrealtor.org/iar/about/advantage.html.

54. Russell Hardin, "Collective Action as an Agreeable n-Prisoners' Dilemma," *Behavioral Science* 16, 5 (1971): 472–481.

55. Paul Edward Johnson, "Unraveling in Democratically Governed Groups," *Rationality and Society* 2 (1990): 4–34.

56. Paul Edward Johnson, "Unraveling in a Variety of Institutional Settings," *Journal of Theoretical Politics* 8 (1996): 299–331.

57. Bob Geary, "Realtors Rankled Over Political Spending," INDYWEEK.com, July 23, 2008, http://www.indyweek.com/gyrobase/Content?oid=oid%3A261337.

58. Andrew S. McFarland, *Common Cause: Lobbying in the Public Interest* (Chatham, N.J.: Chatham House, 1984).

59. Associated Press, "Sierra Club Changes Focus to Avoid Going Bankrupt," *University Daily Kansan,* September 28, 1994, 2.

60. Leslie King, "Ideology, Strategy and Conflict in a Social Movement Organization: The Sierra Club Immigration Wars," *Mobilization: An International Quarterly* 13, 1 (February 2008): 45–61.

61. Richard D. Lamm, "For Sale: The Policies of the Sierra Club," *Social Contract* 17, 1 (2006), http://www.thesocialcontract.com/artman2/publish/tsc_17_01/tsc_17_01_lamm_sierra.shtml.

62. *Substantial* is defined vaguely, but the law allows organizations to spend at least 20 percent of their resources on lobbying.

63. Internal Revenue Service, http://www.irs.gov/charities/nonprofits/article/0,,id=96107,00.html.

64. Bureau of Labor Statistics, "News: Union Members in 2008," press release, January 28, 2009.

65. Daniel Bell, *The End of Ideology: On the Exhaustion of Political Ideas in the Fifties* (Glencoe, Ill.: Free Press, 1960).

66. Orley Ashenfelter and John H. Pencavel, "American Trade Union Growth: 1900–1960," *Quarterly Journal of Economics* 83, 3 (1969): 434–448; Richard B. Freeman and James L. Medoff, *What Do Unions Do?* (New York: Basic Books, 1984).

67. Lyle Scruggs and Peter Lange, "Where Have All the Members Gone? Globalization, Institutions, and Union Density," *Journal of Politics* 64, 1 (2002): 126–153; Paul E. Johnson, "Organized Labor in an Era of Blue-Collar Decline," in *Interest Group Politics,* 3rd ed., ed. Allan J. Cigler and Burdett A. Loomis (Washington, D.C.: CQ Press, 1991), 33–62.

68. David Lowery and Holly Brasher, *Organized Interests and American Government* (New York: McGraw Hill, 2004), 22.

69. Glenn R. Carroll. "Organizational Ecology," *Annual Review of Sociology* 10, 1 (1984): 71–93; Glenn R. Carroll, "Concentration and Specialization: Dynamics of Niche Width in Populations of Organizations," *American Journal of Sociology* 90, 6 (1985): 1262–1283.

70. See David Lowery and Virginia Gray, "The Population Ecology of Gucci Gulch, or the Natural Regulation of Interest Group Numbers," *American Journal of Political Science* 39 (1993): 1–29; Virginia Gray and David Lowery, *The Population Ecology of Interest Representation: Lobbying Communities in the American States* (Ann Arbor: University of Michigan Press, 1996).

71. Virginia Gray and David Lowery, "A Niche Theory of Interest Representation," *Journal of Politics* 58 (1996): 91–111.

72. William P. Browne, "Issue Niches and the Limits of Interest Group Influence, " in *Interest Group Politics,* 3rd ed., 345–370.

73. Anthony J. Nownes and Daniel Lipinski, "The Population Ecology of Interest Group Death: Gay and Lesbian Rights Interest Groups in the United States, 1945–98," *British Journal of Political Science* 35, 2 (2005): 303–319.

74. Hardin, *Collective Action.*

75. Dennis Chong, *Collective Action and the Civil Rights Movement* (Chicago: University of Chicago Press, 1991), 261; Gordon Tullock, "The Paradox of Revolution," *Public Choice* 11 (1971): 89–100; Mark I. Lichbach, *The Rebel's Dilemma* (Ann Arbor: University of Michigan Press, 1998); Olson and Zeckhauser, "Economic Theory of Alliances"; Ostrom, *Governing the Commons.*

76. Edwin C. Banfield, *The Moral Basis of a Backward Society* (New York: Free Press, 1958).

SUGGESTED READING

Chong, Dennis. *Collective Action and the Civil Rights Movement.* Chicago: University of Chicago Press, 1991.

Gray, Virginia, and David Lowery. *The Population Ecology of Interest Representation: Lobbying Communities in the American States.* Ann Arbor: University of Michigan Press, 1996.

Hardin, Russell. *Collective Action.* Washington, D.C.: RFF Press, 1982.

Olson, Mancur Jr. *The Logic of Collective Action: Public Goods and the Theory of Groups,* 2nd ed. Cambridge: Harvard University Press, 1971.

chapter 5

American Pluralism, Interest Group Liberalism, and Neopluralism

by Matt Grossmann

FOR MUCH OF THE HISTORY OF political science, pluralism was the only theoretical approach of note used to study interest groups. Scholars studied interest groups if they thought that groups were the basis of politics. Taking a pluralist approach meant (1) that politics involved cooperating with some in order to compete with others; and (2) that society had more than a single important dividing line. Today, a pure pluralist perspective is rarely invoked as a theoretical framework for empirical research on interest groups. It is commonly considered outdated, normatively suspect, and incomplete.

Yet today's interest group scholarship is never too far removed from the intellectual heritage of pluralism. When Frank Baumgartner and Beth Leech assessed the interest group subfield in 1998, they wrote: "Forty years ago, the group approach to politics was so dominant that it virtually defined the contemporary approach to political science."[1] They tracked the decline of the prominence of interest group studies in political science, finding it inextricably linked to the decline of group-based approaches to the political process. The golden days of interest group research, in other words, were the pluralist days.

Pluralist assumptions also lurk in the background of most contemporary interest group research. Few modern scholars would dispute that politics involves competition among many participants, with some agents, such as lobbyists, acting as representatives of constituencies. And few would challenge the idea that different groups are active in different issue domains. Both of these premises underlie the organization of this volume. They are no longer seriously debated.

Yet the pluralist framework has not offered much utility for contemporary researchers attempting to derive hypotheses for empirical studies of interest organizations. As a result, the pluralist framework has been subjected to many attempts to revise it, with numerous calls to imagine a "neopluralism" with a reformed set of tenets. These attempts at reframing are nothing new in the field. The concept of pluralism was contested from the beginning, with some alleged pluralists disclaiming the title and others enlarging its scope and assumptions. And the word *pluralism* has also been used in both normative and empirical accounts of politics. Furthermore, many of the empirical accounts were largely descriptive and did not introduce testable hypotheses to compare against other theories. Thus, confusion has reigned. Despite numerous attempts, pluralist theory has not been fully resuscitated in a way that enables its usage in contemporary research.

What follows argues that pluralism, at its most basic level, remains a useful theoretical framework for studying the role of interest groups, especially as it employs the empirical strand of pluralist theory to extend group theories of the political process. The chapter begins with a definition and explanation of the pluralist view of politics that largely equates it with group theory. Second, it provides summaries of two foundational texts, *The Governmental Process* by David Truman and *Who Governs?* by Robert Dahl, and their later interpretations. Third, it assesses the contemporary relevance of three primary critiques of pluralist theory found in the community power debate, collective action theory, and studies of institutions and organizations. Fourth, it reviews "interest group liberalism" and "neopluralism," two types of reformulations of pluralist theory. Fifth, it presents some ideas about the utility of the pluralist framework for interest group research, specifying where it is likely to be most and least useful. It compares its utility to the other three theoretical frameworks offered in this volume and establishes some grounds under which researchers can choose among the frameworks for their own studies. Finally, it presents two fundamental sets of interest group research questions that pluralist theory highlights but that remain unanswered.

The goal of the chapter is to provide readers with an understanding of the pluralist framework that allows application to current research. Sometimes this goal requires simplification of intellectual history and the collapsing of many ideas into a few core precepts. Accepting the pluralist framework as a useful starting point for interest group research does not require refighting the debates of the 1960s or ignoring the utility of alternative frameworks. Like all theoretical approaches, pluralist theory and its reformulation highlight important questions and provide ideas about how to find answers. Pluralism can be quite valuable in some contexts, especially in relating interest group studies to larger questions about the political process.

WHAT IS PLURALISM?

Politics is the competition to influence collective decision making; pluralism is the framework for studying politics that assumes that the units of this competition are groups. These groups include identity-based constituencies like ethnicities or religions, economic constituencies like occupations and industries, and ideological or issue-based constituencies that share politically relevant views. The multiplicity of interests and ideas in society is taken as a given and as fundamental to the process in which groups compete to influence elections and policy outcomes in government institutions.

There are four logical alternatives to assuming that the units of political competition are groups. Pluralism is most often compared to elitist or stratification theories, which posit that the units of competition are hierarchically organized classes defined by some combination of income, education, and social status. The most commonly used contemporary alternative, however, takes individuals, rather than groups, as the primary unit of political competition; this perspective is most evident in rational choice theories of politics. A less common alternative assumes that society should be studied as a whole. In this view, the most important political characteristics are shared across society, and the largest differences are found between nations and across time periods. European contexts offer a fourth alternative: the idea that a few important divisions or cleavages (such as class and religion) define politics, with citizens lining up on one side or the other of each divide. The group is the most flexible, and the most amorphous, of these possible basic units of political competition. The groups in group theories of politics often have overlapping memberships and unclear membership lines; the opponents of each group may also be multiple or undefined.

The differences in these approaches are apparent in the debate over national health care in the United States. A pluralist framework would start with a simple question: Which groups care about the policy outcome? Doctors, nurses, insurance companies, hospitals, and sufferers of diseases immediately come to mind. The outcome of the health care debate, under a pluralist framework, would be assumed to have something to do with the competition among groups like these, and many more. Researchers working from a pluralist framework would ask which of these groups are well organized and which have become important constituencies for parties or elected officials. Predictions of policy outcomes would flow largely from the relative influence of these groups and how they line up on the sides of the policy debate.

In contrast, a framework based on social classes would look for differences in the self-evident interests of those at the top and bottom of the socioeconomic spectrum to posit predictions and explanations for health care policy outcomes. Scholars might point to politically important differences between those with and without access to health insurance. A cleavage-based approach would look for basic differences in public ideological predispositions and social affiliation that might be relevant to health care, such as religious identity and attitudes toward redistribution. Scholars might ask how those cleavages play out in the party system and which side has control of government. Those who hold political theories that consider individuals as the units of political competition, in contrast, might specify which individual is most likely to affect the outcome of the policy debate if opinions are placed on a spectrum. They might look to the preferences of the likely sixtieth voter in the filibuster-prone U.S. Senate or the preferences of the median voter in that member's state. Political theories that look to the society as a whole might posit that U.S. political culture is too capitalistic to adopt national health care or that society made the critical health care decisions long ago and will not change them.

Readers should be familiar with each of these types of explanations, as they are commonly used in the casual empiricism of pundit commentary as well as political science scholarship. The group-based perspective has proved to be an enduring framework for studying politics because it stems from one of the basic strands of political interpretation. Yet as a framework, pluralism is a broad umbrella that could incorporate many potential predictions in health care policy or in any other area. The primary similarity in pluralist accounts is to look first at the interests and ideas of diverse groups to examine political competition over policy outcomes.

Table 5.1 lists some other potential explanations of political competition that rely on the pluralist framework. These examples are not exhaustive, but they show how pluralist accounts develop. First, we can identify the groups involved. Second, we can compare the relative advantages of these groups in political mobilization. Third, we can specify how the governing system and the potential policy options under consideration affect the way these groups compete within a policy issue area. These steps have broad potential applications in political analysis.

TABLE 5.1 **Examples of Pluralist Explanations**

	Examples of relevant groups	Potential mobilization dynamics	Potential policy arena dynamics
Health care	Doctors, insurers, hospitals, sufferers of diseases	Business and occupational groups advantaged over patients	Competition for government subsidies
Education	Teachers, parents, contractors, administrators	Teachers attempt to mobilize the most involved parents	Government officials respond to parent concerns
Taxes	High-income earners, business owners, retail sector	Business sectors each mobilize to protect own tax advantages	Wide use of tax credits to appease particular interests
Defense	The Pentagon, military families, contractors	Broad support for large defense budget	Support dependent on perceptions of foreign threats
Environment	Polluting industries, park users, energy companies	Environmentalists line up against businesses	Who wins dependent on high-profile disasters and economy

David Truman: Groups in the Governmental Process

The pluralist approach gained prominence in political science with the 1951 publication of *The Governmental Process* by David Truman. The organization of this famous treatise should be readily understandable to contemporary interest group scholars.[2] It begins with group origins, moves to organizing considerations, specifies multiple tactics of influence, and concludes with normative implications. The main difference between Truman's work and contemporary interest group scholarship is that Truman begins with social groups. For Truman, an interest such as doctors is made up of the occupational constituency, their formal associations, and their allies within government. Truman identifies the American Medical Association as one arena for internal conflicts among doctors and as a manifestation of doctors, as a social group, gravitating toward government involvement via formal organization.

Truman does not outline and test a series of hypotheses about interest groups. In moving from descriptive to analytic accounts, he tends only to list variables that may be relevant to interest group success. For example, he says that three categories of social disturbances help provide the context for interest group organization: socioeconomic change due to technology, mobilization by potential allies or opponents, and changes in government organization or policy. As he actually stated it, this hypothesis is quite weak and vague: he finds examples of interest group organizing in response to all three sets of factors and concludes that they are relevant. Rather than accepting these descriptive observations, later scholars have read stronger hypotheses into Truman. Robert Salisbury says that Truman makes two important predictions: (1) increasing social complexity produces interest group diversification; and (2) mobilized groups face pressure from new mobilization by previously unorganized opposing groups.[3] Even in this stronger form, the hypotheses appear trivially true: many more interest groups have mobilized since Truman wrote, some in response to opposing groups that had previously organized. When Truman is used as a straw man in contemporary reviews, however, these same claims are often taken to a logical extreme that is obviously false. Here is how Jeffrey Berry and Clyde Wilcox reference Truman: "Early observers of interest group politics thought that interest groups formed easily and naturally and that, because of this, any imbalance in interest group politics would naturally lead to its own remedy."[4]

This revisionist intellectual history is unfortunate because most of Truman's book is dedicated to nuanced historical narratives about the many problems interest groups have in organizing to influence government policy. To Truman, it is obvious that some groups are more politically organized than others and that some organized groups are more influential than others. What is difficult to figure out is how some groups gain advantage over others. In Truman's concluding summary, the closest he comes to hypotheses about who succeeds is another vague list of three categories of explanations: "(1) factors relating to a group's strategic position in the society; (2) factors associated with the internal characteristics of the group; and (3) factors peculiar to the governmental institutions themselves."[5] In Truman's view, a large number of factors account for why some groups are more successful: they may begin with advantages in social status; they may succeed at generating cohesion and a political orientation; or they may face a receptive government. Truman does not claim that all groups will succeed or that all policy debates will be equally balanced. Instead, understanding the relative strengths of the political combatants and the reasons for their success or failure constitutes the research agenda that he proposes.

Robert Dahl: Competition in Policy Domains

The most commonly cited pluralist text is *Who Governs?* by Robert Dahl.[6] It is the product of a case study of the political competition in New Haven, Connecticut, in three areas:

political nominations, urban redevelopment, and public education. Dahl finds that different policy areas are associated with different influential actors. He also shows that each actor in political competition has a distinct set of political resources, which they put to use with unequal effectiveness. The book opens with a history of social status in the community and argues that inequalities in notability, economic success, popular support, and government involvement no longer all favor the same social group. The book is then framed as a discussion of how a society with formal political equality, but lots of "dispersed inequalities" in politically relevant resources, governs itself.

Although most interest group scholars have seen Dahl's work as a continuation of Truman's, Andrew McFarland argues that Dahl and later pluralists "rejected group theory."[7] McFarland says that Dahl sees organized interests as playing only a minor role in governing New Haven, pointing to a neighborhood group as the one major example used by Dahl. McFarland's view stems from the contemporary conflation of interest groups in society with organized interests. After all, Dahl devotes much of his book to analyzing the roles of occupational groups, ethnic immigrant groups, religious groups, business entrepreneurs, unions, and government employees, the very units of political competition envisioned by Truman. He portrays public education debates in New Haven as a product of policymaker efforts to build support from teachers, administrators, Catholics, and parent leaders. Dahl also emphasizes the leverage that social and political leaders gain by the perception that they represent public constituencies.

Yet Dahl does add several important observations to the pluralist theoretical framework. Most important, he emphasizes the role of political leadership by elected and appointed officials. He argues that these leaders often have their own ambitions and policy ideas that do not stem from their group affiliations. Their proposals do not necessarily reflect a set of compromises among social groups that the leaders make in order to build an electoral coalition. This point comes through most strongly in Dahl's discussion of urban redevelopment, a major initiative led almost entirely by the mayor and the development administrator. These efforts were a response to federal policy change (grant availability), rather than public or interest group pressure. The mayor had to anticipate how various constituencies would respond to his ideas, but he led and they acquiesced.

This argument is related to Dahl's second major theoretical advance: his emphasis on the dominant role of professionals in political life. As Dahl famously argues, "In liberal societies, politics is a sideshow in the great circus of life."[8] Most citizens are uninvolved and ill informed, which means that political professionals need only to conduct their work with a vague allegiance to democratic participation. They must appear responsive and inclusive, but typically doing so only requires rituals such as forums for public input and advisory committees with members allegedly representing broad constituencies. In Dahl's view, political institutions are not merely arenas for group conflict. They feature a political class that organizes the interests of potential constituencies in the service of their own ends.

Dahl's third major addition to the pluralist framework sowed the seeds of the backlash against it. Dahl held that influence on political institutions and policy outcomes was a process that had to be observed. Relative influence did not follow automatically from the distribution of resources. Researchers had to observe how political leaders built support for policy proposals, how constituencies defined and pursued their own interests, and how public opinions influenced political elite behavior. This was a methodological approach more than a theory of the political process, but the theory and method were combined in later applications.

CLASSIC CRITIQUES AND THEIR CONTEMPORARY RELEVANCE

The pluralist approach has been critiqued extensively since Truman and Dahl wrote. Some scholars have denied its relevance completely, and others have modified or extended its potential application. Figure 5.1 reviews this history in a timeline.

Pluralism was most directly and energetically challenged by elitist theories of community power. Pluralist theory emphasized influence on the political process and policy outcomes. It discussed power as merely an absolute form of influence; one had power if one determined the outcome. In the most cited article in the history of the *American Political Science Review*, Peter Bachrach and Morton Baratz argue that pluralism dealt with only one "face of power."[9] A second face allowed some to manipulate the political process to prevent the grievances of others from ever becoming political issues that required decisions. Some years later John Gaventa argues that a third face of power allowed elites to prevent some constituencies from ever realizing their grievances and seeing them as political issues.[10]

Logically, neither of these ideas is incompatible with group theories of politics. Truman talks extensively of the many reasons why some "potential groups" had not mobilized politically, and Dahl spends much of *Who Governs?* explaining how political elites structure decision making to avoid open conflict. Yet different assumptions about the nature of political power between pluralist and elitist scholars quickly led to irreconcilable arguments about the capacity of social science methods to observe the exercise of power in society. No amount of evidence taken from public political processes can adequately test the theory that most influence on political outcomes stems from the power of

FIGURE 5.1 **A Chronology of Pluralism and its Critics**

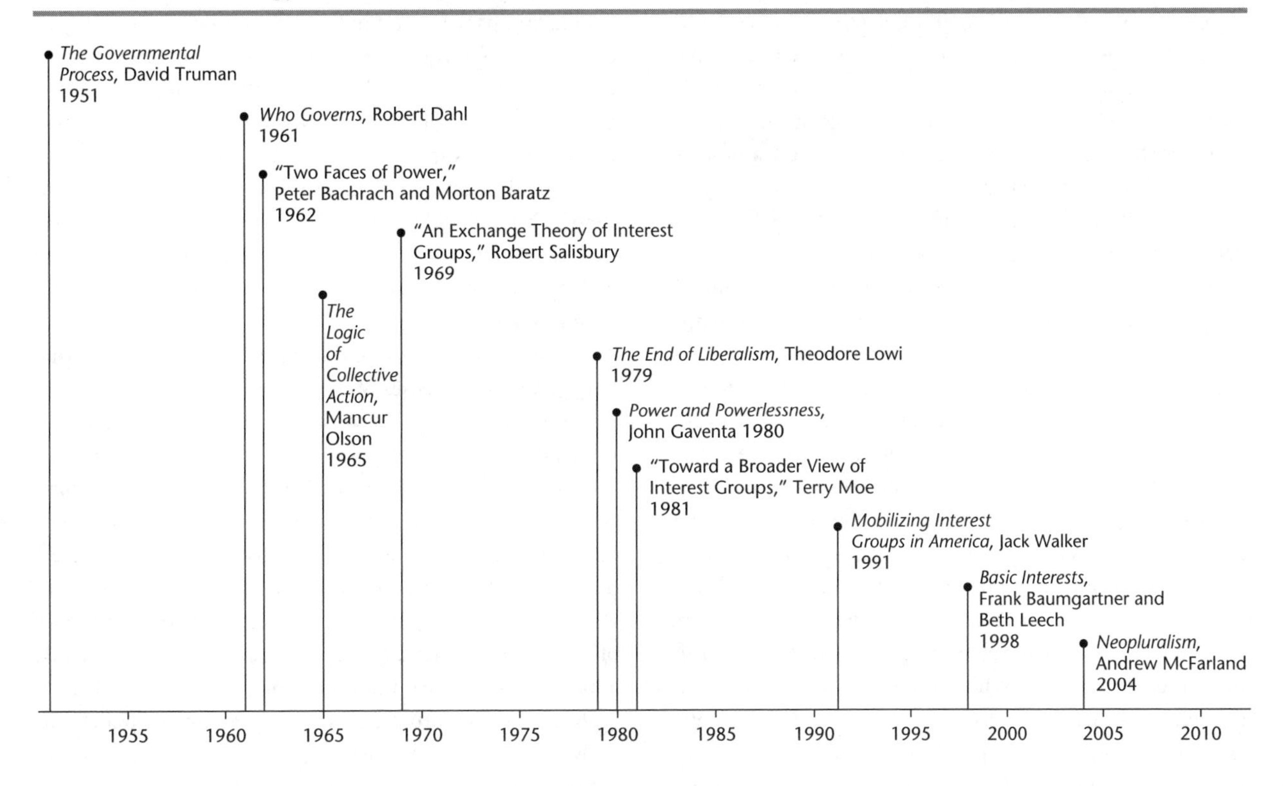

some elites to prevent issues from ever arising and to prevent some groups from realizing their own interests. Likewise, citing examples of interests that some researchers believe could potentially play more fundamental roles in local politics will not convince pluralists that elites exercise power primarily by preventing the emergence of class politics. Strangely, today's scholars rarely mention critiques of pluralism related to community power, even though they more or less led to its official downfall. Contemporary interest group scholarship is no less challengeable on these age-old grounds; studying which lobbyists get their way in Washington policy debates is subject to the same critiques of method leveled at Dahl.

The critique of the pluralist framework that has had a greater impact on interest group scholarship is the one advanced by Mancur Olson in his 1965 book *The Logic of Collective Action: Public Goods and the Theory of Groups.*[11] Olson frames the book as a critique of group theories of politics, famously arguing that individuals with shared interests or ideas do not necessarily have incentives to act collectively to pursue their shared goals. To encourage collective action, according to Olson, leaders of large groups need to provide a set of benefits available only to members. Olson's argument stimulated a large research literature to analyze how organizations generate membership support.[12] Yet most evidence refutes the claim that selective incentives are necessary for membership mobilization.[13] Contemporary scholars credit Olson with opening a research agenda into interest group mobilization, but they use an expanded view of the types of incentives that cause individuals to join organizations.[14] Overall, the modern consensus on group mobilization is at least as consistent with Truman as it is with Olson: multiple factors enable groups to act collectively (see Chapter 4).

Another set of arguments was less direct in its criticism of the pluralist framework, but probably did more to undermine the logic of using the group approach to study interest organizations. Salisbury finds that most interest organizations present in Washington and most of those that participate in policymaking are not membership groups.[15] Instead, they are institutions such as corporations, charities, and professional advocacy groups. Surveys of interest group leaders by Kay Lehman Schlozman and John Tierney and by Jack Walker further elaborate on the diversity of types of interest organizations, the diversity of their mobilization techniques, and the diversity of their tactics for influencing government.[16] Walker reports that organizing and maintaining an interest group is made easier by funding from government and foundations. Schlozman and Tierney find important differences in tactics across organizational types, resource levels, and ideological goals. On the whole, interest organizations without memberships have proliferated and become a permanent part of Washington politics.

Neither Truman nor Dahl argue that membership organizations are the only method of mobilizing constituencies to influence government; in fact, both cite examples of influence by constituency leaders without any official backing by a membership. Yet the emphasis of the new line of research is inconsistent with the pluralist framework. Pluralist theory considers interest organizations to be manifestations of group interests and ideas, whether or not they have membership. Much of the contemporary literature, in contrast, is concerned with the organizations as unitary actors. In this view, the organizations may rely on constituencies, or they may behave independently of them; their behavior is best predicted by characteristics of the organizations themselves, such as the ties between their leaders and government officials. This is an important difference in perspective. If the AARP is best seen as an organization equivalent to all organizations with the same resources, rather than a representation of the political influence of older people, the pluralist framework does not have as much to offer. If allocating money from a corporate budget generates the same results as an equivalent amount of donations from thousands of people who share a common political perspective, pluralist theory is unlikely to generate helpful hypotheses for investigating interest group influence. Curiously, therefore, the most important threat to the utility of the pluralist framework is the emphasis on institutions and organizational behavior in contemporary research, rather than either of the two self-conscious critiques of pluralism: elitism and collective action theory.

Interest Group Liberalism

One of the most important efforts to refine and update pluralist theory is *The End of Liberalism* by Theodore Lowi.[17] It is difficult, however, to discern where Lowi disagrees with the empirical assumptions of the pluralist framework because he conflates empirical and normative theory. He sees pluralism as a combination of theory and ideology, even arguing that all good theories of politics become ideologies. Lowi introduces his own idea of "interest group liberalism" as an ideology about how government should function that is shared across the political spectrum, rather than an empirical theory for use in political science. This shared ideology is an updated version of pluralism. It posits that society features diverse interests that organize to participate in politics and that government should ratify the compromises reached by bargaining among interest group leaders. The only difference between the two major U.S. political parties in their application of this public philosophy is that they disagree on which interest groups have the most legitimate demands.

As a normative theory, Lowi finds fault with pluralism and therefore with its extension in interest group liberalism. The ideology, according to Lowi, assumes that bargaining among groups will result in fair competition and equality of influence. It also equates the aggregation of diverse interests with the public interest. As a result, the ideology of interest group liberalism minimizes direct popular control over government, institutionalizes social privileges in government institutions, and makes government resistant to change. Not coincidentally, these are the same criticisms leveled at Dahl and Truman when scholars perceive them as making normative claims about the superiority of the governing system that they describe.

Lowi's critique of pluralism as an empirical theory, however, mostly focuses on its lack of concern with administration. First, the power of interest group administration means that organizations perpetuate themselves and organizational leaders institutionalize their leadership roles. Although pluralist theory leaves this out, according to Lowi, the addition of this part of administrative theory merely makes it more applicable and predictive. The reason is that whenever interests mobilize, they become permanent parts of the political system. Pluralism's second failure to include administrative theory, however, is more detrimental. Even if a pluralist policy process generates government policy initially, the policy still must be administered. According to Lowi, administration gives government an opportunity to drive future policy change and to perpetuate its own expansion. Government gives itself the legitimacy to pursue its own interests, according to Lowi, by adhering to the ideology of interest group liberalism. In other words, government institutes new policy by claiming that it is responding to a consensus among representative interest groups rather than pursuing policy goals shared by all Americans.

Lowi uses this theory to analyze the history of several policy areas, including agriculture, urban affairs, and social welfare. In each case, administrative agencies and departments were empowered to respond to the professional leaders of organized constituencies and the interests of their own bureaucracies. They created public policy that did not achieve any broad social goals, according to Lowi, even though government seemed to be constantly growing its authority and responding to interest group demands.

The primary difference between Lowi and pluralists, then, is that Lowi is far less sanguine about the policy results of the political process. As an empirical theorist, however, Lowi adds two important claims to the pluralist framework. First, he brings the state back into pluralism, arguing that government pursues its own interests directly rather than as another group in competition with others. Second, he argues that the normative implications of pluralism can be put to use in the service of government because administrators can justify their behavior on the basis of upholding a fair political process rather than pursuing fair policy goals.

NEOPLURALISM

The most recent advances in pluralist theory have taken place around the moniker "neopluralism." David Lowery and Virginia Gray argue that contemporary interest group research points toward a neopluralist theoretical perspective that contrasts with traditional pluralism and economic theories built around the work of Olson.[18] The neopluralist perspective, they argue, is attentive to the many different types of organizations that arise to influence government policy and the multiple ways they compete with one another. It also incorporates the variation in strategies, tactics, and lobbying targets across organizations, which is driven by the uncertainty associated with attempts to influence policy. Finally, neopluralism highlights the connections between mobilization, influence attempts, and policy change. The neopluralist perspective understands, they argue, that every stage of the influence process may produce feedback effects, of which the most obvious is that government programs create mobilization by new constituencies.

In this sense, neopluralism is an effort to accept and incorporate the third critique of pluralism outlined above: the focus on organizational development and behavior. The neopluralist perspective agrees that interest organizations do not always look like archetypal representations of social group interests. It agrees that many aspects of the influence process are driven by idiosyncratic factors related to individual organizations or government officials. The perspective also incorporates parts of administrative and institutional theory, admitting that the context of contemporary interest group competition is the semipermanent results of past political processes: government rules that continue to affect policy results. Yet we are still left with the question of how much the group approach to politics helps answer contemporary questions. Can we divorce the interest groups we see today from the process of relative social group mobilization? Can we divorce their influence from an effort by policymakers to respond to constituency group pressure? In their own research on state interest group populations, Gray and Lowery concentrate on the broad connections between the size and diversity of interest group populations and the characteristics of the state economy and society. This focus implies, but does not specify, some connection between the character of the original social constituencies identified by Truman and today's interest organizations.

In his book *Neopluralism: The Evolution of Political Process Theory*, Andrew McFarland provides a history of pluralist theory and offers a set of theoretical arguments that is similar to those offered by Lowery and Gray.[19] McFarland, however, attempts to integrate many other theoretical frameworks, especially social movement theory and theories of the politics of the policy process. Like Lowery and Gray, he associates neopluralism with a revitalization of pluralist theory that incorporates the many responses to Olson's collective action theory. He cites interest group research as proving that many organizations form, maintain themselves, and influence policy regularly. As a result, most studies of policy areas find involvement by multiple well-organized groups. These findings, according to McFarland, should be combined with attention to collective action theory as well as an acknowledgement that some policy areas can be characterized by the lack of competition among interests found in Lowi's work. Pluralism, in other words, should expand by accepting most of the extensions and critiques proposed by others.

McFarland also hopes to incorporate some alternative approaches from studies of social movements, political institutions, the politics of the policy process, and planning. From social movement theory, he wants to take an expanded view of resource mobilization that explains how new groups mobilize and pays close attention to rhetoric. He appreciates the concept of framing, the process of coming up with policy arguments and rationales for mobilization. From studies of political institutions, he wants to bring back state autonomy, the idea that government agencies and departments can develop policy largely on their own as well as create their own constituencies. This approach is best exemplified by Daniel Carpenter's book *The Forging of Bureaucratic Autonomy*.[20] Carpenter shows that executives at the U.S. Postal Service and the Department of Agriculture developed new policy goals to generate support for their agencies from an array of powerful constituency groups.

From studies of the policy process, McFarland wants to incorporate the advocacy coalition framework that focuses on shared beliefs, goals, and interactions among a group of policy proponents inside and outside of government. Punctuated equilibrium theory, emphasizing that policy history involves long periods of stability and short periods of major change, is also highlighted. From planning theory, he wants to add that multiple competing interests occasionally come together to reach consensus on an approach to policy change. Uniting all these theories is attention to political cycles that appear over long time horizons. McFarland creates his own periodization of interest mobilization and American policy history based on this idea. Rather than seeing all of these theoretical developments as competing, McFarland sees them all as part of the still unfinished development of a theory of the political process that began with pluralism.

Matt Grossmann's discussion of neopluralism notes that the primary difference between traditional pluralist and neopluralist approaches is the contemporary focus on formal interest organizations.[21] Pluralism addresses groups as general constituencies such as occupations or industries, whereas neopluralism emphasizes the fundraising strategies, influence tactics, cooperative and competitive relationships, and policymaking roles of specific organizations. Neopluralist approaches successfully incorporated three segments of organizational theory into pluralist theory: (1) population ecology, the idea that organizations compete with others for resources within particular fields; (2) institutional theory, the idea that organizations can become taken-for-granted embodiments of social values or public interest goals; and (3) network theory, the idea that interpersonal and interorganizational relationships and patterns of interaction among actors may be just as important as formal organizational boundaries. Where neopluralism goes wrong is the separation of studies of interest organizations from analysis of the broader conflicts among social or economic groups with shared interests or ideas. This separation means that interest group scholars interact less with scholars studying interest mobilization and aggregation in other contexts. Scholars studying the mobilization of specific groups in subfields like ethnic politics create their own frameworks rather than build on pluralist theory. The same is true of scholars studying the competition among interests in a specific policy domain in subfields like political economy. Establishing organizations as the only domain of interest group research has led to the fractured development of similar theories about interest mobilization and aggregation across social science; it is this balkanization that McFarland attempts to rectify.

IS NEOPLURALISM OLD WINE IN NEW BOTTLES?

For a new scholar entering the field deciding what theoretical approach to utilize, the lack of consensus among pluralist scholars and the confusion associated with amalgamating a hodgepodge of disparate theories creates a serious detriment to becoming an adherent. Economistic theorists at least agree on first principles; social movement theorists agree on the major categories and concerns of their theory; and theorists of organizations agree on the population under study. Pluralists often disclaim the title, and neopluralists want to incorporate every theoretical advance as their own. What differentiates the (neo)pluralist approach from others? Is there a core set of propositions or insights that new scholars can assess to determine if they buy the general framework?

The differentiated features of the theoretical framework are those that have been with it since the outline of group theory by Truman and the perspective on political competition offered by Dahl. Like all theoretical frameworks, the pluralist approach can incorporate new findings, add ideas from other areas, and adapt to changing circumstances. Yet what differentiates pluralism is still its focus on the multiple actors involved in political competition in each policy area and the assumption that groups with shared interests and ideas are the basic units of political competition. One can accept these premises and still argue that framing is a useful theoretical idea or that the prominent role of foundations in financing organizations is an important empirical finding. Yet it is not particularly useful to argue that either of these ideas is a core tenet of pluralist or neopluralist thought.

Look at the use of findings about how members are encouraged to join interest organizations. One could adapt Olson's theory to incorporate the new findings; Terry Moe does just that, arguing that a reformed Olsonian model incorporating individual nonselective incentives for mobilization is superior to a pluralist model.[22] Moe illustrates how individuals lacking obvious self-interest might join political organizations if they had high levels of efficacy or if they wanted to gain friendship or social acceptance. Moe is not in much empirical disagreement with the neopluralists on the reasons that people join organizations, even though neopluralists use the same findings to argue that Olson's critique of group theory has not held up well. Yet there are some distinctive features of the response of each perspective: economistic approaches argue that the findings require researchers to return to the individual, elucidating the many reasons he or she may join a group, whereas the pluralist approaches argue that the findings imply that many different kinds of social groups may mobilize to influence the political process.

Scholars who agree on the basic precepts of pluralism are unlikely to reach consensus either on the appropriate telling of the post-Dahl intellectual history or the most important recent findings to incorporate into pluralist theory. New scholars wishing to use a pluralist or neopluralist framework will have to accept this ambiguity. Because pluralism was implicated in broad debates about power and how government should be structured, scholars using the approach will also be burdened by heavy normative baggage. Still, this approach retains some real virtues. First, it can help rescue the interest group subfield from its secondary status; the way to make interest group studies more relevant to other subfields is to stop insisting that the organizations themselves are of primary relevance and instead focus on how the organizations reflect broader political competition among social, ideological, and economic sectors. Second, the basic tenets of the framework are readily understandable and easily applied across issue areas and groups, as well as to foreign contexts. Scholars can always look for the groups in competition over policy outcomes.

The idea that interest group liberalism and neopluralism are just examples of old wine in new bottles is meant to make it easier for new scholars to decide whether to adopt the pluralist framework and see how it applies to their field. This also works against the use of traditional group theory and pluralism as straw men in contemporary interest group studies. Just to be clear, no one ever said all groups have equal influence on policy. No one ever said all groups mobilize effectively. No one ever denied that government officials and departments pursue their own interests. No pluralist ever said that lobbying by interest organizations is the only important driver of policy outcomes. And pluralism as an empirical framework is not necessarily associated with any set of normative claims about how politics should be organized. Instead, pluralism is just a starting point for scholarship that (1) asks scholars to look for the groups that are competing to influence policy; (2) suggests that there is likely to be more than one group of importance; and (3) sees the policymaking process as operating in the context of competition among broad social and ideological groups, as well as economic sectors, to influence collective decisions.

WHEN TO USE THE PLURALIST FRAMEWORK

Most social scientists now accept that theoretical progress rarely takes the form of Thomas Kuhn's scientific revolutions.[23] One does not typically see a new theoretical framework entirely dislodge an old framework, leading to discipline-wide consensus on the basic assumptions that should underlie future work. Instead, multiple approaches maintain adherents, and research proceeds from different sets of assumptions. Given the reality of multiple approaches, it is helpful to ask when it is likely to be most appropriate to use a pluralist framework for undertaking interest group research. Three fairly obvious cases emerge, along with two less obvious.

The most straightforward case is a researcher who is interested in a particular group or set of groups. If, for example, she is interested in the organized representation of American Jews or doctors, she would find it helpful to think in terms of the shared interests and ideas of each group in public policy and to compare their representation and policymaking involvement to their likely competitors in policy debates. Focusing on the leaders of a single organization that represents a group or ignoring likely opponents of the group, in contrast, is unlikely to lead to a compelling insight or predictive theory. The researcher would also gain little from divorcing the study of the organizations associated with Jews or doctors from their role as representatives of those constituencies.

The second clear instance where pluralism should be considered as a useful framework is in assessing competition within a policy area in which group competitors can be readily identified. If a researcher can only identify Democrats and Republicans as the policy combatants or believes that the policy area features rough consensus among all participants, he may find a pluralist approach unlikely to yield useful insights. On the other hand, given clear competition among industries, occupations, ethnic groups, or ideologues, he may find it useful to begin by studying how well each group is represented in government and the interest group community.

These two circumstances are related to the third case: when the researcher is studying the relative mobilization or involvement of different groups. If she is interested in why some ethnic groups are better represented than others or how the mobilization of different industries has changed over time, she would benefit from thinking about which groups have clear goals in government policy and which groups mobilize most effectively. In contrast, she may find it less helpful to analyze the histories of each organization representing every group to uncover narratives of how each developed, raised funds, and survived.

A less clear case that might benefit from the pluralist framework is one in which a researcher is relating organizational activity to public political behavior or attempting to assess who gets represented by interest groups. The researcher should not attempt to answer these questions simply by asking who joins organizations or whether interest group arguments are in line with opinions expressed in public opinion polls. Rather, he should analyze whom interest groups claim to represent and whether the ideas of leaders match those of claimed constituents. It would also be helpful for him to know which public groups have not mobilized effectively and which opinions expressed by members of the public are not associated with any organizations to speak on their behalf.

The final instance in which the pluralist framework likely has something to offer researchers is when they consider how policymakers respond to interest organizations. If scholars simply count resources available to different organizations, they may not reach satisfying conclusions about whether policymakers listen to or respond to organizations that claim to speak in behalf of a social group or industry. Instead, scholars need to understand how the representation of constituencies by these organizations affects their influence; in other words, are organizations treated differently based on whom they claim to represent? Likewise, scholars are unlikely to make much progress if they consider organizations as free-floating seekers of resources, policy involvement, or publicity independent of the interests or opinions they seek to represent. We should think of the interaction between interest groups and policymakers as a reflection of how policymakers treat input from the social or economic groups they represent.

COMPARISON TO ALTERNATIVE FRAMEWORKS

In intellectual history, pluralist ideas are most often contrasted with elitist ideas about the distribution of power in society. Yet elitism is not used widely to study interest groups in contemporary politics. Even the notion of "iron triangles," the idea that congressional committees, administrative agencies, and interest groups work together to forward the same interests in some policy areas, has lost favor in interest group research. Today, the primary alternatives to using pluralist ideas to study interest groups are economic modeling of collective action and exchange and theories of organizational development and maintenance. In sociology, the social movement approach is most dominant; many of the same organizations called "interest groups" in political science are commonly referred to as "social movement organizations" in sociology. These four alternative approaches are reflected in this volume. Each approach is reviewed in Table 5.2, which summarizes their foci and most obvious applications.

The contrast between pluralist ideas and economic modeling is the clearest. Pluralist approaches do not start from the individual unit of analysis and do not assume rational choice decision making. Groups may take action based on any number of motivations and may act together to achieve joint goals, even if economic models indicate that rational actors would not behave accordingly. Policymakers may respond to group pressure, even absent a direct *quid pro quo* exchange or clear electoral incentive. The choice between these two frameworks is likely to be driven by a scholar's underlying assumptions about human nature. Pluralist assumptions appear much more consistent with established findings about group formation, identity, and comparison from social psychology and anthropology. The downside is that they do not enable a researcher to move from a few universal assumptions to clear empirical predictions.

The contrast between social movement and pluralist approaches is traditionally cast as a bottom-up versus top-down distinction: social movement theory begins with the realization of a grievance among a segment of the public, whereas pluralist approaches begin with competition in a policy area. This is a reasonable division to guide the use of each approach; social movement theory collapses the debate between interests and within government into a broad category called the "political opportunity structure"; pluralism, on the other hand, does not have much to say about the mechanics of the mobilization process. In practice, the use of each theoretical approach is driven less by their relative strengths and more by which groups are under study. Social movement theory is, for example, the most prominent framework used to study environmentalists, women's groups, and ethnic groups. This topical division is unfortunate, because it does not necessarily correspond to important differences in the behavior of these groups compared to others.

The contrast between pluralist approaches and those that focus on group formation and maintenance is less clear. Traditionally, focusing on the needs and internal processes of interest organizations has been most useful for understanding how groups raise money and how they attempt to influence government. Pluralist approaches instead emphasize the character of the competition among social and economic sectors. More recently, scholars of group formation have begun to import agent-based modeling, an approach using computer simulations to model human interaction. These computer simulations allow the researcher to input any assumptions about individual decisions and interaction patterns. A model might include a city of hundreds of people who talk to their next-door

TABLE 5.2 **Comparing the Frameworks**

	Focus of inquiry	Approach is most relevant	Example of use
Pluralism	Groups in society and economy competing for policy influence	When interested in the groups or when issue area competitors are easy to identify	Analyze strengths in health care debate between providers, insurers, and mobilized patient groups
Economic models of collective action	Strategic considerations based on individual self-interest	When want to identify micro-level mechanisms or when all actors agree on structure of negotiation	Analyze why some types of industry associations are able to mobilize more company members
Social movements	Broad mobilization around political ideas	When large public uprisings pursue change through social protest	Compare the tactics and success of the gay rights movement and the antinuclear movement
Group formation and maintenance	Organizational development and resource mobilization	When want to identify micro-level mechanisms for how organizations form and survive	Model the development of consumer groups and competition for members among them

neighbors about politics, deciding whether to join political groups based on whether their friends are joining. This model is designed to show how these assumptions lead to aggregate results, such as the number of people who join groups. Pluralist assumptions could also be used in this type of model, but modifying economic assumptions is the more common approach. Yet pluralism also allows scholars to take the types of social interests and ideas affected by policy as apparent, rather than explicitly model the development of each group.

Naturally, there are plenty of ways to combine various theoretical insights from all of the approaches. Interest group scholars are rarely asked to place themselves completely in one theoretical corner, enabling them to choose among theoretical ideas in cafeteria style. In interest group studies, merging economistic and pluralist ideas is attempted most often. Yet this amalgamation may be the least fruitful, given the gulf between the basic assumptions of each theory. Combining pluralist and social movement theory might enable a more complete understanding of interest groups that stem from a public mobilization. Explicitly modeling how individuals cooperate in groups to compete with other groups over decision making might flesh out the dynamics of mobilization that remain vague in pluralist theory. A grand synthesis of all of the theoretical approaches presented in this volume may be possible, but it is unlikely to happen anytime soon.

UNANSWERED FUNDAMENTAL QUESTIONS

If the pluralist theoretical perspective is to continue being useful, it will have to help scholars answer some central questions about the role of interest groups in politics and governance. Versions of pluralist theory could be used to answer many typical questions in interest group research. To fundamentally change common ideas about interest groups, however, scholars will have to use pluralist theory to direct their attention to answering the two basic questions that it raises.

First, which social groups and economic sectors are politically mobilized and how are they organized? Interest group scholars have begun to analyze sectors of organizations based on whom they represent or what issue perspective they advocate, but they have a long way to go in analyzing how organizations representing the same broad interests work together or compete. We also have not updated or assessed our lists of allegedly unorganized social groups. The question of whether organizations that represent a social group act differently from those that represent a "public interest" issue also remains largely open. There is still much to explore about the differences between representatives of economic sectors and representatives of social groups. Interest group representation is largely an open field. We know a little about whether group leaders represent members, but there are still many organizations that make untested claims about representing large constituencies or public opinion.

All of these questions assume that interest representation works through the interest group community, but there are other potential routes. Some scholars have begun to see political parties as coalitions of social groups and sectors.[24] Scholars have yet to compare group representation within the parties to group representation by interest organizations. There are also some groups that produce politicians and government officials at disproportionate rates. Scholars of ethnic politics are attentive to all of these dimensions of representation, but we have yet to see how other occupational, ideological, and religious groups compare in their representation in multiple types of political institutions.

A second fundamental question for pluralist investigation is what factors influence the success of some groups relative to others. Interest group research has largely studied which organizational sectors are the largest and which organizational tactics are most effective. We have left more general questions, such as why some groups are more influential than others, to other scholars. A more formal investigation may be helpful. There are multiple reasons for potential inequality in interest representation: (1) more resourceful organizations may arise to represent some groups; (2) organizations representing some groups may be more effective; and (3) organizations representing some groups may enjoy greater receptivity from policymakers. We have studied each of these separately, in terms of individual organizations, but not together in an effort to explain group-level advantages in political influence.

There are likely to be multiple types of advantages that allow some groups to succeed politically more than others. First, some political constituencies have advantages based on their own characteristics, such as education levels. Second, some groups may hold issue positions that face less political opposition, They may hold popular positions or those that require less government action. Third, some groups may have institutional advantages such as allies in government. Fourth, some groups may be better off as a result of history. They may have been influential in the past, or, if not, the status quo may already be structured to benefit them.

We may never come to completely satisfactory answers to these questions. But one reason for the lack of progress may be that we have not tried to answer them in quite a while. Since the days of the primary works by Truman, Dahl, and Lowi, we have largely stopped thinking of politics in pluralist terms. The pluralist perspective, as presented here, left open as many questions as it attempted to answer. One of the great misreadings of pluralist history is to see it as a well-developed explanation for political phenomena with clear hypotheses. When it did produce hypotheses, they were mostly innocuous predictions that stood up against the extreme arguments forwarded by elitists. The most obvious hypotheses were: (1) more than one group influences policy; (2) new groups often mobilize to oppose others; and (3) different groups are most active in each policy area. These ideas can hardly be more than a starting point. We still need to know which groups mobilize politically, what form their mobilization takes, and who wins and loses in policy competition.

CONCLUSION

The pluralist theoretical framework remains useful for studying the role of interest groups in the political process. It asks important questions but leaves many open for further study. It serves as a good starting point for many types of investigations, especially where the policy combatants are easy to identify or the social groups of interest are clear. The pluralist framework has some advantages over alternative perspectives, especially its flexible assumptions and its focus on group competition as a principal element of political life.

As defined here, the pluralist view of politics is an extension of group theory. It begins with the premise that the important actors in political competition are groups with shared interests or ideas. Beginning with David Truman, it sees the differential mobilization of some groups over others as a fact of politics and the waves of mobilization and involvement by different groups as a main source of change. Beginning with Robert Dahl, it sees competition in policy areas as involving multiple actors, including those who claim to speak in behalf of constituencies. It analyzes political competition by examining who is most involved and how they operate.

This baseline theoretical perspective is still the most useful aspect of pluralist theory that differentiates it from other frameworks. Of the original critiques of pluralist theory, elitism and collective action theory have not held up well empirically. Studies of institutions and organizations have successfully challenged the focus of pluralist theory, but are not at all incompatible with its baseline assumptions. The two major attempts to update pluralism have largely extended these assumptions and adapted them based on new findings. Interest group liberalism recognized that governments can institutionalize the role of interest groups, furthering their own interests at the expense of broader public policy goals. Neopluralism added that contemporary findings about how organizations develop and maintain themselves and about how policymakers interact with interest groups can be integrated with pluralist theory.

For scholars thinking about which theoretical framework to use in their work, this complex intellectual history and the normative baggage that accompanies it can be difficult to grasp and stomach. Yet the pluralist perspective remains an important candidate for use in many types of interest group research. It is especially useful for studies of the relative mobilization of particular groups or the competition among readily identifiable combatants in a policy area. Questions about the relationship between public and organized political behavior also cannot be effectively answered without considering a pluralist framework. The same is true of questions about how policymakers respond to organizations that act as representatives of constituencies. It is by no means certain, however, that all scholars are better off using the pluralist framework. Economistic theories are better for those who share rational choice assumptions or want to build predictions from a few universal precepts. Social movement theory is likely to be more useful to people interested in a specific mobilization attempt, rather than competition over a policy outcome. Organizational theories are likely to be useful for studying specific organizations or organizational populations from any of these perspectives.

The pluralist framework may be most useful for its ability to redirect interest group scholars to focus on the larger political competition that frames their investigation of a specific community of organizations in Washington. Somewhere along the way, interest group scholars lost track of broader questions about which groups and economic sectors mobilize to influence politics, how they organize themselves, and which succeed in becoming part of the governing process and influencing policy outcomes. It was these questions that generated the original discipline-wide interest in studies of interest groups. Without a pluralist framework, it is hard to judge where interest organizations fit in the general battles of politics, to evaluate the role of interest groups in "who gets what, when, and how." A pluralist framework can allow scholars of interest groups to relate their work to age-old questions of democratic theory and practice. Pluralist theory offers some ideas about the initial questions that interest group scholars should ask themselves. Its usefulness, however, may relate more to its tendency to view interest organizations as one important manifestation of the broader social conflict over collective decision making.

NOTES

1. Frank R. Baumgartner and Beth L. Leech, *Basic Interests: The Importance of Groups in Politics and Political Science* (Princeton: Princeton University Press, 1998), xv.

2. David B. Truman, *The Governmental Process: Political Interests and Public Opinion* (New York: Knopf, 1951), 506.

3. Robert H. Salisbury, "An Exchange Theory of Interest Groups," *Midwest Journal of Political Science* 13 (1969): 1–32.

4. Jeffrey M. Berry and Clyde Wilcox, *The Interest Group Society,* 5th ed. (New York: Pearson Longman, 2009).

5. Truman, *Governmental Process.*

6. Robert A. Dahl, *Who Governs? Democracy and Power in an American City* (New Haven: Yale University Press, 1961).

7. Andrew S. McFarland, *Neopluralism: The Evolution of Political Process Theory* (Lawrence: University of Kansas Press, 2004).

8. Dahl, *Who Governs?,* 305.

9. Peter Bachrach and Morton Baratz, "Two Faces of Power," *American Political Science Review* 56 (1962): 947–952.

10. John Gaventa, *Power and Powerlessness: Quiescence and Rebellion in an Appalachian Valley* (Urbana: University of Illinois Press, 1980).

11. Mancur Olson, *The Logic of Collective Action: Public Goods and the Theory of Groups* (Cambridge: Harvard University Press, 1965).

12. See Baumgartner and Leech, *Basic Interests.*

13. See Jack L. Walker, *Mobilizing Interest Groups in America: Patrons, Professions, and Social Movements* (Ann Arbor: University of Michigan Press, 1991).

14. Robert H. Salisbury, *Interests and Institutions: Substance and Structure in American Politics* (Pittsburgh: University of Pittsburgh Press, 1992).

15. Robert H. Salisbury, "Interest Representation: The Dominance of Institutions," *American Political Science Review* 78 (1984): 64–76.

16. Kay Lehman Schlozman and John T. Tierney, *Organized Interests and American Democracy* (New York: Harper and Row, 1986); Walker, Mobilizing Interest Groups.

17. Theodore Lowi, *The End of Liberalism: The Second Republic of the United States* (New York: W. W. Norton, 1979).

18. David Lowery and Virginia Gray, "A Neopluralist Perspective on Research on Organized Interests," *Political Research Quarterly* 57 (2004): 163–175.

19. McFarland, *Neopluralism.*

20. Daniel Carpenter, *The Forging of Bureaucratic Autonomy: Networks, Reputations and Policy Innovation in Executive Agencies, 1862–1928* (Princeton: Princeton University Press, 2001).

21. Matt Grossmann, "The Organization of Factions: Interest Mobilization and the Group Theory of Politics," *Public Organization Review* 6 (2006): 107–124.

22. Terry M. Moe, "Toward a Broader View of Interest Groups," *Journal of Politics* 43 (1981): 531–543.

23. Thomas S. Kuhn, *The Structure of Scientific Revolutions* (Chicago: University of Chicago Press, 1962).

24. Marty Cohen, David Karol, Hans Noel, and John Zaller, *The Party Decides: Presidential Nominations Before and After Reform* (Chicago: University of Chicago Press, 2008).

SUGGESTED READING

Baumgartner, Frank R., and Beth L. Leech. *Basic Interests: The Importance of Groups in Politics and Political Science.* Princeton: Princeton University Press, 1998.

Berry, Jeffrey M., and Clyde Wilcox. *The Interest Group Society,* 5th ed. New York: Pearson Longman, 2009.

Dahl, Robert A. *Who Governs? Democracy and Power in an American City.* New Haven: Yale University Press, 1961.

Gaventa, John. *Power and Powerlessness: Quiescence and Rebellion in an Appalachian Valley.* Urbana: University of Illinois Press, 1980.

Grossmann, Matt. "The Organization of Factions: Interest Mobilization and the Group Theory of Politics." *Public Organization Review* 6, 2 (2006): 107–124.

Lowery, David, and Virginia Gray. "A Neopluralist Perspective on Research on Organized Interests." *Political Research Quarterly* 57, 1 (2004): 163–175.

Lowi, Theodore. *The End of Liberalism: The Second Republic of the United States.* New York: W. W. Norton, 1979.

McFarland, Andrew S. *Neopluralism: The Evolution of Political Process Theory.* Lawrence: University of Kansas Press, 2004.

Moe, Terry M. "Toward a Broader View of Interest Groups." *Journal of Politics* 43, 3 (1981): 531–543.

Olson, Mancur. *The Logic of Collective Action: Public Goods and the Theory of Groups.* Cambridge: Harvard University Press, 1965.

Salisbury, Robert H. *Interests and Institutions: Substance and Structure in American Politics.* Pittsburgh: University of Pittsburgh Press, 1992.

Schlozman, Kay Lehman, and John T. Tierney. *Organized Interests and American Democracy.* New York: Harper and Row, 1986.

Truman, David B. *The Governmental Process: Political Interests and Public Opinion.* New York: Knopf, 1951.

Walker, Jack L. *Mobilizing Interest Groups in America: Patrons, Professions, and Social Movements.* Ann Arbor: University of Michigan Press, 1991.

chapter 6

Interest Groups and Social Movements

by Dara Z. Strolovitch and M. David Forrest

"One weekday morning in mid-July," a 2007 *New York Times Magazine* article "Can Lobbyists Stop the War?" by *New Republic* editor Michael Crowley begins, "perhaps two dozen liberal organizers gathered around a conference table in an office building on Washington's K Street. Their mission: American withdrawal from Iraq." Those arranged around the table, the article continues, represented "the new face of the antiwar movement—now one of Washington's most vigorous single-issue lobbies." [1] Noting that the "playbook for opposing a war has changed markedly since the street-protest ethos of the anti-Vietnam movement," Crowley writes, "[t]ie-dyed shirts and flowers have been replaced by oxfords and BlackBerries. Politicians are as likely to be lobbied politely as berated." [2] Instead of a "freewheeling circus managed from college campuses and coffee houses," he continues, the new antiwar movement is a "multimillion-dollar operation run by media-savvy professionals" [3]

If tie-dyes and coffee houses are the prototypical (if also stereotypical and caricatured) images of social movements, conference tables and K Street are the interest group analogues. Although not driven by theoretical considerations, Crowley's equation of "the antiwar movement" with a "lobby" captures many of the empirical and conceptual issues at stake in considering the relationship between interest groups on the one hand and social movements on the other. First, this formulation highlights definitional questions: What are social movements, how can they be distinguished from interest groups, and where, if anywhere, can we draw the line between them? Second, what are the implications of the distinctions we make and the boundaries we draw for each one as an object of study, as well as for our understanding of each one's political and representational roles? Finally, have the answers to these questions changed over time, and if so, why and to what effect?

Guided by overarching concerns about representation, this chapter addresses each of these three broad sets of questions about the relationship between interest groups and social movements, emphasizing movements and organizations involved in national politics and those that represent marginalized groups. The chapter begins by exploring the history and evolution of the definitions of and distinctions between interest groups and social movements. It then examines the ways in which the relationship between the two concepts does and does not map onto distinctions between political insiders and outsiders. Next, it explores alternatives to the interest group/social movement distinction, and then discusses the implications of the ways interest groups and social movements are treated as objects of inquiry by political science and sociology. The chapter concludes with a discussion about the implications of the connections between interest groups and social movements for representative democracy in the United States.

These topics do not, by any means, represent an exhaustive list of the many important questions about the relationship between interest groups and social movements in American politics. Taken together, however, they draw attention to several constellations of questions and concepts that simultaneously illuminate the contours of contemporary group politics while also suggesting some issues that stand to benefit from further inquiry.

EVOLVING DEFINITIONS AND DISTINCTIONS

Contemporary textbook definitions of interest groups and social movements often imply that clear differences distinguish one from the other. An admittedly unscientific sampling of introductory American politics textbooks finds social movements described as "outsider" and "grassroots" groups that "lack the resources, the contacts, or the experience to use other political strategies"[4]; as "large informal grouping[s] of individuals and/or organizations focused on specific political or social issues"[5]; as "amorphous aggregates of people sharing general values and a desire for social change"[6]; and as "public activities designed to bring attention to political causes, usually generated by those without access to conventional means of expressing their views."[7] Interest groups are commonly depicted as groups of people "organized to pursue a common interest or interests, through political participation, toward the ultimate goal of getting favorable public policy decisions from government"[8]; as organizations of people "with shared goals that tr[y] to influence public policy through a variety of activities"[9]; as "organized groups of people seeking to influence public policy"[10]; and as organizations "of individuals who share a common political goal and unite for the purpose of influencing public policy decisions."[11]

As accurate as these definitions might seem in a contemporary context, early considerations of groups in American politics did not typically draw firm distinctions between formal organizations and other, more diffuse, forms of group mobilization such as social movements. Examining the evolution of these distinctions suggests that their source is as normative as it is empirical. In other words, underlying many such distinctions are broad questions and shifting normative assumptions about the appropriate role for nongovernmental but policy-oriented groups in American politics.

Indeed, discussions about "group politics" provide a Rorschach test of the loftiest aspirations for and the most skeptical apprehensions about American politics at particular moments in the nation's history. In explaining his concerns about the "violence of faction" in *Federalist* 10, James Madison describes factions simply as "a number of citizens . . . who are united and actuated by some common impulse of passion, or of interest, adverse to the rights of other citizens, or to the permanent and aggregate interests of the community." Written on the heels of Shays's Rebellion, *Federalist* 10 reflects anxieties about populist uprisings and class divisions—what Madison calls "the various and unequal distribution of property"—which, he writes, are "the most common and durable source of factions" because "[t]hose who hold and those who are without property have ever formed distinct interests in society."[12] While Madison treated groups, in Theodore Lowi's characterization, as a necessary evil in need of regulation, Alexis de Tocqueville lauds political associations as a boon to democracy. Writing almost fifty years after Madison, Tocqueville viewed political associations as essential guards against majority tyranny (see Chapter 2).[13]

If Madison and Tocqueville's treatments crystallize general concerns about U.S. politics, the extent to which and the ways in which they draw distinctions between more formal, elite organizations and more populist and amorphous masses serve as even more fine-grained lenses into an era's particular unease about and hopes for democracy. So, while Madison refers to class divisions as substantive sources of factions, he does not distinguish among their possible forms. The terms *interest group* or *social movement* were not available to him in 1787. He could, however, have distinguished between "mobs" and "associations," but he did not. Such an unwillingness to distinguish between the two highlights Madison's concerns about democracy as a form of government that facilitates the formation of social groups that pursue their own interest at the expense of the public good. Tocqueville, on the other hand, did distinguish between the positive role he ascribes to political associations and his less sanguine characterization of amorphous and unruly "mobs," which might be seen as a precursor to several twentieth-century portrayals of movements. This distinction unveils Tocqueville's fear that the pursuit of equality within democracy will eliminate differences within the polity and tyrannize it, rather than encourage greater opportunities for creation and achievement.

Arthur Bentley and David Truman, often considered the progenitors of interest group theory, were also quite broad and general in their conceptualizations of groups. They intended their group theory to counter what they saw as the tendency of political scientists of the time to treat the state as "an entity above the behavior of individuals . . . [and as] autonomous from influence from everyday political factors."[14] Instead, Bentley argues, politics and government were driven by "group actions seeking interests, with interest defined as economic interest." As Andrew McFarland writes in a 2010 essay, "Bentley's fundamental political reality was the process of group interaction in the pursuit of evolving, often conflicting economic interests." According to McFarland, Truman argues similarly that interactions among political groups are crucial to understanding American politics. In this characterization of group politics, law and political institutions adjudicate "the rules of the process of the group struggle for power" and may create more favorable conditions for some kinds of groups. Once again, however, this conceptualization does not rest on or imply a distinction between interest groups and social movements.[15]

The seeds of the current understanding of interest groups as organized insider associations and social movements as diffuse political instruments used by political outsiders are often seen as having been sown by pluralist accounts of politics in the 1950s and 1960s. Pluralism's general vision of American politics is one of a political system that successfully funnels conflict into government institutions by making power diffuse and power structures permeable, with multiple points of access that are open to all comers.[16] Writing in the context of cold war America, scholars such as Robert Dahl hoped to offer a liberal alternative to Marxist ideas that social structures are set and can be changed only by revolution. Instead, Dahl argues, the seeds of change lie *within* existing institutions. "So long as the prerequisites of democracy are substantially intact in this country," Dahl writes in *A Preface to Democratic Theory*, "it appears to be a relatively efficient system for reinforcing agreement, encouraging moderation, and maintaining social peace."[17]

Dahl also wanted to offer an alternative to C. Wright Mills's argument that the United States was controlled by a "power elite" of government officials, corporate leaders, and military officers. In *Who Governs?* Dahl offers a case study of power in New Haven, Connecticut. He argues that rather than being concentrated in a single power elite, political resources were dispersed, decentralizing power and opening multiple routes to influence. But while Dahl notes that resources such as time and money could be used to form organizations, his pluralism was not "foremost a theory of interest groups; instead, it was an overall theory of power."[18] Within this broader framework, citizens were said to influence policy in part through their ability to mobilize into groups and contribute time, money, and other resources to organizations that could access levers of power alongside other forces such as political parties and government agencies. Although *Who Governs?* did not address social movements explicitly, Dahl's contention that any group sufficiently interested in an issue can and, most important, *should* press its demands *within* formal institutions draws a tacit distinction between the two concepts. In particular, it suggests that protest-oriented, "outsider" social movements are categorically different from the interest groups that form when citizens rationally pursue political goals and policy changes.

In 1965, just four years after Dahl suggested that rational citizens tend to pursue common objectives through the formation of interest groups, economist Mancur Olson claimed that rather than promote mobilization by groups with grievances, rationality in fact served to prevent it. In his foundational work, *The Logic of Collective Action*, Olson argues that the goals pursued by interest groups are almost always "public goods," equally available to everyone in a particular aggregate or class, such as farmers, U.S. citizens, and so forth, regardless of whether they participate in the

FIGURE 6.1 **Number of National Women's, Racial Minority, and Economic Justice Organizations Founded by Decade, 1790s–2000s**

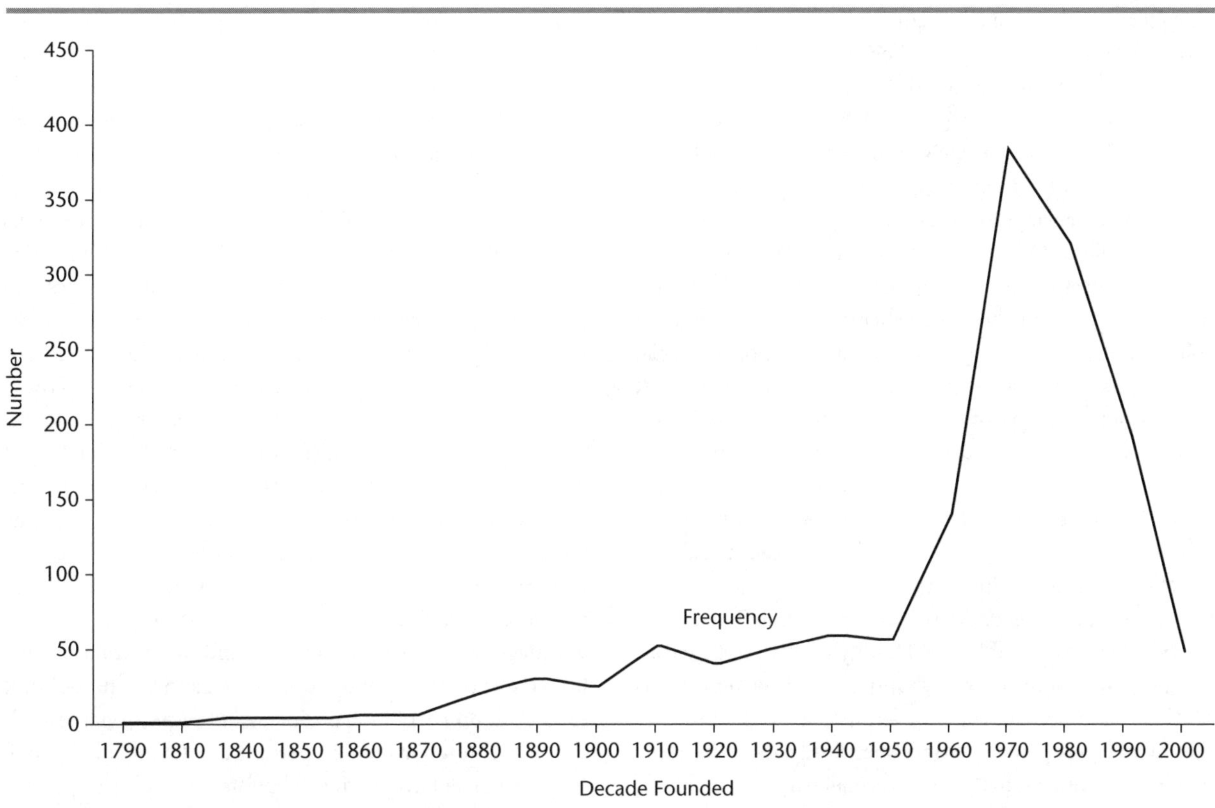

SOURCES: *Associations Unlimited* (Detroit: Gale Research, online); Women's Information Exchange, *Electra Pages*, electrapages.com; *Encyclopedia of Associations* (Detroit: Gale Research, 2000); *Leadership Conference on Civil and Human Rights*, 2000, civilrights.org); *National Directory of Asian Pacific American Organizations* (Washington, D.C.: Organization of Chinese Americans, 1999); *National Directory of Hispanic Organizations* (Washington, D.C.: Congressional Hispanic Caucus, Inc., 1999); *Public Interest Profiles* (Washington, D.C.: Foundation for Public Affairs, 1999); *Washington Information Directory* (Washington, D.C.: CQ Press, 1998, 2005–2006, and online); *Washington Representatives* (Bethesda, Md.: Columbia Books, 1999); *Who's Who in Washington Nonprofit Groups* (Washington, D.C.: Congressional Quarterly, 1995); *Women of Color Organizations and Projects National Directory* (Oakland: Women of Color Resource Center, 1998).

efforts to obtain them. A "rational actor," therefore, would decline the costs of participation, choosing instead to "free ride" and receive the public good without paying any cost unless selective incentives were made available only to participants. As a consequence, Olson claims that rational citizens will not contribute to interest group formation, leaving many group interests unrepresented. According to Olson, this barrier can be overcome only in small groups in which members carry individual responsibility for protecting the group interest or, in the case of large, diffuse groups, if organizations offset the costs of participation with "selective incentives" given only to members. Olson applies his theory to the labor movement, and his framework was later incorporated into many theories of social movement organization. Although this theory departed from earlier ones, it drew similar connections between the rational forms of collective action made possible through selective incentives provided by formal organizations and the irrationality of mobilization among what he called the "forgotten groups," "the unorganized group . . . that has no lobby" "takes no action," and "exerts no pressure."[19] He argues that such "large and latent groups"—a category that included, inter alia, migrant farm workers and taxpayers—could not provide selective incentives. As a consequence, he treated organizing around such issues as illogical and fundamentally different from interest group formation.

The social movements of the "long 1960s" (defined as the period from the late 1950s to the early 1970s) mobilized historically marginalized and excluded groups—in particular, women, racial minorities, and low-income people—giving the lie to Olson's contention that a lack of selective incentives meant that such populations would never mobilize. In the wake of these movements, several accounts of collective action challenged the characterization of social movements as irrational deviations from normal interest group politics. Many of these accounts crystallized their authors' own hopes for social movements and their anxieties about interest groups as political forces. As a consequence, many of them also maintain and, in some cases, solidify the ever-sharpening division between these two varieties of group politics. Frances Fox Piven and Richard Cloward's *Poor People's Movements*, Theodore Lowi's *The Politics of Disorder*, and Michael Lipsky's *Protest in City Politics* all treat protest-based, disruptive social movements as sensible—and perhaps superior—responses to the limits of the interest group system. More specifically, these accounts hold that in contrast to the more formally organized politics of interest groups, protest is a more accessible resource for securing concessions to the demands of marginalized groups and dismantling inequalities (although, for Piven and Cloward especially, such success is contingent upon the existence of political crisis). These protesting groups generally lack access to the money, time, and contacts necessary for the formation of interest groups, but under the right conditions they could create enough disorder to force policymakers to respond to them.[20] In these formulations, the line dividing interest groups and social movements is built less around rationality and logic than around the dominance of elite interests, which tend to control the collective action of interest groups more than they control social movements.

INSIDERS AND OUTSIDERS

The work of scholars such as Piven and Cloward, Lowi, and Lipsky suggests that another way to conceptualize the distinction between interest groups and social movements is "insiders" versus "outsiders." As both the foregoing discussion and the *New York Times* piece quoted at the beginning of this chapter imply, interest groups are typically thought of as elite political "insiders" that operate as recognized "players" in Washington, D.C. In such a conception, the tactics used by interest groups are also seen as distinct from those used by social movements, which are typically associated with "outsider" actions such as protests and other vociferous berating of politicians. In addition to using "outsider" tactics, this conceptualization treats social movement activities as relatively spontaneous and passionate rather than viewing them as calculated and well planned. Finally, in the popular imagination, social movements are commonly associated with marginalized issues and populations—in the *New York Times* story, the antiwar movement.

In this approach, distinctions between interest groups and social movements are linked to central and enduring themes in scholarship about U.S. interest group politics—in particular to concerns about the dearth and relative weakness of organizations that represent marginalized groups such as women, racial minorities, low-income, and LGBTQ (lesbian, gay, bisexual, transgender, queer or questioning) people within the "pluralist heaven" and the consequent dominance of corporate, business, and professional organizations that typically oppose the goals and drown out the voices of these and other disadvantaged groups.[21] In her 2000 Survey of National Social and Economic Justice Organizations, Dara Strolovitch found that organizations representing women, racial minorities, and low-income people have fewer resources and fewer organizational and political tools than do corporate, business, and professional organizations, with fewer than 33 percent employing a legal staff, only 25 percent employing lobbyists, and only 20 percent having political action committees (PACs).[22] In contrast, in their 1986 study of interest groups, Kay Lehman Schlozman and John Tierney found that 75 percent of organizations employed a legal staff, and 54 percent had PACs.[23] In his 1998 research, Kenneth Kollman noted that 64 percent of organizations had affiliated PACs.[24]

UNIONS AS INSIDERS AND OUTSIDERS

Like the antiwar movement described by Michael Crowley in the introduction to this chapter, the labor movement has often straddled the boundaries between insider and outsider status and tactics in ways that have varied among sectors as well as over time. Indeed, throughout the 1960s and 1970s many labor unions, rather than directing their resources toward social movement efforts, instead adopted models of business unionism—a framework driven by institutional bargaining between union leaders and employers rather than directed by member participation and mobilization.

By the 1980s, however, the business unionism model had begun to falter, as membership numbers and institutional power were waning in the wake of the Reagan administration's anti-unionism. In the mid-1990s many unions tried to regain some of the power they had lost by returning to the kinds of grassroots mobilizing that had characterized the Depression-era labor movement. The American Federation of Labor and Congress of Industrial Organizations (AFL-CIO) has followed this path: From the post–World War II period through the 1980s, the AFL-CIO operated mostly on a business unionism model, keeping itself divided from—and even hostile to—left-wing politics and social movements. Faced with its diminished political presence and declining influence, however, in 1989 the AFL-CIO founded the Organizing Institute, intended to train union organizers and revitalize activity among union members. In 1995 members elected John Sweeney as AFL-CIO president. Sweeney, one of the handful of union leaders who had reached out and hired activist organizers during the 1970s and 1980s, shifted the AFL-CIO's efforts to encompass a mix of business unionism and grassroots mobilization, moving $20 million in the budget toward organizing and hiring young progressive activists as staff. The significance of what some have called social movement unionism and the return to organizing remains unclear, however, and scholars continue to investigate the prevalence of such social movement tactics and the efficacy of their use.

SOURCE: Lowell Turner, Harry C. Katz, and Richard W. Hurd, eds., *Rekindling the Movement: Labor's Quest for Relevance in the 21st Century* (Ithaca, N.Y.: Cornell University Press, 2001).

While it is doubtless 14 true that interest group politics has typically been dominated by powerful interests such as business, financial, and professional organizations, the *Times* article also reports that some important shifts have occurred over the last several decades. First, although marginalized groups had few formal political organizations representing their interests in national politics until well into the twentieth century, there was an explosion during the 1960s and 1970s in the number of movements and organizations speaking on behalf of disadvantaged populations. Many of these movements and organizations had grown out of the social and economic justice movements of the "long 1960s," in some cases out of the ashes of grassroots movements that had been decimated by, for example, the FBI's Counter Intelligence Program (COINTELPRO). COINTELPRO was conducted between 1956 and 1971, with the goal of infiltrating and disrupting groups that the FBI regarded as subversive.[25] By the beginning of the twenty-first century, there were more than 700 organizations representing women, racial minorities, and low-income people in national politics.[26] These include more than 40 African American organizations, more than 30 Asian Pacific American organizations, and well over 100 women's organizations.[27]

In addition to the increased presence of organizations representing political "outsiders," who had once mobilized mainly through social movements, the characteristics, tactics, and activities that once seemed to differentiate interest groups from social movements are no longer quite as useful in this regard. First, many social movement organizations have professionalized and nationalized offices inside the Washington Beltway that lobby public officials directly. Although organizations that have their origins in outsider movements remain outnumbered and outspent by organizations representing other, more traditional interests, and although they continue to engage in grassroots mobilization and other unconventional activities, they have also come to resemble political insiders. For example, 61.4 percent of organizations that represent women, racial minorities, and low-income people in national politics have offices in the greater District of Columbia area (Washington, D.C.; Maryland; and Virginia), and many of these are located on or near "Gucci Gulch," the K Street corridor that is home to some of the most powerful lobbying firms and interest groups in the country.[28]

In all of these ways, organizations such as the National Association for the Advancement of Colored People, the National Organization for Women, the Center for Law and Social Policy, the National Council of La Raza, and the Asian American Justice Center have become a significant and visible presence in Washington politics. These and similar organizations now provide an institutionalized voice to and compensatory representation for the concerns of formerly excluded groups that still have insufficient formal representation in national politics, challenging historic patterns of exclusion and altering the American political landscape by publicizing and opposing the dominance of business, professional, and corporate lobbies. Their roots in movements of challengers, however, mean that they straddle the boundary between "insiders" and "outsiders."

Clarissa Martinez de Castro, director of Immigration and National Campaigns at the National Council of La Raza, speaks to reporters after a meeting with President Obama in 2010 to discuss immigration reform.

The possibility of drawing a clear distinction between interest groups and social movements is further muddied by the growth in conservative social movements and by their cross-fertilization of tactics. While many outsiders have adopted insider tactics, many insiders have taken on characteristics, engaged in activities, and made claims that are more commonly associated with outsider movements. During the Obama administration's attempts to overhaul the health care system, interest groups such as FreedomWorks, run by former House majority leader Dick Armey, mobilized much of the grassroots opposition to Democratic plans for reform in town hall meetings across the country.[29] Among formal advocacy organizations, more than 70 percent engage in some amount of direct lobbying activities, 80 percent engage in indirect lobbying through grassroots mobilization, more than 50 percent organize demonstrations, and 67 percent participate in demonstrations.[30] Although often dismissed as "astroturf" when they are associated with business and professional organizations, such activity underscores the extent to which it is difficult to draw broad conceptual distinctions between interest groups and social movements.

DIVISIONS OF INTELLECTUAL LABOR

Thus far, the distinction between interest groups and social movements has been addressed as a substantive one, but it is also an artifact of the ways in which interest groups and social movements are treated as objects of study. As processes and institutions that blend social and political phenomena, interest groups and social movements are examined by both political scientists and sociologists. How each discipline treats them, is, to some degree, a function of each one's respective focus. As David Meyer and Lindsey Lupo write in a 2007 review essay about political science and the study of social movements, if we characterize social movements as permanent organizations engaged in collective action, then sociology seems like the appropriate base of inquiry. A scholar concerned with the policy impact of this collective action, however, would likely turn to frameworks and tools used by political scientists to examine the policy process, policy outcomes, and the connections among organized actors and their interests, state structures, and public policies.[31]

Indeed, much like interest groups and social movements themselves, *scholarship* on interest groups and social movements is in potentially productive tension.[32] Meyer and Lupo write, "Social movements represent a challenge not only to more conventional political action, but also to academic analysis."[33] Social movements are a central focus within sociology, where the focus tends be on questions about mobilization. Sociologists are also interested in interest groups and in social movement organizations, which they often examine under a broader rubric of organizational behavior.[34] Interest groups are integral to the study of American politics, but the study of social movements occupies a more tenuous position within the discipline and the subfield. Although political scientists "engaged the area of social movements very productively in the late 1960s and early 1970s," Meyer and Lupo argue, "by the middle of the 1970s the ground was largely ceded to sociology."[35] The reasons for this concession are varied, but among the most relevant theoretically and for our purposes here are (1) that social movement activity falls precariously between institutions and behavior, the two main branches within the study of American politics; and (2) the path-dependent trajectory set in motion by pluralist scholars.

As suggested in the previous section, pluralist theories imply that if groups with grievances do not try to press their claims through the many possible levels and branches of government, it is because they choose not to, not because they are prevented from doing so. Like the psychologists before them who had treated mass political action as a form of extreme, mob-like behavior and as an irrational response to the breakdown of social norms in the wake of phenomena such as national disasters or massive unemployment, scholars such as Robert Dahl treated extra-institutional activity such as social movements as exceptional, apolitical, and deviant. Portraying political institutions as permeable and as containing the seeds of change, pluralist scholars argued that legitimate political conflicts would and should be channeled into and resolved by political institutions.

Equating movements with riots and the like suggests that pluralists generally drew sharp distinctions between rational political actors who form organizations to lobby officials and discontented individuals who irrationally and spontaneously participate in social movements—not to achieve political goals but to alleviate psychological strains. Such a focus on individuals and on spontaneity tends to ignore and trivialize the political content and import of social movements. As sociologist Doug McAdam writes in his now classic account of the civil rights movement of the 1960s, "[I]f the pluralist portrait is accurate, how are we to explain social movements? . . . Why would any group engaged in rational, self-interested political action ignore the advantages of such an open, responsive gentlemanly political system?"[36]

As McAdam points out, the pluralists' faith in this responsive system led the social sciences to be caught off guard by the "turbulence" of the 1960s. While this surprise stimulated questions about why extant theoretical paradigms had failed to anticipate or explain the rise of mass movements, the main thrust of the resulting political science scholarship drew on economic models and rational choice theories that emphasized strategic incentives such as those inspired by Olson discussed above.[37] Although some of the resulting scholarship in this tradition has examined social movement activity (see, for example, Dennis Chong's 1991 book), the bulk of the work in the American politics subfield of political science has focused on interest groups, leaving sociologists to examine social movements.[38] The consequence of this scholarly division of labor, Elisabeth Clemens argues, is an incomplete understanding of political development.[39]

In addition to being addressed in different ways by sociologists and political scientists, interest groups and social movements do not constitute a discrete area of study, and some of the work in political science that has interesting and important implications for understanding movements and organizations has been written by scholars who do not necessarily consider interest groups or social movements their central object of study. As Meyer and Lupo write, political scientists interested in social movements tend either to "adapt paradigms from other disciplines to their topic, considering interest groups, race and ethnicity, voting, or power analysis in the context of the movement at hand," or to " 'cross over' to other disciplines, including history, anthropology, and particularly sociology, borrowing outside frameworks and speaking back to theory in another discipline."[40] Therefore, many such scholars do not belabor questions about whether and how to distinguish interest groups from social movements. Scholarship about the politics of race, ethnicity, and gender, such as Cathy Cohen's *Boundaries of Blackness*, Jane Mansbridge's *Why We Lost the ERA*, and Janelle Wong's *Democracy's Promise*, provide just a few examples of work that incorporates examinations of interest groups and social movements without being primarily *about* interest groups and social movements.

Similarly, scholars working within "policy feedback" frameworks examine the effects of social movements and advocacy organizations holistically and over time in order to understand the ways in which policy designs "influence the mobilization of organized interests and their interactions with elected officials."[41] Policy feedback approaches are particularly useful for thinking through the complicated interplay among these two concepts, as well as for contemplating the relationships among them and political interests, identities, institutions, and policy outcomes. Andrea Campbell's work, for example, has illuminated a great deal about the movements and organizations involved in the enactment of Social Security in 1935. Campbell traces the policy's role in the political construction of a senior citizen constituency with interests and preferences that policy entrepreneurs, interest groups, and political parties subsequently attempted to represent.[42] Along similar lines, Suzanne Mettler and Christopher Parker demonstrate how the education and training benefits provided to World War II veterans through the GI Bill helped to create the conditions that led returning black veterans to mobilize for civil rights, which led, in turn, to the creation of additional civil rights organizations and eventually to policy changes such as the Civil Rights Act of 1964.[43] Such work exemplifies the idea that, Meyer and Lupo argue, "the focus on institutions, the concern with political organization, the attention to institutional frameworks, and the focus on the policy payoff of different strategies of action . . . contribute mightily to the study of social movements; these are all areas that are underdeveloped in the social movements literature" that is dominated by sociological accounts.[44]

INTEREST ORGANIZATIONS, CONTENTIOUS POLITICS, AND OTHER FRAMEWORKS

Recognizing the difficulty of delineating a hard-and-fast distinction between interest groups and social movements, some scholars have posited conceptual frameworks that flout the disciplinary division of labor and encompass both, while also including other kinds of groups and activities such as political parties, revolutionary movements, and uncoordinated mass resistance. Paul Burstein argues that interest groups, social movements, and political parties are more productively considered under the single heading of "interest organizations," which he defines as formal and informal organizations that help different groups of people achieve political goals in a representative democracy.[45] Other scholars, such as Kenneth Andrews and Bob Edwards, Debra Minkoff, and Dara Strolovitch, adopt the term advocacy organization to capture the ways in which the activities of social movement organizations and interest groups serve to "make public interest claims either promoting or resisting social change that, if implemented, would conflict with the social, cultural, political, or economic interests or values of other constituencies and groups."[46] Scholars who use this term focus most often on organizations pursuing so-called "public interests," such as good government and consumer protection. In a slightly different vein, Minkoff and Strolovitch suggest that advocacy organizations have the institutional capacity to act on behalf of those who do not have the political resources to form their own organizations and express their interests directly.[47]

Charles Tilly, Sidney Tarrow, Doug McAdam, and others have urged scholars to consider social movements within a more synthetic framework that underscores their relationships to a range of collective actions, including not only interest groups but also terrorism, civil war, peasant rebellions, and revolution. This framework is generally known as "contentious politics," the social and political activities through which "actors make claims bearing on someone else's interests, leading to coordinated efforts on behalf of shared interests or programs, in which governments are involved as targets, initiators of claims, or third parties."[48] In the contentious politics framework, social movements are sustained campaigns of contentious claim-making that use repeated and similar collective actions and root themselves in a base of organizations, networks, traditions, and solidarities that make these actions possible. Interest groups act as the formal institutionalization of social movements in which contentious claim-making becomes more conventional and achieves integration into established systems of government.

CONCLUSION: IMPLICATIONS FOR REPRESENTATIVE DEMOCRACY

As evocative as the image of tie-dyes giving way to BlackBerries might be, our discussion about the relationship between interest groups and social movements suggests that the situation is more complicated than that contrast suggests. Indeed, it seems that it is not only, as Crowley writes, that "[p]oliticians are as likely to be lobbied politely as berated,"[49] but also that the same actors may well engage in both the lobbying and the berating. What are the implications of such connections between interest groups and social movements for representation and equality? First, the interest group explosion, of which the rise in organizations representing marginalized groups is a part, vastly increased the numbers of organizations that represent more traditional interests. In addition, some scholars argue that the professionalization of social movement organizations that has facilitated their inclusion within the interest group system has also led to their "capture" and to the prioritization of demands that fit the status quo in ways that reproduce the exclusions that defined the system prior to their inclusion.[50] Moreover, there is some evidence that inequalities are perpetuated by the very organizations that claim to speak on behalf of disadvantaged groups. Strolovitch has shown that although advocacy organizations provide an institutionalized voice for African Americans, women, Asian Americans, and other marginalized groups, these organizations also have tended to mobilize disproportionately around issues that affect the most advantaged members of these groups. To the extent that inclusion has served to incorporate movement interests into the existing interest group system, rather than to disrupt and reorder it, the connections between interest groups and social movements might be creating new, more intractable barriers to democracy and equality.

On the other hand, there is evidence that social movement practices have brought new groups interested in mobilizing common goods, public interests, and the concerns of marginalized citizens into an interest group system that once had been the almost exclusive preserve of groups devoted to protecting the status quo power and market relations.[51] This new focus has enabled greater levels of inclusion in the interest group system and more challenges to the ability of dominant groups to set the policy agenda. To the extent that this inclusion is meaningful—meaning that it allows previously excluded interests to disrupt and reorder the priorities of the political system—it seems to have expanded representation and facilitated increased democratic equality. For example, work on the rise of citizen groups highlights the extent to which these groups have introduced a strong voice for certain social concerns, especially those surrounding environmental protection, within policy debates.[52]

Other research suggests that many organizations are committed to advocating for their most disadvantaged constituents, that many do speak extensively and effectively on behalf of intersectionally marginalized subgroups, and that many provide a meaningful institutional channel for social movement concerns. Advocacy organizations that establish explicit organizational mandates to represent intersectionally marginalized constituents; raise contentious issues in contract negotiations (in the case of unions); collect better information about the relationship between the needs of constituents and the activities of interest organizations, foster ties to state and local organizations that empower nationally overlooked interests; provide greater descriptive representation to the most disadvantaged constituents; mobilize coalitions that transcend usual boundaries of representation; and establish ideological commitments to an interconnected vision of social justice are all more likely to disrupt the status quo in a way that establishes greater possibilities for the pursuit of equality in the interest group system.[53] Practices that address multiple injustices and that better represent the experiences of their constituencies are often pivotal to movement successes.[54]

Whether the increasing imbrications between interest groups and social movements ultimately advance or hinder equality, representation, and democracy in the United States, articles such as the one quoted at the beginning of this chapter suggest that they are here to stay, at least for the foreseeable future. Clear distinctions between the outsider status of social movements and the insider status of interest groups are increasingly untenable—if, indeed, they ever were accurate. But whatever the similarities between interest groups and social movements, to the extent that patterns of exclusion and dominance continue to define their encounters, they cannot simply be treated as a single entity. Rather than conceptualizing interest groups and social movements as either one-in-the same or as completely different species, perhaps they are more accurately understood as two political forces that coexist at a juncture where interest groups principally seek to manage the boundaries of group politics and social movements seek to disturb them.

NOTES

1. Michael Crowley, "Can Lobbyists Stop the War?" *New York Times Magazine*, September 9, 2007, 54.
2. Ibid.
3. Ibid.
4. Benjamin Ginsberg, Theodore J. Lowi, Margaret Weir, and Robert J. Spitzer, *We the People: An Introduction to American Politics*, 7th ed. (New York: Norton, 2009), 256.
5. Kenneth Dautrich and David A. Yalof, *American Government: Historical, Popular, and Global Perspectives* (Belmont, Calif.: Wadsworth Cengage Learning, 2009), 332.
6. Samuel Kernell, Gary C. Jacobson, and Thad Kousser, *The Logic of American Politics*, 4th ed. (Washington, D.C.: CQ Press, 2009), 624.
7. Christine Barbour and Gerald C. Wright, *Keeping the Republic: Power and Citizenship in American Politics* (Washington, D.C.: CQ Press, 2009), 607.
8. Ginsberg et al., *We the People*, 241.
9. Dautrich and Yalof, *American Government*, 328.
10. Kernell, Jacobson, and Kousser, *Logic of American Politics*, 610, 787.
11. Barbour and Wright, *Keeping the Republic*, 578.
12. James Madison, "Number 10," in *The Federalist Papers* (New York: Penguin, 1987 [1788]) 123, 124.
13. Alexis de Tocqueville, *Democracy in America*, trans. George Lawrence (HarperCollins: New York, 2000 [1835; 1840]), 192–195.
14. Andrew McFarland, "Interest Group Theory," in *The Oxford Handbook of American Political Parties and Interest Groups*, ed. L. Sandy Maisel and Jeffrey M. Berry. (London: Oxford University Press, 2010), 38.
15. Ibid., 38–39.
16. As a broad theory of power in American politics, pluralism addresses many issues beyond the role of groups. For more in-depth treatment of pluralism, see the chapters in this volume by Matt Grossman and Kay Lehman Schlozman.
17. Robert A. Dahl, *A Preface to Democratic Theory* (Chicago: University of Chicago Press, 1956), 151.
18. McFarland, "Interest Group Theory," 39.
19. Mancur Olson, *The Logic of Collective Action* (Cambridge: Harvard University Press, 1965), 165.
20. David S. Meyer and Lindsey Lupo, "Assessing the Politics of Protest: Political Science and the Study of Social Movements," in *Handbook of Social Movements Across Disciplines*, ed. Bert Klandermans and Conny Roggeband (New York: Springer, 2007), 114–117.
21. Kay Lehman Schlozman and Traci Burch, "Political Voice in an Age of Inequality," in *America at Risk: The Great Dangers*, ed. Robert F. Faulkner and Susan Shell (Ann Arbor: University of Michigan Press, 2009).
22. Dara Z. Strolovitch, *Affirmative Advocacy: Race, Class, and Gender in Interest Group Politics* (Chicago: University of Chicago Press, 2007), 49.
23. Kay Schlozman and John Tierney, *Organized Interests and American Democracy* (New York: Harper and Row, 1986).
24. Kenneth Kollman, *Outside Lobbying: Public Opinion and Interest Group Strategies* (Princeton: Princeton University Press, 1998).
25. Jeffrey Berry, *Lobbying for the People: The Political Behavior of Public Interest Groups* (Princeton: Princeton University Press, 1977); Strolovitch, *Affirmative Advocacy*.
26. Dara Z. Strolovitch, "Do Interest Groups Represent the Disadvantaged? Advocacy at the Intersections of Race, Class, and Gender," *Journal of Politics* 68 (2006): 894–910.

27. Frank R. Baumgartner and Beth L. Leech, *Basic Interests: The Importance of Groups in Politics and in Political Science* (Princeton: Princeton University Press, 1998); Virginia Gray and David Lowery, *The Population Ecology of Interest Representation: Lobbying Communities in the American States* (Ann Arbor: University of Michigan Press, 1996); Michael T. Heaney, "Outside the Issue Niche: the Multidimensionality of Interest Group Identity," *American Politics Research* 32 (2004): 611–651; Schlozman and Burch, "Political Voice"; Daniel J. Tichenor and Richard A. Harris, "The Development of Interest Group Politics in America: Beyond the Conceits of Modern Times," *Annual Review of Political Science* 8 (2005): 251–270. As Strolovitch notes in *Affirmative Advocacy*, Tichenor and Harris have challenged the characterization of a late twentieth-century explosion in the number of interest groups in the United States as having been brought on by two world wars, New Deal–era government programs, and the movements of the 1960s. In particular, Tichenor and Harris argue that the surveys, interviews, and directories of organizations from which data about political organizations are typically collected tell us little about organizations that died before the 1950s, when directories such as the *Encyclopedia of Associations, Washington Information Directory*, and *Washington Representatives* began publication. They argue that most political science work has therefore ignored the "robust set of organized interests engaged in Progressive Era political life." See Daniel Tichenor and Richard Harris, "Organized Interests and American Political Development," *Political Science Quarterly* 117 (2002–2003): 587–612, 593.

28. Strolovitch, *Affirmative Advocacy*, 49

29. David M. Herszenhorn and Sheryl Gay Stolberg, "Health Plan Opponents Make Voices Heard," *New York Times*, August 3, 2009, A12.

30. Strolovitch, *Affirmative Advocacy*, 145.

31. Meyer and Lupo, "Assessing the Politics," 111.

32. See Dara Z. Strolovitch and M. David Forrest, "Social and Economic Justice Movements and Organizations," in *Oxford Handbook of American Political Parties and Interest Groups*.

33. Meyer and Lupo, "Assessing the Politics of Protest," 111.

34. Kenneth T. Andrews and Bob Edwards, "Advocacy Organizations in the U.S. Political Process," *Annual Review of Sociology* 30 (2004): 480.

35. Meyer and Lupo, "Assessing the Politics of Protest," 111–112.

36. Doug McAdam, *Political Process and the Development of Black Insurgency, 1930–1970* (Chicago: University of Chicago Press, 1982), 6.

37. Andrews and Edwards, "Advocacy Organizations," 480.

38. Dennis Chong, *Collective Action and the Civil Rights Movement* (Chicago: University of Chicago Press, 1991).

39. Elisabeth S. Clemens, *The People's Lobby: Organizational Innovation and the Rise of Interest Group Politics in the United States, 1890–1925* (Chicago: University of Chicago Press, 1997), 62.

40. Meyer and Lupo, "Assessing the Politics of Protest," 113.

41. Joe Soss and Sandford Schram, "A Public Transformed? Welfare Reform as Policy Feedback," *American Political Science Review* 101 (2007): 113.

42. Andrea Campbell, *How Policies Make Citizens* (Princeton: Princeton University Press, 2003).

43. Suzanne Mettler, "Bringing the State Back In to Civic Engagement," *American Political Science Review* 96, 2 (June 2002) 351–365; Christopher Parker, *Soldiers to Citizens* (Princeton: Princeton University Press, 2009), 44; Meyer and Lupo, "Assessing the Politics of Protest," 113.

45. Paul Burstein, "Social Movements and Public Policy," in *How Social Movements Matter*, ed. Marco Giugni, Doug McAdam, and Charles Tilly (Minneapolis: University of Minnesota Press, 1999).

46. Andrews and Edwards, "Advocacy Organizations," 481.

47. Debra Minkoff, *Organizing for Equality: The Evolution of Women's and Racial-Ethnic Organizations in America* (New Brunswick, N.J.: Rutgers University Press, 1995); Strolovitch, *Affirmative Advocacy*, 4.

48. Charles Tilly and Sidney Tarrow, *Contentious Politics* (Boulder: Paradigm, 2007), 4.

49. Crowley, "Can Lobbyists Stop the War?" 54.

50. Ibid., 49–50.

51. Mark E. Warren, "The Political Role of Nonprofits in a Democracy," *Society* (2003): 40, 46–51.

52. Jeffrey M. Berry, *The New Liberalism: The Rising Power of Citizen Groups* (Washington, D.C.: Brookings Institution Press, 1999).

53. Strolovitch, *Affirmative Advocacy*.

54. Sharon Kurtz, *Workplace Justice: Organizing Multi-identity Movements* (Minneapolis: University of Minnesota Press, 2002).

SUGGESTED READING

Berry, Jeffrey M. *The New Liberalism: The Rising Power of Citizen Groups*. Washington, D.C.: Brookings, 1999.

———. "Citizen Groups and the Changing Nature of Interest Group Politics in America." *Annals of the American Academy of Political and Social Science* 528 (1993): 30–41.

Costain, Anne N. "Social Movements as Mechanisms for Political Inclusion." In *The Politics of Democratic Inclusion*, ed. Christina Wolbrecht and Rodney E. Hero. Philadelphia: Temple University Press, 2005.

Geron, Kim, Enrique De La Cruz, and Jaideep Singh. "Asian Pacific American Social Movements and Interest Groups." *PS: Political Science and Politics* 34 (2001): 619–624.

Haider-Markel, Donald P., and Kenneth J. Meier. "The Politics of Gay and Lesbian Rights: Expanding the Scope of the Conflict." *Journal of Politics* 58 (1996): 332–349.

McAdam, Doug. *Political Process and the Development of Black Insurgency, 1930–1970*. Chicago: University of Chicago Press, 1982.

Meyer, David S., and Lindsey Lupo. "Assessing the Politics of Protest: Political Science and the Study of Social Movements." In *Handbook of Social Movements Across Disciplines*, ed. Bert Klandermans and Conny Roggeband. New York: Springer, 2007.

Marquez, Benjamin, and James Jennings. "Representation by Other Means: Mexican American and Puerto Rican Social Movement Organizations." *PS: Political Science and Politics* 33 (2000): 541–546.

Minkoff, Debra. *Organizing for Equality: The Evolution of Women's and Racial-Ethnic Organizations in America, 1955–1985*. New Brunswick, N.J.: Rutgers University Press, 1995.

Staggenborg, Suzanne. *The Pro-Choice Movement*. New York: Oxford University Press, 1991.

Strolovitch, Dara Z. *Affirmative Advocacy: Race, Class, and Gender in Interest Group Politics*. Chicago: University of Chicago Press, 2007.

chapter 7

Economic Models of Interest Groups and Lobbying

by Scott H. Ainsworth and Austin C. Clemens

THE WELL-ESTABLISHED TIES THAT bind economic models to the study of groups reach back to the earliest days of social science. In fact, economists were fascinated by groups long before most political scientists were. Arthur Bentley, often thought of as the first group scholar, considered himself an economist and believed that an understanding of groups would enhance his understanding of his field. "[M]y interest in politics is not primary, but derived from my interest in economic life," he wrote.[1] Indeed, economists played a central role in the debates swirling around various notions related to interest groups and representation in a pluralist society. Mancur Olson, in his *Logic of Collective Action,* introduced important work by numerous economists, including John Kenneth Galbraith. Galbraith, as well as others, evaluated the prospects for groups and associations to play dominant roles in the representation of citizens' interests. For some economists, representation by groups was more finely tuned and more meaningful than representation by formally established government institutions. Olson was less sanguine about the prospects for group representation in a pluralist society because, he argued, some interests were vulnerable to free-riding problems; that is, some groups and interests would remain underrepresented.

This chapter starts with a brief review of Olson's classic treatise from 1965. A discussion of the classic themes in the markets and interest group literature follows. A description of game theory introduces the central sections of the chapter, which address models focused on money and influence, information exchange, and the multiple venues available for pressuring government officials. The final substantive section looks at some of the newest economic models related to interest groups.

Although many of the issues discussed in this chapter have a game theoretic or economic structure to them, others—although grounded in economic reasoning—are more empirically oriented. Introducing a wide range of economic models to the field is important, but it is also valuable to indicate ways in which disparate fields can inform one another.

A BRIEF REVIEW OF THE WORK OF MANCUR OLSON

Aside from Olson's work, few interest group scholars read work that links economics to interest groups and lobbying. Even for Olson, many scholars develop a throw-away line, and then quickly move on to other affairs. The citation is obligatory, but not salutary. Olson was the first scholar to note fundamental contradictions in David Truman's analysis in *The Governmental Process.* Truman had asserted that interest groups make claims upon others; that is, interest groups are narrowly focused on their own well-being, even if that focus creates costs for others. The sense that "groups act to serve their interests presumably is based upon the assumption that the individuals in groups act out of self-interest. If the individuals in a group altruistically disregarded their personal welfare, it would not be very likely that collectively they would seek some selfish common or group objective."[2] In short, if groups pursue narrow self-interests, then certainly the individual members of the groups must be sensitive to their own narrow self-interests. Therefore, individual concerns and individual choice must be incorporated into the analysis of interest groups. Starting with this simple assumption, Olson proceeded deductively to develop his theory of collective action (see Chapter 5).

Olson carefully distinguished between the different kinds of benefits that groups provide in their attempts to attract individuals to join collective efforts. Group benefits are essentially either private or public goods. Private goods are characterized by two conditions: rivalrous consumption and excludability. Both conditions are straightforward. Rivalrous consumption precludes two or more people from using the good at the same time without there being some

The authors thank Sven Feldmann and Bird Loomis for their comments and suggestions. The usual caveats apply.

diminution in the value of the good. Excludability ensures that one can prevent others from using or benefiting from the good. In contrast, public goods have nonrivalrous consumption and are nonexcludable. Many people can consume the same good without any depreciation in the value of the good because they are nonrivalrous. In addition, no one can be prevented from using or benefiting from the good because it is nonexcludable. Free riding allows one to benefit from the provision of a public good or collective effort even if he or she did not contribute any money or effort. There are many public goods all around us. National defense and clean air are public goods. Old-fashioned television broadcasts (as opposed to cable or pay-for-view) are public goods.

Two common misperceptions about public and private goods deserve attention. The first is that everyone values a public good. Analogous to the diverse nature of our demands for private goods, citizens have different preferences for the types of public goods provided and for the level of any public good's provision. Second, the provision of a good is entirely independent of its public or private nature. Certainly, governments do provide public goods, but they also provide many private goods in the form of contracts and entitlements. Consider the bidding process that takes place before any public roads, bridges, or airports can be built. The government's selection of a bid bestows a private good on the chosen construction company, even though the construction project itself may yield a public good. The government's *contracts* for roads, bridges, or stadiums are themselves private goods. In addition, governments are not the only providers of public goods: individuals, private firms, interest groups, and other nongovernmental institutions can also provide public goods.

Given that public goods provided by groups are nonexcludable, individuals' pursuit of narrow self-interest might undermine the ability of groups to organize. In particular, some of the benefits associated with group benefits might be available to joiners and nonjoiners alike. If the benefits a group provides are nonexcludable, then nonjoiners secure the same rewards as joiners. Nonexcludable benefits create an opportunity for individuals to benefit whether or not they contribute to collective efforts—that is, some individuals might free ride on the efforts of others. Although the incentive to free ride in collective action situations can be great, there are stable outcomes, typically referred to as equilibria, in which some individuals contribute while others free ride. In particular, if the threshold for group success has already been met, one would not expect additional joiners to the cause. The first volunteers to arrive at a benefit car wash typically work more than those who arrive later because the latecomers see that the threshold for a successful benefit has already been met. When many people are involved in a collective effort, who contributes and who free rides? As long as the threshold number of contributions is met, there are many equilibria, each with a different mix of individuals who free ride.

The minimum threshold for contributions could be met by individuals playing pure strategies (contribute or free ride) or by playing mixed strategies. Everyone could play the same mixed strategy or different mixed strategies. Some individuals could always play pure strategies while others play mixed strategies. The diversity of equilibria is tremendous. In a setting with an incredibly large number of equilibria, Olson highlighted just one, the one in which everyone free rides. Whenever numerous equilibria exist, an equilibrium selection problem occurs. Which of the many equilibria should a social scientist predict? Olson highlighted the equilibrium in which no one contributed, but the Olsonian equilibrium is not the only one in collective action settings. Other scholars focus on those equilibria that are most likely to occur given the presence of interest group entrepreneurs or focus on those equilibria in which everyone plays the same mixed strategy.

FREE RIDING

The free-rider problem occurs in collective action situations when individuals can enjoy the benefits of collective efforts without contributing. The canonical example is national defense. A nation may defend all of its inhabitants or none of its inhabitants, but it cannot select whom it will defend and whom it will not defend. If inhabitants are not required to contribute, their incentive is to free ride on the efforts and contributions of others. Both public and private interests must cope with free riding. Public interest groups often provide small selective benefits to their members, such as gifts with the group's logo, magazines, or admittance to organized events, to encourage joining. Private firms often focus their lobbying efforts very narrowly so that competitors are not benefited.

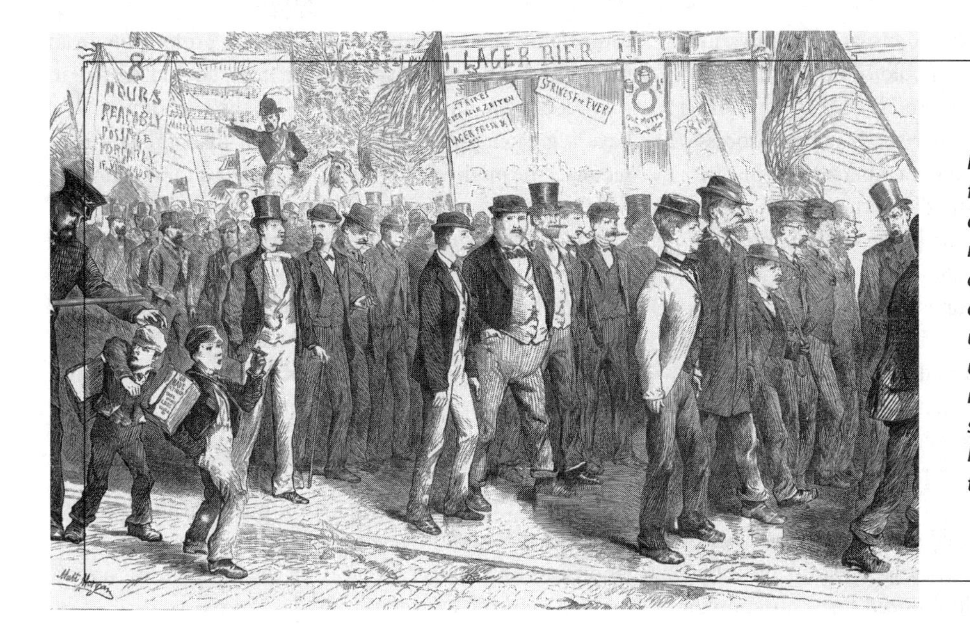

Free riding can take many forms. When labor unions advocated for legislation mandating an eight-hour day and safer workplace conditions, their work ultimately benefited those union members and nonmembers alike. In 1872 striking workers marched in New York City in support of the eight-hour movement.

The free-rider problem can be onerous, but it need not undermine all collective efforts. The question is how can one obviate the free-rider problem? Of Olson's numerous options, we consider two here. Olson wrote of the effects of group size and coercion on the free-rider problem. He argued that the collective action problem would be most onerous for large groups rather than small groups. Automobile manufacturers might avoid the free-rider problem because they are so few in number. They could readily coordinate their actions, and they could see the impact of their efforts because their benefits would be concentrated. In contrast, automobile consumers face much greater obstacles in their collective efforts. Suppose the manufacturers lobby for particular safety standards, but consumers want higher standards. Huge sums of money would be at stake for a small number of producers. Although there are millions of consumers, each of whom might value safer cars, the benefits are widely distributed rather than concentrated. No single consumer is likely to see the impact of his or her contribution to the collective effort for safer cars. Whenever collective benefits are concentrated, collective efforts are easier; and whenever benefits are widely distributed, collective efforts are harder.

Coercion or social pressure, Olson argued, greatly affected individuals' decisions about joining groups. In the United States, labor and trade groups as well as professional societies often seek legal sanctions to make membership in their organizations all but mandatory. Unions seek closed shops, wherein union support is compulsory for all workers. The argument for a closed shop is straightforward. If unions fight for safer work conditions and a higher wage, then all workers benefit whether they are union members or not.

RENT-SEEKING

In the political context, rent-seeking behavior refers to any attempt by economic agents to gain wealth through the manipulation of the political system. Rather than investing in new technologies to produce better widgets, firms shift resources to secure political protection of their (precarious) position in the market. In 1971 Nobel Laureate George Stigler identified ways that a firm might use the political system to manipulate its market position. Subsidies, price controls, barriers to entry for competitors, and taxes on goods that substitute for one's own goods all increase profits. The oil industry, for example, lobbies to increase subsidies and tax benefits for fossil fuel producers while simultaneously lobbying against other means of producing energy that would reduce demand for their own product.

The goods provided are public goods and thereby nonexcludable. Since all benefit, all should be required to support the collective efforts. Some professional societies have secured considerable influence over accreditation processes and licensing procedures, making membership all but necessary for one's professional standing. Many states require practicing lawyers to be members of the state's bar association. The American Medical Association manages most school and hospital accreditation issues. Unions and professional societies are each engaging in rent-seeking, trying to use lobbying pressure to manipulate their market conditions. If professional organizations can secure monopoly rights from the state or be recognized as adjudicators of quality, their market positions are protected by the state (see Chapter 20).

Olson's work tightly focused on a central question for interest group scholars: Which interests organize and which remain latent? But Olson also introduced a new question for interest group scholars: Are like-minded individuals invulnerable to squabbles and internecine competitions? The quest for group affiliation is countered with the quest for individual economic survival. It is not that groups fail to emerge; rather, it is that many more groups could emerge. Groups are not seen as the "automatic fruit" of interests.[3] It is not that group affiliation is irrational, but that it is fragile. Given Truman's assertion that political interest groups make claims upon others, it is only natural to think that groups and group members might be strategic in their pursuits of policy gains. Economic models are particularly well suited to analyzing the strategic pursuit of policy gains.

MARKETS AND POLITICAL ACTIVITY

As noted, Bentley sought to understand economics better by focusing on groups. Truman also tied groups and economics. Truman argued that his disturbance theory showed that bad economic times (a disturbance) led to more interest group growth. Salisbury, citing various shortcomings in Truman's work, also explored the connections between market conditions and group emergence.[4] Salisbury noted that groups were not the automatic fruit of interests. Groups needed entrepreneurs, individuals who were willing to risk capital to secure a profit. Salisbury noted that many of the early agricultural interest group entrepreneurs owned newspapers or magazines. Each separate endeavor, the group and the magazine or newspaper, enhanced and strengthened the viability of the other.[5]

More recently, scholars have explored how lobbying activity fluctuates during good or bad economic times.[6] One question they asked is how much capital should firms devote to lobbying and how much to productive efforts? As the relative value of production goes down, the incentives to engage in lobbying increase because a successful lobbying campaign can yield subsidies or market protections from the government. Moreover, weaker firms should engage in more lobbying, and weaker sectors of the economy should have a greater presence in Washington than the strongest sectors. One might recall Microsoft's delayed foray into politics. Before the possibility of antitrust proceedings, Microsoft had virtually no presence in Washington. The company devoted considerable resources to production and virtually none to lobbying. In contrast, automobile manufacturers have long, established histories of lobbying in Washington for favorable regulations or direct government support. More empirically oriented work evaluates how firms allocate resources across three types of political activity: lobbying, contributing to campaigns, or giving to charities. Many factors affect their allocations, including their market position and their extant relations with the government. The empirical results suggest that firms exploit political opportunities to increase revenues and decrease costs.[7]

GAME THEORY AND INTEREST GROUPS AND LOBBYING

Game theoretic applications to the study of interest groups and lobbying have been among the most controversial of methodological approaches employed. Games require defined sets of players and options or actions available to the players. Depending on the actions chosen by the players, a particular outcome is obtained, and payoffs are distributed. Game theoretic models are often amenable to comparative statics analysis, whereby one can see how changes in some aspect of the game affect players' optimal strategies. Games of incomplete information allow scholars to address players' beliefs. As players' strategies move them along a game tree, they refine their information and update their beliefs about one another. Actions (and inaction) affect those beliefs. Ultimately, scholars focus on those equilibrium results that are consistent with reasonable beliefs.

Testing strategic interactions directly has proven to be much more vexing than testing hypotheses derived from comparative statics. Scholars face a problem related to the independence of observations, which is a crucial assumption in most econometric methods. In a game theoretic scenario, players' choices are seldom truly independent from other players' choices, so our observations of actions taken are no longer independent. Game theoretic methods generally lack random elements, and wholly deterministic processes are less amenable to statistical evaluations. If one proceeds without the derived information from the counterfactuals (that is, the choices not made), the observed variables are vulnerable to selection bias. The dog that did not bark in the night can be as important as observed signals. Switching regressions allow one to derive information that is related to the choices not

GAME THEORY AND EMPIRICAL TESTS

Some games have a dominant strategy, which means that a player's optimal strategy remains the same regardless of the actions of other players. The oft-cited prisoners' dilemma game, which now appears in virtually every introduction to political science, is such a game. Each player has a dominant strategy to defect on the other player. Games more representative of real-life scenarios often display the interdependence of the players' optimal actions; that is, dominant strategies do not exist. In coordination games, one player's optimal actions change as other players' strategies change. During a traffic slowdown, should *everyone* take the alternative route? When a single strategy dominates others, or even when some variation in strategies is observed, it can be difficult to test games empirically because of the deterministic nature of equilibria. R. D. McKelvey and T. R. Palfrey proposed a solution that works by assuming that players sometimes make errors (or, equivalently, are somewhat uncertain about payoffs). Their quantal response model is well suited for statistical testing because it makes probabilistic predictions about outcomes.

made, but switching regressions are not the only route to consider. A small set of scholars has developed new equilibrium concepts and new statistical techniques to address these concerns.[8]

MODELS WITH MONEY AND POLITICS

At least since E. E. Schattschneider's *The Semisovereign People,* political scientists have been concerned with the potential for bias toward groups with greater resources. The models in this section look at how monetary donations can be used to influence elections and policy. Scholars attempt to answer questions such as: What types of candidates are advantaged by interest group giving? What strategies will groups pursue in setting their donation schedules? How will legislation and policy be affected by group giving?

Nobel laureate Gary Becker developed a fairly simple game between taxpayers and subsidized entities. Each group fights to reduce its tax or increase its subsidy. A government budget constraint applies so that the total amount of subsidies equals the total tax revenue. The resources spent on lobbying translate directly into outcomes via an "influence function." Becker assumes that legislators simply transmit, via the influence function, the preferences of interest groups. He thereby removes all institutional and environmental concerns from the process. The legislature in Becker's model is a very dark, black box. Nevertheless, Becker is able to derive interesting hypotheses. Large groups suffer from more free riding, and will be more hard-pressed to mobilize. The relative power of smaller groups is enhanced by the free-riding problems plaguing the larger groups. Small groups, therefore, are not disadvantaged in the process solely due to their size.[9] Becker does not, however, address many of the most interesting questions for political scientists: How do interest groups influence voting behavior? How do legislators and lobbyists interact? Are there currencies other than money that might affect political outcomes? Furthermore, Becker does not attempt to incorporate elections or voters.

B. Douglas Bernheim and Michael Whinston developed a common agency model that has been widely applied within economics to study lobbying.[10] In a common agency setting, there is one agent and multiple principals. The principals are competing to influence the agent's actions. Suppose the agent can split a good into several parts and that the good in this game is tariff policy. Some industries will be protected, and others will not. The principals adjust their bids on each part of the policy.[11] The competing principals are firms within those industries. Each firm wants low tariffs on its own inputs so that manufacturing costs are kept low, and each wants higher tariffs on its outputs to limit the competition from foreign producers. Firms place bids to alter separate elements of the tariff policy. Bernheim and Whinston note that models of this sort have an embarrassment of riches. There are many, many equilibria. To reduce the number of equilibria and fine-tune predictions, most scholars restrict their attention to truthful bids, which results in coalition-proof equilibria.[12]

Arthur Denzau and Michael Munger focus on individual legislators and voters. Legislators set out to maximize votes by appealing for votes as well as contributions. The primary result is that unorganized voters or latent groups are able to exert influence over a legislator via the ballot box. The comparative statics in Denzau and Munger's work suggests that potential groups are still represented even as existing groups work to buy influence. The latent groups can, therefore, mitigate the influence of organized interests. Other models are based solely on bribes.[13] Interests buy votes. The *quid pro quo* in such models may be harsher than in reality, but important implications fall directly from the model. A common result is that bribes are given only to marginal opponents of a policy proposal. Legislators who already support the interest group's position receive no money because their preferences do not need to be swayed.

This result has interesting implications for the empirical studies on PAC giving and roll-call votes. Many scholars presume that there is a linear relationship between money contributed and the probability of a favorable vote. Some of the vote-buying models suggest that those presumptions need to be fine-tuned.

Many scholars are exploring how general policy outcomes are affected by electoral fortunes. Congress takes a back seat in these models, but the presumption is that the winning candidate's platform does affect policy. Candidates in these models have genuine policy preferences, but money can alter those preferences. Candidates may alter policy preferences to secure more campaign funds. Voters fall into one of two categories: informed or uninformed. Candidates face a tradeoff between pandering to uninformed voters with costly advertising and picking policy to appeal to informed voters. Gene Grossman and Elhanan Helpman model a situation in which groups donate money both to win elections and to move stated policies of the candidates in their direction. Groups have an incentive to back more popular candidates. The majority party is therefore more beholden to interest groups.

A similar model developed by David Baron found that the most popular candidate in a race does not need interest group money as much as less popular candidates and therefore will not cater to groups.[14] The differences in the Baron and Grossman and Helpman results center on several factors including their assumptions about informed and uninformed voters as well as candidates' propensities to seek monetary donations.[15] The presence of informed voters who already know how they will vote and uninformed voters who can be swayed may strike some political scientists as hewing closely to reality. Those political scientists who have read V. O. Key's *Responsible Electorate,* however, may feel uneasy about the assumption that uninformed voters are readily swayed by campaign advertisements. Peter Aranson and Melvin Hinich developed one of the first models in this area.[16] Unlike most scholars doing similar work, Aranson and Hinich highlighted the normative implications of their findings. Disclosure laws and contribution limits have been a prominent feature of federal elections since the mid-1970s. Aranson and Hinich contend that many of those laws, and in particular contribution limits, enhance the already considerable incumbency advantage.

INFORMATIONAL MODELS

Money or pressure may not be the only currency of importance to legislators and lobbyists. Many scholars argue that information is the key to lobbyists' success, and many political scientists and economists use signaling games to model the information transmission between lobbyists and legislators. Informational models highlight the communication between lobbyists and legislators. Rather than employing a mechanical influence function, signaling models incorporate legislators as strategic players and highlight important institutional structures. Because the information is valuable to legislators, informational models allow for the possibility that the net effect of lobbying is actually welfare-increasing—something unlikely in the models in the previous sections. Legislators are full-fledged players in most information-based models, so one can consider how legislators might structure their interactions with lobbyists as well as how lobbyists allocate resources to influence legislators. Generally, these models do not attempt to address what kinds of groups are advantaged or disadvantaged by lobbying—another contrast with the models in the earlier sections of the chapter.

The focus on institutions provides opportunities to refine our descriptions of strategic behavior. That is, different stages of a decision-making process in an institution create different strategic concerns for a group. Lobbying to secure a spot on the congressional agenda may be very different from lobbying for votes.[17] Truthful revelation by lobbyists is not presumed, so these models allow us to look at the factors that encourage credible signals. Costly signals tend to be more credible than cheap signals. Scott Ainsworth shows how legislators can structure their interactions with lobbyists to force high cost signals from interest groups. The legislators in models by Ainsworth and by Jan Potters and Frans Van Winden rely on costly signals to regulate their relationship with lobbyists.[18] Other scholars allow the interest group to increase its own costs, to send more credible signals.[19] David Austen-Smith and John Wright allow legislators to audit lobbyists' claims, which also encourages truthful revelation.[20] Audits are more likely in the Austen-Smith and Wright model when legislators receive competing claims from lobbyists. Group competition, therefore, can enhance truthful revelation of information.

Signaling models are more complicated if one imagines both lobbying and electoral activities. Suppose a group can provide legislators with direct campaign contributions or with information that is costly to gather. The information is valuable to legislators, but so are campaign contributions. Campaign money might drive out good—though costly—information.[21] First, suppose that lobbyists cannot lie. They might be concerned about their reputations and their opportunities for continued access to legislators, but many models simply presume that they cannot lie if information is conveyed to legislators. They can, however, choose to remain silent. The information, if it is gathered, may support a group's claims or undermine a group's claims. Now suppose an interest group's search for information is observed by legislators. Legislators can ascertain the substance of that information based on whether the group chooses to share it. If the information supports the group's claim, it will certainly be shared. The group will choose not to share the information only if the information is damning for the group. Legislators recognize this. Not providing information is a signal to the lawmaker that the interest group might have engaged in costly research and found that the data did not support the group's view. Gathering information to share is a risky proposition, so interest groups often prefer to forgo information gathering and give direct campaign contributions instead. This result is rather pessimistic. If lobbyists can subsidize legislators with information and money, the money drives out some of the information.[22] If the interest group could lie, the dynamic of this game would be different, but campaign contributions might still drive out information. Suppose that the groups cannot lie, but they instead provide some sort of range within which the truth lies.[23] Or suppose legislators are able to audit lobbyists' claims. After these modifications, money is still likely to drive out information.

HYBRID MODELS

A raft of new scholarship examines how interests and pressures in one institution or setting affect behaviors in other institutions. Steven Balla and John Wright explore whether the array of interests in Congress is reflected in an agency's advisory councils.[24] Sanford Gordon and Catherine Hafer and Richard Hall and Kristina Miler consider how pressure on legislators can affect agency oversight and agency behavior.[25] Corporations might signal the bureaucracy that they are willing to fight legislative battles by spending a lot of money at the legislative stage, even without the intent of actually influencing policy. Once Microsoft was threatened, it lobbied legislators to have the Department of Justice antitrust budget reduced. Microsoft's efforts signaled that it could impose costs on antitrust agencies. Bureaucratic agencies, therefore, might monitor large political donors less than smaller ones. If a firm's transgressions are readily observable, there is regular public pressure on the agency to act. When a firm's activities are in the public eye, large campaign donations are less likely to alter a bureaucratic agency's behavior. If interest group activities in the first branch of government are designed to illicit behavior in another branch of government, then work that simply lists activities or describes behaviors related to interest groups in Congress requires careful interpretation.

Another set of models explores the connections between access and influence. Susanne Lohmann imagines interest groups first paying for access to legislators and then providing information to those legislators.[26] If a group is closely aligned with the legislator, it can get access for free. This model implies a negative correlation between interest group-lawmaker policy congruence and donations. Austen-Smith notes that the empirical literature has found a positive relationship between policy congruence and donations.[27] To resolve this discrepancy, Lohmann suggests that groups might donate to a friend because if he or she gets elected the group has free access to that lawmaker. Austen-Smith prefers to highlight the role for uncertainty. The lawmaker is uncertain about the interest group's policy position. A contribution signals to the legislator that the interest group has favorable information. Therefore, for Austen-Smith, the value of access increases as preferences and goals converge, so groups have an incentive to donate to those legislators with whom they agree.

The Lohmann and Austen-Smith models yield some interesting ideas about the mechanism driving contributions for access. If Lohmann is correct, one might observe the negative relationship in a subset of elections where the legislator with preferences congruent to the interest group has no hope of winning. An evaluation of the implications from Austen-Smith's work is less direct, but one might hypothesize that newer organizations have more uncertain policy positions than older organizations. Newer organizations, therefore, will have to contribute more money to gain access than established lobbies. In a similar fashion, groups addressing issues that are entirely new to the agenda should have to pay more for access.

NEW (AND OLD) AREAS OF RESEARCH INTO GROUP ACTIVITY

Every area of political science is affected by new trends in research or renewed interests in older trends. The past decade has seen an explosion of scholarship tying sociology to the other social sciences.

Sociology and Economics

Many issues once considered firmly within the sociologist's bailiwick are amenable to economic reasoning and game theoretic modeling. The perception of a rigid dichotomy between sociological and economic models is undermined by recent models of networks and social decisions. Throughout much of his work, Nobel laureate George Akerlof explored the social implications of individuals' decisions. For Akerlof, private decisions are those with no social consequences. As he notes, one can buy an apple or an orange for lunch, and there are few if any social consequences. In contrast, social decisions are those decisions with clear social consequences. "While my network of friends . . . are not affected in the least by my choice between apples and oranges, they will be affected by my educational aspirations, my attitudes and practices toward racial discrimination," or any of myriad other social decisions.[28] Therefore, an individual's choice (say about education) may be affected by the social consequences of that choice. Attention to the social consequences of a choice may help or hurt an individual. In one set of examples, Akerlof considers high school students. Students may underinvest in their education because they are rewarded with an expanded circle of friends. The individual, private returns to education are not independently maximized when strong social rewards for underachievement exist.[29] Akerlof's goal was to assess individuals' behaviors when they are rewarded for their status in society and when they are rewarded for their ability to conform to the rest of society. These models define the bounds of important social interactions because status-seekers attempt to be as different as possible from everyone else and conformers try to mimic everyone else. Akerlof's models provide representations of social distance and show that people overinvest in status and may either over- or underinvest in conformity.

Network analysis crosses many disciplines and subfields. The expansion of a network is often tied to the viability of collective efforts. As networks become more and more inclusive, the self-enforcement mechanisms that facilitate cooperation among their members become strained to the point that networks may collapse upon themselves.[30] Consider that large organizations, whether they are professional organizations, interest groups, or political parties, sometimes have a hard time maintaining their numbers. Often, when a large organization, such as the American Medical Association, shrinks, other smaller professional organizations, such as the American Society of Nephrology or the American College of Cardiology, expand. In other words, networks spin off from one another. Cliques may develop within networks.[31] One might imagine information flowing readily within the separate cliques. As information flows from one clique to another, individuals may develop a clearer sense of the viability of a collective effort within the overall network (see Chapter 4).

Partitioning games provide another means to analyze the opportunities for new group or clique emergence. Igal Milchtaich and Eyal Winter develop a game in which individuals seek to join a group of like-minded individuals.[32] In the spirit of Truman, shared attitudes are the sole basis of joining. Milchtaich and Winter show that if individuals are characterized by a single, one-dimensional attribute, a stable partition always exists. That is, all individuals join a group and are content to remain in that group. If individuals are not one-dimensional, however, the presence of a stable group partition depends on whether there is an upper limit on the number of groups that can be formed. Whenever an upper limit on the number of groups exists, no stable partition exists. Group memberships keep shifting. This formal theoretic result leads one to consider various empirical and normative implications. Can there be a limit on the number of groups in a society? In a number of works evaluating state-level lobbying, Virginia Gray and David Lowery argue that there is a natural limit to the number of groups likely to develop in a state.[33] Some states have a greater "carrying capacity" for groups than others. If Gray and Lowery are correct, then the Milchtaich and Winter result is particularly intriguing. As virtually every interest group text reminds us, Truman argued that groups emerged from disturbances in society; but the work of Milchtaich and Winter suggests that under some circumstances disequilibrium is the norm. The observation of a disturbance may be coincidental to the underlying, ever-present disequilibrium. If one looks hard enough, one sees that there are always disturbances and there are always changes within the group environment.[34]

Joining a group often has social consequences. If a member's sense of belonging is accompanied with a public display or recognition, joining has a social consequence. Indeed, some group members proudly display their affiliations with pins or bumper stickers. Their expressive benefits from joining appear quite tangible. Group membership has both private and public consequences, but scholars have not fully explored this area. When are group memberships private decisions and when are they social decisions? Surely, there are important distinctions between (privately) identifying with an interest and (publicly) mobilizing with a group.[35] In some models, joining is a simple, private exchange. In others, joining publicly signals group viability and facilitates coordination with others, but these signals are of no social consequence for those "outside of the group."[36]

Private Politics

For the last few years, David Baron has explored what he terms private politics.[37] Private politics are demands made through private channels for policy change. Clearly, private politics, as envisioned by Baron, have social consequences. Baron develops a three-stage game in which an activist makes a demand upon a manufacturing firm, and the firm either accepts or rejects it. If the demand is accepted, the firm bears certain costs associated with the policy change. After the firm's decision, the activist either decides to back down and do nothing or boycotts the firm, which is a costly decision for both the activist and the firm. The success of the boycott partly depends on the salience of the issues at hand. Baron's work is helpful for thinking about the motivation of the players—the firm and the activist. Should an activist threaten to boycott a company that is known to have some altruistic motivations? If she does, the boycott is more likely to be successful because the altruistic firm is sensitive to such concerns and more likely to agree to the demands for

Boycotts

When interest groups feel outmatched in the legislative arena, they might engage in private politics. David Baron cites Greenpeace's 2000 campaign to pressure Coca-Cola to eliminate hydrofluorocarbons (HFCs) from vending machines. Greenpeace created graphics with Coca-Cola's iconic polar bears standing on a melting glacier. Members of the public were encouraged to print these images and paste them onto Coca-Cola vending machines. Greenpeace timed their campaign to coincide with the 2000 Olympic Games. Enough publicity was generated to elicit a promise from Coca-Cola to eliminate HFCs from their vending machines. Not all boycotts are so effective. If an issue does not meet with a broadly supportive public and an attentive media, the boycott will likely be ignored.

change. The activist may, however, create a net negative effect if the altruistic firm suffers from a damaged market position. The success of a boycott is partly a function of issue saliency. Some firms levying large costs on society may nevertheless be inappropriate targets for a boycott because there is too little issue saliency. The activist may therefore be tempted to pick targets producing few social costs simply because they are more salient.

Baron's work is quite intriguing in today's world of boycotts and protests, but it is not entirely novel. Truman discussed the circumstances when demands upon others might be settled in private venues and when they might be settled in public forums. Albert Hirschman, in his book *Shifting Involvements*, argued that people blended private marketplace activities with some public and some political demands. The advantage of Baron's work, in contrast to Truman's or Hirschman's, is that all of the assumptions behind Baron's model remain explicit. Baron's approach also reminds us of the central role that interest group entrepreneurs can play. One could revisit Salisbury's exchange-based model and see an entrepreneur risking high opportunity cost to affect an outcome, with the hope of increasing his group membership base. Finally, Baron's work exemplifies how important it is for economists to study interest group literature. Just as economic models can enrich our understanding of interest groups, a careful reading of the interest group literature could strengthen economic models.[38]

CONCLUSION

Why study economic or game theoretic models of interest groups and lobbying? Studies of lobbyists and lobbying, dating back to at least Lester Milbrath's path-breaking work on lobbyists, often list a set of activities in which lobbyists engage.[39] Such lists provide insights into the day-to-day activities of lobbyists, but they do not tell us anything about lobbying strategies per se. Consider a lobbying campaign. Even seemingly inconsequential activities, such as constituent fly-ins, may be important if they are a costly signal of issue salience. A lobbyist's contacting behavior may be a function of both legislators' preferences and other lobbyists' activities. Under different circumstances, lobbyists may engage in activities with an eye toward their opponents or their allies. With an eye toward building and maintaining coalitions, one may create supermajorities to limit the ability of any particular member of a coalition to threaten defection in an attempt to secure additional resources.[40] In a supermajority, no single legislator is crucial, so no legislator can extract excessive rewards for his or her support. Supermajorities may be cheaper to secure and maintain than simple majorities. Typically, scholars link lobbying activities to policy goals, but work on supermajorities suggests that lobbying activities and contacting behaviors may be linked to both policy goals and to coalition maintenance and cost concerns. A simple list of activities fails to explain how some activities reinforce others. Grassroots lobbying and direct lobbying are often used in combination. Scholars increasingly examine the combined effects of lobbying and contributions. The simple point is that lobbying does not occur in a vacuum, so lists of lobbying activities are barely illuminating. Instead of lists, one might consider theories that address what prompts certain types of lobbying activities and consider how those activities interact with one another. Economic and game theoretic models can help in these regards.

NOTES

1. Arthur F. Bentley, *The Process of Government* (Evanston, Ill.: Principia Press, 1949), 210.

2. Mancur Olson, *The Logic of Collective Action: Public Goods and the Theory of Groups.* (Cambridge: Harvard University Press, 1965), 1.

3. Robert H. Salisbury, "An Exchange Theory of Interest Groups," *Midwest Journal of Political Science* 13 (1969): 1–32.

4. Ibid.

5. John Mark Hansen and Scott Ainsworth explore similar themes. See Hansen, "The Political Economy of Group Membership," *American Political Science Review* 79 (1985): 79–96; and Ainsworth, *Analyzing Interest Groups: Group Influence on People and Policies* (New York: W. W. Norton, 2002), chaps. 2 and 3.

6. See Richard Damania, "Influence in Decline: Lobbying in Contracting Industries," *Economics and Politics* 14 (2002): 209–223.

7. Wendy L Hansen and Neil J. Mitchell, "Disaggregating and Explaining Corporate Political Activity: Domestic and Foreign Corporations in National Politics," *American Political Science Review* 94 (2000): 891–903.

8. Thomas Palfrey and the late Richard McKelvey developed the quantal response equilibrium concept. See R. D. McKelvey and T. R. Palfrey, "Quantal Response Equilibria in Normal Form Games," *Games and Economic Behavior* 7 (1995): 6–38; and McKelvey and Palfrey, "Quantal Response Equilibria for Extensive Form Games," *Experimental Economics* 1 (1998): 9–41. Curtis S. Signorino has worked on related statistical techniques. See Signorino, "Strategy and Selection in International Relations," *International Interactions* 28 (2002): 93–115; and Signorino, "Structure and Uncertainty in Discrete Choice Models," *Political Analysis* 11 (2003): 316–344.

9. Gary S. Becker, "A Theory of Competition among Pressure Groups for Political Influence," *Quarterly Journal of Economics* 98 (1983): 385.

10. B. Douglas Bernheim and Michael D. Whinston refer to their model as a menu auction but in related work they use the term common agency. See Bernheim and Whinston, "Menu Auctions, Resource Allocation, and Economic Influence," *Quarterly Journal of Economics* 101 (1986): 1–32.

11. Gene M. Grossman and Elhanan Helpman apply this basic model to evaluate lobbying behaviors. See Grossman and Helpman, "Protection for Sale," *American Economic Review* 84 (1994): 833–850; and Grossman and Helpman, *Special Interest Politics* (Cambridge: MIT Press, 2001).

12. More precisely, one should say "locally truthful." Locally truthful bids have a precise mathematical structure—typically equating marginal bids and marginal valuations.

13. James M. Snyder, "On Buying Legislatures," *Economics and Politics* 3 (1991): 93–109.

14. David P. Baron, "Electoral Competition with Informed and Uninformed Voters," *American Political Science Review* 88 (1994): 34–37.

15. The interested reader should also see David Austen-Smith, "Interest Groups, Campaign Contributions, and Probabilistic Voting, " *Public Choice* 54 (1987): 123–139; and Austen-Smith, "Campaign Contributions and Access," *American Political Science Review* 89 (1995): 566–581.

16. Peter Aronson and Melvin J. Hinich, "Some Aspects of the Political Economy of Election Campaign Contribution Laws," *Public Choice* 34 (1979): 435–461.

17. David Austen-Smith, "Information and Influence," *American Journal of Political Science* 37 (1993): 799–833.

18. Scott Ainsworth, "Regulating Lobbyists and Interest Group Influence," *Journal of Politics* 55 (1993): 41–56; Ainsworth, "The Role of Legislators in the Determination of Interest Group Influence," *Legislative Studies Quarterly* 22 (1997): 517–533; and Jan Potters and Frans van Winden, "Lobbying and Asymmetric Information," *Public Choice* 74 (1992): 269–292.

19. Randolph Sloof and Frans van Winden, "Show Them Your Teeth First! A Game-Theoretic Analysis of Lobbying and Pressure," *Public Choice* 104 (2000): 81–120.

20. David Austen-Smith and John R. Wright, "Competitive Lobbying for a Legislator's Vote," *Social Choice and Welfare* 9 (1992): 229–257; and Austen-Smith and Wright, "Counteractive Lobbying," *American Journal of Political Science* 38 (1994): 25–44.

21. Morten Bennedsen and Sven E. Feldmann, "Informational Lobbying and Political Contributions," *Journal of Public Economics* 90 (2006): 631–656.

22. Richard L. Hall and Alan V. Deardorff, "Lobbying as Legislative Subsidy," *American Political Science Review* 100 (2006): 69–84.

23. For a model of this sort, see Vincent P. Crawford and Joel Sobel, "Strategic Information Transmission," *Econometrica* 50 (1982) 1431–1451.

24. Steven J. Balla and John R. Wright, "Interest Groups, Advisory Committees, and Congressional Control of the Bureaucracy," *American Journal of Political Science* 45 (2001): 799–812.

25. Sanford C. Gordon and Catherine Hafer, "Flexing Muscle: Corporate Political Expenditures as Signals to the Bureaucracy," *American Political Science Review* 99 (2005): 245–261; Gordon and Hafer, "Corporate Influence and the Regulatory Mandate," *Journal of Politics* 69 (2007): 300–319; and Richard L. Hall and Kristina C. Miler, "What Happens after the Alarm? Interest Group Subsidies to Legislative Overseers," *Journal of Politics* 70 (2008): 990–1005.

26. Susanne Lohmann, "Information, Access, and Contributions: A Signaling Model of Lobbying," *Public Choice* 85 (1995): 267–284.

27. Austen-Smith, "Campaign Contributions and Access."

28. George A. Akerlof, "Social Distance and Social Decisions," *Econometrica* 65 (1997): 1006.

29. The interested reader should also see David Austen-Smith and Roland G. Fryer Jr., "An Economic Analysis of 'Acting White,'" *Quarterly Journal of Economics* 120 (2005): 551–583.

30. See Kurt Annen, "Social Capital, Inclusive Networks, and Economic Performance," *Journal of Economic Behavior and Organization* 50 (2003): 449–463; and M. Kandori, "Social Norms and Community Enforcement," *Review of Economic Studies* 59 (1992): 63–80.

31. Michael Suk-Young Chwe, "Communication and Coordination in Social Networks," *Review of Economic Studies* 67 (2000): 1–16.

32. Igal Milchtaich and Eyal Winter, "Stability and Segregation in Group Formation," *Games and Economic Behavior* 38 (2002): 318–346.

33. Virginia Gray and David Lowery, *The Population Ecology of Interest Representation: Lobbying Communities in the American States* (Ann Arbor: University of Michigan Press, 1996).

34. Nicholas R. Miller develops another view of disequilibrium in an interest group society. The continual bargaining in an interest group society and the ever-changing coalitions might provide an element of systemic stability that a stable division with set winners and losers would not provide. See Miller, "Pluralism and Social Choice," *American Political Science Review* 77 (1983): 734–747. Also see Ainsworth, *Analyzing Interest Groups.*

35. Scott S. Gartner and Gary M. Segura, "Appearances Can Be Deceptive: Self-Selection, Social Group Identification, and Political Mobilization," *Rationality and Society* 9 (1997): 131–161.

36. See Scott Ainsworth and Itai Sened, "The Role of Lobbyists: Entrepreneurs with Two Audiences," *American Journal of Political Science* 37 (1993): 834–866; and Susanne Lohmann, "Dynamics of Informational Cascades: The Monday Demonstrations in Leipzig, East Germany, 1989–1991," *World Politics* 47 (1994): 42–101; and Lohmann, "Information, Access, and Contributions."

37. David P. Baron, "Private Politics, Corporate Social Responsibility, and Integrated Strategy, " *Journal of Economic and Management Strategy* 10, 1 (2001): 7–45; and Baron, "Private Politics," *Journal of Economic and Management Strategy* 12, 1 (2003): 31–66.

38. See Frans van Winden, "On the Economic Theory of Interest Groups: Towards a Group Frame of Reference in Political Economics," *Public Choice* 100 (1999): 1–29.

39. Lester W. Milbrath, *The Washington Lobbyists* (Westport, Conn.: Greenwood Press, 1963).

40. Tim Groseclose and James M. Snyder, "Buying Supermajorities," *American Political Science Review* 90 (1996): 303–315.

SUGGESTED READING

Ainsworth, Scott. *Analyzing Interest Groups: Group Influence on People and Policies.* New York: W. W. Norton, 2002.

———. "Regulating Lobbyists and Interest Group Influence." *Journal of Politics* 55 (1993): 41–56.

———. "The Role of Legislators in the Determination of Interest Group Influence." *Legislative Studies Quarterly* 22 (1997): 517–533.

Ainsworth, Scott, and Itai Sened. "The Role of Lobbyists: Entrepreneurs with Two Audiences." *American Journal of Political Science* 37 (1993): 834–866.

Akerlof, George A. "Social Distance and Social Decisions." *Econometrica* 65 (1997): 1005–1027.

Annen, Kurt. "Social Capital, Inclusive Networks, and Economic Performance." *Journal of Economic Behavior and Organization* 50 (2003): 449–463.

Aranson, Peter, and Melvin J. Hinich. "Some Aspects of the Political Economy of Election Campaign Contribution Laws." *Public Choice* 34 (1979): 435–461.

Austen-Smith, David. "Interest Groups, Campaign Contributions, and Probabilistic Voting." *Public Choice* 54 (1987): 123–139.

———. "Information and Influence." *American Journal of Political Science* 37 (1993): 799–833.

———. "Campaign Contributions and Access." *American Political Science Review* 89 (1995): 566–581.

Austen-Smith, David, and Roland G. Fryer Jr. "An Economic Analysis of 'Acting White.' " *Quarterly Journal of Economics* 120 (2005): 551–583.

Austen-Smith, David, and John R. Wright. "Competitive Lobbying for a Legislator's Vote." *Social Choice and Welfare* 9 (1992): 229–257.

———. "Counteractive Lobbying." *American Journal of Political Science* 38 (1994): 25–44.

Balla, Steven J., and John R. Wright. "Interest Groups, Advisory Committees, and Congressional Control of the Bureaucracy." *American Journal of Political Science* 45 (2001): 799–812.

Baron, David P. "Electoral Competition with Informed and Uninformed Voters." *American Political Science Review* 88 (1994): 34–37.

———. "Private Politics, Corporate Social Responsibility, and Integrated Strategy." *Journal of Economic and Management Strategy* 10 (2001): 7–45.

———. "Private Politics." *Journal of Economic and Management Strategy* 12 (2003): 31–66.

Becker, Gary S. "A Theory of Competition among Pressure Groups for Political Influence." *Quarterly Journal of Economics* 98 (1983): 371–400.

Bennedsen, Morten, and Sven E. Feldmann. "Informational Lobbying and Political Contributions." *Journal of Public Economics* 90 (2006): 631–656.

Bentley, Arthur F. *The Process of Government. Evanston, Ill.: Principia Press,* 1949. (Originally published in 1908 by University of Chicago Press.)

Bernheim, B. Douglas. and Michael D. Whinston. "Menu Auctions, Resource Allocation, and Economic Influence." *Quarterly Journal of Economics* 101 (1986): 1–32.

Chwe, Michael Suk-Young. "Communication and Coordination in Social Networks." *Review of Economic Studies* 67 (2000): 1–16.

Crawford, Vincent P., and Joel Sobel. "Strategic Information Transmission." *Econometrica* 50 (1982) 1431–51.

Damania, Richard. "Influence in Decline: Lobbying in Contracting Industries." *Economics and Politics* 14 (2002): 209–223.

Denzau, Arthur T., and Michael C. Munger. "Legislators and Interest Groups: How Unorganized Interests Get Represented." *American Political Science Review* 80 (1986): 89–106.

Galbraith, John Kenneth. *American Capitalism: The Concept of Countervailing Power.* London: Hamish Hamilton, 1952.

Gartner, Scott S., and Gary M. Segura. "Appearances Can Be Deceptive: Self-Selection, Social Group Identification, and Political Mobilization." *Rationality and Society* 9 (1997): 131–161.

Gordon, Sanford C., and Catherine Hafer. "Flexing Muscle: Corporate Political Expenditures as Signals to the Bureaucracy." *American Political Science Review* 99 (2005): 245–261.

———. "Corporate Influence and the Regulatory Mandate." *Journal of Politics* 69 (2007): 300–319.

Gray, Virginia, and David Lowery. *The Population Ecology of Interest Representation: Lobbying Communities in the American States.* Ann Arbor: University of Michigan Press, 1996.

Groseclose, Tim, and James M. Snyder. "Buying Supermajorities." *American Political Science Review* 90 (1996): 303–315.

Grossman, Gene M., and Elhanan Helpman. *Special Interest Politics.* Cambridge: MIT Press, 2001.

———. "Protection for Sale." *American Economic Review* 84 (1994): 833–850.

———. "Electoral Competition and Special Interest Politics." *Review of Economic Studies* 63 (1996): 265–286.

Hall, Richard L., and Alan V. Deardorff. "Lobbying as Legislative Subsidy." *American Political Science Review* 100 (2006): 69–84.

Hall, Richard L., and Kristina C. Miler. "What Happens after the Alarm? Interest Group Subsidies to Legislative Overseers." *Journal of Politics* 70 (2008): 990–1005.

Hansen, John Mark. "The Political Economy of Group Membership." *American Political Science Review* 79 (1985): 79–96.

Hansen, Wendy L., and Neil J. Mitchell. "Disaggregating and Explaining Corporate Political Activity: Domestic and Foreign Corporations in National Politics." *American Political Science Review* 94 (2000): 891–903.

Hirschman, Albert O. Shifting Involvements: *Private Interest and Public Action.* Princeton: Princeton University Press, 2002.

Kandori, M. "Social Norms and Community Enforcement." *Review of Economic Studies* 59 (1992): 63–80.

Key, V. O. The Responsible Electorate. Cambridge: *Harvard University Press,* 1966.

Lohmann, Susanne. "Dynamics of Informational Cascades: The Monday Demonstrations in Leipzig, East Germany, 1989–1991." *World Politics* 47 (1994): 42–101.

———. "Information, Access, and Contributions: A Signaling Model of Lobbying." *Public Choice* 85 (1995): 267–284.

McKelvey, R. D., and T. R. Palfrey. "Quantal Response Equilibria in Normal Form Games." *Games and Economic Behavior* 7 (1995): 6–38.

———. "Quantal Response Equilibria for Extensive Form Games." *Experimental Economics* 1 (1998): 9–41.

Milbrath, Lester W. *The Washington Lobbyists. Westport,* Conn.: Greenwood Press, 1963.

Miller, Nicholas R. "Pluralism and Social Choice." *American Political Science Review* 77 (1983): 734–747.

Milchtaich, Igal, and Eyal Winter. "Stability and Segregation in Group Formation." *Games and Economic Behavior* 38 (2002): 318–346.

Olson, Mancur. *The Logic of Collective Action: Public Goods and the Theory of Groups.* Cambridge: Harvard University Press, 1965.

Palfrey, Thomas R., and Howard Rosenthal. "Private Incentives in Social Dilemmas." *Journal of Public Economics* 35 (1988): 309–332.

Potters, Jan, and Frans van Winden. "Lobbying and Asymmetric Information." *Public Choice* 74 (1992): 269–292.

Salisbury, Robert H. "An Exchange Theory of Interest Groups." *Midwest Journal of Political Science* 13 (1969): 1–32.

Schattschneider, E. E. *The Semisovereign People.* New York: Holt, Rinehart, and Winston, 1960.

Signorino, Curtis S. "Strategy and Selection in International Relations." *International Interactions* 28 (2002): 93–115.

———. "Structure and Uncertainty in Discrete Choice Models." *Political Analysis* 11 (2003): 316–344.

Sloof, Randolph, and Frans Van Winden. "Show Them Your Teeth First! 'A Game-Theoretic Analysis of Lobbying and Pressure.'" *Public Choice* 104 (2000): 81–120.

Snyder, James M. "On Buying Legislatures." *Economics and Politics* 3 (1991): 93–109.

Truman, David B. *The Governmental Process.* New York: Knopf, 1951.

van Winden, Frans. "On the Economic Theory of Interest Groups: Towards a Group Frame of Reference in Political Economics." *Public Choice* 100 (1999): 1–29.

PART III ★ INTEREST GROUPS AND THE GROWTH OF GOVERNMENT

CHAPTER 8	The Growth of Government and the Expansion of Interest Groups	101
CHAPTER 9	Interest Groups and the Courts	113
CHAPTER 10	Interest Groups and the Executive Branch	127
CHAPTER 11	Interest Groups and Political Parties: The Politics of Representation	145

chapter 8

The Growth of Government and the Expansion of Interest Groups

by Beth Leech

ELECTIONS ARE TOUGH TIMES FOR lobbyists. There is nothing like an election to bring out the strongest anti-interest group statements from politicians. During the 2007 Democratic presidential primary, Sen. John Edwards proclaimed:

> In the past 10 years, the number of lobbyists in Washington has tripled to 36,000. That means there are sixty registered lobbyists for each member of Congress and 20 times more lobbyists than people in my hometown of Robbins, North Carolina. That's all you need to know to know that Washington is the problem, not the solution.[1]

Edwards was not the only one to make a point about the large numbers of interest groups, and he is not the only politician to identify lobbyists as the root of all political problems. Candidate Barack Obama tried to ban all lobbyists from employment by his campaign, and President Obama forbade any registered lobbyist from talking to a member of Congress about any project for the Recovery Act of 2009, the federal legislation aimed at boosting the economy during the economic downturn at the time. Registered lobbyists could make formal requests in writing, but not informal requests in person.[2] And during the same year, the nonprofit watchdog group Center for Public Integrity conducted an analysis that observed:

> More than 770 companies and interest groups hired an estimated 2,340 lobbyists to influence federal policy on climate change in the past year, as the issue gathered momentum and came to a vote on Capitol Hill. That's an increase of more than 300 percent in the number of lobbyists on climate change in just five years, and means that Washington can now boast more than four climate lobbyists for every member of Congress.[3]

Not only politicians and watchdog groups have noticed the upsurge. The lobbyists themselves have commented on it. Former U.S. representative Daniel A. Mica, D-Fla., now the president of an interest group that lobbies for credit unions, was quoted just before the 2008 election as saying, "It's going to be a very, very busy year; we might as well brace ourselves for it." His group, the Credit Union National Association, had asked its state affiliates to increase their budgets so that more people could be sent to Washington to lobby on credit union issues. "It doesn't matter which one is president—there is going to be a tremendous need for lobbying," Mica said.[4]

These recent examples are hardly the first time in history that the number of interest groups in Washington has been remarked upon. Political scientist Mark Petracca, in his book *The Politics of Interests: Interest Groups Transformed* (1992), listed a series of quotations from journalists and professors beginning in 1915, all complaining about the large number of interest groups. In 1927 James Pollack was quoted as saying, "Never before have legislative bodies been subjected to such a continuous and powerful bombardment from private interests as at present." A decade earlier Herbert Croly had made a similar observation about "the large number of voluntary associations" that were "devoted to the propagation of special economic interests or special political and social ideas." In the decades that followed, many more journalists and political scientists would again make such observations.[5]

Why are there so many interest groups? Why does the number keep growing? And because it is clear that many politicians and many political observers see this as a problem, what, if anything, can or should be done about it? As is the case with most social and political phenomena, the causal processes involved are far from simple, but two common categories of explanations do exist: the growth can be blamed on interest groups or on government. The first category of explanations suggests that the growth in the interest group population is driven by the desires and actions of interest groups and social movements. These types of explanations go something like this: people want something, so they join an interest group or begin a social movement. The interest group or social movement appeals to (or puts pressure on) government officials, then policy changes. And, because there are always new things to want, more interest groups and more social movements are formed, and the process continues. According to this category of explanation, the only limitation on the number of groups in society is the number of people who want something. This approach can be labeled the interest-driven model. It frames the argument most often when politicians and popular media complain about interest group influence, but it is also common in the scholarly literature, as with economist Mancur Olson's book *Rise and Decline of Nations,* where he argues that the proliferation of interest groups are to blame for the decline mentioned in the title.[6]

The second category of answers looks to government activities to explain the growth in interest groups. According to these explanations, the interest group system grows because government and government officials encourage interest groups to participate in the policy process. This category of explanation includes direct efforts by government itself to create interest organizations, as well as indirect effects of government activities leading to the growth of the interest group population. We will call this approach the government-driven model.

Which of the two models, the interest-driven or the government-driven, more accurately reflects how the interest group system operates and grows? Both models contain a great deal of truth, in that interest groups and government operate symbiotically, each feeding on the other for its own benefit. One grows because the other grows—they coevolve, at times with one leading, at other times the other.

THE SIZE OF THE GROUP SYSTEM

Assessing the reasons behind the growth of the interest group system is hindered by the difficulty in obtaining consistent, accurate counts of such groups over time. For the first century and a half of U.S. history there were no official counts. Researchers have instead relied upon descriptive anecdotes from political observers of the time or from related evidence such as how many interest groups testified at congressional hearings and how many membership groups were listed in historical directories. (See Chapters 1 through 3 for views on the early history of interest groups in the United States.) Neither type of evidence completely answers the question of how many interest groups were active in Washington, however, because not all membership groups lobby, and it is difficult to know what percentage of interest groups testified at hearings and what percentage was left out. Still, each type provides at least a hint of what the interest group population looked like historically.

As far back as 1939, journalist Kenneth Crawford estimated that there were 6,000 lobbyists and 5,000 lawyers in Washington trying to influence policy decisions.[7] Other observers estimated that by World War II there were 12,000 lobbyists in the capital.[8] In addition to such eyewitness observations about lobbying in the early twentieth century, counts of interest groups also can be estimated based on witnesses from interest groups who testified at congressional hearings.[9] Beginning in the 1970s better evidence about the size of the interest group population became available in the form of two directories published by for-profit presses: *Encyclopedia of Associations* and *Washington Representatives.* The *Encyclopedia,* which is designed to provide basic descriptions and contact information for all membership organizations in the United States, shows that the number of associations grew nearly 80 percent between 1975 and 2005, from 12,491 groups to 22,402 groups.[10] The greatest expansion occurred among groups with political leanings: civil rights groups grew during the period by 210 percent (from 273 associations to 838 associations) and ideological groups grew by 149 percent (from 245 associations to 609 associations).[11] Although the *Encyclopedia of Associations* provides insight into which types of groups are becoming more or less prevalent, it is not a perfect measure of interest group activity. It does not include businesses or any organization that does not have members, and many of the associations it lists may not lobby at all. A better measure of lobbying activity per se comes from *Washington Representatives,* which since 1977 has collected information about interest groups active in the capital from numerous sources including phone books, lists of congressional and agency witnesses, and lists of those who have commented on proposed agency rules. The directory provides evidence that the number of interest groups active in Washington doubled between 1981 and 2006, rising from nearly 7,000 to nearly 14,000 organizations.[12] Many of these interest groups employ multiple lobbyists and some of them employ dozens. As was the case with the membership associations listed in the *Encyclopedia of Associations,* greater growth appeared in some areas than others. The most striking change occurred among health-related groups, with an 883 percent increase in the number of groups. Social welfare groups grew by 291 percent, identity groups by 192 percent, and public interest groups by 123 percent.[13] All types of groups increased in numbers, but the growth rate of the aforementioned groups far outstripped the growth of corporations and occupational groups that lobby. Businesses, trade associations, and professional associations saw their relative share of the interest group population fall during this period. Still, political scientist Kay Lehman Schlozman points out that the numbers of such business-related organizations were so great to begin with that they still dominate the interest group population. Corporations still make up about 36 percent of the total interest group population, and trade associations account for another 11 percent. Social welfare groups, by comparison, are less than one-tenth of 1 percent, and even health-related groups make up only about 4 percent of the total. The raw numbers of interest groups also do not take into consideration how much each of these groups is able to spend on lobbying—and therefore the number of lobbyists they can hire. Baumgartner and Leech estimate that spending by businesses and trade associations in 1996 made up more than 78 percent of total spending on lobbying in Washington, more than eight times what citizen groups reported spending.[14] All indications are that this disparity in resources remains.

Beginning in 1946, lobbyists were required to register with the federal government. The law might have resulted in a better count, but it was so narrowly written—requiring registration for just those organizations whose "principal purpose" was lobbying—that the only registrants were lobbyists from professional lobbying firms, not lobbyists who were employed by businesses, trade associations, or other groups. Only 800 to 1,000 firms were registered as lobbyists during the 1960s, but informal counts were much higher.[15] A 1991 Government Accounting Office (GAO) report showed that about half of the lobbyists the GAO identified by using the *Washington Representatives* directory and a brief survey were actually registered as lobbyists.[16] So researchers went back to relying on anecdotes, congressional hearings, telephone books, and directories compiled by private companies. Since 1995, however, the data on the number of interest groups in Washington have become more reliable. The Lobbying Disclosure Act of 1995 required any organization that spends more than $20,000 (now adjusted for inflation) in a six-month period to register with the House and Senate, listing all employees who spend more than 20 percent of their time in lobbying activities. The data still have limitations. Some of the growth in registrations since 1995 is simply the result of organizations learning about the law and finally deciding to register. The way the law is written, organizations that do most of their advocacy inside the bureaucracy or before the courts, rather than within Congress, are often not required to register and are undercounted. Organizations that operate on very small budgets also will be undercounted because they are not required to register, and some organizations may try to avoid registering by taking advantage of accounting tricks to keep their official lobbying spending artificially low.[17] Still, the act provides far more accurate information about the number of interest groups in Washington than ever before.

TABLE 8.1 **The Expansion of Interest Groups, 2004–2009**

Year	Number of groups	Number of lobbyists	Spending on lobbying
2004	13,350	13,105	$2.17 billion
2005	14,418	14,001	$2.43 billion
2006	14,702	14,449	$2.62 billion
2007	15,191	14,798	$2.85 billion
2008	15,481	14,246	$3.3 billion
2009	16,343	13,751	$3.48 billion

SOURCES: Lobbying disclosure reports collected and coded by the Center for Responsive Politics and Timothy La Pira, http://www.opensecrets.org/lobby/index.php.

In 1996, the first year for which data are available, nearly 6,000 separate lobbying organizations registered with the government. Thirteen years later, as shown in Table 8.1, more than 16,000 separate organizations were registered and reported employing a total of 13,751 lobbyists and spending more than $3.5 billion on lobbying. By comparison, total PAC donations to candidates in 2009 by the 4,618 federally registered political action committees totaled only $174 million. Over the years, total spending on lobbying has increased from just over $1 billion, steadily rising up until the present day. Interestingly enough, however, while the dollar amount spent has been steadily increasing, the *number* of lobbyists reached nearly 13,000 by as early as 1999 and

Massachusetts gubernatorial candidates (left to right) Charles D. Baker, Tim Cahill, and Gov. Deval Patrick square off in a debate sponsored by the AARP on October 20, 2010. The AARP, which promotes the interests of senior citizens, ranks among the top ten interest groups in the amount of money it spends on lobbying.

has waxed and waned between 12,000 and 14,000 since then, rising and falling from year to year, suggesting that by 1999 most organizations that should have been registering had finally begun to register. Although the numbers must be interpreted cautiously—especially in the earliest years when there clearly was substantial underreporting—it is clear that the lobbying community is indeed quite large, and that *at least* $3.5 billion is now being spent each year on efforts to influence government policy.[18] In addition, it is important to remember that the definition of a lobbyist included in the Lobbying Disclosure Act—someone who spends at least 20 percent of his or her work time contacting federal elected officials or top agency officials in order to influence policy—excludes many who work in the Washington interest group milieu. Virtually all of these organizations employ support staff, and many employ lawyers, experts on regulatory processes, membership organizers, and public relations personnel—none of whom are required to register as lobbyists even though their efforts help to further the efforts of the lobbyists who are registered. For this reason political scientist James Thurber has put forth the educated guess that the interest group community is three to four times as large as the number of registered lobbyists, suggesting 261,000 as a probable estimate of what he calls the "influence-lobbying complex."[19] The size of the total lobbying population in Washington has been counted and estimated in numerous ways, each of which has its own shortcomings and errors. What remains certain through all of these accountings: the interest group population is large by any standard and it is growing.

THE SIZE OF GOVERNMENT

One way of measuring the growth of government over time is to look at increases in the federal budget. The U.S. national budget in terms of outlays, or spending, totaled more than $3 trillion in fiscal 2009, a thousand-fold leap from the $3 billion budget of eighty years before, when Calvin Coolidge was president. This rise has not been uniformly incremental, with changes occurring equally across all years. Rather, the growth of government is marked by three distinct periods: a postwar adjustment period from the end of World War II until 1956, a period of rapid growth continuing until 1975, then a period of restrained growth continuing until about 1995.[20] Since the start of the Iraq war, spending has entered a new period of rapid growth.[21] Although the U.S. budget as a whole seldom shows extreme shifts one way or another—the many parts of the budget moving up and down tend to even out any abrupt changes—one can see such patterns by looking at the subfunctions of the budget that apply to different specific policy areas. Large changes in these subfunctions were much more common in the growth period of the late 1950s through the early 1970s than in the other two periods. Since the 1960s the federal budget has by and large increased in tandem with the size of the gross domestic product (GDP). Since that time, the budget has grown larger each year, and so has the GDP. Spending as a percent of GDP has fluctuated between 17 percent and 22 percent. By comparison, federal spending in 1925 was only 3 percent of GDP, but that level skyrocketed to 42 percent during World War II before dropping back down to 15 percent in 1950.[22]

The patterns in the growth of the federal government precede, then parallel, what has been called the "interest group explosion" of the 1960s and early 1970s, when a striking increase in citizen groups occurred in Washington, followed by a mobilization of additional business interests in response to that "explosion."[23] It is not surprising that the growth of interest groups has so often been linked to the growth of government: the growth of each closely mimics the other. Figure 8.1 shows another measure of the size of the government—the number of civilian employees—from 1940 until the 1990s and compares that measure to the number of interest groups in the system. The government expanded rapidly during World War II and immediately thereafter, clearly outstripping the growth of the interest group system. The number of interest groups then increased to again roughly parallel the still-growing government. In the decades that followed, the interest group system and the government grew in tandem, trending upward through the 1960s and early 1970s before tapering off and reaching somewhat of a plateau in the mid-1970s and 1980s, which is as far as these data take us. The growth of both show similar, but certainly not identical, patterns.[24]

INTEREST-DRIVEN EXPLANATIONS FOR GROWTH

James Madison observed in *Federalist* 10 that the causes of what he called "factions"—groups of citizens with interests that might be contrary to the interests of the country as a whole—were "sown in the nature of man." That is, because not everyone shares the same opinions or makes his living in the same way or has the same possessions, ideas about the best course of government action will also diverge. The types of factions he described sound very much like some of the best-known interest groups of the modern day: religious groups, ideological groups, creditors, merchants, and landowners. The diversity of the population would lead naturally to faction.

Madison's focus in *Federalist* 10 was on how to structure the government, using divided power, to mute the influence of faction, but his causal explanation for how factions come into being is reflected in much of the early pluralist work on how interest groups come into being. Pluralists viewed interest groups as arising naturally out of the

FIGURE 8.1 **The Size of Government and the Size of the Interest Group Population**

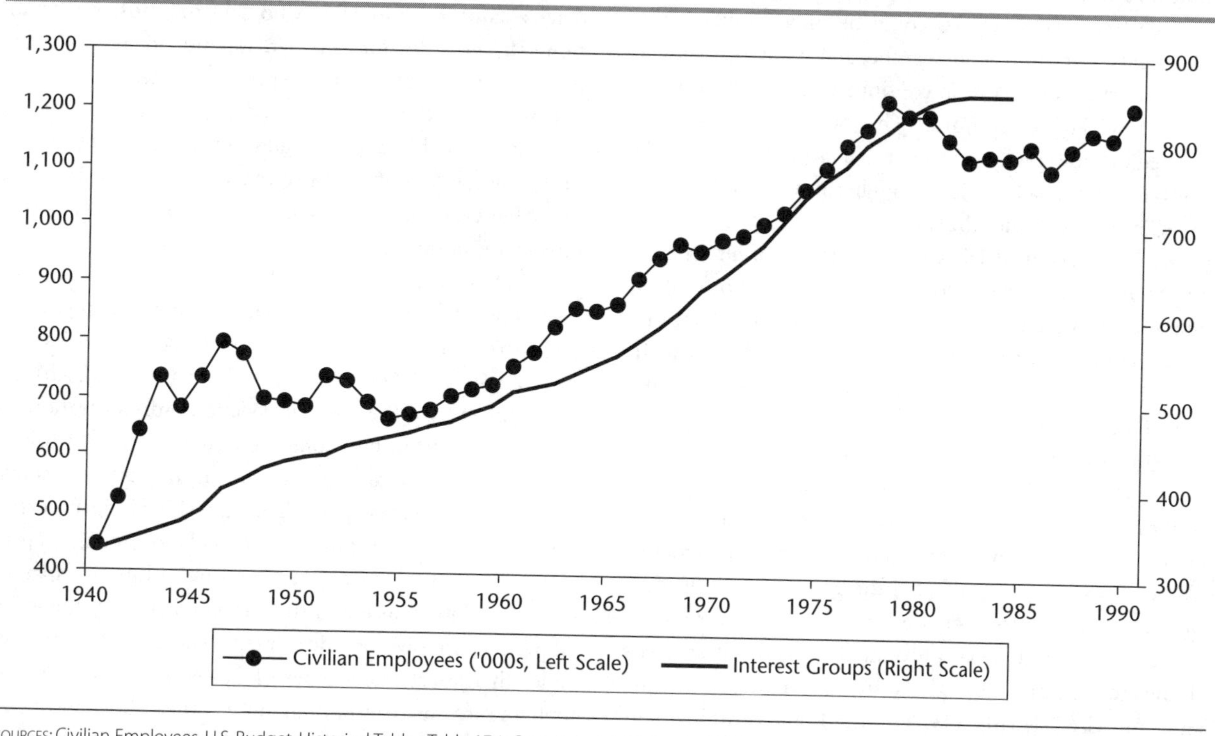

SOURCES: Civilian Employees, U.S. Budget, Historical Tables, Table 17.1; Groups, Jack L. Walker, *Mobilizing Interest Groups in America: Patrons, Professions, and Social Movements* (Ann Arbor: University of Michigan Press, 1991); see Frank R. Baumgartner and Bryan D. Jones, *Agendas and Instability in American Politics* (Chicago: University of Chicago, 1993), chap. 9.

wants, beliefs, and needs of the public. The interest group system would grow because the population grew, the economy grew, and the modern world had become more complex. Those groups would turn to government to solve these disturbances in the status quo, and as government responded to the requests of those groups, the government too would grow.[25] This interest-driven view of growth and mobilization contains at least a few grains of truth. We do see increases in the number of interest groups as economies grow and society diversifies. A study of interest group membership levels also has found that more people tend to join those groups during times of threats to their interests than at other times, suggesting that disturbances to the status quo do trigger mobilization.[26]

Economists refer to these requests by interest groups and the responses by government as rent-seeking. Rent-seeking refers to efforts by interest groups to use the power of the government to gain advantages that they would not be able to achieve alone. The benefits may be in the form of direct payments and subsidies or in the form of regulations such as tariffs and licensing that make it easier for a business to make a profit. Interest groups seek these benefits through government because the government has the ability to tax and to force others to pay those taxes, as well as the ability to use force, if necessary, to get others to follow rules. Businesses, workers, and professionals all can make money in their fields without government involvement, but involving government can possibly make it easier to raise the profit margin. Involving the government also allows an interest group to distribute the costs of a benefit widely, even if the benefit only helps a narrow slice of society. Because of this some economists argue that majoritarian government will inevitably lead to spending levels that are higher than individuals would choose if they had to pay for the benefits directly themselves.[27] The reasoning goes like this: a person may vote in favor of building the new superhighway between two cities when that cost is dispersed among citizens all over the country, but if he had to pay a toll that accurately reflected the cost of the highway each time he used it—a cost that might run into thousands of dollars—he might change his mind about the desirability of the road.

The rent-seeking argument can be extended to social movements as well as economic interest groups. Social movement organizations (SMOs) might mobilize to convince individuals to change or improve something about themselves and the world around them, or they could enlist the government and the rule of law to require others to change. The first route to change is often seen as more difficult and less effective than the second. The Temperance movement of the early twentieth century began with efforts to convince friends, neighbors, and others that alcohol consumption is detrimental to health and to society, using educational campaigns based on pamphlets, press, and public speeches.[28] These efforts could be only as effective as arguments and information can be, and many people who liked to drink were likely to continue to do so, even in the face of societal disapproval. The movement ultimately enlisted the power of government to make it illegal to sell or drink alcohol, resulting in the Eighteenth Amendment to the Constitution and the Prohibition era. The coercive power of government leads interest groups of all types to aim their efforts toward persuading government officials to help them achieve their goals rather than simply attempting to do so directly, without involving the government at all. In this way, the desires of interest groups can result in the growth of government.

In looking for examples of times that interest groups clearly set and changed the government's agenda, we often find examples of successful social movements, such as the civil rights, environmental, and women's movements. These efforts not only affected the government's agenda, but also helped to increase the size of government, because successful social movement pressure often leads to the creation of a new agency, such as the U.S. Commission on Civil Rights (1957), the Equal Employment Opportunity Commission (1964), or the Environmental Protection Agency (1970). Although political interest in an issue area can wax or wane, the newly established agency endures. It becomes a semipermanent part of the federal budget, with an interest group constituency that wants to see it continue. It is possible to trace the formation of SMOs—the interest groups that help to make up the larger social movement—using historic documents and compare the rise of these groups to the rise of issues on the congressional agenda. Congressional attention to all three of these areas—minority rights, women's rights, and environmental protection—was sporadic at best before these social movements began to grow. After the formation of the SMOs and the rise of the movements themselves, congressional attention increased substantially and remained high for two decades or more.[29] Naturally, politics is complex and multicausal. SMOs were not the only reason for the change in the congressional agenda, and the attention to these areas was not guaranteed to endure indefinitely. Beginning in the late 1980s and early 1990s, congressional attention turned away from all three of these issues, and the number of hearings held in each area dropped to levels not seen since before the movements began.[30]

The discussion above describes lobbying for collective goods: in other words, public policies. Changes in public policy affect constituents and industry generally, but interest groups also lobby for private goods, such as line-items, earmarks, and other government actions that benefit a single individual or single corporation. Political scientist Kenneth Godwin and economist Barry Seldon give the example of a defense contractor lobbyist who said the most important thing she ever did for her firm was not to influence any particular vote, but to get a 25 percent increase in the price of a missile her firm made inserted into an omnibus defense bill. Although this line-item addition increased her firm's profits by $50 million over five years (and increased the size of the federal budget by that amount) there was never a vote directly on raising the price.[31]

Because private benefits like this one are often at stake, companies that are highly regulated by the federal government spend more on lobbying than those companies that are not regulated, Godwin and Seldon have found. Airlines are regulated by the Federal Aviation Administration in areas ranging from how long their employees can work to which routes they can fly, and the airlines are very active lobbyists before government. The publishing industry experiences relatively little government regulation, thanks in part to the First Amendment. Although publishing companies do indeed lobby on issues such as whether they should be allowed to also own broadcast media and changes in the tax codes that affect many types of businesses, their levels of lobbying are much lower than those of the airlines and other regulated industries.[32]

Interest-driven views of the growth of the interest group system and the growth of government represent the dominant explanation in the popular media and even in some scholarly writing about politics. It is a perspective that is easy to understand and that makes sense at a gut level. After all, why do interest groups lobby if not to advocate for or against something that government might do? And if the groups lobbying in favor of the new policy win, government will likely grow a bit larger. So the roles of interest groups in the growth of government and their own expansion are important. Still, virtually all serious theories of the topic also take note of the role of the government in this process of growth. The reasons that the government is integral are not as well known as the interest-driven reasons, so it is worth examining them in some detail.

GOVERNMENT-DRIVEN EXPLANATIONS OF GROWTH

Government can be central to interest group growth in several ways. It can provide direct patronage, offering money and support to nascent interest groups as well as to established groups. In addition, new government programs can actually create the incentive for groups to mobilize. Finally, government activity in any policy area provides a signal to interest groups about where to most effectively focus their energies at a given time.

Many theories of social movements contain within them the idea that government actions can encourage mass mobilization.[33] Sociologists and political scientists who study such movements have pointed to the role of what they call the "political opportunity structure" in determining the success or failure of a movement. Such opportunities are not limited to direct subsidy of movements, but include factors such as whether members or leaders of the movement have allies within government, whether government is less likely than it once was to repress dissent, and whether conflict exists among government actors or other elites. Any or all of these can provide a chance for a social movement to make a difference, rather than being ignored or struck down.

Bruce Josten, chief lobbyist for the U.S. Chamber of Commerce, appears on Capitol Hill on August 4, 2009. The Chamber of Commerce is an example of one of the well-known interest groups in the United States that were actually created by—or at least strongly encouraged by—the U.S. government itself.

Direct Patronage

Some of the best-known interest groups in the United States were created by—or at least strongly encouraged by—the U.S. government itself. To govern effectively, officials need information about the world outside of Washington, about what constituents want, and about how particular policy proposals might affect the economy and daily life. The reverse is also true: interest organizations are useful because they can serve as conduits for information from Washington out to their memberships.

Political scientists Jocelyn Crowley and Theda Skocpol argue that one of the reasons for the huge growth in membership groups in the post–Civil War decades in the United States was that in the North the government had encouraged the creation of voluntary organizations to mobilize support for the war effort and conscript soldiers. These structures, once created, made it easier to form new and related voluntary organizations. In the South, the efforts were controlled from the top, and postwar growth of voluntary organizations was more limited.[34] Although voluntary organizations do not necessarily petition the government—and without that advocacy effort they are not interest groups—the most difficult aspect of advocacy is organizing in the first place. Voluntary organizations are assumed to be feeder organizations for the group system, and feeder organizations are the result of government encouragement and support.

Many additional examples can be found throughout U.S. history. The Department of the Army helped create the National Rifle Association in the nineteenth century, in part to make sure that future soldiers would already have experience with firearms. To make use of the information that interest groups can provide, commerce secretaries from a number of presidential administrations from Taft to Ford helped create the U.S. Chamber of Commerce (founded in 1912), the Business Council (founded in 1933), the Business Roundtable (founded in 1972), and a long series of trade associations so that these organizations could advise the government about economic policies. The American Farm Bureau Federation had its roots in a network of advisory committees created, beginning in about 1911, by the Department of Agriculture to help it to bring information and advice to farmers at the county level. A series of government-sponsored conferences on women's rights during the Kennedy administration provided support and start-up funds to feminist groups and ultimately led to the creation of the National Organization for Women (NOW).[35]

These examples are not isolated incidents. Surveys of membership groups conducted by political scientist Jack Walker during the 1980s found that government patronage was essential for the creation of many groups. Walker distinguishes between citizen groups such as the Sierra Club or NOW, whose memberships do not have an occupational basis, and what he calls nonprofit-sector and profit-sector groups. Nonprofit-sector and profit-sector groups have members who join because of their jobs. He mentions the American Lung Association as an example of a nonprofit-sector group, while profit-sector groups include trade associations such as the American Petroleum Institute or the American Forest and Paper Association. For groups founded between 1960 and 1983, government grants were an important funding source for 11 percent of the profit-sector groups, 20 percent of the citizen groups, and 33 percent of the nonprofit-sector groups. For groups with earlier founding dates, government start-up funds were somewhat less important: only about 3 percent of the profit-sector groups and 12 percent of the citizen groups reported receiving such funds. Nonprofit-sector groups founded before 1929 relied on government grants 13 percent of the time, and those founded between 1930 and 1959 relied on such grants

20 percent of the time.[36] These percentages show the importance of government funds for interest group mobilization in the New Deal era as well as increased support during the "interest group explosion" of the 1960s and 1970s, when government also was rapidly expanding into new areas of regulation and programming.

Government contracts and grants for specific interest group services also have led to the growth of interest groups by supporting their day-to-day functions. Ironically, it was a push to make government smaller by delegating many social services to private entities that led to this aspect of interest group growth. Efforts toward "privatization" of government services from the late 1970s on have meant that grants and contracts were offered to those willing to take on some of these functions.[37] Walker found that nearly 10 percent of all budget revenues for nonprofit sector organizations came from government grants and contracts (the comparable figure for profit-sector organizations was 2 percent and for citizen organizations 6 percent). These figures are averages: some groups do not receive grants and contracts, while others rely on them almost entirely. Direct support from government therefore remains an important factor in interest group maintenance in the United States.[38] Even the mighty AARP received $5 million from the federal government in 2009 so that its foundation could provide tax preparation assistance to low- and moderate-income senior citizens.

Government rules and regulations can also help support interest groups. Most interest groups (with the major exception of individual businesses) are exempt from income taxes because the government grants them nonprofit status. Even trade associations—organizations that represent individual businesses in a particular industry—are tax-exempt. Those nonprofit groups that qualify as charitable organizations are not only tax-exempt, but also the government allows anyone who donates money to them to take a tax deduction. Such tax laws are central to the financial well-being of many groups focused on education, research, and service to society.

OLDSTER POWER!

The AARP is the largest citizen group in the United States, boasting 40 million members and spending more than $20 million annually on federal lobbying. It ranks fifth among all interest groups in the amount of money it spends on lobbying, rubbing shoulders with the likes of the U.S. Chamber of Commerce, Exxon, and the American Medical Association. It is the only citizen group among the top twenty interest group spenders; by comparison even a group as reputedly powerful as the National Rifle Association spends only about $2 million a year on lobbying.

Why are senior citizens such a notable force in American interest group politics? Has it always been this way? Taking a closer look at the senior citizen lobby provides a window into how the symbiotic relationship between interest groups and government plays out.

Senior citizens made up about 13 percent of the U.S. population in 2008, more than triple the percentage in 1950. Their numbers are one reason why interest groups that represent the elderly can be so effective—there are plenty of potential members. Perhaps more important, however, is that these members vote, and they vote in much higher numbers than other segments of the population. But senior citizens were not always so politically active, and there is substantial evidence that the growth of interest groups representing senior citizens did not occur until well after the passage of the Social Security Act in 1935. The AARP itself did not come into being until 1958. Political scientist Andrea Campbell connects the increased engagement of older Americans to the growth of Social Security benefits "by connecting their fortunes tangibly and immediately to government action."

Interest groups and social movement organizations were, however, involved in some of the early efforts to create an old-age pension plan funded by the government. Sociologist Edwin Amenta has documented how the Townsend Movement during the Great Depression used a series of dues-paying clubs to advocate for $150 monthly pensions for all nonworking elderly. The Townsend Plan never passed, but its fairly radical proposal ($150 per month was far more than the median family income at the time) is credited with helping set the stage for the passage of the more modest Old Age Assistance program, which was need-based and had benefits of $15 to $30 a month. Was the Townsend Movement the "cause" of OAA or of Social Security? No such direct link seems likely. The modern Social Security system did not come into being until the 1950s, when the Townsend Movement had largely withered. Most of today's senior citizen mobilization did not occur until after the passage of the Older Americans Act of 1965, which authorized a series of grants to states to provide a wide range of services to the elderly.

Because of this historical pattern of mobilization, Campbell argues forcefully that "senior mass membership groups did not create Social Security policy. Rather, the policy helped create the groups." The groups, and especially the strength and size of the groups, were the consequences of the government policies, not the cause of them. Seniors mobilized because they had benefits to protect.

SOURCES: Edwin Amenta, *When Movements Matter* (Princeton: Princeton University Press, 2006); Andrea Campbell, *How Policies Create Citizens* (Princeton: Princeton University Press, 2005); 2010 Statistical Abstract, www.census.gov.

Incentives to Lobby

Interest groups could not lobby if it were not for the government; it is as simple as that. Without the ability and inclination by government officials to do something, there would be little reason for an interest group to lobby. This point is sometimes hard to grasp in an era when government rules and regulations seem to affect almost every aspect of daily life. But imagine an area in which the government does not involve itself, such as the number of days of sunshine a town experiences each year. There is little reason why anyone would spend time and effort mobilizing and lobbying to convince public officials that the town needs more sunshine because those officials have no power to change the sunshine levels. By extension, the more power and more inclination government officials have to legislate or regulate in an area, the more incentive potential interest groups have to lobby in the area. In 2009 the number of organizations lobbying on health care reform bills increased by nearly 300 percent.[39] Why? Because the Obama health care bill was being debated, and every business, organization, and profession that would be affected wanted to weigh in with their views about the potential impact of the bill.

Political scientist Scott Ainsworth has noted that the historical descriptions we have of times of great interest group growth—the 1880s, the 1920s, and the late 1960s and early 1970s—also were times in which government decentralization increased.[40] A more decentralized government offers more opportunities for lobbyists to lobby, because there are more potential sources of power. Likewise, supported by evidence from interest groups at the state level, political scientists Virginia Gray and David Lowery argue that the number of interest groups in a population will be dependent not only on the number of potential members and other resources that the organizations have, but also on the incentives created by potential government goods, services, and regulations. As these potential incentives grow, so will the interest group population.[41]

Once government has actually created a program or policy, the incentives for interest groups to mobilize and to lobby reach their peak. The mobilization of business interests in the 1970s and 1980s is often attributed to a reaction to increasing regulation and business attempts to respond to those regulations. The Tobacco Research Council was founded by tobacco companies in the 1940s to attempt to counteract regulatory efforts encouraged by the American Cancer Society and the American Heart Association in conjunction with officials in the U.S. Public Health Service.[42] Because of psychological tendencies to respond more strongly to the threat of loss than to the possibility of gain, we often see interest group mobilization in response to outside threats (such as that faced by the tobacco companies) or to the threatened loss of an existing government program. It is easier to mobilize to protect an existing program than it is to mobilize to seek a new program.[43] Once a policy benefit has been created, it attracts a constituency that likely will mobilize if necessary to ensure its survival.

"Interests" in politics require both the desires of some group of citizens and the potential actions of public officials.[44] Interests, therefore, are more than just the wants and needs of citizens. Those wants and needs become interests only when the government acts on them. Because interests are created by government actions, interest group mobilization is affected as well. That is, government activity affects lobbying activity. As government becomes more active in a particular area, so too will the corresponding interest groups, meaning that in any given year the types of interests lobbying are strongly related to the types of activity that government officials are working on.

Data made available through the Lobbying Disclosure Act and similar data from the states have made it possible to examine this symbiotic relationship over time, across issues, and over geographic space. The Lobbying Disclosure Act data allow researchers to identify the number of organizations active in Washington in seventy-four government-designated issue areas. When these numbers are linked to information about the issue areas in which Congress is holding hearings, the connection between government action and lobbying reaction becomes clear. The amount of lobbying varies greatly across issue areas. An average of 427 interest groups registered to lobby on health policy issues during one recent five-year period, while only about five interest groups registered to lobby on issues related to the minting of money. Such extreme differences across issue areas exist throughout the fifteen years of the lobbying disclosure reports, but it is also possible to see some variation within particular issue areas from year to year. An increase of about twenty congressional hearings in a year meant about thirty-six more interest groups registering to lobby in that area. That attention from Congress was a more important factor in determining the number of interest groups than government spending in an area. For each *$100 billion* in spending, there was an average increase of only about five registered interest groups.[45] Attention to an issue by the federal government even spurs lobbying at the state level, with congressional hearings in an issue area leading to more interest groups registering in that area across the states. The effect is stronger in areas where the federal government has traditionally been active, such as health, agriculture, education, transportation, and welfare.[46]

Attention and Coordination

The resource in shortest supply in Washington is attention.[47] At any given point in time, the supply of issues that elected officials and interest groups could be working on is potentially limitless. Even when issues make it to the formal legislative agenda, they join more than 8,000 new bills in each two-year Congress, of which only about 400 become law. Any one political actor can put time and effort into only a few. In this situation, it is in the best interest of interest groups to be working on an issue that has some likelihood of moving forward, rather than spinning their wheels and wasting time on an issue where no one else is likely to show an interest.[48]

Government activity in a policy area lowers the risk that an interest group's efforts will be for naught and increases the potential benefits to the group for participating. Most activity is therefore expected to gravitate toward policy areas in which government is already engaged. Government activity provides the signal that a policy area is "ripe" for policy change and provides a reason to focus on one issue rather than another, whether the group's goal is to facilitate change or fight against it. The government activity provides a coordination point where multiple political actors can meet.

As discussed above, interest groups have a role in agenda-setting, but agenda-setting by itself very seldom drives interest group or government growth beyond the existing status quo. A few interest groups may petition government, but large numbers of other interest groups will not join that fight unless there is a probability for action. Why? Because those other interest groups do not want to waste their time on an issue that probably is not going anywhere.

Any time an interest group decides to put effort into lobbying on an issue that is a public policy or collective good, a dilemma is created for other groups. The other interest groups may support the issue, but their resources are not unlimited. In this situation, the primary goal for most interest groups is to ascertain whether any other interest groups or government officials are *also* going to become involved in that issue. If some are involved, then more will become involved. If more are involved, even more may join in. The pattern we see in interest group lobbying across all issues therefore looks something like a ski-slope distribution. There are many, many issues on which either zero or a handful of interest groups are ever active. Then there are a few issues on which hundreds and hundreds of lobbyists are active. Analyses show that the top 5 percent of the issues on which interest groups are active attract nearly half of all of the lobbying activity, while the bottom 50 percent of the issues attract only 3 percent of the lobbying.[49] This seems to be a general principle as very similar patterns of lobbying attention have been demonstrated in multiple years for the federal government, in the American states, and before the Scottish parliament.[50]

The corollary to these findings is that because most interest groups will spend time lobbying on the same issues, not all groups will be lobbying on their most preferred issue. Interest groups, far from being able to dictate government agendas, often end up spending much of their time working on issues that are at the periphery of their missions: these are issues about which they have opinions and preferred outcomes, but not the issues they would have chosen to work on in a perfect world. What policymakers and interest group lobbyists are doing in the early stages of an issue is trying to send signals that this is an issue to watch; this is a bandwagon that others should be ready to jump on. An issue becomes "important" and worth spending time on because others have decided that it is important and worth spending time on, and those decisions are in turn based in large part on the decisions of others before them. Every time someone else agrees to cooperate, the risks and costs decrease for subsequent participants. The hard part is getting the cascade of interest started in the first place.

Some interest groups still will choose to lobby alone, and most interest groups have "most-favored" issues on the back burner to which they devote at least some of their time. Indeed, for some interest groups, the importance of an issue is so great that fighting for years with no hope of immediate success is better than simply ignoring it. Opponents of the death penalty worked for decades in many states with little evidence of policy change until a breakthrough in DNA testing gave them another basis on which to argue their point.[51] Sometimes interest groups lobby alone when leaders of the group have decided that the issue is a priority and a long-term strategy is needed. Sometimes groups lobby alone when the issue is a private good or earmark that benefits the interest group but does not require a general policymaking process. In such cases one or two government officials and the lobbyist can succeed in creating the earmark or granting the waiver, and in such cases lobbying alone is an adequate strategy. To change general policy or to create new programs, however, the behind-the-scenes approach is inadequate. Sustained attention from many policy actors is required.

CONCLUSION

The relationship between government and interest groups is a two-way street, although the government's part in this process is often overlooked. Do interest groups cause the growth in government or does growth in government cause the growth in interest groups? The two are so intertwined that it perhaps is impossible to say. A study of lobbying populations in the states in 1997 attempted to pin down whether the interest groups were the leaders or the followers. The authors compared legislative agendas in 1995, 1997, and 1999 to the number of interest groups registered in various issue areas in 1997. The evidence suggested that interest groups were not reacting to the legislative agendas of two years earlier, nor did the interest group actions in 1997 seem to be causing the legislative agendas of two years in the future. What they found, however, was that lobbying registrations in 1997 were most strongly related to government activity in that same year. Interest group actions were so closely tied to what legislatures were currently doing that the authors described them as "living in the moment." The attention paid to an issue by one side rises and falls with the attention paid by the other.[52]

Advocacy and lobbying have been part of the governmental process since the beginning of U.S. democracy. The First Amendment granted the right to petition government, and organized interests have not been shy about making use of that right. What we have seen since those early days, however, is an increasing professionalization of the interest group community and increasing specialization of these organizations as government has grown alongside. The history of interest group involvement in politics suggests that the number of lobbyists active in Washington is likely to continue growing—at least as long as the scope and size of government legislation and programs continue to grow as well.

NOTES

1. The American Presidency Project, "John Edwards, Remarks in Des Moines, Iowa, July 26, 2007," http://www.presidency.ucsb.edu/ws/index.php?pid=77257.

2. OMB Watch, "White House Announces Changes to Recovery Act Lobbying Memo," http://www.ombwatch.org/node/10069.

3. Center for Public Integrity, "The Climate Change Lobby," http://www.publicintegrity.org/investigations/climate_change/.

4. Quoted in Jeffrey H. Birnbaum, "In a Harsh Climate for Lobbyists, the Forecast Calls for . . . More Lobbyists," *Washington Post*, August 12, 2008.

5. Mark P. Petracca, *The Politics of Interests* (Boulder: Westview, 1992), 22.

6. Mancur Olson, *The Rise and Decline of Nations: Economic Growth, Stagflation, and Social Rigidities* (New Haven: Yale University Press, 1984). For a popular treatment, see journalist Jonathan Rauch's 1994 book, *Demosclerosis: The Silent Killer of American Government* (New York: Times Books).

7. Kenneth G. Crawford, *The Pressure Boys* (Julian Messner, 1939).

8. Wilfred E. Brinkley and Malcolm C. Moos, *A Grammar of American Politics,* 3rd ed. (Knopf [1949] 1958), cited in Petracca, *Politics of Interests.*

9. Daniel J. Tichenor and Richard A. Harris, "The Development of Interest Group Politics in America: Beyond the Conceits of Modern Times," *Annual Review of Political Science* 8 (June 2005): 251–270.

10. Frank R. Baumgartner, Grant Jordan, John McCarthy, Shaun Bevan, and Jamie Greenan, "Tracing Interest-Group Populations in the US and UK," paper presented at the annual meeting of the American Political Science Association, Boston, 2008.

11. Ibid.

12. Kay Lehman Schlozman, "Who Sings in the Heavenly Chorus," in *The Oxford Handbook of American Political Parties and Interest Groups,* ed. L. Sandy Maisel and Jeffrey M. Berry (New York: Oxford University Press, 2010), 405–450.

13. Ibid.

14. Frank R. Baumgartner and Beth L. Leech, "Issue Niches and Policy Bandwagons: Patterns of Interest Group Involvement in National Politics," *Journal of Politics* 63 (2001): 1191–1213.

15. Lester Milbrath, "Lobbying," in *Encyclopedia of the Social Sciences,* vol. 9, ed. David L. Sills (New York: Macmillan, 1968).

16. General Accounting Office, "Federal Lobbying: Federal Regulation of Lobbying Act of 1946 is Ineffective," July 1991.

17. And, in fact, there is evidence that the number of registered lobbyists dropped (but the amount of spending by lobbyists did not) in late 2008 and 2009 after President Obama issued rules limiting participation by lobbyists. See OMB Watch, "Federal Lobbyists Have Increasingly Terminated Their Registrations," http://www.ombwatch.org/node/10541.

18. PAC data are from the Federal Election Commission, www.fec.gov; lobbying data for 1998–2009 come from the Center for Responsive Politics, http://www.opensecrets.org/lobby/index.php; for 1998–2009 and 1996, from Frank R. Baumgartner and Beth L. Leech, http://lobby.la.psu.edu/related.html. Additional analyses contained in Carter Foxgrover, "Temporal Dynamics of Interest Group Activity, 1998–2007," paper presented at the 2010 Midwest Political Science Association meeting, Chicago.

19. Robert J. Samuelson, "Lobbying is Democracy in Action," *Newsweek,* December 13, 2008, http://www.newsweek.com/2008/12/12/lobbying-is-democracy-in-action.html.

20. Frank R. Baumgartner, Bryan D. Jones, and James L. True, "Policy Punctuations: US Budget Authority 1947–95," *Journal of Politics* 60 (January 1998): 1–33.

21. See http://www.policyagendas.org/page/trend-analysis.

22. Congressional Budget Office, "A 125-Year Picture of the Federal Government's Share of the Economy, 1950 to 2075," http://www.cbo.gov/doc.cfm?index=3521.

23. Jeffrey M. Berry, *The Interest Group Society,* 3rd ed. (New York: Longman, 1997).

24. And, in fact, the number of employees underestimates the overall reach of the federal government, according to Paul C. Light's book *The True Size of Government* (Washington, D.C.: Brookings, 1999). Especially since the 1970s, many government functions have been contracted out to businesses and nonprofits. See also Steven Rathgeb Smith and Michael Lipsky, *Nonprofits for Hire: The Welfare State in the Age of Contracting* (Cambridge: Harvard University Press, 1993).

25. David Truman, *The Governmental Process* (New York: Knopf, 1951).

26. John Mark Hansen, "The Political Economy of Group Membership," *American Political Science Review* 79 (February 1985): 79–96.

27. For example, see Gordon Tullock, "Some Problems of Majority Voting," *Journal of Political Economy* 67 (December 1959): 571–579.

28. Peter H. Odegard, *Pressure Politics: The Story of the Anti-Saloon League* (New York: Columbia University Press, 1928).

29. Frank R. Baumgartner and Bryan D. Jones, *Agendas and Instability in American Politics* (Chicago: University of Chicago, 1993); Frank R. Baumgartner and Christine Mahoney, "Social Movements, the Rise of New Issues, and the Public Agenda," in *Routing the Opposition: Social Movements, Public Policy, and Democracy*, ed. David S. Meyer, Valerie Jenness, and Helen Ingram (Minneapolis: University of Minnesota, 2005); Debra Minkoff, *Organizing for Equality: The Evolution of Women's and Racial-Ethic Organizations in America, 1955–1985* (New Brunswick, N.J.: Rutgers University Press, 1995).

30. Baumgartner and Mahoney, "Social Movements."

31. Kenneth R. Godwin and Barry J. Seldon, "What Corporations Really Want from Government," in *Interest Group Politics*, 6th ed., ed. Allan Cigler and Burdett Loomis (Washington, D.C.: CQ Press, 2002), 206; also see Kenneth R. Godwin, Edward J. López, and Barry J. Seldon, "Allocating Lobbying Resources between Collective and Private Rents," *Political Research Quarterly* 61 (June 2008): 345–359.

32. Godwin and Seldon, "What Corporations Really Want."

33. For an overview of these approaches, see Doug McAdam, John D. McCarthy, and Mayer N. Zald, eds., *Comparative Perspectives on Social Movements: Political Opportunities, Mobilizing Structures, and Cultural Framings* (New York: Cambridge University Press, 1996).

34. Jocelyn Elise Crowley and Theda Skocpol, "The Rush to Organize: Explaining Associational Formation in the United States, 1860–1920s," *American Journal of Political Science* 45 (August 2001): 813–829.

35. All described in Jack Walker, *Mobilizing Interest Groups in America* (Ann Arbor: University of Michigan Press, 1991), 30–31.

36. Ibid, 79.

37. Smith and Lipsky, *Nonprofits for Hire.*

38. Walker, *Mobilizing Interest Groups*, 82.

39. Michael Bechel, "Number of Special Interests Vying to Influence Health Reform Legislation Swelled as Debate Dragged On," http://www.opensecrets.org/news/2010/03/number-of-special-interest-groups-v.html.

40. Scott Ainsworth, "Electoral Strength and the Emergence of Group Influence in the Late 1800s: The Grand Army of the Republic," *American Politics Quarterly* 23 (July 1995): 319–338.

41. David Lowery and Virginia Gray, "The Population Ecology of Gucci Gulch, or the Natural Regulation of Interest Group Numbers," *American Journal of Political Science* 39 (January 1995): 1–29.

42. Walker, *Mobilizing Interest Groups*, 28.

43. Daniel Kahneman and Amos Tversky, "Prospect Theory: An Analysis of Decision-Making under Risk," *Econometrica* 47 (March 1985): 263–291. For a discussion, see Walker, *Mobilizing Interest Groups*, and Andrea L. Campbell, *How Policies Make Citizens* (Princeton: Princeton University Press, 2005).

44. John P. Heinz, Edward O. Laumann, Robert L. Nelson, and Robert H. Salisbury, *The Hollow Core: Private Interests in National Policymaking* (Cambridge: Harvard University Press, 1993).

45. Beth L. Leech, Frank R. Baumgartner, Timothy M. LaPira, and Nicholas Semanko, "Drawing Lobbyists to Washington: Government Activity and Interest Group Mobilization," *Political Research Quarterly* 58 (March 2005): 19–30.

46. Frank R. Baumgartner, Virginia Gray, and David Lowery, "Federal Policy Activity and the Mobilization of State Lobbying Organizations," *Political Research Quarterly* 62 (2009): 552.

47. Bryan D. Jones and Frank R. Baumgartner, *The Politics of Attention: How Government Prioritizes Problems* (Chicago: University of Chicago Press, 2005).

48. In this regard, lobbying for earmarks and other private benefits differs from lobbying for collective goods that involve changes in public policy. Earmark grants may require as little as the activities of one interest group and one active member of Congress to come to fruition. Although growing and the subject of great attention and concern, earmarks still are a relatively small portion of the federal budget—less than 1 percent according to the Congressional Research Service—and are a correspondingly small portion of what interest groups in Washington spend most of their time on. See Frank R. Baumgartner, Jeffrey M. Berry, Marie Hojnacki, David C. Kimball, and Beth L. Leech, *Lobbying and Policy Change: Who Wins, Who Loses, and Why* (Chicago: University of Chicago Press, 2009).

49. Holly Brasher, "Configurations of Interest Group Activity and Legislative Success in the U.S. House of Representatives," paper presented at the 2009 American Political Science Association meeting, Toronto, September 3–6.

50. Baumgartner and Leech, "Issue Niches and Policy Bandwagons"; Frederick J. Boehmke, John Wiggs, Sean Gailmard, and Andrew Pettine, "Still Waters or Whirlpools? The Distribution of Lobbying across Governments and Venues," paper presented at the 2009 American Political Science Association meeting, Toronto, September 3–6; Darren Halpin and Graeme Baxter, "Searching for 'Tartan' Policy Bandwagons: Mapping the Mobilization of Organized Interests in Public Policy," paper presented at the 2008 American Political Science Association meeting, August 28–31.

51. Frank R. Baumgartner, Suzanna L. De Boef, and Amber E. Boydstun, *The Decline of the Death Penalty and the Discovery of Innocence* (New York: Cambridge University Press, 2008).

52. David Lowery, Virginia Gray, Matthew Fellowes, and Jennifer Anderson, "Living in the Moment: Lags, Leads, and the Link Between Legislative Agendas and Interest Advocacy," *Social Science Quarterly* 85 (June 2004): 463–477.

SUGGESTED READING

Baumgartner, Frank R., and Beth L. Leech. "Issue Niches and Policy Bandwagons: Patterns of Interest Group Involvement in National Politics." *Journal of Politics* 63 (2001): 1191–1213.

Hansen, John Mark. "The Political Economy of Group Membership." *American Political Science Review* 79 (February 1985): 79–96.

Leech, Beth L., Frank R. Baumgartner, Timothy M. LaPira, and Nicholas Semanko. "Drawing Lobbyists to Washington: Government Activity and Interest Group Mobilization." *Political Research Quarterly* 58 (March 2005): 19–30.

Lowery, David, and Virginia Gray. "The Population Ecology of Gucci Gulch, or the Natural Regulation of Interest Group Numbers." *American Journal of Political Science* 39 (January 1995): 1–29.

Minkoff, Debra. *Organizing for Equality: The Evolution* of *Women's and Racial-Ethic Organizations in America, 1955–1985.* New Brunswick, N.J.: Rutgers University Press, 1995.

Petracca, Mark P., ed. *The Politics of Interests.* Boulder: Westview Press, 1992.

Schlozman, Kay Lehman. "Who Sings in the Heavenly Chorus." In *The Oxford Handbook of American Political Parties and Interest Groups.* Eds. L. Sandy Maisel and Jeffrey M. Berry. New York: Oxford University Press, 2010, 405–450.

Walker, Jack L. *Mobilizing Interest Groups in America: Patrons, Professions, and Social Movements.* Ann Arbor: University of Michigan Press, 1991.

chapter 9

Interest Groups and the Courts

by Karen O'Connor and Alixandra B. Yanus

IN THE SUMMER OF 1869 SUFFRAGIST Susan B. Anthony addressed the annual meeting of the Woman Suffrage Association of Missouri. Its president was Virginia Minor, who was the first woman in Missouri to advocate female suffrage publicly. During that meeting, Minor's husband, Francis, a lawyer, first articulated the belief that the Fourteenth Amendment enfranchised women because they were citizens of the United States. His interpretation of the amendment, set forth in what were called the St. Louis Resolutions, had a profound impact on the direction the National Woman Suffrage Association (NWSA) was to take.

To publicize his views, the full text of the St. Louis Resolutions was printed in NWSA's newspaper, *The Revolution*. Anthony had 10,000 additional copies printed and distributed across the country. Copies were also placed on the desks of all members of Congress. But this publication alone did not create the social and legal change NWSA sought to achieve.

In October, after speaking with Anthony, Francis Minor wrote to the readers of *The Revolution* to ask "if a test case cannot be made at your coming election." Realizing the potential publicity and policy change that a litigation strategy could bring, he continued:

> If this were done, in no other way could our cause be more widely, and at the same time definitively brought before the public. Every newspaper in the land would tell the story. . . . The question would be thoroughly discussed by thousands, who now give it no thought—and by the time it reached the court of final resort, the popular verdict would be in accord with the judgment that is sure to be rendered.

Several judges indicated their agreement with Minor's argument. And, "encouraged by the opinions of able lawyers and judges, . . . [women] promptly made a practical test case of this question by registering and voting during the state and presidential elections of 1871 and '72."[1] NWSA members knew that most voting registrars would prevent them from registering, in part out of fear for their own prosecution if they allowed women to register. The women chose to register anyway, in the hopes that they might bring a legal challenge to the courts. Their efforts to this end were also encouraged by a majority report of the House Judiciary Committee that said a woman's right to vote could be established through test case litigation without any further need for federal legislation or constitutional amendment.

Although the women were successful in bringing such test cases before state and federal courts, none of their efforts resulted in a positive outcome. Anthony was tried and convicted of unlawfully and willfully voting. Federal judge Ward Hunt, in his first case on the bench, not only directed the jury to find her guilty, but also prevented her from testifying in her own defense and even admitted to writing his decision before the trial.

One positive result of NWSA's failed attempt to gain suffrage for women through litigation in the 1870s was the massive publicity the organization garnered. Even antisuffrage publications spoke out against the treatment of the women, increasing the group's visibility and raising sympathy for their cause. The success of the test case litigation strategy from a public relations perspective provided future groups with the hope that if they followed NWSA's template, they might not only increase their visibility, but also create policy change.[2]

The story of the NWSA's attempt to gain suffrage for women shares much with the stories of modern interest groups that have chosen to turn to the courts. It is, however, just one example in a long and varied legacy of interest group activity in the judiciary. To paint a more complete picture of organized interests' efforts to lobby the third branch of the government, this chapter examines what types of groups participate in the courts, how groups participate, why they participate, and when and under what conditions they are successful in their efforts.

Before we begin our exploration of interest groups in the judiciary, we should note that the court system in the United States is a vast entity composed of thousands of tribunals at the state and federal levels of government. Despite the size of this judicial system, much of the scholarship conducted on interest groups in the courts focuses on their involvement before the U.S. Supreme Court. By necessity, then, the Court is also at the center of our discussion here. Where possible, we also briefly discuss interest group participation in lower federal and state supreme courts to round out the story of how interest groups influence the judicial process.

WHO PARTICIPATES IN THE JUDICIARY?

Judicial politics scholars have classified the groups participating before the judiciary in a variety of ways. The simplest distinctions are those between advantaged and disadvantaged groups, or what Marc Galanter calls "the haves and the have nots."[3] The following considers participants before the courts from these perspectives. It also examines research on judicial participation using more traditional group classifications that borrow heavily from the interest group literature: institutions and public interest groups.

Disadvantaged versus Advantaged Groups

In 1938 the Court noted that the judiciary had a duty to protect certain "discrete and insular minorities," although it did not clearly define these groups.[4] Twenty years later, Clement E. Vose was one of the first scholars to document the importance of a disadvantaged group's use of the courts. His examination of the National Association for the Advancement of Colored People (NAACP), and the success of its independent Legal Defense Fund (LDF) in court to end restrictive housing covenants, revealed that litigation was critical because the NAACP had realized that racist views and party politics prevented it from achieving its goals in the legislature or the executive branch.[5] Jack Greenberg's and Richard Kluger's analyses of the LDF's role in the school discrimination cases that culminated in *Brown v. Board of Education* (1954) further underscored the importance of LDF general counsel Thurgood Marshall's decision to turn to the courts to achieve policy change.[6]

The intrinsically interesting nature of these findings led political scientist Richard Cortner to articulate what he dubbed political disadvantage theory. Cortner argued that there were certain classes of interest groups that were especially compelled to turn to the courts because they faced barriers in their ability to successfully attain their goals in the legislative and executive branches.[7] Cortner provided few specific examples of these organized interests, but other scholars recognized the validity of this theory and began to examine the growing litigation efforts of disadvantaged groups—including death row inmates,[8] Mexican Americans,[9] women,[10] and Native Americans.[11]

The "Haves" and "Have Nots"

Following a similar logic but looking at commercial cases instead of those involving constitutional or statutory rights, in 1974 Marc Galanter posited his theory of the "haves" and the "have nots." His "have nots" generally included parties that appeared before the court in but one or two cases. They lacked the resources or interest to pursue a long-term litigation strategy and were often unfamiliar with the practices of the judicial system.

The "haves," on the other hand, were groups that often became repeat players before a particular court, frequently using litigation to resolve conflict and becoming familiar with the legal system and the judges. "Haves," according to Galanter, came in a wide variety of forms, including criminal prosecutors, insurance companies, and landlords. They also included institutions such as businesses, corporations, and state, local, or national governments. The wealth, size, and resources of these groups enabled them to "to pursue . . . long run interests."[12] They also generally had "advance intelligence" that enabled them to build judicial precedent.[13]

The Galanter framework continues to be applied extensively in modern scholarship. Political scientist Donald R. Songer and his colleagues have built a considerable body of research applying Galanter's framework to the U.S. courts of appeals and the Supreme Court. Their research defined "haves" as governments and businesses and consistently found that these groups won more cases over time than "have nots."[14] Other scholars, including Herbert M. Kritzer, have also examined the advantages that accrue to governments, which most scholars view as the ultimate repeat player.[15]

Interest Group Classifications

Interest group scholars have traditionally classified organized interests not exclusively by their political resources, but also by their group type. Labels such as businesses, institutions, governments, membership groups, and trade associations have become common in this literature. With these labels come the attendant expectations about groups' resources and goals. Businesses and institutions are generally expected to have greater financial resources, and membership groups are usually expected to have greater human resources.[16]

It is not surprising that the groups that lobby the judiciary are very different from their counterparts that lobby the elected branches. Research by Kay Lehman Schlozman and John T. Tierney and by Frank R. Baumgartner and Beth A. Leech found that business and trade associations constitute more than half of all groups lobbying the legislature.[17] In contrast, Gregory A. Caldeira and John R. Wright found that corporations and business, trade, and professional organizations constituted only a plurality (roughly 40 percent) of all groups participating before the Supreme Court during its 1982 term. Public interest groups, individuals, and governments were more visible in the Court than in the elected branches.[18]

These findings have been supported by more recent analyses. In one study, Paul M. Collins and Lisa A. Solowiej analyzed all of the groups participating before the Court during its 1995 term. Although businesses and trade groups filed about 40 percent of all briefs in their sample, these groups constituted less than 25 percent of all individual participants—a decline from the data observed by Caldeira and Wright. State governments (8 percent of briefs, 21 percent of groups), public advocacy groups and law firms (30 percent of briefs and 17 percent of groups), and individuals (9 percent of briefs and 22 percent of groups) continued to constitute a much larger percentage of those lobbying the judiciary than the elected branches.[19] This involvement, however, may not be a preferred strategy; in her survey-based study of social and economic justice advocacy groups, Dara Strolovitch found that these groups were quite reluctant to target the federal courts.[20]

HOW DO GROUPS PARTICIPATE IN THE JUDICIAL PROCESS?

In a book published in 1908, Arthur F. Bentley was the first political scientist to note that certain groups lobby the courts to obtain desired policy ends.[21] Since then, a host of scholars have completed detailed examinations of the variety of ways interest groups participate before the judiciary. Among the most common ways interest groups participate are through sponsorship of cases, filing amicus curiae (friend of the court) briefs, participating in the judicial nomination process, and advocacy during judicial elections.

Sponsorship

As discussed in the opening vignette, the NWSA was perhaps the first interest group to formulate and pursue the development of a direct sponsorship strategy, wherein an interest group or groups take primary responsibility for writing briefs and filing a particular case on behalf of a selected plaintiff. This practice is more common than the casual observer might expect. As Cortner has noted, "Cases do not arrive on the doorstep of the Supreme Court like orphans in the night."[22] Litigation is extremely expensive, and most cases involving challenges to constitutional or statutory law either involve the government or another advantaged litigant as the sponsor. These groups may include corporations, governments, or even public interest law firms, who appear before the court frequently and are skilled in developing long-range litigation strategies.

In the early 1900s the National Consumers League (NCL) sponsored cases involving protective legislation every time it was able to persuade parties to allow the league to represent them. Its volunteer counsel, Louis Brandeis, even filed a brief defending the state of Oregon's maximum hour law. That brief, which contained 100 pages of statistical data on the effects of long hours on women's health became known as the "Brandeis Brief," and was made even more famous for the fact that it offered the Court only three pages of legal argument. Still, the Court adopted many of the arguments and facts offered in the NCL's brief in *Muller* v. *Oregon* (1908). The NCL continued to use this type of brief in a series of cases it sponsored before the Supreme Court through 1936.

Amicus Curiae Briefs

The amicus curiae brief was originally conceived to ensure that the Supreme Court was fully informed on any issue it considered. As first envisioned, amicus curiae briefs were expected to present information in a neutral way, but practice before the Court has proven otherwise. Samuel Krislov's seminal 1963 work on the amicus brief documented the changes that have occurred over time and argued that the amicus brief is no longer a "neutral, amorphous embodiment of justice, but is an important participant in the interest group struggle."[23]

Though it may seem intuitive today, scholars at the time were reluctant to accept Krislov's conclusion. In fact, a 1969 study by Nathan Hakman concluded that interest groups participated as amicus curiae only rarely during the Court's 1928–1966 terms. Hakman labeled any scholarly work on amicus curiae briefs as "scholarly folklore."[24]

Hakman's observations stood as fact for more than a decade. His work trivialized Vose's work on both sponsorship and amicus curiae briefs, as he argued that the NAACP LDF's amicus activity was not reflective of any other group's political strategy. In 1982, however, Karen O'Connor and Lee Epstein challenged and finally laid to rest the assertions in Hakman's scholarship. Using Hakman's own coding scheme and methodology, they updated his work by analyzing the Court's 1970–1980 terms. They found that interest group participation as amicus curiae was as high as 90 percent in some issue areas, but that it varied significantly among case types.[25] More recent work, such as that of Ryan J. Owens and Lee Epstein, found that participation across case types is "virtually indistinguishable" and that at least one friend of the court brief is filed in about 90 percent of all cases.[26] Moreover, the number of amicus briefs filed annually at the U.S. Supreme Court has increased substantially over time.[27] Figure 9.1 documents this change.

Scholarly analysis of the volume of interest group participation as amicus curiae in lower courts has been more limited. But one recent study by Wendy L. Martinek illuminated a great deal about participation in the lower federal courts, specifically the U.S. courts of appeals. Martinek found that, like the U.S. Supreme Court, the appeals courts have experienced a notable increase in amicus participation over time. The percentage of cases attracting amicus curiae

FIGURE 9.1 **Average Number of Amicus Briefs Per Case, 1953–2001**

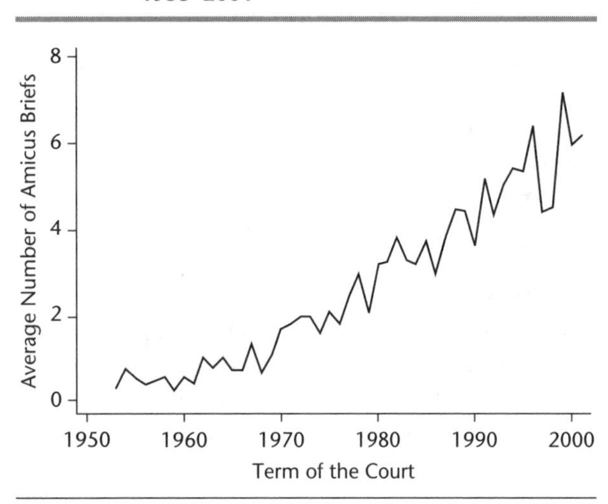

SOURCE: Data from Paul M. Collins, *Friends of the Supreme Court* (New York: Oxford University Press, 2008).

participation in these lower courts, however, is significantly lower than in the Supreme Court. In 1925 interest groups participated in about 1 percent to 2 percent of circuit court cases; by 1995 groups participated in 7 percent to 8 percent of cases.[28]

A 1994 study by Lee Epstein also shed light on interest group participation outside the Supreme Court. Examining state supreme courts, Epstein considered two questions: (1) whether organized interests' participation as amicus curiae in state courts had grown from 1965 to 1990; and (2) whether the kinds of interests participating in state court litigation changed over that time period. She found that from 1965 to 1990, organized interests assumed a heightened presence in state supreme courts and that a wider variety of organized interests participated in cases in 1990 than in 1965.[29]

The Judicial Nomination Process

The U.S. Constitution dictates that the president has the power, with the advice and consent of the Senate, to nominate judges to serve on all federal courts. During the twentieth and twenty-first centuries, this process has become increasingly political, with interest groups and individuals mobilizing to support and to oppose nominees for the Supreme Court, as well as the federal circuit and district courts.

The earliest modern example of interest group involvement in the judicial nomination process is the nomination of Louis Brandeis to the Supreme Court in 1916. Brandeis's work on behalf of the NCL made him a controversial nominee, particularly among business and trade groups. Others opposed Brandeis's nomination because of his religion, Judaism. These groups mobilized an extensive grassroots lobbying campaign. They were joined in this effort by a number of groups, such as labor unions, that supported his nomination.[30]

It took more than four months and many hours of Senate hearings before Brandeis was confirmed. His nomination, however, set a new precedent for group involvement in the nomination process. Although the levels of participation rarely reached the fever pitch of the Brandeis nomination, in 1930 interest groups including the NAACP lobbied successfully to block the nomination of Judge John Parker to the Court because of his controversial views on race. Other interest groups also involved themselves in particularly controversial nominations such as Richard M. Nixon's selections of Judges Clement Haynsworth and G. Harrold Carswell in 1969 and 1970, respectively.[31]

The nominations of Robert Bork (1987) and Clarence Thomas (1990) ushered in a new era in interest group involvement in judicial nominations, and the kind of attention interest groups paid to these nominees continues to be the benchmark today. Each of these judges, however, was criticized for very different reasons. Bork, whose nomination was ultimately withdrawn by President Ronald Reagan, drew fire because many observers viewed him as an ideological extremist. In contrast, Thomas received negative attention because some people considered him less qualified than many other nominees—the American Bar

To express their views on cases being heard by the Supreme Court, interested parties submit amicus briefs in hopes of swaying justices' opinions. Rev. Rob Schenck, president of the Christian group Faith and Action, which had submitted two briefs, prays in front of the Court while the justices hear a case dealing with the display of the Ten Commandments in government buildings.

TABLE 9.1 **American Bar Association Rating of Supreme Court Nominees, 1956–2010**

Nominee	Year	ABA rating (vote)
William Brennan Jr.	1956	Eminently qualified (unanimous)
Charles Whitaker	1957	Eminently qualified (unanimous)
Potter Stewart	1959	Exceptionally well qualified (10–1)
Byron White	1962	Exceptionally well qualified (unanimous)
Arthur Goldberg	1962	Highly acceptable from the standpoint of professional qualifications
Abe Fortas	1965	Highly acceptable from the viewpoint of professional qualifications
Thurgood Marshall	1967	Highly acceptable from the viewpoint of professional qualifications
Abe Fortas (chief justice)	1968	Highly acceptable from the viewpoint of professional qualifications
Homer Thornberry	1968	Highly acceptable from the viewpoint of professional qualifications (unanimous)
Warren Burger	1969	Highly acceptable from the viewpoint of professional qualifications (unanimous)
Clement Haynsworth Jr.	1969	Highly acceptable from the viewpoint of professional qualifications (unanimous)
G. Harrold Carswell	1970	Qualified (unanimous)
Harry Blackmun	1970	Meeting high standards of professional competence, temperament, and integrity (unanimous)
Lewis Powell Jr.	1971	In an exceptional degree meets high standards of professional competence, judicial temperament, and integrity, and is one of the best qualified lawyers available for appointment to the Supreme Court (unanimous)
William Rehnquist	1971	Unanimously qualified (9 well qualified, 3 not opposed)
John Paul Stevens	1975	Meets high standards of professional competence, judicial temperament, and integrity (unanimous)
Sandra Day O'Connor	1981	The committee is of the opinion that Judge O'Connor meets the highest standards of judicial temperament and integrity. Her professional experience to date has not been as extensive or challenging as that of some other persons who might be available for appointment to the Supreme Court of the United States. Nevertheless, after considering her outstanding academic record, her demonstrated intelligence, and her service as a legislator, a lawyer, and a trial and appellate judge, the committee is of the opinion that she is qualified from the standpoint of professional competence for appointment to the Supreme Court of the United States.
William Rehnquist (chief justice)	1986	Well qualified (unanimous)
Antonin Scalia	1986	Well qualified (unanimous)
Robert Bork	1987	Well qualified (10 well qualified, 1 not opposed, 4 not qualified)
Anthony Kennedy	1987	Well qualified (unanimous)
David Souter	1990	Well qualified (unanimous)
Clarence Thomas	1991	Qualified (12 qualified, 2 not qualified, 1 recusal)
Ruth Bader Ginsburg	1993	Well qualified (unanimous)
Stephen Breyer	1994	Well qualified (unanimous)
John G. Roberts Jr.	2005	Well qualified (unanimous)
John G. Roberts Jr. (chief justice)	2005	Well qualified (unanimous)
Harriet E. Miers	2005	No rating
Samuel A. Alito Jr.	2005	Well qualified (unanimous with one recusal)
Sonia Sotomayor	2009	Well qualified (unanimous)
Elena Kagan	2010	Well qualified (unanimous with one abstention)

NOTE: The American Bar Association's Committee on the Federal Judiciary began rating Supreme Court nominees in 1956. At various points in its history, the committee altered its rating categories, making comparisons across time difficult. This table includes the unofficial ratings given to Supreme Court nominees. The American Bar Association does not issue an official list of such ratings. Committee votes are provided when such data are available.

SOURCE: Updated from Lee Epstein, Jeffrey A. Segal, Harold J. Spaeth, and Thomas G. Walker, *The Supreme Court Compendium: Data, Decisions, and Developments*, 4th ed. (Washington, D.C.: CQ Press, 2007). Data compiled from the American Bar Association and numerous secondary sources.

Association gave him a relatively low "qualified" rating, and because he had very little judicial experience. Thomas also was accused of sexual indiscretions, most notably by Anita Hill, who had worked for Thomas at the Equal Employment Opportunity Commission. Despite these accusations, Thomas's nomination was approved, but by a very close vote in the Senate.

Now, let us look at the types of interest groups that participated in these contentious battles. A wide array of liberal interest groups actively opposed Bork's confirmation; these groups included the American Civil Liberties Union, the AFL-CIO, and a number of pro-choice groups. Simultaneously, a coalition of conservative, religious, and criminal justice groups, such as the American Conservative Union and the Moral Majority, mobilized to support him.[32] Both sides focused their initial efforts on grassroots mobilization, asking their members and sympathizers to contact their representatives and senators. They eventually turned to newspaper, radio, and television advertisements to broaden their message.

During the Thomas nomination, many of the most vocal critics were feminist groups, especially the National Organization for Women (NOW). Another critic of Thomas's nomination was the NAACP, which felt that despite his race, Thomas's criticisms of affirmative action policies would hinder their agenda. These criticisms put many black Americans, particularly women, in a precarious position. They favored an African American justice to replace the departing Thurgood Marshall, and they did not believe that President George H. W. Bush would nominate another black American if the Thomas nomination failed. But they questioned Thomas's loyalty to their political agenda and were reluctant to dismiss Hill's accusations.

More recently, the nominations of Chief Justice John G. Roberts (2005) and Justices Samuel Alito (2006), Sonia Sotomayor (2009), and Elena Kagan (2010) have been less controversial and, perhaps as a result, have not garnered a different type of interest group participation from that seen in the Bork and Thomas hearings. Aware of interest group activity and the rigor of Senate hearings, recent presidents have, except for President George W. Bush in his choice of Harriet Miers, vetted their nominees more thoroughly. The result has been less controversy for groups to use in their public relations campaigns.

In addition, the Senate Judiciary Committee has taken greater action to limit the more visible formal role of interest group testimony in the nomination process. During Sotomayor's Senate confirmation process, a record 218 groups submitted some form of testimony; however, representatives from only five liberal and three conservative groups were among the witnesses formally called to testify.[33]

Interest groups have also become increasingly visible in the confirmation hearings for judges nominated to the federal circuit and district courts. Realizing the policymaking power of these judgeships and that these judges often become part of the judicial pipeline, groups have begun to oppose controversial nominees earlier in the process. George W. Bush's nominations of controversial conservative judges, such as Priscilla Owen and Miguel Estrada, attracted a great deal of attention from liberal and conservative groups alike.

Judicial Elections

In the last ten to fifteen years, interest groups have also become active in state supreme court elections. Critics of this activity charge that this growth is one of the most significant factors explaining the rising cost of judicial elections. As retired justice Sandra Day O'Connor stated in a 2008 interview with *Parade* magazine:

> Political pressure is a big problem in a number of our state courts. More than 89 percent of state judges go through some form of election process. Many of these elections recently have become full-fledged political battles, fueled by growing sums of money spent by candidates and special-interest groups to attack, defend and counterattack.[34]

Interest group involvement in a number of states (many of them using partisan judicial elections) has also been criticized for its perceived effect on case outcomes.[35] In 1998 Chief Justice Pascal Calogero of the Louisiana Supreme Court was facing a tight reelection campaign. During this campaign, he received donations from Shintech, a Japanese chemical company that was facing a lawsuit from a group of low-income citizens who wanted to stop the construction of a new plant in their area. Because they were unable to afford their own representation, the citizens initially sought assistance from the law clinic at Tulane University. But, this assistance would be short-lived—in June of 1998, the court on which Calogero served changed the rules regarding the types of parties law clinics could represent in class action lawsuits, effectively eliminating Tulane's ability to represent the concerned citizens and allowing construction of the chemical plant to go forward. Critics of this decision quickly charged that Calogero's action had been bought.[36]

Ten years later, the U.S. Supreme Court was asked to consider the legal and ethical implications of a similar case in West Virginia. During the 2004 elections, A. T. Massey Coal Company spent $3 million on Brent Benjamin's successful bid for a seat on the court. A few months later, a case involving Massey was argued before the Court. Judge Benjamin did not recuse himself. Instead, he cast the deciding vote in a 3–2 decision in favor of Massey, a decision that awarded the company a victory valued at more than $50 million.[37]

The Court's 2009 decision in *Caperton v. Massey* concluded that such cases posed a "serious risk of actual bias—based on objective and reasonable perceptions—when a person with a personal stake in a particular case had a significant and disproportionate influence in placing the judge on the case by raising funds or directing the judge's election campaign when the case was pending or imminent."[38] Therefore, the Court reasoned, Judge Benjamin should have recused himself from the decision. The effects of the decision have not yet been fully realized, although it is unlikely that this decision alone will quell the influence of interest groups in state court elections.

Justice Brent Benjamin of the West Virginia Court of Appeals found himself at the center of a dispute that reached the U.S. Supreme Court. Benjamin had refused to recuse himself from a case involving a coal mining company that had donated heavily to his judicial election campaign. The Court ruled that there was a significant enough risk for bias that Benjamin should have recused himself.

WHY DO GROUPS PARTICIPATE?

As we have discussed, groups make great efforts to influence the composition of the courts. This activity has become common as groups have realized just how significant the judges making the decisions can be to influencing case outcomes. But nominations are not the only venue for interest group involvement in the judiciary. In addition to attempting to influence courts' composition, groups also participate before the courts. Popular wisdom dictates that they do so for two principal reasons: an interest in achieving policy change and the desire to maintain their organization by attracting publicity and membership.[39]

Achieving Policy Change

Influencing policy outcomes is perhaps the primary goal of many groups that participate before the courts.[40] Groups who participate as sponsors and amici have somewhat different strategies and goals. We consider each of these separately.

Sponsorship

Anecdotal evidence throughout this chapter suggests that interest groups' efforts to sponsor litigation campaigns may be a successful way to achieve legal change. The NAACP LDF achieved its goal of desegregating public education through a series of victories before the Supreme Court. Believing that they would achieve more by gradually bringing down the system rather than aiming directly for public elementary and secondary schools, the LDF began its efforts to challenge segregation first in law schools, an issue they felt judges could easily understand, in *Missouri ex rel. v. Canada* (1938) and *Sweatt v. Painter* (1950), and later graduate schools in *McLaurin v. Oklahoma* (1950). It was only after achieving victories in these cases that they turned to elementary and secondary education.

Brown v. Board of Education was part of this carefully planned litigation strategy. The case, as it reached the Court, was a combination of lower court decisions that the LDF had selected and shepherded through the process to show the range of states and individuals facing segregation in education. *Brown* came out of Topeka, Kansas, and the other cases originated in Delaware, South Carolina, Virginia, and Washington, D.C.

The NAACP's successes with desegregation litigation inspired other groups to follow the case sponsorship strategy. During her days at the American Civil Liberties Union's Women's Rights Project, Ruth Bader Ginsburg, who was appointed to the Court in 1993, successfully used case sponsorship and planned litigation in cases such as *Frontiero v. Richardson* (1973), *Weinberger v. Wiesenfeld* (1975), and *Craig v. Boren* (1976) to achieve greater rights for women. Latino/a groups such as the Mexican American Legal Defense and Educational Fund and the League of United Latin American Citizens also have used case sponsorship to win greater rights for Spanish-speaking citizens and immigrants in the areas of voting and education, in cases such as *LULAC v. Perry* (2006) and *San Antonio Independent School District v. Rodriguez* (1973). And, more recently, abortion groups on both sides of the question have used planned litigation and sponsored cases designed to either preserve or erode the Court's decision in *Roe v. Wade* (1973).[41]

Amicus Curiae Briefs

Previous research has found that groups use amicus curiae briefs to try to affect Supreme Court policy outcomes in several distinct ways. One study divides these efforts into two major categories: (1) an informational role and (2) a signaling role.[42] Interest groups wishing to inform the

The NAACP Legal Defense and Educational Fund, started in 1940 under the leadership of Thurgood Marshall, used the courts as an avenue for social and policy change. Their legal victory in the 1954 case of **Brown v. Board of Education**, *was a landmark in the fight against segregation. Here, attorneys George E. C. Hayes, left, Thurgood Marshall, center, and James M. Nabrit, leave the Supreme Court after the* **Brown** *opinion was handed down.*

justices may see amicus briefs as an opportunity to move beyond the issues highlighted in the party briefs. They may provide the judiciary with unique information congruent with the group's ideal policy preferences or provide the Court with additional information about the potential consequences of its decision.

James F. Spriggs and Paul J. Wahlbeck have examined the informational role of amicus curiae at the Supreme Court in substantial detail.[43] They found that more than 60 percent of amicus briefs filed before the Court during its 1992 term contained information not discussed in the party briefs, and 25 percent contained entirely new information. Although the justices did not often cite briefs that contained solely unique information, arguments from briefs that blended information from party briefs were adopted quite frequently. More recent work by Paul Collins has supplemented these conclusions.[44] These results are discussed in greater detail below.

The second role of amicus briefs, that of a signal to the Court, is also significant. At the certiorari stage, when the Court is choosing which cases to hear, justices may be uncertain about which cases most merit review. One or more amicus briefs may help to amplify the significance of a case. This kind of brief solves an information problem for the justices by signaling them about a case's public or political importance, as well as citizens' opinions about these concerns. In an analysis of all certiorari petitions filed during the Court's 1982 term, Caldeira and Wright found further evidence that cases supported by one or more amicus brief at certiorari are more likely than other similar cases to be granted review.[45]

Organizational Maintenance

In addition to policy change, interest groups may also participate before the courts to pursue organizational maintenance by using their involvement in court cases to get publicity, to claim credit, to attract the attention (and money) of constituents, and to solicit new members or donors.[46]

In a survey of interest groups participating before the Supreme Court during its 1982 term, Caldeira and Wright found substantial evidence that organizational maintenance matters to at least some of the groups. More than 30 percent of business, trade, and professional organizations responded that filing an amicus brief was very important to "keeping their members happy." Almost 40 percent said that such participation was essential to avoiding conflict within the organization.[47]

Groups can engage in organizational maintenance activities in connection with any Supreme Court case, but this strategy may be particularly effective in highly salient cases.[48] Constituents are more likely to be aware of salient issues, and groups can more easily mobilize, raise funds, and garner praise in these cases. In fact, the highest levels of interest group participation as amicus curiae (measured both in briefs and individual groups) have been seen in cases that have addressed politically volatile issues and garnered high levels of national attention. Examples include the 1989 abortion case of *Webster v. Reproductive Health Services* and the 2003 affirmative action cases involving the University of Michigan, *Grutter v. Bollinger* and *Gratz v. Bollinger*, both of which set records for their high levels of interest group participation.

Influencing the Composition of the Courts

The joint goals of policy change and organizational maintenance extend to participation in the nomination process. Some scholars have posited that organizational maintenance may be groups' primary motivation for involvement in confirmation hearings.[49] But groups still maintain their goals to creating policy change. By influencing the judges that sit on a court, groups can also influence the decisions made by that court.

TABLE 9.2 **Friends of the Court: Amicus Participation in *McDonald v. City of Chicago* (2010)**

For the Petitioner, *McDonald*	For the Respondent, *City of Chicago*	For Neither Party
Rutherford Institute	Educational Fund to Stop Gun Violence	Brady Center to Prevent Gun Violence et al.
Paragon Foundation	Members of Congress	NAACP Legal Defense and Educational Fund
Heartland Institute	English/Early American Historians	
CATO Institute and Pacific Legal Foundation	Professors of Criminal Justice	
Buckeye Firearms Foundation and the United States	American Cities et al.	
Concealed Carry Foundation	United States Conference of Mayors	
State Legislators	Organizations Committed to Protecting the Public's Health, Safety and Well-Being	
Professors of Philosophy and Criminology	American States	
Members of Congress	Historians and Legal Scholars (2)	
Foundation for Moral Law	Historians on Early American Legal, Constitutional, and Pennsylvania History	
National Shooting Sports Foundation	Law Professor and Students	
Jews for the Preservation of Firearms Ownership	Association of Prosecuting Attorneys and District Attorneys	
Arms Keeper	Illinois Cities et al.	
Academics for the Second Amendment	Board of Education of the City of Chicago et al.	
Center for Constitutional Jurisprudence	Oak Park Citizens Committee for Handgun Control	
American Center for Law and Justice	Anti-Defamation League	
Maryland Arms Collectors' Association		
Calguns Foundation		
State Criminal Justice Officers		
American Legislative Exchange Council		
Goldwater Institute and Wyoming Liberty Group		
Institute for Justice		
Safari Club International		
Gun Owners of America et al.		
Eagle Forum LDF		
International Law Enforcement Educators et al.		
State Governments		
Rocky Mountain Gun Owners and National Association for Gun Rights		
Constitutional Law Professors		
State Firearm Associations		
American Civil Rights Union et al.		
Appellants in *Nordyke v. King*		

Because the Senate has the power of advice and consent during the confirmation process, substantial portions of groups' lobbying efforts are targeted toward members of that body, especially those on the Senate Judiciary Committee. Caldeira and Wright argue that groups have three goals as they try to influence senators' votes. First, groups aim to alter constituent opinion, as senators who vote against the perceived will of voters in their states have often faced electoral consequences. Second, groups want to organize constituents to engage in grassroots lobbying efforts. The volume of contact from citizens helps members to gauge the nomination's importance. Finally, groups provide information directly to senators about the nominee's previous decisions. This informational role includes garnering invitations to appear before the committee as a witness.[50]

Notably, analyses have shown that groups' methods and goals of participation in judicial nominations vary little across courts and time. Regardless of whether the nomination is for a lower federal court, the Supreme Court, or the U.S. Department of Justice, groups appear to engage in similar lobbying activities and to be driven by the same goals of policy change and organizational maintenance.[51]

Are Interest Groups Successful in the Courts?

The findings of studies evaluating interest group success in the courts are as varied as the groups that participate in the judiciary. In the sections that follow, we consider some of

SHOULD INTEREST GROUPS PLAY A ROLE IN THE JUDICIAL NOMINATION PROCESS?

Since the nominations of Robert Bork and Clarence Thomas in the 1980s, interest groups have come to play a greater role in judicial nominations, both at the Supreme Court and appellate court levels. Groups use judicial nominations as an opportunity to influence the composition of the judiciary, alter the course of public policy, and raise visibility for their cause.

Should interest groups play any role at all in the judicial nomination process? On one hand, interest groups provide a voice for citizens in the advice and consent process. They provide senators with important information on citizens' concerns regarding federal judicial nominees—political appointees who serve lifetime terms. Interest groups may also conduct research and consider policy implications that Senate staffers and executive branch officials may not have the time or the expertise to evaluate.

On the other hand, the ideal of blind justice demands that the Senate's approval of judicial nominations should be based on qualifications, judicial skills, and legal knowledge. Public opinion or a nominee's personal beliefs about issues that may come before the courts should be irrelevant. Allowing interest groups to play an active role in the nomination process may encourage greater ideological and political conflict, as evidenced by battles over recent nominees' beliefs regarding abortion and gun control.

the research evaluating groups' success in achieving policy change, carrying out organizational maintenance, and influencing the composition of the courts.

Conventional wisdom, especially in the 1960s and 1970s, suggests that the Supreme Court played a dynamic role in putting issues on the national agenda and creating social change.[52] Gerald N. Rosenberg, however, argued that the Court is a constrained policy actor whose decisions have limited effects. In this view, even if interest groups are victorious, their ability to use their victories to achieve policy change may be an effort in vain.[53] Rosenberg pointed out that the justices are bound by their docket, the rules of the legal system, and the checks and balances of the American political system. To this end, he offered evidence that the Court's decisions do not cause major changes in public opinion, issue salience, or policy. Rosenberg further suggested that because the Court lacks a concrete ability to enforce its decisions, executive and legislative involvement and economic and technological changes are more significant in changing social and political conditions than the decisions of the Supreme Court.

One specific illustration of interest groups' inability to use the Court to influence public policy, according to Rosenberg, occurred in the years following *Roe v. Wade* (1973). Despite the decision's liberalizing effect on abortion policies, Rosenberg found no significant increase in the concrete policy goals pursued by pro-choice groups, such as the percentage of hospitals providing abortions. In addition, using newspaper and magazine coverage from 1940 to 1976, Rosenberg found that the abortion issue's salience did not increase immediately after the Court's decision.[54]

Another vein of scholarship takes a narrower view of interest groups' ability to influence public policies. Rather than looking for evidence of interest group influence on broad areas of public policy, these researchers look for evidence of organizational influence on case outcomes and justices' votes. On the whole, these studies have offered a more positive view on the success of interest groups before the courts.

Paul M. Collins studied the influence of amicus briefs on Supreme Court decision making over approximately fifty years. His analysis showed that regardless of a judge's or interest group's ideology, justices were more likely to vote for a particular party as the number of amicus briefs filed on behalf of that party increased. Collins also demonstrated that a growing number of amicus briefs in a case can compel justices to vote against their traditional policy preferences. Finally, he showed that increasing the number of amicus briefs filed in a case can increase the number of opinions filed by the justices.[55]

Collins's results are consistent with the findings of scholars who examine lower courts. Donald Songer and Ashlyn Kuersten, found that litigants supported by amicus curiae briefs in state supreme courts had greater success than parties that did not have amicus support. These findings held true regardless of whether the amicus supported a petitioner or a respondent.[56]

Organizational Maintenance

Although fewer than 30 percent of Supreme Court cases—and much smaller percentages of lower federal and state court decisions—receive media attention, judicial decisions generally are prime opportunities for groups to reach out to their members.[57] Even cases that do not receive a great deal of media attention, such as procedural corporate law decisions, may be interesting to a small clientele; it is up to the interest groups representing these individuals to lobby the Court and claim credit for their activities. As interest groups participate in about 90 percent of Supreme Court decisions, it is a relatively safe bet that these activities are occurring in earnest.[58]

Groups reap many benefits from attracting members' attention during the judicial deliberation process. Pro-choice groups used the Court's 1989 decision in *Webster v. Reproductive Health Services* as an opportunity to organize a march on Washington, D.C., that was attended by more than 400,000 people. Many of these individuals provided mailing addresses and contact information that groups could use to get in touch with them for years to come.[59]

The judicial process similarly inspired pro-life activists in the months and years following *Webster.* Scholars such as Suzanne Staggenborg have asserted that the growth of the direct action movement at abortion clinics (for example, clinic protestors) was a direct result of the Court's decision. These scholars argue that this decision got the attention of average citizens who would not have otherwise considered the abortion issue at the center of their lives.[60]

More generally, political scientists have demonstrated that at least some Supreme Court decisions can increase the salience and alter public opinion on political issues.[61] These changes in attention and beliefs are essential to groups' broader ability to maintain their existence. The results are far from universal, but they may explain why groups put so much stock in participation in Supreme Court cases dealing with constitutional issues, particularly those relating to civil rights and liberties.

Influencing the Composition of the Courts

It is difficult to evaluate how successful groups are in influencing the composition of the Court, in large part because there are two sides to every nomination battle, and in each, one side must win, and one side must necessarily lose. So, while liberal groups achieved an extraordinary victory in their effort to defeat the nomination of Robert Bork, conservative groups achieved a similar victory in the confirmation of Clarence Thomas.

Groups' ability to use nominations as opportunities for organizational maintenance have much more consistent outcomes. Even the liberal groups that failed to defeat the Thomas nomination, most notably NOW, saw their membership and financial resources increase tremendously as the Senate debated the nomination.[62] Moreover, because abortion has become somewhat of a litmus test for judicial nominees, mentions of abortion groups in the media inevitably rise with each Supreme Court nominee. Media attention provides pro-life and pro-choice groups with a great deal of free publicity that can be used to mobilize old members and attract new ones. Nevertheless, even these results may vary with the visibility of the court and the judge being nominated. Nominees to the Supreme Court garner more attention than nominees to the federal district courts. Controversial nominees also attract more publicity than those who are highly qualified and ideologically neutral.[63]

CONCLUSION

This chapter has explored interest group participation in the judiciary, examining which groups participate, how they participate, and why they participate. The chapter also evaluated organizations' success in lobbying the courts. The evidence indicates that the groups that lobby the judiciary are different in important ways from their counterparts that lobby the executive and legislative branches, often possessing different skills, concerned with unique issues, and performing different cost-benefit analyses.

Although a great deal about interest group involvement in the courts has been learned, there remains much to pursue in the effort to understand interest group litigation. Political scientists studying interest groups and the courts should continue to untangle the nuances of the conditions under which groups are most successful in lobbying the courts, as well as to better understand what drives group participation. Are there, for example, particular issue areas or types of cases in which interest groups are most successful at achieving policy change or organizational maintenance? How do groups measure their own success in lobbying the courts?

One way scholars might begin to answer these questions is by better integrating work about interest groups by judicial politics researchers and interest group researchers. With a few exceptions (such as Walker, Schlozman and Tierney, and Strolovitch), comparatively few researchers who examine interest groups and the courts are primarily scholars of interest groups. As a consequence, the study of interest groups and the courts has become somewhat of a niche pursuit in judicial politics, rather than part of the broader interest groups universe. The dynamics of interest group participation vary across branches, and groups' decisions to lobby the judiciary affect how they lobby other branches; therefore, taking a broader look at many of these questions might also provide us with a different understanding of interest group litigation.

Efforts also should be made to move beyond examinations of how interest groups lobby the Supreme Court to explore groups' attempt to influence lower federal and state courts. With the increasing availability of data on both litigation campaigns and lower courts, studies of these other judicial venues and longitudinal analyses are more possible today than in the past. Understanding if and how groups plan litigation campaigns across courts and time will give us a better idea of how groups allocate their resources in the effort to influence public policy.

Although there is still much to learn about interest groups and the courts, there is also much to admire about the current state of scholarship in this area. A great deal is known about amicus participation before the Supreme Court, for example, and scholars have produced a relatively clear understanding of the incentives that shape groups' participation in the Court. The challenge now is to expand this knowledge to areas such as group success, as well as to broaden explorations across courts and subfields so that we might better comprehend the inputs and outputs of the political system.

NOTES

1. Elizabeth Cady Stanton, Susan B. Anthony, and Matilda Joslyn Gage, eds., *The History of Woman Suffrage*, vol. 2 (New York: Fowler and Wells, 1882), 586.

2. This vignette draws heavily from Karen O'Connor, *Women's Organizations' Use of the Courts* (Lexington, Mass.: Lexington Books, 1980).

3. Marc Galanter, "Why the Haves Come Out Ahead: Speculations on the Limits of Legal Change," *Law and Society Review* 9 (1974): 95–160.

4. *United States* v. *Carolene Products*, 304 U.S. 144 (1938).

5. Clement E. Vose, *Caucasians Only* (Berkeley: University of California Press, 1959).

6. Jack Greenberg, *Judicial Process and Social Change: Constitutional Litigation* (St. Paul: West Publishing, 1977); Richard Kluger, *Simple Justice: The History of* Brown v. Board of Education *and Black America's Struggle for Equality* (New York: Alfred A. Knopf, 1976); Greenberg, *Crusaders in the Courts: How a Dedicated Band of Lawyers Fought for the Civil Rights Revolution* (New York: Basic Books, 1994).

7. Richard C. Cortner, "Strategies and Tactics of Litigants in Constitutional Cases," *Journal of Public Law* 17 (1968): 287–307.

8. Michael Meltsner, *Cruel and Unusual: The Supreme Court and Capital Punishment* (New York: Random House, 1972).

9. Karen O'Connor and Lee Epstein, "A Legal Voice for the Chicano Community: The Mexican American Legal Defense and Education Fund, 1968–1982," *Social Science Quarterly* 65 (1984): 245–256.

10. O'Connor, *Women's Organizations' Use.*

11. Petra T. Shattuck and Jill Norgren, "Political Use of the Legal Process by Black and American Indian Minorities," *Howard Law Journal* 22 (1979): 1–26.

12. Galanter, "Why the Haves Come Out Ahead," 98.

13. Ibid.

14. Donald R. Songer, Reginald S. Sheehan, and Susan Brodie Haire, "Do the Haves Come Out Ahead Over Time? Applying Galanter's Framework to the Courts of Appeals, 1925–1988," in *In Litigation: Do the "Haves" Still Come Out Ahead?* eds. Herbert M. Kritzer and Susan Silbey (Stanford, Calif.: Stanford University Press, 2003), 85–107; Donald R. Songer, Ashlyn Kuersten, and Erin Kaheny, "Why the Haves Don't Always Come Out Ahead: Repeat Players Meet Amici Curiae for the Disadvantaged," *Political Research Quarterly* 53 (2000): 537–556.

15. Herbert M. Kritzer, "The Government Gorilla: Why Does Government Come Out Ahead in Appellate Courts?," *In Litigation*, 342–370.

16. Elisabeth R. Gerber, *The Populist Paradox* (Princeton: Princeton University Press, 1999).

17. Kay Lehman Schlozman and John T. Tierney, *Organized Interests and American Democracy* (New York: Harper Collins, 1986); Frank R. Baumgartner and Beth A. Leech, *Basic Interests: The Importance of Groups in Politics and in Political Science* (Princeton: Princeton University Press, 1998).

18. Gregory A. Caldeira and John R. Wright, "Amici Curiae Before the Supreme Court: Who Participates, When, and How Much?" *Journal of Politics* 52 (1990): 782–806.

19. Paul M. Collins Jr. and Lisa A. Solowiej, "Interest Group Participation, Competition, and Conflict in the U.S. Supreme Court," *Law and Social Inquiry* 32 (2007): 955–984.

20. Dara Z. Strolovitch, *Affirmative Advocacy: Race, Class, and Gender in Interest Group Politics* (Chicago: University of Chicago Press, 2007).

21. Arthur Bentley, *The Process of Government* (Cambridge: Belknap Press of Harvard University Press, 1908).

22. Richard C. Cortner, *The Supreme Court and Civil Liberties Policy* (Palo Alto, Calif.: Mayfield, 1975).

23. Samuel Krislov, "The Amicus Brief: From Friendship to Advocacy," *Yale Law Journal* 72 (1963): 694–721.

24. Nathan Hakman, "Lobbying the Supreme Court: An Appraisal of Political Science Folklore," *Fordham Law Review* 35 (1969): 199.

25. Karen O'Connor and Lee Epstein, "Amicus Curiae Participation in U.S. Supreme Court Litigation: An Appraisal of Hakman's Folklore," *Law and Society Review* 16 (1982): 311–320.

26. Ryan J. Owens and Lee Epstein, "Amicus Curiae during the Rehnquist Years," *Judicature* 89 (2005): 129.

27. Joseph D. Kearney and Thomas W. Merrill, "The Influence of Amicus Curiae Briefs on the Supreme Court," *University of Pennsylvania Law Review* 143 (2000): 748–854.

28. Wendy L. Martinek, "Amici Curiae in the U.S. Courts of Appeals," *American Politics Research* 34 (2006): 803–824.

29. Lee Epstein, "Exploring the Participation of Organized Interests in State Court Litigation," *Political Research Quarterly* 47 (1994): 335–351.

30. Paul A. Freund, "Essays on the Supreme Court Appointment Process: Appointment of Justices: Some Historical Perspectives," *Harvard Law Review* 101 (1988): 1146–63.

31. John Anthony Maltese, "The Selling of Clement Haynsworth: Politics and the Confirmation of Supreme Court Justices," *Judicature* 72 (1989): 339–347.

32. Norman Viera and Leonard Gross, *Supreme Court Appointments: Judge Bork and the Politicization of Senate Confirmations* (Carbondale: Southern Illinois University Press, 1998).

33. Senate Judiciary Committee, "The Nomination of Sonia Sotomayor to be an Associate Justice of the Supreme Court of the United States," http://judiciary.senate.gov/hearings/hearing.cfm?id=3959; Amy Harder and Charlie Szymanski, "Sotomayor in Context: Unprecedented Input from Interest Groups," *National Journal*, August 5, 2009.

34. Sandra Day O'Connor, "How to Save Our Courts," *Parade*, http://www.parade.com/articles/editions/2008/edition_02-24-2008/Courts_O_Connor.

35. Vernon V. Palmer and John Levendis, "The Louisiana Supreme Court in Question: An Empirical and Statistical Study of

the Effects of Campaign Money on the Judicial Function," *Tulane Law Review* 82 (2008): 1291–1314.

36. CBS News, "Justice for Sale," *Sixty Minutes,* March 24, 2000, http://www.cbsnews.com/stories/2000/03/24/60II/main175831.shtml.

37. Gretchen Mae Stone, "U.S. Supreme Court Hears Caperton Case," *The State Journal,* March 5, 2009, http://statejournal.com/story.cfm?func=viewstory&storyid=53651.

38. *Caperton* v. *A. T. Massey Coal Company,* 556 U.S. ______ (2009).

39. See, for example Martinek, "Amici Curiae in the U.S. Courts of Appeals;" Scott A. Comparato, *Amici Curiae and Strategic Behavior in State Supreme Courts* (Westport, Conn.: Praeger Publishers, 2003).

40. Lee Epstein and C. K. Rowland, "Debunking the Myth of Interest Group Invincibility in the Courts," *American Political Science Review* 85 (1991): 205–217; Thomas G. Hansford, "Lobbying Strategies, Venue Selection and Organized Interest Involvement at the U.S. Supreme Court," *American Politics Research* 32 (2004): 170–197; Rorie Spill Solberg and Eric N. Waltenburg, "Why do Interest Groups Engage the Judiciary? Policy Wishes and Structural Needs," *Social Science Quarterly* 87 (2006): 558–572.

41. Not all scholars are convinced that interest groups are important to determining case outcomes. See Steven C. Tauber, "On Behalf of the Condemned: The Impact of the NAACP Legal Defense Fund on Capital Punishment Decision Making on the U.S. Courts of Appeals," *Political Research Quarterly* 51 (1998): 191–218.

42. Victor E. Flango, Donald C. Bross, and Sarah Corbally, "Amicus Curiae Briefs: The Court's Perspective," *Justice System Journal* 27 (2006): 180–190.

43. James E. Spriggs and Paul J. Wahlbeck, "Amicus Curiae and the Role of Information at the U.S. Supreme Court," *Political Research Quarterly* 50 (1997): 365–386.

44. Paul M. Collins, *Friends of the Supreme Court: Interest Groups and Judicial Decision Making* (New York: Oxford University Press, 2008).

45. Gregory A. Caldeira and John R. Wright, "Organized Interests and Agenda Setting in the United States Supreme Court," *American Political Science Review* 82 (1988): 1109–1127.

46. Joseph F. Kobylka, "A Court-Created Context for Groups' Litigation: Libertarian Groups and Obscenity," *Journal of Politics* 49 (1987): 1061–78; Gregory A. Caldeira and John R. Wright, "Why Organized Interests Participate as Amicus Curiae in the U.S. Supreme Court," paper presented at the 1995 annual meeting of the American Political Science Association, Atlanta, Georgia; Stephen L. Wasby, *Race Relations Litigation in an Age of Complexity* (Charlottesville: University of Virginia Press, 1995).

47. Caldeira and Wright, "Why Organized Interests Participate."

48. Hansford, "Lobbying Strategies."

49. Lee Epstein, Rene Lindstadt, Jeffrey A. Segal, and Chad Westerland, "The Changing Dynamics of Senate Voting on Supreme Court Nominees," *Journal of Politics* 68 (2006): 296–307.

50. Gregory A. Caldeira and John R. Wright, "Lobbying for Justice: Organized Interests, Supreme Court Nominations, and United States Senate," *American Journal of Political Science* 42 (1998): 499–523.

51. Gregory A. Caldeira, Marie Hojnacki, and John R. Wright, "The Lobbying Activities of Organized Interests in Federal Judicial Nominations," *Journal of Politics* 62 (2000): 51–69.

52. C. Herman Pritchett, "Equal Protection and the Urban Majority," *American Political Science Review* 58 (1964): 869–875; Kluger, *Simple Justice;* Stephen L. Wasby, Anthony D'Amato, and Rosemary Metrailer, *Desegregation from Brown to Alexander* (Carbondale: Southern Illinois University Press, 1977); O'Connor, *Women's Organizations' Use.*

53. Rosenberg, *Hollow Hope.*

54. Ibid.

55. Collins, *Friends of the Supreme Court.*

56. Donald R. Songer and Ashlyn Kuersten, "The Success of Amici in State Supreme Courts," *Political Research Quarterly* 48 (1995): 31–42.

57. Linda Greenhouse, "Press Room Predictions," *Perspectives on Politics* 2 (2004): 781–784.

58. Kearney and Merrill, "Influence of Amicus Curiae Briefs."

59. Karen O'Connor, *No Neutral Ground: Abortion Politics in an Age of Absolutes* (Boulder: Westview Press, 1996).

60. Suzanne Staggenborg, *The Pro-Choice Movement: Organization and Activism in the Abortion Conflict* (New York: Oxford University Press, 1991).

61. Timothy Johnson and Andrew D. Martin, "The Public's Conditional Response to Supreme Court Decisions," *American Political Science Review* 92 (1998): 299; and Charles H. Franklin and Liane C. Kosaki, "The Republican School Master: The Supreme Court, Public Opinion, and Abortion," *American Political Science Review* 83 (1989): 751–771.

62. Ronald J. Hrebenar, Matthew Burbank, and Robert C. Benedict, *Political Parties, Interest Groups, and Political Campaigns* (Boulder: Westview Press, 1999).

63. Epstein et al., "Changing Dynamics."

SUGGESTED READING

Caldeira, Gregory A., and John R. Wright. "Amici Curiae Before the Supreme Court: Who Participates, When, and How Much?" *Journal of Politics* 52 (1990): 782–806.

Collins, Paul M. *Friends of the Supreme Court.* New York: Oxford University Press, 2008.

Epstein, Lee, Rene Lindstadt, Jeffrey A. Segal, and Chad Westerland. "The Changing Dynamics of Senate Voting on Supreme Court Nominees." *Journal of Politics* 68 (2006): 296–307.

Galanter, Marc. "Why the Haves Come Out Ahead: Speculations on the Limits of Legal Change." *Law and Society Review* 9 (1974): 95–160.

Hansford, Thomas G. "Lobbying Strategies, Venue Selection, and Organized Interest Involvement at the U.S. Supreme Court." *American Politics Research* 32 (2004): 170–197.

Kearney, Joseph D., and Thomas W. Merrill. "The Influence of Amicus Curiae Briefs on the Supreme Court." *University of Pennsylvania Law Review* 143 (2000): 748–854.

O'Connor, Karen, and Lee Epstein. "Amicus Curiae Participation in the U.S. Supreme Court Litigation: An Appraisal of Hakman's Folklore." *Law and Society Review* 16 (1982): 311–320.

Strolovitch, Dara Z. *Affirmative Advocacy: Race, Class, and Gender in Interest Group Politics.* Chicago: University of Chicago Press, 2007.

Vose, Clement E. *Caucasians Only.* Berkeley: University of California Press, 1959.

chapter 10

Interest Groups and the Executive Branch

by Mark A. Peterson

When most people think about interest groups and the federal government, they probably conjure up images of lobbyists plying their trade in the ornate vestibules of Capitol Hill, in the public and private meeting rooms of committees and subcommittees, in the personal offices of members of Congress, and over culinary fare and libations at campaign fund-raising events. But because the executive branch does far more than implement legislative dictates—it is instrumental in galvanizing the congressional agenda, motivating and shaping individual bills, and filling in the expansive interpretive holes in vague statutory language—interest groups have an enormous stake, too, in influencing executive decision making. In turn, officials from the president of the United States on down to career civil servants in the bowels of federal bureaus gain advantage from having allies in the interest group community. The scope and nature of the interactions between interest groups and the executive branch are an all-too-often overlooked, but essential, feature of American government and policymaking.

How interest groups engage executive officials and how those officials relate to group representatives are, to be sure, quite different from what happens in Congress. Despite the increased security at the Capitol and House and Senate office buildings, they remain public spaces. Just about anyone can freely make his or her way to hearing rooms and member offices, or even buttonhole members or their staffs in the hallways. Representatives of corporations, trade associations, professional societies, and advocacy organizations with a significant presence in a legislator's constituency have little difficulty securing access, by appointment or sometimes by just showing up. The White House could not be more different. No one gets past its iron gates without an advance appointment and prearranged clearance. And while the Hill teems with wandering people, be they tourists, constituents, or working lobbyists, the lobby of the White House West Wing is decidedly decorous and muted, from the marine guard in dress uniform who greets one at the door to the quiet splendor of the room itself. In the White House complex, group representatives are often met en masse, channeled to staged forums in grand rooms such as the Indian Treaty Room. One-on-one sessions with presidential aides may be common for favored groups, but are not easily arranged. Even the agencies of the executive branch beyond the Executive Office of the President are far less easily penetrated than the domains in which senators and representatives conduct their business. And yet interest groups do find their way into the executive establishment, and policymaking ultimately reflects this additional pathway into government.

This chapter provides an overview of the two-way "outside-in" and "inside-out" flow in which interest groups interact with and attempt to have sway over decision making in the executive branch, from the office of the president to the myriad departments, bureaus, and independent agencies of the federal government, and executive branch officials seek to exploit these interactions to serve their own purposes.[1] It begins with a description of the resources that organized interests bring to the policymaking and implementation process. These political and programmatic assets ensure that groups cannot be gratuitously ignored in policy deliberations and often make them attractive partners for executive branch officials. They function as the keys to gain access to the parts of the government that require a formal invitation for entrée. With organized interests and officials poised to engage one another, their respective and overlapping objectives, both programmatic and political, which create opportunities for mutual advantage through collaboration and locate the potential points of conflict, are identified in this chapter. The remainder of the chapter examines the specific, strategically driven processes through which interest groups and officials in the executive branch interact, starting with the Executive Office of the President, and then moving to administrative and independent regulatory agencies.

THE INTEREST GROUP DOWRY

In the popular lexicon organized interests are commonly referred to as "special interests" or "pressure groups." Such

Representatives of the United Automobile Workers Union leave a meeting at the White House in 1938 with President Roosevelt. The union informed the president about the state of Michigan's auto workers and asked for millions of dollars of relief funds to Michigan's struggling residents.

terms underscore general perceptions that these organizations attempt to direct public-sector actions and extract taxpayer-financed resources to serve their individual interests—"rent-seeking," the economists call it—regardless of the consequences for the common good. One need only consider the political conduct of oil and coal producers in energy and environmental policy, teachers' unions in education policy, the insurance and pharmaceutical industries in health care policy, the contractors woven into the military-industrial complex in defense policy, among others, to see the resonance, and often legitimacy, of this portrayal. But even for those wishing to pursue the public interest, intent on crafting statutes and regulations that constitute workable and good public policies, many interest groups offer a dowry of valuable attributes that warrant their inclusion in executive branch policy deliberations. Organized interests may be disliked, but they cannot, even should not, be ignored.

To start, few public policies can be effective if powerful stakeholders refuse to participate or cooperate in their ultimate implementation. The productivity of the economy—and therefore the jobs and compensation on which all Americans depend—hinges on the decisions made by private firms large and small. Government, even as embodied in the president of the United States, can entice or discourage certain kinds of business behaviors, but it cannot command them.[2] This need for private-sector cooperation affords business, in particular, considerable leverage in policy deliberations. As with Congress, executive branch officials need to know whether various policy options will stimulate favorable responses from producers and employers or provoke resistance harmful to economic dynamism. For the administrations of Presidents George W. Bush and Barack Obama, preventing the "Great Recession" of the 2000s from becoming the next Great Depression, stemming the collapse of credit and financial institutions essential to economic performance, and finding a route to eventual job creation could not be accomplished without actively engaging the private sector. That is not to suggest that optimal policy necessarily emerges from these interactions, but it would be hard to imagine deriving an effective approach to government economic policymaking that entirely disregarded the likely defiance of the business community.

Moreover, interest groups can tender much more of substantive value to executive branch officials than merely what policy attributes would be necessary to secure their cooperation. In all policy domains, as with their legislative counterparts, presidents, political appointees, and bureaucrats operate in a realm of two kinds of uncertainty: the programmatic uncertainty of how a particular policy approach would actually work in the "real" world and the political uncertainty of how it would be perceived and acted upon by relevant constituencies.[3] Although they are far from having a monopoly on this information, interest groups of all kinds—from Fortune 500 companies to nonprofit service agencies to citizen-oriented advocacy organizations—can help executive branch officials understand the programmatic and political impacts of particular agenda issues, policy options, and regulatory details. As a complement to the analyses and experiential knowledge provided by experts in universities, think tanks, and the bureaucratic agencies themselves, representatives of interest groups can add substantially to the information that executive branch officials need to make effective decisions. Although policymakers should recognize the biases inherent in their perspectives and make the necessary adjustments, they should also acknowledge that school districts, universities, and teachers know something about education; airlines, railroads, truckers, state and local officials, and transit-associated consumer groups know something about transportation; physicians, nurses, hospitals, the AARP, and patient-advocacy organizations know something about health care—and the list goes on.

In addition, all of these interests include individuals who know well the needs, activities, and players relevant to the policy domain by virtue of their senior positions in companies, nonprofit institutions, or subnational governments. When presidential administrations are choosing the people to fill the ranks of political appointees throughout the executive branch, it is only natural that they often turn to individuals from the sphere of interest groups, albeit with predictable predilections: Democratic administrations are more likely to populate the Energy and Interior Departments with people experienced in the environmental movement, and Republicans will select those associated with the energy-producing industries.

Another asset that facilitates access of organized interests to the executive branch is their capacity to deliver political support to executive officials and agencies. Such political assistance can take on many forms. For the president there are certain parallels with members of Congress. Interest groups can direct substantial campaign contributions to a presidential candidate, especially if the public financing of the general election campaign erodes even further than it did in 2008, when Obama chose not to accept public funding. George W. Bush set a particularly striking example. For both his initial election and reelection, his nomination campaigns and inaugural ceremonies were supported by large sums raised from friendly industries and groups.[4] Interest groups also provide political enhancement, as well as protective cover, for presidents as they pursue their representational and programmatic priorities. The political backing that organized interests offer officials and agencies in the rest of the executive branch is necessarily far more nuanced. Not only are campaign dollars not involved, but also strict rules forbid agency officials from accepting anything of any value from groups and their representatives. But interest groups can improve the prospects of legislative ideas originating in executive agencies and give agencies and the existing programs they run credible protection from budgetary or oversight assault in Congress.

While acknowledging the benefits that organized interests can bring to executive branch policymaking, we should also recognize that this access is not uniformly available to all types of interests. As E. E. Schattschneider observed in 1960, formal organization represents a "mobilization of bias" in that organized interests reflect and give political heft to the skewed distribution of resources and capacity for effective organization that exist in the larger society.[5] For reasons addressed elsewhere in this book, petroleum companies are far more certain to come together in collective action, have larger scope for monitoring government actions, and have greater ability to plow money, analysis, and lobbyists into the policymaking process than are consumers of energy or advocates of environmental protections (see Chapters 4 and 7). In each policy domain, some groups remain "latent" without formal organization (consider the unemployed), or possess resource dowries too small to gain entry to the White House or executive agencies or to wield much influence in policymaking.[6] In the absence of laws intended to promote more balanced representation of interests in policy decision making—which do exist in some realms—and an energetic orientation of executive officials to seek out less-endowed interests, interest group engagement with the executive branch in policymaking and implementation risks producing further reinforcement of existing group advantages.

President Barack Obama speaks at the annual dinner of the Human Rights Campaign (HRC) in October 2009. During his campaign, Obama pledged to end the military's "Don't Ask, Don't Tell" policy, against which the HRC fervently lobbied.

OVERLAPPING OBJECTIVES

This summary of the assets that interest groups can bring to the policymaking process begins to reveal the potentially overlapping objectives of groups and executive branch officials. That sets the stage for exploring the various ways they actually interact across different settings within executive establishment.

The goals of interests and officials fall into two categories: programmatic and political. Programmatic objectives involve what the government should, can, and will do. They may entail wanting the government to act or intervene in certain ways or, instead, preferring that it not act and stay out of particular realms of the economy and society. Fulfilling either form of programmatic objectives engages the processes of agenda setting, lawmaking (including new policies pursued by the president using executive orders under the authority of existing statutes), and implementation (all forms of executive decision making that serve to activate and enforce the intent of lawmaking). Political objectives are more inward; they focus on the standing of organized interests and officials. They involve actions taken by other players in policymaking, and building relationships with them, that invigorate or safeguard the status of the interest group, agency, or official in the policymaking setting. The specific political needs of interests and officials vary tremendously across the different types of participants. Table 10.1 summarizes the programmatic and political objectives of organized interests and officials in three broad domains of the executive branch: the White House (shorthand for the Executive Office of the President), executive line-agencies, and independent regulatory commissions.[7]

Programmatic Objectives

Law and policy, as they are experienced by all elements of society, derive from three distinct features of the policymaking process: agenda setting, formal lawmaking, and rulemaking. Each is targeted, but in different ways, by organized interests and executive branch officials.

The Policymaking Agenda

Because their specific interests or their visions for the country are affected by actions of the federal government, organized interests have a strong incentive to try to influence which policy issues the government is actively considering. There are issues that organized interests would like the government to address (such as economic growth and job creation, energy production, strengthened defense, environmental protection, and the like), and other matters that some groups want the government of the day to ignore (such as climate change, regulation of financial institutions, undocumented immigrants, and abortion control). In the modern era, because the president has become the most prominent individual player in setting the agenda, this desire to place issues on or to block them from the policy agenda often means striving to affect presidential decision making. Although there are other influential people, including the Speaker of the House and the Senate majority leader, no other single actor in the system has a comparable capacity to set the agenda for the government in general and Congress in particular.[8] At the same time, chief executives want to leverage their impact on agenda setting as effectively as possible to advance their policy goals. The White House has an incentive to both collaborate with supportive interest groups that have the ears of members of Congress and try to weaken the legislative influence of organizations antagonistic to the president's policy platform. Other parts of the executive branch typically do not participate in establishing the agenda of issues that are under government consideration and therefore are far less likely to interact with interest groups for this purpose.

Lawmaking

A core concern of organized interests and policymakers, including in the executive branch, is lawmaking, the translation of specific policy ideas into law. Getting an issue on the agenda may be a prerequisite for achieving policy change, but it is changing the body of law that actually alters the status quo. At the federal level, laws result from the legislative process and the enactment of statutes (with either

TABLE 10.1 **Programmatic and Political Objectives of Interest Groups and Executive Officials**

Interest Groups	White House	Executive Line-Agencies	Independent Regulatory Agencies
		Programmatic Objectives	
Agenda influence	Agenda control		
Lawmaking influence • Statutory • Executive orders	• Ideas for lawmaking Initiatives (invited/overt) • Support for lawmaking Initiatives (invited/overt)	• Ideas for lawmaking initiatives (reciprocal/quiet) • Support for lawmaking initiatives (reciprocal/quiet)	• Ideas for lawmaking initiatives (reciprocal/quiet)
Rulemaking/Regulatory influence	Compatibility of proposed rules with administration policy positions	Substantive/Technical expertise (workability)	Substantive/Technical expertise (workability)
		Political Objectives	
• Representational credibility • Niche leadership	• Legitimacy • Outreach	• Support in Congress • Public cover	• Sustained autonomy

Congress and the president acting in concert or the two houses of the legislature overturning a presidential veto), but they also consist of provisions dictated unilaterally by the president in executive orders issued in accordance with existing statutory authority. Similar to agenda setting, parties inside and outside of government may want the president to adopt ideas they favor or reject those they oppose.

Although a great deal of federal law was enacted by Congress without substantial involvement of the president, including laws of major policy consequence, presidents actively seek to set the agenda of issues and prescribe the specific features of enacted policy.[9] All modern presidents (other than Eisenhower in his first year in office) have sent Congress "presidential programs" that aggregate initiatives over a wide range of policy areas. Organized interests generally want to influence the process by which presidents formulate their legislative proposals. Presidents and their advisers often reach out to interest groups to invite their policy ideas, gain from their relevant expertise, and solicit their support for presidential initiatives in Congress. They may also pursue strategies to stymie the legislative influence of organized interests hostile to the president's policy designs.

Line-agencies in the executive branch perform the operational functions of the executive branch under presidential management, and they are also often a source of legislative initiatives picked up by members of Congress. Agency officials may contribute directly to the formulation of the president's legislative program or put forward proposals independent of, but judged, through "central legislative clearance," not to be in contradiction to the administration's legislative priorities.[10] Some organized interests have cultivated relationships with permanent civil servants that span multiple presidential administrations. These interests provide ideas and expertise to agency officials and lend support to their initiatives when they reach Capitol Hill. The independent regulatory agencies, however, tend to be more distant from the process of proposing and enacting statutes, although they, too, may be a source of policy ideas.

Rulemaking and Regulations

Anything enacted by Congress, whether of presidential origin or not, must be implemented and enforced by federal agencies, which craft the specific language of rules and regulations. Because statutes passed by Congress are often vague, agency officials frequently must fill in the substantive details, which can be of considerable moment. These gaps provide a crucial opening for interest group involvement, creating opportunities for them to try to shift the weight of the final law more in line with their own preferences. The legislative process is commonly not the end of the battle over what a law will require; rather, it is one stage in a process that extends to agency implementation. In addition, to obtain the technical knowledge they need to write the implementation provisions, bureaucrats may turn to some well-placed interest groups for assistance in the rulemaking process. As noted below, there are formal procedures by which interest groups and others are invited to inform agency decision making. That is also the case for independent regulatory agencies, which, among other activities, are mandated to enforce legal provisions and adjudicate perceived failures of compliance.

These rulemaking and regulatory activities are central to the work of executive branch agencies, but not the White House. There is one crucial caveat. With roots in earlier presidencies, the 1980 Paperwork Reduction Act, and, in particular, President Reagan's Executive Order 12291, the Office of Information and Regulatory Affairs, which lies within the Office of Management and Budget (OMB) in the Executive Office of the President, reviews new regulations proposed by executive agencies. This process gives officials inside the overall White House enterprise the means to block regulatory approaches considered to conflict with administration policy preferences. Under Reagan, for example, responding to the Aspirin Foundation of America, the OMB stopped for a number of years a proposed regulation that would have required Aspirin bottle labels to contain information about the product's links to Reye's syndrome among children.[11] The extent of interest group involvement with these regulatory decisions would be governed by the president's objectives.

Political Objectives

Interactions between organized interests and officials in different parts of the executive branch also have the potential to advance political objectives for all of the entities involved. These objectives overlap, but take on a character specific to each participant.

Where numerous complementary and conflicting interest groups compete with each other, achieving access to, and influence with, executive branch officials confers upon an interest group at least two valuable political assets. The first might be called "representational credibility." The exchanges with the executive branch show that an organized interest is taken seriously as an appropriate and legitimate voice for a particular constituency. Combined with efficacious access to Congress, executive branch interactions show a group's current and potential members, overall supporters, and possible external funders that it is an influential player and worthy of continued support. The second political asset is the opportunity to be identified as a "niche leader."[12] Having tentacles into the executive branch in addition to the legislature elevates the stature of an organized interest among others operating in the same policy domain. Placement at the pinnacle of policymaking from bill enactment to bureaucratic rulemaking makes a group indispensable, or unavoidable, on the issues of interest to it.

The White House can also exploit orchestrated relationships with interest groups to advance political objectives. First, sustained presidential leadership depends on a president being viewed by the public and other policymakers as legitimately wielding the powers of the office on behalf of the nation. Presidents who come into office lacking a majority of the popular vote or under questionable circumstances, or are later tarnished by scandals, can help themselves by building relationships with an array of organized interests that, taken together, represent the broad sweep of American society. Second, politically secure presidents can use interactions with interest groups to reinforce ties to newer elements of their electorate bases, engaging in outreach to bring those interests more firmly into the presidential camp. Examples of these political dynamics will be in evidence when specific White House strategies for liaison with different types of interest groups are discussed below.

Given the role of Congress in establishing federal agencies and financing their operations through the annual appropriations process, executive line-agencies are always subject to legislative decisions and vulnerable to possible legislative interventions—oversight, reductions in funding, and even reversal of agencies' programmatic decisions. Interest groups that have enduring relationships with the members and staff of House and Senate committees of jurisdiction and that may benefit from the programmatic activities of particular agencies can provide overt support in the legislature for the activities of those agencies. When agencies are under challenge in the media and other public forums, groups can provide them with public cover to help ward off congressional challenges.

An important political objective for independent regulatory agencies is to protect their autonomy from both the president and Congress. One of the greatest risks to this independence may be organized interests that perceive themselves harmed by an agency's regulatory decision and use that complaint to seek legislative or presidential intervention. When an agency avoids direct confrontations with influential interests, there are few incentives for interference from the White House or the Hill. The alternative risk, noted below, is that an independent regulatory agency develops such close ties with particular interests, such as a specific industry, that it becomes a case of regulatory "capture"; in this instance, the agency serves the objectives of the industry it is supposed to regulate rather than the public purpose articulated in its establishing legislation.

INTEREST GROUPS AND THE WHITE HOUSE

In one form or another all presidents have had some kind of association and strategic engagement with interest groups, broadly defined. All electoral coalitions that have brought presidents to office constitute an assemblage of interests, be they agrarian, mercantile, slaveholding, populist, ethnic, banking, environmentalist, or whatever the nature of the social and economic divisions that were politically mobilized at the time. But, the significance, complexity, and instrumentality of these relationships—their "density"—took on greater significance once the emergent attributes of the modern presidency fully coalesced with the tenure Franklin Delano Roosevelt.[13] The presidency from FDR on has had three core features relevant to interest groups. The first is a general expectation among other policymakers and the electorate that the president holds a leadership role in addressing all manner of challenges facing the nation, including economic concerns, domestic issues more generally, and foreign relations and national security. Second, the White House is not just a residence but rather a short-hand descriptor that encompasses an advisory and operational establishment, separate from the president's political party organization, that is both beholden to the president and imbued with sufficient staff resources to permit expansive, and often specialized, engagement with a multitude of players in the policymaking process, including organized interests.[14] Third, whatever the president's partisan affiliation and ideological orientation, the White House apparatus will aggressively strive to influence the choices of other policymakers, such as members of Congress, through the use of strategic and orchestrated communication with the public writ large, targeted subgroups of the electorate, and organized interests.

In the political and institutional context of the modern presidency, chief executives and their administrations have employed, to varying degrees and effect, three broad strategies to align relevant domains of interest groups to serve their political and policy purposes: intimidating opponents, promoting and winning friends, and mobilizing allies.[15] Although there are important examples of administrations that pursued the first two strategies, mobilizing allies has become the predominate theme of White House-interest group interactions. It is also the approach over which presidents and their aides have the maximum control. "The enormous range of presidential activity," observes Carol Greenwald, "permits the President to solicit aid from groups when he needs them, and palm them off when the pressure lessens."[16] Every kind of relationship with interest groups, however, constitutes a form of exchange, so the invitation to work with the White House also opens an avenue for influencing policy content.

Intimidating Opponents

Most incoming administrations seem to take the contours of the interest group system as a given, fixed feature of the political environment in which they will have to work. But

President George W. Bush meets with Darfur advocates at the White House in 2006. They include Rabbi David Saperstein of the Religious Action Center of Reform Judaism (far left), Faith McDonnell of the Institute on Liberty and Democracy, and Simon Deng, a former slave in Darfur (right).

not all. Consider President Ronald Reagan, who entered the Oval Office in 1981 having campaigned on the themes of lower taxes, reduced federal spending, deregulation, privatization, and, with the exception of a commitment to a vastly larger defense capacity, an overarching call for smaller government.[17] Under previous administrations, especially those of Democrats Franklin Roosevelt with his New Deal and Lyndon Johnson with his Great Society, but also that of Reagan's fellow Republican Richard Nixon, the scope of responsibilities, activities, and interventions in the market by government had grown dramatically. The obligations and expenditures of the federal government had come to include welfare and food stamps; housing expansion; health care coverage for the elderly, disabled, and categories of the poor; social security; environmental regulation; occupational health and safety; primary and secondary education; legal services; urban mass transit; gun control; among many other issues, almost all of which Reagan wanted to curtail or eliminate.

Government expansion tends to promote the mobilization of new interest groups, and through contracts and grants even finances some of their activities. Reagan and his advisers, including former representative David Stockman, who served as Reagan's OMB director, perceived the flourishing of liberal organized interests to be a product of government largesse and a direct political threat to the administration's commitment to shrink government. The administration launched a campaign across executive agencies to "defund the left," intended to weaken, if not fatally wound, likely interest group opponents to the president's initiatives by cutting off their supply of federal dollars. In the end this strategy proved largely ineffective because the administration misidentified the groups most reliant on federal funding. They were not the suspected liberal activist groups, who actually obtained most of their resources from nongovernmental sources; rather, they were mainstream organizations, assiduously nonpartisan, that represented the nonprofit sector and were major providers of services financed by government contracts. The approach of the Reagan administration ironically tended to incite the antagonism of these previously nonconfrontational groups.[18]

More recently, the George W. Bush administration, with an orientation to government that resembled Reagan's, sought to diminish the political clout of interests with longstanding ties to the Democratic opposition. Women's organizations had enjoyed formal access to the White House during many administrations, but President Bill Clinton had elevated the presence of Democratic-leaning groups by creating the White House Office for Women's Initiatives and Outreach. Bush not only shut down this office, considered to be a platform for feminist organizations, but also shifted White House entrée to explicitly Republican-friendly women's groups and representatives, such as the National Federation of Republican Women, RightNow!, and female corporate CEOs and small-business entrepreneurs. These actions may have closed some doors to liberal women's advocacy organizations, but they hardly endangered their existence. The Bush administration also took a more direct approach to undercutting the stature and influence in government of organized labor, long an ally of Democrats. Labor representatives viewed a number of the administration's policy proposals, such as support for "paycheck protection" (union members would have to formally approve the use of their dues for political activities) and "competitive sourcing" (allowing private firms to compete to perform tasks done by federal civilian positions), as pointed assaults on the very existence of unions. The power of organized labor, however, was far more affected by the steady decline in the percentage of the workforce belonging to unions that had begun decades earlier.[19]

One can easily imagine why employing a strategy of intimidating interest group opponents would be even less efficacious for presidents—especially for liberal Democrats—who push programmatic agendas that are the mirror image of Reagan's or Bush's. The natural adversaries to expanding the role of government to boost investments in social programs or to invigorate regulatory protections of the environment or workplace would be for-profit companies and their trade associations, and perhaps organizations representing "movement" conservatives. These interests are not reliant on government (other than defense contractors) and most have independent capacities to raise revenues and mobilize their memberships or constituencies.[20] As noted, even Democratic administrations often depend on the cooperation of private-sector interests and are not usually in a position to threaten these types of potential interest group opponents.

Promoting and Winning Friends

To foster a community of organized interests more friendly to a president's agenda, it is probably far easier to expand the ranks of those who would be inclined to support an administration's programmatic and political objectives than to undercut opposing groups. Modern presidents have pursued two approaches in this vein. First, they have promoted the formation of new organizations with compatible goals and opened avenues for their access to government. Second, they have sought to shift the perspectives and allegiance of existing interests toward the goals of the administration.

Democratic presidents have generally focused more on the first approach of encouraging new groups or facilitating the access to the executive establishment of existing interests that supported their elections. FDR's 1932 electoral coalition, for example, and the policies of his and subsequent administrations helped to empower and reinforce the political foothold of African American civil rights groups and organized labor. Lyndon Johnson's "war on poverty" included creation of community action agencies under the Economic Opportunity Act of 1964, which contributed to the political training and mobilization of activists who endorsed expanded social policies and years later would become prominent figures in the nation's political leadership.[21] John Kennedy's administration played an even more explicit role in the mobilization of women's groups, such as the National Organization for Women, whose initial leaders were brought together by White House conferences.[22] All of these initiatives altered the interest group landscape in favor of the kinds of policy objectives advanced by Democratic administrations. With the communications technologies of e-mail, the Internet, and various social media such as Facebook and Twitter, the Obama administration sought to transition the millions of electronically connected campaign activists, mobilized in 2008, into a new grassroots force, Organizing for America, to give political lift to the president's initiatives on health care reform, climate change, and "green" energy production. This undertaking, however, proved far less effective than the more traditional interest-promotion activities of past Democratic presidencies.

Republican presidents have been the primary agents behind efforts to swing existing interests from potential resistance to support. President Nixon's administration exploited racial fears, campus unrest, and patriotism associated with American involvement in the Vietnam War to break the Democratic hold on many southern whites and northern blue-collar workers from ethnic communities and gain their loyalty both in the voting booth and in support of administration policies. Reagan turned to abortion, economic dislocation and taxes, and concerns about an emasculated military in the face of the Soviet threat to bring evangelical Protestants, Catholics, upper-middle-class professionals, and various ethnic groups fully into the set of interests favoring his administration and its aspirations.[23] Neither president may have achieved the enduring commitments of all these interests, but they affected the policy successes of their respective administrations. In addition, the Nixon and Reagan administrations helped engineer the political profile of the interest group system that would be in place when George W. Bush arrived in the White House armed with a muscular conservative policy agenda but tainted politically by a contested election and the loss of the popular vote.[24]

Mobilizing Allies

Building collaborations with supportive organized interests is now a routine feature of White House operations and administration activities more broadly. For an incoming administration it begins with the appointment process—the imperative to fill positions within the White House Office, cabinet, and hundreds of subcabinet posts throughout the executive branch. The people chosen for these positions—whether direct presidential appointments, as with a number of close advisory jobs in the White House, or nominations that require Senate confirmation—come from varied backgrounds, but they typically include many individuals with experience working for or connected in other ways to interest groups, from trade associations to professional societies to advocacy organizations. This personnel linkage between the executive branch and organized interests has characterized all presidencies, although some have defined these ties more sharply than others. In George W. Bush's administration, Vice President Dick Cheney had been CEO of a major energy supply company, and more than a couple dozen executive branch officials had previously been executives in energy-producing firms or had represented them in the nation's capital.[25] As one senior executive from an energy company put it, "The people running the United States government are from the energy industry."[26] This pattern of appointments followed the 2000 campaign in which Bush was the top recipient of contributions from this industry.[27] Reflecting a quite different policy perspective and links to a contrary set of interests, Obama's early appointments in the energy domain pleased environmental groups. The appointees had held positions in academia, federal and state government, environmental organizations, and Washington, D.C., law firms; a few came from the industry.[28]

As presidents formulate the initiatives intended to fulfill their programmatic and political objectives, these personnel arrangements can simultaneously facilitate the infusion of interest group perspectives into executive branch decision making and provide an administration with ambassadors for reaching out to allied interests and the coalitions of which they are a part. But to be effective, these and other resources for coordinating with interest groups must be given thoughtful direction through "interest group liaison," the process by which people in the White House decide with which organized interests to speak and for what purpose.[29] Back in Franklin Roosevelt's day, various presidential aides included among their tasks the maintenance of ties with groups important to the Democratic coalition. Although this kind of informal arrangement persisted through many presidencies, communication and orchestration with organized interests became both more routine and often more specialized.[30] Nixon began to institutionalize the function, but it was President Gerald Ford who formally established the Office of Public Liaison (OPL) with the specific mission to "communicate, articulate, and support the President's programs, policies, and priorities in order to mobilize support for them," according to William Baroody, the OPL's first director.[31] The name of the office symbolized making connections to the public through its constituent parts, and it avoided the appearance of creating a specific unit in the White House for special interests.[32]

Since then, the office has been moved around in placement, prestige, and importance within the White House staff structure, even in terms of its centrality as the point of instrumental White House engagement with interest groups. Under Anne Wexler in the Carter White House it helped take the lead in orchestrating campaigns to advance the president's legislative agenda. In the Reagan administration it played more of a supporting role with other offices in the Executive Office of the President. George W. Bush placed the OPL within a new Office of Strategic Initiatives run by Karl Rove, the president's main political adviser, and it reported directly to Rove. At the outset of the Obama administration the Office of Public Liaison apparently disappeared in name, with its functions—and new technological forms of communication and mobilization—subsumed under the broader rubric of Public Engagement, led by Valerie Jarrett, a close friend whom Obama chose as senior adviser and assistant to the president.[33] Even when the OPL dominates White House liaison with groups, many other entities and staffs within the Executive Office of the President enjoy, and exploit, close ties with organized interests.[34]

Whatever the institutional arrangements in the White House, how presidents and their advisers orchestrate these instrumental relationships with organized interests is highly contingent. The emphasis they give to particular forms of interest group liaison is based on strategic calculations that vary across administrations and across issues within a single presidency.[35] As Joseph Pika notes, the interactions are "doubly dynamic," as "both groups and presidents will vary in the value attached to different types of liaison and pursue different strategies in advancing their interests."[36]

The White House approaches used in specific instances reflect the individual ambitions of presidents, their current political standing and needs, the kind of objectives they seek to fulfill with a particular course of action, the existing population of organized interests open to White House overtures, and the specific assets of policy expertise, ideological proximity, and political relevance that different groups possess. To simplify this complex assortment of factors that influence how the White House conducts interest group liaison, presented in Figure 10.1 is a typology of approaches based on two underlying dimensions that encompass a president's objectives and orientation to the interest group system.[37] These two dimensions also help to identify the kinds of organizational attributes that would make groups welcome collaborators.

The first dimension addresses what a president is trying to achieve. Is the objective "programmatic," an undertaking to legislate new policies, to change existing law, or to put into place policies adopted by executive action, such as executive orders? This objective reflects the president as

FIGURE 10.1 **Typology of White House Liaison with Interest Groups**

		Breadth of Group Interactions	
		Inclusive	Exclusive
Purpose of Group Interactions	Representational	Liaison as **Legitimization**	Liaison as **Outreach**
	Programmatic	Liaison as **Consensus Building**	Liaison as **Governing Party**

agenda setter, policy advocate, "legislator in chief," and innovative chief executive. Or is the objective "representational," an act intended to strengthen, confirm, or extend the president's political standing, credibility, even legitimacy before the entire nation or particular constituencies of consequence to the administration. Although in the longer run, efforts to advance this objective may give the president greater leverage in policymaking, in the near term they are about the president as head of state, duly chosen, and wielding rightful authority. Presidents who ran substantive, issue-based election campaigns, who won reasonably decisive victories, and who possess expansive policy agendas would be expected to emphasize programmatic objectives (but not to the exclusion of all other forms of interest group engagement). The White House seeks legislative advantage through what has been called "reverse lobbying" or "lobbying the lobbies."[38] Those presidents whose electoral bases are more precarious, who have been touched by major scandal, or, alternatively, who want to use the mantle of the office to draw new or previously ostracized constituencies into the political mainstream are likely to underscore, in particular, representational purposes.

The second dimension in Figure 10.1 portrays the assessment made by the White House about the character of the relevant interest group community and the availability of different kinds of groups to the president's cause, given what the administration is seeking to accomplish. Is a diverse collection of interests present and likely to be supportive of the president's goals, or at least open to overtures from the White House, permitting the administration to be broadly "inclusive" in its liaison with the group system? Or are there such deep divisions within the interest group community, perhaps aligned with conflict between the two political parties, making it desirable, perhaps necessary, for the administration to pursue "exclusive" interactions with a set of compatible groups? During times of consensus, or occasions of great political vulnerability on the part of the president, one would anticipate pursuit of inclusive relationships with assorted organized interests. When the issues involved are divisive, or prompt an administration to zero in on elements of the president's electoral base, targeted, exclusive White House engagement with selected groups is likely to be more evident.

By putting these two dimensions together, one can identify four distinct approaches to interest group liaison by the White House. Each is described, starting with the two that derive from representational objectives, and illustrated by recent presidencies. These empirical examples tend to show central tendencies within individual presidencies, but every administration at various times, responsive to specific conditions and objectives, has employed all four strategies.

Relatively rarely do presidents feel the need to call upon *liaison as legitimization.* But publicly connecting with diverse groups from across the political spectrum that are well recognized by Americans can be an essential strategy for building, or reestablishing, a chief executive's claims to authority and influence in government. No one understood this dynamic better than Gerald Ford. As an appointed vice president, replacing scandal-ridden Spiro Agnew, Ford became president when his predecessor, Richard Nixon, resigned from office in the wake of the Watergate scandals. Although Ford had been a well-regarded minority leader of the House of Representatives, the constituents of his House district in Michigan were the only part of the American electorate ever to have cast a ballot for him. His pardon of Nixon dramatically eroded his presidential credibility even further. The Ford administration used all kinds of means, including inclusive interactions with organized interests that spanned Republican and Democratic coalitions, to invigorate the president's representational gravitas and garner greater legitimacy.[39]

Following the disputed 2000 election one might well have expected Bush to begin his presidency emphasizing a similar approach to interest groups. When the election results hinged on how to count votes in Florida, the outcome of the election was effectively determined by the appointed U.S. Supreme Court in a 5–4 decision (the five being the justices chosen by previous Republican presidents). With this decision giving Bush Florida and a slim majority in the Electoral College, he was sworn into office as the first president in 118 years to have lost the popular vote. Moreover, he campaigned on the theme of being a "uniter, not a divider," suggesting a desire to bring the nation together after such a traumatic experience and near constitutional crisis.[40] Although the circumstances of the election may have signaled the logic of using inclusive interactions with organized interests to serve the representational interests of the president and augment his legitimacy, Bush's personal orientation and the primacy of his policy objectives overwhelmed these incentives and took him in an entirely different direction (see below).[41]

When presidents seek to realize representational objectives, it is usually in the form of *liaison as outreach.* Many presidents have been elected with the aid of coalitions that included interests relatively new to the political process or fairly recently mobilized and not yet widely accepted as part of the mainstream of American politics with ready access to government. Here the organizations to which the White House reaches out are likely to be fairly new and so far lacking the political armaments associated with conventionally strong interest groups—sizable memberships, stable financing, large staffs made up of experienced insiders, and a presence in electoral politics. Franklin Roosevelt's election helped bring African Americans into greater political prominence. Kennedy and Johnson elevated the place of women as a political constituency. Jimmy Carter was the first to recognize gays and lesbians among his supporters. Reagan welcomed the wave of evangelical Christians newly mobilized to influence the politics and policy of the day, not just the afterlife. In the wake of 9/11, George W. Bush made the most extensive overtures of any president to the Muslim community. All of these presidents used the apparatus of the White House to establish formal points of communication and access for these interests. Although the Bush administration's relationship with Muslims eventually soured, in all of these cases the chief executives were not striving to enhance their own immediate political standing in the face of threats; rather, they were intent on exploiting their representational stature as president—with exclusive, targeted ties to groups—to enhance the presence and position of new elements of their electoral coalitions.[42]

Individuals generally choose to run for president because they want to accomplish something, whether shrinking the scope and impact of government or expanding its capacity to address problems here and abroad. Presidents from Franklin Roosevelt on have typically had expansive legislative agendas. Overall, programmatic objectives tend to dominate representational goals. On occasion a president will serve during times of fairly broad agreement, even consensus, about the challenges to be met and the responsibility of government in meeting them. During the Eighty-ninth Congress in 1965–1966, before the escalation of U.S. involvement in Vietnam would divide the nation and contribute to a weakening economy, the country lined up behind President Johnson's agenda of fighting poverty, investing in schools, promoting housing for the poor, and generally using government to serve social purposes. He turned to the interest group community to help him accomplish his programmatic objectives, finding inclusive ways to link advocates for the poor and industry, in a form of *liaison as consensus building*.[43] That window did not stay open long, and most periods of the modern era have lacked the opportunity for presidents to nurture and exploit a policy consensus. But on specific issues, comparable moments have occurred. Much of what George W. Bush wanted to do was rife with controversy and fought out between contending political forces. Still, the No Child Left Behind Act of 2001 was enacted with bipartisan support and with the White House willing to engage a wider than usual range of interest groups in the education policy arena. The word *consensus* may overstate what occurred, but in the context of the typology, liaison as consensus building is the most apt description.[44]

Most of the time, because of the constitutional separation of powers and the bicameral legislature—a system that Richard Neustadt famously and more accurately described as "separated institutions sharing powers"[45]—consensus does not exist. And it is far from certain that even the most skilled, popular, and persuasive chief executive will be able to get Congress to go along, especially on proposals of considerable scope and complexity, imbued with controversial elements. Moreover, the policymaking challenges for presidents have intensified over the last thirty years as the two political parties in Congress have become more ideologically polarized.[46] To prevail over these institutional barriers and build winning legislative coalitions, presidents and their administrations often employ multitiered strategies of influence. They communicate and negotiate directly with members of Congress and influence them indirectly by activating their constituents through appeals to the public and collaborations with organized interests. In the common environment of contentious policy issues, the incentives are for presidents to press their programmatic objectives in partnerships with an exclusive cluster of organized interests whose policy positions track with those of the president and the administration's largely partisan congressional allies. In this setting the approach to interest groups is one of liaison as governing party, devoted to policymaking and predicated on weaving together a coalition of the like-minded that spans the administration, Congress, and the community of outside interests. The organized interests especially attractive to the White House here are those with memberships or supporters in multiple congressional districts and states and professional staffs well connected to the congressional establishment.[47] These close bonds between an administration and organized interests also open the avenues for enhanced influence by particular organizations, permitting some groups to have greater access to the White House than others. Such interests participate directly in the crafting of presidential proposals and may well compel an administration to add or drop specific policy provisions in exchange for their overall endorsement, active lobbying of Congress, and grassroots mobilization.

When Carter's legislative program became firmly lodged in the quicksand of Congress, the coalition-building imperatives of federal policymaking led the programmatically ambitious president to shed his initial hostility toward interest group politics. Coordinating relationships with supportive organized interests became a central feature of legislative strategies in the Carter White House.[48] When Reagan arrived in the nation's capital with an especially bold agenda to slash the budget, cut taxes, and shred regulations, Republicans in Congress were nearly unanimous in support but too few in number to enact legislation. Officials in the Reagan White House worked assiduously with allied organized interests to influence the House and Senate. In a survey of interest groups at the time, as one would expect with the administration taking an exclusive approach, only 8 percent of organizations had frequent and cooperative interactions with the White House. These groups were decidedly Republican in their orientation, probusiness, with substantial resources, and with congressionally connected staffs, who had considerable experience in actively lobbying Congress. In short, they were well equipped to push the president's initiatives on Capitol Hill.[49] George W. Bush's liaison activities comported with Reagan's governing party model on one issue after another—energy, environment, business regulation, Medicare restructuring, defense, "charitable choice" for faith-based organizations, and the like. All of these linked business interests, the Christian Right, and other conservative organizations with largely unified Republicans in Congress against Democrats and their allies among labor unions, consumer groups, environmental organizations, and civil rights groups. Bush's aspirations and the cohesiveness of congressional Republicans, along with the administration's interest group allies, cast aside any cautions the president might have entertained given the nature of his victory in the 2000 election; and the post–9/11 environment only strengthened his resolve.[50]

Although Carter never really gained the upper hand with Congress, he would have faced even greater difficulties had he not incorporated interest groups into his legislative strategies. The liaison-as-governing party approach fully adopted by Reagan and the younger Bush almost certainly advanced their programmatic objectives, with many issues, such as Reagan's tax and budget cuts and Bush's energy and Medicare plans, decided in Congress by fairly narrow margins, sometimes after drawn-out battles. One of the reasons that President Clinton had a more problematic relationship with Congress, even though he was the first Democratic president in twelve years and initially had fairly healthy Democratic majorities in the House and Senate, is that he and his advisers did not settle on an efficacious approach to the interest group community. Despite the rise of partisan polarization in Congress and within the interest group system, Clinton chose to undertake an ambitious programmatic agenda not within the parameters of liaison as governing party. Instead he pursued a "third way" as a "New Democrat" for which there was no existing, inherent base in the interest group community. Nor was there consensus. Clinton was left without an effective interest group strategy for a programmatically energized president, and then in the 1994 elections the Republicans took over the Congress for the first time in forty years, leaving him without opportunities to push a major policy agenda.[51]

President Obama assumed the powers of the presidency seemingly primed for a *liaison-as-governing-party* strategy.[52] In 2008 he enjoyed the largest first-term popular vote electoral win of any Democratic president since FDR; his party in Congress held a healthy majority, picking up fifty-two seats in the House and fourteen in the Senate in 2006 and 2008; partisan division had reached new heights; and his campaign was fueled by major and specific programmatic commitments to, among other things, stimulate the economy and institute far-reaching financial regulatory reform, enact comprehensive health care reform, promote clean energy, and tackle immigration reform. Organized interests with close ties to the Democratic majority, having battled Bush for eight years, were prepared to help push this expansive policy agenda. And the administration sought to turn its electronically networked campaign volunteers into a policy-oriented grassroots organization, Organizing for America. To a large extent the administration's actions fit the contours of liaison as governing party, but with important caveats. First, Obama had also pledged to try to bridge the deep partisanship evident in Washington by reaching across the aisle. Second, that commitment having failed, the Republican opposition institutionalized the use of the filibuster in the Senate to oppose the president. With all major administration initiatives requiring sixty votes to pass in the Senate over the filibuster, the White House had to reach out to the few moderate Republicans and the conservative Democrats, and therefore the constituencies and interests they represent. Third, after six decades of failure on health care reform, Obama concluded that a winning strategy required allying with, or at least neutralizing, interests not usually associated with Democratic ranks, such as organized medicine and the pharmaceutical and insurance industries. Fourth, Organizing for America proved to be a paper tiger. Finally, in the area of education policy, the administration actually challenged the teachers' unions, core parts of the Democratic coalition. The main White House approach to interest group liaison ended up being programmatically based and targeted, but, unlike with Reagan or George W. Bush, the exclusive set of groups engaged with the administration changed from one issue to the next.

INTEREST GROUPS AND FEDERAL AGENCIES

The congressional arena may be where media and popular attention is most focused on the role of organized interests in policymaking (widely viewed as excessive), and White House interactions with groups may gain exposure due to the star power of the president, but interchange between interests and executive agencies is no less significant and consequential. To start, the implementation process is "an extension of the struggle which began in the legislature."[53] Interest groups are sure to follow. At the same time, the bureaucracy has a considerable amount of independence from other policymakers, with discretion of importance to the outcome of policymaking.[54] Because Congress typically legislates with fairly broad strokes (often to the point of complete ambiguity), and implementation is a continuous process, the bulk of lawmaking actually happens in the departments, agencies, and bureaus. As described by Scott Furlong and Cornelius Kerwin:

> [R]ule making by agencies has eclipsed legislation by Congress as the most important source of lawmaking in at least three ways. In terms of sheer volume there is simply no competition between legislation and rule making. . . . Second, the specificity of command is generally far greater in rules than in statutes. . . . Finally, there is greater immediacy of effect in rules.[55]

Organized interests recognize these fundamental features of modern government. Surveys of interest groups consistently reveal that most of them (more than 75 percent) lobby administrative agencies, meet with government officials, and attempt to influence the drafting of rules and regulations. Moreover, groups place the importance of these activities on par with their efforts to influence Congress and the president, and they consider these endeavors to be effective.[56] Unlike interactions with the White House, and more similar to the situation with Congress, the pattern of communication flows primarily from the organized interests to the executive branch.

Several long-standing characteristics of the executive branch and the procedures that govern agency decision making provide opportunities for organized interests to participate in and influence the rulemaking process. Because many of them characterize administrative agencies, such as the cabinet departments, and separate agencies, such as the Environmental Protection Agency, and independent regulatory agencies not under the managerial authority of the president, such as the Federal Trade Commission (FTC), one can consider both these general types of agencies together in this discussion.

Historically, a number of entities established by Congress within the executive branch are "clientele" based. They are intended to protect and advance the interests of particular groups in the society.[57] One need only consider the cabinet-level Departments of Agriculture (farmers), Commerce (business), Labor, and Veterans Affairs to appreciate the connections. Although not all political appointees and even civil servants in these departments or their decisions have favored the relevant clientele groups, everyone expects that their representatives will seek to exploit these executive venues and thereby shield their interests as well as further their agendas. In addition, the process for selecting political appointees in all agencies has always offered another avenue of influence. Organized interests strive to help shape these choices. Often their own people land in senior positions with departments and agencies, sometimes exemplifying the a virtual "revolving door" between groups and government.[58] Jack Walker's national survey of membership associations among interest groups found that just under a third of them had staff members who had held appointments in the federal government (and about half employed staff who were past civil servants).[59] Such appointments do not settle

IRON TRIANGLES AND ISSUE NETWORKS

Effective power in Washington policy-making is often lodged in what political scientists call iron triangles. An iron triangle is a tight alliance between congressional committees, interest groups or representatives of regulated industries, and bureaucratic agencies; policy is made to benefit the shared interests of these three power centers, not for the benefit of the greater public. Politicians are themselves quite aware of this triangular arrangement. Former secretary of Health, Education, and Welfare John Gardner once declared before the Senate Government Operations Committee, "As everyone in this room knows but few people outside of Washington understand, questions of public policy nominally lodged with the Secretary are often decided far beyond the Secretary's reach by a trinity—not exactly a holy trinity—consisting of (1) representatives of an outside lobby, (2) middle-level bureaucrats, and (3) selected members of Congress."[1]

The metaphor of the iron triangle has been refined by scholars, who speak instead of issue networks.[2] The iron triangle suggests a solid, continuing relationship between a particular interest group and fixed agencies and subcommittees. The network idea suggests that the relationships are more complex than a simple triangle, often involving competing interests. There are thus clusters of interest groups, policy specialists, consultants, and research institutes ("think tanks") that are influential in policy areas. All elements of the cluster can use the courts or can lobbying the executive branch or sympathetic members of Congress to contest the relationships that develop as iron triangles. The number of interests and multiple modes of participation show that the concept of an iron triangle, while powerful, is often overly simple. That is, while the relationships identified by the iron triangle remain important, the full range of politics is frequently better captured by the concept of issue networks.

SOURCE: Adapted from Barbour, Christine and Gerald C. Wright. *Keeping the Republic*, 5th ed. Washington: CQ Press, 2012, 357-358.

1. Quoted in Dennis D. Riley, *Controlling the Federal Bureaucracy* (Philadelphia: Temple University Press, 1987), 43.
2. Hugh Heclo, "Issue Networks and the Executive Establishment," in Anthony King, ed., *The New American Political System* (Washington, D.C.: American Enterprise Institute, 1978), 87–124.

the outcomes of rulemaking, which is more in the purview of the civil servants who constitute what is commonly called the "permanent government," but they afford enhanced opportunities for particular interests to sway the determinations of civil servants within the agencies and bureaus. Finally, various units within the federal executive establishment have for years utilized advisory committees, some established by Congress, to furnish officials with substantive guidance and technical information. By some counts there are currently fifty-two federal agencies that have 915 advisory committees with an aggregate membership of 60,000 individuals, a significant number of whom have been closely tied to interest groups. A third of the groups in Walker's study had executive directors or other staff members who sat on advisory committees. This pathway to influence, however, may have narrowed. In 2009 "[h]undreds, if not thousands, of lobbyists [were] likely to be ejected from federal advisory panels as part of a little-noticed initiative by the Obama administration to curb K Street's influence in Washington."[60]

Modern reforms of the rules of procedure, meeting requirements, and transparency provisions also have facilitated groups' monitoring of agency activities and their gaining access in order to influence the promulgation of rules and regulations.[61] Although these changes were intended to open the backroom decision making of government to public scrutiny, much like the open-meeting requirements for legislative markups by congressional committees, these provisions draw far more attention from interest groups than from average citizens. These mechanisms do not enable organized interests to "initiate rulemaking," but they provide multiple means to influence, even "partner" with agencies in the process.[62] The most important legal-institutional change along these lines is probably the set of requirements put in place by the Administrative Procedures Act (APA) enacted in 1946.[63] Federal agencies must publish in the *Federal Register* all proposed rules, formally designated as a Notice of Proposed Rulemaking, which opens a period for "notice and comment" by interested parties (with organized interests among the most interested). Proposed rules can generate scores of detailed comments—few, if any, from citizens or even academics, but, depending on the agency and the subject of the rule, large numbers from government agencies and interest groups. Commercial interests are particularly well represented, because a new government regulation is most likely to affect them, and their interest groups possess the resources needed to track and provide informed responses to proposed regulations.[64] The agency will weigh the comments and then issue a final rule. To participate in the process, an organization needs to know what is transpiring within the agencies, which gives particular weight to the "specialized knowledge" of organized interests.[65] Groups—especially unions and citizen organizations that often counter business interests—believe that this task has been made easier by "sunshine" laws and the Freedom of Information Act, all passed by Congress in the 1970s to make more public the actions and decisions and federal officials.[66] The rapid rise of electronic communication, from information-rich agency Web sites to digital methods for submitting comments on proposed rules, is sure to ease the burdens of groups trying to monitor agency activities.[67]

If all else fails in the efforts of organized interests to move agency decisions in a desirable direction, they can turn to other institutions for assistance. Because Congress establishes and funds executive branch agencies, and could theoretically terminate them or transfer their programs, agency officials pay attention to legislative signals. Groups with strong allies on the Hill can draw on those relationships to help gain some leverage over executive branch decision makers.[68] In addition, as discussed in Chapter 9, interest groups can and do challenge agency interpretations of statutes in court, at times winning judicial decrees that overturn or supplant the rules and judgments of the agency. Of particular relevance to citizen groups are the numerous laws passed in the 1970s, such as the Consumer Product Safety Act, that broadened the standing for groups to sue.[69]

Have all of these means for groups to interject themselves into agency decision making granted them real power over executive policymaking? There is not a single definitive answer. At one extreme a number of scholars over the years have identified opportunities for private interests to "capture" agencies and, more or less, instruct the agencies to do their bidding. According to Marver Bernstein, whatever broad-based political movement that led to the creation of an agency to regulate a particular industry ultimately dissipates, but the commercial interests remain, well heeled, well organized, and relatively unchallenged. A prime example appeared to be the first independent regulatory agency, the Interstate Commerce Commission, established in 1887 to regulate the railroad industry. For many years it was thought to serve the anticompetitive wishes of the railroads (it was eventually abolished in 1995).[70] This assessment, however, has not been sustained by studies across the range of agencies and over time. With the modern growth of citizen groups and other nonbusiness interests, and the provisions of law that have opened up agency procedures, it is also more difficult for industries to work quietly within hidden seams of government.[71] Tightly closed subsystems of congressional committees, bureaucrats, and commercial interests, to the extent they existed in the past, have given way to far more open and fluid "issue (or policy) networks."[72] It is also not entirely clear just how much influence interest groups have over the conventional rulemaking process, or what types of groups tend to be favored. The lack of clarity is due in part to the wide variety of federal agencies, from administrative bureaus to independent regulatory commissions. Commercial interests, among other groups, are especially active in the process, and they at least report the perception of effectiveness, but the scholarly conclusions are mixed. Some researchers find little impact of comments on final rules, but others, investigating different sets of agencies and using somewhat different methodologies, do detect agency adjustments in final rules, particularly when groups' comments reflect a consensus of views.[73] There is also some evidence that organized interests derive real influence through more informal interactions with agency officials, but by their nature these paths of causation are difficult to observe and measure.[74] These less-than-definitive conclusions underscore the importance of continued study of the relationship between interest groups and executive branch agencies.

CONCLUSION

The frequently reported flow of political action committee contributions to congressional campaigns; the legions of registered lobbyists, activists, and group members who ply the corridors of Congress; and the television ads funded by industry, advocacy organizations, and coalitions that plug positions on various policy issues all focus public and media attention on the nexus between organized interests and the national legislature. Although their interactions are typically less overt, interest groups are comparably insinuated into the executive branch as well. And for good reason. Interest groups possess expertise and capabilities of value to executive branch officials and potentially to informed policymaking. At the same time, those officials make decisions that likely surpass legislative lawmaking in scope, detail, and immediacy, with significant implications for almost every group constituency.

In important respects, however, the nature of exchange between interest groups and the executive branch are different from what is found on Capitol Hill. The president is not just another elected official. A chief executive wields more control over the agenda than anyone else and therefore is a target of particular concern to organized interests. But the president also has far greater capacity to build a shield against group influence and instead orchestrate engagement with the interest group system on terms defined by the administration and in accordance with its objectives. If one looks at the executive branch in terms of the presidency alone, one sees that the arrow of influence typically points outward from the White House to the interest group community, rather than the reverse, although there will always be counter examples.

Shift to the executive branch departments and agencies beyond the White House fence, however, and here organized interests have more opportunities to thrust themselves into executive branch decision making, as clienteles of particular agencies or through means both direct and indirect to influence the policy choices made by political appointees and civil servants. The procedures governing rulemaking, as well as increased openness, have made it easier for organized interests to monitor agency activities and insert their views into deliberations about implementation and administration. It is not clear to what effect, however. Earlier notions about agency capture do not appear sustained by the accumulating evidence, at least as a generalization, but groups certainly do take advantage of the opportunities granted them to convey their voices into the executive policymaking arena.

★

NOTES

1. Kathryn Dunn Tenpas, "Lobbying and the Executive Branch: Outside-In and Inside-Out," in *The Interest Group Connection: Electioneering, Lobbying, and Policymaking in Washington*, ed. Paul S. Herrnson, Ronald G. Shaiko, and Clyde Wilcox (Washington, D.C: CQ Press, 2005), 249–257.

2. Charles E. Lindblom, *Politics and Markets* (New York: Basic Books, 1977).

3. David Austen-Smith and William H. Riker, "Asymmetric Information and the Coherence of Legislation," *American Political Science Review* 81, 3 (September 1987): 897–918.

4. Mark A. Peterson, "Still A Government of Chums: Bush, Business, and Organized Interests," in *The George W. Bush Legacy*, ed. Colin Campbell, Bert A. Rockman, and Andrew Rudalevige (Washington, D.C.: CQ Press, 2007).

5. E. E. Schattschneider, *The Semisovereign People* (New York: Holt, Rinehart, and Winston, 1960).

6. Mancur Olson, *The Logic of Collective Action* (Cambridge: Harvard University Press, 1965); Kay Lehman Scholzman and Sidney Verba, *Injury to Insult: Unemployment, Class, and Political Response* (Cambridge: Harvard University Press, 1979).

7. For the purposes of this section, there is a distinction between "executive line-agencies" that carry out operational functions of the executive branch under presidential management, whether or not they are in cabinet departments, such as the Centers for Medicare and Medicaid Services in the Department of Health and Human Services, or independent, such as the Environmental Protection Agency, and "independent regulatory agencies," which reside outside of cabinet departments, are intended to be free of direct presidential control, and enforce the regulation of particular spheres of the market or political activity, such as Commodity Futures Trading Commission and the Federal Elections Commission, respectively.

8. John W. Kingdon, *Agendas, Alternatives, and Public Policies* (New York: HarperCollins, 1995).

9. Charles O. Jones, *The Presidency in a Separated System* (Washington, D.C.: Brookings Institution, 1994).

10. Richard E. Neustadt, "Presidency and Legislation: The Growth of Central Legislative Clearance," *American Political Science Review* 48 (September 1954): 641–671.

11. Alan B. Morrison, "OMB Interference with Agency Rulemaking: The Wrong Way to Write a Regulation," *Harvard Law Review* 99, 5 (March 1986): 1067.

12. William P. Browne, "Organized Interests and Their Issue Niches: A Search for Pluralism in a Policy Domain," *Journal of Politics* 52 (May 1990): 477–509.

13. Stephen Skowronek, *The Politics Presidents Make: Leadership from John Adams to George Bush* (Cambridge: Harvard University Press, 1993), 30–31. See also Joseph A. Pika, "Interest Groups and the Executive: Presidential Intervention," in *Interest Group Politics*, ed. Allan J. Cigler and Burdett A. Loomis (Washington, D.C.: CQ Press, 1983), 298–323; and Martha Joynt Kumar and Michael Grossman, "The Presidency and Interest Groups," in *The Presidency and the Political System*, ed. Michael Nelson (Washington, D.C.: CQ Press, 1984), 282–312.

14. John Hart, *The Presidential Branch: From Washington to Clinton*, 2nd ed. (Chatham, N.J.: Chatham House Press, 1994); Bradley H. Patterson Jr., *The Ring of Power: The White House Staff and Its Expanding Role in Government* (New York: Basic Books, 1988); and Charles E. Walcott and Karen Hult, *Governing the White House: From Hoover Through LBJ* (Lawrence: University Press of Kansas, 1995).

15. Mark A. Peterson, "Interest Mobilization and the Presidency," in *The Politics of Interests: Interest Groups Transformed*, ed. Mark P. Petracca (Boulder: Westview Press, 1992).

16. Carol S. Greenwald, *Group Power: Lobbying and Public Policy* (New York: Praeger, 1977), 215.

17. See Peterson, "Interest Mobilization and the Presidency," and Mark A. Peterson, "The Presidency and Organized Interests: White House Patterns of Interest Group Liaison," *American Political Science Review* 86 (September 1992): 612–625.

18. Mark A. Peterson and Jack L. Walker, "Interest Group Responses to Partisan Change: The Impact of the Reagan Administration upon the National Interest Group System," in *Interest Group Politics*, 2nd ed., ed. Allan J. Cigler and Burdett A. Loomis (Washington, D.C.: CQ Press, 1986).

19. Peterson, "Still a Government of Chums"; As it turns out, union membership in fact nosed up a bit late in the Bush administration. See "Union Member Summary," Economic News Release, Bureau of Labor Statistics, U.S. Department of Labor, January 28, 2009, http://www.bls.gov/news.release/union2.nr0.htm.

20. Jack L. Walker Jr., *Mobilizing Interest Groups in America: Patrons, Professions, and Social Movements* (Ann Arbor: University of Michigan Press, 1991).

21. J. David Greenstone and Paul E. Peterson, *Race and Authority in Urban Politics* (Chicago: University of Chicago Press, 1976).

22. Walker, *Mobilizing Interest Groups*, 31.

23. Benjamin Ginsberg and Martin Shefter, "The Presidency and Organized Interests," in *The Presidency and the Political System*, 2nd ed., ed. Michael Nelson (Washington, D.C.: CQ Press, 1988).

24. Peterson, "Still a Government of Chums."

25. Ibid.

26. Don Van Natta Jr. and Neela Banerjee, "Bush Policies Have Been Good to Energy Industry," *New York Times*, April 21, 2002, sec. 1, 22.

27. "A Money in Politics Backgrounder on the Energy Industry," Center for Responsive Politics, available at http://www.opensecrets.org/pressreleases/energybriefing.html.

28. Jim Tankersley and Tom Hamburger, "Scientists Cheer Latest Obama Picks," *Los Angeles Times*, December 16, 2008, A15.

29. Peterson, "Interest Mobilization and the Presidency"; and Joseph A. Pika, "Interest Groups: A Doubly Dynamic Relationship," in *Presidential Policymaking: An End-of-Century Assessment*, ed. Steven A. Shull (Armonk, N.Y.: M. E. Sharpe, 1999), 59–78.

30. Bradley H. Patterson, *To Serve the President: Continuity and Innovation in the White House Staff* (Washington, D.C.: Brookings Institution Press, 2008).

31. Robert M. Copeland, "Cultivating Interest Group Support: Public Liaison in the Ford Administration," paper presented at the annual meeting of the Midwest Political Science Association, Chicago, Ill., 1985, 18.

32. Joseph A. Pika, "The White House Office of Public Liaison," *Presidential Studies Quarterly* 39 (September 2009): 549–573.

33. Peterson, "Interest Mobilization and the Presidency"; Peterson, "Presidency and Organized Interests"; Peterson, "Still a Government of Chums;" Pika, "White House Office of Public Liaison"; and "Office of Public Engagement," http://www.whitehouse.gov/administration/eop/ope.

34. Tenpas, "Lobbying the Executive Branch," 252–253.

35. See Walcott and Hult, *Governing the White House*, 120.

36. Pika, "Interest Groups and the Executive," 75.

37. See also Pika, "Interest Groups."

38. Quoted terms are from Ronald G. Shaiko, "Reverse Lobbying: Interest Group Mobilization from the White House and the Hill," in *Interest Group Politics*, 5th ed., ed. Allan J. Cigler and Burdett A. Loomis (Washington, D.C.: CQ Press, 1998); and Hart, *Presidential Branch*, 127.

39. Peterson, "Interest Mobilization and the Presidency."

40. Gary C. Jacobson, *A Divider, Not a Uniter: George W. Bush and the American People* (New York: Pearson Longman, 2007).

41. Peterson, "Interest Mobilization and the Presidency."

42. Ibid.; Peterson, "Presidency and Organized Interests"; Peterson, "Still a Government of Chums."

43. Peterson, "Interest Mobilization and the Presidency."

44. Peterson, "Still a Government of Chums."

45. Richard E. Neustadt, *Presidential Power* (New York: John Wiley, 1960), 33.

46. Sean M. Theriault, *Party Polarization in Congress* (New York: Cambridge University Press, 2008).

47. Peterson, "Presidency and Organized Interests"; and see Mark A. Peterson, "From Trust to Political Power: Interest Groups, Public Choice, and Health Care," in *Uncertain Times: Kenneth Arrow and the Changing Economics of Health Care*, ed. Peter J. Hammer, Deborah Haas-Wilson, Mark A. Peterson, and William M. Sage (Durham, N.C.: Duke University Press, 2003), 276–277.

48. Peterson, "Interest Mobilization and the Presidency."

49. Ibid.

50. Peterson, "Still a Government of Chums."

51. Mark A. Peterson, "Clinton and Organized Interests: Splitting Friends, Unifying Enemies," in *The Clinton Legacy*, ed. Colin Campbell and Bert A. Rockman (Chatham, N.J.: Chatham House, 1999); Stephen A. Skowronek, "The Risks of 'Third-Way' Politics," *Society* 33 (September/October 1996): 33.

52. This paragraph is based on an overall reading of the general media, specialized media, and other forms of general coverage of the first eighteen months of the Obama administration. Useful background information can be found in Jonathan Alter, *The Promise: President Obama: Year One* (New York: Simon and Schuster, 2010); Adriel Bettelheim, "The Shape of the Office," *CQ Weekly*, January 5, 2009, 20–26; Jay Cost, "Three Cheers for Partisanship," RealClearPolitics.com, February 16, 2009, http://www.realclearpolitics.com/horseraceblog/2009/02/three_cheers_for_partisanship

.html; Brian Friel, "Sorting the House: A NJ Analysis Finds House Congressional Districts More Polarized Than Ever Before," *National Journal*, April 24, 2010; Carl Hulse, "Legislative Hurdles in an Era of Conflict, Not Compromise," *New York Times*, June 20, 2010, A18.

53. L. Harmon Zeigler and G. Wayne Peak, *Interest Groups in American Society*, 2nd ed. (Englewood Cliffs, N.J.: Prentice-Hall, 1964), 160.

54. Daniel P. Carpenter, *The Forging of Bureaucratic Autonomy: Reputations, Networks, and Policy Innovations in Executive Agencies, 1862–1928* (Princeton: Princeton University Press, 2001).

55. Scott R. Furlong and Cornelius M. Kerwin, "Interest Group Participation in Rule Making: A Decade of Change," *Journal of Public Administration Research and Theory* 15 (July 2004): 354.

56. Frank R. Baumgartner and Beth L. Leech, *Basic Interests: The Importance of Groups in Politics and in Political Science* (Chicago: Chicago University Press, 1998), 152; Furlong and Kerwin, "Interest Group Participation in Rule Making," 364; Kay Lehman Schlozman and John T. Tierney, *Organized Interests and American Democracy* (New York: Harper and Row, 1986), 150; Walker, *Mobilizing Interest Groups in America*, 109.

57. Edgar Lane, "Interest Groups and the Bureaucracy," in *Bureaucracy and Democratic Government*, ed. James C. Charlesworth (Philadelphia: American Academy of Political and Social Science, 1954), 108.

58. Suzanne J. Piotrowski and David Rosenbloom, "The Legal-Institutional Framework for Interest Group Participation in Federal Administrative Policymaking," in *Interest Group Connection*, 270–272; Ziegler and Peak, *Interest Groups in American Society*, 169.

59. Walker, *Mobilizing Interest Groups in America*, 69.

60. Dan Eggen, "Lobbyists Pushed off Advisory Panels," *Washington Post*, November 27, 2009, A1.

61. An excellent summary is presented in Piotrowski and Rosenbloom, "Legal-Institutional Framework," 258–281. More detail can be found in Cornelius M. Kerwin, *Rulemaking: How Government Agencies Write Law and Make Policy*, 3rd ed. (Washington, D.C.: CQ Press, 2003).

62. Piotrowski and Rosenbloom, "Legal-Institutional Framework," 267, 270–272; and Scott R. Furlong, "Exploring Interest Group Participation in Executive Policymaking," in *Interest Group Connection*, 284.

63. Kerwin, *Rulemaking*.

64. Furlong, "Exploring Interest Group Participation," 282–297; Marissa Martino Golden, "Interest Groups in the Rule-Making Process: Who Participates? Whose Voices Get Heard?" *Journal of Public Administration Research and Theory* 8 (April 1998): 245–270; and Kerwin, *Rulemaking*.

65. Furlong, "Exploring Interest Group Participation," 286.

66. Piotrowski and Rosenbloom, "Legal-Institutional Framework," 272–274; Schlozman and Tierney, *Organized Interests and American Democracy*, 348.

67. Furlong and Kerwin, "Interest Group Participation in Rulemaking," 365–368; Furlong, "Exploring Interest Group Participation."

68. John E. Chubb, *Interest Groups and the Bureaucracy: The Politics of Energy* (Stanford, Calif.: Stanford University Press, 1983); Furlong, "Exploring Interest Group Participation," 284.

69. For an overview of these changes and their impact, see R. Shep Melnick, *Between the Lines: Interpreting Welfare Rights* (Washington, D.C.: Brookings, 1994).

70. Marver Bernstein, *Regulating Business by Independent Commission* (Princeton: Princeton University Press, 1955); see also George J. Stigler, "The Theory of Economic Regulation," *The Bell Journal of Economics and Management Science* 2 (Spring 1971): 3–21.

71. Walker, *Mobilizing Interest Groups in America*, chap. 7.

72. Piotrowski and Rosenbloom, "Legal-Institutional Framework," 276–277. See also Thomas L. Gais, Mark A. Peterson, and Jack L. Walker, "Interest Groups, Iron Triangles, and Representative Institutions in American National Government," *British Journal of Political Science* 14 (April 1984): 161–185; and Hugh Heclo, "Issue Networks and the Executive Establishment," in *The New American Political System*, ed. Anthony King (Washington, D.C: American Enterprise Institute, 1978).

73. Golden, "Interest Groups in the Rule-Making Process"; Susan Webb Yackee, "Sweet-Talking the Fourth Branch: The Influence of Interest Group Comments on Federal Agency Rulemaking," *Journal of Public Administration Research and Theory* 16 (January 2006): 103–124.

74. Yackee, "Sweet-Talking the Fourth Branch," 116.

SUGGESTED READING

Herrnson, Paul S., Ronald G. Shaiko, and Clyde Wilcox, eds. *The Interest Group Connection: Electioneering, Lobbying, and Policymaking in Washington*. Washington, D.C.: CQ Press, 2005.

Peterson, Mark A. "The Presidency and Organized Interests: White House Patterns of Interest Group Liaison." *American Political Science Review* 86 (September 1992): 612–625.

Pika, Joseph A. "Interest Groups: A Doubly Dynamic Relationship." In *Presidential Policymaking: An End-of-Century Assessment*. Ed. Steven A. Shull. Armonk, N.Y.: M. E. Sharpe, 1999), 59–78.

———. "The White House Office of Public Liaison." *Presidential Studies Quarterly* 39 (September 2009): 549–573.

Shaiko, Ronald G. "Reverse Lobbying: Interest Group Mobilization from the White House and the Hill." In *Interest Group Politics*, 5th ed. Ed. Allan J. Cigler and Burdett A. Loomis. Washington, D.C.: CQ Press, 1998.

Yackee, Susan Webb. "Sweet-Talking the Fourth Branch: The Influence of Interest Group Comments on Federal Agency Rulemaking." *Journal of Public Administration Research and Theory* 16 (January 2006): 103–124.

chapter 11

Interest Groups and Political Parties: The Politics of Representation

by Paul S. Herrnson

INTEREST GROUPS AND POLITICAL parties have a storied place in American history, despite the ambivalence the framers of the U.S. Constitution felt about them. Today, many citizens consider interest groups and political parties sources of corruption and abuse. Among those holding these views are individuals who identify with, are members of, and even contribute to a political party or one or more interest groups. Regardless of the level of esteem or disdain with which they have been traditionally and are currently held, interest groups and parties have had and continue to have a major impact on American politics. They influence elections, the organization of government, and virtually every aspect of the policymaking process. By organizing and giving voice to the opinions of citizens and others living in the United States, they ensure that those in government look beyond their own interests when making public policy.

This chapter analyzes the roles of interest groups and parties in the political process, with a special focus on the politics of representation. Parties and groups can be seen in different lights: sometimes they cooperate effectively, often for extended period of time, as do Democrats and labor unions. But they also compete for influence, with groups sometimes working with parties, sometimes working against them, and at other times remaining apart from partisan politics. In short, groups and parties represent their constituencies in distinct ways. To put it mildly, relations between parties and groups are complex and subject to change, as they seek to fulfill their representational roles in American politics.[1] The first section discusses how the Constitution's framers regarded groups and parties, which they called "factions," and the impact their concerns about these organizations had on their blueprint for the government. The second section investigates the breadth of interests that seek to influence politics and the methods they use to pursue their goals, including electioneering and lobbying strategies. The third examines the roles of parties in the representation of citizens' views, including how they contribute to mobilizing voters, organizing the government, and policymaking. The fourth section discusses cooperation among parties and groups in the representation of various interests. Not surprisingly, the discussion of the Democratic Party highlights its relationships with labor unions, environmental groups, women, minorities, and other traditionally underrepresented and liberal groups, and the coverage of the Republican Party draws attention to that party's relationships with the business sector, free market and antiregulation groups, and more conservative elements of society that have been advantaged historically in American politics. The chapter concludes with a discussion of the impact of contemporary interest group and party politics on representation and policymaking.

CONSTITUTIONAL DESIGN AND THE POLITICS OF REPRESENTATION

Interest groups, political parties, and the politics of representation weighed heavily on the minds of the framers of the Constitution. The framers' main concern was that a large group or party—a faction—would become mobilized, unite, and become so obsessed with advancing its own interests that it would seek to pass laws contrary to the common good. Should this faction become large and persistent enough to capture the institutions of government it could result in a tyranny of the majority. Under this scenario, the political representation of minority interests would become insufficient to protect the minority's most basic rights and liberties from intrusion by those who belong to the majority interest.

The influence of the framers' vision for society and of the institutions they created is visible through the tremendous diversity in contemporary American society and the vast numbers of formal and informal groups that represent this diversity of interests. In 2000 there were about 22,000 associations representing various interests ranging from the major auto manufacturing companies to the unions representing their workers to associations representing doctors, lawyers, and other professionals to advocates for foreign, state, and local governments.[2] Whether advancing narrow, specific aims or advocating broad-based conservative, moderate, or liberal causes, interest groups are ubiquitous.

The growth and differentiation of groups have changed their capacity for representation. At present, groups articulate the interests of smaller and smaller slices of the population, as well as broader groups, such as the AARP, which seeks to represent more than 40 million citizens age fifty and over. The proliferation of narrow groups has often come at the expense of larger ones; in the 2009–2010 debate over health care, dozens of specific interests, such as teaching hospitals and nurse practitioners, weighed in on the legislation, a development that reduced the impact of the American Medical Association, which has lost its dominance in representing the medical community over the past fifty years.

The constitutional design has had a major impact on the organization and activities of American political parties as well. In theory, political parties exist to capture as many public offices as possible, suggesting they will organize to contest elections for every office.[3] In reality, neither of the two parties is that effectively organized. Both major parties, however, have decentralized organizations capable of contesting most federal and state offices and many others. Political decentralization has historically contributed to the parties' moderation, but the growing partisan polarization of national politics since the 1980s has diminished these moderating tendencies. Furthermore, the need to win the votes of individuals identifying with a wide array of interests has historically fostered the development of two moderate, broad-based parties. Unlike parties in multiparty systems, U.S. parties build their coalitions among interests before elections occur, rather than constructing coalitions after the election results are known. The constitutional design of the U.S. political system also has important implications for representation in general. The system that was designed to make it difficult for any one interest group or political party to dominate the political process resulted in these organizations flourishing.

The existence of so many political institutions with independent bases of power creates opportunities and, in many cases, expectations that interest groups and political parties will organize around these power centers. Sometimes referred to as access or pressure points, they include the White House, the bureaucracy, Congress, the federal courts, and parallel institutions in state and local governments. The maturation of many of these institutions has resulted in the development of a plethora of access points within them. In the House, Senate, state legislatures, and some local governments, these access points include committees, subcommittees, party leadership organizations, task forces, and formal and informal groups of policy entrepreneurs. The distribution of power within the political system laid down the basic underpinnings for what has developed into a very large lobbying community, which as is discussed later, has had a profound impact on the strategies interest groups and their lobbyists use to influence government.

INTEREST GROUPS

The seeds for a large and diverse interest group community may have been sown during the framing of the Constitution, but it took many economic, political, and sociological changes for those seeds to mature and bear fruit. Contemporary interest groups are involved in many aspects of politics, including elections, the staffing of the government, and policymaking. They contribute to the representation of many societal interests, but their overall involvement, whether as individual groups or as a whole, is not always benign.

Types of Interest Groups

Interest groups can be categorized in numerous ways, including as economic or noneconomic groups, membership or nonmembership groups, by the breadth of their agenda, or whether they represent private or public interests. One of the most frequently used categorizations divides interests into eight types: corporations; trade and other business associations; professional associations; unions; citizens' groups; groups representing specific segments of the population, such as women, the elderly, or disabled; groups advocating civil rights, social welfare, and related causes; and other miscellaneous interests. Among these groups, corporations and trade associations have the biggest presence in Washington, D.C. Roughly one-fifth of all corporations and one-third of all trade associations have offices in Washington. Together they make up about 75 percent of all groups that have established Washington offices. Professional organizations run a somewhat distant third, maintaining about 10 percent of all Washington offices, followed by citizens' groups, which have about 5 percent. Unions and the other types of organizations make up the remainder.[4]

A less complex scheme for categorizing interest groups was developed by the Federal Election Commission (FEC) for the purpose of categorizing political action committees or PACs (part of an interest group that makes contributions to candidates in federal elections).[5] The FEC's classification has the value of allowing one to measure the level of participation of each type of PAC in the financing of federal elections. During the 2006 election season almost 5,100 PACs were registered with the FEC, and they contributed approximately $372.1 million to federal candidates.[6] More than 58 percent of them were associated with business interests, including 38 percent sponsored by corporations and 20 percent sponsored by trade, membership, and health

Table 11.1 **Composition of the PAC Community and its Contributions, 2006 (in millions)**

PAC type	Percentage of PACs	Percentage of contributions
Corporate	35.3	$36.5
Corporations without stock	2.3	1.3
Trade/membership/health	20	27.4
Cooperative	0.8	0.9
Labor	6.1	15
Nonconnected	35.3	18.9
Total number of PACs/Total contributions	5,109	$372.1

organizations. These PACs accounted for almost two-thirds of all PAC contributions given in the 2006 election cycle. Labor unions accounted for a mere 6 percent of all PACs and approximately 15 percent of all PAC contributions. Nonconnected PACs, which had no organizational sponsor other than the PAC itself, are typically made up of citizens who share a deep concern for one or more salient issues. They accounted for the final 35 percent of all PACs and about 19 percent of all PAC donations.

In terms of representation, no matter what method of categorization one uses, the evidence strongly suggests that business interests are the most heavily represented members of the interest group community. That does not mean they always get what they want, but it does offer continuing support to scholar E. E. Schattschneider's famous dictum: "The flaw in the pluralist heaven is that the heavenly chorus sings with a strong upper-class accent." [7]

Another approach to organizing interest groups is by the resources they bring to bear on the political process. Resources include the group's financial clout, expertise, political contacts, leadership, a large membership, and a socially valued cause. Corporations and other business interests obviously have huge financial resources, which they use to help them establish political contacts and develop technical expertise they can deploy when trying to influence government. Many of the wealthiest companies in the United States or foreign companies that have U.S. subsidiaries maintain public relations offices in Washington and various state capitals. Others hire lobbying firms to monitor the activities of various legislative committees and government agencies to present their client's case when the time is ripe for action. Many labor unions also have representatives in Washington and in some state capitals. In addition to possessing significant financial resources, unions gain much of their clout because of their large united memberships that champion the causes of working men and women. Unions are especially influential with politicians whose electoral constituencies include many union members. Most citizens' groups, including those that form PACs, have neither the financial resources of business nor the manpower of labor. Instead, they derive their influence from the moral high ground associated with the causes they seek to advance and the skills of their leaders—as is exemplified by civil rights groups.[8]

Interest Group Strategies and Activities

Interest groups try to make their voices heard in politics in many ways, including participating in elections, using an inside strategy to have direct influence on the policymaking process, using an outside strategy to raise awareness about principal issues, and mobilizing grassroots supporters to pressure the government. The most effective groups choose a strategy that is well suited to their goals and resources and form coalitions with others that can bring additional resources to the table in pursuit of their common objectives. Some, like the representatives of the pharmaceutical industry, possess sufficient resources to use a broad array of strategies and tactics to influence the policymaking process.

Elections

In the United States, unlike in most other democracies, candidates, rather than parties, are responsible for most campaign activities.[9] Candidates are largely self-recruited and must assemble their own campaign organizations and money to run for office, and they need a wide array of sources for campaign assistance. As a result, elections provide an important path to political influence for PACs and other forms of organized interests as well as for individuals and political parties. In fact, most congressional candidates and campaign aides consider interest groups second only to parties in providing campaign assistance.[10]

Interest groups pursue somewhat different objectives when they participate in elections. Business-oriented groups consider elections an important part of a broader campaign to gain access and influence with elected officials. Recognizing that most officials, particularly members of Congress and state legislatures, are usually reelected, they contribute mainly to incumbents. Most of their contributions are financial, but some business-oriented groups provide fundraising assistance, purchase polls, or furnish other in-kind services to candidates. Business-oriented groups rarely make independent expenditures to attack a candidate or recruit candidates to challenge a sitting incumbent out of concern that such efforts would generate anger and undercut their goal of increasing their legislative clout. Still, when national trends are clear, as in 1994 and 2010, business interests may help challengers from one party, in both of those years Republicans, take advantage of the prevailing political winds.

Much of the support business groups provide is given to party leaders, committee and subcommittee chairs, and others in a position to influence legislation that is of importance to the group. Many contributions are made by a

THE PHARMACEUTICAL INDUSTRY PLAYS POLITICS

The pharmaceutical industry is among the most well-represented interests in the United States. Its targeted communications, often spearheaded by the trade association, Pharmaceutical Research and Manufacturers of America (PhRMA), include millions of dollars in spending intended to influence Congress and the executive branch. PACs and individuals associated with the industry contributed more than $70 million to federal candidates and parties during the five elections held between 1998 and 2006.* In addition to lobbying members of Congress and the executive branch, the industry tries to create a sympathetic climate of opinion in Washington, D.C., by advertising in specialized periodicals, including *Roll Call* and *The Hill*, which are widely read by national policymakers. PhRMA attempts to shape public opinion by televising issue advocacy ads and paying for print ads in major newspapers and magazines. The industry is also among the nation's leaders in generating grassroots support for its interests. One of its most effective tactics is to establish shell groups with innocuous names, such as Citizens for Better Medicare, the Seniors Coalition, and the United Seniors Association, to blanket the airwaves with television ads intended to gin up backing for public policies or candidates who support the interests of drug companies.

The pharmaceutical industry has been largely successful in its endeavors, helping to defeat President Bill Clinton's health care reform plan in 1994 and undermine a variety of prescription drug reforms that would have been unfavorable to its interests. One of its most recent triumphs was the enactment of the Medicare Prescription Drug, Improvement, and Modernization Act, which has been criticized by some as providing more benefits to the pharmaceutical industry than to the senior citizens it is supposed to serve.

SOURCE: Paul S. Herrnson, *Congressional Elections: Campaigning at Home and in Washington* (Washington, D.C.: CQ Press, 2008), 278–279.

*Spending figures include soft money contributions to parties during elections from 1998 through 2006. Figures compiled from the Center for Responsive Politics, www.opensecrets.org.

group's lobbyists as a part of laying the groundwork for later lobbying efforts. The basic principle is simple: group representatives seek to become perceived as part of an incumbent's reelection team during the campaign season with the hope of being considered part of an officeholder's policy team when the group's main issues are under consideration. Given their slim prospects for success, challengers rarely receive contributions from business-oriented groups, but candidates for open seats—who have good odds of being elected—often benefit from business PAC contributions, as well as those from outside groups.

Ideological groups, by contrast, perceive elections as an opportunity to change the composition of the legislature rather than to improve their relations with current members. The issues they seek to advance are often linked to values so fundamental that legislators would not be expected to change their views in response to a contribution or a visit by a lobbyist. Therefore, instead of targeting entrenched incumbents for support, they target candidates in competitive races so as to maximize the number of legislators who share their views. Ideological groups typically participate in a broader range of activities than access-oriented groups. They actively recruit candidates who share their views to run for office, try to discourage others, and participate in primary elections. These groups also make campaign endorsements, and contact their members to urge them to support their preferred candidates financially, to work as volunteers, and to vote. Unlike access-oriented groups, ideological groups often make independent expenditures to fund negative ads that discourage voters from backing an opponent. The Club for Growth, championing free markets and opposing taxes and government regulation, is an example of an ideological PAC that carries out a wide array of election activities. It recruits candidates to run for Congress against incumbents of both parties, and makes campaign contributions and independent expenditures, including paying for some extremely negative ads on television. In this instance and many others, money may provide enhanced representation for the voices of those who can raise and spend it.

Some groups, such as labor unions and some trade associations, pursue both access and ideological goals, following "mixed" strategies. These groups are like ideological groups in that they give the vast majority of their support to candidates of one party. Like access-oriented groups, however, they contribute substantial resources to party and committee leaders and other incumbents that occupy positions of power, including some who are very likely to win reelection.

The differences in the electoral behavior of groups that pursue access-oriented, ideological, or mixed strategies are grounded in their objectives for participating in the political process. A lobbyist for a corporation might reap tremendous legislative benefits from meeting with several congressional leaders to make the case for slightly lowering or raising tariffs on imports, but the leader of an ideological group, such as EMILY's List or the Susan B. Anthony List, which hold opposing sides on abortion, is unlikely to anticipate making any headway in persuading members of Congress to change their positions on abortion rights legislation.

Interest groups become involved in elections in a number of ways. By associating themselves with a particular candidate, groups hope to push their own agendas and reap policy rewards should their candidate win. In 2007 Democratic presidential hopeful Christopher Dodd received the endorsement of the International Association of Fire Fighters.

A group that uses a mixed strategy stands to benefit from maximizing the number of seats held by politicians who belong to the party that shares its views and maintaining good relations with party leaders who are in a position to advance its legislative goals. For ideological groups, a strategy that centers on reelecting friends and defeating opponents is usually preferable. For access-oriented groups, a strategy that keeps the doors of an elected official open for negotiating on narrowly based, often economic, matters is ideal. For unions and other groups that use mixed strategies, the best strategy is one that increases the number of elected officials of their preferred party and encourages that party's leaders to be responsive to them.

Inside Strategies

Inside strategies aim to influence one or more aspects of the legislative process, the administrative process, or the judicial process. Groups may testify at hearings, assist with writing legislation, help to formulate legislative strategy, and provide technical information about a bill and its impact on the nation or a legislator's constituents. They provide political information regarding public opinion about a bill and the elected officials and coalitions that make up its backers. They also provide talking points to help a legislator explain a highly visible and controversial roll-call vote to constituents. These efforts generally involve personal contact among lobbyists, members of Congress, and congressional aides. Some lobbyists bring group members whose causes they represent to Washington so these individuals can directly make their case to the members of Congress who represent them. Interest groups use similar tactics in many state capitals.[11]

Interest groups also try to influence cabinet officials, presidential and gubernatorial aides, and other members of the executive branch. They provide these individuals with technical information, participate in hearings, and discuss the ramifications of proposed decisions. Some help draft or provide comments on regulations and guidelines proposed by executive branch agencies. Group members also may serve on various advisory commissions. Influencing presidents and governors is much harder, but the difficulty does not stop groups from trying. Whether a group's lobbying strategy targets the legislature or executive branch in Washington or a state, part of the strategy must be to provide some sort of expertise in order to make the case for its position. A lobbyist who is regarded as a trustworthy and reliable source of information can wield a lot of influence in government circles (see Chapter 26).

The most successful groups in Washington are able to join with congressional subcommittee members and their staffs and with executive branch officials who have expertise in a particular area to form collegial decision-making groups, frequently referred to as "iron triangles," "issue networks," or "policy subgovernments."[12] These clusters of policy experts are small regimes within a government that focus on the minutiae of arcane, highly specialized areas of public policy. Acting below the general public's radar, they have tremendous power.

The judicial branch of the federal government is supposed to be immune to political pressures and resolve conflicts involving plaintiffs.[13] Individuals cannot make campaign contributions to federal judges, who are appointed for life, nor can they buttonhole them in a hallway of a courthouse as they might a member of Congress in the U.S. Capitol. Nevertheless, court rulings can have far-reaching consequences for individuals and societal interests and, as a result, the interest groups that try to influence them.

Interest groups try to influence the judicial process in a variety of ways. First, they try to influence who gets to serve on the courts by recommending potential nominees and endorsing or opposing those who are nominated. Groups such as the National Association for the Advancement of Colored People and the National Organization for Women are among the many recognized for lobbying members of the Senate, especially the Judiciary Committee, to make known their opinions of various nominees. The American Bar Association carries out a number of functions for the legal community, but perhaps its most visible one is vetting federal judicial nominees and giving them a rating ranging from "not qualified" to "well qualified."

Groups also try to influence the judicial process by educating judges and other members of the legal community about various issues through conferences and the publication of scholarly articles. The most direct way groups try to influence the courts is through litigation. Groups sponsor test cases to assess the constitutionality or application of the action of government; they file class action lawsuits representing large numbers of individuals (often group members) with a common complaint; and they file amicus briefs intended to provide a court with legal arguments or information that is pertinent to a case.

Outside Strategies

Interest groups often execute outside strategies to help create a positive political environment. Shaping public opinion so it favors a group's goals can be accomplished in a variety of ways, including talking to journalists and opinion columnists and disseminating television, radio, Internet, and print advertisements. Groups that have small budgets or lack the ability to capture the attention of journalists sometimes resort to public action. A large demonstration or protest can often garner substantial media attention from local and sometimes national news media. Regardless of the tactics used, a group that successfully shapes public opinion is in a strong position to attract the attention of policymakers and press them to support its cause.

A second aspect involves harnessing outside pressure, often referred to as grassroots lobbying, to influence policymakers directly. Labor unions, churches, and other groups with large memberships mobilize their members to pressure their representatives in government through campaigns of letter-writing, telephone calls, and e-mails. Astroturf lobbying occurs when a group's efforts are heavily contrived, such as when it generates letters to members of Congress that bear the names of group members from their states or districts (see Chapter 28). Grassroots and astroturf communications are intended to show legislators that important blocs of voters and their advocates are watching how they vote on specific pieces of legislation.[14] The more authentic a group's homegrown pressure, the more effective it is likely to be.

Interest Groups and the Policymaking Process

For the most part, interest groups have decentralizing effects on the policymaking process. Roughly 35,000 registered lobbyists work in the Washington area.[15] They are assisted by tens of thousands of others in trade associations, public relations firms, and other agencies that work to advance their own particular group's interests. Many others lobby state capitals. The effects of these organizations' jockeying to advance their preferred policies is to pull decision makers in many directions. This is particularly the case for members of Congress and state legislators, who are very sensitive to their constituents' interests.

The impact of interest group pressures is largely conservative in some significant ways. First, the existence of so many groups with diverse and often contradictory agendas and the presence of so many access points where they can make their views heard make it difficult for policymakers to reach the consensus needed to change public policy. Moreover, in situations where a consensus is reached, the original legislation is usually watered down and introduces only modest change. Second, given the financial, informational, and organizational advantages that business interests have over others, it is not surprising that the tax codes, regulations, and many other aspects of public policy in the United States favor business over labor, manufacturers over consumers, and the wealthy over the poor. Third, given the tremendous impact of corporate America on the overall health of the country, it is not surprising that most scholars believe that big business occupies a "privileged position" in American politics.[16]

The federal government's trillion-dollar bailouts of the banking, insurance, and automobile industries following the economic meltdown of 2008 provides substantial evidence to support this view. Still, many diverse interests are represented within the policymaking process.[17] Such extensive representation may well diminish the overall capacity of the political system to respond to serious issues, in that many interests will seek accommodation on any given major policy proposal, such as health care or banking reform.

POLITICAL PARTIES

Despite the framers' intentions, political parties not only took root and survived, but also flourished. The two major U.S. parties are the central contestants in most political battles; however, minor parties are important as well. Minor party (and independent) politicians typically involve placing new issues on the political agenda, introducing organizational innovations, influencing which major party candidate wins an election, and deciding which party possesses a majority in an evenly divided legislature. Parties in the United States are not as dominant or as plentiful as those in other democracies, but their influence is pervasive. Parties affect the political identification, opinions, and voting decisions of most citizens; they have a major impact on the careers of virtually all politicians; they are significant to the conduct of political campaigns; they organize the government; and they are critical players in the policymaking process. Their combined influence in each of these areas makes the parties central institutions for representation. What follows is a brief look at American parties, presented for the purpose of contrasting them with groups in terms of their representational roles.

The Party in the Electorate

The major parties' electoral followings are both large and broad based.[18] Although their memberships fluctuate in response to political events and conditions, each of the parties has attracted the loyalties of about one-third of the electorate over the last few decades. Independent and apolitical voters constitute the remainder. Each party's electoral coalition comprises many different groups of voters.[19] The Democratic coalition includes more people of lower socioeconomic status than does its Republican counterpart.

Significant demographic differences between the parties' electoral followings exist when one looks beyond socioeconomic status. Younger voters and senior citizens tend to identify with the Democratic Party. The middle-aged generally prefer the Republicans, and many remain Republicans as they age.[20] Substantially more women identify with the Democrats than the Republicans, and the men are about equally divided. The Democrats also attract the support of more blacks and Hispanics, while the Republicans benefit from the support of larger numbers of whites. Religion has a significant impact on voters' partisan identification. Republicans attract the support of substantially more Protestants who practice their religion on a regular basis. Reflecting their traditional loyalties to the Democratic Party, practicing Jews consider themselves Democrats

The National Rifle Association has long been a supporter of Republican candidates. Here Sen. John McCain, R-Ariz., addresses the NRA's national convention to rally support during his campaign for the presidency in 2008.

Democratic California gubernatorial candidate Jerry Brown, left, talks with union member Marvin Kropke during a campaign event on September 6, 2010. Much as Republicans rely on support from business and conservative interest groups, Democrats typically count on labor union backing.

by overwhelming numbers. Practicing Catholics, once a bulwark of support for the Democrats, are now evenly divided between Democrats and Republicans. Finally, secular voters (who do not attend any religious services) are substantially more likely to consider themselves Democrats than Republicans.

Voters' political dispositions and attitudes also influence their partisan alignments: most liberals consider themselves Democrats; most conservatives are Republicans; and moderates divide their support equally between the parties. These ideological alignments find expression in Democratic Party and Republican Party identifiers' support for various issues. Most who believe in bigger government and more government services identify themselves as Democrats; those who prefer a smaller government that provides fewer services consider themselves Republicans. Voters who favor government regulation in areas such as environmental protection and gun control tend to support the Democrats; those who hold opposing views tend to support the Republicans. In addition, given the differences in the demographic composition of the parties' coalitions, Democrats tend to attract the support of voters who favor abortion rights, affirmative action for blacks, increased immigration, and allowing gays to enter into marriage or civil union.

In short, the Democratic Party tends to attract more support of less prosperous elements of society, those belonging to traditionally underrepresented groups, and those who are most likely to benefit from government regulations and domestic programs. The Republican Party, on the other hand, derives much of its support from those who have traditionally enjoyed more political and economic power and would prefer to limit the government's ability to change the status quo. One crucial policy area where Republicans prefer more government action and Democrats prefer less is military spending and intervention. Those identifying with the GOP generally support greater defense spending and the use of force; and those who support the Democrats prefer to spend less on the military and are more likely to embrace diplomacy and the distribution of foreign aid.

Party Organizations and Campaigns

Most party campaign activities in the United States are conducted by party organizations that seek to maximize the number of offices under their control. Winning votes is therefore an important first step in advancing a party's interests and representing the individuals and interest groups that are part of its constituency. Party organizations have traditionally carried out a number of activities to help elect their candidates. These activities include associating the party and its candidates with popular issues through writing a platform and setting a political agenda that works to their advantage and directly assisting candidates with their campaigns. The parties' and candidates' reliance on private funding means that their fortunes to some degree rise and fall with their abilities to raise money. The private funding of campaigns creates opportunities for interest groups to have a significant impact on elections and many other aspects of politics.

During the nineteenth and early twentieth centuries political parties were the central actors in elections. Local party bosses and the old-fashioned political machines they headed collected most of the money and supplied the manpower needed to wage a campaign, and they were responsible for mounting those campaigns. Their ability to hand out nominations, distribute government jobs and contracts, and assist their constituents in other ways resulted in the parties holding the keys to electoral success. This concentration of power, however, severely limited the impact of ordinary citizens on the election process. Because most party decisions were made behind closed doors by top leaders, regular partisans had little say in the selection of party nominees, the formulation of campaign issues, or any other aspect of campaigning. Nor could they do much to affect the party's postelection legislative agenda. The lack of representation in party activities and the corrupt nature of party politics led reformers to pass a number of measures intended to weaken parties, including the direct primary, civil service regulations, and campaign finance reforms. The reforms, along with the erosion of the tight-knit ethnic neighborhoods that once formed the core of the machines' constituency, the modernization of mass communications, and the introduction of innovations from the public relations arena to political campaigns, led to a precipitous decline of the parties' roles in electoral politics. By the mid-twentieth century, a new candidate-centered model of elections had emerged. Under this model, self-starter candidates campaigned to secure their party's nomination, raised their own funds, and used their own campaign organizations to contest the general election. Because of the centrality of money in elections, the candidate-centered campaign increased the influence of interest groups in elections.

Following the 1968 presidential election, party reforms introduced by the Democrats' McGovern-Fraser Commission made the presidential nominations process more participatory and demographically representative. Codified into law in many states, the major provisions of these reforms still remain in place, despite tinkering by later reform commissions. The reforms require that party nominations processes, whether primaries or caucuses, be open to the participation of individuals who register to vote as party members. (In some states unaffiliated voters are allowed to participate, and parties in a few states allow for the participation of individuals who register with the opposing party.) Democratic Party rules require the delegations that Democratic state parties select to participate in the party's national convention to be demographically representative in terms of gender, race, and ethnicity. They also tie delegate selection to candidate preferences. That is, most of the delegates to the national convention are selected on the basis of their support for a presidential candidate, and the delegates are expected to vote to nominate that candidate at the convention. This requirement results in the proportional representation of the candidate picks of primary and caucus participants. Contemporary Democratic national conventions offer a broad representational picture of the party's adherents, as opposed to those prior to the 1970s, which were dominated by party bosses and hand-picked white male party activists.

Although Democrats introduced the most far-reaching party reforms, the reform movement also affected the Republican Party. Some state Republican parties put forth reforms similar to those of the Democrats; others were forced to go along when Democratic state legislatures enacted them into law. Nevertheless, although more open and participatory than they were during the pre-reform era, most GOP convention delegates are still white males. Moreover, because of the rules the Republicans use to select delegates, their conventions do not adhere as closely to the principle of proportional representation as the Democrats' conventions.[21]

The next set of party organizational changes took place during the late 1970s and early 1980s, when the parties began to adapt to the candidate-centered election system by raising more money and developing new election programs. First, the Republicans and then the Democrats transformed their national, congressional, and senatorial campaign committees in Washington into major centers of campaign money and political expertise, which they used primarily to help federal candidates involved in closely contested races. The Democratic and Republican congressional and senatorial campaign committees began to give candidates substantial contributions, make large coordinated expenditures on their behalf, and provide them with assistance with campaign management, strategy, communications, fund-raising, issue and opposition research, and other aspects of campaigning requiring technical expertise or in-depth research. They also began to provide candidates with transactional assistance to help them obtain money and other resources from other politicians, political consultants, and PACs. Party assistance became an important factor in determining which House and Senate candidates received the support of PACs, political consultants, and others elites that participated in congressional candidates.[22] Some state party committees underwent similar transformations and began to provide candidates for state offices with comparable assistance.[23]

In addition to campaign services and transactional assistance provided directly to candidates, the national and some state party organizations communicate directly to voters. They use independent expenditures (made without the knowledge or consent of their candidates) to communicate via television, radio, the Internet, or the U.S. mail to build

MAJOR PARTY PLATFORMS, 2008

	Democratic Party	Republican Party
Abortion and reproductive rights	The Democratic Party strongly and unequivocally supports *Roe v. Wade* and a woman's right to choose a safe and legal abortion, regardless of ability to pay, and we oppose any and all efforts to weaken or undermine that right. The Democratic Party also strongly supports access to comprehensive affordable family planning services and age-appropriate sex education which empower people to make informed choices and live healthy lives. We also recognize that such health care and education help reduce the number of unintended pregnancies and thereby also reduce the need for abortions.	[W]e assert the inherent dignity and sanctity of all human life and affirm that the unborn child has a fundamental individual right to life which cannot be infringed. We support a human life amendment to the Constitution, and we endorse legislation to make clear that the Fourteenth Amendment's protections apply to unborn children. We oppose using public revenues to promote or perform abortion and will not fund organizations which advocate it. We support the appointment of judges who respect traditional family values and the sanctity and dignity of innocent human life.
Energy and the environment	[W]e Democrats commit to fast-track investment of billions of dollars over the next ten years to establish a green energy sector that will create up to five million jobs . . . where workers manufacture wind turbines, . . . solar energy generation plants, or . . . in hybrids. . . . [W]e'll create a . . . program to give disadvantaged youth job skills for this emerging industry. We know we can't drill our way to energy independence and so we must invest in research and development, and deployment of renewable energy technologies . . . as well as technologies to store energy through advanced batteries and clean up our coal plants.	If we are to have the resources we need to achieve energy independence, we simply must draw more American oil from American soil. We support accelerated exploration, drilling and development from new oilfields. . . . We will encourage refinery construction and modernization and, with sensitivity to environmental concerns, an expedited permitting process. . . . We must continue to develop alternative fuels, such as biofuels. . . . We must also produce more vehicles that operate on electricity and natural gas, both to reduce demand for oil and to cut CO_2 emissions.
Health care	Democrats are united around a commitment that every American man, woman, and child be guaranteed affordable, comprehensive healthcare. . . . [This] would end cost-shifting from the uninsured, promote prevention and wellness, stop insurance discrimination, help eliminate health care disparities, and achieve savings through competition, choice, innovation, and higher quality care. . . . Health care should be a shared responsibility between employers, workers, insurers, providers and government. . . . We support increased funding into research, care and prevention of HIV/AIDS. . . . We need to invest in	Republicans believe the key to real reform is to give control of the health care system to patients and their health care providers, not bureaucrats in government or business. . . . [We] oppose socialized medicine in the form of a government-run universal health care system. . . . [W]e fully support parental rights to consent to medical treatment for their children including mental health treatment, drug treatment, alcohol treatment, and treatment involving pregnancy, contraceptives and abortion. . . . .[W]e call for a major expansion of research . . . with adult stem cells, umbilical cord blood, and . . . without the destruction of embryonic human life. . . . No health care professional . . . should

support for their candidates or tear down their candidates' opponents. During presidential election years the Democratic and Republican national committees also spend millions to try to set a national political agenda that favors their candidates. The parties' congressional and senatorial campaign committees spend additional sums in presidential and midterm election years to set favorable campaign agendas in the constituencies of their most competitive contestants. Party organizations at all levels seek to identify, register, and mobilize voters that support their candidates. The election programs the parties began to develop during the 1970s and 1980s have enabled them to play important supplemental roles in the campaigns of candidates involved in closely contested elections.

The 2008 elections bear witness to the importance of party activity. Formal party organizations spent approximately $345 million on contributions, coordinated expenditures, and independent expenditures in the contests for president, the U.S. House, and the U.S. Senate. They spent additional sums on issue advocacy advertising, voter mobilization, and other campaign efforts. Party politicians also contributed an additional $50.4 million from their personal campaign accounts and leadership PACs to other candidates.[24] Most of these funds flowed from members of Congress to other members and congressional candidates. Party campaign support, agenda-setting activities, and influence on the campaign decision making of others increased the parties' influence over which candidates get elected. At the

	Democratic Party	Republican Party
	biomedical research and stem cell research. . . . We will end health insurance discrimination against contraception and provide compassionate care to rape victims.	ever be required to perform, provide for, or refer for a health care service against their conscience. . . . We must ensure that taxpayer money is focused on caring for U.S. citizens and other individuals in our country legally.
National security	To renew American leadership in the world, we must first bring the Iraq war to a responsible end. Our men and women in uniform have performed admirably while sacrificing immeasurably. Our civilian leaders have failed them. . . . We will defeat Al Qaeda in Afghanistan and Pakistan, where those who actually attacked us on 9-11 reside and are resurgent. . . . We will fully fund and implement the recommendations of the bipartisan 9-11 Commission. . . We must invest still more in human intelligence and deploy additional trained operatives with specialized knowledge of local cultures and languages. . . We will review the current Administration's warrantless wiretapping program.	Along with unrelenting vigilance to prevent bioterrorism and other WMD-related attacks, we must regularly exercise our ability to quickly respond if one were to occur. . . . We must develop and deploy both national and theater missile defenses to protect the American homeland, our people, our Armed Forces abroad, and our allies. . . . We must increase the ranks and resources of our human intelligence capabilities, integrate technical and human sources, and get that information more quickly to the warfighter and the policy maker. The multi-jurisdictional arrangements that now prevail on Capitol Hill should be replaced by a single Joint Committee on Intelligence.
Taxes	We will expand the childcare tax credit, . . . we'll expand the Earned Income Tax Credit, and raise the minimum wage and index it to inflation. . . . We will . . . create a new American Opportunity Tax Credit to ensure that the first $4,000 of a college education is completely free for most Americans. We will . . . end the tax breaks that ship jobs overseas. . . . We will exempt all start-up companies from capital gains taxes and provide them a tax credit for health insurance. . . . We will restore fairness and responsibility to our tax code. . . . We will shut down the corporate loopholes and tax havens and use the money so that we can provide an immediate middle-class tax cut that will offer relief to workers and their families. We'll eliminate federal income taxes for millions of retirees. . . . We will not increase taxes on any family earning under $250,000 and we will offer additional tax cuts for middle class families.	[We will] tax only to raise revenue for essential government functions. . . . [We] support a supermajority requirement in both the House and Senate to guard against tax hikes. . . . The Republican Party will . . . simplify tax policy, eliminating special deals, and putting those saved dollars back into the taxpayers' pockets. Republicans will advance tax policies to support American families, promote savings and innovation, and put us on a path to fundamental tax reform. We will continue our fight against the federal death tax. . . . We support a major reduction in the corporate tax rate so that American companies stay competitive . . . and American jobs can remain in this country. . . . The mammoth IRS tax code must be replaced with a system that is simple, transparent, and fair while maximizing economic growth and job creation. . . . We support choice in education for all families . . . whether through charter schools, vouchers or tax credits for attending faith-based or other nonpublic schools, or the option of home schooling.

SOURCES: Democratic Party, http://www.democrats.org/a/party/platform.html; and Republican Party, http://platform.gop.com/2008platform.pdf.

same time, the increased activity of groups in raising and spending campaign funds serves both to complement and compete with party funding.

Parties in Government

Parties in government help translate citizen preferences, as expressed in the polling place, into public policies. One essential step in this process involves organizing the government. Members of the majority party in the House caucus select the Speaker, majority leader, majority whip, caucus chair, and a host of lesser officials that will have the responsibility for leading their party. They also select committee and subcommittee leaders and distribute committee assignments to their members. Members of the minority party also select leaders and distribute committee assignments. Party members in the U.S. Senate and most state legislative chambers also caucus to select their leaders. Presidents and governors can select anyone they want to fill their cabinet, executive offices, and other appointed positions, but the vast majority of their selections are almost always members of their party.

Another critical step involves influencing the political agenda. The president is the nation's number one agenda setter, but the president must negotiate with party leaders in Congress because the House and Senate set their own legislative agendas. When one party controls both the presidency and the legislature, it can generally ensure that the issues its supporters care about are considered in the policymaking process. During periods of divided government, the president's priorities are usually paramount, but both parties must compromise for the government to accomplish anything. Still, parties often compete with organized interests for space on a limited legislative agenda; since the 1980s groups have increasingly sought specific spending earmarks outside the regular legislative process, and they are often passed with little partisan consideration.[25]

A third important step concerns steering the policymaking activities of public officials. Members of Congress and state legislators often focus on the parochial interests of their constituents. They also give considerable attention to the interest groups that have supported their campaigns. These centrifugal forces have a major impact on what legislators do in office. Committee assignments, interest-based caucuses, and pressures from lobbyists have a decentralizing effect on the legislative process. Nevertheless, party affiliation is one the best explanations for how members of Congress cast their legislative roll-call votes. There are a number of reasons for the importance of the party connection: politicians who share similar ideologies and policy preferences typically join the same party; electoral districts whose voters that share similar political views typically elect politicians of the same party to office; party campaign assistance can strengthen a politician's proclivities to support their party's goals once in office; elected officials depend on party leaders and their colleagues for committee assignments, mentoring, and other assistance in advancing their policy preferences and careers; and elected officials are well aware that voters judge both their performance as individuals and their party's accomplishments in office when voting in the next election.

Political Parties and Policymaking

Elections are blunt instruments for controlling government, but they are an important foundation for representation, especially in a political system that uses checks and balances to limit the majority party's ability to translate public impulses into policy and creates many opportunities for interest group input. Because both parties seek to maximize the number of votes they win and must overcome the centrifugal pressures that legislators feel from their constituent and interest group supporters, they tend to stake out moderate issue positions. Under most circumstances policymaking is incremental, leading to modest change in the role of government and the rules by which Americans live most of the time. When the Democrats are in power, they seek to introduce programs that improve the lives of working Americans, enact regulations to protect worker safety and the environment, and put in place laws that protect rights and advance opportunities for minorities, women, and other traditionally under-represented groups. They also use foreign aid and diplomacy as major tools for international relations. When Republicans are in control, they seek to enact free market policies that benefit business over labor, reduce workplace safety regulations and environmental protections that may hinder production, overturn programs that advance the interests of women and minorities in favor of conservative social policies, and pursue a muscular foreign policy. The operative word in both parties' policy pursuits is *seek*, as it is often difficult for a party to accomplish its policy goals. Under most circumstances the best they can do is to enact small policy changes in their preferred direction. But even small changes can constitute significant victories for some party constituencies, including supportive interest groups.

The incremental style of policymaking that characterizes "politics as usual" is, however, occasionally punctuated by periods of major policy change. Following the 1929 stock market crash and the onset of the Great Depression, the next two elections led to Democratic takeovers of the previously Republican-controlled House and Senate and the replacement of a Republican president, Herbert Hoover, by Democrat Franklin D. Roosevelt. Once in power, Roosevelt and the Democrats transformed the federal government's laissez-faire economic and social policies with policies that gave the federal government a major role in the economy, including the creation of massive public works projects that produced new jobs and "safety net" programs designed to combat poverty. A second example of massive policy change is President Lyndon Johnson's Great Society initiatives, which sought to eliminate poverty and racial injustice through addressing problems in education, medical care, and the nation's crumbling cities. A third example is important both in terms of what it did and did not accomplish. Following the Republican Party's winning majority control of both the U.S. House and Senate for the first time in forty years in 1994, GOP House leaders, armed with their "Contract with America," sought to eliminate or drastically reduce several social welfare programs and to reduce the size and impact of the federal government. The Republicans were successful in passing most of their agenda in the House, but they were unable to garner enough support in the Senate to enact most of the contract's provisions into law.

For all their ability to set the legislative agendas, parties must also address the highly focused wishes of organized interests. The AARP worked with Republicans to fashion Medicare drug benefits in 2003, but then coordinated their efforts with Democrats in 2009–2010 in efforts to pass health care reform.

INTEREST GROUP-POLITICAL PARTY COLLABORATION AND COMPETITION

Given that interest groups and political parties represent some of the same individuals and societal interests, it is not surprising that they forge alliances and work together in pursuit of their mutual goals. By cooperating, these organizations can improve the representation of their mutual constituents. Labor unions have worked closely with the Democratic Party, and business interests have had strong ties with the Republicans. At the same time, groups and parties ordinarily collaborate and compete with each other. Competition takes place in fund-raising, attracting the allegiances and volunteer efforts of activists, and in the policymaking process. Collaboration occurs in these same areas, and historical circumstances influence the amount of each.

Interest group and party leaders recognize that they can help each other and their preferred candidates in many areas of campaigning, including fund-raising. Given that federal and most state laws limit the amount that an individual, political party, or interest group can contribute to a candidate or a political organization, parties and groups understand it is usually in their best interests, and in those of their preferred candidates, to cooperate with each other in channeling funds to close races. Many interest groups contribute to party organizations and follow party cues when contributing to candidates; some party organizations provide information and other resources to interest groups. Similarly, parties and groups sometimes collaborate with each other in recruiting candidates and providing them with campaign services and assistance. Such cooperation may break down when parties and interest groups back different candidates in a primary or the general election.

Groups and parties also may collaborate or compete for the loyalties of political activists and volunteers. Competition stems from the reality that these individuals possess only so much time to devote to politics and that volunteering for a party-run voter canvass may prevent them from volunteering in a canvass run by an interest group or vice-versa. For example, some of the grassroots supporters who volunteered on the Obama-Biden 2008 election campaign probably would have worked for a union or some other progressive organization had that campaign's outreach efforts not been so extensive. But knowing that an allied organization and its volunteers are working to mobilize part of one's own constituency can lead to coordination and cooperation. Confidence in labor unions' abilities to mobilize union voters frees Democrats to focus on non-union voters, such as women, environmentalists, other Democrats, and independents. Republican Party officials generally devote fewer resources to mobilizing business leaders because they can count on the U.S. Chamber of Commerce, its state and local affiliates, and other trade associations for that purpose. Likewise, social conservative groups and evangelical churches often complement Republican organizations in many states.

The policymaking process is another arena where interest group-political party relations can be characterized by collaboration or competition, depending on the policy area and the relationship between the group and the party. In areas of strong policy agreement, interest groups can work with party leaders in Congress to help write a piece of legislation and generate support for it among party members in the House and Senate. The more broadly based the interest group coalition, the more assistance group members can give party leaders in collecting congressional votes. In policy areas where there is some but not complete agreement among party members in Congress and relevant interest groups, the legislative process is often marked by competition among groups and members who wish to shape the details of a bill. Finally, when powerful interest

The so-called K Street Project, conceived of as a way to garner Republican support amongst interest groups, was named after Washington, D.C.'s, K Street, N.W., home to many lobbying firms.

groups are divided or strongly oppose a bill, they can use the political systems' numerous access points to try to kill it, including opposing it in relevant subcommittees, full committees, on the House or Senate floor, or in the White House. The executive branch offers additional venues for opposing or weakening a policy during the implementation stage of the policy process. Groups also can challenge some policies in the courts. Scholars often use the term *hyperpluralism* when describing the situation in which political pressures emanating from a plethora of particular interest groups work to prevent the government from acting.[26]

In the late 1990s and during much of the George W. Bush administration, GOP congressional leaders pressured many interest groups to work with Republicans as part of an overall "team." Labeled the K Street Project, Rep. Tom DeLay and others aggressively sought to reward their interest group friends and punish their enemies.[27] In the end, however, groups often have interests that are more specific and frequently at odds with the comprehensive agendas of political parties, The K Street Project ultimately failed to form lobbyists and groups into partisan alignments, a stark demonstration of how groups and parties offer distinct kinds of representation.

In general, party leaders have more clout in their relationships with interest groups when their party possesses both legislative and electoral majorities and is strongly united on the issues. When a party is in the minority or its members of Congress are somewhat divided, interest groups can bargain with the congressional party leadership or with other members of the party's caucus to try to accomplish their aims. Under these circumstances, group activity serves to reinforce the pressures felt by members of Congress, and it can weaken or kill a piece of legislation.

CONCLUSION

Interest groups and political parties have had a long and storied history in American politics. Although neither is mentioned in the Declaration of Independence or the U.S. Constitution, these organizations have come to play important roles in representation and governance, including the formation of public opinion, the conduct of campaigns and elections, and various aspects of the policymaking process. The influence of both sets of organizations has been shaped by the broader political environment and by the relative power possessed by the other. When political parties are strong, interest groups tend to be less powerful, and vice-versa. Most would agree that during the late twentieth and early twenty-first centuries interest groups, particularly those that have money, expertise, and a corps of dedicated volunteers, have had the upper hand. However, both parties and groups tend to benefit when leaders of both sets of organizations find ways to collaborate, either through sustained sets of relationships or through more fleeting associations. Still, groups and parties often represent their constituencies in different ways, and as groups have grown in number and power over the 20th century their very density tends to slow down the possibility of broad policy change, even in the wake of substantial partisan electoral victories.

NOTES

1. Christopher Witko, "The Ecology of Party-Organized Interest Relationships," *Polity* 41, 2 (April 2009): 211–234.
2. Frank R. Baumgartner, "The Grown and Diversity of U.S. Associations, 1954–2004," working paper, March 29, 2005.
3. Joseph A. Schlessinger, "The New American Political Party," *American Political Science Review* 79 (1985): 1152– 1169.
4. Kay Lehman Schlozman and John T. Tierney, *Organized Interests and American Democracy* (New York: Harper and Row, 1986), 67.
5. Some PACs also contribute to political parties and make independent expenditures.
6. "PAC Activity Continues to Climb in 2006," Federal Election Commission press release, October 5, 2007, http://www.fec.gov/press/press2007/20071009pac/20071009pac.shtml.
7. E. E. Schattschneider, *The Semisovereign People* (New York: Holt, Rinehart, and Winston, 1960), 35.
8. Schlozman and Tierney, *Organized Interests*, 103–106.
9. This section draws heavily from Paul S. Herrnson, *Congressional Elections: Campaigning at Home and in Washington* (Washington, D.C.: CQ Press, 2008), esp. 132–165.
10. Ibid., 161.
11. Schlozman and Tierney, *Organized Interests*, 289–310.
12. See Gordon Adams, *The Iron Triangle* (New York: Council on Economic Priorities, 1981), 175–180; Hugh Heclo, "Issue Networks and the Executive Establishment," in *The New American Political System*, ed. Anthony King (Washington, D.C.: American Enterprise Institute, 1978), 87–124.
13. Note that in some states judges are elected or selected by governors (often with the approval of the state legislature) and subject to retention elections.
14. Linda L. Fowler and Ronald D. Shaiko, "The Grass Roots Connection," *American Journal of Political Science* 31 (1987): 484–510; James G. Gimpel, "Grassroots Organizations and Equilibrium Cycles in Group Mobilization and Access," in *The Interest Group Connection*, ed. Paul S. Herrnson, Ronald G. Shaiko, and Clyde Wilcox (Chatham, N.J.: Chatham House, 1998), 100–115.
15. Jeffrey H. Birnbaum, "The Road to Riches Is Called K Street," *Washington Post*, June 22, 2005.
16. Charles E. Lindblom, *Politics and Markets* (New York: Basic Books, 1977), 170–188.
17. Jonathan Rauch, *Government's End: Why Washington Stopped Working* (New York: Public Affairs, 1999).

18. On party identification, see especially, Angus Campbell, Philip E. Converse, Warren E. Miller, and Donald E. Stokes, *The American Voter* (New York: John Wiley, 1960).

19. The descriptions of the parties' coalitions draw heavily from Peter F. Galderisi, "Overview of the Electorate," in *Guide to Campaign Politics* (Washington, D.C.: CQ Press, 2005), esp. 116–118.

20. See http://www.cnn.com/ELECTION/2008/results/polls/#USP00p1.

21. See, for example, Byron E. Shafer, *Quiet Revolution: The Struggle for the Democratic Party and the Shaping of Post-Reform Politics* (New York: Russell Sage, 1983).

22. Paul S. Herrnson, *Party Campaigning in the 1980s* (Cambridge: Harvard University Press, 1988); Cornelius P. Cotter, James L. Gibson, John F. Bibby, and Robert J. Huckshorn, *Party Organizations in American Politics* (Pittsburgh: University of Pittsburgh Press, 1989).

23. Herrnson, *Congressional Elections,* 124–126.

24. For more information on candidate-to-candidate contributions see ibid., 104–107; and Paul S. Herrnson, "Party Organizations, Party-Connected Committees, Party Allies, and the Financing of Federal Elections," *Journal of Politics* 71 (2009): 1207–1224. The 2008 figure is from the Center for Responsive Politics.

25. See, for example, Robert Kaiser, *So Damn Much Money* (New York: Knopf, 2009), on earmarks for higher education.

26. Rauch, *Government's End.*

27. See, for example, Burdett Loomis, "Does K Street Run Through Capitol Hill? Lobbying Congress in the Republican Era," in *Interest Group Politics,* 7th ed., ed. Allan Cigler and Burdett Loomis (Washington, D.C.: CQ Press, 2008).

SUGGESTED READING

Berry, Jeffrey M. *The New Liberalism: The Rising Power of Citizen Groups.* Washington, D.C.: Brookings Institution Press, 1998.

Dark, Taylor. *The Unions and the Democrats: An Enduring Alliance.* Ithaca, N.Y.: Cornell University Press, 1999.

Herrnson, Paul S. *Congressional Elections: Campaigning at Home and in Washington,* 5th ed. Washington, D.C.: CQ Press, 2008.

Key, V. O. *Politics, Parties, and Pressure Groups,* 5th ed. New York: Thomas Y. Crowell, 1964.

Sager, Ryan. *The Elephant in the Room: Evangelicals, Libertarians, and the Battle to Control the Republican Party.* Hoboken, N.J.: John Wiley, 2006.

Thomas, Clive S. *Political Parties and Interest Groups: Shaping Democratic Governance.* Boulder: Lynne Rienner, 2005.

PART IV ★ INTEREST GROUPS BY SECTOR AND TYPE

CHAPTER 12	**Agricultural**	163
CHAPTER 13	**Business and Organized Labor**	173
CHAPTER 14	**Defense and Homeland Security**	193
CHAPTER 15	**Civil Rights**	209
CHAPTER 16	**Issue Advocacy Groups and Think Tanks**	223
CHAPTER 17	**Religious Interest Groups**	239
CHAPTER 18	**Women's and Feminist Movements and Organizations**	251
CHAPTER 19	**Public Interest Groups**	261
CHAPTER 20	**Professional Associations**	271
CHAPTER 21	**Elementary and Secondary Education**	283

CHAPTER 22 Energy and the Environment 295

CHAPTER 23 Intergovernmental Lobbying 309

CHAPTER 24 Foreign Lobbying 321

chapter 12

Agriculture

by Adam Sheingate

EVERY FIVE YEARS OR SO, CONGRESS passes a massive farm bill covering a host of programs and policies, including food stamps, land conservation, and rural development. The most contentious and controversial element of all farm policy, however, is the portion authorizing the federal government to boost farm incomes with crop subsidies, loans, and other forms of support. In 2008, the last time Congress enacted farm legislation, it left the basic operation of these commodity programs largely unchanged, despite record high prices for crops and a projection by the Congressional Budget Office that spending for these subsidies would reach $42 billion over the next five years; (in fact, the actual cost likely will be higher; farm spending during the previous five years exceeded $81 billion).[1] Amidst concerns about rising deficits and the high cost of subsidies, President George W. Bush vetoed the 2008 farm bill. Undeterred, Congress set aside its partisan differences as ninety-nine Republicans in the House and thirty-five Republicans in the Senate joined the majority Democrats to override the president's veto and make the farm bill law.[2]

While Congress was extending the system of crop subsidies, the U.S. Department of Agriculture (USDA) was tabulating the results of the 2007 Census of Agriculture. Taken once every five years, the census reported a total of 2.2 million farms in the United States, home to roughly 6.8 million people or just over 2 percent of the population.[3] A closer look at the numbers shows that far fewer truly make a living from farming. Of the nearly 3.3 million farm owners or operators in the United States, less than half listed farming as their primary occupation. The reason is that the vast majority of farms in the United States, nearly 80 percent, have annual sales of agricultural products that total less than $50,000, and 40 percent of all farms sold less than $2,500 in products in 2007. Today, most of our nation's domestic food supply comes from a small number of very large farms. According to the 2007 census, just 125,000 farms accounted for 75 percent of the total value of the nation's agricultural production. At the same time, these largest, most productive farms receive most of the money from government programs. In 2007 more than half of all subsidies went to just over 150,000 farms with annual sales of $250,000 or more.[4]

These developments might strike some as puzzling or troubling or both. At a time when fewer people make a living from farming, the federal government continues to subsidize agricultural production by about $16 billion a year. Moreover, it is not the marginal farmers who receive the bulk of these subsidies, but rather a handful of large producers who make up the most economically viable part of the sector and seemingly have the least need for government support. More cynical readers and most political scientists will immediately point to the power of agricultural interest groups and their influence in Congress as an obvious explanation for this continued government largesse. In large measure, this conclusion would be right: it is the politics that explains the policy.

But the story is more complicated than that, especially if we want to understand why agricultural interest groups continue to enjoy such influence even though they represent ever fewer numbers of farmers. The key is to understand how the characteristics of agricultural policy and the unique features of agricultural production translate into political influence for agricultural interests. In addition, the institutional features of Congress and broader political conditions also help farm groups defend the status quo.

The next section describes the history of agricultural groups in the United States since the nineteenth century. This history provides some context for the discussion that follows as well as illustrating the long involvement of the federal government in agricultural matters—itself an important part of the explanation.[5] Next comes an examination of various sources of interest group power, including the political economy of agriculture, policy effects, institutional characteristics, and political factors that help explain why small numbers of farmers continue to wield a large degree of influence over agricultural matters. The chapter concludes with a consideration of future prospects for agricultural interest groups. As the number of farmers who actually benefit from current farm programs continues to shrink, agricultural interest groups may find their membership and influence declining in the future.

A BRIEF HISTORY OF AGRICULTURAL INTEREST GROUPS

Although American farmers were involved in various agricultural societies since the days of the early Republic, it is in the late nineteenth century when producers first established political organizations. Responding to the challenges of the Industrial Revolution, farmers were among the first occupational groups to call for a stronger government role in the economy. Agrarian discontent intensified with the farm crisis of the 1920s, and, in the midst of the Great Depression, agriculture became a cornerstone of the New Deal. Farmers, through their local organizations, were important for the success of New Deal farm programs, a policy role that translated into political influence as well. Aided by government subsidies, agriculture prospered in the decades after World War II as farm organizations skillfully influenced the policy process in Congress. In recent decades, agricultural interest groups have managed to retain a great deal of influence before Congress, but they also face challenges from groups representing the interests of industry, consumers, and environmentalists.

The power of the Farmers' Alliance to achieve legislation favorable for America's farmers is caricatured in this cartoon from 1891.

Nineteenth-Century Farm Organizations

In 1867 Oliver Kelley, a former clerk of the USDA, established the Order of the Patrons of Husbandry, commonly known as the Grange. Kelley envisioned an organization that would be an adjunct to the Department of Agriculture, with local associations organized into state chapters represented at an annual convention of the National Grange. With the creation of a nationwide organization of farmers, Kelley predicted that "Congress will appropriate a million . . . dollars annually for the Department of Agriculture," adding that "hardly any member of Congress would wish to vote against appropriations that would be called for by the department." [6]

Despite Kelley's enthusiasm, his group's progress was slow until growing resentment toward the railroads led to a rapid rise in membership; at its peak in 1875, 800,000 men and women were members of 20,000 local granges throughout the country. In many state capitals, particularly in the Midwest, the Grange wielded considerable influence on matters such as railroad regulation, and it pushed successfully at the national level for the elevation of the USDA to cabinet status in 1889. On other important issues, such as the tariff, the Grange was internally divided, and with the deteriorating economic condition of agriculture in the 1880s, many local granges ceased operation and membership declined precipitously.[7]

The Farmers' Alliance further demonstrates the organizational limits of nineteenth-century agricultural groups. Organized in the 1880s, the Farmers' Alliance attracted members united by their opposition to railroads and other concentrations of economic power. An innovative system of traveling lecturers spread the organization's message and persuaded many farmers in the South to join cooperatives. When many of the cooperatives failed amid the worsening depression of the 1880s, Alliance leaders called upon the federal government to create a publicly financed system of cooperatives that would permit farmers to store crops, secure loans, and trade in agricultural commodities.[8]

With the call for government intervention in the farm economy, the Farmers' Alliance turned its attention to electoral politics. In 1890 Alliance leaders mobilized to elect sympathetic candidates to Congress. Although more than forty candidates won seats, many proved less supportive than expected. Convinced that farmers would not be heard by the two major parties, the Farmers' Alliance supported Populist Party candidate James Weaver in the 1892 presidential election. But Populist efforts to create a party of farmers could not overcome lingering sectional antipathies, single-member districts, and plurality elections. When the Populist Party swung its support behind William Jennings Bryan and the Democrats in 1896, the Alliance agenda became lost in a campaign dominated by other issues.[9]

The experiences of the Grange and the Farmers' Alliance illustrate the formidable obstacles to the articulation of agricultural interests. Put in the language of interest group theory, farmers alone could not bear the costs of organizational creation and maintenance.[10] In the early twentieth century, agricultural producers found a solution to these problems with a bipartisan organization of farmers, created largely through the efforts and resources of the federal government.

The Rise of the Farm Bureau

During the first decade of the twentieth century, the USDA sent technical advisers throughout the southern United States to combat a boll weevil epidemic. Their success led in 1914 to the Smith-Lever Act and the creation of a national system of county extension agents. By 1918 more than 6,000 agents were at work in 80 percent of rural counties in the United States. One of the county agents' main tasks was to organize farmers into local committees, or farm bureaus, to help disseminate technical information and implement federal extension programs. County agents, in turn, maintained close relations with their local farm bureau, and the dues collected from bureau members often helped to pay their agent's salary.[11]

As the number of county farm bureaus multiplied, several statewide federations formed, and in 1919 leaders from Illinois, New York, and several other states established the American Farm Bureau Federation. From the beginning, the Farm Bureau occupied an ambiguous position between a private interest lobby and a public service organization. Even as the bureau maintained a close relationship with the Extension Service and the USDA, it also employed a Washington lobbyist to press its interests before Congress.[12]

The creation of the Farm Bureau as a political organization coincided with a steep decline in prices for agricultural commodities after World War I. For the next decade, a prolonged farm crisis led to greater calls for government intervention in the agricultural economy. The Farm Bureau emerged as a vocal advocate of farm interests and helped to create a bipartisan farm bloc in Congress. With the bureau's support, members from rural districts pushed for passage of the McNary-Haugen bill, a controversial plan to lift farm prices by allowing the federal government to purchase surplus commodities and sell them on world markets. Congress passed the bill twice, but presidential vetoes killed the measure in 1927 and 1928. The push for government aid, however, continued, along with a deepening depression that extended well beyond agriculture. The election of Franklin D. Roosevelt in 1932, along with Democratic gains in the House and Senate, removed the remaining obstacles to government action, and in May 1933, two months after Roosevelt's inauguration, Congress passed the Agricultural Adjustment Act (AAA). At the heart of the new law was a system of government price supports for farmers who agreed to limit production of basic crops such as wheat, cotton, and corn.[13]

The AAA was a bold step, inaugurating a substantial role for the federal government in the farm economy that continues to the present. To be successful, however, government farm programs required the active participation of farmers themselves; implementation of production controls and price supports depended on careful monitoring for compliance with a host of new rules and regulations. To secure this needed cooperation, Secretary of Agriculture Henry A. Wallace turned to the Extension Service and its local partnership with the Farm Bureau to implement the AAA.[14]

For the Farm Bureau, which had lost nearly half its membership between 1930 and 1933, the AAA presented an opportunity to rebuild the organization. Working closely with county agents, local farm bureaus helped organize farmers into production control committees. In the South, where membership was lowest, bureau organizers used the new committees as a way to get farmers to join the organization. It was not uncommon for county agents to promote New Deal policies as a benefit of Farm Bureau membership. One county agent informed farmers that "for each dollar you invest in Farm Bureau dues, you have received $125 from the government." [15] In sum, the bureau enjoyed a privileged position as a partner in the implementation of agricultural programs. To be sure, the New Deal was good for the Farm Bureau: between 1933 and 1940 its membership more than doubled, making it the largest farm organization in the country.[16] At the same time, the bureau emerged as the recognized representative of agricultural interests before Congress.[17]

Conflict, Compromise, and Commodity Groups

The dominance of the Farm Bureau in agricultural policy matters proved short-lived. By the late 1930s relations between the Farm Bureau and the USDA had grown tense, particularly over government efforts to help poor and landless tenant farmers in the South. Farm Bureau allies in Congress attacked federal policies that threatened a white, landholding elite. Liberals within the USDA responded by cultivating relations to the National Farmers Union, a rival farm organization with close ties to organized labor and the liberal wing of the Democratic Party. Meanwhile, the Extension Service lost its role as the lead agency for the implementation of farm programs, as a growing chorus of critics called for an end to the special relationship between the Farm Bureau and the county agent.[18]

The battle lines over agricultural policy turned increasingly partisan in the years after World War II, as the National Farmers Union grew closer to the Democratic Party and the Farm Bureau became a staunch supporter of Republican

During the Great Depression the American Farm Bureau Federation greatly expanded its reach to become the largest farm organization in the United States. The bureau created a powerful voting bloc in Congress and was integral in passing farm legislation. In 1939 bureau leaders assembled at the White House to present the bureau's legislative program to President Franklin Roosevelt.

farm polices. Through the 1940s and 1950s both parties tried to enact the farm program preferred by its allies. Democrats advocated a system of high, fixed price supports desired by wheat farmers, who faced an uncertain and competitive international market. Republicans, for their part, advocated a system of lower, flexible supports to aid corn and livestock producers in the Midwest, who expected increased domestic demand from affluent postwar consumers. Even so, neither the Farm Bureau nor the Farmers Union completely lost access to the policy process, and both used Congress as a base from which to attack the policies and privileged access of their rivals. In 1949 the bureau orchestrated the defeat of a Truman administration plan for high, fixed supports, as advocated by the union. When the Republicans regained control of the White House in 1952, the Farmers Union and their Democratic allies in Congress renewed their campaign against the Farm Bureau-Extension Service relationship, leading to their official separation in 1954. Ultimately, neither party could make farm policy on a firm partisan basis.[19]

In the 1960s Congress broke the partisan deadlock through a policy change that transformed the politics of agriculture. Traditional price supports lifted farm incomes through government purchases of commodities, which subsequently raised crop prices. In 1962 and 1964 Congress lowered support prices for wheat, cotton, and corn and made up the difference with a direct income support. In other words, income supports came in the form of cash payments from the government rather than higher market prices for crops. The change allowed crop exports to compete on world markets more effectively, lowered prices for consumers, yet still supported farm incomes. The Food and Agriculture Act of 1965 reaffirmed the principle of direct payments and, most important, combined the various provisions governing different crops into a single omnibus bill that authorized farm programs for the next four years.

The policy changes of the 1960s transformed a zero-sum struggle between partisan political forces and their farm organization allies into a cooperative arrangement among rural representatives in Congress. Debates over farm policy no longer pitted wheat farmers who advocated high price supports and production controls against corn farmers who wanted lower supports and greater flexibility. With a shift to direct forms of income support, subsidies for one set of producers did not diminish the profitability of others. As internecine conflict over farm policy diminished, a new politics of agriculture took shape in which specialized commodity groups took the lead from general farm organizations in providing advice and support to the House and Senate agriculture committees responsible for writing multiyear, omnibus farm legislation.[20]

Issue Niches and Interest Fragmentation

The shift to a bipartisan farm policy took place amid other changes in American politics that also had important consequences for agriculture. Supreme Court decisions mandating a more equitable apportionment of House seats and redistricting decisions following the 1970 census reduced farm representation in Congress from 12 percent to 3 percent of the chamber.[21] Meanwhile, congressional reforms strengthened the House leadership and increased the influence of the House Democratic caucus, diminishing the autonomy that individual committees enjoyed over policy. In 1975 veteran representative Bob Poage, D-Texas, chairman of the Agriculture Committee, was one of three committee chairs ousted by the Democratic caucus.

Responding to these changes, rural representatives sought ways to adapt farm policy to new political realities. In 1973 Congress debated a reauthorization of farm programs at a time of mounting consumer concerns about high inflation and rising food prices. Facing pressure to reduce the cost of farm programs and backed by a veto threat from President Richard Nixon, Congress passed the Agriculture and Consumer Protection Act of 1973. The act removed the last vestiges of the price support system for major crops and replaced it with direct payments to farmers when market prices fell below a certain level. Passed during a time of high commodity prices and growing export demand for U.S. farm products, program costs under the new law shrank to historic lows in 1974.[22]

Policy changes in the 1970s illustrated how the constituency for agricultural policy had broadened beyond farmers and their representatives. Nutrition programs such as food stamps became a more important part of farm bill politics as expenditures for these programs grew considerably, eventually exceeding commodity programs as a share of the USDA annual budget. High inflation during the 1970s sparked greater consumer interest in farm policy, while food processing companies emerged as major players in farm bill debates. In the 1980s environmental considerations emerged in farm policy as attention turned toward the adverse effects of intensive agriculture on soil and water quality.[23]

As a result, farm bill reauthorizations became increasingly complex, as Congress had to wrestle with enormous bills that addressed commodity programs, nutrition, trade, and the environment, which illustrates the diversity of interests seeking to shape the legislation. In a study of the 1985 farm bill, political scientist William Browne found that of the most active organizations involved in the legislative process that year, less than a quarter represented farmers.[24] This is not to say that farmers or their representatives had lost their influence; rather, as Browne and others have argued, interest fragmentation reflected the multiplication of issue niches in agriculture. Commodity organizations remained the most important voices in agricultural matters, particularly on the subject of income supports. At the same time, new actors and groups concerned with issues such as land use, conservation, food safety, and energy also found their place at the farm bill table. As deficits came to dominate American politics during the early 1990s, the various interests involved in agricultural policy had to compete with one another over a shrinking pie.

Reform Pressures and Program Resilience

With the politics of deficit reduction center stage, commodity organizations faced a challenging environment, which became clear in 1995 when farm programs came up for reauthorization before a Republican-controlled Congress. Elected on the promise of a balanced budget and intent on showing their fiscal restraint, the Republican leadership insisted that the farm bill include substantial reforms to commodity programs. The result was the Freedom to Farm Act, a proposal to phase out income supports by paying farmers a fixed but declining subsidy regardless of how much they produced. Reformers hailed the act as a market-oriented turn that would gradually wean farmers from government support. Opponents on the agriculture committees and among various producer groups saw the plan as undermining the agricultural safety net in existence since the New Deal. Cotton producers, in particular, responded coolly to the proposal, prompting four southern Republicans from cotton-producing districts to join the minority Democrats and defeat the act in the House Agriculture Committee. Undeterred, the Republican leadership inserted the plan in a mammoth budget reconciliation bill that contained major elements of their "Contract with America" agenda. President Bill Clinton vetoed the bill, but with Republicans on record in support, the Freedom to Farm Act passed as a stand alone bill in 1996.[25]

When first passed, Freedom to Farm seemed to signal a change in policy and politics. The concerns of commodity groups and their allies in Congress appeared to take a backseat to the desires of the Republican majorities and an energized leadership. The change proved short-lived. When agricultural prices declined considerably a few years later, a Republican Congress responded with a series of generous emergency payments to farmers. In 2002 Congress passed a new farm bill that reinstated many of the income-support policies eliminated under Freedom to Farm.[26] In 2008 Congress again passed a farm bill that left much of the subsidy program unchanged, even as commodity prices reached new highs and a growing chorus criticized the adverse economic, health, and environmental effects of agricultural subsidies.[27]

In sum, farmers have been involved in national politics for well over a century. Indeed, the rise of influential farm interests and their persistence in the face of economic and demographic shifts are closely linked to the long-standing federal role in agricultural markets. The complex system of subsidies may face periodic scrutiny, but the programs and its supporters have evolved to meet the challenges of interest fragmentation, declining rural representation, and institutional change in Congress.

UNDERSTANDING INTEREST GROUP INFLUENCE IN AGRICULTURE

What explains the continued influence of agricultural interests in American politics? As discussed below, part of the answer can be found in the unique characteristics of agriculture itself. The nature of agricultural markets, combined with the spatial distribution of commodity production and the institutional fragmentation of the American political system, provides farmers with organizational advantages that translate into continued political influence. In addition, the positive image of farmers as hard-working, patriotic Americans can be a potent weapon in the battle over agricultural programs.

The Political Economy of Agriculture

Perhaps the most straightforward explanation for the pattern of interest group influence in agriculture is found in the work of economist Mancur Olson (see Chapters 5 and 7). According to Olson, smaller groups can more easily overcome obstacles to collective action, such as the free-rider problem, and therefore enjoy political advantages over diffuse interests. As a relatively small group, farmers are more likely to come together and lobby on behalf of government subsidies compared to a relatively large and diffuse group such as consumers or taxpayers who bear the cost of agricultural supports. Adding to this advantage is the concentration of benefits and costs of farm programs. As the number of farmers decline, the benefits of commodity programs become more concentrated and the costs diffused more widely, which helps to explain why farm organizations work so hard to maintain subsidies, and why it is difficult to mobilize broader opposition against them. Although a reduction in subsidies might reduce the income of some farmers by thousands of dollars, the effects of subsidy cuts will be imperceptible among consumers and taxpayers who have little incentive to organize opposition against them.

Apart from the political advantages of relative group size, it is also important to understand how the economic characteristics of agriculture result in persistent demands for government support. Imagine a fictional widget factory. If a market glut causes the price of widgets to decline, the factory can cut production. Conversely, if the demand for widgets rises, the factory can increase output. By contrast, agricultural markets do not work so smoothly. Agricultural land and equipment is not easily converted to other uses, and the constraints and uncertainties of the growing cycle prevent farmers from simply adjusting production levels to meet demand. In addition, most farm commodities are highly inelastic with respect to demand and supply. That is, both the consumption and the production of food are relatively insensitive to price—people do not eat twice as much bread if the price of wheat falls by half. As a result, small changes in output can produce large swings in price, making agriculture subject to boom and bust cycles that leave farm incomes highly unstable and agricultural investments exceptionally risky.[28] Government farm programs are designed to address these market imperfections by providing farmers an agricultural income safety net.

Moreover, the very existence of agricultural policies contributes to farmers' organizational advantages. First, as noted, the relative concentration of benefits and costs of farm programs creates an incentive for producers to organize and lobby on behalf of continued support—just as the benefits of subsidies are concentrated among producers, so are the costs of any cuts in government supports. Second, the successful implementation of government programs requires the coordination of individual producers. As described previously, the inauguration of agricultural supports in the 1930s prompted the federal government to turn to the Farm Bureau as an ally in program management. This partnership was beneficial to the Farm Bureau; in effect, the government helped underwrite the cost of organizational creation and maintenance. Third, the recurrence of agricultural policy issues, especially the periodic reauthorization of farm legislation, prompted rural representatives in Congress to turn to farm organizations for information about program operation and constituency opinions on policy matters, which translates into privileged access for farm groups in policy debates.[29] In sum, there are significant feedback effects in agricultural policy that create powerful interests in favor of continued government support for farmers.[30]

Institutional and Political Factors

Because the most important decisions regarding agricultural policy remain in the hands of Congress rather than the executive, features of congressional structure contribute greatly to the political influence of agricultural interest groups. In particular, the committee system offers distinct advantages to geographically concentrated interests such as agriculture. Indeed, agriculture offers a vivid example of distributive theories of Congress that depict the committee system as an institutionalized practice of logrolling (a continuing set of deals) among various constituency interests. According to this view, members choose to serve on committees that provide policy benefits to their districts; at the same time, chamber deference to committee decisions guarantees that members of various committees will be able to reward their constituents back home. One important implication of this theory is that committees will be unrepresentative of the chamber, or they will be preference outliers, in the language of political science. In the case of agriculture, scholars have largely found that membership on the House Agriculture Committee and the Agricultural Subcommittee on House Appropriations draws heavily from rural districts.[31]

Table 12.1 **District Characteristics, 110th Congress (district averages unless otherwise noted)**

	Farms	Agricultural products sold ($1,000s)	Government payments ($1,000s)
Agriculture Committee	12,475	$2,439,291	$75,241
Agricultural Appropriations	6,862	$1,415,895	$52,020
Other members	4,205	$486,520	$13,082
Committee share (percent)	30%	44%	51%

SOURCE: USDA Census of Agriculture, 2007.

The characteristics of districts represented on the Agriculture Committee and the Agricultural Appropriations Subcommittee during the 110th Congress (2007–2008) support this view (see Table 12.1). According to the 2007 Census of Agriculture, the average district represented on the House Agriculture Committee contained more than 12,000 farms, sold nearly $2.5 billion in agricultural products, and received around $75 million in direct government payments. Members on the Agricultural Appropriations Subcommittee came from districts that averaged nearly 7,000 farms, produced almost $1.5 billion in agricultural goods, and received $50 million in subsidies. By comparison, the remaining House districts averaged around 4,000 farms, sold less than $500 million in agricultural goods, and received just $13 million in subsidies. In total, the districts represented by the fifty-nine members on the House Agriculture Committee and the Agricultural Appropriations Subcommittee account for 30 percent of all farms, 44 percent of all farm products, and 51 percent of all government farm payments.

To illustrate further, consider the First Congressional District of Kansas. Encompassing nearly the entire western two-thirds of the state, an area roughly the size of Illinois, the Kansas First is arguably the most agricultural district in the country. It ranked first in terms of number of farms and the value of agricultural products sold, and it ranked second in terms of government payments received in 2007. It is not surprising, then, that a succession of representatives from this district has held a seat on the House Agriculture Committee for more than forty years. Currently, the "Big First," as the Kansas district is known, is represented by Republican Tim Huelskamp, who was elected to the House in 2010 after his predecessor, Jerry Moran, stepped down to run successfully for the U.S. Senate. Moran, also a Republican, had held his seat on the Agriculture Committee since 1996 when he was elected to replace Pat Roberts, the former chair of the House Agriculture Committee, who stepped down in 1996, also to make a successful run for the Senate. Roberts succeeded Republican Keith Sebelius, who served on the committee for twelve years during his career in Congress. His predecessor was Robert Dole, who also held a seat on the House Agriculture Committee before being elected to the Senate in 1968.

We gain further insight into the importance of congressional structure for agricultural interest groups influence by looking at campaign contributions. Using data from the Center for Responsive Politics and the Federal Election Commission, Table 12.2 shows the average receipts and share of total receipts from agribusiness sources for members of the 110th Congress who ran for reelection in 2008 (agribusiness includes crop and livestock production, food processing, and agricultural service industries). Members of the House Agriculture Committee received more than $150,000 on average from agribusiness sources during the 2007–2008 election cycle, approximately 12 percent of their total campaign receipts. Similarly, members on the Agricultural Appropriations Subcommittee received around $110,000 or 10 percent of their total receipts from agribusiness during this period. By contrast, members who did not have seats on these two House panels received around $37,000 in agribusiness contributions, only 3 percent of their total receipts. Overall, Agriculture Committee and Appropriations Subcommittee members received 38 percent of all agribusiness contributions to House candidates in 2008.

What do these contributions tell us about agricultural interest group influence? First, campaign contributions are not about buying votes or even persuading the undecided; rather, they are intended to keep powerful allies in office. Agribusiness contributions go disproportionately to members on committees with agricultural jurisdiction who overwhelmingly come from agricultural districts. Consequently, these members are almost always in substantial agreement with the policy positions of their contributors. Over time, relationships with well-placed members become quite valuable, and campaign contributions are a comparatively inexpensive way for interest groups to protect an investment.

In fact, campaign contributions pale in comparison to lobbying expenditures by agribusiness groups. According to the Center for Responsive Politics, agribusiness sources spent around $250 million on lobbying in 2007 and 2008, compared to $65 million in campaign contributions during

Table 12.2 **Agribusiness Contributions to House Members, 2007–2008 (district averages)**

	Receipts from agribusiness	Agribusiness share of total receipts
Agriculture Committee	$157,905	12%
Agricultural appropriations	$111,944	10%
Other members	$36,926	3%

SOURCE: Center for Responsive Politics; Federal Election Commission.

the same period. As Richard Hall and Katherine Bradley discuss in this volume (see Chapter 25), these lobbying costs are a form of legislative subsidy; they help allies—particularly those on committees of jurisdiction—make progress on shared policy objectives by providing policy information and political intelligence.

It is important to remember, however, that in this case the focus is on agri*business*. Most of the money spent on contributions and lobbying comes from firms and trade associations involved in food production and processing. Table 12.3 lists the top ten agribusiness spenders, excluding tobacco companies, during the 2007–2008 election cycle. Lobbying expenditures are clearly much greater, although the figures include expenditures on all issues, not just agriculture, as well as costs associated with lobbying executive agencies and departments. Producer organizations, such as the American Farm Bureau Federation or the Dairy Farmers of America are important, but they only spend a third to a half as much as corporate actors such as American Crystal Sugar or Monsanto. An important and growing feature of agricultural politics is the extent of corporate influence.

Farmers and their organizations may not have as much money as these corporate interests, but they do have something that is ultimately just as valuable to members of Congress: votes. Moreover, the concentration of agricultural production coupled with the geographic nature of political representation means that farmers remain a politically important constituency in certain parts of the country. The benefits of government farm subsidies are concentrated in the Midwest and Plains regions of the United States. This concentration of benefits translates into fifteen congressional districts where 75 percent or more of farms receive government payments (ten of these districts are represented on the two agriculture panels in the House). During the 110th Congress, six of these districts were represented by Democrats and nine by Republicans.

Table 12.3 **Top Ten Agribusiness Spenders: Campaign and Lobbying Expenses, 2007–2008**

Campaign contributions		Lobbying expenditures	
American Crystal Sugar	$1,861,650	Monsanto Co.	$13,400,000
Dairy Farmers of America	$924,950	Food Marketing Institute	$7,828,130
Farm Credit Council	$879,807	American Farm Bureau	$7,030,000
Weyerhaeuser Co.	$737,350	American Forest & Paper Assn.	$6,810,000
Safeway Inc.	$721,802	Grocery Manufacturers of America	$6,020,000
UST Inc.	$678,459	Kraft Foods	$6,010,000
Flo-Sun Inc.	$671,000	International Paper	$5,350,000
American Farm Bureau	$666,704	Weyerhaeuser Co.	$4,640,000
California Dairies Inc.	$629,250	CropLife America	$3,993,041
Deere & Co.	$602,366	Tyson Foods	$3,791,433

SOURCE: Center for Responsive Politics.

The Senate magnifies the effects of this concentration. In five states, Illinois, Iowa, Nebraska, North Dakota, and South Dakota, more than 70 percent of farmers receive government payments. These five states, 10 percent of the Senate, accounted for around a quarter of all subsidies in 2007. Again, the partisan balance was evenly divided: in the 110th Congress five Democratic and five Republican senators represented these states.

In other words, both parties depend to some extent on farmers' votes, particularly in those districts and states where government payments are most concentrated. With the recent string of close presidential elections and fairly thin margins separating the two parties in Congress (at least until the 2010 elections), Democrats and Republicans alike have presented themselves as friends of the farmer. Consequently, neither party wishes to challenge the policy status quo. Moreover, when times get tough for agriculture, both parties are tempted to engage in expensive bidding wars with government supports. This is what occurred in the late 1990s. When a financial crisis in Asia led to a sharp drop in farm prices, Congress passed several emergency spending measures. In 1999 Republicans proposed $6.5 billion aid package; Democrats responded with an $11 billion measure; and Congress eventually settled on $10 billion in emergency aid.[32]

One final political advantage deserves mention: farmers remain sympathetic figures in the eyes of many. The image of the hard-working, small family farm is a rhetorical asset that is useful when defending commodity programs. Arguing against critics who claim that agricultural subsidies are wasteful or even harmful, supporters of farm programs often assert that subsidy cuts will endanger America's social fabric by reducing the number of family farms. It is true that some smaller farms would suffer if agricultural subsidies were cut, but the overwhelming share of federal payments go to the largest, economically efficient producers. The point is that farming—or at least an idealized image of it—is a potent weapon in policy debates that makes it harder to line up votes against subsidies.

FUTURE PROSPECTS OF AGRICULTURAL INTEREST GROUPS

A number of factors contribute to the enduring power and influence of agricultural interest groups. These factors include a relationship with the federal government that stretches back more than a century and a set of policies that not only encouraged the development of agricultural groups, but whose benefits continue to be concentrated in a relatively small number of producers and whose costs are distributed widely across the rest of society. Important features of congressional structure, especially the committee system, magnify the influence of rural representatives over farm policy. This feature of the agricultural policy process is further reinforced by campaign contributions and lobbying expenditures that go to those members with the greatest constituency interest in policy debates. Finally, the continued cultural resonance of farming makes it easier to target agriculture as a deserving recipient of government support.

Despite these advantages, agricultural interest groups are not completely immune from economic and political forces that threaten their continued influence. First, the trend toward an increasingly fragmented interest group environment in agricultural policy is likely to continue. Agribusiness—input suppliers, food processors, and retailers—remain the most powerful nonproducer interests in agricultural policy debates. They will continue to lobby on behalf of government programs that reward efficient, large-scale producers of low-cost commodities. Their continued support is, however, far from assured if global pressures to reduce agricultural subsidies peel off agribusiness support. Processors and retailers can always substitute imports for domestic inputs, while machinery and other input suppliers would abandon domestic growers if it means retaining access to foreign markets. Meanwhile, the range of groups engaged in agricultural policy debates continues to expand. Criticism of the environmental costs of industrial agriculture and public health concerns over about food safety and childhood obesity have grown more prominent as advocacy groups draw public attention to the negative consequences of agricultural subsidies.[33] The popularity of books such as Michael Pollan's *The Omnivore's Dilemma* and the growing demand for organic foods and direct-to-consumer markets (farmer's markets and community-supported agriculture) signals a rising consumer awareness and suspicion of industrial agriculture that one day may spill over into the political realm.

Second, the prospect of large long-term deficits will make it more difficult for agricultural interest groups and their allies in Congress to control the policy process. During the 1990s, as described above, deficit-reduction efforts diminished the influence of the agriculture committees in Congress and their interest group allies. In contrast, the 2002 and 2008 farm bills were written at a time when deficit concerns were less pressing and the budget reconciliation process (which can force authorizing committees to cut program costs or face painful consequences) ceased to function. Whether Congress resuscitates the reconciliation process is unclear, but consideration of the subsequent farm bills may well face increasing fiscal pressures.

Third, and most important, as production becomes more concentrated on fewer and fewer farms, so do the benefits of government subsidies. In 2007 only 40 percent of the nation's 2 million farms, around 800,000, received any type of government support. Moreover, for 90 percent of these subsidized farms the average government payment was only $4,700, about twice the size of the average tax return in 2008. At the other extreme, less than 2 percent of farms received more than $75,000 in government payments, which amounted to more than a quarter of all subsidies paid in 2007.[34] In other words, government programs provide substantial benefits to very few farmers. Although it is the largest recipients who are the most influential politically and are likely to remain so, the concentration of government subsidies could eventually weaken constituency support for farm policy among rural representatives in Congress.

How agricultural interest groups will respond to these challenges remains to be seen. Farm groups have shown a remarkable resilience in the face of political challenges. Moreover, a sharp decline in agricultural prices or a tightening of the partisan balance in Congress would diminish the force of these trends and allow the current alignment of interest group power and agricultural policy to continue a bit longer. Another likely scenario is that farm groups and their congressional allies will adapt to the new political realities, perhaps by supporting policy compromises such as caps on subsidy payments to large producers or an increase in government spending to support organic farming.

Still, powerful economic, demographic, and political pressures cannot be held at bay forever. True, the major farm organizations enjoy considerable political advantages and powerful allies in Washington. True, their influence is magnified by congressional structures and maintained by campaign contributions. Yet farm group influence also depends on a claim of representation. As the myth of the family farmer confronts the reality of corporate agriculture, this claim is becoming increasingly untenable. Ultimately, the greatest risk to farm groups is the failure to represent faithfully the interests of the vast majority of farmers.

NOTES

1. Jim Monke, "Farm Commodity Programs in the 2008 Farm Bill," *CRS Report for Congress* (RL34594), July 23, 2008, http://www.ers.usda.gov/Data/FarmIncome/govt_pay/GP9607us.xls.

2. In fact, Congress voted to override President Bush's veto twice. Due to a clerical error, a portion of the bill was not included in the version Bush initially vetoed. Congress voted again on the farm bill; Bush vetoed the complete version; and Congress successfully voted to override the veto. Catharine Richert, "Farm Bill Clears With Wide Support," *CQ Weekly Online,* May 19, 2008, 1354; Aliya Sternstein, "Congress Again Enacts Farm Bill by Overriding Presidential Veto," *CQ Weekly Online,* June 23, 2008, 1716.

3. For purposes of the census, the USDA defines a farm as any place that sold at least $1,000 in agricultural products in 2007.

4. USDA, 2007 Census of Agriculture.

5. This section draws largely from my work in *The Rise of the Agricultural Welfare State: Institutions and Interest Group Power in the United States, France, and Japan* (Princeton: Princeton University Press, 2001).

6. Oliver H. Kelley, *Origins and Progress of the Patrons of Husbandry in the United States: A History of 1866–1873* (Philadelphia: J. A. Wagenseller, 1875), 19, 44.

7. Solon Buck, *The Granger Movement: A Study of Agricultural Organization and Its Political, Economic, and Social Manifestations, 1870–1880* (Cambridge: Harvard University Press, 1913), 40–42, 52–69.

8. Lawrence Goodwyn, *Democratic Promise: The Populist Moment in America* (New York: Oxford University Press, 1976).

9. Elizabeth Sanders, *Roots of Reform: Farmers, Workers and the American State, 1877–1917* (Chicago: University of Chicago Press, 1999).

10. Robert H. Salisbury, "An Exchange Theory of Interest Groups," *Midwest Journal of Political Science* 13 (February 1969): 1–32; Jack L. Walker Jr., *Mobilizing Interest Groups in America: Patrons, Professions, and Social Movements* (Ann Arbor: University of Michigan Press, 1991).

11. Orville M. Kile, *The Farm Bureau Through Three Decades* (Baltimore: Waverly Press, 1948).

12. Ibid., 35–57.

13. John Mark Hansen, *Gaining Access: Congress and the Farm Lobby, 1919–1981* (Chicago: University of Chicago Press, 1991).

14. Christiana McFayden Campbell, *The Farm Bureau and the New Deal* (Urbana: University of Illinois Press, 1962).

15. William J. Block, *The Separation of the Farm Bureau and the Extension Service: Political Issue in a Federal System* (Urbana: University of Illinois Press, 1960), 25.

16. For membership figures from the period, see Robert L. Tontz, "Membership of General Farmers' Organizations, United States, 1874–1960," *Agricultural History* 38 (July 1964): 136–143.

17. Hansen, *Gaining Access.*

18. Block, *Separation of the Farm Bureau and the Extension Service.*

19. Graham K. Wilson, *Special Interests and Policymaking: Agricultural Policies and Politics in Britain and the United States, 1956–1970* (New York: Wiley, 1977).

20. Charles O. Jones, "Representation in Congress: The Case of the House Agriculture Committee," *American Political Science Review* 55 (1961): 358–367.

21. Hansen, *Gaining Access,* 167.

22. Bruce L. Gardner, *American Agriculture: How It Flourished and What It Cost* (Cambridge: Harvard University Press, 2002).

23. William Browne, *Private Interests, Public Policy, and American Agriculture* (Lawrence: University Press of Kansas, 1988).

24. Ibid., 30.

25. Sheingate, *Rise of the Agricultural Welfare State.*

26. Eric M. Patashnik, *Reforms at Risk: What Happens after Major Policy Changes are Enacted* (Princeton: Princeton University Press, 2008).

27. David M. Herszenhorn, "Farm Subsidies Seem Immune to an Overhaul," *New York Times,* July 26, 2007, 1.

28. The classic statement is in Theodore Schultz, *The Economic Organization of Agriculture* (New York: McGraw-Hill, 1953), 175–194.

29. Hansen, *Gaining Access.*

30. Paul Pierson, "When Effect Becomes Cause: Policy Feedback and Political Change," *World Politics* 45 (1993): 595–568.

31. On distributive theories generally, see Kenneth A. Shepsle and Barry R. Weingast, "The Institutional Foundations of Committee Power," *American Political Science Review* 81 (1987): 85–104; and E. Scott Adler and John S. Lapinski, "Demand-Side Theory and Congressional Committee Composition: A Constituency Characteristic Approach," *American Journal of Political Science* 41 (1997): 895–918; on agriculture in particular, see Mark S. Hurwitz, Roger J. Moiles, and David W. Rohde, "Distributive and Partisan Issues in Agriculture Policy in the 104th House," *American Political Science Review* 95 (2001): 911–922.

32. Patashnik, *Reforms at Risk,* 67.

33. Catharine Richert, "Reshaping the Farm Agenda." *CQ Weekly Online,* January 8, 2007, 114–120.

34. See http://ers.usda.gov/Briefing/FarmIncome/govtpaybyfarmtype.htm; http://www.irs.gov/taxstats/index.html.

SUGGESTED READING

Browne, William. *Private Interests, Public Policy, and American Agriculture.* Lawrence: University Press of Kansas, 1988.

Gardner, Bruce L. *American Agriculture: How It Flourished and What It Cost.* Cambridge: Harvard University Press, 2002.

Hansen, John Mark. *Gaining Access: Congress and the Farm Lobby, 1919-1981.* Chicago: University of Chicago Press, 1991.

Hurwitz, Mark S., Roger J. Moiles, and David W. Rohde, "Distributive and Partisan Issues in Agriculture Policy in the 104th House." *American Political Science Review* 95 (2001): 911–922.

Jones, Charles O. "Representation in Congress: The Case of the House Agriculture Committee." *American Political Science Review* 55 (1961): 358–367.

Salisbury, Robert H. "An Exchange Theory of Interest Groups." *Midwest Journal of Political Science* 13 (1969): 1–32

Sanders, Elizabeth. *Roots of Reform: Farmers, Workers and the American State, 1877–1917.* Chicago: University of Chicago Press, 1999.

Sheingate, Adam. *The Rise of the Agricultural Welfare State: Institutions and Interest Group Power in the United States, France, and Japan.* Princeton: Princeton University Press, 2001.

Wilson, Graham K. *Special Interests and Policymaking: Agricultural Policies and Politics in Britain and the United States, 1956–1970.* New York: Wiley, 1977.

chapter 13

Business and Organized Labor

by Susan Orr and Peter L. Francia

THE CLASH OF BUSINESS AND LABOR is something of a classic matchup in American interest group politics. Political pundits often frame political battles between business and labor as the legislative equivalent of a Muhammad Ali versus Joe Frazier epic—"big business" fights "big labor." The heavyweight fight narrative may provide an eye-catching headline and compelling tale, but in most cases it obscures much more than it informs.

Business and labor constitute highly diverse categories, but in keeping with the old adage that politics makes strange bedfellows, labor and business groups do form political alliances on occasion. A contemporary example of such an alliance is the partnership of the Service Employees International Union (SEIU), one of the nation's largest unions, and Wal-Mart, one of the most powerful corporations, to push for a mandate that employers provide workers health insurance as part of the 2009 health care reform bill.[1] This unlikely collaboration attracted the ire of other powerful unions, such as the Teamsters, and influential business groups, including the Chamber of Commerce and the National Federation of Independent Business (NFIB).[2] Although Wal-Mart and SEIU were allies on health care reform, they remain at loggerheads on other political issues. In particular, SEIU stands united with all labor organizations to promote passage of a labor law reform bill, the Employee Free Choice Act (EFCA), and Wal-Mart, in concert with the vast majority of American businesses, vehemently opposes the legislation.

It is also misleading to portray business and labor groups as equally matched in number, size, and political strength. In fact, scholars consistently document a business advantage.[3] Business and labor, however, have disparate assets and resources. The relative power of each is therefore contingent upon the particular policy domain and activity or strategy under consideration. Business groups generally have greater financial resources, and organized labor is better at providing the human resources of campaign workers.

This diversity becomes apparent when exploring the range and variety of business and labor interest groups, as well as the types of political activities they undertake. The activities of interest groups fall into two primary categories: electioneering and lobbying. Business and labor groups each attempt to ensure that their preferred representatives win office, and they endeavor to persuade elected officials, bureaucrats, and the public that their policy preferences are the most desirable. As the quest for election precedes the pursuit of policy, this chapter begins with the activities of business and labor in election campaigns while also exploring the early history and formation of business and labor groups.

THE LOGIC OF COLLECTIVE ACTION

In his 1965 book *The Logic of Collective Action,* Mancur Olson argued that some interest groups would form more easily than others would and that some interests might fail to form groups (see Chapter 4).[4] He posited that groups that offer particularistic benefits to members, apart from their collective political goals, more readily overcome collective action problems. Olson's emphasis on group formation was a response to scholars in the pluralist tradition who offered "disturbance" theories to explain the origin of interest groups (see Chapter 5).[5] They believed that groups in society with shared interests naturally form interest groups and engage in political action to protect their collective interests when they are under threat.

Contrary to the fundamental assumptions of the pluralist perspective, Olson's work showed that organized groups did not necessarily reflect the actual distribution of interests in the general population; rather, they favored those with the resources that could provide the most attractive selective incentives to its membership. Other theorists soon responded to Olson's ideas. Some argued that groups form as a response to the expansion of government programs and regulation, which either exert costs upon or provide benefits to group members (see Chapter 8).[6] Others stressed the role of leaders or political "entrepreneurs" in galvanizing group members into action.[7] Each of these theories has relevance to the formation and political mobilization of labor and business groups.

The power of business interests in Washington has long concerned Americans. This 1881 cartoon by Joseph Keppler depicts Liberty threatened by monopolies as Uncle Sam is asked what he will do about it.

FORMATION AND EARLY HISTORY OF LABOR GROUPS

In 1866 organizers founded the first U.S. labor federation, the National Labor Union (NLU). The NLU advocated for legislation to secure an eight-hour workday, improved workers' housing, the Department of Labor, and government management of railroads, water transportation, and the telegraph.[8] The more successful Noble Order of the Knights of Labor (K of L) formed just a few years later in 1869. The K of L supported similar policy goals, such as an eight-hour workday, but unlike other previous efforts to organize workers, the K of L welcomed all laborers: skilled and unskilled, whites and blacks, males and females, farmers and intellectuals.

These two early groups, however, failed to sustain themselves (the NLU dissolved in 1872, and the K of L's membership dropped from more than 700,000 members in 1886 to under 100,000 by 1890) at least in part for failing to provide the particularistic benefits to members that Olson's work showed was so important. The NLU lost the support of trade unionists because of concerns that the organization was too focused on issues related to broad social change, such as currency reform, rather than on the more immediate economic problems directly affecting workers. Likewise, membership in the K of L dropped dramatically when it failed to deliver on promises, such as the eight-hour workday.

In contrast, the American Federation of Labor (AFL), founded in 1886, focused its efforts on delivering particularistic benefits. The AFL organized skilled workers by craft and used their leverage in the workplace to push for favorable conditions of employment. This strategy, often referred to as "pure and simple" unionism, was the philosophy of Samuel Gompers, the AFL's inaugural president. Gompers rejected calls from more radical labor leaders to challenge capitalism or to engage in broader social reforms; he instead focused the AFL's efforts on winning better working conditions and higher wages for workers. By 1920 the AFL had 4 million members.

As the U.S. economy industrialized, a few union leaders, most notably John Lewis of the United Mine Workers, pushed the AFL and its member unions to promote union organizing on an industrial scale among rank-and-file

The dominance of business interests in Washington is lampooned in this 1894 cartoon by W. A. Rogers. Leading the march of businessmen on the Capitol is steel magnate Andrew Carnegie who charges in front of bowing members of Congress.

workers in manufacturing plants. Lewis advocated political action and engagement with government as a way to aid union organizing. This clash of philosophies within organized labor highlights the role of "political entrepreneurs," or leaders, in the mobilization of organized labor. Ultimately, Lewis led a number of unions out of the AFL and formed the Congress of Industrial Organizations (CIO) in 1935 to focus on industrial-scale organizing. The CIO's organizing drives met with vigorous opposition from corporations, especially steel and auto manufacturers, which prompted Lewis and CIO unions to push hard for government protection of workers' rights to organize. Public support of labor from President Franklin D. Roosevelt, a Democrat, and his administration's help in passing the National Labor Relations Act (NLRA) led Lewis, himself a Republican, to direct union support to the president's reelection in 1936.[9] This successful campaign paved the way for organized labor's continuing political alliance with the Democratic Party and its involvement in electoral politics.[10] In 1955 the AFL and CIO merged to form the AFL-CIO. The Committee on Political Education (COPE) became the campaigning arm of the new federation, and a crucial electoral force for the Democratic Party.[11]

Favorable government policy also aided organized labor. The most dramatic example was passage in 1935 of the NLRA, also known as the Wagner Act in the aftermath of the Great Depression. The NLRA established government protection for workers to organize into unions, which sparked a sharp increase in union membership.[12] Government policy changes also facilitated growth in public sector unionism in the 1960s. President John F. Kennedy established the first rights to unionize at the federal level through Executive Order 10988, and many states loosened their restrictions on public employee unions around the same time.[13] The surge in unionization in the public sector that followed these changes compensated in part for declining private sector union membership that began in the late 1950s.

Some attribute these declines, in part, to government action. Most notably, the Taft-Hartley Act passed in 1947 prevented unions from requiring union membership as a condition of employment in union workplaces. Decades later, President Ronald Reagan's dismissal of about 11,000 striking air traffic controllers in 1981 set the tone for a rise in employer resistance to unions.[14] Union leaders' limited action in the face of falling membership and structural shifts, or "disturbances," in the American economy also contributed to the steady fall in the percentage of workers that are union members from a high of about one-third of the workforce in the mid-1950s to 12.3 percent in 2009.[15]

Finally, it is worth noting that broad social movements and social protests often grow into persistent organizations

William J. Cronin, representing automobile manufacturers, speaks out against the Wagner Labor Act before the Senate Education and Labor Committee in 1939. He detailed the detrimental affect of strikes on automakers and suggested amendments to the legislation. As a visual, he presented police photographs of labor leaders to illustrate their criminal activities.

(see Chapter 6). This phenomenon has further contributed to the formation of unions. A good illustration is the unionization of California farm workers in the 1960s under the leadership of Cesar Chavez, who organized a successful boycott of grapes and lettuce.[16] More recently, "Justice for Janitors," a campaign led by the SEIU, and the "Hotel Workers Rising" campaign of UNITE HERE, which represents hospitality and related workers, have adopted this approach, engaging with civic leaders outside of organized labor and promoting product boycotts to pressure employers into recognizing their workers' right to form a union. Many labor scholars have begun to argue that the social movement approach to union formation is the traditional and most effective way to mobilize workers and have been calling for resurgence in the approach as a way to revitalize the labor movement.[17]

FORMATION AND EARLY HISTORY OF BUSINESS GROUPS

Just as academic theories about interest group formation and mobilization aid our understanding of organized labor, they also shed light on the political engagement of American business groups. During the second half of the nineteenth century, corporate monopolies, railroads, and other related interests exercised their power in American politics through large campaign contributions from wealthy industrialists that critics charged corrupted the political process. Indeed, allegations of vote buying and graft were common during this period and were exposed in stories by investigative journalists known as "muckrakers."

Despite some negative accounts in the press about the role of wealthy individuals, whom some journalists referred to as "robber barons," in the political process, business interests extended their influence by organizing into groups. The National Association of Manufacturers (NAM) and the Chamber of Commerce are two of the oldest and largest general business organizations. Both were formed with the help of political entrepreneurs and the promise of government policy benefits. NAM, created in the 1890s, was in part the product of William McKinley's political campaign efforts. McKinley's political strategist, Mark Hanna, encouraged the nascent NAM so that the campaign could gain support in the South, where Democrats almost exclusively controlled government. He sought to create a business organization outside of the Republican Party, as racial discrimination in the South led to weak support for Republicans, even though many business leaders found their economic policies favorable. NAM appealed to business on a platform of pressing for government policies that would promote

The National Association of Manufacturers was formed in the 1890s and today represents some 11,000 manufacturing companies. This 1940 NAM billboard touts private enterprise as a fundamental american ideal.

commercial development and trade. Although NAM proved helpful to McKinley, particularly in the primaries, the McKinley administration could not deliver the promised economic development policies. This failure to win favorable policy, and that some saw NAM as too closely tied to the GOP, made it difficult for the organization to retain members and to sustain support in the South. As a result, it developed policy positions opposing organized labor and government support of unions, in an attempt to gain and retain members.[18]

Another Republican administration—that of William Howard Taft—was instrumental in the formation of the Chamber of Commerce. Taft, with the help of his secretary of commerce, invited business leaders from all regions and industrial sectors to form a national organization that would offer a unified "business voice," especially on export and trade policy. In this way, Taft administration officials acted as political entrepreneurs and helped business leaders overcome their collective action problems.[19] The chamber's origins were also the result of "disturbances" that helped overcome American business leaders' wariness of government engagement. Its goals were to win favorable policy not only to promote trade, but in the area of labor law as well. The creation of the chamber also was necessitated by some beginning to see NAM as representing a particular segment of the business community. With a view to retaining membership, the Chamber of Commerce does not adopt policy positions on issues pertaining to particular segments of the corporate community that may be irrelevant or even detrimental to other sectors. But over time, especially as government intervention in the economy increased, specialist groups representing particular trades and sectors of business in national politics emerged.

The Semiconductor Industry Association (SIA) is a great example of a specialized business organization forming in response to a looming "threat." In the late 1970s the U.S. economy was struggling. Faced with declining demand, U.S. semiconductor manufacturers found it difficult to compete with their Japanese counterparts who received government support. American manufacturers initiated the SIA to push for more favorable terms of trade—efforts that have resulted in some successes.[20] The small number of semiconductor manufacturers and the ease with which this group formed in the face of an economic "disturbance" support Olson's contention that small groups that can reap significant benefits will readily overcome the difficulties of collective action.

A poor economy and increasing government regulation during the 1970s also sparked a surge in membership in the National Federation of Independent Business (NFIB). The NFIB, formed by a political entrepreneur in the 1940s, is the "political voice" of small business. Meanwhile, the chief executive officers (CEOs) of the nation's largest corporations formed the Business Roundtable in 1972 with the aim of facilitating their input on public policy among government officeholders and the public.[21] Individual corporations choosing to become politically engaged do not face collective action problems, but, as political scientist David Vogel points out, a poor economic climate and perceived threats of regulation galvanized a significant increase in independent corporate activity in politics during the 1970s.[22] Taken together, theories of interest group formation are helpful in explaining not only the genesis and mobilization of business and labor groups, but also the decisions of individual corporations to become politically active.

BUSINESS AND LABOR "BY THE NUMBERS"

All the theorizing about interest group formation and maintenance led to an emphasis in scholarly work on assessing group strength through surveys of groups, often with a view to uncovering a bias toward business. Indeed, scholars who have surveyed membership in the interest group system, regardless of the data source they use, have consistently found that business groups significantly outnumber those with labor interests. Using data collected by the Department of Commerce in 1949, David Truman documented 2,300 business-related groups active in national politics, compared to 200 labor unions. Likewise, in 1970 the *Encyclopedia of Associations* listed 2,753 trade and business-related groups compared to 225 labor unions and federations. By 1995 the respective figures were 3,973 to 246.[23] The Federal Election Commission (FEC) also has collected data on the number of political action committees (PACs) active in federal elections. Again, the numbers demonstrate a considerable business advantage. Since the 1980s corporate groups have outnumbered labor by at least four to one: the 2008 totals were 1,601 corporate PACs to 273 labor PACs.[24] Finally, data made available through lobbying disclosure laws indicate that in 1996, 43 percent of groups lobbying on a range of issues represented business and corporate interests compared to only 2 percent that represented labor.[25]

The "count by numbers" method of assessing the relative influence of groups in politics has led many scholars to conclude that there is a pro-business bias in the interest group system. Many others scholars, while not directly challenging such a conclusion, have pointed to significant flaws in this approach. For example, general counts of politically active groups mask the fact that the number and mix of groups that are politically engaged in policy disputes depends on the issue. Some "all encompassing" issues, such as health care reform or labor and environmental regulation, attract a large number and wide array of groups. Others that deal with specific legislation, such as special tax provisions or subsidies to particular industries, attract only a few groups. The more particularistic issues, which draw fewer groups, generally have a more pronounced bias toward corporate interests, which leads some political observers to suggest that the power of business in politics may be underestimated.[26]

Conversely, scholars have found that highly salient issues, which draw the attention of many groups, are more difficult for corporate interests to influence. The reason is that even though business interests are likely to be unified and active in large numbers on a high-profile issue with wide-ranging impact, so too are opposing groups representing labor and consumer interests. As the public is paying attention to these policy disputes, so too are legislators, who are likely to be attentive to public opinion and the preferences of a broad cross section of their constituents. This finding has led scholars to conclude that business influence works indirectly on salient issues due to the sizable efforts and resources that business groups devote to shaping citizens' policy preferences.[27]

A fundamental difficulty in assessing the political strength of various societal interests is defining the term *interest group*.[28] In fact, different researchers and data sources employ disparate definitions. A common oversight of political observers assessing business influence is that they often overlook the activity of individual corporations in politics. The media and many scholars tend to focus on organizations such as the Chamber of Commerce or the National Association of Manufacturers, which represent "business" interests in broad terms. Large corporations, however, retain in-house lobbyists and political strategists and wield considerable influence that studies and reports of group politics often do not capture.[29] The number of corporations with registered lobbyists and public affairs offices in Washington, D.C., increased rapidly in the 1970s.[30] The number of corporate PACs rose from 89 in 1974 to 950 in 1979. As noted previously, some three decades later, there were more than 1,600 corporate PACs.[31] In addition, powerful corporations such as Microsoft and Wal-Mart have intensified their campaigning and lobbying efforts. Excluding the political activity of corporations may significantly underplay business influence in the interest group system, leading some scholars to appeal for more studies of the political life of individual corporations.[32]

A further weakness of relying on surveys of groups to assess political influence is that researchers use data from a variety of sources that may measure involvement in specific political activities such as campaign donations, but not others such as lobbying. Overlooking lobbying is problematic, as some groups favor certain venues and strategies for political activity and deliberately avoid others. Corporations tend to avoid testifying in public hearings, and some shun campaign donations, seeking to forestall potential adverse publicity; instead, they favor one-on-one meetings with legislators and their staff.[33] Conversely, associations and membership groups favor public hearings to "advertise" their political activity to their members. Given that surveys of groups do not always consider multiple data sources reflecting engagement in different political strategies and venues, they often offer an incomplete picture of group political involvement.

Even more problematic is that researchers have no stable metric against which to assess bias in the interest group system. To establish bias in the interest group system, political observers would need a baseline measure of interests in society against which to compare the range of groups that purportedly represent those interests. Such a baseline does not exist.[34] In truth, we do not know what an "unbiased" interest group system would look like, which is particularly problematic for scholars who attempt to uncover changes in group strength over time with a view to developing theories about group formation and establishing the kinds of factors that affect group power. Not only is there no stable metric of societal interests to use as a baseline, but also there are no comprehensive data on groups active in politics over time and across venues.[35]

All these weaknesses notwithstanding, the available data are consistent in demonstrating that business groups outnumber labor groups across a range of activities and that the number of business groups has increased at a faster rate than the number of labor groups. The more rapid increase in corporate groups has led some scholars to assert that bias toward business in the interest group system has increased over time.[36] But others contest this conclusion, pointing to the rapid rise in "public" or citizen interest groups since the late 1960s, which decreased the percentage of both business and labor in the overall interest group community.[37] As noted earlier, organized labor also has experienced significant declines in the percentage of the workforce it represents, although some scholars contest the extent to which this has diminished labor's political power and influence, especially within the Democratic Party.[38] Ever since the late 1990s the AFL-CIO and its member unions have been responding to the decline in union membership by increasing their political engagement.

In keeping with theories of interest group mobilization, leadership changes prompted the renewal in labor's political action. John Sweeney won the presidency of the AFL-CIO in 1995 after campaigning on a platform of reorienting labor's political operations and revitalizing organizing efforts. Sweeney's leadership met with some success, but it was not sufficient to prevent five of the AFL-CIO's largest member unions from breaking with the federation to establish a rival organization, Change to Win (CtW) in 2005. The split in the labor movement resulted in part from a conflict over the amount of resources to devote to member organizing drives versus political efforts. CtW unions stressed the need to organize more workers to gain political leverage, while the AFL-CIO suggested political clout and a change in labor law were essential for successful organizing.[39]

Despite their disagreements, both federations and their member unions continued to engage aggressively in political mobilization. Furthermore, despite the rift at the national level, member unions of both federations coordinated their political activities through state-level federations and central labor councils. A critical question arising from the division in organized labor and the renewed energy unions are directing toward politics is how it will affect labor's political power, especially given the high level of political activity of business groups.

MEMBERS AS A RESOURCE: MOBILIZING THE ELECTORATE

The AFL-CIO's "Vote 2008" Web site offers an impressive set of statistics related to the organization's voter turnout efforts in the 2008 election. Even though union membership stood at just above 12 percent of the workforce, voters from union households represented 21 percent of the electorate in 2008. Furthermore, 67 percent of union voters supported Barack Obama, the AFL-CIO–endorsed presidential candidate, in contrast to 51 percent of non-union voters.[40] From the AFL-CIO's perspective, these results reflect not only the financial resources they dedicated to the campaign but also their substantial grassroots efforts, which included knocking on 10 million doors, distributing 27 million flyers at worksites, sending 57 million political mailers, and making 70 million phone calls to encourage union voters to go to the polls. Not to be outdone, CtW dedicated 1,500 organizers to their member-to-member voter canvass, made 20 million phone calls, sent 10 million pieces of direct mail, and enlisted the help of 50,000 volunteers on Election Day.[41] These impressive figures do not include the independent campaigning of the two federations' member unions, which are significant. For example, 1,500 members of the SEIU took time off work to campaign in twenty-four battleground states.[42]

Labor's grassroots mobilization efforts in 2008 reflect a shift in strategy that occurred following Sweeney's rise to the presidency of the AFL-CIO.[43] Sweeney and others, some of whom left to form the CtW, argued that labor had to break away from the checkbook-focused political campaigning they had come to rely on and instead return to old-fashioned, pavement-pounding campaigns in which labor's primary asset—its members—were the most important.[44] Organized labor's new strategies included galvanizing members to encourage their fellow workers and family members to vote and to support union-endorsed candidates. In keeping with academic findings on the effects of various "get-out-the-vote" techniques, the AFL-CIO conducted its own studies that demonstrated that face-to-face interactions gave the most "bang for the buck" in terms of new voters per dollar spent.[45] Furthermore, the research showed that members talking to their fellow members and their families about the important issues in elections and the positions of the candidates was better received than union staffers instructing workers about which candidates to support. Accordingly, organized labor has adopted member-driven grassroots campaigns to mobilize its members, their families, and even non-union working-class Americans to vote. To bolster these efforts, an AFL-CIO affiliate organization, Working America, offers memberships to working-class Americans whose workplaces are not unionized.[46] Indeed, despite the split between the AFL-CIO and the CtW, organized labor's grassroots campaigns have remained cooperative and largely coordinated.

This strategy seems to have been successful: turnout among union members and their families has remained quite consistent. Union households made up 23 percent of the electorate in 1996, 26 percent in 2000, 24 percent in 2004, and, as mentioned above, even amid the high turnout

New Jersey members of the Service Employees International Union (SEIU) canvass on Election Day 2009 to encourage voters to support the Democratic gubernatorial candidate, John Corzine.

of the 2008 election, 21 percent of voters came from union households.[47] These aggregate figures are reinforced by academic studies showing that the likelihood of individual union members and members of union households, turning out to vote is higher than that of similarly situated citizens who are not in union households. Labor economist Richard Freeman estimates that union members are 4 percent more likely to vote than nonmembers with the same demographic characteristics and income level.[48] Other scholars have found a slightly greater impact of union membership among lower-income and middle-income voters, estimating that members of union households in the bottom two-thirds of the income distribution are about 7 percent more likely to vote than citizens with the same demographic characteristics who are not members of union households.[49] This difference may be important to the future of organized labor, because even though union membership has, over the last few decades, come to include more middle- and upper-class members (partially due to strong public sector unionism), unions are directing a lot of resources toward organizing new members in the low-income service sector of the economy. In time, unions could benefit from even greater returns for their member mobilization efforts than they currently do.

Beyond getting their members to the polls, unions have been successful in getting their members to vote for their preferred candidates. On the national level, ever since the New Deal, the labor movement has typically supported candidates from the Democratic Party. In fact unions' strong support for Democrats, along with the significant resources they devoted to campaigning for Democratic candidates, led political scientist David Greenstone, writing in the 1960s, to argue that organized labor functioned as the electoral wing of the Democratic Party.[50] More recently, at the presidential level, there have been two notable lows in union member electoral support for Democrats: in 1972 George McGovern captured only 42 percent of the labor vote, and in 1980 Jimmy Carter secured only 50 percent.[51] These lows in part reflect national trends, but they can also be blamed on the failure of the AFL-CIO to endorse McGovern (some unions, including the powerful United Auto Workers, backed his campaign), and the Teamsters Union's endorsement of Reagan, in opposition to the AFL-CIO and most of its member unions who supported Carter. Since 1980 members of union households have supported Democratic candidates at rates around 10 percent higher than their non-union counterparts.[52] The gap between union and non-union voters' support for Democratic House and Senate candidates has generally been slightly higher, averaging between 8 percent and 25 percent since 1988.[53]

Leaders of Change to Win, however, argued that Democrats in Congress were taking union support for granted and giving little in return. As they left the AFL-CIO, the CtW leadership asserted they would no longer serve as the "ATM" for the Democrats and instead would seek out labor-friendly Republicans to support. In reality, that proved quite difficult to do, but in the 2008 election the SEIU, the largest CtW union, held back some of its funds to wage postelection campaigns against Democrats who failed to keep to their election pledges on issues important to labor.

Organized labor's focus on mobilizing union members and their families makes strategic sense. Although, as shown in the next section, corporate groups often have superior financial clout, they generally cannot match unions' human resources. Further, characteristics of union members—namely, that they do not join the group for specifically political purposes and often come from demographic groups with lower levels of political participation—make union efforts to engage members in politics a fruitful endeavor. In contrast, many business groups have a limited number of individual members and draw those they do have from among citizens whose demographic characteristics suggest they are already likely to vote. The Chamber of Commerce claims around 215,000 members, while the Business Roundtable consists of 188 CEOs from the relatively few U.S. corporations with annual revenues exceeding $5 trillion. In comparison, the Department of Labor reports there were 16.3 million wage and salary workers represented by a union in 2010. The relatively small member base of most business organizations leads them to focus more of their attention on using financial resources and in shaping public opinion through grassroots lobbying, public relations campaigns, and sponsoring think-tanks to develop and disseminate research on public policy.[54]

Still, some business groups do engage in member mobilization, and recently individual corporations have been experimenting with get-out-the-vote efforts. The National Federation of Independent Business actively seeks to mobilize its members to turn out to vote on Election Day. In a similar manner to organized labor, the NFIB has found that using its members to encourage small business owners to go to the polls through personal contacts is much more effective than direct mail or telephone campaigns. The organization has selected 20,000 of its approximately 60,000 members to participate in its Value Added Voter Program. Each participant in the program pledges to contact thirteen fellow small business proprietors to encourage their participation on Election Day.[55]

Large companies also have begun to see their employees and stockholders as a political resource and have launched voter registration and education efforts. The Business-Industry Political Action Committee (BIPAC), a business group coalition that provides services to businesses to assist their employee voter education efforts, reported in 2002 that 3,000 companies had begun contacting their workers.[56] Even though federal law prohibits companies from asking hourly employees to contribute to, or vote for,

THE EMPLOYEE FREE CHOICE ACT OF 2009

The Employee Free Choice Act of 2009 has three major components:

1. Card-check: A union becomes certified by the National Labor Relations Board (NLRB) when a majority of employees have signed authorizations (union cards) designating the union as its bargaining representative. Employers would no longer be able to call for a secret ballot election. Secret ballot elections, however, would be held if at least 30 percent of workers requested a secret ballot election.

2. Binding arbitration: Employers and a newly formed union would have ninety days to negotiate a first contract. After ninety days, either side could request mediation by the Federal Mediation and Conciliation Service. If there is no agreement between the two sides after thirty days of mediation, settlement would be reached through binding arbitration. Deadline extensions are possible through mutual agreement.

3. Tougher penalties: Civil penalties would increase to $20,000 per violation against companies that violate workers' rights during an organizing campaign or first contract negotiations. Workers who were the victims of illegal company activity during an organizing drive or first contract negotiations would receive triple back pay. The NLRB also would be required to seek a federal court injunction if there is reasonable cause to believe that an employer violated an employee's rights during an organizing campaign or first contract negotiations.

SOURCE: Library of Congress, http://thomas.loc.gov/cgi-bin/query/z?c111:H.R.1409.

a specific candidate, they can engage in voter education and registration and invite candidates to give talks in the workplace. Generally, employers support Republican candidates, and, even though they do not directly urge their workers to support their favored candidates, their preferences may be apparent.

Wal-Mart caused controversy during the 2008 election when it ran voter registration and education sessions for its employees that included instruction on the possible policy consequences if the Democratic Party won control of the presidency and Congress. In particular, Wal-Mart highlighted the detrimental impact that passage of the Employee Free Choice Act might have on their employees (for an explanation of the legislation). The sessions created consternation among some Wal-Mart workers who felt the company was instructing them on how to vote. It also puzzled political reporters who noted that the demographic characteristics of Wal-Mart workers would make them more likely to support Democratic candidates and observed that the corporation was actively funding Democratic campaigns through its PAC.[57] This seeming inconsistency is explained by considering the strategies and motivations that groups use when directing financial resources to political campaigns.

FINANCIAL RESOURCES: SUPPORTING CANDIDATES' CAMPAIGNS

The regulatory environment has significantly shaped business and labor groups' use of money to influence political campaigns (see Part V of this volume). Prior to the comprehensive framework of campaign finance laws the federal government established in the 1970s, U.S. corporations were prohibited from funding candidates for federal office with passage of the Tillman Act (1907); and unions were barred from using their treasury funds to contribute to federal election campaigns, first under the wartime Smith-Connelly Act (1943), and then permanently with passage of the Taft-Hartley Act (1947). The Federal Election Campaign Act (1971) and its 1974 amendments permitted unions and corporations to establish "separated segregated funds"—the official name for political action committees. PACs are organizations that solicit funds from corporations' or unions' "restricted class" for the purpose of supporting candidates for federal office. In the case of unions, the restricted class is their members; for corporations, it is their executives, shareholders, and their families. All money donated to PACs, as well as given by PACs to campaigns, must be reported to the FEC and is subject to limits. Individual members of PACs' restricted class can give $5,000 per election to their PAC. The PACs themselves are limited to giving $5,000 to a candidate per election. Even though union treasury and corporate money cannot be used for campaign contributions, such funds can be used to cover the operating costs of the PAC.[58]

As mentioned above, since the late 1970s the number of corporate PACs has outnumbered labor PACs by about four to one. During the 2008 electoral cycle, the overall total of PAC money came to $388 million. Of that amount, corporate PACs gave $145 million (37 percent) compared to $61 million from labor (15 percent). These disparities are roughly consistent with previous election cycles.[59] In addition, these figures likely underestimate the total PAC contributions that interests associated with business groups gave, as the FEC classifies PACs connected to trade and health associations, as well as those connected to ideological groups, separately. More than a few of these groups have connections to, and represent, business interests. Indeed, the Center for Responsive Politics (CRP), a think tank that analyzes campaign finance data, breaks down the FEC's categories and reports that business-related PACs contributed 69 percent of all PAC contributions in 2008 compared to labor's 17 percent.[60]

Despite the millions of dollars that corporate and labor PACs give to campaigns, their donations are a quite modest amount of total campaign receipts. In fact, of all the contributions candidates received in 2008, the amount from PACs represented about 33 percent of the total for those running for a seat in the House, and 20 percent for the Senate.[61] Labor and business PACs gave only a proportion of total PAC money, and individual PACs are limited to contributing $5,000 per candidate per election, which means that if a PAC made the maximum contribution possible, it would still amount to a relatively small proportion of the overall resources required for even a modest political campaign. Indeed, the FEC reports that the majority of corporate (67 percent) and labor (56 percent) PACs contributed $100,000 or less to campaigns in 2008; meanwhile, relatively few PACs—sixty corporate and forty-four labor—gave more than $1 million. The CRP reports that nine labor PACs were among the top twenty donors in 2008. These included the International Brotherhood of Electrical Workers ($3.3 million), International Association of Firefighters ($2.7 million), and the Laborers Union ($2.5 million).[62] On the business side, two individual corporations featured in the top twenty PACs—AT&T ($3.1 million) and Honeywell International ($2.5 million)—as did six business-focused groups, including the largest PAC contributor, National Association of Realtors ($4 million), the American Bankers Association ($2.9 million), and the National Beer Wholesalers Association ($2.8 million). The strict limits on the amount of resources that PACs can direct to campaigns led business and labor groups to seek alternative ways to influence elections.

PACs AND INDEPENDENT EXPENDITURES

In addition to contributions made directly to campaigns, PACs registered with the FEC can engage in "independent expenditures" on behalf of candidates in federal races. This type of spending in campaigns came about as a result of *Buckley v. Valeo* (1976), in which the Supreme Court decided that spending on election campaigns is protected free speech (see Chapter 34). The Court upheld regulations on the amount of money individuals and groups could give to candidates campaigns, but ruled against restrictions on the amount of money individuals and groups could spend on their own, on behalf of a candidate, but independently of the candidate's campaign. Independent expenditures made by PACs must be funded by money that is donated to the organization in amounts that comply with federal limits. Unions cannot use treasury funds and corporations cannot use company funds for this type of political engagement. The advantage of this kind of expenditure for PACs is that there are no spending limits. Unlike PAC contributions to campaigns, independent expenditures generally are concentrated on a few critical and often tightly fought races.

In 2008 the FEC reported that PACs spent $135 million on independent expenditures. Of that total, PACs directed $98.8 million toward the presidential campaign and $21.7 million and $14.6 million to support or oppose candidates for the House and Senate, respectively. These amounts are roughly equivalent to the levels of independent expenditures in 2006, but are considerably higher than prior electoral cycles.[63] FEC reports indicate that of all labor and corporate PACs, only a relative few—forty-one labor and twenty-four corporate—engaged in any independent expenditures in 2008. The amount of money corporate PACs spent on independent expenditures is quite low, just $221,000; in contrast, labor PACs spent $58.6 million. Corporate independent expenditures do not represent the entire spending in this category on behalf of business interests, as some of the $44 million spent by groups that fall into the FEC's category of trade, membership, and health PACs are no doubt connected to business. The strong showing of labor groups in this category, in comparison to business, does, however, reflect the two groups' contrasting approaches to financing campaigns. Independent expenditures allow groups to spend large sums in an attempt to get their preferred candidates elected and are therefore more frequently used by interest groups who adopt electoral rather than access-driven strategies.

The Service Employees International Union spent considerably more than any other labor group on independent expenditures in the 2008 electoral cycle—a total of $38 million. Of that, SEIU directed around $31 million to the presidential election and approximately $2.5 million to a few Senate races that were crucial for the Democrats to gain the sixty seats they needed to have a filibuster-proof majority. The SEIU directed the remaining money to House candidates in special elections held prior to the November election and to those in highly competitive races. The United Auto Workers PAC was the next largest source of independent expenditures among labor unions. The UAW spent $4.8 million—with $4.5 million going to the presidential race and the remainder to pivotal Senate races. The last labor-related group among the top ten PACs with respect to independent expenditures is the American Federation of Teachers, which spent all of their $3.8 million in the presidential race. This pattern of independent expenditures accords with the aims of organized labor to help Democrats win and maintain majorities in Congress and control the White House to further a prolabor legislative agenda.

The recent campaign finance case, *Citizens United v. Federal Election Commission* (2010), also deserves mention for its potentially far-reaching implications for corporate and union campaign spending. The case was originally brought by Citizens United, a nonprofit corporation that was prevented by the FEC from distributing a film critical of Hillary Clinton via video on demand in the run-up to the 2008 election. The FEC argued that the film was an advertisement paid for by independent expenditures and therefore under the Bipartisan Campaign Reform Act (BCRA) could not be aired in the thirty days immediately preceding the election (see Chapter 33). Instead of ruling narrowly in the case, the Supreme Court requested a second hearing addressing more expansive questions. The majority of justices then issued a decision that overturned not only parts of the BCRA, but also other long-standing precedents. The *Citizens United* decision ruled that restricting corporate expenditures in elections, provided the expenditures are not given as donations to candidates' campaigns, violates corporations' First Amendment speech rights. The ruling overturned restrictions barring corporations from using their general revenues to finance electoral activity. Even though the case did not directly deal with labor unions, it is widely held that the ruling also applies to them and that consequently they too are free to make unlimited independent expenditures from their treasury funds to promote political candidates.

The long-term impact of the *Citizens United* ruling remains unclear. In the short term, the first groups to take advantage of it were the AFL-CIO and the American Federation of State, County and Municipal Employees (AFSCME), the public service employees union. Both organizations ran advertisements, paid for with independent expenditures, against incumbent senator Blanche Lincoln in a closely contested Democratic primary in Arkansas.[64] To date, corporations seem reticent to take advantage of the opportunity to spend additional money to influence elections—a pattern that comports with the access-oriented approach business adopts toward finance strategy. It is an approach that may change, however. That is why some unions, particularly the SEIU, oppose *Citizens United* and believe that any potential benefit it may offer labor in campaigns will ultimately be swamped by corporate campaign dollars.[65] In response to the decision, the Obama administration has urged Congress to pass legislation that would limit political spending by corporations with large government contracts, or that are owned by foreign entities. The legislation would also require public disclosure about who is financing political advertisements paid for with independent expenditures.[66]

GROUPS KNOWN AS 527s AND 501(c)s

A final way that labor and corporate groups can channel resources to electoral campaigns is through what are called 527 or 501(c) groups (see Part VI). These groups receive their designations from the internal revenue codes that govern their tax status. Following passage of the BCRA, federal law prohibited unions and corporations from giving what was termed "soft money"—contributions that avoid federal restrictions—to political parties to use for electioneering (see Chapter 33). Soft money exploited a loophole in the campaign finance laws that allowed unions and corporations to give money to political parties in unlimited amounts for the purposes of "party building" activities. This money often went toward political ads that did not expressly name a candidate for federal office, but still made it clear to viewers which candidate to support or oppose. Soft money did not have to come from union or corporate PACs; rather, it could be drawn from union treasury funds and corporations directly.

With the outright restriction on soft money that resulted from the BCRA reforms, some of this money has been channeled to 527s and 501(c)s. The 527 groups are established for the specific purpose of engaging in political advocacy, but they do not contribute to candidates for federal office, which is what distinguishes them from PACs. The 527s that are connected with organizations that have PACs and that engage in activities to influence federal elections, such as running campaign ads, must register with the FEC and submit disclosure reports to the commission. The 527s that do not engage in activities to influence federal elections provide financial reporting to the IRS. The 501(c) groups are tax-exempt organizations, such as the Americans for Prosperity Foundation, that, like 527s, cannot contribute to campaigns, but can engage in political activities, such as voter mobilization and education, provided that political activity does not become their primary purpose. When connected to labor groups, these organizations are deemed 501(c)(5)s; if connected to business groups or chambers of commerce, they are 501(c)(6)s.

A crucial difference between 527s and 501(c)s is that 501(c)s do not have to disclose the names of donors from whom they receive money. This may partially explain why labor groups are much more prominent among top spending 527s and business groups favor 501(c)s. Many of the business-oriented, tax-exempt organizations have names that make it difficult to deduce who is funding them or whose interests they represent. For example, Americans for Job Security and the Employee Freedom Action Committee, both among the top 501(c) spenders in 2008, are sponsored by businesses, rather than by individual membership groups, despite popular sounding names.[67] According to the Campaign Finance Institute, spending in the 2008 election by these two types of organizations was more than $400 million—split roughly equally between 527s and 501(c)s. The equal split, however, indicates a significant decline in spending for 527 groups, which had paid out more than $426 million to influence federal elections in 2004, and a rise in 501(c) activity, which increased more than threefold in comparison to 2004 when such groups spent $60 million.

Unions were among the highest spending 527s in the 2008 election cycle. Organizations tied to AFCSME ($32.8 million), SEIU ($29 million), CtW ($13.9 million), and UNITE-HERE ($6.4 million) were all in the top ten according to a study conducted by the Campaign Finance Institute.[68] These groups, along with America Votes, a 501(c) supported by unions and other Democratic-leaning groups that spent $17.6 million, focused their efforts on the "ground war." This means that rather than directing money toward broadcast advertisements and other forms of media, they instead hired organizers and concentrated on voter registration and get-out-the-vote efforts in swing states.

In contrast to 527s, in which labor groups were dominant, 501(c) organizations that spent considerable sums in 2008 were overwhelmingly tied to business groups. The 501(c)(6) allied to the U.S. Chamber of Commerce spent the most ($36.3 million). A 501(c) organization sponsored by the prescription drug industry trade association—America's Agenda: Health Care for Kids—also was among the top five spenders ($13.2 million). Two organizations, the Coalition for a Democratic Workplace ($5 million) and the Employee Freedom Action Committee ($20 million), are business-funded entities that were established for the purpose of defeating the Employee Free Choice Act. The one labor group that made the list of high spending 501(c) organizations was American Rights at Work, which is focused on fighting for passage of the same labor law reform bill. The pattern of spending for the 501(c)s differs from that of 527s as they spent about half of their combined total on media ads. These ads were run predominantly in states with close Senate races, and most focused on the issue of labor law reform. In fact, a spokesman for the Chamber of Commerce and the Coalition for a Democratic Workplace (of which the chamber is a member) made public statements to the effect that their goal was to ensure that the Democrats did not win enough seats to gain a filibuster-proof majority in the Senate.

The Democrats made major gains in the Senate in the 2008 elections, and in April 2009 Sen. Arlen Specter of Pennsylvania switched his party affiliation and joined the Democrats. Several months later, Democrat Al Franken was declared the winner of Minnesota's contested Senate election. He was sworn into office in July 2009, giving Democrats a filibuster-proof majority of sixty seats. This advantage emboldened labor groups, which began a serious push for health care reform and labor law reform; it also provoked an aggressive opposing response from business groups.

BUSINESS VERSUS LABOR IN THE LEGISLATIVE ARENA

Business and labor groups attempt to influence congressional policy by relying on their economic and political resources. Economic resources refer to the methods available to business and labor that can affect economic events and conditions. These economic resources are particularly important to business. Politicians need business to succeed and will cooperate and respond readily to its concerns to avoid disruptions in the economy. This necessity provides business with what Charles Lindblom referred to as a "privileged position."[69] But labor unions also have the ability to affect economic production through collective bargaining, strikes, and slowdowns.[70] Labor's economic resources allow it to gain access to policymakers who are eager to avoid worker disruptions that also can slow or harm the economy.

Political resources, such as campaign contributions and expenditures, political advertising, and grassroots activities designed to mobilize supporters to participate in the political process, allow business and labor to influence elections directly. By investing in these activities, business and labor seek to shape the ideological composition of Congress in their favor. To maximize the impact of their political resources, business and labor follow different strategies when allocating their funds.[71]

Corporate PACs generally adopt what has been deemed an access-driven pattern of PAC contributions. They direct funds largely to incumbents and to members of the majority party in Congress as a way to make sure they are heard by legislators who are making policies that may impact their businesses. PACs that adopt an access-oriented strategy often direct funds to members on committees that oversee the policy areas of interest to them, and will alter the partisan balance of their contributions according to which political party controls Congress. A comparison of donations from PACs associated with business interests in the 2004 and 2008 election cycle illustrates this phenomenon. The Center for Responsive Politics documents that in 2004, when Republicans controlled Congress, business directed 66 percent of its contributions to Republicans and 34 percent to Democrats. By 2008, when Democrats controlled the House and were fighting hard to gain control of the Senate, the corresponding figures were 51 percent to Republicans versus 49 percent to Democrats.

In contrast to business PACs, labor PACs tend to adopt what is referred to as an "ideological" or "electoral" strategy. Labor PACs, put simply, target their contributions to prolabor Democrats, and give special priority to those in close races, whether they are incumbents facing serious challengers or challengers with a chance of winning a seat from an incumbent Republican. On occasion, labor PACs also reward loyal Democrats in safe races with contributions; the little money they direct to Republicans is generally given to incumbents on the committees that oversee policies most relevant to unions.[72] The partisan distribution of campaign contributions from labor PACs in 2004 was 87 percent to Democrats and 13 percent to

Republicans. Even though Republicans were the majority party in Congress in 2004, labor PACs overwhelmingly supported Democrats. The comparable figures for 2008 were 92 percent to Democrats and 8 percent to Republicans.

The different approaches of labor and corporate PACs are further revealed by looking at the relative amounts of money they devote to incumbents, challengers, and candidates in open seat races. According to FEC data for the 2008 cycle, corporate PACs gave $8.8 million to Democratic incumbents and $18.5 million to Republican incumbents. In both categories, they outspent labor PACs, which gave $2.4 million to Democratic incumbents and only $391,150 to sitting Republicans. Labor PACs contributed $2.9 million to Democratic challengers, compared to $642,000 from corporate PACs. The patterns were reversed for Republican challengers, who received $2.1 million from corporate PACs and only $59,000 from labor PACs. In open seat races, Democrats received $1.9 million from corporate PACs and $1.2 million from labor PACs. While corporate PACs gave a similar amount, $1.1 million to Republican candidates, Democrats gave them a mere $20,500.

In the end, electoral assistance may increase the likelihood of a candidate voting with business or labor on at least some congressional roll-call votes.[73] There is, however, greater consensus that the activities of business and labor groups provide them with access to elected officials as well as additional time with legislators.[74] PAC money also can have an effect on legislation before it comes to a vote on the floor of Congress, such as through amendments during committee markups.[75]

Outside of electoral politics, business and labor groups rely on their legislative departments. Within many legislative departments are legislative action committees (LACs), which help educate members about important legislation and policies and about the positions members of Congress have taken on issues affecting the interests of the group. Many local chapters of the Chamber of Commerce have LACs, as do state chapters of the AFL-CIO. LACs help arrange personal meetings with lawmakers, compile voting records of legislators, and organize grassroots lobbying efforts to convey the intensity of their members' opinions.

To maximize grassroots lobbying efforts, business and labor groups sponsor television and radio advertisements, as well as massive e-mail, letter-writing, and postcard campaigns. Business groups run "advertorials" (advertisements to educate the public). They also make efforts to encourage business owners to have their voices heard in the legislative process.[76] The NFIB lists the most pressing issues facing small businesses and offers its members suggestions on its Web site about how best to contact lawmakers; the importance of personalizing letters, faxes, and e-mails; and tips for telephone calls to congressional offices.

In addition to Web sites that members can visit for information, business and labor groups also send legislative updates through e-mail to those subscribed to its activist network. These e-mails typically describe a problem facing the nation and instruct subscribers to contact their members of Congress. Many of the e-mails contain strong rhetoric to attract attention, and they nearly always include instructions for subscribers to contact their friends, family, and co-workers. The AFL-CIO contacts supporters through a mailing list: peoplepower@aflcio.org. In April 2009 it urged members to contact their representatives to voice their support for President Obama's budget resolution for fiscal year 2010. CtW sends its activists e-mail updates and even attaches some with streaming video. In one e-mail, "Wal-Mart's War on Workers," CtW provides a link to a six-minute online minidocumentary about workers' struggles to organize into a union and to win higher wages and benefits. The e-mail encourages the recipient to support Wal-Mart workers and to share the video with friends.

Finally, grassroots efforts include organizing protests and demonstrations.[77] Although this approach is less common, it can generate significant media attention. In 2007 truck drivers with the International Brotherhood of Teamsters made headlines by picketing on the Mexican border crossings in California and Texas. The drivers carried signs that read, "NAFTA Kills" and "Unsafe Mexican Trucks" in protest of a pilot program that allowed up to 100 Mexican trucking companies to haul their cargo anywhere in the United States.[78] On the business side, groups in the insurance industry reportedly organized protests at town hall meetings in 2009 to oppose health care reform—an effort that some critics derided as "astroturfing" for falsely creating an impression that the grassroots opposition was spontaneous.[79] Nevertheless, the insurance industry succeeded in dominating the news coverage on health care reform for much of the summer of 2009.

Although grassroots lobbying often provides useful information to voters and legislators and can have an effect on public policies,[80] the most obvious way that business and labor groups attempt to influence policy is through Washington-based lobbyists, many of whom work on K Street in the nation's capital. These lobbyists meet personally with legislators and their aides and often provide them with press releases and policy papers. In addition, they closely monitor potential legislation or changes in regulations that may affect their interests. Lobbyists for business and labor are active at the local, state, and national levels of government, and they attempt to influence all branches of government, including executive agencies, the legislature, and, in some rare instances, even judges and chief executives.[81]

In 2008 some 642 lobbyists were working on labor, antitrust, and workplace issues at the federal level. Wal-Mart Stores spent almost $6.6 million on lobbying expenditures in 2008, and the AFL-CIO spent $3.1 million. Business

NATIONAL FEDERATION OF INDEPENDENT BUSINESS'S "TIPS ON CONTACTING LAWMAKERS"

TIPS ON TELEPHONING YOUR LAWMAKERS

To find your lawmaker's phone number, use our searchable online congressional directory or call the U.S. Capitol Switchboard at (202) 224-3121 and ask for your senator's and/or representative's office.

Remember that telephone calls are often taken by a staff member, not the member of Congress. Ask to speak with the aide who handles the issue on which you wish to comment.

After identifying yourself, tell the aide you would like to leave a brief message, such as: "Please tell Senator/Representative (Name) that I support/oppose (S.___/H.R.___)."

You will also want to state reasons for your support or opposition to the bill. Let them know how the bill affects your business, giving your related costs, your number of employees (and how they will be affected), and your number of years in business. Ask for your senator's or representative's position on the bill. You may also request a written response to your telephone call.

TIPS ON WRITING TO CONGRESS

If you decide to write an email or fax, this list of helpful suggestions will improve the effectiveness of the letter:

1. Your purpose for writing should be stated in the first paragraph of the letter. If your letter pertains to a specific piece of legislation, identify it accordingly, e.g., House bill: H. R._____, Senate bill: S._____.
2. Be courteous, to the point, and include key information, using examples to support your position. Let your lawmaker know how the bill affects your business, giving your related costs, your number of employees (and how they will be affected), and your number of years in business. Your real-life examples humanize an issue in a way that facts and figures cannot.
3. Address only one issue in each note; and, if possible, keep the letter to one page.
4. Be sure to copy us on your correspondence and any reply you receive from your lawmaker.

You can send an email to your Representative or Senator directly from NFIB.com. Visit our Action Alert Center for current issue alerts that contain language that may be helpful in getting started.

If you have further questions, please contact NFIB Legislative Services at (202) 314-2080.

Addressing correspondence

To a Senator

The Honorable (full name)
__(Rm.#)__(name of) Senate Office Building
United States Senate
Washington, DC 20510

Dear Senator:

To a Representative:

The Honorable (full name)
__(Rm.#)__(name of) House Office Building
United States House of Representatives
Washington, DC 20515

Dear Representative:

Note: When writing to the chair of a committee or the Speaker of the House, it is proper to address them as Dear Mr. Chairman or Madam Chairwoman; or Dear Madam Speaker.

SOURCE: National Federation of Independent Business, http://www.nfib.com/tabid/739/Default.aspx?cmsid=49347.

interests clearly dominate lobbying expenditures. From 1998 to 2009 no group came close to matching the $488.5 million spent by the Chamber of Commerce (see Table 13.1). By comparison, all labor groups combined spent only slightly above $370 million during the same period.

On the most recent controversial labor bill in the 110th and 111th Congresses, the Employee Free Choice Act, business again flexed its financial muscle. Business groups ranging from the American Bankers Association to the International Sleep Products Association opposed the legislation. In 2008 the Chamber of Commerce spent $91.6 million to defeat the measure compared to $38.7 million spent in favor of the bill by all labor groups combined.[82] With Democrats expanding their majorities in Congress and capturing the White House following the 2008 election, the Chamber of Commerce wasted little time in getting television ads ready to pressure members of Congress to oppose the EFCA.

In Pennsylvania, the Chamber of Commerce targeted Senator Specter, a previous EFCA co-sponsor, and succeeded in getting him to back away from his earlier support for the legislation. The chamber then continued to keep the pressure on Specter after he left the Republican Party and joined the Democratic Party. To mount a national campaign in 2009, the Chamber of Commerce also partnered with the Association of Builders and Contractors, Retail Industry Leaders Association, and others to form the Coalition for a Democratic Workplace. Some reports indicate

TABLE 13.1 **Top Spenders on Lobbying, 1998-2009**

Lobbying Client	Total
U.S. Chamber of Commerce	$488,458,180
American Medical Assn.	$208,472,500
General Electric	$183,895,000
American Hospital Assn.	$172,940,431
AARP	$164,072,064
Pharmaceutical Rsrch & Mfrs of America	$154,533,400
AT&T Inc.	$140,516,229
Northrop Grumman	$133,515,253
Edison Electric Institute	$128,645,999
Business Roundtable	$127,980,000
National Assn. of Realtors	$127,977,380
Exxon Mobil	$124,626,942
Blue Cross/Blue Shield	$120,491,385
Verizon Communications	$118,344,841
Lockheed Martin	$115,567,888
Boeing Co.	$108,728,310
General Motors	$104,774,483
Southern Co.	$97,670,694
Freddie Mac	$96,194,048
Altria Group	$88,380,000

SOURCE: Center for Responsive Politics (opensecrets.org).

that the coalition was prepared to spend upwards of $30 million to defeat EFCA. This amount was in addition to $20 million to $30 million that the Chamber of Commerce planned to spend in 2009, as well as tens of millions of dollars from various other probusiness interests such as American Solutions, Employee Freedom Action Committee, Americans for Job Security, Alliance for Worker Freedom, and the Workforce Fairness Institute.[83] These intensive efforts on the business side likely contributed to the eventual failure of EFCA to become law in either the 110th or the 111th Congresses.

Given the massive inequities in financial resources that labor and business devote to lobbying, it is unsurprising that one of the most comprehensive surveys of lobbying to date (encompassing ninety-eight different issue areas) found that the number of lobbyists representing business outnumbered those of labor by 6 to 1.[84] The imbalance of political voices is further illustrated by the fact that the majority of labor lobbyists represented six large unions, while corporate lobbyists came from a much broader range of organizations, many of which specialized in a specific policy area. Labor marshals a competent but small squad of all-purpose players on the lobbying field, who are outnumbered by a much larger corporate squad with lots of special teams. Labor lobbyists are likely to be working on a wide portfolio of issues simultaneously, while corporate lobbyists can afford to work more intensely and focus on a single policy area.

In the congressional arena, this resource imbalance is mitigated because corporate and labor groups almost always work in coalitions when advocating for policy change, and very often different sets of corporate interests take opposing "sides" in a policy dispute. This means that there is greater equity in the resources available to opponents in a policy dispute than is indicated by a raw comparison of business and labor. On almost all legislative issues, therefore, interests representing each side of a debate have the ability to engage in the most common lobbying tactics through one or another coalition member. Such strategies include making direct contacts with legislators and their staff, conducting and disseminating policy research, and drafting policy proposals.[85] Scholars argue, perhaps surprisingly, that in cases where resource imbalances remain, that having more resources does not predict that a lobbying coalition will get the policy change it desires. One reason is Washington's strong bias for maintaining the status quo, which means that those pushing for legislation to change existing policy lose more often than they win. Frequently, such resistance to change advantages business interests because the status quo already benefits them.[86]

Business interests also have an advantage in policy disputes where they are unified and stand opposed to labor groups. In such cases business interests prevail about 80 percent of the time. In contrast, when business is opposed by citizen interest groups, or by labor and citizen groups working together, they succeed only about 50 percent of the time.[87] Business power, although not as monolithic as portrayed in media accounts, does outweigh that of labor in the lobbying arena. In fact, when asked in a recent survey of corporate lobbyists who was their major opposition, not one of them said labor lobbyists.[88]

Emerging scholarship on the growth of corporate lobbying argues that since the mid-1990s corporations have been escalating the resources they devote to lobbying because they are increasingly aware of its potential payoffs.[89] Many corporations therefore have gone from seeing political action as a defensive move to preserve the status quo to one that takes an offensive stance actively seeking benefits from government policy. These benefits may not arise from large policy changes on high profile issues, but rather through small clauses in, and amendments to, legislation. Examples include small changes in the tax code inserted into complex legislation or disputes about *how* government will regulate air pollution, once the question that it should regulate air pollution has been settled.[90] Because of their lower salience, these actions go largely unnoticed, yet offer significant particularistic benefits. For business lobbyists, the delight, not the devil, can often be found in the details.

TELEVISION SCRIPT OF A CHAMBER OF COMMERCE AD TARGETING SEN. ARLEN SPECTER

Person 1: We can't let Congress do this to our economy.

Narrator: Congress wants to strip away the secret ballot, and the bureaucrats dictate to Pennsylvania businesses.

Person 2: Pennsylvania needs jobs. We don't need government mandates. We need jobs.

Narrator: Senator Arlen Specter says it's a particularly bad time to pass card check.

Person 3: Card check won't just take away the secret ballot. Card check will wipe out jobs.

Person 4: Congress needs to fix the economy; not try to worry about trying to bail out the big unions.

Narrator: Tell Senator Specter to keep standing firm against card check.

SOURCE: U.S. Chamber of Commerce, http://www.uschamber.com/wfi/default.

Business resource advantages offer an additional benefit when it comes to executive branch lobbying. The rulemaking process, through which bureaucracies and executive agencies interpret and implement congressional legislation, offers lobbyists a significant opportunity to shape policy. More than 80 percent of political organizations report lobbying during rulemaking, and 75 percent rate it equal in importance to lobbying Congress.[91] The number of rules written by the executive branch far surpasses the volume of legislation from Congress. Despite the a mandatory public comment period in the rulemaking process, which is designed to encourage wide participation, corporate interests have the advantage because monitoring and tracking the procedure across the broad array of agencies in the executive branch requires significant resources. Partly for that reason, studies show that the number of comments submitted by corporate interests (57 percent) far surpasses the number from government sources (19 percent), and other interest groups (22 percent).[92] Recent research demonstrates the payoff for the large volume of business comments is that the content of final rules generally tends to align with their preferences.[93]

A new rule issued by the National Mediation Board (NMB) that was heavily favored by organized labor is a recent exception to this trend. It is one that illustrates the importance and impact of rulemaking. The NMB oversees union organizing in the transportation sector that is governed by the Railway Labor Act (1926). In this role, the NMB manages elections in which workers decide whether they wish to be represented by a union. The Railway Labor Act mandates that the NMB "develop an election procedure that accurately reflects the majority's determination regarding representation," but does not offer any specifics about how the election process should be designed. For seventy-five years, the NMB interpreted their mandate to mean that a majority of workers in a bargaining unit had to vote in favor of the union for it to be certified. Any worker who abstained from voting was automatically counted as a vote against union representation. The rule change alters this interpretation so that a union will become the official representative of workers if a majority of those *participating* in the election vote in favor of the union. The AFL-CIO proposed the rule change arguing that it brought the process in line with common democratic practices. The business community vigorously opposed the change, anticipating it will make organizing workers in the transportation sector easier.[94] So far, the new rule has been upheld at the district level of the federal court system, but is likely to be face further challenges in the judicial arena.

The judicial branch is another important arena for lobbyists, who try to influence court appointments, litigate test cases, and influence court decisions by filing amicus curiae (friend of the court) briefs. The filing of amicus briefs is the most common interest group activity before the courts, and is one that is arguably characterized by more pluralistic participation than others. A study of the 1995 Supreme Court session revealed that corporations participated in 22 percent of the seventy cases in which briefs were filed, and trade associations in 68 percent. In comparison, public advocacy groups submitted briefs in 57 percent of cases, and unions a much smaller 10 percent.[95]

A more contentious judicial arena for labor and business is the appointment of members to the National Labor Relations Board, a semijudicial agency that has been referred to as the Supreme Court of labor law. It is the agency that interprets and adjudicates disputes involving the National Labor Relations Act. The NLRA governs union organizing in the private sector (with the exception of the transportation industry). Appointees to the five-member board are nominated by the president and confirmed by the Senate for five-year terms. The appointment process was relatively free of partisan rancor and lobbying until the late 1970s when the norm of appointing experienced lawyers and scholars from "neutral" backgrounds was broken. Subsequently, first business and then labor have lobbied presidents and senators to nominate and confirm probusiness or pro-union lawyers to the board.[96] In response, and with the urging of organized interests on both sides, senators have frequently filibustered or placed holds on nominees. It has become commonplace for presidents to have to resort to making recess appointments or leave vacancies on the board because it has become so difficult to for nominees to win Senate confirmation.[97] Studies show that there is good reason for significant lobbying on these appointments. Recent decisions reveal a clear pattern: NLRB members whose appointment was supported by business vote consistently in favor of business interests, whereas members whose appointment was supported by labor vote consistently in favor of labor interests.[98]

Even though wrangling over NLRB appointments can be consequential, it is a lobbying activity that often goes unnoticed by the wider public. In contrast, on many issues both business and labor adopt "outside strategies" and deliberately attempt to activate their "grassroots" supporters and the wider public.

CONCLUSION

Business and labor have honed and employed different strategies and techniques to advance their cause. Yet each ultimately is limited in its ability to win its preferred legislative policies based on its political resources. Organized labor's impressive electoral support is difficult to translate into congressional majorities that will support its legislative priorities, and business interests' financial resources are insufficient to secure their policy goals on highly salient policies in the face of strong public opposition. If political battles between business and labor are akin to a heavyweight boxing match, as alluded to at the opening of the chapter, then it seems that neither side can regularly deliver a knockout blow. Even as organized labor has seen its membership fall as a percentage of the workforce in recent decades, it "punches above its weight" in the electoral arena, so that business interests have to remain aware and responsive to the moves of their political opponent.

NOTES

1. Health Care Reform letter, Walmartstores.com, June 30, 2009, www. walmartstores.com/download/3857.pdf.

2. Jeffrey Young, "Wal-Mart Backs Health Benefit Mandate," *The Hill.com,* June 30 2009, thehill.com/business—lobby/wal-mart-backs-health-benefits-mandate-2009-06-30.html. See also Melanie Trottman, "SEIU Health-Care Push Aided by Wal-Mart," *Wall Street Journal,* July 27, 2009, online. wsj.com/article/SB12486533739368 2517.html.

3. See for example, G. William Domhoff, *Who Rules America? Challenges to Corporate and Class Dominance* (Englewood Cliffs, N.J.: Prentice-Hall, 1967); Charles E. Lindblom, *Politics and Markets: The World's Political Economic Systems* (New York: Basic Books, 1977); David Vogel, *Fluctuating Fortunes: The Political Power of Business in America* (New York: Basic Books, 1989); and Patrick Bernhagen, *The Political Power of Business: Structure and Information in Public Policymaking* (New York: Routledge, 2007).

4. Mancur Olson, *The Logic of Collective Action* (Cambridge: Harvard University Press, 1965).

5. David B. Truman, *The Government Process* (New York: Knopf, 1951).

6. Jack L. Walker Jr., *Mobilizing Interest Groups in America: Patrons, Professions, and Social Movements* (Ann Arbor: University of Michigan Press, 1993), 29.

7. Robert H. Salisbury, "An Exchange Theory of Interest Groups," *Midwest Journal of Political Science* 13 (1969): 1–32.

8. Marc Karson, "The National Labor Union and the Knights of Labor," in *Labor and American Politics,* ed. Charles M. Rehmus, Doris B. McLaughlin, and Frederick H. Nesbitt (Ann Arbor: University of Michigan Press, 1978), 68–74.

9. Organized labor's efforts to reelect FDR were officially coordinated through an organization, Labor's Non-Partisan League, which included unions from both the AFL and the CIO. It was the CIO unions and particularly Lewis's UMW that provided most of the direction and resources. The UMW alone directed an unprecedented $600,000 to the political effort. For a comprehensive history of the CIO, see Robert Zieger, *The CIO 1935–1955* (Chapel Hill: University of North Carolina Press, 1995).

10. J. David Greenstone, *Labor in American Politics* (New York: Knopf, 1969).

11. Taylor Dark, *The Unions and the Democrats: An Enduring Alliance* (Ithaca: Cornell University Press, 1999).

12. The extent to which the National Labor Relations Act contributed to a rise in union membership starting in the late 1930s is debated among labor scholars. For a discussion of this point and the role of the state in the formation of unions more generally, see Melvyn Dubofsky, *The State and Labor in Modern America* (Chapel Hill: University of North Carolina Press, 1994).

13. Donald S. Wasserman, "Collective Bargaining Rights in the Public Sector: Promises and Reality," in *Justice on the Job: Perspective on the Erosion of Collective Bargaining in the United States,* ed. Richard Block, Sheldon Friedman, Michelle Kaminski, and Andy Levin (Kalamazoo, Mich.: W. E. Upjohn Institute for Employment Research, 2006).

14. For discussions of the fall in union density in the United States and factors that have contributed to it, see Taylor E. Dark, *Unions and the Democrats,* chap. 1; Michael Goldfield, *The Decline of Organized Labor in the United States* (Chicago: University of Chicago Press, 1987); Nelson Lichtenstein, *State of the Union: A Century of American Labor* (Princeton: University of Princeton Press, 2002)

15. For historical membership figures, see Leo Troy, "Trade Union Membership, 1880–1960," *Review of Economic Statistics* 47 (1965): 93–113. For contemporary data, see Bureau of Labor Statistics, "Union Members Summary," January 28, 2009, www.bls.gov/news.release/union2.nr0.htm.

16. See Cletus Daniel, "Cesar Chavez and the Unionization of California Farm Workers," in *Labor Leaders in America,* ed. Melvyn

Dubofsky and Warren Van Tine (Urbana: University of Illinois Press, 1987).

17. Margaret Levi, "Organizing Power: The Prospects for an American Labor Movement," *Perspectives on Politics* 1 (2003): 45–68. See also Peter L. Francia, "Assessing the Labor-Democratic Party Alliance: A One-Sided Relationship?" *Polity* 42 (2010): 293–303.

18. Cathie Jo Martin, "Sectional Parties, Divided Business," *Studies in American Political Development* 20 (2006): 160–184.

19. Philip A. Mundo, *Interest Groups: Cases and Characteristics* (Chicago: Nelson Hall, 1992), chap. 4.

20. Ibid., chap. 3.

21. Mark A. Smith, *American Business and Political Power: Public Opinion, Elections and Democracy* (Chicago: University of Chicago Press, 2001), chap. 3.

22. David Vogel, *Fluctuating Fortunes: The Political Power of Business in America* (New York: Basic Books, 1989).

23. For data cited here, as well as a comprehensive review of the literature on bias in the interest group system, see Frank R. Baumgartner and Beth L. Leech, *Basic Interests: The Importance of Groups in Politics and in Political Science* (Princeton: Princeton University Press, 1988), chaps. 5 and 6. For a later review of the literature and criticism of this approach to assessing group influence, see David Lowery and Virginia Gray, "Bias in the Heavenly Chorus: Interests in Society and before Government," *Journal of Theoretical Politics* 16 (2004): 5–30.

24. Federal Election Commission, "FEC Records Slight Increase in the Number of PACs," FEC News Release, January 17, 2008, www.fec.gov/press/press2008/20080117paccount.shtml.

25. Frank R. Baumgartner and Beth L. Leech, "Interest Niches and Policy Bandwagons: Patterns of Interest Group Involvement in National Politics," *Journal of Politics* 63 (2001): 1191–1213.

26. Ibid.

27. Smith, *American Business and Political Power.*

28. For a discussion of problems with defining interest groups, see James Yoho, "The Evolution of a Better Definition of 'Interest Group,'" *Social Science Journal* 35 (1998): 231–234. See also Baumgartner and Leech, *Basic Interests,* 25–30.

29. David M. Hart, "Business Is Not an Interest Group: On the Study of Companies in American National Politics," *Annual Review of Political Science* 7 (2004): 47–69.

30. Jacob S. Hacker and Paul Pierson, "Winner-Take-All Politics: Public Policy, Political Organization, and the Precipitous Rise of Top Incomes in the United States," *Politics & Society* 38 (2010): 152–204; see also David Vogel, *Fluctuating Fortunes* (New York: Basic Books, 1989), 196.

31. Federal Election Commission, "FEC Records Slight Increase in the Number of PACs," FEC News Release, January 17, 2008, www.fec.gov/press/press2008/20080117paccount.shtml.

32. Edward Alden and Neil Buckley, "Wal-Mart Becomes Largest Corporate Political Investor," *Financial Times,* February 24, 2004.

33. Jeffrey M. Berry, *The New Liberalism: The Rising Power of Citizen Groups* (Washington, D.C.: Brookings Institution Press, 1999).

34. David Lowery and Virginia Gray, "Bias in the Heavenly Chorus: Interests in Society and Before Government," *Journal of Theoretical Politics* 16 (2004): 5–30.

35. Daniel J. Tichenor and Richard A. Harris, "The Development of Interest Group Politics in America: Beyond the Conceits of Modern Times," *Annual Review of Political Science* 8 (2005): 251–270.

36. Kay Lehman Schlozman and John T. Tierney, *Organized Interests and American Democracy* (New York: Harper and Row, 1986).

37. See Berry, *The New Liberalism.* See also Walker, *Mobilizing Interest Groups.* For a survey of studies on the dynamics of bias, see Baumgartner and Leech, *Basic Interests,* chap. 6.

38. Dark, *Unions and the Democrats;* see also Peter L. Francia, *The Future of Organized Labor in American Politics* (New York: Columbia University Press, 2006).

39. For a comprehensive overview of the split in organized labor, see Marick F. Masters, Ray Gibney, and Thomas J. Zagenczyk, "The AFL-CIO v. CTW: The Competing Visions, Strategies, and Structures," *Journal of Labor Research* 27 (2006): 473–504. See also Tracy Roof, "CTW vs. the AFL-CIO: The Potential Impact of the Split on Labor's Political Action," *International Journal of Organization Theory and Behavior* 10 (2007): 245–275.

40. AFL-CIO, "Working Families Vote," www.afl-cio.org/issues/politics/index.cfm. Exit poll numbers differ slightly from those reported by the AFL-CIO. According to exit polls, 60 percent of union members voted for Obama compared to 37 percent for McCain; see www.cnn.com/ELECTION/2008/results/polls/#val=USP00p3.

41. Change to Win, "Unions Hit the Ground Running After GOP Convention," CtW press release, September 5, 2008, www.changetowin.org/for-the-media/press-releases-and-statements.

42. Jonathan Tasini, "Labor's Election Ground War—And How the Media Is Missing It," *Huffington Post,* August 25, 2008, www.huffingtonpost.com/jonathan-tasini/labors-election-ground-wa_b_121208.html.

43. For a full account of changes in AFL-CIO political activities after Sweeney became president of the organization, see Francia, *Future of Organized Labor.*

44. Steve Rosenthal, "Building to Win, Building to Last: The AFL-CIO Political Program," in *Not Your Father's Labor Movement: Inside the AFL-CIO* (New York: Verso, 1998).

45. Alan Gerber and Donald Green, "The Effects of Canvassing, Telephone Calls, and Direct Mail on Voter Turnout: A Field Experiment," *American Political Science Review* 94 (2000): 653–663.

46. Richard Hurd, "U.S. Labor 2006: Strategic Developments across the Divide," *Journal of Labor Research* 28 (2007): 313–324.

47. Pew Research Center for People and the Press, "GOP Makes Gains among the Working Class, While Democrats Hold on to the Union Vote," August 2, 2005, people-press.org/commentary/?analysisid=114.

48. Richard Freeman, "What Do Unions Do . . . to Voting?" NBER Working Paper Series, September 2003, www.nber.org/papers/w9992.

49. Jan E. Leighley and Jonathan Nagler, "Unions, Voter Turnout, and Class Bias in the U.S. Electorate, 1964–2004," *Journal of Politics* 69 (2007): 430–441.

50. J. David Greenstone, *Labor in American Politics* (New York: Knopf, 1969).

51. Tracy Chang, "The Labor Vote in U.S. National Elections," *Political Quarterly* 72 (2001): 375–385. See also Peter L. Francia, "Wither Labor? Reassessing Organized Labor's Political Power," *International Journal of Organization Theory and Behavior* 10 (2007): 188–212.

52. Pew Research Center for People and the Press, "GOP Makes Gains."

53. Francia, *Future of Organized Labor,* 72–74.

54. Smith, *American Business and Political Power.*

55. Richard M. Skinner, *More Than Money: Interest Group Action in Congressional Elections* (Lanham, Md.: Rowman and Littlefield, 2007).

56. Lorraine Woellert, "Business Vows to Get Out the Vote: A GOP-Industry Push is Taking a Page from Labor's Playbook," *Business Week,* October 7, 2002.

57. Daniel Gross, "Retail Politics: Wal-Mart's Campaign to Influence the Election," *Newsweek,* August 5, 2008.

58. The rules governing corporate and labor PACs are contained in Federal Election Commission guide "Corporations and Labor Organizations," www.fec.gov/pdf/colagui.pdf.

59. Federal Election Commission, "PAC Contributions to Candidates 1996–2008 Election Cycles," www.fec.gov/press/press2009/20090415PAC/20090424PAC.shtml.

60. These data and those for the following section are from Center for Responsive Politics, "The Big Picture: Business-Labor-Ideology Split in PAC and Individual Donations to Candidates and Parties," www.opensecrets.org/bigpicture/blio.php?cycle=2008.

61. Center for Responsive Politics, "The Big Picture 2008: The Price of Admission," www.opensecrets.org/bigpicture/stats.php.

62. All figures have been rounded; complete data available from Center for Responsive Politics, "Top PACs 2008," www.opensecrets.org/bigpicture/toppacs.php?cycle=2008&Type=C.

63. Federal Election Commission, "Growth in PAC Financial Activity Slows," news release, April 24, 2009, www.fec.gov/press/press2009/20090415PAC/20090424PAC.shtml.

64. Suzy Khim, "The Citizens United Effect," *Mother Jones,* June 7, 2010, motherjones.com/politics/2010/06/citizens-united-effect.

65. Ibid.

66. The DISCLOSE Act (the acronym for Democracy is Strengthened by Casting Light on Spending in Elections) would accomplish these goals. It passed the House on June 24, 2010, but has yet to pass the Senate. For details, see David Herszenhorn, "House Approves Legislation that Mandates the Disclosure of Political Spending," *New York Times,* June 24, 2010, www.nytimes.com/2010/06/25/us/politics/25cong.html.

67. National Public Radio, "Secret Money Project: Election 2008," www.npr.org/blogs/secretmoney/about_the_project/.

68. Campaign Finance Institute, "Soft Money Political Spending by 501(c) Nonprofits Tripled in 2008 Election," Campaign Finance Institute Working Paper, February 29, 2009, www.cfinst.org/pr/prRelease.aspx?ReleaseID=221.

69. Lindblom, *Politics and Markets.* For a different perspective, see Smith, *American Business and Political Power.*

70. Dark, *The Unions and the Democrats,* 36.

71. The academic literature on PAC contribution strategies is quite extensive. See David J. Gopoian, "What Makes PACs Tick: An Analysis of the Allocation Patterns of Economic Interest Groups," *American Journal of Political Science* 28 (1984): 259–281; James W. Endersby and Michael C. Munger, "The Impact of Legislator Attributes on Union PAC Campaign Contributions," *Journal of Labor Research* 13 (1992): 79–97; Richard W. Hurd and Jeffrey Sohl, "Strategic Diversity in Labor PAC Contribution Patterns," *Social Science Journal* 29 (1992): 65–86; and Thomas J. Rudolph, "Corporate and Labor PAC Contributions in House Elections: Measuring the Effects of Majority Party Status," *Journal of Politics* 61 (1999): 195–206.

72. Laura I. Langbein, "Money and Access: Some Empirical Evidence," *Journal of Politics* 48 (1986): 1054–62; Theodore J. Eismeier and Philip H. Pollock III, *Business, Money, and the Rise of Corporate PACs in American Elections* (New York: Quorum Books, 1988).

73. See James Kau and Paul H. Rubin, "The Impact of Labor Unions on the Passage of Economic Legislation," *Journal of Labor Research* 2 (1981): 133–145; Gregory Saltzman, "Congressional Voting on Labor Issues: The Role of PACs," *Industrial and Labor Relations Review* 40 (1987): 163–179; Peter F. Burns, Peter L. Francia, and Paul S. Herrnson, "Labor at Work: Union Campaign Activities and Legislative Payoffs in the U.S. House of Representatives," *Social Science Quarterly* 81 (2000): 507–522. For a different perspective, see John R. Wright, "PACs, Contributions, and Roll Calls: An Organizational Perspective," *American Political Science Review* 79 (1985): 400–414; Janet M. Grenzke, "PACs and the Congressional Supermarket: The Currency is Complex," *American Journal of Political Science* 33 (1989): 1–24; Gregory Wawro, "A Panel Probit Analysis of Campaign Contributions and Roll-Call Votes," *American Journal of Political Science* 45 (2001): 563–579.

74. Langbein, "Money and Access." See also Richard L. Hall and Frank W. Wayman, "Buying Time: Moneyed Interests and the Mobilization of Bias in Congressional Subcommittees," *American Political Science Review* 84 (September 1990), 797–820; but see Thomas L. Brunell, "The Relationship between Political Parties and Interest Groups: Explaining Patterns of PAC Contributions to Candidates for Congress," *Political Research Quarterly* 58 (December 2005): 681–688.

75. M. Margaret Conway, Joanne Connor Green, and Marian Currinder, "Interest Group Money in Elections," in *Interest Group Politics,* 6th ed., ed. Allan J. Cigler and Burdett A. Loomis (Washington, D.C.: CQ Press, 2002).

76. Anthony Nownes, *Total Lobbying: What Lobbyists Want (and How They Try to Get It)* (New York: Cambridge University Press, 2006).

77. See Michael Lipsky, "Protest as a Political Resource," *American Political Science Review* 62 (December 1968): 1144–1158.

78. Associated Press, "Drivers Protest Allowing Mexican Trucks in U.S.," www.msnbc.msn.com/id/20625369.

79. Ben Smith, "The Summer of Astroturf," *Politico,* www.politico.com/news/stories/0809/26312.html.

80. Kenneth M. Goldstein, *Interest Groups, Lobbying, and Participation in America* (New York: Cambridge University Press, 1999), 126.

81. Nownes, *Total Lobbying.*

82. Center for Responsive Politics, "Labor and Business Spend Big on Looming Unionization Issue," www.opensecrets.org/news/2009/02/labor-and-business-spend-big-o.html.

83. AFL-CIO, "Who Is Against the Employee Free Choice Act?" www.aflcio.org/joinaunion/voiceatwork/efca/against_list.cfm.

84. Frank R. Baumgartner, Jeffrey M. Berry, Marie Hojnacki, David C. Kimball, and Beth Leech, *Lobbying and Policy Change* (Chicago: University of Chicago Press, 2009).

85. For a summary of multiple studies of common lobbying activities, see Baumgartner and Leech, *Basic Interests,* chap. 8. For a more contemporary survey, see Baumgartner et al., *Lobbying and Policy Change,* chap. 8.

86. Baumgartner et al., *Lobbying and Policy Change.*

87. Ibid., 238.

88. Lee Drutman, "The Business of America is Lobbying: The Expansion of Corporate Political Activity and the Future of American Pluralism" (unpublished dissertation, University of California, Berkeley, 2010), chap. 7, www.leedrutman.com/dissertation.html; cited with author's permission. The corporate lobbyists' most commonly mentioned sources of opposition were: members of Congress (26 percent), "getting visibility" (26 percent), and "other industry lobbyists" (21 percent).

89. Ibid.

90. For a more thorough overview of this argument and additional examples, see Smith, *American Business and Political Power,* chap. 2; and Drutman, "Business of America is Lobbying."

91. Scott R. Furlong and Cornelius Kerwin, "Interest Group Participation in Rule Making: A Decade of Change," *Journal of Public Administration Research and Theory* 15 (2005): 353–370.

92. Jason Webb Yackee and Susan Webb Yackee, "A Bias Towards Business? Assessing Interest Group Influence on the U.S. Bureaucracy,"

Journal of Politics 68, 1 (2006): 128–139. See also, Marissa Martino Golden, "Interest Groups in the Rule-Making Process: Who Participates? Whose Voices Get Heard? *Journal of Public Administration Research and Theory* 8 (April 1998): 245–279.

93. Yackee and Yackee, "A Bias Towards Business?" This study drew its sample of rules from those written by the Occupational Safety and Health Administration, Employment Standards Administration, Federal Railroad Administration, and Federal Highway Administration. The various agencies included in the sample seem especially relevant to questions of business and labor. The findings in this study are contradicted by earlier research that found the greater volume of business comments did not impact the content of final rules. See Golden, "Interest Groups in the Rule-Making Process."

94. A comprehensive description of the rule change along with the substantial number of comments from business and labor groups is available at the National Mediation Board Web site, www.nmb.gov/representation/proposed-rep-rulemaking.html.

95. Paul M. Collins Jr. and Lisa A. Solowiej, "Interest Group Participation, Competition, and Conflict in the U.S. Supreme Court," *Law & Social Inquiry* 32, 4 (2007). See also Gregory A. Caldeira and John R. Wright, "Amici Curiae before the Supreme Court: Who Participates, When, and How Much?" *The Journal of Politics* 52, 3 (1990).

96. Joann Flynn, "A Quiet Revolution at the Labor Board: The Transformation of the NLRB, 1935–2000," *Ohio State Law Journal* 61 (2000). See also Terry M. Moe, "Interests, Institutions and Positive Theory: The Politics of the NLRB," *Studies in American Political Development* 2 (1987).

97. The recent partisan rancor over appointments to the NLRB has forced it to operate with only two members, as first Democrats failed to confirm George W. Bush's appointees, and then Republicans stalled Barack Obama's appointees. The Supreme Court decided in *New Process Steel LP v. NLRB* (2010) that the NLRA as written does not permit a two-member NLRB to issue decisions.

98. Flynn, "A Quiet Revolution."

SUGGESTED READING

Dark, Taylor E. *The Unions and the Democrats: An Enduring Alliance.* Ithaca: Cornell University Press, 1999.

Francia, Peter L. *The Future of Organized Labor in American Politics.* New York: Columbia University Press, 2006.

Greenstone, J. David. *Labor in American Politics.* New York: Knopf, 1969.

Lichtenstein, Nelson. *State of the Union: A Century of American Labor.* Princeton: University of Princeton Press, 2002.

Smith, Mark A. *American Business and Political Power: Public Opinion, Elections and Democracy.* Chicago: University of Chicago Press, 2001.

Vogel, David. *Fluctuating Fortunes: The Political Power of Business in America.* New York: Basic Books, 1989.

chapter 14

Defense and Homeland Security

by Carmine Scavo

To "provide for the common defense," is one of the reasons "we the people" ordained and established the Constitution of the United States. And at each inaugural, the president of the United States takes an oath to "preserve, protect and defend the Constitution." Members of Congress add "against all enemies foreign and domestic" in their oaths of office. These affirmations are reasons enough to consider the functioning of interest groups in national defense and homeland security policy. Another reason is that providing for the common defense costs the U.S. government some $750 billion per year—or about 21 percent of all federal expenditures. Defense and homeland security are therefore both significant and lucrative areas in which interest groups operate.[1]

Defense policy has been an important concern to policymakers since the founding of the Republic. Homeland security, however, is a bit different because it arguably began on September 11, 2001, with the terrorist attacks on the World Trade Center in New York, the Pentagon in suburban Washington, D.C., and the foiled attack on the U.S. Capitol. Although defense and homeland security policy are clearly related, there are significant differences between the two areas to cause them to be treated differently in this chapter.

NATIONAL DEFENSE

Defense policy, and in particular military procurement, is a prime example of distributive public policy. As defined by Theodore Lowi, a distributive policy is "characterized by the ease with which [it] can be disaggregated and dispensed unit by small unit, each unit more or less in isolation from other units and from any general rule."[2] Generally, distributive policies are therefore less controversial and less political than other types of public policies. Additionally, one might think that national (homeland) defense or homeland security might be more "rationally based" than political, that a decision such as which type of new bomber the U.S. Air Force purchases should be made on the basis of rational, technical factors such as range, speed, capacity, or reliability.[3] Although parties may disagree about the importance of these various factors, the decision should not be made on overtly political criteria such as which specific group benefits and who pays.

That said, it would therefore be shocking to find significant interest group activity in defense and homeland security policy, as shocking as finding gambling in Rick's American Café in the classic film *Casablanca.* Organized interest activity in defense and homeland security policy is considerable, and a great deal of competition and conflict among the groups is involved. Modern defense and homeland security allocations are based not only on rational technical criteria but also on overtly political criteria: whose congressional district will get contracts, which contractor will provide equipment, whether formulas allocating funding are weighted more heavily for population or severity of need, and so forth. All of this stems from the larger political battle—how much of the federal budget should go for national defense and how much should be spent on domestic priorities. Or to put it differently, should we fund guns or butter?

In today's national security environment, this last observation sounds quaint, a relic of some bygone era. But the reader need only remember that a permanent, large, (expensive) military is largely a post–World War II phenomenon in the United States. After the First World War, the United States largely disarmed. Defense expenditures that were approximately $170 billion in 1919 (in constant 1958 dollars)—about 15 percent of the gross domestic product—fell to less than 10 percent of that figure by 1922. When World War II ended, defense expenditures also went down steeply from $1.1 trillion in 1945—just over 40 percent of GDP—to 10 percent of that in 1950. But 10 percent of $1.1 trillion is a lot more than 10 percent of $170 billion. And 1950 was something of a local minimum—expenditures in constant 1958 dollars were in the $200 billion to $350 billion range until the Vietnam War neared its end in the 1970s.[4] Since then, defense expenditures have been in the 5 percent

TABLE 14.1 **Top Ten Defense/Aerospace Industry Lobbying Expenditures, 2009**

Boeing Co.	$16,850,000
Lockheed Martin	$13,553,782
United Technologies	$8,100,000
BAE Systems	$4,670,000
European Aeronautic Defence & Space	$2,980,000
Finmeccanica SpA	$1,124,100
Rockwell Collins Inc.	$740,138
Space Exploration Technologies	$563,500
GenCorp Inc.	$470,000
Ducommun Inc.	$440,000

SOURCE: Center for Responsive Politics (opensecrets.org).

NOTE: All lobbying expenditures cited come from the Senate Office of Public Records.

to 8 percent range of GDP, but have gone from a low near 5 percent in 2000 to approximately 8 percent in 2010.[5]

The Military-Industrial Complex

Large expenditures on defense in the late 1940s and 1950s introduced political calculations into defense policy. At first these calculations were largely advocating for higher defense expenditures by a loose confederation of "pro-defense" interests. As he was about to leave office in 1961, President Dwight Eisenhower delivered a speech counseling wariness against what he called the "military-industrial complex." Eisenhower said, "This conjunction of an immense military establishment and a large arms industry is new in the American experience. The total influence—economic, political, even spiritual—is felt in every city, every Statehouse, every office of the Federal government. We recognize the imperative need for this development. Yet we must not fail to comprehend its grave implications. Our toil, resources and livelihood are all involved; so is the structure of our society."[6]

The military-industrial complex can be seen as a superinterest group—a banding together of various organized interests in American society, all of which favor continued or increased expenditures on weapons systems and national defense. When we view defense policy through Lowi's distributive lens, this solidarity of opinion and interest makes a great deal of sense. In this view, specific interest groups that are active in other policy arenas—such as the American Trucking Association or the AFL-CIO—are not identifiable, but organized interests such as the U.S. Air Force or the U.S. Marine Corps can be identified. More recently, however, organized interest activity in defense has moved beyond the aggregate lobbying for more defense spending to arguments advocating specific weapons systems, certain contractors, different types of regional subcontracting expenditures, and so on. It is not an overstatement to say that defense policy has moved from distributive policy to redistributive policy—who wins and who loses has become much more important because there is a relatively fixed sum of funding as compared to a time when funding could be increased to satisfy most demands. As Lowi has noted, the politics of redistributive policymaking is much more conflictual than the politics of distributive policymaking.

Precursors to today's political battles over defense policy and military procurement can be seen in the battles of the 1950s over matters such as air power versus ground-based troops and manned bombers versus missiles. In both of these examples, different branches of the military, different commands within the military, different military contractors, and other organized interests took active positions in the debate and lobbied for their own viewpoint. When Eisenhower became president in 1953, his view of American military power included heavy reliance on nuclear weapons and the airpower capabilities of the Strategic Air Command. The U.S. Army thought his thinking would mean severe

TABLE 14.2 **Top 10 Defense and Aerospace Industry PAC Contributions to Federal Candidates, 2010**

Company PAC	Total contribution	To Democratic candidates	To Republican candidates
Boeing Co.	$2,094,000	$1,139,000	$945,000
Lockheed Martin	$1,875,250	$1,069,500	$800,250
United Technologies	$752,000	$455,500	$292,000
BAE Systems	$729,000	$406,500	$322,000
EADS North America	$178,200	$98,500	$79,700
Triumph Group	$143,000	$70,000	$73,000
Rockwell Collins Inc.	$124,000	$67,000	$57,000
Aerojet & GenCorp Inc.	$91,900	$54,500	$37,400
Dynetics Inc.	$49,500	$2,000	$47,500
Teledyne Technologies	$23,000	$10,500	$12,500

SOURCE: Center for Responsive Politics (opensecrets.org).

NOTE: Based on data released by the Federal Election Commission, December 13, 2010.

President Dwight D. Eisenhower gave his farewell address on January 17, 1961. In this speech he outlined his now-famous warning about ties between the military and private defense industry saying, "In the councils of government, we must guard against the acquisition of unwarranted influence, whether sought or unsought, by the military-industrial complex. The potential for the disastrous rise of misplaced power exists and will persist."

reductions in ground forces and lowered expenditures on the army. They could not, however, counter Eisenhower on rational technical grounds because his reputation as a military leader was virtually unassailable in the public's eye and in Congress. Eisenhower eventually grew tired of the military's sniping dissension with his policies and built up the civilian power of the secretary of defense's office as a counter to the military power of the Joint Chiefs of Staff. This political battle between organized military interests and the president resulted in greater distance between them, perhaps contributing to miscommunications between military and civilian authority in the Bay of Pigs and Cuban missile crises in the Kennedy administration.[7]

In the 1950s and 1960s the United States faced increased competition for military supremacy from the Soviet Union. Fears that the Soviet Union was outpacing the United States in the production of jet-powered bombers capable of carrying nuclear weapons and intercontinental ballistic missiles led to political debates over the existence of a "bomber gap" and a "missile gap." Sen. John Kennedy used leaked (and inflated) air force estimates of the size of the Soviet ICBM fleet in his reelection campaign in 1958 and then in his run for the presidency in 1960, criticizing the Republican Party as being weak on defense. By emphasizing the relative weakness of U.S. strategic forces vis-à-vis the Soviets, Kennedy strengthened arguments by defense advocates to increase spending on new weapons systems and personnel.

The attempt by the marines to re-mission themselves in a nuclear world is another example of this type of organized interest activity. Amphibious landings by marines were a hallmark of the Pacific theater in WWII. And the marine amphibious landing at Inchon was one of the turning points of the Korean War. In a nuclear world, such amphibious landings made less sense as one nuclear weapon could destroy an entire assault group and all its concentrated supporting personnel and equipment. More diffuse attack groups were proposed as an alternative. Helicopters could transport troops ashore from more widely dispersed ships standing farther out to sea, making the assault group less vulnerable to a single nuclear weapon. Advocates for helicopter use by the marines became more active in defense policy, eventually resulting in calls for the development of the V-22 Osprey tiltrotor aircraft. Helicopter advocates worked closely with the marines to influence Congress to fund helicopter delivery systems to replace amphibious vehicles. By the time of the Vietnam War the marines had become adept at using helicopters to transport troops and to engage the enemy.

Defense-related political battles grew in number and intensity as the battle over defense dollars became more severe toward the end of the Vietnam War. The political battles cited above—and others of the same era—do not, however, have the same flavor as those that followed. The interests represented in the earlier battles were either overtly political—Democrats versus Republicans—or internecine—the air force versus the army versus the navy versus the marines. Political conflict in post–WWII defense policy generally involved questions of how much money to spend on defense, whether one form of defending the country was superior to another, and/or which branch of the service was to be ascendant. In this sense, the politics of defense policy was different from the politics of other kinds of policy. It was not until several years later that the politics of defense policy shifted and began to resemble more the typical forms of interest group activity in the United States. The changeover occurred at the end of the Vietnam War in the mid-1970s. Two examples can be used to illustrate this changeover: the B-1 bomber program and the V-22 Osprey. And more recent examples of the F-35 Lightning and the use of contractors in Iraq and Afghanistan bring the story up to date.

"Who's on Who" and the B-1 Lancer Bomber

In the 1960s the B-1 Lancer bomber was originally the supersonic replacement for the aging B-52. The B-1 was a complete rethinking of air force strategic doctrine—moving from the development of bombers with higher operating altitude parameters to low-level operations. Designed by Rockwell International, the B-1's development was stopped and started several times. Growing frustrated with the lack of long-range commitment to the development of the new bomber, Rockwell and the air force developed an overtly political strategy to work for continued B-1 funding. Called "Who's on Who," this strategy used individual lobbyists who were important to members of Congress (MCs) to influence their votes.[8] MCs who represented districts with military bases would be targeted by military personnel, and those with important defense contractors would be targeted by civilians representing those contractors. Lobbyists—whether paid or unpaid—who personally knew certain MCs were assigned to influence them. In addition, to broaden the aircraft's political appeal, Rockwell diversified the subcontracting for the B-1. Individual MCs were shown how many jobs their congressional district would gain should the bomber be fully funded or lost if it was not. As Nick Kotz writes, "... more than five thousand corporations in forty-eight states had at least a small piece of the B-1.... Most of the contracts involved only one or two hundred jobs, but for many local economies those jobs were very important. And local leaders let their congressmen know it."[9]

Meanwhile, the costs of the B-1 continued to grow. By the late 1970s the United States had also developed cruise missile technology, which questioned anew the usefulness of manned bombers in general and the B-1 in particular. Rockwell's political strategy made the B-1 more likely to be funded, while the reduced perceived need for a new manned bomber made it more likely to be canceled.

On June 30, 1977, President Jimmy Carter canceled development of the B-1 but agreed with the air force to develop several prototypes for flight testing. Under increasing pressure from the air force to restart the B-1 program but unwilling to reverse his decision, Carter startled everybody by announcing publicly that the United States was moving into stealth technology and would soon produce the B-2 Spirit stealth bomber built by Northrop.[10] The B-2 represented a new generation of manned bomber technology that threatened to make the B-1 obsolete.

With the election of Ronald Reagan in 1980, the air force saw a chance to get *both* new funding for the development of the B-2 program *and* to restart funding the B-1 program. Partly as a reaction to claims (by Northrop and other interested parties) that the B-1 was "old technology," Rockwell redesigned the bomber as the B-1B, incorporating some stealth technology into the design. On October 31, 1981, President Reagan announced that the United States would build 100 B-1B bombers and 132 B-2 bombers "exactly what the Air Force had proposed from the beginning."[11] There are currently around 70 B-1B and 21 B-2 bombers operational in the U.S. Air Force.

The Rockwell political strategy to fund construction of the B-1 was akin to a full court press in basketball. Rockwell used not only the Who's on Who strategy but also letter-writing campaigns to MCs and MC duck-hunting expeditions on Wye Island in the Chesapeake Bay.[12] Rockwell's campaign for the B-1 eventually led Sen. William Proxmire, D-Wisc., to hold hearings on the company's potentially illegal campaign contributions to the reelection campaign of President Richard Nixon. Several hundred thousand dollars in lobbying expenses were eventually disallowed by the Pentagon's internal auditor.

Rockwell's campaign was successful in securing long-term funding for the B-1 and became "a model for future defense lobbying, including efforts to secure funding for the C-5B transport plane and the MX missile."[13] Evaluating Rockwell's record of success alongside the charges of corruption, one senior Rockwell official said, "Well, we got the B-1 and the space-shuttle contracts, and we've made a lot of friends."[14]

Corporate Lobbying and the V-22 Osprey Tiltrotor

As noted above, the U.S. Marines moved actively into helicopter operations before the beginning of the Vietnam War. As troop delivery vehicles, helicopters have great advantages over fixed-wing aircraft in that they do not need long landing strips and they can operate off much smaller ships than fixed-winged airplanes, which require aircraft carriers. Helicopters have several disadvantages: they lack the speed, range, and carrying capacity of fixed-wing aircraft. Slow speed makes helicopters vulnerable to antiaircraft fire; relatively short range threatens the mission of assault ships lying far off any invasion site; and low carrying capacity means that only small numbers of troops lightly equipped can be delivered at any given moment.

In the 1970s Bell Helicopter began work on tiltrotor technology, which would allow an aircraft to take off like a helicopter but operate like a fixed-wing airplane and have the advantages of both types of aircraft. In 1980 Dick Spivey of Bell convinced Col. Robert Magnus that tiltrotor technology was the answer to the marines' aerial assault dilemma. To broaden its appeal, the tiltrotor was originally proposed as a multibranch weapons system and to have civilian applications.[15] Eventually, however, only the marines showed real interest in it.[16] The V-22 Osprey could be refueled in flight, allowing it to fly to battle zones, fly as fast as fixed-wing aircraft, and have the capacity to carry up to twenty-four fully equipped personnel.

As with the B-1, the costs for development of the V-22 escalated rapidly. The tiltrotor was new and unproven technology and getting it to work properly was difficult. Senior officials—both civilians and in the military—began to

Bell Helicopter led concerted public relations campaigns to raise national awareness of its importance to U.S. defense. Bell's activities included sending representatives to newspapers, performing demonstrations, and encouraging potential contractors to contact their representatives and express their support for continued U.S. spending on the technology's development.

doubt whether the project would ever work. And there were reliability and maintenance questions concerning the V-22.[17] Rather than let the project live or die on its merits, Bell decided to take an overtly political approach modeled on the B-1 Lancer campaign.

Bell termed its marketing strategy for the project, "Keep the Program Sold." Personnel from Bell

> would visit the editorial boards of the *Washington Post, New York Times, Los Angeles Times,* and other newspapers to talk up the tiltrotor. Bell would send the VV-15 [the precursor to the V-22] out into the country to make flight demonstrations. . . . Bell would convene a symposium for potential Osprey subcontractors to school them on the tiltrotor and urge them to tell their members of Congress how important it could be to their company, their local economy, and the nation. . . . Everywhere they went . . . [Bell officials] would emphasize that the tiltrotor wasn't just another aircraft but a "national asset." The goal . . . was to brand that idea into the public and political consciousness within six to nine months: "national asset."[18]

Bell's strategy to keep the Osprey project fully funded succeeded in the face of cost overruns (including the cost of research and development, each Osprey costs approximately $100 million), questions about the Osprey's capabilities, several evaluation flight crashes that killed some three dozen marines, and a great deal of criticism in the media.[19] The political approach to defense policy has now virtually become the norm. One last case of weapons procurement demonstrates this point.

Battling for an Alternate Engine: The F-35 Lightning II Joint Strike Fighter

The F-35 is a new generation of fighter planes currently under development. This fighter is designed to fit the needs of all four military commands as well as those of allied nations (particularly NATO nations but also Australia). Lockheed-Martin is the major contractor building the F-35, and its specifications call for engines made by Pratt and Whitney. Congress has also been funding research and development of an alternative engine built by a joint General Electric-Rolls Royce consortium. President Barack Obama, and President George W. Bush before him, opposed funding for the alternative engine, as has the Pentagon, but powerful MCs were able to get continued funding by arguing that competition in engine development would create economic efficiencies and provide a possible fallback position if the Pratt and Whitney engine does not perform as promised. Many MCs actually want the two-track development of the engines in order to spread the wealth of the several billion dollar engine subcontracts to their congressional districts and states. ABC News has reported that the pivotal congressional backers of the two-track strategy—Democrats and Republicans alike—represent states such as Indiana, Massachusetts, Michigan, and Ohio where GE has important facilities.[20]

The F-35 engine battle has created some strange political positioning by various actors and interest groups. MCs cite a 2007 General Accountability Office (GAO) report that concluded the engine competition would actually wind up saving taxpayers money.[21] Groups outside of government, such as the Lexington Institute and Citizens Against Government Waste, that usually lobby for efficiency, are lobbying against the two-track development process.

The two sets of subcontractors—Pratt and Whitney and GE-Rolls Royce—are using overtly political strategies to advance their positions in this battle. Lexington Institute has engaged in a broad-based media campaign against the two-track strategy, while Citizens Against Government Waste is using a more internal lobbying strategy in its opposition.

In early 2011 the House of Representatives passed amendments to the Defense Department budget, eliminating

Despite opposition from Presidents Bush and Obama and the Pentagon, Congress continued funding of two engine development programs for the F-35 fighter plane. Supporters say that the second engine is necessary in case the first does not perform well. Major lobbying activities have surrounded the issue as considerable money is at stake. This 2010 rally at the U.S. Capitol supported funding for the alternative engine program.

the $450 million in funding for the GE-Rolls Royce alternative engine. The 233–198 vote was broadly bipartisan: 110 Republicans and 123 Democrats voted to eliminate funding, and 68 Democrats and 130 Republicans voted to continue it. The legislation has been referred to the Senate for action. Concerning the potential end to this continuing battle, Rep. John Larson, D-Conn., was quoted as saying, "This is like 'Night of the Living Dead' with this engine."[22]

U.S. Contractors in Iraq and Afghanistan as Interest Groups

The United States invaded Afghanistan to overthrow the Taliban government in 2001 and then invaded Iraq in 2003. Civilian contractors are an important component of both the U.S. military presence and the postwar development of the two countries. A recent Department of Defense presentation concluded that fully 50 percent of Central Command's force was composed of civilian contractors.[23] The media have focused a great deal of attention on civilian contractors such as Xe (formerly Blackwater) that provide base support, security, interpreting, and construction services.

Postwar development contracting is, however, where the real political action has taken place. In an ongoing series of analyses, the Center for Public Integrity has investigated campaign contributions by major U.S. contractors. Between 1990 and 2002 contractors such as General Electric, ($8.8 million), Northrop Grumman ($8.5 million), Bechtel ($3.3 million), and Kellogg, Brown, and Root ($2.4 million) made campaign contributions to presidential and congressional candidates attempting to influence defense policy and to maintain access to Iraq and Afghanistan when military operations are completed there.[24]

Comparison of the Cases

All of these cases show that political activity in defense policy has changed dramatically from the 1950s to the present. Although it is true that specific interest groups cannot be readily identified in lobbying efforts for specific weapons systems, military interests (the air force, the marines), manufacturers (Rockwell, Northrop, Bell-Boeing), and contractors (Kellogg, Brown, and Root, Bechtel) used interest group strategies to advance their positions and interests. They made direct contact with lawmakers, attempted to influence public opinion, made financial contributions to political campaigns, commissioned research studies, and held symposia. They diversified their operations to many different states and congressional districts to demonstrate the direct economic impact their activities had and so to broaden the appeal to MCs. Defense policy has come to resemble domestic policymaking in terms of the political activity influencing those who actually make policy.

It is also clear that various organized interests have learned that a direct strategy of lobbying policymakers is only part of what is needed to succeed. In the B-1 case, Rockwell relied almost completely on direct lobbying, but for the V-22 and the F-35, contractors have also attempted to influence public opinion through sophisticated advertising campaigns, indirectly affecting policymakers. The influence of lobbyists may be difficult for policymakers to resist, but an outpouring of informed and concerned public opinion—especially from constituents—is almost impossible to ignore.

In some ways, the political approach to influencing defense decisions is simpler than an overt policy approach. Opposing the B-1 or the V-22 or mastering the assets and liabilities of the different engine options for the F-35 requires a great deal of technical expertise. This expertise often comes with a high price. Actors often do not possess or cannot afford the necessary expertise to engage in the policy battle and so are forced back on the political strategy that can be pursued at a lower cost. When the U.S. Navy

A civilian contractor in Iraq sorts recyclable materials. U.S. firms involved in providing military support in Iraq and Afghanistan contribute millions of dollars to political campaigns and spend considerable sums on advertising in Washington political publications.

proposed developing an outlying landing field (OLF) for practice aircraft carrier takeoffs and landings in rural northeastern North Carolina, local opponents could not muster the necessary policy expertise to counter the navy's position. They therefore enlisted national political officials—North Carolina senators Elizabeth Dole and Richard Burr—as well as the state's governor and area U.S. representatives to oppose the plan, basically because the people in the area did not want the OLF located there.[25]

The political approach became such a norm in military basing decisions (where to locate new facilities and which facilities to close) that Congress and the president have actually agreed to try to exclude politics from the process of realigning or closing bases. They agreed in 1988 that BRAC (base realignment and closure) decisions would be made by a bipartisan commission appointed by the president and approved by the U.S. Senate. The secretary of defense would provide the BRAC Commission with a list of potential base closings, and the commission would evaluate the closings and make a recommendation to the president, who could then implement the recommendations or send them back to the commission for further study. The recommendations would go into effect unless disapproved by a joint resolution of Congress. This remarkably kludgy process was established for the primary reason of attempting to minimize politics and the role of organized interests in base closing decisions.[26]

The process for assigning new assets—such as the F-35—to existing bases is supposed to be equally nonpolitical, but it too has become political. In 2010 the navy proposed assignments for new squadrons of F-35s and put them out for public comment under environmental rules. Often, public comments involve NIMBY (not in my backyard) approaches like the OLF controversy—too much noise, impacts on bird populations, and so on. In this case, however, the large economic consequences of the navy's F-35 basing decision have led to political competition *for* the new squadrons. The two options for basing the F-35 are for eleven squadrons to be based at Marine Corps Air Station (MCAS) Cherry Point, North Carolina, or splitting the squadrons between MCAS Cherry Point and MCAS Beaufort, South Carolina. In a recent carefully worded news article, the *Havelock News*, the local newspaper for the community surrounding MCAS Cherry Point, informed local residents that the comment period for the basing decision was about to close and advised interested residents to make their voices heard on this decision, if they so desired.[27]

One can see the same pattern of political action replacing policy analysis occurring in homeland security as in defense, although over a much more compressed time line.

HOMELAND SECURITY

In response to the terrorist attacks of September 11, 2001, Congress established the Department of Homeland Security (DHS). The legislation establishing DHS combined some twenty-two federal agencies into the third largest cabinet department. One of DHS's first activities was the development of the National Response Plan (NRP)—an all-hazards plan to respond to domestic emergencies—which was released to the public in January 2005.

From its inception to 2005, DHS focused primarily on counterterrorism. Because of this narrow focus, DHS's—and particularly the Federal Emergency Management Agency's (FEMA)—reactions to Hurricane Katrina in 2005 were deemed a "failure of initiative" by the Select Bipartisan Committee to Investigate the Preparation for and Response to Hurricane Katrina.[28] FEMA's poor response to Katrina refocused attention on the natural disaster element in homeland security policy and caused a major rethinking of federal response to homeland security threats. One result of the federal government's poor response to Katrina was replacement of the NRP with the National Response Framework (NRF) in March 2008. The NRF focuses more heavily on the roles of local government in reacting to disasters and emergencies and pays more attention to low probability-high consequence events, such as major terrorist attacks, and higher probability-lower consequence events, such as natural disasters or epidemic diseases.[29]

There is no consensus as to what homeland security really is. Most people have an intuitive grasp that homeland security means making the United States safer domestically

AGENCIES COMBINED INTO THE DEPARTMENT OF HOMELAND SECURITY (DHS) AND THOSE OMITTED

COMBINED INTO DHS

U.S. Coast Guard
Citizenship and Immigration Services
Customs and Border Protection
Federal Emergency Management Agency
Secret Service
Transportation Security Administration

OMITTED FROM DHS

Federal Bureau of Investigation
Central Intelligence Agency

against a variety of threats. Some of these threats are natural (floods, hurricanes, tornadoes, and epidemics); some are accidental (oil spills, chemical plant explosions); and others are intentional (terrorist attacks and computer hacking). Some of these threats are high probability-low consequence events (a localized tornado), and others are low probability-high consequence events (a bioterrorism attack in a populated area).

The U.S. government's response to all of these potential events is summarized in the phrase "all-hazards approach." Even within this agreed-upon approach, however, there are interests, such as the National Emergency Management Association (NEMA), that think the emphasis should be on natural disasters given that they have a higher probability and those, such as the National Counterterrorism Center, that think the emphasis should be on terrorism because the consequences of a terrorist event could be so severe. And still others think the emphasis should be on military reactions because the military can be efficient in addressing such events.[30] And, finally, there are those, such as the International City Management Association, that think the emphasis should be on civilian reactions because most first responders are civilians.

Generally, the expected outcomes of high probability-low consequence events can be calculated fairly readily. For example, based on previous experience, the predicted costs of a Category 2 hurricane hitting Wilmington, N.C., can be estimated with a fairly high degree of accuracy. The actual probability of some events is, however, largely subjective. The answer to how likely it is for a bioterrorist strike on a major city often tells us more about the preexisting beliefs of the individual or group making the prediction than it does about the actual event. As William Waugh has written, "Media attention can make hazards and disasters seem much worse or more frequent than they really are. . . . Personal and family traumas may create champions for lesser risks. The point is that these less probable or even improbable hazards may be included in the planning. But that's politics and the planning process is, after all, political as well as technical."[31]

Because there is no consensus as to what homeland security is and whether the probability of events or their consequence is more important, the entire field is open to definition. And the competition to define the field becomes very political. A broad definition of homeland security would include at least the five components listed in the box below.

One can easily see the overlaps among these five subsectors and the haziness in some of the dividing lines between them. Where does domestic safety end and counterterrorism begin? Or more practically, how much should the U.S. military be involved in domestic counterterrorism or emergency management? One can also see how some issues span several subsectors. The flooding in New Orleans was an emergency management (hurricane, flood), domestic safety (breakdown in public order, looting), and public health (contamination of water supplies, oil spills) event.

Involved in homeland security policy and politics are interest groups representing businesses and trade, professions, ethnicities, civil rights and civil liberties, and the various subsections of the nation itself. When a homeland security–related event occurs, the number and intensity of opinions expressed by interest groups is simply overwhelming.

Early Interest Group Involvement in Homeland Security Following 9/11

After 9/11 a flood of interest groups took positions related to national security, the threat of terrorism, and counterterrorism. It appeared that every organized interest group (and some newly created ones) had suddenly discovered that their group had an interest in homeland security. The families of the 9/11 victims formed their own interest group—the Family Steering Committee for the 9/11 Commission—which assisted the 9/11 Commission in developing its final report.[32] The Airline Pilots Association renewed calls for the installation of reinforced cockpit doors on commercial planes and the arming of pilots.[33] The International Association of Fire Fighters, International Association of Chiefs of Police, and NEMA all developed positions on 9/11 and the implementation of the 9/11 Commission recommendations. The Arab American Institute put out a statement: "Arab Americans, like all other Americans are transfixed by this tragedy. We have family and friends who worked in the World Trade

FIVE COMPONENTS OF THE HOMELAND SECURITY SECTOR AND SAMPLE INTEREST GROUPS

Counterterrorism: Those activities that are undertaken to prevent, deter, preempt, and respond to terrorism, whether real or implied.

Example: The International Association of Counterterrorism and Security Professionals (IACSP) provides information and educational services for those concerned about the challenges terrorism places on society. Other groups in this subsector include the International Counter-Terrorism Officers Association and different groups whose missions focus more on specific terrorist groups.

National Defense: Military operations against state and nonstate foes of the United States.

Example: The Center for the National Security Interest (CNSI) supports policies that serve to conserve and maintain America's national security strengths and its armed forces. Other groups in this subsector include the National Defense Industrial Association, the National Defense Transportation Association, and various groups representing active duty and retired military personnel.

Emergency Management: Those activities undertaken to mitigate, prevent, respond to, and recover from emergencies and disasters.

Example: The National Emergency Management Association (NEMA) is the professional association of state emergency management directors. Other groups in this subsector are the International Association of Emergency Managers, the Disaster Preparedness and Emergency Response Association, and various state and regional associations. In 2002 NEMA was the initiating partner in the establishment of the National Homeland Security Consortium.

Domestic Safety: Those activities involving law enforcement and infrastructure protection.

Example: The International Association of Fire Chiefs represents the leadership of firefighters and emergency responders. Other groups included in this subsector are the International Association of Chiefs of Police and the Public Safety Employees Association.

Public Health: Those activities involving the prevention and control of infectious diseases, monitoring and improving sanitary measures, and monitoring environmental hazards.

Example: The American Public Health Association (APHA) represents health professionals who work to promote health and prevent disease. In this subsector the Association of Schools of Public Health represents schools and universities; various state and regional associations also are active.

Center. We mourn for those who lost their lives and those who were injured. We mourn, as well, for our country in this time of national trauma."[34] The American Trucking Association added a security component to its training course; the American Institute of Certified Public Accountants developed a brochure on financial information for disaster victims; the Association of Air Medical Services created a "web-based, interactive, geo-coded database of air ambulance resources."[35] The director of the Federation of American Scientists' Project on Government Secrecy—a group that had long lobbied for increased transparency of government projects—said, "I have had to come to terms with the fact that government secrecy is not the worst thing in the world. . . . There are worse things."[36] Various universities came together with representatives of the U.S. military's Central Command in Colorado Springs to form the Homeland Security/Defense Education Consortium to set standards for homeland security education programs. And in December 2001 two security policy professionals, worried that there was no trade association to represent the interests of homeland security contractors, formed the Homeland Security Industries Association.[37]

The broadest conclusion one can draw from interest group reaction to the focusing event of 9/11 is the consensus on the necessity of increased security.[38] In this sense, interest groups in the post-9/11 time period defined the issue of security as a universal issue, an issue that is likely to affect everybody regardless of race, class, age, or ethnicity. Within just a few months of 9/11, however, the initial unanimity of interest group opinion began to disintegrate. Dale Krane captured what happened in the subtitle to his review of federalism in the summer 2003 edition of *Publius*, "Division replaces unity."[39]

Part of the disintegration of the post-9/11 unanimity was the result of the Bush administration's efforts to re-image U.S. homeland security. For example, the establishment of the Department of Homeland Security was widely supported in Congress, but the Bush administration caused controversy when it advocated making DHS exempt from normal government personnel policies. The National Treasury Employees Union and groups representing other federal employees filed suit against the new personnel system. In August 2005 an injunction was issued stopping DHS from implementing the new policy, and in 2008 DHS announced it would not pursue its implementation.[40]

DHS provided a single target for interest groups to approach, and lobbyists responded to this almost immediately.[41] Many groups came away frustrated by their initial experiences in dealing with DHS.[42]

DHS's first major test came in the form of Hurricane Katrina. After the hurricane, an outpouring of position papers, editorials, and research reports similar to those issued after 9/11 came from interest groups, professional associations, and think tanks. The major difference between the post-Katrina reports and the post-9/11 reports was the lack of common purpose in the post-Katrina reports. Fingers were pointed and blame assessed for the poor government reaction at a wide variety of actors including President Bush, Louisiana governor Kathleen Blanco, New Orleans mayor Ray Nagin, the New Orleans Police Department, and FEMA. Preexisting policies also came under criticism—New Orleans residency laws that required police officers to live in the city,[43] Army Corps of Engineers work on the New Orleans levees, racism, "hurricane fatigue,"[44] partisanship,[45] and an example of wrongly applied cognitive heuristics.[46] Division replacing unity could be used more aptly to describe the interest group universe's reaction to Katrina as compared to its reaction to 9/11.

Intergovernmental Policies, Funding, and Interest Group Influence

A full listing of all groups involved in homeland security policy is impossible. Even developing a classification or typology of these groups is a daunting task and beyond the scope of this chapter. Many of the typologies developed in the past do not supply the level of detail that is necessary in the homeland security sector. But there are groups that tend to specialize in one of the five areas described in the box above and those that cross-cut some or all of the areas.

At its heart, homeland security is intergovernmental. Virtually all first responders in the United States are employees of local or state governments where elaborate mutual assistance agreements have been negotiated over the years for one government's personnel to go to the aid of others when needed. Since 2001 homeland security policy has tended to come from the federal government and to be implemented at the state and local level.

Because homeland security is intergovernmental, members of the Big Seven interest groups—Council of State Governments, National Governors Association, National Conference of State Legislatures, National League of Cities, U.S. Conference of Mayors, National Association of Counties, and International City/County Management Association (ICMA)—have been active in attempting to influence homeland security policy.[47] ICMA has become a leader in developing the "networked approach" to emergency and disaster management, in many ways an alternative to enunciated national policy in the Bush administration.[48] States and regional organizations (Southern Governors Association, Coalition of Northeastern Governors, and so forth) also have been active in lobbying for changes in homeland security policy that would benefit specific regions of the country by actions such as refiguring the formula on which DHS grants are provided to states and localities.

To increase the level of preparedness of state and local governments, DHS makes funding available directly to state and local governments—more than $15 billion from 2002 through 2009. The magnitude of this funding draws attention to the formulas on which the funding is based and any potential bias the formulas might contain.[49] From 2003 on, the vast majority of DHS funding for state and local governments came through five programs: the Urban Area Security Initiative, State Homeland Security Program, Law Enforcement Terrorism Prevention Program, Metropolitan Medical Response System Program, and Citizen Corps Program.

Table 14.3 shows the funding for these programs from 2002 through 2009. The two shaded areas in Table 14.3 are discussed below. From 2003 on, the total amount of DHS funding has varied from a high of $2.7 billion to a low of $1.7 billion. More important than the total amount of

TABLE 14.3 **Distribution of Department of Homeland Security Grant Funds, 2002–2009**

Year	Urban Area Security Initiative	State Homeland Security Program	Law Enforcement Terrorism Prevention	Pct of total	Metropolitan Medical Response System program	Citizen Corps Program	Pct of total	Total
2002		$315,700,000						$315,700,000
2003	$596,351,000	$2,066,295,000		98.6%		$37,528,557	1.4%	$2,700,174,557
2004	$671,017,498	$1,675,058,500	$497,050,000	97.2	$46,281,496	$34,793,500	2.8	$2,294,200,994
2005	$854,656,750	$1,062,285,226	$386,285,537	98.2	$28,221,408	$13,485,710	1.8	$2,344,934,631
2006	$710,622,000	$528,165,000	$384,120,000	97.1	$28,808,920	$19,206,000	2.9	$1,670,921,920
2007	$746,900,000	$509,250,000	$363,750,000	97.2	$32,010,000	$14,550,000	2.8	$1,666,460,000
2008	$781,630,000	$862,925,000		96.8	$39,831,500	$14,572,500	3.2	$1,698,959,000
2009	$798,631,250	$861,137,000		96.8	$39,831,404	$14,572,500	3.2	$1,714,172,154

SOURCE: Data assembled from U.S. Census Bureau, *Consolidated Federal Funds Report*, www.census.gov/govs/cffr.

funding, however, is the allocation of funds to the various states and localities. The initial distribution of funds to the states was determined by the USA PATRIOT Act in 2002.[50] Various analyses show that DHS grants to the states from 2002 through 2006 were at least partially determined by political forces rather than need or risk of terrorist attack.[51] Research reported by Michael Greenberg and his associates shows a strong correlation between state population and the total amount of DHS funding (ρ = .94) across the fifty states.[52] In 2006 eligibility for homeland security grants was changed to reduce the "equity" component and to take risk assessment more into account. Regardless of the specific formula, different state governments weighed in with critiques of their share of funding. For example, the new funding formula reduced the amounts available to New York and Washington, D.C.—targets of the 9/11 attacks—while also reducing funds to other high visibility localities such as New Orleans and San Diego.[53] The change in the funding formula pitted region against region and state against state. When the issue was universal or distributive, states lobbied for more funding for homeland security–related functions; when the issue became more redistributive, interstate competition increased, and each state became an interest group in its own right.

Funding for both the general purpose Urban Area Security Initiative and State Homeland Security Program has declined since 2004, although these two grants still receive the vast majority of all DHS funding to state and local governments. This becomes clearer when one considers that the Law Enforcement Terrorism Prevention Program, which was funded separately from the State Homeland Security Program in 2004 through 2007, was combined back into it in 2008. These general purpose grants, which maxed out at over $2.8 billion in 2004, dropped to $1.62 billion in 2008 before bumping up a bit to $1.64 billion in 2009. The Metropolitan Medical Response System Program is a program to fund medical and public health functions specifically, and the Citizen Corps Program is the main FEMA funding mechanism to assist local emergency managers. The total of these two special purpose programs has tended to increase each year since 2005. The trend can be seen in the two shaded columns in Table 14.3: the percentage of all DHS funding going to general purpose projects declined from 98.6 percent of the total to 96.8 percent, while the percentage earmarked for medical or emergency management functions grew from 1.4 percent to 3.2 percent.

Many of the changes in funding can be attributed to the work of groups active in the various subsectors described above. As homeland security funding has become more available, interest groups representing firefighters, police officers, public health officials, and others have discovered how closely intertwined their clientele's interests are with homeland security, which has allowed them to make a relatively larger claim on homeland security funding.

Funding for the homeland security function is also made available through sources other than DHS—through the Department of Health and Human Services, Department of Agriculture, and Department of Justice. The total amount of non-DHS funding in 2006 was approximately $2.8 billion (tracking this funding over time is beyond the scope of this chapter). Samuel Clovis writes, "It is clear special interests have influenced the creation of these grant programs to benefit particular professions rather than to build overall homeland security capability and preparedness."[54]

In an immature policy area like homeland security, basic questions in the field are not yet established. Not only are there disagreements as to what the answers to questions should be but also disagreements about what questions to ask. In 2001 and 2002 questions concerned not just whether local governments should get more federal DHS grants, but what was worth protecting, what was actually being threatened, and by whom. By 2009 the issue area had become more defined, and interest group patterns were becoming more regularized. In the decentralized policymaking environment of the United States, this often means interest groups can peel off portions of the policy pie and claim them as their own, entitling them to federal funding that friendly members of Congress are often all too willing to provide.

Homeland security as a policy area is therefore being defined both through federal dictates and through interest group activity, much of which is not traditional interest group political pressure but the competition between contending ideas. It is apparent that there is a "chicken and egg" problem in who determines homeland security policy. Federal policy determines funding; interest groups, think tanks, and researchers respond to these federal initiatives and release reports showing that new and different approaches are necessary; the federal government responds to these reports by shifting funding incrementally to different areas. These iterations more sharply define the policy area through an evolutionary process that results in a great deal of expert (read interest group) influence in the policy area and claims by the federal government that it is being responsive to the public will (read expert opinion).

Because of the relatively undefined nature of homeland security policy, interest group activity in the early 2000s was not regularized. New groups arose; others disappeared. Groups battled not only to increase their share of the pie but also to define the pie that was being baked, not only to get their fair share of federal funding or to influence policy outcomes but also to define the policy arena. The Bush administration and Congress responded by funding homeland security activities in ways that allowed state and local governments large degrees of discretion in how the funds were expended; and research shows that the initial rounds of federal funding were requested and awarded primarily for the purchase of equipment, for disaster preparedness/mitigation, and for drills and training exercises—the top three areas for which local government own-source funding was also used.[55] Equipment, disaster preparedness/mitigation, and drills were not designated for only one set of local government employees—firefighters, emergency managers, or police officers—but for employees and citizens in general. In fact, much of the equipment purchases—communications systems, for example—were designed to increase interoperability between various legacy systems that had become more and more problematic as time went on.

A specific example of this shaping of homeland security policy concerns the development of the National Incident Management System (NIMS) and the use of 10-codes by local law enforcement and firefighters for communicating to one another.[56] In 2003 President Bush signed Homeland Security Presidential Directive 5 (Management of Domestic Incidents), which directed DHS to develop NIMS. DHS secretary Tom Ridge released NIMS in March 2004. NIMS required all state and local emergency management personnel to undergo training by 2005. A portion of that training was to focus on increasing the clarity of communications between different agencies at different levels of government. Local law enforcement and firefighters had been using 10-codes to communicate since the 1930s. In May 2005 FEMA issued a directive stating that compliance with NIMS meant giving up the 10-codes because they were often not used the same way by different agencies and therefore conflicted with the goal of increasing clarity of communications. Interest groups representing police officers, firefighters, and emergency management officials immediately announced their opposition to this change.

Within a few months of the original FEMA directive, DHS reversed its position. Secretary Michael Chertoff announced to the International Association of Chiefs of Police annual conference in Miami that NIMS compliance no longer would mean giving up 10-codes, but that the meanings of the codes needed to be standardized across agencies and levels of government. His announcement was met with "a warm round of applause from the full house of police chiefs."[57]

Janet Napolitano, Secretary of the Department of Homeland Security, speaks at the annual convention of the International Association of Chiefs of Police in 2009. Advocacy groups representing first responders have played a significant role in influencing homeland security policy since the attacks on September 11, 2001.

Interest Group Activity and the Broadening of Homeland Security Policy

One can see that the maturation of homeland security as a policy area and the regularization of interest group activity have had several effects. First, the federal government's definition of the field—as almost wholly one of counterterrorism—was met by interest group attempts to broaden the definition to encompass preexisting fields: emergency management, public health, and so on. The "all-hazards" approach developed in the 1990s was advocated as better fitting the policy problem than the newly developed—almost *ad hoc*—approaches the federal government proposed. The poor response to Hurricane Katrina was seen as a vindication of this earlier approach. Soon after Katrina hit, Walter Peacock, the director of Texas A&M University's Hazard Reduction and Recovery Center, was quoted in the *Washington Post*, "People were thinking about the possibility of terrorism. They weren't thinking about the reality of a hurricane."[58] Interest group influence, in particular interest groups calling for less centralization and standardization of homeland security policy, caused policy to change: the 10-codes were back in, and the National Response Framework replaced the National Response Plan. Likewise, congressional action allowing the president to call up a state's National Guard (without consulting the state's governor) in times of "natural disaster, epidemic, or other serious public health emergency, terrorist attack or incident" was repealed in 2008 after strong lobbying by the National Governors Association.[59] Furthermore, the U.S. Army's Northern Command's role in establishing the Homeland Security Defense Education Association ended in 2007 when the association morphed into a decentralized, collaboratively run entity for developing standards for homeland security education. President Obama's choice for DHS secretary also indicates the reassertion of state and local governments as interest groups: Obama appointed Janet Napolitano, governor of Arizona, to replace Chertoff, a former U.S. attorney and appeals court judge. We have no accurate estimate of the number of first responders nationwide, but to get some idea, consider that there are approximately 150,000 police officers and 125,000 firefighters. Add into this the number of emergency room hospital workers, public health officials, National Guard troops, and so on, and one can see the large number of individuals involved in directly implementing homeland security policy. Virtually all of these people are employed by the some 50,000 state or local governments. Although overt political action by these organizations and governments is uncommon, the possibility (or threat) of such action is often enough to cause changes in national government policy.

CONCLUSION

There is a natural affinity between defense and homeland security, but there are also divisions. Defense and homeland security are both concerned with the protection of the United States against potential enemies. Some of these enemies are human, and some are natural. Some are internal, and some are external. What separates defense and homeland security? One might argue that the fields are divided by military versus civilian, but as we have seen, civilian contractors provide 50 percent of the forces in Iraq and Afghanistan, and the Bush administration argued that the Department of Defense should be the lead agency in large-scale homeland security events. One might argue that fields are separated as domestic versus foreign, but we now see that foreign terrorist groups operate in the United States and that military personnel engage in domestic relief and the enforcement of some domestic law.[60] There are overlaps in virtually any line of division that one can identify between the two fields.

Yet it is also apparent that interest group activity in the two fields is different. In both policy areas, organized interests are vocal and active. In defense, however, those interests tend not to be groups with names, but contractors/subcontractors and local, state, and regional interests. In homeland security, the groups have names and they have become much more political than they were in the early 2000s, but there still is a battle over ideas—defining the field is a major point of contention. As homeland security matures as a policy area, interest group activity likely will become more "normal" and also more fractious.

It is clear that providing for the common defense is a major constitutionally mandated area of public policy, but it should also be clear that defense and homeland security now vie with other policy areas for federal dollars. As time passes, and images of the Cold War and the 9/11 tragedies recede, the singular importance of defense and counterterrorism seem also to fade. Making an uncontested claim on federal monies becomes more difficult and introduces politics and interest group activity into defense and homeland security calculations. As arguments over the relative size of slices of the federal pie become more heated, interest group activity in defense and homeland security will become more active, sophisticated, and strident in the future.

NOTES

1. Actual estimates of how much the United States spends on national defense vary widely depending on whether one includes or excludes homeland security spending, veterans' benefits, and off-budget spending for the war in Iraq and Afghanistan.

2. Theodore Lowi, "American Business, Public Policy, Case Studies, and Political Theory, *World Politics* 16 (July 1964): 690.

3. See Michael Brown, *Flying Blind: The Politics of the U.S. Strategic Bomber Program* (Ithaca: Cornell University Press, 1992).

4. James Clayton, "The Fiscal Limits of the Warfare-Welfare State: Defense and Welfare Spending in the United States since 1900," *Western Political Quarterly* 29 (1976): 364–383.

5. See www.usgovernmentspending.com.

6. "Military-Industrial Complex Speech, Dwight Eisenhower, 1961," www.h-net.org/~hst306 documents/indust.html.

7. Donald Alan Carter, "Eisenhower versus the Generals," *Journal of Military History* 71, 4 (October 2007): 1169–1199.

8. Although formally forbidden from directly lobbying of Congress, the air force apparently disregarded Title 18 of the U.S.

Code and engaged in one-on-one lobbying. See Nick Kotz, *Wild Blue Yonder: Money, Politics, and the B-1 Bomber* (New York: Pantheon, 1988).

9. Ibid., 128.

10. Brown, *Flying Blind.*

11. Kotz, *Wild Blue Yonder,* 215.

12. See Nick Kotz, "The Chesapeake Bay Goose Hunt, the Beautiful Secretary, and Other Ways the Defense Lobby Got the B-1," *Washington Monthly,* February 1988, 29–38. In at least one case, Rockwell's stimulated letter-writing campaign may have backfired. Rep. Les Aspin, D-Wisc., received several hundred pro-B-1 letters, but his staff discovered that the letters were nearly identical in format and traced them all to one Rockwell subsidiary in Illinois.

13. Ibid., 29.

14. Kotz, *Wild Blue Yonder,* 138.

15. Bell officials told the *Dallas Morning News* that civilian versions of the tiltrotor could be used to ferry forty workers at a time to offshore oil platforms and that the military tiltrotor project could generate some 10,000 jobs in the Fort Worth, Texas, area. See Richard Whittle, *The Dream Machine: The Untold History of the Notorious V-22 Osprey* (New York: Simon and Schuster, 2010), 144.

16. Of the 458 V-22s currently planned for procurement, 360 are slated for the marines, 50 for U.S. Special Operations Command, and 48 for the navy.

17. Jeremiah Gertler, *V-22 Osprey Tilt-Rotor Aircraft: Background and Issues for Congress* (Washington, D.C.: Congressional Research Service, December 22, 2009).

18. Whittle, *Dream Machine,* 145.

19. In January 2001 CBS News ran a series of articles that accused the Marine Corps of falsifying maintenance records on the Osprey. On the Sunday after Inauguration Day, 2001, *60 Minutes* ran an extremely critical story on the Osprey quoting incoming Vice President Cheney telling Congress, the Osprey was "a program I don't need" when he was secretary of defense in 1992 (quoted in Whittle, *Dream Machine,* 313).

20. Matthew Rusk and Brian Ross, "A $3 Billion Government Boondoggle? Congress Pushes Fighter Jet Engine that Military Says it Doesn't Want or Need," ABC News, May 21, 2010, abcnews.go.com/Blotter/joint-strike-fighter-billion-boondoggle/story?id=10692337.

21. General Accountability Office, *Joint Strike Fighter: Progress Made and Challenges Remain,* March 2007, www.gao.gov/new.items/d07360.pdf.

22. Mara Lee, "Pratt Wins F-35 Engine Battle: House Votes to Kill Funding for GE Version," *Hartford Courant,* February 16, 2011.

23. Office of the Assistant Secretary of Defense for Logistics and Materiel Readiness, "Contractor Support for US Operations in the USCENTCOM Area of Responsibility, Iraq and Afghanistan," May 2010, www.acq.osd.mil/log/PS/hot_topics.html.

24. Center for Public Integrity, *Windfalls of War: U.S. Contractors in Iraq and Afghanistan,* 2010, projects.publicintegrity.org/wow.

25. See www.bluenc.com/outlying-landing-field-olf.

26. See "Base Realignment and Closure (BRAC)," www.globalsecurity.org/military/facility/brac.htm; and Jerry Brito, "The BRAC Model for Spending Reform," mercatus.org/publication/brac-model-spending-reform, February 4, 2010.

27. Drew C. Wilson, "Comment Period on F-35 Basing Options Nears an End," *Havelock News,* July 8, 2010.

28. Select Bipartisan Committee to Investigate the Preparation for and Response to Hurricane Katrina, *A Failure of Initiative,* February 15, 2006, www.gpoaccess.gov/katrinareport/mainreport.pdf.

29. See www.dhs.gov/files/programs/editorial_ 0566.shtm.

30. In 2002 Eric V. Larsen and John Peters of the RAND Corporation developed "Understanding Homeland Security," www.fathom.com/course/21701714, a course "to provide the public with the analytical tools . . . to evaluate whether the government is creating a viable homeland security system." In this course, homeland security is defined as "all *military* activities aimed at preparing for, protecting against or managing the consequences of attacks on American soil, including the CONUS and US territories and possessions. It includes all actions to safeguard the populace and its property, critical infrastructure, the government and military, its installations and deploying forces" (emphasis added). This definition stresses both military nature and the human dimension of homeland security policy. A different viewpoint is expressed by Steven Tomisek's writing in *Strategic Forum,* a Web site of the National Defense University at www.ndu.edu/inss/strforum/SF189/sf189.htm. His article "Homeland security: The new role for defense," states "Homeland security should not be viewed as exclusively or even primarily a military task."

31. William Waugh Jr. "Terrorism and the all-hazards model," paper delivered at the IDS Emergency Management On-Line Conference, June 28–July 16, 2004, training.fema.gov/emiweb/downloads/Waugh%20-20Terrorism%20and%20Planning.doc.

32. See M. Kent Bolton, *US Foreign Policymaking and National Security after 9/11: Present at the Re-Creation* (Lanham, Md.: Rowman and Littlefield, 2007).

33. Statement of Captain Duane Woerth, President, Airline Pilots Association, International, before the Committee on Commerce, Science, and Transportation, U.S. Senate, on Aviation Security, September 20, 2001, www.alpa.org/portals/alpa/pressroom/testimony/2002andprior/2001-9-20_Woerth.htm.

34. Arab American Institute, *Healing the Nation: The Arab American Experience after September 11* (Washington, D.C.: Arab American Institute, 2002), 2.

35. American Society of Association Executives, "Sustaining the spirit of post-9/11 efforts, associations intensify civic programs," September 7, 2004, www.asaecenter.org/AboutUs/newsreldetail.cfm?ItemNumber=6808.

36. Robin Toner, "Reconsidering Security, US Clamps Down on Agency Web Sites," *New York Times,* October 27, 2001, B4.

37. Bara Vaida, "Let's Start an Association!" *National Journal,* September 20, 2003, 35, 38.

38. On focusing events, see John Kingdon, *Agendas, Alternatives, and Public Policies* (Boston: Little, Brown, 1984); and Thomas Birkland, *Lessons of Disaster: Policy Change after Catastrophic Events* (Washington, D.C.: Georgetown University Press, 2006).

39. Dale Krane, "The State of American Federalism, 2002–2003: Division Replaces Unity," *Publius: The Journal of Federalism* 33, 3 (Summer 2003): 1.

40. Stephen Barr, "DHS Withdraws Bid to Curb Union Rights," *Washington Post,* February 20, 2008, D1.

41. Philip Shenon, "Cashing in: Former Domestic Security Aides Switch to Lobbying," *New York Times,* April 29, 2003, www.commondreams.org/headlines03/0429-03.htm.

42. Samuel Lowenburg, "Homeland Security Tests Lobbyist Patience," *Politico,* October 3, 2007, www.politico.com/news/stories/1007/6159.html.

43. Thad Allen, "Leadership in Disaster," comments made at the annual Federal Emergency Management Agency Emergency Management Institute, June 6, 2006, Emmitsburg, Md., training.fema.gov/EMIWeb/edu/06conf/Conference%20Agenda%202006.doc.

44. Steven Gray, "Hurricane Fatigue in New Orleans?" *Time*, September 9, 2008, www.time.com/time/nation/article/0,8599,1840053,00.html.

45. Cherie Maestras, Lonna Rae Atkeson, Thomas Croom, and Lisa A. Bryant, "Shifting the Blame: Federalism, Media, and Public Assignment of Blame Following Hurricane Katrina," *Publius: The Journal of Federalism* 38, 4 (Fall 2008): 609–632.

46. Carmine Scavo, "Enablers of Mass Effects: How Terrorists Benefit from the Information Age," in *Threats to Homeland Security: An All-Hazards Approach*, ed. Richard J. Kilroy Jr. (Hoboken, N.J.: Wiley, 2007), 312–340.

47. The Big Seven are powerful interest groups that lobby the federal government for policies that benefit state and local level and also work for "good government" at the state and local level.

48. See International City/County Management Association, *A Networked Approach to Improvements in Emergency Management* (Washington, D.C.: International City/County Management Association, 2006).

49. DHS grant funding is a combination of formula and project grants. The formula determines who is eligible to apply for funding under, for example, the Urban Area Security Initiative.

50. Michael Greenberg, Will Irving, and Rae Zimmerman, "Allocating US Department of Homeland Security Funds to States with Explicit Equity, Population, and Energy Facility Security Criteria," *Socio-Economic Planning Sciences* 43 (2009): 229–239.

51. See R. Morris Coats, Gokhan Karahan, and Robert Tollison, "Terrorism and Pork-barrel Spending," *Public Choice* 128 (2006): 275–287; Tyler Prante and Alok Bohara, "What Determines Homeland Security Spending? An Econometric Analysis of the Homeland Security Grant Program," *Policy Studies Journal* 36, 2 (2008): 243–256; and Holly T. Goerdel, "Politics versus Risk in State Allocations of Federal Security Grants," paper presented at the annual meeting of the Midwest Political Science Association, Chicago, April 3–6, 2009. Also see Shawn Reese, *Risk-Based Funding in Homeland Security Grant Legislation: Analysis of Issues for the 109th Congress*, August 29, 2005, fas.org/sgp/crs/homesec/RL33050.pdf.

52. Greenberg et al., 231.

53. Dan Eggen and Mary Beth Sheridan, "Anti-terror Funding Cut in DC and New York," *Washington Post*, June 1, 2006, www.washingtonpost.com/wp-dyn/content/article/2006/05/31/AR2006053101364.html.

54. Samuel H. Clovis Jr., "Federalism, Homeland Security and National Preparedness: A Case Study in the Development of Public Policy," *Homeland Security Affairs* 2, 2 (October 2006): 15.

55. Carmine Scavo, Richard C. Kearney, and Richard J. Kilroy Jr. "Local Government Managers' Views of Homeland Security," *The Municipal Yearbook, 2006* (Washington, D.C.: ICMA, 2006), 19–26.

56. Ten codes apparently originated in the 1930s when it was important to minimize the amount of time police officers and firefighters spent in radio communications. Each of the codes has a different meaning—for example, 10-4 means "OK" or "Acknowledgement," and 10-10 means "fight in progress." Different agencies use different variations of 10-codes. A fairly thorough listing of the 10-codes approved by the Association of Public Communications Officers can be found at spiffy.ci.uiuc.edu/~kline/Stuff/ten-codes.html.

57. Lon Slepicka, "DHS Secretary: Keep Your 10-Codes," cms.firehouse.com/web/online/News/DHS-Secretary--Keep-Your-10-Codes/46$44881.

58. Susan Glasser and Josh White, "Storm Exposed Disarray at the Top," *Washington Post*, September 4, 2005.

59. John Warner Defense Authorization Act (HR 5122), Section 1076: 333, Paragraph A.

60. On domestic use of U.S. military forces, see Nan D. Hunter, *The Law of Emergencies* (Oxford: Butterworth-Heinemann, 2009), chap. 4.

SUGGESTED READING

Kettl, Donald F. *System Under Stress: Homeland Security and American Politics.* 2nd ed. Washington, D.C.: CQ Press, 2007.

Kilroy, Richard J., Jr. *Threats to Homeland Security: An All-Hazards Approach.* New York: John Wiley and Sons, 2008.

Kotz, Nick. *The Wild Blue Yonder: Money, Politics and the B1 Bomber.* New York: Pantheon, 1988.

Miskel, James. *Disaster Response and Homeland Security: What Works and What Doesn't.* Westport, Conn.: Praeger, 2006.

Whittle, Richard. *The Dream Machine: The Untold History of the Notorious V-22 Osprey.* New York: Simon and Schuster, 2010.

Wilson, George C. *This War Really Matters: Inside the Fight for Defense Dollars.* Washington, D.C.: CQ Press, 1999.

chapter 15

Civil Rights

by Benjamin Marquez

THE CIVIL RIGHTS MOVEMENT OF THE "long 1960s," which reached its zenith in the middle decades of the twentieth century, evokes images of unity, sacrifice, and resistance to social injustices. The decades-long struggle by people of color for equal social and political rights changed the course of American politics. An important aspect of the civil rights movement was its heavy—although not exclusive—reliance on mass participation instead of the more conventional forms of politics such as lobbying or electioneering. Groups like the League of United Latin American Citizens (LULAC), the National Association for the Advancement of Colored People (NAACP), and the Southern Christian Leadership Conference were the titular heads of social movements that attracted people from all walks of life, with many risking their jobs, personal safety, and, at times, their lives, in pursuit of equality and social justice. The organizations that articulated this vision issued a collective challenge to authorities, power holders, and American cultural practices. Combining judicial and legislative approaches with high-profile public events, the civil rights movement helped usher in landmark legislation that changed the landscape of American society, most notably with the passage of the Civil Rights Acts of 1964 and 1968 and the Voting Rights Act of 1965.

After its legislative victories in the 1960s, however, the civil rights movement fragmented. Some groups and principal leaders chose to leverage their political gains by working in partisan and electoral politics, which resulted in some impressive gains. After the protests of the 1960s, African Americans were elected in major cities including Atlanta, Detroit, Los Angeles, and Newark. In 1973 approximately 2,600 blacks held elected office, doubling their numbers in three years. By 1983 the number had jumped to 5,600, and by 1993 it had reached more than 8,000, almost four times the number of elected officials in 1973.[1] The number of Latino elected officials also began to rise after the 1970s. Although severely underrepresented at the statewide and national level, more than 5,000 Latinos held elective office. Chris Garcia and Gabriel Sanchez argue that after the civil rights era, a "major revolution" resulted in Latinos taking seats on county commissions, city councils, and school boards. Since that time, Latinos have been elected mayors in cities including Denver, El Paso, Los Angeles, Miami, San Antonio, San José, and Santa Fe.[2]

The successes of civil rights activism set the stage for a broader spectrum of political work in later decades. Some activists, frustrated by the lack of economic progress accompanying the movement's legislative gains, continued to engage in contentious politics through unions, student groups, and community-based organizations.[3] Others created new, more specialized groups to serve the needs of particular sectors of the minority population, such as entrepreneurs, veterans, professionals, and artists. Many of these organizations now bear little resemblance to the mass-based organizations of the civil rights era, and they have adapted their strategies to improve their ability to influence public policy; that is, they have become interest groups. While some large, broadly based groups such as the NAACP continue to be influential in American policy and politics, many groups focus their efforts on more narrowly defined issue arenas affecting clearly defined groups of people.

EARLY CIVIL RIGHTS ACTION

The civil rights movement had its roots in a long history of struggle against a racial caste system and the political and economic disenfranchisement that went with it. One typically thinks of civil rights and civil rights organizations as those that address issues affecting African Americans and other racial minorities, but civil rights issues involve many other groups and issues, including the rights of lesbian, gay, bisexual, and transgendered (LGBT) people, the disabled, American Indians, Asian Americans, Muslim Americans, and others. Organizations representing these latter groups advocated for change during the second half of the twentieth century and continue to do so today. This chapter focuses on the experiences and development of organizations that represent African Americans and Latinos, but these other groups are brought into the discussion as well.

Early Hispanic Civil Rights Groups

For Mexican Americans, organized resistance to racial discrimination began in the mid-nineteenth century immediately after the U.S.-Mexico War (1846–1848) as a response to a rapidly changing political and racial order. Mexican Americans were then under the political and social dominance of the Anglo rebels. Workers were subjected to a dual wage system, and landowners were rapidly losing their land by force or through fraud.[4] In response to these abuses, labor unions and sociedades mutualistas (mutual aid societies) were formed. The first political organizations advocating on behalf of Mexican Americans argued that people of Mexican origin were bound together by their working-class status, a strong cultural heritage, and status as a defeated people.[5] Groups like La Alianza de Sociedades Mutualistas and Sociedad Morelos Mutua de Panaderos viewed the problems facing Mexican Americans as rooted in labor exploitation reinforced by racial and cultural discrimination. Union organizing and mutual aid societies proliferated at the turn of the twentieth century, as immigration grew in response to increased demand for labor in southwestern agriculture and extractive industries. Unions and mutual aid societies represented Mexican Americans in labor disputes. Mutual aid societies hosted cultural events and provided services such as libraries and credit unions. Both kinds of organizations defended the community in a hostile racial environment, but saw class and cultural issues as transcending national boundaries. Mexican Americans were subject to harsh working conditions and discriminatory wage structures across the Southwest regardless of their immigrant status. Moreover, their efforts to organize across racial lines were rebuffed by Anglo workers, for whom racial hierarchies trumped class-based solidarities. Finally, the Mexican workers were subjugated in an area of the United States that was originally Mexican national territory.[6]

The first Mexican American civil rights organizations, groups whose work centered on the rights of citizenship and formal equality, came at the turn of the twentieth century. LULAC, the most prominent, was established in 1929. It was created by uniting older groups—the Order Sons of America, Order Knights of America, and League of Latin American Citizens—that had been active since the turn of the century. These organizations fought against racism, demanded improved educational opportunities, and sought greater political representation. They argued that American society held great promise to assimilate their people in the way it had with other groups, such as Italian, Irish, and Jewish immigrants. After World War II, LULAC councils intensified their campaign for educational reform and against racial segregation in the public schools. These civil rights organizations broke completely with the immigrants' focus on Mexican politics and were the first to advocate social assimilation. A major element in their political strategy was to combat the view held by Anglos that Mexican Americans

The League of United Latin American Citizens (LULAC) was formed in 1929 through the unification of several existing organizations. They joined to fight with a unified voice against inequalities and injustices endured by Mexican Americans in the United States. President John F. Kennedy and Jacqueline Kennedy, along with Vice President Lyndon Johnson and Lady Bird Johnson, attend a 1963 LULAC dinner in Houston. President Kennedy was named an honorary member of the group.

were properly residents of Mexico and not worthy of American citizenship. To combat these attitudes and to promote social incorporation, LULAC members sponsored Boy Scouts and Girl Scouts troops, 4-H Clubs, and Little League baseball teams, and raised money for charities such as the March of Dimes and Red Cross. LULAC lobbied against segregation by pressuring local school boards and employers. During the 1960s LULAC and the American GI Forum were the two leading proponents of equal civil rights for Mexican Americans.[7]

Early African American Civil Rights Groups

In the twentieth century the NAACP and the National Urban League were the two most important African American organizations advocating for change. Founded in 1909, the NAACP was formed to abolish racial segregation, to promote equal educational opportunities, to enfranchise African Americans as voters, producers, and consumers, and to enforce the provisions of the Fourteenth and Fifteenth Amendments. Its principle strategy in the first half of the century was to lobby for federal legislation and file lawsuits to combat lynching and other forms of racist violence and to institute equal rights for blacks in voting, civil rights, housing, and education.[8] The Urban League was created in 1911 to aid the large numbers of African Americans who fled the South for jobs in northern cities, a demographic shift known as the First Great Migration. The Urban League lobbied business, industry, and unions to create opportunities for black workers. It also lobbied for vocational training, housing, and social work services to the black community.[9] The NAACP and Urban League were the largest but not the only civil rights organizations to emerge in the early twentieth century. Other significant groups such as the National Council of Negro Women and the Brotherhood of Sleeping Car Porters represented black women and workers. Although groups were specialized even in this early era, and the number of groups would grow during the 1960s, they worked to advance the interests of all black people through what Dona Hamilton and Charles Hamilton call the dual agenda. These organizations believed their work benefited all African Americans. They opposed racial discrimination in all areas of life but also fought for social programs that would alleviate the economic problems facing the black community: a nationally administered universal social welfare system and guaranteed full employment policies.[10]

NAACP and LULAC lawyers argued two major legal cases that had profound effects on the course of the civil rights movement. In *Hernández v. Texas* (1954), LULAC lawyers argued that the Fourteenth Amendment's equal protection clause should be extended to groups other than African Americans. Mexican Americans occupied a racial position outside of the black-white binary, but were still subject to the damaging impact of racial discrimination. Under Texas state law they were technically classified as white, but in practice the classification was a legal fiction that precluded relief against segregation and discrimination. In 1950 an all-Anglo jury had convicted Pete Hernández of murder in Texas. Hernández challenged his conviction on

The NAACP used the court system as a principle part of their strategy to establish legal equality for racial minorities. Thurgood Marshall and his team represented Linda and Terry Lynn Brown, above, from Topeka, Kansas, among others, in the landmark Brown v. Board of Education *case, decided in 1954. The opinion stated "that in the field of public education the doctrine of 'separate-but-equal' has no place. Separate educational facilities are inherently unequal."*

grounds that Mexican Americans were systematically excluded from the judicial process, including serving on juries, a practice he argued was unconstitutional because a jury of his peers did not try him. The U.S. Supreme Court agreed that Mexican Americans were systematically excluded from trial juries and gave them legal recognition as a racial "class apart" from non-Hispanic whites.[11] The NAACP argued the landmark decision, *Brown v. Board of Education* (1954), in which the Court declared that state laws mandating segregation of the races to be unconstitutional. The Court ruled that *de jure* racial segregation violated the equal protection clause of the Fourteenth Amendment. Even segregated schools with "equal" facilities and teachers were found to be harmful to black students and therefore unconstitutional.[12]

These legal breakthroughs gave movement lawyers important tools and tactics they could utilize in other settings. *Brown* and *Hernández* dramatically improved the legal situation of African Americans yet stiffened white resolve against integration, which set the stage for the tumultuous decade of activism that followed. Still, civil rights activists were given new hope that long-standing racial hierarchies were vulnerable to change. Other social changes fueled their optimism and resolve for change. Mexican American and black veterans of World War II returned to the United States in hopes of realizing the ideals of equality and freedom at home that they had defended. Moreover, the minority urban population grew dramatically in the postwar period, giving these populations the potential for collective action that was nearly impossible in rural settings. Economic development in the South and Southwest drastically reduced the regions' dependence on manual labor and broke the historic ties of African Americans and Mexican Americans to agricultural labor. The subsequent rise in urban populations increased the capacity of minority communities to establish collective identities and defend themselves through new social networks, political organizations, and media outlets. Changing demographics set the stage for a new wave of civil rights advocacy.

THE CIVIL RIGHTS MOVEMENT AND THE POLITICS OF MASS PARTICIPATION

As the black and Latino populations grew, advances in their occupational attainment and higher incomes improved their capacity to organize. At the same time, rapid industrialization rendered racial hierarchies vulnerable to change through persuasion, the courts, and, one of the most potent social movement tools, disruptive behavior. Among whites, persuasion was more likely to find a receptive audience than the other tactics. Surveys of whites' attitudes reveal that support for formal discrimination and beliefs that racial minorities are innately inferior diminished sharply during and after the 1960s.[13] Industrialization and the mechanization of agriculture disrupted the social order by increasing the salience of class-based politics.[14] The convergence of these trends created a political opportunity through which civil rights organizations could capitalize on favorable public opinion and legal gains to press for further change through direct action.

Mass collective action, such as demonstrations, boycotts, and riots, prompted legislative and social policy

Civil rights leaders (from left to right) Martin Luther King Jr., Whitney Young, and James Farmer, among others, meet with President Lyndon Johnson (center) at the White House in January 1964. President Johnson signed into law the landmark Civil Rights Act of 1964 some seven months later.

reform in three central ways. First, it drew attention to the severity of racial discrimination and to the ways in which racism contradicted the American ideals of freedom and equality. The national media brought the civil rights struggle to the forefront of American politics. Southern police forces suppressed peaceful demonstrations with beatings, dogs, teargas, and mass arrests, combined with the violence of white hate organizations, shocked the conscience of many Americans who had once turned a blind eye to racial disparities. Second, acts of civil disobedience disrupted institutionally regulated cooperation. Protesters risked their livelihood and personal safety by participating in the civil rights movement, but they also undermined the institutions that perpetuated their inequality. With their willingness to use unconventional means to achieve change, civil rights activists threatened political stability, refused to cooperate with the norms of segregation, and threatened the incomes of targeted businesses and slowed investment. Disruptive behavior forced white leaders and business owners to negotiate with civil rights leaders for concessions. Some of the best known civil rights era protests—the Montgomery Bus Boycott (1955), the Freedom Rides (1961), the formation of La Raza Unida Party (1970), and the urban riots of the mid to late 1960s—were rebellious, disruptive acts. They brought attention to injustices, but extracted concessions from economic and political elites by interrupting or stopping ongoing economic and political processes.[15]

Groups such as the Student Nonviolent Coordinating Committee, Black Panthers, La Raza Unida Party, and Crusade for Justice practiced a contentious form of politics that challenged the political and economic status quo. Their work prodded members of Congress to pass several significant and far-reaching pieces of legislation. The Civil Rights Act of 1964 outlawed discrimination in virtually every aspect of public life in the United States, including schools, workplaces, voter registration, public accommodations, and government funding. The Voting Rights Act of 1965 outlawed discriminatory practices in voting procedures and established federal oversight of voting administration in southern states. Title VIII of the Civil Rights Act of 1968 (more commonly known as the Fair Housing Act) strengthened the 1965 law's provisions by specifically targeting home sales, rentals, and financing as well as providing federal enforcement power against discrimination in these areas.

FRAGMENTATION AND FOCUS IN THE POST-CIVIL RIGHTS ERA

The civil rights era dates between 1950 and 1980, but it was after this period that the number of minority political organizations and interest groups increased dramatically. Burdett Loomis and Allan Cigler attribute the growth in the number of interest groups after World War II to increased affluence and education.[16] They cite other factors—the ascendency of a new professional and managerial elite, a growing sense of entitlement, and rising expectations among racial minorities that their lives would improve—that explain the large numbers of new organizations representing people of color. Although such organizations are widely credited with helping to secure many of the advances gained by communities of color, questions remain about whether contemporary configurations of political organizations

The Southern Christian Leadership Conference, Student Nonviolent Coordinating Committee, and other groups organized the 1965 Selma-to-Montgomery march to advocate for voting rights. Led by Rev. Martin Luther King Jr., marchers crossed the Edmund Pettus Bridge on March 21, 1965. Images of police brutally attacking marchers earlier in the month sent shockwaves across the nation. Soon thereafter President Johnson successfully pressed Congress for voting rights legislation.

In February 1970 protesters marched in Los Angeles as part of the Chicano Moratorium, a Latino movement protesting the war in Vietnam, shedding light on institutional discrimination, and promoting social justice.

represent a new wave of innovation and tactical diversity or a breakdown of the racial solidarity demonstrated during the 1960s.[17] Concurrently, socioeconomic progress spurred the creation of business and professional groups whose primary mission was to serve the needs of a new minority middle class. In other words, lower levels of discrimination combined with increased occupational and income mobility can create diverging political interests.[18] Moreover, determining which organizations represent the interests of the minority community presents a research problem. New issues and problems call for new organizations to deal with shifting political grounds. The growth of specialized minority political organizations may actually be an expression of newly acquired power and resources. Conversely, other inequalities rooted in differences in class, gender, and immigration status can promote an interest group universe with little common ground. New political opportunities in government and society for members of racial minorities following the civil rights movement were major accomplishments, but they also channeled protest into less disruptive, more institutionalized channels for politics.[19]

Have contemporary organizations representing the minority community evolved from social movements to interest groups? Do these organizations represent a new, innovative stage in civil rights activism, or do they reflect more fragmented minority populations and/or the cooptation of its leadership cadre?[20] To answer these questions it is important to examine the roles of self-interest and the programmatic goals of outside donors or government agencies on contemporary civil rights advocacy. If growing socioeconomic diversity among people of color erodes group solidarity, the plethora of new organizations may indicate a breakdown of the common cause and volunteerism that marked the civil rights movement.[21] In other words, elite sponsorship and the availability of grants and gifts, rather than the energy of ethnic or racial grievances, can drive a movement's course of action. Funding for specific projects or causes also gives enterprising individuals the freedom to form new organizations in response to those opportunities. The resulting organizations can operate without a membership base and the accountability that goes with it.[22]

The study of contemporary civil rights advocacy presents a theoretical and empirical challenge. The most common definitions of interest groups are necessarily broad and encompass virtually any kind of organized activity. In his classic study, David Truman defined interest groups as "any group that, on the basis of one or more shaped attitudes, makes certain claims upon other groups in the society for the establishment, maintenance, or enhancement of forms of behavior that are implied by the shared attitudes."[23] Definitions of social movements are similarly broad. In an effort to acknowledge the full spectrum of political action, social movements are typically defined as contentious entities whose claims, if fully realized, conflict with another group's interests, reflected in the status quo. Social movements are recognized as collective, organized, sustained, and noninstitutional challenge to authorities, power holders, or cultural beliefs and practices.[24]

These definitions encompass the activities of the NAACP and LULAC. Many of the organizations emerging after the 1960s can be attributed to the work of these flagship organizations. But what made civil rights organizations effective was their independence to act in the face of white resistance or political pressure. Civil rights groups had organizational structures and outside sources of income, but few paid employees. They needed a mass base of voluntary participants to engage in sustained political action and support the group monetarily.[25] The civil rights organizations of the 1960s were better able to challenge the status quo than more insular interest groups because they could count on community-generated resources and institutions. Had they depended on the state, businesses, and other white-controlled institutions for support, they might have found it impossible to engage in disruptive tactics such as boycotts, marches, processions, vigils, rallies, and demonstrations. Without a strong membership base, these organizations could have not mobilized large numbers of individuals willing to accept the consequences of confronting a white power structure that was often willing to resort to violence.[26]

The great sacrifices made by civil rights activists are instructive because they point to the power of racial ties to bind individuals together in a collective effort. The civil rights movement was a complex phenomenon with multiple leaders, organizations, and viewpoints.[27] Unity was maintained through what Michael Dawson calls "linked fate," a deep sense of belonging driven by a common racial and caste status transcending the other social divisions of occupation and income; and racial solidarity helped the movement overcome the "free-rider problem," the collective action paradox identified by economist Mancur Olson, in which participation in any collective activity is irrational if the individuals can enjoy the benefits without participating in it themselves.[28] The question of group solidarity in the modern era is basic to our understanding of the course racial and ethnic politics has taken since that time. Voluntary organizations levy a high cost on individuals in terms of time and emotionally draining work that is difficult to sustain even among the most dedicated activists. Nevertheless, voluntary participation and community-based financial support are important measures of grassroots support and accountability in any organization. Financial self-sufficiency is an extension of what Saul Alinsky, a leading theorist and community activist, called the "iron rule" of community organizing, which is never to do for others what they can do for themselves. Alinsky's insight is important because many of today's minority political organizations rely, sometimes exclusively, on grants and gifts from outside sources. External funding, Alinsky argued, held the potential to undermine the membership's power and decision-making ability and elevate a leadership cadre whose primary skill was not leadership but grant-writing. An organization's capacity to raise money through its membership fosters strong ties to the surrounding community, tests activists' commitments, and ensures leadership accountability.[29]

FOLLOW THE FUNDING TRAIL

As the number of civil rights advocacy groups has grown, so have the kinds of organizations. Many of these new organizations advocate on behalf of the community they serve, but few have dues-paying members or a democratically elected leadership cadre. Even venerable organizations like LULAC and the NAACP receive a large portion of their operating budget from outside sources. They are still active and continue to advocate on behalf of Latinos and African Americans at the national and local levels. Today, instead of heading a disruptive social movement capable of mobilizing mass action, they serve as lobbying instruments and as platforms for advocating equal civil rights and economic advancement. They also sponsor scholarship competitions and cultural events.[30] More significant, however, is that the NAACP and LULAC are no longer the most important groups in minority politics; rather, they have been joined by a large number of specialized organizations advocating for change in particular arenas or providing services to minority populations.[31]

The increased availability of government and private funding for social services and political projects since the 1960s can change civil rights advocacy in ways that redirect and distort their earlier representative function. Many of the new nonprofit groups formed in the wake of the 1960s have their origins in the protests of the civil rights era. The influx of money from government and white-controlled foundations, however, disrupts the relationship between minority populations and their organizations in two ways. First, it contributes to a political environment that rewards moderation and working within established institutional channels. Some large groups like the NAACP always relied on money from white-controlled institutions, but groups like LULAC went to great lengths to avoid taking money from outside groups, especially in its early years. The upsurge in foundation support for social movement organizations after the 1960s tended to go to public interest movements, organizations pursuing broad collective goals through professional advocacy or the provision of social services. J. Craig Jenkins found that 67.5 percent of all foundation money given to social movement organizations went to professionally administered groups offering legal and political advocacy or technical support. Organizations engaged in activist training and direct grassroots actions received only 23 percent of the total. Far less money went to groups whose goals or ideologies could be construed as controversial in any way. Social movement organizations involved in antinuclear activism, LGBT rights, and the peace movement received only 7.5 percent of all grants.[32] The funding climate is especially challenging as corporate donors favor groups promoting education (57 percent) over civil rights activities (12 percent) and legal services (1 percent).[33]

SURVEYING THE NEW UNIVERSE OF MINORITY POLITICAL ORGANIZATIONS WITH GUIDESTAR

There is no authoritative census of civil rights organizations that allows a researcher to make a definitive comparison of their goals or to document the increase in their number over time. But one place to look for these answers is in the world of nonprofit organizations, tax-exempt entities where much of the growth in minority group organizing has occurred. Jeffrey Berry found that between 1977 and 1997 the number of nonprofit organizations grew from 276,000 to 693,000.[1] Most of these organizations are new, but among the organizations serving minority communities, many are groups that survived the civil rights era and have applied for and received nonprofit status. The list of groups filing for nonprofit status through the Internal Revenue Service is a useful proxy for a register of currently active minority political organizations.[2]

To examine the universe of civil rights and minority organizations, one can analyze organizations by their classification with the Internal Revenue Service in the GuideStar database, created by the National Taxonomy of Exempt Entities classification system (NTEE). In the mid-1990s the IRS implemented this system to categorize nonprofit organizations. Once a group has been deemed eligible to receive federal tax-exempt status, the IRS classifies it based on descriptive data in the organization's application.[3] These records consequently provide useful information about the size and diversity of groups advocating for minorities and about civil rights issues.

Examining the organizations in the GuideStar database that speak for or provide services for African Americans and Latinos reveals some important patterns. Although broad-based civil rights organizations are difficult to sustain, the two best known groups from the civil rights era continue to be active. There are currently 1,729 chapters of the NAACP and 839 chapters of LULAC with tax-exempt status in the United States. The GuideStar database contains 3,311 African American and 4,784 Latino advocacy organizations (see Table 15.1).[4] Other tax-exempt entities serving minority communities engage in a broad spectrum of activities, including health care and counseling. It is not only the narrowly tailored groups that survive on outside grants and gifts. Today, some of the most readily recognized civil rights organizations are heavily subsidized by grants of various kinds. For example, the NAACP central headquarters, NAACP Legal Defense and Educational Fund, and National Urban League headquarters are funded almost completely by grants and contributions.[5] Some of the largest Latino political organizations received virtually all of their funding from sources other than their members. The Mexican American Legal Defense and Educational Fund, Southwest Voter Registration and Education Project, Southwest Industrial Areas Foundation, and National Council of La Raza are dependent upon outside funding.[6]

A review of nine NTEE core codes confirms trends documented elsewhere. The number of organizations working on behalf of African Americans[7] and Latinos [8] has grown rapidly. Of the 3,311 organizations working on behalf of African Americans listed in the GuideStar database in 2009, 827 groups were active in the arts and culture, and 687 provided human services. The next largest category of organizations, numbering 503, are the groups that the NTEE categorized as providing a "Public and Societal Benefit." Civil rights organizations and other groups active in the promotion and protection of civil liberties constituted just 15 percent of the total.[9] This is a significant although small proportion of the total. Latinos were represented by 4,784 nonprofit organizations. The largest category within these organizations was the 1,320 human services organizations, a full 28 percent of the total. The next largest category was the 725 groups providing public and societal benefits, which includes civil rights organizations.

Determining how or under what conditions groups involved in artistic or cultural activities have a political impact is beyond the scope of this chapter, but they do merit closer examination by social scientists. Social service agencies and cultural groups can have a political impact by reinforcing racial group solidarity or educating community members. Individuals who head these groups can, and often do, take stands on public policies or pending legislation without threatening the organization's nonprofit status. Internal Revenue Service regulations stipulate that nonprofit organizations must not participate in political campaigns or any activity in support of or opposition to a political party or candidate for public office. IRS regulations do, however, allow nonprofit organizations to engage in

Fueling this expansion is that incorporating as an organization with tax-exempt status is a relatively simple, low-cost process that yields considerable financial advantages. Nonprofit organizations pay no federal, state, and local taxes and can devote more of their resources to achieving their goals. Nonprofit status shields participants from personal liability for the group's actions and offers donors a deduction for federal tax purposes. Nonprofit organizations qualify for special grants and government funding. To retain their tax-exempt status, nonprofit organizations must also restrict the scope of their work to nonpartisan activities. The availability of funding for specialized projects can prompt enterprising organizers to create staff organizations or service agencies that have no dues-paying members and are run by a paid professional staff.[34] Once they are formed, they are independent entities that take on a life of their own, far removed from the mass action tactics of social movements or umbrella civil rights organizations.

The second way that outside money disrupts the relationship between minority populations and their traditional organizations is that it affects solidarity. New funding opportunities may facilitate the formation of new minority organizations, but a considerable body of theoretical and empirical work on social assimilation predicts the gradual breakdown of group solidarity over time. As more and more members of marginalized groups assimilate socially, politically, and economically, group loyalty and solidarity decline.[35] Political reform lowers barriers to integration and more overt political activities by lobbying to influence legislation as long as it is germane to their mission.[10]

The list of contemporary minority organizations is long. Some groups in the Arts, Culture, and Humanities category that serve Latinos and African Americans have a single purpose, such as organizing a yearly cultural event. Others work on historical museums of all kinds and projects in the performing arts—dance, film, music, and theater—all year long. Still other groups sponsor genealogical research and maintain historical archives. Education and Research groups sponsor scholarships, fellowships, and health education programs. Others provide education programs for business owners and professionals. Education and Research groups also include parent-teacher organizations, scholarship societies, preparatory schools, charter schools, hearing and speech centers, as well as family planning centers. There are organizations for minority law social workers, enforcement officers, firefighters, and engineers. Health care providers have their own professional associations. Other health-related groups concentrate their efforts on problems such as AIDS, drug abuse, diabetes, Alzheimer's, family violence, children's health services, and cancer. Others offer allergy and immunization services, psychiatric help, hepatitis outreach, and counseling services. Under the rubric of Human Services, Latino and African organizations have created social and recreation clubs, community centers, charitable organizations, housing associations, wellness clinics, job training, and general social service agencies. Included in this category are adoption societies, marriage counseling, youth mentoring, low-income housing projects, Boys and Girls Clubs, and legal services.

Finally, under the heading of Public Social Benefit, where civil rights organizations are most likely to be categorized, the range of activities is just as varied. This category includes civil rights and liberties associations and groups engaged in various community projects. Also included here are groups that come under the heading of Mutual/Membership Benefit, Philanthropy, Volunteerism, Service, and Voter Education. These groups include women's associations, veterans groups, economic development organizations, and civil rights groups. Tax-exempt status in this category provides for exemption of business leagues, chambers of commerce, real estate boards, boards of trade that are not organized for profit and do not benefit private shareholders or individuals. The mission of these groups is to advance of the interests of a particular trade or community. This category therefore includes nonprofit housing corporations, business and professional groups, chambers of commerce, credit unions, economic development organizations, and neighborhood associations.

1. Jeffrey Berry, "Empowering Nonprofits," paper prepared for the Urban Seminar Series on Children's Health and Safety, Kennedy School of Government, Harvard University, May 2003, www.hks.harvard.edu/urban poverty/Berry.pdf.
2. Several research groups maintain publicly accessible databases on nonprofit organizations. GuideStar USA is generally recognized as the most comprehensive. Its database contains detailed financial information on more than 1.8 million nonprofit organizations. See www2.guidestar.org/Home.aspx.
3. The NTEE-CC classification system divides the universe of nonprofit organizations into twenty-six major groups under ten broad categories: Arts, Culture, and Humanities; Education, Environment, and Animals; Health, Human Services; International; Foreign Affairs; Public, Societal Benefit; Religion; Mutual/Membership Benefit; Business; and Unknown or Unclassified. Each broad category is further broken down by function such as alliances, advocacy, management and technical assistance, research, policy analysis, fundraising, and other types of support. For more information on these categories consult the Urban Institute's guide: nccs.urban.org/classification/NTEE.cfm. Nonprofit organization databases offer new opportunities for the study of racial representation and the consequences of a large number of organizations for minority politics. GuideStar USA's data bank contains IRS 990 forms for almost 2 million nonprofit organizations. Other nonprofit organization data bases include the Foundation Center: fconline.foundationcenter.org/ and the National Center for Charitable Statistics: nccs.urban.org/.
4. All of the organizations included in this count either have minority key words in their name (i.e., Black, African American, Latino, Hispanic, Mexican American) or list serving the black or Hispanic community in their statement of purpose.
5. See IRS 990 forms.
6. Benjamin Marquez, "Bankrolling Mexican American Political Organizations: Corporate and Foundation Sponsorship of Racial Politics," *Social Service Review* 77, 3 (September 2003): 329–346.
7. The search terms used were *African American, Afro American, Black American,* and *Negro.*
8. The search terms used were *Hispanic, Latino, Latina, Chicano, Chicana,* and *Mexican American.*
9. Groups broadly defined as promoting a public and societal benefit.
10. See www.irs.gov/irm/part7/irm_07-025-004.html.

the intensity of group bonds whereby new organizations and political expressions that often extend beyond issues of race or cultural distinctions can thrive.[36] As such, changes in socioeconomic status signal a break with a rigid system of racial hegemony. As people of color are less likely to be thrown together along a single axis of racial domination, they participate in a broader spectrum of social and political life, and their political thinking changes.[37] It is not unusual to find organizations as diverse as community development corporations, environmental justice groups, minority chambers of commerce, and professional associations serving the minority community. The list includes organizations such as the National Black Chamber of Commerce, United States Hispanic Chamber of Commerce, National Latina/o Lesbian Gay and Transgender Organization, National Association of Black Veterans, National Association of Hispanic Journalists, and National Association for Hispanic Health.

This expansion is a relatively new phenomenon, with most of it occurring after the 1960s. Michael Cortés found that fewer than 2 percent of all nonprofit organizations serving Latino populations were granted tax-exempt status by the IRS during the first half of the twentieth century. Paralleling trends in other arenas of interest group activity, the number of organizations representing minority interests rose dramatically. By 1996 half of all Latino nonprofit organizations were less than ten years old.[38] In her 2000 survey of national economic and social justice organizations, Dara

TABLE 15.1 **Black and Latino Advocacy Groups, 2010**

Black advocacy	Arts, culture and humanities	Education and research	Environment and animals	Health	Human services	International	Public and societal benefit	Religion	Business associations	TOTAL
Organizations										
African American	590	371	15	232	513	20	354	57	102	2,254
Negro	30	27	0	0	56	20	25	2	1	161
Afro American	34	6	1	5	16	1	5	2	0	70
Black American	173	103	25	45	102	8	119	16	235	826
Total	827	502	41	282	687	49	503	77	338	3,311
Latino advocacy organizations										
Mexican American	21	13	0	3	29	5	16	1	13	133
Hispanic	273	366	14	222	654	12	436	104	254	2,679
Latino	248	211	15	188	530	14	221	42	34	1,595
Latina	26	23	1	49	97	5	42	6	4	268
Chicano/a	21	11	0	3	10	0	10	3	33	91
Total	589	624	30	465	1320	36	725	156	338	4,784

SOURCE: Data from www.guidestar.org.

Strolovitch found thirty-two national organizations representing Asian Pacific Americans, forty that represent African Americans, forty-three that represent Latinos/as, and thirty-five that represent American Indians. Moreover, 56 percent of these civil rights and racial minority organizations were formed between 1960 and 1999.[39]

The class and occupational composition of minority organizations' membership bases and their sources of income will shape the trajectory of contemporary civil rights politics. A central question among many scholars of race and ethnicity has to do with the ways in which minority social and economic progress drives the new diversity of minority political activism. Even if individuals perceive a high degree of shared fate, in an era of greater civil liberties and social mobility, broad-based volunteer organizations will have more difficulty overcoming the free-rider problem. At the same time, those minority organizations that define their purpose narrowly will find it easier to attract members and serve their needs while exercising more freedom to redefine group goals and commitments. Organizers have wide latitude when creating an organization, and there is a growing literature on political organizing that calls attention to the importance of identity construction and how it can drive group action in unpredictable ways. In other words, reasons for joining a social movement organization are typically viewed in traditional terms: race, class, gender, and ideology. The proliferation of social movements emphasizes the power that other variables such as lifestyle and sexuality can motivate activism or redefine social movements themselves.[40] If this is also true for people of color, then minority political organizations will assume forms that are just as varied and unpredictable as they are in the general population. The challenge is to determine to what extent and in what combination contemporary minority organizations reflect a necessary adaptation to changing circumstances or the growing influence of narrow interests within the minority community.

THE FUTURE OF CIVIL RIGHTS ORGANIZATIONS

A simple catalog and tally of the number of existing minority political organizations cannot answer all of our questions about race and representation in minority advocacy organizations. Nor does the NTEE classification system measure the scope of a group's work or its impact. The oldest civil rights groups, the NAACP and LULAC are still active. The NAACP is the largest by far with 2008 income of more than $24 million. Headquartered in Baltimore, Md., with an office in Washington, D.C., the group lobbies Congress and monitors pending legislation. Through print and electronic media, the NAACP communicates its findings to a national network of affiliates. The NAACP also advances its civil rights agenda through outreach to its local chapters, African American religious leaders, voter education, and get-out-the-vote campaigns. LULAC has a far smaller income, just over $3 million in 2009, and operates on a far smaller scale than the NAACP. The organization hosts a large annual convention and serves as a forum and network for Latino leaders and politicians. Legal advocacy, youth scholarships, and social services are provided through its independent local councils and entities affiliated with the national headquarters: the Mexican American Legal Defense and Education Fund and LULAC National Education Service Centers, Inc.

The newer nonprofit minority organizations merit closer attention because of their contributions and potential to redefine the meaning of a civil rights agenda. Today,

Cardinal Roger Mahony of the Archdiocese of Los Angeles and other supporters of the DREAM Act hold a vigil and procession through downtown Los Angeles in early December 2010. The DREAM Act would ease the legalization process of people who entered the country illegally as children. The act ultimately failed to gain the necessary votes in the Senate a few weeks later.

LEADERSHIP CONFERENCE ON CIVIL AND HUMAN RIGHTS

The Leadership Conference on Civil and Human Rights (LCCHR) is a national coalition focused on preserving the basic civil and human rights of people residing in the United States. Established in 1950, the organization has become a major lobbying organization for civil rights legislation. The LCCHR was founded by A. Philip Randolph, the head of the Brotherhood of Sleeping Car Porters, Roy Wilkins of the NAACP, and Arnold Aronson of the National Jewish Community Relations Advisory Council. These men shared a commitment to civil rights and social justice, and their diverse backgrounds allowed them to extend their influence to many areas of society.

Today the LCCHR is has more than 200 member organizations and represents the interests of an expansive array of civil rights issues, including education, disability rights, health care, housing, immigration, LGBT rights, religious rights, women's rights, and workers' rights. To promote the rights of those they represent, members of the group's leadership, particularly Wade Henderson, the current president, often testify before Congress on a number of policy issues. The LCCHR frequently writes letters to members of the Senate, asking them to vote in a particular way when legislation pertaining to civil rights is up for consideration. The LCCR rates how members of Congress vote on civil rights issues. In 2009 the LCCHR spent close to $900,000 on their lobbying efforts, nearly triple the amount it spent in 2001.

The Leadership Conference seeks to help immigrants overcome and remedy the prejudice and discrimination they face upon entering the United States and ease their assimilation into American society. Of particular interest to the group is access to higher education for young immigrants, regardless of legal status. Over the past decade, the LCCHR has advocated for passage of the DREAM Act, a law that would provide a path to citizenship for undocumented young adults who go to college or serve in the military. In 2007 the organization sent a letter to members of the Senate, urging them to vote in support of the legislation. In 2009 they sent out a similar letter, once again asking for a favorable vote. In 2010 the House passed the legislation, but it did not gain the necessary support in the Senate for passage.

Fair pay and workers' rights are another set of issues the LCCHR has addressed recently. The organization advocates fairness in the workplace, the right to economic advancement, the right to join a union, and a worker's right to file a complaint without facing discrimination or retaliation. The LCCHR also promotes women's rights and for women to have equal pay for equal work. In *Ledbetter v. Goodyear Tire & Rubber Co.* (2007) the Supreme Court ruled that in accordance with Title VII of the Civil Rights Act, women have 180 days to file suit against an employer for denying them a pay raise based on their gender. The LCCHR fought to reverse this ruling, and was influential in the passage of the Lily Ledbetter Fair Pay Act. The LCCHR wrote multiple letters to members of the Senate, saying that passage would greatly help victims of workplace discrimination.

LGBT rights have also been at the forefront of the LCCHR's agenda over the past decade. The repeal of the military's don't ask, don't tell policy, nondiscrimination in the workplace, and legislation pertaining to same-sex marriage have been areas of LCCHR lobbying efforts. The debate over same-sex marriage has been of particular interest to the LCCHR. The conference has lobbied against passage of an amendment to the Constitution that would limit marriage in the United States to the union of one man and one woman, thus denying members of the LGBT community the right to marry and prohibit same-sex partners from receiving spousal benefits. The LCCHR issued numerous press releases regarding the proposed Federal Marriage Amendment, saying it would "use the Constitution to restrict rather than expand rights." When the amendment was defeated in 2006, the LCCHR was strong in its praise, congratulating Congress for ensuring that discrimination would not be part of the Constitution.

instead of a handful of organizations like the NAACP and LULAC speaking authoritatively on behalf of people of color, a multitude of voices now articulate their own visions of minority interests. The solidarity that made many of the gains during the 1960s brought leaders and followers into a close working relationship. In the absence of more pervasive and overt discrimination and with the heightened attention given to civil rights issues, there is far less constraint on claims made by these groups on behalf of American racial and ethnic groups. Activists can exercise a wide latitude and discretion when launching political initiatives without the political constraints or accountability more common in mass-based organizations. New organizations can enter areas of specialization that reflect donor priorities and the personal ambition of group leaders rather than group policy preferences.

Minority political organizations are increasingly specialized, and many represent the interests of the most advantaged sectors of the minority population. At the very least, nonprofit status has the effect of placing formerly independent organizations under the watch of the federal government. The loss of that status can threaten their funding sources and, ultimately, the group itself. Jeffrey Berry and David Arons found that regulation by the federal government had a profound effect on nonprofits' political behavior. Uncertainty about rules governing political behavior and a fear of losing their nonprofit status restricts the scope of their advocacy work. As Berry argues, "A primary reason why the poor and other marginalized constituents are not adequately represented in public policymaking is because the government discourages their representatives from participating."[41]

A better understanding of minority political organizations will require more qualitative and quantitative research. Although minority political representation might be suppressed in one sector, specifying what actually constitutes a minority political organization in the first place is a difficult conceptual problem. Despite the problems minority political organizations face, recent research reveals that race and ethnicity continue to be important mobilizing themes. At the national level, black, Asian, and Latino organizations have lobbied on matters of immigration and social services.[42] Immigrant status and poverty can depress levels of participation in organized politics, but some scholars have found significant levels of group activity especially when it comes to education and civil rights.[43] There is also evidence that groups organizing along nonracial lines or fostering coalitional politics offer promising avenues for minority group advocacy.[44]

Social and economic integration and the emergence of innovative styles of organizing have blurred the distinction between majority and minority interest groups. The post–civil rights era led to the emergence of organizations that organize in minority communities but do not use race as an organizing tool. The best example of this approach is the Industrial Areas Foundation (IAF) network. The IAF is a network of organizations operating in poor and minority communities across the country. Instead of utilizing the rhetoric and strategies of the civil rights movement, it trains and motivates its members on the basis of religious values. Indeed, the group specifically rejects organizing on the basis of race and works to build a multiracial alliance. They train leaders and advocate on behalf of the poor and in communities where virtually all of their activists and constituents are people of color.[45] For the IAF leadership, minority politics is class politics, and, rather than discrimination, poverty and neglect are the foundation of discontent.

CONCLUSION

The civil rights movement changed the course of American politics. The world of minority advocacy groups changed as well. Today it is difficult to make categorical statements about the way minority interests are advanced through interest groups, but serious questions should be raised about the large number of nonprofit groups and how nonprofit status influences their behavior. The NAACP and LULAC have survived to this point, in part, because of their nonprofit status. Although hundreds of affiliates with both organizations have nonprofit status, only a handful report any significant income, and most report no income at all. On the other hand, the national offices of both groups have prospered. For 2007 the national office of the NAACP did far better in this respect, raising 14 percent of its $42,642,584 income from membership dues and assessments. For the same year, LULAC's national office reported a substantial but far more modest income of $2,021,330.[46] How these organizations function as minority representatives raises difficult questions about the way that race and politics are expressed through interest groups. Few of today's civil rights groups could survive on membership dues or fundraising activities.

Civil rights leaders assert that they have utilized the gains of the 1960s to leverage new resources by forming corporate "partnerships" and accepting government grants. The rapid expansion of new organizations, many of which have few overtly political goals, however, casts doubt on this assertion. It is more plausible that grants and gifts extend the life of groups that may have passed from the scene if they were solely dependent on membership dues and volunteers and spawned others with limited community support. If true, the result is a less disruptive civil rights community constantly in search of politically safe strategies.

NOTES

1. Frederick C. Harris et al., *Countervailing Forces in African-American Civic Activism, 1973–1994* (Cambridge: Cambridge University Press, 2006).

2. F. Chris Garcia and Gabriel R. Sanchez, *Hispanics and the U.S. Political System: Moving into the Mainstream* (Upper Saddle River, N.J.: Pearson Prentice Hall, 2008).

3. Frances Fox Piven and Richard A. Cloward, *Poor People's Movements: Why They Succeed, How They Fail* (New York: Vintage Books, 1979); Donald Charles Reitzes and Dietrich C. Reitzes, *The Alinsky Legacy: Alive and Kicking* (Greenwich, Conn.: JAI Press, 1987).

4. David Montejano, *Anglos and Mexicans in the Making of Texas, 1836–1986* (Austin: University of Texas Press, 1987); Richard Griswold del Castillo, *The Treaty of Guadalupe Hidalgo: A Legacy of Conflict* (Norman: University of Oklahoma Press, 1990).

5. Emilio Zamora, *The World of the Mexican Worker in Texas* (College Station: Texas A&M Press, 2000).

6. Vicki Ruiz, *Cannery Women, Cannery Lives: Mexican Women, Unionization, and the California Food Processing Industry, 1930–1950* (Albuquerque: University of New Mexico Press, 1987); Mario T. Garcia, *Mexican Americans: Leadership, Ideology, and Identity, 1930–1960* (New Haven: Yale University Press, 1989); José Amaro Hernández, *Mutual Aid for Survival: The Case of the Mexican American* (Malabar, Fla.: Krieger, 1983); Zaragosa Vargas, *Labor Rights are Civil Rights: Mexican American Workers in Twentieth–Century America* (Princeton: Princeton University Press, 2005).

7. Benjamin Marquez, *LULAC: The Evolution of a Mexican American Political Organization* (Austin: University of Texas Press, 1993); David Gutierrez, *Walls and Mirrors: Mexican Americans, Mexican Immigrants, and the Politics of Ethnicity* (Berkeley: University of California Press, 1995); Craig Allan Kaplowitz, *LULAC, Mexican Americans, and National Policy* (College Station: Texas A&M University Press, 2005).

8. Gilbert Jonas, *Freedom's Sword: The NAACP and the Struggle Against Racism in America, 1909–1969* (New York: Routledge, 2005).

9. Toure F. Reed, *Not Alms but Opportunity: The Urban League and the Politics of Racial Uplift, 1910–1950* (Chapel Hill: University of North Carolina Press, 2008).

10. Dona C. Hamilton, and Charles V. Hamilton, *The Dual Agenda: Race and Social Welfare Policies of Civil Rights Organizations* (New York: Columbia University Press, 1997), 4.

11. Michael A. Olivas, *Colored Men and Hombres Aquí:* Hernández v. Texas *and the Emergence of Mexican American Lawyering* (Houston, Texas: Arte Publico Press, 2006).

12. James T. Patterson, Brown v. Board of Education: *A Civil Rights Milestone and Its Troubled Legacy* (New York: Oxford University Press, 2001).

13. David O. Sears, Jim Sidanius, and Lawrence Bobo, "Race in American Politics: Framing the Debates," in *Racialized Politics: The Debate About Racism in America,* ed. David O. Sears, Jim Sidanius, and Lawrence Bobo (Chicago: University of Chicago Press, 2000), 1–43; Howard Schuman, *Racial Attitudes in America: Trends and Interpretations.* (Cambridge: Harvard University Press, 1988).

14. Jack M. Bloom, *Class, Race, and the Civil Rights Movement.* (Bloomington: Indiana University Press, 1987); Byron E. Shafer and Richard Johnston, *The End of Southern Exceptionalism: Class, Race, and Partisan Change in the Postwar South* (Cambridge: Harvard University Press, 2006).

15. Frances Fox Piven, *Challenging Authority: How Ordinary People Change America* (Lanham, Md.: Rowman and Littlefield, 2006); Joseph E. Luders, *The Civil Rights Movement and the Logic of Social Change* (Cambridge: Cambridge University Press, 2010); Ignacio M. Garcia, *United We Win: The Rise and Fall of La Raza Unida Party* (Tucson: Mexican American Studies and Research Center, University of Arizona, 1989); Carlos Munoz, *Youth, Identity, Power: The Chicano Movement* (London; New York: Verso, 2007); Ernesto B. Vigil, *The Crusade for Justice: Chicano Militancy and the Government's War on Dissent* (Madison: University of Wisconsin Press, 1999).

16. Allan J. Cigler and Burdett A. Loomis, eds., *Interest Group Politics* (Washington, D.C.: CQ Press, 1998).

17. Susan Olzak and Emily Ryo, "Organizational Diversity, Vitality and Outcomes in the Civil Rights Movement," *Social Forces* 85, 4 (2007): 1561–91.

18. William Julius Wilson, *The Truly Disadvantaged: The Inner City, the Underclass, and Public Policy* (Chicago: University of Chicago Press, 1990); Gutierrez, *Walls and Mirrors.*

19. G. William Domhoff, "The Power Elite and Their Challengers: The Role of Nonprofits in American Social Conflict," *American Behavioral Scientist* 52, 7 (March 2009): 955–973.

20. Robert Charles Smith, *We Have No Leaders: African Americans in the Post–Civil Rights Era* (Albany: State University of New York Press, 1996); Benjamin Marquez, *Constructing Identities in Mexican American Political Organizations: Choosing Issues, Taking Sides* (Austin: University of Texas Press, 2003).

21. Marquez, *Choosing Issues, Taking Sides.*

22. See John D. McCarthy, and Mayer N. Zald, "Resource Mobilization and Social Movements: A Partial Theory," *American Journal of Sociology* 82, 6 (1977): 1212–1241; Mayer N. Zald and John D. McCarthy, *Social Movements in an Organizational Society: Collected Essays* (New Brunswick, N.J.: Transaction Books, 1987).

23. David B. Truman, *The Governmental Process: Political Interests and Public Opinion* (New York: Knopf, 1951).

24. Jeff Goodwin, James M. Jasper, and Francesca Polletta, *Passionate Politics: Emotions and Social Movements* (Chicago: University of Chicago Press, 2001).

25. Doug McAdam, *Political Process and the Development of Black Insurgency, 1930–1970* (Chicago: University of Chicago Press, 1982); Aldon D. Morris, *The Origins of the Civil Rights Movement: Black Communities Organizing for Change* (New York: Free Press, 1984); Garcia, *United We Win;* J. Craig Jenkins, *The Politics of Insurgency* (New York: Columbia University Press, 1985).

26. Aldon, *Origins of the Civil Rights Movement.*

27. David J. Garrow, *Bearing the Cross: Martin Luther King, Jr., and the Southern Christian Leadership Conference* (New York: W. Morrow, 1986).

28. Michael C. Dawson, *Behind the Mule: Race and Class in African-American Politics* (Princeton: Princeton University Press, 1995); Mancur Olson, *The Logic of Collective Action: Public Goods and the Theory of Groups* (New York: Schocken Books, 1965); Aldon, *Origins of the Civil Rights Movement.*

29. For an overview of the literature on Alinsky and his organization, Industrial Areas Foundation, see Harry C. Boyte, *CommonWealth: A Return to Citizen Politics* (New York: Free Press, 1989); Ernesto Cortés Jr., "Changing the Locus of Political Decision Making: San Antonio's COPs," *Christianity and Crisis* 47, 1 (1987): 18–22; Ernesto Cortés Jr., "Reweaving the Social Fabric," *Boston Review* 19, 3 (1994); Cynthia Perry, *Organizing for Change: IAF 50 Years: Power, Action, Justice* (San Francisco: Industrial Areas Foundation, 1990); Reitzes and Reitzes, *Alinsky Legacy.*

30. Gary C. Gray and Victoria Bishop Kendzia, "Organizational Self-Censorship: Corporate Sponsorship, Nonprofit Funding, and the Educational Experience," *Canadian Review of Sociology* 46, 2 (May 2009): 161–177.

31. Theda Skocpol, *Diminished Democracy: From Membership to Management in American Civic Life* (Norman: University of Oklahoma Press, 2003).

32. J. Craig Jenkins, "Channeling Social Protest: Foundation Patronage of Contemporary Social Movements," in *Private Action and the Private Good*, ed. Walter W. Powell and Elisabeth S. Clemens (New Haven: Yale University Press, 1998), 206–216.

33. Steven L Paprocki and Robert O. Bothwell, *Corporate Grantmaking: Giving to Racial/Ethnic Populations* (Lanham, Md.: University Press of America, 1994); see Joseph Galaskiewicz and Michelle Sinclair Colman, "Collaboration Between Corporations and Nonprofit Organizations," in *The Nonprofit Sector: A Research Handbook*, ed. Walter W. Powell and Richard Steinberg (New Haven: Yale University Press, 2006), 180–204.

34. J. Craig Jenkins and Abigail Halcli, "Grassrooting the System? The Development and Impact of Social Movement Philanthropy, 1953–1990," in *Philanthropic Foundations: New Scholarship, New Possibilities*, ed. Ellen Condliffe Lagemann (Bloomington: Indiana University Press, 1999), 277–299.

35. Milton Gordon, *Assimilation in American Life* (New York: Oxford University Press, 1964); Robert Dahl, *Who Governs? Democracy and Power in an American City* (New Haven: Yale University Press, 1964); Richard D. Alba, and Victor Nee, *Remaking the American Mainstream: Assimilation and Contemporary Immigration* (Cambridge: Harvard University Press, 2003). See Edward E. Telles and Vilma Ortiz, *Generations of Exclusion: Mexican Americans, Assimilation, and Race* (New York: Russell Sage Foundation, 2008).

36. Howard Winant, *The New Politics of Race: Globalism, Difference, Justice* (Minneapolis: University of Minnesota Press, 2004).

37. Wilson, *Truly Disadvantaged.*

38. Michael Cortés, "A Statistical Profile of Latino Nonprofit Organizations in the United States," in *Nuevos Senderos: Reflections on Hispanics and Philanthropy*, ed. Diana Campoamor, William A. Díaz, and Henry A. J. Ramos (Houston: Arte Publico, 1999), 17–54.

39. Dara Z. Strolovitch, *Affirmative Advocacy: Race, Class, Gender, and Interest Group Politics* (Chicago: University of Chicago Press, 2007). See also Chapter 19, by Kay Lehman Schlozman, in this volume.

40. Jo Reger and Daniel J. Myers, *Identity Work in Social Movements* (Minneapolis: University of Minnesota Press, 2008); Richard Jenkins, *Social Identity* (New York: Routledge, 1996); Alberto Melucci, *Nomads of the Present: Social Movements and Individual Needs in Contemporary Society* (Philadelphia: Temple University Press, 1989); Alain Touraine, *Return of the Actor* (Minneapolis: University of Minnesota Press, 1988).

41. Jeffrey Berry, "Empowering Nonprofits," paper prepared for the Urban Seminar Series on Children's Health and Safety, Kennedy School of Government, Harvard University, May 2003, www.hks.harvard.edu/urbanpoverty/Berry.pdf.

42. Kaplowitz, *LULAC;* Carolyn Wong, *Lobbying for Inclusion: Rights Politics and the Making of Immigration Policy* (Palo Alto, Calif.: Stanford University Press, 2006).

43. See S. Karthick Ramakrishnan and Irene Bloemraad, *Civic Hopes and Political Realities: Immigrants, Community Organizations and Political Engagement* (New York: Russell Sage Foundation, 2008).

44. Rufus P. Browning et al., *Protest Is Not Enough: The Struggle of Blacks and Hispanics for Equality in Urban Politics* (Berkeley: University of California Press, 1984); Strolovitch, *Affirmative Advocacy;* Cristina Beltrán, *The Trouble with Unity: Latino Politics and the Creation of Identity* (New York: Oxford University Press, 2010).

45. Mark R. Warren, *Dry Bones Rattling: Community Building to Revitalize American Democracy* (Princeton: Princeton University Press, 2001); Warren, *Fire in the Heart: How White Activists Embrace Racial Justice* (Oxford; New York: Oxford University Press, 2010).

46. IRS 990 Form, 2007.

SUGGESTED READINGS

Berry, Jeffery M., and David F. Arons. *A Voice for Nonprofits.* Washington, D.C.: Brookings, 2003.

Hero, Rodney. *Latinos and the U.S. Political System: Two-Tiered Pluralism.* Philadelphia: Temple University Press, 1992.

Ramakrishnan, S. Karthick, and Irene Bloemraad, eds. *Civic Hopes and Political Realities: Immigrants, Community Organizations, and Political Engagement.* New York: Russell Sage Foundation, 2008.

Strolovitch, Dara Z. *Affirmative Advocacy: Race, Class, and Gender in Interest Group Politics.* Chicago: University of Chicago Press, 2007.

Wong, Carolyn. *Lobbying for Inclusion: Rights, Politics, and the Making of Immigration Policy.* Palo Alto, Calif.: Stanford University Press, 2006.

chapter 16

Issue Advocacy Groups and Think Tanks

by Richard Skinner

THE TERM "THINK TANK" WAS first used during World War II to describe secure environments where top secret matters could be discussed freely. Paul Dickson elegantly defines a think tank as a "bridge between knowledge and power"; Andrew Rich describes it as an "independent, non-interest-based, nonprofit" institute that produces and relies on "expertise and ideas to obtain support and to influence the policymaking process."[1] Unlike universities, think tanks do not offer undergraduate classes, although a few have bestowed graduate degrees, most notably the RAND Corporation. Think tanks are more intimately involved with the policy process, usually operate on shorter time horizons, and produce work accessible to those outside academia.[2] Unlike most other interest groups, think tanks generally do not have an explicit constituency. Although they may have ideological biases, they do not contribute to campaigns or endorse candidates.[3] Think tanks also may have close links to policymakers and may receive public contracts, but they are not part of the normal governmental structure. Their independence from bureaucratic controls can be a significant asset to think tanks. As Bruce Smith explains:

> Systematic and imaginative policy research generally seems difficult to perform within an agency having responsibility for policy or operations. The pressure-ridden atmosphere of government agencies does not lend itself to the sort of intellectual "climate" conducive for creative policy research. And (what may amount to the same thing in practical terms) the individuals with the requisite research skills are difficult to recruit for direct government employment because they have become acclimated through years of training to an academic-type atmosphere.[4]

Estimates from the past two decades show about 100 think tanks operating in Washington and between 600 and 1,000 nationwide.[5] The most influential institutes are located in Washington, New York, or Los Angeles, but numerous others are located in state capitals and focus on issues facing state government.[6] Think tanks vary greatly in size and scope. Many small think tanks may have only a handful of researchers, rely heavily on outside academics working on contract, and focus on only one issue area. Larger organizations may have about a dozen fellows, writing papers on a limited number of topics. The biggest and best-established think tanks, such as RAND or the Brookings Institution, may have more than 100 fellows and research assistants, covering the full gamut of policy issues.[7]

THINK TANKS AS INTEREST GROUPS

Think tanks have many of the same characteristics as other interest groups. In their early days, they often benefited from outside patrons. Jerome Greene, secretary of the Rockefeller Foundation, was critical to the formation of the Institute of Governmental Research (IGR), a progenitor of Brookings, and Henry "Hap" Arnold, chief of staff of the U.S. Army Air Force, essentially created RAND. Entrepreneurs may assume the costs of starting a think tank and may dominate their organization for years to come. Examples include Wesley Mitchell of the National Bureau of Economic Research and Bob Greenstein of the Center for Budgetary and Policy Priorities. The excellent reputations of these institutions reflect in large part the respect that policymakers held for the integrity and ability of their founders. Other leaders may not have technically created their think tanks, but still may be widely credited with their rise to prominence. William Baroody Sr. and Hamilton Fish Armstrong dominated the American Enterprise Institute and the Council on Foreign Relations, respectively, for a generation each. Both organizations encountered significant difficulty in replacing them.

Like other interest groups, think tanks need to engage in organizational maintenance. To continue functioning, think tanks may need to shift their mission, seek new sources of funding, or adjust to a changing political climate. With the rise of media-savvy conservative research institutes such as the Heritage Foundation in the 1970s and 1980s, established players such as Brookings embraced more aggressive public relations. When the Pentagon reduced its spending on research and development during

MAJOR THINK TANK CONTRIBUTIONS TO POLICY DEBATES

- The Institute for Government Research's work on behalf of an executive budget process, which culminated in the Budget and Accounting Act of 1921.
- The studies conducted during World War II by the Council on Foreign Relations and the Committee for Economic Development on the shape of the postwar world, especially on the development of the global economy.
- The popularization of Keynesian ideas by the Committee for Economic Development in the 1940s and by the Brookings Institution in the 1950s.
- RAND's highly influential work on nuclear strategy in the 1950s, which contributed heavily to actions later taken by the Kennedy administration.
- The work by Brookings and the American Enterprise Institute on the deregulation of trucking, airlines, and telecommunications, which did much to shape policy actions taken in the late 1970s and early 1980s.
- The years of studies by conservative and centrist think tanks on the problems of long-term assistance to the poor, which provided valuable data that informed the 1996 reform of welfare.

the Vietnam War, RAND successfully expanded its mission to include more work on domestic issues. Similarly, when President Ronald Reagan slashed spending for evaluation of antipoverty programs, the Urban Institute expanded its sources of funding to include more overseas clients.

Like other interest groups, think tanks can fail to maintain themselves. A changing political climate may push a research institute out of the mainstream, reducing its capacity to influence public policy or gain favorable publicity. Charges of "fellow traveling" with Communists destroyed the Institute of Pacific Relations in the 1950s and later badly damaged the Institute for Policy Studies. During the New Deal era, the Brookings Institution's reputation for dowdy conservatism alienated foundations and academia, cutting it off from vital sources of funding and personnel.

Think tanks may be unable to replace a charismatic leader. Despite building a respected reputation in progressive circles, the Center for the Study of Democratic Institutions never escaped the shadow of its founder, former University of Chicago president Robert Maynard Hutchins, and it expired within a few years of his death. The center suffered from many problems common among think tanks—insecure funding, extravagant spending, vagueness of purpose, an inability to attract personnel to match its ambitions, a failure to adapt to changing times—but its dominance by Hutchins posed particular problems. Mary Ann Dzuback argues: "The center's demise occurred because Hutchins was so much a part of its definition that when his health failed, there was not enough of a commitment to the idea on which it was based to sustain it."[8] Hutchins had founded the center in 1959 as a spin-off of the Fund for the Republic, a civil libertarian group that was itself an outgrowth of the Ford Foundation. Although the center published a respected magazine and held some well-attended conferences, its "dialogues" among eminent scholars failed to fulfill Hutchins's extravagant visions. Milton Mayer described the center as the "lengthened shadow of Robert Maynard Hutchins"; its uncertain mission kept it from establishing a clear identity independent of its founder.[9] His advanced age and declining health discouraged donor interest in building a long-term endowment, and his successor left office after only a year, after repeated conflicts with the board of trustees, forcing the ailing Hutchins to resume command. After his death in 1977, the center failed to find a lasting leader or a source of funding, and was forced to close.

To continue functioning, think tanks need to secure funding. As of the early twenty-first century, RAND is by far the wealthiest think tank, with an annual budget of about $200 million, overwhelmingly funded by contracts for clients, especially the U.S. government. The Brookings Institution, the Heritage Foundation, and the Hoover Institution each spend more than $30 million a year. Smaller institutes may have budgets of only a million or two.[10] Think tanks have often enjoyed exceptionally close relationships with philanthropic foundations; indeed the two entities can be said to have come of age together. The Carnegie Corporation helped give birth to the National Bureau of Economic Research, and the Rockefeller Foundation was intimately involved in the creation of the Institute for Government Research (IGR). In the 1970s a network of conservative foundations helped create the intellectual infrastructure that contributed to the Reagan administration. The Tax Reform Act of 1969 discouraged such close relationships by increasing a foundation's legal liability when it provided more than one-third of an organization's budget.[11] Wealthy individuals also provide much support for think tanks: Andrew Carnegie and Robert Brookings gave so much that their names now are emblazoned upon research institutes. The Heritage Foundation pioneered the use of direct mail in the 1970s, and conservative think tanks have henceforth remained heavily dependent upon small individual gifts.[12] The federal government began contracting out research to

Members of think tanks can influence policy by sharing their research with Congress. Here, scholars from the Heritage Foundation, Council on Foreign Relations, and the Center for Security Policy speak before the House Armed Services Committee on the national security implications of the potential takeover of six U.S. ports by a company based in Dubai in 2006.

think tanks after World War II. Federal grants remain central to the funding of RAND, the National Bureau of Economic Research, and the Urban Institute.

Some think tanks have internal resources that can support their activities. A few of the largest and oldest think tanks, such as Brookings, have endowments that lend them greater stability even in difficult times. In addition, Brookings is among those think tanks that generate significant income through the sale of books, journals, and monographs, and through the rental of data produced in-house. Think tanks may also make money by providing training and holding conferences for policymakers and business executives.

THINK TANK STRUCTURE AND PERSONNEL

Most think tanks are formally operated by a board of trustees, who are usually prominent figures from the worlds of politics, business, and education. Harold Orlans asserts that these boards "establish, review, and legitimate broad institutional policies and objectives" and "act as an intermediary and a buffer between an institute, sponsors, and the public." [13] They rarely involve themselves in the day-to-day business of a research institute, but they may intervene to redefine its mission or replace its leadership.

The staff of the think tank is headed by a chief executive, usually with the title of president or director. These positions can be both rewarding and demanding. On the one hand, think tank director can operate without the constraints inflicted upon a university president. There are no student protests, no alumni questioning decisions, no state legislature cutting the budget, and no tenured faculty free to criticize on a whim.[14] On the other hand, think tank directors must be administrative managers, public intellectuals, fund-raisers, and chief researchers all at once. As a result, these positions are difficult to fill. Some think tank directors, such as Harold Moulton of Brookings and Ed Feulner of the Heritage Foundation, have stayed in power for decades. By contrast, junior staff, such as those who handle public relations, may experience rapid turnover. Many young people new to Washington may begin their careers as researchers or administrative personnel at think tanks, with the goal of moving on quickly. But the heart of think tanks is their team of research scholars and fellows. They include, among others, academics who prefer a less restrictive setting, former officeholders who enjoy the opportunity to think and write at leisure, and policy specialists who benefit from having institutional support for their research. These are the personnel who publish books, conduct research projects, testify before congressional hearings, answer media queries, and perform all the other tasks central to a think tank's functioning. Many younger, smaller institutes rely heavily on outside researchers, who may lend their expertise by contract, but are not employed by think tanks full-time.[15]

TAX STATUS OF THINK TANKS

Think tanks are usually organized under Section 501(c)(3) of the Internal Revenue Code. This classification is a double-edged sword. Since 1917 contributions to a 501(c)(3) organization have been tax-deductible, providing a potent incentive to donors. But for almost as long, such groups have been generally forbidden to lobby public officials or take part in political campaigns.[16] This is not an idle threat. The American Enterprise Institute was forced to operate with much greater discretion after the IRS accused it of excessive entanglement with Barry Goldwater's 1964 presidential campaign.

WHAT DO THINK TANKS THINK ABOUT?

Think tanks are probably best known for developing policy ideas: defining problems, producing proposals, and gauging the impact of existing programs. Relatively few think tanks produce much original data—it is expensive, time-consuming, and unpredictable—but those that do (such as the Brookings Institution, the Urban Institute, and the Center for Budget and Policy Priorities) often make data production a core area of expertise. Think tanks rarely develop entirely new ideas. More often, they engage in "research brokering," bringing academic concepts to the attention of policymakers, developing proposals in anticipation of the time when enactment might be politically feasible.[17] In essence, think tanks act as middlemen, more practical-minded than academic scholars, less caught up in the moment than officeholders. The independence of think tanks allows them to develop policy ideas without immediate concern for their political impact. As Martha Derthick and Paul Quirk explain, "the indifference of academic analysts to short-term feasibility" helps expand the array of policy changes available in the long term.[18]

Think tanks can market ideas to policymakers, either directly or through the media. The Brookings Institution, the Carnegie Endowment for International Peace, and the Council on Foreign Relations publish influential journals as well as numerous books and monographs. Journalists frequently turn to think tank scholars for commentary on current events, and many institutes expend great effort to place opinion articles in influential outlets. Bruce L. R. Smith notes that policymakers often have little time to read books.[19] Think tanks need to adapt to policymakers' schedules by presenting ideas through in-person briefings or short-form written material.[20] Seminars and conferences can also provide a valuable means of bringing together government officials, academics, journalists, and business executives to discuss policy issues. Andrew Rich argues that think tanks are likely to have their greatest impact early in the policymaking process, defining a problem, proposing possible solutions, and doing the foundational work that those more engaged in the political game may lack the time to do.[21] As the process continues, research institutes lose most of their influence, as the outlines of the debate become set. Think tanks can also serve as part of a career track for policy experts who may have spent time in academia or government, and may return in the near future. They often advise presidential campaigns and transitions, providing them both with policy ideas and future administration appointees.[22] Of course, the think tanks of today have evolved over many decades. What follows is a brief history of this development. This background sheds light on the reasons that some think tanks were able to grow and prosper whereas others lost influence and declined by failing to respond to changing circumstances.

THE BIRTH OF THINK TANKS

As the Industrial Revolution radically altered life in the United States of the late nineteenth century, a new breed of social scientists sought engagement with the problems besetting an industrializing United States.[23] But efforts at social change, even of the most conservative "economy and efficiency" sort, inevitably ran into an obstacle in the inadequacy of the American state. Unlike its European counterparts, the United States had developed popular politics before creating a modern administrative apparatus. Instead, American politics was dominated by party leaders, and government positions mostly went to patronage employees who had proven their loyalty through campaign work. The civil service movement that arose after the Civil War scored some modest victories: the creation of the Civil Service Commission in 1871 and the passage of the Pendleton Civil Service Act in 1883. Some positions were put on the "merit system," examinations were required, salary scales established, but the power and prestige of the career civil service remained limited.[24]

Seeking to ameliorate social conditions (or to improve their image), civic-minded businessmen endowed foundations to pursue "scientific charity": the Russell Sage Foundation (1907, often considered the first "think tank"), the Carnegie Corporation (1911), the Carnegie Endowment for International Peace (1913), and the Rockefeller Foundation (1913).[25] In New York City, Frederick Cleveland and two associates founded the Bureau of Municipal Research (1907), which sought to apply business methods to the study of the public sector.[26] President William Howard Taft, who shared the bureau's emphasis on an executive budget, appointed Cleveland as chairman of the Commission on Economy and Efficiency in 1910. Cleveland assembled a blue-ribbon staff that included Frank Goodnow, an administrative law professor at Columbia, and William F. Willoughby, a prominent statistician who had held a variety of high-level government positions.[27] The "Taft Commission" proposed an executive budget in a 1912 report. But Congress feared such concentration of power in the president's hands and immediately dismissed the idea.

Cleveland, Goodnow, and Willoughby were not willing to let the commission's work die. Cleveland suggested to Jerome Greene, secretary of the Rockefeller Foundation, that the federal government needed a national version of the Bureau of Municipal Research, a nonpartisan institute devoted to government efficiency. Greene rounded up corporate and academic support for the Institute for Government Research; he selected Goodnow as chairman of the board of trustees and Willoughby as director.[28]

As soon as Willoughby took over the institute in 1916, he committed it to the struggle for a national budget. The outbreak of World War I only reemphasized the disorderly condition of the American state. Willoughby organized congressional hearings, drafted bills, and hired public relations specialists in the pursuit of his campaign. President Woodrow Wilson vetoed the first budget legislation over a constitutional issue, but his successor, Warren Harding, signed the Budget and Accounting Act into law in 1921.[29]

WAR, DEPRESSION, AND THE NEED FOR EXPERTISE: THINK TANKS, 1917–1945

After the U.S. entry into World War I, Wilson was forced to bring in academics and business executives to manage the war effort and plan for the postwar settlement. The War Industries Board (WIB), tasked with managing defense production, hired numerous economists and statisticians (including the staff of the IGR) to monitor the nation's financial health. These experts quickly understood the poor state of the federal government's economic data.[30] In September 1917, at Wilson's direction, a planning staff was assembled (soon known simply as "the Inquiry") that included many of the era's leading academics and journalists. Their findings became an important foundation for Wilson's "Fourteen Points."[31]

But after the armistice of November 1918, Wilson quickly disassembled the intellectual apparatus of the American war effort. Many scholars were frustrated by their experience. Frequently, the WIB lacked the necessary data to make economic decisions. Members of the Inquiry found themselves ignored at the Paris Peace Conference and commiserated with similarly alienated members of the British delegation. The two groups quickly found common ground and began plans for a joint Anglo-American institution to study international affairs, but postwar tensions soon made a bi-national organization unlikely.[32] So the group of Inquiry veterans (with the assistance of some influential New Yorkers) created the Council on Foreign Relations in 1921; Hamilton Fish Armstrong, a young journalist, served as the CFR's executive director. He dominated the CFR and its influential journal, *Foreign Affairs*, until his retirement in 1972.[33]

Economist Wesley Mitchell had run the War Industries Board's Price Section, where he was constantly frustrated by the lack of sound statistics. After the war, with funding from the Rockefeller Foundation, Mitchell created the National Bureau of Economic Research, which quickly became the nation's leading source of data on the business cycle. The NBER built a reputation for integrity, nonpartisanship, and high academic standards, which it has maintained to this day.[34]

Similarly, Robert Brookings, a St. Louis businessman, came away from his wartime experience with a new commitment to improved economic research. His friendship with Andrew Carnegie landed him on the Taft Commission and the board of the Institute for Government Research. These activities, in turn, led Wilson to appoint him to the WIB. At war's end, Brookings assumed the chairmanship of the IGR, where he soon became a dominant figure. In 1922 Brookings founded the Institute of Economics and, two years later, the Robert Brookings Graduate School of Economics and Government. The three entities were technically separate, but in fact deeply entangled. Their institutional culture differed substantially, and their leaders clashed frequently. The three entities were merged in 1927 to form the Brookings Institution.[35]

The New Deal led to an unprecedented need for experts in government, and yet it also posed dilemmas for the community of policy intellectuals and the think tanks that housed them. The government was developing its own internal sources of expertise and no longer depended as much on outsiders. Roosevelt's political wheeling-and-dealing and his lack of concern for policy coherence dismayed many Progressives devoted to "good government" and hostile to party machines. Harold Moulton, the economist who served as Brookings president from 1927 to 1952, became deeply alienated from the New Deal, and emerged as a conservative spokesman and an opponent of Keynesian economics. Brookings, while still respected for its technical expertise, was increasingly marginal to academic thinking and political debates.[36]

As with its predecessor, World War II greatly expanded the government's need for technical expertise. Even before the United States entered the war, the Council on Foreign Relations was conducting its War and Peace Studies to develop long-term paths for the nation as a superpower. The studies emerged from meetings in 1939 between the CFR leadership and top State Department officials. The government lacked the capacity for long-term studies of the kind envisaged by the council; to ensure independence, funding came from the Rockefeller Foundation.[37]

The businessmen who created the Committee for Economic Development (CED) thought about the postwar world along similar lines to those followed at the CFR. With the encouragement of Secretary of Commerce Jesse Jones, corporate executives friendly to the New Deal, such as Studebaker president Paul Hoffman and advertising magnate William Benton, created the committee in 1942 as an alternative to more conservative organizations such as the National Association of Manufacturers. Supported by a staff of academic economists, the CED embraced Keynesianism as an alternative both to national planning and to laissez-faire. Its proposals underlay the Employment Act of 1946, which created the Council of Economic Advisers (CEA). Beardsley Ruml, a veteran of the Rockefeller Foundation, the University of Chicago, and the New York Federal Reserve Bank, became the CED's dominant intellectual force, spearheading establishment acceptance of Keynesian ideas.[38] Think tanks were showing their ability to not just to analyze policy, but to shape it, in the manner of other interest groups.

TECHNOCRATIC LIBERALISM AND ITS CRITICS: THINK TANKS, 1945–1969

Henry Arnold, the U.S. Army Air Force chief of staff created Project RAND (short for "research and development") as a subsidiary of Douglas Aircraft in 1946; but the relationship proved uncomfortable, and it was spun off as an independent nonprofit corporation two years later. Franklin Collbohm, a Douglas Aircraft engineer, who served as RAND's president for two decades, quickly established a permissive, individualistic culture that attracted many of the era's leading minds.[39]

RAND rapidly moved beyond a narrow focus on technical issues facing the air force. Its very first report, issued in 1946, proposed the construction of an earth-orbiting satellite.[40] It benefited from steady support at the highest levels of the air force, but it also received funding from the nation's leading foundations and eventually from the Atomic Energy Commission and the National Aeronautics and Space Administration. Financially secure and physically separated from the Pentagon (it was and is headquartered in Santa Monica, California), RAND enjoyed enormous independence and acquired impressive prestige. It absorbed numerous academics interested in the strategic implications of the atomic bomb. Heavily influenced by the polymath John von Neumann, RAND became a pioneer in game theory and computing. Mathematician Edwin Paxson transformed the wartime technique of operations research into the much broader field of systems analysis.[41]

In the 1950s RAND made its greatest contribution through its studies of nuclear strategy. A clique of scientists and mathematicians made it their mission to "think about the unthinkable." This group included political scientists Bernard Brodie and William Kaufmann, physicists Bruno Augenstein and Herman Kahn, and economists Henry Rowen and Andrew Marshall. Kahn's flamboyance would eventually make him by far the most famous (he allegedly served as the model for Dr. Strangelove), but the most influential member of this crowd was mathematician Albert Wohlstetter. In 1953 Wohlstetter produced a study of the vulnerability of Strategic Air Command bases to a surprise Soviet attack. Wohlstetter urged the air force to upgrade its early-warning radar system, to better protect its repair and fueling systems, and to abandon stationing bombers overseas. Not only were Wohlstetter's recommendations adopted, but also his study proved vastly influential in broader contexts. It legitimized nuclear strategy as a field of inquiry. It greatly increased concern about the possibility of a Soviet first strike and it showed the utility of RAND's mode of operations, especially its freedom from bureaucratic control.[42] With its growing prestige, RAND made further contributions in strategic studies as the decade approached an end. Concerned about the possibility of an accidental nuclear war, Wohlstetter devised a "fail-safe" procedure in which bombers would pause at a series of checkpoints to await confirmation of an actual conflict; should no such assurance come, the bombers would return to their bases.[43] RAND scientists also pushed for the development of intercontinental ballistic missiles, and helped conceive the ideas behind the first spy, weather, and communications satellites.[44]

But RAND analysts were especially active in formulating a critique of "massive retaliation": the policy enunciated by President Dwight Eisenhower and Secretary of State John Foster Dulles that the United States might respond to Soviet aggression anywhere on the globe with an enormous atomic attack on the USSR itself. Kaufmann, Kahn, and other members of the RAND clique of strategic thinkers instead offered a policy of "counterforce," using nuclear weapons sparingly against military targets only, while holding a reserve for further action should the Soviets not back down. Thinkers affiliated with the CFR also shared the RANDites' disdain for "massive retaliation," with Henry Kissinger's widely read *Nuclear Weapons and Foreign Policy* (1957) providing the most influential summary of their perspective.[45]

During his 1960 bid for the presidency, John F. Kennedy seized upon many of the ideas of the RAND strategic clique, with Wohlstetter and Marshall advising his campaign on nuclear issues. Kennedy warned of a "missile gap" that would lead to Soviet nuclear superiority; RAND studies, based on air force intelligence, had dwelled on the same (nonexistent) threat. Kennedy appointed Ford Motor president Robert McNamara as his secretary of defense. Quantitatively minded and familiar with operations research from his wartime work for the U.S. Army Air Force, McNamara was a natural ally of think tank intellectuals. He filled the Pentagon with RAND sages rapidly dubbed the "Whiz Kids" who helped him overhaul the defense budget and increase his power over the individual services. RAND analyst Daniel Ellsberg helped in the radical overhaul of the nation's plans for a nuclear war, injecting notions of counterforce and flexible response into what had been a rigid plan for massive retaliation. McNamara's revolution at the Pentagon increased RAND's prestige even

Dr. Louis A. Giamboni and Elaine Renner carry out secret research with the TRAC machine at the RAND Corporation in 1958. During the 1950s RAND carried out influential research, most notably in defense matters.

further, making it the emblematic "think tank," and allowing its alumni to fill critical posts in government, industry, and academia.[46] Kahn himself was too outrageous for government service. But his works *On Thermonuclear War* (1960) and *Thinking About the Unthinkable* (1962) made him a household name, and he soon left RAND to create his own think tank, the Hudson Institute.[47] But RAND's heyday would be brief. Many uniformed personnel (especially, ironically enough, in the air force) came to loath what they saw as the arrogance of the Whiz Kids. Doves found them to be cold-blooded technocrats, cavalierly discussing the deaths of tens of millions. The missile gap proved nonexistent, and two of the RANDites' favorite notions, civil defense and counterforce, found only limited applicability.[48] The Vietnam War increasingly soaked up resources that might have been available to RAND. Many saw the quagmire in Southeast Asia as the ultimate example of the failures of technocratic notions of "limited war." With its Pentagon support on the decline, in the late 1960s RAND looked to diversify its financial support and research agenda. In 1967 economist Henry Rowen replaced Collbohm as RAND's president. The institute won more grants from foundations, foreign governments, and states and municipalities; by 1970, one-quarter of its funding came from nondefense sources.[49]

Despite the rise of RAND, the Council on Foreign Relations retained its prestige in the years after World War II. It increased its professional staff and gained greater support from foundations. The CFR's meetings and publications continued to be leading venues for statements by important policymakers. The council remained a voice of internationalist "establishment" opinion, firmly supporting NATO and the Marshall Plan. It weathered assaults from conservatives and isolationists to retain influence in both Democratic and Republican administrations, especially within the State Department.[50]

The power of think tank intellectuals in postwar America was not limited to foreign policy. If RAND and the CFR were the centers of technocratic liberalism as the United States became a superpower, Brookings performed a similar function as the federal government increased its role in the economy. Economist Robert Calkins, a veteran of the Committee on Economic Development and the Rockefeller Foundation, took over the institution's presidency in 1952. Unlike his predecessor, Harold Moulton, Calkins proved to be a pillar of the liberal establishment, building close ties with prominent foundations and assembling a staff that included several of the nation's leading Keynesian economists. Calkins quickly built strong relationships between Brookings and pivotal bureaucrats, congressional staffers, and policymakers, particularly among liberal Democrats. Brookings's strength in economic research gave it special influence over the Bureau of the Budget and the Council of Economic Advisers during the Kennedy-Johnson era.[51]

The institution's ethos fit an era of "liberal consensus," of optimism about the capabilities of government, of confidence that fundamental ideological questions had been answered. President Lyndon Johnson especially embraced social science as a tool that could inform policymaking. The rapid growth of social services under the Great Society led to a greater need for program evaluation. With skepticism growing about the effectiveness of many new initiatives, Johnson called for the creation of an "urban RAND" that would employ the latest techniques. In 1968 the Urban Institute was created, with funding from three cabinet departments, as well as from the Ford Foundation. The Urban Institute emulated RAND in its dependence on government contracts, and its president, William Gorham, was a veteran of RAND as well as of the Pentagon and the Department of Health, Education, and Welfare. The Urban Institute proved to be anything but a slavish supporter of the Great Society. Many of its analyses of War on Poverty programs found them to be ill-conceived or poorly administrated. By the end of the 1960s, even liberal technocrats were losing faith in the ability of government to solve social problems.[52]

Think tanks were coming under fire from critics all along the ideological spectrum. Through legislation and committee hearings, congressional critics reined in the political activities of foundations. The Vietnam War undermined the reputation of technocratic expertise, especially that of RAND and the CFR, which had supported U.S. involvement in Southeast Asia and provided advice to the government on the conduct of the war.[53] Both entities, traditionally centers of establishment consensus, saw bitter internal disputes as the war persisted. Most notably, Daniel Ellsberg, a quintessential RAND analyst and veteran of McNamara's Pentagon, leaked to the press a top-secret history of the Vietnam War that became known as the "Pentagon Papers." The leak badly damaged RAND's relationship with the military and forced the resignation of RAND president Henry Rowen.[54]

Both sides of the political spectrum developed critiques of technocratic liberalism. The New Left criticized "objective" expertise as simply another element of a soul-crushing social hierarchy and saw many think tanks as tools of the military-industrial complex. These forces had their own research institution in the Institute for Policy Studies, founded by two former Kennedy administration officials in 1963. Funded by wealthy liberals and some small foundations, the IPS became a favorite of many left-leaning intellectuals, the antiwar movement, and the 1972 presidential campaign of George McGovern.[55]

If technocratic liberalism's critics on the Left often received the most publicity, its opponents on the Right proved to be more influential. A small group of right-leaning think tanks gained prominence as the conservative movement increased its political relevance in the late 1960s. Founded as a probusiness advocacy group in 1943, the American Enterprise Association remained little known until General Electric president A. D. Marshall took over its command a decade later. He soon hired two staff economists from the U.S. Chamber of Commerce, William Baroody Sr. and W. Glenn Campbell, to remodel the stagnant organization. Baroody proved to be an organizational wizard and a master fund-raiser, and he made the renamed American Enterprise Institute into the premier exponent of free-market thought in the 1960s. Baroody placed special value on establishing AEI's intellectual respectability and built ties to conservative thinkers such as economist Milton Friedman. But Baroody also was an enthusiastic supporter of Barry Goldwater's 1964 presidential campaign, and his work on its behalf led to investigations by congressional critics and the Internal Revenue Service. AEI was forced into a stance of cautious detachment from the political process, eventually opening room for more engaged think tanks on the Right.

During the First World War, Herbert Hoover became concerned about the need to preserve records from this tumultuous era; in 1919 he gave his budding collection to his alma mater, Stanford University, establishing the Hoover War Library. The archives eventually also encompassed the Second World War and the rise of fascism and communism. At the end of the 1950s Hoover pushed for what had become the Hoover Institution to adopt a stronger conservative, anticommunist ethos. After winning greater independence from Stanford, the institution lured Campbell away from AEI to serve as its president. Campbell made the Hoover Institution into the West Coast equivalent of AEI: a right-leaning think tank with strong academic credentials and valuable ties to the political circles of Barry Goldwater and Ronald Reagan.[56]

AEI encouraged the rise of another conservative think tank in the 1960s. The Center for Strategic and International Studies was founded in 1962 by Adm. Arleigh Burke, former chief of naval operations, and David Abshire, who had worked in turn as a military officer, an academic historian, and a congressional staffer, and would later serve in the Nixon and Reagan administrations. CSIS exuded a more humanistic and tradition-minded ethos than the quantitative orientation of RAND; its conservative, anticommunist politics gave it entrée in Republican circles. Gradually its views became less distinctive, and it became a favorite base for former officeholders such as Secretary of State Henry Kissinger.[57]

THE RISE OF THE NEW RIGHT: THINK TANKS, 1969–1981

Despite the growing prominence of right-leaning think tanks, the Nixon administration found itself dependent on the Brookings Institution, the Urban Institute, RAND, and the Council of Foreign Relations for advice, even though they were often home to veterans of the Kennedy and Johnson administrations. Conservatives inside and outside the administration bemoaned the power of a "permanent government" of high-level civil servants, policy intellectuals, establishment journalists, and congressional staffers.[58] Nixon advisers such as speechwriter Patrick Buchanan urged greater attention to building a conservative intellectual infrastructure that could develop policy alternatives, coordinate media communications, and serve as a "talent bank" for future Republican administrations. The same idea occurred to two conservative Republican staffers on Capitol Hill, Ed Feulner and Paul Weyrich. Both men were frustrated by what they saw as the centrism of the Nixon administration, the nonideological approach of congressional Republican leaders, and by the cautious tone of AEI. In 1973 Feulner and Weyrich first founded the Republican Study Committee and then the Heritage Foundation. Heritage would be a new kind of think tank, an "advocacy think tank" that made no pretense at objectivity and that would use the media aggressively to disseminate its ideological message. Heritage was funded not by the likes of the Rockefeller and Ford Foundations, but by wealthy conservatives such as Richard Mellon Scaife, brewer Joseph Coors, and oilman Edward Noble. It also became the first think tank to employ direct-mail fund-raising.

If Brookings and the CFR tended to produce earnest book-length studies, Heritage preferred backgrounders and bulletins that would pass what Feulner called the "briefcase test": a policymaker could take one out of a briefcase, and digest it while riding to work. Rather than the quasi-academic tone of earlier think tanks, Heritage adopted the traditional methods of lobbyists: pithy, accessible information that supports a specific policy outcome. It built a staff of young conservative intellectuals, who became used to writing on tight deadlines and were more comfortable in Republican congressional offices than in faculty lounges. Heritage quickly equaled or exceeded the influence wielded by AEI and Hoover in conservative circles. As the media noticed the rise of the New Right in the late 1970s, they increasingly turned to Heritage fellows for timely, glib commentary. As more conservative Republicans gained power, they used Heritage's "talent bank" to find potential staffers.[59]

Heritage's success helped fuel an explosion in conservative think tanks in the late 1970s and early 1980s. These included the Institute for Contemporary Studies (1974), the Ethics and Public Policy Center (1976), the Cato Institute (1977), the Manhattan Institute (1978), and the Competitive Enterprise Institute (1984). These organizations owed much of their power to a new network of conservative funders: not only individuals such as Coors, Scaife, and the members of the Koch family (especially important in libertarian circles), but also a number of foundations: John M. Olin, Bradley, Smith Richardson, and Lilly. Much of their giving was coordinated by the neoconservative intellectual Irving Kristol and by former Treasury secretary William Simon.[60]

The growth of the New Right was not limited to new institutions. William Baroody Sr. continued to promote the AEI energetically. If Heritage had outflanked it on the Right, there was still room for AEI to serve as the favorite think tank of establishment Republicans. Many veterans of the Nixon and Ford administrations joined AEI after leaving government service. These included Secretary of Defense Melvin Laird, Federal Reserve chairman Arthur Burns, CEA chairman Herbert Stein, and even former president Ford. At a time when free-market ideas were gaining greater acceptance, AEI amassed an outstanding team of conservative economic thinkers, including James C. Miller III, Murray Weidenbaum, Paul MacAvoy, Antonin Scalia, and Robert Bork. Weidenbaum's *Government Mandated Price Increases* and Bork's *The Antitrust Paradox* proved especially influential in policy debates. AEI also became a popular perch for many neoconservatives, former Democrats disillusioned by what they saw as the party's leftward turn. Irving Kristol joined the institute in 1976 and soon brought along foreign policy thinker Jeane Kirkpatrick and public opinion analyst Ben Wattenberg.[61] AEI served as a means for many neoconservatives to build ties with the Republican Party and the business community.[62] But neoconservatives soon joined other right-leaning think tanks, including the Heritage Foundation and the Ethics and Public Policy Center, as their loyalty to the Democratic Party waned.

Free market thought spread well beyond conservative circles in the 1970s. The role played by Brookings and AEI in bringing economic deregulation to the attention of policymakers is often cited as a prime example of the political impact of policymakers. In the 1950s and 1960s academic economists became increasingly critical of New Deal-era regulations of trucking, telecommunications, and airlines. They argued that these restrictions prevented competition, which in turn led to high prices, poor service, and slow growth. But these regulations served the interests of existing producers and the labor unions that represented their employees, which were able to win the support of policymakers.[63] Between 1967 and 1975 the Ford Foundation funded research on economic regulation at the Brookings Institution, apparently for no other reason than that it was an area that might reward greater investigation. AEI soon began its own studies. The two think tanks held regular conferences and workshops that brought the new academic consensus to the attention of policy experts. These events helped build a cadre of young economists and lawyers, who would later serve in government, especially the CEA and the Office of Management and Budget (OMB).[64] Free market Republicans (notably President Ford) and consumer-minded Democrats (especially Sen. Edward Kennedy, D-Mass.) both embraced greater competition, and, to the surprise of most observers, all three industries were deregulated by the early 1980s. The perceived success of deregulation led to an intellectual consensus among think tank intellectuals in favor of greater competition in telecommunications, which helped lay the groundwork for the Telecommunications Act of 1996.[65]

THE AGE OF IDEOLOGICAL WARFARE: THINK TANKS, 1981–1993

Conservative think tanks had a rare opportunity for influence during the Reagan administration. Drawing upon the experience of Brookings's role during the Kennedy transition, the Heritage Foundation and the Hoover Institution produced guides for beginning a new era of conservative governance: *Mandate for Leadership* and *The United States in 1980,* respectively. Both garnered massive attention from the press and policymakers. Given its strongly conservative cast, the Reagan administration needed to fill policymaking positions with those who possessed substantive expertise and ideological reliability. Think tanks, especially Heritage, Hoover, AEI, and CSIS, could easily fill these requirements, and their alumni were soon walking the corridors of power.

The new era forced existing think tanks to adapt. Just as cutbacks in defense research encouraged RAND to expand its efforts into domestic policy, reductions in federal spending on antipoverty and housing programs led the Urban Institute to seek support elsewhere, especially from foreign governments. Brookings moved away from its traditional emphasis on book-length studies and embraced shorter publications and more aggressive media outreach.[66] RAND continued to branch out, including accepting more overseas contracts, but the hawkish tone of the Reagan years suited it well, as defense spending soared, and many with ties to the Santa Monica beach gained high office. William Baroody Jr. replaced his father as president of AEI in 1978, but proved to be a disaster as a financial manager, and the board of trustees forced him out eight years later. He was replaced by Christopher DeMuth, a former top official at Reagan's OMB, who then led AEI for two decades.[67] Heritage has remained a powerful force among Republicans; its aggressive marketing of conservative proposals made it unusually influential during debates on telecommunications, health care, and welfare during the 1990s.[68] But other think tanks found it more difficult to adapt to changing times. The Institute for Policy Studies was badly damaged by internal disputes in the 1970s, by cutbacks in foundation support in the 1980s, and by an increasingly radical reputation that alienated more mainstream allies.[69] The Hudson Institute nearly collapsed after the death of founder Herman Kahn in 1983. The CFR lost much of its influence as elite consensus on foreign policy evaporated in the wake of Vietnam.[70]

Conservative "advocacy tanks" soon met with counterparts on the center-left, including the Center for Budget and Policy Priorities (1981), the Progressive Policy Institute (1989), the Economic Policy Institute (1985), and the World Policy Institute (1982).[71] More specialized think tanks emerged, particularly in foreign policy (the Institute for International Economics and the Henry Stimson Center)

CRITICISMS OF THINK TANKS

Populist: Think tanks' reverence for expertise produces an elitist ethos that does not easily coexist with popular control or open debate.

Leftist: Think tanks serve the interests of an oligarchy distrustful of democratic politics. They narrow the public agenda to issues that do not threaten the existing socioeconomic hierarchy. The wealthy individuals who serve on think tank boards of trustees and provide their funding have powerful stakes in a capitalist status quo.

Rightist: Think tank intellectuals form part of a "new class" of professionals who, even as they prosper from the fruits of capitalism, nevertheless encourage hostility to the very free enterprise system that supports their work.

and environmentalism (the Worldwatch Institute and the World Resources Institute). The growth in specialized groups reflected a tendency about foundations to prefer grants for narrowly focused projects with clear payoffs.

THINK TANKS TODAY, 1993–PRESENT

Think tanks have continued to move away from the older model of objectivity and generalism. "Vanity tanks" often have little identity apart from that of a founding personality. For example, since its creation in 1988, the Center for Security Policy has been dominated by Frank Gaffney Jr., a former official in Reagan's Defense Department, and his concern with ballistic missile defense. "Legacy tanks" founded by retired policymakers have also joined the ranks of research institutes. Former presidents Richard Nixon and Jimmy Carter founded organizations to pursue their commitments to national security and human rights, respectively. The lines between think tank research, political advocacy, and interest group lobbying have continued to blur. Several free market think tanks have been accused of pursuing research primarily to serve the needs of corporate sponsors. Old guard think tanks still remain the most respected by the media and policymakers; surveys find them holding in highest regard Brookings, CFR, RAND, and the Carnegie Endowment. Even in an ideological era, a reputation for disinterested expertise remains an asset.[72]

Liberals have followed conservatives in developing advocacy tanks. Organized labor sponsored the creation of the Economic Policy Institute in 1985, which has become particularly known for its criticism of free trade and for its biennial study, *The State of Working America.* Jared Bernstein, a longtime scholar at EPI, became chief economic adviser for Vice President Joseph Biden. Jeffrey Faux, a onetime member of Jimmy Carter's CEA, has headed EPI throughout its existence, and former secretary of labor Robert Reich and economics writer Robert Kuttner are among the charter members of the board of trustees who still serve.[73]

Moderate Democrats created the Democratic Leadership Council in 1985 to promote centrist ideas within the party.[74] From the beginning, DLC founder Al From entertained the notion of the organization creating an in-house think tank. After the 1988 election From and fellow DLC staffer Will Marshall planned an organization modeled on conservative advocacy tanks; they actually met with Heritage Foundation founder Ed Feulner to discuss plans for the group. Such a think tank would produce policy proposals accessible to political elites, hold seminars for policymakers, and publish a journal of progressive thought. The Progressive Policy Institute was incorporated in December 1988 and began in its activities the next year. Marshall has headed the PPI throughout its history, and the organization has consistently remained close to the DLC.

Bill Clinton headed the DLC before entering the 1992 presidential election, and his campaigns and administrations made us of DLC/PPI ideas on welfare reform, free trade, and national service. Following in the footsteps of

MAJOR THINK TANKS AND THEIR POLITICAL ORIENTATIONS

Conservative or Center-Right
American Enterprise Institute
Cato Institute
Center for Strategic and International Studies
Heritage Foundation
Hoover Institution
Lexington Institute
Manhattan Institute

Centrist
Aspen Institute
Brookings Institution
Carnegie Endowment
Center for Politics
Council on Foreign Relations
Institute for International Economics
Inter-American Dialogue
Kaiser Family Foundation
New America Foundation
Public Policy Institute of California
RAND Corporation

Progressive or Center-Left
Carter Center
Center for American Progress
Center for Economic and Policy Research
Center on Budget and Policy Priorities
Economic Policy Institute
Joint Center for Political and Economic Studies
Urban Institute

conservative think tanks, the DLC produced an influential guide for the Clinton transition, *Mandate For Change*. Veterans of the two organizations filled numerous positions in the administration. Bruce Reed (once policy director at the DLC, now the council's president) wrote several important Clinton speeches, helped develop Clinton's health care proposal during the 1992 campaign, served as a leading advocate of welfare reform, and eventually became White House domestic policy chief. Elaine Kamarck, once a PPI senior fellow, headed the Reinventing Government initiative. Jeremy Rosner, a health care analyst for PPI, helped promote the version of managed competition that became the centerpiece of the Clinton health care proposal.[75]

Most notably, the Center for American Progress (founded 2003) was created as a "Democratic Heritage" (AEI was once referred to as the "Republican Brookings"). Just as Heritage and AEI have provided holding places for Republican policymakers, CAP was founded by onetime Clinton White House chief of staff John Podesta, who later presided over Barack Obama's transition to power. Other veterans of the Clinton administration, such as CEA chair Laura D'Andrea Tyson and State Department official Morton Halperin, also joined CAP. Gene Sperling, who served as chairman of the National Economic Council under Clinton, joined CAP before later becoming counselor to Secretary of the Treasury Timothy Geithner. Within five years, CAP had acquired 180 employees and a $25 million budget, with much of its funding coming from prominent liberal donors such as financier George Soros and Progressive Insurance founder Peter Lewis. CAP was quick to use the Internet to promote progressive causes, hosting a group blog at ThinkProgress.org, and producing an electronic newsletter, "The Progress Report." It also provides communications material to the Senate Democratic Policy Committee.[76]

Several CAP veterans worked on the presidential nomination campaigns of Hillary Rodham Clinton and Obama. Denis McDonough, a senior fellow at CAP, served as a top foreign policy adviser to Obama during the 2008 election, and later served as chief of staff to the National Security Council.[77] Melody Barnes, a CAP veteran, became chair of the Domestic Policy Council. In his management of the Obama transition, Podesta was able to draw upon CAP's resources, including a variety of policy studies and an experienced staff. CAP produced a twenty-six-page report detailing the day-to-day activities of the early Obama presidency.[78]

Conservative think tanks enjoyed access to the George W. Bush administration much as they did with other Republican presidents. The Heritage Foundation provided advice on personnel during the transition.[79] Economists at the Hoover Institution, many of them veterans of previous Republican administrations, provided advice to Bush's 2000 presidential campaign. In 2005 Bush proposed adding private accounts to Social Security. The Cato Institute had advocated this idea since 1981, when it published Peter Ferrara's *Social Security: The Inherent Contradiction*. In 1998 Ed Crane of Cato met with then-governor Bush and found him to be an enthusiastic supporter of privatization. Andrew Biggs, a former Cato analyst, served as associate commissioner of the Social Security Administration. Other Cato alumni led advocacy groups supporting private accounts.[80]

The American Enterprise Institute, however, received the most attention for its role in the administration. Vice President Dick Cheney had been an AEI fellow in the 1990s. His wife, Lynne Cheney, continued to work there while her husband was in office. Lawrence Lindsey, director of the National Economic Council and principal author of the Bush tax cuts, was another AEI veteran. R. Glenn Hubbard joined AEI after serving as chairman of the Council of Economic Advisers, and John R. Bolton, a former AEI fellow, served in the State Department, and later became ambassador to the United Nations.[81]

But probably the most controversial aspect of AEI's influence was the role that neoconservatives played in the conduct of the Iraq War. AEI had a strong relationship with the neoconservative movement since Irving Kristol joined the think tank in 1976. Michael Ledeen, a veteran of Ronald Reagan's National Security Council, became a resident scholar at AEI, where he advocated a policy of overthrowing dictators, including Saddam Hussein. Richard Perle, a leading neoconservative who had served as a staffer to Sen. Henry Jackson, D-Wash., in the 1970s, and then as assistant secretary of defense for national security policy under Reagan, advocated regime change in the Middle East while based at AEI. David Wurmser, a protégé of Perle at AEI, promoted American support for an Iraqi insurgency against Hussein; he later became a top adviser to Cheney. Laurie Mylroie, a foreign policy scholar once aligned with the 1992 Clinton campaign, promoted the notion that Hussein was involved with the 1993 World Trade Center bombing. Mylroie served as a scholar at AEI and became close to Perle.[82]

Perle, who served as chair of the Defense Policy Board during the early years of the George W. Bush administration, emerged as an early supporter of war with Iraq, as did his fellow neoconservative (and longtime friend) Paul Wolfowitz, who would later join AEI himself after serving as deputy secretary of defense.[83] Perle and Wolfowitz were close allies of controversial Iraqi National Congress leader Ahmed Chalabi, who attended annual AEI conferences.[84] The *Weekly Standard*, founded by William Kristol (son of Irving Kristol), became an important outlet for neoconservatives close to AEI and committed to the ouster of Saddam Hussein. Think tank support for the Iraq War was not limited to conservatives; Will Marshall of the Progressive Policy

Institute and Kenneth Pollack of the Brookings Institution were also among the influential advocates of regime change.[85]

Other AEI veterans in the administration, such as Cheney, Wurmser and Bolton, were also leading hawks before and during the war. David Frum, the speechwriter who coined the phrase *axis of evil* for Bush's 2002 State of the Union address, joined AEI after leaving the White House. Frum was fired by AEI in March 2010 after he criticized Republican strategy on health care legislation; he had previously lambasted Sarah Palin and Rush Limbaugh.[86]

Even in an era of partisan polarization, some issues remain amenable to old-fashioned building of consensus. By the late 1990s both parties were open to a more centrist path on education. Republicans had suffered politically by limiting their education proposals to school vouchers and calling for the abolition of the Department of Education. Democrats were aware of widespread dissatisfaction with the performance of public schools and became more open to a greater emphasis on testing and standards. The Heritage Foundation, Brookings Institution, and Progressive Policy Institute led a new centrist critique that emphasized accountability and teacher quality, eventually influencing the No Child Left Behind Act of 2001.[87] But the influence of education research remains limited, given shaky methodology, accusations of politicization, and a disconnection from policy reality.[88]

The 1996 welfare reform bill offered an unusual opportunity for think tank influence. Few organized interests were active in the debate, allowing experts to supersede lobbyists in influence. Although the debate followed sharp ideological lines, nearly everyone agreed the existing system was not functioning well. Years of research had produced a consensus on the need to reduce long-term dependency. Conservative think tanks had led the criticism of welfare programs, dating back to the Manhattan Institute's support for Charles Murray's influential work *Losing Ground* (1984). The Cato Institute produced a widely read 1995 report arguing that welfare benefits often paid more than low-wage work. A relentless critic of welfare, Robert Rector of the Heritage Foundation, enjoyed great influence among congressional Republicans.[89]

But centrist or left-leaning institutes also shaped the welfare reform debate of the 1990s. The Urban Institute,

Upon the fiftieth anniversary of the Brookings Institution in 1966, President Lyndon Johnson remarked, "You are a national institution, so important to, at least, the Executive Branch—and, I think, the Congress, and the country—that if you did not exist we would have to ask someone to create you." In December 2009 President Barack Obama addressed scholars at the Brookings Institution on his economic policies.

Brookings, and the Center on Budget and Policy Priorities all gained influence through producing works summarizing the state of welfare policy research in a form that was accessible to policy professionals.[90] The CBPP especially benefited from the reputation of Robert Greenstein, its founder, for expertise, integrity, and political acumen. Greenstein had been the most influential advocate of the expansion of the earned income tax credit in the 1980s and early 1990s, a reform to help low-wage workers that appealed to many moderate Republicans and the so-called New Democrats.[91] In 2001 Greenstein helped lead efforts for an expanded child tax credit aimed at lower-income families, which became part of tax cut legislation signed by George W. Bush.[92]

CONCLUSION

Diane Stone argues that it is difficult to evaluate the importance of think tanks, because policymakers are reluctant to share credit for policy ideas. Many worthy reports and research studies may go unread. Much of the work done by think tanks, particularly those of a more ideological stripe, mostly serves to reinforce the existing views of policymakers. Andrew Rich suggests that think tanks have their greatest impact when they engage in "foundational research," defining problems, translating ideas into concrete policy proposals. They also contribute when they produce "hard data" such as cost estimates for proposed legislation, but relatively few institutes have such a capability. Rich suggests that think tanks have been seeing their collective credibility decline in recent years as competition for attention increases and as policymakers disregard work from ideologically hostile institutes. Focusing too much on short-term matters, such as commentary on pending legislation, may bring attention but not influence. When a think tank becomes simply another voice repeating a predictable mantra, it loses much of its "value."[93]

But Frederick Hess notes what he calls the "clarity, focus, and energy" of "advocacy tanks" that can "act and speak with more crispness and agility."[94] Think tanks share many of the characteristics of other interest groups. They need to find the means of keeping themselves in existence: establishing a purpose, raising money, finding supporters, and adjudicating internal conflicts. Leadership is vital to the establishment of a successful think tank: entrepreneurs to found an organization, patrons to provide essential outside support, and staff to manage day-to-day affairs. Think tanks need to build and maintain credibility with policymakers to preserve influence in policy debates. But think tanks do differ from other interest groups in some fundamental ways. Most still at least maintain the pretense of being "objective" seekers of truth, rather than representatives of a specific group with particular concerns. Although think tanks usually have some large individual supporters, and they may even have a number of small donors, they rarely make "member services" a core mission. Given their 501(c)3 status, think tanks, even highly ideological ones, avoid open advocacy for specific legislation. Much like other interest groups, think tanks are most often at the periphery of the policy process, dependent upon their influence on government officials.

NOTES

1. Paul Dickson, *Think Tanks* (New York: Ballantine Books, 1972), 28; Andrew Rich, *Think Tanks, Public Policy, and the Politics of Expertise* (New York: Cambridge University Press, 2004) 11–12.

2. Diane Stone, *Capturing the Political Imagination: Think Tanks and the Policy Process* (New York: Routledge, 1996), 13; Donald Abelson, *A Capital Idea: Think Tanks and U.S. Foreign Policy* (Montreal: McGill-Queen's University Press, 2006), 75–76.

3. Stone, *Capturing the Political Imagination*, 13–14.

4. Bruce L. R. Smith, *The RAND Corporation: A Case Study of a Nonprofit Advisory Corporation* (Cambridge: Harvard University Press, 1966), 243.

5. Andrew Rich, *Think Tanks, Public Policy, and the Politics of Expertise.* (New York: Cambridge University Press, 2004), 14–15.

6. James Allen Smith, *The Idea Brokers: Think Tanks and the Rise of the New Policy Elite* (New York: Free Press, 1991), xiv–xv.

7. David Ricci, *The Transformation of American Politics: The New Washington and the Rise of Think Tanks* (New Haven: Yale University Press, 1993), 1–6.

8. Mary Ann Dzuback, *Robert M. Hutchins: Portrait of an Educator* (Chicago: University of Chicago Press, 1991), 254.

9. Milton Mayer, *Robert Maynard Hutchins: A Memoir* (Berkeley: University of California Press, 1993), 485.

10. Abelson, *Capital Idea*, 9, 18, 45, 48.

11. Stone, *Capturing the Political Imagination*, 53–62.

12. Abelson, *Capital Idea*, 84–88.

13. Stone, *Capturing the Political Imagination*, 65; Harold Orlans, *The Nonprofit Research Institute: Its Origin, Operation, Problems, and Prospects* (New York: McGraw-Hill, 1972), 59–63.

14. Orlans, *Nonprofit Research Institute*, 63–64.

15. Stone, *Capturing the Political Imagination*, 66–68.

16. Jeffrey Berry, *A Voice for Nonprofits* (Washington, D.C.: Brookings Institution Press, 2003), 4.

17. Ricci, *Transformation of American Politics*, 104.

18. Martha Derthick and Paul Quirk, *The Politics of Deregulation* (Washington, D.C.: Brookings Institution Press, 1985), 247–248.

19. B. L. R. Smith, *RAND Corporation*, 277–283.

20. Abelson, *Capital Idea*, 9–18, 45–48.

21. Andrew Rich, *Think Tanks, Public Policy, and the Politics of Expertise* (New York: Cambridge University Press, 2004), 144–151.

22. Abelson, *Capital Idea*, 24–36.

23. Stephen Skowronek, *Building a New American State: The Expansion of Federal Administrative Capabilities, 1877–1920* (New York: Cambridge University Press, 1982), 46.

24. Ibid., 47–84.

25. Abelson, *Capital Idea,* 56–59; Leonard Silk and Mark Silk, *The American Establishment* (New York: Basic Books, 1980), 104–108, 153–160.

26. Donald Critchlow, *The Brookings Institution, 1916–1952: Expertise and the Public Interest in a Democratic Society* (DeKalb: Northern Illinois University Press, 1985), 17–28.

27. Skowronek, *Building a New American State,* 177–184; Critchlow, *Brookings Institution, 1916–1952,* 28–32.

28. Skowronek, *Building a New American State,* 194–206; Critchlow, *Brookings Institution, 1916–1952,* 28–33.

29. Critchlow, *Brookings Institution, 1916–1952,* 36–40.

30. Ibid., 41.

31. Robert Schulzinger, *Wise Men of Foreign Affairs: The History of the Council on Foreign Relations* (New York: Columbia University Press, 1984), 2–4; Ronald Steel, *Walter Lippmann and the American Century* (Boston: Little, Brown, 1980), 116–133.

32. Steel, *Walter Lippmann,* 150; Schulzinger, *Wise Men of Foreign Affairs,* 2–11; Abelson, *Capital Idea,* 71–74.

33. Schulzinger, *Wise Men of Foreign Affairs,* 5–11.

34. J. A. Smith, *Idea Brokers,* 62–67.

35. Abelson, *Capital Idea,* 59–64; Critchlow, *Brookings Institution, 1916–1952,* 56; Silk and Silk, *American Establishment,* 153–166.

36. Critchlow, *Brookings Institution, 1916–1952,* passim.

37. Schulzinger, *Wise Men of Foreign Affairs,* 33–43, 60–51, 81–94, 102–106.

38. John B. Judis, *The Paradox of American Democracy: Elites, Special Interests, and the Betrayal of the Public Trust* (New York: Routledge, 2001).

39. B. L. R. Smith, *RAND Corporation,* 49–65, 154–157.

40. Ibid., 49–65; Alex Abella, *Soldiers of Reason: The RAND Corporation and the Rise of American Empire* (Orlando: Harcourt, 2008), 19–20.

41. Fred Kaplan, *The Wizards of Armageddon* (New York: Simon and Schuster, 1983), 85–110; B. L. R. Smith, *RAND Corporation,* 6–8, 67–74; Orlans, *Nonprofit Research Institute,* 108–122; Abella, *Soldiers of Reason,* 57–63; Paul Dickson, *Think Tanks* (New York: Ballantine Books, 1972), 61–64, 67–71.

42. Kaplan, *Wizards of Armageddon,* 74–110, 125–43. B. L. R. Smith, *RAND Corporation,* 199–240.

43. Abella, *Soldiers of Reason,* 86–87.

44. Kaplan, *Wizards of Armageddon,* 111–124. B. L. R. Smith, *RAND Corporation* 108–114; Dickson, *Think Tanks,* 69–71.

45. Schulzinger, *Wise Men of Foreign Affairs,* 150–157; Kaplan, *Wizards of Armageddon,* 185–200, 232–247.

46. Kaplan, *Wizards of Armageddon,* 241–257; B. L. R. Smith, *RAND Corporation,* 14–20, 125–147.

47. Kaplan, *Wizards of Armageddon,* 220–32.

48. B. L. R. Smith, *RAND Corporation,* 283–296.

49. Abella, *Soldiers of Reason,* 168–187, 200–202; Orlans, *Nonprofit Research Institute,* 108–122; Dickson, *Think Tanks,* 75–85.

50. Schulzinger, *Wise Men of Foreign Affairs,* 113–115, 125–129, 136–141, 148–149, 177–193.

51. J. A. Smith, *Idea Brokers,* 122–166; Critchlow, *Brookings Institution, 1916–1952,* 166–10.

52. Berry, *A Voice for Nonprofits,* 11–15. Ricci, *Transformation of American Politics* 42–43; J. A. Smith, *Idea Brokers,* 146–66; Abelson, *Capital Idea,* 76–77.

53. Schulzinger, *Wise Men of Foreign Affairs,* 166–175; Dickson, *Think Tanks,* 55, 67; Abella, *Soldiers of Reason,* 168–187.

54. Abella, *Soldiers of Reason,* 213–216.

55. Ricci, *Transformation of American Politics,* 153; J. A. Smith, *Idea Brokers,* 159–165; Dickson, *Think Tanks,* 277–289.

56. Abelson, *Capital Idea,* 64–71.

57. Ibid., 88.

58. Ricci, *Transformation of American Politics,* 152–153; Silk and Silk, *American Establishment,* 153–160, 174–177.

59. Sidney Blumenthal, *The Rise of the Counter-Establishment* (New York: Crown, 1986), 46; Ricci, *Transformation of American Politics,* 160–162.

60. Rich, *Think Tanks,* 53–56; Judis, *Paradox of American Democracy.*

61. Ricci, *Transformation of American Politics,* 160–162; J. A. Smith, *Idea Brokers,* 180–184, 190–202; Blumenthal, *Rise of the Counter-Establishment,* 29–47.

62. Justin Vaisse, *Neoconservatism: The Biography of a Movement* (Cambridge: Belknap Press of Harvard University, 2010), 204; Murray Friedman, *The Neoconservative Revolution: Jewish Intellectuals and the Shaping of Public Policy* (New York: Cambridge University Press, 2008), 131–132.

63. Derthick and Quirk, *Politics of Deregulation,* 29–35.

64. Ibid., 36–37.

65. Rich, *Think Tanks,* 40–41.

66. Ibid., 67–71.

67. Abelson, *Capital Idea,* 80–84; J. A. Smith, *Idea Brokers,* 204.

68. Rich, *Think Tanks,* 171–172, 181–196.

69. Ricci, *Transformation of American Politics,* 218–219; Rich, *Think Tanks,* 70–71.

70. Schulzinger, *Wise Men of Foreign Affairs,* 210–242.

71. Ricci, *Transformation of American Politics,* 219.

72. Abelson, *Capital Idea,* 170–176; Abella, *Soldiers of Reason,* 304.

73. Paul Taylor, "Analyzing Alternatives in Labor's Think Tank; Liberal Economists Study Government's Role," *Washington Post,* February 19, 1987, A25.

74. Kenneth S. Baer, *Reinventing Democrats: The Politics of Liberalism From Reagan to Clinton* (Lawrence: University Press of Kansas, 2000), 65–92.

75. Ibid., passim. Rich, *Think Tanks,* 169–170.

76. Charlie Savage, "Shepherd of a Government in Exile," *New York Times,* November 7, 2008, A22; Eliza Newlin Carney, "Extreme Makeover," *National Journal,* February 26, 2005, 598–603.

77. Marisa Katz, "In the Tanks," *National Journal,* August 4, 2007, 39–31.

78. John P. Burke, "The Obama Presidential Transition: An Early Assessment," *Presidential Studies Quarterly* 39, 3 (September 2009).

79. Paul Krugman, "In the Tank?" *New York Times,* December 13, 2000, A5.

80. Jeffrey H. Birnbaum, "Private-Account Concept Grew from Obscure Roots," *Washington Post,* February 22, 2005, A1; Richard W. Stevenson, "For Bush, A Long Embrace of Social Security Plan," *New York Times,* February 27, 2005, 1.

81. Gregg Sangillo, "Intellectual Infrastructure," *National Journal,* October 15, 2005.

82. Jacob Heilbrunn, *They Knew They Were Right: The Rise of the Neocons* (New York: Doubleday, 2008), 219–240.

83. Ibid., 250–277.

84. Vaisse, *Neoconservatism,* 247–251.

85. Ibid., 251–255.

86. Howard Kurtz, "Conservative David Frum Loses Think-Tank Job after Criticizing GOP," *Washington Post,* March 26, 2010.

87. Patrick McGuinn, *No Child Left Behind and the Transformation of Federal Education Policy, 1965–2006* (Lawrence: University Press of Kansas, 2006).

88. Frederick M. Hess, ed., *When Research Matters: How Scholarship Influences Education Policy* (Cambridge: Harvard Education Press, 2008).

89. R. Kent Weaver, *Ending Welfare As We Know It* (Washington, D.C.: Brookings Institution Press, 2000), 213.
90. Ibid., 105–143.
91. Ibid., 199–201.
92. Rich, *Think Tanks,* 199–201.
93. Ibid., 153–154.
94. Frederick M. Hess, "Conclusion," in *When Research Matters,* 247.

SUGGESTED READING

Abella, Alex. *Soldiers of Reason: The RAND Corporation and the Rise of American Empire.* Chicago: Houghton Mifflin, 2008.

Abelson, Donald. *A Capital Idea: Think Tanks and U.S. Foreign Policy.* Montreal: McGill-Queen's University Press, 2006.

———. *Do Think Tanks Matter? Assessing the Impact of Public Policy Institutes.* Montreal: McGill-Queen's University Press, 2009.

Critchlow, Donald. *The Brookings Institution, 1916–1952: Expertise and the Public Interest in a Democratic Society.* DeKalb, Ill.: Northern Illinois University Press, 1985.

Derthick, Martha, and Paul Quirk. *The Politics of Deregulation.* Washington, D.C.: Brookings Institution Press, 1985.

Dickson, Paul. *Think Tanks.* New York: Ballantine Books, 1972.

Judis, John B. *The Paradox of American Democracy: Elites, Special Interests, and the Betrayal of the Public Trust.* New York: Routledge, 2001.

Kaplan, Fred. *The Wizards of Armageddon.* New York: Simon and Schuster, 1983.

Orlans, Harold. *The Nonprofit Research Institute: Its Origin, Operation, Problems, and Prospects.* New York: McGraw-Hill, 1972.

Ricci, David. *The Transformation of American Politics: The New Washington and the Rise of Think Tanks.* New Haven: Yale University Press, 1993.

Rich, Andrew. *Think Tanks, Public Policy, and the Politics of Expertise.* New York: Cambridge University Press, 2004.

Schulzinger, Robert. *Wise Men of Foreign Affairs: The History of the Council on Foreign Relations.* New York: Columbia University Press, 1984.

Skowronek, Stephen. *Building a New American State: The Expansion of Federal Administrative Capabilities, 1877–1920.* New York: Cambridge University Press, 1982.

Smith, James Allen. *The Idea Brokers: Think Tanks and the Rise of the New Policy Elite.* New York: Free Press, 1991.

Stone, Diane. *Capturing the Political Imagination: Think Tanks and the Policy Process.* New York: Routledge, 1996.

chapter 17

Religious Interest Groups

by James L. Guth

SINCE ITS FOUNDING, THE UNITED STATES has been one of the most religious nations in the developed world. Therefore, it should not be surprising that religious groups have long played a role in American politics. Historians have painted a rich picture of that involvement, but political scientists have been slower to study religious organizations. Most overviews of interest group politics ignore them entirely, and textbooks usually give only brief notice. Indeed, political science generally has exhibited indifference to religious factors, and religion and politics scholars often fail to connect their work to theoretical issues central to the discipline.[1]

This chapter offers a review of religious politics that intersects the concerns of interest group scholars, but it also identifies gaps in our understanding of religious groups. It uses evidence from studies of religious groups and from less-systematic observation, providing a guide to what is known, and still needs to be known, about their activity in American politics.[2] It considers first the development and maintenance of religious interest groups, discusses some of the differences between institutional and membership groups, and then turns to an extended consideration of their political strategies.

DEVELOPMENT AND MAINTENANCE OF RELIGIOUS GROUPS

Like other interest groups, religious groups have grown in number, exhibited greater diversity in sponsorship, and proliferated in type. A 1950 survey found only a handful of religious lobbies in Washington, D.C., with most representing denominations. During the advocacy explosion of the 1960s, however, they multiplied rapidly, so that by 1980 scholars could identify at least seventy-four national religious lobbies, dominated by liberal religious denominations and causes. In the 1980s the Christian Right diversified representation by spawning a complex of specialized lobbies, evoking counter-mobilization by "religious left" groups. In 1994 scholars counted 120 Washington offices, including many membership organizations devoted to particular causes. Despite the lack of a recent systematic inventory, there is no sign that numbers are diminishing. *New York Times* reporters found that 413 religious groups lobbied Congress in 2005. A few years later Laura Olson identified more than 70 "religious left" organizations alone, and another close observer found 225 religious lobby offices in Washington.[3]

Several factors have contributed to this proliferation. First, the same social factors that encourage interest organizations generally have operated here as well: higher education, greater discretionary incomes, and new communications technologies have created expanded markets for groups and facilitated contact with potential members. Second, a more diverse "religious ecology" has also supported additional groups, exemplified by lobbying organizations for Muslims, Hindus, Buddhists, and other religious minorities. In a related vein, the growth in the nonreligious has created a constituency for organizations such as the Secular Coalition for America, American Atheists, and the Atheist Alliance International.

The representational spurt also reflects another form of religious diversity: new theological divisions in older communities. As mainline Protestant churches split into liberal and conservative factions, complete with distinct political agendas, new organizations emerged to speak for conservative minorities, often competing with official denominational lobbies. For example, the Institute for Religion and Democracy has encouraged conservative challenges to the theological and political liberals leading the United Methodist Church and the Presbyterian Church (U.S.A.).[4] Catholics of varied theological persuasions support pro-life groups: Catholics for Choice, Call to Action, Catholic Answers, Pax Christi, Catholics United for the Common Good, and other organizations, aside from the official U.S. Conference of Catholic Bishops (USCCB), that lobby for Catholic institutions such as hospitals or religious orders.[5]

A changing political agenda also encouraged group proliferation, as issues previously negotiated elsewhere

RELIGIOUS INTEREST GROUPS IN WASHINGTON

Religious lobbies in Washington vary considerably in size and resources. The U.S. Conference of Catholic Bishops has long been one of the best staffed religious lobbies, representing the institutional interests of the Roman Catholic Church and addressing broader public policy issues since World War I. The National Council of Churches speaks for the larger mainline Protestant churches, but also includes some black Protestant and Orthodox denominations. Founded as the Federal Council of Churches in 1908 as a voice for the Social Gospel movement, the NCC still lobbies for progressive social welfare policy and liberal internationalism. Its work is often supplemented by (but sometimes conflicts with) that of mainline denominational lobbies, most notably those of the United Methodist Church and the Presbyterian Church (U.S.A.). Both the council and mainline offices have suffered from shrinking resources, as the membership and financial contributions of constituent churches have declined. The Friends Committee on National Legislation and the Mennonite Central Committee have long represented the "peace churches" on international issues, with some impact. Founded in 1973 by Lutheran pastor Arthur Simon, Bread for the World is a formidable presence on Capitol Hill on hunger and international development issues.

Conservative Christian groups have been somewhat more transient, but the Family Research Council, founded in 1983 and reinvigorated by Reagan staffer Gary Bauer and radio psychologist James Dobson in 1988, has been a consistent presence in Washington and has been led by Tony Perkins since 2003. Dobson eventually detached his interest from the council and created Focus on the Family Action, as the political arm of his popular Christian radio ministry. Beverly LaHaye's Concerned Women for America has fought for conservative social policies since 1979 and has extended its interest into international issues. The Traditional Values Coalition, founded by Louis P. Sheldon in 1980, usually takes a hard-line conservative position on culture war issues and represents individual Protestant congregations. Finally, the Ethics and Religious Liberty Commission of the Southern Baptist Convention, the nation's largest Protestant denomination, has played a growing role in Washington. The ERLC is led by Dr. Richard Land, who has wide connections among conservative Christian groups and was an influential voice in the George W. Bush White House on religious issues.

shifted to Washington. Prior to the 1960s and 1970s religious exercises in public schools, abortion, gay rights, and other "moral" issues were dealt with in states and localities. Since then, federal courts have moved these issues to a national forum, giving birth to the so-called culture wars, thereby drawing religious interests to Washington. Similarly, federal antiterrorism policy after 9/11 encouraged a greater lobbying presence for religious minorities such as Muslims.

Like other American institutions, religious organizations have often felt the growing reach of the regulatory state, affecting individual churches, denominations, parochial schools, hospitals, and social service agencies. In a slightly different way, the growth of earmarking by national legislators has allowed religious groups to exploit government programs that may have only a tangential relationship to religious concerns, but offer financial aid.

Finally, the heightened availability of entrepreneurs, patrons, and sponsors has played a vital role. Christian Right organizations, from the old Moral Majority to the Christian Coalition to Focus on the Family Action, are notable examples. Each grew out of ministries established for religious purposes by Jerry Falwell, Pat Robertson, and James Dobson, exploiting new communication technologies to build a religious audience. Although their motivations varied, all three entrepreneurs then used part of their organizational surplus to subsidize political activity. Intellectual entrepreneurs, such as the late Rev. Richard John Neuhaus of *First Things* and Princeton law professor Robert George, helped create a sophisticated ideational basis for conservative group activity. Secular conservative foundations and patrons also contributed to the formation and maintenance of religious lobbies, sometimes abetted by Republican Party organizations.[6]

Entrepreneurs, patrons, and political sponsors have fostered the "religious left" as well. People for the American Way was founded by TV producer Norman Lear in 1981 to counter the growth of the religious Right and from the beginning depended on major foundation and patron sponsorship. Later in the 1980s the liberal Interfaith Impact benefited not only from mainline Protestant denominational funding, but also from foundation grants for projects such as voter mobilization. The Interfaith Alliance, created in 1994 to fight the Christian Coalition, received start-up funds from the Democratic Congressional Campaign Committee. Other liberal religious groups were byproducts of Barack Obama's campaign to mobilize religious voters in 2008 or were sponsored by the Democratic National Committee. These new groups, like their secular liberal allies, have used Web-based technologies for mobilization and communication with an inherently diverse religious constituency.[7]

The role of entrepreneurs and patrons suggests continued expansion of the religious lobbying sector. In his classic article on group entrepreneurs, Robert Salisbury noted that each successive organizing wave within a sector is often led by personnel "trained" in the previous one.[8] The growth of religious interest groups certainly fits this pattern, drawing experienced potential entrepreneurs from the pioneering (if sometimes unsuccessful) Christian Right or religious Left groups, sometimes by way of a stint in government or party organizations. Although this pattern does not predict the success of any particular entrepreneurial vehicle, it certainly suggests continued "start-ups" of new groups.

Naturally, such outside help can sometimes be a mixed blessing, especially if it makes the group excessively sensitive to the patron's political concerns. The Christian Coalition was often caught between founder Pat Robertson's pre-occupations and the more conservative views of grassroots members.[9] In some cases, subsequent withdrawal of sponsorship or patronage precipitates the demise of an organization, as with Interfaith Impact in the 1990s and the Christian Coalition a decade later. But outside support can also keep a foundering lobby alive: the liberal National Council of Churches (NCC), the peak association for mainline Protestant, black Protestant, and Orthodox denominations, now depends more on foundation support than on denominational assessments or individual contributions.[10]

TYPES OF RELIGIOUS LOBBYING ORGANIZATIONS

Religious lobbying certainly confirms Salisbury's argument that the politics of institutions may be quite different from those of membership organizations.[11] First, denominational lobbies have institutional interests to protect: they are concerned with IRS treatment of ministerial housing allowances, the tax status of auxiliary enterprises, "conscience clauses" in regulation of Catholic hospitals, and so on. Second, when these institutions do speak for individual members, that is, parishioners, on broader issues, they often do so with a considerable degree of freedom. This is especially true of denominational and "peak association" lobbies such as the NCC or the National Association of Evangelicals (NAE). Most Americans do not join churches to advance public policy and may be unaware of their denomination's "official" platform or that the church leaders often take stances that differ from those of their members. A long-standing critique of mainline Protestant churches is that officials constantly lobby for liberal policies opposed by conservative laity. Indeed, one writer memorably tagged religious lobbyists as "generals without armies," a phrase that has become part of the conventional wisdom—although not without challenge from other scholars.[12]

The Catholic Church provides another intriguing case of institutional politics. Not only does the USCCB have one of the best staffed religious lobbies, but also it "represents" about one-quarter of all Americans and has more claim to authoritative status than its Protestant counterparts. Like them, however, the USCCB often lacks membership support when it ventures beyond institutional concerns. In part, the lack of support reflects the uneasy nexus between the Catholic Church's social teachings and American political alignments. Because the church is conservative on moral questions, liberal on social welfare, and cooperative internationalist on foreign policy, it confronts a divided internal constituency on almost every issue. Invariably, liberals and conservatives battle to bring the bishops around, albeit without the internal democratic mold that allows Protestant dissidents to challenge denominational policies.[13]

Although political scientists have almost entirely neglected the question of how denominations and peak associations make political decisions, they have studied one critical organizational element: the clergy. In general, evidence shows that mainline Protestant clergy are more liberal than their laity and that political liberalism increases as one rises in mainline hierarchies, while Evangelical clergy are more in line with their congregations.[14] Yet, these findings have not been integrated into an understanding of institutional politics: few have explored the dynamics of denominational decision making. Nor has there been much rigorous work on the impact that clerical attitudes, whether liberal or conservative, have on laity.[15] Close observation of mainline Protestant denominations suggests that on public policy matters they are really a hybrid of institution, where decisions are dominated by constituted authorities, and membership organization, where member opinion may have some effect.

In this respect, sociologists have long debated whether internal political conflicts have even influenced church membership. Some argue that liberal political postures have contributed to ongoing membership "exits" from the Episcopal Church, the Presbyterian Church (U.S.A.), the United Methodist Church, and other mainline bodies, perhaps in favor of more conservative ones, such as the Southern Baptist Convention, Assemblies of God, and other Evangelical denominations. What little evidence we have is mixed, but it shows that some parishioners are not entirely indifferent to the politics of denomination leaders.[16]

Although denominational lobbies and church federations remain visible institutional actors in Washington, D.C., an increasing proportion of religious lobbies take the form of nondenominational parachurch organizations, emerging from the efforts of individual or organizational entrepreneurs and patrons. As membership organizations, they face rather different constraints than institutional lobbies do. They typically emphasize purposive or policy incentives and constantly struggle to attract and keep dues-paying or contributing members, often by exploiting "the political crisis of the month."[17] This tactic may be effective when in opposition, but more difficult to maintain when political allies are in power. Christian Right groups, notably, found it much easier to attract resources during the Clinton era than during the George W. Bush years, when several fell on hard times or actually failed, at the very time that new religious Left groups were sprouting and prospering.

Membership groups invariably face a classic problem that institutional lobbies have already largely solved: how to transform the entrepreneurial into the bureaucratic. Although such groups benefit enormously from the sponsorship and patronage of their founders, relatively few negotiate the transition to routinized leadership and institutional permanence. Bread for the World, a liberal antihunger lobby, is much admired for building an active and stable membership base, drawn from a wide range of churches. But other parachurch lobbying organizations have struggled to stay afloat. The Moral Majority, Christian Coalition, and even Focus on the Family remained quite dependent on their founders and major patrons—and either disappeared or declined in their absence. A similar dependence might be seen in some liberal groups, such as Jim Wallis's Call to Renewal, and in the new religious lobbies spawned by the Obama campaign, such as the Matthew 25 Network. Even successful recruiting of highly motivated, purposive members is a mixed benefit: the Christian Coalition was stymied in expanding its agenda beyond conservative social issues by the fierce resistance of members, who withheld contributions or dropped out.[18] Although transient organizations may still have political impact, as demonstrated by Christian Coalition's high rank among influential lobbies in the 1990s, they eventually fail to enjoy the political advantages of institutional permanence.

ELECTORAL INVOLVEMENT OF RELIGIOUS ORGANIZATIONS

It is clear that religious groups replicate the strategies used by secular interests.[19] Many religious organizations have stressed electoral strategies and, even though the media have often reported on actions such as endorsing candidates, distributing voter guides, and mobilizing grassroots activists, political scientists have done few systematic studies. There is research that indicates Christian Right groups have infiltrated the Republican Party, recruited and supported primary contestants, and influenced party platforms at all levels.[20] Similarly, electoral intervention by some Catholic bishops has recently been a focus of attention, but many other official and unofficial Catholic groups have also participated in campaigns. Electoral engagement by black Protestant clergy, churches, and denominations is widely recognized, but little studied in the context of interest group activity. And there has been little scholarly scrutiny of electoral efforts by liberal religious groups, although the visibility of religious Left leaders in the 2008 Democratic campaign and the rise of new religious groups supporting Obama suggest that religious interests work both sides of the partisan street.[21]

Although religious groups occasionally raise money for candidates, political action committees have never been central to their strategies, diverting scarce resources away from organizational needs. Rather, religious groups focus on mobilizing sympathetic voters, by methods that have changed over time and with experience. Christian Right

Focus on the Family, an Evangelical Christian group, displays sample advertisements designed to encourage their base to vote. These ads mention controversial issues such as abortion and same-sex marriage to rally like-minded voters without endorsing a particular candidate.

organizations in the 1980s stressed pastor-centered efforts to register voters, endorse candidates, and mobilize parishioners. Later, these tactics gave way to organizing influential laity in selected churches, encouraging face-to-face persuasion of fellow parishioners. In the same way, mass distribution of voter guides was gradually replaced by more sophisticated communications, such as phone banks, e-mails, and Web site links. Although churches cannot endorse candidates, contribute institutional resources to campaigns, or otherwise show favoritism in campaigns without endangering their tax exempt 501(c)(3) status, many are still the focus of considerable campaigning.

Studies of elections from 1996 to 2008 reveal the ebb and flow of religious mobilization strategies. Voter registration and get-out-the-vote efforts were most common, followed by political advice from fellow parishioners. Direct contact from religious interest groups came in third, increasing in frequency over time, but voter guides—often the center of media accounts—declined in prominence. Pastoral endorsements were always rare, despite the suspicions of reporters (and the IRS). Electoral targets varied: black Protestants usually were subject to the most religious (and perhaps, secular) contacts, followed closely by traditionalist Evangelicals. Catholic traditionalists also were reached quite often, but liberals generally were left alone. Indeed, conservative groups far outperformed their liberal rivals, even in 2008.[22]

Do electoral contacts work? It is difficult to sort out the independent effects of religious mobilization: the GOP and secular conservatives often target the same constituencies as the Christian Right, just as Democratic and liberal groups aim at black Protestants, already subject to a host of religious influences. Nevertheless, when everything is taken into account, religious contacts do bolster turnout, but seem not to influence vote choice.[23] Still, given the scope of religious mobilization and the size of religious communities, such contacts compare favorably with numbers produced by candidate, party, and other interest organizations.

Lobbying Congress

Electoral strategies are designed to facilitate legislative access. Religious lobbyists have been the subject of several fine studies, although we lack systematic data on their tactics. There is scholarly consensus on certain aspects of religious lobbying, some notable gaps in the literature, and vigorous arguments about its efficacy.

Scholars agree that religious lobbyists have a distinctive style, or perhaps, a distinct conception of their role. Although those representing institutional interests may adopt the same pragmatic mien as other lobbyists, many religious lobbyists exhibit a prophetic style. On the Right, this style entails condemnation of the moral decline of America and the failure of public policy to reverse that decline, and on the Left, a broad critique of social injustice and government's unwillingness to serve the poor or marginalized. Although some scholars argue that this style hinders the legislative fortunes of religious groups, both Right and Left, others see it as a salubrious counterweight to the economic bias of the interest group system. But even the latter observers concede that religious groups often adopt policies too extreme to be viable and neglect the detail work necessary for effective lobbying.[24]

Another point of consensus is that religious lobbying is almost invariably coalition politics: religious groups constantly engage in alliances that shift from issue to issue. Yet there has been little effort to apply rigorous theories of intergroup behavior to explain the patterns. Most often, cooperation is simply attributed either to scarce resources—religious lobbies are too small and poorly resourced to sustain their broad political agendas alone—or to the desire to share specialized expertise of niche groups.

Ideological compatibility probably explains as much alliance behavior as resource limitations, ambitious agendas, and specialization. The polarization of the interest group universe in the 1980s certainly shaped the major religious coalitions: a liberal alliance of mainline and black Protestant denominations, the NCC, membership groups such as Bread for the World, and several Jewish lobbies confronts a conservative alliance of the National Association of Evangelicals, Focus on the Family, the Family Research Council, Concerned Women for America, the Eagle Forum, the Southern Baptist Convention, pro-life organizations, and other traditionalist groups.[25] Although elements of each alliance sometimes cooperate with the other—even to the point of "détente" between the two—in-group relations are certainly more intensive. But ideological compatibility does not always overcome personal rivalries, organizational competition for members and resources, and conflicting strategic visions, as both alliances experience persistent internal tensions.[26]

The two alliances also stress different influence strategies. Just as conservative groups usually outperform liberal rivals in electoral mobilization, they have demonstrated the ability to mobilize grassroots support for legislation. Media accounts abound on the power of Focus on the Family or the Family Research Council to jam phone lines, fax machines, and e-mail boxes on Capitol Hill. Conservative groups also have institutionalized entrée into the House GOP conference in caucus form: the Family Values Action Team of sympathetic members. Although this group seldom includes GOP influentials, it has reliably transmitted group demands to the party leadership, a nexus enhanced by the fact that most team members come from religious traditions dominant in the conservative alliance. Liberal organizations, on the other hand, cultivate sympathetic legislators directly, reinforced by contacts from activist liberal pastors and lay leaders, rather than from more conservative laity.[27] (Naturally, such contacts may have more impact when they do reflect the laity's views, and not just those of local and national elites.) Even then, observers are often skeptical about the liberal coalition's influence.[28]

Catholic lobbyists remain independent from both coalitions, at times working with each. The distinctive theological tradition of the church, its mixed ideology, Catholics' importance as a swing voting bloc, and a natural constituency of Catholic legislators on both sides of the aisle, give the church operational flexibility unmatched by other religious lobbies. In addition, substantial staff resources permit church representatives to deal knowledgeably with issues, often bolstered by relevant practical experience of Catholic institutions, from hospitals to Catholic Charities to overseas development groups. Still, as already noted, USCCB lobbyists frequently lack grassroots support and may face competition from other Catholic voices.

The thorniest question for interest group scholars is whether religious groups wield much power in legislative settings. None of the extant studies of religious lobbying in Washington has attempted a rigorous assessment of effectiveness.[29] Even in the best case, religious lobbying would be only one influence over members, who must also take into account their own religious values and those of their constituents, in addition to their partisanship and ideological perspective, lobbying by secular groups, and the wishes of the president and party leaders. With all factors accounted for, the impact of religious lobbying may be quite modest.[30]

Another approach in assessing influence might be to aggregate case studies to make broader, if qualitative, judgments. Here we have some fine examples: James Findlay's account of mainline church lobbying on 1960s civil rights legislation, Matthew Moen's study of early Christian Right efforts in Congress, Allen Hertzke's review of the religious campaign for the International Religious Freedom Act of 1998, and Steven Tipton's analysis of religious liberal lobbying in the 1990s.[31] These studies present a mixed picture of influence: Findlay found that mainline Protestant lobbies were critical to the passage of civil rights legislation, but in special circumstances not likely to be repeated; Moen showed that the Christian Right influenced the congressional agenda, but failed to change public policy; Hertzke saw group effects on both agenda and statute; and Tipton concluded that the liberal coalition failed to shape either Bill Clinton's agenda or policy, merely riding the legislative waves of stronger forces. Even a more comprehensive review of case studies would not cumulate to a full picture of group activity. Nor, for that matter, does sustained scholarly attention always produce conclusive judgments about effectiveness: studies of Jewish groups' lobbying power still produce contrary findings.[32] As Hertzke has concluded, "A weak link in the literature is systematic analysis of policy impact." [33]

Religious Groups in the Courts

Throughout the twentieth century religious organizations have participated in the judicial system, from a Catholic order defending religious education (*Pierce v. Society of*

Culture Wars Timeline

- 1962–1963. The Supreme Court rules that religious exercises, such as prayers and Bible reading are unconstitutional establishments of religion in *Engel v. Vitale* (1962) and *Abington School District v. Schempp* (1963).

- 1973. The Court rules in *Roe v. Wade* that restrictive state laws on abortion violate the Constitution, eliciting a wave of religious activism, first from the Catholic Church, joined later by a wide range of other religious groups, especially evangelical Protestants. The abortion issue reshapes national party coalitions and influences legislative deliberations on policies ranging from international development aid to national health care reform.

- 1980–1985. The Court prohibits the posting of the Ten Commandments in classrooms (*Stone v. Graham*, 1980) and strikes down an Alabama law requiring teachers to open each school day with a moment of silence (*Wallace v. Jaffree*, 1985). These cases are merely one stream in the Court's increasingly separatist interpretation of the establishment clause of the First Amendment.

- 1993–2009. Hawaii state courts open the door to the legalization of same-sex marriage in the state, but are preempted in 1998 by an amendment to the state constitution. In 1996 President Bill Clinton signs the Defense of Marriage Act, denying federal recognition of same-sex marriage. The legal campaign for same-sex marriage nevertheless continues, and in 1999 the Vermont Supreme Court rules that the exclusion of same-sex couples from marriage benefits violates the state constitution. This case is followed by similar litigation in a number of states, with success in Massachusetts (2003), California (2008), and Iowa (2009). The movement elicits counter-mobilization by opponents, who sponsor state constitutional amendments, especially during the presidential election year of 2004, but continuing thereafter, succeeding in thirty states. This issue, along with related gay rights questions, remains strongly contested by religious groups into the Obama administration.

JAY SEKULOW

The new-found legal sophistication of Christian Right organizations in the 1990s resulted in large part from the efforts of Jay Alan Sekulow, a Jewish convert to Christianity who has long served as chief counsel for the American Center for Law and Justice (ACLJ). The ACLJ is a litigating organization sponsored originally by televangelist Pat Robertson to counter the separationist litigation of the American Civil Liberties Union (ACLU). By 2005 Sekulow had taken twelve cases to the Supreme Court and assisted in four more. Of these cases, he prevailed in ten, making him one of the most prominent and successful church-state litigators in the country. During the George W. Bush administration he was also an important adviser to the Justice Department on a wide range of religion-related issues and has been credited with introducing a strong element of pragmatism and professionalism to conservative religious litigation strategies.

Jay Sekulow (center), chief counsel for the American Center for Law and Justice, speaks to the media outside of the U.S. Supreme Court in 2004. Sekulow argued before the Court in support of the Child Online Protection Act of 1998.

Sisters, 1925) to Jehovah's Witnesses fighting mandatory flag salutes in schools (*Minersville School District v. Gobitis*, 1940). Indeed, by mid-century a few religious interest groups "organized and structured the litigation of constitutional questions with a considerable degree of proficiency."[34] The American Jewish Congress (AJC), American Civil Liberties Union (ACLU), and Americans United for Separation of Church and State brought litigation challenging establishment clause violations, sometimes assisted by Seventh-Day Adventists and the Baptist Joint Committee. Although these groups had distinct constituencies, sometimes preferred different cases, and often battled over strategy, they formed a loose separationist alliance, leaving accommodationist arguments to state officials whose policies were under challenge or, occasionally, to lawyers from the Catholic Church. (Separationist groups insist on strict separation of religion and public institutions, while accommodationist groups favor more interaction.) Few accommodationists exhibited the expertise, strategic acumen, or litigating skills of the separationist specialists, often seminal legal thinkers such as the AJC's Leo Pfeffer.[35]

Like representation before Congress, religious group litigation changed dramatically after 1980, as the rise of the Christian Right made the legal universe not only more diverse, but also more confrontational. Replicating the trajectory of their separationist foes, accommodationists first wrote amicus briefs, but soon moved on to case sponsorship and other tactics.[36] As the accommodationist campaign mounted, more cases saw religious groups on *both* sides, as separationists lost the virtual monopoly of representation they enjoyed earlier.

The accommodationist lobby quickly took on a diversity of its own. At its core was the American Center for Law and Justice (ACLJ), sponsored by Pat Robertson as a conservative rival for the ACLU. Headed by experienced litigator Jay Sekulow, the ACLJ sponsored cases taking a free speech approach to free exercise issues, one pioneered by John Whitehead's Rutherford Institute. Several other organizations specialized in areas of legal politics, with older groups such as the Christian Legal Society and the National Association of Evangelicals still preferring amicus briefs. Indeed, after 1990 no religion case before the Supreme Court lacked at least one such brief. A few groups preferred less confrontational strategies, working with states and private parties to resolve religious issues without litigation. Eventually, Christian Right leaders created the Alliance Defense Fund (ADF) as a "United Way" for litigation. The ADF also has gone beyond joint fund-raising to training Christian Right lawyers and initiating its own cases.[37]

Thus, the religious agenda before the courts is now contested by two distinct ideological coalitions: the old separationist alliance (now part of the liberal legislative coalition discussed above) and a new coterie of Christian

Right organizations. Although organizations have their constituencies, patrons, ideological formulations, and strategies, their presence assures lively litigation over religious issues. Assessing the impact of group litigation is difficult, but Christian Right organizations claim notable victories in state and federal courts. Independent observers agree that when they can make a case for accommodation on free speech grounds, they have often won, most notably in *Rosenberger v. University of Virginia* (1995). On establishment clause issues, however, separationist groups still have a better track record.[38]

Success or failure is, however, often beyond the control of interest group litigants: legal doctrine and the composition of the federal courts constrain their influence. Recognizing this, conservative and liberal religious groups focused more energy on presidential judicial nominations, either by contesting Senate confirmations or by trying to influence the nominations themselves. There are few studies of these efforts to sway judicial nominations, but it is clear that opposition from conservative religious groups hastened the withdrawal of Harriet Miers as George W. Bush's nominee to the Supreme Court.[39]

Religious Interests and Executive Politics

Nowhere is the literature on religious groups more anecdotal than in the area of executive politics. Although journalists are often intrigued by ties between the White House and religious groups, there is little scholarly analysis of how the president and executive office personnel interact with religious interests and how responsive they are to those groups. There is even less on efforts to influence bureaucratic decisions, reflecting the assumption that unlike business, labor, and agricultural organizations, religious groups have no natural clientele agency, no bureaucracy devoted to protecting their interests.

Like other groups, religious interests have welcomed the larger and more specialized presidential staff, which offers "new avenues and institutions for mutual interaction between the president and religious interests."[40] Every president since Lyndon Johnson has designated at least one staffer as a liaison with religious groups, and recent administrations have even more elaborate structures. Naturally, administrations coordinate with organizations representing significant parts of their electoral coalition: Republicans provide access to religious conservatives and, sometimes, Catholic officials, while Democrats listen to mainline Protestant lobbyists, Jewish leaders, liberal Catholic groups, and black Protestants.

Still, the variations are significant. Ronald Reagan's White House cultivated Christian Right leaders, ignored mainline Protestants, and had rather testy relationships with the Catholic bishops—given their lobbying against Reagan's Central American policy and their liberal pastoral letters on nuclear arms and the economy. George H. W. Bush's administration, on the other hand, kept its distance from both liberal and conservative coalitions, trying to avoid polarization. The Clinton White House, after briefly wooing religious conservatives, opened the door wide to mainline and black Protestants and Catholic liberals, providing unprecedented access, if not always influence. George W. Bush and his staff pointedly ignored mainline Protestants—including leaders of his own United Methodist Church—preferring regular consultations with Evangelical and Catholic officials.[41]

The Obama White House has gone even further toward institutionalizing religious access by creating the Advisory Council on Faith-based and Neighborhood Partnerships, which draws from an unprecedented range of denominations, religious service institutions, and traditions, from Muslims to Jews to Southern Baptists. The council emerged from Obama's effort to broaden the Democratic religious base and from his aspirations for a new consensus on abortion, gay rights, health care, and international economic development. Joshua DuBois, who led the Obama campaign's religious outreach, was named to head this office. Whether this formal liaison structure can bridge the chasm between conservative and liberal religious lobbies is uncertain, as is the staff's ability to negotiate the wide diversity built into its membership.

One council assignment is to advise on the restructuring of George W. Bush's faith-based initiative, a controversial program designed to expand religious organizations' role in providing social services. Bush's original proposals stalled legislatively over the right of religious groups receiving federal money to hire only within their faith, with the dividing line largely—though not entirely—between the conservative and liberal religious coalitions. As a result of the legislative stalemate, the Bush administration expanded government-religious group partnerships by administrative action, earning mixed reviews.[42]

This controversy highlights a larger reality of federal policy: the government has long fostered cooperative ties with religious organizations in implementing its social welfare programs, relationships encouraged by the 1996 welfare reform law. Although these interactions generally do not approach the clientele relationships sometimes depicted as the model for agency-group relations in agriculture, water policy, or public works, they do merit further attention. Government grants and contracts with Catholic Charities, Lutheran Social Services, Salvation Army, and other religious providers constitute an important aspect of government programs—and major budget shares for service organizations.

International relief and development programs also have a long and intricate relationship with religious

President of the U.S. Conference of Catholic Bishops, Bishop William Skylstad, meets with President George W. Bush at the White House in 2005.

organizations. Since World War II the government has often relied on private agencies, and the American Friends Service Committee, Church World Service, Oxfam, World Vision, and Catholic Relief Services became mainstays of implementing foreign aid through contracts, grants, and subsidies, while adding substantial private funds to complement government programs. Over time, these agencies established lobbies to support their operational units, sometimes in concert with secular nongovernmental organizations. As in domestic policy, this interest group community was initially dominated by traditional Jewish, mainline Protestant, and Catholic denominational agencies, but more recently Evangelical parachurch organizations, such as World Vision, Samaritan's Purse, and others, have surpassed them, buttressed by the lobbying of older groups such as the NAE, which has increasing interests in global policy developments.[43]

Growing religious involvement on international issues has created new points for group entrée into the bureaucratic process. The International Religious Freedom Act of 1998, sponsored by a religious coalition dominated by Evangelicals, established an office in the State Department to report on the status of religious freedom around the world and the U.S. Commission on International Religious Freedom specifically designed to pressure the State Department. The commission has been filled by religious leaders, with Evangelicals especially well represented and, as expected, has continually prodded a reluctant bureaucracy to take a more aggressive line on religious freedom, with mixed results to date.[44]

Religious interest groups are becoming major players in the bureaucratic (and legislative) politics of foreign policy. Greater numbers of religious Americans are personally engaged in international religious missions; they have increasing interest in international affairs; and their religious institutions have growing ties across international boundaries.[45] In addition, religious minorities in the United States often have natural ethnic connections abroad, creating strong incentives for involvement, just as Jewish organizations have long stressed Middle East policy.[46] Finally, greater partisan and ideological cleavages over foreign policy provide entrée for religious groups, as these divisions may be shaped by religious factors.

CONCLUSION

The religious interest group sector has experienced many of the trends seen among other groups, but exhibits some distinctive characteristics as well. Like other groups, they have proliferated over the past three decades, represent a wider range of interests, and are shaped by government involvement with almost every aspect of American life. Although this sector includes nearly every organizational form, today it is dominated less by institutional interests, such as denominations, and more by membership associations. Entrepreneurs and patrons have played a vital role in creating these new groups, which often speak for religious populations and interests previously underrepresented.

Although religious interest groups use the same influence techniques as others, many emphasize electoral mobilization and, in recent years, litigation. To influence Congress, they often work in coalitions, but their prophetic legislative style and lack of grassroots support may reduce their impact. They have been less involved in bureaucratic politics, but that tendency may be eroding, especially in areas such as social services and foreign policy. On the whole, long-term social and political trends suggest future vitality for this sector of interest groups.

NOTES

1. Kenneth D. Wald and Clyde Wilcox, "Has Political Science Rediscovered the Faith Factor?" *American Political Science Review* 100 (November 2006): 523–529.

2. A valuable review is Allen D. Hertzke, "Religion and Interest Groups in American Politics," in *The Oxford Handbook of Religion and American Politics*, ed. Corwin E. Smidt, Lyman A. Kellstedt, and James L. Guth (New York: Oxford University Press, 2009), 299–329.

3. Laura Olson, "The American Religious Left, 2008," communication with the author; Steven M. Tipton, *Public Pulpits: Methodists and Mainline Churches in the Moral Argument of Public Life* (Chicago: University of Chicago Press, 2007), xii; Allen D. Hertzke, "The Religious Advocacy Explosion," *Pew Forum on Religion and Public Life*, 2010.

4. For these theological and political divisions, see Robert Wuthnow, *The Restructuring of American Religion* (Princeton: Princeton University Press, 1988); and Tipton, *Public Pulpits*.

5. Peter Steinfels, *A People Adrift: The Crisis of the Roman Catholic Church in America* (New York: Simon and Schuster, 2003).

6. Clyde Wilcox and Gregory Fortelny, "Religion and Social Movements," in *Oxford Handbook of Religion*, 266–298.

7. For the campaign's encouragement of these organizations, see James L. Guth, "Religion in the 2008 Election," in *The American Elections of 2008*, ed. Janet M. Box-Steffensmeier and Steven E. Schier, (Lanham, Md.: Rowman and Littlefield, 2009), 117–136.

8. Robert H. Salisbury, "An Exchange Theory of Interest Groups," *Midwest Journal of Political Science* 13 (February 1969): 1–32.

9. Joel D. Vaughan, *The Rise and Fall of the Christian Coalition* (Eugene, Ore.: Resource Publications, 2009).

10. Foundations supporting the NCC are found at www.ncccusa.org/about/invest.html.

11. Robert H. Salisbury, "Interest Representation: The Dominance of Institutions," *American Political Science Review* 78 (March 1984): 64–70.

12. James L. Adams, *The Growing Church Lobby in Washington* (Grand Rapids, Mich.: Eerdmans, 1970); Hertzke, "Religion and Interest Groups."

13. Thomas J. Reese, *A Flock of Shepherds: The National Conference of Catholic Bishops* (Kansas City, Mo.: Sheed and Ward, 1992), 187–224; David Yamane, *The Catholic Church in State Politics* (Lanham, Md.: Rowman and Littlefield, 2005).

14. James L. Guth, John C. Green, Corwin E. Smidt, Lyman A. Kellstedt, and Margaret M. Poloma, *The Bully Pulpit: The Politics of Protestant Clergy* (Lawrence: University Press of Kansas, 1997).

15. An exception is Paul A. Djupe and Christopher P. Gilbert, *The Political Influence of Churches* (New York: Cambridge University Press, 2009).

16. Although sociologists are skeptical about the role of political dissension in restructuring church membership, "political switching" does occur. See John C. Green and James L. Guth, "From Lambs to Sheep: Denominational Change and Political Behavior," in *Rediscovering the Religious Factor in American Politics*, ed. David C. Leege and Lyman A. Kellstedt, (Armonk, N.Y.: M. E. Sharpe, 1993), 100–120.

17. James L. Guth, John C. Green, Lyman A. Kellstedt, and Corwin E. Smidt, "Onward Christian Soldiers: Religious Activist Groups in American Politics," in *Interest Group Politics*, 4th ed., ed. Allan J. Cigler and Burdett A. Loomis, (Washington, D.C.: CQ Press, 1995), 55–76.

18. Vaughan, *Rise and Fall of the Christian Coalition.*

19. Compare, for example, the assessment of lobbyist activities in four policy sectors by John P. Heinz, Edward O. Laumann, Robert L. Nelson, and Robert H. Salisbury, *The Hollow Core: Private Interests in National Policy Making* (Cambridge: Harvard University Press, 1993); Kay Lehman Schlozman and John T. Tierney, *Organized Interests and American Democracy* (New York: HarperCollins, 1986).

20. John C. Green, Mark J. Rozell, and Clyde Wilcox, eds., *The Values Campaign: The Christian Right in the 2004 Elections* (Washington, D.C.: Georgetown University Press, 2006).

21. Amy Sullivan, *The Party Faithful: How and Why Democrats Are Closing the God Gap* (New York: Scribner, 2008). Religious Left support for Democratic candidates is hardly new. See Shaun A. Casey, *The Making of a Catholic President* (New York: Oxford University Press, 2009).

22. The evidence in this section is from James L. Guth, Lyman A. Kellstedt, John C. Green, and Corwin E. Smidt, "Getting the Spirit: Religious and Partisan Mobilization in the 2004 Elections," in *Interest Group Politics*, 7th ed., ed. Allan J. Cigler and Burdett A. Loomis (Washington, D.C.: CQ Press, 2007), 157–181. See also Jon A. Shields, *The Democratic Virtues of the Christian Right* (Princeton: Princeton University Press, 2009), 115–146, for similar conclusions from different data.

23. Guth et al., "Getting the Spirit."

24. For a thorough exposition, see Daniel J. B. Hofrenning, *In Washington But Not of It: The Prophetic Politics of Religious Lobbyists* (Philadelphia: Temple University Press, 1995). For further discussion, see Hertzke, "Religious Interest Groups," and Tipton, *Public Pulpits.*

25. Jack Walker, *Mobilizing Interest Groups in America: Patrons, Professions, and Social Movements* (Ann Arbor: University of Michigan Press, 1991), 144–150.

26. For the liberals, see Tipton, *Public Pulpits;* for the conservatives, Napp Nazworth, "The Institutionalization of the Christian Right" (unpublished Ph.D. dissertation, University of Florida, 2006).

27. Laura Olson, "Mainline Protestant Washington Offices and the Political Lives of Clergy," in *The Quiet Hand of God: Faith-Based Activism and the Public Role of Mainline Protestantism*, ed. Robert Wuthnow and John H. Evans (Berkeley: University of California Press, 2002), 54–79.

28. For these assessments, see Hertzke, "Religious Interest Groups," Tipton, *Public Pulpits*, and Hofrenning, *In Washington But Not of It.*

29. Frank R. Baumgartner and Beth L. Leech, *Basic Interests: The Importance of Groups in Politics and Political Science* (Princeton: Princeton University Press, 1998), suggest models for such a study. The only approximation in this sector is David Yamane and Elizabeth Oldmixon, "Religion in the Legislative Arena: Affiliation, Salience, Advocacy, and Public Policy," *Legislative Studies Quarterly* 31 (August 2006): 433–460.

30. Barry C. Burden, *The Personal Roots of Representation* (Princeton: Princeton University Press, 2007), 112–136; James L. Guth, "Religion and Roll Calls: Religious Influences on the U.S. House of Representatives, 1997–2002," presented at the annual meeting of the American Political Science Association, Chicago, August 30–September 2, 2007; Elizabeth Oldmixon, "Religion and Legislative Politics," in *Oxford Handbook of Religion*, 497–517.

31. James F. Findlay, *Church People in the Struggle: The National Council of Churches and the Black Freedom Movement, 1950–1970* (New York: Oxford University Press, 1993); Matthew Moen, *The Christian Right and Congress* (Tuscaloosa: University of Alabama Press, 1989); Allan D. Hertzke, *Freeing God's Children: The Unlikely Alliance for Global Human Rights* (Lanham, Md.: Rowman and Littlefield, 2004); and Tipton, *Public Pulpits.*

32. Consider the massive controversy created by John J. Mearsheimer and Steven M. Walt, *The Israel Lobby and U.S. Foreign Policy* (New York: Farrar, Straus and Giroux, 2007).

33. Hertzke, "Religious Interest Groups," 321.

34. Frank Sorauf, *The Wall of Separation: The Constitutional Politics of Church and State* (Princeton: Princeton University Press, 1976), 4.

35. Gregg Ivers, *To Build A Wall: American Jews and the Separation of Church and State* (Charlottesville: University of Virginia Press, 1995).

36. Gregg Ivers, "Please God, Save This Honorable Court: The Emergence of the Conservative Legal Bar," in *The Interest Group Connection,* ed. Paul S. Herrnson, Ronald G. Shaiko, and Clyde Wilcox, (Chatham, N.J.: Chatham House, 1998), 289–301.

37. Steven P. Brown, *Trumping Religion: The New Christian Right, The Free Speech Clause, and the Courts* (Tuscaloosa: University of Alabama Press, 2002); Hans J. Hacker, *The Culture of Conservative Christian Litigation* (Lanham, Md.: Rowman and Littlefield, 2005).

38. Steven P. Brown reviews the success of the free speech strategy in *Trumping Religion*, chapters 5 and 6.

39. Dan Gilgoff, *The Jesus Machine: How James Dobson, Focus on the Family, and Evangelical America Are Winning the Culture War* (New York: St. Martins Press, 2007), 228–241.

40. Harold F. Bass and Mark J. Rozell, "Religion and the U.S. Presidency," in *Oxford Handbook of Religion*, 487.

41. Tipton, *Public Pulpits;* James L. Guth, "Clinton, Impeachment and the Culture Wars," in *The Postmodern Presidency: Bill Clinton's Legacy in U.S. Politics,* ed. Steven E. Schier (Pittsburgh: University of Pittsburgh Press, 2000), 203–222; and Guth, "George Bush and Religious Politics," in *High Risk and Big Ambition: The Presidency of George W. Bush*, ed. Steven E. Schier (Pittsburgh: University of Pittsburgh Press, 2004), 117–144.

42. Amy E. Black, Douglas L. Koopman, and David K. Ryden, *Of Little Faith: The Politics of George W. Bush's Faith-Based Initiatives* (Washington, D.C.: Georgetown University Press, 2006).

43. J. Bruce Nichols, *The Uneasy Alliance: Religion, Refugee Work, and U.S. Foreign Policy* (New York: Oxford University Press, 1988); and Rachel McCleary, *Global Compassion: Private Voluntary Organizations and U.S. Foreign Policy Since 1939* (New York: Oxford University Press, 2009).

44. Thomas F. Farr, *World of Faith and Freedom: Why International Religious Liberty Is Vital to American National Security* (New York: Oxford University Press, 2008).

45. Robert Wuthnow, *Boundless Faith: The Global Outreach of American Churches* (Berkeley: University of California Press, 2009).

46. Compare Eric M. Uslaner, "American Interests in the Balance: Do Ethnic Groups Dominate Foreign Policy Making?" in *Interest Group Politics,* 7th ed., 301–321.

SUGGESTED READING

Cleary, Edward L, and Allen D. Hertzke, eds. *Representing God at the Statehouse: Religion and Politics in the American States.* Lanham, Md.: Rowman and Littlefield, 2006.

Deckman, Melissa M. *School Board Battles: The Christian Right in Local Politics.* Washington, D.C.: Georgetown University Press, 2004.

Djupe, Paul A., and Laura R. Olson, eds. *Religious Interests in Community Conflict: Beyond the Culture Wars.* Waco, Texas: Baylor University Press, 2007.

Ebersole, Luke. *Church Lobbying in the Nation's Capital.* New York: Macmillan, 1951.

Hertzke, Allen D. *Representing God in Washington: The Role of Religious Lobbies in the American Polity.* Knoxville: University of Tennessee Press, 1988.

Noll, Mark A., and Luke E. Harlow, eds. *Religion and American Politics: From Colonial Times to the Present.* 2nd ed. New York: Oxford University Press, 2007.

Pratt, Henry J. *The Liberalization of American Protestantism: A Case Study in Complex Organizations.* Detroit, Mich.: Wayne State University Press, 1972.

Wuthnow, Robert, and John H. Evans, eds. *The Quiet Hand of God: Faith-Based Activism and the Public Role of Mainline Protestantism.* Berkeley: University of California Press, 2002.

chapter 18

Women's and Feminist Movements and Organizations

by Anne N. Costain

SOCIAL MOVEMENTS ARE OFTEN GIVEN credit for bringing about the historic changes that have taken place in the treatment of women and in policy toward gender more generally in the United States.[1] This development is not surprising, considering the frequency with which American movements addressing women and gender-related issues occur. Scholars typically identify three "waves" of women's movements, stretching from the mid-nineteenth century to the present, and accompanied by many other change-oriented movements that have pursued and continue to pursue these issues.[2] Among the allies and adversaries of women's rights were and are the abolition, temperance, progressive, peace, labor, civil rights, reproductive choice, pro-life, and gay rights movements. Yet, since the first American women's movement, dramatic aspects of movement politics from the massive marches of suffragists in New York City and the nation's capital to the imprisonment of suffrage leaders and their resulting hunger strikes have often overshadowed the enduring, continuous, incrementally innovative actions of formal organizations—interest groups and lobbying organizations—that have similarly advocated for policy change. This chapter presents a shift in focus from women's movements to women's interest groups to consider the closely related yet surprisingly different set of gender issues addressed over the years by organized groups and social movements.[3] The argument is not that group processes have necessarily been more important than movement processes in determining the outcomes of gender issues; rather, it emphasizes an aspect of feminist activism that has often been given short shrift.

REINTERPRETING THE FIRST TWO WAVES OF FEMINISM

A main impetus for the shift in emphasis from women's movements to women's interest groups is the rich new body of research that reexamines the periods leading up to and following the achievement of American woman suffrage in 1920.[4] These writings reframe a dominant narrative that had previously held that success in winning the vote resulted from a type of social movement politics that restricted feminist goals to suffrage (hence a movement labeled suffrage rather than feminist). This story identified voting as an overarching theme that mobilized and united supporters by tying attainment of the vote to winning full citizenship for women. Suffragists argued that citizenship in the context of American institutions would lead to achievement of other desired objectives even in the absence of a clear political strategy after its adoption.

The new scholarship challenges this interpretation by situating its narrative in the historic context of party decline and interest group rise following the American Civil War. The new frame shifts the focus from successful social movement politics leading to institutional change to an emphasis on the burgeoning number of active and powerful interest groups working on women's issues during a period of rising opportunity for group politics. Gathered from research in history, sociology, and political science, this story begins with the proliferation of women's groups arising out of the legacy of antebellum female benevolent societies and abolitionist groups. It examines how these presuffrage organizations paved the way for the women's club movement, civic associations, good government groups, and ultimately a style of lobbying centered on education—a style that transformed early twentieth-century lobbying and institutional politics in America.[5]

This reinterpretation of the first feminist wave suggests a parallel reexamination of the second wave. Much of the writing about the mid-twentieth-century women's liberation/women's rights movement (second wave feminism) has begun, either explicitly or by inference, by interpreting this movement as a response to work undone and mistakes made by the first women's movement.[6] This explanation, like the dominant narrative about achieving suffrage, has stressed that the second wave of the women's movement mobilized around a single issue: adding an Equal Rights Amendment (ERA) to the Constitution to guarantee legal equality for women. The ERA, like suffrage, was rather naïvely thought to be the route to solidifying women's first-class citizenship in the United States by embedding this status in the Constitution and thereby prohibiting laws treating males and females unequally. The experiences of the two waves of the feminist movement begin to diverge in 1982 following the failure of the ERA to win ratification by the required number of states. While the first wave of feminism fragmented as a kind of victim of its own success, the second wave splintered due to failure to achieve its primary goal.

Following attainment of the vote in 1920, the suffrage movement reorganized itself to pursue a second goal, but without the same consensus that had existed in support of suffrage. Foreshadowing the dominant goal of the second feminist movement, some leaders and organizations concentrated on amending the Constitution to secure equal rights for women. Others pursued aims of their allies in the progressive movement, working to perfect democratic governance through expansion of direct democracy (town meetings, initiative and referendum voting, and recall elections), citizen participation in politics, and stronger laws against government corruption. In contrast, members of the second wave of feminism were left in the position of searching for what seemed to them to be second-best solutions, having failed to achieve their primary goal of amending the Constitution. Some began campaigns to add ERAs to state constitutions, while others focused on reproductive rights, broad social justice concerns, and how sexual orientation fits into public recognition of families.

In spite of these differences, the new scholarship points to strong similarities between the two waves of feminism. Each operated in a climate characterized by party decline, interest group proliferation, and the growing power of interests. The focus of extant scholarship on social movements to the neglect of interest group activities has, however, de-emphasized these important continuities. Adding to the research on the expansion of women's organizations following suffrage, Dara Strolovitch has documented an explosion of women's groups between 1960 and 1999, with 65 percent of the national women's organizations at the end of this period having started within it.[7] At the end of the twentieth century, a third wave of feminism began to emerge, building on the cultural successes in language, shifting values, and social justice of the second wave movement, but criticizing the lack of diversity and overemphasis on unity within earlier women's movements.

Second and third wave feminisms continue to coexist (albeit largely with different generations of adherents), resulting in an unprecedented diversity within women's groups. By refocusing on changes within the community of women's and feminist organizations in the wake of the success of the first women's movement, and arguably the partial failure of the second and uncertain future of the third wave of feminism, we can identify issue and organizational patterns that seem to provide different possibilities for issues of gender as dialogues and institutional change in response to a political climate that favors interest groups over parties and, perhaps, movements as well.

Frances Willard was a tireless late-nineteenth-century advocate for the temperance movement and women's suffrage. She led the National Women's Temperance Union, National Council of Women, and the Women's Christian Temperance Union.

THE FIRST WAVE REINTERPRETED

The new scholarship on groups within the first wave of feminism shows how they succeeded in altering institutions through innovative challenges to the status quo. Elisabeth Clemens has demonstrated how women's groups employed collective action during the more than seventy-year period between the women's rights convention at Seneca Falls in 1848 and the achievement of national suffrage in ways not previously seen in America.[8] Although women's exclusion from the vote could have pushed them to embrace lobbying or other methods of political participation that were—unlike voting—open to them, they mounted a fierce critique of pressure group politics, echoing the sentiments of the progressive movement about the threat lobbyists posed to the public interest. As their campaign for suffrage progressed, lacking the vote and access to important sources of institutional power, they began to use lobbying without lessening their critique of the way it was routinely practiced early in the twentieth century. The women's club movement at the turn of the twentieth century shows how women kept up sharp attacks on special interest groups, but turned some of these groups' methods to their own purposes. Unlike men's clubs, such as the Masons and the Odd Fellows, women's clubs eschewed exclusivity and secret societies with political goals and instead became models of open membership and democratic practices. Even those women's clubs that seemed most distant from politics discussed civic affairs, but, unlike men's clubs, avoided partisanship even while devoting much energy to criticizing the smoke-filled backroom dealings of political bosses. Women's civic associations, such as the Wisconsin Women's Progressive Association and Los Angeles's Friday Morning Club, adopted the organizational trappings of urban political clubhouses and redesigned them to recruit the largely middle- and upper-class women who had the education and leisure to challenge government dishonesty.[9] Taking lessons from those they wished to displace from power, women and their progressive allies met, recruited, organized, and became educated about how to win electoral office. Theda Skocpol has observed that "classic voluntary federations taught people how to run meetings, handle moneys, keep records, and participate in group discussions."[10] These practices helped to create opportunities for all women, including blue-collar and lower-level white-collar women to acquire skills for political leadership. Michael Young has furnished data on the pre–Civil War auxiliary societies supporting temperance and the abolition of slavery, showing that women's activism even in this early period was quite significant. In 1837, one out of every ten auxiliary antislavery societies was formally designated either as a women's society or a woman-led children's society.[11] It is likely that temperance auxiliaries contained even more women leaders.

There were numerous advantages for women in adopting forms from voluntary organizations rather than joining political parties, which were often, in any case, hesitant to receive them. One of the greatest social barriers for women was the widespread belief that men should operate in the public sphere and women should exercise their influence through the private sphere. Voluntary associations in the early twentieth century occupied a gray zone between these two spheres. As Clemens notes, "Without directly challenging the fundamentally fraternal character of political life, women drew on domestic and religious models of action to begin to craft a public role for themselves."[12] These groups and their leaders often described their work as teaching and

On College Day in February 1917 women representing various schools gathered outside the White House to appeal to the president for the right to vote.

WOMEN'S GROUPS AND THE NEW LOBBYING IN THE 1920s

Political scientist Pendleton Herring wrote in 1929 of the significant change from old to new Washington lobbying, which he characterized as a shift from a medieval concept of representation based upon class and estate to a new emphasis on shared beliefs and interests. Rather than banding together to protect one's fellow workers, religious congregants, and neighbors, interests were shifting to associations of like-minded people. In Herring's words: "The emphasis has shifted from the individual. The voice harkened to by legislators is not the lone voice of the citizen crying in a wilderness of individual opinions, but the chorus of a cause organized for a purpose and directed by a press agent."[1]

Herring singled out women's groups as the forefront of this revolution in group representation before Congress. He described their number in Washington, D.C., as second only to those representing industry. Women's groups were notably diverse, encompassing the Federated Farm Women of America, National Women's Trade Union League, Women's Christian Temperance Union, National League of Women Voters, Daughters of the American Revolution (DAR), and Women's International League for Peace and Freedom (WILPF). Although women's groups often worked as allies, organizations such as the DAR and the WILPF frequently battled on opposite sides of issues, including national defense.

Herring noted that in the 1920s few national women's societies failed to become involved with some aspect of legislation. Most came to Washington frequently and operated there in a consistent manner. Women's lobbyists saw their role as providing information to clarify misunderstood points on issues, consulting with supporters of particular bills, helping to arrange hearings, keeping their members informed about congressional activity on issues of interest, and "sit[ting] for weary hours in the gallery of House or Senate whenever these measures are likely to come up and thus get[ting] first hand knowledge of the tactics of opponents and the support given by friends."[2]

This type of lobbying practiced and, in some cases invented, by women's lobbyists would be easily recognized on Capitol Hill today.

1. Pendleton Herring, *Group Representation Before Congress* (Baltimore: Johns Hopkins University Press, 1929), 7.
2. The *Woman Citizen*, March 30–31, 1927, as quoted in ibid., 191.

applying the moral authority of wife and mother within the family to solve social problems.[13] This approach resonated with some of the party politics of the day. William Jennings Bryan, three times the presidential nominee of the Democratic Party, declared, "The world needs the brain of woman as well as the brain of man, and even more does it need the conscience of woman."[14] Pietistic partisan politics were in vogue as was the belief in the general moral superiority of women—particularly mothers. Bryan became a late but fervent supporter of temperance and suffrage. Michael Young has noted that within the temperance movement, the "attack against special sins [most notably alcohol abuse and slavery] provided women the opportunity to move aggressively against male institutions."[15] Women's civic associations of the period issued even more straightforward attacks on men's political clubs. Despite their political purpose, however, women's organizations were careful to distinguish between their nonpartisan advocacy for the public interest and against corruption and sin and the self-interested wheeling and dealing of partisan political bosses against whom they fought.

This blending of the public and private was also combined with an educational approach to political change rather than using threats and rewards to pressure politicians to adopt particular issue positions—a strategy that represented an important innovation in the organizational repertoires of interest group politics and one that has contemporary analogues. Corporate lobbying groups unconsciously imitate postsuffrage women's groups when they pose as educators and defenders of the public interest by using slogans such as "Truth about Global Warming," when their actual purpose is to block stricter federal laws on auto emissions. The women's interests of the first wave overcame obstacles to their inclusion in politics, as they broke down barriers between politics and private life. Their effectiveness is evident in Pendleton Herring's classic analysis *Group Representation in Congress*, in which he characterizes lobbying by women's groups as remarkably diverse and engaged with an exceptionally broad range of policy issues. The durability of this pattern of lobbying is reflected in its reappearance in one of the most widely circulated slogans of second wave feminism, "The personal is political."

ANALYZING SECOND WAVE FEMINISM

As areas of government regulation grew in the 1960s and 1970s, there was a corresponding rapid growth of women's groups, as there was of groups and lobbying generally.[16] These groups included not only those representing business and industry, although they were the most numerous and organized most quickly, but also public interest and social movement-initiated organizations. Andrew McFarland explains the simultaneous emergence and growth of business and public interest groups as part of a neopluralist view of American politics. He writes, "We can expect movements to spin off citizens groups to act in the policymaking process as a countervailing power to producer groups." [17] Just as the first wave woman's movement mobilized in a time of heightened government regulation, booming interest group politics, and decline of political parties, wave two emerged and grew in a similar time of change and offered similar opportunities for influence. Tracing this interest group ancestry reveals a pattern of development, issue interests, and political impact different from the narrative on women's social movements that is most prevalent in the existing literature.

Although the lineage stretching from the radical wing of first wave feminism to the beginning of the second wave is clear—personified by Alice Paul and the National Women's Party she founded and continued to lead during this period—the more diverse and scattered remnants of interest organizations that were either part of or grew out of the suffrage movement are also readily discoverable. Published research, including the author's, provides evidence of ongoing group ties between the two women's movements.[18] Of the fourteen organizations dedicated to representing women's interests in Washington during the 1970s, eight had strong ties to first wave feminism. Some of these groups preceded the first wave movement, later becoming active in it, and some arose either out of the movement or its aftermath.[19] A few examples of these "wave-spanning" organizations reveal their diversity and common purposes. A small number of women college graduates who wanted to encourage women to get a college education to better utilize the talents of women for the benefit of "humankind" founded the American Association of University Women in 1881. The League of Women Voters began as an auxiliary of the National American Woman Suffrage Association, but eventually became the League of Women Voters of the United States in 1946 with the mission of promoting the political education of enfranchised women. The General Federation of Women's Clubs was founded in 1868 to unite and advance common interests of women's clubs in fields ranging from arts and education to international and public affairs. It was a leader in the club movement following woman suffrage. The National Council of Jewish Women was organized in 1893 during the Parliament of Religions at the Chicago World's Fair as a service organization and to advance women's status in society and combat sexism. The National Council of Business and Professional Women (BPW) grew out of efforts by the U.S. government in 1918 to engage women in the war effort. In 1919 it became the BPW/USA with its first president a member of the National Woman's Party. The United Methodist Women came into existence when fourteen missionary societies joined together in 1869 to spread the gospel through service ministries and advocacy for women and children.

Because social movements are an important part of the process of issue definition within the American system, it is not surprising that first wave groups still had major goals to achieve even after the movement ended; it is also not surprising that those goals were still relevant in the 1960s and 1970s.[20] Because the woman suffrage movement did not articulate a clear strategy for political action after attaining the vote, women remained second-class citizens who had far less policy impact than men in spite of their new rights to vote and run for office. In national elections, women did not begin to vote at rates equaling or exceeding men until 1980 (see Table 18.1). Sex continued to be a significant category in granting or denying legal rights in employment, service on juries, obtaining financial credit, and owning or disposing of property.[21]

The diverse array of groups growing out of the first wave of the movement was an important contributor to early successes in interest group lobbying. The League of Women Voters trained lobbyists from the National Organization for Women (NOW) and the National Women's Political Caucus (NWPC). Experienced lobbyists such as Olya Margolin of the National Council of Jewish Women used her entrée as a trusted ally of organized labor to get women's movement groups invited as witnesses in important congressional committee hearings. By the early 1970s there was a convergence of left, right, and center groups working on gender issues. Organizationally, this linking brought together enough resources, especially from the long-established groups, to mount a plausible challenge to the status quo.[22]

TABLE 18.1 **Gender Differences in Voter Turnout in Presidential and Midterm Congressional Elections, 1964–1994**

Year	Women	Men
1964	67%	72%
1966	53	58
1968	66	70
1970	53	57
1972	62	64
1974	43	46
1976	59	60
1978	45	47
1980	59	59
1982	48	49
1984	61	59
1986	46	46
1988	58	56
1990	45	45
1992	62	60
1994	45	45

SOURCE: This table combines voting data from the U.S. Census reported in M. Margaret Conway, Gertrude A. Steurnagel, and David W. Ahern, *Women and Political Participation: Cultural Change in the Political Arena* (Washington, D.C.: CQ Press, 1997), 79–80.

Women browse literature at the National Organization for Women's (NOW) fourth annual conference in 1970. The organization was planning a national strike of women that summer to protest gender discrimination.

The new social movement also gave rise to feminist organizations such as NOW, NWPC, and the Women's Equity Action League that, along with state and local groups, played critical but somewhat different roles in creating stories that made women's discontent clearer and in communicating these narratives to the media and thereby to the public.[23] As many have observed, Betty Friedan's book, *The Feminine Mystique* grabbed the public's attention by exposing widespread discontent among women and labeling this phenomenon a problem with "no name." [24] Providing a narrative, story, or "frame" to make sense out of these feelings was an essential precursor to effective lobbying on behalf of women in the second wave.

DEVELOPING AGENDA OF THE SECOND WAVE

An under-explored aspect of this coordinated lobbying effort on behalf of feminism is how it moved beyond the second wave movement issues related to the ERA—sex discrimination and civil rights—to find goals of relevance to its members that would attract public attention and sustain the movement. Earlier research by the author and two collaborators using *New York Times* data to track the evolution of a feminist agenda found that prior to the emergence of the second women's movement in the mid-1960s, most women's coverage by the *New York Times* focused on their increasing numbers in the paid labor market.[25] The most evident demographic shift from the mid-1950s to the mid-1960s was the number of women either remaining in the workforce after marrying or reentering the job market while married with children. The second most common topic of articles dealt with the changing nature of families in this period. Much of the shift resulted from more women working outside the home, but women's general discontent with their lives also began to be acknowledged in print. Equal rights appeared as a distant third source of subject matter. These articles often referred to the United Nation's sponsored convention on political rights for women, proposals for an equal rights amendment in the U.S. constitution, and links between the black civil rights movement and women's rights.

Between 1965 and 1974 the emergence of an identifiable women's movement became evident in the *Times*. The largest proportion of articles in this period examined women and work with women's legal rights running a close second. The overlap between these two subjects is significant. Articles featured issues ranging from unequal pay to differential promotion opportunities, conditions of employment, and sexism in the workplace (not yet clearly identified as sexual harassment). In addition, coverage of the debate over the ERA appeared often. The third most prominent subject was women in families. These articles debated the appropriate roles of fathers and mothers in the socialization of children. Women, work, and the family continued to be important concerns, with lack of availability of quality childcare a serious worry.

At the peak of the women's movement from 1975 to 1984, there was as close to a single theme as can be found throughout this period. Fully three-quarters of the articles on women dealt with their legal rights, and more than half of these stories discussed the ERA. For the first time, work dropped in importance. Still, women and work appeared in a majority of the articles, many featuring women's legal rights as employees. Families were the third largest topic. A number of these articles examined the likely effect of the ERA on families. Others were personal stories of individuals balancing work and family.

By the period between 1985 and 1995, it was clear that although the ERA had been successfully added to a number of state constitutions, it would not be added to the U.S. Constitution. In the *New York Times* more than eight in ten of the articles concerning women dealt with women and employment, and two-thirds of these featured the family. Again, there was a great deal of overlap, with concerns about women, work, and family commanding the most space. Work and family had never ceased to be important. A change reflecting the increasing entry of women into the workplace was that articles no longer examined men's feelings about women's workforce participation, but were more likely to consider the implications associated with women as continuing to bear primary responsibility for taking care of the home and children while also participating in the paid labor force. Frequent topics were domestic violence, the rising divorce rate, and how women's rapid entry into the labor market had contributed to both. A strong argument can be made that the second wave movement, with its focused agenda on women's legal rights, held sway only for roughly a ten-year period, with the predominant gender discussion outside that period remaining women, work, and family.

As illustrative as they are of the evolution of the feminist agenda, these data do not address relationships between a movement unified in its effort to achieve legal equality for women and the organized interests within it supporting a wider range of issues spanning family, social roles, and jobs and employment. To assess the role of feminist interest groups in shaping an agenda, nine movement-linked interest groups were identified based on their wide-ranging engagement in political actions on behalf of the movement.[26] Articles were pulled directly from the *New York Times* using Lexis-Nexis as the searching mechanism.[27]

This data set spanned the period from 1980, when most feminists recognized that there was little chance that the Equal Rights Amendment would be ratified, to 1996, when the second wave movement was clearly in decline. The most prevalent issues discussed by these feminist groups were abortion, education, work and economics, and civil rights/women's legal rights. Because the countermovement opposing the second wave most frequently framed women's issues in the context of the family, articles mentioning family were also analyzed.

Analysis of the *New York Times* articles showed that reporting on employment and the economy and education remained both high and relatively constant throughout the period, but coverage of women's legal rights and abortion varied widely. Throughout the 1980s large numbers of articles dealt with women's legal rights. Even after the defeat of the ERA in 1982, the number of articles grew, peaking in 1984. By 1990, however, legal rights had the fewest mentions in the data set. Abortion largely replaced women's legal rights in coverage. Second wave feminist groups were adamant about objecting to family as a frame, arguing that women should be viewed autonomously. In contrast, the countermovement groups interviewed in these articles argued that a liberal individualistic perspective of this sort would destroy conventional families and family life in America. The issues most frequently looked at in a family context were abortion, education, and employment. Civil rights rarely included a family perspective.

The *Times* evidence demonstrates that even the second wave groups linked most closely to the feminist movement pursued a broader agenda than is commonly assumed. Their agenda also appears more reflective of *Times* coverage generally. There is a clear split between the more liberal and the more conservative women's groups over how to frame these issues, with conservative preference for handling women's issues in the context of family, and liberals seeking to avoid family frames when possible.[28]

THE THIRD WAVE BROADENS THE FEMINIST AGENDA

Adding to the diversity of women's groups and the issues they have contested is the third wave women's movement that took root in the 1990s. This most recent wave was initiated mainly by women in their twenties and thirties at the time, who had grown up with the benefits of the political gains won by first and second wave movement activists. The younger generation's activism was stimulated by their questioning of several assumptions and actions of their second wave forebears, by concerns about the antifeminist backlash that had taken root in the 1980s, and by events such as the rape trial of William Kennedy Smith and the confirmation of Clarence Thomas to the U.S. Supreme Court in spite of accusations of sexual harassment.[29] The term "third wave" first appeared in an essay, "Becoming the Third Wave," by Rebecca Walker and published in *Ms.* magazine in 1992.[30] Walker, the daughter of author Alice Walker, along with Shannon Liss, Amy Richards, and others founded the Third Wave Foundation in 1992 to reach young feminists, male or female, between the ages of fifteen and thirty. Third wavers have used numerous ways to communicate with each other and the public, including "zines," pages of handwritten and typed material photocopied and distributed through informal networks, Internet blogs, "Riot Grrrl Press," a nonprofit distribution and printing service for underground women writers cofounded with the members of the punk band Bikini Kill, and published anthologies with personal accounts by young feminists of their experiences positive and negative with feminism.[31] These individual stories about attempts to navigate the ideals and contradictions of second wave feminism placed the third wave in the cross-hairs of the culture wars. The conservative right embraced their pointed critiques of the second wave of feminism, and many on the left chided them for their limited historical perspective and sometimes naïve embrace of pop culture.

Although the third wave and its agenda are difficult to delineate and define, many of its driving concerns were anticipated by second wave feminists of color, lesbian feminists, and others who pushed the movement to address issues of race, class, and sexuality. In addition to continued attention to long-standing issues such as reproductive rights, employment discrimination, educational opportunity, sexual harassment, and rape, at the core of the third wave have been challenges to what some critics have characterized as feminism's essentialist and universalizing assumptions about women that many argued privileged the experiences and interests of white, heterosexual, and middle-class women. As such, many third wave feminists advocate, either explicitly or implicitly, an "intersectional" framework that emphasizes the meeting points among various forms of marginalization: race, ethnicity, class, sexuality, and gender identity.[32] To these ends, many third wave feminists are engaged with issues and movements associated with lesbian, gay, transgender, and intersex rights as well as with anti-racist, anti-imperialist, and economic justice movements.[33] In addition to its intersectional approach, third wave feminism also has a strong cultural focus. Rebecca Walker explains this best in criticizing what many young feminists see as the unreachable and unappealing ideal feminist of the second wave. "For many of us it seems that to be a feminist in the way that we have seen or understood feminism is to conform to an identity and way of living that doesn't allow for individuality, complexity, or less than perfect personal histories. We fear that the identity will dictate and regulate our lives." [34] The third wave's insistence on a "fun" feminism that is open to Barbie dolls, *Buffy the Vampire Slayer,* high fashion, and sexual experimentation challenges both societal and second wave feminist norms.[35] It is, however, consistent with culturalist understandings of social movements. Noted social movement theorist Alberto Melucci has written, "Contemporary movements are prophets of the present." [36] The third wavers may well be giving voice to social change that has already taken place—a new reality created by the laws, policies, and opportunities opened through state responses to the women's movement of the sixties and seventies.

Where third wave feminism does appear to diverge most from earlier feminist waves is in its small number of organized groups. The reexamined histories of the suffrage and women's rights movements demonstrate the value of groups in maintaining a broad feminist agenda in the face of powerful movement and political pressures to stick with one consistent goal, whether it is suffrage or legal equality. Cyberspace, Web sites, the blogosphere, or communication through the music and messaging of pop culture may be the modern versions of preserving an agenda broad enough to sustain movement activists and pressure political institutions. But because the state and its political institutions are notoriously slower to change than social and economic institutions, the lack of robust groups to challenge the status quo is likely to prove problematic.

CONCLUSION

Stepping back from emphasizing a social movement focus (or implied focus) when exploring issues of gender opens the possibility of understanding more fully the emerging complexity and ambiguity of gender politics in the twenty-first century. The importance for social movements of maintaining a consistent message with broad acceptance and an emotionally appealing narrative can make it difficult to sustain the multiple perspectives that allow issues to transmute, attract new followers and allies, and remain culturally relevant in times of rapid change and unusual interest group power and influence.

The relationships between feminists and the relatively sympathetic Obama administration (after working as outsiders through the eight years of the George W. Bush presidency) reveal the complexity of maintaining a broad agenda with relatively limited conventional organizational and economic resources. From the first months of the Obama administration to the present, feminist and GLBT (gay, lesbian, bisexual, transgender) groups have bounced back and forth between organizing grassroots protests and letter-writing campaigns to get followers to pressure the administration to back away from unfavorable decisions on issues such as stripping $200 million out of the economic stimulus package to fund state purchases of contraceptives for poor women, to celebrating President Barack Obama's quick and decisive action to rescind "the global gag rule." That shift in government policy once again allows U.S. foreign aid to go to health clinics that perform and give advice on abortion. Groups joined together to challenge Congress to repeal the "don't ask, don't tell" policy in the military under which service members discovered to be gay are discharged. At the end of 2010 Congress passed and President Obama signed legislation that repealed this provision. The bill requires the president and his top military advisers to certify that repealing the ban will not harm troops' ability to fight. When this certification is issued, gay service members for the first time will be able to serve openly in the U.S. military. Many of these same groups mobilized and advocated confirming federal judge Sonia Sotomayor and Solicitor General Elena Kagan to the Supreme Court. At the same time, they expressed their anger at the president's reluctance to take steps to repeal the federal Defense of Marriage Act (DOMA) that limits marriage to a man and a woman. In February 2011 Attorney General Eric Holder announced that the Department of Justice would no longer defend DOMA in court. President Obama has stated that his position on gay marriage is "constantly evolving," but he has not yet shifted from supporting civil unions for same sex couples to endorsing gay marriage.

Balancing support for a president who shares many of the same values as movement groups, while maintaining a sufficient presence to advance a solid feminist agenda, will require a sophisticated political understanding, resources, and access to decision makers. Whether the remnants of the second wave of women's organizations can combine effectively with the energy and issues of the third wave to mount this kind of campaign is unclear. Broad agendas compel attention on many fronts. The widening circle of allies and advocates of gendered issues holds promise for legislative reform, but puts a premium on the organizational skill needed to balance the multiple interests necessary to pass new laws.

NOTES

1. The term *gender* is used to broaden consideration from just biological sex (women and men) to encompass social and cultural understandings of appropriate behavior within the continuum of masculinity and femininity as well.

2. Use of the term *wave* to identify the suffrage and contemporary women's movements has been criticized for imposing artificial boundaries, for universalizing what takes place "within" a wave, and for neglecting activity that takes place between waves, such as the contributions of labor union women. The criticism has spurred an effort by academic historians to recapture that history and "re-wave" public understanding of feminist reform. This chapter attempts to use the term *wave* not in its narrower meaning, but in its more inclusive meaning, arguing that there was more to the suffrage movement than claiming the vote and more to the women's movement of the 1960s and 1970s than its work on the Equal Rights Amendment (ERA) and legal equality. For a discussion of these issues, see Dorothy Sue Cobble, *The Other Women's Movement: Workplace Justice and Social Rights in Modern America* (Princeton: Princeton University Press, 2004).

3. Paul Burstein has made the point that in the past too much effort has been expended defining political interests either as social movements, interest groups, or political parties, which creates fragmented literatures within important issue areas such as the environment, public interest, civil rights, and gender. Burstein, "Interest Organizations, Political Parties, and the Study of Democratic Politics," in *Social Movements and American Political Institutions*, ed. Anne N. Costain and Andrew S. McFarland (Lanham, Md.: Rowman and Littlefield, 1998), 39–56. While acknowledging Burstein's concern about the resulting fragmentation of important literatures on social movements, this chapter seeks to illuminate the contrasting goals, targets, and mechanisms addressed by women's interest groups and organizations as compared with social movements during more than a hundred years of U.S. political history.

4. Ellen Carol Dubois, *Feminism and Suffrage: The Emergence of an Independent Women's Movement in America 1848–1869* (Ithaca, N.Y.: Cornell University Press, 1978); and Dubois, *Woman Suffrage and Woman's Rights* (New York: New York University Press, 1998); Kristi Anderson, *After Suffrage: Women in Parties and Electoral Politics before the New Deal* (Chicago: University of Chicago Press, 1996); Elisabeth Clemens, "Organizational Repertoires and Institutional Change: Women's Groups and the Transformation of U.S. Politics, 1890–1920," *American Journal of Sociology* 98 (January 1993): 755–798; and Clemens, *The People's Lobby: Organizational Innovation and the Rise of Interest Group Politics in the United States, 1890–1925* (Chicago: University of Chicago Press, 1997).

5. Clemens, "Organizational Repertoires."

6. See Janet Boles, *The Politics of the Equal Rights Amendment* (New York: Longman, 1979); Anne N. Costain, *Inviting Women's Rebellion: A Political Process Interpretation of the Women's Movement* (Baltimore: Johns Hopkins University Press, 1992); and Jane Mansbridge, *Why We Lost the ERA* (Chicago: University of Chicago Press, 1986).

7. Dara Z. Strolovitch, *Affirmative Advocacy* (Chicago: University of Chicago Press, 2007), 16–17.

8. Clemens, "Organizational Repertoires."

9. Clemens, *People's Lobby*, 184–234.

10. Theda Skocpol, "Voice and Inequality: The Transformation of American Civic Democracy," *Perspectives on Politics* 2 (March 2004): 10.

11. Michael Young, "Religious Origins of U.S. National Social Movements," *American Sociological Review* 67 (October 2002): 660–688.

12. Clemens, "Organizational Repertoires," 776.

13. Young, "Religious Origins," 683.

14. Michael Kazen, *A Godly Hero: The Life of William Jennings Bryan* (New York: Knopf, 2006), 257.

15. Young, "Religious Origins," 683.

16. Strolovich, *Affirmative Advocacy;* and Jeffrey M. Berry, *The Interest Group Society*, 3rd ed. (New York: Longman, 1997): 17–43.

17. Andrew S. McFarland, *Neopluralism: The Evolution of Political Process Theory* (Lawrence: University Press of Kansas, 2004), 66.

18. See Anne N. Costain, "Representing Women: The Transition from Social Movement to Interest Group," *Western Political Quarterly* 34 (March 1981): 100–113; and Sarah Slavin, ed., *U.S. Women's Interest Groups: Institutional Profiles* (Westport, Conn.: Greenwood Press, 1995).

19. Information reported on these groups came from structured interviews conducted by the author between 1974 and 1975 and lasting from forty-five minutes to two and a half hours with representatives of the organizations. Specific criteria for selecting groups to interview were that (1) each had an on-going interest in women's rights that was central to the organization's purpose; (2) each made a systematic effort to influence congressional policy relating to women; and (3) each had an office in Washington, D.C., during the period when the interviews were conducted. Two other groups seeming to fit these criteria declined to be interviewed (the National Council of Negro Women and the National Council of Catholic Women). The groups covered were: American Association of University Women, November 19, 1974, and August 11, 1975; B'nai B'rith Women, November 19, 1974; Federally Employed Women, December 30, 1974, and May 7, 1975; Federation of Organizations for Professional Women, January 3, 1975, and July 30, 1975; General Federation of Women's Clubs, October 17, 1974; League of Women Voters, October 8, 1974, and August 14, 1975;

National Council of Jewish Women, November 1, 1974; National Federation of Business and Professional Women's Clubs, September 20, 1974, and October 1, 1974; National Organization for Women, October 31, 1974, and August 5, 1975; National Woman's Party, January 23, 1975; National Women's Political Caucus, October 22, 1974; United Methodist Women, November 4, 1974; Women's Equity Action League, November 1974; and Women's Lobby, December 3, 1974. Slavin, *U.S. Women's Interest Groups,* was consulted when additional information about group histories was needed.

20. McFarland, *Neopluralism,* 74.

21. Judith A. Baer and Leslie Friedman Goldstein, *The Constitutional and Legal Rights of Women: Cases in Law and Social Change,* 3rd ed. (Los Angeles: Roxbury Press, 2006); and Katherine T. Bartlett and Deborah L. Rhode, *Gender and Law: Theory, Doctrine, Commentary,* 4th ed. (New York: Aspen Publishers, 2006).

22. In this period, the most active national lobbying groups arising out of the second wave women's movement were the National Organization for Women, National Women's Political Caucus, Federally Employed Women, Women's Equity Action League, and Women's Lobby.

23. Costain, *Inviting Women's Rebellion.*

24. Betty Friedan, *The Feminine Mystique* (New York: W. W. Norton, 1963).

25. Anne N. Costain, Richard Braunstein, and Heidi Berggren, "Framing the Women's Movement," in *Women, Media, and Politics,* ed. Pippa Norris (New York: Oxford University Press, 1997), 205–220.

26. The following second wave feminist groups were selected for this search: National Organization for Women (NOW), National Women's Political Caucus, Women's Equity Action League (WEAL), Federally Employed Women (FEW), Congressional Caucus on Women's Issues, Society to Cut Up Men (SCUM), Redstockings, Older Women's League (OWL), and National Abortion and Reproductive Rights Action League (NARAL). All of these groups have self-identified as feminist and were formed during the time of the emergence of the second wave women's movement. See Anne Costain and Heather Frazier, "Media Portrayal of 'Second Wave' Feminist Groups," in *Deliberation, Democracy, and the Media,* ed. Simone Chambers and Anne Costain (Lanham, Md.: Rowman and Littlefield, 2000), 155–174.

27. Between 1980 and 1996, the *New York Times* published 1,852 articles mentioning these nine second wave feminist organizations. Half referenced NOW, the largest feminist group throughout the period.

28. Ronnee Schreiber, *Righting Feminism: Conservative Women and American Politics* (New York: Oxford University Press, 2008).

29. Catherine M. Orr, "Looking for the Third Wave" *Hypatia* 12 (Summer 1997): 30.

30. Rory Dicker and Alison Piepmeier, eds. *Catching a Wave: Reclaiming Feminism for the 21st Century* (Boston: Northeastern University Press, 2003), 10–26.

31. Among the best-known anthologies are Rebecca Walker, ed., *To Be Real: Telling the Truth and Changing the Face of Feminism* (New York: Anchor Books, 1995); Barbara Findlen, ed., *Listen Up: Voices from the Next Feminist Generation* (Seattle: Seal Press, 1995); and Leslie Heywood and Jennifer Drake, eds., *Third Wave Agenda: Being Feminist, Doing Feminism* (Minneapolis: University of Minnesota Press, 1997).

32. See, for example, Kimberlé Crenshaw, "Mapping the Margins: Intersectionality, Identity Politics, and Violence Against Women of Color," in *Theorizing Feminisms,* ed. Elizabeth Hackett and Sally Haslanger (New York: Oxford University Press, 2006), 159–173; bell hooks, *Ain't I a Woman* (Boston: Southend Press, 1981); and Strolovitch, *Affirmative Advocacy.*

33. Charlotte Kroløkke and Anne Scott Sorensen, *Gender Communication Theories and Analyses: From Silence to Performance* (Thousand Oaks, Calif.: Sage, 2006).

34. Walker, *To Be Real,* xxxiii.

35. Ann Braithwaite, "The Personal, the Political, Third-wave and Postfeminisms," *Feminist Theory* 3 (December 2002): 338–340.

36. Alberto Melucci, *Challenging Codes: Collective Action in the Information Age* (Cambridge, UK: Cambridge University Press, 1996), 1.

SUGGESTED READING

Andersen, Kristi. *After Suffrage: Women in Partisan and Electoral Politics before the New Deal.* Chicago: University of Chicago Press, 1996.

Clemens, Elisabeth. *The People's Lobby: Organizational Innovation and the Rise of Interest Group Politics in the United States, 1890–1925.* Chicago: University of Chicago Press, 1997.

Costain, Anne N. *Inviting Women's Rebellion: A Political Process Interpretation of the Women's Movement.* Baltimore: Johns Hopkins University Press, 1992.

Freeman, Jo. *The Politics of Women's Liberation: A Case Study of an Emerging Social Movement and in Relation to the Policy Process.* New York: Longman, 1975.

Heywood, Leslie, and Jennifer Drake, eds. *Third Wave Agenda: Being Feminist, Doing Feminism.* Minneapolis: University of Minnesota Press, 1997.

Minkoff, Debra. *Organizing Equality: The Evolution of Women's and Racial-Ethnic Organizations in America, 1955–1985.* New Brunswick, N.J.: Rutgers University Press, 1995.

Orr, Catherine M. "Looking for the Third Wave." *Hypatia* 12 (Summer 1997): 29–45.

Schreiber, Ronnee. *Righting Feminism: Conservative Women and American Politics.* New York: Oxford University Press, 2008.

Skocpol, Theda, "Voice and Inequality: The Transformation of American Civic Democracy." *Perspectives on Politics* 2 (March 2004): 3–20.

Strolovich, Dara Z. *Affirmative Advocacy.* Chicago: University of Chicago Press, 2007.

Walker, Rebecca, ed. *To Be Real: Telling the Truth and Changing the Face of Feminism.* New York: Anchor Books, 1995.

Woliver, Laura R. *From Outrage to Action: The Politics of Grass-Roots Dissent.* Urbana: University of Illinois Press, 1993.

chapter 19

Public Interest Groups

by Kay Lehman Schlozman

THE ORGANIZATIONS ACTIVE IN Washington span an astonishing range. They encompass organizations based on how people earn a living, how they spend their leisure, and how they define themselves in religious or ethnic terms. They range from organizations that have billions in assets to others that live from hand to mouth and from those with liberal views to those with conservative views. Within this diverse set of organizations, public interest groups—the American Automobile Association, Defenders of Wildlife, and Amnesty International USA are well-known examples—have grown in number and importance in Washington politics since the late 1960s. These are organizations that represent broad public interests that are generally beneficial to all in society, with objectives such as safer streets or safer consumer products, cleaner water or cleaner government, and enhanced domestic security or reduced domestic violence. While everyone has a stake in such broad public interests, relatively few people care intensely about them or give them the highest political priority. Not surprisingly, public interest groups are less numerous than other kinds of organized interests—especially organizations that represent citizens' work-related economic interests. Yet, they are often influential in policymaking.

WHAT ARE PUBLIC INTERESTS? WHAT ARE PUBLIC INTEREST GROUPS?

Many political organizations claim to be acting in the public interest. The president of General Motors once told a Senate committee "For years I thought what was good for our country was good for General Motors and vice versa."[1] The "vice versa" presents a problem for conceptions of the public interest; that is, what is good for General Motors may be good for the country, but it is likely to be particularly good for those with a special stake in GM's prosperity—among them GM's executives, shareholders, workers, dealers, and suppliers. For this reason, public interest groups can be defined as "organizations that seek policy goals that, if achieved, would not confer a selective benefit on the leaders, the activists, or the members of the organization."[2] Another way to conceptualize the objectives of public interest groups is in terms of public goods. As defined by economists, the characteristic of a public good is that if it is available to some member of a society, it cannot be withheld from everyone else.

In the vast array of organized interests, public interest groups are not especially numerous. As shown in Table 19.1, they constituted only 4.1 percent of the nearly 14,000 organizations listed in the 2006 *Washington Representatives* directory as having a presence in national politics—either by maintaining an office in the capital or by hiring Washington-based consultants or counsel to manage their government relations activities.[3] Although the number of organizations that advocate on behalf of public goods is dwarfed by the

TABLE 19.1 **Organized Interests in Washington Politics**

Distribution of organizations[1]	
Public interest groups	4.1%
Corporations[2]	36.1
Trade and other business associations	10.7
Occupational associations	5.2
Unions	.8
Education	5.4
Health	4.4
Identity groups[3]	3.8
Social welfare or poor	.9
State and local governments	11.8
Foreign	6.5
Other	8.6
Don't know	1.7
Total	100.0%
N[4]	13,777

SOURCE: Washington Representatives Study.

1. Distribution of organizations listed in the 2006 *Washington Representatives* directory (Bethesda, Md.: Columbia Books and Information Services, 2006).
2. Includes U.S. corporations, U.S. subsidiaries of foreign corporations, and for-profit firms of professionals such as law and consulting firms.
3. Includes organizations representing racial, ethnic, or religious groups, elderly, women, or LGBT.
4. Total number of organizations listed in the directory.

number that are organized around economic matters, especially business, the causes advocated by public interest groups are remarkably diverse. The top portion of Table 19.2 gives examples of various kinds of public interest groups. Most of the names make clear the organization's main objective, but a few might be puzzling: the Close Up Foundation sponsors educational programs in the nation's capital that encourage civic engagement; the Death with Dignity National Center advocates on behalf of laws allowing "a terminally ill, mentally competent adult the right to request and receive a prescription to hasten death under certain specific safeguards;"[4] and Americans for Divorce Reform supports modifications to state-level no-fault divorce laws that would make it more difficult for married couples to divorce. The bottom portion of Table 19.2 shows the distribution of such organizations and makes clear their diversity. In fact, the largest category of public interest groups is a polyglot set of single-issue organizations that advocate on behalf of causes having no obvious ideological tendency.

The undisputed political benefit that can accrue from making claims in the public interest leads to a number of misconceptions.[5] In spite of the occasional efforts by those who run public interest groups to wrap themselves in a mantle of civic sainthood, those who advocate on behalf of public interests have no monopoly on democratic virtue. What is more, there is no such thing as a single "public interest." In any controversy involving a public interest on one side, there is usually a competing public interest on the other.[6] Those who adduce publicly interested foreign policy or environmental concerns to promote an energy tax may be opposed by equally public interested consumer advocates for low energy costs. Similarly, the environmentalists who argue for wilderness and wildlife preservation may be opposed by other public interest advocates who champion the freedom for snowmobilers to enjoy the national parks in winter. That there are almost inevitably competing public interests at issue in any political conflict does not necessarily mean that the sides are evenly balanced. Many political conflicts find supporters of public and private goods on the same side. The consumer-minded supporters of low energy costs would find many privately interested allies, among them energy producers and processors.

The list of organizations in Table 19.2 underscores a corollary to the observation that there is rarely only a single public interest at stake in any political controversy: contrary to the stereotype, public interest groups are not inevitably liberal. It is extremely difficult to extract a bottom line that summarizes the ideological balance between competing visions of the public interest. Overall, the set of organizations representing public goods leans somewhat to the left, but the representation of conservative public interests is considerable. In fact, explicitly ideological public interest groups, such as anti- or pro-gun control groups on the domestic front or pro-national security or pro-peace groups in the international domain, are fairly evenly balanced between conservative and liberal. Moreover, many of the public interest groups in various presumptively liberal categories are, in fact, either ideologically neutral or conservative. Examples include consumer groups like the American Motorcyclist Association, which advocates against restrictions on youth motorcycle riding and for the freedom to ride on public lands; wildlife organizations like Pheasants Forever, an organization "dedicated to the conservation of pheasants" that brings together "a diversified group of

TABLE 19.2 **Examples and Distribution of Public Interest Groups in Washington Politics**

Examples of public interest groups	
Consumer	
Center for Auto Safety	
Consumer Federation of America	
National Association of Investors Corporation	
Environmental and wildlife	
Environmental Working Group	
Greenpeace, USA	
Izaak Walton League	
Government reform	
Campaign Reform Project	
Citizens against Government Waste	
Project on Government Oversight	
Civil liberties	
American Civil Liberties Union	
Council on Religious Freedom	
Electronic Privacy Information Center	
Citizen empowerment	
Center for Voting and Democracy	
Close Up Foundation	
Speak Out! USA	
Other liberal groups	
Amnesty International	
Death with Dignity National Center	
Religious Coalition for Reproductive Choice	
Other conservative groups	
American Security Council	
Americans for Tax Reform	
Citizens for Law and Order	
Other	
Americans for Divorce Reform	
Federation for American Immigration Reform	
National Safety Council	
Distribution of public interest groups[1]	
Consumer	6.4%
Environmental and wildlife	22.0
Government reform	4.5
Civil liberties	1.3
Citizen empowerment	3.5
Other liberal groups	18.8
Other conservative groups	14.2
Other	29.3
Total	100.0%

SOURCE: Washington Representatives Study.

1. Organizations listed in the 2006 *Washington Representatives* directory (Bethesda, Md.: Columbia Books and Information Services, 2006).

IS DUCKS UNLIMITED A PUBLIC INTEREST GROUP?

Public interest groups can be defined as organizations that seek policy goals that, if achieved, would not confer a selective benefit on the leaders, the activists, or the members of the organization. Even though the definition seems clear, it is often difficult to discern in practice whether an organization is a public interest group.

Consider Ducks Unlimited, which, according to its Web site, "is the world's leader in wetlands and waterfowl conservation." With more than 1 million supporters, "by any measure, DU is one of the largest conservation/environmental groups in the world . . . DU supporters have raised nearly $1.6 billion for conservation since 1937."

Among its policy concerns are the "threats to wetlands that are no longer covered by the Clean Water Act . . . areas [that] are vital not just for waterfowl and wildlife, but also for clean drinking water as well." Visitors to the Web site can click on links to information about "Land Protection," "Oil Spill Response," and "Waterfowl Habitat."

According to a study conducted by Mediamark Research, however, 91 percent of the readers of the Ducks Unlimited Newsletter are hunters, and 64 percent of them hunt on public land. Visitors to the Web site can also click on links to information about "Retriever Training," "Hunting Tips," "Duck Calling," "Decoy Strategies," and "Shooting Tips."

Wetland and waterfowl conservation are clearly public goods, but duck hunters clearly have a selective interest in preserving the wetlands that serve as waterfowl habitats. Is Ducks Unlimited a public interest group?

Graduate student Dawn Plattner carries out research sponsored by Ducks Unlimited to track black duck populations around Long Island.

SOURCE: All information was taken from the Web site of Ducks Unlimited, http://www.ducks.org.

NOTE: Out of concern not to undercount the proportion of public interest groups among all organizations active in Washington politics, our research team coded Ducks Unlimited as a public interest group concerned with wildlife and animals.

hunters, non-hunters, farmers, ranchers, landowners, conservation enthusiasts and wildlife officials"[7]; and foreign policy organizations like the anti-Castro Cuban American National Foundation; or government reform organizations like the Citizens against Government Waste.

Furthermore, compared to advocates of liberal public interests, conservative public interest organizations are more likely to find themselves on the same side of a policy controversy as an intense private interest—for example, a corporation or trade association representing real estate developers or the manufacturers of infant car seats.

Another important qualification to the understanding of what is meant by the public interest is that even though the public goods on behalf of which public interest groups advocate are available to all, they are not equally valued or equally accessible to all. Those on opposite sides of the controversy over the rights of smokers care differentially about the competing public goods at issue: the liberty to pursue a pleasurable habit and the public health benefits of a smoke-free environment. Although available to all, a newly created federal wilderness area will be valued differently by hikers than by opera buffs or, especially, supporters of low taxes, and will be more accessible to lovers of the outdoors who live in a nearby city than to people who live far away.

A final caveat is that many public interest groups are not groups at all. In fact, the majority of organizations in the pressure system are not associations of individuals. Like American Airlines, Ford Foundation, University of Nebraska, or American Ballet Theatre, they may be what Robert Salisbury calls "institutions" and have no members at all.[8] Or they may, like the National Association of Children's Hospitals or the Snack Food Association, be membership associations whose members are not individuals but are, instead, institutions. Among public interest groups, many, such as the Sierra Club, are membership associations with individuals as members, but many others are not groups at all. One example is the Washington Legal Foundation (WLF), a public interest law firm that according to its Web site seeks to "strengthen America's free enterprise system." Although the WLF does not have members in the ordinary sense, it has 501(c)3 tax-exempt status and accepts donations from contributors whose names are kept confidential.

WHY SO FEW PUBLIC INTEREST GROUPS? THE FREE-RIDER PROBLEM

To understand why, if the interests espoused by public interest groups are widely shared, there are, at least in relative terms, so few of them, it helps to review several strands of explanation of the origins of interest groups.[9] The once-dominant analysis of American politics, interest group pluralism, placed interest groups at the center of policymaking and emphasized the low barriers to entry to, and the fluid nature of, the organized interest system.[10] Organized interests, therefore, supposedly emerge more or less automatically in response to disturbances in the political environment and regularly enter and leave the pressure system as dictated by their concerns about the particular issues at stake in politics at any given time. Because of the ease of entry and exit from pressure politics, the relatively small numbers of public interest groups would have been interpreted as an indication of an absence of political concern about the public goods on behalf of which they might advocate.

The interest group pluralist argument about the absence of barriers to the emergence of political groups sustained its most formidable challenge from Mancur Olson, whose analysis would explain the small number of public interest groups.[11] Olson contended that the rational individual has an incentive not to spend scarce resources of money and time in support of favored causes but rather to free ride on the efforts of others. According to Olson, we can expect organizations to emerge only if they are able to coerce potential free riders to support group efforts or are able to provide selective benefits available only to those who assist in the collective effort. Moreover, contrary to the understanding common in democratic theory that the larger the jointly interested constituency, the more likely it will be represented by organization, the free-rider problem is exacerbated when the potential group is large. Therefore, according to Olson, large, diffuse groups lacking the capacity to coerce cooperation or to provide selective benefits—of which public interest groups are examples—often face severe collective action problems that prevent them from organizing on behalf of their collective political concerns.

In response to Olson, political scientists have pointed to several pathways around the free-rider problem. Clearly, the political arena contains many public interest groups that are not in a position to force members to join and that do not provide selective benefits of significant economic value. Moreover, ongoing public interest groups that do offer selective benefits to induce membership had to overcome the free-rider problem at the outset to get off the ground. Why are there any public interest groups at all? For one thing, those who seek to found a membership group or keep one going can provide a broader array of selective benefits in place of material ones—in particular, social and psychological benefits such as the pleasure of working with others and enjoying their fellowship and esteem and the satisfaction associated with working on behalf of a cherished cause.[12] Another factor is that entrepreneurs are critical in founding and nurturing new organizations.[13] Moreover, organizations may have external patrons—for example, foundations or government—that encourage and subsidize the founding of new organizations, especially organizations that seek public goods.[14] Potentially even more important than external patrons are large donors among the members.[15] Because they are more likely to value the fellowship and recognition that accompany organizational involvement and leadership, large donors are more likely than outside patrons to stick around for the long run.

THE GROWING NUMBER OF PUBLIC INTEREST GROUPS

The pluralist perspective emphasizes that organizations go in and out of pressure politics depending upon the significance of their business with the government at any particular time; and the free-rider problem points to the barriers to the formation of new organizations, especially large ones. It is nevertheless clear that the number of public interest groups active in Washington politics has increased substantially in recent decades. The number of organizations listed in the Washington Representatives directory more than doubled in the quarter century between 1981 and 2006—rising from 6,681 to 13,777 for an increase of 106 percent. Starting from a much smaller base, the number of public interest groups rose at a slightly more rapid rate from 254 to 578 for an increase of 126 percent over that same period. In the process, the share of the pressure system occupied by public interest groups grew very slightly from 3.8 percent to 4.1 percent.

The net increase in organizations active in Washington politics reflects not simply an excess of organizational births over organizational deaths but also the complex processes by which organizations enter and leave the pressure community. In contrast to populations of plants and animals, however, the set of organizations that constitute the pressure system at any given moment represents the results of organizational politicization as well as of organizational births and deaths. That is, new entrants into pressure politics can be either entirely new organizations or, more likely, existing organizations that have been outside politics. Similarly, organizations that exit from pressure politics may continue as organizations outside politics, or they may go out of business altogether.

The public interest groups listed in 2006 were distinctive in being younger than most of the organizations in the directory. More than half the public interest groups—compared to less than one-third of the all organizations in the directory—had been founded since 1980.[16] In addition, while only one in eight of the public interest groups was around in 1920, more than one-third of all the organizations in the 2006 directory were.

A DOZEN PUBLIC INTEREST GROUPS: WHAT THEY SUPPORT AND WHAT THEY DO

	A sample issue	A sample tactic
Americans for Tax Reform	Flat tax or lower taxes	Rating legislators
Association for Airline Passenger Rights	Flight quality (e.g., delays, baggage fees)	Grassroots lobbying
Center for Auto Safety	Vehicle safety (e.g., airbags, rollover)	Providing expert opinions and data
Committee on the Present Danger	Confronting terrorism	Testifying in congressional hearings
Council for a Livable World	Stopping nuclear proliferation	Endorsing candidates
Friends of the Earth	Global warming	Providing policy analysis
Innocence Project	Exonerating the wrongfully accused or convicted	Representing convicted prisoners in court
Mountain States Legal Foundation	Private property rights	Filing suit
OMB Watch	Government transparency and accountability	Monitoring government actions
Project Vote!	Increasing voter turnout	Disseminating results of research
U.S. English	Making English the national language	Providing model legislation
World Wildlife Fund	Protecting animal and plant habitats	Testifying before administrative agencies

SOURCE: All information taken from the Web sites of the organizations.

Considering the subsequent histories of the organizations listed in the 1981 directory indicates a similar distinctiveness for public interest groups. Contrary to the received wisdom that "Once in politics, always in politics," organizations often leave the political arena. In general, however, when organizations exit the pressure system, they leave politics, but are very unlikely to go out of business entirely. The pattern is somewhat different for public interest groups, however. Perhaps because the causes they espoused were eventually eliminated from the political agenda, a relatively large share of the public interest groups from 1981 that were not in the 2006 directory were not only politically inactive but also no longer extant as organizations.

When the data about public interest groups are put under a microscope, it becomes clear that the growth has been uneven across subcategories. Table 19.3 divides the public interest category into its constituent parts. The rate of increase was particularly sharp for "other public interest groups"—both domestic organizations such as the Air Bag and Seat Belt Safety Campaign, Security on Campus, and Coalition for the Prevention of Alcohol Problems, and, especially, nonideological organizations focused on problems abroad. In contrast, growth in the numbers of consumer and civil liberties organizations, traditionally an important component of the public interest community, has been very limited. Table 19.3 also indicates that the increase in other liberal public interest groups has outpaced the growth in other conservative public interest groups. Even more finely grained analysis demonstrates that the divergence occurred during the five years at the end of the period—between 2001 and 2006—a time when the Republicans controlled both the presidency and Congress, and liberals were feeling besieged.[17]

WHAT PUBLIC INTEREST GROUPS DO

The federal governing structure was deliberately designed by the founders to establish multiple, often overlapping institutions and, therefore, multiple points of access for those who seek a hearing by policymakers. Organizations seeking to influence policy get involved in a variety of ways. Using 2001 as the base year, data about the resources and political activities of organizations active in national politics were assembled from the 2001 Washington Representatives directory, organizational Web sites, congressional sources, the Federal Election Commission, Supreme Court records, opensecrets.org, and politicalmoneyline.com. This data set, known as the Washington Representatives Study, permits researchers to measure whether organizations got involved in a particular way and, if so, how much they did with respect to the following: using their Web sites to inform potential supporters about policy issues and to urge them to take political action; lobbying Congress; testifying at congressional hearings; filing amicus briefs; and making donations to political action committees (PACs).[18] It is clear that strategic considerations and resource constraints imply that different kinds of organizations are active in different arenas and, therefore,

Amnesty International sponsored this 2008 protest against the treatment of detainees at Guantánamo Bay, Cuba.

TABLE 19.3 **Growth in Numbers of Public Interest Groups, 1981–2006**

	Relative increase	...Absolute ...increase
Consumer	12%	4
Environmental and wildlife	116%	67
Government reform	179%	17
Civil liberties	–8%	–1
Citizen empowerment	486%	17
Other liberal groups	160%	67
Other conservative groups	84%	41
Other public interest groups	200%	112

SOURCE: Washington Representatives Study.

that the policymakers in different institutional settings hear different mixes of messages.

A large number of resources, ranging from an appealing message to a large and engaged membership to skilled personnel on staff, are relevant for political advocacy. The *Washington Representatives* directories contain a valuable surrogate measure of an organization's political capacity, the number of in-house lobbyists it has on staff, and the number of outside law, public relations, or consulting firms it hires. Washington lobbyists are often characterized as having bottomless war chests to fund their political operations, but nearly three-quarters, 74 percent, of all the organizations in the directory—and two-thirds of the public interest groups—were what could be characterized as low capacity, either hiring only a single outside firm or having only one or two people on staff in Washington and hiring no outside firms.

A number of factors might predispose an individual organization to choose in-house or outside representation: the limitations it faces in locating its headquarters, the extent to which political representation is central or peripheral to its mission, and the volume of its business with the federal government. Organizations with autonomy in choosing the location of their headquarters and organizations for which Washington politics are a central focus are more likely to maintain an office or locate their headquarters in the capital. The organizations for which involvement in federal politics is secondary to the main organizational purpose may employ an outside firm or two to conduct their political business in the capital and work with their hired guns from home.

Politics is obviously at the center of organizational mission for public interest groups, so it is not surprising that they are relatively likely to have offices in Washington and not to rely on outside counsel or consultants to manage their government relations affairs. On average, public interest groups have 1.9 people on staff in their Washington offices and hire .5 outside firms. The analogous figures for all organizations in the directory are .9 and 1.2.

One time-honored tactic of organizational political influence is grassroots lobbying—mobilizing members and other supporters to get in touch with public officials in support of favored political causes. The Internet has expanded the possibilities for political involvement in that organizations can use its enormous capacity to communicate with interested individuals—informing them of pending political issues and encouraging them to take action when appropriate. Policy issues obviously go to the heart of what public interest groups are about, and public support is a crucial resource for their effectiveness in politics. As expected, public interest groups are quite likely to use their Web sites to keep potential supporters up-to-date about policy issues of concern and to facilitate political involvement by urging them to take political action, encouraging them to sign up for e-mail updates, or helping them to register or vote.[19] As shown in Table 19.4, nearly all of the public interest groups, 84 percent, discuss political issues on their Web sites, and 66 percent otherwise facilitate political action. In contrast, the figures for all organizations for which a Web site could be found behave very differently: 37 percent discuss current political issues, and 22 percent use their Web sites for political activation.

For each organization in the 2001 directory, archival sources were used to code information about the extent of involvement in four forms of Washington political activity: spending on lobbying in 2000 and 2001, as reported in the lobbying registrations filed with the Senate's Office of Public Records[20]; testifying before congressional committees and subcommittees; filing amicus briefs before the Supreme Court; and making PAC donations. Of the four activities considered, spending on lobbying is the one that permits an organization to use its financial resources at its own initiative, constrained only by the requirement to register and the restrictions on lobbying by nonprofits. Because organizations are required to divulge only their expenditures on lobbying and not the amounts spent on political activities such as grassroots lobbying, conducting and publicizing research, or filing amicus briefs, the spending disclosed through lobbying registrations is only a partial measure of the funds spent by an organization activity in pursuit of political influence.

Organizations that spend less than $10,000 in a six-month period are not required to file reports, so lobbying expense data omit the expenditures of relatively inactive organizations and small and impecunious ones. In addition, unless they establish a parallel, non-tax-deductible 501(c)4 arm, organizations that fall into the 501(c)3 designation in the tax code—that is, nonprofits for which contributions are tax deductible—are legally enjoined from undertaking significant lobbying, but not from engaging in many other kinds of political activity.[21] Many public interest groups are either 501(c)3s, or small and resource-deprived, or both. Therefore, it is not surprising that while 61 percent of all organizations spent at least $10,000 on lobbying in 2000 and 2001, only 39 percent of public interest groups did so.

Organizations retain control over whether and how much they lobby, but the initiative when it comes to congressional testimony rests with senators and representatives and their staffs. Testifying before a congressional committee entails costs, especially if travel is involved. In contrast to spending on lobbying, however, the sums never reach stratospheric heights. Because it is a form of voice for which the initiative rests with the people's elected representatives, congressional testimonies seem to be more receptive to statements from organizations representing public goods: 32 percent of the public interest groups, compared to 18 percent of all organizations listed, testified before congressional committees or subcommittees.

Although they cannot engage in conventional lobbying of judges and their clerks, public interest groups that seek to influence federal judicial outcomes have several options. They can focus on nominees to the bench and attempt to have an impact on Senate confirmation processes. They can file suit. Or they can file an amicus curiae brief. An amicus brief can make arguments that litigants cannot make, inform the court of the broader implications of the case, provide additional background information, indicate the lineup of political and social forces concerned about the case, and clarify who besides the immediate litigants might be affected by the outcome.[22] Filing amicus briefs remains a relatively rare activity, but, as Table 19.4 shows, public interest groups are relatively likely to do so. Only 8 percent of all organizations used this technique, but 15 percent of public interest groups—including 42 percent of the small number of civil liberties groups—filed briefs.

TABLE 19.4 **Public Interest Group Activity in Washington Politics**

	Public interest groups	All organizations[1]
Web site discusses political issues[2]	84%	37%
Web site facilitates political action[3]	66%	22%
Spent at least $10,000 on lobbying[4]	39%	61%
Testified in Congress[5]	32%	18%
Filed an amicus brief[6]	15%	8%
Made a PAC donation[7]	7%	10%

SOURCE: Washington Representatives Study.

1. Figures are for all organizations in the 2001 *Washington Representatives* directory (Bethesda, Md.: Columbia Books and Information Services, 2001).
2. Figures are for all organizations in the 2001 directory for which Web sites could be found in spring 2008; state and local governments have been omitted.
3. Web site encourages individuals to take specific political action; invites submission of an e-mail address in order to receive a newsletter or periodic updates about policy matters; or includes links to facilitate voter registration.
4. Spent a total of at least $10,000 on lobbying in 2000 and 2001.
5. Testified before a congressional committee or subcommittee in 2001 or 2002.
6. Filed an amicus brief with the Supreme Court during the 2000–2001 or 2001–2002 terms.
7. Made a PAC donation in a federal election between 1999 and 2002; figure for all organizations does not include candidate or party PACs.

Organizations often supplement their attempts to influence policy through direct communications to public officials with actions targeted at elections. The most common organizational strategy for electoral action is making contributions to candidates and parties. In making such a contribution, an organization may have the objective of influencing the outcome of the election and thereby retain an officeholder who is congenial to its policy goals or replace one who is hostile. An organization that seeks to affect who holds office will focus its donations on competitive elections in which additional resources have the potential to make a difference in who wins. But organizations often make contributions to sure winners—even to candidates who have no opposition at all. Such contributions have a second objective: to influence what the eventual winner will do once in office rather than to have an impact on who wins. To gain a hearing for a political story that they inevitably believe to be persuasive and fair, organizations seek to ensure their access to elected officials who will be dealing with policy matters that affect the organization and its stakeholders. Campaign contributions—especially campaign contributions with a recognizable policy agenda and return address attached—are considered to be a means of facilitating access.

The vehicle used to collect campaign contributions from individuals and stamp it with the organization's imprimatur is the PAC. Ordinarily, PACs are affiliated with organizations such as unions, professional associations, or corporations that are constituted for some other purpose. Many public interest PACs, however, are stand-alone organizations, established to permit those with a special concern about a particular public good—for example, environmental preservation or a vigorous national security policy—to make strategic campaign donations. Even so, making PAC donations is quite uncommon. Only 7 percent of public interest groups made a PAC donation during either the 1999–2000 or 2001–2002 electoral cycle—a figure not much different from the 10 percent of all organizations that did so (see Chapter 31).

THE DISTRIBUTION OF ORGANIZED INTEREST ACTIVITY

Over the past generation, the increase in the number of public interest groups active in Washington politics has meant that public officials are exposed to a set of perspectives that otherwise might not be voiced in the political process. Systematic evidence shows that the presence of such organizations makes a difference.[23] Still, the rate of growth since 1981 in the number of public interest groups, while somewhat more rapid than the growth rate for all organizations, is not especially remarkable.

Moreover, when we consider the total bundle of political activity arising from organized interests in listed Table 19.5, we see that across the various domains of activity, public interest groups are responsible for only a small share of the total activity. Table 19.5 shows for each of these forms of organizational activity the percentage of the activity that comes from public interest groups and, for purposes of comparison, the percentage that comes from business groups.[24] In interpreting the figures in Table 19.5, it is important to keep in mind that only in the top row, which shows the distribution of organizations in the 2001 *Washington Representatives* directory, is the organization the unit of analysis. Other rows show the distribution of the number of dollars spent on lobbying, testimonies before congressional committees and subcommittees, signings of amicus briefs filed before the Supreme Court, and dollars of PAC spending.[25] Within any particular institutional arena, the weight of activity coming from public interest groups and business organizations is a function of the number of organizations in a particular category, the likelihood that they are involved in that arena, and the average amount of activity for organizations that are involved.

Table 19.5 makes clear that with respect to each form of involvement, public interest groups contribute only a small share of the political input. Reflecting IRS rules about lobbying by tax-exempt organizations and the small budgets of many public interest groups, they spend a minuscule 2 percent of the lobbying dollars. The underrepresentation is less notable when it comes to testifying before Congress or filing amicus briefs. Still, even for these forms of organized interest involvement, less than one-sixth of the activity arises from public interest groups. In contrast, business organizations invariably account for a larger share—usually a much larger share—of activity than do public interest groups. The disparities are especially striking when it comes to the forms of activity in which the metric is dollars rather than acts: lobbying and PAC spending. That public interest groups are responsible for only a small portion of organized interest activity reflects the relatively small number of such organizations rather than low levels of activity by public interest groups. Although it is useful to compare the share of public interest activity in any realm with the share of public interest organizations, it is critical not to reify the distribution of organizations in the top row of Table 19.5. The set of organizations active in Washington cannot be considered any kind of natural population. Although it is impossible to specify what a representative distribution of organizations would look like, it is clear that public interest organizations are relatively scarce and business organizations are numerous in pressure politics, with implications for the amount of activity emanating from each sector.

TABLE 19.5 **Share of All Activity from Public Interest Groups and Business Organizations**[1]

	Public interest groups	Business organizations[2]
All organizations[3]	5%	53%
Spending on lobbying[4]	2%	72%
Congressional testimonies[5]	11%	30%
Amicus briefs[6]	13%	14%
PAC donations[7]	9%	48%

SOURCE: Washington Representatives Study.

1. Percentage of all activity of a particular kind attributable to public interest groups or to business organizations; if a column were added for all other organizations, then the three figures would add across to 100 percent.
2. Includes U.S. and foreign corporations, U.S. subsidiaries of foreign corporations, for-profit firms of professionals such as law and consulting firms, U.S. and foreign trade and other business associations, and business-affiliated research organizations.
3. Includes all organizations in the 2001 *Washington Representatives* directory (Bethesda, Md.: Columbia Books and Information Services, 2001).
4. Includes all spending on lobbying in 2000 and 2001 by organizations in the 2001 *Washington Representatives* directory.
5. Includes all testimonies by organizations (regardless of whether the organizations were listed in the 2001 *Washington Representatives* directory) before congressional committees or subcommittees in 2001 or 2002.
6. Includes all amicus briefs filed by organizations (regardless of whether the organizations were listed in the 2001 *Washington Representatives* directory) with the Supreme Court during the 2000–2001 or 2001–2002 terms.
7. Includes all donations by PACs (regardless of whether the PACs or their sponsoring organizations were listed in the 2001 *Washington Representatives* directory) in a federal election between 1999 and 2002; does not include donations by candidate or party PACS.

CONCLUSION

Over the last generation political observers have noted the increasing number and importance of organizations advocating on behalf of broad public interests. By calling attention to concerns that otherwise might find no organizational voice, public interest groups play a critical role in broadening the political discourse in American politics, bringing new issues into the political arena, and representing points of view that might not be heard.

Systematic empirical data indicate that some widely held understandings about public interest groups are insufficiently nuanced. In any real political controversy, there are usually competing broad public interests at stake, which means that any claim to represent *the* public interest should be treated skeptically and that there are conservative public interest groups as well as liberal ones and those with no obvious ideological coloration. Furthermore, public interest groups are not necessarily groups. Many of them—for example, think tanks and public interest law firms—take on other institutional forms. In addition, although their numbers have increased substantially in recent decades, the number of organized interests active in Washington politics has also grown over the period. Hence, public interest groups still form only a very small portion of the organizations active in Washington. Even though the rate of growth for public interest groups is somewhat more rapid than the rate of growth for the pressure system as a whole, it has not outpaced that of a number of other kinds of organizations.

Because political action and advocacy tend to be quite central to the organizational mission of most public interest groups, they tend to have offices, even headquarters, in Washington and are more likely to use in-house staff for political representation instead of outside counsel or consultants. Organizations for which political advocacy is a secondary pursuit may move in and out of politics as needed; in contrast, public interest groups tend to enter pressure politics not as previously existing organizations that have been politically mobilized but as newly hatched organizations. Similarly, when they leave the political fray, they are relatively likely to go out of business altogether rather than to continue to exist as organizations outside politics.

In terms of their political activities, because they tend to have messages that are legitimately framed in terms of the good of all, to be resource-strapped, and to be subject to limitations on lobbying imposed by nonprofit tax status, public interest groups are more likely than other organizations in pressure politics to engage in activities entailing the public statement of clearly articulated messages: using their Web sites as a tool for discussing policy issues, testifying before Congress, and filing amicus briefs with the Supreme Court.

NOTES

This work draws on research on inequalities of political voice in American democracy currently being conducted with Sidney Verba and Henry Brady. Collection of the data used in this chapter was supported by Boston College and Harvard University. This enterprise has benefited from the industry, enthusiasm, and talents of an extraordinary group of research assistants: Will Bacic, Jeremy Bailey, John Barry, Patrick Behrer, Traci Burch, Ageliki Christopher, Lauren Daniel, Joshua Darr, Sarah Debbink, Lee Drutman, Lauren Escher, Glen Feder, John Gattman, Daniel Geary, Heitor Gouvea, Gail Harmon, Caitlyn Jones, Philip Jones, Lora Krsulich, Samuel Lampert, Jeremy Landau, Kate Letourneau, Miriam Mansury, Katie Marcot, Timothy Mooney, Rafael Munoz, Janice Pardue, Michael Parker, Robert Porter, Nathaniel Probert, Karthick Ramakrishnan, Veronica Roberts, Amanda Rothschild, Julia Schlozman, Ganesh Sitaraman, Dorothy Smith, Kathryn Smith, Martin Steinwand, Emily Thorson, Clay Tousey, and Jill Weidner.

1. Charles Erwin Wilson quoted in John Bartlett, *Familiar Quotations,* 16th ed. (Boston: Little Brown, 1992), 680.

2. This definition is drawn from Jeffery M. Berry's in *Lobbying for the People* (Princeton: Princeton University Press, 1977), 7. It differs in one respect, however. Berry specifies that the achievement of the organization's goals "will not selectively or materially benefit the membership or activists of the organization." The definition offered here permits a nonselective, but material, benefit such as low taxes or low consumer prices to be considered a form of public interest.

3. These numbers are based on an enumeration of the organizations listed in the 2006 *Washington Representatives* directory (Bethesda, Md.: Columbia Books and Information Services, 2006). The directory is the most nearly comprehensive listing of politically active organizations in Washington.

4. Quotation is taken from the organization's Web site: www.deathwithdignity.org/aboutus.

5. This section draws on Kay Lehman Schlozman and John T. Tierney, *Organized Interests and American Democracy* (New York: Harper and Row, 1986), 28–32.

6. This point is made by Andrew S. McFarland, *Public Interest Lobbies* (Washington, D.C.: American Enterprise Institute, 1976), chap. 2.

7. Taken from the organization's Web site, www.pheasantsforever.org/page/1/mission.jsp.

8. On this point, which is often overlooked in discussions of organized interest politics, see Robert H. Salisbury, "Interest Representation: The Dominance of Institutions," *American Political Science Review* 78 (1984): 64–76; and David Lowery, Virginia Gray, Jennifer Anderson, and Adam J. Newmark, "Collective Action and the Mobilization of Institutions," *Journal of Politics* 66 (2004): 684–705.

9. Helpful discussions of the various explanations for the emergence of interest groups can be found in Anthony J. Nownes, "The Population Ecology of Interest group Formation: Mobilizing for Gay and Lesbian Rights in the United States, 1950–1998," *British Journal of Political Science* 34 (2004): 49–58; and Andrew McFarland, "Neopluralism," *Annual Review of Political Science* 10 (2007): 53–57.

10. Among the most significant works from an interest group pluralist point of view are Arthur F. Bentley, *The Process of Government* (Chicago: University of Chicago Press, 1908); David B. Truman, *The Governmental Process: Political Interests and Public Opinion*, 2nd ed. (New York: Knopf, 1951); Earl Latham, *The Group Basis of Politics* (Ithaca, N.Y.: Cornell University Press, 1952); and Robert A. Dahl, *A Preface to Democratic Theory* (New Haven: Yale University Press, 1956). These authors differ from one another in important respects, and no single work serves as the definitive text for interest group pluralism. Therefore, the brief rendition of the interest group pluralist perspective in this paragraph is a caricature that, although frequently set up as a straw man by detractors, was never espoused by interest group pluralists. In particular, Robert A. Dahl, *Who Governs?* (New Haven: Yale University Press, 1961) gave a less central place to interest groups in his understanding of political contestation and never subscribed to the belief that the competing pressures comprise the sum total of political forces in making policy. For a discussion of the many uses of the term "pluralism," see McFarland, "Neopluralism."

11. Mancur Olson, *The Logic of Collective Action: Public Goods and the Theory of Groups* (Cambridge: Harvard University Press, 1965).

12. James Q. Wilson, *Political Organizations* (New York: Basic Books, 1973), esp. chaps. 2 and 3.

13. See, for example, Robert H. Salisbury, "An Exchange Theory of Interest Groups," *Midwest Political Science Review* 13 (1969): 1–32; and Norman Frohlich, Joe A. Oppenheimer, and Oran R. Young, *Political Leadership and Collective Goods* (Princeton: Princeton University Press, 1971).

14. Jack Walker, *Interest Groups in America: Patrons, Professions, and Social Movements* (Ann Arbor: University of Michigan Press, 1991), esp. chap. 5.

15. Anthony J. Nownes, "Patronage and Citizen Groups: A Reevaluation," *Political Behavior* 17 (1995): 203–221.

16. For several reasons, corporations and foreign organizations are not included in the calculations on which the figures in this paragraph are based.

17. Dara Strolovitch shows a similar pattern for other kinds of citizens' groups in *Affirmative Advocacy* (Chicago: University of Chicago Press, 2007), 17. She found that the period between 1960 and 1999 saw the formation of 56 percent of civil rights and racial minority organizations, 79 percent of economic justice organizations, and 65 percent of women's organizations that existed in 2000.

18. Thus, data were generated about attempts to influence through the electoral process as well as through the direct expression of preferences. Unfortunately, there was no analogous source that would allow the aggregation of data about organizational activity in the executive branch.

19. Unfortunately, this data collection did not take place until spring 2008. Even then, it was possible to find Web sites for 78 percent of the organizations listed in the 2001 directory or 83 percent of the 2001 organizations not known to be out of existence. Because their Web sites are used to inform the public about the issues currently under consideration, state and local governments are not included in this analysis.

20. Information about lobbying expenses is contained on the publicly accessible Web site of the Center for Responsive Politics, opensecrets.org. The center discusses its sources and coding methods at www.opensecrets.org/lobbyists/methodology.asp. If opensecrets.org did not have any information about the lobbying spending of an organization, we also consulted the data contained at politicalmoneyline.org (now CQ MoneyLine).

21. See Jeffrey M. Berry, with David F. Arons, *A Voice for Nonprofits* (Washington, D.C.: Brookings, 1999).

22. See Bruce J. Ennis, "Effective Amicus Briefs," *Catholic University Law Review* 33 (1984): 606; Gregory A. Caldeira and John R. Wright, "Organized Interests and Agenda Setting in the U.S. Supreme Court," *American Political Science Review* 82 (1988): 1111; Donald Songer and Reginald S. Sheehan, "Interest Group Success in the Courts: Amicus Participation in the Supreme Court," *Political Research Quarterly* 46 (1993): 351–352; Kevin T. McGuire and Barbara Palmer, "Issue Fluidity on the Supreme Court," *American Political Science Review* 89 (1995): 696; James F. Spriggs II, and Paul J. Wahlbeck, "Amicus Curiae and the Role of Information at the Supreme Court, *Political Research Quarterly* 50 (1997): 371–373; Luther T. Munford, "When Does the Curiae Need an Amicus?" *Journal of Appellate Practice and Process* 1 (1999): 281–282; and Paul M. Collins, "Friends of the Court: Examining the Influence of Amicus Curiae Participation in U.S. Supreme Court Litigation," *Law and Society Review* 28 (2004): 813.

23. See Jeffrey M. Berry, *The New Liberalism: The Rising Power of Citizen Groups* (Washington, DC: Brookings, 1999).

24. Business organizations include U.S. and foreign corporations, U.S. subsidiaries of foreign corporations, for-profit firms of professionals such as law and consulting firms, U.S. and foreign trade and other business associations, and business-affiliated research organizations.

25. For congressional testimonies, amicus briefs, and PAC spending, we used archival sources to document the involvement of all organizations that undertook a particular activity—including organizations not listed in the 2001 *Washington Representatives* directory.

SUGGESTED READING

Berry, Jeffery M. *Lobbying for the People.* Princeton: Princeton University Press, 1977.

———. *The New Liberalism: The Rising Power of Citizen Groups.* Washington, D.C.: Brookings, 1999.

Berry, Jeffrey M., with David F. Arons. *A Voice for Nonprofits.* Washington, D.C.: Brookings, 2003.

Kollman, Ken. *Outside Lobbying: Public Opinion and Interest Group Strategies.* Princeton: Princeton University Press, 1998.

McFarland, Andrew S. *Public Interest Lobbies.* Washington, D.C.: American Enterprise Institute, 1976.

Olson, Mancur. *The Logic of Collective Action: Public Goods and the Theory of Groups.* Cambridge: Harvard University Press, 1965.

Rothenberg, Lawrence S. *Linking Citizens to Government: Interest Group Politics at Common Cause.* Cambridge: Cambridge University Press, 1992.

Schlozman, Kay Lehman, and John T. Tierney. *Organized Interests and American Democracy.* New York: Harper and Row, 1986.

Walker, Jack. *Interest Groups in America: Patrons, Professions, and Social Movements.* Ann Arbor: University of Michigan Press, 1991.

Wilson, James Q. *Political Organizations.* New York: Basic Books, 1973.

chapter 20

Professional Associations

by Christopher M. Witko

Some professional associations are well known and often disliked for their political activities, while hundreds of professional associations are virtually unknown to the public. No matter how much or little they use their influence, professional associations have long been important political actors in the United States. This chapter discusses the historical development and current political activities of professional associations and the controversies surrounding some of their political and governmental activities.

The first section of this chapter begins with a discussion of what a professional association is and distinguishes it from other types of organized interests that share similarities. Next is a brief examination of the historical development of professional associations. The chapter then discusses their political and governmental activities, highlighting the ways that professional associations are similar and dissimilar to other types of organized interests. The last section turns to the matter of just how powerful professional associations are in the politics of the United States.

WHAT IS A PROFESSIONAL ASSOCIATION?

The question of what a professional association is seems obvious when one thinks of specific groups, such as the American Medical Association (AMA) or the American Bar Association (ABA), but the lines of demarcation between these groups and other types of organized interests are not always so clear. A professional association is an organization composed of individuals who practice a common profession. Such groups form for a variety of purposes, including professional education and training, setting professional standards of practice, and socialization and networking among members. Another purpose—and often a fundamental one—is to influence politics and public policy, which is the focus of this chapter. The relative balance in emphasis between political and nonpolitical activities depends on the specific association in question and the extent to which the political agenda touches upon the interests of a profession at a given time.

Professional associations have similarities with other types of organized interests in terms of organizational structure, membership, and goals. Professional associations are similar to trade or industry groups in that they are organized around economic activity, and the difference between an industry and a profession is not always clear. Unlike trade or industry associations, professional associations are generally made up of individuals rather than institutions (such as firms). Some organizations, however, such as the National Automobile Dealers Association, allow both individual membership and institutional membership, blurring the lines between trade or industry associations and professional associations.[1]

Because professional associations represent individual members of particular professions and often advocate on their behalf before government and employers, they clearly share some similarities with labor unions. Indeed, unions in professions such as teaching often developed from professional associations. The National Education Association, which collectively bargains for educators in many states where doing so is permitted by law, retains "association" in its title.[2] Members of unions and associations pay dues or membership fees, and members often derive important economic benefits. The path of the National Football League Players Association shows the functional similarities between associations and unions. In 1989 the players went from being a union, to an association, and back to being recertified as a union in 1993.[3] According to federal and state labor laws, unions in the United States generally have the right to bargain collectively with employers on behalf of their members, but professional associations generally do not have this legal right. The legal procedures for forming and maintaining a labor union are more rigorous than for a professional association.

Defining professional associations in the abstract is not simple, but most people are familiar with the examples presented in Table 20.1. Among them are the AMA and the ABA, two unusually well known and unusually politically active groups. Many other professional associations are virtually unknown, but still are active in politics. As the title of

TABLE 20.1 **Selected Professional Associations by Economic Sector**

Sector	Association name
Academia/science	American Physical Society American Economic Association American Chemical Society National Social Science Association
Business/financial services	American Institute of Certified Public Accountants Society for Human Resource Management United Professional Sales Association National Association of Insurance and Financial Advisors Institute of Management Consultants National Society of Tax Professionals
Computers/technology	Association of Information Technology Professionals Independent Computer Consultants Association Technology Professional Services Association
Ethnic/racial/gender	National Association of Hispanic Journalists National Black Nurses Association National Association of Asian American Professionals National Association of Women in Construction
Healthcare	American Medical Association American Dental Association American Nurses Association American Society of Anesthesiologists American Podiatric Medical Association American Optometric Association
Legal	American Bar Association American Association for Justice (formerly American Trial Lawyers Association) National Association of Legal Assistants National Association of Property Tax Attorneys

this chapter indicates, professional associations represent every profession from attorneys to zoologists, along with racial, ethnic, and gender-based associations within particular professions. Their prominence in public affairs varies greatly, as one can see from a Lexis-Nexis search of media mentions of three organizations in Figure 20.1.

Ever since Alexis de Tocqueville published his observations, students of American society have observed that the United States has a rich associational life. It should not be surprising, therefore, that there are numerous professional associations in America and that these organizations often attempt to influence politics. Indeed, one of the first organized interest groups to lobby the federal government can be viewed as a forerunner of the modern professional association. The Society of the Cincinnati represented the claims of Continental Army officers before the federal government during the early days of the new nation. The society was viewed with deep suspicion by much of the public, a pattern that continues to this day.[4]

In the early part of the nineteenth century, organizations representing the professions shared aspects of traditional guilds, labor unions, and modern professional associations. Craftsmen such as hatmakers and cobblers formed organizations, which performed many of the functions that would come to be associated with professional associations. They provided a forum within which craftsmen could discuss political issues relevant to the profession, institute apprentice systems to regulate entry into the profession and ensure professional competence, and join together to represent the interests of these professions before government.[5]

The later proliferation of numerous diversified professions requiring specialized knowledge created the conditions for the growth of professional associations. In the early 1800s a customer could get a haircut and have a tooth pulled by the same person; by the late 1800s barber and dentist were different occupations. Some of the well-known professional associations formed during this time period: the AMA in 1847 and the ABA in 1878. As the economy continued to become larger and more complex, with well-defined professions, and as the intervention of the government in the economy increased throughout the late nineteenth and twentieth centuries, the number of associations representing these occupational groups before government also rose. Jack Walker reports that the first professional associations were founded in the mid-1800s and that half of those listed in his 1983 sample of Washington lobby groups had been founded by World War II.[6]

The creation of the American Bar Association is a good example of the process of the founding of many other professional associations. Early in American history there were few legal restrictions on who could practice law and no clear consensus on what kind of training was needed to be a lawyer. The ABA was created to promote the practice of law as a profession and to help define the training and requirements for practice. The organization increased opportunities to socialize and to disseminate professionally useful information and, in the realm of politics, to seek uniform state laws that were relevant to the legal profession and the practice of law.[7] These purposes—socialization/networking and professional education and development and a desire to influence public policy relevant to the profession—can be seen in other organizations that formed during this era, such as the American Political Science Association.[8] The stated mission of the American Medical Association is "to promote the art and science of medicine and the betterment of public health." [9] These goals require the AMA to be

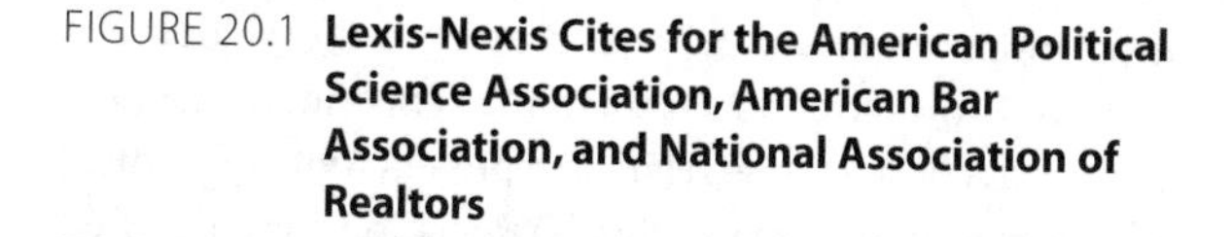

FIGURE 20.1 **Lexis-Nexis Cites for the American Political Science Association, American Bar Association, and National Association of Realtors**

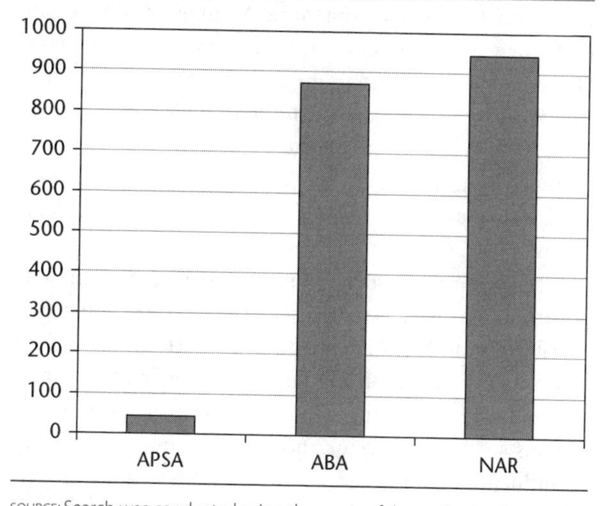

SOURCE: Search was conducted using the name of the professional association in the category of "major U.S. and world publications" for the period from June 10, 2007, to June 10, 2009.

involved in government and politics. Influencing politics and policy was central to the founding of many professional associations and continues to be an important aspect of the activities of modern professional associations.

PROFESSIONAL ASSOCIATION ACTIVITIES IN MODERN POLITICS

As David Lowery and Virginia Gray point out, individual studies of organized interests have usually focused on one aspect of interest group activity, or one stage in what they call the "influence production process." [10] Following the way these various stages are viewed in the interest group literature, this section examines the activities of professional associations beginning with their mobilization and maintenance, continuing with their place in the broader interest group community, and ending with a discussion of how professional associations attempt to influence government and politics and the extent to which they succeed.

Association Mobilization and Maintenance

Becoming mobilized and securing the resources necessary to stay in existence are serious problems for many organized interests. Following from Mancur Olson's work, scholars have taken the threats to interest group mobilization and maintenance very seriously. There are impediments to the mobilization of interests in the pursuit of collective goods and professional benefits, let alone the good of the public.[11] In reality, individual group leaders are sometimes willing to act as entrepreneurs to bear the costs of organization, and this was the pattern with many professional associations.[12] Dr. Nathan S. Davis devoted a considerable amount of his time and energy to the founding and maintenance of the AMA over a half-century time period.[13] Leaders can be driven by many things in their quests to form groups, including money, status, professional interests, and social benefits. The scholars following from Olson necessarily view these people as driven by self-interest, but it seems probable that the founders of at least some groups engaged in these activities with relatively selfless goals in mind.

Once formed, mortality rates for organized interests are very high and therefore acquiring resources to maintain the organization is a critically important task for all groups.[14] To stay in existence as a viable group, an organization needs resources, including money and the time of volunteers. Emotional and identity-based attachments to professional associations are probably weak compared to some other types of groups, such as racial or ethnic groups. Still, professional associations have numerous means of offering selective incentives to prospective members to join the organization, which undoubtedly helps them to maintain memberships and the dues that usually accompany them. At the extreme in professions such as the law, states may require that a person join a professional association to be licensed to work.

Even where professional associations lack this much power, other incentives include discounted professional insurance or reduced costs for professional continuing education and journal subscription, which can be very effective in attracting additional members, especially where state law requires continuing education.[15] (The state laws mandating continuing education are often advocated by professional associations.) Critics have charged that some of the more powerful professional associations in the medical or legal fields act essentially in the same way as guilds did in the Middle Ages: restricting the supply of certain professionals via their control over access to the field enabled by state legislation, which would drive up the cost of professional services.[16] In the absence of state laws that help to maintain membership, associations can offer networking, socializing, and other selective benefits such as cheaper insurance from pooled rates.

Selective incentives and state laws encouraging or even mandating membership in the professional associations make it difficult for members to resign, which should lead to a large amount of continuity for professional associations once formed. Indeed, as the Walker study found, many professional associations are very old. The difficulty of quitting also undoubtedly influences the internal dynamics of professional associations. Rather than simply exiting the organization when they disagree with the leadership, professional association members are more likely to try to influence the direction of the organization.[17] The leadership may, however, be less responsive because dissatisfied members cannot easily exit. Although selective benefits are an important and perhaps primary reason to belong to professional associations, Gail Lee Cafferata found in a study of a medical professional association that rank-and-file members were more satisfied with their group when they perceived that it was achieving collective goals, including political influence.[18] Because political goals were often important for the founding of these organizations, and members often derive satisfaction from the achievement of political goals, politics remains central to many professional associations.

Professional Associations in the Interest Group Community

Different types of interest organizations face different problems in mobilizing and maintaining themselves, which in turn helps to shape the composition and population of the interest group system, along with factors such as the size and scope of government.[19] Certainly, as government has become larger and more complex, professional associations have proliferated, but determining an exact number of professional associations is not simple because, unlike lobbying organizations or political action committees (PACs), professional associations are not required to register. Based on listings contained in reference books such as *The National Trade and Professional Associations of the United States and Encyclopedia of Associations,* there are hundreds of groups that are active in the United States. A disproportionate number are headquartered in Washington, D.C., and Virginia, indicating the importance of national politics to many of these organizations. According to the 2008 edition of *National Trade and Professional Associations of the United States,* 1,058 trade and professional associations were headquartered in Washington, and 881 in Virginia; the next largest number was 623 in Illinois.[20]

Even with more precise figures, the total of professional associations would tell us only so much about the number of professions being represented. The reason is that professions like medicine and law have several different professional associations representing different specialties or subprofessional groups, with larger umbrella associations representing the specialists and the entire profession (see Table 20.1). The AMA is well known because it represents more than 270,000 doctors, while a much smaller group, the National Association of Managed Care Physicians, represents approximately 15,000 medical professionals.[21]

Research by Kay Lehman Schlozman shows that in the early 1980s professional associations were 6.9 percent of the organizations being represented in the Washington lobbying community, and 14.8 percent of the organized interests having their own office in Washington. More recently, Frank Baumgartner and Beth Leech found that professional associations made up 5.79 percent of the organizations registered to lobby in Washington.[22] This figure marks a small reduction in the relative representation of professional associations. Professional associations are also well represented in the PAC system in Washington, which indicates their willingness to contribute money to candidates. Determining the precise numbers of professional association PACs is difficult because the Federal Election Commission categorizes professional associations with trade, membership, and health PACs. (The activities of some professional association PACs are discussed in more detail below.)

Professional associations tend to be active in state governments. Because state governments are often primarily responsible for regulating the various professions (see Chapter 35), professional associations have an obvious interest in legislation regulating the licensing of occupations such as physicians and lawyers. They may also try to influence more broad-based legislation, which affects certain professions, both at the state and federal level.

Seeking Influence: Political and Government Activities of Professional Associations

Professional associations engage in activities that are similar to other organized interests, such as lobbying or supporting candidates in elections, but they have somewhat different means of influencing politics and government compared to other types of organized interests. For example, political actors such as elected officials and bureaucrats have created their own professional associations, and some bureaucrats in the professions employed in government belong to one. For these individuals, professional associations can provide a venue through which policy information is spread and membership can promote the diffusion of policy innovations across the country. Finally, in many jurisdictions, quasi-governmental functions are delegated to professional agencies by the government, powers denied to most organized interests.

Professional Associations as Just Another "Wealthy Special Interest"

Like any other organized interest, a professional association seeks to shape policy by influencing the decisions of bureaucrats and elected officials and by supporting candidates that are favorable toward the association's interests. As one might expect given the stereotypes, professional associations often expend many resources pursuing relatively narrow policy aims of importance to their members, but of only limited salience for the general public. In other cases, however, they take positions and become active on broader issues of more concern to the mass public. When members of academic professional associations lobby for more National Science Foundation grant money for their discipline, the benefit for the profession is clear, but it may not have much immediate effect on the public or the federal budget. Similarly, sometimes professional associations can be involved in somewhat obscure debates over professional turf. In California, associations representing podiatrists and orthopedists disagreed over which specialists had the exclusive right to operate on ankles.[23]

Professional associations are understandably quite active on laws and policies relating to the regulation of their profession. Almost every state has laws requiring attorneys to pass the state bar exam to have a law license, and the vast majority of states require licensed lawyers to attend law school. Similar laws exist for the medical profession and many others. Professional associations were instrumental in getting these laws passed, and the ABA continues to pressure jurisdictions that do not require lawyers to attend law school to adopt such laws.[24] The laws affect the public good by having a potentially more rigorous set of standards for all entrants into the profession, but detractors view them as attempts to restrict entry into the profession and thereby reduce competition, which increases fees.

In terms of tactics, professional associations are, on average, more likely to use insider approaches, such as direct lobbying and contributing to electoral campaigns, than some other types of organized interests. This capacity stems from the economic resources that these organizations have by virtue of representing a profession, although clearly the range of resources can vary. Favoring insider tactics may also reflect the professional identity that many leaders have, which leads to a bias against participating in more controversial activities such as street protests or demonstrations.

Although professional associations are extremely active in electoral politics and in lobbying government, their expenditures and efforts need to be kept in perspective. The AMA has more than 1,000 employees and an annual budget of approximately $200 million, with more than 2,000 local and regional medical societies under its umbrella. The ABA claims to represent more than half of the practicing lawyers in the United States, or about 400,000 individuals, and it has an annual budget of more than $100 million. The National Association of Realtors (NAR) has an annual budget of approximately $54 million and has 1,800 local boards and affiliates in every state.[25] Even though these huge organizations devote a relatively small portion of their total resources to political activity, they can and do outspend smaller professional associations. As a sector, however, professional associations are certainly not as well resourced as business interests such as corporations or trade associations.

Nevertheless, professional organizations are quite active in politics, and a handful of them have a very large resource base that can be used to influence politics. According to the Center for Responsive Politics, the AMA spent more than $20 million lobbying the federal government in 2008 and well over $200 million on lobbying between 1998 and 2008. These amounts trail only the U.S. Chamber of Commerce in terms of organized interest lobbying expenditures during this time period. The NAR also spent a large amount on lobbying, with expenditures of approximately $17 million in 2008 and approximately $118 million between 1998 and 2008, putting it in the top ten in terms of expenditures for the period. State subsidiaries of federated associations also spend many thousands of dollars on lobbying activities at the federal, state, and local levels. Because these organizations are so large and so politically active, most of their lobbying expenditures go to pay their in-house lobbyists rather than to contract lobbyists or lobbying firms. These associations are obviously extreme outliers in terms of their lobbying activity; many other professional associations spend very little on lobbying, as can be seen in Table 20.2, which shows variation in political expenditures for a diverse set of professional associations.

The same is true of contributions to politicians. Many professional associations give very little or nothing to candidates for office, but a few are quite active. It should not be surprising that some of the more active professional associations in terms of lobbying are also active when it comes to political contributions. According to the Center for Responsive Politics, the NAR political action committee has given more money to candidates for federal office than any other professional association PAC. In 2005–2006 it gave $3.8 million to candidates for federal office, and in 2007–2008, just over $4 million. The AMA's PAC contributed nearly $1.5 million to federal candidates in 2007–2008. Associations that were not particularly active in lobbying also contributed large amounts of money to candidates: the National Association of Insurance and Financial Advisers contributed $2.3 million to federal candidates in 2007–2008. The ABA does not contribute money to politicians, but a PAC representing trial lawyers called American Association for Justice has distributed hundreds of thousands of dollars to federal candidates in recent elections.[26]

Some professional associations that are not very politically active belong to organizations of professional associations that lobby on their behalf. The American Political Science Association and other professional scholarly associations representing social scientists belong to the Consortium of Social Science Associations. This organization spent $160,000 on lobbying the federal government on issues related to federal funding for the social sciences in recent years.[27]

The partisan preferences demonstrated by these PACs depends not only on the politics of the particular professional association but also on the political environment. Associations of home builders, auto dealers, and physicians have tended to favor Republicans, presumably because they want fewer regulations on these industries. Academic

TABLE 20.2 **Membership and Political Expenditures of Selected Professional Associations, 2007–2008**

Association	Membership (approximate)	Lobbying Expenditures (2008)	PAC Contributions (2007–2008)
National Association of Realtors	1,100,000	$17,340,000	$4,020,900
American Medical Association	240,000	$20,550,000	$1,464,450
American Bar Association	400,000	$1,080,000	No PAC sponsored
Nat'l Community Pharmacists Assn.	23,000	$590,000	$940,549
Nat'l Assn of Social Workers	150,000	$842,194	$836,019
Nat'l Society of Accountants	30,000	$40,000	$37,033
American Physical Society	46,000	$510,000	No PAC sponsored
American Library Assn.	65,000	$163,360	No PAC sponsored
American Inst. of Architects	83,000	$850,000	$240,688
Nat'l Assn. of Insurance and Financial Advisors	200,000	$315,000	$2,333,554

SOURCES: For data on lobbying expenditures and PAC contributions, Center for Responsive Politics (opensecrets.org); for membership data, www.realtor.org/library/virtual_library/membershipcount; www.abanet.org/about/; www.medpagetoday.com/MeetingCoverage/AMA/14691; www.ncpanet.org/membership/index.php; www.socialworkers.org/pressroom/features/general/nasw.asp; www.nsacct.org/about_nsa.asp?id=642; www.aps.org/about/history/index.cfm; www.guidestar.org/pqShowGsReport.do?partner=justgivews&ein=36-2166947; Scott Frank, director of Media Relations, American Institute of Architects, 5/7/10; and www.naifa.org/join/.

studies of the AMA PAC find that it gives more money to Republicans and members of Congress with important institutional positions than to other candidates.[28] In contrast, in recent election cycles the NAR has pursued a pragmatic bipartisan strategy, dividing its contributions almost evenly between the two parties, but modestly favoring the majority party in any given cycle. The close association between trial lawyers and the Democratic Party can be seen in the trial lawyer PAC money going almost exclusively to Democratic candidates.

Another approach to politics is to use information to influence both mass and elite opinions. Like many other types of organized interests, professional associations seek to influence the public policy debate by engaging in research and publicizing the results. Professional associations may enjoy an information advantage relative to other types of interests because some degree of specialized knowledge is inherent to the idea of being a professional, and, given the complexity of some of the daily activities of the various professions, these associations probably enjoy the benefits of informational asymmetries when dealing with other political actors.

Professional Associations for Policymakers and the Bureaucracy

As the above discussion indicates, professional associations and other types of organized interests share some core similarities in the tactics they use to influence the political process, but there are also important differences in professional associations and how they influence government and policy. One difference is that in many cases bureaucrats and even elected officials belong to professional associations, which allows these organizations to have direct influence on the implementation of laws through the activities of their individual members. Examples of professional associations representing elected or appointed officials include the National Governors Association, National Association of Insurance Commissioners, and State and Territorial Air Pollution Program Administrators.[29] These organizations can play an important role in the policymaking process and in the process of policy diffusion across different political jurisdictions. A detailed study of one policy area finds that states whose insurance commissioners were on the Accident and Health Insurance policy committee of the National Association of Insurance Commissioners were most likely to adopt a particular health maintenance organization (HMO) law.[30] The organizations representing government officials are obviously different from other professional associations in that their members are insiders, but in other respects they are quite similar. For example, organizations representing judges will often lobby for professional autonomy and pay increases and attempt to protect their status as expert professionals, much like doctors or lawyers would do.

Other professional associations are more general in their orientation and not limited to government officials but still have large numbers of members working in the public sector. The American Public Health Association has members in academe and the public and private sectors. Social workers employed by government agencies may belong to the National Association of Social Workers. Many professional associations promulgate voluntary standards for the conduct of members of the profession, which can affect the policies of the agencies hiring them to the extent that employees can shape agency rules and norms. The Children's Division of the American Humane Association makes caseload recommendations for child protective workers, and the International Association of Firefighters makes recommendations for the appropriate number of firefighters working on engines, ladders, and so forth. Other organizations have called for specific goals to be met by governments, such as the American Public Health Association, which has precise numerical targets it wishes to achieve for rates of smoking, salmonella outbreaks, and other similar public health problems.[31]

Professional associations for government officials can influence policy from within when their members are present in the policymaking areas of government or they can influence politics through the political activities of the rank and file like any other group. Traditionally, laws such as the federal Hatch Act (1939) and "little Hatch Acts" in the states have served to limit the political activities of individuals employed by government. Although on-the-job partisan political activity is still prohibited, in recent years laws have been revised to permit government employees to participate in most political activities.[32] That many of these professionals are government employees gives them a unique ability to shape the formulation and implementation of government policy. This insider status can provide representation for the beneficiaries of government programs administered by social workers and similar professionals, who are unlikely to be politically powerful or to have many resources of their own with which to influence the government.

Self-regulation and Other Quasi-governmental Functions

Another difference between professional associations and some other types of organized interests is that the government delegates regulatory and other types of governmental authority to these groups, and they function in some respects as limited-purpose government bodies. When organizations, such as bar or medical associations, take the lead in developing guidelines for admission to the profession, disciplining members for poor conduct, and the like, they are performing an essentially government function known as self-regulation. This delegation of regulatory authority is based on the argument that "lawyers, and other specialized professions, possess complex and esoteric knowledge and skills" and therefore they alone are capable of understanding their profession's problems and supplying penalties and remedies.[33]

As early as the 1870s some states were delegating these functions to professional associations in areas such as medicine. Russell Gruen, Steven Pearson, and Troyen Brennan write of a social contract between the public and the medical professions where "society grants the medical professions—comprising individuals and their collective associations—special social status and certain privileges such as monopoly use of knowledge, practice autonomy and the right to self-regulate."[34] In almost every state, the legislature has delegated the authority to regulate the legal profession to the profession itself. In these states, it is often mandatory to join the bar association to practice law: lawyers determine standards of admission to the bar and oversee any disciplinary hearings or investigations. This level of authority can be especially justified for this profession

Dr. Morris Fishbein (left), president of the American Medical Association, talks to Sen. Allen Ellender, D-La., in 1939 during Senate hearings on a major health care bill proposed by Sen. Robert Wagner, D-N.Y. The AMA testified at the hearings and strongly opposed the legislation, which did not move past the committee.

Beginning in 1956 the American Bar Association's Committee on the Federal Judiciary began rating Supreme Court nominations. The ABA found nominee William Brennan (left, with President Eisenhower) to be "eminently qualified" following his nomination in 1956.

because lawyers should be independent of the executive branch, with which they often clash during criminal and civil trials, but self-regulation extends to many other professions as well. Medical associations in many states play a similar role as bar associations in the regulation of the medical profession.[35]

The need for specialized knowledge to regulate effectively leads governments to delegate regulatory authority to the professions, but it also raises the possibility that a profession will use this regulatory authority to advance itself at the expense of the public interest. Indeed, it is often charged that professional associations act in a self-protective manner rather than in the interest of the public. William Gallagher argues that the California Bar Association has not always been vigilant in protecting the public good during disciplinary hearings for its members.[36] Although other professions have asserted the right to self-regulation, only a relatively select few currently practice the right, as courts and legislatures denied the right to many professions in the early 1900s.[37]

Professional associations have the authority to engage in other governmental activities in a way that few other organized interests do. At least one type of professional association—again the state bar—participates in an important constitutionally or statutorily defined activity, the selection of judges. In states that have the merit plan of judicial selection, the law often dictates that the judicial selection commissions who nominate judges must contain several lawyers, and these lawyers are in turn often chosen by the state bar association. Other organized interests often participate in nominations for all sorts of elective and appointive offices, but a statutorily or constitutionally defined role in the selection of officials of one of the three coequal branches of government is fairly unusual. At the federal level, the ABA typically interviews judicial candidates and rates them, yet this group has no ability to accept or reject nominees, or even exert any influence on the Senate's final confirmation decisions.[38] It is clear that lawyers' associations have quite a bit of governmental authority delegated to them, mostly likely stemming from the large number of lawyers active in state legislatures.

THE POLITICAL POWER OF PROFESSIONAL ASSOCIATIONS

Professional associations engage in many of the same tactics as other organized interests, but the special role in the governmental and regulatory process that some enjoy provides them with opportunities to protect their interests that many other groups lack. Indeed, most professional associations do not have such power. Therefore, it is appropriate to assess the political power of professional associations in the same manner as other organized interests.

The ability of an interest to influence politics is shaped by its resources. Professional associations are relatively well endowed, but certainly no more so than other prominent organized interests such as corporations or trade associations. John Schmidhauser and Larry Berg write, however, that professional associations do have three resources that other groups may lack: (1) the possession and even monopoly of specialized knowledge; (2) a perceived commitment of service to society that "transcends individual self-interest"; and (3) the ability to regulate their own professional conduct.[39] As noted above, the third factor they cite seems to be almost unique to professional associations, while the first would seem to apply to numerous institutions that are active in politics, such as corporations. A perceived commitment to society is probably true of many good government groups as well. Overall, professions that have the authority to regulate themselves are necessarily influential within their narrow area of regulatory authority. In other policy areas, whether or not they succeed in influencing policy probably depends on the same factors as other groups, given that the resources they possess are by no means unique.

Based on a large body of research conducted over the last few decades, one can conclude that just how influential professional associations are should vary depending on factors such as the involvement of other opposing organized interests and the salience and partisanship of the issue. The interest group literature shows that organized interests, on average, are most influential on low-salience, nonpartisan technical issues, which should enable the success of professional associations on their issues of narrow concern. Many issues of concern to professional associations are relatively low salience and technical, such as the dispute noted earlier between the two medical associations. On this kind of issue, a professional association must necessarily be influential.[40] Even on issues that do not pit associations against one another, technical issues should allow professional associations to leverage their expertise into influence on policy.

On issues of broader importance to the general public, the ability of professional associations to influence policy is limited by the context in which they operate. The American Library Association has vigorously objected to provisions of the USA PATRIOT Act that allow government access to citizens' library records, but this lobbying has not succeeded because of the larger political dynamics surrounding the issue.[41] The involvement of the AMA in universal health care, and its changing political clout on this issue, is instructive in showing how the context constrains the ability of professional associations to influence policy. The AMA clearly has all of the resources that should make any organized interest successful; it also has a monopoly on specialized information. Traditionally, doctors have also enjoyed great public prestige, undoubtedly linked to their claim to value the public good above self-interest. These resources have been powerful weapons for the AMA at times. During the late 1940s and early 1950s the AMA raised and spent money on a "national education campaign" and donated funds to opponents of national health insurance.[42] It cannot necessarily be attributed solely to the AMA efforts, but public and political support for national health insurance weakened.

Since its heyday, the AMA's clout has decreased. It was unsuccessful in defeating the Medicare bill in 1965. Part of this effort, dubbed "operation coffee cup," involved the

The American Library Association became a vocal critic of the government's demands for library records under the USA PATRIOT Act as part of investigations.

distribution of a recording to AMA ladies' auxiliaries by actor Ronald Reagan in which he spoke out against "socialized medicine." [43] Mark Peterson writes that the AMA was met with countervailing interests and a loss of trust in the late 1960s, which led to a decline in its power over the subsequent years.[44] Additionally, in the early 1990s the AMA was not as active in derailing the Clinton health care reform bill. Although the AMA continues to play an important role in political issues related to its profession, it is not as powerful as it once was.[45] In the most recent attempts at health insurance reform, the AMA joined the private health insurance industry in opposition to any health care reform that created a public insurance plan for those not already covered by Medicare or Medicaid.[46] As desired, the so-called public option was not included in the health insurance reform legislation, but it is not clear whether the exclusion is attributable to the AMA's opposition. Most professional associations will never approach the power that the AMA had or still has. For the most part, on issues of broader importance, professional associations are able to influence but rarely determine outcomes because of the range of interest groups active in Washington on these types of issues.

Professional associations also lobby in the broader public interest. Medical associations (somewhat belatedly, critics might note) have lobbied in favor of restrictions on tobacco use, and their action likely furthered government attempts to regulate tobacco more vigorously by giving proponents the support of well-respected experts. Some physicians also recommend that doctors' organizations take the lead in attempts to expand access to health care and control costs.[47] The AMA did not oppose the final health care reform legislation enacted by Congress and signed by President Obama.

Most people think about organized interests in terms of their influence in policy and elections, but associations also may affect other political outcomes of importance. In his work on social capital, Robert Putnam argues that membership in voluntary associations increases trust and political participation. Even though associational life in America is declining, survey data indicate that membership in professional associations is increasing, according to Putnam.[48] Furthermore, while professional association membership has potential career and economic benefits, it may also lead to the acquisition of the same types of political skills as membership in other types of organizations. This effect may not be as great because members of professional associations are already highly educated and already possess these skills.[49] Finally, membership in professional associations provides an avenue for important information about relevant political issues for association members, which subsidizes the costs of remaining informed about politics. Unlike influence on legislation and policy, this type of influence is not nearly as controversial, explaining the relative dearth of studies into these questions.

CONCLUSION

The large number of professional associations in existence is testament to the often-cited American penchant to join voluntary organizations. Voluntary organizations of professionals have been forming and seeking to influence government and politics since the beginning of American history. Truly modern professional associations began to proliferate around the time of the Civil War with the development of the modern division of labor, and they have been an important political force ever since. Well-known and highly influential professional associations are often active in the U.S. campaign finance and lobbying systems, and are well represented in the halls of government. In many ways, professional associations are similar to other interest groups, and much of what can be said of any organized interests also applies to professional associations, but there are some important differences. Because professional organizations arise out of economic activity, they should generally have an easier time of maintaining themselves once they are formed, compared to some other types of groups. In some cases, they also perform important quasi-governmental functions, which other types of organized interests do not perform and which create the possibility that groups will use this influence for their own narrow ends.

The right of self-regulation and the use of abundant material resources in the pursuit of the interests of the profession for some groups means that controversy over the role of professional associations in politics is bound to exist. On one hand, the ability of professional associations to engage in self-regulation and their activities on many notable pieces of legislation reinforces the negative views toward organized interests held by the public. On the other, the public tends to rely on the legitimate professional expertise of these groups, expertise that can potentially be used for self-serving aims, but is also recognized as essential to the public good.

NOTES

1. National Automobile Dealers Association, www.nada.org/Membership.

2. Marjorie Murphy, *Blackboard Unions, the AFT and the NEA, 1900–1980* (Ithaca, N.Y.: Cornell University Press, 1990).

3. *National Trade and Professional Associations of the United States* (Bethesda, Md.: Columbia Books, 2008).

4. Minor Myers Jr., *Liberty without Anarchy: A History of the Society of the Cincinnati* (Charlottesville: University of Virginia Press, 1983).

5. Melvyn Dubofsky and Foster Rhea Dulles, *Labor in American History*, 6th ed. (Wheeling, Ill.: Harlan Davidson, 1999).

6. Jack L. Walker, "The Origins and Maintenance of Interest Groups in America," *American Political Science Review* 77 (1983): 390–406, 394.

7. John R. Schmidhauser, with Larry L. Berg, "The American Bar Association and the Human Rights Conventions: The Political Significance of Private Professional Associations," *Social Research* 38, 2 (1971): 362–410.

8. John G. Gunnell, "The Founding of the American Political Science Association: Discipline, Profession, Political Theory and Politics," *American Political Science Review* 100, 4 (2006): 479–486.

9. American Medical Association, www.ama-assn.org/ama/pub/about-ama/our-mission.shtml.

10. David Lowery and Virginia Gray, "A Neopluralist Perspective on Research on Organized Interests," *Political Research Quarterly* 57, 1 (2004): 164–175.

11. Mancur Olson, *The Logic of Collective Action: Public Goods and the Theory of Groups* (Cambridge: Harvard University Press, 1965).

12. Anthony J. Nownes and Grant Neeley, "Public Interest Group Entrepreneurship and Theories of Group Mobilization," *Political Research Quarterly* 49, 1 (1996): 119–146.

13. American Medical Association, www.ama-assn.org/ama/pub/category/12982.html.

14. David Lowery and Virginia Gray, "The Population Ecology of Gucci Gulch, or The Natural Regulation of Interest Group Numbers in the American States," *American Journal of Political Science* 39, 1 (1995): 1–29.

15. Sally Conway Kilbane and John H. Beck, "Professional Associations and the Free Rider Problem: The Case of Optometrists," *Public Choice* 65 (1990): 181–187.

16. J. A. C. Grant, "The Gild [*sic*] Returns to America, I," *Journal of Politics* 4, 3 (1942): 303–336; George J. Stigler, "The Theory of Economic Regulation," *Bell Journal of Economics and Management Science* 2, 1 (1971): 3–21.

17. Maryann Barakso and Brian F. Schaffner, "Exit, Voice, and Interest Group Governance," *American Politics Research* 36, 2 (2008): 186–209.

18. Gail Lee Cafferata, "Member and Leader Satisfaction with a Professional Organization: An Exchange Perspective," *Administrative Science Quarterly* 24, 3 (1979): 472–483.

19. Lowery and Gray, "Population Ecology of Gucci Gulch."

20. *National Trade and Professional Associations of the United States* (Bethesda, Md.: Columbia Books, 2008).

21. Ibid.

22. Kay Lehman Schlozman, "What Accent the Heavenly Chorus? Political Equality and the American Pressure System," *Journal of Politics* 46, 4 (1984): 1006–1032; Frank C. Baumgartner and Beth L. Leech, "Interest Niches and Policy Bandwagons: Patterns of Interest Group Involvement in National Politics," *Journal of Politics* 63, 4 (1996): 1191–1213.

23. Jay Michaels and Dan Walters, *The Third House: Lobbyists, Power and Money in Sacramento* (Berkeley, Calif.: Berkeley Public Policy Press, 2002).

24. G. Jeffrey MacDonald, "The Self-made Lawyer: Not every attorney goes to law school. Seven states allow another path to law practice—the same one that Abe Lincoln took," *Christian Science Monitor*, June 3, 2003.

25. *National Trade and Professional Associations.*

26. Center for Responsive Politics, www.opensecrets.org.

27. Consortium of Social Science Associations, www.cossa.org.

28. Karen Gutermuth, "The American Medical Political Action Committee: Which Senators Get the Money and Why? *Journal of Health Politics, Policy and Law* 24, 2 (1999): 357–382; John D. Wilkerson and David Carrell, "Money, Politics, and Medicine: The American Medical PAC's Strategy of Giving in U.S. House Races," *Journal of Health Politics, Policy and Law* 24, 2 (1999): 335–355.

29. *National Trade and Professional Associations.*

30. Steven J. Balla, "Interstate Professional Associations and the Diffusion of Policy Innovations," *American Politics Research* 29, 3 (2001): 221–245.

31. David N. Ammons, "The Role of Professional Associations in Establishing and Promoting Performance Standards for Local Government," *Public Productivity and Management Review* 17, 3 (1994): 281–298.

32. Joanne J. Thompson, "Social Workers and Politics: Beyond the Hatch Act," *Social Work* 39 (1994): 457–465.

33. William T. Gallagher, "Ideologies of Professionalism and the Politics of Self-Regulation in the California State Bar," *Pepperdine Law Review* 22 (1995): 485–628, 489.

34. Russell L. Gruen, Steven D. Pearson, and Troyen A. Brennan, "Physician-Citizens—Public Roles and Professional Obligations," *Journal of the American Medical Association* 291, 1 (2004): 294–298.

35. Monica Noether, "The Effect of Government Policy Change on the Supply of Physicians: Expansion of a Competitive Fringe," *Journal of Law and Economics* 29, 2 (1986): 231–262.

36. Gallagher, "Ideologies of Professionalism."

37. Grant, "Gild Returns."

38. R. Townsend Davis Jr., "The American Bar Association and Judicial Nominees: Advice without Consent," *Columbia Law Review* 89, 3 (1989): 550–579.

39. Schmidhauser and Berg, "American Bar Association and the Human Rights Conventions."

40. Michaels and Walters, *Third House.*

41. American Library Association, www.ala.org/Template.cfm?Section=ifissues&Template=/ContentManagement/ContentDisplay.cfm&ContentID=76879.

42. Jill Quadagno, "Why the United States Has no National Health Insurance: Stakeholder Mobilization against the Welfare State, 1945–1996," *Journal of Health and Social Behavior* 45 (2004): 25–44.

43. Laura K. Altom, and Larry R. Churchill, "Pay, Pride, and Public Purpose: Why America's Doctors Should Support Universal Healthcare," *Medscape General Medicine* 9, 1 (2007): 40.

44. Mark A. Peterson, "From Trust to Political Power: Interest Groups, Public Choice and Health Care," *Journal of Health Politics, Policy and Law* 26, 5 (2001):1146–63.

45. Jeffrey Young, "State Physician Groups, AMA Target GOP Senators over Medicare Votes," *The Hill.com*, July 1, 2008.

46. Robert Pear, "Doctors' Group Opposes Public Insurance Plan," *New York Times*, On-line edition, June 11, 2009.

47. Gruen, Pearson, and Brennan, "Physician-Citizens—Public Roles."

48. Robert D. Putnam, *Making Democracy Work: Civic Traditions in Modern Italy* (Princeton: Princeton University Press, 1993).

49. Henry E. Brady, Sidney Verba, and Kay Lehman Schlozman, "Beyond SES: A Resource Model of Political Participation," *American Political Science Review* 89, 2 (1995): 279–294.

SUGGESTED READING

Balla, Steven J. "Interstate Professional Associations and the Diffusion of Policy Innovations." *American Politics Research* 29, 3 (2001): 221–245.

Merton, Robert K. "The Functions of the Professional Association." *American Journal of Nursing* 58, 1 (1958): 50–54.

Olson, Mancur. *The Logic of Collective Action: Public Goods and the Theory of Groups.* Cambridge: Harvard University Press, 1965.

Schmidhauser, John R., with Larry L. Berg. "The American Bar Association and the Human Rights Conventions: The Political Significance of Private Professional Associations." *Social Research* 38, 2 (1971): 362–410.

Walker, Jack L. "The Origins and Maintenance of Interest Groups in America." *American Political Science Review* 77 (1983): 390–406, 394.

chapter 21

Elementary and Secondary Education

by R. Kenneth Godwin

EDUCATION POLICY LIES at the intersection of three enduring clusters of questions: First, how much should a child's parents determine her opportunities in life? Second, should it be parents or the government who determine the ideas to which children are exposed? Third, to whom should the producers of education services be held accountable? The importance of these questions, combined with the huge government expenditures on public and secondary (K-12) education, virtually guarantee that education will be a battleground for competing interest groups.[1]

The United States spends a higher proportion of its gross domestic product on education than any country in the world.[2] It also has the highest per pupil expenditures.[3] In fiscal year 2006 government expenditures on public elementary and secondary education were $529 billion.[4] Adjusted for inflation, per pupil expenditures for K-12 education have increased by more than three percent per year from 1890 to 2005. In other words, real per pupil expenditures have almost doubled every twenty years.[5] K-12 education constitutes the largest expenditure of state and local monies. The average per pupil cost of education is more than $9,000 annually.[6] In 2008 Americans spent an additional $42.8 billion on private schools.[7]

These enormous expenditures make education an important political issue and a target for interest groups. Between 1959 and 1995 the number of national interest groups involved in education grew from 563 to 1,312.[8] The number of organizations involved in state and local education is many times that. Lobbying expenditures on education issues have more than doubled since 1998.[9]

Three additional aspects of education make it important to organized interests. First, Americans view education as *the* key to providing equality of opportunity to all children. Civil rights and ethnicity-based groups see increasing educational opportunities for disadvantaged students as essential to achieving an equitable society. Second, local citizens consider public education as an opportunity to socialize students to America's fundamental principles and values. Because Americans do not agree over what should be included in these principles and values, schools have become major battlefields in the nation's culture wars. Third, the publication in 1983 of *A Nation at Risk: The Imperative for Educational Reform* by Ronald Reagan's National Commission on Excellence in Education made education reform an important political issue.

CATEGORIES OF INTEREST ORGANIZATIONS

Prior to 1983 the producers of education—teachers, principals, and school district superintendents—controlled education policy. Today, the battle over how to reform education pits groups representing those producers against well-organized groups that want to hold districts, schools, and individual educators responsible for student outcomes.

Producer Groups

In 1959 Wisconsin opened the door to education interest group activity when it passed the first state law allowing public sector employees to bargain collectively. It was a strike in 1960 by New York City teachers, however, that proved to be the watershed moment for collective bargaining by teachers. The strike forced New York to allow collective bargaining for teachers. The union members voted to go on strike again in 1962, and Gov. Nelson Rockefeller found $13 million in state funds to help New York City meet the teachers' demands for a $995 pay raise and a duty-free lunch period.[10] Numerous states followed Wisconsin and New York in allowing public employee unions, and teacher strikes across the nation increased dramatically. In 1964 there were nine teacher strikes; in 1967 there were 105; and during the 1975–1976 school year 203 strikes took place. The rise in the number of unionized teachers, collective bargaining agreements, and teacher strikes helped to increase the average annual salaries of teachers (in current dollars) from $5,264 in 1961 to $43,262 in 2001.[11]

The "production" of education involves numerous organizations that represent individuals working in elementary and secondary education. The most powerful of these producer groups are the two major teachers' unions, the National Education Association (NEA) and the American Federation of Teachers (AFT). These organizations are extraordinarily influential at the national, state, and local levels.[12] In fact, political scientists who study interest groups rank teachers' unions as the most influential interest group in state politics.[13] These unions have 4 million dues-paying members, and their political action committees (PACs) contributed more than $56 million in campaign contributions between 1989 and 2008. Ninety-five percent of these contributions went to Democratic Party candidates.[14] In addition to teachers' unions are the organizations that represent school principals, nonprofessional school staff such as clerical staff and maintenance workers, school social workers, and school district superintendents. Each of the national organizations has state organizations, and many have local chapters in large school districts. Moreover, the National Association of Elementary School Principals (NAESP) has an individual in each state responsible for lobbying that state's congressional delegation and for organizing NAESP's grassroots lobbying campaigns.[15] Although the PTA (National Parent Teacher Association) is officially an organization that represents parents and teachers, teachers are the organization's dominant force and control its political agenda.[16]

Producer organizations in education are similar to any other special interest; they pursue policies that advance the interests of their members while claiming that the policies are in the interests of students and the public. Teachers' unions favor policies such as tenure for classroom teachers, smaller class sizes, hiring teacher aides, and teacher autonomy in the classroom. Most important, unions favor costly time-consuming procedures for dismissing poorly performing teachers. They strongly oppose any teacher accountability measures based on gains in student performance and any policy that allows school districts to hire teachers who have not completed certification programs from schools of education. The *bête noire* of teacher organizations is a voucher program that allows public funds to support private education.

Teachers' unions have an extraordinary advantage over most other labor unions. In the private sector, labor's representatives bargain with the representatives of management. In public education, teachers typically bargain with representatives they have chosen in state and local elections. Teachers' organizations often are the only organized interest providing campaign workers and funding to candidates for local school boards. As Terry Moe has shown, the support of teachers' unions is the most important variable predicting the electoral outcomes of school board election.[17] In addition, teachers' organizations can count on the support of other labor organizations, civil rights groups, liberal interest groups, and the Democratic Party in political struggles over education policy.

Business Organizations

Business associations constitute the second set of interests involved in K-12 education. Business groups generally support policies that will provide a competent labor force and that are cost effective. The difficulty for business interest groups is that they are concerned with many issues other than education. Education becomes a priority only when a crisis occurs in the local schools. When this happens, business organizations, such as the local Chamber of Commerce and individual local firms, participate on ad hoc, short-term committees formed to address the crisis.[18] When the crisis passes or a critical election is over, the business community's interest fades, and participants narrow their focus to conventional education issues: containing costs, eliminating unbusinesslike practices such as tenure, and reducing excessive bureaucracy.[19] Business interests want to keep taxes and spending low and to root out inefficiency, and they generally support reforms such as school choice and accountability testing. Despite the sporadic nature of their involvement, business groups provide a major restraint on the political effectiveness of education producer groups.

Educational Equity Organizations

The third category of interest organization consists of civil rights organizations and groups representing disadvantaged populations. Among the more influential organizations when it comes to education policy are the National Association for the Advancement of Colored People (NAACP), the NAACP Legal Defense and Educational Fund, National Urban League, National Council of La Raza, Mexican American Legal Defense Fund, and Native American Rights Fund. Groups that have proven important in guaranteeing equal educational opportunities for girls and women include the National Organization for Women, National Coalition for Women and Girls in Education, and Association for Women in Science. More recently, a growing number of groups have worked on behalf of lesbian, gay, bisexual, and transgendered students. One such group is the Gay, Lesbian and Straight Education Network.

Starting with the landmark *Brown v. Board of Education* decision in 1954, civil rights groups have pressed for school desegregation.[20] These groups also advocated for programs such as Head Start that provide additional educational opportunities for minority and low-income students. Civil rights organizations have worked with groups representing students with special needs. These groups include the American Association of People with Disabilities and the Disability Rights Education and Defense

Fund. Also active are organizations representing specific disability conditions such as the National Center for Law and the Deaf.

Religious and Ideological Associations

Ideological and religious groups have become an important force in education politics. The rise of the Christian Right within the Republican Party, and in politics more generally, has had a significant impact on K-12 politics.[21] Focus on the Family, Family Research Council, 700 Club, and Christian Coalition are among the most active religious groups that lobby for socially conservative policies. These groups have proven particularly adept at using talk radio and the Christian Broadcasting Network to advocate their positions on education policy. Primary issues for social conservatives include family values, sex education, prayer in the public schools, and teaching "intelligent design" as a legitimate scientific alternative to evolution. They oppose multicultural education, particularly educational programs that teach respect for gay and lesbian rights and for nontraditional families.

Liberal groups are also active in education politics. People for the American Way is particularly vigorous in its fight against school vouchers and the teaching of intelligent design. The National Council of Churches, American Civil Liberties Union, American Center for Law and Justice, Southern Poverty Law Center, and the now-defunct ACORN (Association of Community Organizations for Reform Now) have been effective advocates for teaching tolerance and multiculturalism in public school.

Because more than 80 percent of private school students attend Catholic schools, Catholic organizations have a strong interest and impact in education politics. Catholic interest groups include the National Catholic Education Association, Federation of Catholic Teachers, Knights of Columbus, Education Committee of the United States, and the U.S. Conference of Catholic Bishops. These organizations advocate for Catholic education, school vouchers, tax credits for private schools, and other issues directly relevant to the Catholic schools in the United States. Other religions with private schools also support greater public support for private education. Although most Jewish organizations oppose school vouchers, some, such as Aguduth Israel, which is affiliated with Orthodox Judaism, lobby for greater public assistance to private schools and for school vouchers.

Ideological foundations and think tanks have provided important support to liberal and conservative interest groups. Although many of these organizations profess to be nonpartisan and claim 501(c)(3) tax status, their research and grant-giving activities usually are ideologically motivated.[22] The Heritage Foundation, American Enterprise Institute, Lynde and Harry Bradley Foundation, Walton Family Foundation, and Olin Foundation support conservative research and publication on education issues. Liberal foundations that support education-related research include the Ford and Rockefeller Foundations as well as smaller regional foundations such as New England's Nellie Mae Education Foundation.

FIGURE 21.1 **Factors Affecting Student Learning**

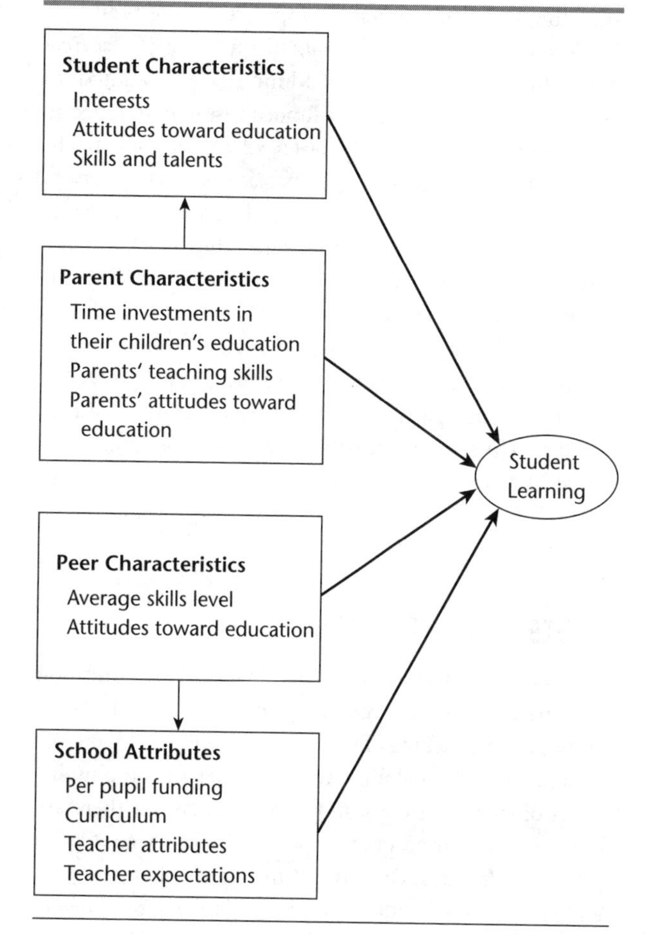

Government Organizations

The final category of education-related interest organizations consists of those that represent governments. The National School Boards Association represents the interests of state boards of education and local school boards, and the Council of Great City Schools represents large, urban school districts. The National Governors Association has been an effective advocate for federal aid to education. Colleges of education in public universities have multiple advocacy groups including the American Association of Colleges for Teacher Education. The National Institute of Child Health and Human Development has been a participant in the battle between conservative and liberal groups advocating different reading programs.[23] Finally, the U.S. Department of Education (ED) has been a powerful advocate in Congress for education programs supported by the president. The ED also affects policy through its funding of research. When the George W. Bush administration wanted to increase school choice, the ED funded research designed to evaluate the effectiveness of charter schools, school vouchers, and programs designed to increase parents' ability to choose schools appropriate to their children. The ED also funded provoucher interest groups including Black Alliance for Educational Opportunities and Hispanic Council for the Reform of Educational Options.[24]

In sum, there is no shortage of interest groups in education. As we shall see below, most of the groups involved in education issues participate in relatively stable coalitions that have either a liberal or a conservative orientation to politics. On most issues, conservative organizations align with the Republican Party, and liberal organizations side with the Democratic Party.

ISSUES AND INTERESTS

Four interrelated issues have dominated K-12 education since the 1950s: (1) desegregation and educational opportunity; (2) the teaching of values; (3) school choice; and (4) educational accountability. All four issues fit the pluralist model of interest groups and public policy—as there are competing organized interests with sufficient resources to lobby policymakers. On three of the issues, liberal organizations have allied with the Democratic Party to compete with a coalition of conservative groups aligned with the Republican Party. The benefits of this ideological and partisan activity are that almost all citizens receive organized representation and informed political debate occurs on every issue. The cost of this partisanship is a polarization of education policy that reflects and reinforces deep conflicts within communities.[25]

Desegregation and Educational Opportunity

A major policy issue in American education is how to reduce ethnic and racial differences in standardized test scores, high school graduation rates, and college attendance rates.[26] The educational outcomes of African Americans and Latinos have lagged far behind those of Anglos and Asians. As shown in Figure 21.1, four broad sets of variables affect educational outcomes: the individual student's attributes, the characteristics of the student's family, the characteristics of the student's classmates and peer groups, and the inputs of the school. In the short term, few policy instruments can affect student and family variables. The state cannot dictate that students will start school ready to learn or that students will value education and work hard. Similarly, the state cannot require parents to be involved in their child's education. But education policymakers can choose policies that affect the quality of a student's classmates, and policymakers can change the level and types of resources available to schools.

Although the *Brown* decision that mandated school desegregation was written more than a half century ago, American schools remain highly segregated by race, ethnicity, and income.[27] Low-income and minority students are concentrated in inner-city schools, and middle-class, white students living in the suburbs remain largely isolated from other ethnic groups. Substantial research demonstrates that desegregating schools greatly improves the educational outcomes of low-income and minority students.[28] One reason that segregation harms disadvantaged students is that the skills and educational attitudes of a student's classmates affect how much he or she learns. On average, low-income students begin school with fewer skills, and their parents often do not have the time or resources to assist their children with their schoolwork. In addition, low-income parents are less likely to be involved in their children's education.[29] For these reasons, school assignment policies that concentrate low-income students in a school reduce those students' educational opportunities.

Another reason that segregation reduces the educational opportunities of low-income and minority students is that relatively few teachers want to teach in schools with high percentages of low-income students.[30] Because teachers with more experience often transfer to schools with a lower percentage of at-risk students, less advantaged students are far more likely to have inexperienced teachers. In states where school districts depend on local property taxes for funding, students in districts with little wealth receive substantially lower per pupil funding.

The problem for policymakers is that housing in metropolitan areas is highly segregated by income, race, and ethnicity, which means that effective desegregation policies cannot use neighborhood attendance zones to assign students to schools. Instead, effective desegregation policies often require a district to use mandatory busing or ethnic quotas when assigning students to schools. Such policies are unpopular and create intense political conflicts. In addition, the federal courts are unlikely to allow a district to use student ethnicity to assign students to schools. In its most recent school desegregation case, *Meredith v. Jefferson County Bd. of Education* and *Parents Involved in Community Schools v. Seattle School District No. 1* (2007), the Supreme Court ruled that the Fourteenth Amendment prohibits school districts from using race as a factor in assigning students to public schools. More than 100 interest organizations filed amicus curiae briefs. As the box above indicates, the majority of these briefs supported the right of school districts to use race and ethnicity in school assignment to achieve desegregation and to improve the educational outcomes of minority students.

AMICUS CURIAE BRIEFS IN *MEREDITH V. JEFFERSON COUNTY BD. OF EDUCATION AND PARENTS INVOLVED IN COMMUNITY SCHOOLS V. SEATTLE SCHOOL DISTRICT NO. 1* (2007)

Amicus Curiae Briefs Supporting the Use of Race and Ethnicity in School Assignment

Lawyers' Committee for Civil Rights of the San Francisco Bay Area; National Collegiate Athletic Association and National Basketball Retired Players Association; American Council on Education; Swann Fellowship, Former School Board Members, Parents and Children from the Charlotte-Mecklenburg Schools; Caucus for Structural Equity; Leadership Conference on Civil Rights and Leadership Conference on Civil Rights Education Fund; National Women's Law Center and National Partnership for Women & Families; Council of the Great City Schools; Magnet Schools of America; Public Education Network; United States Conference of Mayors; National Parent Teacher Association; Human Rights Advocacy Groups; International Law Professors; Commonwealth of Massachusetts; American Educational Research Association; National School Boards Association; Black Women Lawyers' Association of Greater Chicago; National Lawyers Guild; Media & Telecommunication Companies; Sens. Edward M. Kennedy and Barack Obama; Massachusetts Association of School Superintendents and Massachusetts Association of School Committees, Inc.; National Urban League; Asian American Legal Defense and Education Fund and Chinese for Affirmative Action; Civil Rights Clinic at Howard University School of Law; Campaign for Educational Equity; NAACP Legal Defense and Educational Fund, Inc.; Puerto Rican Legal Defense and Education Fund; Former Chancellors of the University of California; Housing Scholars and Research and Advocacy Organizations in Support of Respondents; 553 Social Scientists; Coalition to Defend Affirmative Action, Integration, and Immigrant Rights and Fight for Equality by Any Means Necessary and United for Equality and Affirmative Action Legal Defense Fund; Rep. Jim McDermott et al.; American Psychological Association; National Education Association; Louisville Area Chamber of Commerce; the states of New York, Connecticut, Illinois, Iowa, Kentucky, Maine, Maryland, Missouri, New Jersey, New Mexico, North Carolina, Oregon, Rhode Island, Utah, Vermont, Washington, Wisconsin, and the District of Columbia and the Commonwealth of Puerto Rico; former U.S. secretaries of Education and secretaries of Health, Education, and Welfare who served five former presidents; Asian American Justice Center; Asian Law Caucus; Asian Pacific American Legal Center; and Asian American Institute et al.; American Civil Liberties Association.

Amicus Curiae Briefs Opposing the Use of Race and Ethnicity in School Assignment

U.S. Government; Merits of Mountain States Legal Foundation; Center for Individual Rights; Asian American Legal Foundation; Florida governor John Ellis "JEB" Bush and the State Board of Education; various school children from Lynn, Massachusetts, who are parties in *Comfort v. Lynn School Committee;* Pacific Legal Foundation; American Civil Rights Institute; Center for Equal Opportunity; American Civil Rights Union and National Association of Neighborhood Schools; Competitive Enterprise Institute; Project on Fair Representation, National Association of Scholars, and law professors; American Civil Rights Institute; Center for Equal Opportunity.

Another equity issue concerns the costs of achieving equality of educational opportunity for students with disabilities or special needs. The costs of educating a severely disabled student can be many times greater than the average per pupil expenditure. Low-income students are more likely to have special educational needs, and children of new immigrants are more likely to need special language classes. These factors place substantial financial burdens on inner-city school districts and on districts with large numbers of immigrants.

The interest groups involved in equity issues typically divide along traditional party lines. The Democratic Party has campaigned for school desegregation and for policies that support children with special needs. Coalitions of civil rights organizations have lobbied to end racial, ethnic, and income segregation in public schools. The NEA has joined civil rights organizations to support desegregating the schools and is on record supporting unpopular policies such as mandatory busing and ethnic quotas in school assignment. The Republican Party has helped create coalitions to defeat these assignment policies. Although no politically significant interest organizations have publicly advocated maintaining segregated schools, groups such as Concerned Parents for Neighborhood Schools and Parents Against Forced Busing have decried busing and ethnic quotas as unproven and ineffective social experiments. Rather than lobbying openly against desegregation, conservative groups have lobbied for policies that require districts to allow students to attend their neighborhood schools.

Various conservative foundations, such as the Heritage Foundation, Pacific Legal Foundation, American Civil Rights Institute, John Locke Foundation, Center for Individual Rights, and Washington Legal Foundation, have brought court cases to end mandatory busing and ethnic quotas in school assignment policies. By 2007 the courts had prohibited or severely limited the use of such policies.[31] Unless the U.S. Supreme Court eventually reverses its previous decisions, conservative groups would seem to have won the battle over achieving desegregation through school assignment policies.[32]

Because the courts have ended the use of race and ethnicity in school assignment plans, civil rights and disability organizations have championed the "education adequacy" movement. Education adequacy requires that all students receive an education that allows them to become economically independent and to participate fully in democratic government. Because students differ in their abilities and socioeconomic backgrounds, it costs significantly more to provide an adequate education to some students than to others. Advocates of education adequacy include not only the groups that lobbied for school desegregation, but also organizations such as ACCESS (Access Quality Education: School Funding, Litigation, Policy, and Adequacy), Rural School and Community Trust, and Broader, Bolder Approach to Education. These groups have formed coalitions to lobby Congress and state legislatures.[33] The coalitions maintain that current education finance and expenditure patterns violate the equal protection clause of the U.S. Constitution and the education adequacy provisions in state constitutions.[34]

Education and the Culture Wars: Whose Values Will Public Schools Teach?

As was the case with equity issues, the battle over whose values schools will teach follows partisan lines. Hot-button issues—school prayer, sex education, tolerance for nontraditional families, and the teaching of intelligent design—have divided state boards of education, local school boards, and the citizens these institutions represent. Often these issues pit the rights of parents to limit the ideas to which their children are exposed against the rights of the state to socialize students in ways chosen by the majority of voters or their elected representatives. Some parents believe that their public schools are teaching ideas that could result in the eternal damnation of their children. At the same time, the public officials who are responsible for preparing students to become citizens of a democracy have decided that not exposing students to ideas such as tolerance and respect for gays and lesbians would discourage the development of political tolerance that is essential to a multicultural and democratic society.

The Christian Right and the Republican Party have led the effort to prevent schools from teaching respect for nontraditional families and gays and lesbians. Focus on the Family, an interest group that represents Christian Evangelicals, maintains that "American public schools have become a frontline in efforts by gay activists to indoctrinate our children to believe dangerous and misleading messages about homosexuality, bisexuality, and transgender identity issues." [35] Focus on the Family, the Traditional Values Coalition, and other similar organizations argue that the U.S. education policies violate Article 26 of the United Nation's Universal Declaration of Human Rights.[36] Article 26 declares that elementary and secondary education should be free and compulsory and that "parents have a prior right to choose the kind of education that shall be given to their children."

Socially conservative groups are not the only interest organizations that believe public schools are teaching objectionable ideas and values. Liberal organizations lobby against the teaching of the antievolution theory of intelligent design.[37] Secular humanist organizations such as Center for Inquiry and Council for Secular Humanists maintain that public education teaches values slanted in favor of religion.[38] Interest groups representing Muslims, Hindus, and Buddhists maintain that public education often favors the Judeo-Christian tradition. Along with many Jewish organizations, such as American Jewish Congress and the National Council of Jewish Women, these groups argue for a stricter separation between public education and religious values.[39] Some Christian organizations such as the National Council of Churches and the Alliance of Baptists also argue that public education should not give preference to Judeo-Christian beliefs.

Education Accountability and School Choice

Education reform has been an important national policy issue since the publication in 1983 of *A Nation at Risk: The Imperative for Educational Reform.* The report, prepared by President Reagan's National Commission on Excellence in Education, helped change Americans' understanding of the performance of their public schools. The report concluded that American students were becoming increasingly noncompetitive with students in other countries. Over the next decade, numerous reports found that despite large increases in per pupil expenditures, the test scores of high school students were not improving. Other research suggested that private schools were doing a better job of teaching low-income, minority students than were the public schools.[40] *A Nation at Risk* and the research it spawned pushed education reform to the top of the nation's domestic agenda.

Proposals to reform education fall into two general categories: those supported by teachers' unions and other producer groups and the policies designed to increase accountability of schools and teachers. The first reforms following publication of *A Nation at Risk* closely followed its three major recommendations: (1) that all high schools provide a more rigorous curriculum; (2) that districts extend the length of the school day and the school year; and (3) that teaching be improved with higher salaries and enhanced preparation and professionalization.[41] An important attribute of these reforms is that they do not challenge the educational control of teachers, principals, and district superintendents. Numerous states adopted these reforms at the urging of business groups and community organizing groups such as the Industrial Areas Foundation and Communities Organized for Public Service.

The second reform category centers on expanding school choice and accountability testing. School choice proposals include: (1) increasing the number of magnet and thematic schools; (2) encouraging the development of charter schools; and (3) providing parents vouchers that they can use in either public or private schools. The pro-voucher interest group coalition includes the organizations of the Christian Right, the Heritage, Fordham, Olin, and Hudson Foundations, and libertarian foundations and research institutes including the Cato, Manhattan, and American Enterprise Institutes. The coalition also includes private school organizations, and centrist organizations such as the Progressive Policy Institute and the Center for American Progress. The George W. Bush administration used the Department of Education to encourage the formation of provoucher minority groups, including the Black Alliance for Educational Options and Hispanic Council for Reform and Educational Options.[42]

The provoucher coalition follows a three-pronged strategy: (1) persuade state legislatures to fund vouchers; (2) use initiative and referenda to put the voucher issue on the ballot; and (3) show the effectiveness of vouchers by using private funding to give vouchers to low-income children. Several Republican governors have backed voucher legislation in their states, and provoucher forces obtained sufficient signatures to put voucher initiatives on state ballots in California, Colorado, and Michigan. Congress funded a short-lived voucher experiment in Washington, D.C., and a voucher program for students displaced by Hurricane Katrina.

Producer organizations, led by the National Coalition for Public Education (NCPE) and the Leadership Conference on Civil Rights, have defeated most voucher proposals. NCPE is composed of sixty groups.[43] The Leadership Conference includes the traditional ethnic- and race-based rights organizations including the NAACP and the Urban League as well as liberal interest groups such as People for the American Way. Other antivoucher groups include Americans United for Separation of Church and State, a coalition of groups opposed to public funding for sectarian schools. As the NEA and the AFT are the Democratic Party's largest contributors of voluntary workers and two of its major sources of campaign funds, the party has played the pivotal role in killing voucher programs and proposals. Only the Milwaukee and Cleveland programs have survived the antivoucher lobbying effort.

The voucher movement has achieved two political victories. In *Simmons-Harris v. Zelman,* the Supreme Court ruled that the Cleveland voucher program was constitutional. The Court also set out the characteristics of a voucher program that would make it constitutionally acceptable.[44] The second accomplishment was the inclusion of private providers of supplementary services in No Child Left Behind (NCLB) legislation.

The rapid development of charter schools in the United States has been the most important development for the education-choice movement. Charter schools receive

Gov. Bill Richardson of New Mexico, campaigning for the Democratic presidential nomination, addresses the National Education Association's annual meeting in the summer of 2007.

public money, but they have fewer rules and regulations than other public schools. In exchange for this reduced regulatory burden, charter schools guarantee they will follow the practices set forth in each school's charter. Supporters of charter schools expect them to improve public education by introducing competition for students and by reducing the regulatory burdens on schools.[45] Major organizations supporting charter schools include for-profit school management firms such as EdisonLearning and numerous not-for-profit firms, including New Schools Venture Fund and National Alliance for Public Charter Schools.

At the same time that school choice was becoming a highly visible political issue, so too was accountability testing, the third school reform movement. *A Nation at Risk* strongly advocated the adoption of rigorous and measurable standards for student outcomes and the development of accountability mechanisms for schools, principals, and teachers. Unlike other education issues, the accountability movement has not followed partisan lines. Instead, a bipartisan coalition formed that included liberal, conservative,

NATIONAL EDUCATION ASSOCIATION PRINCIPAL ISSUES FOR THE 111TH CONGRESS, 2009–2010 (IN ALPHABETICAL ORDER)

- Child nutrition
- Education funding/jobs
- Educator pension protection
- Pension protection
- Educator tax relief
- Funding for higher education
- Funding for special education and for children with disabilities
- Revise No Child Left Behind
- Social Security offsets (GPO/WEP)
- Union rights
- Universal health care
- Vouchers

SOURCE: National Education Association, http://www.nea.org/home/LegislativeActionCenter.html.

libertarian, and government organizations. These organizations included the Council of Chief State School Officers, National Governors Association, National Urban League, NAACP, the Reagan and Bush administrations, and moderate Democratic organizations such as the Democratic Leadership Council. This coalition advocated reforms that would hold schools and teachers directly accountable for what their students did not learn.[46] Two moderate Democratic governors, Ann Richards of Texas and James Hunt of North Carolina, introduced accountability testing in the early 1990s. Over the next few years, students in those two states showed significantly greater improvement on the National Association of Educational Progress test scores than did students in states without accountability testing.[47]

The major producer groups—AFT, NEA, Council of the Great City Schools, and National Association of School Boards—strongly opposed all objective accountability measures.[48] Many conservative Republicans in Congress joined the producer organizations in opposing national accountability policies. These legislators saw the accountability movement as having the potential to put the federal government in charge of education.

Presidents George H. W. Bush and Bill Clinton supported the accountability movement. President George W. Bush, in conjunction with the National Governors Association, prepared *Goals 2000*. This document included the goal of students demonstrating competency through accountability tests in grades four, eight, and twelve. Congress later ratified these goals in the Educate America Act of 2004. This act was a bipartisan effort led by moderates in both parties, and organizations representing low-income and minority families strongly supported the legislation.

The culmination of these efforts to use standardized testing and accountability measures was the 2001 reauthorization of the Elementary and Secondary Education Act of 1965, better known as No Child Left Behind.[49] Leadership for the adoption of NCLB was remarkably bipartisan, coming from President George. W. Bush, Democratic representative George Miller of California, and Democratic senator Edward Kennedy of Massachusetts. NCLB made federal aid to states dependent upon the states adopting accountability testing. The legislation requires schools that consistently fail to meet their adequate yearly progress (AYP) goals to allow students to transfer to other public schools. If a school does not meet its AYP goals for four consecutive years, NCLB requires the state to close the school, reconstitute it as a charter school, or take over the school's operation. NCLB also allows school districts to use federal funds to employ private contractors to provide tutoring to low-performing students in low-performing schools. Finally, NCLB labels as *low-performing* any school that does not meet AYP goals for a number of demographic subgroups: students eligible for free or reduced-cost lunch, African American students, and Latino students.

After initially supporting No Child Left Behind, the AFT eventually joined the NEA in 2008 in opposing its reauthorization.[50] The NEA and the AFT have spent enormous sums to elect Democratic members of Congress who oppose the accountability testing portions of NCLB. The unions fear that if states can track the education growth scores of students in an individual teacher's class, then principals and district superintendents can compare the effectiveness of individual teachers. If this occurs, it could become much easier to fire a teacher for poor performance. Because a major priority for any union is preventing union members from losing their jobs, accountability testing is anathema to the teachers' unions. The box above provides the NEA's other legislative priorities for the 111th Congress.

REPUBLICAN ATTACKS ON TEACHERS' COLLECTIVE BARGAINING RIGHTS

In 2011 the collective bargaining rights of teachers emerged as a major education issue. Public employee unions, especially teachers' unions, have followed a risky political strategy: they formed an electoral alliance with the Democratic

Party. The teachers' unions are the largest contributors to Democratic candidates in state and local elections, and these contributions go overwhelmingly to Democrats. Their support of Democrats makes the unions politically vulnerable during periods of Republican control. The nationwide recession that began in 2008, the resulting state budget crises, and the landslide Republican victories in the 2010 elections led several Republican governors to support limitations on the collective bargaining rights of public employees. Wisconsin, the first state to allow collective bargaining by public employee unions, became the first state to reduce those rights. On March 9, 2011, Wisconsin dramatically limited the collective bargaining rights of public employee unions. The bill prevents the automatic deduction of union dues from workers' paychecks, limits the issues on which public employee unions can bargain, and limits their salary increases. If other states follow Wisconsin's lead, the political power of state and local teachers' unions would be substantially reduced, and the Democratic Party's fundraising would suffer.

CONCLUSION

Five factors influenced the explosion of interest groups active in education policy: (1) the social movements of the 1960s and 1970s called attention to inequalities in educational opportunities and outcomes; (2) changes in state laws allowed teachers to organize and to use collective bargaining to improve their working conditions; (3) the growth in public expenditures for K-12 education; (4) America's culture wars and the perception that K-12 education is important to the socialization process; and (5) the increasing federal role in funding and regulating public education.

Interest groups involved in education generally have divided along the traditional liberal-conservative ideological dimension. Producer organizations have allied with other liberal groups and with the Democratic Party to promote school desegregation, reduce inequalities in educational outcomes, increase school funding, and teach the value of social diversity. This coalition has fought school vouchers and accountability measures that include standardized test scores. A conservative coalition, including the Christian Right, libertarian groups, and, on some issues, the business community, has opposed the liberal coalition. These groups generally have worked with the Republican Party in support of test-based accountability, increased school choice, and a reduced role of the federal government in education policy decisions. Because education issues involve enduring questions of politics, it is unlikely that any of these issues will be resolved.

NOTES

1. Interest group involvement in American education generally splits into those groups active in elementary and secondary education (K-12) and organizations active in postsecondary education. Teachers' unions are the dominant interest group in elementary and secondary education, but faculty unions in most states are not a significant force in higher education. For a review of the interest groups and issues in higher education, see Constance Cook, *Lobbying for Higher Education: How Colleges and Universities Influence Federal Policy* (Nashville, Tenn.: Vanderbilt University Press, 1998).

2. OECD Historical Statistics, www.nationmaster.com/graph/edu_tot_exp_as_of_gdp-education-total-expenditure-gdp.

3. Department of Education, National Institute for Educational Statistics, Indicator 43, per student expenditure on education, nces.ed.gov/Pubs/eiip/eiipid43.asp.

4. Department of Education, National Institute for Educational Statistics, nces.ed.gov/fastfacts/display.asp?id=66.

5. Eric A. Hanushek and Steven G. Rivkin, "Understanding the Twentieth-Century Growth in U.S. School Spending," *The Journal of Human Resources* 33 (2002): 40–68; National Center for Education Statistics, nces.ed.gov/pubs2007/npefs13years/chapter4a.asp.

6. U.S. Department of Education, www2.ed.gov/about/overview/fed/10facts/edlite-chart.html.

7. Bruce Baker, *Private Schooling in the U.S.: Expenditures, Supply, and Policy Implications,* National Education Policy Center (Boulder: 2009), epicpolicy.org/publication/private-schooling-us.

8. Frank Baumgartner and Beth Leech, *Basic Interests: The Importance of Groups in Politics and in Political Science* (Princeton: Princeton University Press, 1998), cited in Julie McDaniel, Celia Sims, and Cecil Miskel, "The National Reading Policy Area: Policy Actors and Perceived Influence," *Educational Policy* 15, 1 (January 2001): 92–114. The growth in education-related organizations mirrors the "explosion" in other sectors as well. See, for example, Jeffrey Berry, *Lobbying for the People* (Princeton: Princeton University Press, 1977), 34; Dara Strolovitch, *Affirmative Advocacy* (Chicago, University of Chicago Press, 2007); and Kay Lehman Schlozman, Chapter 19 of this volume.

9. Darleen Opfer, Tamara Young, and Lance Fusarelli, "Politics of Interest: Interest Groups and Advocacy Coalitions in American Education," in *Handbook of Education Politics and Policy.* ed. Bruce Cooper, James Cibulka, and Lance Fusarelli (New York: Routledge, 2008).

10. Richard Kahlenberg, "The History of Collective Bargaining among Teachers," in *Collective Bargaining in Education,* ed. Jane Hannaway and Andrew Retherham (Cambridge: Harvard Education Press, 2006).

11. Ibid., 18.

12. In right-to-work states in the South, where unionization of public employees is very difficult or impossible, the NEA and the AFT organize their members into professional associations. These associations are powerful political actors at the state and local levels, but lack the two attributes that are critical to labor organizations: the right to strike and the right to compel workers to pay dues.

13. Clive S. Thomas and Ronald J. Hrebenar, "Interest Groups in the American States," in *Politics in the American States,* ed. Virginia Gray and Herbert Jacobs, 7th ed. (Washington, D.C.: CQ Press, 1999).

14. Center for Responsive Politics Top All-Time Donors, www.opensecrets.org/orgs/list.php?order=A.

15. National Association of Elementary School Principals provides a list of each state's leading advocacy official, www.naesp.org/resources/1/Pdfs/FRC9-8.pdf.

16. Charlene Haar, *The Politics of the PTA* (Somerset, N.J.: Transaction, 2002); Terry Moe, "Union Power and the Education of Children," in *Collective Bargaining in Education: Negotiating Change in Today's Schools,* ed. Jane Hannaway and Andrew Rotherham (Cambridge: Harvard Education Press, 2006).

17. Terry Moe, "Teachers Unions and School Board Elections," in *Besieged: School Boards and the Future of Education Politics,* ed. William G. Howell (Washington, D.C.: Brookings Institution Press, 2005).

18. Clarence N. Stone, Jeffrey R. Henig, Bryan D. Jones, and Carol Pierannunzi, *Building Civic Capacity: The Politics of Reforming Urban Schools* (Lawrence: University Press of Kansas, 2001).

19. Clarence N. Stone, "Civic Capacity and Urban Education," *Urban Affairs Review* 36 (May 2001): 595–619.

20. *Brown v. Board of Education of Topeka,* 347 U.S. 483 (1954).

21. The Christian Right is a loose consortium of interest organizations supporting conservative positions on social issues. Among the groups involved are Eagle Forum, CEO America, National Right to Life, Focus on the Family, Traditional Values Coalition, Christian Seniors Association, and Family Research Council.

22. In the Internal Revenue Service Code, Section 501(c)(3) prohibits organizations claiming this status from engaging in any election activity or legislative lobbying.

23. McDaniel, Sims, and Miskel, "The National Reading Policy Arena, Policy Actors, and Perceived Influence," *Educational Policy* 15 (2001): 92–114.

24. Janelle Scott, Christopher Lubienski, and Elizabeth DeBray-Pelot, "The Ideological and Political Landscape of School Choice Interest Groups in the Post-*Zelman* Era," in Cooper, Cibulka, and Fusarelli, *Handbook of Education Politics and Policy.*

25. Howell, *Besieged.*

26. Christopher Jencks and Meredith Phillips, *The Black-White Test-Score Gap* (Washington, D.C.: Brookings Institution Press, 1998).

27. Gary Orfield and John T. Yun, *Resegregation in American Schools* (Cambridge: Harvard Civil Rights Project, 1999), w3.uchastings.edu/wingate/PDF/Resegregation_American_Schools99.

28. Eric A. Hanushek, John F. Kain, and Steven G. Rivkin, "New Evidence about *Brown v. Board of Education*: The Complex Effects of School Racial Composition on Achievement," Working Paper W8741, National Bureau of Economic Research, December 2002.

29. Samuel Bowles and Henry M. Levin, "The Determinants of Scholastic Achievement: An Appraisal of Some Recent Evidence, *Journal of Human Resources* 3 (1968): 3–24; Grace Kau and Jennifer S. Thompson, "Racial and Ethnic Stratification in Educational Achievement and Attainment," *Annual Review of Sociology* 29 (2003): 417–442.

30. Heather G. Peske, and Kati Haycock, *Teaching Inequality: How Poor and Minority Students are Shortchanged on Teacher Quality* (Washington, D.C.: The Education Trust, 2006).

31. See *Milliken v. Bradley,* 418 U.S. 717 (1974), and *Belk v. Charlotte-Mecklenburg Board of Education,* 211 F.3d 853 (4th Cir. 2000), for limits on busing, and *Meredith v. Jefferson County Bd. of Education* and *Parents Involved in Community Schools v. Seattle School District No. 1,* 551 U.S. 701 (2007), for racial preference in school assignment.

32. School districts can use income as an assignment criterion, but only a small number of districts have chosen to do so.

33. To examine the membership of these coalitions, go to www.schoolfunding.info/ and www.boldapproach.org/who.html.

34. John G. Augenblick, John L. Myers, and Amy Berk Anderson, "Equity and Adequacy in School Funding," *The Future of Children* 7, 3 (Winter 1997): 63–78.

35. Focus on the Family, Education, www.citizenlink.org/fosi/education/.

36. Universal Declaration of Human Rights, www.un.org/en/documents/udhr/index.shtml#a26.

37. Intelligent design argues that the observed order in the universe is best explained by an intelligent cause rather than natural selection, an undirected process. Leading proponents of the intelligent design movement are associated with the conservative Discovery Institute.

38. Council for Secular Humanism, www.secularhumanism.org/.

39. For example, see the Council for Islamic Education and the Institute of Islamic Information and Education.

40. James S. Coleman, Thomas Hoffer, and Sally Kilgore, *High School Achievement* (New York, Basic Books, 1982); James S. Coleman and Thomas Hoffer, *Public and Private High Schools* (New York: Basic Books, 1987); William Sander and Anthony Krautmann, "Catholic Schools, Dropout Rates and Educational Attainment," *Economic Inquiry* 33 (1995): 217–233.

41. School Reform, education.stateuniversity.com/pages/2400/SchoolReform.html#ixzz0LAC95FV8&D.

42. For a full discussion of minority groups supportive of the voucher movement, see Thomas C. Pedroni, *Market Movements: African American Involvement in School Voucher Reform* (New York: Routledge, 2007).

43. Scott, Lubienski, and DeBray-Pelot, "Ideological and Political Landscape."

44. *Simmons-Harris v. Zelman,* 536 U.S. 639 (2002).

45. For a discussion of the expectations of supporters and critics of charter schools, see Michael Mintrom, "Innovation: Does Choice Encourage Improvement in the Ways that Schools are Organized or Managed?" Michigan State University, Department of Political Science, www.epc.msu.edu/publications/DEBATE/SECTION4.PDF.

46. Maris A. Vinovskis, *From a Nation at Risk to No Child Left Behind: National Education Goals and the Creation of Federal Education Policy* (New York: Teachers College Press, 2009).

47. Eric Hanushek and Margaret Raymond, "Does School Accountability Lead to Improved Student Performance?" Working Paper, National Bureau of Economic Research, July 2004.

48. Vinovskis, *From a Nation at Risk,* 34–35.

49. No Child Left Behind is actually the 2001 Reauthorization of the Elementary and Secondary Education Act first passed in 1965.

50. See the AFT position on NCLB at www.unionvoice.org/afteactivst/legislative_action_center3.html.

SUGGESTED READING

Cook, Constance. *Lobbying for Higher Education: How Colleges and Universities Influence Federal Policy.* Nashville, Tenn.: Vanderbilt University Press, 1998.

Green, Jay. *Education Myths: What Special-Interest Groups Want You to Believe About Our Schools and Why it Isn't So.* Lanham, Md.: Rowman and Littlefield, 2006.

Haar, Charlene. *The Politics of the PTA* Somerset, N.J.: Transaction, 2002.

Hannaway, Jane, and Andrew J. Rotherham, eds. *Collective Bargaining in Education: Negotiating Change in Today's Schools.* Cambridge: Harvard Education Press, 2006.

Howell, William G., ed. *Besieged: School Boards and the Future of Education Politics.* Washington, D.C.: Brookings Institution Press, 2005.

Itkonen, Tiina. *The Role of Special Education Interest Groups in National Policy.* Amherst, N.Y.: Cambria Press, 2009.

McDonnell, Lorraine M. "No Child Left Behind and the Federal Role in Education: Evolution or Revolution?" *Peabody Journal of Education* 80 (2005): 19–38.

chapter 22

Energy and the Environment

by Christopher Bosso

No study of interest groups is complete without an examination of the thousands of organizations that advocate on behalf of environmental and energy causes. Indeed, everything you have read in preceding chapters about group formation, organizational maintenance, members and leaders, strategy and tactics, and policy impacts applies to these organizations. Moreover, important insights about group mobilization and maintenance, including Mancur Olson's collective action problem, were derived in part by examining groups advocating for environmental and energy causes.[1]

We consider environmental and energy groups together because *any* method for generating energy—oil, coal, hydropower, nuclear fission, even wood and biomass—has an environmental impact. The roots of environmentalism lie in nineteenth-century concerns about the conservation and managed use of natural resources, as industrialization and urban growth fed demands for energy production. These tensions heightened through the twentieth century and came into focus in the 1960s, when opposition to a hydropower development on Storm King Mountain in New York, fights over oil production in waters off the California coast, and disputes over nuclear power plant sites helped to ignite the contemporary environmental movement. These conflicts grew sharper in the 1970s as oil price shocks brought on by political tremors in the Middle East reshaped the global economy and openly pitted goals of energy availability and price against environmental protection and wildlife preservation. And these tensions resonate today, as evidenced by the fallout over the Deepwater Horizon oil disaster in the Gulf of Mexico, arguments over the environmental impacts of corn-based ethanol, or the push for "green jobs" in solar and wind power generation. So one cannot talk about energy without talking about the environment.

It is impossible to succinctly survey the immense expanse of environmental and energy advocacy organizations. In the United States alone such a survey would cover thousands of groups of varied size, location, focus, organizational characteristics, and activity. Typing the term *environment* in the search engine provided by Guidestar.org, the nonprofit philanthropy database, returns 62,000 entries; typing in *energy* results in nearly 7,000. Combining the terms still results in 1,600 hits. These groups range from large and internationally known professionalized organizations such as Greenpeace and the World Wildlife Fund, which work on issues like global warming and preservation of the Amazonian ecosystem, to the small volunteer group seeking to protect a local watershed or stop construction of a liquefied natural gas storage plant. For the sake of tractability, this chapter examines the origins, evolution, and current state of the national environmental advocacy community.[2] Focusing on these groups reveals quite a bit about environmental and energy groups overall without reducing a vast and diverse array of groups into an artificial "movement" that began with the first Earth Day (April 22, 1970). As we shall see, organized environmentalism is broader and more diverse than common imagery suggests.

GROUP FORMATION

Strip away everything else about interest groups and one comes back to a basic point: they are created to achieve goals not otherwise being met by the political system, particularly by the major political parties that dominate electoral politics. More on that point later. For now, it is essential to note that specifics of any particular group's origins—how it was founded, by whom, where, and so forth—are rooted in the social and political contexts that sociologist Elisabeth Clemens calls "the complexity of social organization." [3] With that in mind, this chapter begins by examining eras in American environmentalism, placing the formation of representative organizations within the contexts that shaped their origins, and then looking at how these groups evolved over time, with the evolution of environmentalism itself.

Environmental Groups in the Progressive Era

The formation of the earliest U.S. environmental organizations reflected growing concerns among social and political elites about the rapid depletion of the nation's natural resources and the despoliation of its landscape owing to rapid industrial and urban development in the late nineteenth century. The groups created in this period were small and regionally based, elite in membership composition, and, as environmental historian Sam Hays argues, reflected Progressive Era ideals of scientific expertise, professional management, and the need to conserve natural resources for use by later generations.[4]

Two groups created during this period stand out: the San Francisco–based Sierra Club (1890) and New York–based National Audubon Society, a federation of state societies with origins in the founding of the Massachusetts Audubon Society in 1896. Sierra and Audubon started as groups of local activists seeking to work with and, if necessary, put political pressure on government officials to counteract the power of business interests in state legislatures and the U.S. Congress. The Sierra Club was formed by San Francisco–area professionals led by naturalist John Muir to lobby federal and state governments to preserve the recently created Yosemite National Park and protect the Sierra Nevada range in the face of pressure for development by mining, timber, and hydropower interests. In the East, the Audubon Societies grew out of local women's clubs engaged in letter-writing campaigns to state and federal officials seeking to stop the slaughter of birds for their plumage; the clubs soon expanded their focus to preserving bird habitats. Both also began as membership groups, with the Sierra Club establishing chapters throughout California and the Audubon Society evolving as a federation of state affiliates. These grassroots connections would aid each organization's longevity over the next century.[5]

Early conservationist and Sierra Club founder John Muir and President Theodore Roosevelt shared a love of the wilderness. During a trip to Yosemite Valley in 1903, Muir successfully persuaded Roosevelt to return the park to federal control.

Environmental Groups Between the Wars

The period between the two world wars represents a pivotal moment in organized environmentalism.[6] Compared to the Progressive Era, the driving focus during the 1920s and 1930s shifted away from the scientific management of nature or appreciation of its aesthetic virtues and toward its recreational opportunities. As a result, this period saw the formation of organizations focused on wildlife management in support of recreational hunting and fishing and on the creation of parks and other wilderness areas to enable urban dwellers to enjoy nature—often by driving to it in their new automobiles.[7]

Moreover, organizations created in this period typically originated in Washington, D.C., a shift attributable to an emerging nationalization of public policy as the federal government became more active in resource management and, with the New Deal, promoting economic development.[8] As with the founding of the Sierra Club decades before, many of these organizations were created *in response to* government actions, such as the creation of the National Park System in 1916, to maintain and expand on those initiatives.

Finally, the organizations created in this period were often sponsored by government officials to serve as external allies in fighting legislative and bureaucratic battles with the promoters of economic development and resource exploitation. The first director of the National Park Service helped to create the National Parks Association; officials in the U.S. Fish and Wildlife Service organized the National Wildlife Federation; and leaders in the U.S. Forest Service founded—and financially supported—the Wilderness Society.[9] Unlike the Sierra Club and Audubon Society, few of these organizations initially maintained a membership base in any real sense, and none would have survived without the patronage of their government sponsors.

Environmental Groups in the Postwar Period

Most environmental groups were dormant during World War II, as members left to serve in the military and war priorities dominated the national agenda. At war's end, a new cohort of activists—such as the Sierra Club's David Brower, who served in Italy with the Tenth Mountain Division—came back from the war sensitized to the loss of wilderness and wildlife in the Old World.[10] Veterans like Brower constituted a new wave of outdoors enthusiasts, new members for groups such as the Sierra Club who also reawakened tensions between those favoring development of nature for economic and recreation purposes versus those concerned about the disappearance of wilderness.[11] These tensions also affected formerly close relationships with federal officials as preservation-minded advocates began to express opposition to the developmental ethos of the National Park Service and the federal Bureau of Land Management in particular.[12]

More important for the environmental era to come, wartime had turned the nation into the "arsenal of democracy," leading to accelerated depletion of natural resources, destruction of wildlife habitats for war industries and agriculture, and dramatically increased air and water pollution. These conditions and the concerns about the side effects of the postwar boom in petrochemicals prompted growing alarm about the impact of pollution on wildlife populations and human health.[13] Older groups, influenced by greater general awareness about *environmental* degradation, began to express a more openly ecological focus. In the late 1940s the Audubon Society warned of possible ecological harm from unchecked use of a new synthetic chemical pesticide, DDT.[14] The National Wildlife Federation, despite its conservative reputation and ties to business, pushed for a cleanup of environments degraded by war production.[15]

Reflecting this context, the organizations created in this period typically were formed by scientists and educators with the support of scientific and professional organizations such as the New York Zoological Society and the Ecologists Union to raise public awareness about the degradation of nature, preserve endangered areas, and enhance the organizational capacity of conservation itself. These organizations reflected the strategic thinking of their creators: support research and education (Conservation Foundation), buy threatened ecosystems (Nature Conservancy), agitate for animals (Defenders of Wildlife), or act as a fundraising vehicle for research and conservation (World Wildlife Fund). Compared to groups formed during the period between the wars, these groups worked *outside* government by supporting research, educating the public, and, where necessary, purchasing land to keep it from being developed or degraded.

Environmental Groups in the Environmental Era

The reformist impulses unleashed during the 1960s reshaped American environmentalism.[16] "Measured in terms of changes in government and legislation," writes Michael Lacey, "it has been a time of extraordinary ferment, so durable and multifaceted as to make earlier times of great upheaval (the Progressive Era and the New Deal years, for example), seem simpler, if no less important, by comparison." [17] That "ferment" generated a wave of new groups dedicated to noneconomic or "public" interests. Jeffrey Berry notes that two-thirds of the public interest organizations he surveyed in 1972–1973 were formed after 1959, and most in the late 1960s.[18] This surge in citizen activism, says Andrew McFarland, grew out of middle-class political mobilization and skepticism about conventional politics, aided by economic prosperity and technical advances in communications, particularly television.[19]

The new groups benefited from a concurrent transformation in the "political opportunity structure"—the legal, institutional, and political lay of the land that gives shape to advocacy strategies and tactics.[20] The loosening of judicial rules on the right to sue in court—the notion of "standing"—and establishment of the legal concept of "class action" [21] gave lawyers representing public interests unprecedented opportunities to use lawsuits as tools against major hydropower and nuclear projects. Moreover, as Shep Melnick observes, judges more readily interpreted federal law "to guarantee a wide variety of groups the right to participate directly in agency deliberations as well as to bring their complaints to court." [22] These trends coalesced in the 1971 *Calvert Cliffs* ruling, in which a federal judge stopped the Atomic Energy Commission from licensing a nuclear power plant until it considered the plant's "environmental impact" under the National Environmental Policy Act (NEPA) of 1969.[23] The *Calvert Cliffs* decision put teeth into NEPA, enabling activists to force federal officials to show that they had considered environmental criteria in authorizing new energy projects.[24]

The new organizations that were to typify the "environmental movement" also enjoyed financial and logistical support by private foundations and older conservation organizations. The Ford Foundation bankrolled many of the "public interest law" organizations that were to forge environmental law, in particular the Environmental Defense Fund (EDF), the Natural Resources Defense Council (NRDC), and the Sierra Club Legal Defense Fund (now Earthjustice).[25] The latter, formally independent of the Sierra Club, often pursued a more militant stance than its parent organization was willing or able to take.[26]

For their part, older organizations took on new issues, such as pesticides, air pollution and nuclear power, and found themselves awash in new members, leading in turn to major changes in organizational mission and strategies. Some, like the Sierra Club, created legal defense funds and non-tax-exempt affiliates to complement established tax-deductible "educational" activities, adapting to new opportunities in ways that allowed environmentalists to expand their legal and legislative efforts. Nearly all for the first time established offices in the nation's capital and created a sense of greater overall permanency for organized environmentalism.[27]

A dramatic example of such a transformation occurred in 1966, when the Internal Revenue Service ruled that a Sierra Club newspaper advertising campaign against a proposed hydropower dam in the Grand Canyon constituted overt lobbying, grounds for revocation of its tax-deductible

USING THE COURTS

The ability of environmental groups to use the courts for policy change was enabled by developments in the courts themselves—developments that were often prompted by lawsuits brought by environmental groups.

The first such development was a dramatic lowering of barriers to judicial access. In *Scenic Hudson Preservation Conference v. Federal Power Commission* (1965), a federal court of appeals ruled that a coalition of environmental groups and local towns could be considered "aggrieved parties" in a suit aimed at stopping the construction of Storm King Mountain, a hydropower plant on the Hudson River. This ruling, later affirmed by the Supreme Court, broadened the concept of "standing" beyond the traditional need to show direct and adverse injury. As a result of this ruling, a plaintiff need only show that the interests in question, including aesthetic or nonmaterial interests, were covered by a relevant statute or constitutional guarantee that were in some way affected by defendants' actions.

The second development was the establishment of the concept of *class action* by the federal courts. In *Sierra Club v. Hickel* (1970) the U.S. Court of Appeals for the Ninth Circuit ruled that plaintiffs could file suit on behalf of entire sectors of society, even if those "represented" knew nothing about the dispute. Plaintiffs no longer needed to name each party to the suit; instead, they could now claim damages on behalf of society itself.

Finally, federal courts increasingly interpreted statutes "to guarantee a wide variety of groups the right to participate directly in agency deliberations as well as to bring their complaints to court."[1] Judicial insistence that federal officials incorporate environmental concerns into their actions began most noticeably with the decision in *Calvert Cliffs Coordinating Committee v. U.S. Atomic Energy Commission* (1971), in which Judge J. Skelly Wright of the federal district court halted federal licensing of a nuclear power plant after determining that the government had failed to consider its environmental impact. The purpose of the National Environmental Policy Act of 1969, Wright declared, "was to tell federal agencies that environmental protection is as much a part of their responsibility as is protection and promotion of the industry they regulate." After *Calvert Cliffs* the onus fell on administrators to show that they had weighed all relevant criteria in approving new projects—and environmental groups were ready to go to court to make sure that they did.

These decisions enabled environmentalists to use the courts to force government and business to take environmental considerations seriously. The expanded role for the judiciary was not popular with business and its conservative allies, and later efforts by Republican presidents Ronald Reagan and George H. W. Bush to appoint conservative judges to the federal judiciary eventually paid off in narrowing access to the courts. By the early 2000s federal courts had become stingier in granting standing to environmental claimants. In *Lujan v. Defenders of Wildlife* (1992) the Supreme Court ruled that plaintiffs must be able to show evidence of some direct and material harm, not one that is indirect and more conjectural. At about the same time, in *Chevron U.S.A. v. Natural Resources Defense Council* (1994), the Court gave more discretion to the Environmental Protection Agency in interpreting the meaning of ambiguous statutory language.

Taken together, these rulings narrowed the range of opportunities for using lawsuits as policy tools. The ability to sue remains important but, except for environmental law firms such as Earthjustice (originally the Sierra Club Legal Defense Fund), the use of lawsuits as a strategy is less central for most environmental groups. Even the two original "science and law" organizations, the Environmental Defense Fund and the Natural Resources Defense Council, now use lawsuits as only one part of their tactical toolbox, employing them less than direct lobbying, scientific research, and public communication.

SOURCES: *Chevron U.S.A. v. Natural Resources Defense Council,* 467 U.S. 837 (1984) at 843–845; *Lujan v. Defenders of Wildlife,* 504 U.S. 555 (1992); R. Shep Melnick, *Regulation and the Courts: The Case of the Clean Air Act* (Washington, D.C.: Brookings Institution Press, 1983); Rosemary O'Leary, "Environmental Policy and the Courts," in *Environmental Policy: New Directions for the 21st Century,* ed. Norman Vig and Michael Kraft (Washington, D.C.: CQ Press, 2002): 151–174; *Scenic Hudson Preservation Conference v. Federal Power Commission,* 354 F.2d 608 (2nd Cir. 1965); *Sierra Club v. Hickel,* 433 F.2d 24 (9th Cir. 1970); *Calvert Cliffs Coordinating Committee v. U.S. Atomic Energy Commission,* 449 F.2d 1109 (1971).

1. R. Shep Melnick, *Regulation and the Courts: The Case of the Clean Air Act* (Washington, D.C.: Brookings Institution Press, 1983), 10.

status. Rather than crippling the Sierra Club, however, the controversial IRS action sparked a flood of contributions from sympathetic citizens, in the process changing the way the club financed itself. Thereafter, the Sierra Club Foundation, a tax-exempt affiliate, continued to pursue gifts directed toward education and other tax-exempt purposes, while the now non-tax-deductible Sierra Club aggressively sought out donations from tens of thousands of supporters through direct mail and newspaper advertising.[28] Membership doubled, transforming the club into a national mass-membership organization. Such rapid changes also created internal tensions over executive director David Brower's leadership, prompting his ouster. In response, Brower went on to found a new organization, Friends of the Earth (FoE).

Other older groups underwent similar transformations. National Audubon Society broadened its agenda and used direct mail to expand its base, which caused tensions with traditional bird-watching members.[29] National Wildlife Federation for the first time recruited its own members in recognition that annual dues were a more dependable source of income compared to merchandise sales and sporadic large donations.[30] Cultivating such mass memberships required that organization leaders pay attention to mass communications, so most at this time created or revamped their magazines (*Sierra, National Wildlife,* and *Audubon*) as tools for member communication, new member recruitment, and advertising revenue.[31] Organizations that for decades had relied on a small base of relatively elite supporters now were sustained by direct-mail-generated, magazine-linked national memberships. This transformation caused internal divisions over organizational mission and tactics, but in the end enabled these older groups to adapt to the challenges and opportunities posed by the environmental era, a story often overlooked in the attention given to the new organizations founded at this time.

And *many* new major environmental groups were created between 1967 and 1977 (see Table 22.1). Primary among them were pioneering "science and law" organizations like EDF and NRDC, which joined older counterparts like the Sierra Club, Audubon Society, and National Wildlife Federation in becoming what Ron Shaiko labeled "full service" environmental groups—multi-issue advocacy organizations supported by a mass base of dues-paying supporters.[32] Others, like Friends of the Earth and Greenpeace, distinguished themselves by establishing affiliates around the world to advocate on behalf of increasingly global environmental and energy issues, chief among them opposition to nuclear power.

Today's Environmental Community: Filling in the Niches

As is clear from Table 22.1, the contours of today's national environmental community were essentially in place by the early 1970s. Any organizations created thereafter would need to fit into whatever advocacy niches were left unfilled or underexploited by existing broad-spectrum organizations. As a result, groups created in the subsequent period followed one of two developmental patterns.

The first were *dissidents*, organizations created because a leader or group of leaders left a group over differences in priorities, tactics, or management style. A prime example is Friends of the Earth, formed by Brower after his ouster at the Sierra Club, and purposefully made different from it: nonmember, non-tax-exempt, and therefore able to be more agile and aggressive in attacking polluters. Brower later split with FoE over leadership issues similar to those that had led to his earlier dismissal; he went on to found yet another group, Earth Island Institute.

The other pattern involves *niche-seekers*, groups created because policy entrepreneurs, including leaders of existing organizations, saw opportunities in unoccupied policy, ideological, or tactical niches. Some, such as American Rivers (1973) and Ocean Conservancy (1972), filled policy niches not being dominated by established major groups. Others were created after the emergence of a new issue onto the policy agenda: concerns over the destruction of tropical rainforests led to the creation of Rainforest Action Network (1985), Rainforest Alliance (1986), and Conservation International (1987). Still others were created in response to changes in the federal income tax code: Earth Share, a United Way-type workplace-giving plan for environmental groups. Some were created to take advantage of new technologies: the Environmental Working Group (1993) specializes in deep analysis of government data, a tactic made possible only with the availability of powerful and inexpensive personal computers.[33]

Finally, a few groups were created to address "environmental justice" issues their founders felt were ignored by established groups. An example is the Center for Environmental Health and Justice, formed in 1981. The CEHJ was founded as the Citizens Clearinghouse for Hazardous Waste by "former housewife" Lois Gibbs and other veterans of the fight to obtain compensation for working-class residents whose health and home values were harmed by a previously undisclosed toxic waste dump in the Love Canal neighborhood of Niagara Falls, N.Y.[34] The CEHJ coordinates the work of grassroots environmentalists who frame toxic waste and other local hazards in social justice terms, particularly for the low-income and minority residents who are most frequently exposed to industrial pollutants. Social justice activists are especially critical of major environmental organizations, such as the National Wildlife Federation and the Nature Conservancy, that accept donations from companies whose activities they claim degrade the health and livability of neighborhoods like Love Canal or in Louisiana's "chemical alley" along the Mississippi River.

In sum, the environmental era produced broad-spectrum organizations like the Environmental Defense Fund and Friends of the Earth, and during the subsequent period these groups were surrounded and often complemented by clusters of more narrowly focused advocacy "boutiques."[35] The result is an environmental advocacy domain characterized by an unexpectedly wide range of groups of varying goals, identities, ideological orientations, strategic visions, tactical strengths, and resources. The variety and density of groups dedicated to environmental and energy issues in fact reflect the variety and density of issues and values found under the environmental tent.

ORGANIZATIONAL MAINTENANCE

Table 22.1 also suggests an often-overlooked fact about advocacy organizations in American politics in general and about environmental groups in particular: most of these groups are still exist decades—even a century—after being founded. Moreover, in most cases they have grown and, at least in terms of gross revenues (see Table 22.2), prospered. The key to their survival, as suggested above, is their capacity to adapt to changing issues and contexts in successive eras in environmental and energy politics. How else does one explain the ability of the Sierra Club to reconstitute itself from a regional preservation group to a national, even global, environmental advocate focusing on a wide array of issues and fueled by the donations of hundreds of thousands of supporters? Like its peers, the Sierra Club adapted to new challenges, new issues, and new

TABLE 22.1 **Environmental Group Origins**

Organization	Year	Where	Facts of origin
Progressive Period			
Sierra Club	1892	Calif.	San Francisco outdoorsmen
National Audubon Society	1905	N.Y.	Group of Boston Women (1896)/NAS formed in N.Y.
Interwar Period			
National Parks Conservation Assn.	1919	D.C.	Organized by National Park Service official
Izaak Walton League	1922	Ill.	Chicago area outdoorsmen/first mass membership environmental group
The Wilderness Society	1935	D.C.	Founded by Interior Dept. official to preserve roadless wilderness
National Wildlife Federation	1936	D.C.	Organized by federal official/D.C. lobbying arm of wildlife movement
Ducks Unlimited	1937	D.C.	Finances wetlands restoration; works with Fish and Wildlife Service
Postwar Era			
Defenders of Wildlife	1947	D.C.	Focuses on endangered species in U.S.
Conservation Foundation	*1948*	*N.Y.*	*Education, organizational capacity/Merged with WWF in 1985*
The Nature Conservancy	1951	D.C.	Land conservancy/purchases "sensitive ecosystems"
World Wildlife Fund–U.S.	1961	D.C.	International focus/1989: merged with Conservation Foundation
Environmental Era			
Environmental Defense (Fund)	1967	N.Y.	First environmental "law firm"/Audubon and Ford Foundation support
Friends of the Earth	1969	Calif.	Spinoff from Sierra Club/1990: merged with Oceanic Society and EPI
Environmental Action	*1970*	*D.C.*	*Created to organize first Earth Day/Closed in 1996*
Natural Resources Defense Council	1970	N.Y.	"Science and Law" organization/Ford Foundation
League of Conservation Voters	1970	D.C.	Co-founded by FOE to influence election outcomes
Earthjustice Legal Defense Fund	1971	Calif.	Originally the Sierra Club Legal Defense Fund
Clean Water Action	1971	Mich.	Loose national coalition of state clean water advocacy organizations
Greenpeace USA	1971	D.C.	"Direct action" oriented / 2000: merged with Ozone Action
"Post-Movement" Period			
Environmental Policy Center	1972	D.C.	*FOE dissidents/education and lobbying/merged with EPI/FOE in 1989*
Trust for Public Land	1972	Calif.	Land conservancy/acquires land for public use
Center for Marine Conservation	1972	D.C.	Changed name to Ocean Conservancy in 2002
American Rivers	1973	CO	Focuses on pollution/preservation issues related to rivers
Environmental Policy Institute	1974	D.C.	*Created by EPC/later merged with EPC and rejoined FOE in 1989*
Sea Shepherd Conservation Society	1977	Calif.	Greenpeace dissidents–"direct action" against overfishing, whaling
Center for Health, Environment, & Justice	1981	D.C.	Started by Love Canal activist Lois Gibbs; focuses on toxic wastes
Earth Island Institute	1982	Calif.	Founded by ex-FOE head Brower; focuses on public education and advocacy
National Park Trust	1983	D.C.	NP Calif. spinoff/acquires private land in/near national parks
Conservation Fund	1985	D.C.	Land Conservancy/leverages donations into public/private partnerships
Rain Forest Action Network	1985	Calif.	International focus/founded by Earth Day organizer and Earth First! Co-founder
Conservation International	1987	D.C.	Founded by ex-Nature Conservancy, WWF staff/used "debt-for-nature" swaps
Earth Share	1988	D.C.	Created by environmental organizations to foster workplace giving
Environmental Working Group	1993	D.C.	Research organization/foundation supported

NOTE: D.C. includes the Virginia and Maryland suburbs; organizations in italics no longer exist.

opportunities, displaying an organizational resiliency often overlooked in scholarly studies of interest groups.

Exceptions to this story of successful adaptation are instructive. Perhaps the most telling is Environmental Action (EA), founded in 1970 by the student organizers of the first Earth Day as a non-tax-exempt advocacy group on the left on the ideological spectrum. Its countercultural ethos and connections to Earth Day initially enabled EA to attract thousands of supporters and to expand its agenda into an array of antipollution, energy, and social justice issues, with an emphasis on grassroots mobilization. In spite of its growth and high profile, however, EA was soon at a severe disadvantage. For one thing, it had a lot of company in its neighborhood. Other new groups—including Friends of the Earth, League of Conservation Voters, Natural Resources Defense Council, Ralph Nader's Public Interest Research Group, and Greenpeace—in one way or another overlapped with EA in terms of ideological orientation, issue agendas, tactics, and, most important, potential appeal to a particular segment of supporters.[36]

Moreover, from the beginning EA was on shakier financial ground than these other organizations. The foundations that supported research, legal action, and institutional capacity building were reluctant to fund grassroots mobilization and social protest, particularly after congressional conservatives pushed through the Tax Reform Act of 1969 to force foundations to assume "expenditure responsibility" over their recipients. Although IRS guidelines

Lois Gibbs, president of the Love Canal Homeowners Association, stands with President Jimmy Carter and Rep. John La Falce, D-N.Y. (right) during a 1980 speech by New York governor Hugh Carey. Carter and Carey signed an agreement to create a federal-state program to relocate residents of the Love Canal neighborhood, the site of a massive toxic waste dump. Gibbs went on to found the Center for Environmental Health and Justice, a grassroots environmental advocacy group.

eventually shielded foundations and their grantees from penalties so long as they served the "public good," most so-called liberal foundations soon shied away from supporting controversial social justice goals and protest-oriented tactics.[37] For their part, individual donors who funded Friends of the Earth and the League of Conservation Voters were wary of EA's comparative lack of professionalism: for many years it continued to function as a collective, with staff members earning identical salaries and decisions arrived at only after lengthy meetings. To an increasingly buttoned-down world of professional environmental advocacy, EA seemed like a throwback—ardent, but amateur.

EA even ran into problems when it tried to emulate its peers. In the 1980s, for example, it belatedly tried to broaden its membership base through direct mail, but found it so difficult to differentiate itself from competitors that it suspended the effort before it lost too much money in the process. Internal disputes over goals and strategies, particularly whether EA should continue to focus on social protest or become a more professional advocacy organization, led to the departure of its more policy-oriented staff.

But EA's leaders labored on, backed by a dedicated cohort of supporters. By the mid-1980s they had restructured the organization's operations and narrowed its agenda into areas such as citizens' right to know about toxic substances in their communities, waste disposal—in particular bottle deposit bills and recycling—and, following a merger with the Energy Conservation Coalition, nuclear power. Even then, however, EA found it hard to differentiate itself: the Center for Health and Environmental Justice was already known for its work on toxic substances, as was the NRDC for its work on recycling and the EDF on issues concerning citizens' "right to know" about chemicals. EA's efforts to influence elections by disseminating the environmental records of candidates were overshadowed by the League of Conservation Voters, to the point that its innovative "Dirty Dozen" list of members of the Congress with the worst voting records on environmental issues was better known than the organization producing it.

Overall, then, EA was too small to compete with the major organizations, too broadly focused to compete with better-situated niche organizations, and, in some respects, too purist to exploit many of the funding sources, such as paid advertising in its magazine, used by other groups. Although widely respected, and a steady source of talent for other environmental organizations, EA could not sustain itself. It shut its doors in October 1996, leaving behind an array of college campus and foreign spin-offs.[38] In a final irony, its "Dirty Dozen" campaign endures, carried on by the League of Conservation Voters.

"MASS MEMBERSHIP" ENVIRONMENTALISM

One should not see EA's demise as an aberrant case of leadership myopia or ineptitude. Every environmental group

TABLE 22.2 **Support for Selected National Environmental Groups, in millions**

Organization (by year founded)	Supporters	Revenues FY 2009	Web site
Sierra Club	1,400,000	$84.7	sierraclub.org
National Audubon Society	600,000	$81.5	audubon.org
National Parks Conservation Association	325,000	$23.9	npca.org
Izaak Walton League	38,000	$4.0	iwla.org
The Wilderness Society	500,000	$34.6	tws.org
National Wildlife Federation	4,000,000	$82.4	nwf.org
Ducks Unlimited	715,000	$136.1	ducks.org
Defenders of Wildlife	1,000,000	$32.1	defenders.org
The Nature Conservancy	1,000,000	$547.2	nature.org
World Wildlife Fund–U.S.	1,200,000	$221.4	worldwildlife.org
Environmental Defense Fund	500,000	$134.0	environmentaldefense.org
Friends of the Earth	26,000	$4.9	foe.org
Natural Resources Defense Council	1,300,000	$113.1	nrdc.org
League of Conservation Voters	40,000	$10.8	lcv.org
Earthjustice	140,000	$34.6	earthjustice.org
Clean Water Action	1,200,000	$9.6	cleanwateraction.org
Greenpeace USA	250,000	$26.3	greenpeaceusa.org
Trust for Public Land	45,000	$187.6	tpl.org
Ocean Conservancy	500,000	$16.7	oceanconservancy.org
American Rivers	65,000	$12.1	amrivers.org
Sea Shepherd Conservation Society	35,000	$4.0	seashepherd.org
Center for Health, Environment, & Justice	27,000	$1.3	chej.org
Earth Island Institute	10,000	$11.1	earthisland.org
National Park Trust	33,000	$0.5	parktrust.org
Conservation Fund	16,000	$192.5	conservationfund.org
Rainforest Action Network	35,000	$3.9	ran.org
Conservation International	70,000	$232.9	conservation.org
Environmental Working Group	n/a	$3.5	ewg.org

SOURCE: Annual reports and IRS Form 990.

NOTE: "Supporters" is a comparatively expansive term that includes "members" and other "supporters" as claimed by the organization in 2010–2011 or where possible to estimate from published sources.

has struggled through fiscal traumas, internal disagreements over strategy and tactics, abrupt changes in leadership, and total reorganization. Some merged with kindred organizations. Why was EA the rare one that actually expired?

Answering this question requires that we flip it on its head: that is, how did the *other* organizations manage to survive, and even thrive, despite often sharp and sudden changes in external conditions, including economic recessions, shifts in public issue agendas, and changes in partisan control of the relevant federal institutions? And what does the answer to this question tell us about the suitability of our understanding of interest group politics generally?

Looking back, it seems clear that the key to survival for most environmental groups is their ability to develop and maintain a mass base of supporters, initially through direct mail and advertising and more recently through Internet communications and donations. This dynamic is particularly notable for "science and law" organizations like the EDF and NRDC that once depended on foundation grants, government contracts, legal fees, or the financial patronage of a few large donors. Today, their viability is tied to donations from hundreds of thousands of supporters of varying types, even if, compared to older groups like the Audubon Society or the Sierra Club, these supporters are not "members" in the classic sense of the term.

"Mass membership environmentalism" prompts criticism, particularly when groups are accused of "sensationalizing" complex environmental issues (chemical pesticide residues on apples) to generate donations or, conversely, of over-emphasizing visually compelling causes (cute animals or aesthetically pleasing landscapes) at the expense of more difficult and less easily imagined ones (environmental justice issues affecting urban populations). Such criticisms have merit. Yet, when compared to other sources, reliance on mass support may be the least problematic way to maintain an organization. Receiving financial support from corporations eager to display their environmental awareness is acutely problematic, even for nonconfrontational wildlife and land conservation groups like the National Wildlife Federation and the Nature Conservancy, which accept donations from energy producers Chevron Texaco and BP.

Critics see such funding as a cynical ploy by companies seeking to "greenwash" their public images, and the Conservancy was severely criticized for its ties to and fiscal support from BP following the Deepwater Horizon oil disaster in the Gulf of Mexico.[39]

Most important, their need to maintain a member base forces groups to cultivate, communicate with, and respond to a grassroots constituency, blunting charges that environmentalism is an elite and unrepresentative value system. In the aggregate sense at least, the size and breadth of this constituency, even more than the funds it generates, enables organized environmentalism to position itself at the center of the political system and to serve as a counterweight to the capacity of business and their conservative political allies to routinely get their way on environmentally problematic energy issues, whether ramping up "clean coal" production or obtaining clearance to drill for oil in the Arctic National Wildlife Refuge (ANWR).[40]

The long-standing battle over ANWR offers a fitting case study of this dynamic. No matter how hard and how many times it tried, and even when dramatic increases in imported oil opened political windows of opportunity, the George W. Bush administration could not overcome the opposition of environmental groups that were able to mobilize their supporters against opening up ANWR to drilling. The Sierra Club, National Audubon Society, and National Wildlife Federation, operating through their state chapters and affiliates, urged members to contact their members of Congress to counteract the pressure from prodrilling forces. Wilderness Society staff coordinated efforts with coalitions of native tribes and religious groups opposed to drilling on "sacred" ground, an effort that included organizing trips to Washington to enable local activists to meet with their representatives and senators and to create a local face to opposition to drilling even as Alaskan officials expressed their support.[41] NRDC and Defenders of Wildlife used phone banks and e-mail networks to generate millions of e-mails and faxes to Congress and the White House.[42] Defenders, NRDC, and the Audubon Society created new ANWR-specific Web sites to "educate" the public and stimulate opposition, and more than a dozen environmental organizations, ranging ideologically from Greenpeace to the World Wildlife Fund, collaborated to create a "virtual" organization (www.saveourenvironment.org) to harness "the power of the Internet to increase public awareness and activism on today's most important environmental issues." [43]

Proponents of opening ANWR to oil production used pretty much the same range of tactics to shape public opinion and mobilize support. The Bush administration and its allies emphasized "common sense" talking points developed by Republican pollster Frank Luntz, arguing that "energy development and the environment can and must co-exist, and this balance must be part of a truly comprehensive, long-term solution that reduces American dependence on foreign oil."[44] Industry associations pursued aggressive newspaper and television advertising campaigns, put together their own coalitions (Arctic Power, the Alliance for Energy and Economic Growth), and created prodrilling Web sites, while labor unions motivated by the prospect of new jobs in the energy sector used their members to make phone calls to potential supporters in crucial states. Energy and natural resource sector industries made donations to the campaign coffers of friendly candidates; in the 2002 election cycle alone, by one measure more than $40 million to Republicans and $15 million to Democrats.[45]

Yet despite considerable (and expensive) efforts over three decades, ANWR remains off-limits to oil production. Proponents of drilling are not giving up; they argued in the wake of the Deepwater Horizon disaster that it was safer to produce oil on land in the Arctic than in the deep waters of the Gulf of Mexico. Environmentalists come away with a much different lesson: the folly of continued and unconstrained dependence on petroleum. Which of these arguments gains traction with the public will depend, as always, on who can better frame the fundamental debate about the energy/environmental nexus.

ARE GROUPS EFFECTIVE?

Environmental organizations have adapted to changing conditions by building politically and fiscally potent mass memberships. But have they made a difference? On one level—stopping drilling in ANWR, for example—the answer is clearly yes. More broadly, one can argue that had these organizations not adapted, it is unlikely that the policy gains made during the early days of the environmental era would have been sustained or that environmentalism as a value system would occupy its current position as a legitimate critique of economic and political orthodoxy.

At another level, however, the answer is less clear. In October 2004, two young environmental activists, Michael Shellenberger and Ted Nordhaus, issued "The Death of Environmentalism," a blistering indictment of failures by mainstream environmentalism to translate apparent overall support for "green" values into substantive policy successes. In their view, environmentalists were too content to focus on problems easily defined as "environmental," to craft narrowly technical solutions, and to sell those solutions to lawmakers through conventional means, such as letter-writing campaigns and direct lobbying. In the case of global warming, for example, that strategy might involve encouraging consumers to buy fluorescent light bulbs and hybrid cars, forging coalitions with business leaders, and lobbying

Congress to adopt carbon cap-and-trade programs. None of these solutions, Shellenberger and Nordhaus argue, tackles the problem head on. Even worse, they advanced the environmental agenda, thereby exposing environmentalism's impotence as a force for social transformation.[46]

Many saw "The Death of Environmentalism" as dramatic and needlessly divisive, but many also agreed that environmentalists had not harnessed the potential power of public opinion. As Carl Pope of the Sierra Club admitted, "We have inadequately mobilized public concerns and values to create political pressure. As a result decision makers have not been forced to confront the need for fundamental changes in the way our society uses carbon (and other greenhouse gasses)."[47] Indeed, with public opinion polls showing generalized (if fluctuating) public support for combating global warming and promoting alternative energy sources, the comparative inability to turn that support into policy action vexes everyone in the environmental community.

Part of this mismatch is rooted in political structure; that is, environmental and other U.S. "public interest" groups operate within a system of formal representation that typically advantages their economic and ideological opponents. As other chapters in this volume remind us, the U.S. constitutional system enshrines representation into distinct geographic constituencies (congressional districts and states) and through an electoral system where the winner-take-all election rules create a bias toward two broad political parties. The rules of the game—rather than some idiosyncrasy of American culture—explain the absence of a viable Green Party, much less *any* viable alternatives to the Democratic and Republican parties that have dominated American electoral politics since the 1850s. As a result, interest groups in the United States play disproportionately central roles in educating, organizing, and mobilizing citizens for action, particularly when compared to parliamentary systems in which political parties typically perform these tasks. In the American context, interest groups are quasi-parties, and provide for supporters all but that last core function of parties in parliamentary systems—organizing and running government.[48]

How *well* a particular group fulfills these functions varies with sector and issue. In general, groups aligned with geographically concentrated constituencies, such as timber workers and coal miners, can speak to, aggregate, and mobilize their adherents in a more sustained and targeted fashion than groups whose supporters are spread out and whose causes are more diffuse.[49] Consider the difficulty of mobilizing citizens on the comparatively abstract and far away problem of global warming versus the ability of an automobile company to energize its workers, their communities, and their elected officials on the possibility of losing jobs should Congress enact tougher automobile fuel efficiency (or CAFE) standards. Such concentrated population distributions of farmers, industrial workers, and workers in extractive sectors like oil and coal parallels the geographically based system of representation in Congress. In a sense, then, locally situated extractive interests enjoy a built-in representational advantage.

As a result, environmental groups, in spite of their capacity to thwart "bad" policies like drilling in ANWR, invariably struggle to sustain effective political coalitions that can match those assembled by industrial and extractive industries. For one thing, environmental benefits such as clean air or ecosystem preservation typically are perceived as diffuse, long-term, and intangible, while jobs in manufacturing or coal mining are local, immediate, and tangible. By default, those defending the economic *status quo* have the easier political task, particularly when the *costs* of policy change are up front and appear to land disproportionately on those whose livelihoods are threatened. Using this logic, it not surprising that elected officials from coal states typically oppose any energy policy characterizing coal as a "dirty" energy source, nor that President Barack Obama promotes "clean coal" technology in the face of skepticism expressed by environmentalists. Jobs, and consequently votes, are at stake.

The composition of the typical environmental organization is also a factor. Few, except for older groups like the Sierra Club, National Audubon, and the National Wildlife Federation, maintain local or state chapters. As a result, groups like Friends of the Earth or Natural Resources Defense Council are easily caricatured as outsiders with little legitimacy among those whose lives are most directly affected by changes in energy production policies. It does not help that many environmental groups have not broadened their base beyond the educated and largely white middle class that historically constitutes their political, ideological, and financial support. As a result, their advocacy for stricter CAFE standards and against oil production in ANWR too easily feeds into a narrative that environmentalism is antijobs, if not antiworker—an image easily manipulated by self-interested corporations and free market ideologues.[50] As a consequence, the George W. Bush administration counted major unions among its allies in fights with environmentalists over the Kyoto Protocol on global climate change, drilling in ANWR, and automobile mileage standards, despite the administration's problematic relationship with organized labor overall.

NEW ALLIANCES

The problem of global climate change and the intersecting need to develop "green energy" technologies and jobs presents environmentalists with an opportunity to reframe the overarching narrative about environmentalism and energy, and to forge politically effective coalitions with old adversaries, labor unions in particular.

Recognition of common goals (and common foes) led to the formation of several so-called "blue-green" coalitions. The Apollo Alliance, founded in 2003, brought together the Sierra Club and National Wildlife Federation and major unions such as United Mineworkers, United Autoworkers, and United Steelworkers to promote a national effort to create "green" American manufacturing jobs—in "clean coal" technologies, hybrid automobiles, and transportation infrastructure in particular—and to mount a united effort to promote global "fair trade" agreements that would benefit American workers.[51] Another such coalition is the Blue Green Alliance, a coalition of the Sierra Club and Natural Resources Defense Council, on one side, and the United Steel Workers and Communications Workers of America on the other, representing some 4 million people in a partnership designed to promote job-creating solutions to global warming. This coalition, formed in 2006, focuses on building grassroots alliances in pivotal labor union states: Michigan, Minnesota, Ohio, Pennsylvania, Washington, and Wisconsin. The coalition helped Obama win these states in the 2008 election.

The groups involved in these efforts range from the ideologically center-right (National Wildlife Federation) to center-left (Sierra Club)—as opposed to critics of free market capitalism like Friends of the Earth—and they shy away from debates over consumer culture and materialism that tend to alienate working-class Americans. Instead, they focus on promoting "progressive" trade policies and investing in new generations of "green jobs," themes more likely to appeal to their labor partners.[52] In doing so, they are seeking to reframe the seemingly abstract issue of climate change away from a narrative of individual sacrifice and lowered living standards and into an *opportunity* for a national investment in science and technology, new jobs, and the promise of a prosperous and environmentally sustainable future. For its part, the 2008 Obama campaign framed its environment and energy platform under the rubric of "New Energy for America," which Obama announced in Lansing, Michigan, a city devastated by the loss of auto industry–related jobs. The administration's economic stimulus package also put heavy emphasis on developing jobs in energy conservation and new energy technologies, including some, like "clean coal," not particularly loved by environmentalists.[53]

Other alliances reflected tactical assessment of political roadblocks. Confronted with federal inaction during the Bush administration, environmentalists worked with state governors—including less doctrinaire Republicans like California governor Arnold Schwarzenegger—to foster innovations and jobs in energy conservation and transportation.[54] Federal inaction also led to the creation of new state-focused organizations and reformulation of older ones. Of note is Environment America, a federation of state advocacy organizations formed in 2007 by two dozen "public interest research groups" (PIRGs) with origins in Ralph Nader's early 1970s group, Public Citizen.[55] The effort to reshape the

EVANGELICALS AND ENVIRONMENTALISM

Environmentalism is an expansive value system, encompassing a broad range of diverse issue priorities, views on individual lifestyles, and opinions about the role of government in promoting and protecting those values. One notable cleavage is religion, with particular frictions between "new age" believers and Christians, who regard the new age reverence and worship of nature as outright paganism. Evangelical Christians—as well as Catholics, Muslims, and some elements within Orthodox Judaism—also oppose proposals for population control. As a result, many evangelicals have historically avoided, if not openly opposed, joining in environmental causes.

Evangelical Christians are not uniform in their views, however, and the emergence of the Evangelical Environmental Network (EEN) in the 1990s reflected growing concerns among less conservative evangelicals that ecosystem destruction violated injunctions in the book of Genesis about being good stewards of the Earth. The EEN therefore promotes "Creation Care," an overarching theology dedicated to "stopping and preventing activities that are harmful (e.g., air and water pollution, species extinction), and participating in activities that further Christ's reconciliation of all of creation to God." More recently, EEN took an especially controversial step in expressing support for action on climate change, and its executive director joined with other religious leaders in attending the 2009 United Nations summit on climate change in Copenhagen. Secular environmentalists long wary about partnerships with any particular religious community now see opportunities to build politically influential bridges. The camps still disagree about issue priorities, tactics, and values—evangelicals retain a deep wariness of direct government action—but they have converged on the need to act now for the sake of future generations.

SOURCES: John Houghton, *The Christian Challenge of Caring for the Earth*, John Ray Initiative, 1996, www.jri.org.uk/brief/christianchallenge.htm; Evangelical Environmental Network, www.creationcare.org/.

PIRGs into an integrated federation of state environmental groups focused on state-level efforts to promote clean energy made a virtue out of necessity during the Bush years and produced a more politically potent coalition of support for policy change once Obama's election created new opportunities at the federal level.

Other nascent coalitions are more philosophical and have important policy ramifications. In February 2006 more than eighty evangelical Christian leaders, a group historically hostile to what many of them had previously considered the pagan underpinnings of environmentalism, announced an "Evangelical Climate Initiative" to fight global warming.[56] The initiative expressed support for market incentives to reduce greenhouse gases and for an educational campaign designed to convince believers that combating global warming was a moral issue sanctioned by the biblical injunction for Christians to be good stewards of the Earth. Partial funding for this campaign came from the Pew Charitable Trusts, Hewlett Foundation, and Rockefeller Brothers Foundation, which saw an unique opportunity to create new alliances in a common effort to combat global warming and to build political support for policy change among conservatives in Congress and in the states.[57]

THE FUTURE OF ENVIRONMENTAL ADVOCACY

The economic crisis that paved the way for Obama's victory in 2008 in many ways ended a thirty-year era of deregulation and skepticism about government action that began with Ronald Reagan and endured through George W. Bush. It also may have marked the end of late twentieth-century environmental and energy politics characterized by the ideological standoff between liberals and conservatives. Yet current debates about energy and environment, punctuated in profound ways by the Deepwater Horizon disaster, raise fundamental questions about what environmentalism in the twenty-first century will look like. Will it continue to be viewed by average Americans as important in the abstract yet peripheral to their central economic concerns, or will it (finally) be integrated more seamlessly into the fabric of daily life? The heightened focus on sustainability, with its attention to economic concerns, promises to reframe the energy/environment nexus, although few are sanguine about the ease of reshaping the role of energy in contemporary life when so many depend on the energy status quo.

At a tactical level, will the future of environmental advocacy be a variation on late twentieth-century environmentalism, with its array of large national advocacy groups positioned in their diverse policy and tactical niches, or will it be reshaped by "virtual" multi-issue groups like MoveOn.org, its adherents connected via social networking software and mobilized by an online call to arms? It will probably be some combination of the two, with resultant effects on the ability of some groups to survive. Environmental groups have shown remarkable capacity to change with the times and technology, but it is not yet clear how the organizations that dominated late twentieth-century environmental advocacy will complete with or accommodate leaner, more agile organizations supported by Web-generated microdonations.

Such questions are variations on old themes. Indeed, as suggested at the start of this chapter, the story of American environmental groups is the story of all interest groups. They were created out of the recognition of new problems or through reconceptualizing old problems. Their tactics reflected new opportunities to act or were made possible by new technologies. Once created, they struggled to maintain themselves by nurturing a base of consistent support and seeking out coalitions beyond. And they reside within and seek to shape issue domains that rarely stay stable for long, in turn affecting the future opportunities for these groups as actors in the larger political system. Beneath seeming stability lies constant flux, a challenge to both these groups and to our own capacity to understand the forces that shape them.

NOTES

1. Mancur Olson, *The Logic of Collective Action* (Cambridge: Harvard University Press, 1965).

2. See Christopher Bosso, *Environment, Inc: From Grassroots to Beltway* (Lawrence: University Press of Kansas, 2005).

3. Elisabeth S. Clemens, *The People's Lobby: Organizational Innovation and the Rise of Interest Group Politics in the United States, 1890–1925* (Chicago: University of Chicago Press, 1997), 2.

4. Samuel Hays, *Conservation and the Gospel of Efficiency: The Progressive Conservation Movement, 1890–1920* (Cambridge: Harvard University Press, 1959).

5. Michael Cohen, *The History of the Sierra Club, 1892–1970* (San Francisco: Sierra Club Books, 1988); Frank Graham, *The Audubon Ark: A History of the National Audubon Society* (New York: Knopf, 1990).

6. Paul S. Sutter, *Driven Wild: How the Fight against Automobiles Launched the Modern Wilderness Movement* (Seattle: University of Washington Press, 2002), 13; Stephen Fox, *John Muir and His Legacy: The American Conservation Movement* (Boston: Little, Brown, 1981), 148–182.

7. Fox, *John Muir*, 158.

8. Clemens, *People's Lobby*, 302.

9. George Hoberg, *Pluralism by Design: Environmental Policy and the American Regulatory State* (Westport, Conn.: Praeger, 1992).

10. Richard Cohen, *Washington at Work: Back Rooms and Clean Air*, 2nd ed. (Boston: Allyn & Bacon, 1995), 84.

11. Ibid., 85.

12. Grant McConnell, "The Conservation Movement—Past and Present," *Western Political Quarterly* 7 (1954): 467.

13. Christopher Bosso, *Pesticides and Politics: The Life Cycle of a Public Issue* (Pittsburgh: University of Pittsburgh Press, 1987).

14. Graham, *Audubon Ark*, 186.

15. Thomas B. Allen, *Guardian of the Wild: The Story of the National Wildlife Federation, 1936–1986* (Bloomington: Indiana University Press, 1987), 50.

16. Samuel P. Huntington, *American Politics: The Promise of Disharmony* (Cambridge: Harvard University Press, 1981).

17. Michael J. Lacey, "The Environmental Revolution and the Growth of the State," in *Government and Environmental Politics: Essays on Historical Developments Since World War Two*, ed. Michael J. Lacey (Baltimore: Johns Hopkins University Press, 1991), 2.

18. Jeffrey Berry, *Lobbying for the People* (Princeton: Princeton University Press, 1977), 34; Dara Strolovitch, *Affirmative Advocacy* (Chicago, University of Chicago Press, 2007).

19. Andrew McFarland, *Public Interest Lobbies: Decision Making on Energy* (Washington: American Enterprise Institute, 1978), 4–5.

20. David S. Meyer and Douglas R. Imig, "Political Opportunity and the Rise and Decline of Interest Group Sectors," *Social Science Journal* 30 (1993), 253–270.

21. *Sierra Club v. Hickel*, 33 F.2d 24, 33 (9th Cir. 1970); *Sierra Club v. Morton*, 405 U.S. 727_(1972).

22. R. Shep Melnick, *Regulation and the Courts: The Case of the Clean Air Act* (Washington, D.C.: Brookings Institution, 1983), 10.

23. *Calvert Cliffs Coordinating Committee. v. U.S. Atomic Energy Commission*, 449 F.2d 1109 (1971).

24. Richard A. Liroff, *A National Policy for the Environment: NEPA and its Aftermath* (Bloomington: Indiana University Press, 1976).

25. Ford Foundation, *Annual Report, 1979*, 15.

26. Robert Gottlieb, *Forcing the Spring: The Transformation of the American Environmental Movement* (Washington, D.C.: Island Press, 1993), 149.

27. *National Journal*, July 24, 1971, 1557.

28. Cohen, *History of the Sierra Club*, 360.

29. Graham, *Audubon Ark*, 228.

30. Allen, *Guardian of the Wild*, 69.

31. Graham, *Audubon Ark*, 227.

32. Ronald G. Shaiko, "More Bang for the Buck: The New Era of Full-Service Public Interest Organizations," in *Interest Group Politics*, 3rd ed., ed. Allan J. Cigler and Burdett Loomis (Washington, D.C.: CQ Press, 1991).

33. Stephen G. Greene, "Technology Helps Small Environmental Group Get Big Results," *Chronicle of Philanthropy*, January 11, 2001, philanthropy.com/free/articles/v13/i06/06001001.htm.

34. Adeline Gordon Levine, *Love Canal: Science, Politics, and People* (Lexington, Mass.: Lexington Books/D.C. Heath, 1982).

35. Shaiko, "More Bang for the Buck," 109–129.

36. Gottlieb, *Forcing the Spring*, 134–136.

37. Robert Holbert, *Tax Laws and Political Access: The Bias of Pluralism Revisited* (Beverly Hills, Calif.: Sage Publications, 1975); Daniel Faber and Deborah McCarthy, eds., *Foundations for Social Change: Critical Perspectives on Philanthropy and Popular Movements* (Lanham, Md.: Rowman and Littlefield, 2005).

38. Don Hopey, "Earth Day Group Near its Last Days, *Pittsburgh Post-Gazette*, December 16, 1996, A12.

39. Joe Stephens, "Nature Conservancy Faces Potential Backlash from Ties to BP," *Washington Post*, May 24, 2010, A1.

40. Deborah L. Guber and Christopher Bosso, "Framing ANWR: Citizens, Consumers, and the Privileged Position of Business," in *Business and Environmental Policy*, ed. Michael Kraft and Sheldon Kamieniecki (Cambridge: MIT Press, 2006), 35–59.

41. Robert Schlesinger, "Two Tribes Split on Alaska Oil Plan," *Boston Globe*, February 25, 2002; Wilderness Society, *Annual Report 2002*, 2.

42. Defenders of Wildlife, *Annual Report 2002*, 7.

43. See Guber and Bosso, "Framing ANWR"; Bosso, *Environment, Inc.*, chap. 5.

44. Luntz Research Companies, *Straight Talk*, 2002, 107.

45. Federal Election Commission data for the 2002 election cycle, as compiled by the Center for Responsive Politics, www.opensecrets.org/industries/indus.asp?Ind=E.

46. Michael Shellenberger and Ted Nordhaus, "The Death of Environmentalism," www.thebreakthrough.org/PDF/Death_of_Environmentalism.pdf, and as elaborated in *Break Through: From the Death of Environmentalism to the Politics of Possibility* (Boston: Houghton Mifflin, 2007).

47. Carl Pope, "And Now for Something Completely Different," January 13, 2005, www.grist.org/news/maindish/2005/01/13/pope-reprint/index.html.

48. Robert A. Dahl and Charles E. Lindblom, *Politics, Economics, and Welfare* (New York: Harper and Row, 1953), 336; Strolovitch, *Affirmative Advocacy*.

49. William P. Browne, *Private Interests, Public Policy, and American Agriculture* (Lawrence: University Press of Kansas, 1988).

50. Guber and Bosso "Framing ANWR."

51. See www.apolloalliance.org.

52. Press Release, "Blue Green Alliance Grows to More Than Four Million," October 9, 2008, *PR Newswire*, via Lexis-Nexis. See www.bluegreenalliance.org.

53. See my.barackobama.com/page/content/newenergy.

54. Barry Rabe, *Statehouse and Greenhouse: The Emerging Politics of American Climate Change Policy* (Washington, D.C.: Brookings Institution, 2004).

55. See www.environmentamerica.org.

56. Laura Goodstein, "Evangelical Leaders Join Global Warming Initiative," *New York Times*, February 28, 2006. See also christiansandclimate.org.

57. "Polls Show Strong Backing for Environmental Protection Across Religious Groups," Pew Forum on Religion and Public Life, December 20, 2004. See www.pewtrusts.org/our_work_report_detail.aspx?id=23028.

SUGGESTED READING

Allen, Thomas B. *Guardian of the Wild: The Story of the National Wildlife Federation, 1936–1986*. Bloomington: Indiana University Press, 1987.

Bosso, Christopher J. *Environment, Inc: From Grassroots to Beltway*. Lawrence: University Press of Kansas, 2005.

Cohen, Michael. *The History of the Sierra Club, 1892–1970*. San Francisco: Sierra Club Books, 1988.

Duffy, Robert J. *The Green Agenda in American Politics: New Strategies for the Twenty-First Century*. Lawrence: University Press of Kansas, 2003.

Dunlap Riley E., and Angela G. Mertig, eds. *American Environmentalism: The U.S. Environmental Movement, 1970–1990*. Philadelphia: Taylor and Francis, 1992.

Fox, Stephen. *John Muir and His Legacy: The American Conservation Movement*. Boston: Little, Brown, 1981.

Gottlieb, Robert. *Forcing the Spring: The Transformation of the American Environmental Movement*. Washington, D.C.: Island Press, 1993.

Graham, Frank Jr. *The Audubon Ark: A History of the National Audubon Society*. New York: Knopf, 1990.

Hays, Samuel P. *Beauty, Health, and Permanence: Environmental Politics in the United States, 1955–1985*. New York: Cambridge University Press, 1987.

Rogers, Marion Lane. *Acorn Days: The Environmental Defense Fund and How it Grew*. New York: Environmental Defense Fund, 1990.

Shabecoff, Philip. *Earth Rising: American Environmentalism in the 21st Century*. Washington, D.C.: Island Press, 2000.

Shaiko, Ronald. *Voices and Echoes for the Environment: Public Interest Representation in the 1990s and Beyond*. New York: Columbia University Press, 1999.

Wapner, Paul. *Environmental Activism and World Civic Politics*. Albany: State University of New York Press, 1996.

chapter 23

Intergovernmental Lobbying

by Beverly A. Cigler

States and local governments do a great deal of lobbying in the American political system. The best-known government-to-government lobbying comes from national institutional membership-based organizations that represent generalists in state and local government, that is, governors, mayors, county executives and commissioners, legislators, and other state and local elected officials. The National Conference of Mayors is one such group. Sometimes these groups are called the "executive coalition" because elected executives are their leading spokespersons. This set of organizations, representing somewhat different interests, shares broadly similar policy concerns and operates within the interest group sector that takes stands on broad issues such as health, welfare, employment, consumer protection, energy and the environment, and civil rights, among others.[1]

Traditionally called the "Big Seven," the intergovernmental lobby primarily consists of the National Governors Association (NGA), National Conference of State Legislatures (NCSL), Council of State Governments (CSG), National League of Cities (NLC), U.S. Conference of Mayors (USCM), National Association of Counties (NACo), and the International City/County Management Association (ICMA). ICMA represents nonelected officials such as county and city managers and does not lobby. The CSG does not lobby either and is unique in representing officials from all branches of government—executive, legislative, and judicial. It has dozens of affiliate organizations, generally tied to functional policy areas. The other five organizations do lobby and are sometimes helped by the nonlobbying of ICMA and CSG in weakening perceptions that the generalist officials are "just another special interest."

The National Governors Association is perhaps the most prominent and most sophisticated of the intergovernmental lobbying organizations. Formed in 1908 to mediate interstate conflict and coordinate state policy on water rights, the NGA did not emerge as a national lobbying force until the 1960s.[2] The NGA is singular among the intergovernmental lobby organizations because there are only fifty governors, compared to the state legislatures conference with an aggregate membership of 7,400 legislators plus thousands of staff. Within the NGA are separate associations for the Democratic and Republican governors, and the NGA's affiliate organizations represent groups like the governors' policy advisers and lieutenant governors. The larger NCSL includes affiliate organizations to represent various legislative staff, such as budget specialists. Similarly, NACo has numerous county organization affiliates that represent the so-called row officers (sheriff, district attorney, register of wills, clerk of courts, jury commissioners, controller, treasurer, and recorder of deeds), who may be independently elected. Individual counties can join NACo, but its membership tilts toward larger counties that can afford the membership fees. The NCSL represents small and medium-sized cities, and the USCM's membership consists of large cities.

The intergovernmental associations often label themselves as public interest groups (PIGs, an unfortunate acronym) because they pursue benefits not limited to their members. On the other hand, others, including some national government officials, sometimes use the acronym PIGs in a pejorative way to argue that the intergovernmental groups operate in a cozy closed subsystem or as part of an iron triangle in which they work with congressional committees and subcommittees and executive branch agencies to develop policies of mutual benefit.[3]

The groups that make up the intergovernmental lobby do far more than lobby. The associations monitor and report on legislative and executive actions, develop and analyze policies, communicate formally and informally with policymakers, and mobilize political support. The levels of sophistication among the groups vary widely, with some mostly doing information sharing and dissemination and others conducting research through surveys. NACo, for example, collaborates with the University of Georgia, and together they have formed the National Center for the Study of Counties, which conducts survey research on timely topics. Political scientist Robert Salisbury would describe these as "service organizations" engaged in state and local government "interest representation."[4] Their reach extends further than domestic issues, as they are also active on so-called "intermestic issues," which have components of both domestic and international policy.

Timothy Conlan and Paul Posner addressed the eroding capacity of the U.S. intergovernmental system to systematically assess changes it confronts, noting the loss of intergovernmental analytic capacity in the White House, the Office of Management and Budget, and the congressional committee system, all of which have downgraded intergovernmental emphases in recent years.[5] The most significant example of the loss of intergovernmental expertise is the demise of the Advisory Commission on Intergovernmental Relations (ACIR), which was abolished in 1996. ACIR was a major source of data and analysis on intergovernmental issues. The death of ACIR and the decline of adequate assessment capacity at the top for policymaking have major implications for the fate of states and local governments in a federal system. In many ways, the intergovernmental lobby fills some of the gaps in the continuing loss of analytic capacity in the intergovernmental system.

Looking at analytical capacity issues from the subnational perspective provides a somewhat more optimistic view. The National League of Cities not only represents and lobbies for its members, but also it has affiliate state organizations, usually called state municipal leagues. NACo membership is by individual county, and it does not have affiliate organizations in the same sense as the NLC. But the forty-eight states that have counties also have state-level county associations that generally include all their counties as members. The county association executive directors from the states meet with each other and work cooperatively with NACo, as do each state's county associations. The U.S. Conference of Mayors represents large cities, compared to the medium and small city membership of NCSL. The large cities do not have state associations; instead, large cities and counties often have their own single jurisdiction offices, with lobbying resources, in Washington, D.C., in addition to relying on the USCM.

All these organizations perform research, build collaborative relationships among their members, and provide a host of services for them. Other groups, such as NARC (National Association of Regional Councils) and NATaT (National Association of Small Towns and Townships) are significant intergovernmental lobbying forces, prompting some to designate the main intergovernmental lobby as the "Big Eight" or the "Big Nine." Collectively, these organizations also include dozens of affiliate groups, and some serve as the secretariat for other groups. In addition to their Washington, D.C., offices, the NCSL and CSG have offices in Denver and Lexington, Kentucky, respectively, and the CSG also has regional offices. Many of the intergovernmental organizations have offices in the Hall of the States, a facility of the States Services Organization, located a few blocks from the U.S. Capitol building. Having offices in the same place facilitates contact with each other and the members of Congress who represent all their constituent governmental units.

The remaining sections of this chapter deal with intergovernmental lobbying by examining the major groups in the field as well as single jurisdiction lobbying. The chapter does not focus more broadly on all types of state and local "interest representation" in the American political system, as outlined by Beverly Cigler's typology, which includes the activities of the Big Seven, other public interest organizations of public officials, specialist associations organized and lobbying around subject matter expertise, and single jurisdictional representation lobbyists such as state, city, and county offices in Washington.[6] The two organizations within the Big Seven that do not lobby, ICMA and CSG, are excluded here precisely because they do not lobby.

EMPIRICAL RESEARCH ON THE INTERGOVERNMENTAL LOBBY

Although there is a substantial literature on interest groups and lobbying, as reviewed in this book, the empirical research or theory development focused on governments lobbying governments is sparse. Allan Cigler and Burdett Loomis highlighted the importance of intergovernmental lobbying decades ago.[7] Mancur Olson's collective action work provided an early explanation for why subnational governments participate in membership organizations such as the NGA, NCSL, and NLC, organizations that offer attractive collective benefits, such as a unified voice speaking on intergovernmental issues, that are denied to nonmembers.[8] These intergovernmental organizations also offer their members a mix of selective benefits, including publications and research. Olson's work also helps explain why the mix of collective and selective benefits for members may not be sufficient. What each individual member wants most for itself, such as funding or special treatment on a mandate, are selective benefits that these organizations cannot readily provide. As a result, states and cities sometimes create their own single representation Washington offices. Olson helps with understanding that subnational governments may seek both collective and selective benefits, sometimes from different sources.

Whether these organizations of public officials are effective in lobbying at the national level for their members is debatable.[9] Because the Big Seven and other organizations often compete with each other on major issues, lobbying success varies widely, and may depend on the issue. It is in the realms of information production, sharing, and dissemination, and the provision of other membership services that the organizations have solid performance records. The groups, however, are "not just another special interest group," as they deal with issues of broad public interest and consequence.[10] They are major generators and disseminators of information to their membership, with conferences, publications, and consultations that provide opportunities for exchanging information and building potentially significant interaction across states and municipalities. Their information, moreover, is shared widely across the political system for the general public and decision makers. Similarly, the affiliate, parallel organizations in the states that lobby state legislatures provide state-specific programs, conferences, research, and other information exchange. In the states, these organizations shape much of state-local and intermunicipal relations, supplementing the work of state and local employees who belong to and network through subject matter organizations.[11]

RISE OF THE INTERGOVERNMENTAL LOBBY

The growth of government and the proliferation of intergovernmental groups are linked. The generalist associations are a twentieth-century phenomenon, with new organizations forming with increased frequency during the New Deal era in the 1930s and again in the 1960s and early 1970s, when the Great Society programs were initiated and expanded, all of which required cooperation among governments at the national, state, and local levels.[12] As noted, the NGA formed in 1908; the NCSL was founded in 1948 for state legislators and staff; the NLC in 1924; and NACo in 1935.

Richard Flanagan argued that the USCM, founded in 1933 to give big city mayors an effective organizational base for lobbying Congress and for coordinating with executive branch agencies, was a major force during the New Deal and that it has been largely overlooked by theorists of American federalism and intergovernmental relations.[13] His account of the New Deal revealed both cooperation and conflict, with cities turning to Washington for help with myriad policy needs, after being rebuffed by the states. In turn, the national government often bypassed states to deal directly with cities because states so often resisted New Deal initiatives. Even in the twenty-first century, the three local government generalist organizations within the Big Seven are sometimes called the "urban lobby."

Flanagan explained that USCM lobbying built support for stronger urban programs and national-city linkages during the New Deal. In effect, the USCM served as an informal extension of the national bureaucracy that offered program information to local jurisdictions and feedback about implementation and policy impact to the national bureaucracies that dealt with urban issues. President Franklin D. Roosevelt had close ties to the USCM, which established a pattern of politics in national urban policy that persisted until the early 1980s, according to Flanagan.

This depiction of intergovernmental lobbying does not dovetail with other assessments. Samuel Beer argued that the intergovernmental lobby was a response to the Great Society, which greatly expanded the national grant-in-aid system and led to the rise of specialists—civil servants—who attempted to undercut the power of generalist elected

THE "BIG SEVEN" INTERGOVERNMENTAL ASSOCIATIONS

Association (current title)	Date founded	Membership
National Governors Association (NGA)	1908	Incumbent governors
Council of State Governments (CSG)	1933	Direct membership by states and territories; serves all branches of government; has dozens of affiliate organizations of specialists
National Conference of State Legislatures (NCSL)	1948	State legislators and staff
National League of Cities (NLC)	1924	Direct membership, by cities and state leagues of cities
National Association of Counties (NACo)	1935	Direct membership by counties; loosely linked state associations; affiliate membership for county professional specialists
United States Conference of Mayors (USCM)	1933	Direct membership by cities with population over 30,000
International City/County Managers Association (ICMA)	1914	Direct membership by appointed city and county managers, and other professionals

officials.[14] Beer saw governments lobbying the federal government in the 1960s as a major change in the system of national representation. It is accurate that lobbying by mayors, governors, and county executives was a 1960s phenomenon, but the USCM was active and influential in the 1930s, 1940s, and 1950s. Therefore, the expansion of the intergovernmental lobby was not as radical a departure from the past as Beer suggested; rather, it reflected its growth and extension.

Flanagan's careful historical analysis challenged the notion that significant intergovernmental lobbying was a response to the programs of the Great Society, when an infusion of national funds began to flow to subnational governments.[15] More accurate is the conclusion that the intergovernmental lobby arose simultaneously with, and helped create, the development of New Deal urban programs—in municipal financing, public housing, and work relief. The USCM in the 1930s had resources such as votes, financing, and information, but it also possessed stature in Washington politics because of its access to the Roosevelt administration. While the USCM helped cities and the administration, Roosevelt used it as a tool to support his programs for cities and worked with New York mayor Fiorello LaGuardia, who was president of the USCM from 1935 to 1945.

Several scholars have provided valuable descriptions of the intergovernmental lobby in the 1960s and performed case study research that focused on specific legislation or programs. Suzanne Farkas examined the urban lobby and the emergence of an urban issues network in national policymaking in the 1960s.[16] Donald Haider examined the intergovernmental lobby from the New Deal to the early 1970s and sorted out three phases.[17] The first period, from the New Deal to 1964, was characterized by the presence of big city mayors who wanted to bypass the states and deal directly with the national government. At the time, governors were not interested in a national presence in state affairs. This account dovetailed with Flanagan's depiction of the USCM.[18] Haider's second period extended from 1964 to 1968 and coincided with President Lyndon Johnson's administration and the growth of national programs. Governors were actively involved in competing for national initiatives and funding, as were mayors and other local government officials. The third phase came with President Richard Nixon's New Federalism initiatives, highlighted by general revenue sharing. Anne Marie Cammisa described this phase as one in which states and local governments received more money with fewer strings attached.[19]

Cammisa's research consisted of interviews and case study analysis of three major pieces of legislation and the roles of the NGA, NCSL, NLC, USCM, and NACo. She added a fourth phase to Haider's work, from President Jimmy Carter's later years in office to 1995. She argued that Carter's anti-Washington candidacy was linked to the eventual decline in national funding for states and cities at the end of his presidency, a trend that continued with President Ronald Reagan's policies.

In 1980 the USCM received 64.3 percent of its budget from national government contracts.[20] Early in his administration, however, Reagan began to reduce the bureaucracy's capacity to deal with urban issues and curtailed the significant financial commitments to cities. The USCM's role as an extension of the national government ended, and the USCM lost its national government contracts.[21] Charles Levine and James Thurber reported that just 34.3 percent of the USCM's budget came from national government contracts in 1985, or almost a 50 percent cut in five years.[22] The staff was reduced from 120 to about 65 by the end of Reagan's second term, and technical services for the USCM were cut.[23] Overall, the Reagan administration slashed national funding to cities and states and broke the direct relationship with cities.

TURNING TO THE LEGAL SYSTEM

The intergovernmental lobby resembles other interest groups in its increasing use of the courts to deal with policy issues of greatest concern. The Academy for State and Local Government (ASLG) was founded in 1971 by the Big Seven. The ASLG is a small nonprofit policy group, which houses the State and Local Legal Center. The national state and local government associations are active in filing amicus curiae briefs before the U.S. Supreme Court to promote their policy initiatives regarding federalism. Until the early 1980s, states and local governments rarely filed briefs and were generally not successful when they did. The legal center was created to aid states in filing briefs and to coordinate the advocacy of state and local governmental associations in litigation before the Court.[24]

Edward Laverty and Kenneth Palmer reviewed thirty-seven cases between 1995 and 1998 in which the associations were active and six high-profile federalism cases during the period when the center was generally less involved.[25] They found that the associations were more unified in raising technical issues, such as intergovernmental policy and program implementation, and prevailed in 68 percent of the cases during the period of study. In addition, the national government and state and local government interest groups usually supported similar positions before the Court on highly technical issues. The associations succeeded less frequently when dealing with major federalism disputes, but in cases in which both the states and national government filed briefs, the states fared better than the national government.

Another intergovernmental organization, the National Association of State Attorneys General, which deals primarily with state issues, moved its headquarters to Washington in the early 1980s and began engaging in national issues more often than it did in the past. This group has become a powerful force in American litigation, with a large number of states joining together for important lawsuits. Attorneys general from nearly two dozen states have filed lawsuits against the national health care law that was passed in 2010, including the claim of interference with interstate commerce.

A 1992 Supreme Court ruling, *Quill Corp. v. North Dakota*, held that a state cannot force a company to collect that state's sales taxes from consumers unless the company has either property or employees there. In addition, the ruling said that state sales taxes cannot extend beyond state lines because they are too complex. States have worked together through the Streamlined Sales Tax Project to make their sales tax systems simpler, and they are using that effort to win congressional authorization for states to extend their sales tax to on-line and catalogue sales. Congress has shown little interest, so it is likely that *Quill* will be challenged in the courts again. Colorado, New York, North Carolina, and Texas have been aggressive in pursuing Amazon.com and other on-line retailers to force them to voluntarily report and collect sales taxes for on-line purchases. The companies argue that revealing their sales through itemized lists is a First Amendment issue not only for customers, but also for the retailers because the names of some on-line companies and interest groups can suggest overt religious, political, or expressive affiliations.

IDEOLOGICAL INTEREST REPRESENTATION IN THE INTERGOVERNMENTAL LOBBY

The Big Seven is not without competitors. Arguing that the National Conference of State Legislatures was too liberal, conservatives created the American Legislative Exchange (ALEC) in 1973. ALEC's principal founder was Paul Weyrich, a leading "movement conservative" and head of the Free Congress Foundation. Weyrich also cofounded the leading national conservative think tank, Heritage Foundation, in 1973. ALEC is currently the largest network of individual state legislators, with more than 2,000 state legislative members of the roughly 7,400 state legislators in the United States, and it works as a well-coordinated network on a broad set of issues. The network writes model laws to promote conservative positions, such as antitax legislation and taxpayer bill of rights (TABOR) laws, and to oppose civil rights laws and consumer, labor, and environmental initiatives. ALEC links state legislators with right-wing think tanks, many of which are located in state capitals.

Unlike the NCSL and the other intergovernmental lobby organizations within the Big Seven, ALEC seeks corporate members who pay dues of up to $50,000 per year and extra to sit on task forces that draft ALEC's legislative initiatives. ALEC is a major success within the conservative movement, but generally works out of public view. Members of ALEC include about three dozen state Speakers of the House, half of the state Senate presidents, and more than thirty state Senate and thirty state House leaders. The members lobby state legislatures and the national government, and the organization has taken credit for passing hundreds of laws. Although ALEC is a conservative interest group that works through an intergovernmental and state lobbying effort, it has most recently looked to the local level for its organizing on policy issues.

As a response to ALEC, the American Legislative Issues Campaign Exchange (ALICE) was created, with its origins in the Center on Wisconsin Strategy, the Economic Analysis and Research Network, and other progressive groups. ALICE, a fledgling organization, serves as a clearinghouse of information and legislation for local governments as they lobby state government. Their goal is to support and assist 10,000 progressive local elected officials. Yet another organization, the Progressive Legislative Action Network (PLAN), was created in 2005. Similar to ALEC, PLAN also develops model legislation and uses grassroots activists. The emergence of ideological groups to advance causes in state legislatures is a new development and one that may lessen the overall effectiveness of the NCSL, which provides nonpartisan advice and research to state legislators. It is not yet known whether the individual-based memberships in these groups achieve more allegiance from the legislators than does NCSL.

STATE OFFICES IN WASHINGTON, D.C.

In 1941 Gov. Herbert Lehman of New York created the first federal-state relations office in Washington, D.C., to seek national funding for projects and to lobby against strong regulations. Other states created federal state offices, mostly in the mid- and late 1960s, and with the rise of the Great Society programs of President Johnson and the New Federalism programs of President Nixon. By 1985, thirty states had offices in Washington. A few state legislatures also created D.C. offices, but most relied on the NCSL. State activism continued to increase in Washington in the 1980s until a recession led to a dwindling of national funds going to subnational governments. Between the late 1980s and late 1990s, the number of state offices in the capital peaked at thirty-six, but dropped to thirty-one by 1998 and has not grown. On the other hand, state and local governments have increased their utilization of other ways to lobby the national government: they hire lobby firms, trade associations, law firms, and other groups to do specialized work in issue monitoring, tracking legislation, and anything else that might help their governments influence national activities. The Center for Responsive Politics tracks the government lobbying activities on its Web site, opensecrets.org. In 2009 the center found that states, territories, and local governments spent $83.5 million in lobbying the national government, but the spending dropped to around $60 million in 2010, as governments at every level responded to a major recession. Nearly 1,000 government entities hire approximately 1,000 lobbyists per year to lobby the national government. In addition, individual state agencies, including state universities, hire lobbyists to work for them in Washington.

Lobbying by individual states has a checkered history of success, with some state offices better funded, more effective at lobbying, and generally more successful than others, as several scholars have found. David Cingranelli interviewed Washington office directors in 1981–1982 and focused on describing communication patterns.[26] John Pelissero and Robert England examined the roles, services, and strategies that the Washington offices of states and local governments ran during Reagan's first term, a time of major changes in intergovernmental relations.[27] Darby Morrisroe updated Cingranelli's early assessment and examined offices in Washington and in state capitals.[28] She asked why some states do not establish offices in Washington and found the reasons to be political. Entrepreneurial, aggressive governors tend to establish offices in Washington. Of major importance is that a governor makes the decision to establish an office, but there is not a systematic explanation for governors' decisions in the aggregate. John Nugent attempted to understand states' Washington offices as a way to maintain balance with a perceived encroaching of the national government on the original safeguards of federalism.[29] He viewed the state offices as a successful attempt to protect state interests and their constitutional roles. Troy Smith used case studies of Medicaid reform, crime policy, and welfare reform to assess the ability of governors and state legislators to represent and defend their interests before Congress.[30] Smith noted that Washington offices are one of several means used by governors to lobby the national government, but did not judge them to be effective.

The most substantial research on states' Washington offices was conducted by Jennifer Jensen, who adapted Robert Salisbury's exchange theory (see Chapter 4) of interest groups to explain why some states mobilize and create Washington lobbying offices and others do not.[31] She expanded Salisbury's theory by considering environmental factors that could affect mobilization, and she interviewed approximately seventy directors and former directors of federal-state liaison offices in Washington, D.C., or state capitals. Jensen found substantial differences between states with Washington offices and those with only state-federal relations offices in their state capitals. Relying on Salisbury, Jensen expected to find that benefits of Washington offices would be the prevailing explanation for their establishment; she found, instead, that office costs were more important. Governors' preferences led to the creation of the Washington offices and, sometimes, the political costs were a disincentive. Media and officials from other political parties complained about spending for the offices, and some state legislators, who recognized the visibility advantages for a governor, as well as an increased ability to secure national funds, were likewise critical.

INTERGOVERNMENTAL LOBBY RESOURCES AND COHESION

The collection of organizations known as the intergovernmental lobby lacks resources such as political action committees and does not participate collectively or individually in election campaigns. The intergovernmental associations do, however, possess the same types of resources as do many other organized interests, including size, status and prestige, access, organizational structure, leadership skill, organizational cohesion, and intensity.

There are more than 87,000 governments in the United States. Just one is the national government, leaving the others to be represented by the intergovernmental lobby of state and local associations. Not all local governments can afford the membership fees of NACo or the NLC, but large majorities at least belong to a state municipal league or county association. Each of the national organizations has dozens of staff members and operating budgets in the millions. The associations at the national and state levels enjoy recognition and a measure of legitimacy with the media, enhancing their ability to influence policy. But conflict often occurs within the intergovernmental lobby—state versus city or county, counties versus cities, large jurisdictions versus smaller jurisdictions, and more. National legislators sometimes are at odds with the municipal or county groups in their states. Groups within the intergovernmental lobby vary greatly in their status and prestige. The prestige and importance of fifty governors in the NGA may offer more clout than that of small-city mayors or counties slow to modernize.

In terms of cohesion and intensity, the intergovernmental associations have significant drawbacks. Thousands of very different jurisdictions are represented, and, depending on the issue, the intergovernmental associations may be internally fragmented. The agendas of USCM's large city mayors are different from those of the small and medium-sized municipalities represented by NCSL. Democratic and Republic governors have differing agendas relating to highly ideological issues, such as government regulation on climate change. Another area of partisan contention is the role of the national government, compared to the private sector's, in the health care system, as is the role of the national versus state governments in health care. Many Republican governors have joined in lawsuits with state attorneys general in suing the national government over provisions in the national heath care reform legislation that was passed in 2010.

The organizations also vary in their membership size and organizational finances. NACo offers a good example of the fragmentation and resource differences. Two-thirds of American counties are rural, meaning that, traditionally, the organization has emphasized public works, especially highways, and agricultural issues. Counties, however, are evolving into major providers of human services and becoming more important when regional approaches are needed. Public health, social welfare, mass transit, solid waste, county modernization, and other issues expand the county agenda and increase conflict among diverse counties. Conflicts ensue over responsibilities and revenues.

As policymaking becomes more partisan, some state legislative officials argue that the National Council of State Legislatures is too liberal in its views and ineffective in influencing Congress. As a result, there is tension in state legislatures between those lawmakers favoring the NCSL and those favoring ALEC's ideological conservative thrust. While the NCSL traditionally has been more active in congressional lobbying than ALEC, tensions hamper policy consensus because of the size and diversity of NCSL membership and the requirement to vote as state, not individual legislators. As a result, the NCSL's primary role, it can be argued, has become more informational than political, while ALEC is very active in congressional lobbying on highly targeted issues and brings formidable resources to bear. This lobbying took place with the balanced budget amendment in 1980 and more recently with taxpayer bill of rights laws that are promoted in many states each year. Best known is the Colorado law, which voters approved in 1992 and requires that increases in overall tax revenues be tied to inflation and population growth unless larger increases are approved by referendum. Although ALEC was influential in Colorado, in 2005 voters there passed changes to allow for more flexibility. Not housed in the Hall of the States, ALEC is aligned with the Heritage Foundation. The splintering of a major Big Seven activity—legislatures lobbying Washington—causes continuing cohesion problems for the intergovernmental lobby.

With regard to organizational structure and leadership, the intergovernmental lobby again has differing resources. Once again, NACo is a case in point. Its diversity mirrors that of its affiliate associations, which are national organizations that represent specialist officials such as county attorneys, administrators, fiscal officers, and parks and recreation personnel. With generalist and specialist officials under the same umbrella, internal policy conflict can occur, but this breadth can also lead to success in meshing spatial (rural versus urban, for example) and functional interests. Associations that consist only of generalists or specialists, however, can be hampered because of a failure to blend differing perspectives.

ISSUES OF INTEREST TO STATE GOVERNMENT LOBBYING ORGANIZATIONS

Agriculture and rural development
Banking, insurance, and financial services
Budget and taxation
Criminal justice
Economic development, job creation, trade, and cultural affairs
Education, pre-school, K-12, higher education, and vocational education
Energy
Environment and natural resources
Health, homeland security, emergency management, and public safety
Human services and workforce development
Immigration
Labor and employment
Telecommunications and information technology
Transportation and infrastructure

The local associations have varying abilities to help their members respond to new political realities, often as a result of their organizational structure. The NLC's dues-paying state affiliate organizations—state municipal leagues—give it a strong permanent network with which to forge strong linkages with state capitals. The NLC also allows cities of any size to join. In Pennsylvania, the NLC affiliate, the state league of cities, changed its name to include municipalities. As a result, it competes with other state-level associations that represent townships and boroughs. At the state level, the intergovernmental lobby groups, then, can compete with each other on issues and for members. But in a given state, the various intergovernmental associations also usually meet on occasion to determine common ground and coordinate some of their lobbying of the state legislature. Because state associations of counties are not formal affiliates of NACo, they traditionally have had weaker ties to NACo than do municipalities with the NLC.

The NLC and NACo were both founded in Chicago and moved to Washington, D.C., as the national government created closer direct linkages to local governments. In contrast, the U.S. Conference of Mayors' only home has been Washington since it was founded in 1932 with the encouragement of FDR. It has always focused on "big city issues" such as crime, drugs, transportation, housing, education, the environment, hunger, and homelessness. As so-called big city problems evolved to smaller jurisdictions in recent decades, the USCM has attracted more members from smaller cities, including its leadership. The wider membership has created opportunities for coalition building with others in the intergovernmental lobby; still, the USCM remains focused on Washington, not the states.

Financial resources of the various state and local organizations also affect their operations. When governments are hit hard by recession, so are their associations. During the Reagan years, as noted, the associations were dramatically affected by the loss of federal funds. High dues for both the state and local associations cause backlash by states and local governments, as well as reduced participation at annual conferences and other meetings as local media report on "junkets."

TACTICS AND ISSUES

To influence congressional policymaking, the associations within the intergovernmental lobby often use tactics that mirror those used by private organized interests: provide information to support their positions, testify at formal hearings, contact legislators and administrators, and cultivate relations with the media. A number of the executive directors of Big Seven organizations are elected members of the National Academy of Public Administration, the congressionally chartered nonpartisan think tank often turned to for advice by Washington policymakers. This affiliation adds to the prestige of the organizations' stances on issues. The state and local lobby organizations also work closely with the International City/County Management Association to obtain objective information. Part of ICMA is the Center for State and Local Government Excellence, which produces quality research and data on important policy issues, such as the looming pension crisis among state and local governments.

The relative advantage of the national intergovernmental lobbying groups in gaining access to policymakers is not, however, matched by a similar capacity to influence policy decisions. In large part, the lack of success can be traced to the enormous variations in group resources within the intergovernmental arena. In addition, the existence of very broad agendas serves to reduce cohesion among the groups and to produce relatively low intensity of many issue stands. Within individual states, the municipal and/or county associations are often perceived to be among the strongest lobbying groups, and they often find success in part because their agendas are clear and agreed upon.

The national intergovernmental lobby did have several major successes in the 1990s when its members worked together on several issues. They were successful in getting the Clinton administration to change its federalism executive order to be more Tenth Amendment–friendly to the states. President Clinton's executive order, according to the intergovernmental lobby, took power away from the states. The president thought that state powers should be reduced when there was a need for uniform national standards, when decentralization increased the costs of government, or when states were reluctant to impose regulations because of fears that affected businesses would relocate to other states. The strong intergovernmental lobby reaction against the executive order resulted in the president rewriting the order to offer a more states-rights–oriented position. The intergovernmental lobby was largely responsible for the passage of the Unfunded Mandates Reform Act, which requires more accountability from Congress than in the past when passing legislation that shifts greater costs to state and local governments. There were also successes in the 1990s on the preemption by Congress of some state laws and regulations in areas such as product liability, credit reporting, interstate branch banking, and telecommunications.

After the tragic events of September 11, 2001, there has been a centralizing tendency in the federal system. The REAL ID legislation, passed in 2005, prompted the national intergovernmental lobby to work together to argue against it as a largely unfunded mandate. The REAL ID Act modified the law pertaining to the security, authentication, and issuing of state drivers' licenses and identification (ID) cards, as well as various immigration issues pertaining to terrorism. States, which often tie various identification procedures to multiple activities, such as library cards, driver licenses, and welfare and food stamps, worked with their national associations to cost out the legislation and asked the national government for more funding than the national government was willing to offer. By 2008 all fifty states either applied for extensions of the original May 2008 compliance deadline or received unsolicited extensions. By October 2009, twenty-five states approved resolutions or binding legislation not to participate in the program. Janet Napolitano, secretary of the Department of Homeland Security (DHS), had criticized the program when she was the governor of Arizona. DHS is to supposed to be the key in checking REAL ID compliance, but the future of the law is uncertain, with congressional bills introduced to amend and repeal it. Perceived federal intrusions on the states' tax base, such as increases in fuel and tobacco taxes, an inflexible grant system, restrictive regulations, and major health care reform involving still unknown effects on the states, among other issues, are perennial issues for the intergovernmental lobby.

One issue that has energized the intergovernmental lobby to work together is immigration reform. Generally, who is admitted to the United States is the responsibility of the national government, which has used a quota system at times. But so-called illegal immigration is also a state and local government issue. States and cities determine the meaning of *unlawful presence.* In addition to law enforcement, states and cities are responsible for integrating immigrants

ISSUES OF INTEREST TO LOCAL GOVERNMENT LOBBYING ASSOCIATIONS

Agriculture and rural affairs
Children, youth, and family
Community and economic development
Criminal and social justice
Economic development, jobs, and workforce development
Education
Emergency management

Energy, environment, and land use
Finance and intergovernmental affairs
Health
Housing
Human services
International affairs

Labor and collective bargaining
Metropolitan policy
Natural resources
Public lands
Rural policy
Telecommunications and technology
Tourism, arts, parks, entertainment, and sports
Transportation and infrastructure

through community building. The intergovernmental lobby has worked together to bring these issues to the legislative agenda despite disagreements among cities, governors, legislators, and the national government on options for resolving the conflicts.

COALITION BUILDING

Each organization within both the national- and state-level intergovernmental lobby associations has its own base of support in Congress or the state legislature. Although a broader base of support can sometimes be developed by combining efforts, the traditional approach has been for groups to work alone. This approach stems from the great diversity among the organizations and their focus on different issues at any given time. The executive directors of the various organizations do, however, know each other well and meet regularly. This is less the case with their staffs, which are more likely to work closely with staff from the individual association's affiliate organizations. As with the close proximity of many of the intergovernmental organizations in the Hall of the States, some state, municipal, and county associations share facilities. In the Hall of the States, the Big Seven association representatives routinely meet with congressional staffers, state officials, federal agency officials, and even the media, to receive briefings on agency and legislative developments. These information networks serve a valuable purpose in bringing organizations together to work in an intergovernmental environment. At the state level, there are opportunities for coalition building with other broad-based organizations such as the state special districts, municipal authorities, and school boards.

Collaboration among intergovernmental organizations ranges from working toward enactment or defeat of specific legislation to the writing of favorable regulations and the adjustment of deadlines for meeting mandates or obtaining waivers, to less subtle policy influences. Still, turf wars are part of the reality within the intergovernmental lobby. At the state level, the range of tactics extends to collaboration among generalists and specialists in providing civic education to the general public, based on the organizations' shared professionalism and commitment to public service. In some states, for example, there are concerted efforts either to promote or defeat proposals for structural changes in local government operation. These include efforts by state legislatures to encourage local mergers and consolidations, which often are met with hostility by the local associations of all types: municipal or county associations, school districts, or other special districts.

Overall, the most significant activity of the intergovernmental lobby is member services, especially providing factual information on policy issues. Major issues tend to trigger attempts at intergroup collaboration—on health care reforms that involve financial and structural changes at the state level or immigration issues that test states' rights. An example is the unfunded mandate; the generalist organizations cosponsored National Unfunded Mandates Day in 1993 and worked together to obtain legislative change. The organizations also forged coalitions with private sector institutions and interests to determine the finalists for major federal transportation funding for high-speed rail. The 2010 midterm elections, however, have changed the future of high-speed rail funding dramatically. Newly elected Republican governors in Wisconsin and Ohio have rejected the funding awarded competitively, and the U.S. Department of Transportation has rejected the notion of those states using the money for highways instead.

CONCLUSION

The American policymaking system has long been described as consisting of multicentered policy dominance.[32] The intergovernmental lobby, made up of national, state, and local associations, competes with a large number of other groups to find a place to promote their policy ideas. Their efforts lack a strong cohesive policy network and suffer from a service network that has been diminished over many years by the loss of direct funding and a membership base with dwindling resources. The broader information infrastructure dealing with intergovernmental issues in the American system has also eroded. Fragmentation within the intergovernmental policy community that varies from one issue to another is a formidable difficulty, although interdependence in collecting and sharing information has increased in recent years. Ideological differences within the organizations, mirroring divisions in society, also pose significant barriers to collaboration and effectiveness. On the other hand, the strong membership services provided by the intergovernmental lobby supply incentives for steady membership by state and local governments.

The jurisdictional nature of representation by the state and local government associations at both the national and state levels may be the lobby's major problem. Funding patterns in the intergovernmental grant system traditionally have funded people, not places. Problems seldom occur neatly with jurisdictional boundaries. The interests of specific units of local government are not necessarily the same as the interests of the larger metropolitan or regional areas. The policy issues confronted by the intergovernmental lobby involve both a government function (transportation, housing, environmental protection, and the like) and a geographic area (state, county, city). Public policies are usually dealt with in the political system in terms of the clusters of values, objectives, and programs related to basic government functions, so that dealing with the spatial/geographic or jurisdictions' dimension continues to be problematic. Executive and legislative decision making, nationally or in the states, generally breaks along functional, not spatial lines. This poses problems for the intergovernmental lobby, either with its generalist organizations of elective officials, or policy generalists, to penetrate the policy process. Specialists—in housing, employment, and crime education, among many others—do not consistently deal with these issues in ways that take account of their spatial implications. The intergovernmental lobby may not be a forceful interest group sector in the aggregate, but each organization is well known and well respected and has its own policy influence. What remains undetermined are the potential and real effects that the vast informational resources of these organizations have on policymaking.

NOTES

1. David D. Meyer and Douglas R. Imig, "Political Opportunity and the Rise and Decline of Interest Group Sectors," *Social Science Journal* 30 (1993): 253–270.
2. See Donald H. Haider, *When Governments Come to Washington: Governors, Mayors, and Intergovernmental Lobbying* (New York: Free Press, 1974); and Anne Marie Cammisa, *Governments as Interest Groups: Intergovernmental Lobbying and the Federal System* (Westport, Conn.: Praeger, 1995).
3. See B. J. Reed, "The Changing Role of Local Advocacy in National Policies," *Journal of Urban Affairs* 5 (1983): 287–298; George E. Hale and Marian Lief Palley, *The Politics of Federal Grants* (Washington, D.C.: CQ Press, 1981); and Charles H. Levine and James A. Thurber, "Reagan and the Intergovernmental Lobby: Iron Triangles, Cozy Subsystems, and Political Conflict," in *Interest Group Politics,* ed. Allan J. Cigler and Burdett A Loomis (Washington, D.C.: CQ Press, 1986), 202–220.
4. Robert H. Salisbury, "Interest Representation and the Dominance of Institutions," *American Political Science Review* 78 (March 1984): 64–77.
5. Timothy J. Conlan and Paul L. Posner, eds., *Intergovernmental Management for the 21st Century* (Washington, D.C.: Brookings Institution Press, 2008).
6. Beverly A. Cigler, "Not Just Another Special Interest: Intergovernmental Representation," in *Interest Group Politics,* ed. Allan J. Cigler and Burdette A. Loomis (Washington, D.C.: CQ Press, 1995), 131–153.
7. Cigler and Loomis, eds., *Interest Group Politics,* 1986.
8. Mancur Olson, *The Logic of Collective Action: Public Goods and the Theory of Groups* (Cambridge: Harvard University Press, 1971).
9. Troy Smith, "When States Lobby," Ph.D. thesis, State University of New York, Albany, 2008.
10. Cigler, "Not Just Another Special Interest."
11. Beverly A. Cigler, "The County-State Connection: A National Study of Associations of Counties," *Public Administration Review* 54 (1995): 3–11.
12. See Haider, *When Governments Come to Washington.*
13. Richard M. Flanagan, "Roosevelt, Mayors and the New Deal Regime: The Origins of Intergovernmental Lobbying and Administration," *Polity* XXXI, 3 (1999): 415–450.
14. Samual H. Beer, "Federalism, Nationalism, and Democracy in America," *American Political Science Review* 72 (March 1978): 9–21.
15. Flanagan, "Roosevelt, Mayors and the New Deal Regime."
16. Suzanne Farkas, *Urban Lobbying: Mayors in the Federal Arena* (New York: New York University Press, 1971).
17. See Haider, *When Governments Come to Washington.*
18. Flanagan, "Roosevelt, Mayors and the New Deal Regime."
19. Cammisa, *Governments as Interest Groups.*
20. Levine and Thurber, "Reagan and the Intergovernmental Lobby."
21. Rochelle L. Stanfield, " 'Defunding the Left' May Remain Just Another Fond Dream of Conservatives," *National Journal* (August 1, 1975): 1375.
22. Levine and Thurber, "Reagan and the Intergovernmental Lobby."
23. Jonathan Walters, "Lobbying for the Good Old Days," *Governing* 5 (June 1991): 35.
24. Only cases in which there is a consensus among the Big Seven are filed, with the hope that by filing a single brief the groups can achieve more success on issues of federalism.

25. Edward B. Laverty and Kenneth T. Palmer, "State and Local Government Interest Groups Before the Supreme Court: Implications for Intergovernmental Policy," *Public Administration Quarterly* 24, 4 (2001): 522–536.

26. David L. Cingranelli, "State Government Lobbies in the National Political Process" (Albany, N.Y.: Rockefeller Institute reprint series, 1984), 122–127.

27. John P. Pelissero and Robert E. England, "State and Local Governments' Washington 'Reps'—Lobbying Strategies and President Reagan's New Federalism," *State and Local Government Review* 19, 2 (1987): 68–72.

28. Darby Morrisroe, "The State of 'State Offices' in Washington: A Critical Assessment," paper presented at the annual meeting of the American Political Science Association, Boston, September 1998.

29. John D. Nugent, "Federalism Attained: Gubernatorial Lobbying in Washington as a Constitutional Function" (Ph.D. thesis, University of Texas, Austin, 1998).

30. Troy Smith, "When States Lobby" (Ph.D. thesis, State University of New York, Albany, 2008).

31. Jennifer M. Jensen and Jennifer G. Kelkres, "The First State Lobbyists: State Lobbying Offices in Washington During World War II," paper presented at the 40th annual meeting of the Northeastern Political Science Association, Boston, November 13–15, 2008.

32. Farkas, *Urban Lobbying.*

SUGGESTED READING

Beer, Samuel H. "Federalism, Nationalism, and Democracy in America." *American Political Science Review* 72 (March 1978): 9–21.

Cammisa, Anne Marie. *Governments as Interest Groups: Intergovernmental Lobbying and the Federal System.* Westport, Conn.: Praeger, 1995.

Cigler, Allan J., and Burdett A Loomis, eds., *Interest Group Politics.* Washington, D.C.: CQ Press, 1986.

Cigler, Beverly A. "Not Just Another Special Interest: Intergovernmental Representation." *In Interest Group Politics,* eds. Allan J. Cigler and Burdett A. Loomis. Washington, D.C.: CQ Press, 1995, 131–153.

———. "The County-State Connection: A National Study of Associations of Counties." *Public Administration Review* 54 (January/February 1995): 3–11.

Cingranelli, David L. "State Government Lobbies in the National Political Process." Albany, N.Y.: Rockefeller Institute reprint series, 1984, 122–127.

Conlan, Timothy J., and Paul L. Posner, eds. *Intergovernmental Management for the 21st Century.* Washington, D.C.: Brookings Institution Press, 2008.

Farkas, Suzanne. *Urban Lobbying: Mayors in the Federal Arena.* New York: New York University Press, 1971.

Flanagan, Richard M. "Roosevelt, Mayors and the New Deal Regime: The Origins of Intergovernmental Lobbying and Administration." *Polity* XXXI, 3 (1999): 415–450.

Haider, Donald H. *When Governments Come to Washington: Governors, Mayors, and Intergovernmental Lobbying.* New York: Free Press, 1974.

Hale, George E., and Marian Lief Palley. *The Politics of Federal Grants.* Washington, D.C.: CQ Press, 1981.

Hays, R. Allen. "Intergovernmental Lobbying: Toward an Understanding of Issue Priorities." *Western Political Quarterly* 44, 4 (1991): 1081–1098.

Jensen, Jennifer M. "Establishing a State Lobbying Office in Washington: Factors that Matter." Paper presented at the annual meeting of the American Political Science Association, Washington, D.C., August 31–September 3, 2000.

Jensen, Jennifer M., and Jennifer G. Kelkres. "The First State Lobbyists: State Lobbying Offices in Washington During World War II." Paper presented at the 40th annual meeting of the Northeastern Political Science Association, Boston, November 13–15, 2008.

Laverty, Edward B., and Kenneth T. Palmer. "State and Local Government Interest Groups Before the Supreme Court: Implications for Intergovernmental Policy." *Public Administration Quarterly* 24, 4 (2001): 522–536.

Levine, Charles H., and James A. Thurber. "Reagan and the Intergovernmental Lobby: Iron Triangles, Cozy Subsystems, and Political Conflict." In Interest Group Politics. Ed. Allan J. Cigler and Burdett A Loomis. Washington, D.C.: CQ Press (1986), 202–220.

Marbach, Joseph, and Wesley Leckrone. "Intergovernmental Lobbying for the Passage of TEA-21." *Publius: The Journal of Federalism* 32, 1 (2002): 45–64.

Menzel, Donald C. "Collecting, Conveying, and Convincing: The Three C's of Local Government Interest Groups." *Public Administration Review* 50 (May-June 1990): 401–405.

Meyer, David D., and Douglas R. Imig. "Political Opportunity and the Rise and Decline of Interest Group Sectors." *Social Science Journal* 30 (July 1993): 253–270.

Morrisroe, Darby. "The State of 'State Offices' in Washington: A Critical Assessment." Paper presented at the annual meeting of the American Political Science Association, Boston, September 1998.

Nugent, John D. "Federalism Attained: Gubernatorial Lobbying in Washington as a Constitutional Function." Ph.D. thesis, Department of Government, University of Texas, Austin, 1997.

Olson, Mancur. *The Logic of Collective Action: Public Goods and the Theory of Groups.* Cambridge: Harvard University Press, 1971.

Pelissero, John P., and Robert E. England. "State and Local Governments' Washington 'Reps'—Lobbying Strategies and President Reagan's New Federalism." *State and Local Government Review* 19, 2 (1987): 68–72.

Reed, B. J. "The Changing Role of Local Advocacy in National Policies." *Journal of Urban Affairs* 5 (Fall 1983): 287–298.

Salisbury, Robert H. "Interest Representation and the Dominance of Institutions." *American Political Science Review* 78 (March 1984): 64–77.

Smith, Troy. "When States Lobby." Ph.D. diss., State University of New York, Albany, 2008.

Stanfield, Rochelle L. "'Defunding the Left' May Remain Just Another Fond Dream of Conservatives." *National Journal* (August 1, 1975): 1375.

Walters, Jonathan, "Lobbying for the Good Old Days." *Governing* 5 (June 1991): 35.

chapter 24

Foreign Lobbying

by Arnd Jurgensen and Renan Levine

In the early morning hours of June 28, 2009, President Manuel Zelaya of Honduras was awakened in the presidential palace in Tegucigalpa at gunpoint by several soldiers. Within minutes, wearing only his pajamas, he was on a plane leaving the country. Zelaya's former party colleague, Roberto Micheletti, replaced him in the first military coup in Central America since the end of the Cold War. The coup was denounced throughout the international community, including by the American government, which immediately suspended military (though not humanitarian) aid. The OAS (Organization of American States) suspended Honduras pending a return to constitutional democracy, with many members, particularly Venezuela, calling for tougher sanctions. It was obvious to all that crucial to the success of the newly installed government was the position of the United States. Wasting no time, and wanting to leave nothing to chance, Micheletti showed up for negotiations in Costa Rica a week later with Bennett Radcliff, a public relations expert with ties to the administration of former president Bill Clinton. Simultaneously, a Latin American business council supporting the newly installed government hired Lanny J. Davis, who had served as Clinton's personal lawyer and campaigned for Hillary Clinton during her run for the presidency, to lobby congressional leaders on behalf of the new Micheletti government.[1] The strategy of the Micheletti government illustrates the continuing centrality of the United States in hemispheric (if not global) affairs and the growing recognition of leaders around the world of the opportunities for foreign interests to influence U.S. policies outside of formal diplomatic channels. Virtually every country maintains an embassy in Washington, D.C., with staff that regularly communicates with officials at the U.S. Department of State, but these diplomatic connections are only one part of how foreign governments seek to advance their political objectives.

With good reason, foreign leaders like Micheletti are under the impression that political pressure can be brought to bear upon the U.S. government while bypassing the State Department. Foreign governments interested in acquiring weapons from the United States engage the Defense Department or the Department of Homeland Security. They meet with members of Congress to urge revamped efforts to protect the environment and to discuss increases in foreign aid. In other words, foreign interests lobby to achieve their policy objectives much like their domestic counterparts, but such activities often raise the ire of groups concerned that foreign entities' influence is contrary to U.S. national interests.

For this chapter, the term *foreign lobbying* refers to any attempt by a foreign power to influence U.S. foreign policy by means other than traditional diplomacy through the State Department. Lobbying by foreign interests began in earnest at the end of the Second World War, but became particularly pronounced around the end of the Cold War in the late 1980s. Such activities include the broad category of "public diplomacy," where a foreign entity seeks to mobilize a domestic group on behalf of a specific cause by funding public relations campaigns, providing information regarding a specific issue to the media, and other activities designed to indirectly influence political decision makers or mass opinion.[2] As discussed below, foreign lobbying excludes lobbying by domestic groups on foreign policy.

The chapter first covers the legal context for foreign lobbying, which requires additional disclosure requirements when embassies hire K Street firms for lobbying or public relations assistance. Next, it describes the foreign interests that actively lobby the U.S. government and their domestic allies and opponents. Even with such allies, many countries engage in extensive campaigns to influence American public opinion. The success of these efforts is difficult to evaluate.

LEGAL CONTEXT OF FOREIGN LOBBYING

American law treats foreign lobbying similarly to domestic lobbying concerns, but with two exceptions. First, all "persons acting as agents of foreign principals in a political or quasi-political capacity" must register with the Department

COVERT ACTIVITIES AND THE FOREIGN AGENTS REGISTRATION ACT

Historically, "foreign lobbying" was seen as a form of illicit meddling in the affairs of foreign countries. In the 1648 Peace of Westphalia, European states agreed to accept the sovereignty of their neighbors, to refrain from interfering in the internal affairs of other states, and to limit their interactions to the mechanisms of diplomacy. If diplomacy failed, military confrontations must be preceded by a declaration of war. Yet there has always existed a third, traditionally covert, option of influencing the policies of neighboring lands through one's intelligence and counterintelligence capacities. Such activities, in contrast to foreign lobbying, are neither acknowledged by the responsible state nor condoned by the recipient.

In the United States, concerns about covert attempts by communist and fascist governments to influence policymakers and public opinion led to the Foreign Agents Registration Act of 1938 (FARA).[1] FARA made previously covert foreign activities such as propaganda campaigns in the United States overt and legal. The act requires foreign agents to register with the Department of Justice, disclose all contracts with the foreign principal, and provide copies of all "informational materials" to the Department of Justice. All such information must be labeled as being distributed on behalf of the foreign principal, and any agents testifying before Congress must provide a copy of all disclosures. All foreign organizations and individuals, including national and subnational government units, foreign corporations, and political parties, are bound by FARA. The fee paid by a foreign principal to an American agent must not be contingent on the successful realization of a lobbying goal.

These disclosures, including details of how much money the agent earns and spends on behalf of the foreign agent are public documents made available in a report to Congress by the U.S. attorney general every six months. These reports are also available in a searchable database on the U.S. Department of Justice Web site and on a Web site maintained by the private Sunlight Foundation (fara.sunlightfoundation.com/). Criminal penalties are associated with the violation of FARA, but enforcement actions are rare, and the Department of Justice Web site concedes that the department "seeks to obtain voluntary compliance."

1. Foreign Agents Registration Act, 22 U.S.C. § 611 *et seq.*

of Justice.[3] Second, foreign lobbyists are prohibited from making campaign contributions. Other than requiring disclosure for all activities, there are few formal limits on the activities of foreign lobbyists and their agents.

The primary set of rules governing foreign lobbyists is found in the Foreign Agents Registration Act (FARA) of 1938 (see box above). To comply with FARA, all foreign agents, including lobbyists and public relations firms, must register with the Justice Department. The most recent semiannual report to Congress listed 541 foreign principals hailing from 127 different individual foreign nations and territories as clients.[4]

A separate database established by the Lobbying Disclosure Act of 1995 (LDA) is maintained by congressional clerks independent of the Justice Department.[5] Foreign lobbyists, like domestic lobbyists, must disclose their congressional lobbying activities if earned income from lobbying exceeds $3,000 or if the costs of maintaining in-house lobbyists exceed $11,500 a quarter. Unlike under FARA, lobbying firms must disclose the names of the lobbyists working for the client, whether those lobbyists held relevant government jobs in the preceding two years, and the specific issues that the firm is working on for the client. American subsidiaries of foreign companies are also bound by these requirements, so the LDA database is more extensive than FARA's. On the most recent forms, these subsidiaries must disclose whether a foreign entity holds at least 20 percent equitable ownership or otherwise "plans, supervises, controls, directs, finances or subsidizes activities" of the organization. Organizations can be fined for noncompliance, but such enforcement is rare, in part because Congress lacks direct enforcement powers. As a result, observers commonly assume that FARA and the LDA significantly underestimate the amount of foreign lobbying that occurs in the United States.

In 1974 the Federal Election Campaign Act (FECA) banned foreign citizens, governments, corporations, parties, and other organizations from making political contributions (or donations in kind) for any federal, state, or local election. Political action committees (PACs) are required to return any contributions they unwittingly accept from a foreign national. The Federal Election Commission is responsible for enforcing FECA.

Immigrants with green cards may make contributions, as may American subsidiaries of foreign corporations as long as the influence of the foreign parent company or foreign nationals is limited.[6] Like American companies, domestic subsidiaries of foreign corporations can also establish PACs to distribute campaign money. According to the Center for Responsive Politics, the most active "foreign-connected PACs" in 2008 were established by the domestic subsidiaries of large European corporations such as telecommunication giant T-Mobile, financial institutions like Credit Suisse Securities, and pharmaceutical companies like GlaxoSmithKline and AstraZeneca. These companies all compete extensively in the United States in economic sectors with high levels of government regulation and involvement, and these PACs are little different from those established by their domestic competitors.

THE PLAYERS: FOREIGN GOVERNMENTS

Almost every country maintains an embassy in Washington, D.C., headed by an ambassador. Most also maintain consulates in other American cities. These missions look after the needs of their citizens who are living or traveling in the United States, but often include staff who are responsible for promoting trade and tourism between the United States and their country. Some larger countries also post defense liaisons, maintain desks devoted to promoting cultural events and educational opportunities, and disseminate information about their country and the actions taken by their political leaders. Most staff members are civil servants who tend to rotate from other postings every few years. Some appointees, especially the ambassador, typically serve thanks to political connections to their government and change whenever the partisan composition of their government changes. Many embassies also include some permanent staff members, including some American citizens, who can provide lobbying or public relations support.

"In-house" lobbying by these embassies and permanent missions is difficult to gauge systematically because embassy officials are not required to file any disclosures when their own staffers advocate on behalf of their government. Many larger missions, such as France and Germany, do not appear to hire any outside consultants. Some large countries and U.S. trading partners, such as Australia, Canada, Japan, and Mexico, hire outside consultants and maintain internal staff dedicated to public diplomacy and/or lobbying. Small countries, nevertheless, dominate the FARA disclosure list. According to its FARA disclosure form, Azerbaijan hired Melwood Communications to work with their embassy's media section to develop a communication strategy in 2008. Ogilvy Worldwide provided a similar service to the Embassy of Pakistan.[7] The disclosure of these contracts, however, is by no means an indication that these countries rely solely on American consulting firms for lobbying and media relations.

In total, eighty-four nations and territories are listed as clients in the most recent (first half of 2008) FARA disclosures for lobbying activity, media and public relations, or "U.S. policy consultations." About half of these nations and territories have at least one contract that explicitly names the embassy or permanent mission. There are likely other firms that may not realize that the cultural promotion activities they perform on behalf of a foreign client may be subject to FARA disclosures.

Foreign corporations, subnational governments, and trade and business groups from abroad also frequently maintain permanent offices in the United States to promote their interests or occasionally to dispatch representatives. Many of the listings in the FARA database include firms hired to promote tourism or investment for a business or a government, including some subnational governments. For some governments and their corporate interests, these efforts are independent or only casually coordinated on an ad-hoc basis and may be prompted by dissatisfaction with the efforts of the national government's mission. For example, after the United States banned imports of Canadian beef because of concerns over mad cow disease in 2004, the

FOREIGN LOBBYING IN COMPARATIVE PERSPECTIVE

Other than traditional diplomacy, foreign lobbying efforts are exceedingly rare outside of America. Few foreign political systems match the number of opportunities that are available in the United States for public interests to influence legislation and the implementation of government policy. As a result, lobbying many government players is both unfamiliar to many diplomats and traditionally seen as inappropriate interference in the domestic affairs of another country.

The United States is unusual because the Constitution explicitly requires the executive branch to share powers relating to foreign affairs with Congress. Low levels of party discipline and a strong congressional committee system open the legislative process, potentially frustrating control of the policymaking process by the president or the majority party leadership in Congress by making it subject to influence by groups independent of the governing party. Two examples of Congress failing to approve deals made with the president or the Department of State are the Covenant of the League of Nations (1919) and the Inter-American Convention Against Illicit Manufacturing of and Trafficking in Firearms (1997). As a result, efforts by foreign governments to reach agreements with the United States are likely to be far more successful if discussions with the State Department are combined with lobbying efforts targeting members of Congress with influence over particular issues.

In contrast, negotiated agreements with the British prime minister or the French president are much more readily enacted. In these countries, the policy process is less conducive to lobbying, and greater value is placed on direct relations between government representatives.

TABLE 24.1 **List of Foreign Nations and Territories that Have Hired Firms to Lobby, January–June 2008**

Afghanistan	Algeria	Angola	Aruba
Australia	Azerbaijan	Bahamas	Barbados
Benin	Bermuda	British Virgin Islands	Cameroon
Canada	Chad	China (PRC)	Colombia
Congo	Cote D'Ivoire (Ivory Coast)	Croatia	Cyprus
Djibouti	Dominica	Dominican Republic	Egypt
El Salvador	Equatorial Guinea	Ethiopia	Georgia
Ghana	Great Britain	Greece	Guyana
Iceland	India	Iran	Iraq
Isle of Man	Israel	Japan	Jordan
Kazakhstan	Korea, Republic of	Liberia	Libya
Liechtenstein	Macedonia	Malta	Marshall Islands
Mexico	Micronesia	Montenegro	Morocco
Nauru	Nigeria	Norway	Pakistan
Palau	Palestine	Panama	Peru
Philippines	Poland	Qatar	Romania
Russia	Sahrawi Arab Democratic Rep.	Saudi Arabia	Senegal
Serbia	Singapore	Somali Democratic Republic	Sri Lanka
Sudan	Taiwan	Tanzania	Thailand
Trinidad & Tobago	Turkey	Uganda	United Arab Emirates
Vanuatu	Venezuela	Vietnam	

SOURCE: U.S. Department of Justice, "Foreign Agents Registration Act Semi-Annual Report," June 2008.

Canadian province of Alberta sent an official representative to Washington to advocate on behalf of agricultural and energy interests that its government felt had not been effectively represented by the federal Canadian government.[8] In other countries, there is a high level of coordination between different government agencies and private sector representatives, especially from countries where industry and government are accustomed to coordinating through corporatist institutions.[9]

THE PLAYERS: DOMESTIC ALLIES AND OPPONENTS

Some foreign countries—Israel is one—enjoy the support of a large number of American citizens who will fight for what they see are that country's interests. FARA does not apply to these organizations because they are run entirely by American citizens (or permanent residents) with funds from domestic sources. Other countries have found their interests opposed by well-organized domestic constituency, such as the anti-Castro Cuban Americans and the International Campaign for Tibet, which lobbies for changes in China's policy in Tibet.

These interest groups are no different from other organizations of like-minded Americans. Prominent groups such as the American Israel Public Affairs Committee (AIPAC), American Hellenic Progressive Association (AHEPA), and Cuban American National Foundation are nonprofit advocacy groups that do not give money directly to any candidates. Other groups, including the U.S.-Cuba Democracy PAC and JStreetPAC (an organization that promotes Israeli-Palestinian peace negotiations), are formal political action committees that raise money to donate to candidates.

Because groups like AIPAC are periodically criticized for co-opting American foreign policy, it is important to differentiate between foreign lobbying and domestic groups that are active on foreign and defense issues. In the face of such criticism, these groups often go to great lengths to demonstrate their independence from the foreign government they support through their lobbying efforts.[10] This independence may actually lead the foreign government they support to oppose select lobbying efforts. In August 1992 Prime Minister Yitzhak Rabin publicly criticized AIPAC for taking strident positions on issues such as arm sales to Arab countries that Rabin felt adversely affected Israel's relationship with the George H. W. Bush administration.[11]

Most of the prominent groups active on foreign policy are organized and funded by American citizens, but a few groups have benefited from money and organizational support provided by the foreign government, especially in the critical formative stages of organizational life. In the late 1980s and early 1990s, Mexico hired several lobbyists to organize Latino interest groups, hoping that these groups would prove to be important allies when lobbying Congress to pass the North American Free Trade Agreement (NAFTA).[12] The apartheid-era South African government made a futile attempt to establish a group in America sympathetic to their policies in the 1970s. Because of restrictions on foreign campaign contributions, some foreign political

AIPAC AND THE ISRAEL LOBBIES

Jewish Americans established advocacy organizations shortly after major waves of Jewish immigrants came to America in the late nineteenth century. Notably, the American Jewish Committee was established in 1906 to advocate against violent anti-Semitism around the world and later expanded their mission to advocate on a broad range of domestic social issues. Shortly thereafter, Zionist groups like Hadassah, a Jewish women's membership organization, and the Zionist Organization of America (ZOA) formed to support the growing Jewish community in Palestine, which was under British control after World War I. Initially, these American Zionist groups were primarily concerned with material aid, but also engaged in advocacy.

Despite Israel's decision to align with the West in the early years after its independence in 1948, many in the Truman and Eisenhower administrations remained reluctant to become closely associated with the new state to avoid the hostility such association would cause in the Arab world. This stance prompted leaders of many of the largest Jewish communal organizations to establish an umbrella group called the Conference of Presidents of Major American Jewish Organizations to provide a unified voice for the community in relations with the White House and the Department of State in 1954. These efforts gained strength after the 1967 Six-Day War and successfully pushed U.S. foreign policy toward maintaining a close relationship with Israel. The most prominent group to emerge was the American Israel Public Affairs Committee (AIPAC), which became the most recognized voice for Americans supporting the Israeli government. Since then, several other pro-Israel advocacy organizations formed, including some whose views on Israel and its relations with the Palestinians and other countries in the Middle East differ from AIPAC's. All of these groups are financed by American contributors and therefore are not considered to be foreign lobbyists. Despite its acronym, AIPAC is not a political action committee, and it does not make donations to political campaigns.

The Center for Responsive Politics categorized between twenty-eight and thirty-seven political action committees as solely focused on pro-Israel lobbying in every election cycle since 1998. These PACs, including National PAC, the National Action Committee, and the Women's Alliance for Israel, regularly contribute between $2 million and $3.5 million dollars to campaigns each election cycle.

groups, such as the nationalist Viśva Hindu Parishad, will instead establish a presence in America in the form of a charitable organization prohibited from political activities.[13] These charities, however, may establish a community network that might provide the social and financial capital for lobbying.

Most domestic groups active in foreign policy tend to fall into three categories: ethnic, religious, or diasporan identity interest groups; trade and business interests; and ideological allies. The groups that get the most attention are the ones primarily made up of Americans with a strong bond to the foreign country or region. Dating back to before World War I, almost every major group of immigrants to the United States organized on issues of concern to their community, issues that often (but not exclusively) concerned American relations with their homeland.[14] Through groups such as AHEPA, Greek Americans have advocated for solving the dispute between Greece and Turkey over Cyprus. These groups have also engaged in grassroots efforts to build sympathy beyond their community for their policy goals. Pro-Israel lobbying groups often claim credit for the strong levels of support for Israel beyond members of the Jewish community.[15]

Foreign nations that do not enjoy the support of a large community of emigrants or co-religionists, such as Chile or the United Arab Emirates, have found lobbying Congress and efforts at public diplomacy to be extremely difficult and very expensive. Even more onerous is the task faced by countries like Azerbaijan and Saudi Arabia, whose lobbying efforts are actively opposed by interests whose size and strength dwarfs the influence of domestic Azerbaijani American or Saudi American groups. Both Azerbaijan and Saudi Arabia spend large amounts of money for lobbying and media relations support. According to the June 30, 2008, FARA report, Azerbaijan paid the Livingston Group, a firm led by former Republican representative Bob Livingston of Louisiana, $374,904 from August 1, 2007, to January 31, 2008. The Royal Embassy of Saudi Arabia paid Qorvis Communications $1,217,000 for the six-month period ending March 31, 2008, and the Loeffler Group and Hogan and Hartson about $300,000 during roughly the same period.

Countries like Azerbaijan and Saudi Arabia do enjoy some domestic allies despite the antagonism of domestic identity groups. And, although it is identity groups that get the most attention, trade and business interests dominate financial contributions and lobbying on foreign policy much as they do on domestic issues. Thanks to both countries' substantial petroleum deposits, Azerbaijan and Saudi Arabia have cultivated support from American oil industry interests. Previous attempts by Saudi Arabia to buy American weapons systems were aided by lobbyists from the corporations that would benefit from these sales.

On many issues that concern foreign governments at the congressional level, foreign entities can also rely on ideological allies rather than co-religionists or emigrants. Trade

CANADA: BUILDING A NETWORK

Some countries enjoy the active political support of American citizens with ancestral or business ties to their country, but most do not. Without a network of American voters to draw upon, getting access to members of Congress can be difficult. Although many Americans have some Canadian ancestry, and Canada is one of America's closest trading partners, there was no homegrown network of Canadian Americans and firms with interests in Canada. To address this deficiency, Canada began the multimillion dollar Enhanced Representation Initiative in 2003 to better inform and influence American decision makers.

As part of this initiative, Canada built a mailing list of Canadian expatriates in the United States and Americans with educational ties or business interests to Canada. This program, called Connect to Canada, uses the mailing list to distribute fact sheets and position statements on important issues and special events. The Web site also allows members to contact embassy staff people when they notice local media coverage of issues of concern to Canada that requires a response. With this information, the Canadian embassy has been developing a database so that when they do need to meet with legislators about trade and other business issues, they can identify which constituents of that member of Congress are most affected by a piece of legislation.

issues such as proposed free trade agreements with several Latin American countries and periodic renewals of China's most favored nation trading status have engaged business, industry, environmental, and union groups on both sides of the debate. Groups that actively opposed the Central America-Dominican Republic-United States Free Trade Agreement (CAFTA-DR) included the AFL-CIO, Public Citizen, and Sierra Club, and groups that historically favor free trade, such as the U.S. Chamber of Commerce, Business Roundtable, and Democratic Leadership Council, supported CAFTA-DR.

In addition to facing opposition on an issue-by-issue basis, foreign lobbying also must contend with general opposition to involvement by foreign governments in the federal policymaking process. At least one Web site, foreignlobbying.org, funded by the Sunlight Foundation and ProPublica, actively publicizes efforts by foreign countries to influence American policymakers through paid lobbying efforts. This Web site organizes FARA disclosures of foreign contracts into a database with information on reported contacts with members of Congress and executive branch officials. The database is accompanied by a set of links to publications by staffers from these groups. The articles and blog postings are explicitly or implicitly critical of paid foreign lobbying by detailing how these efforts lead to (or prevent) certain policy outcomes, how the public relations firms attempt to cast the client country in a positive light, and how much money is spent on lobbying relative to the country's per capita GDP. When ProPublica and Sunlight Foundation launched the site, they published an article highlighting how Bermuda successfully lobbied for a bill that would indirectly benefit Bermuda's reinsurance industry, Turkey's well-funded attempts to stop Congress from recognizing the killings of Armenians between 1915 and 1923 as genocide, and the multimillion dollar efforts of several African countries.[16]

FOREIGN LOBBYING STRATEGIES

The presence of permanent foreign missions in Washington creates advantages and disadvantages for lobbying. Although budget constraints are frequently an issue for many foreign missions, foreign diplomats never need to worry about the collective action problem faced by interest groups who must rely on selective benefits for members to sustain their efforts to lobby for collective benefits. Unlike permanent missions, interest groups must protect their organizations from competing groups, must worry about retaining key staffers, and ultimately face the prospect of insolvency. Embassy lobbying efforts must confront other challenges. Embassy staffers tend to be trained as general diplomats and are adept at traditional diplomacy, but may not have the skills or the interest to engage in lobbying or public diplomacy. Even after an embassy successfully engages in such efforts, regular turnover in mission staff often results in the embassy losing much of its Washington "know-how" and the personal connections that are necessary for successful lobbying. Despite hosting frequent receptions and parties to forge personal connections, foreign missions enjoy little leverage in persuading members of Congress. Emissaries complain that they enjoy little access to lawmakers and their staffs because priority is given to groups with "votes and/or money"—campaign contributions—two assets foreign missions lack.[17]

Foreign lobbies or their domestic allies have effectively persuaded many members of Congress to join congressional member organizations (CMOs) devoted to their country or region. Formally established in 1995, CMOs are generally bipartisan caucuses and working groups of members who ostensibly share an interest in a particular area. Because there are varying levels of activity and effectiveness, and participation does not guarantee support on important votes, joining relevant CMOs is a low-cost, low-effort

TABLE 24.2 **Top Five Foreign-Connected PACs, 2008**

PAC name	Industry	Country of origin	2008 contributions
Anheuser-Busch	Food and beverage	Belgium	$1,512,722
KPMG LLP	Accounting and consulting	Netherlands	1,206,766
UBS Americas	Financial services	Switzerland	825,000
GlaxoSmithKline	Pharmaceuticals	United Kingdom	793,420
BAE Systems	Defense and aerospace	United Kingdom	711,250

SOURCE: Center for Responsive Politics (opensecrets.org).

activity for many representatives.[18] In the 110th Congress, out of 278 official CMOs, more than 50 are obviously devoted to foreign policy issues, most on particular regions or countries (including several focusing on Israel), but also for issues like human trafficking and religious minorities in the Middle East.

Because these networks infrequently mobilize on their own accord, many embassies engage in many "outside" lobbying strategies.[19] Such strategies may include a wide range of promotional activities designed to foster goodwill among the American public toward their country or its policies.[20] These activities include funding for art, music, or film exhibitions; high-profile visits by foreign heads of state; media outreach efforts; and funding for American leaders to visit the foreign country.[21] Some promotional activities are undertaken by nonconsular groups established or supported (either partially or in full) by the foreign country. Examples of such groups include the Japan Foundation and Federation of Alliances Françaises USA.[22] Countries like Australia and Japan promote and fund study opportunities to American students and professors, and Canada makes grants available to researchers and universities who seek to do research about or in Canada.

These activities are rarely treated as forms of lobbying either by scholars or the Justice Department. But by engaging in such activities, foreign nations hope to promote a positive image for their country, indirectly aiding their efforts to maintain good political relations. Around the world, the United States engages in similar efforts at "public diplomacy" to further American interests indirectly by making foreign publics better informed and more understanding about the United States.[23] At least in theory, the United States is better able to promote its national interest if public opinion is favorably disposed toward it. The same logic applies as well if not more so to influencing policymaking in the United States.

MOTIVATIONS FOR FOREIGN LOBBYISTS

Given the international norms against active intervention in the domestic politics of foreign nations, foreign entities were slow to mount extensive lobbying campaigns in the United States. This reluctance began to evaporate in light of lobbying successes by domestic American groups seeking to influence foreign policy before the end of the Cold War. These successes include the rise of AIPAC since the late 1960s, the successes of business interests seeking to trade with China in the 1970s, and several high-profile political disputes in the 1980s, including the efforts of the Japanese government to build a positive image and maintain access to the American market, the fight over aiding rebels in Nicaragua and Angola, and even the ultimately unsuccessful attempts of South Africa to delay the imposition of sanctions.[24] The successes spawned domestic and foreign imitators who explicitly sought to copy the tactics of those who lobbied for close relations with Israel and China, especially the usefulness of mobilizing a domestic constituency on behalf of their interests.

These successes were especially notable because during the Cold War, foreign policies were largely cemented in place by overriding concerns about containment and deterrence, so there were not many attempts at changes in these policies.[25] The demise of the Soviet Union removed those constraints and made foreign policy less salient to the general public. In the first post–Cold War presidential campaign, Bill Clinton criticized President George H. W. Bush for focusing too much on foreign affairs.[26] For much of his tenure in office, Clinton focused on domestic policy initiatives. As a result, individual members of Congress, such as the leading Republican on the Senate Foreign Relations Committee, Sen. Jesse Helms, R-N.C., enjoyed far greater opportunities to determine the aims, goals, and implementation of foreign policy.

Increased congressional involvement in foreign affairs paralleled the post–Cold War rise in importance of foreign policy issues like trade, human rights, and the environment that overlap with domestic interests. Foreign policy issues have always overlapped with domestic concerns, but the overlaps have grown as a result of global economic integration, the expansion of communications technology, transboundary environmental issues, travel, terrorism, and other recent developments. These "intermestic" issues motivate many foreign interests to lobby the United States because the end of the Cold War has made the United States the most powerful and important global player, both militarily and economically.

The expansion of global trade and capital markets and the corresponding increase in the importance of intermestic issues have had a twofold effect. First, U.S. domestic policy has a greater impact on interests outside of the country. After the American real estate bubble burst in 2008, causing repercussions in almost every other economy around the world, few nations could afford to take a disinterested view of essentially "domestic" U.S. financial regulations. Likewise, consumer safety regulations in the United States affect manufacturers in China and elsewhere and may constitute nontariff barriers to trade if foreign manufacturers cannot meet American standards. Because these domestic policies have a direct impact on foreign business and the market is too large for many to ignore, foreign players have a growing incentive to try to shape these regulations. According to the Center for Responsive Politics' analysis of Congressional Records, nearly 1,000 clients lobbied Congress on trade issues. For many U.S. trading partners, much of the formal lobbying is carried out by corporations and trade organizations, not directly by their governments.

Second, executive agencies other than the State Department have begun to play significant roles outside of U.S. territory. Howard Wiarda's 2000 study of U.S. foreign policy toward Mexico offers one of the best illustrations of this phenomenon. Wiarda argues that the United States does not have one foreign policy toward Mexico; rather, it has dozens, one for every bureau, agency, or department active there.[27] The EPA focuses on environmental issues; money laundering is handled by the IRS, the Treasury Department, and the FBI. Before the establishment of the Department of Homeland Security, one agency, the Drug Enforcement Agency, was primarily responsible for combating illegal drugs coming across the border from Mexico, and a second, the Immigration and Naturalization Service, focused on immigration.

The overlap between policies is considerable (drugs and money laundering, for example), and in some cases the policies operate at cross-purposes. The number of players involved in shaping these policies is enormous, including not only the president, the top policymakers in the executive branch departments, and the relevant committees in Congress. Because many of the issues involved do not reach the threshold of congressional or presidential attention, however, lower-level bureaucrats often set policy and decide how to allocate resources. Empowering these officials creates more access points for lobbyists.

Another factor explaining lobbying efforts is geopolitical or ethnic rivalry. Describing domestic interest groups, Lester Milbrath observed that "nearly every vigorous push in one direction stimulates an opponent or coalition of opponents to push in the opposite direction."[28] On intermestic issues like trade or arms sales, if domestic opposition was engaged in high-profile lobbying, then foreign interests and their allies would likely need to respond or suffer certain defeat. Before NAFTA was implemented, domestic opponents, including many unions, began a fierce lobbying campaign, which spurred supporters tied to Mexican and Canadian interests.[29] The lobbying efforts on behalf of Israel by AIPAC prompted Saudi Arabia and Egypt, among others, to become involved in similar efforts. A more recent example is the relationship between Armenia, Turkey, and Azerbaijan. Lobbying efforts by Armenian Americans (led by the Armenian Assembly of America and the Armenian National Committee of America) successfully petitioned Congress in 2007 to pass a bill declaring the massacre of Armenians during World War I to be a genocide, despite White House opposition. Their efforts attracted almost 150 members of the House of Representatives to the Congressional Caucus on Armenian Issues. To counter the large domestic Armenian lobby, both Turkey and Azerbaijan lobbied the Bush White House and cultivated relationships with House members in the Congressional Caucus on Turkey and Turkish Americans and the Congressional Caucus on Azerbaijan. Azerbaijan's successful courting of the Bush White House enabled them to secure annual executive waivers from a congressional bill from the early 1990s that excluded Azerbaijan from receiving aid targeted to former Soviet republics.[30]

The threat of a trade sanction has also been a strong stimulus to lobbying activity, because of the danger to a foreign agent's interests. Such sanctions prompted apartheid South Africa to increase their lobbying efforts in the 1980s. More recently, Canada and others engaged in a flurry of lobbying to head off a "Buy American" provision in the economic stimulus bill under Barack Obama. A further illustration is the extensive lobbying campaign that was launched by Switzerland in 2009 in response to U.S. pressure to release banking information, coupled with threats of possible sanctions for failure to do so.[31] Members of the international community have, it appears, recognized that even if some American citizens are helped by trade sanctions, others are hurt by them. Under the threat of injury to their livelihoods, these Americans can be mobilized to oppose these policies even if they are not members of a cohesive identity group.

Dependence on the United States for the sale of arms or for foreign aid is another factor that explains lobbying activities. According to FARA, the largest recipients of aid as well as arms are among the most active lobbying states. No country can count on Congress renewing this aid in perpetuity given other budgetary pressures. The threat of losing American aid prompted the lobbying efforts on behalf of the newly installed government of Honduras described in the introduction. The largest recipient of U.S. military and humanitarian aid in the Western Hemisphere is Colombia, a controversial recipient because of its undistinguished human rights record. As a result, Colombia's lobbying and media relations efforts include staffers specifically assigned to human rights issues who communicate with often-critical NGOs.[32]

DETERMINANTS OF SUCCESS

Success of foreign lobbying, especially public diplomacy efforts, is very difficult to gauge, especially in terms of policy outcomes. In 1987 a subsidiary of Toshiba, a Japanese electronics company, sold advanced submarine technology to the Soviet Union in violation of American restrictions on the distribution of weapon technology. Even after Toshiba and the Japanese government waged an intensive lobbying and public relations campaign, both houses of Congress passed a bill that banned the subsidiary from exporting any products into the United States for three years and prevented the parent company from selling to the federal government for three years (worth about $200 million). This outcome would seem to be a lobbying failure. It could have been worse, however: the initial bill passed by the Senate banned all exports by the company for five years, and some legislators proposed a permanent ban. Instead, it was able to salvage its brand name and reputation to enable it to continue selling products directly to American consumer long after the Soviet Union ceased to exist.[33]

Evaluating the success of diplomatic efforts like Toshiba's often requires using counterfactuals: What would have been the penalty for Toshiba if the company (and the Japanese government) had not lobbied for a lighter penalty? The Senate demonstrated a willingness to impose much tougher sanctions, but President Ronald Reagan made it clear that he opposed any penalty that would endanger U.S.-Japanese relations and signaled that he would veto the original Senate bill if it passed the House. If the White House maintained its resolve in the face of strong public opinion favoring penalties, then Toshiba's efforts were largely unnecessary.

We asserted earlier that Hugo Chavez's attempts to improve attitudes toward Venezuela by providing discounted heating oil seem to have had little impact on influencing policymakers in Washington. From an alternative vantage point, however, the United States has not invaded Venezuela or funded groups intent on overthrowing Chavez's military regime, two actions the United States has historically taken toward unsympathetic leftist regimes in Latin and Central America.

Mohammed Ahrari, as well as Patrick Haney and Walt Vanderbush argue that lobbying by domestic identity groups is most successful when these efforts are congruent with government policy or national strategic interests. But Trevor Rubenzer found that such congruence was neither necessary nor sufficient and argues that such congruence may be the product of lobbying efforts, especially public diplomacy efforts, intended to convince public opinion or policymakers that these foreign interests are consistent with American national interests.[34]

The impact of such efforts at public diplomacy is especially difficult to gauge for three reasons. First, Americans do not have strong opinions one way or another about every country or the people within it, so polls about American attitudes toward, say, Paraguay, would be suspect. Second, when Americans do have a strong opinion about a country, such opinions can often be traced to intrinsic opinion sources, such as their religious beliefs.[35] This makes it especially difficult to attribute any changes in opinion toward a country to the particular messaging efforts engaged in by the foreign country, especially if the news about it is unfavorable at the same time. Third, drawing connections between these changes in public opinion and decisions by policymakers is tenuous, and decisions by policymakers may more often drive public opinion.[36]

Some efforts have been made to examine very specific causes and effects of public diplomacy. Robert Albritton and Jarol Manheim looked at the amount of coverage a country receives and whether such coverage is positive, and they found that nations that hired public relations firms saw improvements in both the amount of coverage they received and its tone.[37] Paul Brewer, Joseph Graf, and Lars Willnat found that showing an article about a nation to subjects in a laboratory shaped how those subjects viewed those foreign nations.[38] Vanderbush argued that policymakers in Washington gave exiles from Iraq and Cuba an inordinate amount of deference because they were presumed to be experts on their home country, helping these exiles win support for the invasion of Iraq and continuing (or extending) the embargo of Cuba.[39]

HUGO CHAVEZ'S PECULIAR PUBLIC DIPLOMACY

Under the current government of Hugo Chavez, Venezuela has had a tenuous relationship with the United States. Many Venezuelan business elites enjoy close ties and high-level contacts in the United States, but most are hostile to the Chavez government. In the absence of domestic allies in the United States through which to influence U.S. policy toward Venezuela, the Chavez government launched one of the more unusual attempts at public diplomacy. Through the oil and gas distributor CITGO, which the Venezuelan government owns, Venezuela sold heating oil at subsidized prices in low-income neighborhoods throughout the United States. Unfortunately for Chavez, this method of public diplomacy has not so far borne much fruit in ending U.S. hostility toward the Venezuelan regime.

CONCLUSION AND IMPLICATIONS

Foreign lobbying remains very controversial, despite the lack of strong evidence that it has much of an influence on policymaking. All interest group activity tends to raise concerns that special interests dominate government at the expense of the general interest of the public, but these concerns become even more emotional when discussing the efforts of foreign governments and their domestic allies. Critics fear that when foreign interests persuade the American government to choose a particular course of action, it means that government is favoring foreigners over its own citizens and may even be compromising America's national interests. These concerns are especially pronounced for foreign policy issues, especially relations with Israel or Cuba, which are very important to relatively small segments of the population that have established effective organizations to lobby for them. According to this view, opposing such groups is a near-silent majority. But when these lobbyists are clearly working on behalf of Americans exercising their rights as citizens to whom government is responsive (rightly or wrongly), there need not be any special discussion of the implications of these groups in a discussion about lobbying.[40]

If the policies are spurred by a foreign nation, then much of these concerns are mitigated by the separation of powers on foreign policy, as members of Congress are loath to support any concern that does not benefit some of their constituents. In a diverse nation, any policy is sure to create winners and losers. Whether more or fewer constituents would benefit as a result of some initiative is always difficult to ascertain, especially when identity politics is in play. Consider a proposed arms sale to Saudi Arabia. Such a sale would benefit American companies and their employees who directly profit from the sale. Those who think America should pay more attention to threats to the energy reserves controlled by Saudi Arabia would likely offer strong support to such an initiative. But such a sale would likely antagonize supporters of Israel and those who see Israel's security as consistent with America's national interest. Such arms sales would also be contrary to the interests of the domestic opposition to Saudi Arabia's authoritarian government and therefore to U.S. citizens concerned about the promotion of democracy and human rights. Both sides could plausibly claim to be advocating for America's strategic interests, and it is arguably impossible to conclude objectively that any of these groups' concerns would outweigh the gains in trade as a result of the sale.

In the case of Honduras, with which this chapter began, the lobbying efforts of the newly installed (and since replaced) government illuminate some of the problems with foreign lobbying. The ability of the narrow elites who supported Micheletti's government to access expensive public relations firms and well-connected lobbyists may have been able to overpower the poorer less-connected supporters of the overturned democratically elected government and thereby trump Washington's long-stated (but often half-heartedly pursued) policy of democracy promotion. Events in Iran and Nicaragua in 1979 are prominent reminders that Honduras would not have been the first time that efforts of democratic promotion conflicted with investment and trade interests endangered by the ascension of a hostile government. In such situations, American national interests are unclear and contested. Impeding democratization might be in the short-term interest of American business interests whose investments and trade interests will remain protected, but may ultimately result in friendly authoritarian governments being replaced by hostile revolutionary regimes. In short, both those who supported Roberto Micheletti and those who wished to restore Manuel Zelaya could argue that supporting their objectives would be consistent with the American national interests.

Commentators who believe that there is an objectively defined national interest prioritize that interest over any other without necessarily taking into account the size of a fungible interest or the relative salience of a concern. Especially since the end of the Cold War, however, it is doubtful whether anyone can ascertain America's objective national interest. America's foreign policy priorities, much like America's domestic policies, are hotly contested. As the lines between domestic and foreign interests have blurred, foreign countries and their domestic allies have increasingly joined the debate. Nonetheless, there is little evidence to suggest that such efforts decisively influence American policy.

NOTES

1. Ginger Thomson, "Honduran Rivals See U.S. Intervention as Crucial in Resolving Political Crisis," *New York Times*, July 12, 2009.

2. We define public diplomacy broadly as attempts to influence the attitudes of the public with respect to a foreign power. This would include efforts to promote cultural awareness through institutions such as the Alliance Français or the Goethe Haus, in the case of France and Germany, respectively.

3. U.S. Department of Justice, www.usdoj.gov/criminal/fara.

4. U.S. Department of Justice, www.usdoj.gov/criminal/fara/reports/June30-2008.pdf; The term, *nations and territories*, is used by the authors based on how the Department of Justice categorizes clients. The list of territories classified separately that are either not sovereign or not recognized by the United States include Palestine, the Sahrawi Arab Democratic Republic, Hong Kong, Tibet, several territories of the United Kingdom, the Netherlands Antilles, and Nagorno-Karabagh. Somewhat arbitrarily, organizations representing Gibraltar, Northern Cyprus, Kurdistan (or the Kurdish Regional

Government), Nagaland, and the Order of Malta are classified under Great Britain, Cyprus, Iraq, India, and Italy, respectively, as are separatist groups like Khalistan (India), Hmong Freedom League (Laos), and Sinn Fein (U.K., but classified as Ireland). The total of individual nations and territories also does not include at least three multinational organizational clients (Arab League, Caribbean Tourism Organization, and European Commission to the United States). From the original list, two separate listings were combined because they represented the same national unit (Serbia and Yugoslavia; and Great Britain and the United Kingdom).

5. Lobbying Disclosure Act of 1995, 2 U.S.C. § 1601.

6. Federal Election Commission, www.fec.gov/pages/brochures/foreign.shtml.

7. Michael Kunczik, *Images of Nations and International Public Relations* (Mahwah, N.J.: Lawrence Erlbaum and Associates, 1997); Jarol B. Manheim, *Strategic Public Diplomacy and American Foreign Policy: The Evolution of Influence* (New York: Oxford University Press, 1994).

8. Interview with Colin Robertson, June 30, 2009; and Government of Alberta International and Intergovernmental Relations, www.international.alberta.ca/553.cfm.

9. Mark Leonard, *Public Diplomacy* (London: Foreign Policy Centre, 2002); Seong-Hun Yun, "Toward Theory Building for Comparative Public Diplomacy from the Perspectives of Public Relations and International Relations: A Macro-Comparative Study of Embassies in Washington, D.C." (Ph.D. diss., University of Maryland, 2005).

10. Jason A. Kirk, "Indian-Americans and the U.S.-India Nuclear Agreement: Consolidation of an Ethnic Lobby?" *Foreign Policy Analysis* 4 (2008): 275–300.

11. David Horovitz, *Shalom, Friend: The Life and Legacy of Yitzhak Rabin* (New York: Newmarket Press, 1996).

12. Todd A. Eisenstadt, "The Rise of the Mexico Lobby in Washington: Even Further from God and Even Closer to the United States," in *Bridging the Border: Transforming Mexico-U.S. Relations*, ed. Rodolpho O. De la Garza and Jesus Velasco (Lanham, Md.: Rowman and Littlefield., 1997), 89–124.

13. Prema Kurien, "Who Speaks for Indian Americans? Religion, Ethnicity, and Political Formation," *American Quarterly* 59, 3 (September 2007):759–783, 1045.

14. Alexander DeConde, *Ethnicity, Race, and American Foreign Policy* (Cambridge: Harvard University Press, 1992); Yossi Shain, "Multicultural Foreign Policy," *Foreign Policy* 100 (Autumn 1995): 69–87.

15. Eric Uslaner, "American Interests in the Balance? Do Ethnic Groups Dominate Foreign Policy Making?" in *Interest Group Politics,* 7th ed., ed. Allan J. Cigler and Burdett Loomis (Washington, D.C.: CQ Press, 2007), 301–322.

16. Anupama Narayanswamy, Luke Rosiak, and Jennifer LaFleur, "Opening the Window on Foreign Lobbying," August 18, 2009, www.propublica.org/feature/opening-the-window-on-foreign-lobbying-718; Narayanswamy, Rosiak, and LaFleur, "Adding it Up: The Top Players in Foreign Agent Lobbying," August 18, 2009, www.propublica.org/feature/adding-it-up-the-top-players-in-foreign-agent-lobbying-718.

17. Interview with Colin Robertson, June 30, 2009.

18. James M. McCormick and Neil J. Mitchell, "Commitments, Transnational Interests, and Congress: Who Joins the Congressional Human Rights Caucus?" *Political Research Quarterly* 60, 4 (2007): 579–592.

19. Ken Kollman, *Outside Lobbying* (Princeton: Princeton University Press, 1998).

20. Evan Potter, *Branding Canada: Projecting Canada's Soft Power Through Public Diplomacy* (Montreal and Kingston: McGill-Queen's University Press, 2008); Yun, "Toward Theory Building for Comparative Public Diplomacy"; Jarol B. Manheim and Robert B. Albritton, "Changing National Images: International Public Relations and Media Agenda-Setting," *American Political Science Review* 78 (1984): 641–657.

21. Julie A. Corwin, "U.S.: Confirmation Row Shows Power of Diaspora Lobbies," *Radio Free Europe/Radio Liberty,* August 2, 2006; Jian Wang and Tsan-Kuo Chang, "Strategic Public Diplomacy and Local Press: How a High-Profile 'Head-Of-State' Visit Was Covered in America's Heartland," *Public Relations Review* 30, 1 (March 2004): 11–24.

22. Ronald J. Hrebenar, Valerie Ploumpis, and Clive S. Thomas, "What Happened to the Japanese Lobby in Washington? The Decline of the Japan Lobby and the Rise of the New China Lobby," in *Interest Group Politics,* ed. Allan J. Cigler and Burdett A. Loomis, (Washington, D.C.: CQ Press, 2007), 322–339.

23. Public Diplomacy Alumni Association, www.publicdiplomacy.org/1.htm.

24. Norman J. Ornstein, "Review: Lobbying for Fun and Policy," *Foreign Policy* 28 (Autumn 1977): 156–165; Tony Smith, *Foreign Attachments: The Power of Ethnic Groups in the Making of American Foreign Policy* (Cambridge: Harvard University Press, 2000).

25. Stephen A. Garrett, "Eastern European Ethnic Groups and American Foreign Policy," *Political Science Quarterly* 93, 2 (1978): 305–306.

26. Ernest J. Wilson III, "Interest Groups and Foreign Policymaking," in *The Interest Group Connection,* ed. Paul Herrnson, Ronald G. Shaiko, and Clyde Wilcox (Chatham, N.J.: Chatham House, 1998), 238–257.

27. Howard Wiarda, "Beyond the Pale: The Bureaucratic Politics of United States Policy in Mexico," *World Affairs* 162, 4 (Spring 2000).

28. Lester W. Milbrath, *The Washington Lobbyists* (Chicago: Rand-McNally, 1963).

29. Frederick W. Mayer, *Interpreting NAFTA* (New York: Columbia University Press, 1998).

30. Corwin, "U.S.: Confirmation Row."

31. Lynnley Browning, "UBS Digs in Its Heels on Clients' Names," *New York Times,* July 17, 2009.

32. Embassy Web site, colombiaemb.org/index.php?option=com_content&task=view&id=314&Itemid=181.

33. Jeffrey D. Hobbs, "Treachery by Any Other Name: A Case Study of the Toshiba Public Relations Crisis," *Management Communication Quarterly* 8, 3 (February 1995): 323–346.

34. Mohammed E. Ahrari, "Conclusions" in *Ethnic Groups and U.S. Foreign Policy,* ed. Mohammed E. Ahrari (New York: Greenwood Press, 1987); Patrick J. Haney and Walt Vanderbush, "The Role of Ethnic Interest Groups in U.S. Foreign Policy: The Case of the Cuban American National Foundation," *International Studies Quarterly* 43 (1999): 341–361; Trevor Rubenzer, "Ethnic Minority Interest Group Attributes and U.S. Foreign Policy Influence: A Qualitative Comparative Analysis," *Foreign Policy Analysis* 4 (2008): 169–185.

35. Jody C. Baumgartner, Peter Francia, and Jonathan S. Morris, "A Clash of Civilizations? The Influence of Religion on Public Opinion of U.S. Foreign Policy in the Middle East," *Political Research Quarterly* 61 (2008): 171–179; Corwin Smidt, "Religion and American Attitudes toward Islam and an Invasion of Iraq," *Sociology of Religion* 66 (2005): 243–261.

36. Robert B. Albritton and Jarol B. Manheim, "Public Relations Efforts for the Third World: Images in the News," *Journal of Communication* 35 (1985): 3–59.

37. Paul R. Brewer, Joseph Graf, and Lars Willnat, "Priming or Framing: Media Influence on Attitudes toward Foreign Countries,"

Gazette: The International Journal for Communication Studies 65, 6 (December 2003): 493–508.

38. Walt Vanderbush, "Exiles and the Marketing of U.S. Policy toward Cuba and Iraq," *Foreign Policy Analysis* 5 (2009): 287–306.

39. Lawrence R. Jacobs and Robert Y. Shapiro, *Politicians Don't Pander: Political Manipulation and the Loss of Democratic Responsiveness* (Chicago: University of Chicago Press, 2000); Richard Sobel, *The Impact of Public Opinion on U.S. Foreign Policy since Vietnam: Constraining the Colossus* (New York : Oxford University Press, 2001); but see Jason A. Kirk, "Indian-Americans and the U.S.–India Nuclear Agreement: Consolidation of an Ethnic Lobby?" *Foreign Policy Analysis* 4 (2008): 275–300.

40. James M. Lindsay, "Getting Uncle Sam's Ear: Will Ethnic Lobbies Cramp America's Foreign Policy Style?" *Brookings Review* (Winter 2002): 37–40.

SUGGESTED READING

DeConde, Alexander. *Ethnicity, Race, and American Foreign Policy.* Cambridge: Harvard University Press, 1992.

Kirk, Jason A. Indian-Americans and the U.S.-India Nuclear Agreement: Consolidation of an Ethnic Lobby? *Foreign Policy Analysis* 4 (2008): 275–300.

Landy, Marc. "Zealous Realism: Comments on Mearsheimer and Walt." *The Forum* 4, 1 (2006).

Lindsay, James M. "Getting Uncle Sam's Ear: Will Ethnic Lobbies Cramp America's Foreign Policy Style?" *Brookings Review* (Winter 2002): 37–40.

Manheim, Jarol B., and Robert B. Albritton. "Changing National Images: International Public Relations and Media Agenda-Setting." *American Political Science Review* 78 (1984): 641–657.

Mathias, Charles McC., Jr. "Ethnic Groups and Foreign Policy." *Foreign Affairs* 59, 5 (Summer 1991): 975–998.

Mayer, Frederick W. *Interpreting NAFTA.* New York: Columbia University Press, 1998.

Richardson, Jeremy. "Government, Interest Groups and Policy Change." *Political Studies* 48, 5 (2000): 1006–25.

Risse-Kappen, Thomas. "Public Opinion, Domestic Structure, and Foreign Policy in Liberal Democracies." *World Politics* 43, 4 (July 1991): 479–512.

Smith, Tony. *Foreign Attachments: The Power of Ethnic Groups in the Making of American Foreign Policy.* Cambridge: Harvard University Press, 2000.

Wilson, Ernest J. III. "Interest Groups and Foreign Policymaking." In *The Interest Group Connection.* Ed. Paul Herrnson, Ronald G. Shaiko, and Clyde Wilcox. Chatham, N.J.: Chatham House, 238–257.

PART V ★ INTEREST GROUPS AND LOBBYING: TACTICS, TECHNIQUES, AND REGULATION

CHAPTER 25	Lobbying and Legislation Strategy	335
CHAPTER 26	Lobbyists: Who Are They? What Do They Do?	347
CHAPTER 27	Lobbying: Techniques and Impact	359
CHAPTER 28	Grassroots, Astroturf, and Internet Lobbying	371
CHAPTER 29	The First Amendment and the Regulation of Lobbying	381

chapter 25

Lobbying and Legislative Strategy

by Katharine W. V. Bradley and Richard L Hall

LOBBYISTS ARE NOT WELL REGARDED by the American public. In a 2006 CBS News/*New York Times* poll, 77 percent of registered voters said that lobbyists bribing legislators is just "the way things work in Congress," and 57 percent believed that "at least half of all members of Congress accept bribes or gifts that influence their votes."[1] These are astonishing numbers, not only for the consensus they reflect but also for the reality they misrepresent. To be sure, lobbyists are important players in shaping the large and small policy decisions that find their way onto the congressional agenda, but vote-buying is rarely the mechanism used to influence legislation. This chapter explores the mechanisms that are used.[2] What rules must lobbyists follow? What resources do they bring to bear in pursuing the goals of the groups they represent? What strategies do they employ and with what effect? Do resource-rich interests get over-represented and, if so, to what degree?

LOBBYING CONGRESS: FOLLOWING THE RULES

That lobbyists are rarely agents of outright corruption does not mean that lobbying is ethically unproblematic. Indeed, the ethical principles that govern the lobbyist-legislator relationship have changed considerably over the last two decades and remain the subject of serious debate. Each chamber has imposed on itself detailed rules that constrain the exchanges between lobbyists and their clients on the one hand and legislators and their staffs on the other.

The most significant of these rules were adopted by Congress with the Lobbying Disclosure Act of 1995 and the amendments to that act in 2007.[3] Taken together, these reforms created more precise and more inclusive definitions of persons required to register as lobbyists; strict and enforceable requirements regarding disclosure, including the filing of quarterly reports on lobbying activity and expenditures; and requirements regarding disclosure of campaign contributions and the "bundling" of contributions.[4] Perhaps most significant were the strict limitations on the gifts, services, and reimbursements that registered lobbyists can provide to members or their staff. Prior to 2007 only gifts up to $50 were permitted under Senate rules, but significant loopholes existed for travel, meals, and other benefits connected to a member's official duties. The abuse of these loopholes was highlighted by a 2005 scandal involving lobbyist Jack Abramoff, who sought legislative favors for his clients by providing members of Congress and their staff with vacations, skyboxes at sporting events, and dinners at *Signatures*, Abramoff's own high-end restaurant in Washington, D.C. Congress responded to the scandal by effectively prohibiting all gifts from lobbyists and imposing strict limits on the provision of, or reimbursement for, travel, food, or lodging expenses for a member or her staff by interest groups, even if connected to a legislator's official duties. Limitations on meals are sufficiently strict that a member or her staff can eat finger foods at an organization's reception but cannot accept a paid sit-down meal.

The value of these reforms is not that they prevent members of Congress from selling their integrity for an occasional dinner or weekend getaway, however. Rather, the rules limit the much greater *access* that a group's lobbyist receives by virtue of buying a legislator dinner or accompanying him on a trip. Access—the opportunity to meet with, talk to, exchange messages with, or assist a legislator and his staff—is a precondition for influencing legislation; it is therefore something that lobbyists covet when they lack it and nurture when they have it. The rules explicitly recognize the ethical implications of lobbyist-provided dinners and travel as a means of gaining access. Senate rules prohibit a private organization or its lobbyists from paying for a trip that was "planned, organized, or arranged by or at the request of a lobbyist," or when the lobbyist accompanies the member on "any segment" of an otherwise permissible one-day event, or if a lobbyist accompanies the member "at any point" of any other trip.[5] The House of Representatives created even stricter regulations on paid travel and the use of noncommercial carriers by members and staff.[6]

Campaign Contribution Rules

The most widely reported and allegedly unethical interactions between lobbyists and legislators concern campaign contributions, which are regulated under the Federal Election Campaign Act (FECA) adopted in 1974 and most recently revised in 2002. No public campaign finance system exists for congressional elections, so incumbents and challengers must rely on private donations to finance their increasingly expensive campaigns. Corporations and labor unions are prohibited from contributing directly to legislators' campaigns, but they can create and organize political action committees (PACs). The PAC raises funds from the organization's members or employees, deposits them in a fund that is segregated from other organizational resources, and allocates those funds to candidates. An organization's lobbyists often play important roles in distributing PAC contributions to particular candidates, and, as noted below, campaign contributions are widely thought to be important instruments of lobbyist influence in the legislative process.

PAC contributions to federal candidates are restricted to $10,000 per election cycle ($5,000 for the primary election; $5,000 for general election). Those limits have not been adjusted since first enacted in the 1974 FECA, however, so the $10,000 maximum today is worth less than half of what it was in 1974 dollars. And as a fraction of an average campaign, the maximum gift is greatly diluted. The average cost of a 1974 reelection campaign for the U.S. House was about $50,000; for a Senate reelection campaign, it was about $500,000. In 2008 the average for the House was $1.34 million—a twenty-five-fold increase; in 2008 the average for the Senate was $7.8 million—a fifteen-fold increase. PACs still provide a nontrivial share of congressional campaign funds—about a fifth of the money raised by Senate candidates and about a third of the money raised by House candidates in 2008—but that share will almost certainly decline given the increase in individual contribution limits.

The Price of Advocacy

If PAC money has become less significant in congressional campaigns, the same cannot be said of the money that interest groups spend on direct lobbying. That amount is large and growing larger. Because of the 1995 Lobbying Disclosure Act, we now have some idea of just how much is being spent.[7] The adoption of stricter regulations on lobbying apparently has not diminished the degree to which interest groups engage in it. As Figure 25.1 shows, for the 111th Congress, lobbying expenditures totaled $7 billion. That is more than double the lobby expenditures only a decade earlier. Interest groups spent more on lobbying than they contributed to all federal candidates combined. In

FIGURE 25.1 **Lobbying Expenditures at the Federal Level, 1998–2010**

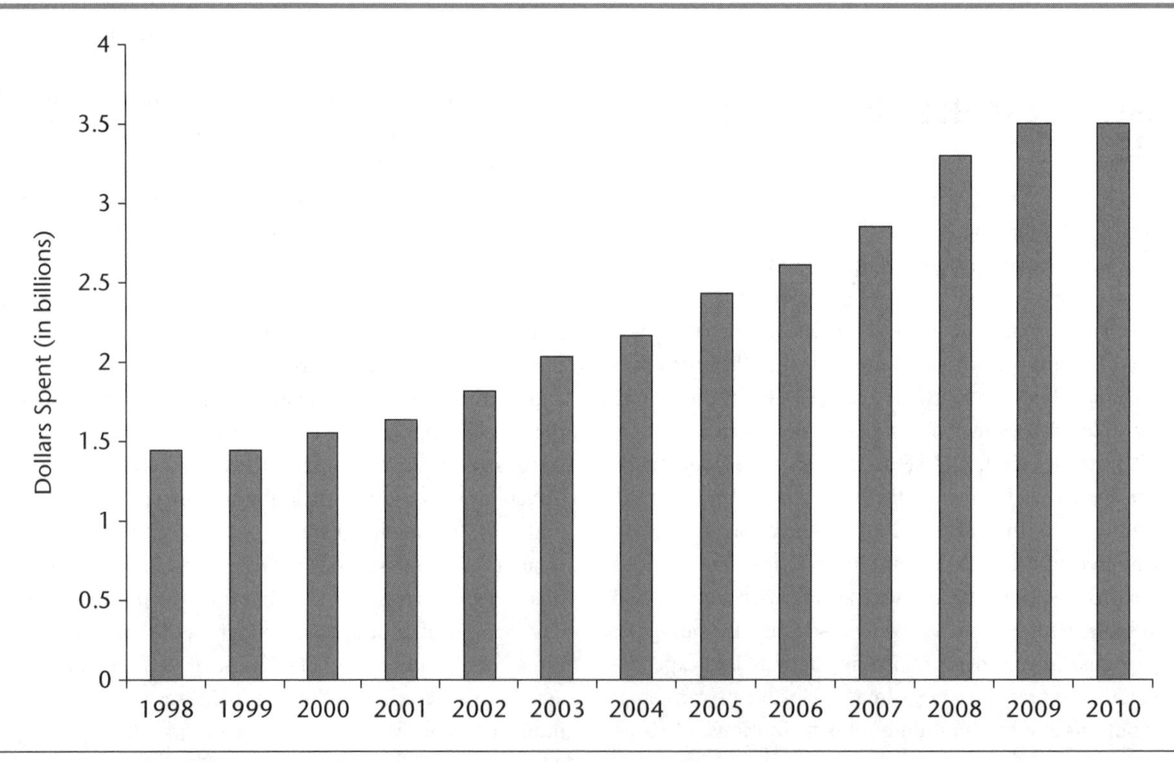

SOURCE: Based on data provided by the Center for Responsive Politics (opensecrets.org).

2007–2008 they did so by a factor of fifteen to one. In 2009 federal lobbying expenditures set yet another new record, rising by more than 8 percent to $3.5 billion.

Even on issues likely to be salient among voters, the ratio of lobbying expenditures to campaign contributions remains high. The 2003 Medicare prescription drug legislation provides a good illustration. The bill heavily subsidized private prescription drug insurance for Medicare recipients while prohibiting the federal government from negotiating discounted drug prices with pharmaceutical companies. It therefore promised revenue windfalls for the pharmaceutical and insurance industries, which together spent $240 million on direct lobbying in that one year, while contributing a far lower (but still substantial) $18 million to campaigns in the prior two-year cycle. These lobbying expenditures, moreover, are almost certainly underreported, in that they do not necessarily include all of the substantial expenditures that interest groups make on issue advertising, policy research, and related activities used to support their inside lobbying efforts.

The variation in lobbying expenditures across groups active on similar issues is often striking, as the Medicare prescription drug bill illustrates. For the year in which Congress considered this legislation, six of the top twenty organizations in annual lobbying expenditures were organizations whose primary focus was passing the bill. Together they spent more than $90 million, and no group opposed to the bill ranked in the top twenty. The anti-Medicare D group that spent the most was the AFL-CIO, which in that Congress lobbied on some two-dozen issues other than the prescription drug bill and still spent only a fourth as much on lobbying as PhRMA, the pharmaceutical trade association.

THE PRACTICE OF LOBBYING

As ethics reformers have learned, lobbying is not easy to define (see Chapter 27). Lobbyists themselves are not good at doing so. Their tendency is to define lobbying as whatever it is that people we call lobbyists do. This is not terribly helpful. Lobbyists engage in a multitude of specific activities, but reproducing them in a list does not illuminate the mechanisms by which lobbyists influence legislators. We want to know what is central, not incidental, to their work.

Lobbying is best defined as a class of strategies for influencing the decisions of legislators. It can have two alternative purposes: (1) to change legislators' positions or keep them from being changed, and (2) to mobilize legislative allies or demobilize legislative opponents. Lobbyists have several means by which they might accomplish those objectives. We focus on each of three instruments of their influence: money, information, and constituency pressure.

Lobbying and Campaign Contributions

Judging from the polling data cited in the introduction, the public believes that lobbying works through the negotiation of some mutually beneficial deals between legislators and special interests. The survey questions presuppose that unscrupulous lobbyists are out to buy legislators' votes and unprincipled legislators are out to make money. This is a decidedly cynical view, at least partly explained by the fact that the polling occurred during the media uproar over the

Rep. Randy Cunningham (R-Calif) admitted to taking over two million dollars worth of goods and cash in exchange for using his seat on the Appropriations Committee for the benefit of defense contractors. He resigned in December 2005 and was sentenced to over eight years in prison.

Jack Abramoff scandal (which eventually did implicate three or four members of Congress). But something close to this view is evident both in the reports of investigative journalists and the systematic research of political scientists. Lobbyists care about legislation; legislators care about reelection. The former give the latter contributions to aid reelection campaigns, the latter promise the former favorable votes. No legislator changes sides on something clearly against her ideology or injurious to her constituents, but she leans toward contributors when she can.

The claim that lobbyists use campaign contributions to buy legislators' votes, it turns out, rests on evidence that can best be described as mixed. Journalists and good government groups that make this assertion too often confuse correlation and causation.[8] If a member of Congress receives PAC contributions from a group and consistently votes in favor of policies preferred by that group, it could be that the member's votes have been bought. But it is far more likely that groups contribute to the campaigns of members they want to see (re)elected, namely, those who vote in ways that the interest group likes.

In fact, PAC managers often say that they do this, and PAC contribution patterns in many policy areas bear it out.[9] As Table 25.1 illustrates, if the two parties have distinct positions on issues that a group cares about, its PAC will favor heavily the sympathetic party's candidates. Labor union and environmental PACs give almost exclusively to sympathetic Democrats, while business associations and oil industry groups give mostly to Republicans. On issues of individual rights, anti-abortion PACs and gun rights groups give predominantly to religious Right Republicans, and gun control and pro-choice groups give to Democrats at rates greater than ten to one. Indeed, many of these PACs would have a hard time raising funds from their organization's members if they gave much of their money to legislators indifferent or opposed to the organization's mission.

Not all PACs exhibit this pattern, however. Indeed, most private sector PACs, such as those involving health professionals, insurance, or transportation, give fairly evenly to the two parties. Contrary to popular belief, however, very rarely does a PAC try to "hedge its bets" by giving to both parties' candidates in a single race.

In light of these patterns, numerous social science studies have examined the connection between campaign contributions and legislators' roll call votes, applying sophisticated methods to disentangle cause and effect. One well-designed study of the farm lobby found that donations from agricultural PACs increased when major agriculture bills came to the floor and that campaign contributions given both before and after floor action influenced members' votes.[10] But this study is one of the few methodologically sound studies that support the vote-buying hypothesis. One of the most comprehensive and compelling studies to date found that PAC donations have no discernible effect on congressional voting decisions.[11] In a review of forty studies of the relationship between PAC contributions and congressional votes, likewise, Stephen Ansolabehere and colleagues concluded that "the evidence that campaign contributions lead to a substantial influence on votes is rather thin," adding that "contributions explain a minuscule fraction of the variation in voting behavior in the U.S. Congress."[12]

TABLE 25.1 **PAC Contributions to Party Candidates, 2008 Election Cycle**

Issue category	Percentage to Democrats	Percentage to Republicans
Labor unions	91%	9%
Business associations	21	71
Abortion policy, pro-choice	90	10
Abortion policy, pro-life	2	98
Gun control	94	6
Gun rights	20	80
Environment	87	13
Oil and gas	25	75

SOURCE: Data reported by the Center for Responsive Politics (opensecrets.org).

There are good reasons why we should not be surprised by money having a weak effect on roll call votes, the cynic's charges notwithstanding. Members' votes are typically over-determined: the influence of party, constituency, and ideology usually point a member in the same direction, making it hard for even large PAC contributions to make much difference. And, as we noted above, the value of even the maximum PAC contribution is tiny relative to the size of today's campaigns, and only 6 percent or 7 percent of all PAC contributions reach that maximum. If votes can be bought so cheaply, groups should be raising and giving more money to more members.

That does not end the matter of money's influence, however. The view that lobbying works through exchange has also been used to explain why legislators become active on particular issues that come before their committees. Interest groups make campaign contributions to buy the time or effort of legislators on issues that groups care about, but they do so selectively. Only their allies, those biased in their favor, will they want to "mobilize." Using statistical techniques similar to those used in the analysis of vote-buying, one study found that PAC donations to supportive legislators induce those legislators to participate more actively in promoting the policy favored by their contributors.[13] That same study also identified a weak "demobilization effect"; in other words, campaign contributions to unsympathetic legislators led them to work less vigorously against their contributors' interests. There is, however, no similar evidence that campaign contributions induce members of Congress to engage in legislative "entrepreneurship," which involves high levels of effort to push a policy initiative onto the congressional agenda and move it through the process.[14]

In summary, the popular view that legislators are regularly bought off by big campaign contributors exaggerates a slim body of evidence. Even when PAC money influences legislators' votes, moreover, it does not necessarily mean that it buys them. PAC contributions may simply signal the legislator that the group agrees with his or her policies, so that the member can more confidently rely on information the group provides.

Information as Persuasion

A second and more important mechanism of lobbyist influence is the provision of information. Lobbyists use information in several different ways. One of these is persuasion, defined as the use of information to change legislators' preferences over policies. Indeed, one of the most prominent scholars on the subject of lobbying, John R. Wright, defines lobbyists' influence almost exclusively in these terms:

> Ultimately, interest groups hope to determine legislators' policy stands, but . . . to do so they must first manipulate the beliefs that determine legislators' policy preferences and their perceptions of the electoral implications of the positions they take. The purpose of a lobbying message is to introduce information that will alter or affect these beliefs. The point at which access ends and influence begins is the point at which legislators adjust their beliefs on the basis of lobbying information.[15]

Wright's emphasis on the persuasive power of information is well placed.[16] Legislators must take a position on scores of complex policy issues, and they cannot possibly know very much about most of these issues. As a result, their decisions about which proposals to support are often subject to considerable uncertainty. Is this policy consistent with my primary goals and values? Will the policy be effective? At what cost? With what unintended consequences? In answering these questions, legislators turn to a number of different sources, including party leaders and colleagues, but interest groups are often well positioned to provide such information. Relative to legislators, lobbyists are specialists. They traffic in facts, arguments, and expertise with respect to that subset of policies that affect their organization, industry, or client. The largest lobbying operations commission their own policy analysis, hire consultants, or pull individuals with relevant expertise from their organization's ranks. In their 2008 lobbying disclosure reports, PhRMA listed thirty-two in-house lobbyists and payments to forty-six lobbying, media, and political consulting firms.[17] Likewise, the nonprofit public interest group Natural Resources Defense Counsel boasts more than 100 experts as program staff covering every possible environmental issue.

More important than policy expertise is the political information that lobbyists can provide—information about the "electoral implications of the positions they take," as Wright puts it. Students of Congress have long observed that members of Congress feel "unsafe at any margin."[18] They go to great lengths to reduce political vulnerability by minimizing the downside risk of a particular vote. Interest groups often reduce risks by providing legislators with information about voter preferences that the legislator does not have. Indeed, John Mark Hansen argues that political information is the key to interest group influence.[19] Because legislators operate under a great deal of uncertainty, "Interest groups offer to help. In exchange for serious consideration of their policy views, they provide political counsel for members of Congress. They offer political intelligence about the preferences of congressional constituents, and they provide political propaganda about the performances of congressional representatives."[20] To the extent that groups have significant memberships within particular states or districts, they have a comparative advantage in generating credible information about the issues to which those constituents are paying attention.

One way that groups provide information about constituent preferences is by holding "lobby days" or constituent "fly-ins," whereby rank-and-file members of the group that reside in particular members' districts are brought to Washington, D.C., given a scripted message, and sent to prearranged meetings with their respective representatives or senators. A closely related tactic is for the lobbyist to accompany "superconstituents"—prominent business people or local officials who may be opinion leaders back in the district—to meetings with a member of Congress or his or her staff. This tactic was especially effective in lobbying for repeal of the estate tax during the George W. Bush administration. Lobbyists for small business owners and conservative groups promoting repeal brought to Washington individuals whose family businesses were in danger of being sold off to pay the estate tax.[21]

Persuasion and Counteractive Lobbying

The view that lobbying works through persuasion has at least one important implication: lobbyists should concentrate their efforts on legislators not already firmly committed to a particular position. This same implication follows if lobbyists are looking to buy votes. The cheapest votes will come from legislators whose positions need to move only a short distance from nay to yea or vice versa.

We have already observed, however, that interest group PACs give heavily to their allies, not to those legislators likely to be on the fence when an issue of concern to the group comes to the floor. The same pattern holds for lobbying—lobbyists primarily lobby legislators who already agree with them. Raymond Bauer, Ithiel de Sola Pool, and Lewis Dexter reported this tendency in their classic 1963 study of business lobbying on trade policy.[22] Lobbyists target those "who will give them the best reception," such that "direct persuasion of uncommitted or opposed congressmen was a minor activity."[23] Recent studies have uncovered similar patterns. The number of contacts between lobbyists and their already committed allies far exceeds lobbyists' contacts with undecided legislators, by large margins.[24] This pattern is borne out in survey data collected from interest group advocates who lobbied on the legislation to provide prescription drug coverage for Medicare recipients at a projected ten-year cost of $400 billion. The data in Figure 25.2 show the number of contacts that lobbyists reported having with the offices of all 100 senators during the ten-month consideration of the bill. On average, lobbyists met two to three times with opponents and fence-sitters, but they met almost three times as often—almost eight contacts on average—with legislators they considered firm allies.

If lobbying is solely or primarily a strategy of persuasion, this behavior is puzzling indeed. Why would highly paid, savvy political strategists waste their time trying to convert the already converted? The simple answer is that lobbying involves much more than attempts to win new supporters. One purpose is to keep current allies from changing their positions. Therefore, they lobby their soft allies when opposing lobbyists target them and try to pull them over to their side. David Austen-Smith and John Wright call this technique "counteractive lobbying."[25] The lobbyist provides additional or more credible information to nullify claims made by opposing lobbyists looking to pick up a few votes. Counteractive lobbying occurs in the competition for votes in the days leading up to a floor roll call. It should be especially vigorous when crucial votes are likely to be close.

FIGURE 25.2 **Lobbying Allies in the U.S. Senate: The Medicare Prescription Drug Bill of 2003**

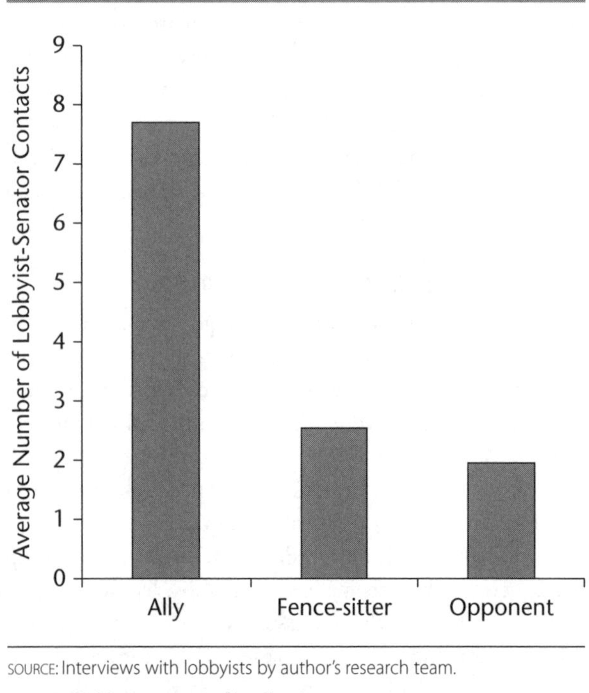

SOURCE: Interviews with lobbyists by author's research team.

NOTE: N of lobbyists = 29; N of legislators = 100.

INFORMATION AND FRAMING

Providing credible information about a bill's policy or political implications is one important way that lobbyists make persuasive appeals. Another strategy—less often effective but potentially powerful—is to define or redefine an issue in a distinctive way. Students of political communication call it "framing." Framing is a rhetorical strategy that selects some attribute or dimension of a policy and makes it salient in the thinking of others.[26] It is less an argument about a policy's consequences than an argument about what the policy is about, which in turn implies which consequences the legislator should care about. Lobbyists pay considerable attention to framing their arguments in ways that have persuasive effects.[27]

The debate over health care reform in the 2008 presidential campaign and in the first year of the Obama administration addressed the best means to extend health insurance coverage to the 40 million citizens without it. Insofar as the initiative was understood as a proposal for universal coverage, large majorities of Americans were supportive. Opponents therefore sought to reframe the debate. They did so by focusing on two aspects of the bill, exaggerating their implications in ways that rendered them salient to many voters. The first was a frame that opponents had used effectively for almost a century.[28] The Obama plan for government to subsidize private insurance was recast as a proposal for "socialized medicine" and the rationing of health care, both of which are unacceptable to the general public.[29] The second frame focused on otherwise obscure provisions regarding end-of-life care counseling, recasting them as attempts to establish "death panels" that would encourage euthanasia for the severely disabled and elderly.[30] In both cases, salience was elevated by appeals to citizens' fears, an especially effective emotional appeal when the goal is to persuade individuals to reconsider their beliefs.[31] As long as these two redefinitions of the debate captivated the public, the prospects for reform faltered. For legislators who wanted to oppose reform on other grounds, the reframing gave them political cover for taking a position too unpopular to adopt without an explanation considered plausible by their constituents.

It is not easy to change the terms of a policy debate, however. In their recent book, Frank Baumgartner and his colleagues report that only four policy issues of the ninety-eight studied were partially or completely reframed during the period of study. The effectiveness of any framing strategy is subject to several limiting factors, including competition among different frames. Several studies of framing show that competing frames at least partially cancel each other's effects.[32] Another limiting factor is whether an issue exhibits "ripeness" or urgency; if it does not, efforts to frame or reframe an issue tend to be ineffective.[33]

Persuasion in its several forms cannot fully explain the extensive contacts that lobbyists have with their most committed allies, however. Such legislators do not need to be lobbied regarding how they should vote. And they are not good targets for lobbying by the opposing side. So why do lobbyists spend so much time with them?

The answer lies in the distinction, discussed above, between members' positions and their priorities. Lobbyists' main purpose in lobbying their allies is mobilization, not persuasion. They want legislative allies to be active on the issue their group cares about, not some other matter about which the member or her constituents (or some other group) might care. The main mechanism by which lobbyists get their allies to become active, however, is not the financial inducements they can offer through contributions to members' campaigns. Rather, they provide legislative assistance. Lobbyists "subsidize" the legislative work of their congressional allies, enabling them to promote (or obstruct) progress on a measure that both lobbyist and legislator support (or oppose).[34]

Providing information is the principal form of this assistance. A "subsidy" in this context refers to the time and effort that a lobbyist saves the legislator and his staff. The lobbyist acquires and assimilates complex policy information and helps the like-minded legislator with the labor-intensive work of turning information into press releases, talking points, speeches, and politically relevant arguments. One congressional staff member made this point while discussing a bill that would become part of the House health care reform proposal in 2009:

> On these issues we agree completely with [this organization]. . . . So [their lobbyist] is writing the section by section summaries of the bill, the fact sheet, and the dear colleague letter. I'm just going to edit them a little, put them in my boss's voice, and a lot of the work will be done. . . . We couldn't get this thing put together without [this] help. He's [also] the guy I'm frantically emailing in the middle of the meeting to get information for my boss. [He gives] 30 second turnaround almost all day long on all questions. Of course it only has to do with the [issues of interest to] his organization.[35]

In addition to providing policy information, lobbyists also engage in political intelligence-gathering: they keep track of a bill's progress and provide headcounts to their allies who need such information in planning a floor strategy.[36] In fact, many of the contacts that lobbyists have with both allies and nonallies is not so much about giving information as getting it. Wright captures this part of the lobbyist's job:

> In the normal course of establishing and maintaining access to legislators, [lobbyists] may learn about the scheduling of hearings, markups, floor debates, and votes; procedural strategies that committee or subcommittee chairmen will employ in markup sessions; positions that legislators have taken or are thinking about taking; and amendments that other legislators or groups might offer. . . . [Such knowledge] . . . is an important resource that can be used to shape perceptions about the viability of various policy options.[37]

The practice of subsidizing the time and information costs of an office does not appear to have changed in the last half century. In classic studies published in the 1960s, Bauer, Pool, and Dexter and Lester Milbrath found that lobbyists mainly served as "adjuncts to staff."[38] Assuming that influencing legislators occurred only through persuasion, however, they incorrectly concluded from these patterns that lobbyists were wasting their time. Supporting the efforts of allies is rarely a waste of time; instead, the reverse is closer to the truth. "A good lobbyist is simply an extension of a congressional member's staff," one lobbyist observed. "If they want information and they trust you, they'll call *you* for information."[39]

In sum, providing information is an important means for persuading members to change their positions or for keeping those positions from being changed, but it can also affect how active legislators will be. That lobbyists spend most of their time lobbying their allies suggests that their influence more often works through the latter mechanism than the former.

OUTSIDE PRESSURE AND INSIDE LOBBYING

Grassroots advocacy—what Ken Kollman refers to as "outside lobbying"—is a time-honored instrument for enhancing the effectiveness of inside lobbying.[40] Outside lobbying consists of attempts to mobilize citizens to pressure their representatives to support the group-preferred policy. Letters, e-mail, phone calls, participation at a legislator's town hall meetings, even protests in front of a representative's office, count as outside lobbying activities. Interest groups can provoke such behavior through membership networks, by generating attention to their issue in the media, and through paid issue advertisements.

Outside lobbying works through two specific processes, both of which have implications for its inside effects.[41] Kollman labels the first one signaling. By generating phone calls or mail to a congressional office, a group effectively signals a legislator that attentive citizens in her state or district hold views consistent with the group's. In this way, outside lobbying can facilitate the representation of the member's constituents, or at least some subset of them. A second, related process is conflict expansion, whereby interest groups increase the salience or importance of the issue to constituents. The impact of outside lobbying, Kollman demonstrates, depends on both. Even if it were easy to show that voters agree with the policy favored by the group, it is usually difficult to establish that the member's behavior on this issue will weigh heavily in voters' minds the next time they go to the polls. Public support for health reform as a general goal was consistently high throughout the first year of the Obama administration, but groups supporting the administration's efforts had trouble demonstrating that large segments of the voting population would punish their representatives for failing to back the Democrats' particular plan.

Like information, outside lobbying can affect both the positions members take and how legislatively active they will be. For example, groups might target their outside lobbying in a way that puts pressure on legislators who are undecided. "With grassroots tactics being used in pursuit of a legislative objective, it is the middle that matters," Ken Goldstein argues. "Lobbyists should target undecided legislators."[42] Although somewhat unusual, grassroots efforts can also pressure a member to reverse his position entirely. The ire of senior citizens was arguably instrumental in changing the position of many legislators on the Medicare Catastrophic Coverage Act in 1989. After enactment in 1988, the insurance premium costs and the efforts of interest groups to mobilize seniors caused a groundswell of opposition. In one instance, this opposition manifested in an angry mob surrounding the Ways and Means Committee chairman, Dan Rostenkowski, a longtime supporter of the act, in his home district in Chicago. The image of senior citizens pounding on the chairman's car became a symbol of the power of grassroots activism and the electoral importance of Medicare. The act was repealed sixteen months later.[43]

Outside lobbying can also motivate a group's allies to play a more active and visible role on an issue. One of the most important activities in which members engage to win reelection is "credit claiming," which David Mayhew defines as "acting so as to generate a belief in a relevant political actor (or actors) that one is personally responsible for causing the government, or some unit thereof, to do something that the actor (or actors) considers desirable." [44] Active participation in the legislative fight is what makes a particular claim credible, but such claims do a member little good if constituents are not paying attention. Outside lobbying can get their attention by raising the salience of the issue.

One specific, expensive, but commonly used form of outside lobbying is issue advertising. Issue ads are ads run by advocacy groups intended to shape viewers' attitudes and behavior with respect to an issue important to the group. Issue ads appear both in print and broadcast form, but most of the print advertising appears in Washington, D.C., outlets, such as *Roll Call*, *The Hill*, or the *Washington Post*, and is targeted at Capitol Hill staffers. A study by the Annenberg Institute estimated spending on issue advertisements in the Washington media market alone came to over $400 million dollars during the 108th Congress.[45] Of ten organizations given closer analysis, all spent more on Washington issue ads than their PACs spent on congressional campaigns.

Most issue ads are broadcast on television, target a larger audience, and serve a different purpose than print ads. These ads attempt to change public attitudes about pending legislation and encourage viewers who are sympathetic to a group's position to contact their representatives and advocate the group's position. During the fight over health care reform in the Clinton administration, the health insurance industry ran ads depicting two ordinary citizens, Harry and Louise, who sat at their kitchen table worrying out loud about how the Clinton plan would restrict their choice of doctor and harm the quality of their care. Journalists and politicians at the time widely asserted that the insurance industry's advertising campaign killed health care reform.

In the last decade and a half, the use of issue advertising has grown significantly. Back on the national agenda in 2009, health care reform generated issue advertising that bordered on the ubiquitous, including ads featuring the original Harry and Louise, but this time they were in favor of reform. Other issue areas, such as energy, environment, and economic policies, likewise generated major advertising campaigns. In President Obama's first 100 days, according to TNSMI/CMAG, $91 million was spent on television issue advertising, more than ten times what was spent in the first 100 days of George W. Bush's presidency.[46]

That issue advertising is at once widely used and expensive has troubled many critics of the role of money in American politics. The degree to which it can be used to manipulate public opinion in a way that influences the legislative process remains unknown, however. We now know that the effects of the original Harry and Louise ads were overstated.[47] We also know that in the years since, the groups using issue advertising have grown in number and diversity and that the competition among ads may diminish the effectiveness of a media campaign by any one side. In any case, the near future of political advertising by private interests will almost certainly look different from the recent past. In *Citizens United v. Federal Elections Commission* (2010) the Supreme Court struck down the government's ban on corporate spending in candidate elections. Among its other implications, this ruling will make it easier for corporations to promote policies by connecting them with specific candidates.

LOBBYING IN COALITIONS

Interest groups often work in collaboration with other groups as part of an ad hoc or an ongoing lobbying coalition. There are many advantages to lobbying in coalitions. Coordinated support for (or opposition to) a policy tends to have a greater impact on legislative decision making. Members of a lobbying coalition can pool their resources and benefit from other members' relative strengths, thereby circumventing the practical limits on a group's legislative agenda. In addition, groups with similar but slightly varying interests may be more likely to be granted access to a legislator if they strategically choose a common goal than if they individually insist on their preferred policy details.

There is broad consensus that lobbying in coalitions has become more common and even more necessary as the number of interest groups grows. But coalitions do not always form where their interests overlap. All groups are more likely to form alliances if they encounter organized opposition, but the tendency to form lobbying alliances depends on the type of groups involved.[48] In particular, advocacy groups representing citizen interests are more likely to form alliances than are corporate interests.[49] At the same time, corporations often work through industry trade associations that operate like coalitions, as pharmaceutical interests form a coalition through PhRMA.

Examples of coalition formation abound in recent history, with large coalitions often developing on both sides of an issue. The larger and more diverse the coalition, the more likely it is that the goals of some coalition members will conflict with the goals of others. The American Iron and Steel Institute (AISI) had represented domestic steel interests before Congress for some ninety years when in the late 1990s foreign steel producers started dumping cheap steel onto the international market. Plummeting steel prices greatly benefited steel-consuming manufacturers, but they bankrupted some of the largest U.S. steel producers. When protectionist trade legislation came before Congress in 1999, AISI could do little more than sit on its hands. From 1999 to 2002, its advocacy budget fell by half.

To return to an earlier example, the Alliance to Improve Medicare, a coalition of insurance companies, pharmaceutical manufacturers, hospitals, and doctors, developed a united front to help win passage of the Medicare prescription drug bill in 2003, while opposition groups failed to coalesce. In contrast, groups in favor of health care reform in 2009 were divided into a multitude of coalitions with only partly overlapping agendas. Better Health Care Together, Coalition to Advance Health Care Reform, Faithful Reform in Health Care, Health Care First, the National Coalition on Health Care, Leadership Conference for Guaranteed Health Care, and Health Care for American Now! all claimed dozens of organizations as members. When health insurance reform was passed in 2010, most of these groups celebrated, but some were bitterly disappointed.[50]

LOBBYING AND REPRESENTATION

One of the most troubling aspects regarding the practice of lobbying is that some interests are able to run multimillion dollar inside and outside campaigns while others lack the access and resources to engage in effective lobbying. Indeed, the larger the number of individuals a group would represent, the more difficult is it to organize for collective action,[51] much less finance the high costs of lobbying on Capitol Hill. Is the interest group system, as E. E. Schattschneider observed half a century ago, biased in favor of individuals and interests already rich in resources?[52]

In twenty-first-century Washington, lobbyists seeking to affect legislative outcomes represent multiple sectors of the economy and a wide range of groups in civil society. This volume includes several chapters on different types of interest groups, including private for-profit interests, nonprofit organizations, think tanks, professional associations, religious groups, and others, all of which are interested in maximizing their influence on legislation. Indeed, the last several decades have seen a proliferation of public interest groups and nonprofit advocacy organizations that might, in principle, counterbalance the upper-class bias of the interest group system.

In some respects, this proliferation has been dramatic. Registered tax-exempt nonprofits increased from 130,000 in 1940 to 1.5 million at the end of the twentieth century.[53] They have continued to increase in number and in political importance since then. Both the Reagan administration and members of the Republican revolution of the 1990s expended considerable effort in delegating functions formerly associated with government to a wide array of social service nonprofits, increasing their presence in public policymaking.[54]

The specific roles that nonprofits play in lobbying Congress depend partly on their legally defined tax status, which can carry restrictions regarding the allowable levels and types of lobbying. Because donations to them are tax-exempt, IRS regulations prohibit charities and foundations from conducting more than an "insubstantial" amount of lobbying.[55] These groups are often labeled by the their location in the tax code as 501(c)(3) organizations. The ability of 501(c)(3) nonprofits to circumvent their restrictions lies depends in part on an allowance for "education" in the tax code, as opposed to "lobbying."

Nonprofits organized as 501(c)(3)s can therefore provide expertise and subsidize the information costs of legislators, even when they lack the lobbying flexibility and resources of other organizations. They may even enjoy greater access to certain legislators than other types of organizations based on their reputations for expertise.[56] An example is the Center on Budget and Policy Priorities, one of the most prominent and well-respected public interest groups on the left. As a 501(c)(3) nonprofit organization, the center has no PAC, nor can it legally create one. It has no large membership base that it might mobilize through outside tactics. It has no organizational presence anywhere outside of Washington, D.C. And it primarily represents individuals who themselves are resource-poor and underrepresented. Nevertheless, many liberal legislators look to it for guidance about whether they should support proposals related to the center's social welfare mission. On the right, think tanks such as the Cato Institute and the Heritage Foundation have been increasingly important in supplying Republican legislators with conservative proposals, policy analysis, and commentary.

The influence of these particular organizations is no doubt exceptional, but they illustrate how other tax-exempt organizations can be effective, if to a lesser degree. Exactly how much has not yet been closely studied. Many nonprofits do not understand or are overly cautious about lobbying restrictions on 501(c)(3)s and may needlessly dampen their advocacy efforts.[57] Jeffrey Berry also acknowledges, however, the extreme heterogeneity of nonprofits and nonprofit behavior, and he points out that even 501(c)(3) organizations can choose to become "H electors," an IRS classification that allows them perform more lobbying activity than conventional nonprofits without losing the tax subsidy associated with charity status.

Other public interest groups organized with a 501(c)(4) tax status cannot attract deductible contributions, and as a result they need worry little about lobbying restrictions. Indeed, groups such as MoveOn.org have demonstrated how aggressive these groups can be in shaping important public policy debates through new technologies, such as online organizing. Furthermore, MoveOn.org and many other nonprofits retain separate Section 527 PACs that are explicitly partisan.[58]

The growth of activist public interest groups and nonprofit advocacy should not, however, lead one to be sanguine about the importance of money and resources in advocacy at the federal level. Corporations, trade associations, and professional associations still spend more on lobbying by huge margins than public interest groups or nonprofits. If a legislator looks to a group either for voting cues or legislative assistance, the chances are much higher that private sector groups will be available to fulfill that purpose.

So too with outside lobbying. The conventional view is that large membership organizations, by mobilizing at the grassroots, can provide a democratic counterweight to special interests. This view is probably wrong. Kollman observes that outside lobbying "reinforces inequalities in access to representatives that accrue from campaign contributions and other less edifying activities of interest groups."[59] These inequalities have only been exacerbated by the growing reliance on television issue advertising. That advertising is highly expensive greatly favors private sector interests. A 2005 Annenberg study found that almost 80 percent of all Washington-area issue ads were run by corporations, a 5-to-1 advantage over citizen or cause advocacy groups (some of which are themselves probusiness). Likewise, business far outpaces labor unions in the use of this instrument. The Annenberg study reports a gigantic 100-to-1 business to union ratio in issue ad spending.[60]

CONCLUSION

Most citizens view legislators and lobbyists as parties to a corrupt relationship in which legislators sell out to the special interests that finance their reelection campaigns. The best systematic research suggests that this view is highly exaggerated. Campaign contributions play a decidedly minor role in legislative decision making, and flat-out corruption is highly unusual.

This is not to say that money does not matter on Capitol Hill; it simply means that the money spent in campaign contributions is less significant when compared to the other ways in which money matters for effective advocacy. Lobbying and the support services that go with it, such as policy analysis, political intelligence-gathering, polling, and political consulting, are expensive undertakings, and private sector interests spend billions of dollars on lobbying every year. The generation of constituency pressure is likewise expensive—interest groups now spend hundreds of millions of dollars on issue advertising alone.

More important to the influence of lobbying on legislation is the information that lobbyists gather and provide to legislators, especially those legislators who already share their policy objectives. The extent to which a group represents citizens in a member's district or can mobilize those citizens likewise gives it a decided advantage. In this respect, special interest groups are not so "special"; they can actually facilitate the representation of voters and voter interests on Capitol Hill between elections. To paraphrase what the cartoon character Pogo once said: "We have met the special interests and they is us."

Pogo notwithstanding, to what extent do special interests, as commonly conceived, affect public policy at the national level? To what extent, that is, do resource inequalities in the private sphere reappear as political biases in the policies that Congress adopts? In the most comprehensive study of lobbying in decades, Baumgartner et al. conclude that resource-rich interest groups tend to be very effective at protecting the status quo policies that favor them, but they are remarkably ineffective at changing policies that do not.[61] The main reason for this, however, is that the status quo is itself the cumulative consequence of private sector power in generations past. Preserving it is to preserve policies that may be unrepresentative of what the citizenry wants but that are extremely difficult to change. The rub for those who historically have been unorganized politically is that Madisonian government makes significant policy change difficult. Well-financed interests can stop what they do not like by winning at any one of several legislative stages. Groups that have been historically underrepresented, even if they are now well organized and well financed, still face substantial barriers to achieving their policy goals.[62]

NOTES

1. Reported on the Public Citizen Web site: www.citizen.org/congress/govt_reform/ethics/congethics/articles.cfm?ID=14945.

2. This chapter draws on Richard L. Hall and Alan V. Deardorff, "Lobbying as Legislative Subsidy," *American Political Science Review* 100, 1 (2006): 69–84. For a more general treatment on which this chapter also draws, see John R. Wright, *Interest Groups and Congress* (Boston: Allyn & Bacon, 1996).

3. For a good summary of the lobbying and ethics rules in Congress, on which we draw here, see Jack Maskell, *Lobbying Law and Ethics Rules Changes in the 110th Congress* (Washington, D.C.: Congressional Research Service, September 18, 2007 ([updated]).

4. *Bundling* refers to the practice whereby a single lobbyist collects checks from multiple individuals or PACs and presents them as a package to a legislator, thereby crediting the lobbyist with assisting the member's campaign far more than the $10,000 per-PAC maximum that federal law allows for one election cycle.

5. S.1. Section 544, new Senate Rule XXXV, paragraph 2(d). Cited in Maskell, "Lobbying Law and Ethics Rules Changes," 9.

6. Ibid.

7. We cannot tell precisely how much is being spent on lobbying Congress, however, as the disclosure reports do not separate expenditures on lobbying the executive branch from expenditures on lobbying Congress.

8. For example, Philip Stern repeatedly makes this mistake in *The Best Congress Money Can Buy* (New York: Pantheon Books, 1988), esp. 43–56. In a subsequent edition, he defends himself in a footnote, but his defense demonstrates that he completely misunderstands his mistake. See Stern, *Still the Best Congress Money Can Buy* (Washington, D.C.: Regnery Gateway, 1992), 71.

9. See Larry J. Sabato, *PAC Power: Inside the World of Political Action Committees* (New York: W. W. Norton, 1985).

10. Thomas Stratmann, "The Market for Congressional Votes: Is Timing of Contributions Everything?" *Journal of Law and Economics* 41, 1 (1998): 85–114.

11. Gregory Wawro, "A Panel Probit Analysis of Campaign Contributions and Roll-Call Votes," *American Journal of Political Science* 45, 3 (2001): 563–579.

12. Stephen Ansolabehere, John M. de Figueiredo, and James M. Snyder Jr., "Why is There so Little Money in U.S. Politics?" *Journal of Economic Perspectives* 17, 1 (2003): 116. Analyzing the same set of studies, however, another prominent scholar concludes that they do provide evidence that money influences votes. See Thomas Stratmann, "Some Talk: Money in Politics. A Partial Review of the Literature," *Public Choice* 124 (2005): 135–156.

13. Richard L. Hall and Frank W. Wayman, "Buying Time: Moneyed Interests and the Mobilization of Bias in Congressional Committees," *American Political Science Review* 84, 3 (1990): 797–820.

14. Gregory Wawro, *Legislative Entrepreneurship in the U.S. House of Representatives* (Ann Arbor: University of Michigan Press, 2000).

15. Wright, *Interest Groups and Congress,* 81.

16. This section draws directly on ibid., chap. 4.

17. As reported on the Center for Responsive Politics Web site, www.opensecrets.org.

18. Thomas E. Mann, *Unsafe at Any Margin: Interpreting Congressional Elections* (Washington, D.C.: American Enterprise Institute, 1978).

19. John Mark Hansen, *Gaining Access: Congress and the Farm Lobby, 1919–1981* (Chicago: University of Chicago Press, 1991).

20. Ibid., 5.

21. See Michael J. Graetz and Ian Shapiro, *Death by a Thousand Cuts: The Fight over Taxing Inherited Wealth* (Princeton: Princeton University Press, 2005).

22. Raymond A. Bauer, Ithiel de Sola Pool, and Lewis A. Dexter, *American Business and Public Policy: The Politics of Foreign Trade* (New York: Atherton Press, 1963).

23. Ibid., 442.

24. See Frank R. Baumgartner, Jeffrey M. Berry, Marie Hojnacki, David C. Kimball, and Beth L. Leech, *Lobbying and Policy Change: Who Wins, Who Loses, and Why* (Chicago: University of Chicago Press, 2009); Marie Hojnacki and David C. Kimball, "Organized Interests and the Decision of Whom to Lobby in Congress," *American Political Science Review* 92 (November 1998): 775–790; Hojnacki and Kimball, "The Who and How of Organizations' Lobbying Strategies in Committee," *Journal of Politics* 61 (December 1999): 999–1024.

25. David Austen-Smith and John R. Wright, "Counteractive Lobbying," *American Journal of Political Science* 38 (February 1994): 25–44. See also Wright, *Interest Groups and Congress,* 96–105.

26. Robert M. Entman, "Framing: Toward Clarification of a Fractured Paradigm," *Journal of Communication* 43, 4 (1993): 51–58.

27. See Baumgartner et al., *Lobbying and Policy Change;* Richard A. Smith, "Interest Group Influence in the U.S. Congress," *Legislative Studies Quarterly* 20 (1995): 89–139.

28. On the use of this frame in the twentieth-century history of health care reform, see Colin Gordon, *Dead on Arrival: The Politics of Health Care in Twentieth-Century America* (Princeton: Princeton University Press, 2003).

29. See Jim Rutenberg and Jackie Calmes, "As Health Care Debate Rages, Obama Takes to the Stump," *New York Times,* August 11, 2009.

30. See Jim Rutenberg and Jackie Calmes, "False 'Death Panel' Rumor Has Some Familiar Roots," *New York Times,* August 13, 2009.

31. Ted Brader has shown how appeals to fear in political advertising increase voter attentiveness and openness to new information. See his *Campaigning for Hearts And Minds: How Emotional Appeals in Political Ads Work* (Chicago: University of Chicago Press, 2006).

32. Dennis Chong and James N. Druckman, "A Theory of Framing and Opinion Formation in Competitive Elite Environments," *Journal of Communication* 57, 1 (2007): 99–118.

33. Baumgartner et al., *Lobbying and Policy Change.*

34. Hall and Deardorff, "Lobbying as Legislative Subsidy."

35. From interview with authors, July 2009.

36. Wright, *Interest Groups and Congress,* 92–95.

37. Ibid., 92.

38. Raymond A. Bauer, Ithiel de Sola Pool, and Lewis A. Dexter, *American Business and Public Policy: The Politics of Foreign Trade* (New York: Atherton Press, 1963); Lester Milbrath, *The Washington Lobbyists* (Chicago: Rand McNally, 1963).

39. Quoted in Wright, *Interest Groups and Congress,* 88.

40. Ken Kollman, *Outside Lobbying: Public Opinion and Interest Group Strategies* (Princeton: Princeton University Press, 1998), 3.

41. The following discussion draws on Kollman, *Outside Lobbying;* and Kenneth M. Goldstein, *Interest Groups, Lobbying, and Participation in America* (Cambridge: Cambridge University Press, 1999).

42. Goldstein, *Interest Groups,* 46.

43. Jonathan Oberlander, *The Political Life of Medicare* (Chicago: University of Chicago Press, 2003).

44. David R. Mayhew, *Congress: The Electoral Connection* (New Haven: Yale University Press, 1974).

45. Erika Falk, Erin Grizard, and Gordon McDonald, "Issue Advertising in the 108th Congress," Annenberg Public Policy Center, 2005.

46. "100 Days of Issue Advertising," The Spot: A Political Ad Blog by TNSMI/CMAG, May 4. 2009, tnsmi-cmag.blogspot .com/2009/05/100-days-of-issue-advertising.html.

47. With benefit of better data and systematic methods, social scientists would later debate the effectiveness of those ads. See Karen Goldsteen, James H. Swan, and Wendy Clemeña, "Harry and Louise and Health Care Reform: Romancing Public Opinion," *Journal of Health Politics, Policy and Law* 26, 6 (2001): 1325–1352; Lawrence R. Jacobs and Robert Y. Shapiro, "Questioning the Conventional Wisdom on Public Opinion toward Health Reform," *Political Science and Politics* 27, 2 (1994): 208–215.

48. Kevin W. Hula, *Lobbying Together: Interest Group Coalitions in Legislative Politics* (Washington, D.C.: Georgetown University Press, 1999).

49. Marie Hojnacki, "Interest Groups' Decisions to Join Alliances or Work Alone," *American Journal of Political Science* 41, 1 (1997): 61–87.

50. Jacqueline Salmon, "Pulling Together on Health Care," *Washington Post,* July 25, 2009.

51. See Mancur Olson, *The Logic of Collective Action: Public Goods and the Theory of Groups* (Cambridge: Harvard University Press, 1965). Jack Walker finds that public interest groups representing large constituencies compensate for their collective action problem by securing funding from rich "patrons," such as foundations and wealthy activists who support their mission. See Jack L. Walker, *Mobilizing Interest Groups in America* (Ann Arbor: University of Michigan Press, 1991).

52. E. E. Schattschneider, *The Semisovereign People* (New York: Holt, Rinehart, and Winston, 1960).

53. Peter D. Hall, "A Historical Overview of Philanthropy, Voluntary Associations, and Nonprofit Organizations in the United States, 1600–2000," in *The Nonprofit Sector: A Research Handbook,* 2nd ed., ed. Walter W. Powell and Richard Steinberg (New Haven: Yale University Press, 2006).

54. Ibid.

55. Erika Lunder, "Tax-Exempt Organizations: Political Activity Restrictions and Disclosure Requirements," Congressional Research Service Report for Congress, Doc 2007-4488, September 11, 2007.

56. Jeffrey M. Berry, *The New Liberalism: The Rising Power of Citizen Groups* (Washington, D.C.: Brookings Institution Press, 1999).

57. Jeffrey M. Berry, *A Voice for Nonprofits* (Washington, D.C.: Brookings Institution Press, 2003).

58. Elizabeth Wasserman, "Nonprofits Walk Fine Line on Political Activity," MSNBC, July 25, 2008, www.msnbc.msn.com/id/ 25838144/.

59. Kollman, *Outside Lobbying,* 5.

60. Falk, Grizard, and McDonald, "Issue Advertising," 16.

61. Baumgartner et al., *Lobbying and Policy Change.*

62. Ibid., 256.

SUGGESTED READING

Ansolabehere, Stephen, John M. de Figueiredo, and James M. Snyder Jr. "Why is There so Little Money in U.S. Politics?" *Journal of Economic Perspectives* 17, 1 (2003): 105–130.

Austen-Smith, David, and John R. Wright. "Counteractive Lobbying." *American Journal of Political Science* 38 (1994): 25–44.

Bauer, Raymond A., Ithiel de Sola Pool, and Lewis A. Dexter. *American Business and Public Policy: The Politics of Foreign Trade.* New York: Atherton Press, 1963.

Baumgartner, Frank, Jeffrey M. Berry, Marie Hojnacki, David C. Kimball, and Beth L. Leech. *Lobbying and Policy Change: Who Wins, Who Loses, and Why.* Chicago: University of Chicago Press, 2009.

Berry, Jeffrey M. *The New Liberalism: The Rising Power of Citizen Groups.* Washington, D.C.: Brookings Institution, 1999.

Hall, Richard L., and Richard Anderson. "Issue Advertising and Legislative Advocacy in Health Politics." In *Interest Group Politics.* Ed. Alan Cigler and Burdett Loomis. Washington, D.C.: CQ Press, 2011.

Hall, Richard L., and Alan V. Deardorff. "Lobbying as Legislative Subsidy." *American Political Science Review* 100, 1 (2006): 69–84.

Hansen, John Mark. *Gaining Access: Congress and the Farm Lobby, 1919–1981.* Chicago: University of Chicago Press, 1991.

Hojnacki, Marie, and David C. Kimball. "Organized Interests and the Decision of Whom to Lobby in Congress." *American Political Science Review* 92, 4 (December 1998).

Kollman, Ken. *Outside Lobbying: Public Opinion and Interest Group Strategies.* Princeton: Princeton University Press, 1998.

Wright. John R. *Interest Groups and Congress.* Boston: Allyn & Bacon, 1996.

chapter 26

Lobbyists: Who Are They? What Do They Do?

by Rogan Kersh

TOYOTA FACED A CRISIS. In 2009 reports of bizarre accidents began popping up around the United States and then in the automaker's home country, Japan. The gas pedal on various Toyota models, drivers reported, was sticking at high speeds, and there appeared to be no way to slow or stop the car. Toyota officials initially reported the problem as improperly fitted floor mats. But by early 2010 accident reports increasingly pointed to a malfunctioning accelerator. Angry customers threatened lawsuits, Congress organized high-profile hearings, and the company's stock plunged—losing a fifth of its value, or $30 billion, in just two weeks.

What to do? Along with recalling thousands of cars to fix the problem, Toyota went shopping . . . for U.S. interest group lobbyists. As the crisis mounted, Toyota added to its stable of thirty-one Washington lobbyists, hiring dozens of additional representatives: some lobbyists who knew the auto industry well, others with ties to important legislators and Obama administration members, and still others with expertise in crisis management and public relations.

By March 2010 Toyota's immediate troubles had abated. Well-scripted appearances on Capitol Hill by Toyota's CEO, Akio Toyoda, along with an elaborate series of public apologies in the media and a surge of calls to congressional offices by Toyota auto workers and dealers around the United States, helped to curb Washington officials' outrage. Toyota returned to selling cars—their sales were up 41 percent for the month, and continued to rise through early summer—and the company's stock price stabilized.

Engineers and car lovers will continue to debate the details of Toyota's mechanical woes. Students of public policy have a different set of questions: Who were those lobbyists Toyota turned to as alarms mounted? What benefits did they provide? And why does a single auto company need thirty-one lobbyists in Washington during ordinary times, anyway?

This chapter looks closely at the who and why of lobbying in America's "interest-group society."[1] Toyota is by no means alone: virtually every major corporation doing business in the United States has lobbying representatives on its payroll. But American politics is not just a corporate-lobbying playground, by any means. An enormous range of interests—including environmentalists and pro-life activists, nurses in Oregon and nannies in New Jersey, and foreign governments from Afghanistan to Zimbabwe—also hire advocates to professionally represent their concerns in Washington, D.C., state capitals, and cities large and small. In short, interest group representatives are everywhere, deeply ingrained in the U.S. system of government and policymaking. Little wonder that Toyota's reflexive action, when faced with a major public issue, was to call in the lobbyists.

WHO ARE THE LOBBYISTS?

The lobbying industry employs more than 100,000 people in Washington, D.C.[2] Hundreds of thousands more represent private and public interests across U.S. cities and states. Beyond this set of professionals, millions of Americans are engaged occasionally in lobbying work, defined broadly as organized attempts to influence government. As a student, did you ever join a high school or college group on a "Lobby Day" in your state legislature, meeting with public officials to encourage low student loan interest rates or streamlined visa policies for graduate students or more state financial support? You were, at least for a day or two, a lobbyist.

The focus here, however, is on those whose primary employment involves working for one or more interest groups. Looking back to the mid-1960s, there were far fewer lobbyists active in the nation's capital—less than a tenth of the total number today. Back then most lobbyists were generalists, serving a range of clients. Today the lobbying world is much more clearly stratified, divisible into four main types of professionals: single-firm, public interest, trade association, and "hired guns."

Along with more professional specialization and increasing numbers, the portrait of Washington lobbyists has changed substantially. Demographically, over the past

TYPES OF PROFESSIONAL LOBBYISTS

SINGLE-FIRM

Lobbyists who work for one company, such as Microsoft or Toyota. Some of the largest such corporations retain dozens of lobbyists, who divide the work of Washington representation by issue expertise, party affiliation (most firms have both Republican and Democratic lobbyists), and branch of government (Congress-focused lobbyists often divide their worlds further, between House and Senate).

GRASSROOTS/PUBLIC INTEREST

Lobbyists representing an issue-based or public concern, often on behalf of large membership organizations. Examples range across the political spectrum: the AARP looks after the interests of retired Americans; the National Rifle Association and the Brady Campaign square off about the rights and dangers of gun ownership; and groups like the Sierra Club or Greenpeace lobby for environmental causes.

TRADE ASSOCIATION

Many industries featuring multiple organizations band together and hire one or more lobbyists to represent their collective interests in Washington or state capitals. Some trade association lobbyists represent large groupings: the national Chamber of Commerce counts 3 million businesses as members, and has fifteen lobbyists in Washington, D.C., to look after their interests. Others look after smaller groups: the Election Technology Council represents the six main U.S. companies that provide the voting machines for American elections. In larger trade groups, association lobbyists often have to spend as much time settling differences between their members as they do promoting their "shared" concerns to lawmakers.

INDEPENDENT/"HIRED GUNS"

Some lobbyists choose to strike out on their own, usually after building a record of success while lobbying in a company or trade association. A "hired gun" (a term most independent lobbyists dislike) may open a lobbying organization of their own with one or two partners, or simply take on clients. They also sometimes work within large law-lobbying firms. It was to many of the best-known independent lobbyists that Toyota, like other organizations that need expert advice swiftly, turned in their time of political need.

five decades lobbyists have on average become wealthier, better educated, and more diverse. In terms of required skills, the typical lobbyist has shifted from a genial "fixer" and provider of gifts, meals, and campaign cash to a skilled political and policy analyst, providing well-researched information to lawmakers. (They may also disperse campaign funds, though under much more tightly regulated rules than fifty years ago.)

In short, the overall portrait of lobbying today—especially in the nation's capital—is one of rising professional status. Lobbying was long viewed as an unsavory occupation, dominated by fixers, schmoozers, and swindlers.[3] Today well-respected U.S. universities run popular graduate programs on how to lobby. Jobs in "government relations" or "public affairs" (often-used synonyms for "lobbyist") are actively sought by former members of Congress and White House officials, by their top staff members, and by talented graduates of public administration, law, and business schools. Americans who believe passionately in a political or policy cause flock to work in public interest organizations, most of which long ago exchanged marching in the streets for sophisticated inside-lobbying activities (see Chapter 19). Far from operating in the shadows, many Washington lobbyists today are intermingled with the public officials they seek to influence: they attended the same colleges, worked together on Capitol Hill and in presidential administrations, live in the same leafy neighborhoods, send their children to the same schools, and socialize regularly. In a policymaking environment of increasing size, technical sophistication, and importance to many Americans' daily lives, replacing old-fashioned political hacks with well-trained professionals has transformed lobbying into a legitimate and even desirable profession.

Lobbyist Demographics

Based on the current issue of *Washington Representatives*, a comprehensive reference book chronicling lobbying in the nation's capital, about three-quarters of today's lobbyists have a professional degree, most often in law. The equivalent figure for the 1950s–1960s is harder to estimate, but one report from the period notes that typical Washington lobbyists either had a law degree or skipped college and were "schooled directly" in politics.[4] Many in the latter group had a background similar to Bobby Baker, a South Carolinian who left high school at age fourteen in 1942 to serve as a page to his home-state senator, Burnet Maybank, and never returned to school. In the Senate young Baker eventually became attached to a powerful patron, Majority Leader Lyndon Johnson; by the late 1950s, his ability to help handle Johnson's wheeling and dealing led Baker to be nicknamed the "101st Senator." Subsequent investigations into Baker's lobbying activities, including evidence that he had traded money and arranged sexual favors to broker political deals involving the Kennedy administration, were cut short in 1963, reportedly due to a timely intervention by Attorney General Robert F. Kennedy himself.[5]

Some members of Congress, given their experience, move into lobbying after they retire. Former majority leaders Tom Daschle, D-S.D., and Bob Dole, R-Kans., both worked as lobbyists after they left the Senate.

Baker became a wealthy man thanks to his connections and ability to fix political problems, but lobbyists of his era typically were not highly compensated. After the advocacy explosion of the 1960s (see Chapter 8), lobbyist pay began rising steadily. By the 1990s a handful of top hired gun lobbyists earned more than $2 million a year. Today the lobbying industry rewards many of its employees quite well. More than seventy heads of trade associations made $1 million or more in salary in 2009. An assistant to a corporate lobbyist—spending his or her time researching issues and tracking political information, as well as handling administrative tasks—makes an annual $60,000, on average. Public interest lobbyists are not usually paid as handsomely as their private counterparts, but they too have also seen a steady rise in compensation. The Environmental Defense Fund, to take one example, pays its chief executive nearly $500,000 per year.[6]

As professional lobbyists' status and pay has improved, a commensurately larger swath of American society is drawn to this realm. In Bobby Baker's day, his fellow lobbyists—as well as nearly all the lawmakers they sought to influence—were white middle-aged or older men. That profile has changed as well.

A Man's World?

Interest group expert Jeffrey Berry's comprehensive look in 1997 at the U.S. "interest group society" termed lobbying a "man's world," though he noted that "barrier[s] to equal employment seem to be eroding." Many recent academic studies continue to observe that a vast "lobbying gender gap" remains in the nation's capital. But in many issue areas, including health—the sector with the highest total spending on lobbying over since 2005—women lobbyists are approaching numerical parity. Of all the individuals registered to lobby on health care issues in 2008–2009, an estimated 48 percent (up from 42 percent just five years earlier) were women: 53 percent of nonprofit health lobbyists and 39 percent of corporate interest group representatives. It is difficult to track these figures back in time, but a 1990 study

TWO LOBBYISTS, PAST AND PRESENT

Heidi Wagner is a vivacious, highly talented health care lobbyist representing a large California biotech firm with dozens of concerns before government, from stem-cell use to tax breaks for genetic research. Wagner is a single-firm lobbyist: although she collaborates with many other health care lobbyists, joining coalitions like the Health Leadership Council, ultimately her services are performed for—and salary paid by—one employer. In 2009, when her company was bought by the Swiss health/pharmaceutical giant Roche, her day-to-day work remained the same. The issues she tracks, legislative benefits she seeks, long hours she puts in: all of these are on behalf of one employer, with a fairly coherent set of interests. And she started young: Wagner was in her early thirties when she moved from Capitol Hill to biotech lobbying.

A different style was presented by Red Cloud, the best-known Native American tribal leader of the late nineteenth century. A legendary Lakota warrior, after the Civil War Red Cloud signed the Fort Laramie Treaty, ceding some land to the government in exchange for hunting rights and removal of U.S. military forts. Frustrated by American government officials' failure to uphold their promises, Red Cloud visited Washington ten times, meeting first with President Ulysses S. Grant in 1870, who dubbed him "Chief Lobbyist," and White House officials in three subsequent administrations. "We have been driven far enough," Red Cloud told Interior Secretary Jacob Cox in 1872. "We want what we ask for." The Lakota warrior turned federal lobbyist for his people died in 1909, aged eighty-eight.

For all their differences, from personal to technological to temporal, these two talented advocates provide largely the same services: delivering information from their clients to Washington decision makers on Capitol Hill and in the executive branch.

put the total proportion of female lobbyists in Washington at 22 percent.[7]

Women are not just claiming a higher proportion of lobbying jobs; they are also moving up the ladder of influence. An informal guide to Washington lobbying power is a periodic "Top Lobbyists" listing in *The Hill*, which surveys a wide range of insiders to compile lists of leading lobbyists in each of the four areas listed in the box above. Of the ninety-four most prominent corporate and independent (hired gun) lobbyists named in their 2009 survey, a total of nineteen, or 20 percent, are women. In the Top Lobbyists rankings four years earlier, the proportion of women was 8 percent (six of seventy-six). In 2007 *Washingtonian* magazine's similar ranking of the capital's fifty most prominent lobbyists featured six (12 percent) women.[8]

Who are some of these powerful women lobbyists? Again, looking specifically at the health sector, the president/CEO of America's Health Insurance Plans (AHIP), the chief lobbying association for health plans and insurance companies, is Karen Ignagni, who played a central role in the health reform battles of 2009–2010. Also vitally involved in that debate were other high-profile women, including Kate Sullivan Hare, the lead Wal-Mart health representative (and former chief Chamber of Commerce representative on health issues); Mary Grealy, president of the powerful Healthcare Leadership Council, an association of two dozen top health-related companies; and Linda Tarplin, a leading Republican voice in the health debate and one of the three women founders of the lobbying firm Tarplin Downs & Young. The lobbying offices of two of the largest pharmaceutical companies, Pfizer and GlaxoSmithKline, are also headed by women. Outside the health realm, but relevant to this chapter's opening, another woman, Josephine Cooper, heads Toyota's group of thirty-one "regular" lobbyists—those already employed by the company before the malfunctioning accelerator crisis hit in late 2009.

State capitals also feature more women in prominent lobbying positions, in health care and other issue domains, than when the subject was investigated in a 1998 study, "Female Lobbyists: Women in the World of 'Good ol' Boys.'"[9] As the number of women lobbyists grows at both the federal and state level, questions arise about whether their lobbying styles—or the issues they emphasize—is demonstrably different from those of male lobbyists. There are not yet definitive answers, but this issue bears watching as more women enter the lobbying corps.

Along with becoming more female, the world of Washington lobbying is growing younger. Ethnic and racial minorities, however, have not made as great strides as have women: *Washingtonian*'s list of fifty top lobbyists included only one African American and one Latino. The rarity is partly a supply-side issue: relatively small proportions of members of Congress and top congressional staff, the primary source of Washington lobbyists, are black or Latino. These numbers have been rising in recent years, and as those experienced political insiders leave for lobbying positions, a more diverse lobbying community is the likely result.

Oglala Lakota leader Red Cloud traveled to Washington on a number of occasions to advocate on behalf of Native American issues. In 1870 Red Cloud met with President Ulysses S. Grant and gave a speech at New York's Cooper Union detailing wrongs committed against Native Americans.

WHAT DO LOBBYISTS DO?

A familiar, if cynical, view among Americans holds that lobbying groups spend money: on campaign contributions, on influence-peddling, even on corrupt activities. After a year of closely studying interest group involvement in congressional policymaking in the mid-1970s, journalist Mary Clay Berry concluded, "Money has everything to do with lobbying. . . . It is all very well to insist, as most politicians do, that the campaign contributions guarantee the donor no more than access. In lobbying, access is everything."[10]

Lobbyists do spend substantial amounts to help get their views across. But dispensing money to buy favors is far from the centerpiece of most lobbying work. Their principal activity involves tracking political and policy developments, reporting on their findings to their interest group clients or membership, and devising a strategy for advancing those clients/members' interests. Whether in Washington, D.C., state capitals, or city government, the main focus of lobbying is the legislative branch. Table 26.1, drawing on direct observational research of a group of health care lobbyists, breaks down the time they spend on legislative activities: concerning Congress, for this set of national lobbyists.[11]

Evident from the table is that nearly half of these health care lobbyists' legislative activity involves managing information. Looking more closely at this category will help illuminate professional lobbyists in action. The focus will then shift to two other broad categories of lobbyist activities: spending money to advance their clients' interests and helping shape policy decisions—in part by influencing who occupies important administration (executive branch) positions. Occasionally, lobbyists wind up serving in those positions themselves.

Managing Information

Interest group lobbyists devote hours most workdays to absorbing, discussing with colleagues, and analyzing in written memos the substantive and political aspects of the issues they are paid to influence. Their research often starts with daily briefings summarizing relevant legislation—*CQ Roll Call*, *POLITICO*, *National Journal*, and the Bureau of National Affairs are popular sources—as well as national media and reliable blog reports, journals covering Capitol Hill, and various congressional and executive branch reports. Lobbyists also utilize their extensive network of fellow advocates, exchanging written summaries of issues, often based on private analysis. Less often do lobbyists consult academic studies in their policy analyses, unless such material has been summarized or otherwise restated in easily digestible form.

Lobbying therefore centrally involves searching for, analyzing, and presenting information. The results are widely utilized. Interest group reports and issue summaries are vitally important to government officials, and by extension to the millions of people they serve, as well as to lobbyists' clients. Among grassroots groups, clients means members—again numbering in the millions. Not all lobbyist information is created equal, however. Knowing what qualifies as valuable—to policymakers and also to clients and fellow lobbyists—is critical to successful lobbying, as is the ability to obtain and communicate the most useful information.

As the health reform debate heated up in the summer and fall of 2009, one study tracked the spread among a network of health lobbyists and public officials (mostly congressional staff, but also a coterie of Obama administration staff members working on health care) of a specific set of health policy ideas. Those ideas—such as the "Cadillac tax" on high-cost insurance policies, which eventually was included in the final bill—that moved most swiftly through the network were advanced in important part by lobbyists in three ways. First, lobbyists helped disseminate policy ideas among lawmakers, utilizing their extensive network of contacts across Washington's health policy community either to build support for or opposition to a proposal. Second, lobbyists for membership groups and trade associations worked to mobilize their members around the country in part by promoting (or vehemently opposing) some of these ideas. And third, lobbying organizations prepared fact sheets that explained the policy in detail, helping to educate the public—and public officials—about policy matters.[12]

Although lobbyists are commonly viewed as masters of manipulation, selectively applying information to serve particular (and, in the popular imagination, usually nefarious) purposes, most of the information they present is relatively unbiased. It is also remarkably consistent: legislative allies and foes, Democratic and Republican officials all receive similar briefing papers and talking points. "Spin" is certainly present, but much more often in the oral presentations that accompany printed or broadcast information. The substantive messages that lobbyists communicate to policymakers are little changed across different congressional or executive branch offices.[13]

Presenting policy information also requires deft political interpretation and positioning. Public interest and trade association lobbyists must present a unified front to public officials from a membership that may have deep internal division. Environmental lobbyists have struggled in recent years to reconcile or at least bridge vastly divergent positions among their supporters about so-called cap and trade approaches to reducing carbon emissions.[14] Because individual companies are loath to go on record as opposing an initiative supported by a congressional committee chair or White House official, they often give that task to the trade association lobbyist who speaks on "behalf of the membership," without putting any CEO or president in the hot seat.

TABLE 26.1 **Washington Health Care Lobbyists' Legislative Activities, 1999–2008**

Type of activity	Legislative time (percent)
Build relationships with members of Congress (MCs)/staff	24.5%
Research/analyze legislative information	24.3
Provide/seek information to/from MCs' offices	19.8
Inform/mobilize the public on congressional issues	12.0
Attend/help organize fundraisers for MCs	6.1
Prepare client(s) for congressional hearings/MC meetings	6.1
Build coalitions including MCs/staff	4.3
Organize conferences/policy discussions	1.7
Draft/amend congressional legislation	1.2
Serve on legislative commissions	0.2

SOURCE: Author's database of lobbying observations.

In all this work to obtain, analyze, and present information, lobbyists serve a valuable role in a sprawling American system of national democratic policymaking. It is difficult for a House member—who on average now represents nearly 700,000 people—to communicate with many of them; senators can represent as many as 37 million constituents, as in California. Interest groups help streamline this two-way line of communication between citizen and policymaker. In summary, lobbyists are essential to maintaining the flow of ideas, arguments, and findings that fuels policymaking in the contemporary United States. Whether this is a positive or negative feature of American governance, especially from a democratic standpoint, is taken up in this chapter's conclusion.

Spending Money

All that information—and developing expertise about when and to whom to deliver it—costs money, as do the other activities in which lobbyists engage. Interest groups large and small, from investment banks to Michigan asparagus growers, spend more than $8 billion each year attempting to influence Washington policymaking. This amount does not include spending on political campaigns: for more information on that thorny subject, consult Part VI of this book.

The $8 billion figure is inexact, it must be noted. Official Senate and House records indicate that registered lobbyists reported spending nearly $3.5 billion on registered lobbying activities in 2010 (see Figure 26.1). But many of the people who seek to influence Congress never bother to register as lobbyists. The best estimates suggest that total spending is at least twice the amount indicated in lobbying registrations.[15]

Who provides the funds that lobbyists spend? For public interest groups such as the Sierra Club or National Taxpayers Association, the members do. If you have ever joined an advocacy group, part of your dues went to support the organization's lobbying efforts. If you are a college student, a small portion of your tuition dollars likely helps pay for your school's lobbying efforts. Private lobbyists are funded either directly by their firms—Toyota pays its in-house representatives a salary—or by required annual contributions from members of a trade association.

The $8 billion spent on lobbying each year covers lobbyists' salaries and personal expenses, research costs, the expense of running a Washington office, and travel. Table 26.2 lists the top-spending lobbying clients for 2010. Note the various sectors represented: health care; oil/gas (BP was among the top spenders in 2009, but halted most contributions after the company's Gulf of Mexico oil spill that began in spring 2010); military contractors (Boeing, Northrop Grumman); public utilities (Pacific Gas & Electric); telecommunications; and soft drinks (American Beverage Association). Most but not all are corporate interests.

FIGURE 26.1 **Registered Lobbyist Spending, 2000-2010**

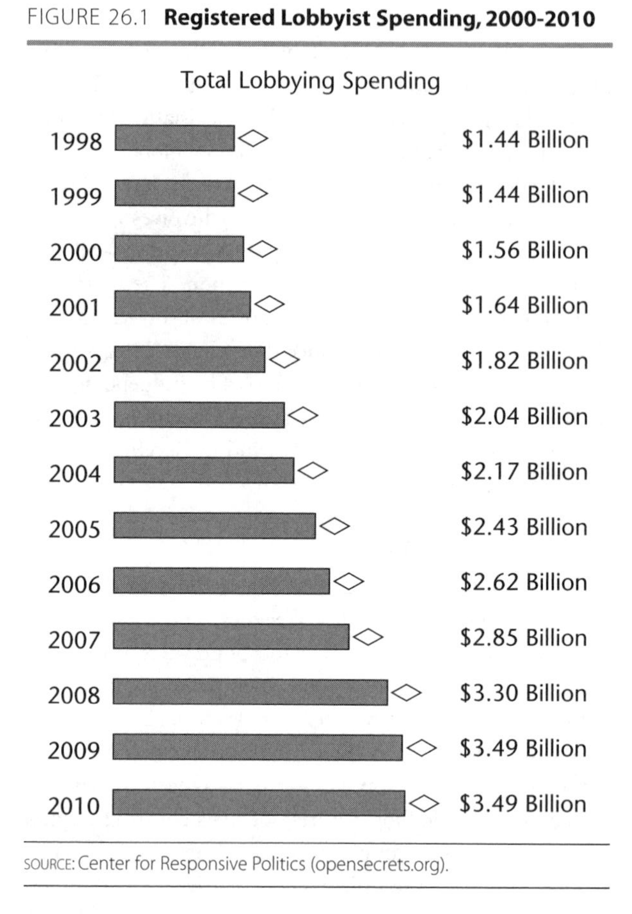

SOURCE: Center for Responsive Politics (opensecrets.org).

Toyota's lobbying adventures in 2009–2010 reflect a basic truth about interest group activity. When an issue of great importance arises in Washington, affected groups tend to boost their spending dramatically. In 2009–2010 a major climate change bill, designed to reduce Americans' use of coal and oil, was promoted by President Obama and debated on Capitol Hill. Sharp spending increases on lobbying were reported by oil companies, coal-mining industries, and electric utilities, which burn thousands of tons of coal each year to produce electricity. One lobbying firm for utilities, Edison Electric Institute, boosted spending on lobbying activities in 2009 to $10.5 million—a nearly 40 percent increase. Analysts who view lobbying as essentially a "money game" look at these hikes in spending and conclude that they add up to real influence in politics.

But the truth is more complicated. What did the energy industry get for all their spending? No climate change law passed in 2009–2010, but was that because of lobbying opposition? Or was it that legislators devoted their attention to other issues such as job creation and health reform? It is more telling when a firm or public interest group manages to shift outcomes in their direction. Energy companies successfully pushed to include an "offset program" in climate change legislation, which allowed them to invest in projects to remove carbon

TABLE 26.2 **Clients' Spending on Lobbying, 2010**

Lobbying client	Total
US Chamber of Commerce	$132,067,500
PG&E Corp	45,460,000
General Electric	39,290,000
FedEx Corp	25,582,074
American Medical Assn	22,555,000
*AARP	22,050,000
Pharmaceutical Rsrch & Mfrs of America	21,740,000
Blue Cross/Blue Shield	21,007,141
ConocoPhillips	19,626,382
American Hospital Assn	19,438,358
Boeing Co	17,896,000
National Cable & Telecommunications Assn	17,710,000
National Assn of Realtors	17,580,000
Verizon Communications	16,750,000
Northrop Grumman	15,740,000
AT&T Inc	15,395,078
United Technologies	14,530,000
National Assn of Broadcasters	13,710,000
Pfizer Inc	13,330,000
Southern Co	13,220,000

SOURCE: Center for Responsive Politics (opensecrets.org).

*AARP, formerly known as the American Association of Retired Persons.

dioxide from the atmosphere if they were not able to meet new targets for reduced emissions (from burning coal) at the smokestack.

Spending increases do seem to help during urgent situations, like that faced by Toyota in the winter of 2009–2010. Crisis management, public relations campaigns, and marshaling forces like Toyota employees across congressional districts may well have a political impact; in times of real urgency, lobbyists (especially seasoned veterans who know the right buttons to push) can sometimes shift official Washington in their favor. This combination of forces requires a great deal of time and energy and therefore is utilized rarely; it can also be quite expensive in practice. Toyota paid $1.4 million to lobby the federal government during the fourth quarter of 2009, as reports of its mechanical problems spread, an amount nearly 20 percent more than in the previous quarter. This spending was followed by a Toyota quarterly record lobbying payout of $2.2 million in the first quarter of 2010. And this amount did not include expensive political activities such as having the Toyota president testify on Capitol Hill.

Lobbyists also spend a large proportion of their funds on responding to the clients who hire them. They communicate with clients via regular, often daily, phone calls and e-mails about Washington developments, compile detailed reports summarizing relevant policy changes, and travel to meet clients or escort them on trips to Washington to make their company's or members' case to lawmakers in person. Grassroots lobbyists (see Chapter 28) additionally must mobilize member support for their policy campaigns. Trade associations engage in similar mobilization activities with their business members.

Whatever their professional affiliation, all lobbyists aim to shape the public policies most relevant to the set of issues on which they are hired to lobby. Gathering and spreading information is a fairly minimal means of influencing policy outcomes, as are donating to a few congressional campaigns. Seasoned lobbyists pursue additional routes in hope of winning legislative changes—or, more often, to maintain a favorable status quo, especially when new government regulations are threatened.

Shaping Policy Outcomes

In 2003, following six years of efforts, Congress approved a broad expansion of the Medicare program, adding a prescription drug benefit to the existing array of health insurance benefits for American senior citizens. The bill seemed doomed to failure until summer 2003, when the nation's largest lobbying group for seniors, AARP (formerly known as the American Association of Retired Persons), threw its weight behind the legislation. Bill Novelli, CEO of AARP, received considerable praise (as well as criticism, from opponents of the new law) for his role as a pivotal actor in passage.[16]

Few lobbyists receive the kind of attention that Novelli did in the prescription drug battle, even in an age when increasing numbers of media organizations, such as the *New York Times* and Bloomberg News, among others, have one or more reporters assigned specifically to cover interest group lobbying in Washington. Far more common is that hundreds or even thousands of lobbyists toil to achieve incremental changes to every significant measure arising on Capitol Hill without much notice from the media. In 2009–2010 more than 4,500 lobbyists were paid to influence the massive health reform legislation that passed in March 2010. Perhaps a half-dozen of this large group will be mentioned by name in forthcoming policy histories of how the final bill was assembled and passed.

Although lobbyists collectively receive billions of dollars to influence members of Congress and administration officials, it is impossible to know how well that money is spent. Most lobbyists are very talented at "credit claiming," or crafting tales for their clients in which they appear, like Novelli in 2003, as the prime movers in major policy battles.[17] More empirically measurable is the success of lobbyists to have members of Congress each year insert an earmark financially benefiting their client into the right appropriations bills as they move through the House and Senate. (The new Republican-majority House in 2011 announced a ban on earmarks, but Washington insiders noted relatively little slowdown in this time-honored practice.) Similarly, a lobbyist may arrange to slip a favorable provision into complex legislation—tax bills are a favored

With a constituency of older Americans, the AARP took a keen interest in the Medicare reforms of 2003. Here the organization's CEO, Bill Novelli (left), and President James Parkel speak in favor of the most significant changes to the program since its inception in 1965.

vehicle—that can save or earn a client millions of dollars.[18] But those "rifle shots," as insiders term them, typically do not affect the significant pieces of legislation that attract Americans' attention.

Are lobbyists, to quote an old Texas adage, "all hat and no cattle" when it comes to influencing U.S. policy outcomes on major issues in a meaningful way? They may not single-handedly block or advance bills, but in three principal ways their work often does matter. First, as Table 26.1 suggests, lobbyists devote considerable time to building relationships on Capitol Hill; they also work to get to know White House and executive branch officials. As a result, over time lobbyists develop networks of overlapping connections across the Hill and presidential administrations. These connections do not automatically translate into direct legislative influence, but they do allow seasoned lobbyists a chance to have their say as policy campaigns develop. It is difficult to determine conclusively, but evidence suggests that well-constructed networks are more valuable when lobbyists seek access than are campaign contributions or other financial sources of support to lobbyists' access.[19]

Second, the information lobbyists provide to lawmakers and their staff sometimes has substantial value. Occasionally, lobbyists' ideas and phrases are incorporated directly into legislation; more often the detailed issue reports they provide are used by harried Capitol Hill or administration staff members to inform their understanding of a policy proposal, at times winding up in drafts of congressional floor speeches or executive branch rules. This type of assistance constitutes a form of "legislative subsidy" (see Chapter 25).

A third way in which lobbyists can directly shape policymakers' activity is use of the "revolving door" between public service and lobbying. What better way to influence policy directly than to work in government or provide advice to newly arriving officials? During the early days of the George W. Bush administration, report after report detailed industry or ideological groups' access in particular policy sectors. High-tech executives and lobbyists, for example, were "poised to profit from what turned out to be a smart bet on Bush," with top industry lobbyist Jim Barksdale (former CEO of Netscape) affirming that "our industry will have more influence than it's ever had in the past."[20] Eight years earlier, newly arrived Clinton White House staffers complained that "lobbyists know their way around this place . . . better than we do." President Clinton's second chief of staff, Leon Panetta, remarked that lobbyist-donors "are the kind of big players who are always around . . . there is without question a greater sensitivity to the issues that they are involved with. Does [lobbying] control policy? Not necessarily, but it sure as hell has an impact as far as decisions that are made."[21] And despite Barack Obama's much-covered campaign pledge to ban lobbyists from his White House, a year into his presidency, at least fifty former lobbyists had been hired in high-ranking positions, including Attorney General Eric S. Holder, a former lobbyist for the telecommunications firm Global Crossing.[22]

The revolving door turns even more rapidly on Capitol Hill. In 2010, 278 former members of Congress were working as Washington lobbyists. The Center for Responsive Politics keeps track of former House and Senate committee staffers now serving as lobbyists and vice versa—lobbyists who have returned to important Capitol Hill staff positions. The Senate Judiciary Committee counts at least 104 former staffers still in Washington, often lobbying their former colleagues.[23]

In summary, interest group actors of various types—association, single-firm, grassroots, "hired guns"—are essential to disseminating, and often creating, the flow of information and ideas that fuel American government and policymaking. Lobbyists spend plenty of money to do so, both in appealing directly to lawmakers (and helping finance their campaigns) and by seeking to mobilize popular support for their views. And they help determine who occupies key government positions, sometimes by filling those positions when the revolving door swings in the right direction. What does all this work add up to? Are lobbyists, as Americans since the founding generation have warned, dangerous figures whom we would be better off without?

DO LOBBYISTS CORRUPT AMERICAN GOVERNMENT?

The Toyota example that opened this chapter can be read two ways. One view is benign: practically all actors in the United States, corporate and public interest alike, now maintain a Washington presence, and they beef it up in times of scrutiny. Just as Toyota hired additional lobbying help when congressional hearings loomed, environmental groups retained more economics experts when cap and trade became part of Congress's agenda after 2006.

Others see lobbyists' saturated presence in Washington as a real problem, with the Toyota case one manifestation. Since the very beginning of the Republic, political leaders and many citizens have expressed concerns about the influence that "special interests" wield in Washington and state capitals. We have always had a love-hate relationship with lobbying, epitomized by James Madison's stern warnings against "factions"—interest groups by a different name—in *Federalist* 10. Concern about lobbyists has surged periodically since Madison's warning. Jacksonian Democrats, Progressives, New Dealers, sixties radicals: all were inspired in their mass movements for change by a fear that a few select groups (usually business) were enjoying undue influence in policymaking.

In 2005–2006 the high-profile GOP lobbyist Jack Abramoff was discovered not only to have flouted restrictions on lobbyist-lawmaker relations, but also to have bilked his clients (many of them Native American tribes) out of tens of millions of dollars.[24] A fresh cascade of outrage about interest group activity poured down on Washington. Members of Congress, even as they scrambled to rid themselves of campaign donations from Abramoff, drew up tough new regulations on lobbying. Three *Washington Post* reporters won the 2006 Pulitzer Prize for a series of articles exposing Abramoff's misdeeds. Democrats surged into the House and Senate majority during the fall 2006 elections, running on an honest government platform. And officials of both parties as well as media pundits described Abramoff's actions as normal Washington practice.[25]

Are shady dealings like Abramoff's still part of lobbyists' everyday practices, similar to the more free-wheeling days of Bobby Baker? The Abramoff example will be cited for years to demonstrate the essential corruption of interest group lobbying. According to a Rasmussen Reports survey a few months after the exposure, only 15 percent of Americans thought Abramoff did "anything different than what lobbyists typically do." Forty-seven percent said that Abramoff's actions were "the norm among lobbyists," and the other 38 percent were not sure.[26]

Yet Abramoff seems much more an exception than rule in contemporary American politics. As three political scientists, all longtime Washington observers, note: "Political reforms have *reduced* the level of corruption in American politics, including the level of bribery, quid pro quo, and special payoffs that involve special interests" (emphasis added).[27] Abramoff's case seems truly exceptional in several respects; most notably, the sheer scale of his thefts and other misdeeds was far greater than any other lobbying scandal of the past three decades, topping $100 million and involving fraud, bribing public officials, and money-laundering.

Ultimately, critics of a deeply "corrupt" world of lobbying may miss the mark. Abramoff in fact is not an example of business as usual. Instead, two tectonic shifts in how interest group lobbyists perform their work have taken place, and they are likely to prove very difficult to roll back.

One shift may stem from the decline in Washington policymaking of what might be termed ordinary virtues: tact, civility, or what President George H. W. Bush used to call "prudence." From organizing lavish fund-raisers to rotating from campaign staffer back to lobbying firm to mingling socially with lawmakers as close companions (not to mention spouses), many lobbyists engage in actions that once raised eyebrows but are now routinely accepted. These actions are all legal—and, indeed, it is hard to imagine how regulators could formally monitor such norms and practices. Clearly a line of reckoning, legally invisible but no less disturbing for that, has been crossed.

Closer associations between lobbyists and lawmakers do not represent a shift back to the bad old days of cash on the barrelhead lobbying. Ties between the two have grown tighter in part due to the professionalization of lobbying described in this chapter. This marks a second major change in Washington since the 1980s. And, just as with what counts as "normal" practices, it may be impossible to tease apart the elaborate networks of professional connections between lobbyists and public officials.

If the effort to police Abramoff's excesses have a long-lasting effect, it could come in focusing public attention on the extent to which lobbyists and lawmakers are intertwined. Initial reform calls following the Abramoff revelations concerned banning campaign contributions or ending privately financed trips for members of Congress and staff. But contributions are well protected by the First Amendment, as the Supreme Court has repeatedly affirmed. And "junkets," every detail of which must be disclosed publicly, are (sadly) often the only way policymakers travel and learn something about the rest of the United States and the globe. Instead, a beneficial result of the Abramoff scandal may lie in restoring a sense—which may have to be largely self-generated—of propriety and balance to the complex relationships between lawmakers and the tens of thousands of lobbyists who seek knowledge about and influence over their decisions.

NOTES

1. Jeffrey M. Berry and Clyde Wilcox, *The Interest Group Society*, 5th ed. (New York: Longman, 2008).

2. Anthony Nownes, *Total Lobbying: What Lobbyists Want (And How They Try To Get It)* (New York: Cambridge University Press, 2006).

3. Jeffrey H. Birnbaum, *The Lobbyists: How Influence Peddlers Get Their Way in Washington* (Washington, D.C.: Crown, 1992), chap. 2.

4. Lester W. Milbrath, "The Political Party Activity of Washington Lobbyists," *Journal of Politics* 20 (1958): 339–352.

5. Evan Thomas, *Robert Kennedy: His Life* (New York: Simon and Schuster, 2000), chaps. 13 and 14.

6. "By the Numbers: Salaries of 514 Top Executives," *National Journal*, April 3, 2010.

7. Berry, *The Interest Group Society* (1997 ed.), 108; Michael G. Bath, Jennifer Gayvert-Owen, and Anthony J. Nownes, "Women Lobbyists: The Gender Gap and Interest Representation," *Politics & Policy* 33, 1 (2005): 136; Kay Lehman Schlozman, "Representing Women in Washington: Sisterhood and Pressure Politics," in *Women, Politics, and Change*, ed. Louise A. Tilly and Patricia Gurin (New York: Russell Sage Foundation, 1990). On women's increasing presence in lobbying, see Denise Benoit, *The Best-Kept Secret: Women Corporate Lobbyists, Policy, and Power in the United States* (New Brunswick, N.J.: Rutgers University Press, 2007).

8. "Top Lobbyists: Corporate" and "Top Lobbyists: Hired Guns," *The Hill*, May 14, 2009 (compare *The Hill*, April 27, 2005); Kim Eisler, "Hired Guns: The City's 50 Top Lobbyists," *Washingtonian*, June 2007.

9. Anthony J. Nownes and Patricia K. Freeman, "Female Lobbyists: Women in the World of 'Good Ol' Boys,'" *Journal of Politics* 60, 4 (1998): 1181–1201; compare Benoit, *Best-Kept Secret*.

10. Amihai Glazer, "Rewarding Political Supporters," *Public Choice* 126 (2006): 454; Mary Clay Berry, "The Case for Public Financing," *APF Reporter* 9 (1977): 2.

11. For more details on types of lobbying activities, see Rogan Kersh, "Corporate Lobbyists as Political Actors," in *Interest Group Politics*, 6th ed., ed. Allan J. Cigler and Burdett A. Loomis (Washington, D.C.: CQ Press, 2002).

12. Rogan Kersh, "The Role of Lobbyists in Disseminating Policy Ideas," unpublished 2010 paper on file with author.

13. For more detail on lobbyists' use of information, see Rogan Kersh, "Lobbyists and the Provision of Political Information," in *Interest Group Politics*, 7th ed.

14. Fred Krupp, "Climate Change: Don't Forfeit the Game," *Science* 317 (2007): 1864–1866. On lobbyists maintaining internal coherence among their members, see Sanford C. Gordon and Catherine Hafer, "Collective Signaling and Political Action," unpublished 2010 paper on file with author.

15. James A. Thurber, "Lobbying Reform: Accountability through Transparency," Testimony before the House Committee on Rules, March 2, 2006.

16. Barbara T. Dreyfuss, "The Seduction: AARP and the Medicare Drug Bill," *American Prospect*, June 2004.

17. For more on lobbyists claiming credit with their clients, see Kersh, "Corporate Lobbyists."

18. Brian Kelleher Richter, Krislert Samphantharak, and Jeffrey F. Timmons, "Lobbying and Taxes," *American Journal of Political Science* 53:4 (2009), 893–909.

19. Kersh, "Lobbyists and the Provision of Political Information."

20. Scott Harris, "Political Dividends for Bush Backers," *The Industry Standard*, January 15, 2001.

21. *New York Times*, January 18, 1993; Panetta quoted by Charles E. Walcott, Shirley Anne Warshaw, and Stephen J. Wayne, "The Office of Chief of Staff," in *The White House World: Transitions, Organization, and Office Operations*, ed. Martha Joynt Kumar and Terry Sullivan (College Station: Texas A&M Press, 2003), 133.

22. Timothy P. Carney, "Obama, Who 'Excluded Lobbyists,' Has Appointed 50," *Washington Examiner*, March 31, 2010.

23. See www.opensecrets.org/revolving.

24. Peter H. Stone, *Heist: Superlobbyist Jack Abramoff, His Republican Allies, and the Buying of Washington* (New York: Farrar, Straus, and Giroux, 2006).

25. For details, see Rogan Kersh, "Ten Myths About Health-Care Lobbying," in *Health Politics and Policy*, 4th ed., ed. James A. Morone, Theodor J. Litman, and Leonard S. Robins (New York: Delmar, 2008).

26. "Americans Not Shocked by Abramoff," *Rasmussen Reports*, January 21, 2006.

27. Paul S. Herrnson, Ronald G. Shaiko, and Clyde Wilcox, "Only Permanent Interests? Creating and Sustaining Interest Group Connections in Changing Political Environments," in *The Interest Group Connection: Electioneering, Lobbying, and Policymaking in Washington*, 2nd ed., ed. Herrnson, Shaiko, and Wilcox (Washington, D.C.: CQ Press, 2004), 389.

SUGGESTED READING

Baumgartner, Frank R., Jeffrey M. Berry, Marie Hojnacki, David C. Kimball, and Beth L. Leech. *Lobbying and Policy Change: Who Wins, Who Loses, and Why.* Chicago: University of Chicago Press, 2009.

Bergan, Daniel E. "Does Grassroots Lobbying Work?" *American Politics Research* 37, 2 (2009): 327–352.

deKieffer, Donald E. *The Citizen's Guide to Lobbying Congress.* Chicago: Chicago Review Press, 2007.

Hall, Richard, and Alan Deardorff. "Lobbying as Legislative Subsidy." *American Political Science Review* 100, 1 (2006): 69–84.

Leech, Beth. "Lobbying and Influence." In *Oxford Handbook of American Political Parties and Interest Groups.* Ed. L. Sandy Maisel and Jeffrey M. Berry. New York: Oxford University Press, 2010.

Loomis, Burdett A., and Allan J. Cigler. "The Changing Nature of Interest Group Politics." In *Interest Group Politics,* 7th ed. Ed. Allan J. Cigler and Burdett A. Loomis. Washington, D.C.: CQ Press, 2006.

Lowery, David. "Why Do Interest Groups Lobby?" *Polity* 39 (2007): 29–54.

Kaiser, Robert. *So Damn Much Money: The Triumph of Lobbying and the Corrosion of American Government.* New York: Knopf, 2009.

chapter 27

Lobbying: Techniques and Impact

by Gary Andres

THE SUBTITLE OF THIS CHAPTER SOUNDS a little like a golf instructional DVD: "Keep your head down, relax, follow through." Not bad advice for a duffer—or a lobbyist either, for that matter.

But that is about where the similarities end. There is a temptation to reduce advocacy to a recipe: "Do these three things and get your bill passed into law."

But just as watching an instructional video will not turn you into Tiger Woods, following a formula does not guarantee lobbying success. It is difficult to shrink advocacy to one-size-fits-all mechanics. Sometimes the same techniques produce wildly different impacts. And certain approaches work best depending on the type of policy being advocated and the stage of the legislative process. Finally, the tactics and tools needed to protect the status quo often differ from those required to enact significant policy change.

Still, lobbying is also more than random acts. Cataloguing techniques allows us to evaluate the power and effectiveness of various methods and understand why some work and others do not. This chapter outlines the techniques of modern lobbying and assesses their efficacy.

LOBBYING DEFINITIONS

Part of the reason lobbying is widely misunderstood stems from definitional confusion.[1] The notion of lobbyists as influence peddlers trying to persuade policymakers through a variety of legal or even illegal means is fixed in the public psyche. Well before the now-infamous Jack Abramoff affair unfolded, the *Washington Post* wrote in a 1983 story about lobbying, "the storied tools of the trade have been booze, broads and black bags."[2] Ironically, in the summer of 2009, the *Post* was engaged in its own embarrassing lobbying controversy when word got out the newspaper planned to sell access to private "salon dinners" with its editors and reporters along with policymakers and other private interests and lobbyists. The newspaper quickly canceled the events once the practice was reported.[3]

Not only do the media reinforce the stereotype, but so do politicians. President Barack Obama has routinely railed against the evils of special interests and lobbyists, while at the same time coordinating closely with lobbyists from organized labor, trial lawyer, and environmental groups to help enact the White House agenda. The constant demonizing of lobbying helps sell newspapers and sounds good in political speeches, but it also fosters negative and misleading stereotypes. This cynical view implies the existence of a single and objective "public interest," which lobbyists either seek to protect or erode.

The real world of lobbying is different. As one recent study concluded, "The central questions of what lobbyists do, why they do it, and how, deserve reconsideration. . . . Political, technological, competitive and public policy trends have transformed the structure, style, strategies and substantive methods of the influence business over the past forty years."[4]

So what is lobbying? It is defined broadly and simply in this chapter as any activity aimed at influencing the actions of public policy decision makers. Why is a straightforward and expansive definition important? First and foremost, it is a more accurate description of lobbying. Influence can take on many forms other than direct, person-to-person advocacy. Moreover, it begins to clear up some misconceptions. With apologies to conventional wisdom, advocacy is a lot more than some fat-cat lobbyist plying members of Congress with three-martini lunches and campaign cash.

Finally, many forget that lobbying is a constitutionally protected endeavor. Just as the First Amendment provides protections for the media and the exercise of religion, it also guarantees the right to "petition the Government for a redress of grievances." When citizens come together or act as individuals to change, comment on, or influence the actions of public policy decision makers, they are not only "lobbying" but also engaging in a constitutionally protected activity. Syndicated columnist Charles Krauthammer even suggested lobbyists consider changing their name to reflect this constitutional protection and call themselves "grievance petitioners."[5]

Understanding lobbying, therefore, requires defining it in these broader terms. From a tactical perspective, petitioning techniques take on many forms and change along with technology and assessments of what works and what does not. Techniques also change as laws and regulations adjust over time. Lobbying under this definition includes direct approaches to policymakers, media strategies, mobilizing citizens (grassroots), strategic research, and yes, money. Each of these dimensions is explored in more detail in this chapter.

This broad set of advocacy tools—and their dynamic nature—also contribute to confusion about lobbying. Lobbying is challenging to understand when its methods are constantly in flux. Over time, the menu of lobbying tactics continues to grow and change. Often public and media misunderstanding of these transformations adds to the confusion about the techniques and impact of lobbying.

Even current law reflects this definitional problem—further contributing to confusion about what lobbyists do and even who they are. Consider two hypothetical interest groups, Citizens Against Dirty Air and People for Clean Water. They both have an interest in H.R. 10, a bill that appropriates $20 billion a year to provide pollution control equipment for lakes and rivers in America. Citizens Against Dirty Air hires a firm to advocate amending the bill to add money for air pollution cleanup. The firm registers for the client, arranges twenty meetings with the pivotal lawmakers in Washington, D.C., and receives a $100,000 fee from the group. Members of People for Clean Water take a different tactical approach. They hire a firm for the same amount of money to help organize grassroots activity in favor of H.R. 10 and to place ads in local newspapers of selected members of Congress. Although both firms are engaged in advocacy, and each organization spent exactly the same amount of money to influence the legislation, the first firm is required to register as a lobbyist, and the second is not. Both engaged in advocacy, but only one was subject to rules regulating lobbying activities.

This example underscores not only why lobbying is misunderstood but also why it is difficult to define. This chapter examines advocacy in a broader way. Despite current law not defining advocacy advertising or grassroots mobilization as lobbying, our broader definition puts them squarely into the lobbying business.

These definitional problems notwithstanding, lobbying is a big and growing business in Washington. One way to measure lobbying growth is by simply counting the number of pages in *Washington Representatives,* a publication that lists interest groups along with the internal and external advocates that represent them. Figure 27.1 underscores the growth in the lobbying field since 1977.

FIGURE 27.1 **Number of Pages in *Washington Representatives*, 1977–2008**

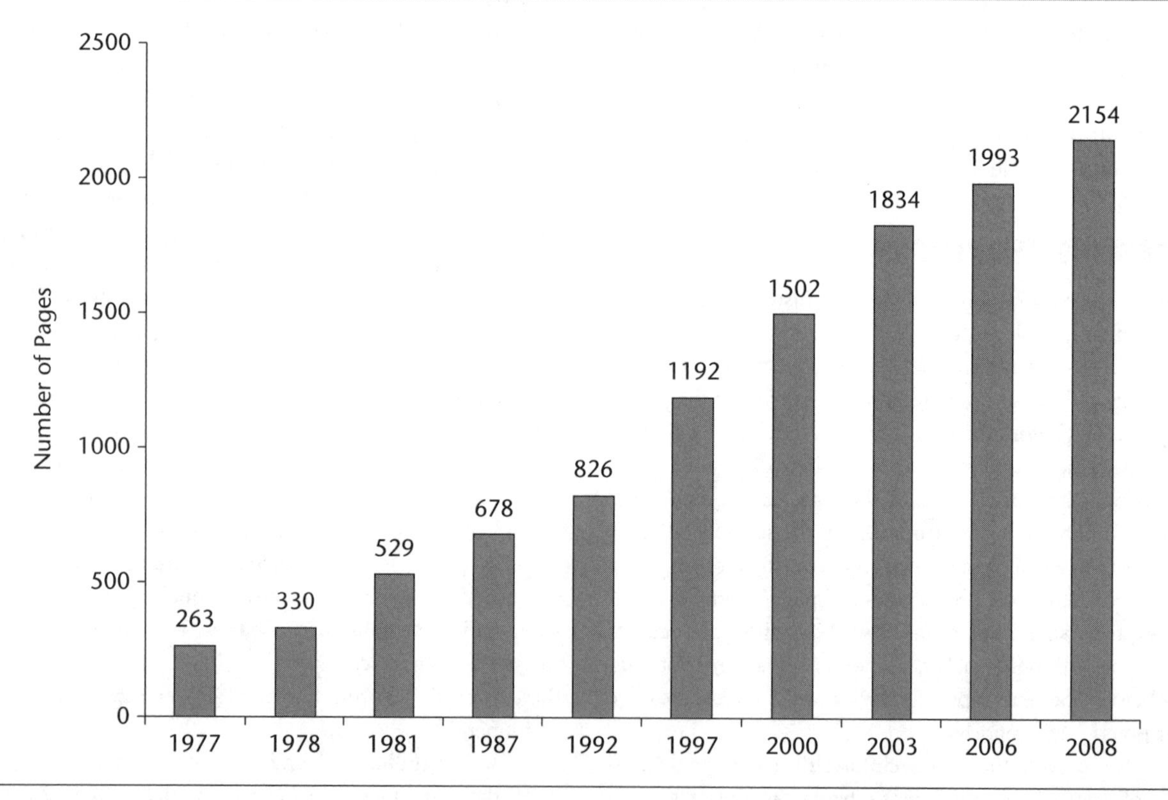

SOURCE: Compiled by the author from *Washington Representatives* (Bethesda, Md.: Columbia Books and Information Services, 2009).

LOBBYING TOOLS AND TECHNIQUES

Lobbying takes on many forms, ranging from direct advocacy to grassroots, as well as a host of activities to support advocacy, such as research and paid media. Each has an important role. Increasingly, lobbyists use multiple tools to conduct integrated advocacy campaigns. The image of the well-connected influence peddler is being replaced by highly organized, multidisciplined campaigns. As noted, direct lobbying will always play a big role in advocacy; it is just not the only role.

Direct Lobbying

When people think of lobbying, direct advocacy usually comes to mind. Lobbyists are hired to shape public policy by engaging directly with decision makers. How is this done? At the basic level, it is through various forms of communication: formal in-person meetings, informal conversations as lawmakers walk from their offices to the Capitol building, e-mail communications, and telephone calls.

But what makes these direct communications effective? After all, policymakers are busy and hear from many different people. Why should decision makers care what lobbyists have to say? As former Republican National Committee chairman Ken Mehlman has said, "Washington is a place with a wealth of information and a poverty of attention."[6]

The best lobbyists have superior information—political, policy, and procedural—which is why former congressional staffers and members of Congress often find lobbying firms to be a welcoming job market once they leave the public sector. They understand the game and all its dimensions.

Having information about how the process works, how challenges have been resolved in the past, or what opponents or proponents might be up to are all incredibly useful in the contemporary process. Information is power.

The metaphor of lobbyists as information brokers is well understood on Capitol Hill. Hill staffers tend to be young and overworked. Similarly, lawmakers are busy and pulled in many different directions. Lobbyists provide an efficient way to understand a problem, its impact in a lawmaker's district or state, and even what the opposition might be saying.

Political scientists Richard Hall and Alan Deardorff develop this concept of "lobbyist as information broker" further, suggesting advocacy is best conceived as a "legislative subsidy."[7] They argue that the public's view of advocacy needs to expand. Instead of thinking about it only as either "exchange" (vote buying) or "persuasion" (information signaling), they suggest legislative subsidy is a more apt metaphor. They describe this subsidy as a "matching grant of policy information, political intelligence, and legislative labor to the enterprise of strategically selected legislators."[8] They argue further that "the proximate political objective of this strategy is not to change legislators' minds but to assist natural allies in achieving their coincident objectives." Another observer, who analyzed lobbying during a much earlier period, comes to the same conclusion. J. McIver Weatherford, in his book *Tribes on the Hill*, writes, "Lobbyists play a permanent part in the congressman's career as information broker."[9]

Direct lobbying on Capitol Hill is one way that lobbyists can ensure that their message is heard by policymakers. Here, David Blankenship (left), a lobbyist for the National Federation of Independent Business, meets with Rep. Darrell Issa, R-Calif.

Effective direct lobbying also requires gaining policymakers' trust. There is a corollary in the advocacy world to the old adage, "You only get one chance to make a first impression," and it is this: *You only get to lie once in your lobbying career, because that will end it.* The best direct lobbying provides policymakers with timely, accurate, and trustworthy information about legislation, procedures, and other political intelligence. Successful direct advocacy can take on many forms. Some lobbyists are policy experts: they know more about a subject than lawmakers and staff. Other lobbyists might be procedural or coalition specialists, understanding the intricacies of parliamentary procedure or winning floor votes. In the midst of the health care reform battle in 2009, many interests hired lobbyists with expertise about the Senate budget reconciliation process to help them understand how that arcane procedure might affect the fate of reform legislation.

Those involved in direct lobbying also know the culture of the policymaking process extremely well. They understand the legislative schedule, the controversies of the day, and the rhythms of the process. As Patrick Griffin, a former White House staffer said, "The best lobbyists don't stand outside the process, but they are actually an integral part of it."

In the aftermath of the Jack Abramoff lobbying scandal, Congress and more recently the Obama White House instituted new rules on disclosure, gifts, and even whether lobbyists can attend meetings with executive branch personnel.

Much of this chapter's discussion emphasizes new modes of advocacy and a more integrated approach to lobbying, but some—like Abramoff—still saw the value of old school techniques. It is probably accurate to say buying drinks or lunches or even arranging golf excursions to Scotland never "bought a vote" or caused a lawmaker to cast a vote in conflict with constituent wishes. From the lobbyists' perspective, however, restricting meals, trips, or other forms of interaction does curtail an important source of information gathering and communication. In a post–lobbying reform world, there is still a need for information and communication.

Regulating a part of the First Amendment—petitioning the government for redress of grievances—will never be outlawed. Although some believe gift bans and other lobbying limits will end direct advocacy, in reality, they just change the venue. The three-martini lunch may be dead, but it has been replaced by coffee at Starbucks or e-mail communications.

Direct lobbying of lawmakers will always be an important part of the advocacy industry. After all, much of the influence business is based on personal relationships, conducting face-to-face meetings, and interacting over the phone or via e-mail. But these advocates need new tools because interest groups continually experiment with innovative ways to shape public policy decisions. The tools to support or go beyond direct advocacy are explored in the next sections.

Research

Can you imagine a major business embarking on a campaign to sell a product without any research on consumer preferences? How will potential buyers respond to a sales pitch? What is the competition selling? Whose market share will suffer as a result of a new business entrant? In the corporate world, this type of research is taken for granted.

And as the lobbying world evolves and becomes more sophisticated, an increasing number of advocacy firms rely on an array of research tools to help advance their causes. Whit Ayres, a well-respected Republican pollster, provided evidence of this trend in an interview with *Roll Call*, revealing how the greater use of research has affected his business: "Ten years ago, three-quarters of the business was polling for political candidates, with one-quarter for corporate and trade association clients. Now that ratio has flipped: 75 percent of the business is issue advocacy polling."[10]

President Obama's staff, like that of previous administrations, uses polling data and focus groups to help shape a persuasive message. "I mean, I'm looking at polling data, like, all the time," a top White House adviser told the *Washington Post*.[11] "I believe the more we know about underlying values and attitudes, and those deeply held attitudes that shape what people think, what they bring to the table, the more we can fine-tune a message," another one of Obama's political advisers said.[12]

Think tanks and internal issue experts are also a growing part of the advocacy world, as more corporations, labor unions, environmental groups, and trade associations employ people to provide policy analysis, research, or "issue management." These individuals may never set foot inside the U.S. Capitol, the White House, or a regulatory agency, but they play a major role in the advocacy process. They shape the language of policy proposals or responses to legislative and regulatory initiatives. They can help put together critiques and the positive messages associated with public policy ideas. These individuals are integral parts of the persuasive process. "Research renders all opinions unequal," said one longtime Washington political and public affairs expert.[13]

And as lobbying has evolved, so has the use of research as part of the advocacy process. "The days of back slapping, 'You help me, I help you' quid pro quo lobbying are long gone," the late Dan Dutko, founder of Dutko Worldwide, once said.[14] In other words, information and research in today's environment represent a form of policy power. The best lobbyists recognize this new reality and add research into their advocacy toolbox.[15]

An unusual industry has developed in Washington that caters to lobbyists and others with a stake in congressional affairs. Above, a couple is paid to wait in line outside of a hearing room on behalf of lobbyists wishing to attend, but not wanting to spend time in line themselves.

The increasing use of research-based message development by various sides in lobbying debates also fuels the growth of the advocacy industry overall. One major theme of this chapter is that lobbying has become more sophisticated. Interest groups need more than "shoe-leather" advocates. These lobbyists need supporting material and resources. Using more research is just one example.

Yet another explanation for growth is that mobilization and countermobilization by various "sides" in legislative and policy debates have helped fuel the overall size of the advocacy industry. As soon as one side in a legislative or policy battle has some powerful research findings, the other side needs to respond. Taken together, these collective actions fuel more advocacy activities and a bigger lobbying industry.

Grassroots/Grass Tops

A 2009 article from *Politico* underscores how and why grassroots is growing as a lobbying tool. Reporter Andie Collier wrote:

> In the future, everyone will be a lobbyist for 15 minutes. And they'll have President Barack Obama to thank for it.

The commander in chief may have no love for K Street, but his aversion to traditional lobbying tactics has combined in the public mind with the extraordinary grassroots campaign that helped propel him to the presidency to produce a result he probably did not foresee: a new enthusiasm for grassroots campaigns among lobbying firms and their clients.[16]

Most major advocacy campaigns inside the Beltway now incorporate a grassroots dimension. Collier interviewed a number of people involved in the lobbying world who underscored this point. One summed it up well:

> Everybody kind of gets it that if you want to make changes in what [legislators are] doing, you've got to get the consumer to speak up, that they're going to be the ones who are going to be affected. . . . That's what Congress wants to see right now. That's who everybody wants to hear from. That's just where we are as a country right now.[17]

Organizing grassroots is a tricky business. Lobbyists know that producing constituent support for their positions helps to persuade lawmakers, but these communications cannot seem manufactured or contrived by interest groups. Some in Washington call contrived grassroots support "astroturf," implying that it is artificial and ineffective. Sen. Harry Reid, D-Nev., brought a piece of plastic Astroturf to a press conference in the summer of 2009, charging that Republicans were manufacturing opposition to President Obama's health care reform efforts.

The most effective grassroots programs identify potential activists or interested individuals, educate them about the consequences of possible congressional or other policy action, and provide them the tools and information to communicate with policymakers. As discussed in more detail below, the Internet now serves as an effective tool to identify potential activists and provide them with easy means to engage with policymakers and their staff.

Since the early 1990s those involved in the advocacy business have added another form of citizen lobbying to their toolkit: "grass tops." This approach mobilizes elite constituents to add their voices to advocacy campaigns.

Grass-tops lobbying might include mayors, governors, or other elected officials. If grassroots promises *quantity* of contacts, grass tops promises *quality*. Lots of letters, e-mails, and phone calls can help demonstrate support or opposition for an issue, but if the mayor of a city or local business leader calls to weigh in, policymakers will listen closely.

Ideally, an advocacy campaign will include both. The most successful lobbyists count on grassroots and grass-tops reinforcements to help bolster their message and make a persuasive sale.

Paid Media

Paid media is one of the most misunderstood parts of the new world of lobbying. Conventional wisdom suggests that the goal of advertising is persuasion. In the public policy context, this suggests that paid media is intended to convince policymakers of the virtues of an interest group's position on an issue. In reality, advertising is important when it comes to advocacy, but persuasion is not the top priority.

Advocacy advertising has grown dramatically since 1969. Washington-based publications such as *National Journal*, *Roll Call*, and *Politico*, to name a few, have all grown in readership and circulation. And as the reach of these publications has expanded, so has the use of issue advertising on their pages. Figure 27.2 demonstrates the dramatic growth in this tactic.

Although you might think advertising is all about persuasion, it is not. Yet that does not diminish its importance. It can also help lobbyists make their case in other ways. And the audience for most issue advertising is also different from you might think.

Air Cover

Members of Congress need to believe the policies they support or oppose are receiving the requisite amount of visibility. Paid advertising can provide that kind of exposure to an issue.

A former member of the congressional leadership used to tell lobbyists when they came into his office, "You can't expect my members to walk the plank for you unless you give them air cover." Paid advertising helps reinforce the positions an interest group takes, explaining the advocates' position to a broader audience with a compelling message.

Many advocacy organizations run issue ads only inside the Beltway, on shows such as *Meet the Press* and *Fox News*

FIGURE 27.2 **Issue Advertisements in *National Journal*, 1969–2009**

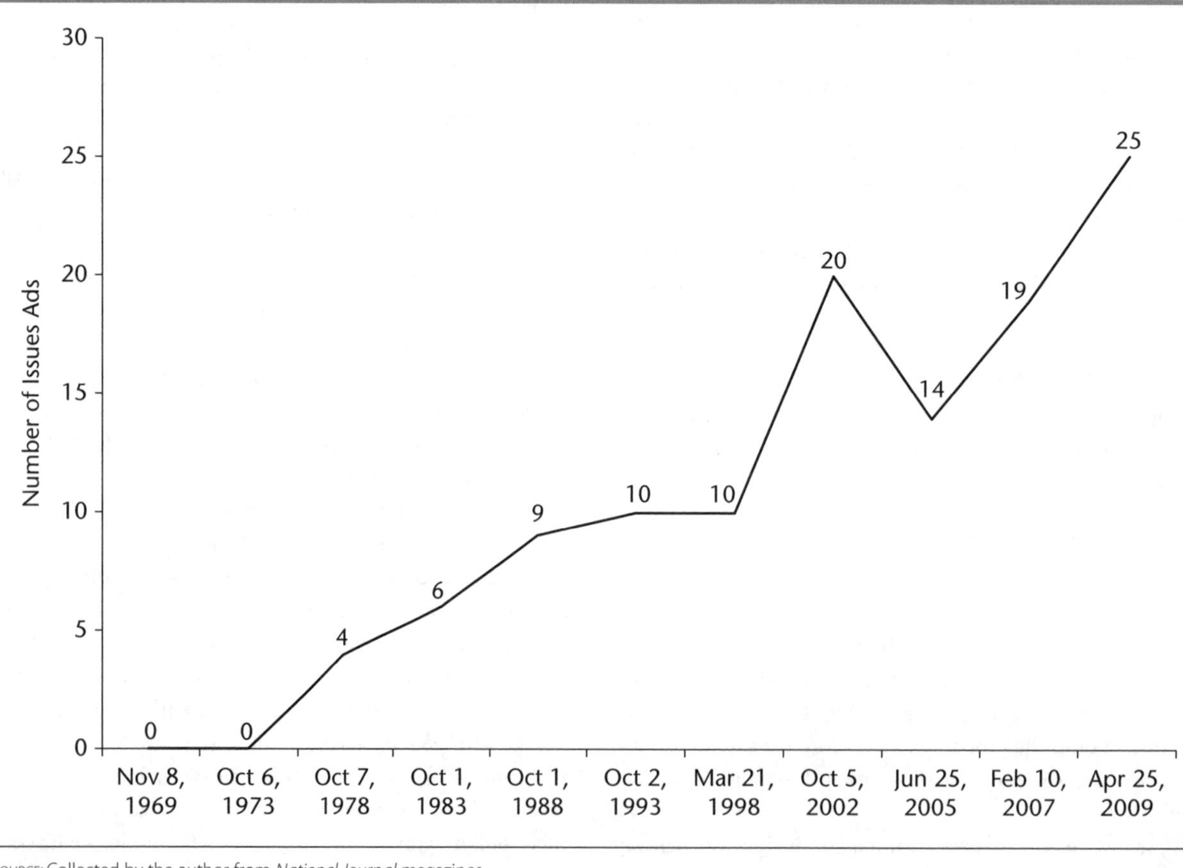

SOURCE: Collected by the author from *National Journal* magazines.

Sunday that opinion leaders watch. The ads help send a message to lawmakers and staff: "This issue is important, and we're investing money in a campaign to help build public support."

The constituents of most House members and senators never see these ads, but they send a signal, as well as a message to help frame the debate inside the Beltway and project a position of strength.

To communicate with policy elites, such as lawmakers, administration officials, and key staff, inside-the-Beltway paid advertising is usually run in widely read Hill publications, including *National Journal, Weekly Standard, Roll Call,* and *Politico.* Ads similar to the one on page 360 will also run on popular Web sites and cable programming.

Start the Chatter

Advocacy success often depends on getting on the agenda. Paid advertising, especially using the media, can help communicate important messages about an issue while projecting an image that the interest group's reach is broad and growing. The nonpolitical advertising industry recognizes the importance of starting "water cooler" conversation about an issue or a product. Inside-the-Beltway advocacy advertising does the same thing for a lobbying campaign.

Advertising can also do much more than communicate a message to someone who happens to see it. It can keep the conversation going among policymakers and staff. A well-crafted ad stimulates conversations among staff on the Hill. "I didn't know how bad the nursing shortage was. Maybe my boss should introduce a bill or look into the subject." Or, "Did you see that new Ford ad featuring all the *American Idol* finalists in the car in front of the Capitol?" Bringing new information or creativity to the policy process can sometimes help an issue's appeal grow more than could legions of shoe-leather lobbyists stalking the halls of Congress. Or, it can certainly help those engaged in direct advocacy sell their message by giving their product more visibility and buzz.

Respond to Opponents

Paid media is also an effective tool to respond to the charges of opponents. Sometimes a narrative catches fire on Capitol Hill. Consider this hypothetical case: H.R. 1 makes it easier for cable companies to get into the telephone business and offer consumers lower prices. "Not so fast," their telephone company competitors say. "We have a study that shows the opposite." Paid advertising can help get this alternative message out in an efficient manner. Not only do staffers read the ads, but also an interest group's lobbyists can e-mail them to the relevant contacts on the Hill. Again, in well-coordinated campaigns, paid media can work in tandem with the individual lobbyists to help disseminate a message quickly as a public debate unfolds.

Identify and Mobilize a Support Base

In the old media world, communications flowed one way. Advertisers did commercials or placed print ads, and that was that. In the new media world, advertising is more accountable, interactive, and does more than send a message—it can identify and mobilize supporters. Advertisers today send a message and ask for help. "Call Congress. Tell them not to cut Medicare benefits!" These types of ads began in the 1980s and have proliferated ever since.

The Internet propels mobilization and accountability to an even higher level. Advertisers now know not only how many people view an ad, but also who takes actions such as contributing money, sending an e-mail address, or volunteering to communicate with a policymaker. Given the power of new technology, paid advertising can spur grassroots action. "We now judge ads not only on what they communicate, but how they motivate people to take action," a campaign consultant turned public affairs manager told me. "Ads now not only ask people to do something, they give them the means to do it. People can point and click on an ad and send a message to Congress at the same time," he said.

Paid media include many dimensions beyond just trying to persuade a public audience. But even with their additional features, paid media can do only so much in a fragmented and often distracted new world of communications. Lobbyists today do more than just pay for media exposure; they now try to "earn" their way into stories that can further help their cause.

Earned Media

Lobbyists also use earned media in their arsenal of lobbying tactics. As opposed to paid media, earned media represents a favorable mention of a particular group in a media story. The more fragmented media environment has created both new challenges and opportunities for lobbyists—earned media helps overcome the challenges and exploit the opportunities.

In a more fragmented media milieu it is hard to get people to pay attention to your message. With the proliferation of cable channels and the Internet, it has become difficult to get concentrated viewership compared to the days when there were only three major broadcast networks. In the 1960s network paid media could saturate a market and drive home a message. No more.

Today, advocacy organizations need other ways to break through. Experts in the lobbying field note a growing trend toward advocates trying to get earned media stories as a way to pierce the clutter. "Most of the stories you read in *Roll Call, The Hill,* or *Congress Daily* were promoted specifically by someone trying to get a favorable process story about an issue gaining momentum or broader support, or trying to frame the debate. They are usually part of the spinning process," Greg Crist, a former communications

WHO ARE THE
9.2 MILLION
AMERICANS WHOSE
JOBS
ARE SUPPORTED
BY THE OIL &
NATURAL GAS
INDUSTRY?

i'm one

Bettina J.
Environmental, Health
and Safety Technician

Bettina is an environmental, health and safety technician for an oil and natural gas company. She is one of 2.1 million Americans working directly in a job that brings you the oil and natural gas you depend on. But that's only part of the story. The industry's $1 trillion lift to the U.S. economy each year actually supports another 7.1 million jobs in other sectors, from logistics to manufacturing to research to retail. All in all, that's real fuel for America's recovery.

Let's discuss the state of American energy at **EnergyTomorrow.org**

Source: *The Economic Impacts of the Oil and Natural Gas Industry on the U.S. Economy*, PricewaterhouseCoopers LLP, September 2009 (Sponsored by API)

© 2011 American Petroleum Institute (API)

THE *people* OF AMERICA'S OIL AND NATURAL GAS INDUSTRY

Advertisements such as this one from the American Petroleum Institute often appear in Washington professional publications as a way of disseminating information on a particular policy issue.

SOURCE: **Reproduced courtesy of the American Petroleum Institute.**

EARNED AND PAID MEDIA

In the world of political consultants and lobbyists, the words *paid media* and *earned media* get thrown around a lot. Paid media is pretty straightforward: it includes any time an interest group pays to place an advertisement in any form of media—whether print, TV, radio, or Internet. Earned media is a little more complicated, but considered more powerful by many insiders, and it refers to any time an interest group gets a favorable mention of its issue in a press story—"Group X advances its agenda because it aligns with powerful Congressman Y," or "Corporation A's CEO a big hit during recent round of Capitol Hill meetings." Stories like this get reported all the time in Washington, and they usually do not happen by accident. Somewhere in an interest group's strategy, someone considered how to promote its cause to a reporter who did a favorable story. Successful earned media stories can be powerful advocacy weapons.

director on Capitol Hill, said.[18] Further reflecting on how interest groups use earned media strategies, Crist added, "Right now people who do this [pursue earned media] are more artisans than scientists. But for those looking to what gives them an edge over their competitors, getting this kind of 'pull through' on their story really gives them a leg up.[19] In other words, it helps lobbyists break through the clutter and fragmentation and get their message on to the radar screens of busy policy makers."

So how is this done? It might be through pitching a new think tank study, or persuading a reporter to write a story about how an interest group is making progress moving its agenda, or maybe a piece focusing on a human interest side of a Washington lobbying battle (how H.R. 1 could help or hurt lawmakers' constituents), or giving a media outlet an exclusive on new polling or focus group research.

Advocates also use the demand for more content in the fragmented media environment as a way to pitch earned media stories. The need for material, along with the proliferation of media outlets, is a two-edged sword. Earned media addresses reporters' continual demand for new stories as well as the need for content interesting enough to break through the clutter.

UNDERSTANDING THE IMPACT OF LOBBYING

New and traditional lobbying tools are both being applied in dynamic and diverse political environments. The final part of this chapter focuses on assessing their impact and providing some insights to help students and scholars better understand how lobbying really works.

Integration

Do some of these tools and techniques work better than others? Probably. But the best lobbying strategies often integrate them all together, much like an effective political campaign—strong, research-based messaging, delivered by multiple, trusted messengers, followed by persuasive and creative media, and all punctuated by positive earned media.[20] Trying to isolate one piece of the lobbying process and evaluate its efficacy without regard for other factors and forces is a mistake.

Research by political scientist Frank Baumgartner and his colleagues underscores this point. Describing the impact of lobbying on public policy change, they write: "We see complex interdependencies, interactive effects of many variables, strategic actors responding to one another; we don't see a single actor or key explanatory variable, even money, that explains a large percentage of what occurs, on its own. Simple explanations come up short." [21] The bottom line in evaluating effectiveness: do not try to single out one tool and measure it. All of these tactics fit together and should be viewed as a whole, even if every one is not used in every situation.

Mobilization/Countermobilization

In addition to the interdependency of all these lobbying tactics, there is another reason why individual advocacy tools are difficult to evaluate: mobilization/countermobilization. This phenomenon provides another important insight into the way lobbying works in the real world.

Mobilization/countermobilization simply means this: most lobbying actions by one side in a debate create a reaction by the other side. And for this reason, gauging the impact of individual tactics is nearly impossible because they take place in an ever-shifting environment.

Here is an example. One interest group commissions a poll that demonstrates overwhelming support among voters for its position. If the survey were allowed to stand by itself, we could evaluate its persuasive impact. Yet once lobbyists for the interest group start circulating the information, the other side produces a poll of its own—countermobilization. The new poll asks questions slightly differently and perhaps adds some more background detail, and consequently new results emerge. Now the lobbying narrative shifts from a discussion about a poll to a debate about two polls. Which one asked the questions in an unbiased way?

Then the debate shifts again. The first group decides to invest in a paid advertising campaign further highlighting its poll results. Doing so gives much broader exposure to the survey and perhaps reestablishes an edge for the first interest group. Will the second group countermobilize again? Perhaps with an even broader and more effective paid media campaign of its own?

This dynamic of mobilization/countermobilization plays out every day in lobbying. Much like a political campaign that includes ups and downs and back and forth between the candidates, with each side using different tools and tactics to gain political advantage, lobbying campaigns include the same kind of give and take. Understanding this dynamic helps not only to explain how lobbying works, but also to underscore why it is nearly impossible to single out one particular tactic at a specific point in time and draw firm conclusions about its efficacy.

Money

Money is another misunderstood part of the lobbying and advocacy equation. The media drive most of the confusion by constructing an assumed nexus between campaign contributions and congressional votes—connections that are spurious at best and slanderous at worst. A *Washington Post* story provided just one small link in a long chain of dubious attempts to join votes and money.

> On June 19, Rep. Mike Ross of Arkansas made clear that he and a group of other conservative Democrats known as the Blue Dogs were increasingly unhappy with the direction that health-care legislation was taking in the House.
>
> Five days later, Ross was the guest of honor at a special "health-care industry reception," one of at least seven fundraisers for the Arkansas lawmaker held by health-care companies or their lobbyists this year, according to publicly available invitations.[22]

It is hard to prove a negative. The tone of the story suggests that Mr. Ross—like other lawmakers before him—traded votes or policy positions for money. This is a gross exaggeration, but a difficult one to refute given the media's commitment to this narrative and the public's predisposition to believe it.

In reality, this is a chicken and egg problem. Do lawmakers support interest groups because of contributions, or do contributions flow because of the positions members of Congress choose to take—with or without the money? Despite the many preconceptions about lobbying, the latter occurs a lot more than the former. In other words, lawmakers take the positions they do, with or without the money.

Contributions often flow because an interest has a plant or business facility in a member's district. The lawmaker supports the interest more because of the firm's employment numbers in his or her district, not because of a $1,000 political action committee (PAC) check.

Washington-based fund-raising events are also often misunderstood. Lobbyists may attend because they know their competitors will attend. Participation is intended more for a lobbyist to gather information and coordinate with like-minded lobbyists rather than ply a lawmaker with campaign cash in exchange for a vote.

Context

Considering context when measuring lobbying's effectiveness is also critical. Stopping an initiative is always easier than enacting comprehensive change. As a result, lobbyists playing defense may look effective, powerful, or successful as opposed to those pushing for major policy change. But it is actually the context of the change being sought—offense or defense—that is more determinative.

Partisanship also fits into context. Successfully convincing a majority member to do something or not could have a bigger impact (particularly in the House) than persuading a lawmaker in the minority. The minority does not completely lack power. The majority just has more.

Finally, where the president comes down on a measure also matters. Research demonstrates that when the president weighs in on a subject, all other things being equal, the chances of a successful change increase.[23]

Lobbying Impact: Hard to Quantify

Does deploying more advocacy tools guarantee increased success? Not necessarily. The impact of lobbying on the public policy process is more nuanced. Thinking that just investing more in lobbying produces more influence or power is a mistake.

But here again, this conclusion is inconsistent with conventional wisdom. The idea that bigger-spending interests "get" more is firmly embedded in the psyche of many and certainly is a well-worn media narrative. The problem is it just does not fit reality.

Political scientists discovered a similarly anomalous relationship between money and winning congressional elections. It turns out that the more incumbent representatives or senators spend, the worse their electoral performance.[24] Why? Competition. When incumbent lawmakers face stiff rivalry and believe they will have a close race, they raise and spend more money. Lawmakers with little competition do not have to spend very much to rack up large winning margins. From an empirical perspective this pattern produces a perverse outcome: the more you spend, the worse you do. But it makes good sense. Representative A, in a tight race, spends $3 million and wins by one point. Representative B with a weak competitor spends $1,000 and wins with by a landslide. Why did the candidate who spent so little money generate such overwhelming results? We know the reason has much to do with the level of competition.

Lobbying has parallels here. If an interest group is under fire in the policy process, it might spend money—tons of it. But so will its competitors. If the railroads gear up, the truckers respond. If banks invest in lobbying tools to gain a competitive advantage, the insurers may try to stop them. When large pharmaceutical companies protect patents and brand name products, the generic drug industry tries to trump them.

As a result, advocacy can sometimes take on the characteristics of an arms race. Each side spends as much as possible and stops only at its own peril. But policy debates include winners and losers—even if it means just maintaining the status quo. And spending a lot does not guarantee success.

Examples abound of groups spending large sums on lobbying and losing. This finding obviously confounds the causal link, much like the case of money in elections. More often than not, groups invest because they are about to lose or are under some policy threat. If they do lose, it looks as if all their spending had no impact. That is not necessarily the case. It may have had an impact or minimized the damage. But it could also have caused a countermobilization by the group's competitors that produced more harm.

When it comes to assessing the impact of lobbying, the bottom line is: it's hard to say. Researchers who investigate the relationship between money and lobbying success enter a complicated web that is difficult to untangle, with too many factors playing out simultaneously. Students and scholars, however, need to remember that just like money in elections, there is no linear relationship between spending money and lobbying success. Many other factors intervene.

Lobbying battles also never end. An interest group may avoid a new tax or onerous regulation this year, but the issue could easily reemerge in the next Congress. An interest might lose a legislative battle, but ameliorate the problem when it is implemented. A lobbyist might face defeat, but get the negative provision changed or repealed in a later Congress.

Lobbying and advocacy is an ongoing, iterative process where a lot of learning and adaptation takes place. Most issues are politically eternal: they have no beginning or end.

Finally, despite the ongoing importance of personal relationships in the advocacy world, success in lobbying is more than just gaining access through relationships. Advocacy professionals bristle most at the notion that their only skills are "who they know." Many lobbyists say these connections do not guarantee success. The following sums up the attitude shared by many involved in the lobbying business: "If anyone thinks hiring a former staffer for [Max] Baucus or [Charles] Schumer or Blanche Lincoln is going to get them what they want, they are crazy," said one health care lobbyist who previously worked on the Senate Finance Committee, referring to several important Democratic senators. "If we were being judged on that, a lot of us should be fired." [25]

LOBBYING: MORE THAN INFLUENCE

Here is one more insight about advocacy. Although this chapter catalogued some tools of influence and gauged their effectiveness, to better understand lobbying, students and scholars must recognize that it is about more than influence.

Given the growth of government, the fragmentation of the media, the increased specialization of policymakers, and partisan polarization, lobbying is more akin to a business consultancy service. Advocates help interest groups understand the political/policy environment and anticipate changes before they happen. They use a broad set of tools to try to shape/understand/respond to the dynamics public policy world.

Part of the lobbyist's job is to gather information and intelligence about what is coming down the pike and help position the client to deal with those realities. Sometimes this information leads a lobbyist to recommend an advocacy strategy using all the tools laid out in this chapter. Sometimes it means employing a more limited set of tactics. Sometimes it means doing nothing. Many interest groups hire lobbyists just to know what is happening in the government environment—not necessarily always trying to influence it.

Lobbyists also help to raise money, mobilize employees, and share information about the impact of government actions on an interest group's members. They can provide information for advertisements or help with new ideas to solve thorny public policy problems.

The days of the individual influence peddler, plying lawmakers with a three-martini lunch are over. But even in those days, lobbyists also relied on other tools and techniques. Misconceptions have always shrouded what lobbyists do, why they do it, and how they conduct their business.

NOTES

1. For a broader discussion about why lobbying is misunderstood, including these definitional problems, see Gary J. Andres, *Lobbying Reconsidered: Under the Influence* (New York: Pearson Longman, 2009).

2. Paul Taylor, "One Stop Shopping," *Washington Post*, August 1, 1983, A1.

3. *Politico* reporter Mike Allen broke this story and wrote several articles in the newspaper and on its Web site on July 2 and July 3, 2009. For a good review of the series of events, see www.politico.com/news/stories/0709/24441.html.

4. Andres, *Lobbying Reconsidered*, 21.

5. Charles Krauthammer, "Grievance Petitioners," *National Review Online*, February 29, 2008.

6. This is a paraphrase of a quote by Mehlman in Mark Halperin and John F. Harris, *The Way to Win: Taking the White House in 2008* (New York: Random House, 2006), 221.

7. Richard L. Hall and Allan V. Deardorff, "Lobbying as Legislative Subsidy," *American Political Science Review* 100, 1 (February 2006): 69–84.

8. Ibid. See also Andres, *Lobbying Reconsidered*, 99.

9. J. McIver Weatherford, *Tribes on the Hill: U.S. Congress Rituals and Realities*, rev. ed. (South Hadley, Mass.: Bergin and Garvey Publishers, 1985), 119. See also Andres, *Lobbying Reconsidered*, chap. 5, for a more detailed discussion of this concept of lobbying as legislative subsidy.

10. Kate Ackley, "Pollsters: Lobbying's Next Frontier," *Roll Call*, September 25, 2007.

11. Michael D. Shear, "Polling Helps Obama Frame Message in Health-Care Debate," *Washington Post*, July 31, 2009, A10.

12. White House pollster Robert Benenson, giving a speech in 2009 at the Economic Club of Canada, as quoted in ibid.

13. Andres, *Lobbying Reconsidered*, 142.

14. Ibid.

15. For more information and examples of how research is used in the modern lobbying world, see ibid., 142–147.

16. Andie Collier, "A President Obama Accident: A Nation of Lobbyists," *Politico*, July 24, 2009.

17. Ibid.

18. Andres, *Lobbying Reconsidered*, 148.

19. Ibid., 149.

20. Ibid., 205–206.

21. Frank R. Baumgartner, Jeffrey M. Berry, Marie Hojnacki, David C. Kimball, and Beth L. Leech, *Lobbying and Policy Change: Who Wins, Who Loses, and Why* (Chicago: University of Chicago Press, 2009).

22 Dan Eggen, "Industry is Generous to Influential Bloc," *Washington Post*, July 31, 2009, A1.

23. Baumgartner et al.,

24. Gary C. Jacobson, "The Effects of Campaign Spending in Congressional Elections," *American Political Science Review* 72, 2 (June 1978): 469–491.

25. Quoted in Dan Eggen and Kimberly Kindy, "Familiar Players in Health Bill Lobby," Washington Post.com, July 6, 2009.

SUGGESTED READING

Andres, Gary J. *Lobbying Reconsidered: Under the Influence*. New Jersey: Pearson, 2009.

Baumgartner, Frank R., Jeffrey M. Berry, Marie Hojnacki, David C. Kimball, and Beth L. Leech. *Lobbying and Policy Change: Who Wins, Who Loses, and Why*. Chicago: University of Chicago Press, 2009.

Cigler, Allan J., and Burdett A. Loomis. *Interest Group Politics*, 7th ed. Washington, D.C.: CQ Press, 2007.

Hall, Richard L., and Allan V. Deardorff. "Lobbying as Legislative Subsidy." *American Political Science Review* 100, 1 (February 2006): 69–84.

Herrnson, Paul S., Ronald G. Shaiko, and Clyde Wilcox. *The Interest Group Connection: Electioneering, Lobbying and Policymaking in Washington*. 2nd ed. Washington D.C.: CQ Press, 2005.

Kersh, Rogan. "Lobbyists and the Provision of Political Information." In *Interest Group Politics*. 7th ed. Ed. Allan J. Cigler and Burdett A. Loomis. Washington, D.C.: CQ Press, 2007.

McGrath, Conor. *Lobbying in Washington, London and Brussels: The Persuasive Communication of Political Issues*. London: Mellen Press, 2005.

chapter 28

Grassroots, Astroturf, and Internet Lobbying

by Dennis W. Johnson

AFTER THE NOVEMBER ELECTIONS in 1938, Speaker of the House William B. Bankhead, D-Ala., spoke with newly elected members of Congress, including C. Estes Kefauver, D-Tenn., giving them sage advice about their impending legislative careers and urging them to think ahead about the prospects of reelection. "Your votes and speeches may make you well known and give you a reputation," Bankhead said, "but it's the way you handle the mail that determines your reelection." [1]

That advice, given more than seventy years ago, applied to the days of the penny postcard and the rare long-distance telephone call; it applies with even greater force in today's world of sophisticated online communications, where lawmakers are inundated with millions of constituent e-mails and besieged by bloggers, twitterers, and social networkers. The lesson is fundamental and universal: elected lawmakers must know how to respond to genuine constituent needs and concerns, and they must be able to tell the difference between genuine concerns and hyperbole, between the real and the manufactured.

Legislators respond to constituent demands and other pressure in one of three basic ways: as delegates, trustees, or politicos. As first outlined by English philosopher and parliamentarian Edmund Burke in the late eighteenth century, then refined and updated by twentieth-century political scientists, lawmakers will vote either according to what they perceive as the wishes of their constituents, their own sense of right without regard to the input of constituents, or they will vote in a combination that responds to external pressure but also takes into account the lawmakers' own sense of what is right.[2] The fundamental genius of an elected representative government, with its constitutionally mandated frequent elections, is that legislators have to be reelected and consequently will do what they can to both understand the wishes and needs of their constituents and do their bidding. The dilemma facing them, however, is trying to balance the competing forces and voices, to make the necessary choices that serve the interests and desires of their constituents.

COMPETING PRESSURES

Lawmakers are confronted with competing pressures. They must be responsive to their party leaders, their own party caucus, to the White House (or resist the executive branch pleas), and to members of their state's congressional delegation. They must listen to and be responsive to organized interests, party power brokers, important constituencies within their state or district, and ideally, to the needs of all citizens. Legislators must also be able to tell the real from the manufactured and to discern the difference between the loudest voices and the best needs of their constituents. Above all, they must be able to gauge salient issues, even when unspoken or unarticulated by constituents.

Interest groups will try their best to reach their lawmakers through a variety of direct or indirect appeals. The direct approach is often characterized by the stereotypical well-heeled, well-fed lobbyist who plies the halls of Congress, committee rooms, and after-hours fund-raising receptions. The lobbyist might be accompanied by the client—the head of government relations of a trade association, the chief executive officer of a corporation, the labor union chief, the head of a civic or nonprofit organization—all claiming to represent the best interests of the local citizens, district, state, or the nation.

In many circumstances, this direct approach will be the most effective. Members of Congress learn firsthand the problems and opportunities facing the interest group, and they will be given talking points and briefing materials, and in many cases, even draft legislation tailored to the interest group's needs and goals.

In many cases, however, direct lobbying is not enough. It needs to be supplemented by the indirect approach. Lawmakers may also need (and want) to be assured that there are active, vigilant citizens and groups back home who are knowledgeable about the issue at hand, are motivated to act, and willing to support them at reelection time. In addition, the lawmaker must also know that an active and involved citizenry can be a double-edged sword; it may consist of mobilized citizens, grateful that the lawmaker will act decisively on their behalf, or irritated citizens, angered by the inattention or wrong-headed decisions of their member of Congress.[3]

The communication and pressure coming from citizens and groups from back home can be powerful reminders of the lawmaker's responsibilities. This is where grassroots lobbying enters the picture.

GRASSROOTS LOBBYING

The term *grassroots lobbying* applies to that broad spectrum of lobbying activity that emanates from constituent groups and is usually generated, orchestrated, and funded by lobbying and law firms, labor unions, corporations, and a whole variety of interest groups. Organizations and interest groups, large and small, engage in grassroots activities. The AFL-CIO, the nation's largest labor union federation, has an entire unit devoted to generating grassroots support from its union affiliates and their members, and it can wield enormous amounts of leverage during elections and while lobbying for or against federal, state, and local policy choices. Virtually all large, sophisticated interest groups employ grassroots techniques. So, too, do smaller groups that focus on a narrower range of issues. For example, the Cat Fanciers' Association, Inc., a nonprofit organization dedicated to the preservation of pedigreed cats, urges its members to organize at the local level to fight against the efforts of animal rights activists.[4]

Grassroots lobbying describes a wide range of activities that involve both groups and individuals who have stakes in policy outcomes: employees, suppliers, and shareholders of corporations; city and county officials; citizens who live in a certain locale affected by change; ideological, civic, cultural, and religious groups, and many more.

Grassroots activities focus on timely, effective communication with members of Congress, state legislators, and other elected officials. Such communication ranges from mass meetings, demonstrations, picketing, and mass telephone and mail campaigns to e-mail barrages, blog postings, text messaging, and other forms of online communications.

On the rare occasion, a grassroots organization will spring to life on its own, filling a perceived issue vacuum. That was the case when Wes Boyd and Joan Blades in 1998

The Tea Party Patriots, a grassroots movement that criticized excessive government spending, had a significant impact on the 2010 primary and general elections. Their rallies attracted considerable crowds, like at this Delaware stop of the Tea Party Express on October 31, 2010, in support of Republican Senate candidate Christine O'Donnell.

founded MoveOn.org and created a political forum for like-minded citizens who were fed up with the attempt to impeach Bill Clinton. The conservative Tea Party Patriots, particularly vocal during 2009, President Barack Obama's first year in office, sees its mission as attracting, educating, informing, and mobilizing like-minded citizens to fight against what they perceived as excessive government spending.[5] The Tea Party Patriots actively sought out candidates for the House and Senate elections in 2010, and because of their activism, several incumbent legislators, including Michael Castle of Delaware, were defeated in the Republican primaries.

In the end, most grassroots activity is generated, coordinated, financed, and orchestrated by established interest groups. When the policy issues involve the federal government and Congress, there is a strong chance that the grassroots activity is being managed by grassroots coordinators working at Washington-based law firms, lobbying shops, government affairs offices, or a whole range of communications offices at interest groups. In 1991 David Rehr, longtime political operative and then president of the National Beer Wholesalers Association, conceded: "Not many grassroots movements begin outside of Washington, D.C."[6]

Grassroots lobbying has existed for many decades. One of its more aggressive early uses occurred in 1948, when the American Medical Association hired veteran political consultants and poured millions of dollars into grassroots efforts to defeat President Harry Truman's bid for national health care. By the 1970s businesses and corporations were testing the potential for grassroots lobbying in what later was characterized as the "new corporate activism."[7] By the 1980s grassroots activities were firmly established in Washington and in state capitals as important tools to educated constituents and persuade lawmakers. A 1983 study of 175 Washington lobbying firms found that 84 percent had developed letter-writing campaigns and 80 percent used grassroots lobbying. A survey conducted in the late 1990s found that 56 percent of interest groups regularly mobilized their members.[8]

GRASS TOPS LOBBYING

A special category of grassroots activity is known as *grass tops lobbying,* the term given to local power brokers, business elites, and other influential citizens, who weigh in on a policy issue with letters, telephone calls, personal visits, and e-mails to lawmakers. Timely, well-crafted arguments from mayors, city council members, local chamber of commerce officials, and business leaders, the argument goes, can sway the opinion of elected officials. These communications, too, often are not written spontaneously, but orchestrated by interest groups that have identified in advance the principal influential individuals in a legislator's district or state.

Grassroots lobbying involves three sets of players. First, is the interest group itself, which devises and coordinates the grassroots campaign; second are the grassroots constituencies; and third are the targeted elected officials.

Group strategists know that a full-bore grassroots effort is something that can be attempted only sparingly throughout a legislative session. In fact, it may be years between the time that an organization flexes its full grassroots muscle and puts its reputation on the line by asking lawmakers to go to bat for it. Pulling out all the stops is of enormous consequence, a decision that involves a group's senior policy officials, its government affairs staff, as well as its communications, political, and grassroots specialists. Successful grassroots operations also require substantial background efforts. Interest organizations must prepare in advance their grassroots populations: employees, shareholders, group members, political, ideological and commercial allies, and grass tops supporters. These populations have to be identified, nurtured, and given basic information and updates on policy developments. As seen below, these activities have become vastly easier in the digital age.

The key to effective grassroots lobbying is having the right constituent groups or individuals contact the right elected officials, with the right message, at the right time. Failure on any one of these counts can easily mean a waste of resources and effort by the interest group. Lawmakers will respond to citizens living in their districts (and presumably voters), but will be far less inclined to respond to blanket appeals from individuals outside their districts or states. A grassroots appeal might be misdirected to a lawmaker who is firmly committed to another position and will not be swayed; or the appeal could be sent to a lawmaker whose committee jurisdiction has nothing to do with the pending legislation or who is already firmly committed to interest group's cause. The message received by lawmakers an from grassroots appeals must be succinct, be factual, and present a solid reason why the legislator should act or vote to the benefit of the group. Grassroots messages that threaten lawmakers rarely work and usually cause more friction and alienation than they are worth. The message must be delivered in a timely fashion. A million e-mails flooding a lawmaker's electronic inbox the day after a crucial vote is a wasted grassroots opportunity and a sure sign of bad planning and worse execution.

Grassroots constituents need to be prepared for action. They need to know the issues, know whom to contact, and know what to say. Frequent newsletters or e-mail alerts help to inform members or constituent groups, and many organizations take advantage of their Web sites to host Take Action pages. Many interest group organizations, as seen in the example below of the Sierra Club, will craft specific language that members can use in sending communications to lawmakers, while simultaneously encouraging members to use their own words and stories.

Grassroots and Health Care Reform

When members of Congress went home for summer break in August 2009, they were confronted with some angry, placard-waving citizens, who bellowed out their disapproval of the health care proposals coming from Congress and the White House. This was not the first time that health care reform had brought out vociferous grassroots opposition.

In November 1945 President Harry Truman strongly endorsed national health insurance, calling for health security for every American. Republican leaders and the American Medical Association (AMA) quickly labeled the president's program a "socialist scheme." [1] National health insurance legislation languished for the next two years, but after Truman's surprising presidential victory in 1948 and a reinvigorated Democratic majority in Congress, health care was back at center stage. In his 1949 State of the Union address, Truman forthrightly asked Congress to "spare no expense" and pass a comprehensive health care plan.

To fight against federal health care, the AMA turned to California-based political consultants Clem Whitaker and Leone Baxter, who had earlier helped the California Medical Association defeat a state-sponsored health insurance care proposal offered by Gov. Earl Warren. Whitaker and Baxter set up shop in Chicago, where the AMA had its headquarters, and with a staff of thirty-seven they spent nearly $5 million in the next three years, using the most sophisticated grassroots and direct lobbying techniques of the day. Whitaker and Baxter gathered 8,000 endorsements from nonmedical organizations, such as patriotic groups, women's organizations, and service and business organizations, both large and small, to oppose the president's plan. The consultants solicited favorable newspaper, magazine, and radio editorials against the plan, and they distributed some 40 million to 50 million pieces of literature in doctors' waiting rooms and hospitals throughout the country, warning patients of the perils of so-called socialized medicine.

In Washington, the AMA spent an additional $1.5 million in 1949 and $1.3 million in 1950 to fight against national health care. Up to this point in American history, no organization had ever spent so much money lobbying in Washington. The AMA then spent another $1 million in the two-week period before congressional elections, and $2 million more was spent by organizations allied with the AMA. National health insurance never stood a chance. The proposed legislation was shelved and did not resurface until four decades later.

Nearly a half century later, when President Bill Clinton took office in 1993, national health care became a high-profile, high-priority agenda item. First lady Hillary Rodham Clinton was put in charge of the effort to formulate and sell the package to Congress and the American people. But the Clinton proposal, adopted without serious congressional consultation, turned out to be an unwieldy, complex 1,342-page document, which was little understood by the public. The Clinton administration failed to sell its proposal to the people. In one telling episode, citizens assembled in focus groups had the Clinton proposal described to them. Seventy percent of the participants approved of the plan. But when the name "Clinton" was attached to it, the approval from participants dropped by thirty or forty points.

Health care opponents were quick to spot an opening. One of the biggest critics was the Health Insurance Association of America, which launched a $15 million issue advocacy campaign against the Clinton plan. Its television advertising, called Harry and Louise, featured a married, well-read, middle-class couple, sitting in their kitchen struggling over the complexities and seemingly unintelligible features of the Clinton plan.[2] This ad did not determine the fate of the Clinton bill, but it did indicate the industry's capacity to mobilize the grassroots.

More recently, during their long August recess in 2009, members of Congress got an earful from constituents who were venting their anger over the proposed national health care ideas that were being formulated by the Obama administration and Congress. Some lawmakers, as they made their way from one town hall meeting to another, were stunned at the hostility and bitterness they found. There were highly visible placards labeling President Barack Obama a Nazi, Stalin lover, or a socialist. In many cases, police had to be called in to make sure matters would stay calm. Much of the organizing for such protests came from conservative talk radio show hosts, bloggers, and astroturf organizations headquartered in Washington.

Later, thousands of conservative protestors came to Washington. The main organizer of the march on Washington was FreedomWorks, headed by former member of Congress Richard K. Armey, R-Texas.[3] FreedomWorks (formerly Citizens for a Sound Economy) is not required by law to disclose its donors, but the president of the organization insists that no money came from corporations fighting against President Obama's health care proposals.

One legacy of the Obama presidential campaign was the enormous e-mail file of supporters and friends. This database was put to use under a new organization, Organizing for America, based in the Democratic National Committee. Many of the tools of the presidential campaign were deployed in the health care debate: e-mail updates, pleas to send messages to members of Congress, solicitation of funds so that issue ads could be aired on television, updates on the www.barackobama.com Web site, and messages urging supporters to volunteer, join forces, and rally behind the president's health care plan.

1. On Truman and the fight for national health insurance, see Monte Poen, *Harry S. Truman versus the Medical Lobby* (Columbia: University of Missouri Press, 1979), 144–145; Stanley Kelley Jr., *Professional Public Relations and Political Power* (Baltimore: Johns Hopkins University Press, 1966), 67–106; and Dennis W. Johnson, *The Laws that Shaped America: Fifteen Acts of Congress and Their Lasting Impact* (New York: Routledge, 2009), 339–142.
2. The Harry and Louise ads were created by political consultant Ben Goddard of Goddard/First Tuesday, a California-based firm. See Robin Toner, "Harry and Louise and a Guy Named Ben," *New York Times*, September 30, 1994, A22; also Darrell West, Diane Heath, and Chris Goodwin, "Harry and Louise Go to Washington: Political Advertising and Health Care Reform," *Journal of Health Politics, Policy and Law* 21 (1996): 35–36.
3. Ben Pershing, "Armey's Army Marches Against Obama," *Washington Post*, September 27, 2009, A8.

ASTROTURF LOBBYING

Astroturf is the evil twin of grassroots lobbying. The label *astroturf* has been given to fake or manufactured grassroots activities. Just as AstroTurf, that synthetic grass used in playgrounds, football fields, and, originally, in the Astrodome Stadium in Houston, Texas, is artificial, so too, is astroturf lobbying, which journalist William Greider described simply as "democracy for hire."[9] Despite its dubious label and the questionable practices associated with it, astroturf lobbying, particularly in the online communications age, is flourishing. As political reporter Ben Smith observed during the summer of 2009, Washington, D.C., is a town "paved in Astroturf."[10]

Astroturf comes in several forms. The most common is the use of front groups—organizations, often with innocent or lofty sounding names, that hide the true membership, funding, and purpose of the lobbying effort. For example, several telecommunications front groups that fought policy battles in New Jersey included Consumers for Cable Choice (funded by Verizon Communications and AT&T), New Millennium Research Council (funded by Verizon Communications), and Keep It Local New Jersey (funded by the New Jersey Telecommunications Association).[11] In the field of the environment and conservation of western lands, the so-called "Wise Use" movement often used front organizations. People for the West! labeled itself a grassroots organization and received nearly all its funding from mining and other corporate interests.[12] During the 1993 health care debates, astroturf organizations such as Rx Partners and Coalition for Health Insurance Choices, funded by health and insurance organizations, had their messages and campaigns orchestrated by Washington-based public relations firms.

Astroturf organizations flourished during the 2009 health care debate. One such group was Americans for Stable Quality Care, which backed the Obama administration's health care agenda and was funded by the Service Employees International Union, the Pharmaceutical Research and Manufacturers of America (the lobbying arm of the drug industry), and other organizations. In summer 2009 it spent more than $12 million in twelve selected states in television advertising to convince citizens that President Obama's health care proposals would improve their lives.[13] Such a campaign is extremely lucrative to the lobbying firms that put them together, and over the past twenty to thirty years, many prominent Washington-based firms have prospered from their ability to manufacture grassroots movements.[14]

A more controversial kind of astroturf lobbying comes in the form of outright deception and lying. This happens infrequently, and if the wrongdoing is uncovered, the consequences are certainly counterproductive to both the public relations firm and its client. In one instance in 1995, some 600,000 telegrams were sent to Congress in support of long-distance telephone companies. About half of those telegrams were sent without proper authorization, according to Beckel Cowan, the public relations firm handling the account for the Competitive Long Distance Coalition.[15] In 2009 at least six forged letters were sent to Rep. Tom Perriello, D-Va., from minority organizations located in his district claiming their opposition to the American Clean Energy and Security Act of 2009. The letters, using the logo, name, and address of the Albemarle-Charlottesville NAACP and Creciendo Junto, a nonprofit network serving the Hispanic community in Charlottesville, were all fake, and had been sent by Bonner and Associates, a well-known Washington-based firm that has managed grassroots campaigns throughout the fifty states for corporations and nonprofit organizations. The two Charlottesville nonprofits, understandably, were outraged that their names and identities had been used falsely.

Congress has made several federal attempts to regulate grassroots lobbying, particularly to demand disclosure of the organizations behind astroturf groups. The Lobbying Disclosure Act of 1995, designed to bring some transparency to lobbying and influence seeking, created several new registration and reporting requirements. Earlier versions of the bill required political consulting and public relations firms that engaged in astroturf lobbying to register and report their expenditures. But those provisions were stripped out in committee and never became part of the lobbying reform law.[16] In late 2005 Sen. John McCain, R-Ariz., proposed similar grassroots disclosure provisions. Two years later, however, McCain joined Sen. Bob Bennett, R-Utah, and twelve other co-sponsors to strip a grassroots lobbying disclosure provision out of the Legislative Transparency and Accountability Act of 2007. Conservative organizations argued against the disclosure provisions. Pioneer direct mail specialist Richard Viguerie at GrassrootsFreedom.com said that the Senate was trying to make "exercising your First Amendment rights a crime." OMB Watch, a nonprofit, nonpartisan organization that promotes government transparency, argued in favor of grassroots disclosure, stating that "disclosure of big dollar grassroots campaigns will bring transparency to the process, so the public will know who speakers are and whose interests they represent."[17] In the end, no grassroots disclosure requirement won approval.

ONLINE LOBBYING

During the last several months of 1998, the United States was seized with the emotionally laden, partisan drive to impeach President Clinton. Special counsel Kenneth Starr issued his report on the investigation of alleged presidential misconduct by releasing it to the public via the Internet in September. Undoubtedly, for many people, both in the United States and worldwide, this was probably one of the first times they had downloaded a report from an Internet site. It was anticipated that the traffic would be so great that seven different government Web sites as well as the major media sites posted the report. Both controversial and titillating, the report was downloaded by millions throughout the world.

At roughly the same time, Blades and Boyd, California software entrepreneurs, were creating MoveOn.org, which served as a rallying point for persons who were fed up with the Republican-led drive to impeach the president. More than a half-million persons signed an online petition urging that Clinton be censured and that the country "move on" to more important things. Thousands of e-mails landed in the computer terminals of individual members of Congress. There had been earlier attempts to lobby through e-mail, but now a whole new set of opportunities was opening up online. In January 1999, during the height of the impeachment proceedings, House offices were averaging about 1,000 e-mails a week, and some Senate offices were receiving more than 10,000 e-mails a week.[18]

MoveOn.org continued its online activism and became an important communications vehicle for progressive voices. MoveOn.org donated $2.5 million to opponents of the impeachment managers; in 2002 it created a virtual phone bank to help get out the vote for antiwar candidates for office; and during much of the George W. Bush administration, fought against the wars, Bush policies, and Bush supporters in Congress. By late 2008 MoveOn.org claimed more than 4 million members.[19]

Blogs, action alerts, viral e-mails, text messages, and tweets have all become part of the arsenal of online communications that interest groups, large and small, have taken advantage of to inform and educate their members, friends, and like-minded groups, to raise funds, and to send urgent missives to lawmakers, urging them to take or block certain actions.

Many other advocacy groups, of all partisan and ideological stripes, quickly moved into the digital age. The advantages of online communications were immediately evident: lower price, faster speed, and better control. Interest groups can develop action alerts for their members, keep them apprised of moving legislation or policy activities, and urge them to communicate online or by regular mail or telephone with their lawmakers. Moreover, they can do so at a fraction of the cost of old-style grassroots activities. The second great advantage is speed, the ability to send the online messages at the optimum time to be effective. The turnaround must often be within a matter of days or even hours; e-mail and other forms of online communication make such responses possible, even routine. The third advantage, degree of control, cannot be

People gather at New York's Columbus Circle for a "We Can't Afford To Wait" vigil for health care reform, sponsored by MoveOn.org, in 2009.

overstated as an important vehicle. An organization can generally know which members and allies have sent online messages, and can assemble a team of faithful, consistent message writers who can be tapped again and again.

ONLINE ADVOCACY

Two examples show the range of online advocacy. The Sierra Club, like so many membership-based interest organizations, features a Take Action section on its Web site.[20] It encourages members to write to national leaders to protect the Tongass National Forest in Alaska, to stop the wall across the U.S.-Mexican border, to protect Colorado's roadless areas, and to save the critical habitat for the Florida panther. Altogether, the Sierra Club had an open call for action on thirty-two policy issues. For each, the organization gives a short description of the issue involved, offers a draft letter to be e-mailed to members of Congress or other elected officials, and encourages Sierra Club members to add their own personal comments to these communications. By asking its own members to fill in their names and addresses, the Sierra Club also has a good way of knowing who has sent online messages and identifying reliable members who can be called upon to send other messages. The Sierra Club also maintains three virtual sites—Climate Crossroads, Sierra Club Trails, and Sierra Student Coalition—where readers can share ideas, enter blog accounts, and discuss other opportunities.

A second example comes from a newer organization, FairTaxNation.org, a grassroots effort that seeks to abolish the Internal Revenue Service and replace all federal taxes on income with a new national sales tax. The organization backs legislation sponsored by several conservative Republicans.[21] Borrowing from the civil rights marches of the 1960s, FairTaxNation.org sponsored Fair Tax Freedom Rides, with teams of local motorcycle bikers and other supporters participating in their own "Ride of the Patriots" to Washington, D.C., to show their support for this legislation. FairTaxNation.org members communicate with one another and organize through their blogsite.

Groups do not need to develop their own online capacity. Private sector vendors can be hired to assist interest groups to track legislation, identify their allies, contact members, and conduct online lobbying campaigns. One of the most prominent is Capitol Advantage, which through its CapWiz software provides grassroots online communication services to more than 1,500 clients. Through its software products, 19.3 million constituent e-mails were sent to elected officials in 2008.[22] Capitol Advantage assists clients by helping them send to elected officials e-mails, faxes, and regular mail; to cover all bases, it will hand-deliver and mail items to the offices of legislators. Another Washington-based firm, 720 Strategies, provides clients with tools to improve social networking capabilities, develop viral marketing techniques, and assist them in getting the most visibility and impact for their blog sites.[23] Many other firms have also entered into the online communications business to assist interest groups get the most out of digital advocacy, a field that continues to grow quickly.

DO GRASSROOTS, ASTROTURF, AND ONLINE LOBBYING WORK?

The critical question is: Does grassroots lobbying, either traditional or online, actually work? Moreover, are lawmakers swayed by such communications? And do certain kinds of communications have more impact than others?

The congressional staffers who answer the telephones or manage the incoming e-mail in House and Senate personal offices at times gain a real insight into the frenetic nature of grassroots communications. Sometimes all outside telephone lines are jammed with calls from irate citizens who were stirred up by a talk radio host who rants against some particular policy or legislation, announces the lawmaker's public telephone number, and urges listeners to call in to the legislator to complain.

At other times, an interest group will hire a telemarketing firm to call its members, explain the urgency of particular legislation, and ask them if they want to speak directly to their member of Congress. The interest group member, now worked up, says, yes, I do, and then is patched through directly to the lawmaker's office.

The experience of Capitol Hill staffers who have served in the front lines of office communications is that the phone calls—generated by talk show jockeys or orchestrated by telemarketers—disrupt the flow of normal communications, cause more irritation than enlightenment, and often come from rude and belligerent callers, many of whom simply have little or no understanding of the issues being discussed.

Certainly astroturf lobbying runs the risk of alienating the lawmakers and the public. Outright falsification and lying, as seen in the example of the Charlottesville nonprofit organizations, is likely to permanently stain the reputation of a telemarketing, phone bank, or mail order firm and the organizations behind such activities. Such falsification is the exception to the rule. Still, astroturf lobbying thrives in the creation of fronted operations, where powerful organized interests use organizations with innocuous names to hide their true character, although policymakers soon understand the linkage.

By the end of 2001, more than a million e-mails a day were being received in congressional offices. The number of e-mails had spiked during the impeachment trial of Bill Clinton, and instead of tapering off after impeachment proceedings were over, they remained unusually high. During

COMMUNICATING WITH CONGRESS: BY THE NUMBERS

One hundred million American adults communicated with Congress from 2002 to 2007

- 44 percent of Americans had contacted a member of Congress or a U.S. senator.
- 43 percent had used the Internet as their means of communication.
- 62 percent of those Internet users who contacted their legislators did not believe that the lawmakers cared what they said.
- 46 percent of those Internet users were dissatisfied with the responses they received from their lawmakers.
- 84 percent of those who sent messages to Congress were asked to do so by a third party.

SOURCE: Kathy Goldschmidt and Leslie Ochreiter, *Communicating with Congress: How the Internet Has Changed Citizen Engagement* (Washington, D.C.: Congressional Management Foundation, 2008), vi.

the decade 1995 through 2004, the number of communications coming in to Congress had increased fourfold. In 2004 Congress received more than 200 million items, with 182 million of those communications coming via the Internet. The fourfold increase was all attributed to Internet-based communications. Yet, during this same time, staffing levels in personal offices of members of Congress had not increased to cope with the increased volume of messages.[24]

To try to manage the flow of e-mails coming into congressional offices, nearly all of the personal and committee offices now use filters, such as Write Your Rep, which require citizens to fill out a form asking for their postal ZIP code, and permitting only those e-mails from ZIP codes within a lawmaker's congressional district.

One research organization that has been studying the relationship of electronic communication between citizens and their legislators is the Congressional Management Foundation (CMF), a nonpartisan, nonprofit organization based in Washington, D.C. In a series of reports, CMF examined the extent and impact of online communications between citizens and federal legislators. In an early report, CMF found many lawmakers reluctant to accept e-mail, particularly if it was suspected to be automated or manufactured, as legitimate as regular mail. Many members of Congress also preferred answering e-mails with regular mail, with letterhead stationery and the member's signature affixed. But after the 9-11 terrorist attacks and the anthrax scare on Capitol Hill, regular mail was suspended for a time, and in many congressional offices, e-mail spiked by 400 percent.[25]

Members of Congress and their staffs are besieged with millions of e-mails each year, together with more traditional forms of communication, such as letters, telegrams, telephone messages, and personal visits. Clearly, it is far easier and more convenient for citizens and groups to send electronic messages to Congress, but the CMF concluded in a 2008 study that "less actual communication is occurring" and that "communications between citizens and Members of Congress are in peril."[26]

Are grassroots campaigns necessary? Nearly every major interest group and many smaller ones that vie for the attention of Congress have adopted some form of grassroots activity, knowing they need as many weapons and methods of persuasion as possible to get their views across to policymakers.

Do such campaigns work? Unfortunately, there have been few political communications or political science studies on the impact of grassroots campaigns. One study of grassroots campaigning at the state legislature level found a "substantial influence" on legislative voting behavior. But other recent scholarly analyses suggest that the effectiveness of such campaigns is at best anecdotal.[27] One of the problems of trying to determine the effectiveness of a particular grassroots campaign is that sophisticated lobbying techniques usually include a combination of communication and persuasion tools, in the form of both direct and indirect lobbying.

CONCLUSION

What is the most effective way to reach members of Congress and their staff with the hope of influencing them on pending or probable legislation? The convincing message might have come from a last minute telephone call from a highly paid Washington lobbyist, who offers a new, compelling twist on the issue. It could have come from the stern warning the members received from their party's leadership caucus meeting about the importance of voting a certain way. Perhaps it was the visceral negative reaction the lawmaker experienced at the town hall meetings just held during the summer recess or the visit to the lawmaker's old political mentor, the mayor of her hometown, who explained how critical the vote was going to be. The member of Congress may have been convinced by the 1,000 telephone calls that jammed up her office lines for three days straight or something her spouse said before they retired the night before. The telephone call from the White House might have been the key. Perhaps, it was the delegation of 100 blue-collar workers who took a day off work at no pay and drove 400 miles to Washington to plead their case. It might have been the 1,500 letters and telegrams received last week or the 4,000 e-mails received during the same time. Or perhaps the lawmaker simply used her own best judgment and political intuition, and, despite the protestations and arm-twisting, did what she thought was best, no matter the political consequences.[28]

No matter how difficult it is to discern the true impact of grassroots lobbying, in whatever form it takes, interest group organizations will continue to use these tools to communicate with their members, gather support, and convey their messages to elected officials.

Increasingly, grassroots lobbying combines online communication techniques with traditional methods. E-mails, blog messages, and social networking communications lead to alert and concerned citizens showing up at town hall meetings, meeting face-to-face with lawmakers, or telephoning them to complain or voice their concern. Lawmakers, attuned to electoral survival and meeting the expectations of their constituents, rely on such citizen feedback. In one way or another, lawmakers must discern what the people back home think and, before voting, know who is concerned about the issue and to what degree of intensity they are concerned.

Astroturf lobbying continues to flourish. Not so much the blatant, and ultimately self-defeating, misrepresentation found in forged letters or misleading communications, but through the campaigns of organizations camouflaged through innocent-sounding front groups. Attempts to force disclosure of the organizations behind such front groups have met with resistance, particularly (but not exclusively) from conservative voices who wrap their argument around the First Amendment right to petition and right to free speech.

Alert congressional staffers and members of Congress will see through such organizations and can readily discern manufactured letter-writing or e-mail campaigns. This is not particularly so with the general public, who will not know true origins of television commercials, Internet pop-up ads, and other communications. This is where astroturf lobbying thrives, in an atmosphere of nontransparency.

Grassroots lobbying in all its forms is one of the arrows in the quiver of interest groups. Grassroots campaigns, orchestrated at the right time, with the right message, sent by the right people to the right elected officials can make the difference between success and failure. They can supplement more direct forms of appeal, or they can be at the forefront of an interest groups communications efforts. Grassroots lobbying in the end is the robust reflection of a dynamic democratic system, where free speech, the freedom to petition, and the clash of ideas thrive.

NOTES

1. C. Estes Kefauver and J. Levin, *A Twentieth-Century Congress* (New York: Duell, Sloan and Pearce, 1947), 171–172.

2. John Wahlke, Heinz Eulau, William Buchanan, and LeRoy Ferguson, *The Legislative System* (New York: John Wiley, 1962), 267ff. Eulau, Wahlke, Buchanan, and Ferguson, "The Role of the Representative: Some Empirical Observations on the Theory of Edmund Burke," *American Political Science Review* 53 (September 1959): 742.

3. One study that examines the decision to lobby either directly or use grassroots approaches is Marie Hojnacki and David C. Kimball, "The Who and How of Organizations' Lobbying Strategies in Committee," *Journal of Politics* 61, 4 (November 1999): 999–1024.

4. Cat Fanciers' Association, "Unraveling the Mysteries of Grassroots Lobbying," www.cfainc.org/articles/legislative/grassroots-lobbying.html.

5. From the Tea Party Patriots official Web site, teapartypatriots.ning.com.

6. Quoted in Elizabeth Drew, "Bush's Weird Tax Cut," *New York Review of Books,* August 1991.

7. Edward A. Grefe and Martin Linsky, *The New Corporate Activism: Harnessing the Power of Grassroots Tactics for Your Organization* (New York: McGraw-Hill, 1995).

8. The 1983 study was by Kay Lehman Schlozman and John T. Tierney, "More of the Same: Washington Pressure Group Activity in a Decade of Change," *Journal of Politics* 45, 2 (1983): 351–377; the example from the late 1990s was from Ken Kollman, *Outside Lobbying: Public Opinion and Interest Group Strategies* (Princeton: Princeton University Press, 1998). See other examples in Daniel E. Bergan, "Does Grassroots Lobbying Work? A Field Experiment Measuring the Effects of an Email Lobbying Campaign on Legislative Behavior," *American Politics Research* 37, 2 (2009): 327–352.

9. William Greider, *Who Will Tell the People? The Betrayal of American Democracy* (New York: Simon and Schuster, 1993).

10. Ben Smith, "The Summer of Astroturf," *Politico,* August 21, 2009.

11. Dionne Searcy, "Consumer Groups Tied to Industry," *Wall Street Journal,* March 28, 2006, B4.

12. Samantha Sanchez, "How the West Is Won: Astroturf Lobbying and the 'Wise Use' Movement," *The American Prospect* 25 (1996): 37–42.

13. "The Ad Campaign: Americans for Stable Quality Care," *New York Times,* August 15, 2009.

14. "Astroturf," SourceWatch Encyclopedia, www.sourcewatch.org/index.php?title=AstroTurf. SourceWatch is a project of the Center for Media and Democracy, a nonprofit, nonpartisan public interest organization based in Madison, Wisconsin.

15. David Segal, "PR Firm Retreats on Telegrams; Phone Companies' Lobbying Tarnished," *Washington Post,* September 16, 1995. A subcontractor, NTS Marketing, Inc., a telemarketing and fundraising firm, had responsibility for calling individuals and getting permission to send out telegrams to Congress on their behalf.

16. Thomas P. Lyon and John W. Maxwell, "Astroturf Lobbying," *Journal of Economics and Management Strategy* 13, 4 (Winter 2004): 561–597.

17. "Misinformation Campaign Defeats Grassroots Lobbying Disclosure in Senate," *OMB Watch,* January 23, 2007, www.ombwatch.org/node/3151.

18. Dennis W. Johnson, *Congress Online: Bridging the Gap Between Citizens and Their Representatives* (New York: Routledge, 2004), 3–4; and background on MoveOn.org from the organization's Web site, www.MoveOn.org.

19. MoveOn.org Political Action, "Celebrating 10 Years of People Power," pol.moveon.org/10years.

20. Sierra Club Web site, action.sierraclub.org.

21. Fair Tax Act of 2009, S.296, sponsored by Saxby Chambliss, R-Ga., would "promote freedom, fairness and economic opportunity by repealing the income tax and other taxes, abolishing the Internal Revenue Service, and by enacting a national sales tax to be administered primarily by the states." The legislation was introduced on January 22, 2009. Companion legislation, H.R.25, was introduced by Rep. John Linder, R-Ga.

22. From the Capitol Advantage Web site, capitoladvantage.com. The author has served as a paid consultant to Capitol Advantage and its affiliate companies.

23. 720 Strategies Web site, http://www.720strategies.com/capabilities. This firm was formerly called e-Advocates.

24. Brad Fitch and Kathy Goldschmidt, *Communicating with Congress: How Capitol Hill is Coping with the Surge in Advocacy* (Washington, D.C.: Congressional Management Foundation, 2005), 4–5.

25. Johnson, *Congress Online,* 120–122; Kathy Goldschmidt, *E-Mail Overload in Congress: Managing a Communications Crisis* (Washington, D.C.: Congress Online Project, 2001).

26. Congressional Management Foundation, *Communicating with Congress: Recommendations for Improving the Democratic Dialogue* (Washington, D.C.: Congressional Management Foundation, 2008), i.

27. Bergan, "Does Grassroots Lobbying Work?" Bergan's study of grassroots coalitions on state legislative behavior show "substantial influence" on legislative voting behavior.

28. Johnson, *Congress Online,* 48.

SUGGESTED READING

Congressional Management Foundation. *Communicating with Congress: Recommendations for Improving the Democratic Dialogue.* Washington, D.C.: Congressional Management Foundation, 2008.

Johnson, Dennis W. *Congress Online: Bridging the Gap between Citizens and their Representatives.* New York: Routledge, 2004.

Kollman, Ken. *Outside Lobbying: Public Opinion and Interest Group Strategies.* Princeton: Princeton University Press, 1998.

Lathrop, Douglas A. "Political Consultants, Interest Groups and Issue Advocacy Work." In *Routledge Handbook on Political Management.* Ed. Dennis W. Johnson. New York: Routledge, 2008, 450–460.

Rosenthal, Alan. *The Third House: Lobbyists and Lobbying in the States.* 2nd ed. Washington, D.C.: CQ Press, 2001.

Schlozman, Kay Lehman, and John T. Tierney. *Organized Interests and American Democracy.* New York: Harper and Row, 1986.

Thurber, James A., and Colton C. Campbell, eds., *Congress and the Internet.* Upper Saddle River, N.J.: Prentice Hall, 2003.

West, Darrell, and Burdett Loomis. *The Sound of Money: How Political Interests Get What They Want.* New York: W. W. Norton, 1998, 1.

chapter 29

The First Amendment and the Regulation of Lobbying

by Ronald J. Hrebenar and Clive S. Thomas

Congress shall make no law respecting an establishment of religion, or prohibiting the free exercise thereof; or abridging the freedom of speech, or of the press; or the right of the people peaceably to assemble, and to petition the Government for a redress of grievances.

—U.S. Constitution, First Amendment

The First Amendment to the U.S. Constitution and the various laws, regulations, and legal cases based on it provide the essential rules of the game for understanding what limits can be placed on political speech in American politics. Every clause in the amendment has had an impact on types of political speech, including the broader processes of joining together in association and lobbying.[1] The words of the First Amendment to the U.S. Constitution seem to be quite clear and absolute in their prohibition against Congress passing any laws that would inhibit Americans from joining interest groups or lobbying the national government. As with many other provisions of the Bill of Rights, however, exceptions have been enacted over the years, and those exceptions are important for understanding the nature of lobbying and interest group politics in the United States.

The real question is what types of regulations on the practice of lobbying will be seen as acceptable protections for the society and its political processes without imposing a significant negative impact on the speech, assembly, and petition foundations of the lobbying process. Is requiring that all lobbyists register with the government unit they lobby enough to inhibit an individual's or organization's constitutional rights of speech, petition, and assembly? If registration is acceptable, then what about additional reporting requirements regarding lobbying expenditures? Then, what about limitations on how an individual or organization can use money to influence the political process? Once the politicians and judges accepted the idea that some regulation could be done without significantly undermining constitutional rights, the question becomes where does one draw the line?

All the clauses of the First Amendment have some type of impact on the lobbying process. The religion clauses give organized religions a special place in the American social and political process, and one of the continuing concerns of reformers and politicians over the years has been to be wary of any restrictions on lobbying that would have a negative impact on religion and religious activities. The freedom of speech and the press clauses are the foundations for all political activities and generally have been given the highest levels of protection by the Supreme Court. Although the speech and press clauses are very important for the lobbying process, this chapter concentrates on the last two clauses that directly related to the process of lobbying and interest group politics. These so-called "rights ancillary to freedom of speech" support the broader rights of freedom of speech and press.[2]

FIRST AMENDMENT PROTECTIONS: A LEGAL HISTORY

The First Amendment's guarantee of the right to petition the government has resulted in relatively few cases where the Supreme Court has explained just what that clause means. The clause has its historic origins in the British *Magna Carta* of 1215 and a 1669 statement by the British Parliament stating that citizens in England possessed the right to present petitions to Parliament. Then in 1689 the English Bill of Rights contained the right of the king's subjects to petition the king.[3]

The meaning of the right of petition has expanded beyond a redress of grievances to include political issues and matters involving the interest and financial prosperity of the petitioners. The right also has been expanded beyond the legislative and executive branches to include administrative agencies and the courts. The right to petition first became significant in American political history in the 1830s when petitions against slavery in the District of Columbia challenged Congress on that divisive issue. In 1840 the House adopted a standing rule that such slavery petitions would no longer be received.[4] John Quincy Adams, a former president of the United States, was then a member of Congress, and he strongly opposed the rules as direct violation of the right to petition government under the First Amendment. That restriction was repealed in 1844. But when security issues were hotly debated, as in World War I, petitions sent to Congress objecting to military recruiting even resulted in the imprisonment of the petitioners.[5]

The combining of petitions with marches or mass demonstrations has had mixed results in Washington, D.C. In 1894 Jacob S. Coxey led an army of unemployed men on a march to Washington and presented petitions, but the leadership was arrested for unlawfully walking on the Capitol's grass. A march of army veterans on Washington in 1932 demanded bonuses, but the Hoover administration called out the U.S. Army to expel the bonus marchers and burn their camps.[6] In the latter half of the twentieth century, marches and mass demonstrations became much more frequent, much more accepted as legitimate and constitutionally protected forms of political speech, and often were carefully coordinated with the Washington police.[7]

The right to assemble means not only the right to participate in some political action but also the right to belong to an organization that engages in politics. *United States v. Cruikshank* (1874) was the first right of assembly case heard by the U.S. Supreme Court. The case involved a massacre of black Republicans in Louisiana in 1873 by an armed white militia organization and a federal law that was passed to limit the Ku Klux Klan's acts of violence. The Court did not apply the First Amendment to the states, but ruled that the two rights (assembly and petition) are an "attribute of national citizenship . . . and guaranteed by the United States." [8] While this decision made the right of association a secondary right to the right of assembly, this difference has eroded over the years.

The First Amendment does not directly state that Americans have a right to join associations, but the right to assemble clause has been interpreted to mean a right to associate or to join together in groups to engage in political action and speech. The right to association was tested in a Supreme Court case regarding membership lists and other documents of the National Association for the Advancement of Colored People.[9] The justices ruled in favor of the right of association and the privacy rights of associations regarding their membership lists.

The application of the First Amendment to corporations expanded the number of actors beyond individual citizens who participate in lobbying. The Court initially affirmed the right of corporations to pay for electoral campaigns in *First National Bank v. Bellotti* (1978). Writing for the majority, Justice Lewis Powell explained that giving cash to influence the outcome of an election "is the type of speech indispensable to decision making in a democracy, and this is no less true because the speech comes from a corporation rather than an individual." [10] Indeed, under the prevailing interpretation of the Constitution, corporations have the same rights as individuals. This was not always the case: American corporations gained these protections in the nineteenth century, when the Court, in a series of rulings, defined the relationship between business and the state. Those rulings shielded companies from government regulation and thereby allowed the corporation to become the dominant form of economic organization. But in a landmark case, *Santa Clara County v. Southern Pacific Railroad* (1886), the Court, invoking the Fourteenth Amendment, defined corporations as "persons" and ruled that California could not tax corporations differently from individuals. It followed that as legal "persons," corporations had First Amendment rights as well.[11] Conservatives have long sought to expand the rights of corporations in American politics.

In 2010 the Supreme Court in a 5–4 decision further expanded the political speech rights of corporations and interest groups in *Citizens United v. Federal Election Commission*. This landmark decision appears to fully extend to corporations and interest groups the First Amendment's freedom of speech protections.[12]

Historically, the assembly, association, and petition/lobbying clauses have not been sites for government regulation, but in the twentieth century, Congress tried to place some restrictions on lobbying and the use of money in federal elections that impacted on political speech and lobbying.

THE FIRST AMENDMENT AND EARLY CONGRESSIONAL EFFORTS TO REGULATE LOBBYING

From the founding of the new national government in 1789 to the 1930s, Congress passed no laws that limited the practices of lobbying on the national level. Beginning in the early 1900s, reformers in Congress introduced bills to control lobbying, but without success. President Theodore Roosevelt in 1905 tried to ban all political contributions by corporations. He also supported public financing of federal candidates. Congress passed the Tillman Act (1907), which prohibited corporate monetary contributions to federal candidates, but the legislation had no enforcement mechanism or public disclosure requirements and its ban on corporate contributions was ignored. The Federal Corrupt Practices Act of 1925 (based on an earlier version, the Publicity Act of 1910) served as the federal level's basic campaign finance law until 1971. The act had no real enforcement power, and no federal candidate was ever prosecuted for violating it.[13]

In the 1930s Congress for the first time passed several laws that placed some limitations on particular lobbies. The first two such laws reflected congressional reactions to powerful lobbies that aggressively sought federal government preferences. Scandals involving the America's maritime shipping industry and the electric power generating industry motivated Congress to pass the first laws that placed some legal restrictions on lobbying. The maritime industry scandal resulted from excessive lobbying by certain companies seeking U.S. postal service contracts. The electric power industry had flooded Congress with millions of communications opposing laws that would impact its operations. Congress enacted the Public Utilities Holding Company Act of 1935, which required financial reports by power companies' lobbyists seeking to influence Congress. A year later, the Merchant Marine Act required lobbyist reports by maritime industries receiving federal subsidies. The legislation required monthly reports of the lobbyists' incomes, expenses, and lobbying interests. Both laws were fatally flawed. First, they were limited to only two of the many industries that lobby the federal government. But even more serious was the federal government's lack of interest in enforcing the laws. For example, one of the goals of the law was to publicize the acts of lobbying by these industries, but the reports were kept secret.[14]

The third lobby restriction law involved the registration of agents of foreign interests who attempted to affect American government decision making. In 1938 Congress became concerned with the possible lobbying and propaganda activities of agents of German and Italian interests. The Foreign Agents Registration Act sought to register anyone representing a foreign government or organization. The act was only occasionally enforced and usually against agents of communist nations. Congress reduced the law's scope in 1966, and agent registration fell off sharply after that. Exemptions to registration were given by narrowing the definition of the term *agent.* Lawyers were exempted if they engaged in routine legal activities for their foreign clients. The legal redefinition of agent greatly increased the burden of proof for government prosecutors, and even though the Justice Department was given some new tools of enforcement, such as civil injunctions, neither injunctions nor prosecutions have been used since the amendments were enacted in 1966. There are thousands of lawyers working in Washington, D.C., for foreign organizations, and many have never registered under this act.[15]

LOBBIES AND THE INTERNAL REVENUE SERVICE CODE

Two other laws passed in the 1930s have also had an impact on lobbying, as they have used the tax system to address the freedom of organizations to lobby on the federal level. Sections of the Revenue Acts of 1938 and 1939 denied tax exemptions to corporations that devoted a "substantial part" of their activities to propaganda and lobbying and denied income tax deductions to taxpayers for contributions to charitable organizations devoting "substantial parts" of their activities to lobbying. Both of these laws are important because they limit an organization's resources that can be used to lobby. Frequent contemporary references to IRS Code sections 501(c)(3) and 501(c)(4) relate to restrictions on organizations to conduct largely educational activities or to allow for substantial lobbying. Therefore, 501(c)(3) organizations, such as the American Red Cross, Salvation Army, and United Way, fall under the category of religious, educational, charitable, scientific, or literary organizations and are quite limited in their abilities to effectively lobby on the national level. Jeffrey Berry has argued that these 501(c)(3) groups could be more aggressive in their political advocacy, but they are restrained by their leaders' perhaps overly cautious interpretation of the limits on lobbying imposed by the IRS rules.[16] Donations made to these organizations are tax deductible, but the organizations are to be largely nonpolitical. In contrast, 501(c)(4) organizations, such as the AARP, League of Conservation Voters, and National Rifle Association, operate exclusively for the promotion of social welfare or for charitable, educational, or recreational purposes. They have an unlimited ability to lobby for legislation and the ability to participate in political campaigns and elections and contributions made to them are not tax deductible. These IRS code sections divide organizations into two sets of groups: some able to lobbying without significant limits and others prohibited from lobbying in any substantial way.

Another section of the IRS code—Section 527—has become an important part of the contemporary lobbying game, and it addresses tax-exempt organizations that seek to influence the nomination or election of public officials. The rise of the 527 groups in the 2002 and 2004 elections brought demands for regulation. Unlike political action committees (PACs), 527s are not regulated by the Federal Election Commission (FEC), but have only a reporting requirement to the IRS. These groups may not advocate the election or defeat of a candidate for federal office, but they may "educate" the public. During a campaign the 527s run television and radio ads that seek to "inform" the voters on a given issue. The ads ordinarily discuss a political issue and then urge the watchers to communicate with the candidate. There is a prohibition on coordinating the issue campaign with any candidates' campaigns. The best-known 527s include the Swift Boat Veterans for Truth, which ran a media campaign against Sen. John Kerry; America Coming Together; Progress for America; and Moveon.org. These four 527s spent about $160 million in the 2004 federal elections. All together, almost $440 million was spent by 527s in 2004.[17] Their spending declined

WHAT IS THE DIFFERENCE BETWEEN 501(C)(3) AND 501(C)(4) ORGANIZATIONS?

The ACLU comprises two separate corporate entities, the American Civil Liberties Union and the ACLU Foundation. Although both the American Civil Liberties Union and the ACLU Foundation are part of the same overall organization, it is necessary to have two separate organizations to enable us to do the broad range of work necessary to protect civil liberties.

—ACLU.org

Although there is some overlap in the work done by each organization, certain activities the ACLU does to protect civil liberties must be done by one organization and not the other. This division is primarily in the area of lobbying. The American Civil Liberties Union engages in legislative lobbying. As an organization that is eligible to receive contributions that are tax-deductible by the contributor, federal law limits the extent to which the ACLU Foundation may engage in lobbying activities. Therefore, most of the lobbying activity done by the ACLU and discussed in this Web site is done by the American Civil Liberties Union. By contrast, most of the ACLU's litigation and communication efforts are done by the ACLU Foundation. Thus, the ACLU is a 501(c)(4) group and may engage in substantial lobbying, but donors may not receive tax deductions for their contributions; while the ACLU Foundation, a 501(c)(3) group, does give donors tax deductions, but is very limited in its political activities.

to about $260 million in 2008. Efforts made in 2005 to regulate 527s by placing them under FEC jurisdiction and limit contributions to them failed as Republicans and Democrats could not agree on which party the 527s seemed to help more. The decline in 527s expenditures from it peak in 2004 may be linked with the enhanced capacities of political parties and candidates to raise huge sums for their own campaigns (see Chapter 30). *Citizens United* appears to have encouraged greater corporate participation in federal elections, but not through direct expenditures on electioneering. Rather, in the 2010 midterm elections corporate and other conservative interests made large contributions to 501(c) (4) groups that spent tens of millions of dollars supporting Republicans in their successful campaign to regain control of the House of Representatives.

Congress Enacts Broad Lobby Registration Laws: The 1946 Reforms

In 1946 Congress passed a major legislative reorganization act that for the first time included a broad-based lobby registration law. The Federal Regulation of Lobbying Act of 1946 (FRLA) was aimed at the whole category of lobbyists working in Washington, D.C., not just those of a few industries or agents working for foreign interests. Only a couple of pages in length, the FRLA was added on to the reorganization law as an afterthought. It provided for the registration of any person hired by someone else for the purpose of lobbying Congress and required quarterly financial reports of lobbying expenditures. These provisions were challenged in *United States v. Harriss* (1954), and the Supreme Court ruled several of the act's most significant parts unconstitutional.[18] The legislation was too vague to meet the requirements of the Fourteenth Amendment's due process requirements, and the reporting and registration provisions violated First Amendment rights, the justices said. The Court concluded the law applied only to those individuals or organizations whose principal purpose is to influence legislation and covered only direct communications with members of Congress on pending or proposed pieces of legislation.

Overall, the FRLA was seriously flawed from the beginning. Many lobbyists refused to register because they claimed that lobbying is not their "principal purpose." Several of the most powerful Washington lobbying organizations for decades refused to register. No grassroots or indirect lobbying was covered by the act. None of the multimillion dollar massive grassroots lobbying operations run to support or kill legislation in Washington were ever reported (see Chapter 27). Only direct contacts with Congress had to be reported, and therefore the law excluded activities such as testifying before congressional committees and the preparation of that testimony. Other groups claimed that their contacts with Congress were purely informational and not lobbying as defined by the act. The focus on direct contacts with members of Congress meant that lobbying of the congressional staff of the individual representative or the professional staffs of a committee was not covered. Furthermore, the law covered only congressional lobbying, so that lobbying the White House, executive departments, regulatory agencies, courts, or any other government organization was exempted. Decisions on what to report were basically left up to the lobbyist to determine. Some lobby organizations reported all of their lobby-related expenditures to Congress; others reported almost nothing. All of these loopholes severely reduced the law's effective regulation of lobbying, and it was further rendered impotent by the failure to provide for any real instruments of enforcement. In the end, the Justice Department largely gave up any attempts to enforce an unenforceable law. Nor did the

David Bossie, president of Citizens United and producer of Hillary: The Movie, *found himself at the center of a landmark Supreme Court case,* Citizens United v. Federal Election Commission *(2010). The Court found that campaign finance restrictions infringed upon corporations' free speech rights, thereby freeing them to spend money in political campaigns.*

responsible offices in the two chambers of Congress, the Clerk of the House and the Secretary of the Senate, perform any monitoring activities after the reports were filed.[19]

Clearly, the first attempt to produce a constitutional and effective lobby regulation law was a failure. Most lobbyists in Washington never registered, and the vast majority of lobbying expenditures still went unreported. Another fifty years would pass before a serious effort was made to correct some of the loopholes of the 1946 law. A rarity in the U.S. Congress, this controversial law was never formally *amended.* It was repealed and then replaced by a new law passed in 1995.

The 1995 Lobbying Regulation Reforms

After a half-century of attempts to repair the flaws of the FRLA, a major reform was accomplished in 1995. The Lobbying Disclosure Act dealt with many of the loopholes of the 1946 law, but still failed to deal with some major ones. It incorporated many of the provisions from previous lobbying laws under a single, uniform statute. Congress passed rules that restrict gifts from lobbyists. Both chambers agreed to end the "fruit baskets" left in the members' offices, the lavish dinners, and free recreational ski trips for members and their staffs with lobbyists. The rules barred senators and representatives from accepting all gifts, meals, and trips except those from family members and friends. The Senate allowed gifts of value of less than $50 with $100 total limits from a single source in a year. The House allowed no gifts of any value from a lobbyist. The law allows exceptions for trips and attendance at events connected to the lawmakers' official duties, such as throwing out the first ball at a baseball game. The exception for trips proved to be a big loophole in that it allowed all-expense-paid trips for fact-finding or associated with official duties, such as "to speak on Congress" before a convention. International trips are limited to seven days and domestic trips to four days, excluding travel time. These changes were important steps toward effectively reducing the role of money in creating access. Finally, registration and disclosure of lobbying incomes and expenditures were greatly improved under the 1995 law, and the American public now has a much clearer set of data to examine regarding the nature of lobbying in Washington.

Many, but not all, of the 1946 loopholes were closed. The new law required better reporting of lobbying activities and extended coverage to the executive branch and the independent regulatory agencies. Because many argued that attempts to limit grassroots lobbying and religious lobbying would infringe too much on the First Amendment rights to petition Congress and the freedom of religion, grassroots lobbying and lobbying by religious groups were excluded from the provisions of the new law. These two exceptions are huge because so much significant lobbying involved grassroots campaigns, and in recent decades lobbying by religious groups has become frequent and powerful. So strong were the objections to the creation of effective lobbying regulations that many compromises had to be made to ensure passage. One major provision that was dropped from the final bill was the creation of an independent enforcement agency. Other major provisions, such as a ban on high-level federal employees to lobby for foreign governments, were also dropped from the bill. The final vote in the House of Representatives was 421–0. Because many members had little or no interest in an effective lobbying regulation law, the unanimous vote indicates the largely symbolic nature of the reform law.

The 2006–2008 Lobbying Reforms

Lobby reform does not happen because it is needed to make the American political system better; it happens almost always in response to a scandal and legislators' perceptions that they need to adopt new regulations or pay the price at the next congressional elections. This is exactly what happened in 2006.

Three well-publicized lobbyist scandals generated tremendous pressure on both parties to deal with some of the perceived excesses disclosed during the 2005–2006 run up to the 2006 elections. The biggest scandal involved the superlobbyist Jack Abramoff's huge expenditures for luxurious golf trips to Scotland, various sporting and entertainment events for congressional leaders paid for on the lobbyist's credit card, along with overcharging his Native American clients by almost $80 million in lobbying fees, while often playing one tribe off against another and diverting his lobbying fees to powerful politicians. In 2005 Rep. Randy "Duke" Cunningham, R-Calif., traded defense contracts for at least $2.4 million in bribes from lobbyists. Cunningham, a former Navy fighter pilot, resigned his seat in Congress and was sentenced to jail. About the same time, Rep. William Jefferson, D-La., a graduate of Harvard Law School and Louisiana's first black member of Congress since Reconstruction, was targeted by federal investigators for taking money to use his congressional clout to arrange business deals in the United States for various African businessmen. Jefferson denied that he had done anything improper, but FBI agents searched his home and found $90,000 in cash in his freezer. He was convicted of receiving bribes in August 2009.

There were so many loopholes to close after the 1995 reforms that the 2006 reformers had numerous items to choose from. They could have banned free travel by government officials on corporate jets; banned excursions to foreign and domestic resorts paid for by lobbyists; established a strong watchdog agency to monitor and enforce lobby laws; prohibited all gifts from lobbyists to government officials and lengthened from one year to two years the period of time a member of Congress, staffer, or executive branch official had to wait to begin lobbying after leaving government service. Congress was controlled by Republicans, who worried about losing control of the House and Senate if they did not act on lobbying reform after controlling the former for twelve years and the latter on and off for most of the same period. The Republican Speaker called for reforms, but did not produce a strong bill. The House version did not include a ban on gifts, did not extend the waiting period to two years, did not eliminate the "earmarks" so beloved by lobbyists and members, did not extend existing reporting requirements to grassroots lobbying campaigns, and did not provide for any enforcement agency. It did require members and their aides to attend ethics training classes and attempted to regulate the 527 nonprofit groups. The Republicans at that time sought to limit 527s because they perceived them to be more supportive of the Democratic Party. The bill died before the 2006 elections, and when the Democrats took control of both chambers of Congress in 2007, they were more aggressive in enacting lobbying reforms to fulfill some of the campaign promises.

WHO IS JACK ABRAMOFF, AND WHY IS HE THE MOST (IN)FAMOUS LOBBYIST EVER?

Jack Abramoff was convicted and sent to prison in 2006. Prior to this turn of events, Abramoff had perhaps the greatest run of success of any lobbyist in American history. There are more than a few lobbyists in Washington, D.C., who earn more than $1 million a year in lobbying compensation, but how many have charged a handful of clients $80 million in fees? In addition, Abramoff owned an exclusive restaurant and used it to wine and dine the city's political elite. He took powerful members of Congress on golf vacations in Scotland and seemed to have the ear of many powerful Washington officials, including even some in the White House.

Abramoff combined a fine education with powerful friends connected to the Republican Party and conservative movement into a very successful political career. In late 1994 he joined Preston Gates Ellis & Rouvelas Meeds LLP, the lobbying arm of a law firm. The Republicans had just captured control of the House of Representatives for the first time in forty years, and the firm wanted a conservative Republican with close ties to the party. Abramoff claimed to be close to several of the new GOP leaders: Newt Gingrich, Dick Armey, and Tom DeLay.

The following year, Abramoff struck pay dirt. He acquired as clients several Native American tribes that were part of the growing world of Indian casinos and gambling. Abramoff worked with DeLay to defeat a bill that threatened to tax Indian casinos. Abramoff's next big client was the Commonwealth of the Northern Mariana Islands, which paid millions to Abramoff and his law firm for getting exemptions to U.S. immigration and labor laws for the island's low-paid labor force that was very attractive to several U.S. apparel brands.

In January 2001, as George W. Bush was about to occupy the White House, Abramoff left Preston Gates and joined the government relations part of another conservative Republican firm. When he changed jobs, he apparently took millions of dollars worth of clients to his new firm. Between 2000 and 2003, six Indian tribes paid Abramoff more than $80 million in fees. This world of power and influence fell apart when Abramoff was sentenced to six years in prison on criminal charges, including tax evasion and fraud. Abramoff also was convicted and sentenced in late 2008 on charges of evading federal taxes. By the time the cases had concluded, associates of Abramoff, members of Congress, Bush executive branch administrators, congressional staff members, and some private businessmen had been convicted of various related crimes.

SOURCES: SourceWatch, "Jack Abramoff," www.sourcewatch.org; James Harding, "Jack Abramoff: The Friend Tom DeLay Can't Shake," *Slate*, slate.com/toolbar.aspx?action=print&id=2116389.

Jack Abramoff, seen here leaving federal court in 2006, realized incredible financial success as a Washington lobbyist, but later became the poster child for political corruption.

With the Democrats in charge, Congress adopted new ethics rules in 2007.[20] Each chamber has its own distinct ethics rules and history of how such rules may be enforced. Both chambers of Congress have adopted internal rule changes that addressed five general areas of lobbying reforms: (1) broad and detailed disclosures of lobbying activities conducted by lobbyists; (2) greater restrictions on the "gift culture" of lobbyists giving gifts including free travel to members of Congress and their staffs; (3) new restrictions on "revolving door" employment patterns of government officials retiring to the private sector to become lobbyists and then often returning government service as policymakers; (4) reform of government pension rules impacting members of Congress who have been convicted of crimes related to their positions of trust; (5) and greater transparency of the internal legislative process with special emphasis on accountability in adding earmarks to pieces of legislation.[21]

Some of the major loopholes were closed by the 2007 legislation, but some serious problems remained. The system for electronic disclosure of the lobbying reports is still very difficult for citizens to access and the enforcement provisions are still inadequate. In 2008 the House authorized the new Office of Congressional Ethics (OCE). An eight-member OCE board was appointed (half by the Democratic Speaker and half by the ranking House Republican), but it is not clear how effective the enforcement powers will be with this new office. It has no power of subpoena and can only recommend possible further investigations to the House Ethics Committee. In its 2010 first quarter report, the OCE noted that during the 111th Congress, it had conducted forty-eight preliminary investigations: twenty-two were closed, and twenty-six warranted further investigation.[22]

CAMPAIGN FINANCE LAWS AND THEIR IMPACT ON LOBBYING

Money used to influence American elections is a special concern of reformers. Congress, usually in response to scandals, has passed several significant laws that attempted to regulate the role of money in federal election campaigns, and cases testing these laws have led to several very important First Amendment decisions by the Supreme Court. The use of interest group money in federal elections is important because it is a principal way that groups ensure their access to government officials. Early laws prohibited labor unions and corporations from directly contributing to such campaigns. In 1971, 1974, and 1976, Congress passed and amended the Federal Elections Campaign Finance Act (FECA). The law established the Federal Elections Commission to regulate federal elections and especially the role of money in these elections. It set up federal funding with a tax check-off system for citizen contributions to the fund and a matching system for subsidizing federal candidates' campaigns. It tried to place limits on how much a candidate could spend of his or her own money in a campaign and set limits on how much money individuals and organizations could contribute to federal campaigns. The law was challenged in court as an unconstitutional violation of First Amendment rights. The Supreme Court ruled in *Buckley v. Valeo* (1976) that most of the FECA was constitutional and that spending money was a constitutionally protected form of political speech, but overturned several parts.[23] Declared unconstitutional were limits on how much money a candidate could spend of his or her own money in campaign and general limits on campaign spending.

The FECA seemed to limit the donations an interest group could give to a candidate for federal office to $5,000 per election per year. But, as usual, the money seemed to find a way to the candidates regardless of the law. "Bundling" of individual contributions from members of a group or organization was a way to avoid the limitations. Under the bundling tactic, many members of an interest can combine their donations, and a bundler, often a lobbyist, could deliver the collected checks to the candidate, and the interest would get full credit for the donation in the politician's eyes.

The next major campaign finance law Congress passed was the McCain-Feingold Act or the Bipartisan Campaign Reform Act of 2002 (BCRA). It amended the FECA of 1971, and it was fast-tracked to the Supreme Court for decisions on several parts that were considered as possible violations of the First Amendment. Major provisions of BCRA were a ban on unrestricted ("soft money") donations made directly to political parties and limits on the advertising by labor unions, corporations, and nonprofit organizations for a period of sixty days prior to a federal election. The Court in *McConnell v. Federal Election Commission* (2003) issued a very complicated 5–4 decision running more than 270 pages in length. It upheld the bans on soft money and advertising prior to federal elections. It held that the restrictions on freedoms of speech were minimal. Justice Clarence Thomas noted in dissent that the decision was the "most significant abridgement of the freedoms of speech and association since the Civil War."[24] In a follow-up decision in 2007, the Court ruled in *Federal Election Commission v. Wisconsin Right to Life, Inc.*, that organizations engaged in a genuine discussion of issues were entitled to a broad exemption from the election communications provisions of BCRA.[25] The ruling signified a retreat from BCRA's regulation of such ads paid for by interest groups and opened the door to the *Citizens United* appeal, in which the Court ruled that corporate funding of independent political broadcasts in candidate elections cannot be limited under the First Amendment. In essence, the *Citizens United* decision gave corporations the same freedoms of political speech as those held by individual American citizens.

ETHICS RULES IN THE EXECUTIVE BRANCH

Another set of rules that act to regulate and often restrict lobbying have been enacted by both houses of Congress and the White House. They can often be found under the label of "ethics rules" and encompass a range of prohibitions on what elected and appointed officials can receive from lobbyists and in what manner these officials can interact with lobbyists as well as their possible future employment as lobbyists.

New White House ethics rules were much in the news early in the Obama administration. Actually, Barack Obama's attempts to limit the influence of lobbyists on his organization began in his presidential campaign with a well-publicized prohibition on lobbyists, political action committees, or corporations contributing money directly to his campaign. During the transition period (November 2008 to January 2009) Obama placed a $5,000 limit on interest groups and lobbyists giving money to partially fund the transition process. The transition process had a budget of $12 million of which $5 million came from the taxpayers and the other $7 million was raised privately. The director of the transition team, John Podesta, stated that Obama had banned lobbyists from the process. Podesta said, "These are the strictest ethics rules ever applied." Any lobbyist who joined the transition team was banned from working on the team in his or her area of lobbying.[26]

Despite stating during the campaign that lobbyists would not be getting jobs and operating in his White House, Obama soon discovered that staffing an administration in Washington, D.C., could not be done without inviting more than a few interest group leaders and lobbyists onto the team.

One of Obama's first presidential orders after the inauguration was to issue a set of ethics rules for his administration. The Executive Order on Ethics Commitments by Executive Branch Personnel included a prohibition on accepting gifts from lobbyists; a ban on former lobbyists participating in decisions related to their former employment for two years; and a prohibition on communicating with a former executive agencies for lobbying purposes for two years after leaving an executive branch agency. The official White House statement attached to this executive order said its purpose was to "rein in the influence of lobbyists in Washington" and to shut down the "revolving door that carries special interests in and out of government."[27]

These ethics rules generally met with widespread public support, but also with some significant doubts as to how effective they would be in the day-to-day process of politics. Moreover, there were always some doubts about whether the rules seriously infringed on the constitutional rights of lobbying and association, but no immediate constitutional challenges were made to test these aspects of the White House ethics code.

LOBBY REGULATIONS AND THE FIRST AMENDMENT

The seemingly absolute position of the First Amendment regarding lobbying has been modified by many of the laws, rules, and regulations that have been discussed so far in this chapter. The courts and legislature have wrestled with the protection of the rights of speech, assembly, association, and petitioning against the growing demands by reformers for laws that seek to limit the tools that lobbyists, individuals, and organizations can use to influence public policy. By and large, there is relatively little real interest in lobby regulation among the major actors in the Washington political game. The business of government involves the allocation of trillions of dollars in the federal policymaking process, and anything that stands in the way of successful lobbying is fought tooth and nail by the lobbyists and most of the elected officials.[28] The battles are also fought in the fifty state capitols, and state lobbying laws have become important elements in the policymaking game.[29]

Nearly every reform has been opposed in the legislative and judicial processes as violations of the First Amendment. Ultimately, the Supreme Court has tried to balance the First Amendment guarantees against the government's desire to hold fair elections and honest and transparent lobbying. Following recent scandals, the new rules of the House and Senate and the new ethics rules of the White House and the executive branch will contribute to a more open and transparent American politics. Much like squeezing a balloon, however, the problems associated with lobbying will soon bulge out in another part of the political system, and the reform battles over lobby laws and the First Amendment will start again. The tensions between the First Amendment and the rules of the American lobbying game seem never to be resolved.

NOTES

1. There are many useful books on the First Amendment and its focus on political speech. Anthony Lewis, of the *New York Times,* has written a book with a popular approach to the question of political speech: *Freedom for Thought We Hate: A Bibliography of the First Amendment* (New York: Basic, 2010). Recent First Amendment books in the more academic category include Daniel A. Farber, *The First Amendment: Concepts and Insights* (Eagan, Minn.: Foundation Press, 2003); Kathleen M. Sullivan and Gerald Gunther, *First Amendment Law,* 4th ed. (New York: Foundation Press/Thomson, 2010); Thomas L. Telford et al., *Freedom of Speech in the United States* (State College, Pa.: Strata Publishing, 2009); and Vikram D. Amar, *The First Amendment, Freedom of Speech: Its Constitutional History and the Contemporary Debate* (Amherst, N.Y.: Prometheus Books, 2009).

2. Sullivan and Gunther, 369–397 and 398–416.

3. Cornell University Law School, "Rights of Association," www.law.cornell.edu.

4. William Lee Miller, *Arguing About Slavery: John Quincy Adams and the Great Battle in the United States Congress* (New York: Vintage Books, 1995), 112.

5. The Supreme Court has said the rights to petition are not absolute. See *McDonald v. Smith,* 472 U.S. 451 (1985). See also Adam Newton, "The rights to petition," Firstamendmentcenter.org.

6. Paul Dickson and Thomas B. Allen, *The Bonus Army: An American Epic* (New York: Walker, 2004).

7. "First Amendment," www.law.cornell.edu.

8. *United States v. Cruikshank,* 92 U.S. 542 (1876).

9. "Association," www.law.cornell.edu. See *NAACP v. Alabama,* 357 U.S. 449 (1958), and also three cases that clarified how groups have control to determine who can be members: *Roberts v. United States Jaycees,* 468 U.S. 609 (1988); *Hurley v. Irish-American GLB Group of Boston,* 515 U.S. 557 (1995); and *Boy Scouts of America v. Dale,* 530 U.S. 640 (2000). In *Yates v. United States,* 354 U.S. 298 (1957), the Court ruled that the First Amendment protected radical speech unless it posed a "clear and present danger."

10. *First National Bank of Boston v. Bellotti,* 435 U.S. 765 (1978); *Lafayette Insurance Company v. French,* 59 U.S. 404 (1855).

11. *Santa Clara County v. Southern Pacific Railroad,* 118 U.S. 394 (1886).

12. *Citizens United v. Federal Election Commission,* 558 U.S. 50 (2010).

13. Robert H. Sitkoff, "Politics and the Business Corporation," Northwestern University School of Law, Law and Economics Papers, 2004. No. 24.

14. Ronald J. Hrebenar, *Interest Group Politics in America* (Armonk, N.Y.: M. E. Sharpe, 1999).

15. Ronald J. Hrebenar and Bryson B. Morgan, *Lobbying in America* (Santa Barbara, Calif.: ABC-CLIO, 2009), chap. 10.

16. Jeffrey Berry, "Non-Profits as Interest Groups: The Politics of Passivity," *Interest Group Politics,* ed. Allan J. Cigler and Burdett A. Loomis (Washington, D.C.: CQ Press, 2006).

17. Opensecrets.org, "527s: Advocacy Group Spending in the 2008 Elections," www.opensecrets.org/5272/index.php.

18. *United States v. Harriss,* 347 U.S. 612 (1954).

19. Cleanupwashington.org, "Lobbying Reform and Influence Peddling Laws."

20. The House Leadership and Open Government Act of 2007 amended parts of the Lobbying Disclosure Act of 1995.

21. Public Citizen, "Detailed Comparison of the Lobbying Laws and Ethics Rules Approved by the 110th Congress," www.citizen .org. Also see Congressional Research Reports, "Lobbying Law and Ethics Changes in the 110th Congress," openers.com/document/ rl34166/2007-09-18.

22. Office of Congressional Ethics, OCE First Quarter 2010 Report, oce.house gov/.

23. *Buckley v. Valeo,* 424 U.S. 1 (1976).

24. *McConnell v. Federal Election Commission,* 540 U.S. 93 (2003).

25. *Washington Times,* "Obama Bans Lobbyists from Transition," November 12, 2008.

26. *Federal Election Commission v. Wisconsin Right to Life, Inc.,* 551 U.S. 449 (2007).

27. White House, "Executive Orders," www.thewhitehouse.gov.

28. For a worldwide perspective, see Raj Chari, John Hogan, and Gary Murphy, *Regulating Lobbying: A Global Perspective* (Manchester, UK: Manchester University Press, 2010).

29. Also see Scott Harden, *Lobbying Ethics and Reform* (Hauppauge N.Y.: Nova Science Publications, 2006).

SUGGESTED READING

Chari, Raj, John Hogan, and Gary Murphy. *Regulating Lobbying: A Global Perspective.* Manchester, UK: Manchester University Press, 2010.

COGEL Council on Governmental Ethics Laws, www.cogel.org.

Farber, Daniel A. *The First Amendment: Concepts and Insights.* 3rd ed. Eagan, Minn.: Foundation Press, 2010.

Harden, Scott T. *Lobbying Ethics and Reform.* Hauppauge N.Y.: Nova Science Publications, 2006.

Hrebenar, Ronald J. "Lobby Laws: The Tension between Reform and the First Amendment." In *Interest Group Politics in America.* 3rd ed. Ed. Ronald J. Hrebenar. Armonk, N.Y.: M. E. Sharpe, 1997.

Lipsak, Adam. "Justices, 5–4, Reject Corporate Spending Limit." *New York Times,* January 21, 2010. This article reviews the landmark U.S. Supreme Court decision overturning limits on corporate funding of political broadcasts in candidate elections because the rule violated the First Amendment. For the full decision, see *Citizens United v. Federal Election Commission* (2010).

Sullivan, Kathleen M., and Gerald Gunther. *First Amendment Law.* 4th ed. New York: Foundation Press/Thomson, 2010.

Thomas, Clive S. "Transparency in Public Affairs: Lessons from the Mixed Experience of the United States." In *Challenge & Response: Essays on Public Affairs & Transparency.* Ed. Tom Spencer and Conor McGrath. Brussels: Landmarks Press, 2006, 41–48.

Thomas, Clive S., et al. "Concerns About Interest Groups: Questions of Democracy, Representation, Bias and Regulation." In *Research Guide to U.S. and International Interest Groups.* Ed. Clive S. Thomas. Westport, Conn.: Praeger Publishers, 2004, 357-390.

Woodstock Theological Center. *The Ethics of Lobbying: Organized Interests, Political Power, and the Common Good.* Washington, D.C.: Georgetown University Press on Behalf of Woodstock Theological Center, 2002.

PART VI ★ INTEREST GROUPS, CAMPAIGNS, AND ELECTIONS – AND MONEY

CHAPTER 30	Interest Groups and Federal Campaigns Before the Federal Election Campaign Act	393
CHAPTER 31	PACs, 527s, and other Groups in Congressional Elections	403
CHAPTER 32	Interest Groups in Presidential Elections	419
CHAPTER 33	Regulating and Reforming Group-Based Electioneering	431

chapter 30

Interest Groups and Federal Campaigns Before the Federal Election Campaign Act

by Allan Cigler and Heather Yates

EXTENSIVE INTEREST GROUP INVOLVEMENT in federal-level campaigns and elections, with some notable exceptions, is of relatively recent vintage. Early in the nation's development, nationally oriented political associations were nonexistent. Interests were latent, and organizations representing them at the federal level were not needed. Farmers had no political or economic reason to organize when they worked just to feed their families. Workers typically labored in small family enterprises. When interests needed to organize for political purposes, it was typically done in an ad hoc manner, with the focus on state and local decision makers, who made the most relevant policies.

Campaigning for federal office, including the presidency in the nation's early years, was largely an individual endeavor, and public campaigning for an office like the presidency was generally regarded as unseemly. The cost of running for federal office was modest, and campaign resources typically came from family and friends. With mass enfranchisement and the development of the political party as an organization, associated with the Jacksonian era beginning in the mid- to late 1820s, the resources needed for running for federal office escalated; patronage employees and wealthy individuals, as well as party members, became important in underwriting campaign activities.

By the middle of the nineteenth century, the impact of the Industrial Revolution and confrontation over slavery had demonstrated the close connection between economic and social/moral concerns and national public policy, and a number of interests became manifest in the form of political associations for the first time. A variety of social movements were spawned as well, ranging from efforts to abolish slavery to reform efforts that sought to curb the excesses of industrial capitalism and corruption in the electoral process.

Interest groups, even those that lobbied significantly during the mid-nineteenth to the early twentieth century, typically stayed out of direct involvement in electoral politics. This was a period, labeled the "golden age" of political parties by historian Arthur Schlesinger Jr., when party organizations stood supreme and had a monopoly in the electoral process.[1] Nominations were the prerogative of party leaders in a closed convention process. Funding in presidential campaigns was dominated by wealthy "fat cat" contributors, those connected to banks, corporations, and railroads, rather than groups per se. Parties dominated congressional campaigns as well; party workers raised money and disbursed funds, which came overwhelmingly from patronage employees and party workers. Organized interests focused largely on state-level elections, including a growing number of attempts to bypass the legislative process by actively participating in initiative and referendum campaigns.[2]

The twentieth century, however, witnessed an ever-increasing involvement of interest groups in national-level elections. That group attention turned to decision making in Washington made sense, given the expanding role of the federal government. The twentieth century also witnessed the continuing organizational decline of political parties, which gradually lost their monopolistic control over nominating candidates and running electoral campaigns, creating a window of opportunity for increased group activity.

The onset of the New Deal in the 1930s was a major turning point in the evolving role of interest groups in campaigns, as the number of interest groups proliferated, parties as organizations continued to decline, and at the same time the need for political resources was accelerating rapidly. Sparked by a technological revolution in how political messages were delivered to voters, by midcentury, campaigns came to rely less on the ranks of party operatives and more on the "new media, the new technology and the new people with the new skills."[3] Interest groups and interest group money now became crucial to campaigns, where individual candidates were typically in charge of their own efforts and group support was actively courted.

By the early 1970s, in the wake of both internal party reform and campaign finance reform, interest groups were beginning to seriously challenge political parties as the most influential factor in presidential and congressional elections. The challenge continues unabated.

GROUPS AND FEDERAL CAMPAIGNS PRIOR TO THE NEW DEAL

Political parties and interest groups in the United States emerged separately as mediating institutions, linking citizens to their government. Parties, as active mobilizers of the mass public, began to develop their organizational form in the late 1820s and early 1830s, and they reached the apex of their electoral influence during the period after the Civil War, until the Progressive reform movement began to take its toll around the turn of the century (see Chapters 3 and 4).

The rise of interest groups as formal organizations paralleled historically the ascent of parties. In the early 1830s the first national organizations representing groups of individuals with common interests, such as the Elks, came into being, typically for social reasons; organization for distinctly political purposes would come later. Group formation "tends to occur in waves" and is greater in some periods than in others.[4] The period after the Civil War was one of those characterized by a proliferation of groups with an interest in national policy. Improvements in communications and technology made national organizations viable, and a variety of social forces, including the increasing economic and social complexity stemming from the Industrial Revolution, created new interests and redefined old ones with stakes in national policy. Coupled with growing government involvement in the conduct of the nation's business, these forces encouraged a mushrooming of interests with incentives to formally organize and actively attempt to influence decision makers.

Although active in the lobbying process, the newly formed groups rarely encroached on party business or challenged party domination of campaigns. Advantaged groups typically worked directly within the policy process, not through elections, and disadvantaged groups found the parties too closed and entrenched for meaningful change. On occasion, they sought to create third party alternatives, such as the Populists.

Agriculture and Labor

One of the first interest sectors to organize on a broad scale was agriculture (see Chapter 12). The National Grange, formed in 1867, initially proved quite successful in shaping banking and railroad legislation, but eschewed direct involvement in campaigns.[5] When the Granger movement declined in the mid-1870s, elements of it and farm groups like the Farmer's Alliance and other small groups joined together to confront the growing political strength of banks and railroads; for the first time farmers turned to the electoral process to address their grievances. Believing the two major parties to be captured by moneyed interests and unconcerned with rural well-being, farmers' efforts typically took the form of a third political party, at times in an alliance with industrial workers, such as the Greenback-Labor Party in the 1870s and 1880s (for a time holding fourteen congressional seats) and the Peoples or Populist Party in the 1890s. In 1892 the Populist candidate, former Greenbacker James B. Weaver, collected 8.5 percent of the vote and 22 of the 444 electoral votes. Not until the mid-1890s did organized farm interests extensively work within a major party, capturing the Democratic presidential nomination for William Jennings Bryan in 1896 and imposing their policy goals upon the platform. From Bryan's third presidential bid in 1908 until the New Deal, however, organized farm interests largely kept a nonpartisan posture in campaigns, as the increasing specialization within farming and the growth of new specialized groups reflecting such diversity made it difficult for farmers to act in a homogenous, partisan manner in elections. Even the most important agriculture interest groups of the era, the American Farm Bureau Federation (AFBF), so instrumental in developing the farm bloc in the 1920s, "did next to nothing in political campaigns."[6] Money and grassroots campaigning in elections were not part of AFBF's strategy for gaining access to decision makers; instead, mobilizing the constituencies of legislators during the policy process was far more important.

The history of the American labor movement after the Civil War reflects a comparable tendency for emerging interest groups to forswear working with the two major parties (see Chapter 13). Still, labor had been long involved in electoral politics, primarily at the local level. In 1828 Philadelphia labor leaders formed the Workingman's Labor Party, and by 1834 labor parties could be found in fifteen states.[7] But in terms of federal elections, neither major party was especially sympathetic to labor interests; mutual suspicion characterized relations between major parties and the labor movement. In some areas, parties and developing labor organizations were competitors for working-class loyalties, at times leading to outright hostility and violence.[8]

The first major attempt to organize workers nationally after the Civil War, by the Knights of Labor, largely avoided involvement in partisan electoral politics, as the group viewed such the activity as too organizationally disruptive. The Knights of Labor faced the challenge of uniting a broad national constituency, even attempting at one point to incorporate business interests, but that effort ultimately proved unsuccessful. The American Federation of Labor (AFL), founded in 1886 in Ohio and composed of trade craft workers, represented the first meaningful attempt by labor interests to get involved in national electoral politics on a sustained, comprehensive basis. The AFL actively lobbied government officials from early in its history, but its involvement in political campaigns was infrequent, and even then might involve only local union affiliates operating selectively, as its charter required the AFL's activity to be nonpartisan. Its leaders concentrated on the internal survival matters that faced a loosely knit federation, made up of a diverse collection of local unions in a context characterized by outright hostility by business interests and unfriendliness from both major parties. The AFL, led by its organizational architect Samuel Gompers, "remained nonpartisan in fact as well as theory . . . from its founding in 1886 to 1906."[9]

By the turn of the century, however, it would have been hard not to notice that the Democratic Party was emerging as much more sympathetic to labor interests than the Republican Party, with its ties to wealth and large businesses. Labor's gravitation toward the Democratic Party and the ongoing participation in elections was made easier by the ethnicity factor, as many union and party leaders on the East Coast shared a common Irish/Catholic cultural heritage. Issues were at the core of the affinity of the AFL's attraction to the Democrats.[10] In 1906 the union leadership presented to Congress and President Theodore Roosevelt a "bill of grievances," which forced lawmakers to go on record as opposing strike-breaking injunctions and the application of antitrust provisions to unions. Most Republicans opposed the federation position, while a strong majority of Democrats took a prolabor stance. Although the federation did not officially endorse Democrats in 1906 (a substantial number among the membership were still Republicans or Socialists at the time), the leadership made a concerted effort to inform its membership of those members of Congress who were prolabor, the overwhelming number of whom were Democrats.

The 1908 federal elections brought the AFL leadership and the Democrats even closer together; the federation engaged in active campaigning among its membership for the first time exclusively on behalf of one party's candidates.[11] These elections presented union leaders a clear choice between two issue-distinctive, relatively homogenous political parties. The Republicans nominated the "injunction judge" William Howard Taft, a hard-liner against worker rights. Gompers and his hand-picked associates appeared before the platform committees of both parties. Republicans were unsympathetic to including union issues in the party platform, and federation leaders suspected the antiunion National Manufacturers Association's president was instrumental in drafting the final document. In contrast, the Democratic Party included a number of prolabor planks in its platform. Campaign activity on behalf of the Democrats took a variety of forms. In 1908 Gompers and AFL leaders were involved in speaking tours on behalf of Democratic candidates, funded by contributions from about 1,100 of its member unions.[12] The executive committee of the federation met with the Democratic National chairman, and Gompers met several times with presidential nominee William Jennings Bryan. The organization's publication, *The American Federalist,* emerged as an

The strictly nonpartisan American Federation of Labor (AFL) became increasingly supportive of Democratic candidates in the early twentieth century. Here, AFL president Samuel Gompers casts his ballot.

important propaganda disseminator of partisan material. Four state party headquarters had federation representatives as part of their in-house operations.[13] Although still claiming to be "nonpartisan" and avoiding official endorsement of candidates, AFL affiliates were active in grassroots campaigning among the membership, distributing literature highlighting the pro- or antilabor voting records of members of Congress, and organizing parades on behalf of certain candidates.[14]

The next two presidential elections further strengthened ties between the Democratic Party and the AFL.[15] Labor officials in 1912 wrote the prolabor plank in the national party platform, and in 1916 the federation all but endorsed the reelection of Woodrow Wilson on official AFL Executive Committee stationary. The federation was quickly evolving from an ad hoc participant in campaigns to having an infrastructure for year-round involvement in elections. By 1920 its primary political committee, the Nonpartisan Campaign Committee, had organized itself around separate speakers, publicity, and information bureaus, each operating on a permanent basis.

Although the AFL continued to be active in disseminating campaign literature focusing on the voting records of legislators in the 1920s, normally in favor of Democratic candidates, the federation's ties to the presidential wing of the Democratic Party were not as strong as during the Wilson presidency. The party platform in 1920 reflected a conservative, less reformist direction, and in 1924 the Democrats selected the probusiness, Wall Street lawyer John W. Davis as their standard bearer, and the federation endorsed Sen. Robert La Follette's third party, Progressive candidacy as a consequence. In 1928 the federation remained officially neutral, not endorsing Al Smith, although virtually all union affiliates were active on behalf of the Democratic nominee. Franklin D. Roosevelt, the Democratic nominee in 1932, was not endorsed.

Prior to the New Deal, it is fair to say that although the federation had a strong pro-Democratic bias in its campaign efforts, it remained independent of the party organization, as it focused on mobilizing its own members. Labor, while typically a Democratic Party ally, had yet to be integrated within the party's campaign operations. This would begin to change during the mid-1930s.

Prohibition Advocates

No discussion of interest group activity in campaigns prior to the New Deal would be complete without a discussion of the tactics and role played by Prohibition forces, particularly the Anti-Saloon League (ASL). The league has been widely studied by political scientists and historians, and it represents the power and passion a single-issue group can have in setting a national political agenda, similar in ways to the single-issue groups that have characterized contemporary politics.[16]

As early as the 1830s churches were engaging in grassroots mobilization, mounting social awareness and citizen education campaigns reporting the harms associated with alcohol. The primary focus was on the distribution of internally published literature to educate voting-eligible citizens (at the time, white males) on the evils of alcohol.

The ASL was officially organized in 1893 in Ohio as a state committee against the sale of alcoholic beverages.[17] In 1895 it reorganized for the same purpose, with a goal to expand into more states beyond Ohio. As an organization, the ASL worked primarily through the Methodist Church, which it relied upon for its budget and membership base, and it never collaborated with the National Prohibition Party, which had been established in 1869. The ASL considered itself nonpartisan, and it worked closely with state party organizations of both major parties. It rejected being exclusively connected to one party, so it would be amenable to the diverse political cultures in several states. Strategically, however, the ASL worked with the dominant party in single-party states such as Kansas, Maine, Michigan, Pennsylvania, and Wisconsin. The ASL controlled a large number of voters of its church constituency, which proved highly influential when working with state parties. The united bloc of ASL voters enabled the group to nominate Prohibition candidates. By the early twentieth century, state parties came to rely upon ASL support and grassroots support for electoral success.[18]

The ASL's grassroots get-out-the-vote campaigns operated exclusively through churches. The group gained open access to church congregations at the pulpit, and local clergy were turning into something akin to political bosses for campaigns, to the extent that Prohibition Party officials often referred to the ASL as the "Methodist Political Machine."[19] The group organized local Anti-Saloon Sunday rallies. Women and children were encouraged to escort husbands and fathers to the ballot box to "vote right or not vote at all."[20] Publications such as voter guides were distributed to church congregations. There is little evidence to suggest direct ASL endorsements (at least with contributions attached), but the group was very skillful in informing voters of "satisfactory dry" candidates through its literature. The group printed leaflets that listed candidates, including a brief synopsis of their record on Prohibition, making the choice for the devout Christian voter obvious.

Between 1903 and 1917, twenty-four states adopted Prohibition laws. In 1917 Congress, which was becoming increasingly dry, in part because of ASL grassroots agitation, submitted the Eighteenth Amendment to the states. Within a year and a half, all but two states had passed the amendment. As sometimes happens when a single-issue group

THE FEDERAL CORRUPT PRACTICES ACT OF 1925

Coming on the heels of the Teapot Dome Scandal, in which oil developers offered gifts to federal officials responsible for granting oil leases, and the Supreme Court's 1921 decision in *Newberry v. United States* which limited Congress's ability to regulate primary elections, Congress passed The Federal Corrupt Practices Act in February 1925. The law required House and Senate candidates, as well as multi-state political committees to report all contributions of $100 or more in election and nonelection years. The law placed spending limits of $25,000 for a Senate candidate, and $5,000 for a House candidate, unless a state had a lower limit. The Act provided the basic structure for campaign finance regulation until the Federal Election Campaign Act came into force in the early 1970s.

The 1925 Act defined the terms "contribution" and "expenditure" as follows:

(c) The term "contribution" includes a gift, subscription, loan, advance, or deposit, of money, or anything of value, and includes a contract, promise, or agreement, whether or not legally enforceable, to make a contribution;

(e) The term "expenditure" includes a payment, distribution, loan, advance, deposit, or gift of money, or any thing of value, and includes a contract, promise, or agreement, whether or not legally enforceable, to make an expenditure.

This Act proved largely unworkable, in large part due to court decisions which rendered it unenforceable.

SOURCE: Quoted material from Federal Corrupt Practices Act, 1925, 43 Stat. 1070 (February 28, 1925).

enjoys policy success, its organization disintegrates.[21] Such was the case with the ASL throughout the 1920s. Although Congress itself remained dry, opposition elements grew in influence, especially the urban, immigrant Catholic voting bloc. After the election of 1932, dry forces no longer constituted a majority in the Congress. With the arrival of the Depression, the wet/dry issue lost its salience, and Prohibition was repealed.

Besides the Eighteenth Amendment, the ASL left another legacy. Its activities contributed to the adoption of the Federal Corrupt Practices Act of 1925, which basically remained the law of the land until the Federal Election Campaign Act (FECA) and its amendments were adopted in 1971 and 1974. One of the major provisions of the act was to target campaign activity and expenditures by groups such as the ASL, which by the 1920s had become very active in federal elections. The new definition of a political committee stated: "(1) any committee, association or organization which accepts contributions or makes expenditures . . . to influence the elections of candidates . . . (2) whether or not in more than one state if such committee . . . is a branch or subsidiary of a national committee, association, or organization."[22]

Although weak and largely unenforced, disclosure laws were on the books prior to this law, but the ASL did not file any reports on the grounds it was a an "educational, scientific, and charitable organization." Once it started filing reports, ASL ran into difficulty because it greatly understated its financial expenditures in election years. At times the money could be substantial. In 1928 dry forces, including the ASL, spent an estimated $2 million in an effort to defeat Al Smith, the "wet" candidate for president.[23] In 1930 the ASL's national superintendent admitted publicly that "more than 90% of the Anti-Saloon Leagues activities cluster around elections" and that such activities are the heart of the organization.[24] Nevertheless, neither the ASL, nor any other group, was ever prosecuted under the law.

THE NEW DEAL TO FECA: THE RISE OF INTEREST GROUP MONEY AND ACTIVITY

Until the New Deal, the few groups that did get involved in federal elections concentrated on their own members; direct campaign contributions to parties and candidates by groups was rare. The New Deal ushered a new era for groups in campaigns, led by labor unions.

Despite labor's affinity for Democrats, until the 1930s labor still fought most of its own battles, typically facing business interests allied with government no matter which party was in control. But a range of New Deal policies created a firm bond between labor and the Democrats, as the party supported workers' rights to organize and provided the means to enforce the newly gained rights. Republican opposition was nearly universal. Indebted to the Roosevelt administration, and believing the Democratic Party's policy concerns were compatible with working-class interests, labor "took the party's interest in winning elections as its own."[25] Appreciative of pro-union support by the Roosevelt administration, by the mid- to late 1930s much of organized labor had become fervently partisan, not just active in mobilizing its own members, but reaching out to the working class generally, as well as furnishing large amounts of money to the Democrats.

Labor's financial activity in elections became especially controversial. Prior to the 1936 election, direct labor contributions to candidates and parties had been negligible. During the 1936 election this changed: labor organizations raised and spent more than $750,000 in direct contributions, and the main contributor was the United Mine Workers, which gave $469,000.[26] The Congress of Industrial Organizations (CIO), a federation of aggressive industrial unions that broke off from the AFL in 1935, created the first modern political action committee (PAC) in 1943, and the AFL followed with its own PAC in 1947. When the federations reunited eight years later, the two PACs combined to form the Committee on Political Education (COPE).

The labor PACs did more than just raise and disburse funds collected from union members. By the mid-1940s PAC funds were underwriting party-like, grassroots activities such as registration drives in working-class areas, distributing pro-Democratic literature, and conducting get-out-the-vote programs on Election Day. Organized labor, with its endorsement of candidates, also acted as a cue for other liberal and progressive groups that were increasingly becoming involved in elections, such as the National Association for the Advancement of Colored People, Americans for Democratic Action, and the American Civil Liberties Union. Although such groups played virtually no role in campaigns per se, they often endorsed labor-preferred candidates and widely publicized their choices.

Perhaps because it was so visible and widely covered by the press, labor campaign activity ultimately became controversial, especially after a series of wartime strikes turned public opinion against the unions in the early 1940s. Over President Roosevelt's veto in 1943, Congress passed the Smith-Connally Act, which extended the Tillman Act's 1907 ban on direct corporate contributions to candidate and party committees to include unions. In 1947 the Taft-Hartley Act made it illegal for union treasury money to be used in the party nomination process or the general election.

By 1950 organized labor had become the preeminent interest group player in campaigns, but financial support for both parties still largely came from wealthy individuals. Labor money did help, however. It was estimated that in 1952 and 1956 "one-seventh of the direct expenses of national-level, pro-Democratic committees were met with labor money."[27] But it was extensive grassroots activity, difficult to measure in financial terms, that set unions apart from other groups. In 1960, when unions across the nation actively supported John Kennedy, it was reported that in just one day 407 union canvassers in Missouri registered more than 85,000 new voters; and in Spanish-speaking parts of southern California, 100,000 registrants were added to the voting rolls.[28] With the Democratic Party increasingly lacking the patronage to build a strong organization and the ability to attract money and party workers, it needed labor's grassroots contributions to remain competitive.

However helpful organized labor was to the Democrats, it did not normally infringe on the party's organizational structure or its long-standing role in running the nomination process and campaigns. There were exceptions. In Detroit COPE was so strong it essentially functioned as the party organization; the United Auto Workers operated powerful congressional district COPE organizations, which functioned as "standing political caucuses" within the regular Democratic Party.[29] One study found that more than three-fourths of the party officials in Wayne County (Detroit) were union members.[30] Here, at least, the interest group *was* the party.

Where party organizations remained strong, however, labor organizations continued to defer to nonlabor party officials by recognizing that parties and interest groups had distinct roles and that labor's distinct economic interests limited its aggregating role in elections.[31] Nonlabor party officials still controlled the selection of delegates to the presidential nominating convention, and labor officials appeared underrepresented given the money and manpower efforts labor supplied to the party. At the 1948 Democratic National Convention union representatives made up only 2.1 percent of the delegation, and in 1952 only about 200 delegates or alternates were in attendance.[32] Union representation at conventions did expand considerably after 1952 through 1968, as party officials, with the power to appoint delegates, increasingly recognized labor officials.

The relationship between the Republican Party and groups oriented toward their policies was far different from that enjoyed by the Democrats. The few efforts to duplicate labor's efforts at grassroots mobilization were largely unsuccessful.[33] Republican-oriented trade associations commonly made endorsements, but they were largely targeted toward their own membership in organization publications and the like. The overwhelming bulk of direct contributions to the party and its candidates continued to come from the wealthy and from business/corporate officials acting as individuals, thereby avoiding the ban on corporate contributions to political committees.

Republican-oriented interest groups started to have an effect on campaigns in the early 1960s when they learned to utilize the PAC vehicle. In 1962 the conservative American Medical Association formed a PAC with the hope of raising funds among its members to elect legislators opposed to government intrusion into the health care system. The National Association of Manufacturers formed the first business PAC, the Business-Industry Political Action Committee (BIPAC), the next year. Like COPE, BIPAC was and remains today a "lead" PAC, acting as a cue to other conservative groups and wealthy individuals wanting to target their direct campaign contributions. Together the two conservative PACs spent $600,000 in 1964, a figure they doubled in 1968.[34] Their expenditure totals in 1968 matched that of COPE. The number of federally registered, probusiness PACs grew from 11 in 1964, to 33 in 1968, and to 200 by the time of the 1972 election.[35] The number of Democratic Party–oriented PACs did not keep pace.

The post–New Deal era also for the first time saw the rise of a few ideological independent electoral interest groups, groups whose primary purpose was to collect and distribute campaign funds to targeted candidates, typically on the basis of their ideological perspective. Lobbying was not part of their mission. One of the first organizations of this type to form was the National Committee for an Effective Congress (NCEC), initially founded in 1948 with the purpose of financially aiding those candidates supportive of the progressive domestic and foreign policy agenda of the New Deal.[36] The group can be viewed the forerunner of today's independent PACs or nonconnected PACs, whose small groups of "members" have a working staff that solicits funds from the general public to use for electoral purposes. The NCEC, from its inception, limited its membership to no more than fifty, typically well-known individuals with liberal credentials, who were really more honorary than governing members; by the mid-1960s the NCEC had roughly 35,000 sponsors or contributors.[37] Initially, the NCEC was a very pro-Democratic group, but it occasionally supported Republicans who shared the group's ideology. In the 1964 elections, for example, the group supported sixty-five Democrats and twenty-three Republicans.[38]

GROUP CHALLENGES TO THE PARTIES

Overall, the interest group campaign activity that took place from the New Deal to the end of the 1950s was dominated by occupational groups like unions and trade associations. The 1960s, however, ushered in a new era for interest groups in elections, one with an expanded role for groups of all sorts, which encroached on the dominant role of parties.

Many factors were involved, but paramount was the decline of party organizations in campaigns. During the late nineteenth and early twentieth centuries, the parties' capacity to control the nominating and campaigning functions began to slowly erode; the incentives for party involvement began to dwindle as the number of patronage positions decreased (leading to a decline in party money as well as workers); and reform movement effects such as the introduction of the direct primary and secret ballot and nonpartisan elections weakened the parties' monopoly over nominations. By the early 1960s the influence of the mass media, particularly television, and the existence of increasingly educated and individualistic voters were creating a context hostile to partisanship. Campaigns became largely candidate-centered rather than party-centered, and campaigning was starting to become the domain of technical specialists—campaign consultants, pollsters, direct mail practitioners, and communications/advertising specialists, all of which escalated the costs of running for office.

The 1960s witnessed a greatly expanded group universe and an increased involvement of groups in campaigns, especially near the end of the decade. Many of the new groups challenged "politics as usual." Although specialization contributed to the growth in the number of occupational and economic interests, the nature of this advocacy universe was being fundamentally altered. A participation revolution was going on as the nation was evolving from an industrial to postindustrial society. Especially noteworthy was the growth of citizens' groups—those organized around an idea or cause with no occupational basis for membership. National policymaking during the decade rose to a level not seen since the 1930s, creating winners and losers in the process; new groups formed to obtain, maintain, and expand benefits, while additional groups organized in opposition. The 1960s were also characterized by a series of social movements on the left of the political spectrum, from the civil rights movement early in the decade, to women's, consumer, and antiwar movements at the end, all of which themselves spawned a multitude of groups.

A number of older organizations also altered their political mission as a result of the turmoil of the decade. For example, the once-docile National Rifle Association (NRA) became energized politically in the face of gun restrictions passed in the wake of the assassination of presidential nomination contender Robert Kennedy in 1968.[39] Within a decade the NRA would become a major force in electoral campaigns.

On the political right, there was not a notable rise in group campaign activity, although Arizona senator Barry Goldwater's capture of the Republican presidential election in 1964 proved a notable exception. Groups like the John Birch Society, motivated by an almost paranoid fear of the nation's threat from internal communism, and the libertarian Young Americans for Freedom, were crucial to Goldwater's success in wining a majority of Republican National Convention delegates.[40] Members of such groups worked through the party delegate–selection process within states to garner the delegates Goldwater needed, overcoming opposition from the Republican establishment.

But it was the 1968 Democratic nomination contest that had the most profound effect on interest group activity in campaigns. The decade preceding the 1968 elections had been especially difficult for the parties, mainly Democrats, whose organizational structure still reflected domination by its working-class, New Deal base. Parties, strongest at the local and state levels, proved incapable of addressing national needs and expectations that were reflected in a new political agenda. Parties were unwilling or unable to accommodate the aspirations of newly "entitled" social interests such as women, youth, and nonwhite minorities, who were challenging traditional authority. The groups focused largely on the governing Democratic Party, and those challenging the system argued that the party had failed to address the complicated matrix of economic, social, and cultural issues (including an unpopular war) that had emerged by the mid-to-late 1960s.

At the 1968 Democratic convention in Chicago, Hubert Humphrey won the Democratic presidential nomination, beating back a challenge by leftist reformist elements that had arisen to challenge the domination of party regulars, elected officials, and their organized labor allies. The central issue of the 1968 nomination contest was the Vietnam War, but the party split was more extensive. Differences arose over lifestyles, the meaning of equality, concern for the environment, and the role of youth, women, and minorities in the political process. Interest groups involved in the challenge, such as the Vietnam Moratorium Committee, or student groups, such as Students for a Democratic Society, were not traditional membership organizations or occupational groups. They were loosely organized issue or cause groups, often without a formal organizational structure or much in the way of financial resources; protest was often the major political resource, and decision making the prerogative of a small number of intense activists.

Humphrey won the nomination but lost the general election, despite a massive effort by organized labor. Theodore White elaborates on the labor effort:

> The dimension of the AFL-CIO effort, unprecedented in American History, can be caught only by its final summary figures: the ultimate registration, by labor's efforts, of 4.6 million voters; the printing and distribution of 55 million pamphlets and leaflets out of Washington and 60 million more from local unions; telephone banks in 638 localities, using 8,055 telephones, manned by 24,551 union men and women and their families; some 72,255 house-to-house canvassers; and, on election day, 94,457 volunteers serving as car-poolers, materials distributors, baby-sitters, poll-watchers, telephoners.[41]

While failing to deny Humphrey the nomination, reform elements did win a major concession; the convention mandated the creation of a commission to address the party structure and how delegates to the nominating convention were chosen. In a period characterized by democratic/participatory impulses, the nomination rules were an anachronism.

Humphrey had accumulated enough delegates to win the nomination without entering a single primary. But even in states where primaries existed, typically they were "beauty contests," unrelated to delegate selection. Only sixteen states had primaries in 1968; only nine had a presidential preference poll attached to them; and in only three of these states were the results binding. The majority of delegates were either party officials or persons chosen by party officials. State conventions and caucuses, where most delegates were chosen, were usually restricted to party insiders. The system appeared as it was: closed, undemocratic, and unrepresentative of the party rank and file.

The commission mandated by the convention, popularly named by the McGovern-Frazier Commission (1968–1972), was to represent a broad range of "groups," including various demographic categories, such as women, youth, and racial minorities; party officials; and formally organized interest groups, such as labor unions and civil rights organizations.[42] The commission's final composition had a bias toward change, with reformers outnumbering party regulars by nearly two to one.[43] Labor, feeling underrepresented on the commission and still angry over Humphrey's defeat, which they blamed on divisiveness created by reform elements, eventually opted out of the deliberations.

The commission's recommendations, including new rules that made state and local parties subject to national party guidelines, were adopted and put in place beginning with the 1972 Democratic presidential selection process. Most important, delegate selection would now have to be done through primaries or a caucus system open to all party registrants, essentially eliminating appointment by state central committees and the party establishment. Incentives were created for selection at the local level, and representation quotas were set to be enforced according to race, gender, and age. No longer in effect was the "unit rule," which had bound all of a state's delegates to vote for the choice of the majority of the delegates; delegate ballots now were counted individually.

Although the Republican Party did not endorse such changes, it also became somewhat more open over time. State parties frequently found themselves under the same laws mandating primaries or caucus systems. As a more middle-class, homogeneous party, Republicans did not find themselves under as much pressure from groups as did Democrats.

The changes resulting from the McGovern-Frazier Commission had a lasting impact on interest group participation in campaigns, especially in Democratic presidential nominating contests, where candidate strategies have been affected. To win the nomination prior to 1972 a candidate was compelled to construct a majority coalition of state party delegations. Since 1972 the strategy has been to construct a coalition of issue publics and their interest group representatives. As Byron Shafer observes, the new strategy has "produced a political arena crowded with interest groups and issue organizations, seeking and being sought, demanding rewards and offering support, while both presidential aspirants and interested partisans tried to secure the maximum benefit from these negotiations."[44] Even groups that had previously been inactive in partisan politics, such as the National Education Association (NEA), became activist organizations.[45] In 1976 the NEA was instrumental in Jimmy Carter's 1976 nomination, and by 1980 the group represented nearly 8 percent of the delegates at the convention and almost 16 percent of the number needed to win the nomination. It was now interest groups rather than parties that increasingly dominated the presidential nomination process and campaigns.

Interest group activity exploded in congressional campaigns as well. The catalysts were the 1974 amendment provisions to the Federal Election Campaign Act of 1971 and how they were interpreted by the Federal Election Commission. The reform measure, passed after the Watergate debacle, although designed primarily to limit the unseemly huge contributions of wealthy "fat cats" to candidates and parties, ironically had the effect of encouraging and enabling a range or groups to become major campaign contributors, whose money was highly sought after by those running for office. In addition to setting limits on a party's contribution to its own candidates, the law cleared away any legal uncertainties about PAC creation and administration.[46] The FEC ruled that money from an organization's treasury could now be used to create, maintain, and control the operations of a PAC (direct contributions to candidates and parties still had to come from funds raised from donors). Previous to the ruling, startup and overhead funds could come only from solicited donations, which, in practice proved to be a barrier to both initial formation and the maintenance of a PAC. As political party scholar Frank Sorauf has noted, the FEC opinion "removed the final impediment to the race of groups to organize PACs and enter electoral politics." [47] The decade after the FECA amendments were passed, the number of federal PACs increased from just over 600 to more than 4,000. Interest group money was now a major factor in congressional election and widely considered a more serious problem than money from wealthy individuals.

NOTES

1. Arthur M. Schlesinger Jr., *The Cycles of American Politics* (Boston: Houghton Mifflin, 1986), 256–276.

2. See for example, Steven L. Piott, *Giving Voters a Voice: The Origins of the Initiative and Referendum in America* (Columbia: University of Missouri Press, 2003).

3. Frank J. Sorauf, *Money in American Elections* (Boston: Scott, Foresman, 1988), 4.

4. David B. Truman, *The Governmental Process,* 2nd ed. (New York: Alfred A. Knopf, 1962), 50.

5. Ibid., 87–93.

6. John Mark Hansen, *Gaining Access: Congress and the Farm Lobby, 1919–1981* (Chicago: University of Chicago Press, 1991).

7. Robert F. Bonitati, "Labor Political Clout in the 80's," *Campaigns and Elections* 1 (April 1980): 58.

8. See, for example, Steven Erie, *Rainbow's End; Dilemmas of Urban Machine Politics, 1840–1981* (Berkeley: University of California Press, 1990).

9. Charles M. Rehmus and Doris B. McLaughlin, *Labor and American Politics* (Ann Arbor: University of Michigan Press, 1967), 12.

10. J. David Greenstone, *Labor in American Politics* (New York: Vintage Books, 1969), 30.

11. Ibid.

12. Marc Karson, *American Labor Unions and Politics 1900–1918* (Carbondale: South Illinois University Press, 1958), 61.

13. Ibid.

14. Rehmus and McLaughlin, *Labor and American Politics,* 14; Greenstone, *Labor in American Politics,* 32.

15. Karson, *American Labor Unions and Politics,* 57–59.

16. See Peter H. Odegard, *Pressure Politics* (New York: Columbia University Press, 1928); Austin K. Kerr, *Organized for Prohibition: A New History of the Anti-Saloon League* (New Haven: Yale University Press, 1985).

17. Odegard, *Pressure Politics,* 1–9.

18. Ibid.

19. Kerr, *Organized for Prohibition,* 68–89.

20. Austin Kerr, "Organizing for Reform: The Anti-Saloon League and Innovation Politics," *American Quarterly* 32 (March 1980): 37–53.

21. This is particularly the case when a group seeks a collective benefit. See James Q. Wilson, *Political Organizations* (New York: Basic Books, 1973), 295.

22. Louise Overraker, *Money in Elections* (New York: MacMillan Company, 1932), 247.

23. Raymond La Raja, *Small Change: Money, Political Parties, and Campaign Finance Reform* (Ann Arbor: University of Michigan Press, 2008), 31.

24. Overraker, *Money in Elections,* 247–249.

25. Greenstone, *Labor in American Politics,* 48.

26. Louise Overacker, *Presidential Campaign Funds* (Boston: Boston University Press, 1946), 50.

27. Alexander Heard, *The Costs of Politics* (Chapel Hill: University of North Carolina Press, 1960).

28. Nicholas Masters, "Organized Labor Bureaucracy as a Base of Support for the Democratic Party," *Law and Contemporary Problems* 27 (June 1962): 262–265.

29. Samuel J. Eldersveld, *Political Parties: A Behavioral Analysis* (Chicago: Rand McNally, 1964), 156.

30. Ibid.

31. Greenstone, *Labor in American Politics,* 200–209.

32. V. O. Key, *Politics, Parties, and Pressure Groups,* 4th ed. (New York: Thomas Y. Crowell, 1958), 73.

33. See, for example, Andrew Hacker and Joel D. Aberbach, "Businessmen in Politics," *Law and Contemporary Problems* 27 (Spring 1962): 266–279.

34. Herbert E. Alexander, *Financing the 1968 Election* (Lexington, Mass.: Lexington Books, 1971), 195, 200–202.

35. Herbert E. Alexander, *Financing the 1972 Election* (Lexington, Mass.: D. C. Heath, 1976), 461, 504.

36. Harry M. Scoble, *Ideology and Electoral Action* (San Francisco: Chandler Publishing Company, 1967).

37. Ibid., 197.

38. Ibid., 85.

39. Kelly Patterson, "The Political Firepower of the National Rifle Association," in *Interest Group Politics,* 4th ed., ed. Allan J. Cigler and Burdett A. Loomis (Washington, D.C.: CQ Press, 1998), 119–144.

40. William Rusher, *The Rise of the Right* (New York: National Review Books, 1993); John Andrews, *The Other Side of the 1960s:*

The Rise of the Contemporary Right (New Brunswick, N.J.: Rutgers University Press, 1997).

41. Theodore H. White, *The Making of the President, 1968* (New York: Pocket Books, 1970).

42. Byron Shafer, *Quiet Revolution* (New York: Russell Sage Foundation, 1983), 3–40.

43. Ibid., 95.

44. Byron Shafer, *Bifurcated Politics* (Cambridge: Harvard University Press, 1988), 108.

45. Michael Malbin, "The Conventions, Platforms, and Issue Activists," in *The American Elections of 1980,* ed. Austin Ranney (Washington, D.C.: American Enterprise Institute, 1981), 99–141.

46. Frank J. Sorauf, "Political Action Committees," in *Campaign Finance Reform: A Sourcebook,* ed. Anthony Corrado et al. (Washington, D.C.: Brookings Institution Press, 1997), 121–164.

47. Ibid., 124.

SUGGESTED READING

Greenstone, David. *Labor in American Politics.* New York: Vantage Books, 1969.

Karson, Marc. *American Labor Unions and Politics.* Carbondale: Southern Illinois University Press, 1958.

Odegard, Peter. *Pressure Politics.* New York: Columbia University Press, 1928.

Overraker, Louise. *Money in American Politics.* New York: MacMillan Company, 1932.

Scoble, Harry M. *Ideology and Electoral Action.* San Francisco: Chandler Publishing Company, 1968.

Shafer, Byron. *Quiet Revolution.* New York: Russell Sage Foundation, 1983.

chapter 31

PACs, 527s, and Other Groups in Congressional Elections

by Michael M. Franz

Americans head to the polls every two years to elect a new Congress. At stake are all 435 seats in the House of Representatives and one-third of the seats in the Senate. These biennial rituals are critical occasions for all Americans, but especially for organized interest groups. Who gets elected determines who sits on important committees, who occupies the principal leadership posts, and more broadly, which party dictates the agenda. Naturally, presidential elections are always important too, but it is Congress that provides organized interests multiple points of entry into the policymaking process. Congress appropriates money to run the government, and a range of committees and subcommittees in both chambers perform oversight of the bureaucracy and the private sector. Put simply, organized interests have a stake in who in Congress makes these decisions and in how they are made.

As a consequence, interest groups in contemporary American politics invest a lot of resources in the electoral process. They contribute to candidates, both with monetary and in-kind gifts. They also advocate directly for the election or defeat of congressional candidates with expenditures on television ads, grassroots mobilization, get-out-the-vote efforts, and polling, among other labors. This chapter explores the role of interest group electioneering in the context of congressional elections and considers three questions. Which types of groups invest in the electoral process? What goals motivate their efforts? And, are interest groups successful in achieving these electoral goals?

The focus of the chapter is the modern period of American campaigns—that is, post–campaign finance reform in the 1970s. Prior to this period the rules concerning campaign finance were a patchwork characterized by weak enforcement. The post-Watergate reforms, in contrast, signified a more coherent campaign finance structure. It should be noted, too, that interest groups have always participated in the electoral process, and Chapter 30 in this volume explicitly discusses these efforts. But in the last thirty or so years, interest groups have been particularly aggressive campaigners, and their efforts intensify with each passing election cycle.

WHAT TYPES OF GROUPS INVEST IN ELECTIONS?

Defining an interest group is not easy. Any group of citizens with like interests or passions—whether organized and formalized—can constitute an interest group. For that reason, there is no existing list of all groups interested in affecting the political process writ large. Those interest groups that engage specifically in electoral politics, however, fall into a number of defined categories, making them relatively easy to find and track (although many challenges remain). This section identifies three broad categories of groups: political action committees (PACs), Section 527s, and nonprofit 501(c) organizations. In contemporary American elections, these three types of groups are most relevant.

Political Action Committees

By far the most common electioneering group, and the most studied, are political action committees. PACs are relatively simple organizations to understand. They are merely formalized ways for other organizations and collections of like-minded citizens to donate legally to federal candidates or spend independently on their behalf. PACs were first used by labor unions in the 1940s to collect donations from union members and direct them to federal candidates. The organizational form of the PAC in that case was a clever maneuver to avoid a congressional ban (initiated with the Taft-Hartley Act of 1947) on direct labor contributions to candidates.

The PAC was legalized when Congress passed campaign finance reform in the early and mid-1970s. The reform permitted corporations (which had been banned from directly contributing to candidates since 1907), unions, and other interests to form transparent committees to contribute to candidates. Congress placed limits on the size of contributions to federal candidates and parties, however, and they mandated that PACs register with the newly created Federal Election Commission, report receipts and expenditures on a regular basis, and conform to standards in the raising and spending of campaign cash.

PACs fall into two broad categories. Labor unions, corporations, or trade associations hoping to contribute to or spend independently on behalf of federal candidates are called connected PACs. They conduct electioneering activity separate from their sponsor's general treasury (although general treasury money can fund the administrative costs of running the PAC). These connected PACs are split into different subcategories depending on their sponsor: labor union, corporation, or trade association.[1] Consider the beverage industry as an example. Pepsi Company has its own corporate PAC, as does Coca-Cola. The Teamsters Union has a labor PAC, as does the United Food and Commercial Workers International Union, both of which represent the employees of soda producers. American Beverage Licenses is a trade association that funds a PAC to represent beverage retailers, and the American Beverage Association PAC represents producers and distributors.

Any other interest group seeking to influence federal elections, but without a sponsor, is also required to form a political committee. These nonconnected PACs are often called ideological PACs because they regularly organize to advocate for specific issue agendas. KidsPAC is a nonconnected political committee concerned with public policies affecting children and families. To continue the beverage example, the health concerns surrounding soda might presumably motivate part of its advocacy and support for candidates.

There are extensive regulations concerning how both connected and nonconnected PACs can raise campaign money. Connected PACs can raise funds only from their "restricted class." This means that corporations can solicit contributions only from executive and administrative personnel, as well as from stockholders; there are also limited opportunities to solicit from additional corporate employees who are not executives or administrative personnel. Labor can solicit only from dues-paying members and its executive and administrative personnel. Trade association PACs can solicit funds from their executive and administrative personnel, as well as (in limited cases) from the employees of their corporate members. These restrictions on connected committees stand in contrast to solicitation rules for nonconnected PACs, which can accept contributions from any American citizen.

There are also limits on PAC expenditures. For most PACs, direct contributions are capped at $5,000 per candidate per election and $15,000 to a national party committee per election cycle.[2] All PACs, however, can spend unlimited amounts on independent advocacy of federal candidates. Independent expenditures are often television or radio advertisements that expressly urge viewers or listeners to vote for or against a federal candidate, but PACs also spend these funds on direct mail and mass telephone calls, among other things.[3]

Since the passage of campaign finance reform in the 1970s, PACs have had a consistent presence in campaigns. According to the FEC, there were 722 registered PACs in 1975. By 1980 there were 2,551, and by 2000 there were 3,706. Between 1975 and 1984 PACs increased at a rate of about 20 percent per year. They have remained fairly steady in number since then. The rate of PAC increase was particularly strong for corporate PACs in the late 1970s and early 1980s. They numbered 139 in 1975, and ten years later there were more than 1,700 corporate-sponsored PACs. Nonconnected PACs grew from 110 in 1977 to about 1,000 in 1984 and 1,300 in 2007. Trade association PACs totaled about 500 in the late 1970s but grew to nearly 1,000 by 2007. Labor PACs in contrast have consistently numbered between 300 and 400 since 1980.[4]

Most relevant for this chapter, PACs are especially important in congressional elections. In 2008 PACs directly contributed more than $300 million to House candidates and $100 million to Senate candidates. These numbers were historic highs. In 2006 PACs contributed $292 million to House candidates and $89 million to Senate candidates (at the time a new high). In fact, since 1980—the first year with PAC contribution breakdowns—PACs have contributed larger amounts of money to House and Senate candidates in each successive election cycle. To put the growth of PAC contributions in perspective, in 1980 PACs contributed $39 million to House candidates and $19 million to Senate candidates. The election cycle totals for PAC contributions to congressional candidates between 1980 and 2008 are shown in Table 31.1; Table 31.2 shows contribution limits for the 2009–2010 election.

In contrast to contributions, PAC independent expenditures in each election cycle are much lower, as Table 31.1 shows. In 1980 PACs spent $2.5 million on independent advocacy for House and Senate candidates, a mere fraction of the total dispensed as candidate contributions. On the other hand, independent expenditures reached noteworthy levels in 2008: $25 million for House candidates and $17.5 million for Senate candidates. This total is still only 10 percent of the contribution total, but the rise in independent expenditures reflects the changes in campaign finance laws passed in 2002. The Bipartisan Campaign Reform Act of 2002 (BCRA) put new restrictions on how public communications by interest groups could be funded (as discussed in the next section). The new restrictions attempted to rein in interest groups that were using loopholes in existing laws to fund advertisements that were not reportable to the Federal Election Commission. These more aggressive restrictions consequently compelled many groups to use the more regulated category of independent expenditures.

It should be noted that the amount of PAC money contributed to presidential candidates is always very low. (Presidential elections are covered in far more detail in

TABLE 31.1 **Interest Group Investments in Congressional Races, 1980–2008**

	PAC contributions	PAC independent expenditures	Interest group TV ads w/o "express advocacy"	Electioneering communications
1980	$57,995,677	$2,488,543	n/a	n/a
1982	86,794,537	5,827,086	n/a	n/a
1984	109,534,727	5,966,038	n/a	n/a
1986	137,656,050	9,358,171	n/a	n/a
1988	157,507,308	7,113,380	n/a	n/a
1990	161,582,944	5,149,075	n/a	n/a
1992	190,352,000	6,627,799	n/a	n/a
1994	192,821,493	5,089,388	n/a	n/a
1996	217,359,944	8,683,378	n/a	n/a
1998	219,502,297	9,357,695	$5,111,518	n/a
2000	256,803,373	16,928,577	33,672,041	n/a
2002	289,025,500	16,769,528	17,482,158	n/a
2004	316,842,818	14,994,305	12,173,166	$11,577,165
2006	381,120,218	38,101,722	n/a	10,506,998
2008	420,698,168	42,730,263	38,408,710	76,652,295

SOURCE: Data in the first, second, and fourth columns are from the FEC. Data in the third column are from the Wisconsin Advertising Project and account for the top seventy-five media markets only.

NOTE: Totals are not adjusted for inflation.

Chapter 32.) PACs contributed only about $5 million to presidential candidates in 2008 and about $3.2 million in 2004; that amount represents only about 1 percent of the PAC investment in congressional candidates. To influence presidential elections, then, PACs have relied on independent expenditures almost exclusively.[5]

Section 527 Organizations

The story of 527s is best told as an evolution from PACs. PACs, as is clear from the previous section, abide by strict rules in the raising and spending of campaign dollars. The rules had two consequences for groups interested in aggressively advocating for a particular candidate: the $5,000 candidate contribution limit is likely too low to make any real difference in the outcome of an election, and independent expenditures, although unlimited, have traditionally been paid for by contributions to the PAC, which are themselves limited. (The rules for PACs in that regard changed somewhat in 2010, and the changes are discussed below.) In practical terms, then, the regulations governing PACs formally prevented collections of wealthy donors, as well as union and corporate interests, from pooling their considerable resources to bankroll candidate advocacy efforts.

To compensate, certain interests in the late 1990s and early 2000s established organizations based on a section of the U.S. tax code. Section 527 in fact covers all political organizations, including PACs, but not all 527 groups must register with the FEC and abide by campaign finance reporting requirements.[6] Most relevant for this chapter, 527s that purchase public communications, such as advertisements, direct mail, and mass telephone calls, that mention or picture federal candidates *but do not expressly advocate their election or defeat* can essentially raise or spend as much money as they want, without limit. As a brief point of explanation, express advocacy is typically defined as public communications that contain certain words, such as *vote for, vote against, elect, defeat, support,* and *reject,* which were first listed in the Supreme Court's 1976 campaign finance ruling in *Buckley v. Valeo*. If an advertisement avoids those words, the communication is alternatively defined as nonexpress advocacy, or issue advocacy, which is generally unregulated by the Federal Election Commission.

Section 527 groups first appeared on the political radar during the presidential primary season of 2000. During the Republican primary, a 527 group called Republicans for Clean Air ran advertisements in California, New York, and Ohio criticizing Sen. John McCain but stopping short of telling viewers to vote for George W. Bush.[7] The 527s proliferated thereafter and funded extensive electioneering in the elections from 2002 to 2008. According to the Campaign Finance Institute and the Center for Responsive Politics, 527s in total spent more than $125 million in 2002 (on congressional races), $440 million in 2004 (on the presidential and congressional elections), just above $200 million in 2006, and more than $250 million in 2008.[8]

Majority Action is a pro-Democratic 527 largely bankrolled by labor unions. The group spent $2 million dollars during the 2006 election and $4 million in 2008. Many labor unions fund liberal 527s such as Majority Action (and with very large contributions), but they also often form their own 527 committees to fund unregulated electioneering. In fact, one labor-sponsored 527—the Service Employees International Union (SEIU)—spent nearly $28 million from its 527 account in the 2008 election cycle. This was above and beyond the regulated funds it raised and spent through its PAC.[9]

On the other side of the aisle, Americans for Honesty on Issues is a pro-Republican 527 group that was active in 2006 and spent more than $2.8 million on broadcast ads attacking Democratic congressional candidates. Its principal donor was Texas homebuilder Bob Perry, who contributed $3 million to the organization in September and October of 2006. The Club for Growth is a conservative antitax group that spent more than $7.5 million in 2006 and $5 million in 2008 from its 527 account. It received large contributions in 2008 from Perry ($650,000), investor John Childs ($250,000), and businessman and philanthropist John Templeton ($200,000), among others.[10]

All told, contributions to Section 527s are often large donations from individuals and organized interests. According to one report, of all 527s active in federal

TABLE 31.2 **Contribution Limits for 2009–2010**

Donors	Recipients: Candidate committee	Recipients: PAC[1]	Recipients: State, district, and local party committee[2]	Recipients: National party committee[3]	Special limits
Individual	$2,400* per election[4]	$5,000 per year	$10,000 per year combined limit	$30,400* per year	Biennial limit of $115,500* ($45,600 to all candidates and $69,900[5] to all PACs and parties)
State, District, and Local Party Committee	$5,000 per election combined limit	$5,000 per year combined limit	Unlimited transfers to other party committees		
National Party Committee	$5,000 per election	$5,000 per year	Unlimited transfers to other party committees		$42,600* to Senate candidate per campaign[6]
PAC Multicandidate[7]	$5,000 per election	$5,000 per year	$5,000 per year combined limit	$15,000 per year	
PAC Not Multicandidate	$2,400* per election[8]	$5,000 per year	$10,000 per year combined limit	$30,400* per year	

SOURCE: Federal Election Commission, www.fec.gov.

NOTES: * These limits are indexed for inflation in odd-numbered years.

1. These limits apply both to connected and nonconnected political action committees (PACs). Affiliated committees share the same set of limits on contributions made and received.
2. A state party committee shares its limits with local and district party committees in that state unless a local or district committee's independence can be demonstrated. These limits apply to multicandidate committees only.
3. A party's national committee, Senate campaign committee, and House campaign committee are each considered national party committees, and each have separate limits, except with respect to Senate candidates—see Special Limits column.
4. Each of the following is considered a separate election with a separate limit: primary election, caucus, or convention with the authority to nominate, general election, runoff election, and special election.
5. No more than $45,600 of this amount may be contributed to state and local parties and PACs.
6. This limit is shared by the national committee and the Senate campaign committee.
7. A multicandidate committee is a political committee that has been registered for at least six months, has received contributions from more than fifty contributors and—with the exception of a state party committee—has made contributions to at least five federal candidates.
8. A federal candidate's authorized committee(s) may contribute no more than $2,000 per election to another federal candidate's authorized committee(s). 2 U.S.C. §432(e)(3)(B) and 11CFR 102.12(c)(2).

elections in 2006, 45 percent of their funds came from individuals contributing more than $100,000, and 36 percent came from labor unions.[11] A similar pattern of large contributions was present in the receipts of 527s for the 2008 cycle.[12] The longevity of specific 527s is an open question, as they have been aggressive spenders in federal elections only in the last decade. Some committees, such as Club for Growth and EMILY's List, have been consistent spenders in the previous three election cycles, but others have been present in only one cycle: Swift Boat Veterans for Truth in 2004, September Fund in 2006, and Alliance for New America in 2008.

There was a particular concern after the passage of BCRA in 2002 that groups that formally funded parties with unregulated donations (what was called "soft money," a funding source for parties that was eliminated in 2002) would shift their large contributions to partisan 527s. In other words, some worried that 527s would become "shadow" parties that raised unregulated funds.[13] The initial evidence is somewhat supportive of this assertion, particularly for pro-Democratic interests. In the 2004 elections specifically, many wealthy pro-Democratic donors and unions gave aggressively to liberal 527s, such as America Coming Together and The Media Fund—a trend that continued into 2006 and 2008.[14] Flush with these large donations, liberal 527s used the money in turn to fund political ads and grassroots efforts that criticized Republican candidates for federal office. Wealthy pro-Republican individuals were also aggressive donors to conservative 527s, such as the Swift Boat Veterans and Progress for America (which went on the attack against Democratic candidates), but corporations and trade associations were less likely to give to these groups in 2004–2008, preferring candidate advocacy in other forms (discussed below).[15]

It is important to be clear about the development of Section 527 groups. Before BCRA was passed in 2002, *any* organization could fund nonexpress advocacy ads at any point in the election cycle. During the 2000 campaign, the

EMILY's List president, Stephanie Schriock, speaks about the organization's "Sarah Doesn't Speak for Me" campaign in the summer before the 2010 midterm elections. The campaign was a reaction to Sarah Palin's highly publicized support for conservative congressional candidates. EMILY's List supports pro-choice, Democratic female candidates for public office.

AFL-CIO used its general treasury money to fund nearly 10,000 procandidate ads in the final two months of the election; Planned Parenthood aired almost 6,000 ads. Some probusiness groups also sponsored ads—nearly 11,000 from Citizens for Better Medicare (backed the pharmaceutical industry), 7,500 from the U.S. Chamber of Commerce, and more than 4,500 from Business Roundtable, a coalition of probusiness interests. Labor, liberal, and probusiness groups were also active in the 2002 congressional elections.[16]

The permissive standard for procandidate advocacy changed after 2002 when BCRA created a new category of public messages called "electioneering communications." This new category included widely broadcast public communications (on radio or television) that mentioned or pictured federal candidates and aired within sixty days of a general election or thirty days of a primary. The new law mandated that such communications be funded only by PACs. The goal was clearly designed to expand what was considered express advocacy, and to close the loophole that had left many ads unregulated in previous elections. Nevertheless, there were some ambiguities in the law, especially as to whether Section 527 groups could continue to fund electioneering communications without being regulated. The FEC did not issue clear guidance on the question in the run-up to the 2004 elections, which in turn motivated their expansion in that cycle.[17]

Nonprofit Groups

Just as 527s can be understood as deriving from certain limitations of PACs, nonprofit groups engaged in electoral politics are outgrowths of limitations in Section 527 organizations. For one thing, not everyone agreed in 2004 (when new rules were being written to implement BCRA) that 527s were beyond the reach of FEC regulations. Existing FEC rules, for example, demand that any organization whose "major purpose" is the election of federal candidates must register with the commission. The FEC argued retroactively in 2006 that some 527s active in the presidential election of 2004 were primarily interested in the outcome of the election and therefore subject to FEC regulation.

To that effect, in late 2006 the FEC levied more than $600,000 in fines against MoveOn.org, Swift Boat Veterans for Truth, and League of Conservation Voters for their section 527 electioneering in the presidential contest, arguing that they should have registered with the FEC as PACs.[18] The commission at this time also established more guidelines about what activity by 527s, such as how they solicit money, might constitute coming under FEC regulatory guidelines.[19] In that sense, the pressure grew more intense and the spotlight focused more on them in the aftermath of the 2004 elections.

In response to these developments, some organized groups sought cover under a different section of the tax code, 501(c). Section 501(c) covers nonprofit organizations of a diverse type. The groups coming under 501(c)(3) are religious, charitable, or educational nonprofit organizations, such as United Way and Red Cross. These groups are restricted in the political realm only to nonpartisan voter education, and any partisan slant in its political activity can cost the group its tax-deductible status. The 501(c)(4) are social welfare nonprofits. Some examples include Defenders of Wildlife Action Fund, Focus on the Family, and League of Conservation Voters. Labor unions operate 501(c)(5) organizations, and business associations, such as chambers of commerce, run 501(c)(6) groups.

The 501(c)(4) groups are growing more important in federal elections. These groups can sponsor a PAC and even air independent expenditures that remain unregulated. One justification for this latter electioneering comes from a critical, if obscure, Supreme Court case from 1986: *FEC v. Massachusetts Citizens for Life* (MCFL). In that case, the Court decided that some 501(c)(4) groups can sponsor express advocacy communications (without having to form a PAC) if the ads are paid for by individuals (Condition 1) and the primary purpose of the group was not political electioneering or lobbying (Condition 2).[20]

The MCFL exemption was rarely used prior to 2002 because nonexpress advocacy communications were permitted by any group, including corporations and unions. After BCRA passed in 2002, 527s became the organizational vehicle used primarily for nonexpress advocacy. But with new focus on regulating 527s after 2004, the Court's twenty-year-old ruling in MCFL became particularly relevant for the 2006 and 2008 elections.[21]

The 501(c)(4) groups were further empowered in 2010 because of the Supreme Court ruling in *Citizens United v. Federal Election Commission,* which overturned many restrictions on who could sponsor independent candidate advocacy. The Court decided that the MCFL exemption should apply to all 501(c)(4)s, essentially eliminating Condition 1. This point is discussed in more detail below. The 501(c)(4) groups have one additional benefit: unlike the rule for PACs and 527s, contributions to these groups are not disclosed. Therefore, a 501(c)(4) group can air ads that mention or picture candidates and not publicly make known the source of the organization's funding.[22]

All 501(c) groups have limitations, however. Most notably, these groups cannot be interested *primarily* in elections, which is Condition 2 of the MCFL test. This restriction was not changed by the Court's ruling in 2010. As such, were a 501(c)(4) organization to organize only in the context of an impending election (appearing to be its only purpose) and sponsor broadcast ads that expressly support or attack candidates for office, the IRS might pursue sanctions against the sponsors of the group. The IRS in particular has stepped up its monitoring of 501(c) groups in recent years.[23]

GROUP SPENDING IN CONGRESSIONAL ELECTIONS

How much have 501(c) groups and 527s spent in recent congressional elections? This question is difficult to answer. Unlike PAC independent expenditures, which are disclosed in detail to the FEC, electioneering by 501(c) groups is not systematically tracked. Although 527 groups are mandated to disclose the purpose of their expenditures, they often do so in vague terms, and they almost never identify whether the money was spent for presidential, congressional, or local races. In the previous section, it was noted that 527s spent an estimated $250 million in 2008. Much of this money was devoted to procandidate electioneering, but millions were also spent on administrative costs and genuine issue advocacy and education. Indeed, assigning such expenditures to specific congressional races is impossible with current IRS disclosure rules for 527s. As for 501(c) groups, the Campaign Finance Institute has devoted considerable efforts to tracking expenditures in recent years, but its estimates (by their own admission) are likely low. Nonetheless, the institute reported about $90 million in 501(c) political expenditures in 2006 and more than $195 million in 2008.[24]

Two other sources of detailed data shed light on interest group investments in advertising during congressional elections. The FEC does track one particular type of unregulated public message, the electioneering communication: broadcast ads aired within sixty days of a general election and thirty days of a primary that feature or picture a federal candidate. The FEC mandates that expenditure of this kind be reported even if there are no restrictions on their funding. Almost all PAC expenditures attacking or supporting candidates are classified as independent expenditures, meaning that the electioneering communication database is a rough proxy of advertising totals for non-PACs such as 527s and 501(c)s. Data of this kind are available for the 2004, 2006, and 2008 elections. The category was created after the 2002 elections. Another method of tracking interest group electioneering is the Wisconsin Advertising Project, which monitors all political advertisements from candidates, parties, and interest groups (including PACs) in top media markets. These data are available for 1998, 2000, 2002, 2004, and 2008.[25]

Total expenditures on electioneering communications in congressional races are included in Table 31.1, as are interest group advertising dollars for ads that avoid express advocacy. A few clarifying points are needed. In general, totals for independent expenditures in this table are distinct from the advertising totals and from the electioneering communication totals. The advertising and electioneering communication columns do, however, contain some overlap, as both tap expenditures for television ads.[26]

Overall, the totals in Table 31.1 show nontrivial investments from interest groups in recent congressional elections. Organized interests spent more than $33 million on procandidate issue advocacy on television in 2000, $17.5 million in 2002, and $12.1 million in 2004. Groups also sponsored $10.5 million in election-time procandidate ads

FIVE INTEREST GROUPS ACTIVE IN 2008

Americans for Job Security—a 501(c)(6) business association that sponsored more than 4,000 television ads on behalf of Republican candidates in five Senate races. The ad buys totaled almost $2 million.

Freedom's Watch—a 501(c)(4) group that spent more than $5 million for more than 11,000 ads on behalf of Republicans in seven House races and four Senate races. One of its motivating issues was support for the Iraq War and the Bush troop surge in 2007.

Patriot Majority—a Section 527 group that aired more than 7,000 ads for Democratic candidates in eight House races and six Senate races. The cost for the ads was nearly $5 million. The group received significant financial support from organized labor.

VoteVets.org—a 501(c)(4) group that also sponsors a PAC; both spent almost $1 million for 2,000 ads touting Democrats in four Senate races and two House races. The group opposed the Iraq War and candidates who supported the war; their ads featured veterans.

Citizens for Strength and Security—a 527 group that spent more than $790,000 for four Democratic Senate candidates. Like the Patriot Majority, the group was largely bankrolled by unions.

SOURCE: Wisconsin Advertising Project.

in 2006. Note the general decline between 2000 and 2006, which is likely the consequence of interest groups over this period diversifying their advocacy efforts to include nonbroadcast expenditures, such as grassroots mobilization and mass telephone calls. There is some evidence that groups (particularly labor unions) in recent years found these ground efforts to be more effective.[27] An added bonus is that such electioneering is often outside the scope of FEC reporting requirements (even after the BCRA) if the messages avoid express advocacy.

Of particular interest is the significant jump in broadcast expenditures for 2008, reversing the decline from 2000. Not only did interest groups spend unprecedented amounts on independent expenditures in 2008, but also they spent $38.4 million on television ads that avoided express advocacy and more than $76 million on radio and television electioneering communications. Almost all of these latter expenditures were funded outside of the regulatory process, and through 527s and 501(c) groups. In a recent article, one political scientist noted the dearth of interest groups electioneering in the 2008 presidential general election, calling them "the barking dog that didn't bite."[28] It seems apparent that the same cannot be said of interest group electioneering in congressional races—it reached unprecedented levels that year. This phenomenon is discussed in the next section, but it seems that much looser regulations concerning the funding of broadcast ads was a primary reason for the significant jump.

Neither data set allows for tracking congressional electioneering that take other forms, such as mass telephone calls and direct mail—making them underestimates of interest group electioneering totals—but they offer some insight into the broad scope of some groups' efforts. The box to the left considers the expenditures of five groups in 2008 that appear in Wisconsin Advertising Project data.

All told, the Wisconsin data identify close to sixty groups with active advertising campaigns in House and Senate elections in 2008. Two were labor unions (AFSCME and SEIU) that combined for nearly $4 million in congressional ads. The rest were a mix of liberal and conservative advocacy groups, such as Americans United for Change, Defenders of Wildlife, and U.S. Term Limits, and pro-business groups, such as the U.S. Chamber of Commerce, National Federation of Independent Business, and Employee Freedom Action Committee.

IMPORTANT DEVELOPMENTS

Understanding PACs, 527s, and 501(c)(4) groups is crucial to knowing the parameters of interest group electioneering, but a few final points are worth discussing briefly. They are likely to be quite relevant in future election cycles.

First, despite all of Congress's attempts to rein in nonexpress advocacy, and the Federal Election Commission's pursuit of 527s after 2004, the Supreme Court, under Chief Justice John Roberts, has signaled a much lower interest in campaign finance regulations. In 2007 the Court ruled in *Wisconsin Right to Life v. FEC* that a pro-life group's ads in the 2004 election, urging viewers to contact Sen. Russ Feingold, D-Wisc., about his position on late-term abortion, should not be regulated because they were genuine issue advocacy arguably unrelated to the election or defeat of Feingold, who was up for reelection that year. The Court more generally argued that nonexpress advocacy ads could be regulated only if the ad was unambiguously election related.

In practical terms, this meant that any group (corporation, union, 501(c), 527) could construct an ad that appeared to tout issues but also attacked candidates. The ruling allowed many of these groups a safe haven in the design of their ads. The example in the previous box of Americans for Job Security and its ads in 2008 (the first year that *Wisconsin* was in effect) is relevant here. As a 501(c)(6), and as such the likely beneficiary of corporate funding, it is not eligible for the MCFL exemption and might typically (post-BCRA) be investigated for improperly funding election-related advertisements outside of its PAC. The *Wisconsin* case, however, allowed it to construct ads that avoided such scrutiny. As alluded to above, this ruling seems principally responsible for the significant jump in 2008 in interest group TV advertising.[29] The lesson of the *Wisconsin* ruling was this: the rules concerning electioneering by 527s and 501(c) groups were confused in the immediate aftermath of BCRA, a lack of clarity amplified by the indecisiveness of the FEC regarding 527s. After *Wisconsin*, however, the Court seemed poised to impose clarity: avoid unambiguous express advocacy, and almost any group can campaign without limit (in source or amount) for or against federal candidates.

One feature of the *Wisconsin* ruling did preserve a level of uncertainty, however: What does it mean to avoid unambiguous express advocacy? That is, when is a group "safely" airing an issue ad that features a candidate, and when does it cross the line to express advocacy that was still regulated? The Court ended that debate in 2010 with its landmark ruling in *Citizens United v. FEC*, in which five justices struck down all restrictions on candidate advocacy from any interest group.

On the one hand, the ruling ended the debate over what types of messages fell under the increasingly complicated regulatory structure. On the other hand, advocacy groups hardly needed the ruling to clear a path for electoral investments. Unions had already found numerous paths to entry (through 527s and 501(c)s, for example), and corporations have generally preferred to fund 501(c) groups (to avoid disclosing their investment) over 527s and historically steered clear of the very visible independent expenditure option.[30] Nevertheless, the justices in *Citizens United* signaled an interest in rethinking many features of campaign finance law. The box below includes a discussion of the recent evolution of campaign finance regulations concerning interest groups and highlights the apparent trend toward deregulation in this area.

The 2010 congressional cycle was the first following the *Citizens United* decision, and interest groups were very aggressive in their electioneering, sponsoring more than $100 million in television advertisements in House and Senate races.[31] This level of investment was higher than in any previous election (outpacing the numbers in Table 31.1, in fact). Because parties and candidates also spent significantly more in 2010, however, the proportion of interest group television advertising remained roughly comparable to previous elections.[32] In other words, although some predicted emboldened interest groups, such as corporations, to spend in the hundreds of millions, this did not happen. Interest groups concentrated their efforts on certain House and Senate races, but their total investments in Senate races (as a proportion of all television spending) were similar to 2008 and lower than in 2000 for House races.

DEVELOPMENTS IN CAMPAIGN FINANCE LAWS FOR INTEREST GROUPS

Recent congressional actions and Supreme Court decisions have altered a number of regulations concerning interest group participation in elections. The overall trend is toward deregulation of interest group restrictions. Consider some changes in the following areas:

- **Sponsorship of television and radio ads.** The Bi-partisan Campaign Reform Act in 2002 established new rules for interest groups' ads airing in the final days of a primary or general election, putting stricter restrictions on how such ads could be funded. In 2004 the FEC failed to apply these rules explicitly to 527s, prompting their proliferation in that cycle and in 2006. In 2007 the Supreme Court further exempted all ads interpreted by "any reasonable person" as issue related. In 2010 the Court threw out all restrictions on group-sponsored ads and advocacy efforts that are uncoordinated with a candidate or party.

- **Contributions to PACs making only independent expenditures.** One limit on PACs is the amount of money they can accept from contributors. Two plaintiffs in different court cases, however, have argued that independent expenditures from nonconnected PACs should not be subject to contribution limits. In other words, a nonconnected PAC should be able to pool large contributions for the purposes of airing ads or contacting voters. These cases are *EMILY's List v. FEC* and *Speechnow.org v. FEC*. The D.C. Circuit Court of Appeals in April 2010 agreed with this logic in its ruling in the latter case, and a number of groups took advantage of this new allowance in the 2010 elections

- **Contributions to political parties.** In 2009 the Republican National Committee challenged restrictions (established by the Bipartisan Campaign Reform Act in 2002) on large donations to political parties meant to help nonfederal candidates. These donations, called "soft money," came to prominence in the 1990s as a means for corporations and unions to invest in party-sponsored efforts to indirectly influence federal elections. The case, *RNC v. FEC*, was appealed to the Supreme Court, but the justices in 2010 chose not to hear the challenge.

- **Disclosure of expenditures and contributions for procandidate advocacy.** Congress has responded to such developments with the only weapon it considers beyond reproach, disclosure mandates. Congress considered whether to force all interest groups, including 501(c)s, corporations, and unions, that air procandidate ads to disclose to the FEC their large donors and to compel these donors to appear in procandidate ads to "endorse" the message, as federal candidates are currently required to do. The House passed such a bill in 2010, but it stalled in the Senate. Reformers are still pressing the issue, however.

The biggest impact in 2010 was the migration of 527s and 501(c) groups into express advocacy. Prior to *Citizens United*, only PACs (and some MCFL 501(c)(4) groups) could sponsor these express advocacy messages. After *Citizens United*, any group can do this, and a number of interest groups formed as 501(c)s and 527s, with union and corporate backing, to air ads that directly called for the election or defeat of federal candidates.

In many ways, then, the 2010 elections were not a dividing line between more or less spending; rather, they were part of an emerging trend of more interest group spending in congressional elections that extends back at least fifteen years.

WHAT MOTIVATES INTEREST GROUPS TO PARTICIPATE?

Once we understand which groups participate in congressional elections, and the extent to which they invest in these elections, the next question is obvious: What exactly do these groups hope to attain? The interest group literature focuses predominantly on two electoral goals, which are most often applied to the allocation of PAC money: access to sitting members of Congress during policymaking, or replacement of unfavorable members of Congress during elections.[33] With the development of 527s and 501(c) groups, we might also add a third goal: issue salience. Certainly, some electoral behavior, such as issue advocacy campaigns, might be motivated to put issues or policy proposals on the agenda during an election campaign.

Access goals are derived from the monetary needs of candidates running for office. As campaigns have become more expensive since the 1960s, mostly as a consequence of the rising cost of television ads, incumbent candidates have sought out PACs for contributions. PAC limits are higher than contributions from individuals, and they have more funds to dispense to candidates than most voting citizens. In other words, it is simply easier to raise funds from PACs—whose purpose is contributing money to candidates—than from individuals, who have less to give. (This might be changing, however, as noted below.) PACs, acting in their self-interest, are more than happy to contribute, but often in exchange for access to the elected official when relevant policy is debated in Congress. Robert Kaiser's provocative book, *So Damn Much Money*, discusses the development of lobbying as a profession, and he spends considerable time highlighting the role of campaign cash in facilitating such lobbying.[34] See again the ever-growing PAC contribution totals in Table 31.1. They indicate that access politics is as strong as ever.

Elections, however, are also opportunities for PACs and other groups to create more directly a policymaking environment that reflects the desires of participating interests. That is, some contributions and other electioneering efforts are not so much designed to curry favor in the halls of Congress but to move votes at the ballot box. Replacement tactics can take many different forms: campaign contributions and independent spending; grassroots mobilization and get-out-the-vote efforts; endorsements, recruitment, and training of potential candidates; and direct mail and mass telephone calls. In general, interest groups can use their resources to make direct appeals to voters on behalf of or in opposition to particular candidates.

For the most part, the explicit goal of interest group electoral participation is rarely known; that is, no PAC or interest group telegraphs its goal in clear terms. One can make inferences from patterns in the data, however. The vast majority of PAC contributions flow to incumbents, the actual policymakers. And it is clear that PACs tend to favor influential policymakers (committee and party leaders) over backbenchers. It also seems reasonable to assume that such contributions are designed to secure access.[35] There is also evidence that interest groups consider district- and state-level factors, such as the percentage unionized or per capita income, when seeking access to members representing relevant constituencies.[36] Labor surely wants access to legislators who represent constituencies with a high number of union workers. When PACs give to competitive incumbents, challengers, and candidates in open seats, however, these contributions are presumably replacement-inspired.[37] Furthermore, independent expenditures and electioneering communications from 527s and 501(c) groups most often appear in competitive races and are likely motivated by replacement goals.

What drives a PAC to favor access over replacement in its contributions? What motivates 527s and 501(c)s to view competitive elections as worthwhile investments? The standard approach is to examine differences across group types. Unions and advocacy groups are considered more ideological and therefore more likely to invest in open seats, competitive races, and so forth. Labor groups in particular contribute mostly to (and spend independently for) Democratic candidates with a strong chance of defeating vulnerable Republican incumbents. Corporations are seen as more pragmatic and are therefore more likely to contribute highly visible PAC dollars to both parties in the hopes of gaining access, but on balance, corporate interests more often prefer Republicans. As was already discussed, some procorporate interests invest in elections with 501(c)s, mostly with the goal of helping Republicans win close races.

One factor that is not often discussed in the literature on PACs, however, is the role of the larger partisan context in explaining changes in interest group electioneering. More than two decades ago one PAC scholar argued, "The conventional wisdom holds that corporations are inclined towards bipartisanship in their PAC activity for a variety of reasons, including the likelihood of having to deal with a Democratic-controlled House, and the sharp ideological schism in the ranks of the Democrats which renders many conservative Democratic candidates palatable to corporation interests."[38] Brooks Jackson additionally recounts the story of how Tony Coelho, former chairman of the Democratic Congressional Campaign Committee (and Al Gore's campaign manager in 2000), persuaded many corporate PACs in the 1980s to contribute to Democrats under the assumption of long-term Democratic control of the House.[39]

All of this changed in the mid- to late 1990s, when control of Congress was no longer certain in each election cycle. In addition, parties in the late 1990s grew more ideologically polarized and homogeneous. Figures 31.1 and 31.2 show the change visually for House and Senate elections between 1978 and 2008. Each graph has two lines. The solid line is a measure of ideological polarization between the parties. It is derived from Keith Poole and Howard Rosenthal's estimates of incumbent members of Congress, which places each member of the House and Senate on a scale from -1 (liberal) to 1 (conservative).[40] The numbers reported in both figures are calculated as follows: the median Democrat and Republican in each chamber is divided by the standard deviation of each party's members; the resulting two measures are then differenced. Larger numbers indicate more ideological distance between the two parties and homogeneity within the two parties. In both the House and Senate, polarization has grown steadily in the last thirty years; the measures in both chambers increased by almost 100 percent over this time. The other line in each graph shows the number of seats the majority party is expected to win in each cycle, excluding highly competitive elections. (These numbers come from *Congressional Quarterly's* assessments, done in October of election years, of competitive congressional elections and combine safe, leaning, and favored seats for the majority party.) In both contexts, the majority party is at threat of losing its control of the chamber for most elections after 1992. There is more variability in Senate elections, but the general pattern holds.

In 1978, for example, the Democrats held a huge lead over Republicans in the House and Senate—meaning the elections that year posed no threat to their status as the majority party—and the two parties were moderately polarized (the Democratic median was –0.304 and the GOP median was 0.228). By 2006 the Republican majority in the House and Senate was at serious risk, and the two parties were more ideologically polarized than at any other time in the previous generation: the Democratic median was –0.406

FIGURE 31.1 **Control of the House is Less Certain in Recent Elections and Features More Polarized Parties**

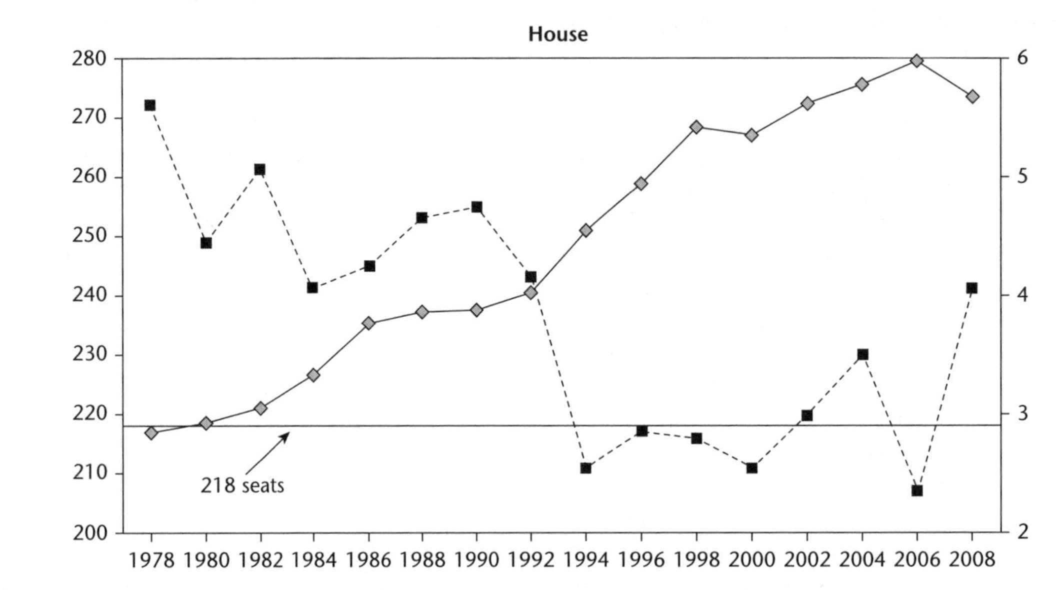

SOURCE: "Expected Seats" is derived from *Congressional Quarterly's* October election-year assessments of House elections. The total shown here is the combined number of safe, leaning, and favored races for the majority party. The number of seats needed to control the chamber is 218. Ideological polarization uses Keith Poole and Howard Rosenthal's (voteview.com/) DW-Nominate scores, which places incumbent House members on a scale of –1 (most liberal) to 1 (most conservative). The number reported here is derived as follows: the Democratic median is divided by the standard deviation of all Democrats; the same is done for Republicans. The Democratic number is then subtracted from the Republican number.

FIGURE 31.2 **Control of the Senate is Less Certain in Recent Elections and Features More Polarized Parties**

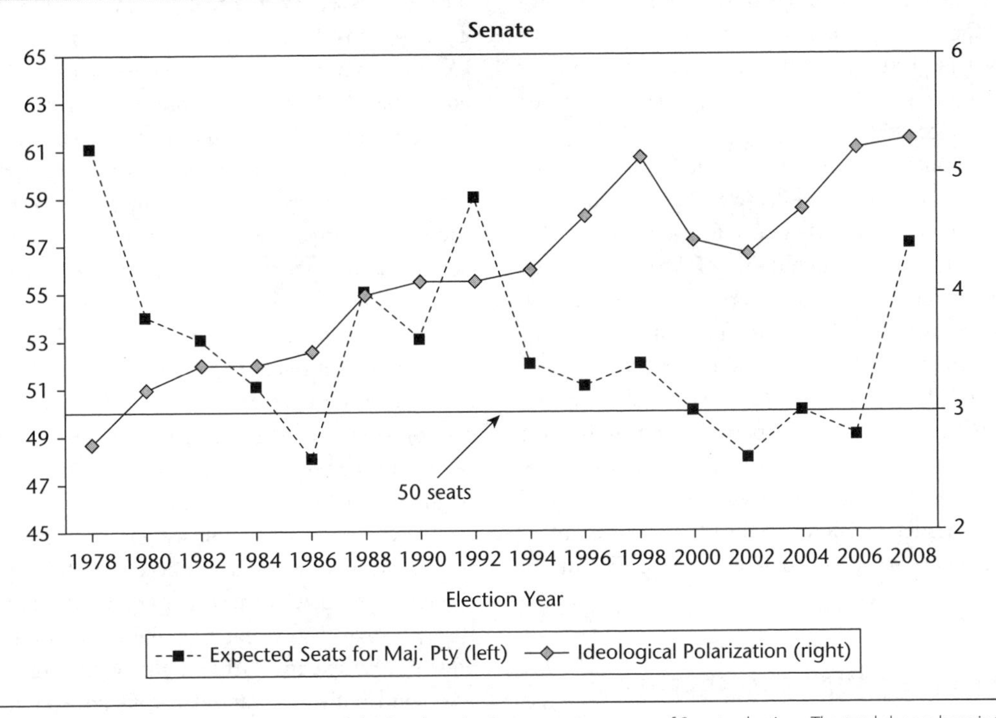

SOURCE: "Expected Seats" is derived from *Congressional Quarterly's* October election-year assessments of Senate elections. The total shown here is the combined number of safe, leaning, and favored races for the majority party. The number of seats needed to control the chamber is 51. Ideological polarization uses Keith Poole and Howard Rosenthal's (voteview.com/) DW-Nominate scores, which places incumbent Senate members on a scale of −1 (most liberal) to 1 (most conservative). The number reported here is derived as follows: the Democratic median is divided by the standard deviation of all Democrats; the same is done for Republicans. The Democratic number is then subtracted from the Republican number.

and the Republican median was 0.535. The 2006 election was not unique, however. Between 1994 and 2006 congressional elections featured ever more polarized parties in the context of fragile majority control.

The change in the partisan context is likely the chief causal variable in the development of 527s and 501(c)s. In short, changes in the partisan and ideological context compelled many groups to pursue replacement goals, helping the candidates in either party pursue control of Congress. This demanded the development of tactics that allowed for the infusion of more cash into competitive races—hence the discovery of 527s and 501(c)s. Keep in mind, as Chapter 33 notes, interest groups barely utilized nonexpress advocacy advertisements before 1996. Groups pursued procandidate electioneering almost exclusively through PACs in the 1980s and early 1990s. Moreover, there is even some evidence in the existing scholarship that the change in the partisan context compelled many PACs in recent years to spend more aggressively in competitive congressional races, ramping up the use of regulated dollars for the purpose of pursuing replacement goals.[41] As Table 31.1 shows, independent expenditures reached unprecedented levels in 2006 and 2008.

The partisan context is not the only motivating force that explains why some groups electioneer with 527s and 501(c)s. Chapter 33 discusses differences across groups (short-lived versus long-standing groups, for example) that motivate some to pursue electioneering ads and others to utilize grassroots mobilization or direct mail. In addition, pushing issue agendas and/or raising the profile of the group might reasonably be more important to some interests than influencing voter decisions on Election Day. All told, however, as congressional elections have become more competitive in the last fifteen years, interest groups have pursued replacement goals more aggressively.

The 2008 elections deserve some mention here. Figures 31.1 and 31.2 show that incumbents in the House and Senate were incredibly polarized in 2007 and 2008, but control of Congress was comfortably in Democratic hands—they were expected to win at least 240 seats in the House and 57 seats in the Senate. With Congress a safe Democratic institution once again, why were interest groups so active in congressional races in 2008? Some of this activity was motivated by the incredibly permissive legal context. As the Court continues to break down barriers in what is permissible electioneering, many wealthy interests will use their resources to tip close races where possible. In that sense, replacement tactics are not abandoned simply because control of Congress is more certain. At the same time, because ideological polarization in Congress is so intense, liberal and conservative groups see each competitive election as incredibly important. Liberal groups see opportunities to pursue wider margins in both chambers, and conservative groups are forced to participate to guard against deeper losses. This held particular relevance in the Senate during the 2008 election when Democrats hoped to win 60 seats for the first time since 1976.

But we should not focus only on the implications for majority control in single election cycles. The consequences of a particular cycle can reverberate in future elections. The 2012 and 2014 elections highlight this: of the sixty-six Senate seats to be contested in both years, the Democrats are incumbents in forty-two of them (64 percent), which suggests the potential for GOP gains and continued struggles for control of the chamber. This situation conceivably might also have motivated some participation by interest groups in 2008 and 2010,[42] to help lay the groundwork for a more favorable 2012 and 2014. Here too the primacy of majority control suggests increased investments from interest groups that are strongly allied with one of the two major parties.

ARE INTEREST GROUPS SUCCESSFUL?

Understanding what motivates organized interests to participate with PAC contributions or 527s and 501(c) groups conveys only half of the story. An important follow-up question seems evident: Are interest groups successful in their efforts? The conventional wisdom says yes; in other words, why would there be so much money in the system if it was not successful? Most everyone has an anecdote of how money seems to influence the development of health policy or economic policy. Put simply, lobbyists roam the halls of Congress with PAC cash to dispense—surely it must matter.

In the arena of congressional policymaking, however, there is surprisingly little evidence that PAC contributions lead consistently to certain voting patterns. Some research suggests that PAC contributions can influence floor voting, but overall only sporadic evidence that members of Congress *change* their voting habits *after* receiving campaign contributions. Political scientist Richard Smith reviewed the literature on the relationship between roll call votes and PAC contributions and discerned that contributions are likely to affect roll calls only under certain circumstances, such as when the issue is not salient with the national electorate.[43] Another study took a similar approach and concluded that the existing scholarship leaves only a thin trail of a money-for-votes relationship in policymaking.[44] The growing consensus in the scholarship then is that PAC money follows congressional voting behavior instead of leading it; that is, PACs contribute to incumbents already inclined to support their interests.

This consensus does not end the debate, however. In the previous section, the goal of "buying votes" was not even listed—almost no scholarship starts from the premise that PACs seek out members of Congress to bribe. Instead, it was noted that PAC behavior is motivated in large measure to secure access to policymakers. In this regard, the evidence is more affirming. PAC contributions seem related to levels of participation by members of Congress on certain policies and in committee work on those policies.[45] But access does not guarantee policymaking success, and there is hardly overwhelming evidence that access to policymakers results in policies different from a process without their input. Once organized interests get a seat at the table, though—a situation more common for campaign contributors than noncontributors—their perspective is very likely to be considered in the resulting legislation. This is an outcome that might reasonably concern many.

If access is often a consequence of making contributions (and more work is still needed in this area), it is not evident that replacement tactics are successful. In fact, there is surprisingly little research on the success of interest group efforts in campaigns.[46] At first glance, it seems obvious that PAC contributions to candidates will have fewer impacts on election outcomes—$5,000 can buy very few political ads. But what of the success of independent expenditures and electioneering bankrolled by 527s and 501(c) groups? Do aggressive ads from groups move enough votes to alter election outcomes? Are interest group negative ads more successful than candidate-sponsored attacks? There are no clear answers to these questions.

This is not to say that evidence does not exist. Plenty of commentators assert a relationship between interest group efforts and election outcomes. Bill Clinton argued that electioneering by the National Rifle Association in 2000 tipped Arkansas for George W. Bush, effectively costing Al Gore the election.[47] The Swift Boat Veterans are often credited with derailing the election of John Kerry in 2004. Surely, interest group electioneering in close races contributes to some election outcomes, but more controlled studies that look for specific effects are needed. If any area of interest group scholarship needs more rigorous empirical work, this is it.

WHAT ROLE SHOULD INTEREST GROUPS PLAY?

The empirical evidence reviewed above may suggest that organized interests are unlikely to have "bought and sold" elections and public policies, but many still worry about their influence in ways that cannot be easily measured. What happens in the halls of Congress that citizens cannot see and that lobbying and campaign finance disclosure laws do not make clear? There are two important correctives against these standard claims of undue influence. First, organized interests are exercising a First Amendment right to associate freely and to pressure government. This right cannot easily be constrained, nor should it be. To that end, James Madison in *Federalist* 10 first argued that the best way to counter the influence of "factions" was not to limit them but to encourage still more factions, thereby reducing the influence of any single group. This is the essence of a pluralist polity. Second, organized interests do serve a valuable function in providing elected officials with expertise in crafting policy to address complex issues. Who better to advise Congress on the design of new Medicare policy than groups advocating for senior citizens (who can speak specifically to what works and does not work in current policy) and prescription drug companies (who are on the front lines of innovative treatments), among others?

To be sure, such arguments might not successfully counter the assertion that organized interests have a pernicious effect on American policymaking. After all, E. E. Schattschneider noted a long time ago that organized interests reflect an "upper-class" bias, in that many interests, such as low-income citizens, never get organized to pressure for policy changes. This bias skews the policies considered in Congress away from unorganized interests. His observation is as apparent and relevant today as it was in 1960.[48]

Nevertheless, a few final points might more effectively serve to allay concerns about interest group dominance. First, and counterintuitively, the influence of special interest money might actually be on the decline. To that end, contribution limits for individuals are indexed to inflation (a change made with BCRA), but PAC contributions limits are not. As such, in the 2010 cycle, an individual could contribute $2,400 to a candidate per election—up $400 since 2004 (and up $1,400 over the pre-BCRA $1,000 limit). PAC contributions remain at $5,000, a limit unchanged since 1974—still higher in fact (and still attractive to candidates running for office) but declining in relative terms.

This has had the practical effect of boosting candidates' contribution totals from individual citizens. To demonstrate, Figure 31.3 shows the percentage of contributions from individuals to House and Senate candidates between 1986 and 2008.[49] In 1986 individuals accounted for 60 percent of contributions to Senate candidates, and only 37 percent of contributions to House candidates. By the 2008 elections, individuals contributed 70 percent of Senate candidates' budgets (down from near 80 percent in 2004 and 2006), and 56 percent of House candidates' budgets. The trend upward is particularly apparent for House candidates, while the percentage was always high(er) for Senate candidates. There is an apparent bump in both the House and

FIGURE 31.3 **Contributions from Individuals to House and Senate Candidates**

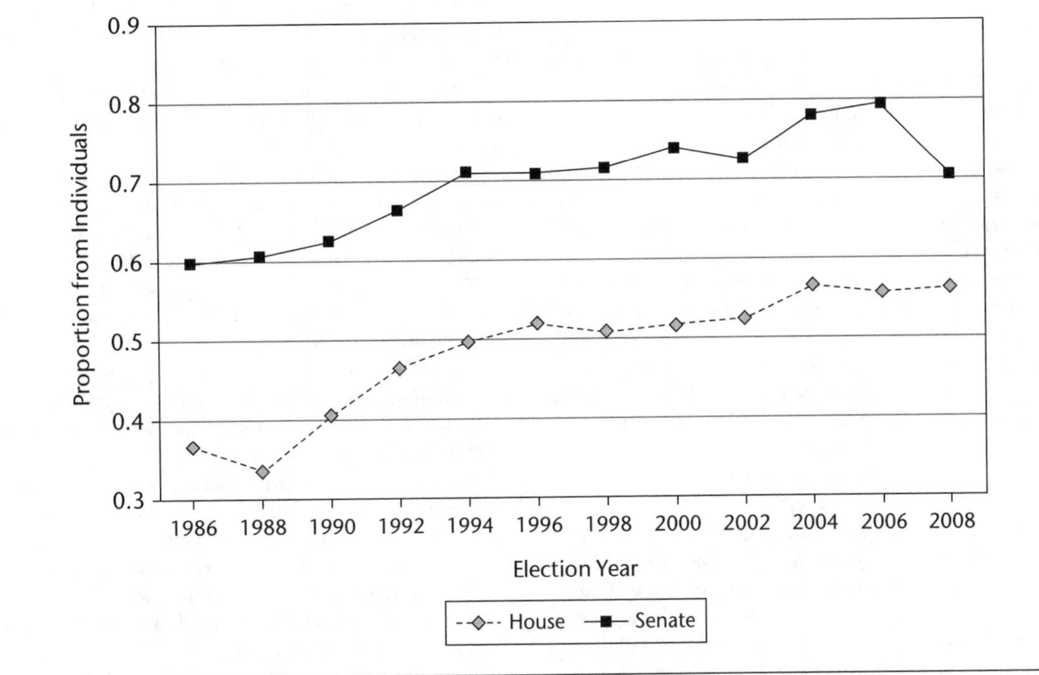

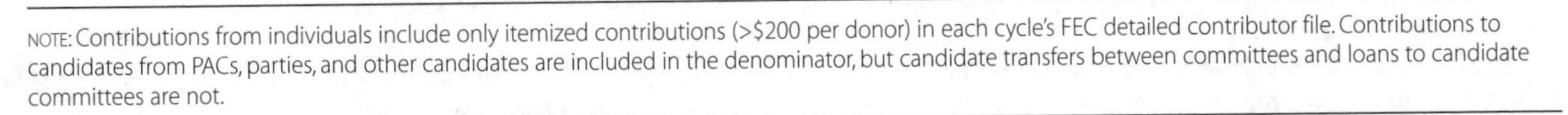
NOTE: Contributions from individuals include only itemized contributions (>$200 per donor) in each cycle's FEC detailed contributor file. Contributions to candidates from PACs, parties, and other candidates are included in the denominator, but candidate transfers between committees and loans to candidate committees are not.

Senate trends after 2002 when individuals' limits were raised, but the trend was sloping upward even before BCRA. This is likely the consequence (among other things) of the development of the Internet, which greatly facilitates fundraising from regular citizens. To be sure, the influence of PAC dollars is higher for some candidates than others (especially incumbents and senators from smaller states), but such influence is on the whole waning.

Second and relative to the influence of 527s and 501(c) groups, by two opponents of BCRA worry in a recent book about the migration of unregulated soft money from parties (a feature of campaign finance practices in the 1990s) to such independent groups.[50] In their view, contributions are more accountable when they go to political parties than when they enter the coffers of largely unknown or short-lived advocacy organizations. This is certainly true—strong parties are in general counterweights to the power of organized interests—but there is almost no evidence that 527s and 501(c)s have had a damaging impact on the behavior of sitting elected officials. Most of this money goes into public communications, which voters are free to accept or reject. Put simply, there is almost no evidence that TV ads from 527s lead to corrupting access in the halls of Congress.

CONCLUSION

Organized interest groups are permanent features of American politics. They play a particularly large role in congressional elections, one that increased and diversified in the late 1990s as Congress grew more polarized and control was up for grabs. Their success, however, is hard to pinpoint. Very little evidence shows that PACs buy votes on the floor of the House and Senate, and there is very little research on the effects of group electioneering efforts on the outcomes of elections. On this last point, then, the gloom and doom suggested by much commentary in the aftermath of the *Citizens United* decision seems potentially overblown. Interest groups have worked hard to locate loopholes in election law, and the Court merely ended the parlor game of byzantine congressional regulation followed by loophole discovery. More still, just as groups have increased their investments in congressional elections, so too have individuals, who account for ever-growing percentages of campaign budgets. All of these points might lead to one reassuring inference: interest groups are active in politics and elections, which is what a pluralistic political process demands, but no single group or industry holds determinative sway on the outcomes of elections or the policy process.

NOTES

1. There are two other connected PAC types: cooperatives and corporations without stock. These are much rarer, however.

2. These limits refer to multicandidate PACs, a classification for any PAC (connected or nonconnected) that receives contributions from more than fifty people and makes contributions to more than five federal candidates. PACs that do not classify as multicandidate can only contribute $1,000 to candidates, but can give $20,000 to national party committees.

3. Sponsors of connected PACs can also spend general treasury funds on direct candidate advocacy if the message is distributed only to its restricted class.

4. These numbers are from a 2008 FEC press release.

5. PACs can also contribute to party committees, who can in turn use those funds to advocate for presidential and congressional candidates.

6. IRS guidelines for 527s can be accessed at: www.irs.gov/charities/political.

7. John Mintz, "Texan Aired 'Clean Air' Ads; Bush's Campaign Not Involved, Billionaire Says," *Washington Post*, March 4, 2000, A6.

8. See www.opensecrets.org/527s/index.php for totals in 2004, 2006, and 2008. The total for 2002 is from Stephen Weissman and Kara Ryan, "Soft Money in the 2006 Election and the Outlook for 2008," Campaign Finance Institute, 2007, 1, www.cfinst.org/pr/prRelease.aspx?ReleaseID=132.

9. Many interest groups have both a PAC and 527 account. This is also true for nonprofit 501(c) organizations.

10. Information on specific 527s is from the Center for Responsive Politics searchable database, www.opensecrets.org/527s/index.php.

11. Weissman and Ryan, "Soft Money," 2.

12. Campaign Finance Institute, "Soft Money Political Spending by 501(c) Nonprofits Tripled in 2008 Election," www.cfinst.org/pr/prRelease.aspx?ReleaseID=221.

13. Richard Skinner, "Do 527's Add Up to a Party? Thinking About the 'Shadows' of Politics," *The Forum* 3, 3 (2005).

14. David Magleby and Kelly Patterson, "War Games: Issues and Resources in the Battle for the Control of Congress," in *The Battle for Congress: Iraq, Scandal, and Campaign Finance in the 2006 Election*, ed. David B. Magleby and Kelly D. Patterson (Boulder: Paradigm Publishers, 2008), 22–24.

15. Robert Boatright et al., "Interest Groups and Advocacy Organizations after BCRA," in *The Election after Reform: Money, Politics and the Bipartisan Campaign Reform Act*, ed. Michael J. Malbin (Lanham, Md.: Rowman and Littlefield, 2006).

16. Interest group totals for ads in 2000, and the claim about 2002, are taken from ibid., Table 6.3. The presence of some probusiness ads in these totals is important, because it indicates that although corporations have been risk averse in funding conservative 527s, as was noted, they are more comfortable with procandidate advocacy if funded by other probusiness entities, particularly those in which there is no disclosure. See also Jennifer Steen, "Financing the 2008 Congressional Elections: A Prospective Guide," *The Forum* 6, 1, (2008): 6–7.

17. Stephen Weissman and Ruth Hassan, "BCRA and the 527 Groups," in *Election after Reform*, 79.

18. From FEC press release: www.fec.gov/press/press2006/20061213murs.html.

19. Weissman and Ryan, "BCRA and the 527 Groups," 3-6.

20. The totals for independent expenditures in Table 31.1 include such MCFL-sponsored expenditures. They account for only a small portion of the total before 2008 and about 15 percent of the total in 2008.

21. Weissman and Ryan, "BCRA and the 527 Groups," 6–10.

22. There is one caveat on this statement. If a 501(c)4 group sponsors an independent expenditure or an electioneering communication, it must disclose to the FEC donations to the group made explicitly for the production and distribution of the ad. This is also true for 527s. In practical terms, this rarely clarifies who is behind the ad because these groups can claim that no particular donation was made to the group for that explicit purpose.

23. Steen, "Financing the 2008 Congressional Elections," 14–15.

24. See Campaign Finance Institute, "Soft Money Political Spending."

25. The "electioneering communications" data are reported by the FEC, and the advertising data were generously provided by the Wisconsin Advertising Project. Data on the project are available at wiscadproject.wisc.edu. There are a few limitations to the data that deserve mention. The FEC electioneering communication database often does not list the candidate that is mentioned in the broadcast ads—presumably because more than one federal candidate was the subject of a reported ad buy. This makes it hard to isolate ads for congressional candidates from ads for presidential candidates. The Wisconsin advertising data reported an estimated cost for each ad buy, not the actual cost. The estimates are based on the market and time of day, but the actual costs could be higher or lower.

26. The overlap is not complete, however. TV ads in Table 31.1 include ads aired outside the sixty-day and thirty-day windows, while electioneering communication totals include radio ads.

27. Peter Francia, *The Future of Organized Labor in American Politics* (New York: Columbia University Press, 2006), 111.

28. David Kimball, "Interest Groups in the 2008 Presidential Election: The Barking Dog That Didn't Bite," **The Forum** 6, 4 (2008).

29. Another relevant factor was the lack of investment in the presidential election, freeing up resources for congressional races. Interest groups who in 2007 were gearing up for aggressive electioneering in 2008 were dissuaded to invest in the presidential election because of the fundraising prowess of Barack Obama and the disapproval of such electioneering by John McCain.

30. The totals in Table 31.1 do not break down independent expenditures by type, but corporate PACs rarely sponsor them. Procorporate efforts of this kind are usually funded with trade association PACs.

31. This number comes from the Wesleyan Media Project, which tracked advertising in the 2010 elections. See election-ad.research.wesleyan.edu/.

32. Michael Franz, "The *Citizens United* Election? Or Same as it Ever Was?" *The Forum* 8, 4 (2010).

33. Diana Evans, "Oil PACs and Aggressive Contribution Strategies," *Journal of Politics* 50, 4 (1988): 1047–1056; Larry Sabato, *PAC Power* (New York: Norton, 1984).

34. Robert Kaiser, *So Damn Much Money* (New York: Alfred Knopf, 2009).

35. David Gopoian, "What Makes PACs Tick? An Analysis of the Allocation Patterns of Economic Interest Groups," *American Journal of Political Science* 28, 2 (1984): 259–281; Janet Grenzke, "Candidate Attributes and PAC Contributions," *Western Political Science Quarterly* 42, 2 (1989): 245–264; Keith Poole, Thomas Romer, and Howard Rosenthal, "The Revealed Preferences of Political Action Committees," *American Economic Review* 77, 2 (1987): 298–302; Thomas Romer and James Snyder, "An Empirical Investigation of the Dynamics of PAC Contributions," *American Journal of Political Science* 38, 3 (1994):745–769.

36. Frank L. Davis, "Sophistication in Corporate PAC Contributions: Demobilizing the Opposition," *American Politics Quarterly* 20, 4 (1992): 381–410; John Wright, "PACs, Contributions, and Roll Call: An Organizational Perspective," *American Political Science Review* 79, 2 (1985): 400–414.

37. James Endersby and Michael C. Munger, "The Impact of Legislator Attributes on Union PAC Campaign Contributions," *Journal of Labor Research* 12, 4 (1992): 79–97; James Herndon, "Access, Record, and Competition as Influences on Interest Group Contributions to Congressional Campaigns," *Journal of Politics* 44, 4 (1982): 996–1019; Michael Malbin, "Of Mountains and Molehills: PACs, Campaigns, and Public Policy," in *Parties, Interest Groups, and Campaign Finance Laws*, ed. Michael Malbin (Washington, D.C.: American Enterprise Institute for Public Policy Research, 1980); Candice Nelson, "The Money Chase: Partisanship, Committee Leadership Change, and PAC Contributions in the House of Representatives," in *The Interest Group Connection: Electioneering, Lobbying, and Policymaking in Washington*, ed. Paul Herrnson, Ronald G. Shaiko, and Clyde Wilcox (Chatham, N.J.: Chatham House Publishers, 1998).

38. Gopoian, "What Makes PACs Tick?" 262

39. Brooks Jackson, *Honest Graft: Big Money and the American Political Process* (Washington, D.C.: Farragut Publishing, 1990).

40. I use first-dimension DW-NOMINATE scores,voteview.com/.

41. Michael Franz, *Choices and Changes: Interest Groups in the Electoral Press* (Philadelphia: Temple University Press, 2008), esp. chap. 4.

42. In 2010 there was also the more immediate goal of winning control of Congress. In the run-up to that election, the House was considered more winnable for Republicans, while the Senate was considered a long shot.

43. Richard Smith, "Interest Group Influence in the U.S. Congress," *Legislative Studies Quarterly* 20, 1 (1995): 89–139.

44. Stephen Ansolabehere, John de Figueiredo, and James Snyder, "Why Is There so Little Money in U.S. Politics?" *Journal of Economic Perspectives* 17, 1 (2003): 105–130.

45. Richard Hall and Frank Wayman, "Buying Time: Moneyed Interests and the Mobilization of Bias in Congressional Committees," *American Political Science Review* 90, 4 (1990): 797–820. John Wright, "Contributions, Lobbying, and Committee Voting in the U.S. House of Representatives," *American Political Science Review* 84, 2 (1990): 417–438.

46. In total, there are only a handful of studies that look at sponsorship effects in advertising persuasion. See, for example, G. M. Garramone, "Effects of Negative Political Advertising: The Roles of Sponsor and Rebuttal," *Journal of Broadcasting and Electronic Media* 29 (1985): 147–159; L. L Kaid and J. Boydston, "An Experimental Study of the Effectiveness of Negative Political Advertisements," *Communication Quarterly* 35 (1987): 193–201; Michael Pfau et al., "Issue-Advocacy Versus Candidate Advertising: Effects on Candidate Preferences and Democratic Process," *Journal of Communication* 52 (2002): 301–315.

47. William Clinton, *My Life* (New York: Alfred Knopf, 2004), 928.

48. E. E. Schattschneider, *The Semisovereign People: A Realist's View of Democracy in America* (New York: Holt, Rinehart and Winston, 1960).

49. In actuality, these percentages are low because they exclude unitemized contributions from individuals giving less than $200 to a candidate. The trend goes back only to 1986 because this is the first cycle that the FEC makes available its "miscellaneous" file of all contributions and transfers between any registered committees.

50. Peter Wallison and Joel Gora, *Better Parties, Better Government: A Realistic Program for Campaign Finance Reform* (Washington, D.C.: American Enterprise Institute Press, 2009), 52–54.

SUGGESTED READING

Berry, Jeffrey M., and Clyde Wilcox. *The Interest Group Society.* New York: Pearson Longman, 2009.

Francia, Peter. *The Future of Organized Labor in American Politics.* New York: Columbia University Press, 2006.

Franz, Michael. *Choices and Changes: Interest Groups in the Electoral Press.* Philadelphia: Temple University Press, 2008.

Kaiser, Robert. *So Damn Much Money.* New York: Alfred Knopf, 2009.

Sabato, Larry J. *PAC Power.* New York: Norton, 1984.

Schattschneider, E. E. *The Semisovereign People: A Realist's View of Democracy in America.* New York: Holt, Rinehart and Winston, 1960.

Wallison, Peter, and Joel Gora. *Better Parties, Better Government: A Realistic Program for Campaign Finance Reform.* Washington, D.C.: The American Enterprise Institute Press, 2009.

chapter 32

Interest Groups in Presidential Elections

by Clyde Wilcox and Elliott Fullmer

In January 2005, nearly four years before the November 2008 presidential election, candidates were already busy courting the support of interest groups. These candidates hoped that group leaders would lend their support in raising money and in communicating with group members. Over the next four years, candidates made frequent appearances at national, state, and local meetings of interest groups, appealing for support by stressing issues central to the organization's agenda.

Most candidates focused heavily on interest groups in Iowa and New Hampshire, the first caucus and primary states for each party's nomination process. Rep. Tom Tancredo campaigned in Iowa on July 7–9, 2005, including visits to four house parties organized by the Christian Coalition of Iowa. On July 18 Gov. Bill Richardson spoke at a fundraiser for the Iowa Trial Lawyers Association. On August 19 Sen. John Edwards spoke to the Iowa Federation of Labor's annual convention at the Five Sullivan Brothers Convention Center at Waterloo, and the next day he delivered remarks to the Iowa Farmers Union at the Best Western Hotel in Marshalltown. On October 8 Sen. Sam Brownback was the featured speaker for Iowa Taxpayers' Day, sponsored by Iowans for Tax Relief, at The Embassy Suites Hotel in Des Moines.[1]

Sometimes candidates braved potentially hostile audiences to try to win group support. In the 2000 presidential campaign, Sen. John McCain had denounced Christian Right leaders Jerry Falwell and Pat Robertson as "agents of intolerance," but in May 2006 McCain addressed students at Falwell's Liberty University. After the speech, Falwell hosted a dinner for McCain and 250 Christian conservative leaders—pastors of large churches and leaders of citizen's groups, where McCain had a chance to make a personal pitch to influential leaders.

In other cases, interest groups invited candidates to meet members, but not to make a speech. In 2007–2008 the Service Employees International Union (SEIU) sponsored a "Walk a Day in My Shoes" program in which a candidate would spend a day working with a union member. All of the Democratic candidates—and no Republican candidates—took part. Sen. Chris Dodd aided a Head Start teacher; Sen. Joe Biden helped a school custodian; and Sen. Barack Obama worked with a homecare worker.[2]

Candidates seek interest group support because they think it will help them win their party's nomination and ultimately the general election. Groups frequently contribute money to candidates; they also communicate directly with their members to endorse or encourage support for a candidate. Many groups are willing to do far more for preferred candidates, helping them win the votes of citizens who do not belong to the organization.

In the 2008 presidential campaign, many groups gave money to candidates through their PACs, encouraged members to contribute to a candidate, or hosted fundraisers. Group members canvassed neighborhoods, registered voters, tried to persuade voters to support candidates, and helped get voters to the polls. Groups ran advertisements on television, radio, and the Internet, and mailed persuasive material to their members and to others who might be influenced by the mailings. They called voters on the phone to persuade them to vote for candidates and to remind them to vote. Some were active in the nomination process, while others waited until the parties had chosen their candidates to get involved.

This chapter addresses several important concepts regarding the role of interest groups in presidential elections. First, it probes the various motivations that groups have for getting involved at different stages of presidential campaigns. It then provides a detailed overview of the major activities undertaken by groups to influence the nomination and general phases of presidential elections. These activities include publicly endorsing candidates, producing voter guides and other mailers, contributing money to candidates, and registering, mobilizing, and persuading voters. In describing these activities, this chapter discusses the ways groups organize and distribute their resources given various campaign finance regulations. Finally, it also documents new and innovative ways that interest groups are using the Web to achieve their goals.

CANDIDATES "WALK IN THE SHOES" OF EVERYDAY WORKERS

Over the course of presidential campaigns, organizations often sponsor initiatives encouraging candidates to demonstrate their support for their ideas. In doing so, interest groups are able to create attention and exposure for their respective issue(s). In addition, they can pressure candidates into supporting their agenda *on the record,* making it politically difficult for them to backtrack in the future.

The Service Employees International Union (SEIU) is one of the most politically active labor unions. It represents about 2 million workers in more than 100 occupations. Its clientele consists primarily of hospital, home care, nursing home, and property service (janitors and security officers) employees.[1]

As the 2008 presidential campaign commenced in early 2007, SEIU knew its endorsement was highly coveted by each Democratic candidate. Not only could the group mobilize its massive member base behind a candidate, but also it planned to spend large sums of money on voter mobilization, ad campaigns, and direct mail.

In January 2007 SEIU announced that as a prerequisite for its endorsement, candidates would need to spend a day working with an SEIU member. The program, named "Walk a Day in My Shoes," would bring candidates into the homes and workplaces of janitors, home-care workers, and nurses. SEIU President Andy Stern argued, "If presidential candidates understand the struggles workers face each day, they will be better able to offer the solutions this country needs."[2]

Candidates in both parties were invited to participate, but only Democrats chose to do so. By summer 2007, six candidates, including front-runners Hillary Clinton, Barack Obama, and John Edwards, had "walked a day" in the shoes of an SEIU-represented worker.

Obama worked with a homecare worker, Pauline Beck, as she assisted an eighty-six-year-old client in his Oakland, California, home. Obama arrived at Beck's home for an early morning breakfast before a long day of mopping floors, doing laundry, washing dishes, changing sheets, and performing other duties. He also spoke to Beck about his policy proposals regarding labor and other relevant issues, such as health care. Afterward, he issued high praise for the program, saying, "Walking just one day in Pauline's shoes was probably the best experience I've had on this campaign so far."[3]

SEIU endorsed Obama in February 2008, several months before he secured the Democratic nomination. Through the primaries and the general election, the union committed considerable resources to his bid for the presidency. More than 100,000 union members volunteered for the campaign. Collectively, SEIU knocked on nearly 2 million doors, made more than 4 million phone calls, sent 2.5 million pieces of mail, and registered over 85,000 new voters.[4]

1. Service Employees International Union, www.seiu.org/our-union/index.php.
2. Organized Labor and the 2008 Presidential Primary Campaign, www.gwu.edu/~action/2008/interestg08/labor08.html.
3. See www.walkadayinmyshoes2008.com/obama-and-beck.
4. See http://www.cnsnews.com/node/40959.

INTEREST GROUPS AND PRESIDENTIAL ELECTIONS

Interest groups are involved in many types of elections, including congressional elections, contests for state and local office, and those wishing the passage of referenda.[3] Groups that seek to gain particularistic benefits from government, such as contracts, exemptions from regulation, and special tax breaks, are especially focused on Congress (see Chapter 31). But groups that focus on broad macroeconomic or ideological policies frequently concentrate their attention on presidential elections because of the president's role in agenda setting, implementing policies, and appointing judges. Groups make a standing decision to be involved in presidential elections, but they may change this decision in response to political events.[4]

Candidates and interest groups enter into relationships with somewhat divergent motives. Presidential candidates seek support from groups because they have resources that can help them win their party's nomination and/or the general election. Groups support candidates to further their policy agenda. They prefer that candidates openly promise to support their main policy agenda, so that they can hold them accountable. Candidates seek to appeal to a broad range of voters, some of whom may not support the group's agenda. They therefore prefer to make broader or more general public statements of support, perhaps with private promises on specific policies.

Some interest groups primarily support candidates of one political party and in some cases may be thought of as elements in the party network.[5] Labor unions and environmental groups are reliable members of the Democratic Party's coalition. Some are part of a social movement that seeks to influence party nominations and platforms.[6] Organizations such as Americans for Tax Reform and National Right to Life actively seek influence within the Republican Party, urging voters, candidates, and officeholders to adopt reliably conservative positions on their respective issues. These groups are usually very active in the long and complex presidential nomination campaign.

Some groups are active in the primaries and caucuses because the nomination phase dramatically narrows the field and in doing so helps define the party's agenda. At the start of the nomination process for the 2008 elections, ten candidates were seeking the Democratic nomination, and twelve candidates were seeking the Republican nomination.

Labor unions historically have been stalwart supporters of Democratic candidates. The American Federation of State, County and Municipal Employees endorsed Democratic senator Hillary Clinton's bid for the presidential nomination in 2008.

Within each party, candidates took different positions on major issues including the Iraq War, the torture of prisoners, health care, the environment, taxes, and immigration. Believing the differences between the candidates were significant, some groups chose to play an active role on behalf of or against a particular candidate. The Club for Growth, an organization of fiscal conservatives, targeted former Arkansas governor Mike Huckabee in numerous negative television spots. Huckabee, the group argued, had established an unacceptable record of increasing taxes while governor. Similarly, the Log Cabin Republicans, an organization of conservatives who support homosexual rights, ran negative ads against former Massachusetts governor Mitt Romney. The group argued that other GOP candidates, such as former New York City mayor Rudy Giuliani, would be more favorable toward its issues than Romney.[7]

Moreover, the usually chaotic nomination process invites interest groups' extra effort, which may affect the outcome. By influencing the nomination process, groups may also influence the party platform. Some organizations have great interest in the content of party platforms, for both symbolic and substantive reasons.[8]

Seeking to shape the Republican platform every four years, Americans for Tax Reform asks candidates to sign a pledge promising that he or she will not increase taxes as president. In 2008 each Republican agreed to the pledge except Fred Thompson and John McCain, who nevertheless was able to secure the GOP nomination.[9]

Other interest groups are active only once the party nominees are selected. They may always support the candidate of one party or in some cases work to elect the candidate who seems the most likely to further their issue agenda. The United Auto Workers (UAW) chose to stay neutral during the 2008 Democratic primaries, opting instead to conserve their resources and help elect the nominee once chosen.[10] In some cases groups may choose to withhold support from both candidates, as the National Rifle Association (NRA) did in 1996 when it determined that neither represented the group's view of Second Amendment rights.

There are many types of interest groups, with different resources that can be used in elections. Large membership organizations such as the AFL-CIO and the NRA have millions of members who can vote for a candidate, contribute to their campaigns, and volunteer their time to persuade others to support the candidate. Some organizations, such as the Sierra Club and Focus on the Family, have a reputation that allows them to reach far beyond their members to larger constituencies—in this case, environmentalists and Christian conservatives. Corporations and trade associations rely less on members and more on their executives and stockholders who have many connections and personal resources. Some membership and ideological organizations have a number of wealthy activists who can invest their own money in campaigns. Some groups have substantial political expertise, acquired through years of campaign activity, including experienced field operatives.

Campaign finance and tax laws help determine which resources groups may use in elections and how they may be used. To allow themselves greater flexibility, many interest groups have created separate funds or structures to conduct various campaign activities.[11] Groups that wish to contribute directly to candidates must form political action committees (PACs), which can collect contributions of up to $5,000 from members of the organization and contribute up to $5,000 to any presidential candidate in any election.[12] They can establish a 501(c)(3) tax-exempt charity to accept large contributions from supporters and to develop persuasive materials and hone their membership lists; however, funds from these committees cannot be used in electioneering. They can also sponsor a 501(c)(4) or 501(c)(6) committee that can accept large contributions, and can do some electoral advocacy so long as this is not the principle purpose of the organization. They can sponsor a 527 committee that can use treasury funds and large contributions from members or supporters to mobilize voters and to run issue ads that do not explicitly endorse a candidate, but are clearly intended to sway voters (see Chapter 31). Recent Supreme Court decisions have allowed for the creation of independent expenditure committees that can accept large contributions from individuals and groups and produce ads to support or oppose a candidate. Although these committees must disclose their donors to the FEC, the donors may be 501(c) organizations that do not disclose *their* donors.[13]

The list of interest groups that are active in any particular election includes many that are not ongoing, permanent organizations. Some are not groups at all, but rather organizational shells formed to use resources in particular ways. In the 2000 nomination process, a group called Republicans for Clean Air created TV ads for the New York primary that attacked McCain's environmental record while praising that of George W. Bush. This "group" had no members or even a permanent mailing address, but was instead a mechanism for two Texas brothers to spend substantial sums to help Bush win the election, using a name designed to lead voters to believe that the ad had been produced by an environmental organization. Other groups are formed by political activists for a particular election only. In the 2004 campaign, liberal interest group leaders came together to create large 527 committees that played distinctive roles in the campaign, primarily funded by a single donor. Many of these groups were disbanded after the 2004 election, and some paid fines for coordinating with the candidate's campaigns.[14]

ENDORSEMENTS AND VOTER GUIDES

Of all activities undertaken by interest groups in presidential elections, endorsements require the least financial commitment. Some groups do not endorse candidates, even though they may provide other types of support. Citizens groups that are organized as nonprofit charities are barred by tax law from endorsing candidates. This category includes churches, which are free to discuss the issues of the campaign but not to endorse candidates if they wish to retain their tax-exempt status.[15] In the 2008 campaign, however, a number of churches explicitly endorsed McCain from the pulpit and sent videotapes of their activities directly to the IRS. Alliance Defense Fund, a conservative Christian law firm, promised to defend all of the churches against potential IRS action. Corporations are allowed to endorse candidates but seldom do so, both because their endorsement would seem self-interested and therefore not sway many voters and because it might cost them customers of the other party.

But many other organizations do endorse candidates, both in the nomination phase and/or the general election. During the 2008 Democratic nomination process, labor unions endorsed different candidates. The American Federation of State, County and Municipal Employees (AFSCME), American Federation of Teachers, Sheet Metal Workers International Organization, and National Association of Letter Carriers endorsed Sen. Hillary Clinton. The SEIU, UNITE HERE, and the International Brotherhood of Teamsters endorsed Barack Obama, and the Transport Workers Union of America, United Steelworkers, and United Mine Workers of America gave early endorsements to John Edwards. During the general election campaign, all of these unions endorsed Obama against McCain.[16] At times, ideological organizations may find it difficult to choose between two or more candidates who are strong supporters of their agendas. In 2008 NARAL Pro-Choice America, the UAW, the AFL-CIO, and the NRA declined to endorse candidates during the primaries. Each of these groups endorsed a candidate in the general election.

If tax law forbids an organization from endorsing candidates, that organization can create a separate political committee that can endorse and engage in electioneering. Focus on the Family is a tax-exempt religious ministry that is part of the Christian Right, but the affiliated Focus on the Family Action is a political arm that can participate in elections as well as contribute money. In other cases, the leaders of an organization may personally endorse a candidate, and although they do not officially speak for the organization, the endorsement may sway group members. During the 2008 GOP primaries, Christian Right and pro-life groups and leaders were divided in their endorsements and conveyed them in different ways. The National Right to Life Committee endorsed Fred Thompson, and American Values

★ 2008 Christian Coalition ★

VOTER GUIDE

PRESIDENTIAL ELECTION

John McCain (R)	ISSUES	Barack Obama (D)
Supports*	Education vouchers that allow parents to choose public or private school for their children	Opposes*
Opposes*	Sex education for children in kindergarten through 12th grade	Supports*
Opposes*	Increase in federal income tax rates	Supports*
Supports*	Appointing judges that will adhere to a strict interpretation of the Constitution	Opposes*
Opposes*	Further restrictions on the right to keep and bear arms	Supports*
Opposes*	Public funding of abortions, (such as govt. health benefits and Planned Parenthood)	Supports*
Supports*	Parental notification for abortions by minors	Opposes*
Supports*	Legislation mandating health care for infants surviving abortions	Opposes*
Opposes*	Granting sexual preference a protected minority status under existing civil rights laws	Supports*
Opposes*	Allowing adoption of children by homosexuals	Supports*
Supports*	Enforcing the 1993 law banning homosexuals in the military	Opposes*
Supports*	Prohibiting public funding for art that is pornographic or anti-religious	Opposes*
Supports*	Tax credits for purchasing private health insurance	Opposes*
Supports*	Allowing federal funding for faith-based charitable organizations	Opposes*
Supports*	Tax credits for investment in renewable sources of energy, (such as wind, solar & biomass)	Supports*
Supports*	Legislation to enact a "cap & trade" system to reduce carbon dioxide emissions	Supports*

www.johnmccain.com www.barackobama.com

Each candidate was sent a 2008 Federal Issues Survey by mail and/or facsimile machine. When possible, positions of candidates on issues were verified or determined using voting records and/or public statements, articles or campaign literature. An asterisk (*) indicates such information was used to determine positions and sources are available on request.

Paid for and authorized by the Christian Coalition; PO Box 37030 - Washington, DC 20013

The Christian Coalition is a pro-family, citizen action organization. This voter guide is provided for educational purposes only and is not to be construed as an endorsement of any candidate or party.

Please visit our web site at www. cc.org

★ Vote on November 4 ★

★ Vote on November 4 ★

Dear fellow American Christian,

You are holding one of the most powerful tools Christians have ever had to impact our society during elections – the Christian Coalition voter guide. This simple tool has helped educate tens of millions of citizens across this nation as to where candidates for public office stand on key faith and family issues.

I want to assure you that your church or civic group has every right to distribute these non-partisan voter guides, and distributing them poses no threat whatsoever to any organization's tax-exempt status. In fact, Christian Coalition is the only organization whose voter guides are prepared in accordance with IRS approved guidelines for distribution in churches.

I encourage you to help spread this important information to others by making additional copies for distribution. You can make voter guides available in every way possible – in churches, at Christian bookstores, as neighborhood handouts and even outside your local polling station. You can also visit our web site at www.cc.org to find links to this guide which you can forward via email to others. They can then download and print directly from our web site.

Also, please be in prayer for our nation, as we continually need God's hand of mercy and protection.

This is a crucial election and too much is at stake for God's people to sit on the sidelines. Be sure to make your vote count by going to the polls this coming Election Day!

Thank you for the stand you are taking as a Christian citizen and may God bless America!

Sincerely,
Roberta Combs
President, Christian Coalition

★ Please go to www.cc.org and help support our 2008 Voter Guide Project ★

The Christian Coalition published this voter guide prior to the 2008 presidential election. Although it does not endorse a particular candidate, it spells out the positions of both candidates on issues of importance to the organization and its members.

president Gary Bauer endorsed McCain. Christian Coalition president Pat Robertson endorsed Rudolph Giuliani, but Focus on the Family founder James Dobson proclaimed that he would advise his supporters to back a third party if Giuliani were the nominee. Dobson was primarily opposed to Giuliani's pro-choice stance on abortion. Dobson and Beverley LaHaye, founder of Concerned Women for America, personally endorsed Huckabee.

Occasionally, the local arm of an interest group and the national organization will prefer different candidates. In 2008 the National Organization for Women endorsed Obama, but the president of the organization's Los Angeles wing publicly supported McCain. The local president, Shelly Mandell, was influenced by McCain's choice of Alaska governor Sarah Palin as his running mate.[17]

Interest groups endorsements, however, do not always sway group members. In 1984 the AFL-CIO took the then-unusual step of endorsing Democrat Walter Mondale in the primaries and worked hard for him in the general election. Yet exit polls showed that nearly half of union members voted for Ronald Reagan.[18] But endorsements can affect nominations even if they do not determine the voting choices of all group members. First, endorsements may lead some group members to work harder on behalf of a candidate. Second, endorsements by interest groups influence voters who do not belong to the organization. The Sierra Club's endorsement probably sways the votes of members of other environmental organizations, and an endorsement by the NRA is likely a voting cue for other gun enthusiasts. Finally, it may be that the information conveyed by the endorsement is part of an information stream that influences partisan choices.[19]

Endorsements matter more if the interest group makes a major effort to distribute the announcement to its members, and even beyond the membership to other sympathetic voters. The NRA and Sierra Club distribute their endorsements through their Web pages, magazines, and newsletters and by mailing materials to members' homes. In closely contested states, they may organize phone banks to call members and other interested citizens to convey their endorsement. Groups may also ask members to distribute materials to their neighbors and thereby expand the impact of the endorsement.

Some groups produce voter guides that show the positions of candidates on issues important to group members. In the 1990s the Christian Coalition distributed tens of millions of voter guides in conservative churches across the United States. These guides did not endorse candidates, but the selection of the issues and the description of candidate positions consistently made it clear that the group preferred GOP nominees. In 1992 the coalition claimed to distribute 40 million voter guides that left no doubt about the group's preference for George H. W. Bush over Bill Clinton. Voter guides allow their readers to see how candidates differ on a variety of issues. Groups can also provide voters with sample ballots to carry into the polling booth, where they can compare the names on the ballot with those endorsed by the organization.

CONTRIBUTING CASH

Interest groups are a major source of funding for congressional candidates. Many corporations and trade associations sponsor PACs that contribute to candidates as part of a larger lobbying effort (see Chapter 31). PAC contributions primarily go to incumbent candidates with some agenda control over committees that affect the group.[20] Some interest groups also bundle contributions of their members, meaning that they collect donations from numerous individual members and present the pooled funds to a campaign. Many encourage their members to contribute directly to candidates as well.[21] In this way, PACs can contribute far more than the legal maximum of $5,000.

In presidential elections, PACs play a much smaller role.[22] During the 2008 nomination process, Hillary Clinton and John McCain both received approximately $1.4 million in direct PAC contributions. As both candidates raised more than $200 million overall, PAC contributions were only slightly more than 1 percent of their overall funds. Obama refused PAC contributions, and the Center for Responsive Politics reports that his campaign received slightly less than $1,800 from PACs, a tiny sum compared to the more than $400 million he raised in the nomination phase.[23]

The small sums from PACs do not mean that interest groups are not important in raising funds for presidential campaigns. Corporate executives contribute as individuals to presidential candidates, and may encourage their employees to do so as well.[24] They may host fundraising events and ask their friends and others to contribute. The Center for Responsive Politics reports that employees of Goldman Sachs gave more than $900,000 to Obama's presidential campaign, nearly $400,000 to Clinton's campaign, and more than $200,000 to McCain. Many interest group leaders volunteer to raise a certain amount for a candidate from individual contributions.[25] In the 2008 campaign, EMILY's List is credited with providing $855,000 to Hillary Clinton's campaign through bundled contributions.[26] From 1980 through the 2000 election, interest groups could also give large "soft money" contributions to political parties. Although these funds could technically not be spent to elect specific candidates, presidential candidates were in fact the major solicitors of soft money and could dictate how the money was spent. Corporations, labor unions, and wealthy individuals were increasingly pressured to give larger and larger sums to presidential campaigns.[27] These soft money contributions were banned under the Bipartisan Campaign Reform Act (BCRA) in 2002, but interest groups and wealthy patrons can contribute large sums to 527 committees and 501(c) committees. In the 2004 presidential elections, George Soros contributed more than $30 million to various 527 committees working to help elect John Kerry.

REGISTERING AND MOBILIZING VOTERS

Interest groups may devote considerable resources to registering and mobilizing voters who support a particular candidate. Frequently, close elections hinge on the turnout of various sectors of the population, and this is especially true during the nomination phase in caucus states. Interest groups therefore work hard to get their members to register and to participate in caucuses or vote on primary day. In the 2000 and 2004 general elections, interest groups and parties devoted enormous energy and spent large sums mobilizing votes.

A strong turnout by group members or by the group's constituency can send a strong signal to candidates and parties. Although unions constitute a small and declining portion of the labor force, union members and families vote in higher numbers than other citizens—something that is obvious to Democratic and Republican candidates (see Chapter 13). Moreover, in close elections, group leaders may be specially courted to mount turnout efforts. In the 2004 election GOP strategist Karl Rove set a goal of increasing turnout among white Evangelicals, and Democratic strategists sought to increase minority and labor turnout.

Groups that are organized as nonprofit charities can register and mobilize voters so long as they do not endorse a candidate in the process. But if the group begins with a list of voters deemed very likely to support a particular candidate, then nonpartisan voter mobilization can have very partisan consequences. For all groups, lists of potentially sympathetic voters are a crucial element in voter mobilization.

The logical starting place for most organizations is with their membership. Labor unions have for decades sponsored centers where union members call other members to urge them to register and vote. Other large membership organizations, such as the NRA and Sierra Club, also have a long history of mobilizing their members. In doing their best to get members registered, groups sometimes "bounce" their membership lists off of voter registration lists compiled by others. Groups may also maintain a list of their most active members and encourage them to volunteer in campaigns or train to be field operators.[28]

But even the largest organizations have too few members to influence presidential elections in all battleground states. In the late 1990s a number of interest groups began developing strategies to register and mobilize nonmembers. Many organizations begin with potential group members—the broad constituency that the group represents. This serves the dual function of increasing the clout of the organization and its constituency and identifying potential members. In the 1990s many conservative organizations worked hard to develop voter contact lists beyond their members. The Christian Coalition's goal in the 1992 election was to identify 1 million "pro-family" voters through volunteers who worked to canvass neighborhoods. Many Christian Coalition activists worked to register members of conservative churches and to add their names to the master list, although the group fell far short of its goal. Before the election, the group contacted potential voters on this list through phone calls and postcards, using volunteers within the organization and a paid firm.

Similarly, the National Association for the Advancement of Colored People (NAACP) through its political arm, National Voter Fund, claimed to have registered some 200,000 new voters in 2000. It also built a list of 3.8 million African Americans who were "infrequent voters" and devised different combinations of live and recorded phone calls and get-out-the-vote (GOTV) mailers to get them to the polls. The group managed to increase turnout, but at a relatively high cost.[29] In 2008 EMILY's List, a pro-choice PAC that seeks to elect pro-choice women, endorsed Clinton and set up a Web site, appropriately called yougogirl.com, which provided first-time caucus-goers with information about the process.[30]

By the 2000s the Republican Party had built its own large voter contact lists and had moved voter mobilization efforts in the general election to within the party. Where once the Christian Coalition had built a list and contacted voters, in 2004 the Bush-Cheney campaign asked pastors and church members to provide copies of membership directories to add to the GOP contact list.[31] Many pastors who supported Bush balked at the request, however.[32] In 2004 the Republican Party also contacted religious conservatives using "microtargeting," a technique that begins with a large voter registration file and adds additional information gathered by the party through phone calls and canvassing. Finally, it adds on consumer data such as what type of car the person drives and what magazines he or she reads. From these data, the party created a predictive model to help identify conservative Christian voters, whom it then contacted using special messages.[33] These same lists helped create the "72-hour plan," in which party activists and volunteers contact all potential voters in targeted districts and states. Not all voter mobilization is conducted within the party, however. In 2008 business groups made a major effort to register and mobilize small business owners and their employees.

The Democratic Party relies far more on liberal and labor groups than on party operatives to mobilize voters. In the 2000s liberal groups began cooperating in voter registration, list building, and contacting voters. Much of this activity was done through newly created 527 committees. Coordinating these new groups was a coalition called America Votes; members donated $50,000 and agreed to participate in a disciplined sharing of efforts. During the 2004 presidential campaign in Florida, the Sierra Club canvassed in Tampa, the League of Conservation Workers canvassed in Orlando, and EMILY's List canvassed in Miami-Dade County.[34]

The AFL-CIO, having conducted focus groups and surveys to assess its member mobilization campaign in 2000, spent $45 million mobilizing its members, including sending volunteers across state lines. But the AFL-CIO also joined other unions in helping form America Coming Together in 2004, which claimed to have registered 85,000 new voters in Ohio, had more than a million personal conversations with potential voters, and knocked on more than 3 million doors.

Liberal groups have worked to create their own version of the 72-hour plan. The principal source of voter contact lists for many groups in 2008 was Catalist, a company that has thus far operated at a loss while building and refining large progressive contact lists. Planned Parenthood Action Fund, the SEIU, and Sierra Club have each credited Catalist with building a targeted list of supporters for them to contact.[35] Catalist helps groups not only identify potential voters but also study through experiments the best mobilization tools for different subsets.

Although groups differ in the types of contacts they make with their members and with other potential voters, the volume of this activity has reached staggering proportions in recent campaigns. Potential voters are contacted repeatedly through the mail, by phone, and by volunteers knocking on their doors. As the election approaches, they

MOVEON.ORG USES VIDEO TO PREVENT THE "NIGHTMARE SCENARIO"

Since the late 1990s MoveOn.org has been one of the leading groups advocating progressive causes and Democratic candidates in presidential elections.

Originally created to defend President Bill Clinton against his impeachment at the hands of a Republican Congress, MoveOn.org has since used technology to vault itself into a formidable group in political campaigns. It uses e-mail as its main method for communicating with supporters, often sending videos, audio downloads, and images to its members hoping to mobilize them behind a particular candidate or cause.

In 2008 MoveOn.org allowed its members to vote (via e-mail) on the group's presidential endorsement. Barack Obama won the vote handily with 70 percent support.[1] The group then played a particularly active role in supporting Obama's bid, spending more than $30 million and registering more than 500,000 voters in the months preceding the election.[2]

In October 2008, following the collapse of several large financial firms, numerous polls indicated that Obama was well positioned to defeat Republican nominee John McCain. The greatest concern for progressives was complacency—the idea that voters would become convinced that Obama would win handily and therefore not show up at the polls and vote.

Seeking to prevent this "nightmare scenario," MoveOn.org sent an e-mail message to its 3.5 million member list. The e-mail included a video link featuring a hypothetical postelection newscast revealing the name of a person whose failure to vote led to McCain's victory by one single vote.

The unique feature of the two-minute video was that the pivotal nonvoter's name was customized to each e-mail recipient. Therefore, an e-mail to a MoveOn.org member by the name of Robert Baker would feature a series of clips displaying a newspaper headline, a church sign, a graffiti-sprayed wall, a Facebook group, and TV news captions all blaming Baker *personally* for Obama's one-vote defeat.[3]

For example, the newspaper headline read, "Nonvoter Identified: Robert Baker"; the church sign said, "All God's Children Welcome (Except Robert Baker)"; the graffiti-sprayed wall, "Robert = loser"; the Facebook group, "10 Million Strong against Robert Baker"; and the TV news caption said, "Republicans Praise Baker."

MoveOn.org's Peter Koechley said the video was intended to "raise the specter of shame and humiliation." The group decided to make the video humorous "to make the pressure go down easier." While Koechley believed most MoveOn.org members intended to vote, he hoped that they would send the video to friends, family, and colleagues whose commitment to participating was less solidified.[4]

Recipients were therefore encouraged to forward it to others, automatically customizing it to the new receiver(s). Within a few days, the e-mail was being forwarded about thirty to thirty-five times per second. Ultimately, only about 17 percent of the recipients were MoveOn.org members. MoveOn.org estimated that more than 21 million people were eventually exposed to the video.[5]

1. Politico, www.politico.com/blogs/bensmith/0208/MoveOn_endorses_Obama.html.
2. Reuters, www.reuters.com/article/pressRelease/idUS239501+05-Nov-2008+PRN20081105.
3. Personal Democracy Forum, techpresident.com/node/6496.
4. Ibid.
5. *New York Times*, thecaucus.blogs.nytimes.com/2008/10/30/using-the-blame-game-to-get-out-the-vote/.

may receive several interest group mailings a day and several live or recorded phone calls. In states that allow early or easy absentee voting, interest group activists try to persuade citizens to cast a vote before Election Day.

The Internet has allowed interest groups to do even more to contact their members and others interested in their issues. Many groups sent e-mails to members before the 2008 balloting, often with embedded video or links to deeper content on the Web page. Several large groups designed Web pages that helped their members (and other site visitors) apply for absentee ballots.

Perhaps the most interesting voter mobilization tool in 2008 was a viral video distributed by MoveOn.org. The group sent to its members a customizable video clip that they could then distribute to their friends. For example, if Sam sent the e-mail to Ellie, the news clip would use Ellie's name when she viewed it. The story is set on the day after the election, when the Republicans had won the election by a single vote—and reporters had identified Ellie as the nonvoter who made the difference.[36]

PERSUADING VOTERS

Many interest groups invest in their own advertising campaign to help elect presidential candidates. The distinction between voter mobilization and voter persuasion is not absolute—often voters are mobilized by messages that persuade them about the relative merits of the major candidates. Moreover, some persuasive messages in television ads are actually designed to reduce turnout among supporters of one candidate, by raising doubts about that candidate.[37]

The most visible voter persuasion by interest groups comes in television advertising. The rules regarding these ads have changed and remain in flux. Interest groups produce their own ads for a variety of reasons. Campaign finance law limits the amount of money that groups can directly give to candidates and parties, but it does not limit the amount that they can spend on advertising. Moreover, by creating their own ads, groups can help to focus public attention on their most important issues. In Chapter 33

Robert Boatright mentions a small ad campaign by Defenders of Wildlife criticizing Palin's support of the hunting of wolves—a campaign that had little impact on Palin's electoral chances, but did garner media attention for the issue. Interest group issue ads can also seek to frame issues that are debated in the campaign, as many groups did in 2008 on environmental issues and health care.

But more often interest group advertising campaigns are aimed at swaying voters. Most of the organizations that run television advertising are aware of and coordinate with other groups supporting the same candidate. Groups cannot coordinate with the candidate, but they can coordinate with one another. They do regular polling to determine the impact of their ads, pretest the ads in focus groups and on the Internet, and share the results of their polling with allied groups.

Beginning in the late 1970s, interest groups could air electioneering ads through their PACs as independent expenditures. These could not be coordinated with the candidate, but groups could usually find a way to help a candidate without explicitly coordinating. Independent expenditure ads are often financed by PACs (which can accept only $5,000 from any single member). This means that groups cannot use large contributions from wealthy supporters. Since the mid-1990s, however, interest groups have been permitted to air "issue advocacy" ads that do not explicitly call for the election or defeat of a particular candidate, but that nevertheless serve as campaign ads. The advantage of issue ads is that they can be financed by a handful of generous donors.[38]

Issue advertising by groups occurs during both the nomination and general election contests, such as the ads that attacked McCain's environmental record and praised Bush's. In 2008 the Club for Growth aired a number of ads during the nomination process attacking Huckabee's record on taxes and spending. AFSCME aired television and radio ads in 2008 criticizing Obama's health care plan and praising Clinton as a candidate "ready to lead."[39]

Issue ads produced by interest groups had striking results in the 2004 general election. A newly formed organization called Swift Boat Veterans and POWs for Truth launched a series of ads attacking John Kerry's military record and his later denunciation of the Vietnam War, eventually spending some $22 million. Political scientists have reported that consultants for both parties believe these ads were very effective.[40] That same year, the Media Fund, a

NRA MOBILIZES AGAINST OBAMA

The National Rifle Association (NRA) has played an active role in presidential elections for several decades. Although the group is nonpartisan, it has become a reliable supporter of Republican presidential candidates in recent years. It spent millions campaigning against Democratic nominees Al Gore and John Kerry in 2000 and 2004, respectively. In 2008 the NRA was again aggressive, putting aside $15 million to attack Barack Obama for his support of gun-control measures.[1]

Throughout the final weeks of the campaign, television ads were aired in battleground states such as Florida, Ohio, Pennsylvania, and Virginia.[2] In addition, the group sent direct mail to its nearly 4 million members. It even established a new Web site, www.GunbaNObama.com, aimed at raising money and tracking Obama's statements and positions against gun rights.[3]

The NRA sent a mailer to its members arguing that Obama would be "the most anti-gun president in American history." On its reverse side, it claimed that Obama supported a handgun ban, an ammunition ban, increased registration requirements, and restrictions on one's right to carry a firearm in public. Obama denied several of these claims, but the group argued that he was simply contradicting past statements and votes.

The NRA also distributed yard signs, such as the one below. Its words were inspired by a highly publicized comment Obama made during the Democratic primaries regarding "bitter" voters and their tendency to "cling to guns or religion" when they feel as though their government is not serving them.[4]

Following his selection as Obama's running mate in August 2008, Joe Biden often returned to his birth state, Pennsylvania, and spoke proudly of his middle-class, Scranton roots. Pennsylvania was considered a swing state in the election, and the Obama campaign undoubtedly saw Biden's background as an asset. In response, the NRA ran television ads in Pennsylvania arguing that Biden did not share the values of the state's many gun-owners. Specifically, the group cited his history of votes in favor of firearm restrictions, including an assault weapons ban signed by President Clinton in 1994.[5]

1. Politico, www.politico.com/news/stories/0608/11452.html.
2. *Los Angeles Times*, latimesblogs.latimes.com/washington/2008/10/nra-plans-a-new.html.
3. *Palm Beach Post*, www.palmbeachpost.com/politics/content/shared/news/stories/2008/10/NRA_ELECTION19_PBP.html.
4. NRA Institute for Legislative Action, www.nraila.org/actioncenter/grassrootsactivism.aspx?id=68.
5. *Washington Post*, voices.washingtonpost.com/44/2008/09/23/nra_to_target_obama-biden_in_e.html; NRA Political Victory Fund, www.gunbanobama.com/Default.aspx?NavGuid=430d7335-d158-44f5-aab6-bb7d1226f3fa.

pro-Democratic 527 group, spent more than $57 million on television and radio advertising.

In the 2008 general election, there was less interest group television advertising than in 2004, in part because both McCain and Obama discouraged independent group spending.[41] But ideological groups, unions, and the Chamber of Commerce still spent tens of millions of dollars in television advertising in battleground states in the final weeks of the campaign. In North Carolina, two union-backed groups, Citizens for Strength and Security and Healthcare for America Now, and MoveOn.org and the League of Conservation Workers spent a combined $860,000 on advertising, while Freedom's Watch spent $220,000 on behalf of McCain.[42]

Many groups in 2008 produced ads on the Internet and e-mailed links to their members and to the press, hoping that the ads would be watched and spread virally. MoveOn.org announced a contest for college students to produce ads for Obama. The best were posted on the Internet, and the winning ad was run on television in battleground states. Many students who submitted entries also posted their ads on their Facebook pages or on YouTube. It is difficult to estimate the value of these Internet ads, but one study of all YouTube viewings (including those sponsored by the candidates) reported that in the eighteen months before the general election, Obama benefited from 14,548,810 hours of viewing, compared to just 488,093 for McCain.[43] Groups can also distribute video on DVDs. In 2004 a new organization called Let Freedom Ring produced a video extolling the religious values of George W. Bush and distributed the DVD to churches in battleground states.

Interest groups also try to persuade voters through the mail. In 2000 the NRA created a list of United Mine Workers members who had hunting licenses in West Virginia and mailed a packet that urged them to "vote your jobs, vote your guns." The packet included quotes from Gore's environmental book *Earth in the Balance.* In battleground states, voters frequently received a number of mailings every day from various groups. Considerable research goes into designing persuasion mail and matching messages to the characteristics of people on the list. Some groups mailed packets to their members to distribute to their neighbors. In a few cases, these volunteers carried ads on their iPods or other devices.

CONCLUSION

Nearly every adult U.S. citizen encounters the efforts of an interest group during a presidential election. Seeking attention for their cause(s) and support for candidates, groups air hundreds of television ads, send millions of direct mail pieces and voter guides, and make countless phone calls in pursuit of their goals. They post signs, issue bumper stickers, and host public events with candidates, sometimes years before an election takes place. Given the multimillion dollar effort of groups, even a disinterested observer finds it difficult to avoid their electioneering activities.

Groups, however, participate in notably different ways. Some merely endorse candidates or make financial contributions, while a network of groups and activists supporting each of the parties does much more. Some are very active in the nomination process, while others participate only during the general election. Groups that are very involved in elections generally cooperate with allied groups and study the impact of their efforts both during and after the campaign. They carefully plan how to use technology such as the Internet and often develop creative electoral tools.

Many longtime groups, including the NRA, Sierra Club, AFL-CIO, and the Chamber of Commerce, continue to exist across elections. Other organizations are formed by interest groups to help coordinate their efforts, such as America Votes. Some are primarily conduits for electoral efforts of individuals, such as Republicans for Clean Air. The boundaries between groups and political parties are porous, and many activists have careers that include several stints in both camps.

Groups are regulated by various campaign finance rules. Contribution limits regulate the amount of money a PAC can accept from an individual donor or give to a presidential candidate. But other entities, such as 527 committees, have fewer restrictions and allow wealthy individuals to give unlimited sums of money and have a major influence on election efforts. These relatively unrestrictive laws, combined with an ever-growing number of organized interests, assure that groups will continue to play a central role in presidential elections in years to come.

NOTES

1. George Washington University, "Iowa Caucuses. Democracy in Action—P2008," August 31, 2009, www.gwu.edu/~action/2008/chrniowa08.html.

2. Service Employees International Union, "Candidates Walk a Day in SEIU Members' Shoes," 2008, www.walkadayinmyshoes2008.com/walkadaytour.

3. Mark J. Rozell and Clyde Wilcox, *Interest Groups in American Campaigns: The New Face of Electioneering* (Washington, D.C.: CQ Press, 1999).

4. Michael J. Malbin, Clyde Wilcox, Mark Rozell, and Richard Skinner, "New Interest Group Strategies: A Preview of Post McCain-Feingold Politics?" *Election Law Journal* 1, 4 (2002): 541–555.

5. Gregory Koger, Seth Masket, and Hans Noel, "Partisan Webs: Information Exchange and Party Networks," *British Journal*

of Political Science 39, 3 (2009): 633–653; Richard Skinner, "Do 527s Add Up to a Party? Thinking about the 'Shadows' of Politics," *The Forum* 3, 3 (2005).

6. John C. Green, Mark J. Rozell, and Clyde Wilcox, "Social Movements and Party Politics: The Case of the Christian Right," *Journal for the Scientific Study of Religion* 40, 3 (2001): 413–426; John C. Green, James L. Guth, and Clyde Wilcox, "Less Than Conquerors: The Christian Right in State Republican Parties," in *Social Movements and American Political Institutions*, ed. Anne N. Costain and Andrew S. McFarland (Lanham, Md.: Rowman and Littlefield, 1998); Clyde Wilcox, "Of Movements and Metaphors: The Co-Evolution of the Christian Right and the Republican Party," in *Evangelicals and American Politics*, ed. S. Brint and J. R. Schroedel (New York: Russell Sage Press, 2009).

7. George Washington University, "Interest Group Campaign Ads—2008 Presidential Primaries, Television and Radio Advertising," www.gwu.edu/~action/2008/ads08/tvads08i.html.

8. John C. Green and James L. Guth, "The Christian Right in the Republican Party: The Case of Pat Robertson's Supporters," *Journal of Politics* 50, 1 (1988):150–165; Denise L. Baer and David A. Bositis, *Elite Cadres and Party Coalitions: Representing the Public in Party Politics* (Contributions in Political Science) (Westport, Conn.: Greenwood Press, 1988).

9. "McCain, Thompson, All Dems Fail to Make No-Tax Pledge," Reuters, January 4, 2008.

10. "Chief Says UAW Will Help Elect Dem, Won't Favor Clinton, Obama," Associated Press, February 3, 2008.

11. Stephen R. Weissman and Kara D. Ryan, "Soft Money in the 2006 Election and the Outlook for 2008," in *Campaign Finance Institute Report* (Washington, D.C.: Campaign Finance Institute, 2007); and Weissman and Ryan, "Nonprofit Interest Groups's Election Activities and Federal Campaign Finance Policy," in *Campaign Finance Institute Report* (Washington, D.C.: Campaign Finance Institute, 2006).

12. When a candidate accepts private contributions instead of federal funds for the general election, as Obama did in 2008, PACs can contribute a second time because the nomination process and general election count as two distinct elections.

13. David B. Magleby and Kelly D. Patterson, "War Games: Issues and Resources in the Battle for Control of Congress," in *Center for the Study of Elections and Democracy Report* (Salt Lake City: Center for the Study of Elections and Democracy, 2007).

14. Steve Weissman, "Soft Money Political Spending by 501(c) Nonprofits Tripled in 2008 Election" (Washington, D.C.: Campaign Finance Institute, 2009); Weissman and Ryan, "Nonprofit Interest Groups's Election Activities."

15. Churches can endorse candidates at any time if they are willing to give up the tax-exempt status.

16. George Washington University, "Endorsements by National Organizations in the 2008 Presidential Primaries," 2008, www.gwu.edu/~action/2008/cands08/endorse08org.html.

17. Jake Tapper, "LA NOW Prez on Palin: 'America, This is What a Feminist Looks Like,'" ABC News, October 6, 2008.

18. Rozell and Wilcox, *Interest Groups in American Campaigns.*

19. Marty Cohen, David Karol, Hans Noel, and John Zaller, "The Invisible Primary in Presidential Nominations, 1980–2004," in *The Making of Presidential Candidates 2008*, ed. W. G. Mayer (Lanham, Md.: Rowman and Littlefield, 2008).

20. Jeffrey M. Berry and Clyde Wilcox, *The Interest Group Society* (New York: Pearson Longman, 2007); Paul S. Herrnson, *Congressional Elections: Campaigning at Home and in Washington* (Washington, D.C.: CQ Press, 1995).

21. Candice J. Nelson, "Women's PACs in the Year of the Woman," in *The Year of the Woman: Myths and Realities*, ed. E. A. Cook, S. Thomas, and C. Wilcox (Boulder: Westview, 1994).

22. Stephen J. Wayne, "Presidential Elections: Traveling the Hard and Soft Money Roads to the White House," in *The Interest Group Connection: Electioneering, Lobbying and Policymaking in Washington*, ed. Paul S. Herrnson, Ronald G. Shaiko, and Clyde Wilcox (Washington, D.C.: CQ Press, 2005).

23. Center for Responsive Politics, "Banking on Becoming President," 2009, www.opensecrets.org/pres08/index.php.

24. Clifford W. Brown, Lynda W. Powell, and Clyde Wilcox, *Serious Money: Fundraising and Contributing in Presidential Nomination Campaigns* (New York: Cambridge University Press, 1995).

25. Center for Responsive Politics, "Banking on Becoming President."

26. National Journal, www.nationaljournal.com/magazine/can-emily-s-list-get-its-mojo-back—20080628.

27. Clyde Wilcox, "Follow the Money: Campaign Finance and Reform," in *Understanding the Presidency*, 3rd ed., ed. J. Pfiffner and R. H. Davidson (New York: Longman, 2003).

28. David B. Magleby, J. Quin Monson, and Kelly D. Patterson, "Introduction," in *Dancing Without Partners: How Candidates, Parties, and Interest Groups Interact in the Presidential Campaign*, ed. Magleby, Monson, and Patterson (Lanham, Md.: Rowman and Littlefield, 2007).

29. Donald P. Green, "Mobilizing African-American Voters Using Direct Mail and Commercial Phone Banks: A Field Experiment," *Political Research Quarterly* 57, 2 (2004): 245–255.

30. Ramona Oliver, "EMILY's List to Democratic Women of Iowa—You Go Girl!" EMILY's List, November 26, 2007, www.emilyslist.org/news/releases/iowa_women_vote.

31. Magleby, Monson, and Patterson, "Introduction."

32. Clyde Wilcox and Carin Robinson, *Onward Christian Soldiers: The Christian Right in American Politics*, 3rd ed. (Boulder: Westview, 2006).

33. J. Quin Monson and J. Baxter Oliphant, "Microtargeting and the Instrumental Mobilization of Religious Conservatives," in *A Matter of Faith: Religion in the 2004 Presidential Election*, ed. D. E. Campbell (Washington, D.C.: Brookings, 2007).

34. Magleby, Monson, and Patterson, "Introduction."

35. Weissman, "Soft Money Political Spending."

36. Nancy Scola, "Shame Works, But Funny Gets Forwarded: MoveOn's 'Non-Voter' Ad Might Be Most Viral Political Video Ever," Personal Democracy Forum, November 7, 2008, techpresident.com/node/6496.

37. Researchers have come to mixed conclusions as to whether negative advertisements do decrease turnout, but some interest group leaders admit that some of their ads have this purpose.

38. Michael J. Malbin, Clyde Wilcox, Mark Rozell, and Richard Skinner, "New Interest Group Strategies: A Preview of Post McCain-Feingold Politics?" *Election Law Journal* 1, 4 (2002): 541–555.

39. George Washington University, "Interest Group Campaign Ads."

40. Magleby, Monson, and Patterson, "Introduction."

41. David C. Kimball, "Interest Groups and the 2008 Presidential Election: The Barking Dog that Didn't Bite," *The Forum* 6, 4 (2008).

42. Eric S. Heberlig, Peter Francia, and Steven H. Greene, "The Conditional Party Teams of the 2008 North Carolina Federal Elections," in *The Change Election: Money, Mobilization, and Persuasion in the 2008 Federal Elections*, ed. David B. Magleby (Salt Lake City: Center for the Study of Elections and Democracy, Brigham Young University, 2009).

43. Diana Owen, "The Campaign and the Media," in *The American Elections of 2008*, ed. Janet M. Box-Steffensmeier and Steven E. Schier (Lanham, Md.: Rowman and Littlefield, 2009), 9–31.

SUGGESTED READING

Berry, Jeffrey M., and Clyde Wilcox. *The Interest Group Society*. New York: Pearson Longman. 2007.

Burbank, Matthew J., Ronald J. Hrebenar, and Robert C. Benedict. *Parties, Interest Groups, and Political Campaigns.* Boulder: Paradigm Publishers, 2008.

Cohen, Marty, David Karol, Hans Noel, and John Zaller. *The Party Decides: Presidential Nominations Before and After Reform.* Chicago: University of Chicago Press, 2008.

Franz, Michael M. *Choices and Changes: Interest Groups in the Electoral Process.* Philadelphia: Temple University Press, 2008.

Magleby, David B., ed. *The Change Election: Money, Mobilization, and Persuasion in the 2008 Federal Elections.* Salt Lake City: Center for the Study of Elections and Democracy, Brigham Young University, 2009.

Magleby, David B., J. Quin Monson, and Kelly D. Patterson, eds. *Dancing Without Partners: How Candidates, Parties, and Interest Groups Interact in the Presidential Campaign.* Lanham, Md.: Rowman and Littlefield, 2007.

Malbin, Michael J., Clyde Wilcox, Mark Rozell, and Richard Skinner. "New Interest Group Strategies: A Preview of Post–McCain-Feingold Politics?" *Election Law Journal* 1, 4 (2002): 541–555.

Rozell, Mark J., and Clyde Wilcox. *Interest Groups in American Campaigns: The New Face of Electioneering.* Washington, D.C.: CQ Press, 1999.

Wayne, Stephen J. "Presidential Elections: Traveling the Hard and Soft Money Roads to the White House." In *The Interest Group Connection: Electioneering, Lobbying and Policymaking in Washington.* Ed. P. S. Herrnson, R. G. Shaiko, and C. Wilcox. Washington, D.C.: CQ Press, 2005.

Wilcox, Clyde. "Follow the Money: Campaign Finance and Reform." In *Understanding the Presidency,* 3rd ed. Ed. J. Pfiffner and R. H. Davidson. New York: Longman, 2003.

chapter 33

Regulating and Reforming Group-Based Electioneering

by Robert G. Boatright

In October 2008 Pennsylvania television viewers were exposed to a wide variety of advertisements discussing presidential candidates Barack Obama and John McCain. Among the ads running at the time was one that asked, "Senator Obama, you tell us you're ready to lead America? Why didn't you choose to lead Illinois? Why, senator, were you so consistently afraid to take a stand?"[1] During the spring of 2008 another political ad ran in Pennsylvania. This one showed former vice president Al Gore's home and announced, "Al Gore wants to cut our energy use, putting our jobs and our future in jeopardy. . . . Without affordable energy, hundreds of millions of people won't have any future at all."[2]

Both of these advertisements were sponsored by interest groups, both made reference to politicians, and both discussed issues relevant to the 2008 presidential campaign. Yet most observers would contend that the first ad aims to discourage voters from supporting the Democratic presidential candidate, while the second is primarily a means of discussing an issue, not of influencing vote choice. The first ad is known as an "electioneering" advertisement, but the second is not. But what distinguishes these two ads? Neither, after all, recommends that voters choose a particular candidate, and both clearly do have some issue content. Where does one draw the line? Must ads mention a candidate for office to count as electioneering? Must they run at a particular time? Herein lies the dilemma for those who would restrict interest groups' election-related communications with the public while still protecting the rights of groups or citizens to discuss issues of concern.

Interest groups use several tools to influence elections. Most prominent among these tools are contributing money to candidates, mobilizing voters, and trying to influence voters' opinions. Despite the explosion in the number of choices Americans have concerning what to watch and listen to, advertising on television and radio remains one of the best ways to persuade voters. Citizens who reside in competitive congressional districts, in states with competitive Senate races, or in states whose electoral votes are up for grabs can expect to see campaign advertisements from a wide array of sources—from the candidates, from the party campaign committees, and from outside groups. One study found that the average citizen of Missouri saw more than twelve campaign ads every day during the state's 2002 Senate election.[3] Although few interest groups have the means and the motivation to engage in electioneering, those that do spend lots of money. In some races, interest groups spend more than candidates or parties.

This chapter first considers the legal context of electioneering advertisements—what groups are permitted to do in their communications with the public, how groups' legal options changed with the passage of the Bipartisan Campaign Reform Act (BCRA) of 2002, and how these options changed again following the Supreme Court's 2010 *Citizens United v. FEC* decision. It then covers the rise of electioneering as a political strategy during the 1980s and 1990s and how BCRA influenced interest group activities in the elections of the 2000s. Following this history, it analyzes the goals they have in their electioneering communications and how these goals have changed in recent election cycles. The chapter closes with a discussion of the future of electioneering and the normative consequences of electioneering regulation.

THE LEGAL CONTEXT OF REGULATION

From 1976 through 2002 nonparty organizations were required, in accordance with the Federal Election Campaign Act (FECA), to disclose their identity in their political advertisements, but there were essentially no limits on what groups could spend. Federal campaign finance law did, however, make two important distinctions in its consideration of interest group advocacy. First, does the content of the group's message directly advocate a vote for or against a particular candidate? Second, are the group's expenditures on the advocacy message coordinated in any way with the expenditures of a candidate or party?

AN ELECTIONEERING ADVERTISEMENT BEFORE THE BIPARTISAN CAMPAIGN REFORM ACT (BCRA)

"PIONEERS"

Announcer: They came to South Dakota to make a life on the land, and left that land to us to use and to protect. But today South Dakota's environment faces new threats—especially to our water.

And John Thune isn't helping.

Voting twice to allow more arsenic in drinking water.

(On screen: Arsenic in drinking water. H.R. 4635, #304, 6/21/00; H.R. 2620, #288, 7/27/01)

And opposing efforts to clean up South Dakota's 161 polluted lakes and rivers.

(On screen: Source: Environmental Protection Agency: H.J. Res. 105, 7/18/00)

It makes you wonder, when it comes to clean water, who is John Thune really representing?

(On screen: Paid for by League of Conservation Voters Action Fund. Not authorized by any candidate or candidate's committee.)

SOURCE: CNN Transcripts, http://transcripts.cnn.com/TRANSCRIPTS/0207/03/ip.00.html.

HILLARY CLINTON'S 2008 "3 AM" AD: CANDIDATE ADVERTISING WITHOUT "MAGIC WORDS"

"CHILDREN"

Announcer [voiceover]: It's 3 a.m., and your children are safe and asleep.

But there's a phone in the White House, and it's ringing. Something's happening in the world.

Your vote will decide who answers that call—whether it's someone who already knows the world's leaders, knows the military, someone tested and ready to lead in a dangerous world.

It' 3 a.m., and your children are safe and asleep. Who do you want answering the phone?

Hillary Clinton [voiceover]: I'm Hillary Clinton, and I approve this message.

(Text on screen: www.HillaryClinton.com; Vote March 4th; Attend your Precinct Convention at 6:45 PM on March 4th; Paid For By Hillary Clinton For President)

SOURCE: Ariel Alexovich, "Clinton's New National Security Ad," *New York Times*, February 29, 2008.

As to the first distinction, the Supreme Court has held since its 1976 *Buckley v. Valeo* decision that certain words clearly constitute express advocacy for a candidate: these words include *vote for, vote against, elect, defeat, support,* and *reject.*[4] The Court's definition, however, excludes speech that leaves little doubt about the speaker's preferences, but does not use such words. It leaves open the possibility of running a message such as the one shown in the box above, sponsored by the League of Conservation Voters (LCV) in 2002. Few people would construe this ad as anything other than an encouragement to vote against John Thune, but the ad does not explicitly *tell* voters to vote for or against anyone. This message, then, is one of issue advocacy, not express advocacy. It has been noted by many researchers that few citizens make distinctions between issue advocacy messages such as the LCV ad and express advocacy messages. In addition, many candidate advertisements do not meet the Court's express advocacy standard; Hillary Clinton's well-known "3 A.M." advertisement from the 2008 Democratic primaries included a voiceover and on-screen text at the end stating that the ad was paid for by the Clinton campaign, but the narration of the ad did not use express advocacy language or even mention the candidates by name.

Second, interest groups cannot coordinate their advocacy campaigns with political parties or candidates unless the communication is paid for with political action committee (PAC) money and disclosed to the Federal Election Commission (FEC) as an in-kind contribution, subject to the $5,000 PAC contribution limit. This low limit prohibits virtually all advertisements from being plausible in-kind contributions. The coordination restrictions do not, however, prevent groups from engaging in express advocacy for a candidate; they merely require that such advocacy be conducted without discussions between the candidate and the group. Express advocacy, then, has generally been disclosed by groups as an independent expenditure, paid for with PAC funds but not subject to any limits.

Most interest group leaders insist that they scrupulously adhere to the restrictions on coordination. In practice, however, the restrictions on coordination do not present an insuperable barrier for groups and candidates seeking to understand each other's strategies. Groups may simply observe a candidate's message and play into it without communicating about it with the candidate (for example, they may adopt language talking about "the need for a change"). Targeting strategy follows a similar logic.

Issue advocacy thus represented an opportunity for corporations, labor unions, and other groups to engage in speech that was virtually synonymous with campaign activity, but to do so using money that could not be contributed

TABLE 33.1 **Permissible Political Activities of PACs and Nonprofit Organizations**

	PACs	527 groups	Nonprofit 501(c)(4), (5), and (6) groups	501(c)(3) charities
Tax status	Contributions are tax exempt but not tax deductible	Contributions are tax exempt but not tax deductible	Contributions are tax exempt but not tax deductible	Contributions are tax deductible
Contribution limits	PACs, parties, and individuals limited to $5,000 per year. Corporate and union contributions prohibited.	None	None	None
Campaign activities:				
Express advocacy	Unlimited	Prohibited by BCRA, now permissible	Prohibited by BCRA, now permissible	Prohibited
Electioneering communications (broadcasts within 60 days of general election or 30 days of primary election)	Unlimited	Prohibited by BCRA, now permissible as long as it is not the "primary purpose" of the organization	Prohibited by BCRA, now permissible as long as it is not the "primary purpose" of the organization	Prohibited
Other electioneering activity		Permitted as long as it is not the "primary purpose" of the organization	Permitted as long as it is not the "primary purpose" of the organization	Prohibited, except for nonpartisan voter registration and education

SOURCE: Adapted from Public Citizen's Congress Watch, www.citizen.org/documents/PermissibleActivitiesofPACsChart.pdf.

to candidates. For corporations and labor unions, this meant that treasury funds could be used for political purposes. For nonprofit 501(c)(4) groups, money raised from member contributions could also be used for this purpose, as long as political activity was not the group's "principal purpose," as defined by IRS regulations. Table 33.1 shows the regulations campaign finance law places on different types of groups according to their legal status as defined by the FEC and the IRS.

THE BIPARTISAN CAMPAIGN REFORM ACT

The Bipartisan Campaign Reform Act, which took effect the day after the 2002 election, was in part an effort by Congress to regulate electioneering. The BCRA defined an electioneering communication as a broadcast, cable, or satellite communication (radio or television) that is aired within thirty days of a primary election or sixty days of a general election, refers to a candidate for federal office, and is targeted at that candidate's electorate. Corporations and labor unions were prohibited by BCRA from using treasury funds for such communications, but they were permitted to use PAC funds to do so. The groups known as 501(c)(4) organizations—meaning that they are nonprofit and not entirely political in nature, but engage in some political activity—are defined as corporations according to the law unless they can certify that they receive no contributions from corporate or labor sources.[5] BCRA also increased the civil and criminal penalties established by FECA for willful violation of the law regarding permissible electioneering.[6] Because express advocacy can be done only with hard money, the electioneering restrictions penalized groups without ample hard money resources by forcing them to abandon their advertising or change the content of their advertising at an earlier time than they would have previously.

A coalition of labor, corporate, and advocacy groups challenged BCRA, and all of the major components of it were upheld by the Supreme Court in its December 2003 *McConnell v. FEC* decision. Since that time, three other features of campaign finance law have loomed large in determining interest groups' responses to the BCRA prohibitions. First, the Court's 1986 decision in *FEC v. Massachusetts Citizens for Life* (MCFL) held that if 501(c)(4) organizations could demonstrate that they received contributions solely from individuals, they were not required to use PAC funds for express advocacy. With the passage of BCRA, groups with an MCFL exemption now fell outside of the scope of the electioneering restrictions and could continue to engage in electioneering communications. In practice, very few 501(c)(4) groups can claim this exemption, but some of the larger and more active issue advocacy groups of the 1990s, such as Planned Parenthood and the League of Conservation Voters, do have this exemption.

Sen. Russ Feingold, D-Wisc., left, and Sen. John McCain, R-Ariz., were instrumental in the passage of the Bipartisan Campaign Reform Act of 2002, commonly known as McCain-Feingold. The legislation set new regulations on campaign donations. Under the act, corporations, unions, and individuals could no longer give unregulated contributions to national political parties.

Second, groups that file under section 527 of the tax code are not mentioned in the law. This omission sparked a temporary growth in 527 groups in the 2004 election as a means of gathering individual contributions for the purpose of airing electioneering advertisements. Subsequent to the 2004 election, however, the FEC heavily penalized several such groups on the grounds that their activities amounted to illegal coordination with the parties.[7] Third, the Court's decision in *Citizens United v. FEC* (2010) struck down BCRA's electioneering restrictions in their entirety and reversed *Austin v. Michigan Chamber of Commerce* (1990), which had prohibited corporations from using treasury funds for direct advocacy. The consequence of the Court's decision is that groups can not only resume the sorts of advertisements they engaged in prior to BCRA, but also they may purchase unlimited amounts of advertising that can encourage voters to vote for or against a candidate.

A BRIEF HISTORY OF ELECTIONEERING

Most studies of electioneering point to the 1994 and 1996 elections as the first instances where group advertising about candidates was widespread. Trevor Potter and Kirk Jowers note that the Supreme Court had ruled in favor of permitting some types of candidate-specific newspaper advertising about candidates as far back as 1980.[8] They argue, however, that television and radio electioneering became widespread only after the successful "Harry and Louise" ads, which featured a married couple expressing unhappiness with President Bill Clinton's health care proposal.[9] Although these advertisements, sponsored by the Health Insurance Association of America, were run far enough in advance of the 1994 election that they clearly were issue ads, their success inspired many groups to create advertisements for the 1996 election. According to one analysis, as much as $150 million was spent on issue advocacy in 1996 by thirty-one different groups. This total included $35 million spent by the AFL-CIO and $17 million spent by the Coalition: Americans Working for Real Change, a group that included several peak business organizations.[10]

A diverse array of groups began advertising in 1996. Many newly formed advocacy groups, such as U.S. Term Limits, made issue advocacy a part of their mission from their inception and developed few other means of communicating with voters. Longer-lived organizations such as the Sierra Club, the National Rifle Association, and the LCV had a history of PAC contributions and advocacy work in various media, but rapidly expanded the budgets of their 501(c)(4) wings in order to advertise.[11] And the back-and-forth advertising between the AFL-CIO and the Coalition demonstrated the speed with which labor unions and business associations could marshal the resources necessary for issue advocacy. The AFL-CIO advertisements were particularly controversial because they aired primarily in the districts of first-term Republican incumbents and because they touched upon issues, such as education, that were not necessarily priority issues for organized labor. Political scientist Gary Jacobson concluded that incumbents who were the targets of AFL-CIO ads received an average of 4 percent fewer votes than similar incumbents who were not targeted.[12] The problem for the AFL-CIO's attempt to "take back Congress," however, was that it set off an arms race of electioneering ads, and the groups that fought back, such as the Coalition, had the ability to see what and where the AFL-CIO had advertised and air contrary messages in the same markets.

As Table 33.2 shows the number of electioneering advertisements had increased by 2000. In that year, eighteen different groups aired more than 150 candidate-specific advertisements in the seven largest media markets; 82 percent of all advertisements were run within sixty days of the general election.[13] Included among the groups running ads were Planned Parenthood, which had not been a major campaign advertiser previously but had

TABLE 33.2 **Candidate-Specific Broadcast Television Advertisements Purchased by Nonparty Organizations, 2000–2004**

2000			2002			2004		
Organization	**Top 75 markets**	**Top 75 within 60 days**	**Organization**	**Top 75 markets**	**Top 75 within 60 days**	**Organization**	**Top 75 markets**	**Top 75 within 60 days**
LABOR			LABOR			LABOR		
AFL-CIO	17,050	9,779	AFL-CIO	4,244	2,945	AFL-CIO	5,642	0
NEA	511	511	NEA	194	194	NEA	3,783	63
American Family Voices	447	0	Others	405	397	UAW	1,754	1,754
Others	59	0				SEIU	1,206	979
						Others	1,263	580
Subtotal	**18,067**	**10,290**	**Subtotal**	**4,843**	**3,536**	**Subtotal**	**13,648**	**3,629**
LIBERAL			LIBERAL			LIBERAL		
Planned Parenthood	5,916	5,916	Sierra Club	1,611	1,078	Media Fund	40,430	5,000
Emily's List	3,514	3,445	Emily's List	896	0	MoveOn	24,257	3,944
Handgun Control	2,867	2,443	LCV	830	830	New Democratic Network	5,755	5,546
Sierra Club	2,245	1,715	Reform Voter Project	665	419	Citizens For a Strong Senate	3,830	3,830
LCV	1,705	1,705	NARAL	386	386	LCV	3,182	2,861
Campaign for a Progr. Future	1,262	979				Emily's List	2,399	851
Others	1,160	566	Others	478	478	Others	2,959	2,836
Subtotal	**18,669**	**16,769**	**Subtotal**	**4,866**	**3,191**	**Subtotal**	**82,812**	**24,868**
BUSINESS			BUSINESS			BUSINESS		
Citizens for Better Medicare	10,876	10,753	United Seniors Association	10,915	9,055	Americans for Job Security	2,290	133
Americans for Job Security	6,069	5,007	Americans for Job Security	1,615	1,615	United Seniors Association	1,470	6
US Chamber of Commerce	7,574	7,574	American Medical Association	915	725	National Asoc, of Realtors	922	922
Business Roundtable	4,884	4,571	National Assoc. of Realtors	200	200	American Medical Assoc.	442	442
Others	1,434	1,040	Others	400	131	Others	297	191
Subtotal	**30,837**	**28,945**	**Subtotal**	**14,045**	**11,726**	**Subtotal**	**5,421**	**1,694**
CONSERVATIVE			CONSERVATIVE			CONSERVATIVE		
US Term Limits	978	37	Club for Growth	1,574	817	Progress for America	8,960	7,433
Americans for Limited Terms	535	195				Swift Boat Veterans	5,077	4,078
NRA	395	358				Club for Growth	4,760	1,602
						Others	2,102	1,621
Subtotal	**1,947**	**629**	**Subtotal**	**1,574**	**817**	**Subtotal**	**20,899**	**14,834**
TOTAL 2000	**68,470**	**56,633**	**TOTAL 2002**	**25,328**	**19,270**	**TOTAL 2004**	**122,782**	**45,025**

SOURCE: Derived from data supplied by the Wisconsin Advertising Project; adapted from Robert G. Boatright, Michael J. Malbin, Mark J. Rozell, and Clyde Wilcox, "Interest Groups and Advocacy Organizations after BCRA," in *The Election after Reform: Money, Politics, and the Bipartisan Campaign Reform Act*, ed. Michael J. Malbin (Lanham, Md.: Rowman and Littlefield, 2006), 112–140.

received a large donation from the Turner Foundation, and the NAACP, which likewise received a large, one-time donation, that came from an anonymous source.[14] The NAACP advertisements received particular attention because they coincided with a get-out-the-vote campaign established by a separate 501(c)(4) organization, the NAACP National Voter Fund, and because of the content of the ads themselves. One NAACP ad discussed George W. Bush's failure to enact hate crimes legislation while he was governor of Texas, accompanied by a graphic description of the murder of James Byrd Jr.[15] Such hard-hitting ads, while likely to leave an impression on viewers, raised concerns that issue advocacy messages might overshadow candidate discourse.

The 2002 campaign season represented a "last hurrah" for groups seeking to use unrestricted contributions for advocacy purposes during the campaign, and spending was far higher than in the previous midterm election of 1998. Many of the groups active in 2000 were far less visible in the 2002 campaign, in part because midterm elections attract less money, in part because of the one-time nature of the contributions that fueled some of the advocacy campaigns in 2000, and in part because many larger groups, such as the AFL-CIO, had begun to conclude that issue advocacy was not as effective a use of group resources as targeted communications. The departure of some of these groups from the playing field, however, meant that organizations that continued to advertise could do so in an environment with less clutter. By far the biggest advertiser in 2002 was the United Seniors Association, which, like Citizens for Better Medicare in 2000, purported to be a grassroots organization but was funded by the major pharmaceutical companies. United Seniors advertised heavily in a small number of House districts during the final two weeks of the 2002 campaign, including in the only two districts where Democratic incumbents were defeated.

Although BCRA's electioneering regulations were expected to reduce the number of interest group advertisements in 2004, the number of such ads actually increased from 2000 to 2004. The nature of the groups running the advertisements changed, however. Ongoing advocacy groups were largely absent from the airwaves during the final two months of the election, with the exception of groups that had MCFL exemptions or groups that were able to spend PAC money on their ads. The absence of ongoing organizations was more than made up for by the rise of 527 organizations such as the Media Fund, New Democratic Network, Swift Boat Veterans for Truth, and Progress for America. Although these groups disclosed their identities at the close of their advertisements, their names likely meant little to the average viewer. The partisan or ideological leanings of organizations such as Planned Parenthood or the Sierra Club would be readily identified by most viewers, and such groups also have long-term interests to protect. A vague, potentially misleading name such as those adopted by 527s or corporate front groups provides little information to viewers about the agenda behind the advertisements or the characteristics of group members.

Although Congress did not act to close the 527 "loophole" after the 2004 election, the number of issue advocacy advertisements declined in 2006 and 2008. In 2006 the major 527 organizations were connected to large, ongoing groups and were somewhat chastened by FEC rulings that punished some of the major 527 groups active in 2004.[16] In 2008 the volume of spending by the candidates and the party campaign committees was high enough that many interest groups turned their attention elsewhere. Michael Franz estimates that total issue advocacy spending in 2006 was $21.9 million, down substantially from the $134 million spent in 2004, and down slightly from the $25 million spent in 2002, the last pre-BCRA election.[17] Although figures for 2008 are hard to come by, most analysts agree that spending

Following enactment of regulations under the Bipartisan Campaign Reform Act of 2002, the nature of organizations running campaign advertisements changed. The 527 group Swift Boat Veterans for Truth ran the now-famous advertisement criticizing presidential candidate John Kerry's military service in Vietnam.

A SAMPLE POST-BCRA AD, WITHOUT REFERENCE TO CANDIDATES

"ANYTHING'S POSSIBLE"

Man #1: Things are about to get a lot better in this country.

(Text on screen: Paid For By American Family Voices Voters' Alliance; www.afvvotersalliance.org)

Man #2: It's been a tough couple of years. But just remember who we are.

Woman #1: We're the country that walked on the moon, that invented the light bulb, the airplane, the Internet.

Woman #2: Don't tell me that we can't change our course in Iraq. . . .

Man #2: . . . find an alternative to oil. . . .

Woman #1: . . . . .and demand leaders who give us hope instead of selling us fear.

Woman #2: We're Americans.

Woman #1: Our parents changed the world.

Man #2: We changed the world.

Woman #2: We can do anything.

Man #1: Together.

Man #2: Together.

Woman #1: We can do anything. Together.

(Text on screen: A New Direction; A New Beginning; New Leadership In Washington)

SOURCE: National Journal Ad Spotlight, www.nationaljournal.com/members/adspotlight/2006/11/1106afvva1.htm.

in 2008 was also far lower than in 2004.[18] A number of smaller, state-focused 527 groups advertised in both elections, and groups with substantial hard money reserves available, such as the Club for Growth and some labor unions (although not the AFL-CIO), continued to advertise and run independent expenditure campaigns.

Effective electioneering campaigns in the 2006 and 2008 elections had three characteristics. First, they were narrowly targeted. The Club for Growth, which often uses hard money to run independent expenditure campaigns in House and Senate primaries, maximized the effectiveness of its ads by selecting races in inexpensive media markets where it is the only active outside group. Second, many groups spent money on advertising immediately outside the sixty-day window, as a means of introducing issues into the campaign, and directed viewers to their Web sites in subsequent ads for candidate-specific information. And third, in some circumstances groups can make their preferences known without using the names of the candidates. In 2006 American Family Voices, a 527 organization funded by AFSCME (American Federation of State, County and Municipal Employees) ran ads that did not mention candidates but played up Democratic criticisms of the Bush administration and called for "change." One such ad is shown in the box above. Ads such as this one do not necessarily count as "electioneering," and they likely would not work in all elections, but they can be effective in circumstances where the viewer already knows what the group is talking about. By the 2010 election, the *Citizens United* decision had rendered these sorts of strategic calculations unnecessary, resulting in an increase in group advertising during the final weeks of the campaign and an increase in the number of ads that urge viewers to vote for or against particular candidates.

WHO BUYS ELECTIONEERING ADS?

Research on the effectiveness of television advertising has shown that issue advertisements are less consequential for shaping elections than are the more targeted means of communication. Face-to-face communications have been shown to be far more effective than advertising.[19] As a result, groups that have memberships large enough and concentrated enough in swing states or districts may prefer to talk to their members rather than purchase advertisements. In addition, groups that value access to legislators of both parties are more likely to pursue their goals through lobbying or other less confrontational techniques than through electoral activity. In short, electioneering may change voters' minds, but it is unlikely to change legislators' minds.

The groups that have spent heavily on electioneering have tended to be groups with substantial financial resources, but not necessarily with large memberships, and they tend to be groups with overtly partisan or ideological goals. Many groups on the list of major pre-BCRA advertisers, such as Sierra Club, Planned Parenthood, and Handgun Control, fit both of these criteria. These are organizations that rarely, if ever, support Republican candidates, and they are groups whose issues of concern—the environment, reproductive rights, or gun control—hold appeal for a large number of nonmembers. The Sierra Club has a relatively large membership for an advocacy group (1.3 million members), but this is a small percentage of the citizens who would be receptive to environmental appeals, and the group's membership is dispersed enough that personal appeals only to members would be unlikely to matter in elections.

The AFL-CIO does not fit the first of these criteria, as its membership is substantial (approximately 11 million members) and represents a large enough proportion of the electorate in some regions of the country to make a difference without bringing in non-union voters. Therefore, although unions did spend heavily on electioneering in the 1990s, some union political directors concluded that such spending was not the most effective use of group resources. AFL-CIO advertising declined substantially following 1996, as the group concentrated more of its resources on member communications.[20] Union spending on electioneering is partly a reflection of the amount of money many of the larger unions commit to elections (they have the ability to pursue a variety of different strategies) and partly a reflection of efforts in parts of the country where unions are not as influential. To take two examples, the United Auto Workers (UAW) has been credited with turning out votes crucial to the Senate victory of Michigan Democrat Debbie Stabenow in 2000, but advertising was not as crucial to this effort as was the UAW's get-out-the-vote campaign among members. In contrast, the AFL-CIO advertised heavily in North Carolina congressional districts in 1996, 1998, and beyond; North Carolina and South Carolina have some of the lowest percentages of union members in the nation, so in these states advertising is a more sensible strategy than in Michigan.

Many corporations do have substantial resources but are not necessarily highly partisan in their goals. Individual businesses are often reluctant to antagonize even politicians with whom they frequently disagree. Business organizations can insulate their members from criticism somewhat: they can engage in electioneering to support probusiness candidates without linking particular companies to these campaigns in the eyes of voters or politicians. The Sierra Club has little to lose from being linked by voters to Democratic candidates, but Wal-Mart may suffer from being linked by its potential customers to any sort of political ideology. The Chamber of Commerce or the Business Roundtable can play a role in elections that their member companies are reluctant to play. This is even more evident in the case of "shadow" groups such as Citizens for Better Medicare, United Seniors Association, or Americans for Job Security. The vague names of these groups belie their funding sources and give a patina of grassroots support to advertisements funded by businesses.

The turn to 527 groups by many large donors in 2004 and the prohibition on corporate and labor funding created a new class of groups that were not true interest groups at all—organizations such as the Media Fund or Progress for America are more accurately described as a temporary pooling of money by wealthy individuals rather than as groups with an ongoing agenda. Among more established groups, BCRA made it difficult for small-membership, large-treasury groups to advertise because groups were required to rely on hard money to advertise during elections. Groups that continued to advertise, such as the Club for Growth or EMILY's List, were organizations that have a large number of members capable of giving $5,000, as opposed to having a handful of members willing to make contributions of $1 million or more. A wealthy benefactor is more likely to turn to 527 groups than to advocacy groups if he or she wishes to fund an advertising campaign. Again, groups with MCFL exemptions, such as the League of Conservation Voters, were able to continue to advertise as before.

WHY PURCHASE ELECTIONEERING ADS?

Many of the critics of electioneering have assumed that the primary goal of such ads is to influence election outcomes. Leaders of many interest groups have responded that their goal is to raise issues, and they have further argued that they can most effectively raise these issues in the context of an election, where citizens are primed by candidates and political parties to think about major political issues.[21] Both arguments have some merit; in reality, however, electioneering ads have a variety of purposes that are not necessarily limited to these two perspectives.

The most instructive means of looking at group goals is to begin with ads that do have a strong issue content. The Sierra Club has traditionally begun its election-year advertising as early as April. It is unlikely that a television viewer in April would remember an ad when he or she votes in November, but the intent of such early ads, according to the group, is to introduce issues into the campaign. By April it is clear in most instances which races will be competitive and who the contestants will be, so ads that mention an incumbent's record on the environment can compel the candidates to discuss the environment or lead voters to pay particular attention to such issues. Early issue ads can also influence the scrutiny voters—and perhaps candidates—give to congressional votes during the spring and summer. In 2008 groups concerned with health care, defense policy, and reproductive rights advertised early as well.

Groups can also advertise in order to call attention to themselves. The Club for Growth aired an advertisement in South Dakota featuring bobble-head dolls of Sens. Tom Daschle, Edward Kennedy, and Hillary Clinton during the spring of 2002.[22] The intent of this ad was to link Daschle, who would not face reelection until 2004, to two well-known liberals, but the humorous nature of the advertisement was a means of signaling to group members that the Club for Growth would be active in seeking to defeat Daschle and to garner media attention. In the long run, an ad such as this might attract new members to the group. Similarly, in 2008 Defenders of Wildlife, a relatively small environmental group that had not engaged in electioneering before, ran an ad through its 501(c)(4) arm, the Defenders Action Fund, discussing Republican vice presidential nominee Sarah

Palin's support for aerial hunting of wolves in Alaska, replete with footage of a wolf bleeding to death after being shot. The group only spent $100,000 on the ad, and the ad ran in only three small media markets, albeit in competitive states.[23] The goal of the advertisement was not so much to influence the election, but to garner media attention for the issue and for the group itself. The ad may not have made a difference in the 2008 election, but it may well have heightened the group's profile and helped fund its issue campaigns in 2009.

Finally, a small number of groups run what they call "soup to nuts" campaigns, in which issue advertisements are one component of a comprehensive election plan. The Club for Growth, MoveOn.org, and the League of Conservation Voters are three groups that have selected House races early in the election cycle and used early advertising to promote nonincumbent candidates as a means of raising their visibility and helping them raise money. Although such advertisements are not explicitly coordinated with the candidates, they can provide candidates with a crucial early advantage. In 2006 the Club for Growth ran ads in Iowa's first congressional district supporting Republican candidate Mike Whalen; the Club also "bundled" contributions for Whalen (that is, collected contributions to Whalen from individual members and forwarded them to the campaign) and engaged in other independent expenditures. The early ads may well have helped Whalen break out of a crowded Republican primary field. The Club did the same in several other multicandidate primaries in 2006 and 2008. MoveOn .org coupled issue advertisements with Internet-based appeals backing primary challenger Donna Edwards in suburban Maryland Democrat Albert Wynn's House district in 2008, and the LCV ran ads touting Republican candidate Joe Schwarz in Michigan in 2004. In all of these districts, electioneering ads may well have been influential because the groups had little competition, because the ads were combined with other types of group appeals, and, with the exception of the Edwards' ads, ran in relatively inexpensive media markets.

The electioneering advertisements that have most clearly raised the ire of reformers, however, have been those run late in the general election and focus more on the candidates than on issues. Clearly, ads such as the anti-Obama ad discussed at the beginning of this chapter provide limited information to voters, but there is no easy way to draw the line between valid issue content and attempts to influence an election. Groups advertising late in the campaign have the luxury of understanding which races are still up in the air—either by virtue of their own research or from observing the spending priorities of the party campaign committees. There have been instances when candidates or parties were "blindsided" by large-scale electioneering campaigns, but in many instances the sheer volume of advertising by the candidates and the parties makes it difficult to measure the effectiveness of late interest group ads. It is this sort of late advertising that may increase following the *Citizens United* decision; however, groups that truly seek to influence election results can wait until they are certain where they can get the best return for their advertising expenditures.

Groups that are contemplating purchasing electioneering ads must consider how to use their resources most effectively to achieve their political goals. For many groups, electioneering makes little sense. For groups with adequate resources, few other means of influencing elections, and an interest in influencing elections rather than gaining access to politicians, electioneering is a viable political strategy. BCRA changed the type of resources that could be devoted to electioneering, which in turn changed the types of groups that air ads. With the removal of BCRA's electioneering restrictions, more groups now have the ability to advertise, but it is still doubtful that it will be to the advantage of very many groups to do so.

NORMATIVE CRITERIA FOR THINKING ABOUT ELECTIONEERING

The issues raised regarding the sponsors and goals of issue ads are important considerations for understanding the values at stake in the debate about regulating electioneering. Reformers have discussed whether a distinction should be made between groups that represent grassroots sentiment and groups that represent narrower interests; whether a distinction should be made between educating the public about issues and merely helping to elect or defeat particular candidates, and whether the tone of some types of electioneering advertisements can be harmful. Among the normative questions raised by group electioneering ads are the following:

Who should set the issue agenda in election campaigns? Some critics of BCRA dubbed the bill the "Incumbent Protection Act." For these opponents, BCRA insulated incumbent officeholders from having to address issues that they would prefer to avoid. Because congressional incumbents outraise their opponents by hefty margins—an average, in 2008, of more than five-to-one in House races, and eight-to-one in Senate races[24]—some have argued that their advantage enables them to avoid controversial issues. Congressional challengers often do not have the resources to present their policy views to the public, and advertising by outside groups may be a means of holding incumbents accountable. Those who support restricting electioneering have countered that in contested races, the candidates and their party committees tend to have enough resources to get their message across.

It is valid to ask, however, whether restricting group advertising can take off the table issues that neither party wishes to discuss. Groups favoring term limits, for example, claim to have undertaken advertising campaigns in races where neither candidate had devoted time to discussing the issue, and to have therefore forced the candidates to take a position on term limits. Likewise, anti-abortion groups have at times run advertisements in races where neither candidate had made abortion a focal point of the campaign. For many groups, the relevant question is whether the issues discussed in the campaign should be only those the candidates wish to discuss.

Are electioneering campaigns truly independent from the campaigns of candidates? That some group advertisements discuss issues on which the candidates are silent raises the possibility that interest groups will do the "dirty work" for candidates—that they will bring up issues that candidates fail to do not because they do not think they are consequential for their campaigns, but because they do not wish to be associated with the sorts of attacks made in these ads. Two obvious examples here are the Swift Boat advertisements run in 2004 and various group advertisements discussing Obama's connections with Bill Ayers, Tony Rezko, and Rev. Jeremiah Wright in 2008. These ads were all run independently of the candidates, but the sponsors received money from people who had also contributed to the candidates these ads benefited, and the ads ran in states that were being vigorously contested by both candidates. Most groups do take seriously the injunction against overt coordination with the candidates, but a *de facto* form of coordination is almost inevitable. For some, this is evidence that any effort to prohibit coordination is likely to be relatively inconsequential.

How can the accuracy of electioneering ads be monitored? Advertising by political candidates often degenerates into debates about whether the candidates' claims about each other are true or false. If a candidate makes a false claim, his or her opponent can generally confront it directly, and it can be harmful to a candidate to be accused of lying in a campaign. It is rare, however, for candidates to take issue with interest group ads. Many supporters of BCRA spoke of candidates being subject to misleading interest group ads late in their campaigns and of being unable to respond. Interest groups often do not have the same incentive to be honest in their ads that candidates do, and, in particular, groups that do not have an ongoing brand name or reputation to protect have little incentive to stick to making verifiable claims. Television stations can refuse advertisements they deem to be misleading or in poor taste, but it is clearly more difficult to monitor electioneering ads by groups than it is to monitor party or candidate ads, and any efforts to do so risk calling attention to the ads themselves.

How much should the public know about the sponsors of electioneering advertisements? BCRA included a "stand by your ad" provision, which required candidates to state in their ads that they "approved this message." Advertisers other than candidates are likewise required to include a printed statement and a voiceover claiming responsibility for the advertisement. Although this provision makes it clear to the public whether the ad was created by a candidate, the acknowledgment that an outside group is responsible for the ad does not necessarily provide meaningful information about the group itself. In the case of 527 ads, the name of the sponsor often conveys little about the group's agenda or funding source. Disclosure requirements about group contributions can help researchers untangle this somewhat, but the average television viewer is unlikely to have easy access to this information. What is a television viewer to make of the knowledge that "Republicans for Clean Air" or "the Media Fund" paid for an advertisement? Prompt disclosure laws can help the media to understand the motivation behind some ads, but there are few legal options to strengthen public knowledge beyond this.

THE FUTURE OF ELECTIONEERING

BCRA's electioneering restrictions applied only to radio and television advertisements. As a consequence, it had no effect on the proliferation of Internet-based electioneering, and it may even have abetted the movement of groups to the Internet. In some cases, groups have used television or radio ads to direct citizens to their Web sites. Many groups have also sought to create online advertisements that make far more pointed statements about the candidates than these groups might make on television or radio. Doing so is not only more cost-effective for groups because they do not have to pay for advertising time, but also it is advantageous in that particularly catchy ads can be distributed virally, potentially reaching a far larger audience than would television or radio ads. In addition, groups can target viewers more effectively by advertising on Web sites that draw people with particular issue interests. The downside of Internet advertising for groups, however, is that it becomes harder for them to reach persuadable voters. An advertisement placed on a Web site frequented by environmentalists or gun-rights activists might be effective in raising money for a group, but it is unlikely to reach citizens who are not already relatively well informed or who have not already made up their minds about how to vote. Internet advertising has become a standard component of groups' election efforts, but it is best seen as a prelude to advertising on television or radio. Groups such as MoveOn.org have sent links of their advertisements to members, encouraging them to share the ads with others and to help fund the group's effort to buy television or radio time for the ads.

Many who seek to reduce the role groups play in elections have also argued for decreasing restrictions on candidate fundraising or providing public subsidies for candidates to air their own advertisements. In other words, they prefer not to further limit groups, but to help underfunded candidates. If regulation is no longer an option—either because of the Supreme Court or because of the impossibility of keeping up with technology, one option simply may be to keep candidates and parties from being drowned out by groups.

CONCLUSION

Television advertising remains one of the most potent tools in the arsenal of organized interests. For all of the attention it has received, however, only a small number of groups have the resources and motivation to engage in advertising on television. In addition, advertising on television and radio will continue to decline in effectiveness as the audiences continue to diminish and fragment. As this chapter makes clear, BCRA changed the priorities of some groups that have traditionally relied on advertising, but it did not significantly decrease the amount of electioneering.

Writing in 2000, Darrell West noted that there were three potential responses to the rise of interest group electioneering: increase disclosure, increase regulation, or do nothing.[25] New disclosure laws and regulations on issue ads have been imposed, with some effect on who advertises but little effect on the volume of electioneering. It is now clear, however, that the Supreme Court will take a dim view of future efforts to regulate electioneering, and that reformers must concentrate upon increasing disclosure. For the time being, many of those who would limit electioneering are in wait-and-see mode, attempting to figure out how much electioneering will increase following the *Citizens United* decision and how they can work to influence the decision-making calculus of those who might wish to engage in electioneering.

NOTES

1. Let Freedom Ring, www.youtube.com/watch?v=geaYuQq5Gag.
2. Juliet Eilperin, "Gore Launches Ambitious Advocacy Campaign on Climate," *Washington Post*, March 30, 2008.
3. David B. Magleby, J. Quin Monson, and Kelly D. Patterson, *Dancing Without Partners: How Candidates, Parties, and Interest Groups Interact in the New Campaign Finance Environment* (Provo, Utah: Center for the Study of Elections and Democracy, Brigham Young University, 2005), 28.
4. For discussion, see Trevor Potter and Kirk L. Jowers, "Speech Governed by Federal Election Laws," in *The New Campaign Finance Sourcebook*, ed. Anthony Corrado, Thomas E. Mann, Daniel Ortiz, and Trevor Potter (Washington, D.C.: Brookings Institution, 2005), 207.
5. Michael J. Malbin, "Assessing the Bipartisan Campaign Reform Act," in *The Election After Reform: Money, Politics, and the Bipartisan Campaign Reform Act*, ed. Michael J. Malbin (Lanham, Md.: Rowman and Littlefield, 2006), 1–18.
6. Donald J. Simon, "Current Regulation and Future Challenges for Campaign Financing in the United States," *Election Law Journal* 3, 3 (2004): 474–498.
7. Kate Phillips, "Group Reaches Settlement with FEC Over 2004 Campaign Advertising." *The New York Times*, March 1, 2007, A16.
8. Potter and Jowers, "Speech Governed by Federal Election Laws," 210.
9. Ibid., 217.
10. Darrell M. West, "How Issue Ads Have Reshaped American Politics," in *Crowded Airwaves: Campaign Advertising in Elections*, ed. James A. Thurber, Candice J. Nelson, and David A. Dulio, (Washington, D.C.: Brookings Institution, 2000), 153.
11. David B. Magleby, "Interest-Group Election Ads," in *Outside Money: Soft Money and Issue Advocacy in the 1998 Congressional Elections*, ed. David B. Magleby, (Lanham, Md.: Rowman and Littlefield, 2000), 41–61.
12. Gary C. Jacobson, "The Effect of the AFL-CIO's 'Voter Education' Campaign in the 1996 House Elections," *Journal of Politics* 61 (1999): 185–194.
13. Robert G. Boatright, Michael J. Malbin, Mark J. Rozell, and Clyde Wilcox, "Interest Groups and Advocacy Organizations after BCRA," in *The Election after Reform: Money, Politics, and the Bipartisan Campaign Reform Act*, ed. Michael J. Malbin (Lanham, Md.: Rowman and Littlefield, 2006), 122–123.
14. Wisconsin Advertising Project, *Final Report on the 2000 Election* (Madison: Wisconsin Advertising Project, 2001).
15. See the George Washington University political advertisement archive, www.gwu.edu/~action/ads2/adnaacp.html.
16. Stephen R. Weissman and Kara D. Ryan, *Soft Money in the 2006 Election and the Outlook for 2008: The Changing Nonprofits Landscape* (Washington, D.C.: The Campaign Finance Institute, 2007); Robert G. Boatright, "Situating the New 527 Groups in Interest Group Theory," *The Forum* 5, 2 (2007).
17. Michael M. Franz, "The Interest Group Response to Campaign Finance Reform," *The Forum* 6, 1 (2008): 11.
18. Wisconsin Advertising Project, "Presidential TV Advertising Continues to Grow: Over $28 Million Spent from September 28–October 4" (Madison: Wisconsin Advertising Project, October 8, 2008).
19. Donald P. Gerber and Alan S. Gerber, *Get Out the Vote: How to Increase Voter Turnout* (Washington, D.C.: Brookings Institution, 2004).
20. Peter Francia, *The Future of Organized Labor in American Politics* (New York: Columbia University Press, 2006), 60–65.

21. See, for example, Steven Rosenthal, "Response to Malbin et al.," *Election Law Journal* 1 (2002): 546–547.

22. Sheryl Gay Stolberg, "Hunting Mr. Democrat," *New York Times*, August 1, 2004.

23. Jimmy Orr, "Sarah Palin Blasts Defenders of Wildlife for new Anti-Palin Campaign," *Christian Science Monitor*, February 4, 2009.

24. Center for Responsive Politics, www.opensecrets.org/overview/incumbs.php.

25. West, "How Issue Ads Have Reshaped American Politics," 161–167.

SUGGESTED READING

Boatright, Robert G., Michael J. Malbin, Mark J. Rozell, and Clyde Wilcox. "Interest Groups and Advocacy Organizations after BCRA." In *The Election after Reform: Money, Politics, and the Bipartisan Campaign Reform Act.* Ed. Michael J. Malbin. Lanham, Md.: Rowman and Littlefield, 2006, 112–140.

Devine, Tad. "Paid Media in an Era of Revolutionary Change." In *Campaigns on the Cutting Edge.* Ed. Richard J. Semiatin. Washington, D.C.: CQ Press, 2008, 27–47.

Franz, Michael M. *Choices and Changes: Interest Groups in the Electoral Process.* Philadelphia: Temple University Press, 2008.

Franz, Michael M., Paul B. Freedman, Kenneth M. Goldstein, and Travis N. Ridout. *Campaign Advertising and American Democracy.* Philadelphia: Temple University Press, 2008.

Jacobson, Gary C. "The Effect of the AFL-CIO's 'Voter Education' Campaign in the 1996 House Elections." *Journal of Politics* 61 (1999): 185–194.

Magleby, David B., and Jonathan W. Tanner. "Interest Group Electioneering in the 2002 Congressional Elections." In *The Last Hurrah? Soft Money and Issue Advocacy in the 2002 Congressional Elections.* Ed. David B. Magleby and J. Quin Monson. Washington, D.C.: Brookings Institution, 2004, 63–89.

Potter, Trevor, and Kirk L. Jowers. "Speech Governed by Federal Election Laws." In *The New Campaign Finance Sourcebook.* Ed. Anthony Corrado, Thomas E. Mann, Daniel R. Ortiz, and Trevor Potter. Washington, D.C.: Brookings Institution, 2005, 205–231.

West, Darrell M. "How Issue Ads Have Reshaped American Politics." In *Crowded Airwaves: Campaign Advertising in Elections.* Ed. James A. Thurber, Candice J. Nelson, and David A. Dulio. Washington, D.C.: Brookings Institution, 2000, 149–169.

PART VII ★ GROUPS AND LOBBYING BEYOND THE BELTWAY

CHAPTER 34	Interest Groups and State Politics	445
CHAPTER 35	Local Interest Groups: Forgotten but Still Influential?	457
CHAPTER 36	Lobbying in the American Style around the World	467

chapter 34

Interest Groups and State Politics

by Anthony J. Nownes

NO ONE KNOWS FOR CERTAIN how many interest groups operate at the state level in the United States. But one thing is certain: *the number is very large.* In one study, political scientists Virginia Gray and David Lowery found well over 30,000 organizations registered to lobby in the American states during the 1990s.[1] That number is surely larger now. Whom do all these groups represent? What do they do? What do they want, and how successful are they at getting what they want? Drawing on extant work on interest groups in state politics, this essay will address these questions.

ORGANIZATIONS ACTIVE IN STATE POLITICS

Six types of organizations are particularly active in state politics: business firms, trade associations, professional associations, governmental organizations, labor unions, and citizen groups.[2] This section touches on all these types of groups. But first, it is worth noting that many of the interest groups that lobby state governments are state, local, or regional chapters or affiliates or subsidiaries of national or regional organizations. Many of the prominent labor unions in state politics, such as the National Education Association, participate through their state affiliates. Similarly, many citizen groups, such as the Sierra Club and National Right to Life, are active through their state chapters. Still, some important state interest groups are freestanding, such as the Howard Jarvis Taxpayers Association (California), Hospital and Healthsystem Association of Pennsylvania, Michigan Retailers Association, and many others.

Business Groups

Business firms come in all shapes and sizes, and in virtually every state many different kinds of business firms lobby state government. In most states, business firms in the state's leading industries are particularly active. In Nevada many gaming firms (Boyd Gaming Corporation and Harrah's Entertainment) and mining firms (Coeur D'Alene Mining and Newmont Mining Corporation) are registered to lobby state government.[3] Similarly, in Michigan, many automotive firms, such as Ford and General Motors, actively lobby.[4] In states that have widely diverse economies (California), all kinds of business firms lobby state government. Many businesses lobby in one state or just a few, but the large and diverse firms (Altria Client Services, Inc., the parent company of Philip Morris; Anheuser-Busch Companies; and Coca Cola Company) lobby in multiple states.

Trade Associations

Trade associations, or groups of businesses, are generally considered among the most active types of interest groups in most states.[5] State and/or local chambers of commerce are especially active. In Minnesota the Duluth Area Chamber of Commerce is registered to lobby state government, as are chambers from many other cities.[6] In virtually every state, more specialized trade associations also lobby. In Texas these associations include the Wholesale Beer Distributors of Texas and the Texas Automobile Dealers Association, which represent their respective interests.[7]

Professional Associations

Professional associations represent practitioners in specific occupations and are likewise prominent in state politics. In all fifty states, doctors and lawyers are represented by powerful professional associations. For example, the Maine Medical Association lobbies on behalf of physicians, and the Maine State Bar Association advocates on behalf of lawyers.[8] And many other professionals have formed associations to represent them. Alabama's certified public accountants are represented by the Alabama Society of Certified Public Accountants, and optometrists have their own association.[9]

Governmental Associations

Governmental organizations, either individual units or groups of government entities, are also active in state politics. Local governments are well represented before their

In 2010 New Jersey governor Chris Christie, who was a registered lobbyist from 1999 to 2001, signed an executive order barring state agencies from hiring lobbyists to lobby the state.

state governments. In Kansas several cities, including Dodge City and Hays, are registered to lobby state government, as are many counties, school districts, and special districts.[10] In addition, the League of Kansas Municipalities and the Kansas Association of Counties represent cities and counties, respectively, at the state capital.[11] Moreover, and somewhat surprisingly, state-level government entities also lobby state government. Executive branch agencies lobby other parts of state government, especially the legislature. Arizona's Department of Education is registered to lobby state government, as are several other executive agencies.[12] Executive branch agencies are similarly well represented in other states.

Labor Unions

Labor unions are prominent actors in all states' politics. Teachers unions, such as the National Education Association and the American Federation of Teachers, are particularly important, but many other types of unions are active as well. In Michigan, as would be expected, the International Union, United Automobile, Aerospace and Agricultural Implement Workers of America, better known as United Auto Workers, is prominent, and in Nevada, where hotels and casinos are plentiful, several hospitality-related unions, including the Culinary Workers Union and the Laborers International Union, are active.[13]

Citizen Groups

Finally, active in all fifty states are citizen groups, made up of like-minded individuals. Groups concerned with abortion (on both sides of the issue), civil rights, the environment, gay and lesbian rights, good government, gun rights and gun control, property rights, taxation, and a wide variety of other "causes" are part of the mix of state politics. In California practically every imaginable constituency has an interest group working on its behalf. NARAL, Pro-choice America, and Planned Parenthood represent abortion rights supporters; Concerned Dog Owners of California represents its interested constituents; the Environmental Defense Fund, the Nature Conservancy, and the Sierra Club represent environmentalists; and the National Rifle Association and the California Rifle and Pistol Association represent gun enthusiasts.[14]

Table 34.1 lists the six major types of interest groups active in the states and provides a few examples of each type. Most state interest groups fit into one of these six categories, but not all. Studies show that charities,[15] churches,[16] colleges and universities,[17] political action committees (PACs),[18] think tanks,[19] and other types of interest groups also thrive in state politics.

COMMUNITIES OF STATE INTEREST GROUPS

Once we have identified the types of state interest groups, it is worth asking: What does the entire body of state interest groups—or communities of groups—look like? Fortunately, state interest group scholars Virginia Gray, David Lowery, and their colleagues have been addressing this question for two decades. Their findings have taught us a great deal about what these communities look like and how and why they differ across states. Four of their findings are particularly important.

First, state interest group communities vary tremendously in size.[20] Gray and Lowery find that some states have large numbers of interest groups, while others have relatively few groups. They report that by the end of the 1990s California and Texas each had more than 2,000 registered interest groups, but Delaware, Hawaii, New Hampshire, Rhode Island, and Wyoming had fewer than 300.[21] The numbers in other states fell in between these extremes.

So what accounts for these variations? Using a population ecology framework, Gray and Lowery zeroed in on three particularly important determinants of community size. First is the *size of the state's economy*. Specifically, Gray and Lowery find that states with larger economies tend to have more interest groups than states with smaller economies. The reason is that a state with a larger economy has a "larger number of potential members or sponsors of all interest organizations."[22] It is not the case, however, that

Casino owners and the unions that represent their employees, including the Culinary Workers Union, represent powerful interests in Nevada.

there is a direct and linear relationship between the size of state's economy and the size of its interest group community.[23] This is so because in relatively crowded interest group communities, fewer interest groups are born and more of them die. In other words, states appear to have set "carrying capacities" for interest groups; once a state reaches its carrying capacity, numbers stop growing.

Lowery and Gray also identify the *level of party competition* in a state as an important determinant of state interest group community size. Specifically, they find that states with competitive party systems—that is, with two political parties that are relatively evenly matched, as opposed to a system in which one party dominates state politics—tend to have more interest groups than states with noncompetitive party systems.[24] Lowery and Holly Brasher explain how party competition affects the size of state interest group communities. They note that "[n]o matter how salient an issue is to potential members or sponsors," few people or patrons will contribute money to or join an organization working on that issue if "there is no chance that the political system will address it."[25] They further note that people and patrons satisfied with the status quo will not mobilize to protect it unless there is some threat to it. Therefore, they argue, "the prospect of policy change matters. . . . If the out-party has a good chance of becoming the in-party at the next election, then old policies may be overturned and new policies actively considered."[26]

There is also evidence that the *number of constituents* affects the size of interest group communities. Lowery and Gray find that in general the supply of interest groups in a state grows with demand.[27] If the number of environmentalists in a state grows, we can expect the number of environmental groups to grow as well. Similarly, if the number of business firms in a state grows, we can expect the number of trade associations and business firms that lobby state government to grow. It is important to note here, however, that the relationship between the number of constituents and number of interest groups is operative within individual interest group guilds or sectors. So it is possible that group numbers may grow in one sector (say, the health care sector) and simultaneously decline in another (say, the construction sector). Differences in overall group numbers across states are a function of differences in the sizes of various interest group sectors.

Second, state interest group communities vary in their level of diversity. Gray and Lowery and their colleagues also show that some state interest group communities are more diverse than others. Overall, they conclude that state interest group communities are quite diverse—that is, in all fifty states a wide range of substantive interests is represented—but some states have far more diverse interest group communities than others. States with relatively diverse interest group communities include California, Illinois, and Louisiana, and those with more uniform

TABLE 34.1 **Six Types of Interest Groups that are Particularly Active in the States**

Type of interest group	Examples
Business firm	Altria Client Services Inc.; Newmont Mining Corporation
Trade association	Duluth (Minnesota) Area Chamber of Commerce; Texas Automobile Dealers; Indoor Tanning Association
Professional association	Maine Medical Association; Alabama Society of Certified Public Accountants
Governmental organization	Arizona Department of Education; Dodge City, Kansas
Labor union	Culinary Workers Union Local 226; Maine Education Association
Citizen group	California Rifle and Pistol Association; Environmental Defense Fund, Planned Parenthood Affiliates of California

interest group communities include Delaware, Florida, and North Dakota.[28] What accounts for these variations in diversity? Two factors appear to be particularly important: *economic diversity* and *economic size.* Not surprisingly, states with diverse economies (such as California) tend to have more diverse interest group communities than states with more concentrated economies (such as New Hampshire). States with larger economies tend to have more interest group diversity. "The disincentives to organization facing very small and very large groups," Gray and Lowery argue, "are mitigated somewhat in larger state economies, leading to more diverse interest group systems in these states."[29]

Third, business interests predominate in state interest group communities. Gray and Lowery find that diversity is substantial in many states, but they also conclude that business interests dominate interest group communities. In other words, most groups active in the states represent what they call "profit-oriented" organizations.[30] This does not mean that business interests always get what they want from state governments. Indeed, Gray and Lowery find that nonbusiness organizations that often tangle with business interest groups—labor unions and citizen groups—are anything but powerless in state lobbying communities.[31] Nonprofit-oriented groups of workers, government employees, environmentalists, gun enthusiasts, and others lobby hard, and they often win in state politics. Nevertheless, the predominance of business organizations in state interest group communities means that in very few political battles do these interests go completely unheeded. Substantively, this means that policies opposed by large numbers of businesses or one large corporation within a state are not easily adopted.

Fourth, institutions predominate in state interest group communities. Beyond describing the six different kinds of interest groups active in state politics, interest group scholars also use a simpler typology to classify groups. Specifically, they distinguish between *institutions,* which are interest groups without members, and *membership organizations.* The most common types of institutions active in state politics are business firms. Other types of institutions include government entities (cities, counties, towns, and government agencies), universities and colleges, and think tanks. Gray and Lowery found that by the end of the 1990s, "institutions comprised 57.81 percent of all organizations registered to lobby in the states."[32] In other words, the majority of interest groups active in the states have no members at all.

LOBBYISTS IN STATE POLITICS

When interest groups attempt to affect state government decisions, they generally (but not always) use lobbyists. There are not many studies of state lobbyists, but those few that exist provide a reasonably good idea of what state lobbyists are like.

Types of State Lobbyists

State lobbyists fall into three general categories—contract lobbyists, in-house lobbyists, and volunteer (or amateur) lobbyists. Contract lobbyists, also known as "outside" lobbyists, are professional, for-hire lobbyists who work for themselves or consulting firms, law firms, lobbying firms, or public relations firms. Contract lobbyists advocate on behalf of whoever hires them and constitute the "hired guns" of lobbying lore. The prototypical contract lobbyist is well connected, with years of experience in state politics.[33] Many contract lobbyists have state government experience, perhaps as legislators or legislative staffers, and many are either political experts in the legislative process or executive rulemaking process, or they are policy experts on one or more issues.[34] No one knows for certain what percentage of state lobbyists are contract lobbyists, but one recent study estimates that they make up less than 15 percent of lobbyists in most states.[35]

In-house lobbyists are professional lobbyists who work for a single organization. Many contract lobbyists lobby all or most of the time, but the typical in-house lobbyist is a "Jack or Jill of all trades" who performs various activities for an organization.[36] In the ranks of in-house state lobbyists are organization heads, such as CEOs, executive directors, and presidents, who lobby as part of their jobs, and "middle managers" in business firms and government agencies, and other organizational employees in citizen groups, professional associations, and trade associations, who lobby part of the time. The typical in-house lobbyist is a policy expert with specialized knowledge about the issues his or her group works on. An in-house lobbyist for a state medical association is therefore likely to be an expert on state health care policy and the state health care system. An in-house lobbyist for a development company will likely have specialized knowledge about legislation, regulations, rules, and court decisions concerning land use. Studies suggest that among professional lobbyists, in-house lobbyists outnumber contract lobbyists by a wide margin in the states.

Finally, there are volunteer lobbyists. Also known as amateur, cause, or citizen lobbyists, they are usually ordinary citizens who advocate on behalf of the organizations that they either belong to or work for. Members of citizen groups or labor unions often volunteer to lobby state government officials on behalf of their organizations. Similarly, a business firm's employees may lobby state government officials for their firm. Some small, underfunded citizen groups use volunteer lobbyists because they cannot afford in-house or contract lobbyists. Other groups, however, use volunteer lobbyists in addition to their paid lobbyists, thinking that state government officials are particularly responsive to the demands of ordinary citizens.

TABLE 34.2 **Characteristics of State Lobbyists in Colorado, Ohio, and West Virginia**

Characteristics/trait		N
Age (median)	52	355
Female	32%	362
Have government experience	56%	371
Highest level of education		371
Some high school	.5%	
High school diploma	1.3%	
Some college	5.9%	
College degree	25.6%	
Some graduate or professional school	13.7%	
Graduate or professional degree	52.8%	
Income (median)	$90,000	292
Part-time lobbyist	55%	369
Racial/Ethnic Identity		371
Caucasian/White	94.6%	
Hispanic/Latino	2.4%	
African American/Black	.8%	
Native American	.8%	
Asian/Pacific Islander	.5%	
Other	.8%	
Years of lobbying experience (mean)	12.8	361

SOURCE: The data come from a survey of lobbyists in Colorado, Ohio, and West Virginia, conducted by the author in 2006. N = the number of lobbyists who responded to the survey item in question.

The Characteristics of State Lobbyists

No one knows for certain how many lobbyists there are in the states, but fragmentary data do exist and they are suggestive. The Washington–based think tank Center for Public Integrity occasionally counts lobbyists in the states, and in their latest tally (2006) they found that approximately 40,000 professional lobbyists were registered to lobby in the states.[37] The actual number of lobbyists is probably much larger, as volunteer lobbyists are generally not required to register. Moreover, some states' laws do not require lobbyists who work for certain types of organizations to register. So the actual number of people who lobby state government in the course of any given year is most likely well above 50,000.

Lobbyists stand at the center of state interest group representation, but we know surprisingly little about who they are. Indeed, there are virtually no comprehensive studies of the composition of state lobbyist communities. Still, we do have some information from a 2006 survey of professional lobbyists in three states: Colorado, Ohio, and West Virginia.[38] The survey queried lobbyists on a number of matters, including their personal characteristics and professional activities. The three states are not necessarily representative of all the states, and only some of the lobbyists completed the survey. Still, the results are suggestive. What do they tell us?

First, women, as well as racial and ethnic minorities are underrepresented in state professional lobbyist communities. As Table 34.2 shows, two-thirds of responding state lobbyists are men, and almost 95 percent are white. Overall, 50.7 percent of the U.S. population is female, and 65.6 percent are non-Hispanic whites.[39] Second, few state lobbyists are young. The median age among responding lobbyists is fifty-two. Third, state lobbyists are an affluent and well-educated group. Ninety-two percent of responding lobbyists graduated from college, compared to approximately 25 percent of adult Americans.[40] The median lobbyist annual income is $90,000, compared to a 2007 median household income of $50,740 for all Americans.[41] Fourth, the average lobbyist is quite experienced, with 12.8 years of lobbying experience. Fifth, most respondents lobby only part-time, while holding additional nonlobbying positions in the organizations for which they work. Finally, most professional state lobbyists have some government experience.

In sum, nonwhites, women, young people, the less well-educated, and those without government experience are underrepresented in communities of professional state lobbyists. Some critics believe the lack of diversity undercuts the legitimacy of representative democracy in the states. Such a critic might argue that homogeneous state lobbyist communities underrepresent the views of nonwhites, poor people, women, political "outsiders," and other traditionally disadvantaged groups in American society. To the extent that state lobbyists affect government decisions—and there is no doubt that they do—this could bias these decisions against the interests of large numbers, perhaps even a majority, of people. Others may argue, however, that the lack of diversity in state lobbyist communities does not matter much. Just because most lobbyists are well-off white men, the argument goes, does not mean that the interests of others are not represented, that a rich white man is perfectly capable of representing the interests of the poor or the homeless.

WHAT DO THESE GROUPS AND LOBBYISTS DO?

The previous two sections make clear that there are tens of thousands of interest groups and lobbyists active in state politics. This simple fact raises the following question: What are all these lobbyists and interest groups doing? The short answer to this question is attempting to influence government decisions.

Lobbying Is About Information

Lobbying does not have a particularly good reputation. Indeed, most Americans tend to think that lobbyists are sleazy fixers who use bribes and shady tactics to get what they want from government.[42] The truth of the matter, however, is quite mundane. Lobbying, it turns out, is mostly (though not solely) about *providing information.* In short, in most instances when a lobbyist lobbies, he provides information to the target of his lobbying effort in an attempt to convince the target that his position is correct on a given issue.[43] Let us assume that a legislature is considering increasing the state sales tax by one-half of 1 percent. A lobbyist for an antitax group—let us call it Citizens against Taxes (CAT)—wishes to convince state legislators that the tax is a terrible idea and should not be adopted. To make her case, she meets personally with as many state legislators and state legislative staffers as possible and testifies before state legislative committees. If the CAT lobbyist can, she also meets with the governor and his or her aides. To make her antitax case, she presents these government decision makers with information suggesting that the tax increase would hurt the state's economy. Specifically, the lobbyist reads from or summarizes papers written by well-known economists showing that tax increases tend to depress economic growth or increase unemployment. Such actions are essentially what lobbyists do when they lobby—they present information designed to persuade the recipients of the information to do something (in this case, vote against a bill) the lobbyist wants them to do. Naturally, in our hypothetical example, while the CAT lobbyist is hard at work trying to defeat the tax increase, a protax advocate, perhaps a lobbyist for a state employees union, is working hard to enact it. The protax lobbyist may argue that a tax increase is necessary to fund popular state government services, and he may present information to legislators predicting how many citizens would suffer without these programs. In both cases the lobbyists' basic strategy is the same—try to convince government officials that they are correct.

The Techniques of Lobbying

Studies of lobbying demonstrate several different ways that lobbyists can present information in an effort to get what they want. The box below, which is based on research on lobbying in the states, lists fifteen techniques that are commonly used by professional state lobbyists.[44] The first five techniques are used by almost all state lobbyists at one time or another, and the next ten are employed by large numbers of state lobbyists in the course of a given year.

The lists suggest several general conclusions about lobbying in the states. First, the techniques are aimed at all three branches of state government. Although many of the most widely utilized lobbying techniques focus on the legislature (testifying before legislative committees, and meeting with legislators), others are directed at the governor's office (interacting with liaison offices within the

TECHNIQUES COMMONLY USED BY PROFESSIONAL STATE LOBBYISTS

Five things that almost all state lobbyists do

- Help to draft legislation
- Meet personally with executive agency personnel
- Meet personally with state legislative staff
- Meet personally with state legislators
- Testify at legislative hearings

Fifteen things that most state lobbyists do

- Engage in informal contacts with state legislators
- Enter into coalitions with other organizations/lobbyists
- Help to draft regulations, rules, or guidelines
- Inspire letter-writing, telephone, or e-mail campaigns to state legislators
- Interact with liaison offices within the governor's office
- Issue press releases
- Meet personally with members of the governor's staff
- Submit written comments on proposed rules and regulations
- Submit written testimony to legislative committees
- Talk with people from the media

SOURCES: Anthony J. Nownes and Krissy Walker DeAlejandro, "Lobbying in the New Millennium: Evidence of Continuity and Change in Three States," *State Politics and Policy Quarterly* 9 (2009): 429–455; Anthony J. Nownes and Patricia Freeman, "Interest Group Activity in the States," *Journal of Politics* 60 (1998): 86–112.

governor's office, meeting with members of the governor's staff) or executive branch agencies (meeting with executive agency personnel, and helping to draft regulations, rules, or guidelines). The judiciary receives far less attention than the other two branches of government, but it too receives some attention. Second, state lobbyists lobby the public as well as government officials. Lobbying members of the public, which is also known as "grassroots" or "outside" lobbying, is a common tactic in the states. Interest groups and their lobbyists know that regular citizens have the ability to affect government decisions by voting and by contacting government officials via e-mail, letter, or telephone, and this is why lobbyists target the public. Third, state lobbying is a personal business. The most widely utilized techniques still entail face-to-face contact with government decision makers. Technological advances and citizen participation notwithstanding, lobbyists rely heavily on personal contacts with government officials and their aides to make their cases. Fourth, surveys show that money is less important in state lobbying than information.[45] Many state lobbyists (more than half in one recent survey) make monetary contributions to elected government officials, primarily state legislators, but contributing money remains far down the list of the most utilized lobbying techniques. Finally, most lobbyists are generalists who rely on a wide variety of techniques to make their cases. The box above does not go into any detail about how many techniques state lobbyists use when they try to affect government decisions, but studies show that the typical state lobbyist does not specialize in one or a few lobbying techniques, but rather uses many different ways to make a persuasive case.[46]

Group Influence

The question of how much power interest groups wield over government decisions is notoriously difficult to answer. There are three primary reasons why. First, every government decision has numerous causes, not just one. Most state government decisions involve many (sometimes hundreds or thousands) political actors, and each of them has a unique mixture of beliefs and motives. When a state government decides to increase its sales tax, many government actors are involved, including the governor, numerous state legislators, many gubernatorial and legislative staffers, and scores of lobbyists (for and against). Given the many participants, it is difficult to determine precisely how much influence any single actor wields. Second, it is often impossible to distinguish influence from agreement. State government officials may do exactly what lobbyists want simply because they are in agreement. If a state enacts a new law easing controls on gun ownership, the decision may mean that many legislators dislike gun control. It is not *prima facie* evidence that the "gun lobby" controls the state legislature. Finally, activity does not mean influence. In other words, just because interest groups are numerous, active, and well heeled does not mean they are influential. Journalists and many citizens mistakenly assume that because there are large numbers of lobbyists and they are very busy, they are influential. This is not the case. The tobacco industry has always been one of the most politically active industries in

Texas state senator Kirk Watson, right, speaks during a July 2008 news conference about wind energy. He was joined by Greg Wortham, director of the West Texas Wind Energy Consortium. Both urged regulators to increase the state's capacity to transmit electrical energy from rural West Texas wind generators to the state's major population centers.

the United States, but that did not stop tobacco companies from suffering truly devastating (for them) political losses in the 1990s.[47]

Power in the States

In the end, all of this means that political scientists do not (and cannot) fully understand precisely how much influence interest groups have in state politics. But that does not mean it is impossible to know *anything* about how much power interest groups wield. Indeed, studies of state interest group politics provide a number of insights about the power of state-level groups. These insights, however, are more general and tentative than they are definitive. So what have we learned about interest group power in the states?

Interest Groups Are Sometimes Influential.

People who study state interest groups agree on one thing: interest groups are sometimes successful at getting what they want from state government.[48] In his book *The Third House: Lobbyists and Lobbying in the States*, state interest group expert Alan Rosenthal concludes, "On the many issues that state legislatures handle . . . lobbyists can and do play an important role."[49] Sometimes gun lobbyists ask state governments to liberalize gun laws, and state governments do just that. Sometimes insurance companies ask state governments to ease regulations, and state governments respond by doing so. The flipside of these examples is that sometimes lobbyists do not get what they want; in some cases gun lobbyists and insurance companies ask for things and state governments ignore them. In short, interest groups win some and they lose some.

Interest Group Influence Is Situational.

Simply concluding that interest groups and their lobbyists are sometimes influential and sometimes not is deeply unsatisfying. A number of studies go beyond this general conclusion and stipulate more specifically where and when we can expect state interest groups to be influential. Rosenthal concludes that interest groups are most likely to be influential when they lobby on "issues of narrow scope, with little salience to the broader state community." "On minor issues," Rosenthal continues, "the lobbyist's influence is likely to be central, and may occasionally carry the day."[50] What exactly constitutes an issue of narrow scope? First, it is one that few people care about. For example, there is little general interest in the ways state governments regulate massage therapists, so whenever states consider regulations on these professionals, lobbyists—especially those representing professional associations of massage therapists—are likely to be influential (because no one else really cares). Second, narrow issues are often technical and complex, such as state governments' regulation of state-chartered banks. The regulations under which these banks operate are often arcane and complex, and not well understood by most people. Not surprisingly, lobbyists who work for state-chartered banks are quite familiar with the regulations and likely to wield influence when regulations are considered.

Interest Groups Are More Influential in Some States Than in Others.

In their multiyear, fifty-state study of interest group power in the states, interest group scholars Ronald Hrebenar and Clive Thomas show that interest groups tend to be more influential in some states than others.[51] They report that in some states interest groups "have an overwhelming and consistent influence on policymaking."[52] In these states active interest groups ask for things and generally receive them. In their latest review of interest group power, Hrebenar and Thomas conclude that interest groups are dominant in Alabama, Florida, Hawaii, and Nevada. In no states, Hrebenar and Thomas conclude, are interest groups impotent—that is, consistently "subordinated to other aspects of the policymaking process."[53] In Kentucky, Michigan, Minnesota, South Dakota, and Vermont, however, groups do not loom particularly large in state policymaking.[54] Instead, other political actors, particularly political parties and government officials—state legislators and the governor—tend to be quite powerful, and groups play a more subordinate role. In fifteen states, according to Hrebenar and Thomas's latest rendering (among them, Colorado, Montana, New York, and Washington), interest groups play a complementary role to other political actors, sometimes exercising a great deal of influence, and sometimes not. In twenty-six other states, such as Alaska, Missouri, New Mexico, and Virginia, interest groups tend to be influential on most issues, but occasionally take a back seat to other political actors.

Two factors in particular appear to determine how influential interest groups are in a state. First is *strength of political parties.* States with strong, active political parties have less powerful interest groups than states with weak, inactive, and indolent political parties.[55] Second is *political culture.* States with traditionalist political cultures, that is, cultures "rooted in an ambivalent attitude toward the marketplace and the commonwealth," and those in which citizens tend to think that the "purpose of government . . . is to maintain the existing social and economic hierarchy," tend to have more powerful interest groups than states without such cultures.[56] In these states, levels of political participation tend to be relatively low. Most of the states with traditionalist political cultures are found in the South, and interest groups tend to be more powerful in southern states than elsewhere.

Some Types of Interest Groups Are More Influential in State Politics Than Others.

Hrebenar and Thomas also find that all interest groups are not created equal; rather, some types of groups are much

TABLE 34.3 **The Most Powerful Interests in the States**

Interest Type	Example
1. General business organizations	"Peak" trade associations
2. Schoolteachers' organizations	State affiliates of the National Education Association (NEA)
3. Utility companies and associations	Individual utilities and trade associations of utilities
4. Manufacturers	Manufacturing firms and trade associations of manufacturing firms
5. Hospital and nursing homes associations	Trade associations of hospitals
6. Insurance: general and medical	Individual insurance companies and trade associations of insurance companies
7. Physicians	State medical associations
8. Contractors, builders, and developers	Individual development firms and builders
9. General local government organizations	"Peak" coalitions of municipalities
10. Lawyers	State bar associations and professional associations of trial lawyers

SOURCE: Adapted from Anthony J. Nownes, Clive S. Thomas, and Ronald J. Hrebenar, "Interest Groups in the States," in *Politics in the American States: A Comparative Analysis*, 9th ed., ed. Virginia Gray and Russell L. Hanson (Washington, D.C.: CQ Press, 2008), 117.

more influential than others. Table 34.3 lists the ten types of interests that Hrebenar and Thomas find most powerful in state politics, although influence varies across states and groups. In almost all the states, according to Thomas and Hrebenar, state government decision makers hear groups representing the general interests of the business community loud and clear. We should not jump to conclusions about the overall power of business, however, for at least two reasons. First, the business community, which in most states is large and diverse, is also divided on many issues. The primacy of general business organizations does not mean that these broad interests always win. On many issues, businesses are pitted against each other, with some winning and some losing. Second, the top-ten list of influential interests also contains teachers, local government organizations, and lawyers, whose interests frequently do not match those of business.

CONCLUSION

Tens of thousands of lobbyists represent tens of thousands of interest groups active in the American states. Studies of state-level interest groups and lobbying have taught us a great deal about the activities and roles of interest groups in state politics. Most notably, we know that interest groups are powerful players in the politics and policymaking of all fifty states.

Three general observations about interest group politics in the states are worth making. First, although interest groups have always been numerous in the states, today there are probably more than ever before. No one knows for certain precisely how many interest groups exist today compared to, say, 1960, but all the available evidence suggests that state interest group communities are larger than they ever have been. As the research of Gray and Lowery suggests, we cannot expect state interest group communities to grow forever. But clearly the number of interest groups in the states has grown for years, and is now relatively large. Second, state interest group communities resemble the Washington, D.C., interest group community. State lobbying has become more professional; grassroots techniques and technology-driven tactics are common; and the bad old days of lobbyists courting government officials largely with entertainment, food, and money are over. Third, state interest group communities are diverse. Although business interests predominate in most state interest group communities, groups representing all sorts of citizens—from antitax tea partiers to environmentalists to animal lovers—are now influential political players in many states.

NOTES

1. Virginia Gray and David Lowery, "The Expression of Density Dependence in State Communities of Organized Interests," *American Politics Research* 29 (1985): 374–391.

2. For substantive information on the types of interest groups active in all fifty states, the Hrebenar and Thomas edited volumes are invaluable. See Ronald J. Hrebenar and Clive S. Thomas, eds., *Interest Group Politics in the Midwestern States* (Ames: Iowa State University Press, 1993); *Interest Group Politics in the Northeastern States* (University Park: Pennsylvania State University Press, 1993); *Interest Group Politics in the Southern States* (Tuscaloosa: University of Alabama Press, 2002); and *Interest Group Politics in the American West* (Salt Lake City: University of Utah Press, 1987).

3. Nevada Legislative Counsel Bureau, *Lobbyist Employer List—75th Session* (Carson City: Nevada Legislative Counsel Bureau, 2009), www.leg.state.nv.us/Lobbyist/reports/LobbyistEmployerList.cfm?Session=75.

4. Michigan Department of State, *Registered Lobbyist/Lobbyist Agent Search* (Lansing: Michigan Department of State, 2009), miboecfr.nicusa.com/cgi-bin/cfr/lobby_srch.cgi.

5. Clive S. Thomas and Ronald J. Hrebenar, "Interest Groups in the States," in *Politics in the American States: A Comparative Analysis*, 6th ed., ed. Virginia Gray and Herbert Jacob (Washington,

D.C.: CQ Press, 1996), 122–158; Thomas and Hrebenar, "Interest Groups in the States," in *Politics in the American States: A Comparative Analysis*, 7th ed., ed. Virginia Gray, Russell L. Hanson, and Herbert Jacob (Washington, D.C.: CQ Press, 1999), 113–143; Thomas and Hrebenar, "Interest Groups in the States," in *Politics in the American States: A Comparative Analysis*, 8th ed., ed. Virginia Gray and Russell L. Hanson (Washington, D.C.: CQ Press, 2004), 100–128.

6. Minnesota Campaign Finance and Public Disclosure Board, *Lobby Lists* (St. Paul: Minnesota Campaign Finance and Public Disclosure Board, 2009), www.cfboard.state.mn.us/lob_lists.html.

7. Texas Ethics Commission, *2009 Registered Lobbyists with Employer/Client Contracts* (Austin: Texas Ethics Commission, 2009), www.ethics.state.tx.us/tedd/LobCon09.xls.

8. Maine Commission on Governmental Ethics and Election Practices, *Lists of Lobbyists and Clients* (Augusta: Maine Commission on Governmental Ethics and Election Practices, 2009), www.mainecampaignfinance.com/public/entity_list.asp?TYPE=LCB.

9. Alabama Ethics Commission, *2009 Registered Lobbyist List* (Montgomery: Alabama Ethics Commission, 2009), ethics.alabama.gov/news/2009Lobbyists_Principals.pdf.

10. Kansas Department of State, *2009 Legislative Lobbyist Directory by Client (Authority)* (Topeka: Kansas Department of State, 2009), www.kssos.org/elections/lobbyist_directory_by_Client_display.asp.

11. Ibid.

12. Arizona Department of State, Office of the Secretary of State, *Arizona Secretary of State Lobbyist System* (Phoenix: State of Arizona, 2009), www.azsos.gov/scripts/Lobbyist_Search.dll.

13. Michigan Department of State, *Registered Lobbyist/Lobbyist Agent Search*; Nevada Legislative Counsel Bureau, *Lobbyist Employer List.*

14. California Secretary of State, *Lobbying Activity: Employers of Lobbyists* (Sacramento: California Secretary of State, 2009), calaccess.ss.ca.gov/Lobbying/Employers/.

15. Marcia Avner, *The Lobbying and Advocacy Handbook for Nonprofit Organizations: Shaping Public Policy at the State and Local Level* (Saint Paul, Minn.: Amherst H. Wilder Foundation, 2001).

16. See, for example, David Yamane, *The Catholic Church in State Politics: Negotiating Prophetic Demands and Political Realities* (Lanham, Md.: Rowman and Littlefield, 2005).

17. See, for example, Randall Brumfield and Michael T. Miller, "A Review of the Literature Related to Government Relations in Higher Education," (unpublished manuscript, Fayetteville: University of Arkansas, 2008), www.eric.ed.gov/ERICDocs/data/ericdocs2sql/content_storage_01/0000019b/80/42/d0/07.pdf.

18. See, for example, Stacy B. Gordon and Cynthia L. Unmack, "The Effect of Term Limits on Corporate PAC Allocation Patterns: The More Things Change. . . " *State and Local Government Review* 35 (2003): 26–37; James D. King and Helenan S. Robin, "Political Action Committees in State Elections," *American Review of Politics* 16 (1995): 61–77; King and Robin, "Party Committees, Nonconnected PACs, and Affiliated PACs in State Elections: Same Species or Different Political Animals?" *Southeastern Political Review* 22 (1994): 559–572; Joel A. Thompson and William Cassie, "Party and PAC Contributions to North Carolina Legislative Candidates," *Legislative Studies Quarterly* 17 (1992): 409–416.

19. John A. Hird, *Power, Knowledge, and Politics: Policy Analysis in the States* (Washington, D.C.: Georgetown University Press, 2005).

20. Virginia Gray and David Lowery, *The Population Ecology of Interest Representation: Lobbying Communities in the American States* (Ann Arbor: University of Michigan Press, 1996).

21. David Lowery and Holly Brasher, *Organized Interests and American Government* (Boston: McGraw Hill, 2004), 76–77.

22. Ibid., 87.

23. David Lowery and Virginia Gray, "The Density of State Interest Group Systems," *Journal of Politics* 55 (1993): 191–206.

24. David Lowery and Virginia Gray, "The Population Ecology of Gucci Gulch, or the Natural Regulation of Interest Group Numbers in the American States," *American Journal of Political Science* 39 (1995): 1–29.

25. Lowery and Brasher, *Organized Interests and American Government*, 84.

26. Ibid., 86.

27. Lowery and Gray, "Population Ecology of Gucci Gulch."

28. Virginia Gray and David Lowery, "The Diversity of State Interest Group Systems," *Political Research Quarterly* 46 (1993): 81–97.

29. Ibid., 93.

30. Virginia Gray and David Lowery, "The Institutionalization of State Communities of Organized Interests," *Political Research Quarterly* 54 (2001): 265–284.

31. Ibid., 272.

32. Ibid.

33. Alan Rosenthal, *The Third House: Lobbyists and Lobbying in the States*, 2nd ed. (Washington, D.C.: CQ Press, 2001), chap. 2.

34. Ibid.

35. Anthony J. Nownes, Clive S. Thomas, and Ronald J. Hrebenar, "Interest Groups in the States," in *Politics in the American States: A Comparative Analysis*, 9th ed., ed. Virginia Gray and Russell L. Hanson (Washington, D.C.: CQ Press, 2008), 110.

36. Rosenthal, *Third House*, 18.

37. Center for Public Integrity, *Ratio of Lobbyists to Legislators 2006* (Washington, D.C.: The Center for Public Integrity, 2007), projects.publicintegrity.org/hiredguns/chart.aspx?act=lobtoleg. New York had the most lobbyists registered in 2006 with 5,117, and North Dakota had the fewest with 154.

38. For more details about how the survey was conducted, see Anthony J. Nownes and Krissy Walker DeAlejandro, "Lobbying in the New Millennium: Evidence of Continuity and Change in Three States," *State Politics and Policy Quarterly* 9 (2009): 429–455.

39. U.S. Census Bureau, *USA Quick Facts* (Washington, D.C.: U.S. Census Bureau, 2009), quickfacts.census.gov/qfd/states/00000.html.

40. Ibid.

41. Ibid.

42. Public Citizen, Congress Watch, *Recent Public Opinion Polls on Ethics in Government* (Washington, D.C.: Public Citizen, 2006), www.citizen.org/congress/govt_reform/ethics/congethics/articles.cfm?ID=14945.

43. See especially John R. Wright, *Interest Groups and Congress: Lobbying, Contributions, and Influence* (Needham Heights, Mass.: Allyn & Bacon, 1996).

44. Nownes and DeAlejandro, "Lobbying in the New Millennium."

45. Ibid.

46. Anthony J. Nownes and Patricia Freeman, "Interest Group Activity in the States," *Journal of Politics* 60 (1998): 86–112.

47. The culmination of these defeats was the Tobacco Master Settlement Agreement, which required tobacco companies to pay hundreds of billions of dollars to state governments.

48. See, for example, Margery M. Ambrosius and Susan Welch, "State Legislators' Perceptions of Business and Labor Interests," *Legislative Studies Quarterly* 13 (1988): 199–209; American Political Science Association, Committee on American Legislatures, and Belle Zeller, *American State Legislatures: Report* (New York: Crowell, 1954); Cynthia J. Bowling and Margaret R. Ferguson, "Divided Government, Interest Representation, and Policy Differences: Competing Explanations of Gridlock in the Fifty States," *Journal of Politics* 63 (2001): 182–206; Elisabeth R. Gerber, *The Populist Paradox: Interest Group Influence and the Promise of Direct Legislation* (Princeton: Princeton University Press, 1999); Charles W. Wiggins, Keith E. Hamm, and Charles G. Bell, "Interest-Group and Party Influence Agents in the Legislative Process: A Comparative State Analysis," *Journal of Politics* 54 (1992): 82–100.

49. Rosenthal, *Third House*, 216–217.

50. Ibid., 217, 218.

51. Thomas and Hrebenar, "Interest Groups in the States," in *Politics in the American States,* 8th ed., 100–128; Nownes, Thomas, and Hrebenar, "Interest Groups in the States," 110.

52. Nownes, Thomas, and Hrebenar, "Interest Groups in the States," 120.

53. Ibid.

54. Ibid., 121.

55. American Political Science Association, Committee on American Legislatures, and Zeller, *American State Legislatures*; Wiggins, Hamm, and Bell, "Interest-Group and Party Influence Agents."

56. Daniel J. Elazar, *American Federalism: A View from the States*, 3rd ed. (New York: Harper and Row); Virginia Gray, "The Socioeconomic and Political Context of States," in *Politics in the American States,* 9th ed., 21.

SUGGESTED READING

Gray, Virginia, and David Lowery. *The Population Ecology of Interest Representation: Lobbying Communities in the American States.* Ann Arbor: University of Michigan Press, 1996.

———. "The Diversity of State Interest Group Systems." *Political Research Quarterly* 46 (1993): 81–97.

Hird, John A. *Power, Knowledge, and Politics: Policy Analysis in the States.* Washington, D.C.: Georgetown University Press, 2005.

Hrebenar, Ronald J., and Clive S. Thomas, eds. *Interest Group Politics in the Southern States.* Tuscaloosa: University of Alabama Press, 2002.

King, James D., and Helenan S. Robin. "Political Action Committees in State Elections." *American Review of Politics* 16 (1995): 61–77.

Lowery, David, and Virginia Gray. "The Population Ecology of Gucci Gulch, or the Natural Regulation of Interest Group Numbers in the American States." *American Journal of Political Science* 39 (1995): 1–29.

Nownes, Anthony J., and Krissy Walker DeAlejandro. "Lobbying in the New Millennium: Evidence of Continuity and Change in Three States." *State Politics and Policy Quarterly* 9 (2009): 429–455.

Nownes, Anthony J., and Patricia Freeman. "Interest Group Activity in the States." *Journal of Politics* 60 (1998): 86–112.

Nownes, Anthony J., Clive S. Thomas, and Ronald J. Hrebenar. "Interest Groups in the States." In *Politics in the American States: A Comparative Analysis.* 9th ed. Ed. Virginia Gray and Russell L. Hanson. Washington, D.C.: CQ Press, 2008, 98–126.

Rosenthal, Alan. *The Third House: Lobbyists and Lobbying in the States*, 2nd ed. Washington, D.C.: CQ Press, 2001.

chapter 35

Local Interest Groups: Forgotten but Still Influential?

by Eric Heberlig and Suzanne Leland

One Monday in September 2008, there was an unusually crowded city council meeting in Charlotte, North Carolina. In addition to the leaders and activists from interested neighborhood and community groups that typically attend such meetings, forty-six city sanitation employees dressed in bright orange uniforms were there, a few holding up a large American flag. They were there for one purpose only: to lobby city council members and the mayor to protect their jobs. An internal audit of city services had suggested privatizing the East Zone's garbage and recycling pick-up to lower costs and improve service. Bids were solicited, and the city's Privatization and Competition Advisory Committee recommended awarding the contract to a Florida-based company, which had submitted a bid that was $537,989 less than the next lowest, which came from the city's solid waste department. The winning bidder also promised it would use a new fleet of larger-capacity collection trucks, which would save fuel costs and help the environment by reducing existing trips to the landfill on trash collection routes and that it would implement single-stream recycling collection at no cost to the city.[1]

One promise the private company could not make, however, was jobs for the forty-six East Zone city employees. Company officials would go no further than giving existing city employees priority consideration. That did not sit well with the sanitation workers. "You need people in Charlotte to keep working," said James Locklear, a twenty-three-year veteran with the city.[2]

In the end, only two council members voted in favor of awarding the contract to the private vendor. Instead, the majority voted to go against the advice of the privatization council and typical protocol regarding sanitation bids. As this story illustrates, lobbying goes on at city hall, and groups—in this case, city workers—can be extremely influential on specific issues.

In many ways, the potential for this type of grassroots "people power" is tantalizing at the local level. From Alexis de Tocqueville to the present, observers of American democracy have favorably documented ordinary people's ability to organize themselves to address collective concerns.[3] Moreover, because political units in which concentrated demographic shifts can produce significant changes in the electorate and therefore in political representation, local officials have reason to pay close attention to unorganized blocs of voters. Racial and ethnic voters have received the greatest attention from scholars. Although unorganized and episodically organized residents might have greater potential influence at the local level than the national or state level, studies find that the distribution of group power is similar at all levels: groups that are "institutionally organized" and have regular access to government officials because of their economic power have major advantages in influencing government. Which groups have influence, and the conditions under which they have it, have long been the focus of the study of local interest group politics.

FROM CLASSIC COMMUNITY POWER STUDIES TO THE BACKWATER OF POLITICAL SCIENCE

In the 1960s the classic community power studies examined interest groups with a focus on local government. Scholars wanted to test the distribution of power and influence in American politics, such as theories of elitism and pluralism, and local politics was an easily accessible forum to do so. A decade earlier power elite theorists such as C. Wright Mills viewed the urban political system as dominated by a privileged minority and relatively closed to the average citizen.[4] This theory suggests that a small number of business groups influence elected officials in local communities to further their self-interest. Sociologists such as Floyd Hunter used the reputational approach to study the city of Atlanta, Georgia. Hunter asked knowledgeable observers to identify who were the most influential decision makers in town. He found that policymaking was dominated by a few principal business interests.[5]

Robert Dahl's *Who Governs?* challenged these findings by taking a broader and more inclusive approach. He

GROUPS IN LOCAL POLITICS

INSTITUTIONAL GROUPS

Groups organized mainly for nonpolitical purposes that can use their resources and stature in the community to gain regular access to public officials.

Examples: Developers, banks, major employers, public employee unions, universities.

EPISODIC GROUPS

Groups that can organize politically to confront a common concern, often spurred by a perceived threat or crisis. Their desire and ability to access public officials is situational.

Examples: Neighborhood organizations, faith-based organizations, racial or ethnic organizations, homeowners associations, not in my back yard groups, taxpayer groups.

DEMOGRAPHIC GROUPS

Groups sharing a demographic trait, particularly a racial or ethnic identity. The group can be organized (frequently in an episodic group), but its influence is usually in its potential to organize, to vote cohesively, and/or to gain representation from one of its members in official positions.

Examples: African, Asian, Hispanic, Irish, and Italian Americans, and others.

observed and interviewed participants on three issues (education, urban renewal, and party nominations) in New Haven, Connecticut, and found that the groups that were active and influential varied on each issue.[6] Unlike Hunter, Dahl concluded that political resources may be unequally distributed, but that the political system is open and made up of diverse interest groups. Politics in New Haven, according to Dahl, was very democratically responsible, competitive, and not dominated by one particular group.

Pluralist theory was immediately challenged by scholars such as William Domhoff, who asserted that the elite still had power behind the scenes because they were careful to keep specific issues off the agenda.[7] Such "nondecisions" were just as important as public decisions in determining policy.

Although their conclusions varied regarding the number and diversity of influential groups in city politics, the community power studies made local interest groups and their interactions with local government officials the core of political science. Unlike later studies of interest groups (mostly at the national level), which examined how groups organized and what tactics they used, the community power studies focused on the critical questions of whether and, if so, how interest groups were influential.

After the community power studies had run their course, the debate in urban politics about community power shifted to urban political economy. Scholars, such as Paul Peterson in his seminal work *City Limits*, assert an economic viewpoint—one where economic factors constrain city decision making; these scholars reject the classic debate between pluralism and elitism.[8] This position asserts that the mobility of capital causes local government officials to acquiesce to business interests even in the absence of a visible business elite. Cities simply cannot afford the risk of losing jobs and revenues if businesses leave because of tax rates or dissatisfaction over economic development policies. Critics of Peterson, such as Steven Elkin and Clarence Stone, argue that Peterson overstates these interests and there is an informal public-private governing arrangement called a "regime" or a durable alliance among local officials, business interests, property owners, and bureaucrats.[9] They also argue that pluralist theory is flawed because it assumes that groups have equal access to the decision-making process.

Conversely, they develop an urban regime theory, which posits that there is a stable alliance between the public and private sectors to make local policy decisions. The private sector controls resources (money and jobs), and the public sector has the ability to cultivate public legitimacy. The word *regime* is used to describe the informal arrangements that surround and complement the formal workings of governmental authority. The regime acts as a mediator between both the public and private sectors. This theory builds upon Hunter's earlier work by making a distinction between favored and disfavored groups. Favored groups (businesses) are those concerned with distributive policies (mainly economic growth), and disfavored groups (other groups) are concerned with redistributive policies (such as assistance to the poor).

Other critics of pluralism who have moved the power debate to the larger politico-economic forces are John Logan and Harvey Molotch. Like Peterson and the regime theorists, they also elaborated on the idea of *Who Governs*, by asking the question, for what? They find that the issue of growth separates local elites from the people who use the city as a place to live and work. The desire for growth tends to create consensus among elites no matter how split they are on other issues. The elites utilize this consensus surrounding growth to eliminate any other alternative purpose of government.[10]

Attention has also focused on the impact of changing demographics on local power, particularly the rise and fall of power of racial and ethnic groups rather than the influence of interest groups per se. Stephen Erie conducted multiple case studies on classic Irish political machines and found support for the pluralist argument regarding the political, but not economic, assimilation. He asserts that although the Democratic machines of the late nineteenth century offered impressive channels of advancement for individual Irish contractors and politicians, they could do only so much for Irish *group* mobility. Erie also contends that since the 1970s the baton of urban group power has been passed to third and fourth generation ethnic groups such as blacks, Hispanics, and Asians. As these minorities mobilized, they searched for viable strategies. The machine model is problematic for these groups because they were kept out of the city trenches in the 1960s. When minority groups finally made enough political gains, the old-style party organizations were already in a state of decline.[11]

Rufus Browning, Dale Marshall, and David Tabb studied black and Hispanic minority group power in ten northern California cities. Their research found that for such groups to achieve power, political incorporation must occur. They define political incorporation as the extent to which the group is represented in important and sometimes dominant coalitions in policymaking institutions. Such incorporation is positively related to responsiveness to black concerns and interests and results in more minority contracts, improved service delivery in minority neighborhoods, the creation of police review boards, and the appointment of more minorities to boards and commissions.[12] These studies analyze "group politics" by examining how demographic groups organize themselves to win political power rather than the traditional focus on specific organizations dedicated to influencing specific election and policy outcomes.

Peter Burns counters, however, that political incorporation is insufficient for minorities to achieve representation.[13] Parties often place patronage before policy responsiveness, and minority elected officials often place the party agenda before the specific concerns of their demographic group. Officials, moreover, are regularly chosen by local party leaders rather than the ethnic community. Burns's case studies of four Connecticut cities reveal that community groups and neighborhood organizations can be important venues for minority interest representation if these groups are able to present a unified voice to public officials.

The trend of the research shows that local interest groups were once at the center of political science while the focus was on urban politics, but then political science began moving away from urban politics. As the population began to shift to the suburbs and federal aid to urban areas declined, political scientists shifted their focus to politics at the federal level. Even within the study of local politics, traditional interest group organizations have lost their caché. Local governments have been the primary innovators in the federal system on gun control and smoking restrictions, yet the role of interest groups in their creation has garnered little attention.[14] Popular urban texts such as Bernard Ross and Myron Levine's *Urban Politics: Power in Metropolitan America*[15] and Ronald Harrigan and John Vogel's *Political Change in the Metropolis*,[16] for example, do not devote a chapter to local interest groups nor do they even get a listing in the index. Texts that cover state and local government are more likely to include them, but typically confine the discussion of interest group politics to the state level (see Virginia Gray and Peter Eisinger's *American States and Cities)*.[17] In contrast, interest groups are a standard chapter in introductory texts on American national politics.

THE CHALLENGES OF STUDYING LOCAL INTEREST GROUPS

The turn in focus away from local interest groups has to do with both the changing theoretical interests of political scientists and the shifts in power in American politics. Political scientists interested in studying power now tend to focus their attention on institutions where power currently seems to reside. The federal government dramatically expanded its direct dealings with cities during the New Deal. This trend reached its height in the 1960s and early 1970s under general revenue sharing where money flowed from Washington to local governments with few strings attached. Federal aid to large cities began to dwindle in the late 1970s, however, and by 1986 general revenue sharing had ended. These changes had significant consequences. In 1977, the year before federal aid contraction began, cities received about 17.5 percent of their total revenues from the federal government. By 1990 federal assistance had decreased to only 5 percent.[18] In 2000 it rose slightly, but only to 5.4 percent. As Table 35.1 shows, the total percentage changes in federal aid dropped by almost 60 percent from 1977 to 2000.[19] City governments can spend only what they raise, and what they raise is controlled by state law. At the same time the federal government was tightening its purse strings, it began to rely more on accomplishing objectives through mandates. Unfortunately for cities, many of these orders to comply with federal law were and are still unfunded.

When power and resources began to shift away from cities in the 1960s, so did the potential for influence of local interest groups. An "influential" local group either participated in a local governing regime that had limited power to do much because it relied on resources (and attendant constraints) from the national and state governments or because it was able to coordinate its activities across multiple government jurisdictions. Robert Lowry and Matthew Potoski find that the number of local organizations positively affects the amounts of federal grants received by local governments.[20]

In addition, economic changes have shifted power structures in cities since the community power studies of the 1950s and 1960s. As the complexity of the economy and the competition for industry between cities increased,

TABLE 35.1 **The Decline of Federal Aid to Cities, per capita**

	1977	1990	2000	1977–2000
Average aid	$86.24	$28.17	$35.04	
Percent change		–67.3%	24.4%	–59.4%
Percent revenue	17.5%	5%	5.4%	

SOURCE: Bruce Walin, "Budgeting for Basics: the Changing Landscape of City Finances," discussion paper, Brookings Institution, 2005, 5.

power shifted from neighborhoods, wards leaders, and even elected officials to professional staffs and special districts. Quasi-public redevelopment corporations were created to handle economic development projects. Business communities often fragmented as local businesses became part of the national and international economy and decisions were made elsewhere. Businesses' commitment to serving as civic boosters for the local communities became highly uncertain. To the extent that governments or civic-minded business elites no longer make the important decisions about local issues, it is worth expanding this analysis of interest group targets beyond attempts to influence local government.

Studying interest groups at the local level is also fraught with challenges posed by their diverse nature. Local governments vary substantially in the role they play in each state. Counties are typically the largest administrative unit in states that deliver essential services such as public works, public safety, education, and human services, but counties may not even exist in some states (Connecticut) or may imitate a small city department (Kansas). Municipalities are often the unit of government that provides services in densely populated areas, but they may not exist in rural areas or in an urban territory where a strong county government prevails. In some areas, special purpose governments (governments that have been created to perform a single function) deal with specific problems ranging from transportation to the provision of sewers and water. In a nation as populous and geographically large as the United States, local governments face different problems, various public service demands, and fiscal responsibilities. Such diversity is illustrated in the area of education. In Hawaii local government does not provide elementary and secondary education; instead, it is left to the state. In Maine schooling can be provided by the state, municipalities, townships, or separate school districts. In Alabama it is provided exclusively by local governments.[21] In short, the focus of a study of interest group influence on education depends upon exactly where the policy is made.

This diversity challenges interest group scholars in studying the topic systematically because of a lack of a consistent unit of analysis. Local governments are "creatures of the state," in the words of Judge John F. Dillon, and their powers vary based on what state government has delegated to them. It is possible that in some parts of the United States, a local government may lack the experience, ability, or even legal authority to engage in a particular policy issue. Variation in institutional power provides an opportunity for research to assess their consequences for the activities of participants in the political process and policy outcomes. In practice, however, the variation makes it more difficult to identify which units of governments are the relevant units to study or to collect comparable data on them. The variation in authority of local governments and the variation in integration of units of local governments create barriers for interest groups working across different types of local governments to affect policy. It creates parallel barriers to studying local interest groups. As a consequence, studies are usually based on place—urban versus suburban versus rural politics—or the issue itself—transportation or water resources or poverty—rather than interest groups per se. Discussions of interest groups are often derivative of other foci of the study (issues, local government structures).

The irony of all of this is that as local governments have lost the focus of political scientists, they have grown greatly in size and scope and provide multiple access points for lobbying to occur. According to the most recent census of governments, there are 87,525 units of local government in the United States: 3,034 counties, 19,429 municipalities, 16,504 townships or towns, 13,506 school districts, and 35,052 special districts.[22] Like states, local governments have increased their capacity greatly since the 1980s. They are more trusted than federal and state government and are considered to be more responsive to citizens' needs.[23] The numbers of local governments do not include private governments, such as business improvement districts or homeowners associations, that also provide services such as street lighting to sidewalks. Their actual numbers are difficult to track and are not even listed in the census of governments. Despite the assets and opportunity provided by the pervasiveness, power, and variety of local governments, scholars have barely scratched the surface in researching how and why groups seek to influence them.

INSTITUTIONAL VERSUS EPISODIC LOCAL GROUPS

The political economy and regime theories provide a clear dichotomy between two types of interest groups that are involved in city politics: "institutional" and "episodic" groups. Both theories emphasize the institutional groups, which have long-standing, prominent presences in community life and have a relatively permanent place on the municipal agenda. They are well integrated into local government decision-making processes and structures. Their views are at least consulted before decisions are made on issues that affect them. Their members often sit on advisory boards and commissions. The most prominent examples are land use organizations (especially developers), local banks, contractors, and government employees (and their unions).

Institutional groups have an advantage in local politics because they are already organized for economic purposes.[24] They have their networks of "members" (especially employees, but potentially suppliers, customers, and stockholders as well) and existing communications structures that can be used to contact governments or send messages regarding the effectiveness and responsiveness of candidates for local office. Their "permanence" makes them attractive coalition partners for local officials, as the benefits of their relationships can accrue for many election or budget cycles. More important, local governments depend on them to produce jobs and tax revenues. Often they are "partners" with government in big development projects, but at the least they have leverage because of their ability to move and take jobs and revenue with them.

In fact, many cities and special districts are formed because businesses groups, such as developers and manufacturers, want to establish new jurisdictions with tax rates, regulations, and services that are more amenable to them.[25] Suzanne Leland and Kurt Thurmaier find that the consolidation of city and county governments is also heavily influenced by local business groups. In their analysis of twenty-six city-county consolidation attempts in the last three decades, they find that business groups (in particular the chamber of commerce, and local real estate developers) have been pivotal in defining the economic development vision for the community to convince voters of the benefits of city-county consolidation.[26]

One note of caution comes from Jeffrey Berry, Kent Portney, and Ken Thomson's study of group agenda setting and influence on local government.[27] They found that business organizations were the least successful sector in winning policy conflicts they initiated. In contrast, neighborhood groups, which are traditionally seen as much less powerful, did well: winning on half the conflicts they initiated and attaining a compromise on the rest. But, Berry et al. also found that on the most critical development issues, business almost always wins. On these projects, city hall is usually a co-initiator and uses the resources at its command to make sure the project gets done. When it has allies in the regime, business wins; when it goes alone, it is less likely to get what it wants.

Members of institutional groups are also potentially important donors in local elections. Given the low level of public attention and participation in local elections, the few who participate by providing volunteers and financial resources may exert considerable influence on grateful local officials (particularly because donors often face fewer legal restrictions than they do at the national level).[28] Logan and Molotch note the importance of the real estate industry as sources of campaign funds in local elections and posit that this is one reason for the power of the prodevelopment regime in city politics.[29] Several recent studies have examined campaign contributors in local elections. These studies conclude that the local campaign finance system is pluralistic but biased. Donors are not representative of the mass public—wealthier occupations and neighborhoods predominate—but no one interest dominates, and a wide array of participants contribute. Labor unions spend heavily with independent expenditures, such as direct communications from the union to the electorate regarding candidates for public office, in cities where such spending is permitted. Most contributors live within the city.[30]

Unions can also be players in "growth machines."[31] Construction unions benefit from the jobs and the wage pressures of a competitive construction market, and public employee unions benefit from the tax revenues and demand for city services generated by growth. As illustrated by the anecdote that opened this chapter, the livelihoods of public employees are particularly dependent on the decisions of local government officials, giving public employees substantial incentive to endorse, canvass, vote, and lobby local officials. Evidence shows that public employee unions are able to mobilize significantly higher levels of turnout from their members than the general public and cue their members to vote for union-endorsed candidates.[32] When pay raises are at stake in the city or education budgets, unions make sure that the hearing rooms are packed with their members. They also have an incentive to bargain for favorable work rules for themselves that may not result in better service or performance for the public.[33] Given the low levels of participation and low levels of interest generally in local elections, unions can have substantial advantages over an unorganized and inattentive public.

There are few studies of interest groups in local politics outside of cities. An exception is William Browne's analysis of rural politics.[34] Browne views farm groups as the dominant institutional group in rural politics and, given the potential diversity of interests in rural areas, asks why other organizations are not more active and influential. He concludes that farmers were the easiest rural residents to organize. Once they were organized, they, along with the government agencies that served them (Agriculture Departments and Extension Services), were able to position themselves as the spokespersons for rural interests. As other rural constituencies were unorganized, farm groups were able to co-opt their issues. The only way "other issues" were addressed was by passing resources through existing farm programs. In short, Browne's analysis of rural politics places farm organizations as the key interest organizations in rural regimes. The limitation of Browne's work for our purposes is that his focus is on rural interests and policy developed at the national level, where farm subsidies are the dominant

Members of the Cleveland, Ohio, teacher's union hold a rally in May 2011 as a show of solidarity with the more than 600 educators laid off by the school district. Teacher's unions have significance at all levels of government.

rural issue. Because farm subsidies are not a local government issue, it may be that farm organizations are not quite as dominant a player in local rural governments, which face similar economic development, land use, and education issues as all local governments. Consistent with Browne, however, Mark Lubell et al. find that agricultural employment (as a proxy for interest group activity) is related to the formation of regional watershed partnerships as farmers seek to "capture" institutions that will affect their water usage and pollution runoff.[35]

Episodic groups, as the name implies, are involved in discrete issues on an irregular basis. By and large, they are citizen groups whose involvement depends on the interest and energy of their volunteers. Unlike most institutional groups, they face persistent collective action problems in organization, maintenance, and stability. They are generally seen as outsiders that must spend a substantial portion of their efforts to gain access to and be taken seriously by local decision makers. Christopher Cooper and Anthony Nownes surveyed citizens groups in seven cities and found that they are less active than institutionalized groups, active in narrower policy niches, and more reactive to the policy initiatives raised by other groups or by government.[36]

Berry, Portney, and Thomson provide the most in-depth analysis of neighborhood groups.[37] They studied seven cities that had delegated significant decision-making authority to neighborhood councils and provided them with administrative and staff support. As such, their findings are likely to present the maximum effectiveness of citizen groups, as opposed to ordinary local politics. When groups were able to achieve high levels of face-to-face contact with city officials, the citizens' evaluations of the perceived responsiveness of city government increased. They concluded that cities with greater participation tended to make decisions that were consistent with larger proportions of the public, including poorer citizens who are traditionally not well represented.

Neighborhood organizations frequently are sparked to organize on land use issues.[38] Berry et al. found that neighborhoods were particularly influential on land use and planning issues.[39] Similarly, anecdotal evidence shows that NIMBY (not in my back yard) groups can eliminate or relocate unwanted facilities.[40] In interviews with local land use lobbyists, Nownes finds that NIMBY groups and neighborhood associations are frequently active in land use politics and that lobbyists spend considerable effort meeting with citizens groups and offering them concessions so that they will not turn out en masse at city council or planning board meetings.[41] Contrary to the view that developers dominate local politics, the lobbyists believed that the default position in many localities was "no growth" and approval of projects was difficult if significant public opposition was apparent. In a study of zoning decisions in the Atlanta metropolitan region, Arnold Fleischmann and Carol Pierannunzi found that local governments overwhelmingly followed the recommendations of their appointed planning commissions.[42] Pressure from developers and citizen protests had little influence on the outcomes, but citizen protest was related to the withdrawal of zoning petitions before they reached a final vote. Also unclear is the extent to which developers or citizen groups influenced the planning commissions before they made their recommendations to elected officials. Lubell et al. found that both the construction industry and environmentalism affected development in Florida and that the

TABLE 35.2 **Perceived Influence of Local Groups on Land Use Policy by Planners at the Local Level**

Group Types	Very influential	Somewhat influential	Little influence	No influence	Total respondents
Economic development agencies	17% (136)	46% (371)	28% (225)	9% (71)	803
Neighborhood associations	19% (155)	44% (350)	29% (230)	8% (66)	801
Local realtor associations	8% (65)	32% (255)	43% (339)	17% (136)	795
Local business owners	22% (179)	56% (449)	19% (156)	2 (18)	802
Environmental groups	9% (75)	44% (351)	36% (290)	11% (87)	803
Home builders association	18% (148)	40% (319)	30% (237)	12% (94)	798
Nonprofit community organizations	5% (41)	40% (315)	44% (354)	11% (88)	798

SOURCE: Dustin Read and Suzanne M. Leland, "A Survey of American Planning Association Members," conducted by the University of North Carolina Center for Real Estate, 2009.

development was conditioned by the type of local government structure: mayors were more responsive than city managers to the desire of wealthier citizens for environmental amenities. They did not measure interest group activity directly, however.[43]

In a nationwide survey of planners in July 2009, Suzanne Leland and Eric Heberlig found that many different groups were perceived as influential in the planning process at the local government level.[44] When asked how influential different groups were in making land use policy, planners believed local business owners had the most influence, followed by neighborhood associations, economic development agencies, and home builders associations, as illustrated in Table 35.2. Environmental groups, local realtors associations, and nonprofit community organizations were viewed as less influential.[45]

Nonprofit agencies and community development corporations (CDCs) are potentially potent advocates with city hall as governments increasingly rely on them to deliver social services and economic development projects. The conventional wisdom is that CDCs have become less involved in citizen mobilization since their heyday in the 1970s as they became more professionalized and focused on maintaining financial support from local officials.[46] Jeffrey Berry and David Arons surveyed directors of nonprofits and conclude that the federal tax code restrictions on election activity by nonprofits (and nonprofits' confusion about these restrictions) inhibit advocacy on behalf of their clients.[47] They also find that local officials are often accessible to nonprofits as the officials find them to be an effective way to reach out to neighborhood and ethnic groups.

Michael Owens studied church-based CDCs in New York City. The pastors he interviewed started CDCs because black politicians were ineffective in assuring the responsiveness of city government to black neighborhoods, contrary to the "political incorporation" thesis.[48] Owens concludes that neighborhoods with CDC projects saw increases in private investment, household incomes, and property values (although the precise contribution of the CDCs was not measured), which were important to the middle-class property owners in the neighborhoods. Still, compared to the rest of the city, these neighborhoods continued to have higher rates of single female–headed households, higher poverty, and lower median incomes.

Other case studies of community organizations present examples of policy successes.[49] If the case studies show nothing else, it is that these (often small) victories come after a long, difficult road. They do little to overturn the general observation of regime theory that the influence of local groups is episodic. Even if they succeed in joining the regime, they face the same challenges as local governments—commitments do not necessarily last because decisions made elsewhere constrain their options and resources.

BUILDING CITIZENS

Beyond direct influence on government policy, local interest groups can have a potentially important influence on citizens themselves. Sidney Verba, Kay Schlozman, and Henry Brady document the importance of community organizations in generating political participation by giving them opportunities to develop civic skills, exposing them to political discussions, and making them available to receive requests to participate in political activities from their colleagues.[50] The role of the African American church has been given particular attention in generating political engagement.[51] Berry, Portney, and Thomson find that overall levels of participation in their sample cities with active neighborhood organizations are not different from other cities. At the same time, they find that people who live in neighborhoods with strong organizations participate more and those without organizations participate less.[52] They also find that participation in neighborhood organizations increases perceptions that local government is responsive and increases knowledge about local government, especially for citizens of low socioeconomic status. They conclude that community organizations are particularly important agents in decreasing civic inequalities because low-income citizens need the additional efforts to engage them politically, while people with higher incomes and education do not.[53]

Civic organizations are important training and recruiting grounds for the infrastructure of local political organizations. They are sources of candidates for public office, local political party officers, and election volunteers.[54] Groups recruit candidates for public office as well and, as nonpartisan slating teams or party factions who dominate primary elections, can play an important role in screening candidates based on their demographic characteristics and ideological commitments.[55] To the extent that experience in local government is often an asset in attaining state or federal offices, local organizations are important to the development of an American governing class.[56] Groups can further provide important voting cues on local ballot initiatives by providing voters information on the geographic and normative distribution of costs and benefits of the proposal.[57]

The role of local citizens organizations as civic educators and recruiters is at risk, however, if fewer people are joining them.[58] Likewise, to the extent that people tend to join organizations that reinforce their existing political philosophies or social identities, the potential civic benefits of learning to work together to overcome political, racial, or class differences is diminished. If local groups are seen as promoting single-issue extremism, moderate members of the community may decline to join them or to attend public forums in which these groups participate.[59]

Eric Oliver does not analyze the role of interest groups directly in his study of participation in local politics, but he does offer several intriguing observations that could be developed as hypotheses. Oliver conjectures that cities suffer from a "bystander effect," in which everyone thinks someone else will step up to take care of the problem. Because there are often many advocacy groups in cities, they may stimulate participation among members, but stimulate bystander effects in everyone else.[60] Oliver and James Gimpel et al. also find that greater diversity (partisan, ideological, economic) leads to greater levels of civic interest and knowledge.[61] Locales with less diversity have few "controversies" to draw people into public life, and the dominant interests of the citizens can be represented by the dominant political party. If so, there may be fewer, or less diverse, interest groups in these areas, as the need for them is weak.

VENUES FOR FUTURE RESEARCH

Like much of the interest group field, the study of local groups is dominated by case studies or studies using a small number of cases that make it difficult to compare results and to generalize with confidence.[62] Local jurisdictions provide considerable varieties of government structures, economic infrastructures, and citizen demographics, but scholars have largely failed to assess how and why interest groups can mobilize and affect policy at the local level. Nor have scholars developed theories of contexts or theories of conditions that might help us develop research questions and research designs to take advantage of the tremendous variety of opportunities for research at the local level. Much of the research on local interest groups focuses on urban groups and urban governments. Why might the dynamics of big city politics create different interest group politics than smaller towns or rural areas? Why might the varieties of local governments create different interest groups politics? How and why do interest groups that attempt to work across multiple government jurisdictions differ from those who target a single institution? Under what conditions do citizen activists work independently or with groups that target single government jurisdictions or are multifaceted in their venues and tactical approaches?

Public meetings, open via state sunshine laws, and technology have led to additional access points and change for local government interest groups. Since the 1960s many local governments have required advance public notice of meetings that any citizen can attend and required minutes, transcripts, or recordings of the meetings for little or no cost. The rise of I-Government (putting information on the Internet) has made information readily available to citizens. It has also allowed interest groups greater access to monitoring local government policymaking. The Internet itself may have an equalizing effect by allowing neighborhood and citizen groups to drum up support on a local issue. Many neighborhood associations now have their own Web pages, blogs, and listservs to keep members of the community instantly informed about important issues affecting them. How have these changes in public information and public access changed local politics? Have they empowered individual citizens or the organizations that have the personnel to monitor city government? Have they made it easier for "extremist voices" to shout at one another or the sharing of information necessary to build consensus?

The community power studies placed interest groups at the heart of local politics and political science. Much has changed since the 1960s, both in terms of the activities of local governments and of interest groups as participants in them. City politics may not be "groupless," as Peterson argues, but it is hardly a pluralist nirvana either. Local officials, institutional groups, and citizens groups all are operating under shifting pressures from the external political, economic, and social environment. Understanding how they adjust will indicate much about the vitality of grassroots democracy and how it is practiced today.

NOTES

1. Susan Stabley, "City Balks at Trash Contract," *Charlotte Business Journal*, September 26, 2008.

2. M. E. Pellin, "City Council Trash Talk," Rhino Times.com. 2008, charlotte.rhinotimes.com/Articles-c-2008-09-29-185288.112113_City_Council_Trash_Talk.html.

3. Alexis de Tocqueville, *Democracy in America*, ed. J. P. Mayer (Garden City, N.Y.: Anchor, 1966; originally published in 1850).

4. C. Wright Mills, *The Power Elite* (New York: Oxford University Press, 1956).

5. Floyd Hunter, *Community Power Structure: A Study of Decision Makers* (Chapel Hill: University of North Carolina Press, 1953).

6. Robert A. Dahl, *Who Governs? Democracy and Power in an American City* (New Haven: Yale University Press, 1961).

7. G. William Domhoff, *Who Really Rules? New Haven and Community Power Reexamined* (New Brunswick, N.J.: Transaction, 1978).

8. Paul E. Peterson, *City Limits* (Chicago: University of Chicago Press, 1981).

9. Clarence N. Stone, *Regime Politics: Governing Atlanta 1946–1988* (Lawrence: University of Kansas Press, 1989); Steven L. Elkin, *City and Regime in the American Republic* (Chicago University of Chicago Press, 1987).

10. John R. Logan and Harvey L. Molotch, *Urban Fortunes: The Political Economy of Place* (Berkeley: University of California Press, 1987).

11. Stephen P. Erie, *Rainbow's End: Irish-Americans and the Dilemmas of Urban Machine Politics, 1840–1985* (Berkeley: University of California Press, 1988).

12. Rufus P. Browning, Dale R. Marshall, and David H. Tabb, *Protest Is Not Enough* (Berkley: University of California Press, 1984).

13. Peter F. Burns, *Electoral Politics Is Not Enough: Racial and Ethnic Minorities and Urban Politics* (Albany: SUNY Press, 2006).

14. Marcia L. Godwin and Jean R. Schroedel, "Policy Diffusion and Strategies for Promoting Policy Change: Evidence from California Local Gun Control Ordinances," *Policy Studies Journal* 28 (2000): 760–776; Charles R. Shipan and Craig Volden, "Bottom-Up Federalism: The Diffusion of Antismoking Policies from U.S. Cities," *American Journal of Political Science* 50 (2006): 825–843.

15. Bernard Ross and Myron Levine, *Urban Politics: Power in Metropolitan America*, 7th ed. (Belmont, Calif.: Wadsworth, 2005).

16. Ronald K. Vogel and John J. Harrigan, *Political Change in the Metropolis*, 8th ed. (New York: Pearson/Longman, 2008).

17. Virginia Gray and Peter Eisinger, *American States and Cities* (New York: Longman, 1997).

18. Peter Eisinger, "City Politics in an Era of Federal Devolution," *Urban Affairs Review* 33 (1998): 308–325.

19. Bruce Wallin, "Budgeting for Basics: the Changing Landscape of City Finances," paper prepared for the Brookings Institution Metropolitan Policy Program, 2005.

20. Robert C. Lowry and Matthew Potoski, "Organized Interests and the Politics of Federal Discretionary Grants," *Journal of Politics* 66 (2004): 513–533.

21. Robert Reischauer, "Governmental Diversity: Bane of the Grants Strategy in the United States," in *American Intergovernmental Relations*, ed. Laurence O'Toole (Washington, D.C.: CQ Press, 2006).

22. U.S. Department of Commerce, *Statistical Abstract of the United States* (Washington, D.C.: U.S. Government Printing Office, 2008).

23. U.S. Council on Intergovernmental Relations, "Why Categorical Grants?" in *American Intergovernmental Relations.*

24. Mancur Olson, *The Logic of Collective Action* (Cambridge: Harvard University Press, 1965).

25. Nancy Burns, *The Formation of American Local Governments: Private Values in Public Institutions* (New York: Oxford University Press, 1994).

26. Suzanne Leland and Kurt Thurmaier, eds. *Case Studies of City-County Consolidation: Reshaping the Local Government* (Armonk, N.Y.: M. E. Sharpe, 2004).

27. Jeffrey M. Berry, Kent E. Portney, and Ken Thomson, *The Rebirth of Urban Democracy* (Washington, D.C.: Brookings Institution, 1993).

28. Brian E. Adams, *Buying the Grassroots: Campaign Finance and the Unrealized Potential of City Elections* (Boulder: First Forum Press, 2009).

29. Logan and Molotch, *Urban Fortunes*, 230–231.

30. Adams, *Buying the Grassroots;* Arnold Fleishmann and Lara Stein, "Campaign Contributions in Local Elections," *Political Research Quarterly* 51 (1998): 673–689; Timothy B. Krebs, "Money and Machine Politics: An Analysis of Corporate and Labor Contributions in Chicago City Council Elections," *Urban Affairs Quarterly* 41 (2005): 47–64; Timothy B. Krebs, "Urban Interests and Campaign Contributions: Evidence from Los Angeles," *Journal of Urban Affairs* 27 (2005): 165–175.

31. Logan and Molotch, *Urban Fortunes.*

32. Herbert B. Asher, Eric S. Heberlig, Randall B. Ripley, and Karen C. Snyder, *American Labor Unions in the Electoral Arena* (Lanham, Md.: Rowman and Littlefield, 2001); Terry M. Moe, "Political Control and the Power of the Agent," *Journal of Law, Economics and Organization* 22 (2006): 1–29.

33. Terry M. Moe, "Collective Bargaining and the Performance of the Public Schools," *American Journal of Political Science* 53 (2009): 156–174.

34. William P. Browne, *The Failure of National Rural Policy* (Washington, D.C.: Georgetown University Press, 2001).

35. Mark Lubell, Mark Schneider, John T. Scholz, and Mihriye Mete, "Watershed Partnerships and the Emergence of Collective Action Institutions," *American Journal of Political Science* 46 (2002): 148–163.

36. Christopher A. Cooper and Anthony Nownes, "Citizen Groups in Big City Politics," *State and Local Government Review* 35 (2003): 102–111.

37. Jeffrey M. Berry, Kent E. Portney, and Ken Thomson, *The Rebirth of Urban Democracy* (Washington, D.C.: Brookings Institution, 1993).

38. John R. Logan and Gordana Rabrenovic, "Neighborhood Associations: Their Issues, Their Allies, and Their Opponents," *Urban Affairs Quarterly* 26 (1990): 68–94.

39. Berry, Portney, and Thomson, *Rebirth of Urban Democracy.*

40. Michael E. Kraft and Bruce B. Clary, "Citizen Participation and the NIMBY Syndrome: Public Response to Radioactive Waste Disposal," *Western Political Quarterly* 44 (1991): 299–328; Barry G. Rabe, *Beyond NIMBY: Hazardous Waste Facility Siting in Canada and the United States* (Washington, D.C.: Brookings Institution, 1994).

41. Anthony J. Nownes, *Total Lobbying: What Lobbyists Want (and How They Try to Get It)* (New York: Cambridge University Press, 2006).

42. Arnold Fleischmann and Carol A. Pierannunzi, "Citizens, Development Interests, and Land-Use Regulations," *Journal of Politics* 52 (1990): 838–853.

43. Mark Lubell, Richard C. Feiock, and Edgar E. Ramirez de la Cruz, "Local Institutions and the Politics of Urban Growth," *American Journal of Political Science* 53 (2009): 649–665.

44. Dustin Read and Suzanne M. Leland, "A Survey of American Planning Association Members" (Chapel Hill: University of North Carolina Center for Real Estate, 2009).

45. The survey was sponsored by the American Planning Association to develop a better understanding of the beliefs of local government planners about interest group influence, public-private partnerships, and metropolitan cooperation. The survey was run on Surveyshare and distributed by state planning association directors and the American Planning Association's monthly newsletter. There were 1,418 respondents.

46. Stephen Macedo et al., *Democracy at Risk: How Political Choices Undermine Citizen Participation and What We Can Do About It* (Washington D.C.: Brookings Institution, 2005); Marion Orr, ed. *Transforming the City: Community Organizing and the Challenge of Political Change* (Lawrence: University of Kansas Press, 2007).

47. Jeffrey M. Berry, with David F. Arons, *A Voice for Nonprofits* (Washington D.C.: Brookings Institution, 2003), 114–120.

48. Rufus P. Browning, Dale R. Marshall, and David H. Tabb, *Protest Is Not Enough* (Berkley: University of California Press, 1984); Michael Leo Owens, *God and Government in the Ghetto: The Politics of Church-State Collaboration in Black America* (Chicago: University of Chicago Press, 2007).

49. David J. O'Brien, *Neighborhood Organization and Interest Group Processes* (Princeton: Princeton University Press, 1975); Orr, *Transforming the City;* John Clayton Thomas, *Between Citizen and City: Neighborhood Organizations and Urban Politics in Cincinnati* (Lawrence: University of Kansas Press, 1986); Mark R. Warren, *Dry Bones Rattling: Community Building to Revitalize American Democracy* (Princeton: Princeton University Press, 2001).

50. Sidney Verba, Kay Lehman Schlozman, and Henry E. Brady, *Voice and Equality: Civic Voluntarism in American Politics* (Cambridge: Harvard University Press, 1995), chap. 13.

51. Allison Calhoun-Brown, "African American Churches and Political Mobilization: The Psychological Impact of Organizational Resources," *Journal of Politics* 58 (1996): 935–953; Fredrick C. Harris, *Something Within: Religion in African American Political Activism* (New York: Oxford University Press, 1999); Eric L. McDaniel, *Politics in the Pews: The Political Mobilization of Black Churches* (Ann Arbor: University of Michigan Press, 2008).

52. Berry, Portney, and Thomson, *Rebirth of Urban Democracy,* 95.

53. Verba, Schlozman, and Brady, *Voice and Equality;* Steven J. Rosenstone and John Mark Hansen, *Mobilization, Participation, and Democracy in America* (New York: Macmillan, 1993).

54. Thomas A. Kazee, ed., *Who Runs for Congress? Ambition, Context, and Candidate Emergence* (Washington, D.C.: CQ Press, 1994); Gary F. Moncrief, Peverill Squire, and Malcolm E. Jewell, *Who Runs for the Legislature?* (Saddle River, N.J.: Prentice Hall, 2001); Kenneth Prewitt, *The Recruitment of Political Leaders: A Study of Citizen-Politicians* (Indianapolis: Bobbs-Merrill, 1970); Joseph A. Schlesinger, *Ambition and Politics: Political Careers in the United States* (Chicago: Rand McNally, 1966); Samuel J. Eldersveld, *Political Parties: A Behavioral Analysis* (Chicago: Rand McNally, 1964).

55. Luis Richardo Fraga, "Domination Through Democratic Means: Non-partisan Slating Groups in City Electoral Politics," *Urban Affairs Quarterly* 23 (1988): 528–553; Seth E. Masket, *No Middle Ground: How Informal Party Organizations Control Nominations and Polarize Legislatures* (Ann Arbor: University of Michigan Press, 2009).

56. Gary C. Jacobson and Samuel Kernell, *Strategy and Choice in Congressional Elections*, 2nd ed. (New Haven: Yale University Press, 1983).

57. Elizabeth R. Gerber and Justin H. Phillips, "Development Ballot Measures, Interest Group Endorsements, and the Political Geography of Growth Preferences," *American Journal of Political Science* 47 (2003): 625–639.

58. Robert D. Putnam, *Bowling Alone: The Collapse and Revival of American Community* (New York: Simon and Schuster, 2000); Theda Skocpol, *Diminished Democracy: From Membership to Management in American Civic Life* (Norman: University of Oklahoma Press, 2003).

59. Morris P. Fiorina, "Extreme Voices: A Dark Side of Civic Engagement," in *Civic Engagement in American Democracy,* eds. Theda Skocpol and Morris Fiorina (Washington, D.C.: Brookings Institution, 1999).

60. J. Eric Oliver, *Democracy in Suburbia* (Princeton: Princeton University Press, 2001), 57.

61. Ibid.; James G. Gimpel, J. Celeste Lay, and Jason E. Schuknecht, *Cultivating Democracy: Civic Environments and Political Socialization in America* (Washington, D.C.: Brookings Institution, 2003).

62. Frank R. Baumgartner and Beth L. Leech, *Basic Interests: The Importance of Groups in Politics and in Political Science* (Princeton: University of Princeton Press, 1998).

SUGGESTED READING

Berry, Jeffrey M., Kent E. Portney, and Ken Thomson. *The Rebirth of Urban Democracy.* Washington, D.C.: Brookings Institution, 1993.

Browning, Rufus P., Dale R. Marshall, and David H. Tabb. *Protest Is Not Enough.* Berkeley: University of California Press, 1984.

Dahl, Robert A. *Who Governs? Democracy and Power in an American City.* New Haven: Yale University Press, 1961.

Logan, John R., and Harvey L. Molotch. *Urban Fortunes: The Political Economy of Place.* Berkeley: University of California Press, 1987.

Peterson, Paul E. *City Limits.* Chicago: University of Chicago Press, 1981.

Stone, Clarence N. *Regime Politics: Governing Atlanta 1946–1988.* Lawrence: University of Kansas Press, 1989.

chapter 36

Lobbying in the American Style around the World

by Conor McGrath

IN THE EARLY 1980S THE EUROPEAN Commission sought to improve the rights of employees. The commission proposed what was known as the Vredeling directive, under which multinational corporations would be obliged to consult their European subsidiaries about future business plans. The European Council of American Chambers of Commerce, known as AmCham, launched an "all out attack" on the directive, flying in "an airplane of Washington lawyers to confront Eurocrats and threaten U.S. retaliatory action."[1] The result was disastrous for U.S. interests, and created a lasting difficulty for American companies in Brussels. AmCham learned the lessons of this fiasco—to the point that today it is regarded as one of the most effective lobbying organizations in Brussels—but the episode illustrates that lobbying styles do differ around the world.

While superficially the lobbying industry in the European Union (EU) looks quite similar to its Washington counterpart, under the surface there are definite differences. Many of the American interests that began to lobby overseas starting in the 1980s assumed their Washington-tested tactics would work as well elsewhere. They found, at a cost, that this is not so. To take one very basic difference, the legislative process in Washington makes it easier to kill a legislative proposal than to proactively get a bill passed; by contrast, in Brussels, once twenty-seven national governments have painstakingly arrived at a consensus on an issue, they are very reluctant to reconsider that position.

It is not a novel idea to note the paradox that although more is known about interest groups in the United States than in any other political system, America is an exceptional rather than a typical case. Lobbying *is* different in the United States for reasons of historical constitutionalism, scope and scale, political culture, and institutional design. A point made much less frequently, however, is that lobbying is different everywhere, for similar reasons. Each nation has an exceptional interest group system. That is not to say that lobbying techniques and tactics are not similar in most locations, for they are, and increasingly so. In every interest group community—to greater or lesser extents and to greater or lesser degrees of effectiveness—lobbyists talk directly to policymakers, join coalitions, stimulate grassroots efforts, undertake policy research and frame policy issues, use the media to advance issues, and so on. These activities, if not entirely universal, are quite common. What is exceptional about every lobbying environment is the political, cultural, and institutional framework within which those ubiquitous activities occur.[2]

Consider the range of entry points by which lobbyists can access the policymaking process, the funding of political parties and electoral campaigns, the autonomy and expertise of bureaucracies, term limits on elected officeholders, and the capacity of the judicial system to challenge official decisions. All these factors, and more, determine the scope and effectiveness of interest group behavior in any given political system. In the United States the right to lobby is a constitutional right—based on the freedoms to petition government for the redress of grievances and to join associations. Moreover, the U.S. Supreme Court has held political contributions are a form of protected speech. By contrast, lobbying continues to be less accepted in France even today, partly due to laws that were in place between 1791 and 1901 that severely limited freedom of association, or what legislation termed "intermediary interests" coming between the individual and the state. Just as relatively widespread perceptions in many East European nations that political participation is ineffective can be viewed as a "hangover" from the communist era, so too can the common suspicion of lobbying in France be partly attributed to the enduring effect of these laws on the development of political culture there. Such national differences make it impossible to generalize about the actual role of interest groups. Every political system is distinct, and so every lobbying or interest representation system is different. But it is certain that institutional arrangements matter enormously to lobbying behavior.

This chapter begins by examining a range of factors that affect how lobbying practices develop in any particular

CULTURAL AND POLITICAL INFLUENCES ON LOBBYING PRACTICES

Cultural

- America is often described as a "nation of joiners," a predilection toward collective (and self-interested) action noted in 1835 by Alexis de Tocqueville, who was struck even then by the prevalence of "associations" in American political culture. In many East European and Latin American nations today, the relatively recent experience of living under dictatorial regimes accounts for much greater reluctance by many people to join advocacy groups.

- There is substantially greater and more regular movement of people among the business, official, and political worlds in the United States than in most other nations, where the "industry of politics" is not yet so well developed, although France and Japan are notable exceptions to this rule.

- National capitals in which the political, media, and business elites are all present can affect lobbying practices, but not all capitals are designed that way. Although New York and Los Angeles are clearly important cities in their own right, more organizations are headquartered or permanently staffed in Washington, D.C. In contrast, Brussels has a tremendous concentration of the European political class, but relatively few media or business leaders, and Canberra is a town largely built around government, but business and media firms are based primarily in Sydney and Melbourne. The geographical separation can help lobbying agencies to recruit clients who want to hire advisers "on the ground," but also make grassroots lobbying techniques more difficult as people may have to travel considerable distances to lobby politicians in person.

Political

- Money in the political process has a direct impact on lobbying activities. Its most obvious manifestation is in campaign contributions to politicians from interest groups. Political advertising in the United States is bought on a commercial basis in the same way that TV ads for breakfast cereal are bought, and as a consequence election campaigns are extremely expensive affairs that oblige candidates and parties to raise substantial funds from organized interests. By contrast, in the United Kingdom each political party is allocated a certain amount of free public service airtime each year, and the amounts that parties are permitted to spend on election campaigns are both regulated and set at relatively low levels.

- Moreover, in America, money tends to flow from interest groups to government in the form of campaign contributions; this position is largely reversed in many other political systems where funds are provided by government to interest groups. In Brussels the European Commission has been known to encourage financially the creation of consultative bodies made up of outside interests. In other nations, such as Germany, government contracts out the provision of some social welfare programs to organized interests and pays them to undertake that work.

- There is an emphasis in many nations—particularly in smaller countries and in those that have undergone relatively recent transitions to democracy—on the traditional notion of lobbying individual policymakers through personal contact. Although that certainly is done in the United States, it is also accompanied there by more sophisticated public and media campaigning around issues.

- A much greater diversity of political and ideological views held by parliamentarians is evident in most nations than is true in the United States; in many countries, having five or six major parties is not uncommon, and they may well span a spectrum encompassing greens, fascists, communists, liberals, conservatives, and regional interests.

nation. It then details some of the most common U.S. lobbying tactics and techniques and considers how these activities are undertaken elsewhere.

FACTORS INFLUENCING LOBBYING BEHAVIOR

Each nation has its own legal and informal "rules" that determine how lobbyists can operate. There is a great deal of literature on individual political systems, but no cohesive body of comparative research analyzes lobbying and interest groups across a number of nations.[3] Some of the most significant factors are discussed below, with examples from a range of countries.

The structure of the U.S. government—with its separation of powers, checks and balances, and federalism—ensures that interest groups can utilize multiple entry points into the policymaking process. In *Federalist* 10 James Madison noted the inevitability of what he termed "factions"—essentially interest groups such as farmers and merchants—and asserted that the proposed Constitution would control factions. In reality, as we see every day, the United States in some ways now resembles a government of interest groups, by interest groups, for interest groups: Woodrow Wilson (the only American president to have been a political science professor and whose own scholarship dealt in part with lobbying) declared in a 1912 campaign speech, "The government of the United States is a foster child of the special interests."[4]

Although it is often remarked that the United States presents an ideal political system for interest groups, there are systems in which organized interests are even more intimately intertwined with government. The organized interest system stands at the very heart of politics in Macao, a special administrative region of China. There, groups receive substantial financial subventions from government and provide the most important channel of political participation. Macao's chief executive is, in fact, elected not

INSTITUTIONAL FACTORS THAT INFLUENCE LOBBYING PRACTICES

■ The relationships between the various branches of government in any nation have a fundamental impact on how lobbyists operate. The dominance of the executive in Canada, Japan, and the United Kingdom naturally means that the bulk of public policy is conceived by ministers and officials and therefore interest groups focus much of their attention on the government rather than on the parliament. Where legislatures are more powerful, as in the United States, groups devote more resources to lobbying their elected representatives.

■ Interest groups that wish to become "insiders" (regularly and quietly consulted by government in the policy formulation process) may decide to emphasize direct advocacy rather than very public and vocal grassroots or media campaigning and can feel constrained from publicly opposing government policy. Executive-dominated systems may find it possible to "capture" interest groups by inhibiting them from employing tactics that could jeopardize their long-term relationship with policymakers.

■ Most national parliaments have more internal party discipline than is the case in the United States, and parliamentarians have a greater sense of belonging to their party than members of Congress do. Because American politicians are much less reliant on a party machine for their election and career progression, they have greater latitude to vote as they choose rather than as their party whips dictate. Washington lobbyists therefore must seek to convince politicians on an individual basis, while their counterparts in other nations may be able to persuade a single minister whose party will be able to turn out hundreds of votes in the parliament.

■ Transparency varies from system to system. Some institutions are more secretive than others (notably, the European Council of Ministers operates largely behind closed doors) and so can be harder to lobby.

■ Corporatist systems in which major interest groups are given some formal consultative role in the policymaking process clearly afford those groups significant privilege.

■ A federal structure of government, as in the United States, clearly allows groups to access government at many different levels to promote their interests, while more centralized systems (such as authoritarian and theocratic regimes) offer fewer venues for lobbyists.

through direct democracy, but through an election committee that is itself largely elected by interest groups. Additionally, interest group leaders occupy almost all the seats on Macao's Executive Council.[5]

Examining another factor, that of lobbying regulation, the presence or absence of a regulatory regime conditions the activities of lobbyists. Indeed, that is the fundamental purpose of such regulation. One can see an extraordinary spectrum in this regard. In most nations around the world, lobbying is entirely unregulated (including in Latin America and Africa, but also in long-established democracies such as India, Ireland, Japan, and Spain). Tentative steps have been taken in the United Kingdom (UK), where some lobbyists have attempted to exercise self-regulation, and in the EU, which recently introduced a voluntary and rather loosely defined model of regulation. There are also those nations, such as Lithuania and Poland, that have enacted lobbying reforms with significant flaws in their drafting and implementation so that the reforms are not entirely rigorous. A small number of nations (Australia, Canada, and the United States) have quite precise and strict statutory regulation of lobbying.[6]

It is worth noting that many (unregulated) Latin American lobbyists may behave with utter propriety while some U.S. lobbyists will deliberately break every rule. Regulation can only retrospectively punish corruption rather than entirely prevent it, as the Jack Abramoff affair in the United States demonstrated. Nevertheless, it remains true that regulation varies enormously around the world and that those variations shape the general pattern of lobbying behavior. Lobbying is different in the UK as compared with Brazil, Lithuania, or the United States, in part because of the different modes of regulation.

Another conditioning factor, the nature of the state-civil society relationship, further illustrates the point. EU institutions combine both a philosophical belief in the virtue of public participation and engagement with a practical need to lean on the expertise of outside groups in formulating policy. In France there is an ingrained tradition of state authoritarianism and a more conflictual and splintered relationship between the state and private actors, which contrasts with the German corporatist tradition of formal involvement with policy institutions by external interests. As the nations of Central and Eastern Europe have transitioned toward democracy, many initially developed corporatist-style arrangements that encouraged the formation of sectoral associations enjoying a monopoly on interest representation in their area. A more recent trend toward pluralist competition between associations is becoming apparent, for example, in Croatia and Hungary. In a different vein, most Latin American nations were actively hostile to the emergence of interest groups until relatively recently.

THE FUNDAMENTALS OF LOBBYING ACTIVITY AROUND THE GLOBE

Despite these national differences, a number of similar lobbying activities are undertaken in most nations around the world. Tactics may be used in greater or lesser extents in particular countries for the reasons noted in the box above, but the repertoire of techniques available to lobbyists is similar everywhere. One constant worth noting is that public perceptions of lobbying and lobbyists are universally poor. Although little empirical evidence in this regard has been gathered, it is clear anecdotally that ordinary citizens instinctively mistrust lobbying and have as their default position the belief that lobbying is illegitimate, seeking to further privilege already well-resourced groups at the expense of the public interest.[7]

Direct Advocacy

Personal contact between a lobbyist and a legislator is a crucial element of the lobbying process in every political system. Ultimately, the effectiveness of a lobbying campaign depends in large measure on the personal relationships between interest representatives and public representatives. The extent to which lobbyists interact directly with policymakers, however, varies from nation to nation. In-house lobbyists everywhere will always be highly involved in advocacy, but contract lobbyists often say that this is something they do relatively infrequently, instead preferring that their client communicates with politicians and civil servants, while the hired lobbyist takes a secondary role (deciding who should be approached, with what arguments, and effecting introductions between the principals).

Most lobbyists in Washington personally and regularly engage with legislators and administration officials, although it is possible that this practice will diminish somewhat over time, depending on the long-term implications of President Barack Obama's 2009 ban on administration officials meeting with registered federal lobbyists to discuss projects to be funded by his almost $800 billion economic stimulus package. Although this policy was later softened, it may convince some U.S. lobbyists that their clients should in the future be more active in lobbying exercises.[8] Direct representation is quite accepted in Brussels, though it is still significantly less routine than in Washington. The size of the European Union, coupled with the fact that few major companies or organizations are headquartered in Brussels, means that clients are simply not on hand to conduct their own lobbying on a day-to-day basis, and because EU officials need to maintain regular contact with interests, this vacuum is filled by contract lobbyists. In the UK, lobbyists generally meet personally with policymakers much less frequently, as politicians and officials have a decided preference for dealing direct with an organization rather than with its hired agents. And in Israel, formal advocacy is relatively rare and unsystematic, while in Japan direct advocacy is generally left by individual companies to their trade associations. In short, the American pattern undergoes substantial modification, depending on circumstances.

Coalitions

Lobbying coalitions develop when groups with a common interest in a particular policy outcome cooperate with each other (generally on a short-term temporary basis) to work for its advancement. Participation in coalitions is one of the most common activities in U.S. lobbying, with surveys indicating that upwards of 80 percent to 90 percent of lobbyists regularly take part in coalitions.[9] Perhaps the defining value of lobbying coalitions is that by uniting around an issue, they can better enable organizations to present their case in terms of the broad public interest, rather than of each group's narrow interest. Coalitions can also prove useful as far as the targets of their activity are concerned. Decision makers are able to communicate and negotiate efficiently

Criticizing the relationship between the European Union Trade Commission and the lobbying organization BusinessEurope, two protesters hold a mock wedding in Brussels outside of the European Commission headquarters.

with a coalition, and coalitions reduce risk for decision makers.

Coalitions have long been a feature of lobbying in Washington and the American states, but they are less common in other nations, although their usage appears to be growing in London and Brussels. At the EU level they tend to differ from American counterparts, in that coalitions in Brussels are often permanent alliances between groups, rather than *ad hoc* arrangements. For example, the pharmaceutical industry's national trade associations in all twenty-seven member states may form a pan-European association in Brussels to work at the EU level. Commonly known as European Federations, these coalitions constitute one of the most prevalent of all lobbying models in Brussels. Given that these federations tend to represent entire industries, however, it is still relatively rare that they would feel the need to reach out more widely to other groups to create a temporary coalition on a particular policy. Studies have shown that perhaps only 10 percent to 20 percent of Brussels lobbyists have experience in short-term coalitions in the American mode.[10] In a number of recent or developing democracies (such as Argentina and South Africa), nongovernmental organizations (NGOs) have successfully built coalitions by drawing on the expertise and experience of established transnational networks. In 2000 several global charities, including Oxfam and the Environmental Justice Foundation, helped to bring together local groups into a new body, the Fisheries Action Coalition Team, to campaign on behalf of fishing communities in Cambodia.

Grassroots Lobbying

In practical terms, grassroots lobbying involves an interest group persuading its own members or supporters to lobby politicians by contacting the lawmakers to urge that they support or oppose a policy proposal (see Chapter 28). Grassroots campaigns often involve large, national issues that could affect many people. Therefore, some organizations have automatic advantages.

- They may be based on a mass individual membership and therefore have ready access to large numbers of potential activists. A prime example is the AARP, which brings around 40 million members to its campaigns to improve the quality of life of those over age fifty.

- Their membership may be geographically widespread and provide legitimate access to large numbers of legislators. The American Federation of Teachers has close to 3,000 local chapters, with members in every community across the United States.

- Their issue may be one that directly affects large numbers of people or inspires intense commitment by many. Examples are health care, abortion, and gun rights.

The fundamental reason why grassroots campaigns are so common and can be so effective in the United States is that they connect to the electoral imperative that drives politicians in the U.S. institutional framework. Crudely put, elections and grassroots lobbying both involve motivated and active voters. Grassroots efforts are utilized in other nations, but nowhere are they either as prevalent or as sophisticated as in the United States. As grassroots campaigns are based on the responsiveness of politicians to their constituents, it is certainly true that a more rigid party structure and more rigorous party discipline, as in Britain, makes for a less fertile environment for grassroots campaigns than is the case in the United States. Yet even in the UK, there are marginal seats, and a correlation between the marginality of a constituency and the effectiveness of grassroots lobbying in the UK was noted more than fifty years ago (with legislation that had been the subject of grassroots campaigns receiving significant levels of support from politicians in marginal districts).[11] Despite this, British interest groups generally fail to devise effective grassroots strategies. Some groups commonly ask their supporters to sign a petition or to mail a postcard to their member of Parliament (MP), but rarely do they organize a more structured and nuanced letter-writing campaign. Similarly, they may ask supporters to rally outside Parliament, but rarely train their members in how to lobby or encourage them to seek a meeting with their MP.

Grassroots activity is even less sophisticated in the EU, where one study suggests that only 1 percent of Brussels lobbyists have encouraged their organizations' members to participate in grassroots lobbying campaigns.[12] This finding points toward a hypothesis that grassroots lobbying will be low in those political systems that have relatively weak levels of democratic accountability and where ordinary voters see institutions of government as unresponsive. Conversely, grassroots lobbying may be quite common and useful in political systems where personal relationships with legislators are extremely important and policy decisions can depend as much on contacts as on sophisticated interest group communities. So, for example, one survey reveals that almost all (94 percent) of respondents reported that grassroots lobbying is undertaken in Lithuania.[13] Although grassroots efforts are reasonably common in Australia and Canada, most nations probably see the use of grassroots lobbying on a sporadic rather than regular basis. Almost 80 percent of Danish interest groups report occasionally encouraging their supporters to contact decision makers, but less than 5 percent of groups do so very often.[14]

Mass Rallies/Protests

On occasion, a lobbying tactic is more common in the rest of the world than in the United States. Although large-scale rallies and protests take place in America—including the

Cadbury employees gathered outside of Britain's Houses of Parliament in February 2010. The workers were lobbying Parliament to act on their behalf to keep jobs and factories running in Britain after the company was purchased by Kraft Foods.

1963 March on Washington for Jobs and Freedom, the 1999 "Battle of Seattle" protesting against World Trade Organization policies, and the 2011 demonstrations against Wisconsin governor Scott Walker's antiunion legislation—they are tactics that U.S. interest groups are usually reluctant to employ. In many other nations, organized interests regularly (in some cases, routinely) generate popular protests in which tens of thousands of people take to the streets in an effort to pressure government. Throughout Latin America, rallies are an accepted tactic, and the same is true in France and much of Africa. A 2003 rally protesting the war in Iraq was the largest ever seen on the streets of London, with around 1.5 million marchers. Other sizable rallies were held in the UK in 2010 and 2011 against public expenditure cuts. And 2011 will long be remembered as the year in which large-scale revolutionary demonstrations, known as the "Arab Spring," spread across North Africa and the Middle East. In a sense, mass rallies are the crudest form of grassroots lobbying: they provide a graphic demonstration to government of the strength of public opinion as regards a particular policy. It is true, however, that particularly in Latin America, but in other nations (such as Nepal) as well, interest groups regularly organize protests as an end in themselves rather than as a carefully thought-out element of a broader lobbying effort. While a rally may provide a highly visible and symbolic event that allows an interest group to appear active and militant, in the end it may have little impact on public policy—indeed, all too often rallies take place precisely because groups have been unable to influence government.[15]

Media Relations/Advertising

American lobbyists are particularly aware of the importance of integrating their private lobbying messages with mass media publicity and public relations. The idea of newspaper advertorials (opinion pieces paid for as advertising) as a vehicle by which companies can spread their views on policy issues is by now well established in the United States. Mobil Oil began running ads on a weekly basis in the *New York Times* in 1974 as a way to influence elite opinion in the political, media, and business worlds in favor of the corporation's public policy preferences. This technique has now morphed into an industry, and issue advocacy advertising by interest groups continues to increase. Issue advertising remains a fairly limited concept in most other nations. Some interest groups may from time to time place advocacy ads in publications that policymakers read, but these ads are not used as a tool by which policy issues are framed for the general public.

Public relations (PR) and lobbying are closely connected in the United States, with most lobbying organizations acutely conscious of the need to deal proactively with the media. This integrated approach to communication has now spread to most other liberal democracies, as lobbyists seek to influence public opinion through the mass media in support of their lobbying campaigns. One notable exception is the EU; in Brussels, PR tends to be accorded a relatively low priority, partly because the only media outlet widely read by policymakers across all twenty-seven member states is the *Financial Times* and partly because the complex and technical nature of many EU regulations makes it difficult for lobbyists to generate a high media profile for their issues. Too often, even in well-developed Western democracies, a media relations component of a lobbying effort means that the interest group has issued a couple of press releases, but in some nations lobbyists do engage proactively in sustained and strategic national and local media campaigns. Chilean NGOs in social areas such as child welfare have embraced the media as a forum for raising consciousness, and lobbying campaigns in Australia have begun to include PR and media components on a much greater scale than before.

Electoral Campaigns

Perhaps the most controversial aspect of interest groups' lobbying activities is their involvement in election campaigns. Clearly, elections are of crucial importance to organized interests because they determine who holds office and therefore what policy agenda will be pursued. But lobbyists can too often and too easily be tarred with the accusation that they subvert democracy, particularly in terms of the money they contribute to candidates and parties. Financial contributions by lobbyists and interest groups occur in many countries, but generally on a much more modest scale than in the United States. In many nations, groups will buy tables at events held by political parties or have an exhibit stall at a major party convention, but making or arranging substantial campaign donations is not something lobbyists in most countries do. Indeed, in many countries—for example, France, Malaysia, and the UK—sizable contributions are prohibited by law, and other nations—such as Australia, Canada, and Italy—are more permissive but still require donations to parties to be declared transparently.

What generally goes unacknowledged in media reporting of interest groups' electoral donations is that money is by no means the most valuable resource that groups can contribute to candidates. Many interest groups in the United States owe their influence not to the cash they can provide, but rather to the number of voters in each district that they can deliver to a candidate. This is particularly important because U.S. political parties are relatively weak at the local level and because interest groups are able to marshal their members into doing much of the necessary mechanics of an election campaign, such as direct mail, "get out the vote" efforts, distributing yard signs, and so on. In addition, interest groups can potentially influence significant numbers of votes by endorsing one candidate over another and encouraging their own members and supporters to vote for that person. This practice is now beginning to spread around the world: in 2007 the two major party leaders in Australia addressed representatives of Christian churches in an attempt to win their endorsement during a general election campaign.

CONCLUSION

Interest groups exist in all political systems and undoubtedly exercise a degree of influence over public policy. Moreover, they tend to draw on broadly similar techniques and activities, which have generally been developed and perfected in the United States. But the extent to which particular lobbying tactics are employed in any given nation, and the effectiveness of each tactic, do vary from country to country. Political, cultural, and institutional contexts ensure that each nation presents lobbyists with a unique interest group system. So, even though the U.S. interest group system is not transferable to other countries in its entirety, some elements of U.S. interest group activity are being adapted (rather than adopted wholesale) by lobbyists in other jurisdictions. Relatively little comparative work on lobbying is currently available, but there is by now a sizable body of work that examines interest group behavior in a range of individual nations, making it possible to begin the analysis of lobbying activity across nations.[16] And there do still remain political systems that are so dissimilar to that of the United States (such as China and Iran) that it is problematic to pinpoint evidence of lobbying convergence.

In very simplistic terms, it appears that "insider" lobbying (or direct contact) is more or less common to all political systems, but that "outsider" lobbying (such as grassroots efforts, media relations, and advocacy advertising) is substantially less frequently employed outside the United States. The reason may be that a nation's institutional framework renders a lobbying technique inappropriate or ineffectual; in other cases, the variation may be due to cultural factors. The relative reluctance of citizens in East European nations such as Estonia and Latvia to join associations is due in part to a lingering sense from their recent communist experience that government is unresponsive.

One current trend worth noting is that political systems and political cultures change over time, and we are beginning to see signs around the world of a convergence of lobbying and advocacy practices. Slowly—but surely—lobbyists in a diverse range of nations are finding ways of employing ever more sophisticated techniques. A good illustration lies in the EU, which has traditionally been centered around private direct lobbying of political and bureaucratic elites. More recently, new patterns of interest group activity have emerged, often driven by nonprofits rather than by corporations, involving grassroots, coalitions, and public opinion.[17] In another context, some interest groups in Tanzania have developed relatively quickly a quite comprehensive range of lobbying tactics, including direct advocacy, researching and drafting legislation, serving on advisory committees, building policy coalitions, and undertaking PR campaigns.[18] American lobbying techniques and skills are being adapted and modified so that they become suitable for use in other nations, which should have the effect of stimulating a new wave of comparative studies.

★

NOTES

1. Maria Green Cowles, "The EU Committee of AmCham: The Powerful Voice of American Business in Brussels," *Journal of European Public Policy* 3, 3 (1996): 339–358.

2. Clive S. Thomas and Ronald J. Hrebenar, "Comparing Lobbying Across Liberal Democracies: Problems, Approaches, and Initial Findings," paper presented at the annual meeting of the American Political Science Association (1996). Also see Cornelia Woll, "Lobbying in the European Union: From *Sui Generis* to a Comparative Perspective," *Journal of European Public Policy* 13, 3 (2006): 456–469.

3. There are some notable exceptions. See Gabriel A. Almond, "A Comparative Study of Interest Groups and the Political Process," *American Political Science Review* 52, 1 (1958): 270–282; Alan R. Ball and Frances Millard, *Pressure Politics in Industrial Societies* (Basingstoke: Macmillan, 1986); Graham K. Wilson, *Business and Politics: A Comparative Introduction*, 2nd ed. (Basingstoke: Macmillan, 1990); Ulrike Liebert, "Parliamentary Lobby Regimes," in *Parliaments and Majority Rule in Western Europe*, ed. Herbert Doring (Frankfurt: Campus Verlag, 1995), 407–447; Philip Norton, ed., *Parliaments and Pressure Groups in Western Europe* (London: Routledge, 1999); and Christine Mahoney, *Brussels Versus the Beltway* (Washington, D.C.: Georgetown University Press, 2008).

4. Woodrow Wilson, quoted in Karl Schriftgiesser, *The Lobbyists: The Art and Business of Influencing Lawmakers* (Boston: Little, Brown, 1951), 35.

5. Bill K. P. Chou, "Interest Groups in Macao: From Corporatism to Cronyism," in *Interest Groups and Lobbying in Latin America, Africa, the Middle East, and Asia*, ed. Conor McGrath (Lewiston, N.Y.: Edwin Mellen Press, 2009), 317–339.

6. Raj Chari, John Hogan, and Gary Murphy, *Regulating Lobbying: A Global Comparison* (Manchester: Manchester University Press, 2010); Craig Holman and Thomas Susman, *Self-Regulation and Regulation of the Lobbying Profession* (Paris: Organisation for Economic Co-operation and Development, 2009); and OECD, *Governance Arrangements to Ensure Transparency in Lobbying: Comparative Overview* (Paris: Organisation for Economic Co-operation and Development, 2006).

7. A 2007 Gallup poll in the United States found that lobbyists were the lowest ranked when people were questioned about the ethics of a range of professional groups. Only 5 percent of respondents thought that lobbyists' honesty and ethics were high or very high, while 58 percent said they were low or very low. Gallup, "Lobbyists Debut at Bottom of Honesty and Ethics List," December 10, 2007, www.gallup.com/poll/103123/lobbyists-debut-honesty-ethics-list.aspx.

8. Office of Management and Budget, "Interim Guidance Regarding Communications with Registered Lobbyists about Recovery Act Funds," memorandum M-09-16, April 7, 2009, www.whitehouse.gov/omb/assets/memoranda_fy2009/m-09-16.pdf. Not coincidentally, the other important lesson Washington lobbyists learned from President Obama's repeated denunciations of their industry is that it is advantageous, if at all possible under the law, not to be officially registered as a federal lobbyist. By some estimates, the number of registered lobbyists has fallen by close to 50 percent since the start of 2009.

9. Surveys of lobbying activity, including coalitions, are available in many academic studies. See, for example, Kay Lehman Schlozman and John T. Tierney, *Organized Interests and American Democracy* (New York: Harper and Row, 1986); John P. Heinz, Edward O. Laumann, Robert L. Nelson, and Robert H. Salisbury, *The Hollow Core* (Cambridge: Harvard University Press, 1997); Anthony J. Nownes and Patricia Freeman, "Interest Group Activity in the States," *Journal of Politics* 60, 1 (1998): 86–112; Ken Kollman, *Outside Lobbying* (Princeton: Princeton University Press, 1998); and on the United Kingdom, Michael Rush, ed., *Parliament and Pressure Politics* (Oxford: Clarendon Press, 1990).

10. Mahoney, *Brussels Versus the Beltway.*

11. J. D. Stewart, *British Pressure Groups: Their Role in Relation to the House of Commons* (London: Oxford University Press, 1958).

12. Mahoney, *Brussels Versus the Beltway.*

13. Ronald J. Hrebenar, Clive S. Thomas, Courtney H. McBeth, and Bryson B. Morgan, "The Problems of Developing Interest Group Politics in Post-Communist Eastern Europe: Learning from Lithuania," in *Interest Groups and Lobbying in Europe*, ed. Conor McGrath (Lewiston, N.Y.: Edwin Mellen Press, 2009), 235–259.

14. Anne Binderkrantz, "Interest Group Strategies: Navigating Between Privileged Access and Strategies of Pressure," *Political Studies* 53, 4 (2005): 694–715.

15. Susan Eckstein, ed., *Power and Popular Protest: Latin American Social Movements* (Berkeley: University of California Press, 2001).

16. One useful attempt to pull together a conceptual framework by which interest group lobbying can be compared between nations is found in *First World Interest Groups*, ed. Clive S. Thomas (Westport, Conn.: Greenwood Press, 1993).

17. Marco Althaus, "Discovering Our (Corporate) Grassroots: European Advocacy 2.0," in *Routledge Handbook of Political Management*, ed. Dennis W. Johnson (New York: Routledge, 2009), 477–494; Simon Titley, "How Political and Social Change Will Transform the EU Public Affairs Industry," *Journal of Public Affairs* 3, 1 (2003): 83–89.

18. Ginger L. Elliott-Teague, "Public Interest Group Behavior in Tanzania," in *Interest Groups and Lobbying in Latin America, Africa, the Middle East, and Asia*, 139–160.

SUGGESTED READING

Althaus, Marco. "Discovering Our (Corporate) Grassroots: European Advocacy 2.0." In *Routledge Handbook of Political Management.* Ed. Dennis W. Johnson. New York: Routledge, 2009.

Mahoney, Christine. *Brussels Versus the Beltway.* Washington, D.C.: Georgetown University Press, 2008.

Mahoney, Christine, and Frank Baumgartner. "Converging Perspectives on Interest Group Research in Europe and America." *West European Politics* 31, 6 (2008): 1253–1273.

McGrath, Conor, ed. *Interest Groups and Lobbying in Europe.* Lewiston, N.Y.: Edwin Mellen Press, 2009.

———, ed. *Interest Groups and Lobbying in Latin America, Africa, the Middle East, and Asia.* Lewiston, N.Y.: Edwin Mellen Press, 2009.

———, ed. *Interest Groups and Lobbying in the United States and Comparative Perspectives.* Lewiston, N.Y.: Edwin Mellen Press, 2009.

Thomas, Clive S., ed. *Research Guide to U.S. and International Interest Groups.* Westport, Conn.: Praeger, 2004.

★ ILLUSTRATION CREDITS AND ACKNOWLEDGMENTS

1. The Evolution of Groups and Lobbying In 18th Century America

12 Library of Congress 15 The Granger Collection, NYC 16 Library of Congress

2. Interest Groups And Lobbying In The 19Th Century: De Tocqueville's America

23 The Granger Collection, NYC 27 Library of Congress 29 Library of Congress 30 Library of Congress

3. Groups in Industrializing America and The Origins of Popular Interest Group Politics

37 Library of Congress 39 Library of Congress 42 Library of Congress

4. Group Formation and Maintenance

53 Library of Congress 56 Roger L. Wollenberg/UPI /Landov

6. Interest Groups and Social Movements

82 AP/Alex Brandon

7. Economic Models of Interest Groups and Lobbying

89 The Granger Collection, NYC

8. The Growth of Government and The Expansion of Organized Interests

103 AP/Bizuayehu Tesfaye 107 AP/Susan Walsh

9. Interest Groups and The Courts

116 AP/J. Scott Applewhite 119 AP/Bob Bird 120 Associated Press

10. Interest Groups and The Executive Branch

128 Library of Congress 129 Richard Clement/Reuters /Landov 133 AP/Gerald Herbert

11. Interest Groups and Parties: The Politics of Representation

149 AP/Susan Walsh 151 David R. Lutman/Reuters /Landov 152 AP/Jason Redmond 157 iStockphoto/Alan Eisen

12. Agriculture

164 Library of Congress 166 Library of Congress

13. Business and Organized Labor

174 Library of Congress 175 Library of Congress 175 Library of Congress 176 Library of Congress 179 David Jolkovski/ The Jersey Journal/Landov

14. Defense and Homeland Security

195 The Dwight D. Eisenhower Presidential Library and Museum 197 Dept. of Defense/ Petty Officer 3rd Class Scott Pittman, U.S. Navy 198 Jeff Malet Photography/Newscom 199 U.S. Army photo/ Spc. Emily Walter 204 AP/Ed Andrieski

15. Civil Rights

210 AP/Houston Chronicle, Ted Rozumalski 211 Carl Iwasaki/Time & Life Pictures/Getty Images

212 Yoichi Okamoto/LBJ Library and Museum 213 AFP/Getty Images 214 David Fenton/Getty Images

16. Issue Advocacy Groups and Think Tanks

225 AP/Dennis Cook 229 AP/HF 235 Mark Wilson/UPI /Landov

17. Religious Interest Groups

242 Reuters/Rick Wilking/Landov 245 AP/ Evan Vucci 247 AP/White House, Krisanne Johnson

18. Women's and Feminist Movements and Organizations

Library of Congress 253 Library of Congress 256 AP/JLP

19. Public Interest Groups

263 AP/Ducks Unlimited, Kelli Alfano 266 AP/PRNewsFoto/Amnesty International

20. Professional Associations

277 Library of Congress 278 Associated Press 279 iStockphoto/Chris Schmidt

21. Elementary and Secondary Education

289 Associated Press

22. Energy and The Environment

Library of Congress 301 AP/Jim McKnight

25. Lobbying and Legislative Strategy

337 AP/Lenny Ignelzi

26. Lobbyists: Who Are They? What Do They Do?

349 AP/Susan Walsh 350 The Granger Collection, NYC 354 AP/Susan Walsh

27. Lobbying: Techniques and Impact

361 Congressional Quarterly/Newscom 363 AP Photo/Susan Walsh 366 Reproduced courtesy of the American Petroleum Institute

28. Grassroots, Astroturf, and Internet Lobbying

372 Michael Reynolds/EPA /Landov 376 Sipa/AP Images

29. The First Amendment and The Regulation of Lobbying

385 AP Photo/Evan Vucci, File 387 AP Photo/Gerald Herbert

30. Interest Groups and Federal Campaigns Before The Federal Election Campaign Act

395 Library of Congress

31. Pacs, 527S, and other Groups in Congressional Elections

407 Roger L. Wollenberg/UPI /Landov

32. Interest Groups in Presidential Elections

421 Joshua Lott/Reuters /Landov 423 Christian Coalition

33. Regulating and Reforming Group-Based Electioneering

434 AP/Dennis Cook 436 Reuters/HO/ Swiftvets.com /Landov

34. Interest Groups and State Politics

446 AP/Mel Evans 447 Carol Highsmith/ Library of Congress 451 AP /Harry Cabluck

35. Local Interest Groups: Forgotten But Still Influential?

464 Gus Chan/The Plain Dealer /Landov

36. Lobbying in The American Style Around The World

470 AP/Yves Logghe 472 Toby Melville/ Reuters /Landov

INDEX

Abington School District v. Schempp (1963), 244
Abortion, 119, 120, 122, 148, 244, 409-410
Abramoff, Jack, 335, 337-338, 355-356, 359, 362, 386, 387
Academy for State and Local Government (ASLG), 312
Adams, John Quincy, 382
Adequate yearly progress (AYP), 290
Administrative Procedures Act (1946), 140
Advertisement:
- congressional elections, 405 (table), 408-409
- electioneering reform, 431-433, 434-441
- lobbying techniques, 342, 364-367
- *See also* Information management

Advisory Commission on Intergovernmental Relations (ACIR), 310
Aerojet & GenCorp Inc., 194 (table)
Afghanistan, 198, 199
African Americans:
- abolitionist movement, 24, 27, 29-31
- advocacy organizations (2010), 218 (table)
- civil rights groups, 209-210, 211-212, 213, 215, 216, 217, 218, 219, 220
- social movements, 81, 212-213
- *See also* Racial minorities

Agency model, 91
Agricultural Adjustment Act (1933), 165
Agricultural interest groups, 163-172
- agricultural census, 169, 174
- bipartisan policy, 165-167
- campaign contributions, 169 (table), 170 (table)
- commodity organizations, 166-167
- Democratic Party, 163, 164, 165-166, 167, 170
- electioneering development, 394
- Farm Bureau creation, 165
- future prospects, 170-171
- historical development, 164-167
- institutional factors, 168-170
- legislation, 165, 166, 167
- nineteenth-century associations, 32-33, 38, 164-165
- policy compromise, 166
- policy conflict, 165-166
- policy influence, 168-170
- policy reform, 167
- political districts, 169 (table)
- political economy, 168
- political factors, 168-170
- Republican Party, 163, 165-166, 167, 169, 170
- *See also specific organization*

Agricultural Subcommittee on House Appropriations, 168-169
Agriculture and Consumer Protection Act (1973), 167
Agriculture Committee, 167, 168-169
Alabama, 244, 445, 452, 460
Alaska, 452
Alito, Samuel A., Jr., 117 (table), 118
Alliance for New America, 406
Altria Group, 186 (table)
America Coming Together, 406
American Anti-Slavery Society (AASS), 29-30
American Association for Labor Legislation, 41
American Association of People with Disabilities, 284-285
American Association of Retired Persons (AARP):
- direct mail response, 55
- federal patronage, 108
- lobbying expenditures (1998-2009), 186 (table)
- lobbyists, 353, 354
- nonprofit tax status, 57
- organizational expansion, 108
- patronage theory, 53
- political debate (2010), 103

American Automobile Association, 261
American Bankers Association, 182, 186
American Bar Association:
- collective action, 51-52
- judicial system, 116-117
- Lexis-Nexis cites, 273 (figure)
- political expenditures (2007-2008), 276 (table)
- professional associations, 271, 272, 275, 278
- representational politics, 150
- Supreme Court nominations (1956-2010), 117 (table)
- tax deductions, 58

American Beverage Licenses, 404
American Bible Society, 23
American Board of Commissioners of Foreign Missions, 23
American Cancer Society, 109
American Center for Law and Justice (ACLJ), 245, 285
American Civil Liberties Union (ACLU), 262 (table)
- education, 285
- judicial system, 117, 119
- public interest organization, 54
- religious interest groups, 245
- tax status, 384

American Clean Energy and Security Act (2009), 375
American Conservative Union, 117-118
American Enterprise Institute (AEI), 223, 224, 226, 230, 231, 232, 233, 234-235, 285, 289
American Family Voices, 435 (table), 437
American Farm Bureau Federation, 38, 43, 107, 165-166, 168, 394
American Federalist, The, 395
American Federation of Labor (AFL), 32, 41, 42, 174-175, 394-396, 398
American Federation of Labor-Congress of Industrial Organizations (AFL-CIO), 81, 372, 400
- electioneering, 407, 421, 423, 425, 435 (table), 436, 437-438
- judicial system, 117
- organized labor, 175, 178, 179, 180, 183, 185-186, 188

American Federation of State, County, and Municipal Employees (AFSCME), 183, 184, 421, 422, 427, 437
American Federation of Teachers (AFT), 182, 284, 290, 422
American Forest and Paper Association, 107
American Heart Association, 109
American Home Missionary Society, 23
American Hospital Association, 186 (table)
American Institute of Architects, 276 (table)
American International Automobile Dealers Association, 58
American Iron and Steel Institute (AISI), 343
American Israel Public Affairs Committee (AIPAC), 324, 325, 327
American Legislative Exchange (ALEC), 313, 315
American Legislative Issues Campaign Exchange (ALICE), 313
American Library Association, 276 (table), 279
American Lung Association, 107
American Medical Association (AMA):
- collective action, 51-52
- economic models, 90, 94

electioneering development, 398
establishment, 42
grassroots lobbying, 373, 374
lobbying expenditures (1998-2009), 186 (table)
political expenditures (2007-2008), 276 (table)
professional associations, 271, 272-273, 274, 275-276, 277, 279-280
tax deductions, 58
American Motorcyclist Association, 262
American Nurses Association, 58
American Odd Fellows, 25
American Petroleum Institute, 107, 366
American Physical Society, 276 (table)
American Political Science Association, 272, 273 (figure), 275
American Political Science Review, 66-67
American Public Health Association, 276-277
American Revolution (1776), 15, 38
American Rights at Work, 184
American Rivers, 299, 300 (table), 302 (table)
American Security Council, 262 (table)
Americans for Divorce Reform, 262
Americans for Honesty on Issues, 405
Americans for Job Security, 183, 409, 435 (table), 438
Americans for Tax Reform, 262 (table), 265, 420, 421
American States and Cities (Gray and Eisinger), 459
American Sunday School Union, 23
American Temperance Society, 27, 28-29, 30
American Tract Society, 23
American Values, 422-423
America's Agenda: Health Care for Kids, 184
America Votes, 184, 425
Ames, Oakes, 26, 27
Amicus curiae briefs, 115-116, 119-120, 267, 268 (table), 286, 287, 312
Amnesty International, 261, 262 (table), 266
Ancient and Accepted Free Masons, 23, 25, 38
Ancient Order of B'nai B'rith, 25
Ancient Order of Hibernians, 25
Angola, 327
Anheuser-Busch, 327 (table)
Anthony, Susan B., 113
Anti-Masonic Party, 37
Anti-Saloon League (ASL), 396-397
Antitrust lobbying, 89, 93
Arctic National Wildlife Refuge (ANWR), 303
Argentina, 471
Arizona, 446
Armenia, 328
Armey, Dick, 82
Articles of Confederation, 15
Asian Pacific Americans, 81
Aspen Institute, 233
Association for Airline Passenger Rights, 265
Astroturf lobbying, 82, 363, 375, 379
A.T. Massey Coal Company, 118
Atheism, 239
Atomic Energy Commission, 297, 298
AT&T, 182, 186 (table)
Austin v. Michigan Chamber of Commerce (1990), 434
Australia, 323, 327, 469, 471, 473
Azerbaijan, 323, 325, 328

Bachrach, Peter, 67 (figure)
BAE Systems, 194 (table), 327 (table)
Baker, Bobby, 348-349
Baker, Charles D., 103
Bank of the United States, 23, 25
Baptist, 241, 243, 288
Baratz, Morton, 67 (figure)
Barksdale, Jim, 354
Basic Interests (Baumgartner and Leech), 67 (figure)
Bauer, Gary, 422-423
Baumgartner, Frank, 67 (figure)
Bechtel, 198
Beecher, Lyman, 28
Belgium, 327 (table)
Bell Helicopter, 195, 196-197, 198-199, 206n23
Benjamin, Brent, 118, 119
Bentley, Arthur, 49-50
Bernstein, Jared, 233
Biddle, Nicholas, 23-24
Biden, Joe, 419
Big Seven lobby:
homeland security, 202, 207n55
intergovernmental lobbying, 309, 310, 311, 312, 315, 316, 317
Bipartisan Campaign Reform Act (2002), 183, 388, 406-407, 408, 410, 415, 416, 424, 431, 433-434, 436, 439, 440
Blackmun, Harry, 117 (table)
Blades, Joan, 372-373
Blankenship, David, 361
Bloomberg News, 353
Blue Cross/Blue Shield, 186 (table)
Blue-green coalitions, 305
Board of Trade (London), 11, 12, 13, 14, 18
Boeing Company, 186 (table), 194 (table)
Bork, Robert, 116, 117-118, 123
Bossie, David, 385
Boundaries of Blackness (Cohen), 83
Boycotts, 95
Boyd, Wes, 372-373
Brandeis, Louis, 115, 116
Brandeis Brief, 115
Bread for the World, 240, 242, 243
Brennan, William, Jr., 117 (table), 278
Breyer, Stephen, 117 (table)
British Petroleum (BP), 295, 302, 303, 352
Brookings Institution, 223, 224, 225, 226, 227, 229-230, 231-232, 233, 234-236
Brown, Jerry, 152
Brownback, Sam, 419
Brown v. Board of Education (1954), 114, 119, 120, 211, 212, 284
Bryan, William Jennings, 164, 394, 395
Buckley v. Valeo (1976), 182, 387, 405, 432
Budget and Accounting Act (1921), 227
Bureau of National Affairs, 351
Burger, Warren, 117 (table)
Bush, George H. W., 246, 424
educational policy, 290
environmentalism, 298
foreign lobbying, 327
lobbyists, 355
Bush, George W., 56, 118
agricultural policy, 163, 172n10
educational policy, 286, 289, 290
environmentalism, 303, 304
grassroots lobbying, 376
homeland security, 201, 202, 204
interest group relations, 128, 129, 133, 134-135, 136, 137, 138
lobbying and legislative strategy, 339, 342
lobbyists, 354
national defense, 197
presidential elections, 422, 425, 427, 428
religious interest groups, 241-242, 245, 246, 247
representational politics, 158
think tanks, 234, 236
Business and organized labor, 173-192
business group development, 176-177
campaign contributions, 181-182
collective action, 173
Democratic Party, 175, 176, 178, 180-181, 182-183, 184-185, 186
education, 283-284, 290-291
electorate mobilization, 179-181
501(c) organizations, 183-184
527 organizations, 183-184
independent expenditures, 182-183
influential growth, 177-179
interest group defined, 178
labor group development, 174-176
legislation, 173, 175, 181, 183, 184, 186-187, 188
legislative action committees (LACs), 184-189
political action committees (PACs), 177, 180-1785
Republican Party, 175, 176-177, 180-181, 184
social movements, 175-176
state politics, 445, 446, 448 (table)
See also specific organization
Business-Industry Political Action Committee (BIPAC), 180-181, 398
Business Roundtable, 186 (table), 407, 435 (table), 438
By-product theory, 51-52, 55-57
Bystander effect, 464

Cadbury, 472
Cahill, Tim, 103
California, 176, 244, 275, 289, 352, 459
state politics, 445, 446, 447-448
California Bar Association, 278
California State Grange, 40-41
Call to Renewal, 242
Calogero, Pascal, 118
Calvert Cliffs Coordinating Committee v. U.S. Atomic Energy Commission (1971), 297, 298
Cambodia, 471
Campaign contributions:
agricultural interest groups, 169 (table), 170 (table)
business groups, 181-182
economic models, 92
First Amendment rights, 387-388
501(c) groups, 183-184
527 groups, 183-184
labor unions, 181-182
lobbying and legislative strategy, 336, 337-339
See also Congressional elections; Electioneering reform; Political action committees (PACs); Presidential elections; specific organization

Campaign Finance Institute, 183, 184, 408
Campaign Reform Project, 262 (table)
Canada, 323-324, 326, 327, 328, 469, 471, 473
Caperton V. Massey (2009), 118
Capitol Advantage, 377
Carnegie, Andrew, 175
Carnegie Endowment for International Peace, 224, 226, 233
Carpenter, Dan, 69
Carswell, G. Harrold, 116, 117 (table)
Carter, Jimmy:
  business and organized labor, 180
  electioneering development, 400-401
  environmentalism, 301
  interest group relations, 135, 136-137, 138
  intergovernmental lobbying, 312
  national defense, 196
  think tanks, 233
Carter Center, 233
Castro, Clarissa Martinez de, 82
Catalist, 425
Catholicism:
  education, 285
  religious interest groups, 25, 239, 240, 241, 243, 244-245, 246, 247
Cato Institute, 231, 233, 234, 235, 289
Center for American Progress (CAP), 233, 234, 289
Center for Auto Safety, 262 (table), 265
Center for Economic and Policy Research, 233
Center for Environmental Health and Justice (CEHJ), 299, 301
Center for Health, Environment, & Justice, 300 (table), 302 (table)
Center for Marine Conservation, 300 (table)
Center for Politics, 233
Center for Public Integrity, 101
Center for Responsive Politics (CRP):
  business and organized labor, 182, 184
  congressional elections, 405
  foreign lobbying, 322-323, 325
  intergovernmental lobbying, 313-314
  presidential elections, 424
  professional associations, 275
Center for Security Policy, 225, 233
Center for Strategic and International Studies (CSIS), 230, 232, 233
Center for Voting and Democracy, 262 (table)
Center on Budget and Policy Priorities (CBPP), 223, 226, 232, 233, 235-236
Central Pacific Railroad, 25
Change to Win (CtW), 178, 179, 180, 184, 185
Chavez, Cesar, 176
Chavez, Hugo, 329
Chevron U.S.A. v. Natural Resources Defense Council (1994), 298
Child Online Protection Act (1998), 245
Childs, John, 405
Chile, 325, 472-473
China, 324, 325-326, 327, 328, 468-469
Christian Coalition, 240, 241, 242, 285, 419, 423, 424, 425
Christian Right, 239, 240-243, 244, 245-246, 285, 288, 289, 422-423
Christie, Chris, 446
Citizen Corps Program, 202-203
Citizens Against Government Waste, 262 (table)
Citizens for Better Medicare, 435 (table), 436, 438
Citizens for Law and Order, 262 (table)
Citizens for Strength and Security, 409, 428
Citizens United v. Federal Election Commission (2010), 182-183, 342-343, 382, 384, 385, 388, 408, 410, 411, 431, 434, 437
City Limits (Peterson), 458
Civil rights, 209-222
  advocacy organizations (2010), 218 (table)
  African Americans, 209-210, 211-212, 213, 215, 216, 217, 218, 219, 220
  collective action, 212-213, 214
  free-rider problem, 215
  gays and lesbians, 209, 217, 219
  group funding, 215-218
  GuideStar database, 216-217, 218 (table)
  historical development, 209-212
  Latin Americans, 209-211, 213, 214, 215, 216, 217, 218, 220
  leadership, 210, 211, 212, 213, 219
  legislation, 83, 209, 212, 213, 219
  organizational prospects, 218, 220
  post-civil rights era, 213-215
  women, 219
  See also specific organization
Civil Rights Act (1964/1968), 83, 209, 212, 213
Civil War, 31, 38, 226
Clean Water Action, 300 (table), 302 (table)
Clinton, Bill:
  agricultural policy, 167
  educational policy, 290
  foreign lobbying, 321, 327
  grassroots lobbying, 372-373, 374, 375-376, 377-378
  health care reform, 49
  interest group relations, 133, 138
  intergovernmental lobbying, 312
  lobbying and legislative strategy, 342
  lobbyists, 354
  presidential elections, 424, 425, 426, 427
  religious interest groups, 241-242, 244, 246
  think tanks, 233-234
Clinton, Hillary, 183, 420, 421, 422, 424, 432, 438
Close Up Foundation, 262
Cloward, Richard, 80
Club for Growth, 405, 406, 421, 427, 435 (table), 437, 438, 439
Coalition for a Democratic Workplace, 184, 186-187
Coalitions:
  blue-green coalitions, 305
  Democratic Party, 133, 134, 135, 136, 138
  global lobbying style, 470-471
  lobbying and legislative strategy, 343
  Republican Party, 133, 134, 136, 137-138
Coca-Cola Company, 95, 404
Coelho, Tony, 412
Cohen, Cathy, 83
Collective action:
  business and organized labor, 173
  civil rights, 212-213, 214
  economic models, 87-90
  group formation and maintenance, 50-53, 54, 59-60
  interest group politics, 36
  public interest groups, 264
  social movements, 80, 84
Colombia, 328-329
Colorado, 56-57, 289, 310, 313, 315, 449 (table), 452
Colt's Firearms Manufacturing Company, 25-26
Committee for Economic Development (CED), 224, 227-229
Committee on Political Education (COPE), 175, 398
Committee on the Present Danger, 265
Common Cause, 54, 56
Communications:
  electioneering communications (1980-2008), 405 (table), 408-409
  electioneering reform, 431-433, 434-441
  ten-code communication policy, 204, 207n64
  See also Information management
Community development corporations (CDCs), 463
Concerned Parents for Neighborhood Schools, 287
Conflict expansion strategy, 342
Congress Daily, 365
Congressional Budget Office, 163
Congressional elections, 403-418
  contribution limits (2009-2010), 406 (table)
  electioneering communications (1980-2008), 405 (table), 408-409
  501(c)(3) organizations, 407-416
  501(c)(4) organizations, 407-408
  527 organizations, 405-416
  group contributions (1980-2008), 405 (table)
  group effectiveness, 414
  group expenditures (1980-2008), 405 (table), 408-409
  group role, 414-416
  important developments, 409-411
  judicial system, 405, 409-411
  legislation, 404, 406-407, 410, 415, 416
  participation motivation, 411-414
  political action committees (PACs), 403-405, 408-416
  See also Electioneering development
Congressional Management Foundation (CMF), 378
Congressional member organizations (CMOs), 326-327
Congressional Quarterly, 366, 412
Congress of Industrial Organizations (CIO), 175, 398
Connecticut, 65-66, 459, 460
Conservation Foundation, 297, 300 (table)
Conservation Fund, 300 (table), 302 (table)
Conservation International, 299, 300 (table), 302 (table)
Constitutional Convention (1787), 15
Consumer Federation of America, 262 (table)

Consumer Product Safety Act, 140
Contentious politics, 84
Continental Congress, 15
Contract with America, 156, 167
Cooper, Josephine, 350
Coors, Joseph, 55
Corruption:
 astroturf lobbying, 375
 lobbyists, 335, 337-338, 355-356, 359, 362, 386, 387
Corzine, John, 179
Costa Rica, 321
Council for a Livable World, 265
Council of Great City Schools, 285, 290
Council of State Governments (CSG):
 homeland security, 202
 intergovernmental lobbying, 309, 311
Council on Foreign Relations (CFR), 223, 224, 225, 226, 227, 228, 229, 230, 231, 232, 233
Council on Religious Freedom, 262 (table)
Counteractive lobbying, 339-340
Counter Intelligence Program (COINTELPRO), 81
CQ Weekly, 366
Craig v. Boren (1976), 119
Crawford, K. G., 43-44
Credit claiming strategy, 342, 353
Crédit Mobilier of America, 26, 27, 32
Credit Union National Association, 101
Croatia, 469
Cronin, William J., 175
Crowding effect, 51
Cuba, 324, 329
Cunningham, Randy, 337, 386
Cutler, Manasseh, 16, 18

Dahl, Robert, 63, 65-66, 67 (figure), 78-79, 457-458
Daschle, Tom, 349, 438
Davis, John W., 396
Death with Dignity National Center, 262
Deepwater Horizon oil spill, 295, 303
Defenders Action Fund, 438-439
Defenders of Wildlife, 261, 297, 298, 300 (table), 302 (table), 303, 407-408, 426-427, 438
Defense of Marriage Act (1996), 244, 258-259
Delaware, 119, 372, 373, 446, 447-448
Democracy in America (Toqueville), 21, 22, 24
Democracy's Promise (Wong), 83
Democratic Leadership Council (DLC), 233-234, 290
Democratic Party:
 business and organized labor, 175, 176, 178, 180-181, 182-183, 184-185, 186
 contacting lawmakers, 186, 378
 defense industry contributions, 194 (table)
 educational policy, 284, 286, 287, 289, 290-291
 electioneering development, 395, 396, 397, 398, 399-400
 electioneering reform, 434, 438, 439
 energy and environmental advocacy, 154, 303, 304
 executive branch influence, 133, 134, 135, 136, 138
 First Amendment rights, 384, 386, 387
 grassroots lobbying, 374
 intergovernmental lobbying, 309, 314
 lobbying and legislative strategy, 338
 lobbyists, 351, 355
 national defense, 194 (table), 195-196, 197-198
 party platforms (2008), 154-155
 presidential elections, 419, 420-421, 423, 424, 425, 426, 427-428
 professional associations, 276, 277
 religious interest groups, 240, 242, 243-244, 246
 representational politics, 145, 149, 151-158
 think tanks, 229-230, 235, 236
 See also Congressional elections; specific administration
Democratization:
 nineteenth-century interests, 25, 26-27, 28, 29
 social movements, 84-85
Demographic groups, 458
Deng, Simon, 133
Dewey, John, 35
Direct lobbying, 361-362, 470
Disability Rights Education and Defense Fund, 284-285
Disabled. *See* People with disabilities
Dissident environmental groups, 299
Disturbance theory, 90
Dobson, James, 240, 423
Dodd, Christopher, 149, 419
Dole, Robert, 169, 349
Dominican Republic, 326
Donations, 93
Douglass, Frederick, 24
DREAM Act, 219
Ducks Unlimited, 263, 300 (table), 302 (table)
Ducommun Inc., 194 (table)
Duer, William, 17
Dynetics Inc., 194 (table)

EADS North America, 194 (table)
Earned media, 365, 367
Earth Day, 300
Earth in the Balance (Gore), 428
Earth Island Institute, 300 (table), 302 (table)
Earthjustice Legal Defense Fund, 297, 300 (table), 302 (table)
Earth Share, 299, 300 (table)
Ecological theory, 59
Economic models, 87-98
 agency model, 91
 boycotts, 95
 campaign contributions, 92
 collective action, 87-90
 disturbance theory, 90
 donations, 93
 exchange theory, 95
 excludability, 87-90
 framework comparison, 72
 free-rider problem, 88-89, 91
 game theory, 90-91
 hybrid models, 93
 informational models, 92-93
 labor unions, 89
 model development, 91-95
 network analysis, 94
 partitioning games, 94
 prisoner's dilemma, 91
 private goods, 87-90
 private politics, 94-95
 public goods, 87-90
 rent-seeking, 89
 rivalrous consumption, 87-90
 signaling models, 92-93
 sociological models, 93-94
 subsidization, 91
 vote-buying model, 91-92
Economic Opportunity Act (1964), 134
Economic Policy Institute (EPI), 232, 233
Edison Electric Institute, 186 (table)
Educate America Act (2004), 290
Education, 283-293
 accountability, 288, 289-290
 adequate yearly progress (AYP), 290
 business organizations, 284
 cultural values, 288
 Democratic Party, 284, 286, 287, 289, 290-291
 desegregation, 114, 119, 120, 211, 212, 284, 286, 287
 educational equity organizations, 284-285
 educational opportunity, 286-288
 executive politics, 286, 289, 290
 gay and lesbian rights, 284
 government organizations, 285-286
 interest group categories, 283-286, 291n9
 labor unions, 283-284, 290-291
 people with disabilities, 284-285, 287
 pluralism, 65 (table)
 political action committees (PACs), 284
 producer groups, 283-284
 racial minorities, 114, 119, 120, 211, 212, 284, 286-288, 289
 religious interest groups, 285, 288, 289, 292n29
 Republican Party, 285, 286, 287, 288, 290-291
 school choice, 288-289
 school vouchers, 288-289
 student learning factors, 285 (figure)
 think tanks, 285, 287, 289
 women, 284, 288
Edwards, John, 101, 419, 420, 422
Egypt, 328
Eighteenth Amendment, 41, 396-397
Eighteenth-century interests, 11-19
 American Revolution (1776), 15, 38
 Articles of Confederation, 15
 Board of Trade (London), 11, 12, 13, 14, 18
 British connections, 11-15
 colonial legislatures, 13-14
 Constitutional Convention (1787), 15
 Continental Congress, 15
 executive branch, 16-17
 factions, 11, 17, 22
 Federalists, 15-17, 22
 First Amendment rights, 11, 15-16
 Glorious Revolution (1688), 11
 historical timeline, 11-17
 House of Burgesses (Virginia), 13
 land speculators, 16, 18
 majority faction, 11
 Massachusetts, 14, 15
 New Jersey, 17
 Pennsylvania, 14
 petitions, 16
 public opinion, 15
 Shay's Rebellion (1786-1787), 15
 South Carolina, 12, 14
 special interests, 17
 theory and practice, 14-17
 U.S. Constitution, 11, 15-17, 18-19
 Virginia, 13, 14
Eisenhower, Dwight:
 national defense, 194-195

professional associations, 278
think tanks, 228
Eisinger, Peter, 459
Electioneering development, 393-402
agricultural interest groups, 394
Democratic Party, 395, 396, 397, 398, 399-400
executive politics, 394, 395, 396, 397, 398, 399, 400-401
judicial system, 397
labor unions, 394-396, 397-398
legislation, 397, 401
New Deal era, 397-399
political action committees (PACs), 398-399
political party challenges, 399-401
pre-New Deal era, 394-397
Prohibition advocacy, 396-397
Republican Party, 395, 398-399, 400
See also Congressional elections; Presidential elections
Electioneering reform, 431-442
Democratic Party, 434, 438, 439
electioneering communications, 431-433, 434-441
501(c)(3) organizations, 433 (table)
501(c)(4) organizations, 433 (table), 434, 435, 438-439
501(c)(5) organizations, 433 (table)
501(c)(6) organizations, 433 (table)
527 organizations, 433 (table), 434, 436-438
future prospects, 440-441
historical development, 434-437
judicial system, 431, 432, 433, 434, 437, 441
legislation, 431, 433-434, 436, 439
normative developments, 439-440
political action committees (PACs), 432, 433 (table)
regulation legalities, 431-433
Republican Party, 434, 437, 438-439
Electorate:
business group mobilization, 179-181
labor union mobilization, 179-181
presidential elections, 423-428
religious interest groups, 242-247
representational politics, 151-152
voter guide, 423, 424
voter mobilization, 179-173, 424-426
voter persuasion, 426-428
voting rights, 113, 119, 252-253
Electronic Privacy Information Center, 262 (table)
Ellender, Allen, 277
EMILY's List, 406, 407, 424, 425, 435 (table), 438
EMILY's List v. FEC, 410
Employee Free Choice Act (2009), 173, 181, 184, 186-187
Employee Freedom Action Committee, 183, 184
Employment Act (1946), 228
Encyclopedia of Associations, 102, 177, 274
End of Liberalism, The (Lowi), 67 (figure), 68
Energy and environmental advocacy, 295-308
blue-green coalitions, 305
Democratic Party, 154, 303, 304
dissident groups, 299
environmental era, 297-299, 300 (table)
environmental justice groups, 299
evangelicalism, 305, 306
executive politics, 296, 298, 301, 303, 304, 305, 306
future prospects, 306
green energy, 304-305
group development, 295-299
group effectiveness, 303-304
group maintenance, 299-301
group origins, 300 (table)
group revenues (2009), 302 (table)
group support, 302 (table)
Internet websites, 302 (table)
interwar period, 296, 300 (table)
judicial system, 297, 298
labor unions, 305
legislation, 297, 298, 300-301
mass membership environmentalism, 301-303
new alliances, 304-306
niche groups, 299
nuclear energy, 297, 298
oil industry, 295, 302-303, 329, 352, 366, 472
pluralism, 65 (table)
post-movement period, 300 (table)
postwar era, 296-297, 300 (table)
Progressive era, 295-296, 300 (table)
Republican Party, 154, 303, 304
taxation, 297-298, 300-301
See also specific organization
Energy Conservation Coalition, 301
Engel v. Vitale (1962), 244
English Bill of Rights (1689), 381
Environmental Action (EA), 300, 301
Environmental Defense Fund (EDF), 297, 298, 299, 300 (table), 301, 302 (table)
Environmentalism. *See* Energy and environmental advocacy; *specific organization*
Environmental Working Group, 262 (table), 299, 300 (table), 302 (table)
Environment America, 305-306
Episcopalian, 241
Episodic groups, 458, 460-461, 462-463
Equal Employment Opportunity Commission (EEOC), 106, 117
Equal Rights Amendment (ERA), 251-252, 256, 257
Estrada, Miguel, 118
European Aeronautic Defence & Space, 194 (table)
European Commission, 467, 470
European Council of American Chambers of Commerce (AmCham), 467
European Union (EU), 467, 469, 471, 472
European Union Trade Commission, 470
Evangelical Environmental Network (EEN), 305
Evangelicalism:
energy and environmental advocacy, 305, 306
religious interest groups, 241, 242, 243, 245, 247
See also specific organization
Exchange theory, 52, 54, 95
Exchange Theory of Interest Groups, An (Salisbury), 67 (figure)
Excludability, 87-90
Executive branch:
Democratic coalitions, 133, 134, 135, 136, 138
educational policy, 286, 289, 290
eighteenth-century interests, 16-17
electioneering development, 394, 395, 396, 397, 398, 399, 400-401
energy and environmental advocacy, 296, 298, 301, 303, 304, 305, 306
Executive Office influence, 128, 129, 132-138
Executive Office liaisons, 135-138
federal agency influence, 130 (table), 138-141
First Amendment rights, 382, 388
foreign lobbying, 321, 327, 328, 329
gay and lesbian rights, 129, 136-137
grassroots lobbying, 372-373, 374, 375-376, 377-378
interest group assets, 127-129
interest group objectives, 129-132
intergovernmental lobbying, 311-312, 313, 316
iron triangles, 139
issue networks, 139
lawmaking agenda, 130-131
liaison as consensus building, 135 (table), 137-138
liaison as governing party, 135 (table), 138
liaison as legitimization, 135 (table), 136
liaison as outreach, 135 (table), 136-137
line-agencies, 130 (table), 131
lobbying and legislative strategy, 339, 340, 341, 342, 359, 362
lobbyists, 348, 351, 352, 354, 355
policymaking agenda, 130
political objectives, 130 (table), 131-132
programmatic objectives, 130-131, 135-136, 137-138
racial minorities, 134, 136
regulatory agenda, 131
religious interest groups, 246-247
Republican coalitions, 133, 134, 136, 137-138
rulemaking agenda, 131
think tanks, 226, 227, 228, 230, 231, 232, 233-234, 235, 236
women, 134, 136
See also Presidential elections; specific administration
Exxon Mobil, 186 (table)

Factions:
congressional elections, 415
eighteenth-century interests, 11, 17, 22
global lobbying, 468
interest group growth, 104
lobbyists, 355
majority faction, 11
representational politics, 145
Factory Girls' Association, 26
FairTaxNation.org, 377
Faith and Action, 116
Faith-based initiatives, 246
Falwell, Jerry, 53, 240, 419
Farmer, James, 212
Farmers' Alliance, 32-33, 38-39, 164-165, 394
FEC v. Massachusetts Citizens for Life (1976), 433

Federal Aviation Administration (FAA), 106
Federal Bureau of Investigation (FBI), 81
Federal Corrupt Practices Act (1925), 382, 397
Federal Election Campaign Act (1971), 181, 322, 336, 387-388, 397, 401, 431
Federal Election Commission (FEC):
- business and organized labor, 177, 181-183, 185
- congressional elections, 403, 404, 405, 407, 408, 409-410
- judicial system, 388, 409-410, 411, 433
- representational politics, 146-147

Federal Election Commission v. Wisconsin Right to Life, Inc. (2007), 388
Federal Emergency Management Agency (FEMA), 199, 202, 203, 204
Federalist Papers, 16, 17, 22, 36, 78, 104-105, 355, 415, 468
Federalists, 15-17
Federal Mediation and Conciliation Service, 181
Federal Register, 140
Federal Regulation of Lobbying Act (1946), 384-385
Federation for American Immigration Reform, 262 (table)
Feingold, Russ, 409, 434
Feminine Mystique, The (Friedan), 256
Feminism. *See* Women
Fifteenth Amendment, 39, 211
Financial Times, 472
Finmeccanica SpA, 194 (table)
First Amendment rights, 381-390
- campaign contributions, 387-388
- congressional elections, 415
- Democratic Party, 384, 386, 387
- eighteenth-century interests, 11, 15-16
- ethics rules, 388
- executive politics, 382, 388
- grassroots lobbying, 375, 379
- historical context, 381-387
- judicial system, 382, 384, 385, 387, 388
- legislation, 381-383, 384-388
- lobbying regulation, 381-390
- lobbying techniques, 359, 362
- nineteenth-century interests, 28, 381-382
- Republican Party, 384, 386, 387
- taxation, 383-387

First National Bank v. Bellotti (1978), 382
Fishbein, Morris, 277
501(c)(3) organizations:
- campaign contributions, 183-184
- congressional elections, 407-416
- electioneering reform, 433 (table)
- First Amendment rights, 383, 384
- lobbying and legislative strategy, 343-344
- presidential elections, 422
- think tanks, 225-226

501(c)(4) organizations:
- congressional elections, 407-408
- electioneering reform, 433 (table), 434, 435, 438-439
- First Amendment rights, 383, 384
- presidential elections, 422

501(c)(5) organizations, 408, 433 (table)
501(c)(6) organizations, 408, 422, 433 (table)
527 organizations:
- campaign contributions, 183-184
- congressional elections, 405-416
- electioneering reform, 433 (table), 434, 436-438
- First Amendment rights, 383-384, 386
- lobbying and legislative strategy, 344
- presidential elections, 422

Florida, 136, 427, 447-448, 452
Focus on the Family, 242, 243, 285, 288, 407-408, 421, 422, 423
Focus on the Family Action, 240, 422
Food and Agriculture Act (1965), 166
Ford, Gerald, 135, 136
Ford Foundation, 224, 230, 231-232, 285, 297
Foreign Agents Registration Act (1938), 322, 323, 324, 326, 328, 383
Foreign lobbying, 321-332
- comparative perspective, 323
- congressional member organizations (CMOs), 326-327
- defined, 321
- domestic interest groups, 324-326
- executive politics, 321, 327, 328, 329
- foreign governments, 323-324
- implications, 330
- legal context, 321-323
- legislation, 322, 323, 324, 326, 328
- lobbying nations (2008), 324 (table)
- motivations, 327-329
- political action committees (PACs), 322-323, 324, 325, 327 (table)
- public diplomacy, 321, 329, 330n10
- strategies, 326-327
- success criteria, 329
- *See also* Global lobbying style; specific country

Forging of Bureaucratic Autonomy, The (Carpenter), 69
Fortas, Abe, 117 (table)
Fourteenth Amendment, 113, 211, 212, 382, 384
Fox News Sunday, 364-365
Framing strategy, 340-341
France, 323, 327, 472, 473
Franken, Al, 184
Freddie Mac, 186 (table)
Freedom of Information Act, 140
Freedom's Watch, 409, 428
Freedom to Farm Act (1996), 167
Freedom Works, 82
Free-rider problem:
- civil rights, 215
- economic models, 88-89, 91
- group formation and maintenance, 54-55
- public interest groups, 263-264
- social movements, 80

Free Soil Party, 37
Friedan, Betty, 256
Friends of the Earth, 265, 298, 299, 300 (table), 301, 302 (table), 304
Frontiero v. Richardson (1973), 119

Gag rule, 30
Galbraith, John Kenneth, 87
Game theory, 90-91
Garrison, William Lloyd, 24, 29, 30
Gaventa, John, 67 (figure)
Gay, Lesbian and Straight Education Network, 284
Gays and lesbians. *See* Lesbian, gay, bisexual, transgendered (LGBT)
GenCorp Inc., 194 (table)
General Electric, 186 (table), 197-198
General Electric-Rolls Royce, 197-198
General Motors, 186 (table)
General Union for the Promotion of the Christian Sabbath, 27, 28, 30
Germany, 323, 469
Gibbs, Lois, 301
GI Bill, 83
Gilded Age, 21, 31-33
Ginsburg, Ruth Bader, 117 (table), 119
Giuliani, Rudy, 421, 423
GlaxoSmithKline, 322, 327 (table)
Global Crossing, 354
Global lobbying style, 467-474
- activity fundamentals, 469-473
- coalitions, 470-471
- cultural influences, 468
- direct advocacy, 470
- electoral campaigns, 473
- grassroots lobbying, 471
- influencing factors, 468-469
- institutional influences, 469
- mass demonstrations, 471-472
- political influences, 468
- public relations, 472-473
- *See also* Foreign lobbying; specific country

Glorious Revolution (1688), 11
Goals 2000, 290
Goldberg, Arthur, 117 (table)
Goldman Sachs, 424
Goldwater, Barry, 226, 230, 399
Gompers, Samuel, 174, 395-396
Gooch, William, 13
Gore, Al, 414, 427, 428, 431
Governmental Process (Truman), 50, 63, 65, 67 (figure), 87
Grand Army of the Republic (GAR), 31, 38
Grand United Order of Odd Fellows, 24
Grange, 32-33, 38-39, 40-41, 52, 164, 165, 394
Grassroots lobbying, 371-380
- activities, 372-373, 374
- astroturf lobbying, 363, 375, 379
- competing pressures, 371-372
- conflict expansion, 342
- credit claiming, 342, 353
- Democratic Party, 374
- effectiveness of, 377-378
- executive politics, 372-373, 374, 375-376, 377-378
- First Amendment rights, 375, 379
- global lobbying style, 471
- grass tops lobbying, 363-364, 373
- health care reform, 373, 374
- issue advertising, 342
- labor union support, 375
- legislation, 375, 377, 380n29
- lobbyists, 348
- online lobbying, 375-377
- outside lobbying, 341-343
- public interest groups, 266
- Republican Party, 372, 373
- signaling, 341-342
- social movements, 82
- state politics, 451
- taxation, 377

Grass tops lobbying, 363-364, 373
Gratz v. Bollinger (2003), 120

Gray, Virginia, 459
Grealy, Mary, 350
Great Britain:
  American Revolution (1776), 15, 38
  Board of Trade (London), 11, 12, 13, 14, 18
  eighteenth-century interests, 11-15, 18, 38
  English Bill of Rights (1689), 381
  foreign lobbying, 327 (table)
  lobbying style, 469, 471, 472, 473
  Magna Carta (1215), 381
Great Depression, 164, 166
Great Society, 230, 311, 312, 313
Greece, 324, 325
Greenback Labor Party, 394
Green energy, 304-305
Greenpeace, USA, 262 (table), 295, 299, 300 (table), 302 (table), 303
  boycotts, 95
  membership, 58
  nonprofit tax status, 57
Group formation and maintenance, 49-62
  by-product theory, 51-52, 55-57
  collective action, 50-53, 54, 59-60
  crowding effect, 51
  early research, 49-50
  ecological theory, 59
  exchange theory, 52, 54
  framework comparison, 72-73
  free-rider problem, 54-55
  group privilege, 51
  labor unions, 58-59
  neopluralism, 59
  nonprofit tax status, 57-58
  organizational factors, 53-59
  patronage theory, 52-53
  pluralism, 52
  selective incentives, 51-52, 55-57
  small group effect, 51
Group privilege, 51
Group Representation in Congress (Herring), 254
Grutter v. Bollinger (2003), 120
GuideStar, 216-217, 218 (table)

Hall of States, 310, 317
Hamilton, Alexander, 16-17, 18-19
Handgun Control, 435 (table), 437
Harding, Warren, 227
Hare, Kate Sullivan, 350
Harrigan, Ronald, 459
Hatch Act (269), 277
Haves-and-have-not theory, 114
Hawaii, 244, 446, 452, 460
Hayes, George E. C., 120
Haynsworth, Clement, 116, 117 (table)
Head Start, 284
Health care, 49, 82
  Medicaid, 280
  Medicare, 279-280, 337, 340, 343, 353, 354, 415
  pluralism, 64, 65 (table)
  representational politics, 154-155
Health Insurance Association of America, 434
Hefner, Hugh, 55
Heritage Foundation, 55, 223, 224, 225, 231, 232, 233, 234, 235, 313, 315
  education, 285, 287, 289
Hernandez v. Texas (1954), 211-212
Herring, Pendleton, 254
Hill, Anita, 117
Hill, The, 350, 365
Hirschman, Albert, 95
Hispanics. *See* Latin Americans
Holder, Eric S., 354
Homeland security, 199-205
  all-hazards approach, 200, 206n38
  Big Seven lobby, 202, 207n55
  counterterrorism, 201, 202 (table)
  domestic safety, 201, 202 (table)
  emergency management, 201, 202 (table)
  funding, 202-204, 207n57
  interest group involvement, 200-205
  intergovernmental policy, 202-205
  legislation, 203, 316
  national defense, 201, 202 (table)
  policy reform, 204-205
  public health, 201, 202 (table)
  security grant funds (2002-2009), 202 (table)
  ten-code communication policy, 204, 207n64
  See also National defense
Honduras, 321, 330
Honeywell International, 182
Hoover, Herbert, 156, 230
Hoover Institution, 224, 230, 231, 232, 233, 234
House of Burgesses (Virginia), 13
Huckabee, Mike, 421, 423, 427
Hudson Institute, 229, 232
Huelskamp, Tim, 169
Humphrey, Hubert, 400
Hungary, 469
Hurricane Katrina (2005), 199, 202
Hybrid economic models, 93
Hyperpluralism, 158
Idaho, 445
Ignagni, Karen, 350
Illinois, 170, 274, 447-448
Immigrants, 25
Improved Order of Red Men, 25
India, 469
Informational models, 92-93
Information management:
  lobbying and legislative strategy, 339
  lobbying techniques, 361
  lobbyists, 351-352
  state politics, 450
  See also Communications
Innocence Project, 265
Insider-outsider status, 80-82
Institute for International Economics, 232-233
Institute for Policy Studies, 224, 230, 232
Institute of Government Research (IGR), 223, 224, 226-227
Institutional groups, 458, 460-462
Inter-American Dialogue, 233
Interest group growth, 101-112
  business groups, 177-179
  civilian employee growth, 104, 105 (figure)
  factions, 104
  government attention, 109-110, 112n56
  government coordination, 109-110
  government-driven explanations, 102, 106-110
  government patronage, 107-108
  government size, 104
  group expansion (2004-2009), 103 (table)
  group system size, 102-104
  interest-driven explanations, 101-102, 104-106
  interest group coordination, 109-110
  labor unions, 177-179
  lobbying incentives, 109
  religious interest groups, 239-241
  senior citizens, 108
  social movement organizations (SMOs), 105-106
Interest group liberalism, 68
Interest group politics, 35-45
  African Americans, 39
  agricultural associations, 38-39, 40-41, 43
  California, 40-41
  collective action, 36
  defined, 36, 44
  Democratic Party, 39-40, 41
  democratization, 41
  effective techniques, 40-41
  Industrialization era, 35-36
  labor unions, 41, 42
  nineteenth-century interests, 36-38
  people's lobby, 41-42
  persistence of, 43-44
  political legitimacy, 40
  Republican Party, 37-38, 39-40, 41
  roll call tabulation, 41
  voluntary associations, 38-40
  women's rights, 39, 41, 42, 43-44
  See also Eighteenth-century interests; Nineteenth-century interests
Intergovernmental lobbying, 309-319
  Big Seven, 309, 310, 311, 312, 315, 316, 317
  coalition building, 317
  Council of State Governments (CSG), 309, 311
  Democratic Party, 309, 314
  empirical research, 310-311
  executive politics, 311-312, 313, 316
  group cohesion, 314-316
  group proliferation, 311-312
  Hall of States, 310, 317
  homeland security, 316
  immigration reform, 316-317
  International City/County Management Association (ICMA), 309, 311, 316
  issues, 316-317
  judicial system, 312-313
  legislation, 316
  National Association of Counties (NACo), 309, 310, 311, 312, 314, 315
  National Conference of State Legislatures (NCSL), 309, 310, 311, 312, 314-315
  National Governors Association (NGA), 309, 310, 311, 312
  National League of Cities (NLC), 309, 310, 311, 312, 314, 315
  organizational structure, 315
  Republican Party, 309, 314-315
  resources, 314, 316
  state offices, 310, 313-314
  state power, 316
  tactics, 316-317
  think tanks, 313
  urban lobby, 311-312
  U.S. Conference of Mayors (USCM), 309, 310, 311, 312, 314-316
Internal Revenue Service (IRS):
  civil rights organizations, 216-217, 218 (table)
  GuideStar database, 216-217, 218 (table)
  nonprofit tax status, 57-58
  See also Taxation

International Association of Firefighters, 182, 276
International Brotherhood of Electrical Workers, 182
International Brotherhood of Teamsters, 180, 185, 422
International City/County Management Association (ICMA):
- homeland security, 200, 202
- intergovernmental lobbying, 309, 311, 316

International Religious Freedom Act (1998), 244, 247
Internet resources:
- environmental groups, 302 (table)
- online lobbying, 375-377
- *See also* specific organization

Interstate Commerce Commission, 140
Iowa, 170, 244, 419
Iran, 330
Iraq:
- civilian contractors, 198, 199
- foreign lobbying, 329
- think tanks, 234-235

Ireland, 469
Iron triangles, 72, 139
Israel, 324, 325, 327, 328, 330
Issa, Darrell, 361
Issue advertising, 342
Issue networks, 139
Italy, 473
Izaak Walton League, 262 (table), 300 (table), 302 (table)

Jackson, Andrew, 25
Japan, 177, 323, 327, 329, 469
Jefferson, Thomas, 22
Jefferson, William, 386
Jehovah Witness, 244-245
Jewish Americans. *See* Israel; Judaism
John Birch Society, 399
Johnson, Lyndon:
- civil rights, 210, 212
- interest group relations, 133, 134, 136, 137
- intergovernmental lobbying, 312, 313
- religious interest groups, 246
- representational politics, 156
- think tanks, 230

Joint Center for Political and Economic Studies, 233
Joint Legislative Committee, 41
Josten, Bruce, 107
Judaism, 25, 245, 285, 288
Judicial system, 113-125
- amicus curiae briefs, 115-116, 119-120, 267, 268 (table), 286, 287, 312
- congressional elections, 405, 409-411
- electioneering development, 397
- electioneering reform, 431, 432, 433, 434, 437, 441
- energy and environmental advocacy, 297, 298
- First Amendment rights, 382, 384, 385, 387, 388
- haves-and-have-not theory, 114
- interest group classifications, 114-115
- interest group success, 121-122
- intergovernmental lobbying, 312-313
- judicial elections, 118
- lobbying and legislative strategy, 342-343
- organizational maintenance, 120, 122-123
- participants, 114-115
- participation considerations, 119-123
- participation strategies, 115-118
- policy change influence, 119-120
- racial minorities, 114, 115, 116-117, 119
- religious interest groups, 244-246
- sponsorship strategy, 113, 115, 119
- Supreme Court nomination, 116-118
- Supreme Court nominee influence, 120-121, 123
- Supreme Court nominees (1956-2010), 117 (table)
- women, 113, 119, 122, 123
- *See also* U.S. Supreme Court

Junior Order of United American Mechanics, 25

Kagan, Elena, 117 (table), 118, 258
Kahn, Herman, 228, 229, 232
Kaiser, Robert, 411
Kaiser Family Foundation, 233
Kansas, 114, 119, 120, 169, 396, 446, 460
Kellogg, Brown, and Root, 198
Kennedy, Anthony, 117 (table)
Kennedy, Edward, 438
Kennedy, John F.:
- business and organized labor, 175
- civil rights, 210
- interest group relations, 134, 136
- lobbyists, 348
- national defense, 195
- think tanks, 228-229

Kennedy, Robert F., 399
Kentucky, 310, 452
Kerry, John, 414, 424, 427, 436
Key, V. O., 92
KidsPAC, 404
King, Martin Luther, Jr., 212, 213
Kissinger, Henry, 228
Knights of Labor, 32, 52, 53, 394
Know-Nothing Party, 37
Korean War, 195
KPMG LLP, 327 (table)
Kuhn, Thomas, 50
Ku Klux Klan, 382

Laborers Union, 182
Labor strikes, 89
Labor unions:
- campaign contributions, 181-182
- economic models, 89
- education, 283-284, 290-291
- electioneering development, 394-396, 397-398
- electorate mobilization, 179-181
- energy and environmental advocacy, 305
- grassroots lobbying, 375
- group formation and maintenance, 58-59
- historical development, 26-27, 32, 174-176
- independent expenditures, 182-183
- influential growth, 177-179
- legislative action committees (LACs), 184-189
- nineteenth-century interests, 26-27, 32, 174
- social movements, 81
- state politics, 446, 448 (table)
- *See also* Business and organized labor; specific organization

La Falce, John, 301
La Follette, Robert, 42, 43, 396
LaHaye, Beverley, 423
Land Ordinance (1787), 18
Land speculation, 16, 18
Latin Americans:
- advocacy organizations (2010), 218 (table)
- civil rights groups, 209-211, 213, 214, 215, 216, 217, 218, 220
- judicial system, 119
- social movements, 81, 82, 214
- *See also* specific organization

Law Enforcement Terrorism Prevention Program, 202-203
Leadership Conference on Civil and Human Rights (LCCHR), 219, 289
League of Conservation Voters (LCV), 300 (table), 301, 302 (table), 407-408, 428, 432, 433, 434, 435 (table), 438, 439
League of United Latin American Citizens (LULAC), 119, 209, 210-212, 214-215, 216-217, 218, 220
League of Women Voters, 54
Ledbetter v. Goodyear Tire & Rubber Co. (2007), 219
Leech, Beth, 67 (figure)
Legal Defense Fund (LDF), 114, 115, 119, 120
Legislation:
- agricultural interest groups, 165, 166, 167
- business and organized labor, 173, 175, 181, 183, 184, 186-187, 188
- civil rights, 83, 209, 212, 213, 219
- congressional elections, 404, 406-407, 410, 415, 416
- electioneering development, 397, 401
- energy and environmental advocacy, 297, 298, 300-301
- First Amendment rights, 381-383, 384-388
- foreign lobbying, 322, 323, 324, 326, 328
- grassroots lobbying, 375, 377, 380n29
- homeland security, 203, 316
- intergovernmental lobbying, 316
- lobbying and legislative strategy, 335, 336, 337, 340, 342, 343
- presidential elections, 424
- religious interest groups, 244, 245, 247
- think tank influence, 224, 226, 227, 228, 232, 235
- *See also* specific legislative act

Legislative action committees (LACs), 184-189
Legislative Transparency and Accountability Act (2007), 375
Lesbian, gay, bisexual, transgendered (LGBT):
- civil rights, 209, 217, 219
- education, 284
- executive branch, 129, 136-137
- same-sex marriage, 244, 258-259

Levine, Myron, 459
Lewis, John, 174-175
Lexington Institute, 197, 233
Lexis-Nexis citations, 273 (figure)
Lily Ledbetter Fair Pay Act, 219
Lipsky, Michael, 80
Lithuania, 471
Lobbying and legislative strategy, 335-346
- campaign contributions, 336, 337-339
- coalitions, 343
- counteractive lobbying, 339-340
- Democratic Party, 338

ethical rules, 335-337
executive politics, 339, 340, 341, 342
framing strategy, 340-341
grassroots lobbying, 341-343
information management, 339
judicial system, 342-343
legislation, 335, 336, 337, 340, 342, 343
lobbying defined, 337
lobbying expenditures, 336-337
lobbying expenditures (1998-2010), 336 (figure)
lobbying practice, 337-340
nonprofit organizations, 343-344
outside lobbying, 341-343
political action committees (PACs), 336, 338-340
representation, 343-344
Republican Party, 338, 343
subsidization, 341, 354
taxation, 343-344
think tanks, 344

Lobbying Disclosure Act (1995), 103, 109, 322, 335, 336, 375, 385

Lobbying techniques:
advertisement, 364-367
air cover, 364-365
astroturf lobbying, 363, 375
beyond policy influence, 369
context considerations, 368
conversational strategy, 365
defined, 359-360
direct lobbying, 361-362
earned media, 365, 367
executive politics, 359, 362
First Amendment rights, 359, 362
fund-raising, 368
grass tops lobbying, 363-364, 373
impact of, 367-369
information brokering, 361
integrated techniques, 367
mobilization/countermobilization, 367-368
opponent response, 365
paid media, 364-365, 367
research strategy, 362-363
state politics, 450-453
support base mobilization, 365
See also Global lobbying style; Grassroots lobbying

Lobbyists, 347-357
categories, 348
client expenditures (2010), 353 (table)
corruption, 335, 337-338, 355-356
Democratic Party, 351, 355
demographics, 347-350
executive politics, 348, 351, 352, 354, 355
expenditures, 352-353
expenditures (2000-2010), 352 (table)
grassroots/public interest, 348
independent/hired gun, 348
information management, 351-352
legislative activities, 350-355
legislative activities (1999-2008), 351 (table)
policy influence, 353-355
racial minorities, 350
Republican Party, 351, 355-356
revolving door strategy, 354
rifle shots, 353-354
single-firm, 348
state politics, 448-449
subsidization, 341, 354
trade association, 348
women, 349-350

Local interest groups, 457-466
bystander effect, 464
citizenship impact, 463-464
community development corporations (CDCs), 463
community power research, 457-459
demographic groups, 458
episodic groups, 458, 460-461, 462-463
federal aid, 460 (table)
institutional groups, 458, 460-462
land use policy, 463 (table)
nonprofit organizations, 463
research agenda, 464-465
research challenges, 459-460
See also State politics

Lockheed Martin, 186 (table), 194 (table), 197
Log Cabin Republicans, 421
Logic of Collective Action, The (Olson), 50, 51, 58-59, 67, 79, 87-90, 173
Losing Ground (Murray), 235
Louisiana, 118, 447-448
Love Canal (New York), 299, 301
Lowi, Theodore, 67 (figure), 68, 80
Lujan v. Defenders of Wildlife (1992), 298
LULAC v. Perry (2006), 119

Madison, James, 11, 15-16, 17, 18-19, 22, 78, 104-105, 355, 415, 468
Magna Carta (1215), 381
Maine, 396, 445, 460
Maine Temperance Union, 28-29
Majority Action, 405
Malaysia, 473
Mandell, Shelly, 423
Manhattan Institute, 231, 233, 235, 289
Mansbridge, Jane, 83
Marshall, Thurgood, 114, 117 (table), 118, 120
Marxism, 78

Massachusetts:
eighteenth-century interests, 14, 15
nineteenth-century interests, 22, 23, 24, 26, 27
state constitution, 22, 244

Massachusetts Audubon Society, 296
Massachusetts Citizens for Life v. FEC (1986), 408, 409, 411
McCain, John, 151, 405, 419, 421, 422-423, 424, 426, 427, 428, 431, 434
McConnell v. Federal Election Commission (2003), 388, 433
McDonald v. City of Chicago (2010), 121 (table)
McDonnell, Faith, 133
McFarland, Andrew, 67 (figure), 69
McGovern, George, 180
McKinley, William, 176-177
McLaurin v. Oklahoma (1950), 119
Meany, George, 55
Media Fund, 406, 427-428, 435 (table), 436, 438
Medicaid, 280
Medicare, 279-280, 337, 340, 343, 353, 354, 415
Medicare Catastrophic Coverage Act (1989), 342
Meet the Press, 364-365
Menonnite, 240
Merchant Marine Act (1936), 383
Meredith v. Jefferson County Board of Education (2007), 286, 287
Methodist, 239, 240, 241, 246
Metropolitan Medican Response System Program, 202-203
Mexican American Legal Defense and Educational Fund, 119
Mexico, 323, 324, 328
Mica, Daniel, 101
Michigan, 128, 289, 305, 352, 396, 438, 445, 446, 452
Microsoft, 90, 93, 178, 348
Miers, Harriet E., 117 (table), 118
Military. *See* National defense
Minersville School District v. Gobitis (1940), 244-245
Minnesota, 305, 445, 452
Minor, Virginia, 113
Missouri, 452
Missouri ex rel v. Canada (1938), 119
Moe, Terry, 67 (figure)
Mondale, Walter, 423
Montana, 452
Moral Majority, 52, 53, 117-118, 240, 242
Moran, Jerry, 169
Mott, Lucretia, 24
Mountain States Legal Foundation, 265
MoveOn.org, 306, 344, 372-373, 376, 407, 426, 428, 435 (table), 439, 440-441
Muir, John, 296
Muller v. Oregon (1908), 115
Murray, Charles, 235

Nabrit, James M., 120
Napolitano, Janet, 204, 205, 316

National Association for the Advancement of Colored People (NAACP):
civil rights, 29, 209, 211-212, 214-215, 216-217, 220
education, 284, 289, 290
electioneering, 425, 434-435
judicial system, 114, 115, 118, 119, 120
representational politics, 150

National Association of Counties (NACo):
homeland security, 202
intergovernmental lobbying, 309, 310, 311, 312, 314, 315

National Association of Elementary School Principals (NAESP), 284
National Association of Evangelicals (NAE), 241, 243, 245, 247
National Association of Insurance and Financial Advisors, 275, 276 (table)
National Association of Investors Corporation, 262 (table)
National Association of Manufacturers (NAM), 176-177, 178, 395, 398

National Association of Realtors (NAR), 56, 182, 275
Lexis-Nexis cites, 273 (figure)
lobbying expenditures (1998-2009), 186 (table)
political expenditures (2007-2008), 276 (table)

National Association of Regional Councils (NARC), 310
National Association of School Boards, 285, 290
National Association of Small Towns and Townships, 310
National Association of Social Workers, 276 (table)
National Association of State Attorneys General, 312-313
National Audubon Society, 296, 297, 298, 299, 300 (table), 302 (table), 303, 304
National Beer Wholesalers Association, 182
National Bureau of Economic Research (NBER), 223, 224, 225, 227

National Coalition for Public Education (NCPE), 289
National Committee for an Effective Congress (NCEC), 399
National Community Pharmacists Association, 276 (table)
National Conference of State Legislatures (NCSL):
homeland security, 202
intergovernmental lobbying, 309, 310, 311, 312, 314-315
National Consumers League (NCL), 115, 116
National Cooperative Association of Cordwainers, 26
National Council of Churches (NCC), 240, 241, 243, 285
National Council of La Raza, 82
National defense, 193-199, 205
B-1 Lancer bomber, 195-196, 198-199
campaign contribution (2010), 194 (table)
Democratic Party, 194 (table), 195-196, 197-198
federal expenditures, 193-194, 205n9
F-35 Lightning II Strike Fighter, 197-199
industry lobbying expenditures (2009), 194 (table)
Middle East civilian contractors, 198, 199
military-industrial complex, 194-198
pluralism, 65 (table)
representational politics, 155
Republican Party, 194 (table), 195-196, 197-198
V-22 Osprey tiltrotor, 195, 196-197, 198-199, 206n27
See also Homeland security
National Education Association (NEA), 271, 284, 287, 290, 400-401
National Emergency Management Association (NEMA), 200, 201
National Environmental Policy Act (1969), 297, 298
National Farmers Union, 165-166
National Federation of Independent Business (NFIB), 49, 173, 177, 180, 185, 186, 361
National Female Anti-Slavery Society, 24
National Football League Players Association, 271
National Governors Association (NGA):
education, 285, 290
homeland security, 202
intergovernmental lobbying, 309, 310, 311, 312
National Institute of Child Health and Human Development, 285
National Journal, 351, 364 (figure), 365
National Labor Relations Act (1935), 175, 188-189
National Labor Relations Board (NLRB), 58, 181, 188-189
National Labor Union (NLU), 32, 174
National League of Cities (NLC):
homeland security, 202
intergovernmental lobbying, 309, 310, 311, 312, 314, 315
National Mediation Board (NMB), 188
National Organization for the Reform of Marijuana Laws (NORML), 55
National Organization for Women (NOW), 107, 134, 255, 256, 423
education, 284
judicial system, 118
representational politics, 150
National Parent Teacher Association (PTA), 284
National Parks Association, 296
National Parks Conservation Association, 300 (table), 302 (table)
National Park Service, 296, 297
National Park System, 296
National Park Trust, 300 (table), 302 (table)
National Prohibition Party, 396
National Rifle Association (NRA), 107, 399
electioneering, 414, 421, 423-424, 425, 427, 428, 435 (table)
representational politics, 151
National Right to Life, 420
National Safety Council, 262 (table)
National Society of Accountants, 276 (table)
National Taxonomy of Exempt Entities (NTEE), 216-217, 218 (table)
National Trade and Professional Associations of the United States, 274
National Trades Union, 26
National Wildlife Federation, 296, 297, 298, 299, 302, 302 (table), 303, 304, 305
National Woman Suffrage Association (NWSA), 113, 115
Nation at Risk, A, 283, 288, 289
Native Americans, 335, 337-338, 349, 350, 355-356, 386
Natural Resources Defense Council (NRDC), 297, 298, 299, 300 (table), 301, 302 (table), 303, 304, 305, 339
Nature Conservancy, 297, 299, 300 (table), 302 (table)
Nebraska, 170
Neopluralism, 59, 69-71
Neopluralism (McFarland), 67 (figure), 69
Netherlands, 327 (table)
Netscape, 354
Network analysis, 94
Nevada, 445, 446, 447, 452
New American Foundation, 233
Newberry v. United States (1921), 397
New Deal, 164, 165, 224, 227, 296, 297, 311, 312
electioneering development, 393, 397-399
New Democratic Network, 435 (table), 436
New England Anti-Slavery Society, 29, 30
New Federalism, 312, 313
New Hampshire, 419, 446, 448
New Jersey, 17, 179, 375, 446
New Mexico, 289, 452
New York, 283, 295, 299, 301, 313, 452
New York Times, 77, 80, 81, 256-257, 353, 472
Nicaragua, 327, 330
Niche environmental groups, 299
Nineteenth Amendment, 41
Nineteenth-century interests, 21-34
abolitionist movement, 24, 27, 29-31
African Americans, 24, 27, 29-31
agricultural associations, 32-33, 38, 164-165
antebellum years, 24-27
Civil War era, 31, 38
conservatives, 21
democratization, 25, 26-27, 28, 29
early nineteenth century, 22-24
First Amendment rights, 28, 381-382
gag rule, 30
Gilded Age, 21, 31-33
immigrants, 25
labor unions, 26-27, 32, 174
Massachusetts, 22, 23, 24, 26, 27
patriotic associations, 25
petitions, 30
professional associations, 27
railroads, 25, 26, 27, 31, 32
religious organizations, 25
religious reform movements, 27-31
Sabbatarian movement, 27-28, 30-31
South Carolina, 24, 29-30
temperance movement, 27, 28-29, 30-31
Toqueville's America, 21-22, 24, 33, 36, 38
voluntary associations, 23, 24-31
women's rights, 24, 26, 27, 251-254
Nixon, Richard:
agricultural policy, 167
interest group relations, 133, 134, 135, 136
intergovernmental lobbying, 312, 313
national defense, 196
Supreme Court nominations, 116
think tanks, 231, 233
Noble Order of the Knights of Labor (K of L), 174
No Child Left Behind Act (2001), 137, 235, 289, 290
Nonpartisan Campaign Committee, 396
Nonprofit organizations:
congressional elections, 405-416
local interest groups, 463
nonprofit tax status, 57-58, 216-217, 218 (table), 266-267
See also 501(c)(3) organizations
North American Free Trade Agreement (NAFTA), 324
North Carolina, 56, 198-199, 290, 313, 438
North Dakota, 170, 313, 447-448
Northrop Grumman, 186 (table), 196, 198
Novelli, Bill, 353, 354
Nuclear energy, 297, 298
Nuclear Weapons and Foreign Policy (Kissinger), 228

Obama, Barack, 82, 101
environmentalism, 305, 306
First Amendment rights, 382
foreign lobbying, 328
gay and lesbian rights, 258-259
grassroots lobbying, 373, 374, 375
homeland security, 205
interest group relations, 128, 129, 134, 135, 138
lobbying, 340, 342, 359, 362
lobbyists, 348, 351, 352, 354
national defense, 197
presidential elections, 419, 420, 422, 423, 424, 426, 427, 428, 431, 440

religious interest groups, 240, 242, 246
think tanks, 234, 235
Ocean Conservancy, 299, 302 (table)
O'Connor, Sandra Day, 117 (table), 118
O'Donnell, Christine, 372
Office of Information and Regulatory Affairs, 131
Office of Management and Budget (OMB), 131, 133
Ohio, 305, 396, 425, 427, 449 (table), 462
Ohio Company, 18
Oil industry, 295, 302-303, 329, 352, 366, 472
Olson, Mancur, 50, 51, 58-59, 67, 79, 87-90, 102, 168, 173, 264
OMB Watch, 265, 375
Omnivore's Dilemma, The (Pollan), 171
Online lobbying, 375-377
On Thermonuclear War (Kahn), 229
Order of the Patrons of Husbandry. *See* Grange
Order of the Star Spangled Banner, 25
Order of United Americans, 25
Oregon, 115
Organized labor. *See* Business and organized labor; Labor unions; *specific organization*
Organizing for America, 134, 138
Organizing Institute, 81
Outside lobbying, 341-343, 448
Owen, Priscilla, 118

Pacific Railroad Act (1862), 25
Pakistan, 323
Palin, Sarah, 407, 423, 426-427, 438-439
Paperwork Reduction Act (1980), 131
Parents Against Forced Busing, 287
Parents Involved in Community Schools v. Seattle School District No. 1 (2007), 286, 287
Parkel, James, 354
Parker, John, 116
Partitioning games, 94
Patrick, Deval, 103
Patriotic associations, 25
Patriot Majority, 409
Patronage:
group formation and maintenance, 52-53
interest group growth, 107-108
Pendleton Civil Service Act (1883), 226
Pennsylvania, 14, 186, 305, 396, 427, 445
People for the American Way, 285
People with disabilities:
civil rights, 209
education, 284-285, 287
Pepsi Company, 404
Perry, Bob, 405
Peterson, Paul, 458
Petitions, 16, 30
Petracca, Mark, 101
Pharmaceutical Research and Manufacturers of America (PhRMA), 148, 186 (table), 337, 339, 343
Pheasants Forever, 262-263
Phillips, Wendell, 24
Pierce v. Society of Sisters (1925), 244-245
Piven, Frances Fox, 80
Planned Parenthood, 407, 425, 433, 434-435, 436, 437
Playboy, 55
Pluralism, 52, 63-75
critiques, 66-68
defined, 64
education, 65 (table)
environment, 65 (table)
framework advantages, 71-72
framework comparison, 72-73
governmental process groups, 65
health care, 64, 65 (table)
hyperpluralism, 158
interest group liberalism, 68
national defense, 65 (table)
neopluralism, 59, 69-71
policy domain competition, 65-66
public interest groups, 264
research chronology, 67 (figure)
research questions, 73-74
social movements, 78-79, 83
taxation, 65 (table)
Poage, Bob, 167
Policy feedback approach, 83-84
Political action committees (PACs):
business and organized labor, 177, 180-1785
composition and contributions (2006), 147 (table)
congressional elections, 403-405, 408-416
education, 284
electioneering development, 398-399
electioneering reform, 432, 433 (table)
foreign lobbying, 322-323, 324, 325, 327 (table)
lobbying and legislative strategy, 336, 338-340
presidential elections, 422, 424
professional associations, 274, 275-276
public interest groups, 265-268
representational politics, 146-147, 148, 153, 154
social movements, 80
See also specific organization
Political Change in the Metropolis (Harrigan and Vogel), 459
Politico, 351, 364, 365, 366
Politics of Disorder, The (Lowi), 80
Politics of Interests, The (Petracca), 101
Pollan, Michael, 171
Poor People's Movements (Piven and Cloward), 80
Populist Party, 164, 394
Powell, Lewis, Jr., 117 (table)
Power and Powerlessness (Gaventa), 67 (figure)
Preface to Democratic Theory, A (Dahl), 78-79
Presbyterian, 239, 240, 241
Presidential elections, 419-430
campaign contributions, 424
Democratic Party, 419, 420-421, 423, 424, 425, 426, 427-428
endorsements, 422-424
501(c)(3) organizations, 422
501(c)(4) organizations, 422
527 organizations, 422
interest group involvement, 420-422
legislation, 424
political action committees (PACs), 422, 424
racial minorities, 425
Republican Party, 419, 420-421, 422-423, 424, 425
voter guide, 423, 424
voter mobilization, 424-426
voter persuasion, 426-428
"Walk a Day in My Shoes" (2007), 420
women, 424, 425
See also Electioneering development; Executive branch; specific administration
Pressure Boys, The (Crawford), 43-44
Prince Hall Masons, 24
Prisoner's dilemma, 91
Private goods, 87-90
Private politics, 94-95
Process of Government, The (Bentley), 49-50
Professional associations, 271-282
defined, 271-273
Democratic Party support, 276, 277
economic sector representation, 272 (table)
for government officials, 276-277
interest group community, 274
Lexis-Nexis cites, 273 (figure)
mobilization and maintenance, 273-274
nineteenth-century interests, 27
policy influence, 274-278
political action committees (PACs), 274, 275-276
political activities, 273-278
political power, 278-280
representational politics, 146, 150
Republican Party support, 275-276
selective incentives, 273-274
self-regulation, 277-278
special interests, 274-276
state politics, 445, 448 (table)
tax deductions, 58
See also specific organization
Progress for America, 406, 435 (table), 436, 438
Progressive Legislative Action Network (PLAN), 313
Progressive Party, 42
Progressive Policy Institute (PPI), 232, 233-235, 289
Prohibition, 396-397
Project on Government Oversight, 262 (table)
Project Vote!, 265
Protestantism, 240, 241, 243, 246, 247
Protest in City Politics (Lipsky), 80
Public and Its Problems, The (Dewey), 35
Public goods:
economic models, 87-90
social movements, 79-80, 84
Public interest:
group formation and maintenance, 54, 55
social movements, 84
Public interest groups, 261-270
collective action, 264
defined, 261-263
examples, 262 (table), 265
free-rider problem, 263-264
grassroots lobbying, 266
group proliferation, 264-265
nonprofit status, 266-267
organized interests, 261 (table), 262 (table), 265, 268
pluralism, 264
policy influence, 265-268
political action committees (PACs), 265-268
Publicity Act (1910), 382
Public opinion, 15
Public Policy Institute of California, 233
Public Utilities Holding Company Act (1935), 383

Quill Corp. v. North Dakota (1992), 313

Racial minorities:
education, 114, 119, 120, 211, 212, 284, 286-288, 289

executive branch influence, 134, 136
judicial system, 114, 115, 116-117, 119
presidential elections, 425
representational politics, 150
social movements, 79 (figure), 80, 81, 84
state politics, 449
voting rights, 119
See also specific ethnicity/race
Railroads, 25, 26, 27, 31, 32, 188
Railway Labor Act (1926), 188
Rain Forest Action Network, 299, 300 (table), 302 (table)
Rainforest Alliance, 299
RAND Corporation, 223-224, 225, 228-229, 230, 231, 232, 233
Rational actor theory, 80, 83
Reagan, Ronald, 116, 423
business and organized labor, 175, 180
environmentalism, 298
foreign lobbying, 328
interest group relations, 131, 133, 134, 135, 137
lobbying and legislative strategy, 343
national defense, 196
religious interest groups, 246
think tanks, 224, 232
REAL ID Act (2005), 316
Recovery Act (2009), 101
Red Cloud, 349, 350
Rehnquist, William, 117 (table)
Religious Coalition for Reproductive Choice, 262 (table)
Religious interest groups, 239-249
congressional lobbying, 243-244
cultural values timeline, 244
Democratic Party support, 240, 242, 243-244, 246
education, 285, 288, 289, 292n29
electoral involvement, 242-247
executive politics, 246-247
faith-based initiative, 246
group proliferation, 239-241
judicial system, 244-246
legislative influence, 244, 245, 247
lobbying organizations, 241-242
nineteenth-century, 25, 27-31
Republican Party support, 240, 242, 243-244, 246
See also specific organization or religion
Rent-seeking, 89
Representational politics, 145-159
collaboration and competition, 157-158
constitutional design, 145-146
Democratic Party, 145, 149, 151-158
election strategies, 147-149
electorate followings, 151-152
energy policy, 154
factions, 145
health care policy, 154-155
inside strategies, 149-150
interest group categorization, 146-147
interest groups, 146-151, 157-158
interest group strategies, 147-150
national defense policy, 155
outside strategies, 150
parties in government, 155-156
party campaigns, 152-155
party platforms (2008), 154-155
pharmaceutical industry, 148
policymaking process, 150-151, 156
political action committees (PACs), 146-147, 148, 153, 154
political parties, 151-158
professional associations, 146, 150
racial minorities, 150
Republican Party, 145, 151-158
taxation policy, 155
women, 148, 150, 154
Republican National Committee (RNC), 410
Republican Party:
business and organized labor, 175, 176-177, 180-181, 184
contacting lawmakers, 186, 378
defense industry contributions, 194 (table)
educational policy, 285, 286, 287, 288, 290-291
electioneering development, 395, 398-399, 400
electioneering reform, 434, 437, 438-439
energy and environmental advocacy, 154, 303, 304
executive branch influence, 133, 134, 136, 137-138
First Amendment rights, 384, 386, 387
grassroots lobbying, 372, 373
intergovernmental lobbying, 309, 314-315
lobbying and legislative strategy, 338, 343
lobbyists, 351, 355-356
national defense, 194 (table), 195-196, 197-198
party platforms (2008), 154-155
presidential elections, 419, 420-421, 422-423, 424, 425
professional associations, 275-276
religious interest groups, 240, 242, 243-244, 246
representational politics, 145, 151-158
think tanks, 230, 231-232, 234, 236
See also Congressional elections; specific administration
Republicans for Clean Air, 405, 422
Responsible Electorate (Key), 92
Revolution, The, 113
Revolving door strategy, 354
Rhode Island, 446
Richardson, Bill, 289, 419
Rifle shots, 353-354
Rise and Decline of Nations (Olson), 102
Rivalrous consumption, 87-90
RNC v. FEC (2009), 410
Roberts, John G., Jr., 117 (table), 118
Roberts, Pat, 169
Robertson, Pat, 240, 241, 245, 419, 423
Rockefeller Foundation, 223, 224, 226-227, 228, 229-230, 231, 285
Rockwell Collins Inc., 194 (table)
Rockwell International, 196, 198, 206n20
Roe v. Wade (1973), 119, 122, 244
Roll Call, 342, 351, 362, 364, 365, 366
Romney, Mitt, 421
Roosevelt, Franklin D.:
agricultural policy, 165, 166
business and organized labor, 175
electioneering development, 396, 397, 398
environmentalism, 296
First Amendment rights, 382
interest group relations, 128, 132, 133, 135, 136, 137
intergovernmental lobbying, 311, 312
representational politics, 156
think tanks, 227
Roosevelt, Theodore, 42, 395
Rosenberger v. University of Virginia (1995), 246
Rosenthal, Alan, 452
Rove, Karl, 424
Russell Sage Foundation, 226

Sabbatarian movement, 27-28, 30-31
Salisbury, Robert, 67 (figure)
Salvation Army, 57
Same-sex marriage, 244, 258-259
San Antonio Independent School District v. Rodriquez (1973), 119
Santa Clara County v. Southern Pacific Railroad (1886), 382
Saperstein, David, 133
Saudi Arabia, 325, 328, 330
Scalia, Antonin, 117 (table)
Scenic Hudson Preservation Conference v. Federal Power Commission (1965), 298
Schattschneider, E. E., 91
Schenck, Rob, 116
School vouchers, 288-289
Schriock, Stephanie, 407
Sea Shepherd Conservation Society, 300 (table), 302 (table)
Sebelius, Keith, 169
Second Great Awakening, 23, 30
Sekulow, Jay, 245
Selective incentives:
group formation and maintenance, 51-52, 55-57
professional associations, 273-274
social movements, 80
Semiconductor Industry Association (SIA), 177
Semisovereign People, The (Schattschneider), 91
Senate Judiciary Committee, 121
Service Employees International Union (SEIU), 173, 176, 179, 182, 183, 184, 405
presidential elections, 419, 420, 422, 425
Sexual orientation. *See* Lesbian, gay, bisexual, transgendered (LGBT)
Shays, Daniel, 15
Shay's Rebellion (1786-1787), 15
Shifting Involvements (Hirschman), 95
Shintech, 118
Sierra Club:
electioneering, 421, 423-424, 425, 434, 435 (table), 436, 437, 438
group development, 296-298, 299-300, 302, 303, 304, 305
nonprofit tax status, 57
online lobbying, 377
public interest organization, 54, 55
recruitment, 56-57
Sierra Club Foundation, 298
Sierra Club Legal Defense Fund. *See* Earthjustice Legal Defense Fund
Sierra Club v. Hickel (1970), 298
Signaling models, 92-93
Silver, Gray, 43
Simmons-Harris v. Zelman, 289
Slavery, 24, 27, 29-31, 381-382
Small group effect, 51
Smith, Al, 396, 397
Smith-Connelly Act (1943), 181, 398

Smith-Lever Act (1914), 165
Social movement organizations (SMOs), 105-106
Social movements, 77-86
  African Americans, 81, 212-213
  Asian Pacific Americans, 81
  astroturf movements, 82
  business and organized labor, 175-176
  collective action, 80, 84
  contentious politics, 84
  defined, 77-80
  democratic representation, 84-85
  disciplinary research, 82-84
  framework comparison, 72
  free-rider problem, 80
  grassroots movements, 82
  insider-outsider status, 80-82
  interest group distinction, 77-82
  interest organizations, 84
  labor unions, 81
  Latin Americans, 81, 82, 214
  organizational chronology (1790s-2000s), 79 (figure)
  pluralism, 78-79, 83
  policy feedback approach, 83-84
  political action committees (PACs), 80
  public goods, 79-80, 84
  public interest, 84
  racial minorities, 79 (figure), 80, 81, 84
  rational actor theory, 80, 83
  selective incentives, 80
  socioeconomic status (SES), 79 (figure), 80, 81
  women, 79 (figure), 80, 81
  See also Civil rights
Social Security Act (1935), 83
Society for Establishing Useful Manufactures (SEUM), 17
Socioeconomic status (SES), 79 (figure), 80, 81
Sociological economic models, 93-94
So Damn Much Money (Kaiser), 411
Sons of Liberty, 15
Soros, George, 424
Sotomayor, Sonia, 117 (table), 118, 258
Souter, David, 117 (table)
South Africa, 324, 327, 328, 471
South Carolina, 12, 14, 24, 29-30, 119, 438
South Dakota, 170, 452
Southern Christian Leadership Conference, 209, 213
Southern Company, 186 (table)
Space Exploration Technologies, 194 (table)
Spain, 469
Speak Out! USA, 262 (table)
Spector, Arlen, 184, 186, 188
Speechnow.org v. FEC, 410
Sponsorship strategy, 113, 115, 119
St. Louis Resolutions (Missouri), 113
Stabenow, Debbie, 438
Stanton, Elizabeth Cady, 24
State Homeland Security Program, 202-203
State of Working America, The (Bernstein), 233
State politics, 445-455
  active organizations, 445-446
  business groups, 445, 448 (table)
  citizen groups, 446, 448 (table)
  community diversity, 447-448
  constituent influence, 447
  economic factors, 446-447, 448
  governmental associations, 445-446, 448 (table)
  grassroots lobbying, 451
  group influence, 451-453
  group power, 452-453
  information management, 450
  in-house lobbyists, 448-449
  institutions, 448
  interest group communities, 446-448
  labor unions, 446, 448 (table)
  lobbying practices, 450-453
  lobbying techniques, 450-451
  lobbyists, 448-449
  membership organizations, 448
  outside lobbyists, 448
  party competition level, 447
  professional associations, 445, 448 (table)
  racial minorities, 449
  trade associations, 445, 448 (table)
  volunteer lobbyists, 449
  women, 449
  See also Local interest groups; specific state
Stevens, John Paul, 117 (table)
Stewart, Potter, 117 (table)
Stone v. Graham (1980), 244
Storm King Mountain (New York), 295
Structure of Scientific Revolutions, The (Kuhn), 50
Subsidization:
  economic models, 91
  lobbying, 341, 354
Sweatt v. Painter (1950), 119
Sweeney, John, 81, 178, 179
Swift Boat Veterans for Truth, 406, 407, 414, 427, 435 (table), 436, 440
Switzerland, 327 (table), 328

Taft, William Howard, 177, 226, 395
Taft-Hartley Act (1947), 175, 181, 398, 403
Tancredo, Tom, 419
Tappan, Arthur, 29
Tarplin, Linda, 350
Taxation:
  civil rights organizations, 216-217, 218 (table)
  energy and environmental advocacy, 297-298, 300-301
  First Amendment rights, 383-387
  grassroots lobbying, 377
  group formation and maintenance, 57-58
  lobbying and legislative strategy, 343-344
  national sales tax, 377
  nonprofit tax status, 57-58, 216-217, 218 (table), 266-267
  public interest groups, 266-267
  representational politics, 155
  tax deductions, 58
  think tanks, 225-226
Tax Reform Act (1969), 224, 300-301
Tea Party Patriots, 372, 373
Teapot Dome Scandal, 397
Telecommunications Act (1996), 232
Teledyne Technologies, 194 (table)
Temperance movement, 27, 28-29, 30-31
Templeton, John, 405
Tenth Amendment, 316
Terrorism:
  Pentagon (2001), 193
  World Trade Center (2001), 193, 199, 200-202
  See also Homeland security
Texas, 290, 313, 445, 446, 451
Thinking About the Unthinkable (Kahn), 229
Think tanks, 223-238
  as interest group, 223-225
  criticisms, 232
  Democratic Party, 229-230, 235, 236
  educational policy, 285, 287, 289
  executive politics, 226, 227, 228, 230, 231, 232, 233-234, 235, 236
  historical development, 226-236
  historical development (1917-1945), 227-228
  historical development (1945-1969), 228-230
  historical development (1981-1993), 232-233
  historical development (1993-present), 233-236
  intergovernmental lobbying, 313
  legislative influence, 224, 226, 227, 228, 232, 235
  lobbying and legislative strategy, 344
  personnel organization, 225
  policy analysis, 226
  political orientations, 228-230, 231-232, 233-236
  Republican Party, 230, 231-232, 234, 236
  structural organization, 225
  tax status, 225-226
  See also specific organization
Third House, The (Rosenthal), 452
Thomas, Clarence, 116-117, 118, 123
Thompson, Fred, 421, 422-423
Thornberry, Homer, 117 (table)
Thune, John, 432
Tibet, 324
Tillman Act (1907), 181, 382, 398
Tobacco Research Council, 109
Toqueville, Alexis de, 21-22, 33, 36, 38, 78, 272
Toward a Broader View of Interest Groups (Moe), 67 (figure)
Toyoda, Akio, 347
Toyota, 347, 348, 350, 352, 353, 355
Tribes on the Hill (Weatherford), 361
Triumph Group, 194 (table)
Truman, David, 50, 63, 65, 67 (figure), 87
Truman, Harry, 373, 374
Trust for Public Land, 300 (table), 302 (table)
Turkey, 325, 326, 328
Two Face of Power (Bachrach and Baratz), 67 (figure)

UBS Americas, 327 (table)
Unfunded Mandates Reform Act, 316
Union Pacific Railroad, 25, 26, 27
United American Mechanics, 25
United Arab Emirates, 325
United Auto Workers (UAW), 128, 180, 182, 421, 435 (table), 438
United Mine Workers (UMW), 174-175, 422, 428
United Nations Universal Declaration of Human Rights, 288
United Seniors Association, 435 (table), 436, 438
United States v. Cruikshank (1874), 382
United States v. Harriss (1954), 384
United Technologies, 194 (table)
UNITE HERE, 176, 184, 422
Urban Area Security Initiative, 202-203

Urban Institute, 224, 225, 226, 230, 231, 233, 235-236
Urban lobby, 311-312
Urban Politics (Levine), 459
U.S. Air Force, 194
U.S. Army, 107, 194-195
U.S. Chamber of Commerce, 49, 107, 407
 business groups, 173, 176, 177, 178, 180, 184, 185, 186-187
U.S. Commission on Civil Rights, 106
U.S. Conference of Catholic Bishops (USCCB), 239, 240, 241, 244, 285
U.S. Conference of Mayors (USCM):
 homeland security, 202
 intergovernmental lobbying, 309, 310, 311, 312, 314-316
U.S. Constitution:
 Eighteenth Amendment, 41, 396-397
 eighteenth-century interests, 11, 15-17, 18-19
 Equal Rights Amendment (ERA), 251-252, 256, 257
 Fifteenth Amendment, 39, 211
 Fourteenth Amendment, 113, 211, 212, 382, 384
 national defense, 193
 Nineteenth Amendment, 41
 representational politics, 145-146
 Supreme Court nominations, 116
 Tenth Amendment, 316
 See also First Amendment rights
U.S. Department of Agriculture (USDA), 107, 163, 164, 165, 166, 167
U.S. Department of Education (ED), 285-286, 289
U.S. Department of Homeland Security (DHS), 199-205
U.S. English, 265
U.S. Environmental Protection Agency (EPA), 106, 298
U.S. Forest Service, 43, 296
U.S. Marine Corps, 194, 196, 199
U.S. Navy, 198-199
U.S. Public Health Service, 109
U.S. Supreme Court:
 abortion, 119, 120, 122, 409-410
 campaign contributions, 182-183, 342-343, 405
 education desegregation, 114, 119, 120, 211, 212, 284, 286, 287
 employment, 115
 equal pay, 219
 First Amendment rights, 382, 384, 385, 387, 388
 intergovernmental lobbying, 312, 313
 judicial elections, 118
 jury selection, 211-212
 primary election regulation, 397
 religious interest groups, 244-246
 school vouchers, 289
 women's rights, 119, 120, 122
 See also Judicial system; specific court case
U.S. Term Limits, 434, 435 (table)
USA Patriot Act (2002), 203, 279

Venezuela, 321, 329
Verizon Communications, 186 (table)
Vermont, 244
Vietnam War, 193, 195, 223-224, 230, 400
Virginia, 13, 14, 119, 274, 427, 452
Vogel, John, 459
Voluntary associations, 23, 24-31
Volunteer lobbyists, 449
Vote-buying model, 91-92
VoteVets.org, 409
Voting rights:
 racial minorities, 119
 women, 113, 252-253
Voting Rights Act (1965), 209, 213

Wagner, Heidi, 349
Wagner Act. *See* National Labor Relations Act (1935)
"Walk a Day in My Shoes" (2007), 420
Wallace v. Jaffree (1985), 244
Wal-Mart, 173, 178, 181, 185-186
Washington, 274, 305, 452
Washington, D.C., 119
 Gucci Gulch, 81
 K Street Project, 157, 158
Washington, George, 22
Washingtonian, 350
Washington Legal Foundation (WLF), 263
Washington Post, 342, 355, 359, 362, 368
Washington Representatives, 102, 103, 261, 264, 265, 266, 268, 348, 360 (figure)
Washington Temperance Societies, 29
Watson, Kirk, 451
Weatherford, J. McIver, 361
Weaver, James, 164, 394
Webster, Daniel, 23-24
Webster v. Reproductive Health Services (1989), 120, 123
Weekly Standard, 365
Weinberger v. Wiesenfeld (1975), 119
West Virginia, 118, 119, 449 (table)
Whitaker, Charles, 117 (table)
White, Byron, 117 (table)
Who Governs? (Dahl), 63, 65-66, 67 (figure), 79, 457-458
Why We Lost the ERA (Mansbridge), 83
Wilderness Society, 296, 300 (table), 302 (table), 303
Willard, Frances, 252
Wilson, Woodrow, 227, 396
Wisconsin, 283, 291, 305, 396
Wisconsin Advertising Project, 408, 417n33
Wisconsin Right to Life v. FEC (2007), 409-410
Woman's Rights Convention (Seneca Falls), 24
Women:
 abortion, 119, 120, 122, 148, 244, 409-410
 civil rights, 219
 educational policy, 284, 288
 equal pay, 219
 executive branch influence, 134, 136
 feminist movement, 251-260
 first wave feminism, 251-254, 259n10
 judicial system, 113, 119, 122, 123, 244
 lobbyists, 349-350
 nineteenth-century interests, 24, 26, 27, 251-254
 presidential elections, 424, 425
 representational politics, 148, 150, 154
 second wave feminism, 252, 254-257, 259n10, 260n34
 social movements, 79 (figure), 80, 81
 state politics, 449
 third wave feminism, 252, 257-258, 259n10
 voting rights, 113, 252-253
 See also specific organization
Wong, Janelle, 83
Working America, 179
Workingman's Labor Party, 394
World War I, 193, 227, 230
World War II, 193, 195, 227-228, 230
World Wildlife Fund, 265, 295, 297, 300 (table), 302 (table), 303
Worthern, Greg, 451
Write Your Rep, 378
Wyoming, 446

Yosemite National Park, 296
Young, Whitney, 212
Young Americans for Freedom, 399
YouTube, 428